THE WOMEN'S FOOTBALL ENCYCLOPEDIA

2016 EDITION

NEAL ROZENDAAL

Foreword by **DR. JEN WELTER**

Order this book online at www.nealrozendaal.com/books
or e-mail the author at nealrozendaal@gmail.com

Cover design by Alison Ackerley
Cover photo by Douglas Charland
Cover photo: D.C. Divas quarterback sneak vs. Boston Renegades, 6/13/15
From left: Becky Worsham, Ashley Rozendaal, Rachel Huhn, Allyson Hamlin, Jennifer Gray, Ashley Branch, and Jennifer Dulski

© Copyright 2016 Rozehawk Publishing. All rights reserved.
No part of this publication may be reproduced, stored in a retrieval system, or transmitted, in any form or by any means, electronic, mechanical, photocopying, recording, or otherwise, without the expressed written permission of the author.

Published in the United States of America
ISBN: 978-0-9970637-0-7
First edition (2016)

Rozehawk Publishing
451 Hungerford Drive
Suite 119, #482
Rockville, MD 20850
www.nealrozendaal.com

To women's football players everywhere,
and especially to the one who changed my life forever:
My wife, Ashley.

"Do you know what my favorite part of the game is? **The opportunity to play.***"*
– Mike Singletary, Pro Football Hall of Fame linebacker

Table of Contents

Front Matter
    Table of Contents i
    Foreword by Dr. Jen Welter ii
    Acknowledgments vi
    Introduction viii

Chapter 1   20th Century
    1.1   History of Women's Football in the 20th Century 1
    1.2   Women's Football Teams, 1967-1985 8
    1.3   Confirmed Women's Football Games, 1967-1985 9

Chapter 2   21st Century Leagues
    2.1   History of Women's Football in the 21st Century 12
    2.2   League Database Legend 16
    2.3   Team Code Index 19
    2.4   U.S. Women's Football Leagues – Year-By-Year Results, 1999-2015 21
    2.5   All-Star Game Results 114

Chapter 3   21st Century Franchises and Players
    3.1   Franchise Database Legend 115
    3.2   Alternate Franchise Name List 118
    3.3   Franchise Game-By-Game Records, 1999-2015 119

Chapter 4   Champions and Records
    4.1   Classifying Leagues and League Championships 345
    4.2   Women's Football Championship Listing 348
    4.3   Women's Football Team Record Book 349
    4.4   Women in Men's Football 355

Chapter 5   Lingerie Football
    5.1   The Case Against Lingerie Football 356
    5.2   Mitch Mortaza and the LFL's Exploitation of Female Athletes 360
    5.3   Lingerie Football Leagues – Year-By-Year Results 372

Chapter 6   International Women's Football
    6.1   The International Growth of Women's Football 382
    6.2   International Women's Football Leagues – Year-By-Year Results 384
    6.3   International Exhibitions 401
    6.4   IFAF Women's Championships 402

Foreword by Dr. Jen Welter

Dr. Jen Welter began her 13-year career in women's football with the Massachusetts Mutiny in 2002. After two seasons, she relocated to Dallas, where she played for the Dallas Dragons in the spring of 2004. Welter achieved her greatest playing fame as a linebacker with the Dallas Diamonds from 2004-2013, winning four national championships with the team. She also won two gold medals as a member of Team USA in the IFAF Women's World Championships in 2010 and 2013. Welter finished her playing career as a member of the Houston Energy in 2014.

Jen Welter became the first woman to play running back on a men's professional football team when she was signed by the Texas Revolution of the Indoor Football League (IFL) in 2014. The following spring, she became the first female to coach in a men's pro football league when the Revolution hired her to coach their linebackers and special teams. Then in the summer of 2015, Jen Welter made national headlines when she was hired by the Arizona Cardinals as an assistant coaching intern for their training camp and preseason. That hiring made Welter the first female coach in NFL history, breaking a prominent barrier for women in sports and attracting national attention to the sport of women's football.

I loved football long before I ever knew women's football was a possibility. I grew up in Vero Beach, Florida, where football was like a religion. I had friends who were football cheerleaders, but I knew I couldn't do that myself...I had to be able to watch the game! As a woman, there was never an opportunity to play football. My first love was actually tennis, but generally, I played a lot of different sports. I got into soccer, softball, track – pretty much any sport I could play. I was certified to teach aerobics when I was 18 years old and I have taught it ever since...anything to stay active!

I went to Boston College for my undergraduate degree, and when I got there, I found rugby. It was the closest sport to football that I ever had the opportunity to play, so I jumped on it. I played rugby all four years at Boston College and was even recruited for the under-20 national team.

After I graduated college, I was working in Massachusetts and playing in a flag football league. The general manager of the Massachusetts Mutiny came around, asking if there were any girls on our team who might be successful playing tackle football. The Mutiny gave me an open tryout in the fall of 2001, and I made the team. I played my first two seasons of women's football with the Massachusetts Mutiny in 2002 and 2003.

I moved to Texas after my second season with the Mutiny. In the spring of 2004, I played for a new team, the Dallas Dragons. The Dragons only lasted for one season. In our last game of the year against the Austin Outlaws, we had so many injuries and so many people had quit that we only had 13 healthy players in uniform. Needless to say, I didn't come off the field a whole lot that game! I played on both offense and defense and scored our only touchdown as a running back, but we lost the game, 52-6.

I literally felt like I had been hit by a truck several times. But the Dallas Diamonds played in the fall, and they were getting ready to start their season. They said I should come and try out for the team, so they scheduled my tryout for the Tuesday right after my last game with the Dragons. I showed up and I could barely move. To make matters worse, all I had to wear was a Dallas Dragons helmet, which made me lots of friends. It's always popular to wear the helmet of a rival team at a tryout!

Anyway, in every single drill, I just mysteriously wound up going against one of the Diamonds' very best players. They really wanted to see what this Dragons chick was made of. The Diamonds had terrific players at that time, like K.B. Bowman, Alberta Fitcheard-Brydson, and Karen "Frogger" Padgett. Much later, Frogger told me that the Diamonds vets were rotating in to decide if they wanted to give me their seal of approval, and they all finally came to the conclusion, "Okay, she's not bad."

But the one girl who stood out to me that day was Jessica Springer. I hadn't yet come to realize that she was one of the best – if not the very best – women's football players to ever play the game. She was just such a tough woman. I very distinctly remember running one drill – and again, I really didn't know yet who Jessica Springer was – and I tackled Springer. All I could hear from the vets was, "Oooooh, new girl took down Springer." I'll never forget that. I thought to myself, "Okay, I guess that's a good thing!"

That was without a doubt one of the toughest days I've ever had. Knowing these women the way I do now, I should have expected that! It was definitely a tryout to end all tryouts. All of the great ones who later made the Dallas Diamonds one of the greatest dynasties in women's football history, they all got their shots on me that first day. But I guess I did all right. It was definitely a "welcome to the club" moment, and thankfully in later years, I became one of those welcomers.

Foreword by Dr. Jen Welter

I literally went straight from the Dragons to the Diamonds in 2004. In my rookie season, they thought I was too little to play linebacker, so they put me at safety. That lasted until the very first game. We had one girl who was an outstanding linebacker, but on one of the first plays of the game, she made a tackle and broke her leg. It was a devastating loss for the Diamonds.

The coaches put the player who was backing me up at safety in at linebacker. I don't know what happened on the next play, but it couldn't have been very good. The very next defensive huddle, Springer asked me, "Welter, what position did you play before you got here?" When I told her linebacker, she said, "Oh, thank God. You two switch positions right now." The next time we came off the field, Springer informed the coaches what she had done, and I ended up being one of their linebackers from that point on.

That's Jessica Springer...she was just a leader in all things. I love her with my whole heart; she was one of the best people to play with. Springer rarely came off the field, and for very good reason. She was an incredible running back, and I realized at one point that there were many plays where she just needed one more block and she would have been gone.

I went to our coach and I said, "Coach, I want to play offense." He looked at me like I was nuts; it was not something that was really in my wheelhouse. Coach said, "Welter, you hate offense." I replied, "Let me bring it back. I don't really want to play offense; I just want to block for Springer. We have too many plays where she's right there." Although linebacker was my primary position, I played offense quite a bit during my time with the Diamonds, mostly just to block for Springer. She would go up to the coach and say, "Can I have Welter for a play now? I want to score!" She was such a great player, and I was proud to be able to block for her.

The Dallas Diamonds created an amazing legacy in women's football, and it was mostly because we all loved each other and we would hold each other very accountable. We would set up extra workouts, because we wanted to be the best and we knew we could be the best. We were not satisfied if we were not dominating. We went undefeated two years in a row in 2004 and 2005 and won two national championships. But then in 2006, we lost our first game in three years to the Houston Energy, 24-10. We were so mad about it! This was unacceptable – we were better than that and we knew it. We made it back to the national championship game in 2006, and we won our third straight title by beating Houston in the championship game.

We had so much talent, and again, we also had that accountability to each other and our mutual promise that we would work. I mean, we *worked*. We had Saturday morning practices, practices after work...we were all in, all the time. It was an amazing group to be around. Sometimes you're tired and you want to skip practice, but we knew if we did, we'd miss so much that missing practice was almost torture. It wasn't so much about the coaches calling us out...we would call each other out on stuff. We were very much a family, and we took a lot of pride in what we were doing on that football field.

The Diamonds switched leagues and in 2008, we won our fourth national championship in five years. A lot of great players on the Diamonds retired after that 2008 championship. I have to confess, having had such a dominant team and a dynasty for so long...I considered retirement, too. I thought, "What else is there to play for or accomplish in this sport? What are you trying to prove? We've already done everything that could possibly be done in this game."

Then I heard about the IFAF Women's World Championships. Without a doubt, it was the opportunity to possibly represent my country that showed me there was more I could do in football. I had never even thought something like that would be possible. But the Women's World Championships showed me that there were still opportunities out there I'd never dreamt of, and knowing that, I had to stay in the game.

I remember filling out the application to be a member of Team USA in 2010. It was surreal...I truly believed that making this team would be the most amazing accomplishment of my life. It was historic. I mean, how many times in your life do you have a chance to do something that has never been done before?

When I found out I made the team, I was just in shock and awe. I was so proud and excited, not only to have made the team myself, but for my four Dallas Diamonds teammates who were going with me. Alberta Fitcheard-Brydson was going...she is obviously one of the best to ever play the game and one of my very best friends in football and in life. Springer was going. I wasn't going alone...I was going with teammates who were like family to me.

Training camp for Team USA in 2010 had this incredible aura. We had no idea what to expect, because there was no precedent. We knew that Germany had been playing football for like 20 years and that they were giants. What if they were going to destroy the little Americans? We were going into this unknown and representing our country and our game. We took it so, so seriously. It was that common vision that was able to get 45 women away from the fact that we had all been on separate teams and were trying to kill each other just days or weeks before!

I remember the Dallas Diamonds hosted the Chicago Force in a playoff game three days before we were leaving for the Women's World Championships in Sweden. I was playing linebacker in the game, and I tackled [Chicago Force quarterback] Sami Grisafe hard. She was down on the turf for what felt like forever...it might not have been that long, but it felt like ages. Sami was not only the quarterback for the Force but my teammate and the starting quarterback for Team USA.

Meanwhile, Chicago's head coach, [John] Konecki, is also the head coach for Team USA. He's over on the Chicago sidelines yelling all sorts of not very nice things at me. I remember very distinctly that he was trying to tell the officials it was helmet-to-helmet contact, and I had to laugh and ask how I could go helmet-to-helmet on Sami Grisafe. She's 5'10" and I'm 5'2"! What did I do...jump up in the air and head-butt the girl?

So I remember being on one knee with my teammates, waiting to see if Sami's okay. I told my teammates, "Hey guys, if I just got kicked off of Team USA for that tackle, then we'd better at least win this game. I'm not staying home for nothing!" She turned out to be all right and able to finish the game, but I picked her off with just under two minutes to go to seal a 27-20 victory. Then three days later, I have to go play with her? Like, we're friends now? You've got to be kidding me...we aren't supposed to like each other. And I know I was not a popular person with the Chicago folks! They probably thought I was crazy!

But we got over all of those things very quickly. Coach Konecki and Coach [Anthony] Stone did such an amazing job making us put away our separate team identities and really come together for something bigger. "Coach Mac" [Mark McLaughlin] was just this amazing spirit of a man. There was a lot of forced integration by the coaches, and we quickly realized we were playing for something very important. All of those differences were cast aside, and I think that's because they picked the absolute right coaches for it.

As a team, we were honored to be representing our country by playing our country's favorite sport. We were ambassadors on an international level, and we were so proud to wear the red, white, and blue. I have never listened to the national anthem the same since the first time I heard it there. It's something people often take for granted at American sporting events...we play the national anthem, and that's for everyone. But when you play the national anthem on an international stage, that's what *you're* playing for. The other country's anthem is being played alongside ours, because the other team's playing for something else. That's a surreal feeling.

I loved every minute of playing for Team USA. I won a second gold medal with the team in 2013, but the 2010 team will always be particularly special. We didn't know what it would be like, and there was so much insecurity because it was the first. That was really one of the historic moments in women's football, and all of those women will be my cherished sisters from now until the time we're in our rockers. Those women will always have a special place in my heart, no matter what. We will always share a very special bond. We're family now.

I played the majority of my career with the Dallas Diamonds. When the Diamonds folded in 2013, several players went to play other places, and a lot of them went to play for the Houston Energy. I finished my women's football playing career by playing three or four games with the Houston Energy in 2014 when I wasn't committed to playing with the Texas Revolution.

In 2014, I went to play for a men's team, the Texas Revolution of the Indoor Football League, and the following spring I was asked to join their team as an assistant coach. Playing and coaching for the Revolution felt like a tremendous gift. I'll never forget that Olivia Griswold – one of my teammates on Team USA – reached out to me and told me, "Welter, I'm glad it's you." I asked her what she meant, and she said, "You speak for all of us and represent us so well. Thank you for what you're doing for all of us." To have my sisters like Olivia and other women's football players from all across the country thank me for what I'm doing for them, that's the greatest compliment I could ever receive. I have so many sisters in the game of football – players and coaches – who are such amazing people but who have just flown under the radar. I wanted to tell people that just because you don't know about them doesn't mean they're not fantastic.

When I started with the Revolution, there were a lot of people waiting for that "uh-oh" moment. I knew it was quite a bit of responsibility, because I wanted to be able to show greatness for women in football and hopefully help create opportunities for others in the future. That means you not only have to do it but do it well.

When I got the offer for a coaching position with the Arizona Cardinals of the NFL, again, it was a blessing...but one that came with a lot of responsibility. I will forever be thankful for the trust and support that everyone on the Cardinals gave me – from [head coach] Bruce Arians and the rest of the Cardinals coaches, all the players, and ownership from

Foreword by Dr. Jen Welter

Michael Bidwell on down. They set a tone that said, "This is what we're doing, she's the right girl to do it, and she's qualified to do it."

It was challenging at times because there were a lot of people in the media who wanted to talk to me. But as much as people wanted to know my story, the story was that I had a lot of work to do! I knew the media was talking about me, but I would get all of these messages secondhand, because I didn't even have a TV in my room. I didn't have time; I didn't want to be distracted. I wanted to be very present and very good. I wanted to spend any extra moment I had investing in the players, the coaches, the playbook, and all those things.

My friends would let me know what others were saying…both good and bad. Any time you have a first, somebody is going to say it's just a publicity stunt. But I knew that I had the education and years of experience playing football…and believe me, I didn't take all those hits on the football field just for the sake of publicity! But it was the positive messages that I remember most. I got a message from Odessa Jenkins saying she heard Michael Strahan talking about me, and he said he thought I'd do well because I had played more football than a lot of coaches in the NFL. I was able to further that conversation and let people know a big part of my qualifications was that I've played the game…and, in doing so, I could get them to actually talk about and acknowledge women's football. That was so amazing and exciting to me.

A reporter asked me, "Are you worried some woman will come in and do more than you?" Heck no! I hope they do! I was a lead blocker most of my career…I'm all about opening opportunities for other people. What good is it if one woman gets in and no one else ever does? That would be unfortunate. I don't know what my grand place in this world is yet, but I know that what I've done has created opportunities for other women and girls, and that is just fantastic.

Coaching in the NFL, people would always tell me I was "living the dream". I had to let them know that I wasn't living *my* dream, because as a young girl, this was a dream I was never permitted to have. The beautiful thing is that because of my experience with the Cardinals, other women can actually have that dream in the future. Now a little girl can look at an NFL sideline and say, "I can do that." The best way I can describe it is that we did the impossible and did it well.

To all the young girls out there with the dream of playing or coaching football – work hard and follow your passion. Keep going, even if it is not the popular path. If I would have just followed the path everybody said was for me, I never would have had these opportunities. I want people to know that my path was not one of everybody encouraging me and telling me I should play football and that I'd be great. It was actually the opposite. Playing football as a girl is not a popular decision, and it's probably never going to be. Opportunities are so few and far between, you have to be willing to fight for them. You've got to be willing to take your hits and get back up and do it again. Because that's football; it's not a game for the faint of heart.

There is no limit to how great women's football can become in the future. We still have far to go, but I've seen women's football go to an international scale. There are countries all over the world now that play women's football, and they look to us to be the leaders in what's possible in this game. It's very important for us to recognize that and to keep pushing on all levels to develop the sport. More and more little girls are growing up playing football, so of course, their talent and knowledge of the game is going to continue to go up. Great progress is being made in this game, like Sam Gordon helping to start the first junior girls tackle football league…as those things continue to happen, the sky's the limit for the future potential of women's football.

I think this book is a fantastic project, because for those of us who played women's football for the strict love of the game and the hope that we were in some way helping to shape the future, it's a delightful, refreshing thought to know that our efforts haven't been in vain. It's so rewarding to know that the women who truly put blood, sweat, and tears into this game will be honored for what they did and for building the foundation of this sport.

– Dr. Jen Welter

Acknowledgments

So many people to thank, so little time! After writing three books on the Iowa Hawkeyes, it has been an incredible three-year journey to here. Thank you to everyone who has taken that ride with me, and I thank God I have this opportunity to share another amazing story with you.

This book is dedicated to every woman who has ever put on a pair of football pads and played the game the right way. But for me, one player stands out above the rest. Supporting my wife Ashley is what originally got me involved in women's football in the first place, and I'm so very proud of her and all her achievements. Just as importantly, being an author is fun, but being a writer is hard work. I've spent many long hours researching and writing this book, and I couldn't have done so without a partner who understands when I'm immersed in my latest project and who can keep the household running while I'm tethered to the computer. I appreciate your sacrifices, Ashley, and I love you, babe!

Our little one-year-old daughter, Magnolia, lights up our days with her happy personality and ever-present smile. Magnolia, you don't understand it yet, but you mean the world to me. Never let anyone tell you there's anything you can't do, Maggie June.

On a personal level, I'd like to recognize my parents, Bill and Norma Rozendaal, who shaped me into the person I am today. I'd also like to acknowledge Paul, Dianna, Paul Jr., Chris, and Alison Ackerley for making my wife who *she* is today! Thank you all for your support. My sister Jill, her husband Rob, my nieces Annabelle and Adeline, and my nephew Gabriel – to the Tanzer family, I want you to know how grateful I am to have you in my life. To Seth, who is probably unlikely to read this while off on an Indiana Jones-style adventure – life is never dull when you're around, and I'm thankful to have you as a brother.

To my groomsmen, Mike McGinley and Andy Ver Woert – I don't speak to you as often as I'd like since our lives have evolved, but I want you both to know you're thought of and appreciated. Thanks too to Michael's two ladies, Kelsi and Katka, for keeping him mostly in line. Becky Aftowicz – I love your positive energy almost as much as Theodore does. Thank you for being such a good friend to our family. To all my family and friends I failed to mention, you know how much I appreciate you, and I promise I'll list you by name next time.

Professionally, I've made so many connections through women's football over the past few years – people who I now consider personal friends – that it would be impossible to list them all. But I'm going to give it a shot, anyway!

To Allyson Hamlin – you're the star we all revolve around. Courage is an overused word in sports, but you're a full-fledged superhero. I think the world of you, and I learn so much from our discussions about women's football and its future. (And thanks again to my wife Ashley for allowing me to hijack her quarterback-center relationship in favor of our quarterback-staff writer relationship!)

Becky Worsham and Rachel Huhn – thanks for your friendship over these past few years, for naming me the "o-line husband", and for adopting Magnolia as an honorary member! The whole offensive line typifies selflessness, which all great lines in football need to do. To Jen Gray, thanks to you and Tree Lewis for sticking it out when times got tough. One of my favorite parts of the sport is to see smiling Jen turn into angry Jen when you step on the field!

Kenyetta Grigsby – you are one of the most relentless athletes I have ever seen. How a person as talented as you can be so humble and so smilingly happy off the field is a mystery to me, but a good mystery! I love it when great things happen to great people, so I'm glad Melissa Washington happened to you. Thanks to both of you for being incredibly nice…and for letting me live vicariously through your foodie adventures.

This is a running theme…so many of the D.C. Divas are wonderful people to be around. Tia Watkins, thank you for being such a considerate and genuine person. Missy Bedwell, you are honestly as caring a person as anyone could ever hope to meet. Ashley Whisonant, you're like a cool breeze…I'll always admire how you make every single thing on and off the field look effortless. Okiima Pickett, I've been energized by how much passion you have for this team and this sport and how badly you want to raise the bar for everyone. Callie Brownson, thank you for your steady, unwavering leadership. It puts my mind at ease that the future of this sport is in the hands of people like you.

DeVon Goldsmith and Trigger McNair – you're two of the many reasons I would never play football. It's comforting to know that if I ever went down a dark alley that you two ladies would be on *my* side! Eleni Kotsis – you have the tenaciousness of a bulldog on the field, but what I appreciate most about you is our many conversations about this team, this sport, and how we can make it all better for the next generation. Donna Wilkinson – thank you for providing the public face of the D.C. Divas for so many years and for being willing to show up anywhere, anytime, in any capacity

Acknowledgments

to help promote the sport of women's football. That kind of dedication is uncommon, and the sport needs ambassadors like you.

There are so many Divas players who I appreciate on and off the field – Lindsay Sollers, Dex Walker, Kentrina Wilson, Helen Deer, Lillian Cherry, Cherre Marshall, Asia Hardy, D'Ajah Scott – seriously, I'm shortchanging so, so many of you. No organization is as great as the D.C. Divas without countless women pulling their weight, most of them thanklessly or without the acclaim they deserve. My sincere respect and love goes out to each and every one of you. To all the past and present members of the D.C. Divas, who have become like a second family to me, you ladies inspire me every single day.

Coach Alison Fischer has cheerfully endured every interruption (or disruption) I've caused and gone out of her way to help me. I appreciate it, Coach Fisch! To the rest of the coaches, thanks for your commitment as well. I'm particularly grateful for Tara Kallal and her happy-go-lucky personality, for Konnie Kordish and her boundless enthusiasm, and for Tessa Nelson for being a kind-hearted person who can still lower the boom to make sure the bus is running on time. And to Eric Evans, thank you for coming back and for making everyone you meet better.

To Rich Daniel – if there is someone more invested in the future of women's football, I haven't met them. Your never-ending advocacy for the health of this sport is admirable. If I begin to tire, I remind myself that you're out there somewhere giving 100 percent to this cause and it motivates me to push through and carry on. We have had many long conversations about the Divas and women's football, and it's an honor to be on your team.

I have been unbelievably blessed by my association with the D.C. Divas, and none of that would be possible if Mr. Paul Hamlin hadn't allowed me to become a part of this team three years ago. Mr. Hamlin, I can't imagine a better gentleman to work for...I know I have grown personally from watching your firm but fair leadership running the Divas organization. Women's football can never repay you for all you've given to this sport, and my only hope is that you don't ever think it has gone unnoticed. I applaud you, Mr. Hamlin.

To Allysea Marfull and Monica Livingston – you two don't wear the Divas uniform anymore, but I always enjoy your company whenever you're around. Doug Charland, Nate Lewis, Matt Hamlin, MacRae O'Brien, and the rest of the Gold Club – the Divas literally could not function without you folks. Thank you for your years of dedication! And of course, Jill, Payton, and Molly Cooper are always on all our minds...never forget that while no one can live forever, a few special people in their time can touch so many lives in a positive way that they literally change the world. And that's as close to immortality as any of us can get. We are blessed to have known such people and challenged daily to emulate them.

Outside of the D.C. Divas, I'd like to thank John Konecki, Terry Lister, Mike Ochmanowicz, and Mark Ring for their coaching insights; Backseat Coach and Militia Cheerleader for being avid fans of the wrong team (ha!); Lisa King for tactfully tolerating my often acerbic opinions on this sport and her league; and the many, many, many players from other teams who I've come to respect. Special recognition in that regard needs to be given to Lisa Horton, who I've found to be every bit as polite and gracious as she was rumored to be, and to Dr. Jen Welter, for taking time out of her very busy schedule to write the foreword to this book.

Several sources were consulted to assemble *The Women's Football Encyclopedia*. Numerous newspapers were used to complete the chapter on 20th century women's football. A special mention should be made of the *Toledo Blade* and its excellent coverage of the era's premier team, the Toledo Troopers.

Karen "Boo" Hunter (aka Boo in LA) and her website, Boo's Unofficial Guide to Women's Tackle Football, provided invaluable information on the myriad of early 21st century women's football leagues. The Women's Football Club message board retained a lot of outstanding information on this time period as well. Historical Massey ratings for several leagues housed at masseyratings.com were also extremely useful. Weekly recaps from around the sport posted on the old Women's Tackle Football Group message board provided insight on more recent women's football seasons. The WTFG message board, which was run by Dion Lee, was an excellent source of women's football news and information in its time.

Although all these sources were terrific, compiling an encyclopedia of this magnitude on a sport as scarcely covered as women's football means that there are unavoidably numerous errors and omissions contained herein. While every effort has been made to ensure completeness and accuracy, the responsibility for any incorrect information that may follow is mine and mine alone.

Finally, to all the players, coaches, staff members, and fans of women's football – past, present, and future – this book would not exist without your devotion and loyalty. For that, you have my sincerest gratitude.

– Neal Rozendaal

Introduction

I was first introduced to the world of women's football when my wife Ashley tried out for the D.C. Divas in the fall of 2012. The very idea of women's football seemed revolutionary to me: football is unquestionably America's favorite sport for men and boys. But can football truly be considered our national sport if it is off-limits to half the population? Sports fans accept that women play any number of less-popular sports and play them well…so why *not* football?

As I began to spend time around the sport, the talent, passion, and incredible life stories of women's football players fascinated me. Women's football drew me in, and I soon wanted to help the sport by pursuing one simple, overarching goal: to demystify women's football. I realized that while much time was being spent thinking about the future of women's football – and for good reason – the past and present of the sport are equally as important and often overlooked.

At present, women's football can be confusing to a casual fan, with multiple leagues and nearly 100 teams cluttering the landscape. Moreover, without a universal source of credible data about women's football, misinformation abounds. Teams and leagues often market themselves by concealing (or even bending) the truth, creating confusion among casual fans. The most popular sports in the United States are easy for fans to follow and understand, and women's football will never reach its full potential if it remains difficult for outsiders to comprehend.

At the same time, a definitive history of women's football hadn't been written. Women have been playing football continuously in the United States for nearly two decades, but as time passes, information about numerous defunct leagues and teams is becoming harder and harder to find. It is imperative that we document the past accomplishments of our players, teams, and leagues for posterity before the origins of this sport are lost forever. Preserving the past and elucidating the present of women's football are what this book is all about.

The Women's Football Encyclopedia is designed to be the most authoritative resource of information on women's football ever published. Within these pages, sports fans can find data on dozens of women's football leagues, more than 300 teams, and the results of over 5,000 women's football games. In addition, the names of over 10,000 women's football players since 1999 have been recorded in recognition of their places as pioneers of this burgeoning sport.

While this book is designed to be the most comprehensive encyclopedia on women's football written to date, it is admittedly far from fully complete. I hope that this book becomes a springboard for even greater coverage and research into the history of women's football going forward. Future editions of this book could be improved in several ways:

21st century U.S. games and teams: I estimate that 95 percent of modern women's football games have been recorded in this book. But there are a few leagues, most notably the Women's Football League, that received such scant coverage that some games and game scores were inevitably missed. Filling in the missing pieces from leagues like the WFL would make this encyclopedia a complete resource on 21st century women's football games.

20th century U.S. games and teams: The section on 20th century games and teams is admittedly incomplete. Games that were mentioned in public records such as newspapers have been cataloged, but there were undoubtedly many more games played and teams that existed, both in the NWFL and WPFL, in and around the 1970s. Hopefully more data can be found on women's football from that era.

International women's football: The number of women's football teams internationally is growing at an exponential rate. The section on international women's football in this encyclopedia lists some of the more popular and well-known international leagues, but keeping a record of other international women's football teams as they are being founded should be a priority for researchers.

Athletes and coaches: There is no more important mission in women's football than to make sure we are recording the names of the people who have been a part of this sport. This encyclopedia is a nice first step toward that goal – recording the names of over 10,000 athletes – but these player registers are still incomplete. In addition, further research into the topics of coaches and team owners, league all-stars, and player statistics would all be beneficial to provide a broader picture of the history of women's football.

If you are reading this book, it's quite likely that you or someone you know can help provide some of the information above that would make a future edition of this encyclopedia an even better historical reference on women's football. If you have any additions, corrections, or updates you'd like to submit to be included in a future edition of this encyclopedia, please feel free to email me any time at nealrozendaal@gmail.com.

As always, thanks for reading.

– Neal Rozendaal

History of Women's Football in the 20th Century

Women have been playing football in the United States continuously since 1999. Prior to that year, the sport of women's football endured a long but rocky history. Here is a brief look at the "pre-modern" era of women's football in the 19th and 20th centuries.

1896-1966 – Women's Football Treated As Farce

The first documented instance I have found of women playing football took place in New York City in 1896 outside a casino in Harlem River Park. College football was the dominant version of the game at the time, and the Ivy League ruled the college football world. On November 21, 1896, one Ivy League football rivalry carried over onto the women.

Ten girls were split five to a side, and each side was pinned with the colors of either Yale or Princeton. Representing these two Ivy League schools, the girls participated in a scrimmage, as reported in the *New York Times*:

> *"Princeton won the ball, and a girl in a short black skirt and orange-colored stockings started the game by kicking the ball over into the crowd of onlookers that surrounded the gridiron...the ball was put in play again, and a Yale girl started with it toward Princeton's goal. She hadn't got far before the other nine girls tackled her and all fell into a heap.*
>
> *There was a wild scramble, and the crowd of men looking on, excited by the struggle, closed in with a rush. The men behind pushed against those in front, and it looked as if the girls would be crushed. Police Captain Haughey had been watching the game and keeping close to the players. With a number of policemen, he got in the way of the crowd and drove it back. He then ordered the game stopped, for fear that somebody would be injured by a repetition of the crush."*

This was hardly a complete football game, as these ladies only got a couple of plays off before the police intervened. However, it illustrates how captivating the concept of women's football was to male spectators, even back in 1896. Other recreational "powder bowl" events were held across college campuses in the ensuing decades, but these exhibitions were unusual and unrecurring, and they were universally treated by the press as more farce than competitive football.

When discussing the origins of women's football, many contemporary sources point back to the NFL's Frankford Yellow Jackets in 1926. At intermission of the Yellow Jackets' NFL game against the Chicago Cardinals on November 6, 1926, a team of women dubbed the "Lady Yellow Jackets" provided the halftime entertainment by squaring off against a team of men in a light scrimmage. Largely because of the NFL connection, many narratives list the 1926 Lady Yellow Jackets as a key starting point for women's football when recounting the history of the sport, and over the years, the impact of the Lady Yellow Jackets has been wildly overstated.

In reality, this halftime sideshow was just as trivial as the New York City scrimmage in 1896...and treated with the same amount of seriousness. The ladies danced upon entering the field, and the "team" the Lady Yellow Jackets faced that day consisted of exactly two old men. It was farce, not competition – a comedy act designed to solicit laughs rather than a pure sporting event, which is how it has been misconstrued in recent years.

Perhaps most importantly, there is no evidence that this appearance by the Lady Yellow Jackets was more than a one-time spectacle or that other NFL franchises assembled similar women's football "teams". It was a singular, trivial event that only gained prominence in sports history over the last decade or so when modern women's football teams and leagues began to reconstruct the history of their sport.

Danni Leone wrote an excellent article examining the 1926 Lady Yellow Jackets contest, concluding, "Their game was not the beginning of an evolution of the sport for women. It was merely a fleeting amusement." And in that way, the story of the Lady Yellow Jackets does hold tremendous historical value, because that account is an outstanding example of how the entire notion of women's football was viewed in the first half of the twentieth century.

Reputedly serious attempts were made to assemble legitimate women's gridiron teams throughout the 1930s and '40s. At the height of the fame of the Toledo Troopers in the 1970s, the *Toledo Blade* reported that back in 1930 and 1931, two Toledo-based women's tackle football teams barnstormed throughout the Midwest playing exhibition games against each other. Not only did these teams play games in Toledo, they reportedly traveled and played contests in Detroit, Newport, and Dayton.

According to the *Blade*, the first few games between these teams were financial successes. But while there were sponsors and paying customers supporting the concept, women's football also faced strong opposition. A scheduled game at the University of Detroit was allegedly cancelled due to objections raised by university officials. As the story goes, the two Toledo teams were ultimately disbanded in 1931 when they received a scathing letter from none other than Mrs. Lou Henry Hoover, the First Lady of the United States and wife of President Herbert Hoover, who accused them of exploiting womanhood.

This attempt at assembling women's football teams in Toledo in 1930-1931 – along with the later success of the Troopers in the 1970s – has led some (in Toledo) to label the town as the "birthplace of women's football". That's a suspect claim, at best. It's impossible to tell how organized these teams were and how serious the attempt at launching women's football in Toledo in the 1930s really was. In any event, we know that the women's football movement in Toledo in the 1930s never attacted major press or got past the barnstorming stage; the effort lacked staying power and quickly dissipated, not unlike the numerous powder bowls organized across college campuses from that era.

While Mrs. Hoover is blamed for temporarily putting a halt to women's football in Toledo, California decided to give it a try by the end of the decade. The Hollywood Stars and Los Angeles Amazons – also called the Chet Relph Stars and Marshall Clampett Amazons, after their sponsors – squared off in a women's football contest at Los Angeles' Gilmore Stadium on October 22, 1939. This game was covered by major national outlets such as *Life Magazine* and was the most widely publicized contest the sport had seen to that point.

Life Magazine was complimentary of the level of play exhibited by the women, declaring, "It was no powder-puff battle. The girls were rough and tough. They kicked each other in the stomach, dirtied each other's faces, tackled and blocked savagely, [and] knocked four girls unconscious. And, strangely enough, they played good football, seldom fumbling or running away from their interference."

Women had – "strangely enough" – proven capable of playing the sport well, but again, not everyone was supportive. Dick Hyland, a former U.S. gold medal winner in rugby at the 1924 Olympics and then a sportswriter for the *Los Angeles Times*, loudly decried the Stars-Amazons game. He mercilessly mocked the female players before stating, "I'm wondering if the report of [the game] doesn't belong on the entertainment pages or over with the crime news."

Even *Life Magazine* itself, probably in an effort to provide "balanced" coverage, cited criticism from doctors in their article on the game. "When doctors hear about the game, most of them were horrified. Football, they said, is a dangerous sport for girls. A woman's body is not heavily muscled [and] cannot withstand knocks. A blow, either on the breasts or in the abdominal region, may result in cancer or internal injury. A woman's nervous system is also too delicate for such rough play," *Life* reported.

Yet just two years later, two teams of women in Chicago decided to ignore the cited cancer risks and try their hands at football anyway. The Chicago Rockets and Chicago Bombers planned an exhibition game at Spencer Coal Park in June 1941. The *Chicago Daily News* and *Chicago Herald-American* both ran photos about women's football invading the Windy City. Two photos in particular attracted attention. The first was a photo of three ladies sitting on the bench at practice, with one of them touching up her makeup with a compact. The second photo featured a winsome tackle for the Chicago Bombers proudly displaying a black eye she received in practice. The message was clear: these women were tough, serious football players…but still feminine enough to avoid terrifying the mainstream establishment.

Women's football games of this nature popped up on occasion throughout the first half of the twentieth century. They gained some media coverage over the unusual premise but then quickly disappeared again after one game, provided the "game" took place at all; the media was fascinated by the idea of women's football as an attention-grabbing oddity, but it rarely provided any reports of the games themselves or treated the sport seriously. That was the cycle women's football followed for decades…until 1967, when Sid Friedman and the WPFL truly changed the game forever.

1967-1971 – Sid Friedman and the Birth of Women's Football

Sid Friedman was a public relations agent for the All-Star Theatrical Agency in Cleveland, Ohio. He also had experience as a sports agent; Friedman was a one-time business manager for pro athletes such as baseball All-Star Jimmy Piersall and Pro Football Hall of Famer Bobby Mitchell. In addition, Friedman had spent a fair amount of time around competitive women as the director of several local and state beauty pageants that were preliminaries for the Miss USA and Miss World pageants.

But more than anything, Friedman was a showman, a PR man, and a promoter. He knew how to make waves and generate media attention, and the idea of women's football – which had fascinated spectators since 1896 – would make a lot of headlines in Friedman's hands.

In August 1967, Friedman announced a plan to organize a women's football team that would challenge men's semi-pro teams on a nationwide barnstorming tour. (Some sources have suggested Friedman started the concept as early as 1965, but I have found no evidence of Friedman promoting women's football prior to August 1967.) He named his team the USA Daredevils, although as the sport expanded to other cities, they were synonymously referred to as the Cleveland Daredevils. Friedman later said that he originally envisioned the Daredevils to be, essentially, a women's football version of the Harlem Globetrotters.

Friedman wanted to garner publicity for the Daredevils and establish some football credibility for the team right out of the gate, and his choice for the Daredevils' head coach accomplished both. Friedman hired Marion Motley, a star fullback for the Cleveland Browns from 1946-1953, as the head coach of the Daredevils. Motley was one of the greatest pro football players ever, averaging 5.7 yards per carry during his career, which is still an NFL record for a non-quarterback. He had also been an African-American pioneer in the sport and became just the second black player ever inducted into the Pro Football Hall of Fame when he was elected in 1968.

Despite his remarkable playing career, Motley's attempts to earn a scouting or coaching position in the NFL after his retirement were rejected at every turn. He applied to multiple NFL teams about open staff positions, only to be passed over each time. Even his old club, the Cleveland Browns, repeatedly turned down Motley's attempts to land a permanent coaching position. Motley would later attribute these rejections to blatant racism, stating that the NFL just wasn't ready for an African-American coach. Lacking other alternatives, he accepted Friedman's offer to coach the Cleveland Daredevils on the condition that he be allowed to coach the team like true professionals.

Motley's influence was apparent from the start. The Daredevils played three men's teams in 1967, and while they lost all three games, they were reportedly competitive and respectable in most of their losses. For example, a group of men in Erie, Pennsylvania – who nicknamed themselves the Erie Pussycats in a thinly-veiled sexual allusion to the gender of their opposition – squeaked past the Daredevils, 31-27. The Cleveland Daredevils were the first women's football team to generate substantial national media attention, to display staying power by surviving for over a decade, and to play a schedule of games against multiple different opponents. As such, the Cleveland Daredevils should rightly be regarded as the first women's football team in history, and Cleveland, Ohio, as the true birthplace of women's football.

The Daredevils' contests against the men were rough, physical games that resulted in several injuries to both sides. But the Daredevils played one other game in 1967, this one against a hastily-arranged team of women from Detroit called the Detroit All-Stars. The Daredevils claimed their only victory of the season over Detroit, and Friedman became enthusiastic after watching the Daredevils compete against other women. Public reception to the idea of the Daredevils playing other women was much better than when they played men, too. Friedman immediately launched plans for a four-team women's football league in 1968 – a league he was destined to name the Women's Professional Football League (WPFL).

Friedman wanted teams in Pittsburgh, Detroit, and Erie to join the Daredevils in 1968, but among those three new markets, only Pittsburgh fielded a confirmed team that season. The Pittsburgh All-Stars (sometimes called the USA All-Stars) were coached by Charley Scales, a former running back standout with the Pittsburgh Steelers and Cleveland Browns. Women's football made its debut in Pittsburgh on November 29, 1968, when the Pittsburgh All-Stars played the Daredevils to an 8-8 draw in front of an estimated crowd of 1,600 spectators.

By 1969, Friedman had expanded the WPFL internationally. His third confirmed entry into the league, the Toronto Canadian Belles, was coached by another Cleveland Browns alumnus, lineman Fred Robinson. The Canadian Belles joined the Daredevils and the renamed Pittsburgh Hurricanes in Friedman's league. However, his plans for a four-team league that season collapsed when the proposed Detroit Petticoats failed to launch in 1969.

Like any good showman, Friedman came up with a number of ideas to promote the league. Most notably, in true Yellow Jackets fashion, Friedman envisioned scrimmages between WPFL teams taking place during nationally-televised NFL halftime shows. This promotion never came through, however, and he blamed NFL team bands for sabotaging his plans by refusing to cede the needed time for his teams during intermission.

By 1971, the WPFL finally secured the four franchises it needed to establish a true league – the Cleveland Daredevils, the Pittsburgh Hurricanes, the Buffalo (NY) All-Stars, and a new entry to the league out of Toledo called the Troopers. Moreover, after years of scattered media coverage, the WPFL landed perhaps its greatest publicity ever when clips of a 1971 contest between the Daredevils and Hurricanes were featured on the NFL pre-game show on CBS.

Yet just as it appeared that the Women's Professional Football League was poised to take off, cracks began to appear in the WPFL armor. Friedman's league got the women's football movement started in the 1960s, but sweeping changes within the sport would leave the WPFL behind and push women's football to its highest level of the twentieth century.

1972-1974 – Alliances Challenge Friedman's WPFL

The WPFL was a single-entity league; in other words, Sid Friedman owned both the league and all of the franchises within it. Because Friedman controlled every WPFL franchise, there was a natural limit to how many teams he could oversee and the geographic reach those teams could have. But independently-owned women's football teams began to emerge in 1972, which dramatically changed the face of the sport. As new owners sprang up across the country, the sport grew from a regional footprint to a national one, and for the first time, Friedman's WPFL faced challengers to its supremacy in women's football.

In 1972, the Detroit Fillies and Pittsburgh Powderkegs announced plans for a four-team Alliance that would rival Friedman's WPFL. This Alliance also included the Midwest Cowgirls, which shared the same ownership, the same coaches, and most of the same players as the Detroit Fillies. (Truthfully, the Midwest Cowgirls and Detroit Fillies were essentially the same team operating under two different names.)

Still, the 1972 Alliance made national headlines mostly thanks to the fourth team in the league. The fourth team in the Alliance was the New York Fillies, the first women's football team to represent the Big Apple. A women's football team in New York City attracted national attention and gave the Alliance equal publicity (and equal standing) to the WPFL.

The New York Fillies debuted on May 13, 1972, against the Midwest Cowgirls in one of the most publicized women's football games in history. Unfortunately, the media was relentlessly negative in the aftermath of the Cowgirls' 28-0 victory. Criticism of the poor field conditions and the low quality of play from New York's expansion franchise led newspapers from coast to coast to label the contest a failure. Yet it gave the sport exposure to millions of readers who weren't previously aware of its existence.

In truth, the Alliance had a shaky foundation. The Powderkegs collapsed before the season even began. Saddled with constant criticism from the press, the much-maligned New York Fillies would last only one year before folding. The Midwest Cowgirls and the Detroit Fillies were, for all practical purposes, the same team, and they would rebrand into the Detroit Demons the following year. But with only one functional franchise, the Alliance may have collapsed altogether if not for a trio of brothers and a savior from the WPFL.

Despite having standout teams like the Daredevils and the Toledo Troopers – who compiled an impressive 8-0 record playing a mix of WPFL and Alliance competition – the WPFL had to share the public spotlight with this upstart Alliance in 1972. For the first time since he started the Daredevils five years earlier, Sid Friedman found his women's football league no longer the center of attention in the sport. How serious Friedman was about the level of play in the WPFL is a subject of speculation even today. Friedman confessed that he started the league as a gimmick, but he also claimed to have quickly come around to the notion of the WPFL being true competitive football. Others weren't as convinced.

After the 1972 season, the Toledo Troopers acrimoniously parted ways with the WPFL, which was a bold move for a team Friedman himself founded as a part of his league. A *Michigan Daily* article in 1973 alleged that Friedman believed the Troopers' lopsided blowout victories would cripple interest in the sport, and it quoted a member of the Troopers' front office, Frank Wallace, who accused Friedman of wanting the Troopers to throw games. Whether that accusation had merit or not, the Troopers' dominance wound up having the opposite effect. The Toledo Troopers would soon become the sport's most-publicized team, and losing the Troopers would prove to be a severe blow to the WPFL.

It also provided a lifeline to the WPFL's only competitor, as the Toledo Troopers joined the Detroit Demons in the Alliance. But the other factor that gave the Alliance a major boost was the involvement of the Matthews brothers, who also brought teams into the league. More importantly, because of the Matthews' involvement, 1973 might go down in history as the year that women's football went national.

In February 1973, the Toledo Troopers went south to play the expansion Dallas Bluebonnets, a team owned by Joe Matthews. The Troopers prevailed over Dallas, 37-12, in a game billed as the first true women's football game played in the south. Meanwhile, Joe's brother Robert lived out on the West Coast, so Robert Matthews decided to start a team of his own: the Los Angeles Dandelions. In July 1973, Joe packed up his Bluebonnets team and shipped them out to California to take on his brother's team. The Dallas Bluebonnets defeated the Los Angeles Dandelions, 16-12, in what was called the first true women's football game ever played on the West Coast. Within a year, Joe and Robert's brother, Stan Matthews, would also start his own women's football team, the Fort Worth Shamrocks.

Friedman's WPFL continued to operate, and the league even announced a landmark first: the first women's football championship game. The 1973 WPFL title game was held in the spring of 1974 in Berea, Ohio – the training site of the

Cleveland Browns – and the Cleveland Daredevils defeated the Dayton Fillies to win the first league championship game in women's football history.

But not even Friedman's innovative league title game could push his WPFL back to the forefront of women's football; Sid Friedman's creation had finally outgrown him. In September 1974, representatives from each of the four members of the Alliance held a meeting in Los Angeles with representatives from three new teams. These seven franchises agreed to formally organize into a new elite women's football league called the National Women's Football League (NWFL), beginning play in 1974. The launch of the NWFL made national headlines from coast to coast and ushered in a new era of women's football.

1974-1976 – The National Women's Football League

The NWFL organized in Los Angeles in September 1974 with seven franchises: the Detroit Demons, Toledo Troopers, Dallas Bluebonnets, Los Angeles Dandelions, Fort Worth Shamrocks, Columbus Pacesetters, and California Mustangs. There weren't any formal divisions, but two groups of teams naturally formed in the NWFL in 1974. The four southern teams – Dallas, Fort Worth, California, and Los Angeles – primarily played each other. Toledo, Detroit, and Columbus, on the other hand, used the Buffalo All-Stars and the occasional WPFL team to fill out their schedules.

On the field, the Toledo Troopers used the NWFL's elevated platform to show off their continued dominance within the sport. The Troopers played abbreviated schedules in 1971 and 1973, but nevertheless, they compiled three straight unbeaten seasons from 1971-1973. In the NWFL's debut season in 1974, the Troopers established themselves as the class of the new league, running out to an undefeated record for the fourth year in a row. The Troopers were led by their star running back, Linda Jefferson, and Jefferson soon found herself in the national spotlight...thanks to a little help from her teammates.

A new monthly women's sports magazine, *WomenSports*, began publication in 1974; in the spring of 1975, they held a public poll asking readers to vote for the Female Athlete of the Year. Jefferson's Trooper teammates flooded the community with ballots, and Jefferson ultimately edged volleyball's Mary Jo Peppler as the 1975 *WomenSports* Athlete of the Year. The magazine's article declared that Toledo's "mayor and entire city council sent in votes...and the last batch put Linda Jefferson over the top."

Meanwhile, the NWFL expanded to eight teams in 1975 with the addition of the San Diego Lobos. The acquisition of the Lobos paid immediate dividends, as their first contest against the Los Angeles Dandelions was broadcast on local television in the Los Angeles metro area. The game on August 17, 1975 – which was billed as the first fully televised game in women's football history – ended in a 6-6 tie.

Yet the Toledo Troopers were still the headline attraction in the NWFL's second season. The Troopers rattled off a fifth straight undefeated record, which led to even more publicity for the team and specifically for Linda Jefferson. Jefferson was chosen to compete on the popular *Women's Superstars* television show on ABC, a show which pitted elite athletes from various sports against each other in a series of athletic events resembling a decathlon. The show aired on March 7, 1976, and Jefferson placed fourth in the overall competition, garnering $2,533.00. That television appearance generated a tremendous amount of publicity for Jefferson, the Troopers, the NWFL, and women's football.

All of that publicity must have seemed pretty appealing to Sid Friedman over in the WPFL. Friedman was still cranking along with his own much-lower profile league, but the WPFL suffered a tremendous blow in June 1976. The league hosted their third league title game on June 5, 1976, and while the Cleveland Daredevils had defeated the Dayton Fillies in the first two WPFL championship games, the 1975 WPFL title game pitted the Fillies against the Middletown Mavericks. The Mavericks went on to rout the Fillies, claiming the WPFL title with a 32-6 victory.

It appeared that the WPFL now finally had a second powerful franchise to join the Cleveland Daredevils. However, the Middletown Mavericks immediately accepted an invitation to join the NWFL for their 1976 fall season, a devastating loss for the second-tier WPFL.

The NWFL continued to expand in 1976, adding five more teams for a total of 13 franchises. The NWFL then shook up the sport by announcing that for the 1976 season, the league would split their teams into three divisions and, for the first time, host their own league championship game.

The eastern division consisted of the Toledo Troopers, Detroit Demons, Columbus Pacesetters, Middletown Mavericks (from the WPFL), and the expansion Philadelphia Queen Bees. In the southern division, the Dallas Bluebonnets and Fort Worth Shamrocks merged to become the DFW Shamrocks, and they were joined in the division by four expansion teams: the Houston Herricanes, Oklahoma City Dolls, San Antonio Flames, and Tulsa Babes. Finally, in the western division, the California Mustangs renamed themselves the Pasadena Roses and joined the Los Angeles Dandelions and San Diego Lobos in a three-team western flank.

The 1976 NWFL season started with a bang. The Toledo Troopers, a team that hadn't lost in the five seasons they had been in existence, were the clear favorites to win the first true NWFL championship. But in the Troopers' 1976 NWFL opener, they traveled down to Oklahoma City to meet the expansion Dolls. On August 22, 1976, the Dolls handed Toledo an astonishing defeat in overtime, 14-8. The seemingly indomitable champs were now vulnerable, and for the first time, the Troopers had a legitimate rival. The rest of the 1976 NWFL season was simply a prelude to a rematch. Toledo and Oklahoma City dominated their respective divisions and landed in the first ever NWFL championship game.

The 1976 NWFL championship game was maybe the most highly-anticipated contest in women's football history, and it lived up to the hype. The Troopers and Dolls each scored two touchdowns, but Toledo got the edge by converting an extra point kick. The Dolls, conversely, thought they had knotted the score when a game-tying extra point kick appeared to slide inside the upright, but the attempt was ruled unsuccessful by the officials on the field. The partisan home crowd at Toledo's Glass Bowl loved the call, but the Dolls organization protested vociferously. The controversial play made the difference in the game, and the Troopers were initially awarded a 13-12 championship victory.

Oklahoma City formally protested the outcome with the NWFL, and in an unprecedented move, the league agreed to review the game tape of the contest to settle the controversy. Game film confirmed that the Dolls' extra point attempt did indeed pass through the uprights, and the league officially granted the Dolls the extra point and retroactively ruled the game a 13-13 draw. The Troopers and Dolls were, therefore, the 1976 NWFL co-champions. The controversy and ensuing draw gave the league even more publicity while setting up a compelling storyline for the 1977 season.

1977-1979 – The Dominoes Fall

What should have been the high point in women's football history was quickly marred by the announcement that the western division of the NWFL was breaking away from the rest of the league and forming their own spin-off league called the Western States Women's Professional Football League (WSWPFL). The high travel costs incurred by the West Coast teams were a burden on their involvement in the league; the San Diego Lobos, for example, played just four league games in 1976, all against the Los Angeles Dandelions. Los Angeles was so geographically isolated that they were unable to coordinate a visit from the NWFL's marquee teams, such as the Troopers. As a result, the Dandelions decided to leave the NWFL and anchor the new WSWPFL.

On paper, the WSWPFL was going to consist of the Dandelions, Hollywood Stars, Long Beach Queens, and Southland Cowgirls in California, and the Mesa American Girls, Phoenix Cowgirls, and Tucson Wild Kittens in Arizona. Whether any of these teams actually ever got off the ground is unclear; no concrete evidence exists that any of these teams truly made the jump from the planning stages to competitive play. All of the WSWPFL, including the Los Angeles Dandelions, rapidly folded, and women's football on the West Coast was finished until the twenty-first century.

The NWFL reorganized in 1977 into northern and southern divisions. There were no surprises in the two five-team divisions, with Toledo and Oklahoma City both going undefeated on their way to a rematch in the 1977 NWFL championship game. This time, there would be no controversy. The Toledo Troopers won the title outright with a 25-14 victory over the Dolls. It was a fitting coronation for what most considered to be the greatest women's football team in history; for the first time, the Troopers triumphed in a league championship game.

As the 1978 season approached, Sid Friedman's WPFL was still limping along. But the Cleveland Daredevils were the only remaining team in that league of any consequence, and the WPFL finally decided to surrender and enter into merger talks with the NWFL. As part of those discussions, the WPFL champion Daredevils agreed to two contests against the NWFL champion Troopers in 1978. These games were hyped as the battle of the champions and marked Toledo's first games against a team from the WPFL since their departure from that league in 1972. The two contests were a letdown, however, as Toledo triumphed in both games by a combined 85-0 score.

The NWFL again featured northern and southern divisions in the 1978 season, and one of their playoff games generated substantial media attention. In the 1978 Northern Division championship game between the Troopers and the Columbus Pacesetters, the NWFL made national news by inviting male reporters into the teams' locker rooms for interviews. It was an amusing play on an ongoing controversy at the time about whether or not female reporters should be allowed in the locker rooms of men's professional sports teams. On the field, the Pacesetters nearly shocked the reigning champions, succumbing to a 12-7 defeat as the Troopers advanced to their third consecutive league championship game.

The NWFL gave women's football fans exactly what they wanted in the 1978 NWFL championship game: an Oklahoma City-Toledo contest for the third straight year. This time, however, the Dolls responded with a terrific defensive performance and became the first team to ever shut out the Troopers, winning the 1978 NWFL title with an 8-0 victory. With the win, the Oklahoma City Dolls secured their own place in women's football history. The Dolls were not nearly as well-known or popular as the Troopers, but they were just as proud and successful a franchise, as witnessed by their three meetings in NWFL championship games...which resulted in a record of 1-1-1, each team claiming one victory and one game ending in a tie.

After the 1978 season, the WPFL mercifully collapsed. The remnants of the Cleveland Daredevils franchise reformed as the Cleveland Brewers and became an expansion NWFL team, while the rest of the league folded. Now only the NWFL remained, but little did anyone know, the NWFL was about to suffer a severe blow.

As the 1979 season began, the Troopers and Dolls were, as usual, the favorites in their respective divisions. However, early in the 1979 season, Toledo was soundly defeated by the Columbus Pacesetters, 35-12. It was just the third loss in the Troopers' history and the first by a team other than Oklahoma City. Moreover, it was by far the largest margin of defeat the Troopers had ever suffered, and it signaled that Toledo's dominating run in the sport was over.

Oklahoma City easily won the southern division and advanced to the 1979 NWFL championship game for the fourth straight year. But the Troopers were taken down again in the Northern Division championship game by the Pacesetters. It was a stunning loss, and it took much of the excitement out of the league championship game, which now pitted Oklahoma City against Columbus. In fact, Toledo's absence from the game sapped so much interest out of the contest that the 1979 NWFL championship game was cancelled entirely. The fourth NWFL title game never took place, a sign that the league was in serious trouble.

The cancelled title game was the first of several dominoes to fall that devastated the sport that offseason. In a seemingly innocuous move, the Lawton Tornadoes, a franchise that had just completed its first year in the NWFL, announced that they would not be able to field a team in 1980. But Lawton's folding led to a chain reaction in which, due to a lack of local competition, the entire southern division of the NWFL folded, including the iconic Oklahoma City Dolls. With no local franchises to play, the legendary Dolls were forced to close up shop.

The northern division of the NWFL was now all that remained of women's football. As if the sport hadn't suffered enough that offseason, the Toledo Troopers then announced that they, too, were folding. The NWFL lost its two most successful franchises in the span of months, and the sport of women's football found itself confined to the upper Midwest for the first time since 1973.

1980-1998 – Women's Football Goes On Hiatus

The NWFL tried to carry on in 1980, led by the Columbus Pacesetters and the Daredevils' successors, the Cleveland Brewers. Columbus, which had suffered many lopsided, demoralizing losses for years at the hands of the Toledo Troopers, had finally overcome the Troopers in the 1979 NWFL playoffs. The Pacesetters celebrated their magical triumph only to find that, ironically, their victory led to the cancellation of the league's title game and hastened the collapse of the Troopers, which dealt a crippling blow to the mainstream popularity and recognition of the entire sport.

Cleveland and Columbus formed the foundation of a new regional NWFL and were joined in 1981 by teams in Cincinnati and Battle Creek, Michigan. After limping along for three years, the NWFL attempted a major comeback in 1983. The biggest news for the league was the addition of a new team in Toledo called the Toledo Furies. Made up of a few of the greats from the Troopers' era, the Furies offered a link back to the glory days of the league's past.

Cleveland, Columbus, and Toledo formed the core of the NWFL in 1983 and even staged a championship game, the league's first known championship game since 1978. The Cleveland Brewers claimed the 1983 NWFL title with a 43-6 victory over the Columbus Pacesetters. The following year, the NWFL held their second championship game in a row, and the title went back to a familiar location. The Furies brought the NWFL championship back to Toledo by knocking off the defending champion Cleveland Brewers, 34-6.

By 1985, there were reportedly five teams in the NWFL: the Columbus Pacesetters, Cleveland Brewers, Toledo Furies, Grand Rapids Carpenters, and Lansing Unicorns. The Grand Rapids Carpenters claimed the final NWFL championship in league history in 1985 before the NWFL breathed its last gasp.

The league took a year off in 1986, and the following year the two remaining franchises – the Cleveland Brewers and Columbus Pacesetters – converted into women's flag football teams. With that, full-contact women's football entered a deep freeze for 14 years before returning for good in 1999.

Women's Football Teams, 1967-1985

The following is a list of all known women's football teams from 1967 – the founding of the Cleveland Daredevils, the charter member of Sid Friedman's WPFL – through 1985, the year the NWFL collapsed. Confirmed teams are listed along with the years in which they are known to have played at least one contest. Proposed teams were discussed in the media but have no record of actually playing a game.

Confirmed teams

Team	Years	Notes
Cleveland Daredevils	1967-78	Also known as USA Daredevils (1967-70)
Pittsburgh Hurricanes	1968-74	Known as USA All-Stars (1968); Hurricanes (1969-71, '73-74); Powderkegs (1971-72)
Toronto Canadian Belles	1969-70	
Toledo Troopers	1971-79	
Buffalo All-Stars	1971-74	
Detroit Fillies	1971-72	Midwest Cowgirls (1972) called separate team; had same owner and swapped players
New York Fillies	1972	Renamed Long Island Herricanes (1974); no confirmed games under that name
Detroit Demons	1973-77	
Los Angeles Dandelions	1973-76	Reportedly rejoined NWFL (1980); no confirmed games after 1976
Akron Wildcats	1973-75	Renamed Akron Rams (1975)
Dallas Bluebonnets	1973-74	Merged with Fort Worth Shamrocks and became DFW Shamrocks (1976)
Toledo Roadrunners	1973	Also known as Northwest Ohio Roadrunners (1973)
Columbus Pacesetters	1974-84	
California Mustangs	1974-75	Renamed Pasadena Roses (1975)
Fort Worth Shamrocks	1974-75	Merged with Dallas Bluebonnets and became DFW Shamrocks (1976)
Dayton Fillies	1974	
San Antonio Roses	1974	Renamed San Antonio Flames (1975)
Middletown Mavericks	1975-79	
San Diego Lobos	1975-76	
Columbus Joan of Arks	1975	
Oklahoma City Dolls	1976-79	Failed attempted revival (1982)
DFW Shamrocks	1976-77	Merger of Fort Worth Shamrocks and Dallas Bluebonnets (1976)
Philadelphia Queen Bees	1976	
San Antonio Flames	1976	
Houston Herricanes	1977-79	
Tulsa Babes	1978	
Cleveland Brewers	1979-85	
Lawton Tornadoes	1979	
Battle Creek Rainbows	1981	Renamed Kalamazoo Rainbows (1982); no confirmed games under that name
Cincinnati Mavericks	1981	
Toledo Furies	1983-85	
Lansing Unicorns	1984-85	
Grand Rapids Carpenters	1984-85	

Exhibition teams
San Francisco Busters and San Jose Knockers played a 1974 exhibition game and merged into the San Jose Ravens.

Proposed teams
Detroit Petticoats (1969)
Texas (Fort Worth) Fireflies (1974)
San Jose Ravens (1975)
Chicago Sirens (1976)
Hollywood Stars (1978)
Long Beach Queens (1978)
Mesa (AZ) American Girls (1978)
Phoenix Cowgirls (1978)
Southland (CA) Cowgirls (1978)
Tucson (AZ) Wild Kittens (1978)
Atlanta Angels (1979)
Redmond (WA) Sex Killers (1979)
Seattle Lakers (1979)
Los Angeles Scandals (1984)

Confirmed Women's Football Games, 1967-1985

Below is every confirmed women's football game played from 1967-1985. This is a partial list and several games are assuredly missing, but these are some of the biggest games that were promoted in newspapers and media at the time.

The acronym EDU means that the exact date of the game is unknown. Games that were advertised in the media but where the outcome is unclear (and where it is uncertain if the game ever even took place) are coded as having a score of 1-1. Games where the final score is unknown but where we know which team prevailed are coded as a 1-0 victory for the confirmed victor.

1967-1970
Date	Team 1	Score	Team 2	Score	Notes
11/25/1967	Erie Pussycats Media (men)	31	Cleveland Daredevils	27	
11/29/1968	Cleveland Daredevils	8	Pittsburgh (USA) All-Stars	8	
7/26/1969	Cleveland Daredevils	28	Toronto Canadian Belles	16	
9/14/1969	Pittsburgh Hurricanes	1	Cleveland Daredevils	1	
EDU 1970	Toronto Canadian Belles	1	Pittsburgh Hurricanes	1	
10/18/1970	Toronto Canadian Belles	1	Cleveland Daredevils	1	
10/24/1970	Cleveland Daredevils	32	Pittsburgh Hurricanes	6	

1971
Date	Team 1	Score	Team 2	Score	Notes
EDU 1971	Toledo Troopers	48	Cleveland Daredevils	12	
EDU 1971	Toledo Troopers	46	Cleveland Daredevils	16	
10/16/1971	Pittsburgh Powderkegs	8	Detroit Fillies	0	
10/16/1971	Toledo Troopers	25	Buffalo All-Stars	6	First game played in Toledo, OH
10/23/1971	Cleveland Daredevils	28	Pittsburgh Hurricanes	0	Game clips shown on CBS NFL pre-game show
10/30/1971	Pittsburgh Hurricanes	1	Cleveland Daredevils	1	
11/6/1971	Toledo Troopers	30	Cleveland Daredevils	6	
11/13/1971	Detroit Fillies	16	Pittsburgh Powderkegs	12	
11/27/1971	*Pittsburgh Powderkegs*	--	*Detroit Fillies*	--	*Postponed from 11/20 and cancelled*

1972
Date	Team 1	Score	Team 2	Score	Notes
EDU 1972	Toledo Troopers	36	Cleveland Daredevils	0	
EDU 1972	Toledo Troopers	39	Detroit Fillies	0	
EDU 1972	Toledo Troopers	37	Buffalo All-Stars	16	
EDU 1972	Toledo Troopers	25	Detroit Fillies	0	
EDU 1972	Toledo Troopers	28	Buffalo All-Stars	2	
EDU 1972	Toledo Troopers	34	New York Fillies	0	
EDU 1972	Toledo Troopers	35	Cleveland Daredevils	0	
5/13/1972	Midwest Cowgirls	28	New York Fillies	0	First game played in New York, NY
5/20/1972	*Pittsburgh Powderkegs*	--	*New York Fillies*	--	*Cancelled*
6/24/1972	New York Fillies	1	Detroit Fillies	1	
8/12/1972	New York Fillies	1	Detroit Fillies	1	
11/4/1972	Toledo Troopers	64	Cleveland Daredevils	14	
11/11/1972	Cleveland Daredevils	1	Buffalo All-Stars	1	

1973
Date	Team 1	Score	Team 2	Score	Notes
EDU 1973	Toledo Troopers	20	Dallas Bluebonnets	0	
EDU 1973	Toledo Troopers	43	Detroit Demons	0	
2/18/1973	Toledo Troopers	37	Dallas Bluebonnets	12	First game played in the southern United States
4/28/1973	Dallas Bluebonnets	19	Detroit Demons	0	
6/22/1973	Cleveland Daredevils	6	Detroit Demons	0	
7/22/1973	Dallas Bluebonnets	16	Los Angeles Dandelions	12	First game played in Los Angeles, CA
8/18/1973	Los Angeles Dandelions	25	Detroit Demons	0	Game syndicated and broadcast nationally
9/8/1973	Los Angeles Dandelions	1	Dallas Bluebonnets	1	
9/15/1973	Toledo Troopers	41	Detroit Demons	0	
9/22/1973	Dayton Fillies	1	Akron Wildcats	1	
9/22/1973	Pittsburgh Hurricanes	1	Cleveland Daredevils	1	
10/20/1973	Cleveland Daredevils	34	Akron Wildcats	0	
11/3/1973	Dayton Fillies	1	Akron Wildcats	1	
11/10/1973	Toledo Roadrunners	1	Cleveland Daredevils	1	
12/2/1973	Cleveland Daredevils	1	Dayton Fillies	0	
12/22/1973	Los Angeles Dandelions	1	Dallas Bluebonnets	0	

1974

Date	Team	Score	Opponent	Score	Notes
EDU 1974	Toledo Troopers	30	Detroit Demons	0	
EDU 1974	Cleveland Daredevils	1	Dayton Fillies	0	1973 WPFL Championship Game
1/19/1974	Dallas Bluebonnets	16	Fort Worth Shamrocks	6	
4/27/1974	Fort Worth Shamrocks	1	Dallas Bluebonnets	1	
8/10/1974	Los Angeles Dandelions	20	California Mustangs	0	
8/10/1974	Cleveland Daredevils	28	Dayton Fillies	12	
8/24/1974	Columbus Pacesetters	12	Cleveland Daredevils	0	
9/21/1974	Toledo Troopers	52	Columbus Pacesetters	0	
9/28/1974	Dayton Fillies	1	Akron Wildcats	1	
9/28/1974	Toledo Troopers	69	Columbus Pacesetters	14	
9/29/1974	Los Angeles Dandelions	1	Dallas Bluebonnets	1	
10/12/1974	Pittsburgh Hurricanes	1	Columbus Pacesetters	1	
10/12/1974	Toledo Troopers	47	Detroit Demons	0	
10/26/1974	Toledo Troopers	50	Columbus Pacesetters	0	
11/2/1974	Toledo Troopers	30	Buffalo All-Stars	8	
11/9/1974	San Antonio Roses	6	Fort Worth Shamrocks	0	

1975

Date	Team	Score	Opponent	Score	Notes
EDU 1975	San Diego Lobos	31	Fort Worth Shamrocks	6	
EDU 1975	Toledo Troopers	20	Detroit Demons	18	
EDU 1975	Cleveland Daredevils	1	Dayton Fillies	0	1974 WPFL Championship Game
8/17/1975	San Diego Lobos	6	Los Angeles Dandelions	6	First fully televised game
8/23/1975	Detroit Demons	7	Columbus Pacesetters	7	
8/24/1975	San Diego Lobos	31	Fort Worth Shamrocks	6	
8/30/1975	Toledo Troopers	25	Columbus Pacesetters	6	
9/6/1975	Detroit Demons	33	Columbus Pacesetters	26	
9/7/1975	San Diego Lobos	14	Los Angeles Dandelions	13	
9/13/1975	Middletown Mavericks	1	Dayton Fillies	1	
9/13/1975	Toledo Troopers	44	Columbus Pacesetters	7	
9/14/1975	San Diego Lobos	58	Pasadena Roses	0	
9/20/1975	Toledo Troopers	25	Detroit Demons	6	
9/21/1975	Los Angeles Dandelions	26	San Diego Lobos	6	
9/28/1975	San Diego Lobos	38	Pasadena Roses	0	
10/5/1975	Los Angeles Dandelions	1	Fort Worth Shamrocks	1	
10/11/1975	Middletown Mavericks	1	Akron Rams	1	
10/11/1975	Los Angeles Dandelions	24	San Diego Lobos	18	
10/18/1975	Toledo Troopers	12	Fort Worth Shamrocks	6	
10/25/1975	Toledo Troopers	19	Detroit Demons	7	
11/1/1975	Toledo Troopers	25	Detroit Demons	12	
11/8/1975	Middletown Mavericks	1	Cleveland Daredevils	1	
11/8/1975	Toledo Troopers	26	Columbus Pacesetters	12	
11/22/1975	Middletown Mavericks	1	Columbus Joan of Arks	1	

1976

Date	Team	Score	Opponent	Score	Notes
EDU 1976	Toledo Troopers	6	Philadelphia Queen Bees	0	
EDU 1976	Toledo Troopers	20	Detroit Demons	14	
EDU 1976	Toledo Troopers	26	Detroit Demons	0	
EDU 1976	Toledo Troopers	18	Columbus Pacesetters	0	
6/5/1976	Middletown Mavericks	32	Dayton Fillies	6	1975 WPFL Championship Game
7/24/1976	DFW Shamrocks	7	Oklahoma City Dolls	0	
8/22/1976	Oklahoma City Dolls	14	Toledo Troopers	8	OT; First documented overtime game
8/29/1976	Toledo Troopers	32	Columbus Pacesetters	7	
9/4/1976	Toledo Troopers	12	Detroit Demons	6	
9/5/1976	Oklahoma City Dolls	28	Los Angeles Dandelions	7	
9/11/1976	Toledo Troopers	64	Philadelphia Queen Bees	0	
9/18/1976	Toledo Troopers	44	Detroit Demons	8	
9/26/1976	Los Angeles Dandelions	20	San Diego Lobos	0	
10/2/1976	Toledo Troopers	34	Columbus Pacesetters	6	
10/10/1976	Los Angeles Dandelions	1	DFW Shamrocks	0	
10/24/1976	San Diego Lobos	25	Los Angeles Dandelions	20	
10/30/1976	Toledo Troopers	32	Middletown Mavericks	6	
11/13/1976	San Antonio Flames	1	DFW Shamrocks	1	
EDU 1976	Oklahoma City Dolls	18	DFW Shamrocks	14	NWFL Southern Conference Championship
12/11/1976	Toledo Troopers	13	Oklahoma City Dolls	13	1976 NWFL Championship Game

Confirmed Women's Football Games, 1967-1985

1977
EDU 1977	Toledo Troopers	78	Philadelphia Queen Bees	0
EDU 1977	Toledo Troopers	26	Detroit Demons	6
6/25/1977	Oklahoma City Dolls	22	DFW Shamrocks	14
8/20/1977	Columbus Pacesetters	29	Middletown Mavericks	0
8/27/1977	Toledo Troopers	40	Columbus Pacesetters	0
8/27/1977	Oklahoma City Dolls	34	Houston Herricanes	6
9/17/1977	Toledo Troopers	62	Middletown Mavericks	0
9/24/1977	Toledo Troopers	62	Middletown Mavericks	0
10/1/1977	Toledo Troopers	35	Columbus Pacesetters	6
10/8/1977	Toledo Troopers	59	Detroit Demons	0
10/29/1977	Toledo Troopers	25	Oklahoma City Dolls	14 1977 NWFL Championship Game

1978
EDU 1978	Oklahoma City Dolls	1	Houston Herricanes	1
EDU 1978	Toledo Troopers	52	Cleveland Daredevils	0
EDU 1978	Toledo Troopers	20	Columbus Pacesetters	0
7/29/1978	Oklahoma City Dolls	54	Tulsa Babes	0
8/19/1978	Columbus Pacesetters	30	Middletown Mavericks	0 Exhibition game
8/26/1978	Toledo Troopers	40	Middletown Mavericks	0 Exhibition game
9/16/1978	Columbus Pacesetters	14	Middletown Mavericks	0
9/23/1978	Toledo Troopers	28	Middletown Mavericks	17
9/30/1978	Toledo Troopers	33	Middletown Mavericks	0
10/7/1978	Toledo Troopers	6	Columbus Pacesetters	0
10/14/1978	Toledo Troopers	33	Cleveland Daredevils	0
10/21/1978	Toledo Troopers	12	Columbus Pacesetters	7 NWFL Northern Conference Championship
11/11/1978	Oklahoma City Dolls	8	Toledo Troopers	0 1978 NWFL Championship Game

1979
8/25/1979	Toledo Troopers	1	Middletown Mavericks	0
8/25/1979	Columbus Pacesetters	1	Cleveland Brewers	0 Exhibition game
8/25/1979	Lawton Tornadoes	12	Houston Herricanes	0
9/8/1979	Columbus Pacesetters	30	Middletown Mavericks	14
9/8/1979	Houston Herricanes	7	Oklahoma City Dolls	6
9/15/1979	Columbus Pacesetters	30	Toledo Troopers	12
9/22/1979	Columbus Pacesetters	1	Cleveland Brewers	0 Exhibition game
9/22/1979	Toledo Troopers	20	Middletown Mavericks	8
9/29/1979	Columbus Pacesetters	1	Middletown Mavericks	0
10/6/1979	Toledo Troopers	25	Columbus Pacesetters	7
10/13/1979	Toledo Troopers	1	Middletown Mavericks	0
10/20/1979	Toledo Troopers	1	Middletown Mavericks	0 NWFL Northern Conference Semifinal Playoff
10/27/1979	Columbus Pacesetters	1	Toledo Troopers	0 NWFL Northern Conference Championship
EDU 1979	*Oklahoma City Dolls*	*--*	*Columbus Pacesetters*	*-- 1979 NWFL Championship Game (cancelled)*

1980-1982
EDU 1980	Columbus Pacesetters	1	Cleveland Brewers	1
8/29/1981	Columbus Pacesetters	65	Battle Creek Rainbows	0
9/12/1981	Cleveland Brewers	25	Battle Creek Rainbows	0
9/26/1981	Battle Creek Rainbows	1	Cincinnati Mavericks	0 Forfeit victory
10/3/1981	Cincinnati Mavericks	12	Battle Creek Rainbows	12
10/10/1981	Columbus Pacesetters	52	Battle Creek Rainbows	0
10/18/1981	Cleveland Brewers	25	Battle Creek Rainbows	0

1983-1985
8/27/1983	Columbus Pacesetters	32	Toledo Furies	14
10/15/1983	Columbus Pacesetters	35	Toledo Furies	18
10/22/1983	Toledo Furies	13	Cleveland Brewers	6
11/9/1983	Cleveland Brewers	43	Columbus Pacesetters	6 1983 NWFL Championship Game
8/19/1984	Toledo Furies	32	Columbus Pacesetters	0
8/25/1984	Toledo Furies	36	Grand Rapids Carpenters	0
9/8/1984	Toledo Furies	1	Grand Rapids Carpenters	1
9/29/1984	Toledo Furies	40	Cleveland Brewers	13
10/7/1984	Toledo Furies	26	Lansing Unicorns	3
10/20/1984	Toledo Furies	32	Columbus Pacesetters	0
10/27/1984	Cleveland Brewers	21	Columbus Pacesetters	14
11/3/1984	Toledo Furies	34	Cleveland Brewers	6 1984 NWFL Championship Game
9/9/1985	Toledo Furies	38	Lansing Unicorns	0
9/22/1985	Cleveland Brewers	20	Toledo Furies	19

History of Women's Football in the 21st Century

An Explosion of Leagues (1999-2003)

The modern era of women's football began on October 9, 1999. Two years after the founding of the WNBA and just three months after Brandi Chastain's famous celebration at the '99 Women's World Cup, it was appropriate timing for the relaunch of women's football. Carter Turner and Terry Sullivan, who both had experience in minor league football, recruited female athletes from across the nation and organized an exhibition game at Midway Stadium in St. Paul, Minnesota. The Lake Michigan Minx defeated the Minnesota Vixens, 33-6, before an announced crowd of 2,463.

This exhibition game received a large amount of press – even from national outlets like *Sports Illustrated* and *ESPN the Magazine* – and the response from fans was overwhelmingly positive. The Minx and Vixens then hit the road that autumn. The six-game "No Limits" Barnstorming Tour took the two teams to cities like Chicago and Green Bay before concluding the tour in Uniondale, New York. The Vixens challenged the Long Island Sharks, a well-known area female flag football team, to a full-contact game; the newly-dubbed New York Sharks upset the Vixens, 12-6, on December 11, 1999, in an entertaining contest.

The following year, Turner and Sullivan expanded that barnstorming tour into the first modern women's football league, appropriately called the Women's Professional Football League (WPFL) after Sid Friedman's original venture three decades earlier. The Vixens and Sharks were two of the 11 founding franchises of the WPFL in 2000, but the league nearly collapsed as soon as it began. Expenses exceeded projections and accusations flew as revenues seemed to go missing. Bills went unpaid and road trips were cancelled. A hastily-arranged title game ended the shortened season prematurely, and the WPFL almost crashed after just one season.

In spite of the WPFL's struggles, interest in women's football skyrocketed. Two women's football leagues decided to take the field in the spring, rather than the fall, and these two leagues would go on to develop a major rivalry that continues in many ways to this day.

Catherine Masters founded the National Women's Football League (NWFL), adopting the same name as the other major 20th century women's football league. Masters had originally intended to own a Nashville team in the WPFL, but she disagreed with several aspects of how the league was being run and left to start her own venture. The NWFL's launch followed the WPFL's playbook, with a barnstorming tour in the fall of 2000 setting the stage for a full league debut in the spring of 2001.

The Independent Women's Football League (IWFL) began play with an exhibition season in 2001 and expanded to a full season the following year. Laurie Frederick was one of the league's co-founders and still serves as the IWFL's CEO 15 years later. Frederick was joined some time later in the IWFL leadership group by Kezia Disney, who started with the league as the owner of the IWFL's Oregon Thunder in 2002.

The NWFL and IWFL carved out a foothold on spring women's football. Back in the fall, Carter Turner left his post as commissioner of the WPFL and founded a new league called the Women's American Football League (WAFL). As the WPFL sought to regain its financial footing under the collective ownership of remaining team owners, the WAFL emerged as the dominant fall women's football league in 2001. But the dysfunction that existed within the WPFL followed Turner to his new venture, and after just one season, the WAFL shattered into three pieces.

The WAFL's collapse along with the continued growth of the sport led to an unprecedented surge in the number of women's football leagues. Deep breath – in 2002, there were *nine* documented women's football leagues split between the spring and the fall: the AFWL, the IWFL, the NWFL, the UWFL, the WAFC, the WAFL-WFA, the WFL, the WPFL, and the WSFL. It would be an understatement to acknowledge that having nine different leagues created a fair amount of confusion for fans of the sport. It fractured the support base and split the enthusiasm for women's football across too many organizations.

With that said, the landscape actually cleared up quite quickly. Many of these leagues were designed to be regional in scope in an effort to minimize travel costs. These small regional leagues very rapidly began to chain together and coalesce into three large, national leagues. Within one year, most of these small regional leagues evaporated, leaving only the WPFL, IWFL, and NWFL and ushering in the tri-champions era.

The Tri-Champions Era (2003-2007)

Three leagues had attained prominence in the sport by 2003. The WPFL recovered enough to become the only women's football league that operated in the fall, while the IWFL and NWFL battled for supremacy in the spring. The sport entered a five-year period of relative stability, with these three leagues dominating the landscape.

The biggest change in 2003 was a cosmetic one, driven by a rare instance of women's football actually being acknowledged by the men's side. The National Women's Football League took its name from the premier women's league of the twentieth century, a league that was founded in 1974. This was now the twenty-first century, however, and the NFL expressed concerns in 2003 over the NWFL's name.

With the myriad of women's leagues that cropped up in 2002, the NFL – which didn't and still doesn't formally endorse or support any women's league – feared that the similarity of the NWFL's name to theirs might mislead fans into thinking they had some kind of formal arrangement with that particular league. The NFL also objected to the NWFL's use of the term "SupHer Bowl" as their title game and the similarity of a few team logos to those of local NFL franchises. Under pressure from the NFL, the NWFL agreed to make several changes, including altering their name to the NWFA – the National Women's Football Association.

From 2003-2007, there were three major women's football leagues – the NWFA, the IWFL, and the WPFL – and all three presented dueling dynasties. The NWFA had the largest (and by many accounts, the strongest) league in women's football. Their marquee team, the Detroit Demolition, put together a remarkable run of four consecutive league championships from 2002-2005 and was widely recognized as the top team in the sport.

But the IWFL and WPFL had solid leagues and dominant teams of their own. The IWFL's Sacramento Sirens won three straight championships from 2003-2005, while the WPFL's Dallas Diamonds also pulled off a three-peat from 2004-2006. Fans, naturally, clamored for a don't-call-it-a-SupHer-Bowl between these three teams – particularly between the IWFL and NWFA champions, since those two leagues both operated in the spring. Yet these leagues just couldn't get together to agree on an interleague matchup between their champions, with each league fearful of having their entire organization lose credibility with a lopsided title game loss.

The sport reached a stalemate for several years, with the IWFL, NWFA, and WPFL champions all being regarded as "tri-champions" of women's football. Fans waited for something to break the deadlock and for the emergence of one dominant league within the sport, and by 2008, they would get their wish.

The unification began when the Demolition, the sport's most dominant team and the four-time defending NWFA champions, left the NWFA for the IWFL after the 2005 season. In their absence, the D.C. Divas won the 2006 NWFA championship and promptly left the league as well, chasing the Demolition to the IWFL. In 2007, the Pittsburgh Passion captured the NWFA crown and they, too, immediately bolted for the IWFL.

These three major defections pushed the IWFL ahead of the NWFA in visibility as the sport's premier spring league. NWFA teams reportedly began to bristle under what was seen as autocratic leadership from Masters, and with the arrival of the Passion, the IWFL acquired the winners of the last six NWFA championships. As the IWFL started to establish itself as the dominant spring league competitively, other women's football teams gravitated toward it, which reinforced its position.

At the same time, the WPFL began to falter. Women's football teams and leagues had debated for years over the best season for women's football. Was it the spring and summer months, when women's football could operate without having to compete directly against immensely popular NFL and major college football teams? Or was it the fall and winter, the season that most sports fans already associate with football?

From its inception, the WPFL staked its claim on the fall/winter season, but the spring/summer months were proving far more popular. Operating in the fall and winter became a large burden for the WPFL, which had to compete against the NFL and major colleges for fan attention and attendance and – perhaps more tellingly – found most local high schools and colleges unwilling to share facilities with them while their own seasons were underway. The WPFL, the original modern women's football league, closed up shop after the 2007 season, and fall/winter women's football took its final bow with it.

The IWFL Takes Control and the Advent of Lingerie Football (2008-2010)

For the first time since 2000, there was an undisputed top league in women's football in 2008. The IWFL was the largest league in the sport with over forty active teams, and it also had most of the marquee franchises in women's football. However, the IWFL had a number of newer and less-developed franchises, and the variation in skill levels and financial support among member teams was wide. To combat this problem, the IWFL introduced a two-tiered system of competition. Essentially operating as major and minor leagues, Tier I teams were the league's strongest and most powerful clubs, while Tier II teams were often weaker franchises in smaller markets.

Tier I teams used Tier II teams to fill out their schedules, but Tier II teams competed in a completely separate postseason tournament. Franchises were also given the opportunity for free passage between tiers. A Tier I team that was struggling, on or off the field, could drop down to Tier II without going out of business completely. On the other hand, a dominant Tier II team would have the chance to eventually step up to the top tier. While there was never any formal process for this, it had the potential to provide for the same type of promotion and relegation used in soccer leagues worldwide but virtually unheard of in American sports.

After seeing her league demoted to minor league status within the sport, Catherine Masters shut the NWFA down following the 2008 season. Some of the remaining teams left for the IWFL, but most of the franchises from the old NWFA reorganized into a new league. The new league simply dropped the N and rebranded into the Women's Football Alliance (WFA) for the 2009 season, picking up where the NWFA left off.

With Masters gone, Jeff King, a former semi-pro football player, and his wife Lisa, a women's football wide receiver, took ownership of the WFA. In addition to owning the league as a whole, the Kings started a WFA team in Fresno, California, called the Central Cal War Angels. The WFA began with 35 teams in 2009 but was still well behind the IWFL as the top competitive league in the sport.

The IWFL was the top competitive league but not the most recognized one. Another league popped up in 2009 and began making headlines, though mostly for the wrong reasons. That year Mitch Mortaza started an indoor, seven-player-a-side enterprise called the Lingerie Football League (LFL), introducing a new format of women's football called "lingerie football". While the LFL remains the original and most popular lingerie football league, several other organizations have tried their hands at lingerie football in recent years.

Lingerie football gets far more media attention and draws more fans than traditional women's football, for reasons that can be easily seen and need not be specified. The LFL, in particular, uses the size of its fanbase and the amount of media coverage it generates to suggest that it's the highest level of women's football, an assertion that is patently ridiculous. Not only is the LFL not the highest level of women's football, lingerie football is not even a legitimate sport, as players are vetted first and foremost based on appearance and not football talent.

The LFL is and has always been, on that basis alone, more spectacle than sport – athletic theater more akin to mud wrestling than actual football. (For more information on the abomination known as lingerie football, see Chapter 5 beginning on page 357.) When women's football is discussed in the popular media and elsewhere, a reference or discussion of lingerie football is almost inevitable due to the titillating nature of the faux-sport. Meanwhile, legitimate women's football – with only minor modifications to the popular sport that men play – continues to soldier on with considerably less fanfare.

Back in traditional football, the IWFL and WFA were joined in 2010 by a third league – the Women's Spring Football League (WSFL). Randall Fields, who presided over the original WSFL in its one season in 2002, resurrected his league eight years later. The WSFL had an exhibition season in 2010 before embarking on its inaugural league schedule in 2011. Fields also launched an eight-player division of the WSFL, which was later rebranded as its own league, the W8FL.

Yet the IWFL had the most history, the strongest teams, and the largest membership of any women's football league. The IWFL enjoyed a three-year run from 2008-2010 as the dominant league in the sport, and it looked as though the IWFL was primed for a long period of control. But looks can be deceiving.

The Rise of the WFA and the Current State of Women's Football (2011-2015)

The Supergroup Defection of 2010 completely shifted the balance of power within the sport. At the conclusion of the 2010 season, ten of the IWFL's 18 existing Tier I franchises – referred to by observers as the "Supergroup" – almost simultaneously announced they were departing from the league. These ten teams initially had plans to create their own elite league in women's football that could launch the sport to even higher recognition, but those plans quickly fell through.

After a period of deliberation, the ten former IWFL franchises collectively declared that they would be joining the WFA. Included in the Supergroup were the IWFL's last three league champions and five of their last six conference champions. Bolstered by these additions, the WFA went from being well behind the IWFL in popularity to the sport's showcase league in a single offseason. The IWFL responded to those losses by abandoning their two-tiered format and collapsing their two tiers back into a single league.

Today, there are three main leagues in women's football – the WFA, the IWFL, and the WSFL. There is also a clear hierarchy between the three. Fields sold the WSFL to former Erie Illusion owner Mary Butler in 2014, and under Butler's leadership, the WSFL has announced its intention to rebrand as the United States Women's Football League (USWFL) beginning with the 2016 season. Whether called the WSFL or USWFL, this small developmental league – catering to teams in smaller markets or with limited rosters – remains the #3 league in the sport.

Both in terms of quantity and, more importantly, quality of teams, the IWFL has been the clear #2 league in women's football in the United States since the Supergroup Defection of 2010. The IWFL has a tremendous history, having completed its 15th season of continuous operation in 2015; that makes the IWFL the longest-running women's football league in the history of the sport.

Still, the IWFL has been relegated to minor league status within the sport for the past half-decade, and it has had a hard time swallowing that position. With their history as the top league in women's football from 2008-2010 and with 15 years of established name recognition, the IWFL has never really accepted their secondary role in the sport, continuing to advance misleading marketing slogans like "The Best Play Here". Thanks largely to that marketing, many fans clamor for a WFA-IWFL merger, which would create a single elite league in women's football that everyone in the sport could recognize.

Whether the IWFL and its ardent supporters accept it or not, the Women's Football Alliance is the top league in women's football at the present time. The WFA has enjoyed five seasons as the premier league in women's football, the longest undisputed run atop the sport for any league since the NWFL from 1974-1985. With over forty teams from coast to coast, the WFA is the largest league in the sport. More importantly, the WFA boasts the vast majority of the most dominant, elite, and historic franchises in women's football.

What does the future hold for women's football? That question is impossible to answer. As you can see, the history of women's football has been defined by instability and constant change. Perhaps the most promising sign for the future of women's football is that the quality of play – particularly at the highest level – continues to rapidly improve. The best women's football teams now perform at a level on the field which would be entertaining to a casual fan on television and which is more recognizable as "football" than "women's football". Off the field, these teams have developed small but loyal cult followings, and they maintain a professional image through social media and overall football operations that could set the foundation for major outside support in the future.

On the other hand, the challenge for women's football is expanding the number of elite teams that operate at that level…enough teams to form a truly elite league that would merit a television contract. In the meantime, the sport continues to struggle to find a way – in the absence of major financial support or a broadcast television deal – to attract more attention to the great sport of women's football. The absence of a national platform has made the growth of the sport a slow climb, with a patchwork of regional grassroots efforts on behalf of local clubs fusing together to represent a national movement.

In a sea of change, one thing does appear certain: after 17 continuous seasons, we can finally declare that women's football, in some form or fashion, is here to stay. The women playing football today carry on a proud tradition started by thousands of athletes before them, and in the same way, their efforts will inspire generations of women to come.

League Database Legend

Sixteen of the largest women's football leagues since 1999 are covered in the following chapter. Some smaller leagues, such as the IWFL's Sixxes League (IWFL6) from 2005-2008, the Ladies Tackle Football League (LTFL), the Women's Xtreme Football League (WXFL), and the New Mexico Women's Adult Football League (NMWAFL), among others, are not included in the next section.

Every season since 1999 has been broken down by league and is listed chronologically in the following chapter. Each league season begins with a brief paragraph recap of news and notes from the league that year. This is followed by a line of league data, split into three columns.

The first column of league data is the classification of the competition level of the league that season. Leagues are classified as Major National Leagues, Minor National Leagues, Regional Leagues, or Exhibition Leagues. For the definitions and classifications of each, see page 347.

The second column of league data is the number of teams that participated in the league that season. This number includes all teams associated with the league, including affiliate teams playing limited schedules and independent teams playing the majority of their schedules against league teams. A second parenthetical number often follows the first number, indicating the number of full-member teams involved in the league that season. Full-member teams are non-affiliate teams playing complete schedules who had a full and fair opportunity to compete for the league championship that season. If every team associated with the league that season was a full-member team, only one number will appear.

The third column of league data is the number of games held by the league that season. This number is displayed in half-game increments; every league game counts as one game, while every interleague game counts as a half-game for each league involved. As an example, if a league is credited with 21.5 games, it is possible the league had 21 league games and one interleague game, or that it had 20 league games and three interleague games, for instance. A second parenthetical number often follows the first number, indicating the number of non-forfeit games held by the league that season. If the league went through the season without a single forfeit game, only one number will appear.

After the line of league data, championship game results are listed. These results include the final score of the league title game (if the league held one) as well as the outcomes of all league bowl games, if any.

The championship game results are then followed by a table, showing the league standings for that season. Teams are listed by conference and division, where applicable.

Teams within each division are listed in order of division finish, with division champions listed first. In the rare case that two teams shared the division title, both division champions are listed in all caps. (This has happened on five occasions in women's football history, where two division teams did not play each other in the regular season and both went undefeated, thus sharing the division championship for the regular season.)

Often division champions appear to have a worse win/loss record than teams listed below them in their division. There are multiple reasons for this. First, division championships are *regular season awards*; a team's postseason performance is never factored into the recognition of a division champion. But each team's listed win/loss record includes all games, including postseason games, preseason exhibition games, and games against teams from lower tiers that might be excluded from a division championship determination. Also, many leagues use power rankings rather than straight regular season records to determine division champions, which allows them to factor strength of schedule into their awarding of division championships.

Each team is then parenthetically followed by a two-to-four letter code, which is used in the scoreboard section below. The next two or three columns indicate the team's overall win/loss record on the season. If any team in the league recorded a tie game that season, a column for ties appears as well.

The next column notes the team's postseason results for that season. The term "postseason" includes both the results of playoff games as well as those of bowl games. The following codes are used to indicate a team's postseason results:

LC	won league championship game
C	made league championship game
CC	made conference championship game (or league semifinals)
S	made conference semifinals (or league quarterfinals)
Q	made conference quarterfinals
W	made conference wild card game
BCW	won bowl tournament
BC	made bowl tournament championship
BS	made bowl tournament semifinals
BQ	made bowl tournament quarterfinals
BW	won bowl game
B	made bowl game
--	did not make postseason

These codes can be used in combination using a hyphen, which occurs when bowl games feature teams that were previously eliminated from the playoffs. For example, the 2014 Madison Blaze are listed as CC-BW, which means they lost their conference championship game before playing in (and winning) a postseason bowl game.

The final two columns indicate the team's status the previous and following seasons. These columns show what name the team used the previous season and what league they played in, as well as whether they were coming off of a period of inactivity. A team's first year is marked "expansion", while a team's final season is marked as "folded". Current 2015 teams are listed as current, but please note that any team which missed the 2015 season has been listed as folded until further notice.

After the full-member teams have all been listed, affiliate teams and independent affiliates are then listed as well. An affiliate team is any team that is denoted as ineligible for the league's playoffs, either due to a lack of playing a full league schedule or by mutual agreement between the team and league. Affiliate teams have gone by various names over the years, such as X-teams or Tier III teams, but the concept is the same and all such teams are listed as affiliate teams for this purpose.

An independent affiliate team is any team that considers itself "independent" in a given season but which plays the majority of its schedule against one league's teams. An independent affiliate may have no formal connection to the league itself other than the fact that the majority of its competition comes from members of that league, and as an independent team, it has no right of access to the league's playoffs. Yet an independent affiliate is functionally treated the same as an affiliate team for the purposes of league listings. (Only two teams have completed an independent schedule against a mix of opponents from various leagues: the Utah Jynx in 2011 and the Utah Falconz in 2014. They are listed in their own sections within those seasons.)

Following the league standings is the league scoreboard. Every league game is listed in six columns. The first column indicates the date of the game. The second column indicates the winning team code (which can be found parenthetically following every team name in the league standings above) followed by the winning team score. Next is the losing team code and the losing team score. In the case of tie games, teams are listed alphabetically by team code.

Various leagues often score forfeits differently, but for the purposes of this scoreboard, forfeits are coded as a 1-0 game in favor of the winner. The reason forfeits are coded as 1-0 is because unlike 2-0 or 6-0 (other forfeit code scores used by some leagues), no actual women's football game can conclude with a 1-0 score under common American football rules. Therefore, a 1-0 game can automatically be assumed to be a forfeited match.

All forfeits are coded as a 1-0 final score, including forfeits by actual teams as well as forfeits by "non-existent teams", teams that did not exist in a given season except on paper, where they forfeited all of their games. Forfeits by actual teams are listed as 1-0 scores, while forfeits by non-existent teams are marked with an N in the game code section below.

The sixth and final column in the league scoreboard adds additional detail about the contest (where applicable) using a game code. The following game codes are used on the league scoreboard:

*	indicates overtime
**	indicates double overtime
***	indicates triple overtime
E	indicates preseason exhibition game
I	indicates interleague game (one team code will not appear in league standings above)
N	indicates forfeit by a non-existent team (see previous remarks on forfeits)
C	indicates league championship game
CC	indicates conference championship game (or league semifinal game)
S	indicates conference semifinal game (or league quarterfinal game)
Q	indicates conference quarterfinal game
W	indicates conference wild card game
B	indicates bowl game
BC	indicates bowl tournament championship game
BS	indicates bowl tournament semifinal game
BQ	indicates bowl tournament quarterfinal game

These codes can also be used in combination. For example, IE indicates a preseason interleague exhibition, and CC* denotes a conference championship game that was decided in overtime.

Preseason exhibition games are games played in preparation for the regular season and are played under normal playing and scorekeeping rules. In the early years, teams would often refer to interleague games as exhibitions. New teams and leagues also often called their first trial season under a limited schedule an "exhibition season" and labeled all their games from that year as exhibition games. But only preseason games are coded as exhibition games for the purposes of this scoreboard; all other games are recorded as normal contests.

A concerted effort was made to provide a complete scoreboard for every league, but in a couple of cases, a complete listing of games could not be found. In those cases, a partial scoreboard is provided listing every contest and outcome that could be confirmed.

Team Code Index

Here is the alphabetical list of team codes. If you see a team code you do not recognize in the following section, you can find the team name using the alphabetical list below.

Code	Team	Code	Team	Code	Team
3RX	Three Rivers Xplosion	COUG	Carolina Cougars	HOU	Houston Energy
ALB	Albany Ambush	COV	Colorado Valkyries	HPOW	Houston Power
ALRG	Alabama Renegades	CPAV	Central PA Vipers	HRD	Harlan Red Devils
ALSM	Alabama Slammers	CRW	Carolina Raging Wolves	HS	Hawaii Storm
ALVA	All Valley Attack	CS	Carolina Spartans	HTTC	H-Town Texas Cyclones
ANM	Albany Night-Mares	CSK	Colorado Springs Koalas	HUNT	Huntsville Tigers
ANVA	Antelope Valley Attack	CSV	Colorado Springs Voodoo	HW	Hawaiian Waves
ANVB	Antelope Valley Bombers	CT	Connecticut Wreckers	IA	Iowa Crush
ARA	Arkansas Assassins	CTC	Connecticut Crush	IAS	Iowa Steamrollers
ARB	Arkansas Banshees	CTCS	Connecticut Crushers	IAT	Iowa Thunder
ARK	Arkansas Wildcats	CTL	Connecticut Lightning	IAX	Iowa Xplosion
ARL	Arlington Impact	CVM	Central Valley Mustangs	IC	Indianapolis Chaos
ARR	Arkansas Rampage	DAL	Dallas Elite	ICE	Northern Ice
ASH	Asheville Assault	DALD	Dallas Dragons	INDY	Indy Crash
ATL	Atlanta Phoenix	DALR	Dallas Rage	INS	Indiana Speed
ATLH	Atlanta Heartbreakers	DANG	Detroit Danger	INT	Indiana Thunder
ATLL	Atlanta Leopards	DAY	Dayton Diamonds	ISK	Indianapolis SaberKatz
ATLR	Atlanta Rage	DAYR	Dayton Rebellion	IV	Indianapolis Vipers
ATLX	Atlanta Xplosion	DAZZ	New York Dazzles	JAX	Jacksonville Dixie Blues
AYJ	Austin Yellow Jackets	DB	Daytona Breakers	JAZZ	Louisiana Jazz
AZ	Arizona Assassins	DBB	Daytona Beach Barracudas	JJ	Jersey Justice
AZC	Arizona Caliente	DC	D.C. Divas	JYNX	Utah Jynx
AZKH	Arizona Knighthawks	DCD	Derby City Dynamite	KC	Kansas City Titans
AZT	Arizona Titans	DDA	Detroit Dark Angels	KCS	Kansas City Spartans
AZV	Arizona Venom	DEL	Delaware Griffins	KCT	Kansas City Tribe
AZW	Arizona Wildfire	DEN	Denver Foxes	KEY	Keystone Assault
BAB	Bay Area Bandits	DENT	Denton Stampede	KNOX	Knoxville Lightning
BAL	Baltimore Burn	DET	Detroit Demolition	KNXS	Knoxville Summit
BAND	So Cal Bandits	DETB	Detroit Blaze	KNXT	Knoxville Tornadoes
BING	Binghamton Tiger Cats	DETP	Detroit Pride	KRUN	Kansas City Krunch
BIRM	Birmingham Steel Magnolias	DFC	Desert Fire Cats	KS	Kansas Phoenix
BLAZ	Blaze'n Canes	DFW	DFW Xtreme	KT	Hawaii Kaua'i Thunder
BLXI	Biloxi Herricanes	DIAM	Dallas Diamonds	KYF	Kentucky Force
BNH	Baltimore Nighthawks	DREV	Dallas Revolution	KYK	Kentucky Karma
BOS	Boston Renegades	DSM	Des Moines Courage	KYV	Kentucky Valkyries
BOSM	Boston Militia	DWR	Daytona Waverunners	LA	Los Angeles Amazons
BOSR	Boston Rampage	ECB	Emerald Coast Barracudas	LAL	Los Angeles Lasers
BRW	Baton Rouge Wildcats	ECS	Emerald Coast Sharks	LBA	Long Beach Aftershock
BSW	Bay State Warriors	EMP	Empire State Roar	LCP	Lee County Predators
BX	Boise Xtreme	ERIE	Erie Illusion	LOU	Louisville Nightmare
CAL	California Quake	ETNR	East Tennessee Rhythm	LRW	Little Rock Wildcats
CAR	Carolina Phoenix	ETXS	East Texas Saberkats	LSM	Lone Star Mustangs
CARC	Carolina Cardinals	EUG	Eugene Edge	LV	Las Vegas Showgirlz
CARQ	Carolina Queens	EVAN	Evansville Express	MACH	Minnesota Machine
CCWA	Central Cal War Angels	EVER	Everett Reign	MAD	Madison Blaze
CCY	Connecticut Cyclones	FAYT	Fayetteville Thunder	MADC	Madison Cougars
CDD	Cheyenne Dust Devils	FAYW	Fayetteville Warriors	MASS	Massachusetts Mutiny
CFA	Central Florida Anarchy	FL	Florida Stingrayz	MAUL	Memphis Maulers
CFT	Cape Fear Thunder	FOX	Clarksville Fox	MBM	Monterrey Black Mambas
CHAT	Chattanooga Locomotion	FUEL	Louisiana Fuel	MC	Mass Chaos
CHI	Chicago Force	FWF	Fort Wayne Flash	ME	Maine Freeze
CIN	Cincinnati Sizzle	GAE	Georgia Enforcers	MEM	Memphis Legacy
CLE	Cleveland Fusion	GAG	Georgia Gladiators	MEMB	Memphis Belles
CLNX	California Lynx	GAP	Georgia Peachez	MEMD	Memphis Dynasty
CMR	Central Massachusetts Ravens	GCH	Gulf Coast Herricanes	MF	Manchester Freedom
CMS	Central Maryland Seahawks	GCR	Gulf Coast Riptide	MHB	Mile High Blaze
COF	Colorado Freeze	GEM	New York Gems	MIA	Miami Fury
COL	Columbus Comets	GVV	Grand Valley Vipers	MIL	Milwaukee Momentum
COLF	Columbus Flames	HAR	Harrisburg Angels	MINN	Minnesota Vixens
COLP	Columbus Phantoms	HI	Hawaii Legends	MINX	Lake Michigan Minx
COR	Corvallis Pride	HILL	Hillsboro Hammerheads	MLNX	Maine Lynx
COS	Colorado Sting	HOLY	Holyoke Hurricanes	MN	Minnesota Vixen

MOA	Missouri Avengers	PUEB	Pueblo Pythons	TSW	Tri-State Warriors
MODC	Modesto Magic	RAGE	Austin Rage	TUC	Tucson Monsoon
MODX	Modesto Maniax	RAVE	Atlanta Ravens	TUCW	Tucson Wildfire
MON	Montreal Blitz	RCRS	River City Raiders	TUL	Tulsa Threat
MOPH	Missouri Phoenix	RCRZ	River City Raiderz	TULE	Tulsa Eagles
MOT	Missouri Thundercats	RCW	Rose City Wildcats	TULT	Tulsa Tornadoes
MR	Maine Rebels	REDD	Redding Rage	TVT	Tennessee Valley Tigers
MRE	Monterrey Royal Eagles	RENO	Reno Rattlers	UT	Utah Falconz
MS	Mississippi Rapids	RICH	Richmond Spirit	UTB	Utah Blitz
MSD	Marana She-Devils	RII	Rhode Island Intensity	VALK	Southern Valkyrie
MSS	Muscle Shoals Smashers	RIR	Rhode Island Riptide	VBW	Ventura Black Widows
MTRX	Memphis Matrix	RMTK	Rocky Mountain Thunderkatz	VCW	Ventura County Wolfpack
MUD	Topeka Mudcats	ROAN	Roanoke Revenge	VV	Valley Vipers
NASH	Nashville Dream	ROCH	Rochester Raptors	WCL	West Coast Lightning
NCRH	Nor Cal Red Hawks	ROCK	Rockford Riveters	WI	Wisconsin Warriors
NCS	North County Stars	ROSA	Santa Rosa Scorchers	WID	Wisconsin Dragons
NE	Nebraska Stampede	SA	San Antonio Regulators	WIR	Wisconsin Riveters
NEI	New England Intensity	SAC	Sacramento Sirens	WIW	Wisconsin Wolves
NEN	New England Nightmare	SAV	Savannah Sabers	WM	West Michigan Mayhem
NER	Northeast Rebels	SBH	South Bend Hawks	WP	Washington Prodigy
NES	New England Storm	SCAA	Salt City Arch Angels	WTF	Memphis WTF
NH	New Hampshire Freedom	SCB	Southern California Breakers	WV	West Virginia Wildfire
NJ	New Jersey Titans	SCC	South Carolina Crusaders	WVB	West Virginia Bruisers
NMB	New Mexico Burn	SCO	Sweetwater County Outlaws	WVW	West Virginia Wonders
NMM	New Mexico Menace	SCR	Steel City Renegades	ZYD	Acadiana Zydeco
NO	New Orleans Blaze	SCS	So Cal Scorpions		
NOK	New Orleans Krewe	SCSD	Sin City Sun Devils		
NOM	New Orleans Mojo	SD	San Diego Surge		
NOS	New Orleans Spice	SDN	San Diego Nitrous		
NOVD	New Orleans Voodoo Dolls	SDS	San Diego Sting		
NTF	North Texas Fury	SDSC	San Diego Sea Catz		
NTK	North Texas Knockouts	SDSF	San Diego Sunfire		
NTRO	Northeastern Nitro	SEA	Seattle Majestics		
NV	Nevada Storm	SEAW	Seattle Warbirds		
NY	New York Sharks	SF	San Francisco Stingrayz		
NYG	New York Galaxy	SFT	San Francisco Tsunami		
NYK	New York Knockout	SILV	Silver State Legacy		
NYN	New York Nemesis	SMJ	Southwest Michigan Jaguars		
OAK	Oakland Banshees	SMR	Southern Maine Rebels		
OCB	Orange County Breakers	SMSH	Nashville Smashers		
OKC	Oklahoma City Lightning	SOUL	Memphis Soul		
OKCA	Oklahoma City Avengers	SPAS	Shreveport Aftershock		
OKCW	Oklahoma City Wildcats	SPIT	Southern Tier Spitfire		
ORES	Oregon Sirens	SPOK	Spokane Scorn		
ORET	Oregon Thunder	SPSH	Shreveport Shockhers		
OREU	Oregon Unforgiven	STL	St. Louis Slam		
ORL	Orlando Anarchy	STLC	South Texas Lady Crushers		
ORLF	Orlando Fire	STM	Kansas City Storm		
ORLL	Orlando Lightning	SYR	Syracuse Sting		
ORLM	Orlando Mayhem	TAC	Tacoma Trauma		
ORLS	Orlando Starz	TALL	Tallahassee Jewels		
OUT	Austin Outlaws	TAM	Tampa Tempest		
PAC	Pacific Warriors	TB	Tampa Bay Inferno		
PALM	Palm Beach Punishers	TBF	Tampa Bay Force		
PB	Pacific Blast	TBP	Tampa Bay Pirates		
PCBR	Panama City Beach Rumble	TBT	Tampa Bay Terminators		
PEN	Pensacola Power	TCM	Tri-City Mustangs		
PFF	Portland Fighting Fillies	TCT	Tri-Cities Thunder		
PHI	Philadelphia Firebirds	TCV	Tulare County Villainz		
PHIP	Philadelphia Phoenix	TIDE	Tidewater Floods		
PHX	Phoenix Phantomz	TMAJ	Tacoma Majestics		
PHXP	Phoenix Prowlers	TNH	Tennessee Heat		
PITF	Pittsburgh Force	TNM	Tennessee Mountaincatz		
PITT	Pittsburgh Passion	TNT	Tennessee Train		
PLB1	Philadelphia Liberty Belles (I)	TNV	Tennessee Venom		
PLB2	Philadelphia Liberty Belles (II)	TOL	Toledo Reign		
POR	Portland Shockwave	TOLS	Toledo Spitfire		
PRED	Detroit Predators	TREE	Tree Town Spitfire		
PRWL	Missouri Prowlers	TSB	Tri-State Bruisers		

U.S. Women's Football Leagues – Year-By-Year Results, 1999-2015

1999 Season Review

The 1999 season was the first year in the modern era of women's football, as the sport got underway in Minnesota and Hawaii. Two teams under the WPFL banner traveled the northern United States on the "No Limits" barnstorming tour. Meanwhile, a much less-publicized HWFL began to take shape.

Leagues: 2   Teams: 5 (4)   Games: 7

Women's Professional Football League (WPFL) – 1999 Season

The Minnesota Vixens and Lake Michigan Minx faced each other several times on the "No Limits" barnstorming tour. Although the Vixens were originally assembled to be the dominant team in the series, the Lake Michigan Minx soundly defeated the Vixens at every turn and came away as the first national champions of women's football's modern era.

Minor National League   Teams: 3 (2)   Games: 6
Championship game result: Lake Michigan Minx 30, Minnesota Vixens 27

1999 WPFL Standings

Teams	W	L	PR	Before	After
Lake Michigan Minx (MINX)	5	0	LC	Expansion	Folded
Minnesota Vixens (MINN)	0	6	C	Expansion	Became Minnesota Vixen
Independent Affiliate					
New York Sharks (NY)	1	0	--	Expansion	--

1999 WPFL Scoreboard

10/9	MINX	33	MINN	6		10/23	MINX	41	MINN	37		12/11	NY	12	MINN	6	
10/16	MINX	31	MINN	19		11/9	MINX	23	MINN	21		1/22	MINX	30	MINN	27	C

Hawaii Women's Football League (HWFL) – 1999 Season

The Hawaiian Waves touted themselves as the first women's football team of the modern era, thanks to an intra-squad scrimmage that was held two weeks before the Vixens and Minx first met in 1999. But the first true women's football game held on the islands took place two months later, and it was a blowout victory for the Waves, who would rebrand as the Hawaii Storm the following year.

Exhibition Season   Teams: 2   Games: 1
No Declared Champion

1999 HWFL Standings

Teams	W	L	PR	Before	After
Hawaiian Waves (HW)	1	0	--	Expansion	Became Hawaii Storm
Hawaii Kaua'i Thunder (KT)	0	1	--	Expansion	--

1999 HWFL Scoreboard

11/27   HW   61   KT   0

2000 Season Review

The success of the WPFL's 1999 barnstorming tour had two consequences. First, the WPFL expanded into an 11-team league, the first true women's football league of the modern era. Second, the WPFL's positive reception in 1999 sparked imitators, with the NWFL and WCFL both launching their own test runs at building a women's football league. The NWFL's attempt was successful, with a league taking shape the following spring. The WCFL, however, never got off the ground, and it – like the HWFL – would not return in 2001.

Leagues: 4   Teams: 18 (16)   Games: 47

Women's Professional Football League (WPFL) – 2000 Season

Buoyed by the overall success of the 1999 barnstorming tour, the WPFL launched a full 11-team league in 2000, the first women's football league of the modern era. The result was an unequivocal disaster. The WPFL greatly overestimated their revenues and bills went unpaid. A planned all-star game was cancelled, the season was shortened, and an abbreviated playoff structure was hastily announced. The Houston Energy claimed the first major national championship of the modern era by winning the 2000 WPFL title, but the entire league looked to be on the verge of collapse after just one full season.

Major National League   Teams: 13 (11)   Games: 39.5
Championship game result: Houston Energy 39, New England Storm 7

2000 WPFL Standings

National Conference	W	L	PR	Before	After
East Division					
New England Storm (NES)	6	3	C	Expansion	--
New York Sharks (NY)	5	3	S	--	Left for MIWFA
New York Galaxy (NYG)	0	4	--	Expansion	Folded
South Division					
Daytona Beach Barracudas (DBB)	6	1	CC	Expansion	Folded
Miami Fury (MIA)	3	4	--	Expansion	Left for MIWFA
Tampa Tempest (TAM)	1	6	--	Expansion	--
American Conference					
Central Division					
Minnesota Vixen (MN)	5	1	CC	Were Minnesota Vixens	Left for MIWFA
Colorado Valkyries (COV)	5	2	S	Expansion	Folded
West Division					
Houston Energy (HOU)	7	2	LC	Expansion	--
Austin Rage (RAGE)	2	5	--	Expansion	--
Oklahoma City Wildcats (OKCW)	0	6	--	Expansion	Folded
Affiliate Teams					
Carolina Cougars (COUG)	0	1	--	Expansion	Left for MIWFA
Oregon Sirens (ORES)	0	1	--	Expansion	Folded

2000 WPFL Scoreboard

Date					Date					Date				
10/14	DBB	34	MIA	17	11/4	COV	53	RAGE	0	11/22	DBB	21	MIA	20
10/14	HOU	52	RAGE	25	11/4	MIA	34	TAM	22	11/25	DBB	27	TAM	6
10/14	MN	14	COV	12	11/4	MN	30	HOU	8	11/25	RAGE	13	OKCW	12
10/14	NES	28	NYG	0	11/4	NY	26	OKCW	6	11/26	COV	54	ORES	0
10/21	HOU	30	RAGE	20	11/5	NES	32	NYG	0	12/1	NY	50	GEM	12 I
10/21	MN	63	TAM	0	11/11	DBB	62	TAM	6	12/2	MIA	28	TAM	12
10/22	COV	58	OKCW	0	11/11	HOU	35	RAGE	21	12/2	NES	48	NY	12
10/22	DBB	35	NYG	6	11/11	MN	28	OKCW	0	12/2	RAGE	14	OKCW	8
10/22	NY	16	NES	8	11/11	NY	19	MIA	12	12/2	HOU	13	COV	0 S
10/28	DBB	27	MIA	0	11/18	COV	7	NES	3	12/9	NES	10	NY	7 S
10/28	MN	35	RAGE	19	11/18	HOU	21	OKCW	0	12/9	TAM	8	COUG	7
10/28	NES	3	NY	0	11/18	MIA	33	TAM	0	12/16	HOU	35	MN	14 CC
10/29	COV	62	HOU	6	11/18	NY	41	NYG	0	1/6	NES	29	DBB	26 CC*
										1/20	HOU	39	NES	7 C

Hawaii Women's Football League (HWFL) – 2000 Season

The HWFL had plans for as many as five teams, but it was never able to launch more than two franchises. The Storm and the Thunder were both offered membership into the WAFL for the 2001 season, but they decided to instead pool their resources and merge into one franchise, which was named the Hawaii Legends.

Exhibition Season   Teams: 2   Games: 1
No Declared Champion

2000 HWFL Standings

Teams	W	L	PR	Before	After
Hawaii Storm (HS)	1	0	--	Were Hawaiian Waves	Folded
Hawaii Kaua'i Thunder (KT)	0	1	--	--	Folded

2000 HWFL Scoreboard

5/13   HS   44   KT   0

National Women's Football League (NWFL) – 2000 Season

Following in the WPFL's footsteps, the NWFL tested the waters for a planned full league in the spring of 2001 with a two-team barnstorming series in the fall of 2000. While the six games between the Alabama Renegades and Nashville Dream didn't attract the same media attention as the WPFL's 1999 series, it was successful enough to ensure that the 2001 NWFL season would proceed as planned.

Exhibition Season   Teams: 2   Games: 6
No Declared Champion

2000 NWFL Standings

Teams	W	L	PR	Before	After
Nashville Dream (NASH)	3	3	--	Expansion	--
Alabama Renegades (ALRG)	3	3	--	Expansion	--

Partial 2000 NWFL Scoreboard

10/21   NASH   30   ALRG   15

Women's Continental Football League (WCFL) – 2000 Season

The original plan for the WCFL centered around two teams – the New York Gems and the Triad Angels, based in the Piedmont Triad region of North Carolina. The Angels never got out of the planning stages, while the Gems played just one game against the WPFL's New York Sharks. After a decisive loss, the Gems and their entire league promptly folded.

Exhibition Season   Teams: 1   Games: 0.5
No Declared Champion

2000 WCFL Standings

Team	W	L	PR	Before	After
New York Gems (GEM)	0	1	--	Expansion	Folded

2000 WCFL Scoreboard

12/1   NY   50   GEM   12   I

2001 Spring/Summer Review

After two seasons of women's football in the fall, 2001 brought the first round of spring football in the modern era. Two major leagues were founded and began a duel that continues in many ways to this day. The NWFL, fresh off of a well-received barnstorming tour in the fall of 2000, expanded into a full ten-team spring league. The IWFL stuck its toes in the water for the first time, with four teams playing a limited expansion season. Finally, the Tennessee Heat served to clear the way for a third spring league, the simply-named WFL.

Leagues: 3   Teams: 15 (14)   Games: 52.5

National Women's Football League (NWFL) – 2001 Season

Building off of the success of their 2000 barnstorming tour, the Alabama Renegades and Nashville Dream were joined by eight more teams to form the core of the NWFL. The NWFL got off to an impressive start, splitting these ten teams into two five-team conferences that covered the entire East Coast. The Philadelphia Liberty Belles became the first spring champions of the modern era, soundly defeating the Pensacola Power for the 2001 NWFL title.

Major National League   Teams: 10   Games: 41
Championship game result: Philadelphia Liberty Belles 40, Pensacola Power 7

2001 NWFL Standings

Northern Conference	W	L	PR	Before	After
Philadelphia Liberty Belles (I) (PLB1)	8	1	LC	Expansion	--
Massachusetts Mutiny (MASS)	8	1	--	Expansion	--
D.C. Divas (DC)	3	4	--	Expansion	--
Connecticut Crush (CTC)	2	6	--	Expansion	--
Baltimore Burn (BAL)	0	7	--	Expansion	--
Southern Conference					
Pensacola Power (PEN)	8	1	C	Expansion	--
Alabama Renegades (ALRG)	5	3	--	--	--
Tennessee Venom (TNV)	4	4	--	Expansion	--
Nashville Dream (NASH)	2	7	--	--	--
Chattanooga Locomotion (CHAT)	1	7	--	Expansion	--

2001 NWFL Scoreboard

Date	Team	Score	Team	Score		Date	Team	Score	Team	Score		Date	Team	Score	Team	Score	
4/21	PEN	20	ALRG	0		5/19	ALRG	27	TNV	6		6/16	CHAT	7	NASH	2	
4/21	PLB1	20	CTC	6		5/19	CTC	24	BAL	0		6/16	MASS	52	CTC	0	
4/21	TNV	20	NASH	14		5/19	PLB1	27	MASS	0		6/16	PEN	20	TNV	6	
						5/20	NASH	15	CHAT	14		6/16	PLB1	14	DC	7	
4/28	ALRG	46	NASH	6													
4/28	MASS	19	CTC	0		5/26	ALRG	32	CHAT	12		6/23	DC	52	TNV	0	
4/28	PEN	36	CHAT	7		5/26	DC	20	BAL	8		6/23	MASS	90	BAL	22	
4/28	PLB1	40	DC	0		5/26	MASS	27	CTC	6		6/23	NASH	18	CHAT	7	
						5/26	PEN	22	NASH	9		6/23	PEN	3	ALRG	0	
5/5	MASS	15	DC	8								6/23	PLB1	74	CTC	0	
5/5	PEN	40	NASH	12		6/2	MASS	12	DC	0							
5/5	PLB1	46	BAL	0		6/2	PEN	7	ALRG	6		7/14	PLB1	40	PEN	7	C
5/5	TNV	24	CHAT	18		6/2	PLB1	47	BAL	0							
						6/2	TNV	14	NASH	8							
5/12	ALRG	20	TNV	13													
5/12	DC	10	CTC	6		6/9	ALRG	28	NASH	21							
5/12	MASS	35	BAL	0		6/9	CTC	18	BAL	12							
5/12	PEN	48	CHAT	0		6/9	MASS	13	PLB1	7							
						6/9	TNV	27	CHAT	6							

Independent Women's Football League (IWFL) – 2001 Season

The IWFL, the oldest women's football league still in existence in the United States, launched in 2001 with an exhibition season that featured four teams. Three of these teams went winless, with the Austin Outlaws finishing as the class of the league.

Exhibition Season　　　　　　　　　Teams: 4 (3)　　　　　　　　　Games: 6.5
Declared Champion (by virtue of regular season record): Austin Outlaws

2001 IWFL Standings

Teams	W	L	T	PR	Before	After
Austin Outlaws (OUT)	5	1	0	--	Expansion	--
Arizona Titans (AZT)	0	2	0	--	Expansion	Left for AFWL
Memphis Maulers (MAUL)	0	3	1	--	Expansion	--

Affiliate Team

	W	L	T	PR	Before	After
Tulsa Tornadoes (TULT)	0	0	1	--	Expansion	--

2001 IWFL Scoreboard

5/9	OUT	28	MAUL	0	E	6/30	OUT	22	TNH	6	I	8/25	MAUL	0	TULT	0
6/2	OUT	42	MAUL	12		7/21	TNH	6	OUT	0	I*	9/8	NY	20	AZT	0	I
6/23	OUT	56	MAUL	0		8/18	OUT	32	ORLL	6	I	10/7	HOU	55	AZT	7	I

Women's Football League (WFL) – 2001 Season

Several members of the NWFL's Nashville Dream spun off into their own team, the Tennessee Heat, which began play in 2001. Carrying the banner of the WFL, the Heat completed a respectable ten-game schedule in 2001 as they laid the groundwork for a new league.

Exhibition Season　　　　　　　　　Teams: 1　　　　　　　　　Games: 5
No Declared Champion

2001 WFL Standings

Team	W	L	PR	Before	After
Tennessee Heat (TNH)	2	8	--	Expansion	--

2001 WFL Scoreboard

6/9	TBF	60	TNH	0	IE	7/21	TNH	6	OUT	0	I*	8/25	MIA	16	TNH	6	I
6/30	OUT	22	TNH	6	I	7/28	COUG	18	TNH	0	I	9/1	ORLL	14	TNH	3	I
7/14	COUG	22	TNH	0	I	8/4	TNH	6	ORLL	0	I	9/29	COUG	43	TNH	6	I
						8/11	COUG	10	TNH	0	I						

2001 Fall/Winter Review

The 2001 fall season was overshadowed by the September 11 terrorist attacks in New York City, as schedules had to be completely reconfigured thanks to a dramatic decrease in air travel. Even before that, the WPFL was already in a state of upheaval after a disappointing 2000 season. Just prior to the start of the 2001 WPFL season, several teams defected and played an independent schedule instead, banding together in a temporary alliance of independents called the MIWFA. The WPFL barely survived to play a 2001 season, featuring just four teams. Meanwhile, a new league – the WAFL – was founded and supplanted the WPFL as the top fall league in women's football in 2001.

Leagues: 3   Teams: 26   Games: 114.5 (110.5)

Women's American Football League (WAFL) – 2001 Season

The WAFL featured 16 teams, the largest number of any league in women's football history to that point. These teams were neatly divided into two conferences – one on the West Coast and one in the Southeast. The California Quake prevailed in the West, while the Jacksonville Dixie Blues reigned supreme in the Southeast. The Quake then defeated the Dixie Blues in a title game dubbed Women's World Bowl I.

Major National League   Teams: 16   Games: 84 (82)
Championship game result: California Quake 30, Jacksonville Dixie Blues 14

2001 WAFL Standings

Atlantic Conference	W	L	T	PR	Before	After
Central Division						
Indianapolis Vipers (IV)	6	4	0	S	Expansion	Left for WAFL-WFA
Alabama Slammers (ALSM)	2	7	0	--	Expansion	Folded
New Orleans Voodoo Dolls (NOVD)	2	8	0	--	Expansion	Left for WAFL-WFA
South Division						
Tampa Bay Force (TBF)	10	2	0	CC	Expansion	Left for WAFL-WFA
Orlando Fire (ORLF)	7	6	0	S	Expansion	Left for WAFL-WFA
Jacksonville Dixie Blues (JAX)	6	6	0	C	Expansion	Left for WAFL-WFA
Pacific Conference						
Northwest Division						
Seattle Warbirds (SEAW)	9	1	1	S	Expansion	Folded
Hawaii Legends (HI)	6	4	0	--	Expansion	Left for WAFC
Rose City Wildcats (RCW)	0	8	0	--	Expansion	Folded
Central Division						
Sacramento Sirens (SAC)	7	3	1	S	Expansion	Left for WAFC
Oakland Banshees (OAK)	2	7	0	--	Expansion	Left for WAFC
San Francisco Tsunami (SFT)	0	8	0	--	Expansion	Left for AFWL
South Division						
California Quake (CAL)	11	2	0	LC	Expansion	Left for WAFC
Arizona Caliente (AZC)	8	4	0	CC	Expansion	Left for WAFC
San Diego Sunfire (SDSF)	5	5	0	--	Expansion	Left for AFWL
Los Angeles Lasers (LAL)	3	7	0	--	Expansion	Left for AFWL

Women's American Football League (WAFL) – 2001 Season (continued)
2001 WAFL Scoreboard

Date	Team	Score	Team	Score	Note		Date	Team	Score	Team	Score	Note		Date	Team	Score	Team	Score	Note
6/9	TBF	60	TNH	0	IE		11/24	IV	1	JAX	0			12/29	AZC	50	LAL	28	
9/8	SYR	26	ORLF	13	I		11/24	OAK	34	SFT	6			12/29	CAL	32	OAK	8	
10/6	ORLF	8	RAGE	7	I		11/24	SDSF	24	AZC	7			12/29	ORLF	44	NOVD	0	
														12/29	SAC	21	SDSF	12	
10/27	MN	21	IV	14	I		11/29	HI	34	LAL	28	*		12/29	SEAW	22	HI	0	
10/27	NOVD	6	ALSM	0			12/1	ALSM	12	NOVD	6								
10/27	SAC	29	SFT	0			12/1	CAL	20	SDSF	14			1/3	SEAW	14	HI	7	
10/27	SEAW	37	RCW	0			12/1	ORLF	42	IV	20			1/5	AZC	14	SFT	12	
10/27	TBF	18	ORLF	6			12/1	SEAW	34	RCW	0			1/5	CAL	24	SDSF	8	
							12/1	TBF	31	JAX	14			1/5	HI	16	RCW	8	
11/3	IV	18	MN	7	I		12/2	HI	7	LAL	6			1/5	LAL	46	OAK	6	
11/3	LAL	22	CAL	14										1/5	ORLF	38	IV	14	
11/3	ORLF	28	JAX	22	*		12/8	AZC	6	LAL	0			1/5	TBF	56	JAX	49	
11/3	SAC	43	RCW	22			12/8	CAL	20	RCW	8								
11/3	SDSF	14	AZC	12			12/8	ORLF	36	ALSM	0			1/12	ALSM	1	TBF	0	
11/3	SEAW	41	OAK	0			12/8	SAC	28	OAK	8			1/12	AZC	26	CAL	22	
11/3	TBF	58	NOVD	0			12/8	SEAW	41	SFT	0			1/12	JAX	47	NOVD	7	
														1/12	LAL	20	SFT	19	
11/10	AZC	12	MN	7	I		12/13	HI	40	OAK	6			1/12	SEAW	17	SAC	14	**
11/10	NOVD	14	ALSM	0			12/15	AZC	12	SDSF	10			1/13	HI	57	SDSF	29	
11/10	SAC	42	OAK	0			12/15	CAL	27	LAL	22								
11/10	SDSF	12	LAL	6			12/15	IV	44	ALSM	8			1/19	AZC	18	SAC	15	
11/10	SEAW	28	RCW	8			12/15	ORLF	20	JAX	9			1/19	CAL	36	SFT	6	
11/10	TBF	50	ORLF	6			12/15	SAC	57	SFT	18			1/19	IV	36	ALSM	0	
							12/15	SEAW	12	RCW	0			1/19	JAX	36	NOVD	12	
11/14	CAL	21	HI	18			12/15	TBF	26	NOVD	0								
11/17	CAL	19	AZC	6			12/16	HI	35	OAK	8			1/26	CAL	40	SAC	13	S
11/17	IV	52	ALSM	6										1/26	JAX	38	IV	32	S
11/17	JAX	21	ORLF	10			12/22	IV	44	NOVD	6			1/26	TBF	31	ORLF	20	S
11/17	OAK	34	SFT	14			12/22	JAX	43	ALSM	8								
11/17	SAC	35	RCW	16			12/22	SAC	0	SEAW	0	*		2/2	AZC	24	SEAW	16	S
11/17	SDSF	20	HI	10			12/22	SDSF	28	LAL	13			2/2	JAX	26	TBF	6	CC
11/17	TBF	52	NOVD	0			12/22	TBF	20	ORLF	14								
														2/10	CAL	16	AZC	12	CC
														2/24	CAL	30	JAX	14	C

Major Independent Women's Football Alliance (MIWFA) – 2001 Season

Four members of the WPFL in 2000 – the Minnesota Vixen, the New York Sharks, the Miami Fury, and affiliate member Carolina Cougars – all defected from the WPFL on the eve of the 2001 season. Instead, they formed the MIWFA, a loose temporary alliance of independents that navigated its way through the 2001 fall schedule. These four teams were joined by two expansion teams, the Orlando Lightning and the Syracuse Sting, in a six-team independent block in 2001.

Independent Major Alliance Teams: 6 Games: 15.5
No Declared Champion

2001 MIWFA Standings

Teams	W	L	PR	Before	After
Carolina Cougars (COUG)	7	1	--	Joined from WPFL	Left for WFL
New York Sharks (NY)	6	1	--	Joined from WPFL	Left for IWFL
Miami Fury (MIA)	3	1	--	Joined from WPFL	Left for IWFL
Minnesota Vixen (MN)	1	2	--	Joined from WPFL	Left for WPFL
Syracuse Sting (SYR)	1	3	--	Expansion	Left for WPFL
Orlando Lightning (ORLL)	1	4	--	Expansion	Folded

2001 MIWFA Scoreboard

Date						Date						Date					
7/14	COUG	22	TNH	0	I	8/18	COUG	16	MIA	7		9/8	MIA	48	ORLL	0	
7/28	COUG	18	TNH	0	I	8/18	NY	25	TAM	0	I	9/8	NY	20	AZT	0	I
7/28	NY	20	NES	0	I	8/18	OUT	32	ORLL	6	I	9/8	SYR	26	ORLF	13	I
8/4	COUG	10	NY	8		8/18	NES	20	SYR	0	I	9/29	COUG	43	TNH	6	
8/4	TNH	6	ORLL	0	I	8/25	COUG	12	ORLL	0		10/7	NY	19	NES	0	I
8/11	COUG	10	TNH	0	I	8/25	MIA	16	TNH	6	I	10/27	MN	21	IV	14	I
8/11	NY	34	SYR	6		9/1	MIA	28	COUG	0		11/3	IV	18	MN	7	I
						9/1	NY	21	SYR	14		11/10	AZC	12	MN	7	I
						9/1	ORLL	14	TNH	3	I						

Women's Professional Football League (WPFL) – 2001 Season

The WPFL survived defections and financial difficulties and – against all odds – put on the most geographically-strained four-team league season in women's football history. The Houston Energy and Austin Rage in Texas paired with Florida's Tampa Tempest, while the New England Storm up in Massachusetts filled out the quartet. Somehow, this league still managed to get off a six-to-eight game season for all of its member teams. The Houston Energy claimed their second straight WPFL title, although with all the defections, it was clearly less prestigious than the first.

Minor National League Teams: 4 Games: 15 (13)
Championship game result: Houston Energy 47, Austin Rage 14

2001 WPFL Standings

Teams	W	L	PR	Before	After
Houston Energy (HOU)	8	0	LC	--	--
Austin Rage (RAGE)	4	4	C	--	--
New England Storm (NES)	2	6	--	--	--
Tampa Tempest (TAM)	0	6	--	--	Left for IWFL

2001 WPFL Scoreboard

Date						Date						Date					
7/28	HOU	27	RAGE	13		8/25	HOU	53	TAM	0		9/22	HOU	33	NES	0	
7/28	NY	20	NES	0	I	8/25	RAGE	32	NES	16		9/22	RAGE	1	TAM	0	
8/4	HOU	25	RAGE	0		9/1	NES	41	TAM	0		10/6	ORLF	8	RAGE	7	I
												10/7	HOU	55	AZT	7	I
8/11	HOU	1	NES	0		9/8	HOU	51	TAM	0		10/7	NY	19	NES	0	I
8/11	RAGE	21	TAM	0		9/8	RAGE	30	NES	18		10/20	HOU	47	RAGE	14	C
8/18	NES	20	SYR	0	I												
8/18	NY	25	TAM	0	I												

2002 Spring/Summer Review

Spring and summer began to win out in the women's game over the traditional men's football season; for the first time in modern women's football, more teams took the field during the spring/summer season of 2002 than in the fall of that year. The NWFL expanded after a successful 2001 campaign, while the IWFL took a step forward with the league's first championship game. The WSFL and UWFL were strictly regional leagues, and the UWFL collapsed midseason. Finally, the WFL hosted a few contests late in the summer in anticipation of a full slate of games in 2003.

Leagues: 5   Teams: 52 (49)   Games: 195.5 (188)

National Women's Football League (NWFL) – 2002 Season

Twenty-two teams spread out across five divisions in the NWFL's 2002 season, making it the largest league in history to that point. A dynasty was born when a team named the Detroit Danger captured the 2002 NWFL title over the Massachusetts Mutiny; the Danger would rebrand following the season and become the Detroit Demolition, dominating the sport for years to come.

Major National League   Teams: 22 (21)   Games: 98 (97)
Championship game result: Detroit Danger 48, Massachusetts Mutiny 30

2002 NWFL Standings

Teams	W	L	PR	Before	After
North Division					
Massachusetts Mutiny (MASS)	9	2	C	--	--
Philadelphia Liberty Belles (I) (PLB1)	7	3	CC	--	Left for IWFL
Connecticut Crush (CTC)	5	5	--	--	--
Maine Freeze (ME)	1	9	--	Expansion	--
Mid-Atlantic Division					
Baltimore Burn (BAL)	9	2	S	--	--
D.C. Divas (DC)	6	3	--	--	--
Asheville Assault (ASH)	4	4	--	Expansion	--
Tennessee Venom (TNV)	0	8	--	--	--
Great Lakes Division					
Detroit Danger (DANG)	10	1	LC	Expansion	Became Detroit Demolition
Cleveland Fusion (CLE)	6	3	S	Expansion	--
Southwest Michigan Jaguars (SMJ)	3	5	--	Expansion	--
South Bend Hawks (SBH)	0	8	--	Expansion	Became Indiana Thunder
Central Division					
Alabama Renegades (ALRG)	7	2	S	--	--
Nashville Dream (NASH)	7	2	S	--	--
Chattanooga Locomotion (CHAT)	4	4	--	--	--
Atlanta Leopards (ATLL)	2	6	--	Expansion	--
Knoxville Summit (KNXS)	0	8	--	Expansion	--
South Division					
Pensacola Power (PEN)	9	1	CC	--	--
Biloxi Herricanes (BLXI)	5	3	--	Expansion	Became Gulf Coast Herricanes
New Orleans Spice (NOS)	2	6	--	Expansion	--
Panama City Beach Rumble (PCBR)	1	7	--	Expansion	--
Affiliate Team					
Rochester Raptors (ROCH)	1	6	--	Expansion	--

National Women's Football League (NWFL) – 2002 Season (continued)
2002 NWFL Scoreboard

Date	Team	Score	Team	Score		Date	Team	Score	Team	Score		Date	Team	Score	Team	Score	
3/23	BAL	20	ROCH	0	E	5/18	ALRG	74	KNXS	0		6/15	ALRG	54	KNXS	12	
3/30	BAL	39	ROCH	0	E	5/18	BAL	21	ASH	0		6/15	BAL	40	ASH	0	
4/6	DC	46	ROCH	0	E	5/18	BLXI	22	NOS	14		6/15	BLXI	36	PCBR	14	
4/13	ROCH	12	ME	0	E	5/18	CHAT	14	ATLL	0		6/15	CLE	20	SMJ	14	
						5/18	CLE	18	SMJ	0		6/15	DANG	33	SBH	0	
4/20	ME	13	ROCH	7	E	5/18	DANG	41	SBH	16		6/15	DC	60	TNV	0	
4/20	ALRG	40	CHAT	12		5/18	DC	53	TNV	0		6/15	MASS	28	CTC	19	
4/20	ASH	36	TNV	14		5/18	MASS	47	CTC	15		6/15	NASH	16	ATLL	14	
4/20	BAL	7	DC	2		5/18	PEN	61	PCBR	0		6/15	PEN	41	NOS	0	
4/20	BLXI	40	NOS	34		5/18	PLB1	55	ME	14		6/15	PLB1	60	ME	0	
4/20	CLE	39	SBH	0													
4/20	DANG	34	SMJ	16		5/25	ALRG	32	ATLL	21		6/22	ALRG	34	NASH	19	
4/20	NASH	26	ATLL	12		5/25	BAL	57	TNV	0		6/22	ASH	1	TNV	0	
4/20	PEN	56	PCBR	6		5/25	BLXI	34	PCBR	6		6/22	BAL	6	DC	0	
						5/25	CLE	14	DANG	3		6/22	CHAT	80	KNXS	0	
4/27	BAL	30	TNV	0		5/25	CTC	45	ME	0		6/22	CTC	49	ME	6	
4/27	CHAT	8	ATLL	6		5/25	DC	54	ASH	0		6/22	DANG	51	CLE	20	
4/27	DC	22	ASH	0		5/25	MASS	17	PLB1	12		6/22	MASS	35	PLB1	21	
4/27	MASS	62	ME	0		5/25	NASH	51	KNXS	0		6/22	PCBR	24	NOS	16	
4/27	NASH	48	KNXS	8		5/25	PEN	50	NOS	7		6/22	PEN	63	BLXI	0	
4/27	PLB1	26	CTC	0		5/25	SMJ	20	SBH	0		6/22	SMJ	33	SBH	8	
5/4	ASH	48	TNV	28		6/1	ATLL	79	KNXS	0		6/29	ALRG	22	ATLL	21	
5/4	CHAT	18	KNXS	0		6/1	BAL	12	DC	6		6/29	BLXI	30	PCBR	6	
5/4	CTC	41	ME	0		6/1	MASS	68	ME	12		6/29	CLE	20	SBH	0	
5/4	DANG	20	CLE	6		6/1	NASH	31	CHAT	12		6/29	DANG	48	SMJ	6	
5/4	DC	7	BAL	6		6/1	PLB1	25	CTC	6		6/29	MASS	55	ME	0	
5/4	NASH	24	ALRG	14								6/29	NASH	36	CHAT	6	
5/4	NOS	48	PCBR	38		6/8	ALRG	22	CHAT	12		6/29	PEN	59	NOS	0	
5/4	PEN	42	BLXI	6		6/8	ASH	22	TNV	0		6/29	PLB1	35	CTC	6	
5/4	PLB1	21	MASS	20		6/8	ATLL	77	KNXS	0							
5/4	SMJ	30	SBH	0		6/8	CLE	40	SBH	16		7/6	DANG	47	NASH	0	S
						6/8	CTC	34	ROCH	6		7/6	MASS	45	CLE	0	S
5/11	CTC	19	ROCH	0		6/8	DANG	48	SMJ	6		7/6	PEN	12	ALRG	8	S
						6/8	NOS	36	PCBR	8		7/6	PLB1	21	BAL	20	S
						6/8	PEN	30	BLXI	0							
												7/13	DANG	14	PEN	7	CC
												7/13	MASS	27	PLB1	16	CC
												7/27	DANG	48	MASS	30	C

Independent Women's Football League (IWFL) – 2002 Season

After a successful exhibition season in 2001, the IWFL hosted its first full slate of games in 2002. The Austin Outlaws, who dominated the IWFL's 2001 exhibition season, won the Western Conference, while the New York Sharks claimed the East title. The IWFL held its first championship game, and the Sharks came away with the first (and so far only) national title in their prestigious history.

Major National League   Teams: 16 (14)   Games: 62 (56.5)
Championship game result: New York Sharks 24, Austin Outlaws 4

2002 IWFL Standings

Eastern Conference	W	L	PR	Before	After
New York Sharks (NY)	9	0	LC	Joined from MIWFA	--
Orlando Starz (ORLS)	6	1	--	Expansion	--
Montreal Blitz (MON)	5	3	--	Expansion	--
Bay State Warriors (BSW)	5	4	--	Expansion	--
Tampa Tempest (TAM)	2	5	--	Joined from WPFL	Folded
New Hampshire Freedom (NH)	2	7	--	Expansion	--
Albany Night-Mares (ANM)	1	6	--	Expansion	--

Western Conference	W	L	PR	Before	After
Corvallis Pride (COR)	8	1	CC	Expansion	--
Austin Outlaws (OUT)	8	4	C	--	Left for NWFA
Oklahoma City Avengers (OKCA)	5	3	--	Expansion	--
Memphis Maulers (MAUL)	5	4	--	--	--
Eugene Edge (EUG)	4	4	--	Expansion	--
Oregon Thunder (ORET)	0	8	--	Expansion	Folded
Tulsa Tornadoes (TULT)	0	8	--	--	Folded

Affiliate Teams	W	L	PR	Before	After
Miami Fury (MIA)	2	1	--	Joined from MIWFA	--
Detroit Blaze (DETB)	0	3	--	Expansion	--

2002 IWFL Scoreboard

Date	Away	Score	Home	Score	Notes
3/30	COR	12	EUG	0	
4/6	EUG	35	ORET	20	
4/6	MAUL	24	OUT	14	
4/6	OKCA	44	TULT	0	
4/13	COR	41	ORET	19	
4/13	MAUL	60	TULT	8	
4/13	OUT	24	OKCA	7	
4/20	BSW	48	NH	0	
4/20	COR	8	EUG	7	
4/20	MAUL	28	OKCA	13	
4/20	NY	45	MON	6	
4/20	OUT	45	TULT	0	
4/27	EUG	31	ORET	14	
4/27	MON	12	NH	0	
4/27	NY	40	BSW	0	
4/27	OKCA	46	TULT	0	
4/27	ORLS	34	TAM	6	
4/27	OUT	28	MAUL	0	
5/4	BSW	34	NH	8	
5/4	COR	46	ORET	0	
5/4	MON	24	ANM	13	
5/4	ORLS	20	TAM	6	
5/11	BSW	14	ANM	9	
5/11	COR	14	EUG	6	
5/11	MON	47	NH	22	
5/11	NY	73	DETB	0	
5/11	OKCA	59	MAUL	16	
5/11	ORLS	1	MIA	0	
5/11	OUT	55	TULT	0	
5/18	BSW	14	ANM	6	
5/18	EUG	20	ORET	8	
5/18	MAUL	39	TULT	0	
5/18	MIA	34	TAM	0	
5/18	NY	44	MON	0	
5/18	OKCA	25	OUT	6	
5/25	COR	21	ORET	13	
5/25	MIA	48	TAM	0	
5/25	ORLS	48	TBF	0	I
5/25	OUT	29	MAUL	6	
5/31	TAM	26	NH	0	
6/1	COR	28	EUG	0	
6/1	MON	33	BSW	24	
6/1	NY	34	ANM	6	
6/2	ORLS	27	NH	6	
6/8	EUG	1	ORET	0	
6/8	MAUL	1	TULT	0	
6/8	MON	21	ANM	13	
6/8	NH	22	DETB	0	
6/8	NY	26	BSW	0	
6/8	OUT	7	OKCA	6	
6/8	TAM	14	ORLS	6	
6/15	ANM	22	DETB	0	
6/15	BSW	18	MON	12	
6/15	COR	1	ORET	0	
6/15	NY	64	NH	0	
6/15	OKCA	44	MAUL	0	
6/15	OUT	1	TULT	0	
6/22	NH	12	ANM	7	
6/22	NY	22	BSW	2	
6/22	ORLS	9	TAM	6	
6/22	OUT	42	COR	14	CC
7/6	NY	24	OUT	4	C
9/28	AZKH	1	OUT	0	I

Women's Spring Football League (WSFL) – 2002 Season

The original WSFL was a four-team league in the Pacific Northwest, consisting of the Tacoma Majestics, Portland Shockwave, Boise Xtreme, and Oregon Unforgiven. The Unforgiven had been slated to play in the Oregon Women's Professional Football (OWPF) league in the fall of 2001, but when that team was pulled from the OWPF to the WSFL, the OWPF collapsed under considerable controversy without playing a game. The WSFL changed its name before the season from the Western States Football League to the Women's Spring Football League, but the acronym remained the same. The Majestics won the 2002 WSFL championship over the Shockwave. After one season, the WSFL and the Unforgiven folded, with the other three teams finding a home in the IWFL.

Regional League　　　　　　　　Teams: 4　　　　　　　　Games: 12.5 (11.5)
Championship game result: Tacoma Majestics 14, Portland Shockwave 0

2002 WSFL Standings

Teams	W	L	PR	Before	After
Tacoma Majestics (TMAJ)	7	0	LC	Expansion	Left for IWFL
Portland Shockwave (POR)	4	3	C	Expansion	Left for IWFL
Boise Xtreme (BX)	1	5	--	Expansion	Left for IWFL
Oregon Unforgiven (OREU)	0	5	--	Expansion	Folded

2002 WSFL Scoreboard

Date						Date						Date					
4/13	AZKH	57	BX	0	IE	5/4	BX	39	OREU	0		5/26	TMAJ	38	BX	0	
						5/4	TMAJ	20	POR	6							
4/20	TMAJ	34	BX	8								6/1	TMAJ	15	POR	12	
4/21	POR	42	OREU	0		5/12	POR	63	OREU	0							
												6/15	TMAJ	14	POR	0	C
4/27	POR	18	BX	12	*	5/18	POR	20	BX	13							
4/27	TMAJ	49	OREU	0		5/18	TMAJ	1	OREU	0							

United Women's Football League (UWFL) – 2002 Season

The UWFL was a seven-team, regional league based in Colorado in 2002. The UWFL was a disaster, becoming the first league in modern women's football to fold midseason. A planned championship game was scuttled, and all seven member teams folded right along with the league.

Exhibition Season　　　　　　　　Teams: 7　　　　　　　　Games: 19
No Declared Champion (League folded midseason)

2002 UWFL Standings

Teams	W	L	PR	Before	After
Colorado Springs Koalas (CSK)	5	1	--	Expansion	Folded
Denver Foxes (DEN)	5	1	--	Expansion	Folded
Pueblo Pythons (PUEB)	4	1	--	Expansion	Folded
Tri-City Mustangs (TCM)	2	3	--	Expansion	Folded
Grand Valley Vipers (GVV)	2	3	--	Expansion	Folded
Sweetwater County Outlaws (SCO)	1	4	--	Expansion	Folded
Cheyenne Dust Devils (CDD)	0	6	--	Expansion	Folded

United Women's Football League (UWFL) – 2002 Season (continued)

2002 UWFL Scoreboard

4/13	TCM	43	CDD	2	4/27	DEN	40	TCM	7	5/12	CSK	31	GVV	6
4/14	CSK	63	SCO	13	4/28	GVV	42	SCO	14	5/12	DEN	42	PUEB	19
4/14	DEN	71	GVV	6	4/28	PUEB	6	CDD	0	5/12	TCM	25	SCO	7
4/20	SCO	15	CDD	14	5/5	CSK	44	CDD	14	5/19	CSK	26	TCM	14
4/21	CSK	30	DEN	29	5/5	DEN	30	SCO	0	5/19	GVV	22	CDD	0
4/21	PUEB	35	TCM	6	5/5	PUEB	29	GVV	8					
										5/26	DEN	74	CDD	0
										5/26	PUEB	48	CSK	46

Women's Football League (WFL) – 2002 Season

The Tennessee Heat were joined in the WFL for the 2002 season by the Carolina Cougars and the Fayetteville Warriors. The WFL hedged its bets between the spring/summer and fall/winter women's football seasons by having their three teams play a few exhibition games against each other in the late summer and early fall. This set the stage for the league's first full season in 2003.

Exhibition Season　　　　　　　Teams: 3　　　　　　　Games: 4
No Declared Champion

2002 WFL Standings

Teams	W	L	PR	Before	After
Carolina Cougars (COUG)	4	0	--	Joined from MIWFA	Folded
Fayetteville Warriors (FAYW)	0	2	--	Expansion	Folded
Tennessee Heat (TNH)	0	2	--	--	--

2002 WFL Scoreboard

7/20	COUG	27	TNH	8
8/10	COUG	44	TNH	0
8/24	COUG	14	FAYW	12
9/7	COUG	44	FAYW	8

2002 Fall/Winter Review

The WAFL had supplanted the WPFL as the top fall/winter women's football league in 2001, but in a stunning reversal, the WPFL quickly reclaimed its throne. The WPFL expanded from four teams to 11 teams in 2002, an unlikely resurrection for a league that had been pushed to the brink the year before. Meanwhile, the WAFL fractured into three pieces. The WAFC and WAFL-WFA both inherited five former WAFL teams, while three ex-WAFL teams became the core of the AFWL. All three of these WAFL successor leagues folded after the 2002 season, and by 2003, the WPFL stood alone as the only remaining fall/winter league in women's football.

Leagues: 4   Teams: 32 (30)   Games: 153.5 (117)

Women's Professional Football League (WPFL) – 2002 Season

The WPFL recovered from near-extinction in 2001 to assemble a solid 11-team league in 2002. The structure may have been different, but the results were the same as ever. The Houston Energy captured their third consecutive WPFL championship, this time dispatching the Wisconsin Riveters. The Energy became the first team in the history of women's football to win three straight league championship games.

Major National League   Teams: 11   Games: 47.5 (43)
Championship game result: Houston Energy 56, Wisconsin Riveters 7

2002 WPFL Standings

National Conference	W	L	PR	Before	After
Wisconsin Riveters (WIR)	10	1	C	Expansion	Left for NWFA (2004)
Syracuse Sting (SYR)	4	4	CC	Joined from MIWFA	--
Indiana Speed (INS)	4	4	--	Expansion	--
Minnesota Vixen (MN)	2	3	--	Joined from MIWFA	--
New England Storm (NES)	1	7	--	--	--
Missouri Prowlers (PRWL)	0	7	--	Expansion	--
American Conference					
Houston Energy (HOU)	11	0	LC	--	--
Arizona Knighthawks (AZKH)	8	2	CC	Expansion	--
Dallas Diamonds (DAL)	4	5	--	Expansion	--
Austin Rage (RAGE)	2	5	--	--	Folded
Los Angeles Amazons (LA)	2	9	--	Expansion	--

2002 WPFL Scoreboard

Date	Team	Score	Team	Score		Date	Team	Score	Team	Score		Date	Team	Score	Team	Score	
4/13	AZKH	57	BX	0	IE	8/29	CAL	20	LA	8	I	9/28	AZKH	1	OUT	0	I
						8/31	AZKH	21	DAL	19		9/28	DAL	27	AZT	22	I
7/27	ROSA	6	LA	0	I	8/31	MN	53	PRWL	0		9/28	HOU	1	LA	0	
						8/31	NES	29	INS	28		9/28	RAGE	74	PRWL	0	
8/3	AZKH	46	LA	6		8/31	WIR	34	SYR	8		9/28	WIR	1	NES	0	
8/3	HOU	46	DAL	6		9/7	AZKH	27	LA	0		10/5	AZKH	41	LA	0	
8/3	WIR	32	NES	0		9/7	HOU	40	SYR	6		10/5	HOU	42	RAGE	7	
						9/7	INS	61	PRWL	0		10/5	WIR	26	SYR	22	
8/10	AZKH	48	RAGE	33		9/7	RAGE	34	DAL	26							
8/10	HOU	39	AZT	0	I	9/7	WIR	44	MN	14		10/12	AZKH	16	LA	0	
8/10	MN	54	PRWL	0								10/12	HOU	31	DAL	0	
8/10	SYR	6	NES	3		9/14	LA	14	ROSA	13	I	10/12	INS	37	NES	0	
						9/14	AZT	1	RAGE	0	I	10/12	WIR	67	PRWL	0	
8/17	DAL	26	RAGE	21		9/14	SYR	14	NES	13							
8/17	HOU	1	AZKH	0		9/14	WIR	26	INS	13		10/19	HOU	46	DAL	7	
8/17	SYR	30	INS	0								10/19	INS	55	PRWL	0	
8/17	WIR	33	MN	14		9/21	DAL	79	PRWL	0		10/19	CAL	20	LA	14	I*
						9/21	HOU	59	RAGE	26							
8/24	DAL	39	NES	20		9/21	LBA	1	LA	0	I	10/26	HOU	6	AZKH	0	CC
8/24	INS	11	MN	6		9/21	SYR	40	NES	7		10/26	WIR	31	SYR	6	CC
						9/21	WIR	27	INS	6							
												11/9	LA	8	HI	0	I
												11/9	HOU	56	WIR	7	C

Women's Affiliated Football Conference (WAFC) – 2002 Season

Five teams from the WAFL's 2001 Pacific Conference joined four expansion teams form the WAFC in 2002. The Sacramento Sirens defeated the Arizona Caliente to claim the first league title in their storied history. After one season, the WAFC closed up shop.

Regional League Teams: 9 (7) Games: 38.5 (33.5)
Championship game result: Sacramento Sirens 59, Arizona Caliente 20

2002 WAFC Standings

	W	L	PR	Before	After
Northern Conference					
Sacramento Sirens (SAC)	11	0	LC	Joined from WAFL	Left for IWFL
Oakland Banshees (OAK)	5	6	CC	Joined from WAFL	Left for IWFL
Santa Rosa Scorchers (ROSA)	3	5	--	Expansion	Left for IWFL
San Francisco Stingrayz (SF)	0	11	--	Expansion	Left for IWFL
Southern Conference					
Arizona Caliente (AZC)	8	2	C	Joined from WAFL	Left for WPFL
Pacific Blast (PB)	6	5	CC	Expansion	Folded
California Quake (CAL)	5	5	--	Joined from WAFL	Left for IWFL
Affiliate Team					
San Diego Nitrous (SDN)	0	4	--	Expansion	Folded
Independent Affiliate					
Hawaii Legends (HI)	1	0	--	Joined from WAFL	Folded

2002 WAFC Scoreboard

Date						Date						Date					
6/29	ROSA	52	SF	0	E	9/28	AZC	56	SDN	0		11/2	CAL	1	SF	0	
						9/28	OAK	34	SF	14		11/6	SAC	47	PB	26	
7/20	ROSA	6	SF	0	E	9/28	SAC	62	ROSA	0		11/9	AZC	26	CAL	0	
7/27	ROSA	6	LA	0	I							11/9	LA	8	PB	0	I
						10/2	PB	22	SF	12		11/9	PB	1	SF	0	
8/3	SAC	41	OAK	20	E	10/5	AZC	27	SF	0		11/10	SAC	55	OAK	0	
8/10	OAK	26	SF	6	E	10/5	PB	56	OAK	20							
8/29	CAL	20	LA	8	I	10/5	SAC	52	CAL	19		11/16	AZC	1	SDN	0	
9/7	SAC	45	SF	0		10/12	CAL	41	SDN	0		11/16	SAC	48	SF	12	
9/8	OAK	31	ROSA	6		10/12	SAC	36	ROSA	9							
9/11	PB	46	CAL	6								11/23	AZC	1	PB	0	CC
						10/17	PB	36	AZC	12		11/23	SAC	69	OAK	0	CC
9/14	AZC	36	OAK	12		10/19	AZC	23	PB	6							
9/14	PB	72	CAL	6		10/19	CAL	20	LA	14	I*	12/7	SAC	59	AZC	20	C
9/14	LA	14	ROSA	13	I	10/19	SAC	53	OAK	32							
9/21	AZC	32	CAL	16		10/26	CAL	1	SDN	0							
9/21	OAK	20	ROSA	14		10/26	OAK	24	SF	20							
						10/27	HI	72	PB	7	E						

Women's American Football League-Women's Football Association (WAFL-WFA) – 2002 Season

Five teams from the WAFL's 2001 Atlantic Conference joined three expansion teams to make an eight-team league in 2002. The league had a hard time deciding if it was a continuous league of the 2001 WAFL or not – it was simultaneously called the WAFL and the WFA during the 2002 season. The WAFL-WFA considered itself enough of a successor league, however, to call its championship game Women's World Bowl II, a contest won by the Jacksonville Dixie Blues. The league was plagued by an unusually high number of forfeits, with nearly half of the WAFL-WFA's scheduled games called off. At the conclusion of the season, the WAFL-WFA (and any subsequent World Bowls) was surrendered to history.

Regional League   Teams: 8 (7)   Games: 43.5 (22.5)
Championship game result: Jacksonville Dixie Blues 68, Indianapolis Vipers 20

2002 WAFL-WFA Standings

Central Conference	W	L	PR	Before	After
Indianapolis Vipers (IV)	9	3	C	Joined from WAFL	Folded
Birmingham Steel Magnolias (BIRM)	5	6	CC	Expansion	Folded
Georgia Enforcers (GAE)	2	8	--	Expansion	Folded
New Orleans Voodoo Dolls (NOVD)	0	10	--	Joined from WAFL	Folded
Southern Conference					
Jacksonville Dixie Blues (JAX)	11	1	LC	Joined from WAFL	Left for IWFL (2004)
Orlando Fire (ORLF)	9	2	CC	Joined from WAFL	Folded
South Carolina Crusaders (SCC)	5	5	--	Expansion	Folded
Tampa Bay Force (TBF)	2	9	--	Joined from WAFL	Folded

2002 WAFL-WFA Scoreboard

Date	Team	Score	Team	Score		Date	Team	Score	Team	Score		Date	Team	Score	Team	Score	
5/25	ORLS	48	TBF	0	I	11/2	JAX	40	BIRM	16		12/7	BIRM	1	GAE	0	
						11/2	TBF	1	GAE	0		12/7	IV	1	NOVD	0	N
10/5	ORLF	53	TBF	6		11/3	ORLF	1	NOVD	0	N	12/7	JAX	20	ORLF	0	
						11/3	SCC	54	IV	34		12/7	SCC	1	TBF	0	
10/12	GAE	1	NOVD	0	N												
10/12	IV	20	BIRM	14		11/9	IV	14	BIRM	8		12/14	BIRM	1	TBF	0	
10/12	ORLF	33	JAX	30		11/9	JAX	35	GAE	6		12/14	JAX	33	IV	6	
10/12	SCC	24	TBF	14		11/9	ORLF	35	SCC	0		12/14	ORLF	1	NOVD	0	N
						11/9	TBF	1	NOVD	0	N	12/14	SCC	1	GAE	0	
10/19	BIRM	20	GAE	8													
10/19	IV	1	NOVD	0	N	11/16	GAE	1	NOVD	0	N	12/21	IV	1	TBF	0	
10/19	JAX	41	TBF	8		11/16	IV	20	SCC	15		12/21	JAX	1	NOVD	0	N
10/19	ORLF	18	SCC	12		11/16	JAX	1	TBF	0		12/21	ORLF	1	BIRM	0	
						11/16	ORLF	35	BIRM	0		12/21	SCC	1	GAE	0	
10/26	BIRM	1	NOVD	0	N												
10/26	IV	1	GAE	0		11/23	BIRM	1	NOVD	0	N	1/11	IV	38	BIRM	6	CC
10/26	JAX	40	SCC	13		11/23	IV	1	GAE	0		1/11	JAX	38	ORLF	18	CC
						11/23	JAX	59	SCC	13							
						11/23	ORLF	40	TBF	0		1/18	JAX	68	IV	20	C

American Football Women's League (AFWL) – 2002 Season

This small, five-team, California-based league was formed around three teams that had played the previous season in the WAFL. The Long Beach Aftershock pulled an upset in the championship game, knocking off the previously undefeated San Diego Sunfire for the title. Those two teams then joined the WPFL at the conclusion of the season, while the rest of the league's teams would fold along with the AFWL.

Regional League Teams: 5 Games: 25 (19)
Championship game result: Long Beach Aftershock 12, San Diego Sunfire 7

2002 AFWL Standings

Teams	W	L	PR	Before	After
San Diego Sunfire (SDSF)	9	1	C	Joined from WAFL	Left for WPFL
Long Beach Aftershock (LBA)	8	3	LC	Expansion	Left for WPFL
Los Angeles Lasers (LAL)	5	4	CC	Joined from WAFL	Folded
Arizona Titans (AZT)	2	10	CC	Joined from IWFL	Folded
San Francisco Tsunami (SFT)	1	7	--	Joined from WAFL	Folded

2002 AFWL Scoreboard

Date						Date						Date					
8/10	HOU	39	AZT	0	I	10/12	LBA	46	SFT	0		11/16	AZT	1	SFT	0	
						10/12	SDSF	42	AZT	6		11/17	LAL	35	LBA	6	
9/14	AZT	1	RAGE	0	I												
						10/19	LBA	14	LAL	0		11/23	LAL	56	AZT	0	
9/21	LAL	66	AZT	0		10/19	SFT	1	AZT	0		11/23	SDSF	1	SFT	0	
9/21	LBA	1	LA	0	I												
9/21	SDSF	27	SFT	0		10/26	LAL	1	SFT	0		12/7	LBA	8	LAL	6	CC
						10/26	SDSF	27	LBA	8		12/7	SDSF	55	AZT	0	CC
9/28	DAL	27	AZT	22	I												
9/28	LBA	63	AZT	0		11/2	LBA	12	AZT	0		12/14	LBA	12	SDSF	7	C
9/28	SDSF	17	LAL	14	*	11/2	SDSF	33	LAL	26							
10/5	LAL	48	SFT	6		11/9	LBA	1	SFT	0							
10/5	SDSF	34	LBA	28		11/9	SDSF	30	AZT	0							

2003 Season Review

The era of tri-champions arrived in 2003, with the NWFA, IWFL, and WPFL champions sharing the mantle of the best team in the sport. The newly-named NWFA (rebranded from the NWFL) and the IWFL each crowned co-champions of the sport's spring/summer season, while the WPFL declared the sport's top fall/winter club. The WFL held its first full season, which ended in disaster, and the regrettably-monikered AWFL lived up to its nickname.

Leagues: 5 Teams: 82 (75) Games: 347 (336)

National Women's Football Association (NWFA) – 2003 Season

The NWFL, under pressure from the NFL, made several changes to their league. They changed their name from the NWFL to the NWFA and agreed to stop referring to their championship game as the "SupHer Bowl". Several NWFA teams also rebranded, adopting new logos that were more distinct from their local NFL teams. One of the NWFA franchises that rebranded that offseason was reigning league champion Detroit; after switching nicknames from the Danger to the Demolition, they went on to capture their second straight national title, edging the Pensacola Power in the championship game.

Major National League   Teams: 32 (30)   Games: 140
Championship game result: Detroit Demolition 28, Pensacola Power 21

2003 NWFA Standings

Northern Conference	W	L	PR	Before	After
North Division					
Philadelphia Phoenix (PHIP)	8	2	CC	Expansion	--
Connecticut Crush (CTC)	7	3	Q	--	--
Massachusetts Mutiny (MASS)	5	3	--	--	--
Maine Freeze (ME)	3	7	--	--	--
Rochester Raptors (ROCH)	0	9	--	--	--
Mid-Atlantic Division					
D.C. Divas (DC)	8	2	S	--	--
Baltimore Burn (BAL)	7	3	Q	--	--
Columbus Flames (COLF)	6	3	--	Expansion	Became Columbus Comets
Pittsburgh Passion (PITT)	2	6	--	Expansion	--
Erie Illusion (ERIE)	0	8	--	Expansion	--
Great Lakes Division					
Detroit Demolition (DET)	11	0	LC	Were Detroit Danger	--
Cleveland Fusion (CLE)	7	3	S	--	--
Southwest Michigan Jaguars (SMJ)	4	4	--	--	--
Toledo Spitfire (TOLS)	2	6	--	Expansion	--
Indiana Thunder (INT)	0	8	--	Were South Bend Hawks	--

Southern Conference	W	L	PR	Before	After
Central Division					
Chattanooga Locomotion (CHAT)	11	1	S	--	--
Alabama Renegades (ALRG)	7	4	S	--	--
Asheville Assault (ASH)	5	4	Q	--	--
Nashville Dream (NASH)	5	6	Q	--	--
Tennessee Venom (TNV)	2	6	--	--	--
Knoxville Summit (KNXS)	2	7	--	--	Left for IWFL
Atlanta Leopards (ATLL)	0	8	--	--	--
Gulf Coast Division					
Pensacola Power (PEN)	11	1	C	--	--
New Orleans Spice (NOS)	5	3	--	--	Became New Orleans Blaze
Panama City Beach Rumble (PCBR)	4	4	--	--	Became Emerald Coast Sharks (2005)
Gulf Coast Herricanes (GCH)	0	8	--	Were Biloxi Herricanes	--
Midwest Division					
Oklahoma City Lightning (OKC)	9	2	CC	Expansion	--
Kansas City Krunch (KRUN)	5	3	--	Expansion	--
St. Louis Slam (STL)	3	5	--	Expansion	--
Evansville Express (EVAN)	0	7	--	Expansion	--

Affiliate Teams	W	L	PR	Before	After
Austin Outlaws (OUT)	1	1	--	Joined from IWFL	--
Denton Stampede (DENT)	0	3	--	Expansion	--

National Women's Football Association (NWFA) – 2003 Season (continued)
2003 NWFA Scoreboard

Date	Team1	Score	Team2	Score	Note	Date	Team1	Score	Team2	Score	Date	Team1	Score	Team2	Score	Note
3/22	CHAT	10	ALRG	8	E	5/3	ALRG	20	ASH	19	5/31	ALRG	49	TNV	0	
						5/3	CHAT	56	ATLL	0	5/31	ASH	21	NASH	20	
3/29	BAL	45	KNXS	0	E	5/3	CLE	90	INT	0	5/31	CHAT	44	KNXS	0	
3/29	CHAT	42	EVAN	0	E	5/3	COLF	34	ERIE	13	5/31	COLF	35	ERIE	12	
3/29	ME	7	ROCH	0	E	5/3	CTC	49	ROCH	0	5/31	DC	30	PITT	25	
3/29	PEN	24	NASH	0	E	5/3	DC	32	PITT	7	5/31	DET	81	TOLS	0	
						5/3	NASH	50	KNXS	0	5/31	NOS	39	PCBR	14	
4/5	CHAT	42	EVAN	0	E	5/3	NOS	44	PCBR	27	5/31	OKC	14	OUT	0	
4/5	COLF	13	NASH	0	E	5/3	PEN	82	GCH	0	5/31	PEN	84	GCH	0	
4/5	CTC	30	ME	20	E	5/3	PHIP	34	ME	0	5/31	PHIP	40	CTC	0	
4/5	OUT	47	DENT	0	E	5/3	SMJ	33	TOLS	0	5/31	SMJ	57	INT	0	
											6/1	MASS	42	ME	0	
4/12	ALRG	8	NASH	6		5/10	ASH	47	ATLL	0						
4/12	BAL	7	PITT	0		5/10	BAL	58	ERIE	3	6/7	BAL	28	ERIE	21	
4/12	CHAT	15	ASH	12	*	5/10	CTC	21	MASS	20	6/7	CLE	34	SMJ	0	
4/12	CTC	12	PHIP	7		5/10	DC	30	COLF	22	6/7	CTC	37	ME	12	
4/12	DC	50	ERIE	0		5/10	DET	95	TOLS	0	6/7	DC	8	COLF	7	
4/12	DET	7	CLE	0		5/10	KRUN	16	EVAN	0	6/7	DET	105	INT	0	
4/12	KNXS	34	ATLL	0		5/10	NASH	60	TNV	0	6/7	KRUN	34	EVAN	7	
4/12	KRUN	12	STL	6	**	5/10	OKC	21	STL	6	6/7	OKC	48	STL	13	
4/12	MASS	48	ROCH	0		5/10	PHIP	51	ROCH	0	6/7	PCBR	28	GCH	8	
4/12	NOS	26	GCH	22		5/10	SMJ	81	INT	12	6/7	PHIP	26	MASS	7	
4/12	OKC	97	DENT	0							6/7	TNV	46	ATLL	14	
4/12	PEN	54	PCBR	0		5/17	ALRG	41	KNXS	0						
4/12	TOLS	32	INT	28		5/17	ASH	54	TNV	0	6/14	BAL	22	DC	14	
						5/17	CHAT	41	NASH	8	6/14	CHAT	22	ASH	15	
4/19	ALRG	30	ATLL	0		5/17	CLE	78	INT	6	6/14	COLF	57	PITT	15	
4/19	ASH	26	TNV	0		5/17	COLF	13	BAL	0	6/14	CTC	18	ME	0	
4/19	CHAT	65	KNXS	0		5/17	MASS	24	CTC	7	6/14	DET	33	CLE	19	
4/19	CLE	66	TOLS	0		5/17	ME	15	ROCH	7	6/14	KNXS	13	TNV	6	
4/19	COLF	21	PITT	18		5/17	OKC	84	DENT	14	6/14	NASH	54	ATLL	0	
4/19	CTC	49	ROCH	6		5/17	PCBR	55	GCH	6	6/14	NOS	34	GCH	0	
4/19	DC	24	BAL	0		5/17	PEN	49	NOS	0	6/14	OKC	35	KRUN	14	
4/19	DET	45	SMJ	9		5/17	PITT	20	ERIE	18	6/14	PEN	35	ALRG	0	
4/19	KRUN	20	EVAN	0		5/17	SMJ	41	TOLS	0	6/14	PHIP	34	ROCH	0	
4/19	MASS	32	ME	9		5/17	STL	7	KRUN	6	6/14	STL	35	EVAN	14	
4/19	NASH	20	STL	6							6/14	TOLS	30	INT	8	
4/19	PCBR	60	GCH	8		5/24	ALRG	42	ATLL	6						
4/19	PEN	49	NOS	3		5/24	ASH	48	KNXS	21	6/28	ALRG	27	ASH	13	Q
						5/24	BAL	21	PITT	15	6/28	CLE	28	BAL	19	Q
4/26	BAL	13	COLF	7		5/24	CHAT	85	TNV	0	6/28	DC	76	CTC	0	Q
4/26	CHAT	28	ALRG	26		5/24	CLE	84	TOLS	0	6/28	OKC	28	NASH	21	Q
4/26	CLE	56	SMJ	6		5/24	DC	74	ERIE	7						
4/26	DET	90	INT	18		5/24	DET	70	SMJ	6	7/12	DET	28	CLE	15	S
4/26	MASS	47	ROCH	0		5/24	KRUN	8	OKC	7	7/12	OKC	20	CHAT	6	S
4/26	OKC	19	KRUN	18	*	5/24	ME	19	ROCH	6	7/12	PEN	34	ALRG	12	S
4/26	PCBR	35	NOS	34		5/24	NASH	27	STL	7	7/12	PHIP	36	DC	32	S
4/26	PEN	81	ATLL	0		5/24	NOS	24	GCH	0						
4/26	PHIP	34	ME	0		5/24	PEN	41	PCBR	7	7/19	DET	58	PHIP	14	CC
4/26	PITT	14	ERIE	7		5/24	PHIP	34	MASS	12	7/19	PEN	26	OKC	14	CC
4/26	STL	27	EVAN	20												
4/26	TNV	26	KNXS	0							8/2	DET	28	PEN	21	C

Independent Women's Football League (IWFL) – 2003 Season

Bolstered by the additions of eight West Coast teams from now-defunct regional leagues, the IWFL established itself alongside the NWFA as one of the top two spring women's football leagues. The Sacramento Sirens triumphed over the defending league champion New York Sharks in the 2003 IWFL championship game; the Sirens, who had won the 2002 WAFC championship in December, claimed their second league championship in the span of eight months.

Major National League Teams: 27 (22) Games: 113 (105)
Championship game result: Sacramento Sirens 41, New York Sharks 30

2003 IWFL Standings

Eastern Conference	W	L	T	PR	Before	After
North Atlantic Division						
Bay State Warriors (BSW)	9	1	0	CC	--	--
Montreal Blitz (MON)	4	4	0	--	--	--
New Hampshire Freedom (NH)	3	5	0	--	--	--
Rhode Island Riptide (RIR)	2	7	0	--	Expansion	Became Rhode Island Intensity
Mid-Atlantic Division						
New York Sharks (NY)	9	1	0	C	--	--
Philadelphia Liberty Belles (I) (PLB1)	3	4	0	--	Joined from NWFA	Folded
Albany Night-Mares (ANM)	1	5	0	--	--	Folded
South Atlantic Division						
Miami Fury (MIA)	6	3	0	S	--	Deferred until 2005
Tampa Bay Terminators (TBT)	4	5	0	--	Expansion	--
Orlando Starz (ORLS)	1	8	0	--	--	Became Orlando Mayhem
Western Conference						
Southwest Division						
Chicago Force (CHI)	10	1	0	CC	Expansion	--
Dallas Revolution (DREV)	4	2	0	--	Expansion	Deferred until 2005
Oklahoma City Avengers (OKCA)	1	7	0	--	--	Folded
Pacific Northwest Division						
Tacoma Majestics (TMAJ)	7	2	0	S	Joined from WSFL	--
Corvallis Pride (COR)	6	2	1	S	--	--
Portland Shockwave (POR)	5	4	1	--	Joined from WSFL	--
Eugene Edge (EUG)	2	6	0	--	--	--
Boise Xtreme (BX)	2	8	0	--	Joined from WSFL	--
Pacific Southwest Division						
Sacramento Sirens (SAC)	12	0	0	LC	Joined from WAFC	--
Oakland Banshees (OAK)	5	5	0	--	Joined from WAFC	--
California Quake (CAL)	3	5	0	--	Joined from WAFC	--
Santa Rosa Scorchers (ROSA)	1	9	0	--	Joined from WAFC	--
Affiliate Teams						
Atlanta Xplosion (ATLX)	9	1	0	--	Expansion	--
San Francisco Stingrayz (SF)	4	2	0	--	Joined from WAFC	--
Memphis Maulers (MAUL)	1	3	0	--	--	Left for WFL (2003)
San Diego Sea Catz (SDSC)	0	4	0	--	Expansion	--
Detroit Blaze (DETB)	0	6	0	--	--	Folded

Independent Women's Football League (IWFL) – 2003 Season (continued)
2003 IWFL Scoreboard

Date	Team1	Score	Team2	Score		Date	Team1	Score	Team2	Score		Date	Team1	Score	Team2	Score	Note
3/8	CAL	8	ROSA	0		4/26	CHI	41	DETB	0		5/24	ATLX	35	TNH	6	I
3/8	SAC	64	OAK	14		4/26	COR	12	BX	0		5/24	BX	1	ROSA	0	
						4/26	MIA	26	TBT	13		5/24	SF	80	CAL	3	
3/15	OAK	28	ROSA	12		4/26	MON	40	NH	0		5/24	TBT	43	OKCA	14	
3/15	SAC	62	SF	26		4/26	NY	62	RIR	0		5/25	CHI	55	SDSC	0	
						4/26	OAK	16	CAL	14		5/25	MIA	44	ORLS	14	
3/22	COR	19	EUG	8		4/26	OKCA	1	MAUL	0							
3/22	DREV	36	MAUL	18		4/26	PLB1	14	ANM	0		5/31	ATLX	39	ORLS	0	
3/22	POR	32	BX	8		4/26	SAC	68	SF	22		5/31	BSW	34	NH	0	
3/22	SAC	67	ROSA	6		4/26	TMAJ	12	POR	0		5/31	CHI	41	DREV	6	
												5/31	EUG	39	BX	0	
3/29	CAL	31	OAK	14		5/3	ATLX	25	TBT	6		5/31	MIA	20	TBT	15	
3/29	CHI	49	DETB	0		5/3	BSW	34	PLB1	6		5/31	MON	1	DETB	0	
3/29	COR	26	POR	26		5/3	CHI	47	DETB	0		5/31	NY	41	ANM	0	
3/29	MAUL	16	OKCA	0		5/3	COR	33	EUG	8		5/31	PLB1	8	RIR	0	
3/29	SF	42	ROSA	13		5/3	DREV	18	OKCA	6		5/31	POR	32	OAK	12	
3/29	TMAJ	42	EUG	0		5/3	MIA	30	ORLS	6		5/31	SAC	65	CAL	21	
						5/3	MON	15	RIR	12		5/31	TMAJ	12	COR	0	
4/5	CHI	1	MAUL	0		5/3	NH	19	ANM	0							
4/5	DREV	16	OKCA	0		5/3	POR	34	BX	12		6/7	ATLX	34	FAYT	8	I
4/5	POR	6	EUG	0		5/3	ROSA	6	CAL	0		6/7	BSW	26	RIR	0	
4/5	SAC	67	OAK	8		5/3	SAC	81	SDSC	0		6/7	CHI	1	OKCA	0	
4/5	TMAJ	26	BX	6		5/3	SF	1	OAK	0		6/7	COR	38	BX	6	
												6/7	MON	14	NH	6	
4/12	BSW	12	RIR	0		5/10	BSW	30	NH	0		6/7	NY	20	MIA	6	
4/12	CAL	43	SDSC	0		5/10	COR	20	POR	14		6/7	ORLS	22	DETB	14	
4/12	COR	18	TMAJ	0		5/10	MIA	26	ATLX	21		6/7	TMAJ	28	POR	20	
4/12	DREV	24	OKCA	8		5/10	NY	98	ANM	0		6/9	NY	36	TBT	0	
4/12	EUG	18	BX	16		5/10	OAK	58	SDSC	0							
4/12	NY	52	MON	0		5/10	PLB1	16	RIR	14		6/14	ATLX	40	MIA	6	
4/12	OAK	16	POR	14		5/10	SAC	67	CAL	14		6/14	BSW	28	PLB1	8	
4/12	SAC	42	ROSA	6		5/10	SF	50	ROSA	0		6/14	NH	29	ANM	0	
4/12	TBT	8	ORLS	0		5/10	TBT	20	ORLS	14		6/14	RIR	26	MON	10	
						5/10	TMAJ	26	EUG	7		6/14	TBT	34	ORLS	0	
4/19	ATLX	39	ORLS	0								6/14	SAC	45	TMAJ	0	S
4/19	BSW	30	MON	6		5/17	ANM	34	DETB	28							
4/19	BX	14	ROSA	6		5/17	ATLX	28	TBT	14		6/21	ATLX	50	TNH	0	I
4/19	CHI	40	DREV	8		5/17	BSW	35	MON	0		6/21	BSW	1	MIA	0	S
4/19	NY	48	PLB1	0		5/17	CHI	1	OKCA	0		6/21	CHI	28	COR	14	S
4/19	RIR	21	NH	0		5/17	MIA	20	ORLS	0							
						5/17	NH	20	RIR	14	*	6/28	ATLX	34	MAUL	14	I
						5/17	NY	58	PLB1	0		6/28	NY	20	BSW	6	CC
						5/17	OAK	14	ROSA	0		6/28	SAC	47	CHI	7	CC
						5/17	POR	18	EUG	14							
						5/17	TMAJ	47	BX	8		7/12	SAC	41	NY	30	C

Women's Professional Football League (WPFL) – 2003 Season

Eight new arrivals punctuated the WPFL's impressive comeback in 2003. Five expansion teams plus three teams from other now-defunct fall/winter leagues helped the WPFL establish itself as the premier (and only remaining) fall/winter women's football league. Wisconsin's Northern Ice defeated the Florida Stingrayz at the conclusion of the WPFL's fifth season.

Major National League   Teams: 17   Games: 81 (78)
Championship game result: Northern Ice 53, Florida Stingrayz 12

2003 WPFL Standings

National Conference	W	L	PR	Before	After
East Division					
Syracuse Sting (SYR)	7	2	--	--	--
New England Storm (NES)	3	6	--	--	Folded
Dayton Rebellion (DAYR)	2	8	--	Expansion	Folded
South Division					
Florida Stingrayz (FL)	8	3	C	Expansion	Folded
Houston Energy (HOU)	7	2	--	--	--
Missouri Prowlers (PRWL)	0	11	--	--	Became Missouri Avengers
American Conference					
North Division					
Northern Ice (ICE)	12	0	LC	Expansion	--
Indiana Speed (INS)	6	3	--	--	--
Minnesota Vixen (MN)	3	7	--	--	--
Toledo Reign (TOL)	0	5	--	Expansion	--
West Division					
Long Beach Aftershock (LBA)	8	1	CC	Joined from AFWL	--
Dallas Diamonds (DAL)	7	3	CC	--	--
Arizona Caliente (AZC)	8	2	--	Joined from WAFC	--
San Diego Sunfire (SDSF)	5	5	--	Joined from AFWL	Folded
So Cal Scorpions (SCS)	2	7	--	Expansion	--
Los Angeles Amazons (LA)	2	8	--	--	--
Arizona Knighthawks (AZKH)	1	8	--	--	Folded

2003 WPFL Scoreboard

Date					Date					Date				
8/2	DAL	66	PRWL	0	8/30	AZC	38	SDSF	20	9/27	NES	30	TOL	14
8/2	ICE	47	NES	0	8/30	INS	22	SYR	7	9/27	SCS	24	LA	14
8/2	INS	26	MN	0	8/30	LBA	54	AZKH	0	9/27	SDSF	50	AZKH	0
8/2	LA	8	SCS	7	8/30	NES	28	DAYR	6	9/27	SYR	48	DAYR	14
8/3	LBA	18	SDSF	6	9/6	AZC	14	SCS	0	10/4	AZC	44	AZKH	12
8/9	AZC	45	LA	0	9/6	DAL	72	PRWL	0	10/4	DAL	49	PRWL	0
8/9	DAL	14	HOU	12	9/6	FL	14	LA	2	10/4	FL	84	NES	6
8/9	FL	87	PRWL	0	9/6	HOU	62	SDSF	22	10/4	HOU	1	PRWL	0
8/9	ICE	69	DAYR	6	9/6	ICE	63	MN	7	10/4	INS	40	DAYR	20
8/9	INS	46	MN	13	9/6	SYR	41	DAYR	8	10/4	LBA	41	SCS	10
8/9	LBA	33	AZKH	6	9/13	AZKH	14	LA	7	10/4	SDSF	58	LA	14
8/9	SYR	12	NES	6	9/13	HOU	57	FL	20	10/4	SYR	28	MN	19
8/16	AZC	16	SCS	14	9/13	ICE	80	TOL	0	10/11	DAL	26	FL	22
8/16	FL	6	SYR	0	9/13	INS	35	DAYR	6	10/11	ICE	58	INS	13
8/16	HOU	39	DAL	14	9/13	LBA	25	AZC	19	10/11	LBA	40	LA	6
8/16	ICE	24	INS	10	9/13	SDSF	36	SCS	14	10/11	MN	61	PRWL	12
8/16	LA	26	AZKH	6	9/13	SYR	28	NES	8	10/11	NES	12	DAYR	8
8/16	LBA	34	SDSF	13	9/20	AZC	46	LA	0	10/11	SDSF	20	AZKH	14
8/16	MN	1	PRWL	0	9/20	DAL	65	PRWL	0	10/11	SYR	55	TOL	12
8/23	AZC	27	AZKH	6	9/20	FL	44	INS	21	10/12	HOU	75	SCS	14
8/23	DAYR	30	TOL	18	9/20	ICE	48	DAYR	0	10/18	AZC	41	SDSF	24
8/23	FL	14	NES	0	9/20	MN	61	TOL	0	10/18	DAL	10	HOU	7
8/23	HOU	41	SCS	0	9/20	SCS	27	AZKH	14	10/18	DAYR	48	PRWL	0
8/23	INS	1	PRWL	0	9/20	SYR	41	NES	12	10/18	ICE	61	MN	13
8/23	SDSF	20	LA	12	9/27	FL	33	MN	15	10/25	FL	22	DAL	14 CC
8/24	ICE	61	MN	6	9/27	HOU	38	DAL	27	10/25	ICE	37	LBA	30 CC
					9/27	ICE	77	PRWL	0	11/8	ICE	53	FL	12 C
					9/27	LBA	32	AZC	27					

Women's Football League (WFL) – 2003 Season

After two years of preparation, the WFL was finally ready to expand to a full league season in 2003. But with only three confirmed teams and scant publicity, the league was completely lost in the shuffle of women's football. The Memphis Maulers were set to host the Fayetteville Thunder in the first ever WFL championship game, but a severe thunderstorm in Memphis was blamed for the cancellation of the contest.

Exhibition Season   Teams: 3   Games: 9
Championship game result: Memphis Maulers vs. Fayetteville Thunder (cancelled)

2003 WFL Standings

Teams	W	L	PR	Before	After
Memphis Maulers (MAUL)	4	1	C	Joined from IWFL (2003)	Folded
Fayetteville Thunder (FAYT)	3	3	C	Expansion	Became WPFL's Cape Fear Thunder (2005)
Tennessee Heat (TNH)	0	7	CC	--	Deferred until 2005

2003 WFL Scoreboard

5/17	MAUL	34	TNH	6		6/7	ATLX	34	FAYT	8	I	6/28	ATLX	34	MAUL	14	I
5/24	ATLX	35	TNH	6	I	6/7	MAUL	14	TNH	6		7/19	FAYT	30	TNH	6
5/31	MAUL	8	FAYT	0		6/14	FAYT	28	TNH	20		7/26	FAYT	22	TNH	14	CC
						6/21	MAUL	16	FAYT	0						
						6/21	ATLX	50	TNH	0	I					

American Women's Football League (AWFL) – 2003 Season

The AWFL tried to launch with just three teams in 2003, but the results were, well, awful. After an abbreviated schedule, the AWFL followed the UWFL's lead from the year before and folded midseason.

Exhibition Season   Teams: 3   Games: 4
No Declared Champion (League folded midseason)

2003 AWFL Standings

Teams	W	L	PR	Before	After
Tennessee Mountaincatz (TNM)	3	0	--	Expansion	Folded
Lee County Predators (LCP)	1	2	--	Expansion	Folded
Harlan Red Devils (HRD)	0	2	--	Expansion	Folded

2003 AWFL Scoreboard

4/12	TNM	16	LCP	0
4/19	LCP	6	HRD	0
4/26	TNM	36	HRD	0
5/3	TNM	40	LCP	0

2004 Season Review

All the small regional leagues apparently took the 2004 season off, leaving the sport to the three major women's leagues – the NWFA, IWFL, and WPFL. The two spring leagues, the NWFA and the IWFL, presented dueling dynasties with repeat champions. The WPFL nearly made it three-for-three for defending league champs, but that possibility was derailed by a new power in women's football.

Leagues: 3   Teams: 77 (66)   Games: 326 (313)

National Women's Football Association (NWFA) – 2004 Season

Despite still being contained to the two easternmost time zones of the United States, the NWFA expanded to 34 full-member teams in 2004, a new record in women's football history. On the field, the Detroit Demolition continued their dominance, trouncing the Oklahoma City Lightning in the championship game for their third straight title.

Major National League   Teams: 34   Games: 146 (145)
Championship game result: Detroit Demolition 52, Oklahoma City Lightning 0

2004 NWFA Standings

Northern Conference	W	L	PR	Before	After
North Division					
Philadelphia Phoenix (PHIP)	7	2	Q	--	--
Massachusetts Mutiny (MASS)	6	3	Q	--	--
Connecticut Crush (CTC)	5	3	--	--	--
Maine Freeze (ME)	1	7	--	--	--
Rochester Raptors (ROCH)	1	7	--	--	Folded
Mid-Atlantic Division					
D.C. Divas (DC)	9	1	CC	--	--
Pittsburgh Passion (PITT)	6	2	--	--	--
Baltimore Burn (BAL)	4	4	--	--	--
Erie Illusion (ERIE)	1	7	--	--	--
Roanoke Revenge (ROAN)	1	7	--	Expansion	Folded
Great Lakes Division					
Detroit Demolition (DET)	11	0	LC	--	--
Columbus Comets (COL)	7	3	S	Were Columbus Flames	--
Southwest Michigan Jaguars (SMJ)	7	3	S	--	--
Cleveland Fusion (CLE)	3	5	--	--	--
Toledo Spitfire (TOLS)	3	5	--	--	--
Indiana Thunder (INT)	2	6	--	--	--
Wisconsin Riveters (WIR)	0	8	--	Joined from WPFL (2002)	Folded
Southern Conference					
South Division					
Chattanooga Locomotion (CHAT)	6	2	S	--	--
Nashville Dream (NASH)	7	2	Q	--	--
Asheville Assault (ASH)	5	3	Q	--	--
Tennessee Venom (TNV)	1	6	--	--	--
Atlanta Leopards (ATLL)	0	7	--	--	--
Gulf Coast Division					
Pensacola Power (PEN)	10	1	CC	--	--
Alabama Renegades (ALRG)	6	3	--	--	--
New Orleans Blaze (NO)	5	3	--	Were New Orleans Spice	--
Muscle Shoals Smashers (MSS)	2	7	--	Expansion	Folded
Gulf Coast Herricanes (GCH)	0	8	--	--	--
Midwest Division					
Kansas City Krunch (KRUN)	7	3	S	--	--
St. Louis Slam (STL)	5	3	--	--	--
Evansville Express (EVAN)	0	8	--	--	Folded
Southwest Division					
Oklahoma City Lightning (OKC)	10	1	C	--	--
Austin Outlaws (OUT)	5	3	--	--	--
Dallas Dragons (DALD)	3	5	--	Expansion	Folded
Denton Stampede (DENT)	0	8	--	--	--

National Women's Football Association (NWFA) – 2004 Season (continued)
2004 NWFA Scoreboard

Date	Team	Score	Team	Score
4/3	CHAT	68	ATLL	0
4/3	COL	19	CLE	2
4/3	DALD	32	OUT	31
4/3	DC	70	ROAN	0
4/3	KRUN	59	DENT	0
4/3	ME	12	ROCH	8
4/3	NASH	31	TNV	0
4/3	NO	67	GCH	0
4/3	PEN	56	MSS	0
4/3	PHIP	34	MASS	19
4/3	PITT	22	BAL	19
4/3	SMJ	1	INT	0
4/3	STL	29	EVAN	0
4/3	TOLS	37	WIR	0
4/10	CTC	32	ME	8
4/17	CHAT	49	TNV	0
4/17	DALD	69	DENT	0
4/17	DC	26	BAL	14
4/17	DET	20	COL	7
4/17	MASS	56	ROCH	0
4/17	MSS	46	GCH	0
4/17	NASH	33	EVAN	0
4/17	OKC	32	OUT	6
4/17	PEN	56	ALRG	7
4/17	PHIP	42	CTC	14
4/17	ROAN	12	ERIE	6
4/17	SMJ	64	WIR	0
4/17	STL	6	KRUN	0
4/24	ASH	19	TNV	6
4/24	BAL	36	ERIE	0
4/24	COL	27	CLE	6
4/24	DET	28	SMJ	0
4/24	KRUN	36	EVAN	6
4/24	MASS	40	ROCH	0
4/24	NASH	65	ATLL	0
4/24	NO	28	ALRG	7
4/24	OKC	32	STL	18
4/24	OUT	78	DENT	0
4/24	PEN	62	GCH	0
4/24	PHIP	57	ME	0
4/24	PITT	34	ROAN	26
4/24	TOLS	32	INT	14
5/1	ALRG	19	MSS	0
5/1	ASH	25	ATLL	0
5/1	CTC	34	ROCH	0
5/1	DC	34	ERIE	0
5/1	DET	18	COL	10
5/1	INT	30	WIR	0
5/1	KRUN	32	EVAN	0
5/1	NASH	27	CHAT	24
5/1	OKC	49	DALD	18
5/1	OUT	64	DENT	0
5/1	PEN	35	NO	12
5/1	PHIP	55	ME	0
5/1	PITT	20	BAL	14
5/1	SMJ	66	TOLS	6
5/8	ALRG	46	GCH	0
5/8	COL	50	TOLS	0
5/8	CTC	62	ROCH	0
5/8	DC	46	ERIE	0
5/8	INT	31	WIR	0
5/8	MASS	40	ME	0
5/8	NASH	35	ASH	14
5/8	NO	60	MSS	0
5/8	OKC	65	DENT	0
5/8	OUT	28	DALD	6
5/8	PITT	49	ROAN	0
5/8	SMJ	39	CLE	6
5/8	STL	20	KRUN	14
5/15	ALRG	55	ATLL	0
5/15	ASH	25	TNV	12
5/15	BAL	32	ERIE	0
5/15	CHAT	21	NASH	7
5/15	COL	69	WIR	0
5/15	DALD	57	DENT	0
5/15	DC	70	ROAN	0
5/15	DET	75	CLE	7
5/15	KRUN	27	EVAN	0
5/15	MASS	27	CTC	7
5/15	NO	26	GCH	0
5/15	PEN	70	MSS	0
5/15	PHIP	48	ROCH	0
5/15	TOLS	18	INT	8
5/22	BAL	56	ROAN	6
5/22	CHAT	62	ATLL	0
5/22	CLE	46	INT	8
5/22	COL	34	SMJ	14
5/22	CTC	23	ME	0
5/22	DC	28	PITT	14
5/22	DET	67	WIR	0
5/22	NASH	48	EVAN	12
5/22	NO	55	MSS	0
5/22	OKC	43	STL	12
5/22	OUT	22	DALD	16
5/22	PEN	42	ALRG	18
5/22	PHIP	14	MASS	7
5/29	ALRG	56	MSS	10
5/29	ASH	13	TNV	12
5/29	BAL	24	ROAN	8
5/29	CLE	35	TOLS	0
5/29	CTC	18	PHIP	16
5/29	DET	82	INT	0
5/29	KRUN	28	STL	18
5/29	OKC	42	OUT	6
5/29	PEN	49	GCH	0
5/29	PITT	28	ERIE	0
5/29	ROCH	22	ME	14
5/29	SMJ	77	WIR	0
6/5	ALRG	35	GCH	7
6/5	CHAT	49	ASH	0
6/5	COL	90	INT	0
6/5	DC	42	PITT	14
6/5	DET	55	CLE	0
6/5	ERIE	21	ROAN	0
6/5	KRUN	59	DENT	0
6/5	MASS	57	ME	0
6/5	NASH	50	MSS	0
6/5	OKC	62	DALD	22
6/5	PEN	28	NO	20
6/5	SMJ	74	TOLS	0
6/5	STL	29	EVAN	6
6/5	TNV	29	ATLL	13
6/12	ALRG	21	NO	12
6/12	ASH	19	ATLL	0
6/12	CHAT	28	TNV	7
6/12	CLE	62	WIR	0
6/12	DC	52	BAL	16
6/12	DET	93	TOLS	0
6/12	MASS	27	CTC	7
6/12	MSS	21	GCH	12
6/12	OKC	80	DENT	0
6/12	OUT	52	DALD	6
6/12	PHIP	58	ROCH	0
6/12	PITT	46	ERIE	0
6/12	STL	12	EVAN	0
6/26	COL	7	MASS	6 Q
6/26	KRUN	20	NASH	19 Q
6/26	PEN	60	ASH	0 Q
6/26	SMJ	26	PHIP	6 Q
7/10	DC	30	SMJ	18 S
7/10	DET	41	COL	23 S
7/10	OKC	21	KRUN	7 S
7/10	PEN	35	CHAT	20 S
7/17	DET	20	DC	14 CC
7/17	OKC	37	PEN	13 CC
7/31	DET	52	OKC	0 C

Independent Women's Football League (IWFL) – 2004 Season

The IWFL rolled the dice on ten affiliate teams (which they called "X-Teams") in 2004, the most in women's football history to that point. Just 18 full-member teams vied for the 2004 IWFL title, and the championship came down to the same two teams as the year before. For the second straight season, the Sacramento Sirens edged the New York Sharks for the IWFL crown.

Major National League Teams: 28 (18) Games: 103 (96)
Championship game result: Sacramento Sirens 29, New York Sharks 27

2004 IWFL Standings

Eastern Conference	W	L	T	PR	Before	After
North Atlantic Division						
Montreal Blitz (MON)	6	2	0	--	--	--
Bay State Warriors (BSW)	0	8	0	--	--	--
Mid-Atlantic Division						
New York Sharks (NY)	10	1	0	C	--	--
Chicago Force (CHI)	6	3	0	S	--	--
New Hampshire Freedom (NH)	4	3	1	--	--	Became Manchester Freedom
South Atlantic Division						
Tampa Bay Terminators (TBT)	7	3	0	CC	--	--
Atlanta Xplosion (ATLX)	5	4	0	S	--	--
Western Conference						
Pacific Northwest Division						
Tacoma Majestics (TMAJ)	8	1	0	S	--	--
Corvallis Pride (COR)	7	3	0	CC	--	--
Portland Shockwave (POR)	3	5	0	--	--	--
Boise Xtreme (BX)	2	6	0	--	--	--
Eugene Edge (EUG)	1	7	0	--	--	--
Pacific West Division						
Sacramento Sirens (SAC)	10	1	0	LC	--	--
San Francisco Stingrayz (SF)	6	2	0	--	--	Left for WPFL
Santa Rosa Scorchers (ROSA)	2	6	0	--	--	--
Pacific Southwest Division						
Oakland Banshees (OAK)	8	1	0	S	--	--
San Diego Sea Catz (SDSC)	3	5	0	--	--	Folded
California Quake (CAL)	0	8	0	--	--	--
Affiliate Teams						
Jacksonville Dixie Blues (JAX)	5	1	0	--	Joined from WAFL-WFA (2002)	--
Rhode Island Intensity (RII)	3	5	0	--	Were Rhode Island Riptide	--
Southern Maine Rebels (SMR)	2	4	1	--	Expansion	--
Orlando Mayhem (ORLM)	2	6	0	--	Were Orlando Starz	--
Memphis Matrix (MTRX)	1	1	0	--	Expansion	Folded
Des Moines Courage (DSM)	1	3	0	--	Expansion	--
Knoxville Summit (KNXS)	0	2	0	--	Joined from NWFA	Became NWFA's Knoxville Tornadoes
Detroit Predators (PRED)	0	3	0	--	Expansion	--
Carolina Spartans (CS)	0	4	0	--	Expansion	Folded
Redding Rage (REDD)	0	4	0	--	Expansion	--

Independent Women's Football League (IWFL) – 2004 Season (continued)
2004 IWFL Scoreboard

Date	Team1	Score	Team2	Score		Date	Team1	Score	Team2	Score		Date	Team1	Score	Team2	Score	Note
4/3	CHI	50	DSM	0		5/8	COR	32	EUG	6		6/5	ATLX	22	ORLM	0	
4/3	EUG	6	POR	0		5/8	JAX	46	MTRX	16		6/5	CHI	30	NH	0	
4/3	JAX	34	TBT	20		5/8	NH	20	BSW	0		6/5	COR	34	BX	0	
4/3	NY	28	ATLX	21		5/8	NY	6	CHI	2		6/5	MON	20	BSW	6	
4/3	OAK	41	CAL	0		5/8	OAK	68	REDD	0		6/5	NY	41	RII	16	
4/3	ORLM	72	CS	0		5/8	POR	21	BX	14		6/5	OAK	38	CAL	0	
4/3	SAC	68	ROSA	0		5/8	RII	21	SMR	14		6/5	SAC	33	ROSA	0	
4/3	SF	94	SDSC	0		5/8	SAC	62	SDSC	6		6/5	SDSC	1	SF	0	
4/3	TMAJ	27	BX	0		5/8	TBT	49	ORLM	0		6/5	TBT	1	CS	0	
												6/5	TMAJ	27	POR	0	
4/17	ATLX	47	KNXS	0		5/15	ATLX	1	KNXS	0							
4/17	CHI	63	PRED	0		5/15	CHI	65	PRED	0		6/12	COR	50	EUG	6	
4/17	COR	20	POR	7		5/15	JAX	1	ORLM	0		6/12	MON	24	SMR	14	
4/17	MTRX	30	DSM	0		5/15	MON	26	RII	13		6/12	NH	36	RII	6	
4/17	NY	26	NH	0		5/15	NH	14	SMR	8		6/12	NY	35	BSW	0	
4/17	OAK	40	SDSC	0		5/15	NY	45	BSW	0		6/12	POR	21	BX	14	
4/17	ROSA	43	REDD	0		5/15	OAK	42	SDSC	0		6/12	SAC	1	CAL	0	
4/17	SAC	69	CAL	0		5/15	POR	28	EUG	13		6/12	SF	92	REDD	0	
4/17	SMR	22	MON	0		5/15	ROSA	1	CAL	0							
4/17	TBT	14	ORLM	0		5/15	SF	36	SAC	20		6/26	COR	22	OAK	14	S
4/17	TMAJ	42	EUG	13		5/15	TMAJ	27	BX	6		6/26	NY	40	CHI	0	S
												6/26	SAC	49	TMAJ	20	S
4/24	BX	20	EUG	14		5/22	ATLX	52	ORLM	13		6/26	TBT	21	ATLX	8	S
4/24	CHI	40	DSM	0		5/22	COR	28	POR	14							
4/24	NH	0	SMR	0	*	5/22	JAX	34	TBT	23		7/10	NY	29	TBT	7	CC
4/24	NY	20	MON	0		5/22	MON	12	RII	7		7/10	SAC	43	COR	8	CC
4/24	OAK	54	REDD	6		5/22	NH	7	BSW	0							
4/24	ORLM	54	CS	0		5/22	NY	27	CHI	7		7/24	SAC	29	NY	27	C
4/24	RII	7	BSW	6		5/22	SF	34	ROSA	19							
4/24	SDSC	20	CAL	13		5/22	TMAJ	49	EUG	0							
4/24	SF	86	ROSA	0													
4/24	TBT	7	ATLX	6		5/29	BX	45	EUG	40							
4/24	TMAJ	33	COR	14		5/29	DSM	30	PRED	6							
						5/29	JAX	53	ORLM	0							
5/1	ATLX	14	JAX	12		5/29	MON	28	BSW	0							
5/1	CHI	42	NH	0		5/29	OAK	34	ROSA	19							
5/1	COR	20	BX	8		5/29	SAC	36	SF	30							
5/1	MON	20	SMR	14		5/29	SDSC	18	CAL	0							
5/1	OAK	34	ROSA	0		5/29	SMR	38	RII	19							
5/1	RII	30	BSW	14		5/29	TBT	22	ATLX	8							
5/1	SAC	68	SDSC	0		5/29	TMAJ	7	COR	0							
5/1	SF	1	CAL	0													
5/1	TBT	70	CS	0													
5/1	TMAJ	34	POR	28													

Women's Professional Football League (WPFL) – 2004 Season

With the Detroit Demolition and the Sacramento Sirens repeating as champions of the NWFA and IWFL, respectively, the spring of 2004 was a good season for defending champs. That fall, the Northern Ice, reigning champions of the WPFL, also advanced to their second straight league title game. But their quest for a repeat was derailed at the last minute by the Dallas Diamonds, who crushed the Ice for the first national championship in their illustrious history.

Major National League   Teams: 15 (14)   Games: 77 (72)
Championship game result: Dallas Diamonds 68, Northern Ice 13

2004 WPFL Standings

National Conference	W	L	PR	Before	After
East Division					
Delaware Griffins (DEL)	8	4	CC	Expansion	--
Syracuse Sting (SYR)	4	6	--	--	Folded
New York Dazzles (DAZZ)	0	10	--	Expansion	--
North Division					
Northern Ice (ICE)	10	2	C	--	Folded
Minnesota Vixen (MN)	6	5	S	--	--
Toledo Reign (TOL)	3	7	--	--	--
Indiana Speed (INS)	3	7	--	--	--
American Conference					
South Division					
Dallas Diamonds (DAL)	12	0	LC	--	--
Houston Energy (HOU)	8	4	CC	--	--
Missouri Avengers (MOA)	0	10	--	Were Missouri Prowlers	Folded
West Division					
Long Beach Aftershock (LBA)	8	3	S	--	--
Arizona Caliente (AZC)	6	4	--	--	--
Los Angeles Amazons (LA)	4	6	--	--	--
So Cal Scorpions (SCS)	1	9	--	--	--
Affiliate Team					
Albany Ambush (ALB)	4	0	--	Expansion	--

2004 WPFL Scoreboard

Date					Date					Date				
7/31	AZC	41	SCS	6	8/28	LA	15	MN	0	10/2	DEL	52	TOL	28
7/31	DAL	49	SYR	0	8/28	TOL	1	MOA	0	10/2	LBA	42	SCS	6
7/31	HOU	1	MOA	0	9/4	ICE	49	MOA	12	10/2	MN	35	MOA	20
7/31	ICE	43	TOL	6	9/4	INS	46	SYR	16	10/2	SYR	25	INS	0
7/31	INS	14	MN	12	9/4	LBA	24	AZC	21	10/9	AZC	14	LA	3
7/31	LBA	36	LA	7	9/4	MN	27	TOL	0	10/9	DAL	1	MOA	0
8/7	ALB	53	DAZZ	0	9/11	AZC	17	LBA	12	10/9	LBA	18	HOU	9
8/7	DEL	20	SYR	16	9/11	DAL	67	DAZZ	0	10/9	MN	30	DEL	20
8/7	ICE	33	SCS	27	9/11	DEL	34	TOL	22	10/9	SYR	40	DAZZ	8
8/7	MN	26	INS	24	9/11	HOU	38	MOA	8	10/16	ALB	10	SYR	6
8/7	TOL	88	MOA	12	9/11	ICE	42	INS	20	10/16	DAL	44	SCS	7
8/14	AZC	35	LA	0	9/11	SCS	3	LA	0	10/16	HOU	28	LBA	8
8/14	DAL	28	HOU	26	9/18	DAL	56	AZC	30	10/16	ICE	35	INS	19
8/14	ICE	27	MN	0	9/18	DEL	18	SYR	0	10/16	LA	20	DEL	14
8/14	LBA	36	SCS	0	9/18	HOU	68	DAZZ	0	10/16	MN	1	MOA	0
8/14	SYR	20	DAZZ	0	9/18	ICE	49	TOL	8	10/23	DEL	47	DAZZ	0
8/14	TOL	28	INS	26	9/18	INS	1	MOA	0	10/23	HOU	21	ICE	14
8/21	DAL	90	MOA	0	9/18	LA	6	SCS	3	10/23	LBA	20	LA	0
8/21	DEL	26	SYR	6	9/25	AZC	22	SCS	6	10/23	MN	14	TOL	8
8/21	HOU	64	INS	6	9/25	DAL	68	TOL	0	10/30	DEL	8	MN	6 S
8/21	LA	3	SCS	0	9/25	HOU	50	DEL	6	10/30	HOU	22	LBA	8 S
8/21	LBA	27	AZC	14	9/25	ICE	32	MN	25	11/6	DAL	25	HOU	14 CC
8/22	ALB	33	DAZZ	0	9/25	LBA	57	LA	15	11/6	ICE	15	DEL	12 CC
8/28	AZC	14	SCS	7	9/25	SYR	47	DAZZ	0	11/20	DAL	68	ICE	13 C
8/28	DAL	33	HOU	13	10/2	ALB	23	DAZZ	0					
8/28	DEL	36	DAZZ	0	10/2	DAL	35	AZC	13					
8/28	ICE	71	INS	0										

2005 Season Review

Women's football had reached an impasse by 2005, as all three major women's football leagues saw their defending champions win another title that season. This left fans clamoring for a true title game, principally between the two major spring champions, the Detroit Demolition and the Sacramento Sirens. By the end of the year, a stunning defection looked as though it would finally grant them their wish. The WFL also made an apparent return to action that year, with little fanfare accompanying its first league championship game.

Leagues: 4   Teams: 90 (77)   Games: 386 (355)

National Women's Football Association (NWFA) – 2005 Season

The NWFA did away with divisions in 2005, instead having teams compete in two massive conferences. The structure change didn't affect the Detroit Demolition at all, as they obliterated the Pensacola Power in the championship game for their fourth straight NWFA title. The biggest news to hit the sport in years came after the season, however, when the four-time champions announced their decision to leave the NWFA and join the IWFL, where they could square off against the Sacramento Sirens for supremacy in the sport.

Major National League   Teams: 39 (36)   Games: 156 (144)
Championship game result: Detroit Demolition 74, Pensacola Power 0

2005 NWFA Standings

Northern Conference	W	L	PR	Before	After
DETROIT DEMOLITION (DET)	11	0	LC	--	Left for IWFL
D.C. DIVAS (DC)	9	1	CC	--	--
Massachusetts Mutiny (MASS)	8	2	S	--	--
Southwest Michigan Jaguars (SMJ)	8	2	S	--	Became West Michigan Mayhem
Columbus Comets (COL)	6	3	Q	--	--
Connecticut Crush (CTC)	6	3	Q	--	--
St. Louis Slam (STL)	5	3	--	--	--
Kentucky Karma (KYK)	5	4	--	Expansion	--
Pittsburgh Passion (PITT)	5	3	--	--	--
Cleveland Fusion (CLE)	5	3	--	--	--
Baltimore Burn (BAL)	4	4	--	--	--
Philadelphia Phoenix (PHIP)	4	4	--	--	--
Milwaukee Momentum (MIL)	4	4	--	Expansion	--
Erie Illusion (ERIE)	3	5	--	--	--
Cincinnati Sizzle (CIN)	2	6	--	Expansion	--
Indiana Thunder (INT)	0	5	--	--	Folded
Toledo Spitfire (TOLS)	0	8	--	--	--
Tidewater Floods (TIDE)	0	8	--	Expansion	--
Maine Freeze (ME)	0	8	--	--	--
Indianapolis SaberKatz (ISK)	0	8	--	Expansion	Folded
Southern Conference					
PENSACOLA POWER (PEN)	10	1	C	--	--
NASHVILLE DREAM (NASH)	8	1	S	--	--
Oklahoma City Lightning (OKC)	9	2	CC	--	--
Chattanooga Locomotion (CHAT)	8	3	S	--	--
Dallas Rage (DALR)	6	3	Q	Expansion	--
New Orleans Blaze (NO)	5	4	Q	--	Deferred until 2007
Alabama Renegades (ALRG)	5	3	--	--	--
Asheville Assault (ASH)	4	4	--	--	Folded
Austin Outlaws (OUT)	4	4	--	--	--
Gulf Coast Herricanes (GCH)	4	4	--	--	Deferred until 2007
Kansas City Krunch (KRUN)	3	5	--	--	Folded
Tennessee Venom (TNV)	3	5	--	--	Became East Tennessee Rhythm (2007)
Knoxville Tornadoes (KNXT)	1	7	--	Were IWFL's Knoxville Summit	--
Emerald Coast Sharks (ECS)	0	8	--	Were Panama City Beach Rumble (2003)	Became Emerald Coast Barracudas
Denton Stampede (DENT)	0	8	--	--	Folded
Atlanta Leopards (ATLL)	0	7	--	--	Folded

National Women's Football Association (NWFA) – 2005 Season (continued)
2005 NWFA Standings (continued)

Affiliate Teams

Team	W	L	Division	Notes
Orange County Breakers (OCB)	1	0	Expansion	--
Antelope Valley Bombers (ANVB)	0	1	Expansion	Became Antelope Valley Attack
Shreveport Shockhers (SPSH)	0	2	Expansion	--

2005 NWFA Scoreboard

Date	Team	Score	Team	Score		Date	Team	Score	Team	Score		Date	Team	Score	Team	Score	
4/16	BAL	38	TIDE	8		5/14	KYK	1	INT	0		6/4	OKC	65	DENT	0	
4/16	CHAT	12	ASH	6	*	5/14	MASS	22	CTC	19		6/4	PEN	35	NO	8	
4/16	CIN	43	TOLS	6		5/14	MIL	65	ISK	0		6/4	PITT	53	TOLS	0	
4/16	DC	18	CLE	0		5/14	NASH	51	KNXT	0		6/4	SMJ	34	CLE	19	
4/16	DET	10	COL	7		5/14	NO	33	SPSH	0		6/4	STL	102	ISK	0	
4/16	GCH	58	ECS	25		5/14	OKC	73	DENT	0							
4/16	KYK	20	STL	0		5/14	OUT	39	DALR	24		6/11	ALRG	1	ATLL	0	
4/16	MASS	17	PHIP	0		5/14	PEN	20	CHAT	0		6/11	ASH	22	TNV	14	
4/16	NASH	20	ALRG	6		5/14	PITT	56	CIN	22		6/11	CHAT	38	SPSH	6	
4/16	OKC	47	KRUN	0		5/14	SMJ	40	TOLS	0		6/11	CLE	34	BAL	14	
4/16	OUT	43	DENT	0								6/11	COL	74	TOLS	0	
4/16	PEN	31	NO	26		5/21	ASH	46	KNXT	0		6/11	CTC	30	ERIE	0	
4/16	PITT	54	ISK	0		5/21	CHAT	20	ALRG	6		6/11	DALR	26	OKC	21	
4/16	SMJ	48	MIL	0		5/21	CLE	61	CIN	0		6/11	DC	54	CIN	0	
4/16	TNV	38	KNXT	0		5/21	COL	100	TIDE	0		6/11	DET	40	PITT	14	
						5/21	CTC	44	ERIE	0		6/11	KYK	20	MIL	14	
4/23	ASH	39	KNXT	0		5/21	DC	22	MASS	12		6/11	MASS	48	ME	0	
4/23	CIN	1	INT	0		5/21	DET	42	SMJ	6		6/11	NASH	17	NO	6	
4/23	CLE	65	ISK	0		5/21	GCH	1	ATLL	0		6/11	OUT	42	DENT	0	
4/23	COL	22	BAL	20		5/21	KRUN	52	ISK	0		6/11	PEN	47	GCH	8	
4/23	CTC	39	ERIE	0		5/21	MIL	14	TOLS	6		6/11	PHIP	48	TIDE	12	
4/23	DALR	40	OUT	38		5/21	NASH	28	TNV	0		6/11	STL	42	KRUN	8	
4/23	DC	20	PITT	0		5/21	OCB	18	ANVB	12							
4/23	KRUN	47	DENT	0		5/21	OKC	47	DALR	6		6/18	ALRG	48	ECS	0	
4/23	MIL	21	KYK	12		5/21	OUT	19	DENT	6		6/18	ASH	1	ATLL	0	
4/23	NASH	21	CHAT	16		5/21	PEN	55	ECS	0		6/18	CHAT	1	TNV	0	
4/23	NO	42	GCH	0		5/21	PHIP	62	ME	0		6/18	CLE	1	INT	0	
4/23	PEN	81	ECS	7		5/21	PITT	26	BAL	12		6/18	COL	56	KYK	0	
4/23	PHIP	41	ME	0		5/21	STL	34	KYK	6		6/18	CTC	49	PHIP	27	
4/23	SMJ	47	STL	6								6/18	DALR	24	KRUN	0	
4/23	TNV	50	ATLL	0		5/28	CHAT	20	ASH	0		6/18	DC	36	BAL	0	
						5/28	COL	64	CIN	0		6/18	DET	1	ISK	0	
4/30	ALRG	7	ASH	0		5/28	CTC	92	ME	0		6/18	ERIE	44	TOLS	0	
4/30	BAL	46	TOLS	0		5/28	DALR	12	KRUN	0		6/18	MASS	60	ME	0	
4/30	CHAT	16	TNV	14		5/28	DC	53	TIDE	0		6/18	NASH	30	KNXT	0	
4/30	CLE	29	PITT	28	*	5/28	DET	31	MIL	0		6/18	NO	27	GCH	0	
4/30	COL	75	INT	0		5/28	KYK	37	TOLS	0		6/18	OKC	1	DENT	0	
4/30	CTC	65	ME	0		5/28	MASS	27	ERIE	0		6/18	PITT	49	TIDE	0	
4/30	DALR	58	DENT	0		5/28	NASH	1	ATLL	0		6/18	SMJ	54	CIN	7	
4/30	DET	76	CIN	0		5/28	NO	28	ECS	0		6/18	STL	12	MIL	7	
4/30	KNXT	30	ATLL	8		5/28	OKC	34	OUT	3							
4/30	MASS	42	ERIE	0		5/28	PEN	59	ALRG	6		6/25	CHAT	16	DALR	14	Q
4/30	NO	48	ECS	0		5/28	SMJ	60	ISK	0		6/25	MASS	34	CTC	12	Q
4/30	OKC	69	OUT	7		5/28	TNV	28	KNXT	24		6/25	OKC	61	NO	14	Q
4/30	PEN	44	GCH	6								6/25	SMJ	20	COL	14	Q
4/30	PHIP	47	TIDE	0		6/4	ALRG	38	KNXT	2							
4/30	SMJ	22	KYK	8		6/4	BAL	68	TIDE	0		7/9	DC	36	MASS	6	S
4/30	STL	46	ISK	0		6/4	CHAT	1	ATLL	0		7/9	DET	49	SMJ	6	S
						6/4	DALR	8	OUT	0		7/9	OKC	42	NASH	7	S
5/8	DET	55	CLE	7		6/4	DC	37	PHIP	0							
						6/4	DET	41	COL	23		7/16	PEN	42	CHAT	12	S
5/14	ALRG	36	TNV	6		6/4	ERIE	34	ME	14		7/16	DET	38	DC	16	CC
5/14	BAL	14	PHIP	0		6/4	GCH	22	ECS	15							
5/14	DC	51	TIDE	0		6/4	KYK	36	KRUN	12		7/23	PEN	17	OKC	14	CC*
5/14	ERIE	30	ME	6		6/4	MASS	42	CTC	6							
5/14	GCH	22	ECS	0		6/4	MIL	1	INT	0		7/30	DET	74	PEN	0	C
5/14	KRUN	16	STL	6		6/4	NASH	42	ASH	0							

Independent Women's Football League (IWFL) – 2005 Season

The IWFL featured 30 teams in 2005, including 23 full-member teams, which was the largest roster of franchises the league had boasted to that point. The Sacramento Sirens narrowly captured their third straight league title over the upstart Atlanta Xplosion. But it would be the acquisition of the NWFA's Detroit Demolition that offseason that would leave the IWFL poised to establish itself as the dominant league in women's football.

Major National League Teams: 30 (23) Games: 150 (135)
Championship game result: Sacramento Sirens 9, Atlanta Xplosion 7

2005 IWFL Standings

Eastern Conference	W	L	T	PR	Before	After
North Atlantic Division						
New York Sharks (NY)	11	1	0	CC	--	--
Southern Maine Rebels (SMR)	8	3	0	S	--	--
Bay State Warriors (BSW)	4	7	0	--	--	--
Manchester Freedom (MF)	3	8	0	--	Were New Hampshire Freedom	--
Rhode Island Intensity (RII)	1	9	0	--	--	Became WPFL's New England Intensity
South Central Division						
Atlanta Xplosion (ATLX)	12	1	0	C	--	--
Baton Rouge Wildcats (BRW)	2	8	0	--	Expansion	--
Dallas Revolution (DREV)	0	6	0	--	Returned from 2003	Folded
South Atlantic Division						
Jacksonville Dixie Blues (JAX)	8	3	0	S	--	Left for WFL
Tampa Bay Terminators (TBT)	7	3	0	--	--	--
Orlando Mayhem (ORLM)	0	10	0	--	--	--
Western Conference						
Midwest Division						
Chicago Force (CHI)	8	3	0	S	--	--
Kansas City Storm (STM)	4	5	1	--	Expansion	--
Detroit Predators (PRED)	4	5	1	--	--	--
Pacific Northwest Division						
Tacoma Majestics (TMAJ)	10	2	0	CC	--	Became Seattle Majestics
Corvallis Pride (COR)	8	3	0	S	--	--
Portland Shockwave (POR)	3	7	0	--	--	--
Boise Xtreme (BX)	2	8	0	--	--	Folded
Eugene Edge (EUG)	1	9	0	--	--	--
Pacific Southwest Division						
Sacramento Sirens (SAC)	13	0	0	LC	--	--
Santa Rosa Scorchers (ROSA)	7	3	0	--	--	--
California Quake (CAL)	6	3	1	--	--	--
Oakland Banshees (OAK)	5	4	1	--	--	--
Redding Rage (REDD)	3	7	0	--	--	--
Affiliate Teams						
Connecticut Lightning (CTL)	6	2	0	--	Expansion	Folded
Miami Fury (MIA)	4	4	0	--	Returned from 2003	--
Tucson Wildfire (TUCW)	4	5	0	--	Expansion	Left for NWFA
Des Moines Courage (DSM)	4	6	0	--	--	Became Iowa Crush
Montreal Blitz (MON)	0	4	0	--	--	--
So Cal Bandits (BAND)	0	9	0	--	Expansion	Folded

Independent Women's Football League (IWFL) – 2005 Season (continued)
2005 IWFL Scoreboard

Date	Team1	Score	Team2	Score	Note
4/2	ATLX	41	JAX	16	
4/2	BRW	1	DREV	0	N
4/2	CAL	17	ROSA	6	
4/2	CHI	12	BSW	7	
4/2	COR	41	BX	6	
4/2	DSM	50	STM	20	
4/2	REDD	20	EUG	19	
4/2	SAC	43	OAK	0	
4/2	TBT	24	ORLM	6	
4/2	TMAJ	38	POR	6	
4/2	TUCW	12	BAND	8	
4/9	ATLX	1	DREV	0	N
4/9	CHI	42	STM	0	
4/9	CTL	33	PRED	6	
4/9	JAX	40	ORLM	6	
4/9	MF	26	RII	0	
4/9	NY	41	BSW	12	
4/9	OAK	22	ROSA	12	
4/9	POR	52	BX	7	
4/9	REDD	41	TUCW	0	
4/9	SAC	72	CAL	0	
4/9	SMR	16	MON	6	
4/9	TBT	62	BRW	6	
4/9	TMAJ	13	COR	0	
4/16	ATLX	29	CHI	0	
4/16	BSW	21	RII	6	
4/16	CAL	33	REDD	0	
4/16	COR	9	POR	7	
4/16	CTL	7	MF	0	
4/16	JAX	57	BRW	13	
4/16	NY	32	SMR	6	
4/16	OAK	50	BAND	0	
4/16	PRED	20	DSM	12	
4/16	SAC	68	ROSA	0	
4/16	STM	63	TUCW	6	
4/16	TBT	27	ORLM	0	
4/16	TMAJ	42	EUG	0	
4/23	ATLX	63	BRW	0	
4/23	BSW	18	MF	0	
4/23	CHI	36	DSM	0	
4/23	JAX	58	TBT	27	
4/23	MIA	24	ORLM	0	
4/23	NY	36	CTL	0	
4/23	OAK	32	REDD	7	
4/23	POR	39	EUG	20	
4/23	PRED	20	STM	14	
4/23	ROSA	14	CAL	0	
4/23	SAC	115	BAND	0	
4/23	SMR	14	RII	7	
4/23	TMAJ	26	BX	6	
4/30	ATLX	40	ORLM	6	
4/30	CAL	0	OAK	0	*
4/30	CHI	34	PRED	0	
4/30	COR	34	BX	6	
4/30	CTL	18	RII	0	
4/30	DSM	30	STM	18	
4/30	EUG	7	REDD	0	
4/30	JAX	33	BRW	13	
4/30	NY	28	MF	0	
4/30	SMR	8	BSW	0	
4/30	TMAJ	39	POR	24	
4/30	TUCW	1	BAND	0	
5/7	CAL	1	BAND	0	
5/7	COR	45	EUG	6	
5/7	PRED	26	DSM	14	
5/7	ROSA	20	BX	6	
5/7	SAC	62	OAK	12	
5/7	SMR	18	MF	13	
5/7	TBT	25	MIA	8	
5/14	ATLX	43	BRW	0	
5/14	CHI	16	BSW	0	
5/14	COR	21	TMAJ	6	
5/14	JAX	46	ORLM	9	
5/14	MIA	22	TBT	6	
5/14	NY	40	RII	6	
5/14	POR	42	EUG	12	
5/14	PRED	25	DSM	0	
5/14	ROSA	21	REDD	13	
5/14	SAC	52	CAL	21	
5/14	SMR	22	MF	12	
5/14	STM	1	DREV	0	N
5/14	TUCW	1	BAND	0	
5/21	COR	43	BX	6	
5/21	CTL	12	PRED	7	
5/21	JAX	64	MIA	12	
5/21	MF	18	RII	7	
5/21	NY	9	BSW	0	
5/21	OAK	18	REDD	12	
5/21	ROSA	1	BAND	0	
5/21	SAC	56	POR	13	
5/21	SMR	30	MON	0	
5/21	TBT	14	ORLM	3	
5/21	TMAJ	20	EUG	0	
5/21	TUCW	12	BRW	6	
5/28	ATLX	34	MIA	0	
5/28	CAL	32	TUCW	0	
5/28	COR	20	POR	14	
5/28	ROSA	32	OAK	20	
5/28	SAC	53	REDD	10	
5/28	STM	25	DSM	6	
5/28	TMAJ	26	BX	0	
6/4	ATLX	39	JAX	18	
6/4	BSW	20	RII	0	
6/4	CHI	59	PRED	13	
6/4	COR	1	EUG	0	
6/4	DSM	1	DREV	0	N
6/4	MF	19	CTL	12	
6/4	MIA	22	ORLM	13	
6/4	NY	28	SMR	6	
6/4	OAK	1	BAND	0	
6/4	ROSA	38	BX	8	
6/4	TBT	63	BRW	0	
6/4	TMAJ	42	POR	0	
6/11	ATLX	49	TBT	0	
6/11	BRW	1	DREV	0	N
6/11	BX	1	EUG	0	
6/11	CAL	21	OAK	6	
6/11	CHI	58	DSM	0	
6/11	CTL	28	RII	22	
6/11	JAX	43	ORLM	19	
6/11	NY	43	MF	0	
6/11	REDD	36	TUCW	0	
6/11	SAC	41	POR	7	
6/11	SMR	8	BSW	0	
6/11	STM	20	PRED	0	
6/12	RII	19	MON	0	
6/18	BX	1	EUG	0	
6/18	CAL	59	TUCW	6	
6/18	CHI	30	STM	0	
6/18	CTL	19	BSW	0	
6/18	DSM	1	DREV	0	N
6/18	JAX	40	BRW	14	
6/18	MIA	14	ORLM	7	
6/18	NY	59	RII	0	
6/18	ROSA	26	REDD	0	
6/18	SAC	1	BAND	0	
6/18	SMR	36	MF	3	
6/18	TMAJ	28	COR	0	
6/25	ATLX	12	CHI	0	
6/25	BSW	18	MF	0	
6/25	NY	41	MON	7	
6/25	PRED	6	STM	6	*
6/25	TBT	21	MIA	14	
7/9	ATLX	26	JAX	12	S
7/9	NY	26	SMR	0	S
7/9	SAC	43	COR	22	S
7/9	TMAJ	14	CHI	0	S
7/23	ATLX	3	NY	0	CC
7/23	SAC	36	TMAJ	14	CC
8/6	SAC	9	ATLX	7	C

Women's Professional Football League (WPFL) – 2005 Season

The WPFL continued its dominance over women's fall football, and the Dallas Diamonds made defending league champions three-for-three in 2005. The Diamonds easily handled the New York Dazzles in the WPFL championship game for their second straight national title.

Major National League Teams: 18 (15) Games: 76 (73)
Championship game result: Dallas Diamonds 61, New York Dazzles 8

2005 WPFL Standings

National Conference	W	L	PR	Before	After
East Division					
New York Dazzles (DAZZ)	10	2	C	--	Folded
Albany Ambush (ALB)	4	6	--	--	--
Delaware Griffins (DEL)	3	6	--	--	Left for IWFL
Cape Fear Thunder (CFT)	2	5	--	Were WFL's Fayetteville Thunder (2003)	--
North Division					
Indiana Speed (INS)	7	4	S	--	--
Minnesota Vixen (MN)	6	5	CC	--	--
Toledo Reign (TOL)	6	4	--	--	--
Carolina Queens (CARQ)	0	6	--	Expansion	--
American Conference					
South Division					
Dallas Diamonds (DAL)	11	0	LC	--	--
Houston Energy (HOU)	4	4	--	--	--
New Mexico Burn (NMB)	0	7	--	Expansion	--
West Division					
So Cal Scorpions (SCS)	10	2	CC	--	--
Los Angeles Amazons (LA)	7	4	S	--	--
Arizona Caliente (AZC)	3	4	--	--	Folded
Long Beach Aftershock (LBA)	1	8	--	--	Folded
Affiliate Teams					
Empire State Roar (EMP)	2	4	--	Expansion	--
San Francisco Stingrayz (SF)	0	4	--	Joined from IWFL	Folded
Georgia Gladiators (GAG)	0	1	--	Expansion	Folded

2005 WPFL Scoreboard

Date						Date						Date					
7/30	ALB	35	DEL	24		8/27	AZC	38	NMB	0		10/1	DAL	55	LBA	0	
7/30	CFT	34	CARQ	0		8/27	DAL	49	HOU	31		10/1	DAZZ	20	ALB	6	
7/30	DAL	76	NMB	0		8/27	EMP	21	ALB	0		10/1	LA	20	AZC	14	
7/30	DAZZ	6	EMP	0		8/27	INS	20	DEL	0		10/1	SCS	69	NMB	0	
7/30	HOU	40	MN	0		8/27	LBA	1	SF	0		10/1	TOL	53	CFT	0	
7/30	LA	42	SF	0		8/27	SCS	14	LA	0		10/8	DAL	56	LBA	0	
7/30	SCS	14	LBA	0		9/3	EMP	30	DAZZ	13		10/8	DAZZ	34	CFT	0	
7/30	TOL	26	INS	20	*	9/3	HOU	14	SCS	13		10/8	DEL	6	ALB	0	
8/6	DAL	1	GAG	0	N	9/3	INS	42	CARQ	6		10/8	HOU	76	NMB	6	
8/6	DAZZ	21	DEL	8		9/10	DAZZ	19	DEL	6		10/8	INS	66	CARQ	8	
8/6	LA	1	SF	0		9/10	HOU	58	NMB	6		10/8	MN	39	EMP	14	
8/6	MN	27	TOL	22		9/10	LA	32	LBA	0		10/8	SCS	35	LA	0	
8/6	SCS	33	LBA	16		9/10	MN	18	INS	13		10/15	ALB	20	TOL	14	
8/13	ALB	14	EMP	13		9/10	SCS	43	AZC	0		10/15	AZC	38	LBA	0	
8/13	DAL	56	NMB	0		9/10	TOL	48	ALB	6		10/15	DAL	38	HOU	27	
8/13	DAZZ	27	SF	8		9/17	CFT	20	ALB	8		10/15	INS	26	MN	14	
8/13	DEL	16	CFT	14		9/17	DAL	62	MN	6		10/15	SCS	24	LA	14	
8/13	MN	7	INS	6		9/17	INS	21	TOL	10		10/16	DAZZ	30	DEL	0	
8/13	SCS	28	HOU	13		9/17	LA	20	AZC	0		10/22	AZC	50	NMB	7	
8/13	TOL	56	CARQ	0		9/17	SCS	39	LBA	0		10/22	LA	12	LBA	6	
8/20	ALB	38	DEL	22		9/24	DAZZ	33	ALB	16		10/22	TOL	36	MN	22	
8/20	DAL	21	HOU	18		9/24	DEL	44	CFT	8		10/28	MN	19	INS	14	S
8/20	DAZZ	12	EMP	8		9/24	INS	55	CARQ	8		10/28	SCS	27	LA	14	S
8/20	INS	44	CFT	8		9/24	MN	30	TOL	8		11/5	DAL	48	SCS	19	CC
8/20	LA	20	AZC	8								11/5	DAZZ	14	MN	12	CC
8/20	TOL	34	CARQ	0								11/19	DAL	61	DAZZ	8	C

Women's Football League (WFL) – 2005 Season

After a disastrous, failed title game in 2003, the WFL made an apparent return to the gridiron in 2005. (The league was so poorly covered that it's impossible to rule out that they played in 2004, but no public records of a 2004 WFL season have yet been found.) The WFL planned their second championship game in 2005, and this time, the league pulled it off, with the Mississippi Rapids defeating the Tennessee Heat in a title game the league dubbed as the Superior Bowl.

Regional League Teams: 3 Games: 4 (3)
Championship game result: Mississippi Rapids 8, Tennessee Heat 6

2005 WFL Standings

Teams	W	L	PR	Before	After
Mississippi Rapids (MS)	2	0	LC	Expansion	--
Tennessee Heat (TNH)	2	1	C	Returned from 2003	--
Kentucky Force (KYF)	0	3	--	Expansion	--

2005 WFL Scoreboard

5/21	TNH	14	KYF	0	6/18	MS	1	KYF	0	7/30	MS	8	TNH	6	C
					6/25	TNH	33	KYF	0					

2006 Season Review

With the Detroit Demolition and the Sacramento Sirens finally sharing a league in 2006, fans couldn't wait to see which of them would claim the 2006 IWFL title. Stunningly, the answer was neither. The NWFA continued to roll along without the Demolition, creating an opening for a new champion, but that champion would rock the sport by following in the Demolition's footsteps in more ways than one. Two dynasties dueled for the WPFL title in a thrilling showdown, while a former IWFL team found glory in the WFL.

Leagues: 4 Teams: 81 (71) Games: 317 (301)

Independent Women's Football League (IWFL) – 2006 Season

Who would win a showdown between the three-time defending IWFL champion Sacramento Sirens and the four-time NWFA champion Detroit Demolition? For some reason, the IWFL placed the two titans in the same conference, and in the Western Conference title game, the Demolition dispatched the Sirens to advance to the IWFL championship. But their dreams of winning five straight league titles were dashed when they were upset by the Atlanta Xplosion in the IWFL title game, an Xplosion team the Demolition had handily defeated in the regular season. Atlanta's victory went down as one of the biggest upsets in women's football history, as it handed the Demolition their first loss in over four years.

Major National League Teams: 28 (23) Games: 113 (101)
Championship game result: Atlanta Xplosion 21, Detroit Demolition 14

2006 IWFL Standings

Eastern Conference	W	L	PR	Before	After
North Atlantic Division					
Bay State Warriors (BSW)	7	2	S	--	Became Boston Rampage
Manchester Freedom (MF)	4	4	--	--	--
Montreal Blitz (MON)	3	5	--	--	--
Mid-Atlantic Division					
New York Sharks (NY)	9	1	CC	--	--
Delaware Griffins (DEL)	2	6	--	Joined from WPFL	--
Southern Maine Rebels (SMR)	1	7	--	--	--
South Atlantic Division					
Atlanta Xplosion (ATLX)	10	1	LC	--	--
Miami Fury (MIA)	7	2	S	--	--
Orlando Mayhem (ORLM)	3	5	--	--	--
Baton Rouge Wildcats (BRW)	3	5	--	--	--
Tampa Bay Terminators (TBT)	2	6	--	--	Folded

Independent Women's Football League (IWFL) – 2006 Season (continued)
2006 IWFL Standings (continued)

Western Conference
Midwest Division

Team	W	L			
Detroit Demolition (DET)	10	1	C	Joined from NWFA	--
Chicago Force (CHI)	6	3	S	--	--
Kansas City Storm (STM)	3	5	--	--	--
Detroit Predators (PRED)	2	6	--	--	--

Pacific Northwest Division

Team	W	L			
Portland Shockwave (POR)	7	2	S	--	--
Seattle Majestics (SEA)	5	3	--	Were Tacoma Majestics	--
Corvallis Pride (COR)	5	3	--	--	--
Eugene Edge (EUG)	0	8	--	--	Folded

Pacific Southwest Division

Team	W	L			
Sacramento Sirens (SAC)	7	3	CC	--	--
Santa Rosa Scorchers (ROSA)	6	2	--	--	--
California Quake (CAL)	4	4	--	--	--
Redding Rage (REDD)	2	6	--	--	--

Affiliate Teams

Team	W	L			
Iowa Crush (IA)	4	4	--	Were Des Moines Courage	--
Indianapolis Chaos (IC)	1	6	--	Expansion	Left for NWFA (2008)
Oakland Banshees (OAK)	0	2	--	--	Deferred until 2008
Carolina Cardinals (CARC)	0	5	--	Expansion	Folded
Tucson Monsoon (TUC)	0	6	--	Expansion	--

2006 IWFL Scoreboard

Date						Date						Date					
4/29	ATLX	67	SAC	20		5/20	COR	30	REDD	6		6/10	ROSA	46	TUC	0	
4/29	BSW	32	MON	6		5/20	MF	1	CARC	0		6/10	SAC	53	REDD	6	
4/29	CHI	26	IA	8		5/20	MIA	22	ORLM	13		6/10	SEA	28	COR	0	
4/29	COR	36	EUG	8		5/20	NY	55	SMR	0		6/17	ATLX	1	TBT	0	
4/29	DET	1	DEL	0		5/20	POR	32	SEA	6		6/17	BRW	1	IC	0	
4/29	MF	26	SMR	6		5/20	ROSA	41	EUG	0		6/17	BSW	1	CARC	0	
4/29	MIA	1	BRW	0		5/20	SAC	53	CAL	19		6/17	CAL	28	TUC	0	
4/29	NY	73	IC	0		5/20	STM	1	PRED	0		6/17	CHI	42	STM	0	
4/29	POR	39	REDD	0								6/17	COR	52	EUG	14	
4/29	PRED	14	STM	8		5/27	BRW	21	TUC	14		6/17	DET	65	IA	0	
4/29	ROSA	18	CAL	8		5/27	CHI	36	PRED	8		6/17	MF	32	SMR	0	
4/29	TBT	41	ORLM	13		5/27	DEL	1	CARC	0		6/17	MIA	20	ORLM	14	
						5/27	DET	74	STM	6		6/17	NY	42	MON	27	
5/6	ATLX	77	BRW	0		5/27	IA	50	IC	12		6/17	PRED	22	DEL	20	
5/6	BSW	41	SMR	6		5/27	MIA	14	TBT	12		6/17	REDD	12	OAK	7	
5/6	CAL	59	TUC	6		5/27	POR	19	SEA	13		6/17	ROSA	33	POR	27	
5/6	CHI	30	PRED	0		5/27	REDD	20	EUG	6		6/17	SAC	42	SEA	20	
5/6	COR	28	REDD	8		5/27	ROSA	46	CAL	0							
5/6	DET	60	IA	8								6/24	CAL	22	TUC	0	
5/6	MF	9	MON	0		6/3	ATLX	36	BRW	0		6/24	CHI	27	STM	0	
5/6	MIA	40	ORLM	6		6/3	BSW	7	MF	0		6/24	COR	20	ROSA	18	
5/6	NY	48	DEL	0		6/3	DET	64	PRED	0		6/24	DET	42	ATLX	7	
5/6	SEA	22	SAC	21		6/3	MIA	22	TBT	19		6/24	IA	48	PRED	0	
5/6	STM	77	IC	0		6/3	MON	31	SMR	12		6/24	MIA	1	TBT	0	
						6/3	NY	47	DEL	0		6/24	MON	36	MF	22	
5/13	ATLX	41	ORLM	0		6/3	ORLM	48	CARC	0		6/24	NY	24	BSW	16	
5/13	BSW	32	DEL	0		6/3	POR	6	COR	0		6/24	ORLM	34	BRW	3	
5/13	CAL	49	TUC	12		6/3	ROSA	52	REDD	0		6/24	POR	46	EUG	14	
5/13	DET	19	CHI	0		6/3	SAC	53	CAL	0		6/24	SAC	1	OAK	0	
5/13	IA	14	PRED	6		6/3	SEA	48	EUG	0		6/24	SEA	48	REDD	6	
5/13	MON	34	SMR	0		6/3	STM	85	IC	0		6/24	SMR	1	DEL	0	
5/13	NY	20	MF	0													
5/13	POR	48	EUG	0		6/10	ATLX	41	MIA	6		7/8	ATLX	41	BSW	0	S
5/13	SAC	56	ROSA	14		6/10	BSW	7	MF	6		7/8	DET	20	CHI	0	S
5/13	SEA	21	COR	6		6/10	DEL	24	SMR	0		7/8	NY	14	MIA	8	S
5/13	TBT	62	BRW	0		6/10	DET	47	CHI	0		7/8	SAC	37	POR	27	S
						6/10	IA	28	STM	0							
5/20	ATLX	46	TBT	0		6/10	IC	1	CARC	0		7/15	ATLX	35	NY	14	CC
5/20	BRW	36	IC	12		6/10	NY	53	MON	7		7/15	DET	52	SAC	20	CC
5/20	BSW	9	MON	0		6/10	ORLM	21	TBT	8							
5/20	CHI	20	IA	6		6/10	POR	55	EUG	0		7/29	ATLX	21	DET	14	C

National Women's Football Association (NWFA) – 2006 Season

Even without the Detroit Demolition, the NWFA still had 33 teams and some of the biggest names in the sport. The D.C. Divas broke through the open field to capture their first national championship, topping the Oklahoma City Lightning in the 2006 NWFA title game. The Divas became the first non-Detroit team to claim the NWFA championship since 2001, but the Divas then shocked the sport by announcing that they would take their title and chase the Demolition to the IWFL for the 2007 season.

Major National League   Teams: 33 (27)   Games: 133 (132)
Championship game result: D.C. Divas 28, Oklahoma City Lightning 7

2006 NWFA Standings

Team	W	L	PR	Before	After
Northern Conference					
Northeast Division					
Massachusetts Mutiny (MASS)	8	2	CC	--	--
Philadelphia Phoenix (PHIP)	5	4	Q	--	--
Connecticut Crush (CTC)	4	4	--	--	--
Maine Freeze (ME)	2	6	--	--	--
North Atlantic Division					
D.C. Divas (DC)	11	0	LC	--	Left for IWFL
Baltimore Burn (BAL)	4	4	--	--	--
Tidewater Floods (TIDE)	2	6	--	--	Folded
Harrisburg Angels (HAR)	0	8	--	Expansion	Became Central PA Vipers
North Central Division					
Cleveland Fusion (CLE)	8	2	S	--	--
Columbus Comets (COL)	7	4	CC	--	--
Pittsburgh Passion (PITT)	5	3	--	--	--
Erie Illusion (ERIE)	1	7	--	--	--
Northwest Division					
West Michigan Mayhem (WM)	7	2	Q	Were Southwest Michigan Jaguars	--
Cincinnati Sizzle (CIN)	3	5	--	--	--
Milwaukee Momentum (MIL)	3	5	--	--	--
Toledo Spitfire (TOLS)	2	7	--	--	Became Tree Town Spitfire
Southern Conference					
Southeast Division					
Pensacola Power (PEN)	5	3	S	--	--
Chattanooga Locomotion (CHAT)	6	3	S	--	--
Alabama Renegades (ALRG)	4	4	--	--	--
Emerald Coast Barracudas (ECB)	1	7	--	Were Emerald Coast Sharks	--
South Central Division					
St. Louis Slam (STL)	7	3	S	--	--
Kentucky Karma (KYK)	4	4	Q	--	--
Nashville Dream (NASH)	0	8	--	--	--
Southwest Division					
Oklahoma City Lightning (OKC)	10	1	C	--	--
Austin Outlaws (OUT)	6	3	Q	--	--
Dallas Rage (DALR)	4	4	--	--	--
Shreveport Shockhers (SPSH)	1	7	--	--	Became IWFL's Shreveport Aftershock
Affiliate Teams					
Blaze'n Canes (BLAZ)	1	0	--	Expansion	Folded
Knoxville Tornadoes (KNXT)	0	2	--	--	Folded
Fort Wayne Flash (FWF)	0	3	--	Expansion	--
West Division					
Orange County Breakers (OCB)	8	0	--	--	--
Antelope Valley Attack (ANVA)	4	4	--	Were Antelope Valley Bombers	Became All Valley Attack
Tucson Wildfire (TUCW)	0	8	--	Joined from IWFL	Became Arizona Venom

National Women's Football Association (NWFA) – 2006 Season (continued)
2006 NWFA Scoreboard

Date	Team 1	Score	Team 2	Score		Date	Team 1	Score	Team 2	Score		Date	Team 1	Score	Team 2	Score	Note
4/15	ERIE	8	TOLS	0		5/13	BLAZ	16	ECB	12		6/10	ANVA	20	TUCW	6	
4/15	OCB	32	TUCW	0		5/13	CHAT	16	NASH	13		6/10	BAL	48	TIDE	12	
4/15	OKC	70	SPSH	0		5/13	KYK	14	ALRG	0		6/10	CLE	46	ERIE	0	
4/15	PEN	56	ECB	12		5/13	OKC	35	STL	12		6/10	COL	27	PITT	13	
4/15	STL	36	KYK	14		5/13	OUT	43	DALR	40		6/10	CTC	7	PHIP	3	
						5/13	TOLS	6	FWF	0		6/10	DALR	46	SPSH	6	
4/22	ALRG	48	ECB	0								6/10	DC	61	HAR	0	
4/22	ANVA	42	TUCW	0		5/20	CLE	49	MIL	0		6/10	KYK	23	NASH	0	
4/22	CHAT	74	KNXT	0		5/20	COL	30	WM	7		6/10	MASS	48	ME	0	
4/22	CLE	13	PITT	12		5/20	DC	40	CTC	0		6/10	MIL	26	CIN	18	
4/22	COL	71	ERIE	0		5/20	MASS	35	BAL	0		6/10	OKC	38	OUT	17	
4/22	CTC	61	ME	0		5/20	ME	20	HAR	6		6/10	PEN	18	ALRG	0	
4/22	DC	13	BAL	6		5/20	OCB	14	ANVA	12		6/10	WM	46	TOLS	0	
4/22	MASS	7	PHIP	0		5/20	OKC	45	SPSH	0							
4/22	MIL	42	TOLS	8		5/20	PEN	48	ECB	0		6/17	ALRG	6	KYK	2	
4/22	OKC	35	DALR	20		5/20	PHIP	28	TIDE	8		6/17	CHAT	20	NASH	6	
4/22	OUT	36	SPSH	8		5/20	PITT	44	CIN	0		6/17	CLE	82	MIL	0	
4/22	STL	22	NASH	14		5/20	STL	48	NASH	0		6/17	DC	48	CTC	0	
4/22	TIDE	33	HAR	6								6/17	MASS	20	BAL	16	
4/22	WM	14	CIN	5		5/27	ALRG	30	ECB	8		6/17	ME	21	HAR	12	
						5/27	CIN	27	TOLS	14		6/17	OCB	31	TUCW	0	
4/29	ALRG	1	KNXT	0		5/27	CLE	35	PITT	33		6/17	OKC	21	STL	16	
4/29	BAL	50	HAR	0		5/27	COL	59	ERIE	0		6/17	OUT	31	DALR	29	
4/29	CIN	46	TOLS	22		5/27	CTC	64	ME	12		6/17	PEN	58	ECB	0	
4/29	CLE	43	ERIE	0		5/27	DC	30	BAL	0		6/17	PHIP	50	TIDE	0	
4/29	DALR	32	NASH	10		5/27	MASS	14	PHIP	7		6/17	PITT	55	CIN	20	
4/29	DC	45	TIDE	0		5/27	OCB	28	TUCW	8		6/17	TOLS	8	ERIE	7	
4/29	MASS	37	CTC	0		5/27	OKC	44	DALR	6		6/17	WM	10	COL	0	
4/29	OCB	38	ANVA	28		5/27	OUT	55	SPSH	13							
4/29	OUT	24	PEN	8		5/27	STL	22	KYK	0		6/24	ANVA	28	TUCW	16	
4/29	PHIP	54	ME	0		5/27	WM	53	MIL	0		6/24	CHAT	35	ALRG	6	
4/29	PITT	6	COL	0								6/24	TIDE	10	HAR	0	
4/29	SPSH	6	ECB	0		6/3	BAL	56	HAR	0							
4/29	STL	14	CHAT	7		6/3	CLE	18	COL	7		7/1	OCB	19	ANVA	6	
4/29	WM	21	MIL	20		6/3	CTC	7	MASS	0	*	7/1	CHAT	23	OUT	6	Q
						6/3	DALR	38	NASH	7		7/1	CLE	52	PHIP	13	Q
5/6	BAL	49	TIDE	0		6/3	DC	65	TIDE	0		7/1	COL	17	WM	7	Q
5/6	CHAT	33	FWF	7		6/3	ECB	28	SPSH	26		7/1	STL	27	KYK	8	Q
5/6	CIN	46	MIL	20		6/3	KYK	18	FWF	6							
5/6	COL	21	CLE	13		6/3	MIL	20	TOLS	6		7/8	ANVA	30	TUCW	6	
5/6	DALR	40	SPSH	8		6/3	OCB	44	ANVA	7		7/8	COL	20	PEN	0	S
5/6	DC	76	HAR	0		6/3	OUT	24	PEN	0		7/8	DC	40	CHAT	0	S
5/6	KYK	8	NASH	3		6/3	PHIP	35	ME	7		7/8	MASS	42	STL	14	S
5/6	MASS	75	ME	0		6/3	PITT	54	ERIE	0		7/8	OKC	14	CLE	13	S
5/6	OCB	20	TUCW	6		6/3	STL	34	CHAT	14							
5/6	OKC	41	OUT	20		6/3	WM	42	CIN	14		7/22	DC	32	COL	7	CC
5/6	PEN	22	ALRG	6								7/22	OKC	21	MASS	16	CC
5/6	PHIP	35	CTC	0													
5/6	PITT	45	ERIE	0								8/5	DC	28	OKC	7	C
5/6	WM	31	TOLS	0													

Women's Professional Football League (WPFL) – 2006 Season

The 2006 WPFL championship game was one of the most anticipated in history, pitting two archrivals with championship pedigrees against each other. The Dallas Diamonds, the two-time defending WPFL champions from 2004 and 2005, faced off against the Houston Energy, who won three straight WPFL championships from 2000-2002. It was the first championship game meeting between these two historic franchises, and after a terrific contest, the Diamonds won their third straight national championship by edging the Energy in the title game.

Major National League   Teams: 16 (14)   Games: 59 (58)
Championship game result: Dallas Diamonds 34, Houston Energy 27

2006 WPFL Standings

National Conference	W	L	PR	Before	After
Central Division					
Houston Energy (HOU)	7	2	C	--	--
Wisconsin Wolves (WIW)	6	4	CC	Expansion	--
Minnesota Vixen (MN)	1	6	--	--	--
North Division					
Indiana Speed (INS)	7	2	S	--	--
Toledo Reign (TOL)	4	4	--	--	--
Carolina Queens (CARQ)	2	6	--	--	--
American Conference					
East Division					
New England Intensity (NEI)	6	2	S	Were IWFL's Rhode Island Intensity	Left for IWFL
Empire State Roar (EMP)	4	3	--	--	--
Connecticut Cyclones (CCY)	0	5	--	Expansion	--
West Division					
Dallas Diamonds (DAL)	8	1	LC	--	--
So Cal Scorpions (SCS)	7	3	CC	--	--
Los Angeles Amazons (LA)	4	4	--	--	--
Las Vegas Showgirlz (LV)	2	5	--	Expansion	--
New Mexico Burn (NMB)	0	8	--	--	--
Affiliate Teams					
Cape Fear Thunder (CFT)	1	1	--	--	Left for IWFL
Albany Ambush (ALB)	0	3	--	--	Folded

2006 WPFL Scoreboard

Date					Date					Date				
7/22	CFT	32	CARQ	7	8/12	NEI	20	EMP	0	9/16	DAL	39	LA	16
7/22	DAL	97	NMB	0	8/12	WIW	27	TOL	0	9/16	HOU	45	SCS	17
7/22	MN	32	TOL	8	8/19	DAL	31	HOU	21	9/16	INS	18	TOL	8
7/22	NEI	26	ALB	0	8/19	EMP	31	CARQ	8	9/16	LV	36	NMB	0
7/22	SCS	13	LA	0	8/19	INS	13	TOL	6	9/16	NEI	6	EMP	0
7/22	WIW	20	INS	0	8/19	LV	30	NMB	0	9/16	WIW	32	MN	6
7/29	DAL	42	LA	13	8/19	NEI	34	CCY	0	9/23	DAL	47	WIW	20
7/29	EMP	36	ALB	0	8/19	SCS	34	LA	12	9/23	HOU	66	MN	0
7/29	INS	14	MN	0	8/26	EMP	34	CCY	0	9/23	INS	41	CARQ	0
7/29	SCS	41	LV	0	8/26	HOU	53	LV	6	9/23	LA	26	LV	2
7/29	TOL	36	CARQ	0	9/2	HOU	41	MN	0	9/23	NEI	42	CCY	6
8/5	CARQ	1	ALB	0	9/2	INS	13	WIW	0	9/23	SCS	77	NMB	7
8/5	DAL	80	NMB	0	9/2	SCS	54	NMB	0	9/30	NEI	49	CCY	6
8/5	EMP	54	CCY	0	9/2	TOL	51	CARQ	0	9/30	WIW	24	EMP	0
8/5	HOU	28	SCS	6	9/9	HOU	24	DAL	10	10/7	SCS	30	NEI	0 S
8/5	LA	20	LV	14	9/9	INS	51	CARQ	0	10/7	WIW	20	INS	18 S
8/5	TOL	34	NEI	22	9/9	LA	50	NMB	0	10/21	DAL	34	SCS	3 CC
8/5	WIW	20	MN	0	9/9	SCS	35	LV	8	10/21	HOU	68	WIW	0 CC
8/12	CARQ	20	CFT	8	9/9	TOL	24	WIW	6	11/4	DAL	34	HOU	27 C
8/12	INS	14	MN	7										
8/12	LA	62	NMB	0										

Women's Football League (WFL) – 2006 Season

The Jacksonville Dixie Blues won the WAFL-WFA title in 2002 but had struggled to find much postseason success against teams from outside the Southeast. Jacksonville solved that little problem by leaving the IWFL and joining the microscopic WFL, which only featured teams from the Southeast. As expected, the Dixie Blues easily rolled to the league championship, beating the Tennessee Heat in Superior Bowl II.

Regional League   Teams: 4   Games: 12 (10)
Championship game result: Jacksonville Dixie Blues 54, Tennessee Heat 25

2006 WFL Standings

Teams	W	L	PR	Before	After
Jacksonville Dixie Blues (JAX)	10	0	LC	Joined from IWFL	--
Tennessee Heat (TNH)	1	1	C	--	--
Mississippi Rapids (MS)	1	1	--	--	Folded
Kentucky Force (KYF)	0	4	--	--	Became WPFL's Kentucky Valkyries
Unknown opponents	0	6			

Partial 2006 WFL Scoreboard

4/29	MS	38	KYF	7		5/13	JAX	1	KYF	0		6/24	JAX	1	KYF	0	
5/6	JAX	63	MS	22		6/10	TNH	28	KYF	12		7/15	JAX	54	TNH	25	C

2007 Season Review

The 2007 season would mark the final season of a six-year run of "tri-champions", where three teams collectively shared the national championship of women's football. The IWFL had started to gain an edge over the NWFA with the acquisitions of their last two league champions. Their quest for supremacy in the sport would be complete by the end of 2007, as the NWFA would be victimized by yet another defection. The WPFL, the first women's football league of the modern era, said goodbye, and fall women's football took its final bow with them. Finally, after seven years and six seasons of little acclaim, the WFL signed off as well.

Leagues: 4   Teams: 81 (77)   Games: 339 (304)

Women's Football League (WFL) – 2007 Season

The WFL, the least-publicized women's football league in history, closed its doors after the 2007 season. The Jacksonville Dixie Blues won their second straight championship in the third and final Superior Bowl, this time over the Clarksville Fox. The Dixie Blues and Fox jumped to other leagues, while the rest of the league folded with the WFL.

Regional League   Teams: 3   Games: 10
Championship game result: Jacksonville Dixie Blues 49, Clarksville Fox 6

2007 WFL Standings

Teams	W	L	PR	Before	After
Jacksonville Dixie Blues (JAX)	6	0	LC	--	Left for WFA (2009)
Clarksville Fox (FOX)	4	3	C	Expansion	Left for IWFL2
Tennessee Heat (TNH)	0	1	--	--	Folded
Unknown opponents	0	6			

Partial 2007 WFL Scoreboard

6/9	FOX	40	TNH	22	
7/14	JAX	49	FOX	6	C

Independent Women's Football League (IWFL) – 2007 Season

The D.C. Divas joined the IWFL in 2007, the second straight year that the reigning NWFA champions joined the league. Ultimately, however, the 2007 IWFL title game was a repeat of the year before. The Detroit Demolition avenged their upset in the 2006 IWFL championship game by defeating the Atlanta Xplosion for their first IWFL crown; it was the fifth and final national championship in the Demolition's storied history.

Major National League   Teams: 29 (28)   Games: 120 (114)
Championship game result: Detroit Demolition 17, Atlanta Xplosion 7

2007 IWFL Standings

Eastern Conference	W	L	PR	Before	After
Northeast Division					
Manchester Freedom (MF)	6	3	S	--	Left for IWFL2
Montreal Blitz (MON)	6	2	--	--	Left for IWFL2
Southern Maine Rebels (SMR)	0	8	--	--	Left for IWFL2
North Atlantic Division					
New York Sharks (NY)	7	3	CC	--	--
Boston Rampage (BOSR)	4	4	--	Were Bay State Warriors	Folded
New England Intensity (NEI)	3	5	--	Joined from WPFL	Left for IWFL2
Mid-Atlantic Division					
D.C. Divas (DC)	8	1	S	Joined from NWFA	--
Delaware Griffins (DEL)	1	5	--	--	Folded
Cape Fear Thunder (CFT)	1	7	--	Joined from WPFL	Left for IWFL2
South Atlantic Division					
Atlanta Xplosion (ATLX)	10	1	C	--	--
Orlando Mayhem (ORLM)	6	2	--	--	--
Miami Fury (MIA)	3	5	--	--	--
Palm Beach Punishers (PALM)	1	7	--	Expansion	--
Western Conference					
Midwest Division					
Detroit Demolition (DET)	10	1	LC	--	--
Chicago Force (CHI)	5	3	--	--	--
Iowa Crush (IA)	2	6	--	--	--
Detroit Predators (PRED)	0	8	--	--	Folded
Mid South Division					
Kansas City Storm (STM)	6	3	S	--	Left for NWFA
Shreveport Aftershock (SPAS)	2	5	--	Were NWFA's Shreveport Shockhers	Left for IWFL2
Baton Rouge Wildcats (BRW)	1	6	--	--	Became IWFL2's Louisiana Fuel
Pacific Northwest Division					
Seattle Majestics (SEA)	8	1	S	--	--
Portland Shockwave (POR)	6	2	--	--	--
Corvallis Pride (COR)	2	6	--	--	--
Redding Rage (REDD)	0	8	--	--	--
Pacific Southwest Division					
Sacramento Sirens (SAC)	8	2	CC	--	--
Santa Rosa Scorchers (ROSA)	5	3	--	--	--
California Quake (CAL)	3	5	--	--	--
Tucson Monsoon (TUC)	1	7	--	--	--
Affiliate Team					
Carolina Phoenix (CAR)	5	1	--	Expansion	Left for IWFL2

Independent Women's Football League (IWFL) – 2007 Season (continued)
2007 IWFL Scoreboard

Date	Team1	Score	Team2	Score		Date	Team1	Score	Team2	Score		Date	Team1	Score	Team2	Score	Note
4/28	ATLX	60	BRW	0		5/26	ATLX	62	PALM	0		6/23	ATLX	1	BRW	0	
4/28	BOSR	13	SMR	0		5/26	CHI	21	STM	0		6/23	BOSR	28	DEL	0	
4/28	CFT	6	DEL	0		5/26	IA	26	PRED	8		6/23	CAL	20	TUC	0	
4/28	CHI	27	IA	6		5/26	MON	7	BOSR	0		6/23	CAR	29	CFT	6	
4/28	COR	46	REDD	0		5/26	POR	9	COR	6		6/23	CHI	69	PRED	0	
4/28	DC	70	NEI	0		5/26	SEA	53	TUC	6		6/23	DC	51	NEI	0	
4/28	DET	83	PRED	0								6/23	MF	28	MON	6	
4/28	MON	20	MF	6		6/2	CAR	36	PRED	0		6/23	MIA	7	PALM	0	
4/28	NY	48	MIA	33		6/2	CHI	33	IA	0		6/23	NY	1	SMR	0	
4/28	ORLM	43	PALM	13		6/2	DC	24	DET	22		6/23	POR	60	REDD	0	
4/28	SAC	13	ROSA	6		6/2	DEL	21	CFT	0		6/23	SEA	23	COR	0	
4/28	SEA	19	POR	2		6/2	MF	26	SMR	2		6/23	STM	19	IA	0	
4/28	SPAS	24	CAR	6		6/2	NY	19	NEI	0							
4/28	TUC	30	CAL	23		6/2	ORLM	27	MIA	13		6/30	ATLX	1	MIA	0	
						6/2	ROSA	55	REDD	0		6/30	BOSR	13	SMR	8	
5/5	ATLX	36	MIA	0		6/2	SAC	24	CAL	15		6/30	CAL	50	REDD	24	
5/5	DC	20	NY	14		6/2	SEA	33	POR	13		6/30	DC	38	CFT	3	
5/5	DET	59	IA	0		6/2	STM	47	BRW	0		6/30	DET	21	CHI	6	
5/5	MON	36	SMR	6								6/30	MF	41	NEI	12	
5/5	NEI	34	DEL	0		6/9	ATLX	65	SPAS	0		6/30	MON	1	PRED	0	
5/5	ORLM	55	BRW	0		6/9	CAR	12	DEL	0		6/30	NY	27	DEL	0	
5/5	ROSA	23	CAL	19		6/9	CHI	41	PRED	0		6/30	ORLM	65	PALM	0	
5/5	SAC	48	TUC	16		6/9	DC	70	BOSR	0		6/30	POR	41	COR	6	
5/5	SEA	15	COR	0		6/9	DET	69	IA	0		6/30	SAC	25	ROSA	0	
5/5	STM	12	SPAS	6		6/9	MF	36	SMR	14		6/30	SEA	16	TUC	0	
						6/9	MON	28	NEI	21		6/30	STM	1	SPAS	0	
5/12	CAR	13	CFT	6		6/9	NY	41	MIA	18							
5/12	DET	23	CHI	20		6/9	ORLM	54	BRW	0		7/14	ATLX	28	DC	18	S
5/12	MF	27	MON	7		6/9	PALM	13	CFT	0		7/14	DET	1	STM	0	S
5/12	NEI	13	BOSR	7		6/9	POR	43	REDD	0		7/14	NY	28	MF	0	S
5/12	ORLM	37	PALM	0		6/9	ROSA	6	SAC	0		7/14	SAC	29	SEA	12	S
5/12	POR	28	COR	7		6/9	SEA	28	COR	3							
5/12	ROSA	27	TUC	6								7/28	ATLX	10	NY	7	CC
5/12	SAC	27	CAL	6		6/16	ATLX	7	ORLM	0		7/28	DET	49	SAC	0	CC
5/12	SEA	61	REDD	0		6/16	BOSR	17	CFT	7							
5/12	SPAS	28	BRW	24		6/16	BRW	42	SPAS	6		8/11	DET	17	ATLX	7	C
5/12	STM	25	IA	12		6/16	COR	42	REDD	0							
						6/16	DC	22	NY	0							
5/19	ATLX	14	ORLM	7		6/16	DET	63	STM	0							
5/19	CAL	32	ROSA	26 *		6/16	IA	14	PRED	6							
5/19	CAR	19	PRED	18		6/16	MIA	22	PALM	7							
5/19	DC	77	CFT	0		6/16	MON	27	SMR	0							
5/19	DET	20	CHI	6		6/16	NEI	24	MF	15							
5/19	MF	36	SMR	6		6/16	ROSA	58	TUC	6							
5/19	MIA	63	PALM	0		6/16	SAC	39	CAL	17							
5/19	NY	26	BOSR	6													
5/19	POR	46	REDD	0													
5/19	SAC	32	TUC	20													
5/19	STM	27	SPAS	0													

National Women's Football Association (NWFA) – 2007 Season

The NWFA was rocked by the departures of the Detroit Demolition and D.C. Divas, who had won the last five league championships from 2002-2006. But the league soldiered on and featured 32 full-member teams competing for the 2007 championship. The Pittsburgh Passion claimed their first national championship by defeating the Columbus Comets for the 2007 NWFA title. But the Passion then stamped the IWFL as the clear top league in women's football when they followed in the footsteps of the Demolition and Divas and immediately defected with their title to the IWFL.

Major National League   Teams: 34 (32)   Games: 150 (129)
Championship game result: Pittsburgh Passion 32, Columbus Comets 0

2007 NWFA Standings

Northern Conference	W	L	PR	Before	After
North Division					
Massachusetts Mutiny (MASS)	8	1	S	--	Folded
Connecticut Crush (CTC)	6	3	Q	--	--
Maine Freeze (ME)	2	6	--	--	--
Central Massachusetts Ravens (CMR)	0	8	--	Expansion	Folded
South Division					
Baltimore Burn (BAL)	4	5	Q	--	--
Philadelphia Phoenix (PHIP)	2	6	--	--	--
Richmond Spirit (RICH)	0	7	--	Expansion	Folded
Central Division					
Pittsburgh Passion (PITT)	13	0	LC	--	Left for IWFL
Erie Illusion (ERIE)	7	2	Q	--	--
Cleveland Fusion (CLE)	8	3	CC	--	--
Central PA Vipers (CPAV)	2	7	--	Were Harrisburg Angels	Left for IWFL
West Division					
West Michigan Mayhem (WM)	7	3	S	--	--
Fort Wayne Flash (FWF)	4	4	--	--	--
Tree Town Spitfire (TREE)	2	6	--	Were Toledo Spitfire	--
Milwaukee Momentum (MIL)	1	7	--	--	Folded
Southern Conference					
Central Division					
Chattanooga Locomotion (CHAT)	8	1	S	--	--
East Tennessee Rhythm (ETNR)	4	4	--	Were Tennessee Venom (2005)	Folded
Alabama Renegades (ALRG)	3	5	--	--	--
Nashville Dream (NASH)	2	6	--	--	Folded
South Division					
Pensacola Power (PEN)	7	2	Q	--	--
New Orleans Blaze (NO)	5	4	Q	Returned from 2005	--
Gulf Coast Herricanes (GCH)	2	6	--	Returned from 2005	--
Emerald Coast Barracudas (ECB)	0	8	--	--	--
North Division					
St. Louis Slam (STL)	8	2	S	--	--
Columbus Comets (COL)	9	4	C	--	--
Kentucky Karma (KYK)	4	4	--	--	--
Cincinnati Sizzle (CIN)	0	8	--	--	--
West Division					
Oklahoma City Lightning (OKC)	9	2	CC	--	--
Austin Outlaws (OUT)	5	3	--	--	--
Dallas Rage (DALR)	2	6	--	--	Became North Texas Fury
Pacific West Division					
Phoenix Prowlers (PHXP)	8	1	Q	Expansion	--
Orange County Breakers (OCB)	5	3	--	--	Became IWFL's Southern California Breakers
All Valley Attack (ALVA)	3	5	--	Were Antelope Valley Attack	Folded
Arizona Venom (AZV)	0	8	--	Were Tucson Wildfire	Became Arizona Wildfire

National Women's Football Association (NWFA) – 2007 Season (continued)
2007 NWFA Scoreboard

Date	Team1	Score	Team2	Score	Note
4/7	PITT	14	COL	7	E
4/7	TREE	6	ERIE	0	*
4/14	BAL	6	PHIP	0	
4/14	DALR	34	NO	33	*
4/14	ERIE	25	CPAV	6	
4/14	MASS	34	CTC	0	
4/14	ME	26	CMR	0	
4/14	OCB	29	ALVA	6	
4/14	OUT	49	GCH	6	
4/14	PHXP	1	AZV	0	N
4/14	WM	6	FWF	0	
4/21	CHAT	36	NASH	7	
4/21	CTC	48	CMR	0	
4/21	ETNR	14	ALRG	8	
4/21	FWF	36	MIL	0	
4/21	KYK	7	CIN	6	
4/21	MASS	21	BAL	0	
4/21	OCB	1	AZV	0	N
4/21	OKC	60	DALR	12	
4/21	PEN	40	ECB	0	
4/21	PHIP	41	CPAV	0	
4/21	PHXP	62	ALVA	0	
4/21	PITT	23	CLE	14	
4/21	STL	27	COL	14	
4/21	WM	50	TREE	0	
4/28	ALVA	1	AZV	0	N
4/28	CHAT	52	ALRG	0	
4/28	CLE	24	BAL	8	
4/28	COL	35	FWF	6	
4/28	CPAV	1	RICH	0	N
4/28	CTC	20	PHIP	13	
4/28	KYK	33	MIL	0	
4/28	ME	22	CMR	0	
4/28	NASH	28	ETNR	22	
4/28	NO	30	ECB	0	
4/28	OKC	21	STL	6	
4/28	OUT	68	DALR	24	
4/28	PEN	48	GCH	0	
4/28	PHXP	36	OCB	0	
4/28	PITT	62	CIN	7	
5/5	ALRG	21	NASH	7	
5/5	BAL	1	RICH	0	N
5/5	CHAT	72	ETNR	0	
5/5	CLE	34	WM	6	
5/5	COL	53	CIN	0	
5/5	ERIE	41	CMR	0	
5/5	GCH	22	ECB	13	
5/5	MASS	60	ME	0	
5/5	MIL	13	TREE	6	
5/5	OKC	32	OUT	20	
5/5	PEN	22	NO	7	
5/5	PITT	52	CPAV	0	
5/5	STL	62	KYK	0	
5/12	CHAT	70	ECB	0	
5/12	CLE	78	CPAV	0	
5/12	COL	44	KYK	0	
5/12	ERIE	14	ME	13	
5/12	ETNR	1	RICH	0	N
5/12	FWF	16	TREE	14	
5/12	MASS	14	CTC	7	
5/12	NO	27	GCH	6	
5/12	OCB	32	ALVA	0	
5/12	OKC	43	DALR	20	
5/12	PEN	20	OUT	14	
5/12	PHXP	1	AZV	0	N
5/12	PITT	53	PHIP	7	
5/12	STL	61	CIN	0	
5/12	WM	51	MIL	0	
5/19	BAL	14	PHIP	8	*
5/19	CPAV	1	RICH	0	N
5/19	CTC	52	ME	0	
5/19	DALR	35	ALRG	8	
5/19	KYK	8	CIN	7	
5/19	MASS	49	CMR	0	
5/19	NO	55	ECB	6	
5/19	OCB	1	AZV	0	N
5/19	OKC	48	NASH	6	
5/19	PEN	56	GCH	8	
5/19	PHXP	52	ALVA	0	
5/19	TREE	30	MIL	10	
5/19	WM	14	FWF	5	
5/26	ALRG	33	ETNR	0	
5/26	ALVA	1	AZV	0	N
5/26	CHAT	54	NASH	0	
5/26	CTC	49	ME	6	
5/26	ERIE	39	CPAV	0	
5/26	MASS	34	BAL	14	
5/26	OKC	37	OUT	7	
5/26	PHIP	1	RICH	0	N
5/26	PHXP	50	OCB	0	
5/26	PITT	40	CLE	18	
5/26	STL	26	COL	13	
5/26	WM	41	TREE	0	
6/2	CHAT	62	ALRG	0	
6/2	CLE	62	CPAV	0	
6/2	COL	10	FWF	0	
6/2	CTC	27	PHIP	14	
6/2	ERIE	1	CMR	0	
6/2	ETNR	32	NASH	12	
6/2	MASS	52	ME	0	
6/2	NO	1	DALR	0	
6/2	OUT	57	GCH	8	
6/2	PEN	54	ECB	0	
6/2	PITT	44	CIN	7	
6/2	STL	26	KYK	0	
6/2	WM	49	MIL	0	
6/9	ALRG	1	DALR	0	
6/9	CHAT	70	ECB	6	
6/9	CLE	39	BAL	0	
6/9	COL	28	KYK	0	
6/9	ERIE	12	TREE	8	
6/9	ETNR	1	RICH	0	N
6/9	FWF	22	MIL	0	
6/9	MASS	1	CMR	0	
6/9	NO	19	GCH	12	
6/9	OCB	40	ALVA	0	
6/9	OKC	59	NASH	0	
6/9	OUT	32	PEN	12	
6/9	PHXP	1	AZV	0	N
6/9	PITT	40	PHIP	0	
6/9	STL	56	CIN	0	
6/16	ALVA	1	AZV	0	N
6/16	BAL	1	RICH	0	N
6/16	CHAT	56	ETNR	0	
6/16	CLE	22	WM	6	
6/16	COL	52	CIN	0	
6/16	CTC	1	CMR	0	
6/16	ERIE	42	ME	0	
6/16	FWF	28	TREE	0	
6/16	GCH	32	ECB	0	
6/16	KYK	14	MIL	6	
6/16	NASH	6	ALRG	0	
6/16	OUT	1	DALR	0	
6/16	PEN	37	NO	28	
6/16	PHXP	35	OCB	0	
6/16	PITT	77	CPAV	0	
6/16	STL	7	OKC	0	
6/23	CLE	57	CTC	0	Q
6/23	COL	10	PEN	0	Q
6/23	OKC	42	NO	12	Q
6/23	PITT	63	ERIE	7	Q
6/23	STL	33	PHXP	29	Q
6/23	WM	33	BAL	14	Q
6/30	CLE	12	MASS	7	S
6/30	COL	27	CHAT	8	S
6/30	OKC	33	STL	7	S
6/30	PITT	34	WM	6	S
7/7	COL	9	OKC	7	CC
7/7	PITT	49	CLE	15	CC
7/21	PITT	32	COL	0	C

Women's Professional Football League (WPFL) – 2007 Season

The ninth and final season of the WPFL saw a changing of the guard, as the three-time defending champion Dallas Diamonds failed to make the playoffs. The Houston Energy advanced to their fifth WPFL championship game, but for the second straight year, they fell a game short of a title. The So Cal Scorpions brought the last WPFL championship to San Diego before the league folded. Surviving teams switched over to a spring/summer schedule, and fall/winter women's football became a thing of the past.

Major National League   Teams: 15 (14)   Games: 59 (51)
Championship game result: So Cal Scorpions 14, Houston Energy 7

2007 WPFL Standings

National Conference	W	L	PR	Before	After
Central Division					
Houston Energy (HOU)	8	2	C	--	Left for IWFL (2009)
Wisconsin Wolves (WIW)	6	4	CC	--	Left for IWFL
Minnesota Vixen (MN)	3	5	--	--	Left for NWFA
North Division					
Indiana Speed (INS)	4	5	S	--	Left for WFA (2009)
Toledo Reign (TOL)	3	5	--	--	Left for WFA (2009)
Carolina Queens (CARQ)	1	6	--	--	Left for IWFL2
American Conference					
East Division					
Empire State Roar (EMP)	8	1	CC	--	Folded
New Jersey Titans (NJ)	3	2	--	Expansion	Left for NWFA
Connecticut Cyclones (CCY)	0	7	--	--	Left for IWFL
West Division					
Los Angeles Amazons (LA)	7	2	S	--	Left for NWFA
So Cal Scorpions (SCS)	9	2	LC	--	Left for IWFL (2010)
Dallas Diamonds (DAL)	5	3	--	--	Left for IWFL
Las Vegas Showgirlz (LV)	2	6	--	--	Left for IWFL
New Mexico Burn (NMB)	0	8	--	--	Folded
Affiliate Team					
Kentucky Valkyries (KYV)	0	1	--	Were WFL's Kentucky Force	Folded

2007 WPFL Scoreboard

Date	Away	Pts	Home	Pts		Date	Away	Pts	Home	Pts		Date	Away	Pts	Home	Pts	
8/18	DAL	14	HOU	6		9/15	DAL	41	LV	10		10/13	HOU	33	DAL	12	
8/18	EMP	61	CCY	0		9/15	EMP	28	SCS	6		10/13	MN	7	INS	0	
8/18	INS	16	MN	0		9/15	HOU	1	CCY	0		10/13	NJ	61	CARQ	8	
8/18	LA	64	NMB	0		9/15	MN	13	TOL	6		10/13	SCS	35	LV	18	
8/18	SCS	36	LV	14		9/15	WIW	29	INS	0		10/20	DAL	1	NMB	0	
8/18	TOL	33	CARQ	0		9/22	DAL	1	NMB	0		10/20	EMP	1	CCY	0	
8/18	WIW	1	KYV	0	N	9/22	EMP	40	TOL	0		10/20	HOU	33	WIW	0	
8/25	EMP	20	NJ	6		9/22	NJ	49	CARQ	8		10/20	INS	43	CARQ	0	
8/25	HOU	77	NMB	0		9/22	SCS	23	LA	12		10/20	LA	28	LV	0	
8/25	LA	33	LV	14		9/22	WIW	42	MN	7		10/20	MN	18	TOL	6	
8/25	TOL	20	CCY	0		9/29	CARQ	20	CCY	2		11/3	SCS	7	LA	6	S
8/25	WIW	34	INS	0		9/29	EMP	22	NJ	7		11/3	WIW	27	INS	8	S
9/1	EMP	28	INS	0		9/29	HOU	27	WIW	6		11/17	HOU	35	WIW	8	CC
9/1	LA	15	SCS	13		9/29	INS	20	TOL	7		11/17	SCS	42	EMP	6	CC
9/1	LV	41	NMB	8		9/29	LA	35	MN	0		12/1	SCS	14	HOU	7	C
9/1	NJ	32	CCY	0		9/29	LV	1	NMB	0							
9/1	TOL	28	CARQ	0		9/29	SCS	21	DAL	19							
9/1	WIW	13	MN	10		10/6	DAL	50	LV	20							
9/8	HOU	63	NMB	0		10/6	EMP	51	TOL	7							
9/8	LA	52	MN	6		10/6	HOU	1	CCY	0							
9/8	SCS	34	DAL	14		10/6	INS	53	CARQ	0							
						10/6	LA	1	NMB	0							
						10/6	SCS	35	WIW	14							

2008 Season Review

It was a new era in women's football! For the first time since 2000, women's football began crowning a consensus annual champion of the sport. This established a clear hierarchy within women's football, one that has been maintained over the last eight years. The IWFL was recognized as the undisputed major league in women's football in 2008, and it had so many teams that it was able to establish a developmental league labeled "Tier II". The NWFA, on its last legs after nine seasons, dropped to minor league status in women's football before folding.

Leagues: 3   Teams: 77 (74)   Games: 320 (301)

Independent Women's Football League (IWFL) – 2008 Season

28 full-member teams remained at the top IWFL level to compete for the first consensus national title in women's football since 2000. The 2008 IWFL championship game turned out to be a terrific one. The Chicago Force and the WPFL-import Dallas Diamonds were tied after regulation, making it the first women's football championship game to go into overtime. The Diamonds won the toss in overtime, drove down the field to the end zone, and captured their fourth national championship in team history.

Major National League   Teams: 31 (28)   Games: 124.5 (119)
Championship game result: Dallas Diamonds 35, Chicago Force 29 (OT)

2008 IWFL Standings

Eastern Conference	W	L	PR	Before	After
North Atlantic Division					
Pittsburgh Passion (PITT)	9	1	CC	Joined from NWFA	--
Boston Militia (BOSM)	6	2	--	Expansion	--
New York Sharks (NY)	6	2	--	--	--
D.C. Divas (DC)	4	4	--	--	--
Baltimore Nighthawks (BNH)	2	6	--	Expansion	--
Central PA Vipers (CPAV)	0	8	--	Joined from NWFA	Left for IWFL2
South Atlantic Division					
Orlando Mayhem (ORLM)	7	2	S	--	Left for IWFL2
Atlanta Xplosion (ATLX)	6	2	--	--	--
Miami Fury (MIA)	3	5	--	--	--
Palm Beach Punishers (PALM)	0	8	--	--	Left for IWFL2
Midwest Division					
Chicago Force (CHI)	10	1	C	--	--
Detroit Demolition (DET)	7	2	S	--	--
Wisconsin Wolves (WIW)	4	4	--	Joined from WPFL	Left for IWFL2 (2010)
Wisconsin Warriors (WI)	2	6	--	Expansion	Left for IWFL2
Columbus Phantoms (COLP)	0	7	--	Expansion	Folded
Western Conference					
Mid South Division					
Dallas Diamonds (DAL)	11	0	LC	Joined from WPFL	--
Kansas City Tribe (KCT)	4	4	--	Expansion	--
Iowa Crush (IA)	0	8	--	--	Left for IWFL2
Pacific Northwest Division					
Seattle Majestics (SEA)	9	1	CC	--	--
Corvallis Pride (COR)	5	4	S	--	--
Portland Shockwave (POR)	5	3	--	--	--
Sacramento Sirens (SAC)	4	4	--	--	--
Redding Rage (REDD)	0	8	--	--	--
Pacific Southwest Division					
California Quake (CAL)	8	1	S	--	--
Las Vegas Showgirlz (LV)	5	3	--	Joined from WPFL	Left for WFA
Southern California Breakers (SCB)	4	4	--	Were NWFA's Orange County Breakers	Left for IWFL2
Tucson Monsoon (TUC)	2	6	--	--	Left for IWFL2
New Mexico Menace (NMM)	0	8	--	Expansion	Left for IWFL2

Independent Women's Football League (IWFL) – 2008 Season (continued)
2008 IWFL Standings (continued)

Affiliate Teams

Santa Rosa Scorchers (ROSA)	2	3	--	--		Folded
Oakland Banshees (OAK)	0	3	--	Returned from 2006		--
Connecticut Cyclones (CCY)	0	4	--	Joined from WPFL		Left for WFA

2008 IWFL Scoreboard

Date						Date						Date					
4/12	BNH	55	CPAV	0		5/10	ATLX	37	PALM	0		6/7	ATLX	42	CAR	0	
4/12	BOSM	27	DC	22		5/10	CAL	37	TUC	0		6/7	BNH	49	MF	0	
4/12	CAL	45	TUC	14		5/10	DAL	48	MIA	6		6/7	BOSM	30	MON	20	
4/12	CHI	14	WIW	7		5/10	DET	14	WIW	0		6/7	CAL	35	NMM	0	
4/12	COR	46	REDD	0		5/10	KCT	20	WI	12		6/7	DAL	50	TUC	0	
4/12	DAL	58	KCT	0		5/10	NY	26	BOSM	24		6/7	DET	73	IA	0	
4/12	DET	34	COLP	0		5/10	PITT	38	COLP	0		6/7	LV	24	SCB	6	
4/12	LV	22	SCB	12		5/10	POR	33	ROSA	12		6/7	MIA	52	PALM	2	
4/12	MIA	6	PALM	2		5/10	SCB	48	NMM	0		6/7	NY	14	DC	8	
4/12	ORLM	13	ATLX	7	*	5/10	SEA	25	COR	0		6/7	ORLM	42	FUEL	0	
4/12	SAC	41	ROSA	27								6/7	PITT	54	HOLY	6	
4/12	SEA	14	POR	0		5/17	ATLX	17	ORLM	14		6/7	POR	23	COR	20	
4/12	WI	30	IA	7		5/17	BOSM	28	NY	14		6/7	SEA	22	OAK	0	
						5/17	CHI	8	WI	0		6/7	WIW	13	KCT	7	
4/19	CAL	5	SCB	0		5/17	COR	18	ROSA	6							
4/19	CHI	18	DET	7		5/17	DAL	62	IA	0		6/14	ATLX	40	CARQ	0	
4/19	COR	28	POR	6		5/17	DC	43	CPAV	0		6/14	BOSM	28	BNH	6	
4/19	DAL	91	NMM	0		5/17	DET	38	KCT	0		6/14	CHI	42	WIW	7	
4/19	KCT	19	IA	6		5/17	LV	27	NMM	7		6/14	DAL	49	MIA	0	
4/19	LV	35	TUC	16		5/17	MIA	22	PALM	0		6/14	DET	37	WI	0	
4/19	NY	26	BNH	6		5/17	PITT	28	BNH	0		6/14	KCT	49	IA	0	
4/19	ORLM	21	MIA	0		5/17	SCB	14	REDD	6		6/14	LV	55	NMM	0	
4/19	PITT	62	CPAV	0		5/17	SEA	27	SAC	0		6/14	NY	31	CPAV	0	
4/19	ROSA	28	REDD	0		5/17	WIW	1	COLP	0		6/14	ORLM	33	PALM	0	
4/19	SEA	14	SAC	7								6/14	PITT	17	DC	12	
4/19	WIW	16	WI	13		5/24	ATLX	35	MIA	0		6/14	POR	9	OAK	2	
						5/24	CAL	41	LV	38		6/14	SAC	34	REDD	0	
4/26	CAL	64	NMM	0		5/24	CHI	56	IA	0		6/14	SCB	24	TUC	6	
4/26	CHI	26	WI	14		5/24	COR	21	REDD	0		6/14	SEA	16	COR	7	
4/26	COR	33	SAC	13		5/24	DC	35	CPAV	0							
4/26	DAL	37	ATLX	14		5/24	SAC	13	POR	9		6/28	CHI	8	DET	7	S
4/26	DC	35	BNH	6		5/24	SEA	20	OAK	0		6/28	DAL	69	CAL	3	S
4/26	DET	53	IA	0		5/24	TUC	14	NMM	13		6/28	PITT	41	ORLM	6	S
4/26	NY	40	CPAV	0								6/28	SEA	35	COR	0	S
4/26	ORLM	55	FUEL	0		5/31	BOSM	38	MF	7							
4/26	PITT	34	BOSM	8		5/31	CAL	27	SCB	0		7/12	CHI	8	PITT	7	CC
4/26	SCB	35	TUC	15		5/31	CHI	40	FOX	0		7/12	DAL	38	SEA	6	CC
4/26	SEA	36	REDD	12		5/31	DAL	28	KCT	13							
4/26	WIW	25	COLP	0		5/31	DC	41	BNH	6		7/26	DAL	35	CHI	29	C*
						5/31	DET	34	WIW	7							
5/3	ATLX	44	MIA	0		5/31	ORLM	39	PALM	0							
5/3	BOSM	48	CPAV	0		5/31	PITT	28	NY	21							
5/3	CAL	30	LV	27		5/31	POR	45	REDD	7							
5/3	CHI	1	COLP	0		5/31	SAC	21	LV	14							
5/3	KCT	6	IA	0		5/31	WI	1	COLP	0							
5/3	NY	54	BNH	28													
5/3	ORLM	43	PALM	0													
5/3	PITT	38	DC	34													
5/3	POR	26	SAC	6													
5/3	ROSA	60	REDD	6													
5/3	TUC	20	NMM	7													

Independent Women's Football League Tier II (IWFL2) – 2008 Season

The IWFL grew so large that it started a "Tier II" level for small-market and mid-market teams, and these teams competed for a separate postseason championship amongst themselves. IWFL2 began as a regional league with 11 teams in 2008, and the first IWFL Tier II championship was played between the Montreal Blitz and the Clarksville Fox, who had joined the league from the now-defunct WFL. The Blitz prevailed, becoming the first non-U.S. team to win a league championship in an American women's football league.

Regional League   Teams: 11   Games: 46.5 (44)
Championship game result: Montreal Blitz 26, Clarksville Fox 6

2008 IWFL2 Standings

Northern Conference	W	L	PR	Before	After
Montreal Blitz (MON)	9	1	LC	Joined from IWFL	--
New England Intensity (NEI)	5	4	CC	Joined from IWFL	--
Manchester Freedom (MF)	4	4	--	Joined from IWFL	--
Holyoke Hurricanes (HOLY)	2	6	--	Expansion	--
Southern Maine Rebels (SMR)	1	7	--	Joined from IWFL	--

Southern Conference
Mid South Division

	W	L	PR	Before	After
Clarksville Fox (FOX)	8	2	C	Joined from WFL	--
Shreveport Aftershock (SPAS)	3	4	--	Joined from IWFL	--
Louisiana Fuel (FUEL)	1	7	--	Were IWFL's Baton Rouge Wildcats	--

South Atlantic Division

	W	L	PR	Before	After
Carolina Phoenix (CAR)	7	2	CC	Joined from IWFL	--
Carolina Queens (CARQ)	4	4	--	Joined from WPFL	--
Cape Fear Thunder (CFT)	2	6	--	Joined from IWFL	--

2008 IWFL2 Scoreboard

Date						Date						Date					
4/12	CAR	40	CFT	0		5/10	CARQ	63	CFT	12		6/7	CARQ	34	SPAS	6	
4/12	FOX	30	CARQ	0		5/10	FOX	28	SPAS	6		6/7	FOX	12	WI	6	
4/12	FUEL	12	SPAS	8		5/10	MF	68	HOLY	0		6/7	NEI	44	SMR	0	
4/12	MON	47	HOLY	10		5/10	MON	53	SMR	0		6/14	CAR	41	CFT	0	
						5/10	NEI	1	CCY	0	N	6/14	FOX	1	COLP	0	
4/19	CARQ	51	CFT	0		5/17	CAR	20	CARQ	14	*	6/14	HOLY	1	CCY	0	N
4/19	FOX	66	FUEL	6		5/17	CFT	1	CCY	0	N	6/14	MON	70	SMR	0	
4/19	MON	14	MF	12		5/17	FOX	14	FUEL	0		6/14	NEI	14	MF	7	
4/19	NEI	37	SMR	6		5/17	MF	49	NEI	8		6/14	SPAS	56	FUEL	0	
4/26	CAR	25	PALM	7		5/17	MON	41	HOLY	6		6/21	MF	53	SMR	0	
4/26	FOX	28	SPAS	0		5/24	CAR	50	CFT	0		6/28	FOX	32	NEI	0	CC
4/26	HOLY	38	SMR	30		5/31	CAR	41	CPAV	0		6/28	MON	41	CAR	27	CC
4/26	MON	28	NEI	0		5/31	CARQ	60	CFT	6		7/26	MON	26	FOX	6	C
5/3	CAR	21	CARQ	12		5/31	MON	40	NEI	14							
5/3	CFT	1	CCY	0	N	5/31	SMR	20	HOLY	14							
5/3	MF	70	SMR	8		5/31	SPAS	14	FUEL	0							
5/3	NEI	48	HOLY	0													
5/3	SPAS	36	FUEL	6													

National Women's Football Association (NWFA) – 2008 Season

Although it still featured a healthy number of teams, the NWFA – racked by the losses of their last six league champions – played its ninth and final season in 2008. The expansion H-Town Texas Cyclones, in just their first season, defeated the West Michigan Mayhem for the last NWFA championship. After the season, the NWFA collapsed, with 18 of the league's 35 teams forming the core of the WFA in 2009.

Minor National League   Teams: 35   Games: 149 (138)
Championship game result: H-Town Texas Cyclones 39, West Michigan Mayhem 10

2008 NWFA Standings

Northern Conference	W	L	T	PR	Before	After
Northeast Division						
New York Nemesis (NYN)	8	1	0	S	Expansion	Left for IWFL
Connecticut Crush (CTC)	3	5	0	--	--	Became IWFL's Connecticut Crushers
Maine Freeze (ME)	0	8	0	--	--	Folded
East Division						
Philadelphia Phoenix (PHIP)	9	1	0	CC	--	Became IWFL's Philadelphia Firebirds
New Jersey Titans (NJ)	3	5	0	--	Joined from WPFL	Left for WFA
Baltimore Burn (BAL)	2	6	0	--	--	Left for WFA
Central Division						
Columbus Comets (COL)	7	3	0	S	--	Left for WFA
Cleveland Fusion (CLE)	5	3	0	--	--	Left for WFA
Erie Illusion (ERIE)	4	4	0	--	--	Left for IWFL2
West Virginia Wonders (WVW)	0	8	0	--	Expansion	Folded
Midwest Division						
Fort Wayne Flash (FWF)	5	4	0	Q	--	Left for WFA
Indianapolis Chaos (IC)	1	7	0	--	Joined from IWFL (2006)	Folded
Dayton Diamonds (DAY)	1	7	0	--	Expansion	Left for WFA
North Division						
West Michigan Mayhem (WM)	11	1	0	C	--	Left for WFA
Minnesota Vixen (MN)	6	3	0	Q	Joined from WPFL	Left for IWFL
Tree Town Spitfire (TREE)	2	6	0	--	--	Folded
Southern Conference						
East Division						
Kentucky Karma (KYK)	7	3	0	S	--	Left for WFA
Chattanooga Locomotion (CHAT)	5	3	0	--	--	Left for IWFL2
Cincinnati Sizzle (CIN)	4	4	0	--	--	Left for WFA
Alabama Renegades (ALRG)	2	6	0	--	--	Folded
Southeast Division						
Pensacola Power (PEN)	6	3	0	Q	--	Became WFA's Gulf Coast Riptide
New Orleans Blaze (NO)	5	3	0	--	--	Left for WFA
Gulf Coast Herricanes (GCH)	2	6	0	--	--	Folded
Emerald Coast Barracudas (ECB)	0	8	0	--	--	Left for WFA
Midwest Division						
St. Louis Slam (STL)	8	1	0	S	--	Left for WFA
Memphis Belles (MEMB)	3	4	1	--	Expansion	Left for WFA
Kansas City Storm (STM)	1	7	0	--	Joined from IWFL	Left for WFA
Central Division						
H-Town Texas Cyclones (HTTC)	11	1	0	LC	Expansion	Left for WFA
Oklahoma City Lightning (OKC)	6	3	0	Q	--	Left for WFA (2010)
Austin Outlaws (OUT)	5	3	0	--	--	Left for WFA
North Texas Fury (NTF)	1	6	1	--	Were Dallas Rage	Folded
West Division						
Los Angeles Amazons (LA)	9	1	0	CC	Joined from WPFL	Left for IWFL
Phoenix Prowlers (PHXP)	5	3	0	--	--	Left for WFA
Modesto Magic (MODC)	1	5	0	--	Expansion	Folded
Arizona Wildfire (AZW)	0	6	0	--	Were Arizona Venom	Folded

National Women's Football Association (NWFA) – 2008 Season (continued)
2008 NWFA Scoreboard

Date	Team1	Score1	Team2	Score2		Date	Team1	Score1	Team2	Score2		Date	Team1	Score1	Team2	Score2	Note
4/19	CHAT	44	ALRG	0		5/17	CHAT	20	CIN	6		6/14	BAL	28	NJ	22	
4/19	CLE	22	WVW	0		5/17	CLE	8	FWF	6		6/14	ERIE	1	WVW	0	
4/19	FWF	59	DAY	0		5/17	DAY	14	IC	8		6/14	FWF	67	IC	6	
4/19	HTTC	27	OUT	20		5/17	ERIE	54	WVW	0		6/14	GCH	30	ECB	14	
4/19	KYK	39	CIN	6		5/17	GCH	50	ECB	12		6/14	HTTC	21	OKC	15	
4/19	LA	47	PHXP	14		5/17	HTTC	40	NTF	6		6/14	KYK	14	ALRG	0	
4/19	MODC	20	AZW	6		5/17	KYK	27	ALRG	26		6/14	MN	1	STM	0	
4/19	NJ	50	ME	0		5/17	LA	42	PHXP	0		6/14	NYN	58	ME	8	
4/19	NO	20	PEN	0		5/17	NJ	26	BAL	6		6/14	OUT	41	NTF	0	
4/19	NYN	35	CTC	0		5/17	NYN	60	ME	0		6/14	PHIP	20	CTC	0	
4/19	OKC	23	NTF	0		5/17	OUT	28	OKC	22		6/14	STL	48	COL	23	
4/19	STL	18	COL	16		5/17	PEN	16	NO	6		6/14	WM	68	DAY	0	
4/19	STM	20	MEMB	16		5/17	PHIP	19	CTC	0							
4/19	TREE	1	IC	0		5/17	STL	54	STM	0		6/21	CHAT	19	KYK	0	
						5/17	WM	51	MN	7		6/21	CIN	43	ALRG	6	
4/26	ALRG	60	PEN	58								6/21	ERIE	29	TREE	0	
4/26	CHAT	38	CIN	0		5/24	CHAT	34	ALRG	6		6/21	FWF	27	CLE	0	
4/26	COL	20	CLE	8		5/24	COL	22	CLE	16		6/21	HTTC	43	NTF	6	
4/26	CTC	55	BAL	24		5/24	FWF	62	DAY	0		6/21	IC	12	DAY	6	
4/26	ERIE	15	TREE	0		5/24	HTTC	35	OUT	14		6/21	LA	41	PHXP	14	
4/26	HTTC	46	GCH	0		5/24	KYK	70	WVW	0		6/21	MEMB	52	STM	0	
4/26	KYK	79	WVW	0		5/24	LA	75	AZW	6		6/21	NO	34	ECB	0	
4/26	LA	90	MODC	0		5/24	NJ	40	ME	0		6/21	NYN	40	BAL	18	
4/26	MN	40	IC	0		5/24	NYN	19	CTC	0		6/21	OKC	30	OUT	3	
4/26	NO	38	ECB	7		5/24	OKC	43	NTF	18		6/21	PEN	36	GCH	0	
4/26	OKC	67	STM	0		5/24	PEN	28	GCH	22		6/21	PHIP	1	ME	0	
4/26	OUT	33	NTF	0		5/24	PHXP	64	MODC	0		6/21	WM	21	MN	13	
4/26	PHIP	40	NJ	0		5/24	STL	42	MEMB	0							
4/26	PHXP	72	AZW	0		5/24	TREE	12	IC	0		6/28	COL	14	FWF	7	Q
4/26	STL	51	MEMB	0								6/28	HTTC	26	OKC	0	Q
4/26	WM	7	FWF	6	*	5/31	CIN	28	KYK	14		6/28	KYK	6	PEN	0	Q
						5/31	CLE	1	WVW	0		6/28	WM	31	MN	7	Q
5/3	ALRG	46	CIN	14		5/31	COL	34	ERIE	0							
5/3	CLE	30	ERIE	0		5/31	CTC	44	ME	0		7/5	HTTC	25	STL	13	S
5/3	COL	91	WVW	0		5/31	LA	1	MODC	0		7/5	LA	1	KYK	0	S
5/3	CTC	48	ME	0		5/31	MEMB	36	ECB	33		7/5	PHIP	15	COL	14	S
5/3	LA	62	AZW	0		5/31	MN	62	IC	6		7/5	WM	34	NYN	7	S
5/3	MEMB	52	ECB	0		5/31	NO	27	GCH	16							
5/3	MN	40	TREE	0		5/31	NYN	46	NJ	6		7/12	HTTC	34	LA	14	CC
5/3	NO	36	GCH	0		5/31	OKC	1	STM	0		7/12	WM	21	PHIP	0	CC
5/3	NYN	19	NJ	12		5/31	PEN	40	ALRG	8							
5/3	PHIP	50	BAL	8		5/31	PHIP	49	BAL	0		7/26	HTTC	39	WM	10	C
5/3	PHXP	67	MODC	0		5/31	PHXP	49	AZW	8							
5/3	STL	24	CHAT	7		5/31	STL	21	CHAT	0							
5/3	WM	82	DAY	0		5/31	WM	76	TREE	0							
5/10	CIN	54	DAY	6		6/7	BAL	24	CTC	21							
5/10	COL	48	ERIE	0		6/7	CIN	61	DAY	0							
5/10	FWF	58	IC	0		6/7	CLE	26	ERIE	0							
5/10	KYK	13	CHAT	7		6/7	COL	104	WVW	0							
5/10	MEMB	6	NTF	6		6/7	HTTC	41	GCH	0							
5/10	MN	58	STM	0		6/7	LA	1	AZW	0							
5/10	NYN	42	BAL	8		6/7	MN	41	TREE	0							
5/10	OKC	21	HTTC	13		6/7	NTF	30	MEMB	14							
5/10	OUT	42	NO	6		6/7	OUT	48	NO	0							
5/10	PEN	64	ECB	24		6/7	PEN	38	ECB	12							
5/10	PHIP	56	ME	0		6/7	PHIP	28	NJ	0							
5/10	WM	54	TREE	0		6/7	PHXP	1	MODC	0							
						6/7	STL	1	STM	0							
						6/7	WM	19	FWF	14							

2009 Season Review

The IWFL was once again the undisputed major league in women's football in 2009, and another close championship game ended this time in a stunning upset. IWFL2 continued its healthy growth, becoming a full-fledged national league with 25 teams. The WFA was launched, taking the NWFA's place as the top non-IWFL-affiliated league in women's football. Several former NWFA teams formed the core of the new WFA, and two ex-NWFA franchises squared off for the inaugural WFA championship.

Leagues: 3 Teams: 84 (78) Games: 343 (305)

Independent Women's Football League (IWFL) – 2009 Season

With five teams joining the IWFL from the now-defunct NWFA, 22 of the best teams in the sport competed in the IWFL in 2009. The D.C. Divas reached their second national championship game, but the heavily-favored Divas were upended in a penalty-laden contest by the Kansas City Tribe, who concluded their second season with an IWFL national championship.

Major National League Teams: 24 (22) Games: 96 (93.5)
Championship game result: Kansas City Tribe 21, D.C. Divas 18

2009 IWFL Standings

Eastern Conference	W	L	PR	Before	After
North Atlantic Division					
Boston Militia (BOSM)	9	1	CC	--	--
New York Nemesis (NYN)	5	3	--	Joined from NWFA	--
New York Sharks (NY)	4	4	--	--	--
Philadelphia Firebirds (PHI)	1	7	--	Were NWFA's Philadelphia Phoenix	--
Connecticut Crushers (CTCS)	1	7	--	Were NWFA's Connecticut Crush	Left for IWFL2
Mid-Atlantic Division					
D.C. Divas (DC)	10	1	C	--	--
Pittsburgh Passion (PITT)	7	2	S	--	--
Detroit Demolition (DET)	4	4	--	--	Folded
Baltimore Nighthawks (BNH)	3	5	--	--	--
South Atlantic Division					
Dallas Diamonds (DAL)	8	1	S	--	--
Atlanta Xplosion (ATLX)	7	1	--	--	--
Miami Fury (MIA)	6	2	--	--	--
Houston Energy (HOU)	2	6	--	Joined from WPFL (2007)	--
Western Conference					
Midwest Division					
Kansas City Tribe (KCT)	10	1	LC	--	--
Chicago Force (CHI)	7	3	CC	--	--
Minnesota Vixen (MN)	2	6	--	Joined from NWFA	Left for IWFL2
Pacific Northwest Division					
Seattle Majestics (SEA)	8	1	S	--	--
Portland Shockwave (POR)	4	4	--	--	--
Corvallis Pride (COR)	2	6	--	--	Folded
Pacific Southwest Division					
Los Angeles Amazons (LA)	8	1	S	Joined from NWFA	--
Sacramento Sirens (SAC)	5	3	--	--	--
California Quake (CAL)	4	4	--	--	--
Affiliate Teams					
Oakland Banshees (OAK)	0	1	--	--	Folded
Redding Rage (REDD)	0	1	--	--	Folded

Independent Women's Football League (IWFL) – 2009 Season (continued)
2009 IWFL Scoreboard

Date	Team	Score	Team	Score		Date	Team	Score	Team	Score		Date	Team	Score	Team	Score	
4/11	ATLX	43	FOX	0		5/9	BOSM	39	MON	0		6/6	ATLX	63	TVT	0	
4/11	CHI	54	IA	0		5/9	HOU	40	SPAS	6		6/6	BNH	30	CTCS	8	
4/11	DAL	69	HOU	0		5/9	KCT	58	WI	0		6/6	BOSM	49	NYN	12	
4/11	DC	33	BNH	0		5/9	LA	64	MODX	0		6/6	CAL	26	SCB	20	
4/11	DET	34	WI	6		5/9	NY	40	CTCS	7		6/6	COR	20	MODX	8	
4/11	KCT	45	MN	8		5/9	NYN	34	PHI	3		6/6	DAL	61	HOU	20	
4/11	LA	32	CAL	2		5/9	SAC	34	CAL	14		6/6	DC	34	NY	18	
4/11	MIA	21	ORLM	0		5/9	SEA	35	POR	7		6/6	DET	33	ERIE	7	
4/11	NY	21	NYN	7								6/6	KCT	19	WI	12	
4/11	SAC	71	MODX	0		5/16	ATLX	77	PALM	7		6/6	MIA	18	ORLM	0	
4/11	SEA	34	COR	0		5/16	BNH	32	JJ	6		6/6	MN	14	IA	9	
						5/16	BOSM	60	PHI	0		6/6	PITT	53	PHI	0	
4/18	ATLX	38	HOU	7		5/16	DAL	64	FUEL	0		6/6	SEA	20	POR	7	
4/18	BNH	22	PHI	15		5/16	DC	21	NY	7							
4/18	BOSM	42	MF	0		5/16	DET	21	CHI	19		6/13	ATLX	19	ORLM	14	
4/18	CHI	38	WI	20		5/16	KCT	48	FOX	6		6/13	BOSM	60	NEI	0	
4/18	DAL	27	FUEL	0		5/16	LA	50	NMM	0		6/13	CHI	26	DET	6	
4/18	KCT	62	IA	0		5/16	MIA	27	ORLM	6		6/13	DAL	76	HOU	7	
4/18	NYN	40	JJ	0		5/16	MN	38	IA	20		6/13	DC	63	PHI	0	
4/18	PITT	29	DET	6		5/16	PITT	41	NYN	0		6/13	KCT	65	MN	0	
4/18	SAC	46	CAL	0		5/16	POR	33	COR	0		6/13	LA	20	SAC	19	
4/18	SEA	20	POR	7		5/16	SEA	21	SAC	20		6/13	MIA	53	PALM	0	
												6/13	NYN	28	CTCS	6	
4/24	MIA	44	PALM	0		5/23	ATLX	16	MIA	12		6/13	PITT	34	NY	33	
4/25	ATLX	28	CHAT	6		5/23	CAL	58	MODX	24		6/13	POR	26	COR	6	
4/25	BOSM	21	NY	7		5/23	CHI	53	MN	0		6/13	SEA	55	TUC	0	
4/25	CAL	61	NMM	0		5/23	COR	1	REDD	0	N						
4/25	CHI	55	MN	0		5/23	DC	70	BNH	14		6/20	CTCS	1	CPAV	0	
4/25	DAL	59	SPAS	0		5/23	HOU	49	SPAS	0							
4/25	DC	35	DET	0		5/23	LA	33	SCB	0		6/27	BOSM	34	DAL	14	S
4/25	LA	42	SCB	0		5/23	PITT	34	DET	12		6/27	CHI	28	SEA	14	S
4/25	NYN	14	MON	6		5/23	SEA	14	POR	12		6/27	DC	27	PITT	17	S
4/25	PHI	31	CTCS	12								6/27	KCT	19	LA	14	S
4/25	PITT	49	BNH	0		5/30	BOSM	66	BNH	0							
4/25	POR	20	COR	7		5/30	CAL	42	MODX	14		7/11	DC	27	BOSM	21	CC
4/25	SEA	33	SAC	8		5/30	DAL	41	MIA	8		7/11	KCT	40	CHI	16	CC
						5/30	DC	42	PHI	0							
5/2	BOSM	47	CTCS	0		5/30	KCT	30	CHI	14		7/25	KCT	21	DC	18	C
5/2	CHI	28	KCT	6		5/30	LA	57	TUC	0							
5/2	DAL	32	ATLX	7		5/30	NY	44	NEI	0							
5/2	DC	27	PITT	7		5/30	NYN	13	MON	12							
5/2	DET	13	BNH	0		5/30	PITT	76	CTCS	0							
5/2	LA	36	CAL	21		5/30	SAC	48	COR	0							
5/2	MIA	21	HOU	0													
5/2	NY	33	PHI	14													
5/2	POR	1	OAK	0	N												
5/2	SAC	39	COR	0													

Independent Women's Football League Tier II (IWFL2) – 2009 Season

IWFL2 expanded into a national league with 25 teams in 2009, and the reigning league champion Montreal Blitz again reached the league's championship game. They faced the Wisconsin Warriors, who had dropped down to Tier II after compiling a 2-6 record in the major IWFL league as an expansion team in 2008. That big-market experience might have aided the Warriors, as they dispatched the Blitz for the national championship.

Minor National League   Teams: 25   Games: 104 (98.5)
Championship game result: Wisconsin Warriors 42, Montreal Blitz 14

Independent Women's Football League Tier II (IWFL2) – 2009 Season (continued)

2009 IWFL2 Standings

Teams	W	L	PR	Before	After
Carolina Queens (CARQ)	7	2	S	--	--
Carolina Phoenix (CAR)	8	2	CC	--	--
Montreal Blitz (MON)	7	4	C	--	--
Wisconsin Warriors (WI)	7	4	LC	Joined from IWFL	--
New England Intensity (NEI)	6	3	S	--	--
Chattanooga Locomotion (CHAT)	6	3	S	Joined from NWFA	--
Jersey Justice (JJ)	6	4	CC	Expansion	--
Manchester Freedom (MF)	4	5	S	--	--
Orlando Mayhem (ORLM)	2	6	--	Joined from IWFL	Folded
Tennessee Valley Tigers (TVT)	5	3	--	Expansion	--
Palm Beach Punishers (PALM)	2	6	--	Joined from IWFL	--
Southern California Breakers (SCB)	4	4	--	Joined from IWFL	--
Erie Illusion (ERIE)	3	5	--	Joined from NWFA	--
Tucson Monsoon (TUC)	5	3	--	Joined from IWFL	--
Shreveport Aftershock (SPAS)	2	4	--	--	Folded
Southern Maine Rebels (SMR)	2	6	--	--	--
Clarksville Fox (FOX)	4	4	--	--	--
Central PA Vipers (CPAV)	2	6	--	Joined from IWFL	Folded
Cape Fear Thunder (CFT)	1	7	--	--	Left for W8FL (2011)
Louisiana Fuel (FUEL)	0	6	--	--	--
Iowa Crush (IA)	0	8	--	Joined from IWFL	--
Modesto Maniax (MODX)	0	8	--	Expansion	--
Holyoke Hurricanes (HOLY)	0	8	--	--	--
New Mexico Menace (NMM)	0	6	--	Joined from IWFL	Folded
Louisville Nightmare (LOU)	0	8	--	Expansion	--

2009 IWFL2 Scoreboard

Date	Team1	Score1	Team2	Score2		Date	Team1	Score1	Team2	Score2		Date	Team1	Score1	Team2	Score2	
4/11	CAR	32	LOU	7		5/2	SCB	55	MODX	0		6/6	CAR	55	CFT	8	
4/11	CARQ	66	CFT	0		5/2	TUC	54	NMM	0		6/6	CPAV	48	HOLY	0	
4/11	CHAT	46	TVT	0		5/2	TVT	32	FUEL	27		6/6	FOX	12	LOU	0	
4/11	JJ	8	ERIE	6		5/2	WI	54	MN	16		6/6	NEI	19	SMR	0	
4/11	MF	27	CTCS	15		5/9	CAR	48	CFT	0		6/7	ERIE	1	HOLY	0	
4/11	NEI	34	HOLY	0		5/9	CARQ	1	LOU	0		6/13	CARQ	36	CAR	20	
4/11	SPAS	32	FUEL	18		5/9	JJ	34	CPAV	0		6/13	CHAT	1	LOU	0	
4/11	TUC	8	NMM	0		5/9	NEI	20	MF	8		6/13	CPAV	30	CFT	6	
4/18	CAR	6	ERIE	0		5/9	PALM	28	FUEL	0		6/13	FOX	22	IA	12	
4/18	CARQ	59	CFT	0		5/9	TUC	14	SCB	13		6/13	JJ	36	ERIE	16	
4/18	CHAT	32	TVT	14		5/16	CHAT	60	CFT	0		6/13	MF	19	SMR	6	
4/18	MON	55	SMR	6		5/16	MF	13	SMR	8		6/13	MON	1	HOLY	0	
4/18	NEI	21	CPAV	14		5/16	NEI	53	HOLY	0		6/13	SCB	21	MODX	6	
4/18	PALM	21	ORLM	6		5/16	SCB	32	TUC	6		6/27	CAR	26	CARQ	16	S
4/18	SCB	33	NMM	0		5/16	TVT	53	LOU	0		6/27	JJ	30	NEI	7	S
4/25	CARQ	28	JJ	20		5/17	MON	1	HOLY	0		6/27	MON	68	MF	0	S
4/25	FOX	37	LOU	7		5/23	CAR	14	PALM	9		6/27	WI	32	CHAT	6	S
4/25	MF	47	CPAV	0		5/23	CARQ	30	CHAT	12		7/11	MON	9	JJ	8	CC
4/25	ORLM	28	HOU	7		5/23	CFT	34	LOU	14		7/11	WI	28	CAR	6	CC
4/25	SMR	14	HOLY	0		5/23	MON	41	ERIE	10		7/25	WI	42	MON	14	C
4/25	TUC	12	MODX	8		5/23	SMR	14	CPAV	8							
4/25	TVT	68	CFT	0		5/23	TUC	55	NMM	7							
4/25	WI	30	IA	0		5/23	TVT	23	FOX	0							
5/2	CAR	42	ORLM	15		5/23	WI	42	IA	0							
5/2	CARQ	26	PALM	14		5/30	CAR	8	CARQ	0							
5/2	CHAT	62	SPAS	0		5/30	CHAT	28	FOX	0							
5/2	ERIE	61	CPAV	8		5/30	ERIE	20	MF	13							
5/2	FOX	14	IA	0		5/30	JJ	28	SMR	8							
5/2	JJ	40	SMR	14		5/30	ORLM	41	PALM	25							
5/2	MON	48	HOLY	0		5/30	SPAS	65	FUEL	36							
5/2	NEI	13	MF	0		5/30	TVT	54	LOU	0							
						5/30	WI	38	MN	8							

Women's Football Alliance (WFA) – 2009 Season

The WFA was formed in 2009 with 31 full-member teams. 18 of those teams played in the defunct NWFA the previous season, including the St. Louis Slam and West Michigan Mayhem, who competed in the first WFA championship game. The Mayhem were making their second straight league title game appearance, but once again, they came up a bit short as the Slam clinched the inaugural WFA championship.

Minor National League   Teams: 35 (31)   Games: 143 (113)
Championship game result: St. Louis Slam 21, West Michigan Mayhem 14
International Bowl: New Orleans Blaze 12, Monterrey Royal Eagles 0

2009 WFA Standings

National Conference	W	L	PR	Before	After
Northeast Division					
Philadelphia Liberty Belles (II) (PLB2)	9	1	CC	Expansion	--
New Jersey Titans (NJ)	5	3	--	Joined from NWFA	--
Baltimore Burn (BAL)	5	4	--	Joined from NWFA	--
Keystone Assault (KEY)	4	4	--	Expansion	--
Binghamton Tiger Cats (BING)	2	6	--	Expansion	Left for IWFL2
Connecticut Cyclones (CCY)	0	8	--	Joined from IWFL	Folded
Mid-Atlantic Division					
Columbus Comets (COL)	9	1	S	Joined from NWFA	--
Kentucky Karma (KYK)	5	3	--	Joined from NWFA	--
Cleveland Fusion (CLE)	4	4	--	Joined from NWFA	--
Pittsburgh Force (PITF)	2	6	--	Expansion	--
Cincinnati Sizzle (CIN)	1	7	--	Joined from NWFA	--
Central Division					
West Michigan Mayhem (WM)	10	1	C	Joined from NWFA	--
Indiana Speed (INS)	6	3	S	Joined from WPFL (2007)	--
Fort Wayne Flash (FWF)	4	4	--	Joined from NWFA	Folded
Toledo Reign (TOL)	1	7	--	Joined from WPFL (2007)	--
Dayton Diamonds (DAY)	1	7	--	Joined from NWFA	--
American Conference					
Southeast Division					
Jacksonville Dixie Blues (JAX)	9	1	CC	Joined from WFL (2007)	--
Gulf Coast Riptide (GCR)	6	2	--	Were NWFA's Pensacola Power	Deferred until 2011
Memphis Belles (MEMB)	4	4	--	Joined from NWFA	Left for IWFL2
New Orleans Blaze (NO)	3	6	BW	Joined from NWFA	--
Emerald Coast Barracudas (ECB)	0	8	--	Joined from NWFA	Folded
Midwest Division					
St. Louis Slam (STL)	11	0	LC	Joined from NWFA	--
Minnesota Machine (MACH)	5	3	--	Expansion	--
Iowa Thunder (IAT)	5	3	--	Expansion	--
Kansas City Storm (STM)	2	6	--	Joined from NWFA	Left for WSFL
Missouri Phoenix (MOPH)	0	8	--	Expansion	Became WSFL's Kansas Phoenix (2011)
Southwest Division					
Austin Outlaws (OUT)	7	2	S	Joined from NWFA	--
Lone Star Mustangs (LSM)	6	2	--	Expansion	--
H-Town Texas Cyclones (HTTC)	2	6	--	Joined from NWFA	Left for IWFL
East Texas Saberkats (ETXS)	0	6	--	Expansion	Folded
Pacific Division					
Las Vegas Showgirlz (LV)	8	1	S	Joined from IWFL	--
California Lynx (CLNX)	5	3	--	Expansion	Became Pacific Warriors
Phoenix Prowlers (PHXP)	3	5	--	Joined from NWFA	Folded
Marana She-Devils (MSD)	0	8	--	Expansion	Folded
Affiliate Team					
Monterrey Royal Eagles (MRE)	0	1	B	Expansion	--

Women's Football Alliance (WFA) – 2009 Season (continued)
2009 WFA Scoreboard

Date	Team	Score	Team	Score	Note
4/4	COL	21	BAL	16	E
4/18	BAL	1	CCY	0	N
4/18	CLE	38	KYK	14	
4/18	COL	49	PITF	0	
4/18	IAT	54	MOPH	0	
4/18	INS	62	DAY	8	
4/18	JAX	64	ECB	16	
4/18	LSM	1	ETXS	0	N
4/18	LV	19	CLNX	6	
4/18	MEMB	46	NO	7	
4/18	NJ	21	BING	0	
4/18	OUT	40	HTTC	34	
4/18	PHXP	1	MSD	0	N
4/18	PLB2	47	KEY	24	
4/18	STL	77	STM	0	
4/18	WM	41	FWF	0	
4/25	CLNX	1	MSD	0	N
4/25	GCR	28	NO	0	
4/25	HTTC	1	ETXS	0	N
4/25	IAT	16	MACH	6	
4/25	INS	52	FWF	0	
4/25	KEY	34	BING	20	
4/25	KYK	22	CIN	14	
4/25	MEMB	50	ECB	0	
4/25	NJ	1	CCY	0	N
4/25	OUT	14	LSM	13	
4/25	PITF	34	CLE	28	
4/25	PLB2	43	BAL	8	
4/25	STL	1	MOPH	0	
4/25	WM	47	TOL	0	
5/2	COL	36	CIN	0	
5/2	GCR	66	ECB	8	
5/2	IAT	74	STM	0	
5/2	INS	60	TOL	0	
5/2	JAX	46	NO	0	
5/2	LSM	20	HTTC	12	
5/2	MACH	56	MOPH	0	
5/2	OUT	1	ETXS	0	N
5/2	WM	56	DAY	0	
5/9	BAL	20	KEY	16	
5/9	BING	1	CCY	0	N
5/9	CLNX	27	PHXP	20	
5/9	COL	30	CLE	12	
5/9	FWF	29	DAY	0	
5/9	GCR	20	NO	10	
5/9	JAX	34	MEMB	20	
5/9	LV	1	MSD	0	N
5/9	OUT	28	LSM	14	
5/9	PITF	36	CIN	18	
5/9	PLB2	14	NJ	12	
5/9	STL	28	MACH	0	
5/9	STM	1	MOPH	0	
5/9	WM	57	TOL	0	
5/16	BAL	1	CCY	0	N
5/16	COL	38	PITF	0	
5/16	FWF	47	TOL	0	
5/16	GCR	50	MEMB	8	
5/16	KYK	20	CLE	12	
5/16	LSM	14	HTTC	12	
5/16	MACH	50	STM	0	
5/16	NJ	26	BING	6	
5/16	NO	39	ECB	20	
5/16	PHXP	1	MSD	0	N
5/16	PLB2	14	KEY	12	
5/16	STL	35	IAT	7	
5/16	WM	20	INS	15	
5/23	KYK	8	PITF	6	
5/23	LV	26	PHXP	14	
5/30	CLE	34	PITF	16	
5/30	CLNX	1	MSD	0	N
5/30	HTTC	1	ETXS	0	N
5/30	IAT	65	MOPH	0	
5/30	INS	14	FWF	7	
5/30	JAX	49	GCR	36	
5/30	KEY	32	BING	6	
5/30	KYK	22	CIN	0	
5/30	LSM	28	OUT	14	
5/30	LV	47	PHXP	8	
5/30	MEMB	44	ECB	12	
5/30	NJ	1	CCY	0	N
5/30	PLB2	13	BAL	10	
5/30	STL	88	STM	0	
5/30	TOL	20	DAY	8	
6/6	BAL	46	KEY	22	
6/6	BING	1	CCY	0	N
6/6	CIN	14	PITF	8	
6/6	CLNX	41	PHXP	6	
6/6	COL	20	CLE	7	
6/6	INS	56	DAY	0	
6/6	JAX	1	ECB	0	
6/6	LV	1	MSD	0	N
6/6	MEMB	32	NO	26	
6/6	OUT	42	HTTC	20	
6/6	PLB2	59	NJ	0	
6/6	STL	42	MACH	7	
6/6	STM	1	MOPH	0	
6/6	WM	35	FWF	0	
6/13	BAL	56	BING	6	
6/13	CLE	36	CIN	18	
6/13	COL	23	KYK	8	
6/13	FWF	38	TOL	0	
6/13	GCR	54	MEMB	20	
6/13	JAX	42	NO	0	
6/13	KEY	28	NJ	6	
6/13	LSM	1	ETXS	0	N
6/13	LV	28	CLNX	20	
6/13	MACH	20	IAT	0	
6/13	PHXP	1	MSD	0	N
6/13	PLB2	1	CCY	0	N
6/13	STL	51	MOPH	0	
6/13	WM	55	DAY	0	
6/20	CLNX	1	MSD	0	N
6/20	COL	47	CIN	8	
6/20	FWF	68	DAY	20	
6/20	GCR	1	ECB	0	
6/20	IAT	54	STM	0	
6/20	INS	58	TOL	0	
6/20	JAX	34	MEMB	6	
6/20	KEY	1	CCY	0	N
6/20	KYK	46	PITF	20	
6/20	LSM	31	HTTC	0	
6/20	LV	35	PHXP	8	
6/20	MACH	61	MOPH	0	
6/20	NJ	1	BAL	0	
6/20	OUT	1	ETXS	0	N
6/20	PLB2	53	BING	0	
6/27	CLE	48	CIN	14	
6/27	COL	21	KYK	12	
6/27	DAY	6	TOL	0	
6/27	JAX	37	GCR	14	
6/27	LV	40	CLNX	22	
6/27	MACH	1	STM	0	
6/27	NO	1	ECB	0	
6/27	OUT	29	HTTC	7	
6/27	STL	40	IAT	10	
6/27	WM	21	INS	0	
7/11	JAX	55	OUT	14	S
7/11	PLB2	19	INS	9	S
7/11	STL	30	LV	12	S
7/11	WM	41	COL	12	S
7/25	STL	40	JAX	32	CC
7/25	WM	28	PLB2	21	CC
8/15	NO	12	MRE	0	B
8/15	STL	21	WM	14	C

2010 Season Review

The IWFL remained the major league in women's football for the third straight season, and a new dynasty would brush off an old one for their first national championship. But it would also be the IWFL's last season on top, as several elite IWFL teams would flip the balance of power that offseason. The WFA would be the beneficiaries, and they continued to grow their ranks in their second season. IWFL2 had a repeat champion, while the WSFL, dormant since 2002, re-launched with an exhibition season in preparation for a full schedule in 2011.

Leagues: 4 Teams: 93 (86) Games: 379 (354)

Independent Women's Football League (IWFL) – 2010 Season

At the top level, 19 IWFL teams vied for a championship. The Sacramento Sirens returned to the IWFL title game for the first time in five years, yet it was the Boston Militia who claimed their first national title by decisively handing the Sacramento Sirens their first loss in five championship game appearances. But one of the biggest upheavals in women's football history hit the league after the season; the IWFL's three-year reign as the major league in women's football came to an abrupt end when over half of the league – ten of the IWFL's 19 full-member teams, including the champion Militia – defected en masse to the WFA.

Major National League Teams: 20 (19) Games: 87 (77)
Championship game result: Boston Militia 39, Sacramento Sirens 7

2010 IWFL Standings

Eastern Conference	W	L	PR	Before	After
Northeast Division					
Boston Militia (BOSM)	11	0	LC	--	Left for WFA
New York Sharks (NY)	7	2	S	--	Left for WFA
Pittsburgh Passion (PITT)	4	4	--	--	Left for WFA
New York Nemesis (NYN)	3	5	--	--	Folded
Philadelphia Firebirds (PHI)	1	7	--	--	--
Southeast Division					
D.C. Divas (DC)	6	4	CC	--	Left for WFA
Atlanta Xplosion (ATLX)	7	2	S	--	Became Atlanta Ravens
Miami Fury (MIA)	5	3	--	--	Left for WFA
Baltimore Nighthawks (BNH)	3	5	--	--	--

Western Conference	W	L	PR	Before	After
Midwest Division					
Dallas Diamonds (DAL)	8	2	CC	--	Left for WFA
Chicago Force (CHI)	7	2	S	--	Left for WFA
Kansas City Tribe (KCT)	6	2	--	--	Left for WFA
Houston Energy (HOU)	5	3	--	--	--
H-Town Texas Cyclones (HTTC)	0	8	--	Joined from WFA	Folded
Pacific West Division					
Sacramento Sirens (SAC)	10	1	C	--	--
So Cal Scorpions (SCS)	6	3	S	Joined from WPFL (2007)	Left for WFA
Portland Shockwave (POR)	6	2	--	--	--
California Quake (CAL)	7	2	--	--	--
Los Angeles Amazons (LA)	4	4	--	--	Left for WFA
Seattle Majestics (SEA)	2	6	--	--	--

Independent Women's Football League (IWFL) – 2010 Season (continued)
2010 IWFL Scoreboard

Date	Team 1	Score	Team 2	Score		Date	Team 1	Score	Team 2	Score		Date	Team 1	Score	Team 2	Score	
4/3	ATLX	65	CHAT	0		5/1	ATLX	21	HOU	20		5/22	ATLX	1	MIA	0	
4/3	BNH	54	PHI	0		5/1	BNH	21	CARQ	0		5/22	BOSM	1	PHI	0	
4/3	BOSM	56	NYN	6		5/1	BOSM	42	DC	35		5/22	CAL	34	SCB	14	
4/3	CAL	50	SEA	14		5/1	CAL	40	TUC	8		5/22	CHI	7	PITT	0	
4/3	CHI	42	WI	0		5/1	CHI	14	KCT	12		5/22	DAL	35	KCT	21	
4/3	DAL	34	HOU	12		5/1	DAL	49	MEMB	6		5/22	DC	49	NYN	21	
4/3	KCT	77	IA	0		5/1	MIA	41	PALM	0		5/22	NY	38	BNH	6	
4/3	LA	37	SCS	26		5/1	NY	50	JJ	8		5/22	SAC	10	LA	6	
4/3	MIA	40	PALM	9		5/1	NYN	33	PHI	0		5/22	SCS	41	TUC	0	
4/3	PITT	32	ERIE	0		5/1	PITT	40	ERIE	2							
4/3	SAC	33	BAB	13		5/1	POR	20	SEA	14		5/29	ATLX	56	FOX	0	
						5/1	SAC	68	MODX	0		5/29	DC	49	PHI	3	
4/10	ATLX	54	CARQ	7								5/29	HOU	1	HTTC	0	N
4/10	BOSM	59	CTCS	10		5/8	BOSM	40	NYN	0		5/29	POR	20	LA	6	
4/10	CAL	60	TUC	20		5/8	CAL	62	MODX	0		5/29	SAC	73	TUC	0	
4/10	CHI	62	WIW	0		5/8	CHI	56	MN	0		5/29	SCS	43	BAB	6	
4/10	DC	54	BNH	6		5/8	DAL	23	ATLX	3		5/29	SEA	52	MODX	0	
4/10	HOU	60	FUEL	0		5/8	DC	28	BNH	7							
4/10	KCT	28	DAL	21		5/8	HOU	1	MIA	0		6/5	BOSM	52	DC	36	
4/10	NY	64	PHI	0		5/8	KCT	44	WI	0		6/5	DAL	44	HOU	36	
4/10	SAC	35	SEA	14		5/8	LA	17	POR	0		6/5	KCT	30	CHI	12	
4/10	SCS	22	SCB	0		5/8	NY	12	PITT	8		6/5	LA	39	SCB	14	
						5/8	SCS	41	SEA	14		6/5	MIA	14	PALM	6	
4/17	CHI	30	WI	7								6/5	NY	27	PITT	10	
4/17	LA	48	CAL	36		5/15	ATLX	50	CARQ	0		6/5	NYN	38	MF	0	
4/17	MIA	1	HTTC	0	N	5/15	BOSM	31	NY	0		6/5	POR	7	CAL	6	
4/17	NY	19	DC	13		5/15	CHI	49	WIW	0		6/5	SAC	60	MODX	0	
4/17	NYN	25	CTCS	0		5/15	DAL	1	HTTC	0	N	6/5	SCS	26	BAB	22	
4/17	PITT	49	PHI	0		5/15	HOU	30	FUEL	0		6/5	SEA	56	TUC	6	
4/17	POR	22	MODX	8		5/15	KCT	80	MN	0							
4/17	SCS	54	TUC	0		5/15	MIA	55	PALM	0		6/12	BOSM	26	NY	6	S
						5/15	PHI	49	BING	0		6/12	DAL	27	CHI	20	S
4/24	ATLX	39	MIA	0		5/15	PITT	34	BNH	6		6/12	DC	35	ATLX	7	S
4/24	BNH	7	NYN	6		5/15	POR	20	SEA	14		6/12	SAC	60	SCS	26	S
4/24	BOSM	27	PITT	0		5/15	SAC	55	MODX	0							
4/24	CAL	42	SCS	40								7/10	BOSM	28	DC	0	CC
4/24	DAL	79	MN	0								7/10	SAC	45	DAL	43	CC
4/24	DC	1	PHI	0													
4/24	HOU	1	HTTC	0	N							7/24	BOSM	39	SAC	7	C
4/24	KCT	55	WIW	0													
4/24	NY	65	CTCS	14								9/11	CAL	68	NCRH	12	IE
4/24	POR	22	SEA	7													
4/24	SAC	27	LA	26													

Independent Women's Football League Tier II (IWFL2) – 2010 Season

The third and final season of the IWFL2 again had 25 regulation teams battling for the title, and once again, the Montreal Blitz made it to the IWFL2 championship game. The Blitz appeared in all three IWFL2 championship games from 2008-2010, and they held off the Bay Area Bandits for their second IWFL2 league championship and their first national title. It was the first time in women's football history that a U.S. national championship was captured by a non-U.S. team. At the conclusion of the year, the league consolidated the remaining IWFL2 teams back into the top tier of the IWFL.

Minor National League   Teams: 27 (25)   Games: 106.5 (99.5)
Championship game result: Montreal Blitz 9, Bay Area Bandits 2

2010 IWFL2 Standings

Eastern Conference	W	L	PR	Before	After
Northeast Division					
MONTREAL BLITZ (MON)	11	0	LC	--	Left for IWFL
NEW ENGLAND INTENSITY (NEI)	8	1	S	--	Left for IWFL
Jersey Justice (JJ)	6	1	--	--	Left for WSFL
Erie Illusion (ERIE)	3	5	--	--	Left for WFA
Manchester Freedom (MF)	2	6	--	--	Left for IWFL
Connecticut Crushers (CTCS)	1	7	--	Joined from IWFL	Folded
Southern Maine Rebels (SMR)	1	7	--	--	Became IWFL's Maine Rebels
Binghamton Tiger Cats (BING)	0	8	--	Joined from WFA	Left for WSFL
Southeast Division					
Carolina Phoenix (CAR)	9	1	CC	--	Left for IWFL
Chattanooga Locomotion (CHAT)	4	4	S	--	Left for IWFL
Tennessee Valley Tigers (TVT)	3	4	--	--	Left for IWFL
Louisiana Fuel (FUEL)	3	5	--	--	Folded
Palm Beach Punishers (PALM)	1	7	--	--	Left for WFA
Carolina Queens (CARQ)	1	7	--	--	Left for IWFL (2012)
Western Conference					
Midwest Division					
Wisconsin Warriors (WI)	6	4	CC	--	Left for IWFL
Memphis Belles (MEMB)	5	4	S	Joined from WFA	Left for IWFL
Clarksville Fox (FOX)	5	3	--	--	Left for IWFL
Wisconsin Wolves (WIW)	4	4	--	Joined from IWFL (2008)	Left for WFA
Iowa Crush (IA)	3	5	--	--	Left for IWFL
Minnesota Vixen (MN)	0	8	--	Joined from IWFL	Left for IWFL
Louisville Nightmare (LOU)	0	7	--	--	Folded
Pacific West Division					
Bay Area Bandits (BAB)	7	4	C	Expansion	Left for WFA
Tucson Monsoon (TUC)	1	7	--	--	Left for IWFL
Modesto Maniax (MODX)	1	8	S	--	Left for IWFL
Southern California Breakers (SCB)	1	7	--	--	Left for IWFL
Affiliate Teams					
Nor Cal Red Hawks (NCRH)	0	3	--	Expansion	Left for IWFL
Holyoke Hurricanes (HOLY)	0	2	--	--	Folded

Independent Women's Football League Tier II (IWFL2) – 2010 Season (continued)
2010 IWFL2 Scoreboard

Date	Team1	Sc1	Team2	Sc2	Note
4/3	CAR	26	CARQ	2	
4/3	FOX	36	TVT	6	
4/3	FUEL	1	HTTC	0	N
4/3	JJ	32	MF	0	
4/3	MEMB	1	LOU	0	
4/3	MON	76	BING	0	
4/3	NEI	28	SMR	0	
4/3	TUC	3	SCB	0	
4/3	WIW	73	MN	30	
4/10	BAB	13	POR	0	
4/10	CAR	49	PALM	0	
4/10	ERIE	57	BING	0	
4/10	FOX	30	CHAT	14	
4/10	IA	35	MN	14	
4/10	JJ	26	SMR	8	
4/10	MEMB	28	TVT	0	
4/10	NEI	25	MF	6	
4/17	BAB	42	SCB	7	
4/17	CARQ	13	PALM	3	
4/17	CHAT	14	MEMB	0	
4/17	ERIE	55	BING	0	
4/17	FOX	1	LOU	0	
4/17	IA	16	FUEL	14	
4/17	MON	41	MF	14	
4/24	CAR	58	LOU	0	
4/24	JJ	40	BING	0	
4/24	MEMB	18	FOX	12	
4/24	MODX	12	SCB	0	
4/24	MON	1	HOLY	0	N
4/24	NEI	22	SMR	0	
4/24	PALM	26	FUEL	20	
4/24	WI	19	ERIE	0	
5/1	BAB	26	SCB	6	
5/1	CAR	56	CHAT	0	
5/1	FOX	28	TVT	12	
5/1	FUEL	1	HTTC	0	N
5/1	IA	37	MN	0	
5/1	MF	1	HOLY	0	N
5/1	MON	41	SMR	6	
5/1	NEI	19	CTCS	18	
5/1	WI	50	WIW	12	
5/8	CAR	48	CARQ	0	
5/8	CHAT	22	MEMB	16	
5/8	ERIE	47	LOU	8	
5/8	JJ	38	BING	0	
5/8	MON	22	CTCS	0	
5/8	NEI	20	MF	8	
5/8	SCB	25	TUC	0	
5/8	TVT	30	FUEL	22	
5/8	WIW	12	IA	6	
5/15	BAB	33	LA	22	
5/15	CAR	72	TVT	0	
5/15	FOX	40	LOU	0	
5/15	JJ	22	CTCS	6	
5/15	MF	21	SMR	6	
5/15	MON	20	NYN	0	
5/15	WI	40	IA	0	
5/22	BAB	47	MODX	8	
5/22	CAR	71	PALM	14	
5/22	CHAT	20	CARQ	6	
5/22	CTCS	46	MF	0	
5/22	JJ	38	BING	8	
5/22	MEMB	1	HTTC	0	N
5/22	MON	34	SMR	0	
5/22	NEI	28	ERIE	8	
5/22	TVT	1	LOU	0	
5/22	WI	55	MN	0	
5/22	WIW	22	IA	16	
5/29	VBW	46	NCRH	8	I
5/29	NEI	56	SMR	7	
5/29	TVT	25	LOU	8	
6/5	CAR	22	BNH	20	*
6/5	CHAT	22	CARQ	0	
6/5	FUEL	1	HTTC	0	N
6/5	MEMB	8	FOX	6	
6/5	MON	26	CTCS	0	
6/5	NEI	27	ERIE	20	
6/5	SMR	21	BING	8	
6/5	WI	28	IA	0	
6/5	WIW	20	MN	18	
6/12	BAB	46	MODX	0	S
6/12	CAR	42	CHAT	14	S
6/12	MON	53	NEI	14	S
6/12	WI	36	MEMB	6	S
7/10	BAB	35	WI	2	CC
7/10	MON	19	CAR	14	CC
7/24	MON	9	BAB	2	C
9/11	CAL	68	NCRH	12	E
10/2	VBW	46	NCRH	0	IE

Women's Football Alliance (WFA) – 2010 Season

The WFA continued to grow in its second season, featuring forty teams in 2010. The Lone Star Mustangs, in just their second year, claimed the 2010 WFA championship by defeating the Columbus Comets, who were making their second appearance in a league title game. The WFA, which had spent two seasons as a minor national league in women's football, surged to the top spot in the sport when ten of the IWFL's top teams joined their ranks that offseason.

Minor National League   Teams: 40 (39)   Games: 172 (165)
Championship game result: Lone Star Mustangs 16, Columbus Comets 12

2010 WFA Standings

National Conference	W	L	PR	Before	After
Northeast Division					
Philadelphia Liberty Belles (II) (PLB2)	9	1	S	--	--
New England Nightmare (NEN)	2	6	--	Expansion	--
Southern Tier Spitfire (SPIT)	0	8	--	Expansion	Folded
East Division					
Baltimore Burn (BAL)	6	3	Q	--	Left for WSFL
Keystone Assault (KEY)	6	2	--	--	--
New Jersey Titans (NJ)	2	6	--	--	Left for WSFL (2012)
Mid-Atlantic Division					
Columbus Comets (COL)	11	1	C	--	--
Pittsburgh Force (PITF)	5	3	--	--	--
Dayton Diamonds (DAY)	0	8	--	--	--
South Central Division					
Jacksonville Dixie Blues (JAX)	9	1	S	--	--
Central Florida Anarchy (CFA)	4	5	Q	Expansion	Became Orlando Anarchy
Tampa Bay Pirates (TBP)	4	4	--	Expansion	--
Carolina Raging Wolves (CRW)	0	8	--	Expansion	--
Central Division					
St. Louis Slam (STL)	10	1	CC	--	--
Indiana Speed (INS)	5	3	--	--	Folded
Kentucky Karma (KYK)	2	6	--	--	--
Cincinnati Sizzle (CIN)	0	8	--	--	--
North Central Division					
West Michigan Mayhem (WM)	7	2	Q	--	--
Cleveland Fusion (CLE)	6	3	Q	--	--
Detroit Dark Angels (DDA)	3	5	--	Expansion	--
Toledo Reign (TOL)	1	7	--	--	--
American Conference					
South Division					
Memphis Soul (SOUL)	6	2	Q	Expansion	Became Memphis WTF
New Orleans Blaze (NO)	3	5	--	--	--
Acadiana Zydeco (ZYD)	0	8	--	Expansion	--
Midwest Division					
Minnesota Machine (MACH)	6	3	Q	--	--
Iowa Thunder (IAT)	7	3	S	--	Folded
Kansas City Spartans (KCS)	3	5	--	Expansion	--
Nebraska Stampede (NE)	0	8	--	Expansion	--
Southwest Division					
Lone Star Mustangs (LSM)	13	0	LC	--	--
Austin Outlaws (OUT)	6	4	S	--	--
Houston Power (HPOW)	5	4	--	Expansion	--
Monterrey Royal Eagles (MRE)	0	4	--	--	Folded
North Pacific Division					
Portland Fighting Fillies (PFF)	8	2	Q	Expansion	--
Central Cal War Angels (CCWA)	4	5	--	Expansion	--
Utah Blitz (UTB)	0	7	--	Expansion	--
South Pacific Division					
Las Vegas Showgirlz (LV)	10	2	CC	--	--
Pacific Warriors (PAC)	7	2	Q	Were California Lynx	--
Arizona Assassins (AZ)	3	5	--	Expansion	--
San Diego Sting (SDS)	0	8	--	Expansion	--

Women's Football Alliance (WFA) – 2010 Season (continued)
2010 WFA Standings (continued)

Affiliate Team

Oklahoma City Lightning (OKC)   0   3   --   Joined from NWFA (2008)   Folded

2010 WFA Scoreboard

Date	Team1	Score	Team2	Score		Date	Team1	Score	Team2	Score		Date	Team1	Score	Team2	Score	
4/10	BAL	54	NEN	14		5/1	STL	50	KYK	0		6/5	KEY	28	NJ	8	
4/10	CCWA	26	SDS	18		5/1	WM	45	INS	13		6/5	LSM	51	NO	0	
4/10	CLE	18	TOL	7								6/5	LV	17	PFF	6	
4/10	INS	41	KYK	0		5/8	AZ	42	SDS	0		6/5	MACH	22	KCS	8	
4/10	JAX	41	CFA	13		5/8	CFA	14	TBP	0		6/5	PAC	41	CCWA	18	
4/10	KEY	30	NJ	16		5/8	COL	58	PITF	0		6/5	PITF	12	DAY	6	
4/10	LSM	62	OKC	0		5/8	HPOW	53	MRE	7		6/5	SOUL	20	ZYD	6	
4/10	LV	27	UTB	0		5/8	IAT	28	NE	6		6/5	STL	37	IAT	14	
4/10	MACH	50	NE	0		5/8	INS	54	KYK	6							
4/10	OUT	7	HPOW	6		5/8	JAX	48	CRW	16		6/12	BAL	16	NJ	0	
4/10	PFF	74	VBW	6	I	5/8	LSM	38	OUT	16		6/12	CCWA	1	SDS	0	
4/10	PITF	9	DAY	8		5/8	LV	34	PAC	6		6/12	COL	48	DAY	0	
4/10	PLB2	63	SPIT	0		5/8	MACH	13	KCS	12		6/12	DDA	20	TOL	0	
4/10	SOUL	34	NO	32		5/8	NEN	26	SPIT	8		6/12	IAT	21	MACH	13	
4/10	STL	35	CIN	0		5/8	NO	27	ZYD	0		6/12	JAX	48	CRW	6	
4/10	WM	52	DDA	0		5/8	PFF	14	UTB	7		6/12	KCS	28	NE	6	
						5/8	PLB2	25	NJ	12		6/12	KEY	38	SPIT	0	
4/17	BAL	62	NJ	36		5/8	STL	57	CIN	0		6/12	LSM	38	OUT	7	
4/17	CLE	54	KYK	6		5/8	TOL	7	DAY	0		6/12	PAC	33	LV	21	
4/17	COL	68	PITF	0		5/8	WM	55	CLE	0		6/12	PFF	18	UTB	10	
4/17	IAT	22	KCS	8								6/12	PITF	48	CIN	0	
4/17	INS	40	CIN	0		5/15	BAL	1	SPIT	0		6/12	PLB2	62	NEN	6	
4/17	JAX	29	CFA	7		5/15	CCWA	26	UTB	7		6/12	SOUL	8	NO	6	
4/17	LSM	32	HPOW	13		5/15	CLE	62	TOL	0		6/12	TBP	14	CFA	9	
4/17	LV	26	AZ	6		5/15	COL	36	WM	31		6/12	WM	66	CLE	14	
4/17	NO	33	ZYD	0		5/15	DDA	45	DAY	0							
4/17	OUT	53	MRE	0		5/15	HPOW	63	ZYD	0		6/19	BAL	36	KEY	24	
4/17	PAC	41	SDS	0		5/15	IAT	24	KCS	0		6/19	CFA	19	TBP	0	
4/17	PFF	26	CCWA	21		5/15	JAX	47	CFA	13		6/19	COL	65	TOL	0	
4/17	SOUL	1	OKC	0		5/15	LSM	55	SOUL	0		6/19	IAT	33	KCS	14	
4/17	STL	34	MACH	0		5/15	LV	48	AZ	8		6/19	KYK	20	CIN	14	
4/17	TBP	42	CRW	36		5/15	MACH	34	NE	0		6/19	LSM	1	MRE	0	
4/17	WM	71	TOL	0		5/15	NJ	47	NEN	6		6/19	LV	31	AZ	0	
						5/15	PAC	1	SDS	0		6/19	MACH	13	NE	12	
4/24	AZ	52	SDS	0		5/15	PLB2	35	KEY	12		6/19	NEN	32	SPIT	0	
4/24	CFA	35	CRW	14		5/15	TBP	8	CRW	0		6/19	NO	17	ZYD	6	
4/24	CLE	60	PITF	3								6/19	OUT	48	HPOW	15	
4/24	COL	43	DAY	0		5/22	CCWA	1	SDS	0		6/19	PFF	16	CCWA	14	
4/24	DDA	7	TOL	6		5/22	COL	68	CIN	6		6/19	PITF	13	DAY	0	
4/24	HPOW	39	NO	6		5/22	HPOW	43	MRE	0		6/19	PLB2	42	NJ	0	
4/24	IAT	47	NE	0		5/22	INS	54	DAY	0		6/19	STL	16	INS	14	
4/24	JAX	63	TBP	0		5/22	KCS	32	NE	6		6/19	WM	73	DDA	0	
4/24	KEY	54	SPIT	0		5/22	KEY	34	BAL	24							
4/24	KYK	6	CIN	0		5/22	LSM	1	OKC	0		6/26	COL	67	BAL	8	Q
4/24	PAC	34	CCWA	29		5/22	LV	55	UTB	0		6/26	IAT	20	MACH	12	Q
4/24	PFF	30	UTB	0		5/22	OUT	51	NO	0		6/26	JAX	47	CFA	13	Q
4/24	PLB2	70	NEN	6		5/22	PAC	20	AZ	8		6/26	LSM	38	PAC	14	Q
4/24	SOUL	30	ZYD	6		5/22	PFF	42	VBW	0	I	6/26	LV	34	PFF	6	Q
4/24	STL	13	INS	6		5/22	PITF	32	DDA	14		6/26	OUT	35	SOUL	0	Q
						5/22	PLB2	71	SPIT	0		6/26	PLB2	35	WM	33	Q
5/1	CLE	39	DDA	12		5/22	SOUL	34	ZYD	0		6/26	STL	50	CLE	23	Q
5/1	JAX	45	CRW	6		5/22	STL	70	KYK	6							
5/1	KCS	32	NE	18		5/22	TBP	26	CRW	20		7/10	COL	36	PLB2	7	S
5/1	KEY	56	NEN	6		5/22	WM	64	TOL	0		7/10	LSM	30	IAT	20	S
5/1	LSM	32	HPOW	0								7/10	LV	27	OUT	21	S
5/1	LV	41	UTB	0		6/5	AZ	24	SDS	6		7/10	STL	52	JAX	26	S
5/1	MACH	21	IAT	7		6/5	BAL	28	NEN	20							
5/1	NJ	47	SPIT	2		6/5	CFA	26	CRW	6		7/17	COL	21	STL	14	CC
5/1	OUT	68	ZYD	0		6/5	CLE	34	DDA	14		7/17	LSM	8	LV	6	CC
5/1	PAC	34	AZ	26		6/5	COL	66	KYK	0							
5/1	PFF	19	CCWA	8		6/5	HPOW	34	OUT	13		7/31	LSM	16	COL	12	C
5/1	PLB2	26	BAL	6		6/5	INS	62	CIN	0							
						6/5	JAX	42	TBP	6							

Women's Spring Football League (WSFL) – 2010 Season

The WSFL, a small regional league that folded after one season in 2002, was resurrected in 2010. The first season of the new WSFL in 2010 featured six teams playing a limited exhibition schedule. That set the stage for the league's first full season in 2011.

Exhibition Season   Teams: 6 (3)   Games: 13.5 (12.5)
Declared Champion (by virtue of regular season record): Kansas City Storm

2010 WSFL Standings

Teams	W	L	PR	Before	After
Kansas City Storm (STM)	7	0	--	Joined from WFA	--
Topeka Mudcats (MUD)	3	4	--	Expansion	--
River City Raiders (RCRS)	0	6	--	Expansion	Folded
Affiliate Teams					
Steel City Renegades (SCR)	2	0	--	Expansion	Folded
Ventura Black Widows (VBW)	2	2	--	Expansion	Left for W8FL
West Virginia Bruisers (WVB)	0	2	--	Expansion	Left for W8FL

2010 WSFL Scoreboard

4/10	PFF	74	VBW	6	I	5/22	STM	21	RCRS	15		6/19	STM	30	MUD	7
						5/22	PFF	42	VBW	0	I				
5/1	STM	21	MUD	0								6/26	SCR	18	WVB	6
						5/29	MUD	27	RCRS	0		6/26	STM	30	MUD	6
5/8	MUD	1	RCRS	0		5/29	VBW	46	NCRH	8	I	7/10	MUD	27	RCRS	6
5/15	SCR	22	WVB	0		6/5	STM	36	MUD	0					
5/15	STM	66	RCRS	0								10/2	VBW	46	NCRH	0	IE
						6/12	STM	52	RCRS	8					

2011 Season Review

The WFA emerged as the top league in women's football when ten of the IWFL's top teams – including their last three league champions and five of their last six conference champions – all simultaneously defected to the WFA. This wave of defections swelled the WFA's ranks to a record number of teams and also brought the WFA its newest league champion. The IWFL regrouped by consolidating its top league with IWFL2, and an old team with a new name claimed the title in the IWFL's first season as a minor league. The WSFL suffered through multiple defections to assemble its first full schedule, and it also launched an eight-player division. And for the first time, one team completed a full, truly independent schedule.

Leagues: 4   Teams: 103 (95)   Games: 412 (379)

Women's Football Alliance (WFA) – 2011 Season

In its first season as the major league in women's football, the WFA set a record in the sport with 59 full-member teams. For the first time since consensus women's football champions had begun being crowned in 2008, a team repeated as major national champions. The Boston Militia, who had won the IWFL when it was the top league in 2010, claimed their second straight consensus national title by defeating the San Diego Surge for the 2011 WFA championship.

Major National League   Teams: 59   Games: 254.5 (241)
Championship game result: Boston Militia 34, San Diego Surge 19

2011 WFA Standings

National Conference	W	L	PR	Before	After
North Division					
Boston Militia (BOSM)	11	1	LC	Joined from IWFL	--
New York Sharks (NY)	5	3	--	Joined from IWFL	--
Northeastern Nitro (NTRO)	4	4	--	Expansion	Left for IWFL
New England Nightmare (NEN)	0	9	--	--	--
Northeast Division					
D.C. Divas (DC)	7	2	Q	Joined from IWFL	--
Keystone Assault (KEY)	3	5	--	--	--
Philadelphia Liberty Belles (II) (PLB2)	2	6	--	--	--
Mid-Atlantic Division					
Pittsburgh Passion (PITT)	8	1	Q	Joined from IWFL	--
Cleveland Fusion (CLE)	5	3	--	--	--
Columbus Comets (COL)	5	3	--	--	--
Erie Illusion (ERIE)	3	6	--	Joined from IWFL2	Left for IWFL
Pittsburgh Force (PITF)	0	8	--	--	--
Atlantic Division					
Atlanta Heartbreakers (ATLH)	4	5	Q	Expansion	Left for WSFL (2013)
Carolina Raging Wolves (CRW)	1	7	--	--	--
Savannah Sabers (SAV)	1	7	--	Expansion	--
South Atlantic Division					
Jacksonville Dixie Blues (JAX)	9	1	S	--	--
Orlando Anarchy (ORL)	5	3	--	Were Central Florida Anarchy	--
Gulf Coast Riptide (GCR)	3	5	--	Returned from 2009	--
Coastal Division					
Miami Fury (MIA)	7	2	Q	Joined from IWFL	--
Palm Beach Punishers (PALM)	5	3	--	Joined from IWFL2	--
Tampa Bay Pirates (TBP)	2	6	--	--	Became Tampa Bay Inferno
North Central Division					
Indy Crash (INDY)	8	3	CC	Expansion	--
Detroit Dark Angels (DDA)	6	2	--	--	--
Cincinnati Sizzle (CIN)	4	4	--	--	--
Toledo Reign (TOL)	4	4	--	--	--
Kentucky Karma (KYK)	1	7	--	--	Folded
Dayton Diamonds (DAY)	0	8	--	--	Folded
Central Division					
Chicago Force (CHI)	9	1	S	Joined from IWFL	--
St. Louis Slam (STL)	5	3	--	--	--
West Michigan Mayhem (WM)	3	5	--	--	--

Women's Football Alliance (WFA) – 2011 Season (continued)
2011 WFA Standings (continued)

American Conference
Upper Midwest Division
Minnesota Machine (MACH)	5	4	Q	--	--
Wisconsin Wolves (WIW)	4	4	--	Joined from IWFL2	--
Wisconsin Dragons (WID)	0	8	--	Expansion	--

Midwest Division
Kansas City Tribe (KCT)	8	2	S	Joined from IWFL	--
Iowa Xplosion (IAX)	5	3	--	Expansion	--
Nebraska Stampede (NE)	4	5	--	--	--
Kansas City Spartans (KCS)	3	5	--	--	--

Southeast Division
Memphis WTF (WTF)	8	2	--	Were Memphis Soul	Became Memphis Dynasty
Little Rock Wildcats (LRW)	3	5	--	Expansion	Became Arkansas Wildcats
Tulsa Eagles (TULE)	0	8	--	Expansion	Became Tulsa Threat

Gulf Coast Division
Houston Power (HPOW)	6	3	Q	--	--
New Orleans Blaze (NO)	4	4	--	--	Folded
Acadiana Zydeco (ZYD)	1	7	--	--	--

South Central Division
Dallas Diamonds (DAL)	10	1	CC	Joined from IWFL	--
Lone Star Mustangs (LSM)	5	3	--	--	--
Austin Outlaws (OUT)	3	5	--	--	--

Northwest Division
Portland Fighting Fillies (PFF)	4	6	Q	--	--
Utah Blitz (UTB)	3	5	--	--	--
Spokane Scorn (SPOK)	1	5	--	Expansion	Folded

North Pacific Division
Bay Area Bandits (BAB)	7	3	S	Joined from IWFL2	--
Central Cal War Angels (CCWA)	6	2	--	--	--
Los Angeles Amazons (LA)	1	7	--	Joined from IWFL	--

South Pacific Division
San Diego Surge (SD)	11	1	C	Expansion	--
Pacific Warriors (PAC)	4	4	--	--	--
Las Vegas Showgirlz (LV)	4	6	--	--	--

Southwest Division
Silver State Legacy (SILV)	6	3	Q	Expansion	--
Arizona Assassins (AZ)	6	3	--	--	--
So Cal Scorpions (SCS)	2	6	--	Joined from IWFL	Folded
San Diego Sting (SDS)	1	7	--	--	--

2011 WFA Scoreboard

Date	Away	Pts	Home	Pts	Note
3/26	LV	12	JYNX	8	IE
4/2	BAB	53	LA	0	
4/2	COL	16	CLE	13	
4/2	DC	35	BOSM	20	
4/2	DDA	14	KYK	0	
4/2	GCR	64	ATLH	6	
4/2	HPOW	40	NO	0	
4/2	JAX	52	SAV	6	
4/2	KCT	77	KCS	0	
4/2	LRW	44	TULE	0	
4/2	LSM	16	OUT	0	
4/2	MIA	62	CRW	0	
4/2	NE	52	MUD	0	IE
4/2	NTRO	13	NEN	0	
4/2	NY	34	PLB2	20	
4/2	SEA	14	PFF	0	I
4/2	PITT	30	PITF	0	
4/2	SCS	16	SDS	0	
4/2	TBP	6	ORL	0	
4/2	TOL	61	DAY	0	
4/2	UTB	40	SPOK	0	
4/2	WIW	20	WID	12	
4/2	WM	20	CIN	0	
4/9	AZ	21	SILV	8	
4/9	BAB	36	PFF	0	
4/9	CCWA	38	UTB	0	
4/9	CHI	69	MACH	0	
4/9	COL	55	PITF	0	
4/9	DAL	39	HPOW	14	
4/9	DC	55	KEY	6	
4/9	DDA	33	CIN	7	
4/9	JAX	42	PALM	12	
4/9	KCS	14	NE	12	
4/9	KCT	82	IAX	0	
4/9	MIA	52	GCR	14	
4/9	NO	14	ZYD	8	
4/9	ORL	36	SAV	14	
4/9	OUT	68	TULE	8	
4/9	PAC	40	SDS	0	
4/9	PITT	56	ERIE	14	
4/9	PLB2	52	NEN	0	
4/9	SD	84	LV	0	
4/9	STL	43	INDY	6	
4/9	TBP	26	CRW	6	
4/9	TOL	23	KYK	0	
4/9	WTF	38	LRW	14	
4/16	AZ	39	SCS	0	
4/16	BOSM	28	NY	7	
4/16	CHI	58	WIW	0	
4/16	DC	20	PLB2	0	
4/16	ERIE	20	PITF	8	
4/16	IAX	14	NE	13	
4/16	INDY	36	DDA	6	
4/16	JAX	42	ORL	7	
4/16	KCT	76	KCS	0	
4/16	LSM	33	OUT	3	
4/16	MACH	21	WID	7	
4/16	MIA	72	ATLH	0	
4/16	NO	22	LRW	14	
4/16	NTRO	6	KEY	0	
4/16	PAC	36	LV	0	
4/16	PALM	38	SAV	0	
4/16	PFF	6	UTB	0	
4/16	PITT	26	CLE	8	
4/16	SD	74	LA	0	
4/16	SILV	42	SDS	0	
4/16	STL	70	DAY	0	
4/16	WM	54	TOL	12	
4/16	WTF	54	ZYD	14	

Continued on next page

Women's Football Alliance (WFA) – 2011 Season (continued)
2011 WFA Scoreboard (continued)

Date	Team	Score	Team	Score		Date	Team	Score	Team	Score		Date	Team	Score	Team	Score	
4/23	INDY	60	CIN	21		5/14	KEY	27	NEN	0		6/11	CHI	76	WM	3	
4/30	ATLH	28	CRW	14		5/14	LSM	14	HPOW	6		6/11	CIN	67	KYK	6	
4/30	AZ	47	SDS	6		5/14	LV	14	UTB	0		6/11	DAL	1	TULE	0	
4/30	BAB	11	CCWA	6		5/14	MIA	12	PALM	9		6/11	DDA	57	DAY	0	
4/30	BOSM	72	NTRO	0		5/14	NO	9	WTF	8		6/11	ERIE	20	PITF	0	
4/30	CHI	29	STL	7		5/14	NY	27	PLB2	21		6/11	HPOW	12	LSM	0	
4/30	CIN	51	DAY	12		5/14	PAC	21	SCS	6		6/11	IAX	20	MACH	17	
4/30	CLE	50	ERIE	0		5/14	PFF	22	SPOK	12		6/11	JAX	45	MIA	24	
4/30	DAL	16	LSM	6		5/14	PITT	45	PITF	0		6/11	KEY	14	PLB2	8	
4/30	DC	49	KEY	0		5/14	SD	48	SILV	15		6/11	NE	32	KCS	18	
4/30	HPOW	16	OUT	6		5/21	ATLH	32	CRW	14		6/11	BING	1	NEN	0	I
4/30	IAX	20	WID	0		5/21	AZ	1	SCS	0		6/11	NY	46	NTRO	7	
4/30	INDY	77	KYK	0		5/21	BOSM	43	NY	6		6/11	ORL	30	CRW	0	
4/30	JAX	21	GCR	14		5/21	CCWA	68	LA	0		6/11	OUT	1	ZYD	0	
4/30	KCT	88	NE	0		5/21	CHI	55	STL	24		6/11	PALM	20	TBP	14	
4/30	LV	16	LA	0		5/21	CLE	50	ERIE	0		6/11	PITT	42	CLE	0	
4/30	MACH	27	WIW	6		5/21	DAL	23	LSM	12		6/11	SD	43	PAC	6	
4/30	MIA	32	TBP	0		5/21	DC	42	PLB2	0		6/11	SDS	20	LV	6	
4/30	NO	19	ZYD	0		5/21	HPOW	1	ZYD	0		6/11	SILV	22	AZ	7	
4/30	NY	48	NEN	12		5/21	IAX	44	KCS	22		6/11	UTB	30	SPOK	22	
4/30	PFF	12	SPOK	0		5/21	INDY	77	KYK	0		6/11	WIW	66	WID	0	
4/30	PITT	17	COL	0		5/21	JAX	43	GCR	0		6/11	WTF	30	LRW	8	
4/30	SD	82	PAC	0		5/21	KCT	57	WIW	0		6/18	AZ	26	PAC	6	
4/30	SILV	27	SCS	3		5/21	MIA	34	TBP	21		6/18	CCWA	24	BAB	15	
4/30	TOL	19	DDA	6		5/21	NE	44	WID	0		6/18	CHI	77	INDY	18	
4/30	WTF	66	TULE	6		5/21	NTRO	8	NEN	0		6/18	CIN	34	TOL	25	
5/7	BAB	36	PFF	0		5/21	OUT	52	NO	0		6/18	COL	64	PITF	0	
5/7	BOSM	62	NEN	0		5/21	PALM	35	SAV	0		6/18	DAL	56	OUT	0	
5/7	CCWA	1	LA	0		5/21	PITT	7	COL	6		6/18	DC	38	NY	16	
5/7	CHI	34	KCT	26		5/21	SD	55	LV	0		6/18	DDA	24	WM	14	
5/7	CLE	54	PITF	0		5/21	SILV	35	SDS	0		6/18	GCR	36	CRW	14	
5/7	COL	36	ERIE	7		5/21	SPOK	26	UTB	20		6/18	HPOW	33	ZYD	0	
5/7	DAL	31	OUT	21		5/21	WM	63	DAY	0		6/18	JAX	34	TBP	7	
5/7	DC	77	NTRO	0		5/21	WTF	56	TULE	0		6/18	KCS	30	WID	0	
5/7	INDY	60	CIN	21		5/28	JYNX	43	LV	22	I	6/18	KEY	26	NEN	8	
5/7	LRW	38	ZYD	8		5/28	WTF	36	ARR	0	I	6/18	LA	1	SCS	0	
5/7	LSM	40	TULE	0		6/4	AZ	41	SDS	6		6/18	LRW	1	TULE	0	
5/7	MACH	6	NE	0		6/4	BOSM	70	PLB2	8		6/18	MACH	33	WIW	8	
5/7	ORL	41	GCR	14		6/4	CCWA	30	PAC	8		6/18	MIA	14	PALM	0	
5/7	PAC	56	LV	6		6/4	CLE	76	PITF	0		6/18	NE	19	IAX	14	
5/7	PALM	16	TBP	8		6/4	COL	1	ERIE	0		6/18	ORL	28	ATLH	0	
5/7	PLB2	28	KEY	12		6/4	CRW	32	SAV	13		6/18	PFF	1	SPOK	0	
5/7	SAV	7	CRW	6		6/4	DAL	44	WTF	0		6/18	PITT	47	ERIE	7	
5/7	SCS	12	SDS	6		6/4	DDA	33	TOL	0		6/18	STL	1	KYK	0	
5/7	SD	55	AZ	20		6/4	HPOW	38	NO	6		6/18	WTF	1	NO	0	
5/7	SILV	44	UTB	0		6/4	KCT	77	IAX	0		6/25	BAB	39	PFF	0	Q
5/7	STL	36	WM	6		6/4	KYK	28	DAY	12		6/25	BOSM	37	DC	24	Q
5/7	TOL	63	DAY	0		6/4	LSM	40	LRW	0		6/25	CHI	41	PITT	31	Q
5/7	WIW	20	KCS	8		6/4	LV	1	LA	0		6/25	DAL	21	HPOW	6	Q
5/14	ATLH	22	SAV	19		6/4	MACH	46	WID	0		6/25	INDY	47	ATLH	0	Q
5/14	BAB	19	CCWA	0		6/4	NTRO	12	KEY	6		6/25	JAX	20	MIA	18	Q
5/14	BOSM	42	NTRO	0		6/4	NY	28	NEN	8		6/25	KCT	51	MACH	0	Q
5/14	CHI	15	WM	6		6/4	ORL	26	GCR	14		6/25	SD	41	SILV	7	Q
5/14	CIN	42	KYK	0		6/4	PALM	34	ATLH	6		7/9	BOSM	50	CHI	23	S
5/14	CLE	16	COL	6		6/4	SD	42	BAB	13		7/9	DAL	23	KCT	20	S
5/14	DAL	64	LRW	0		6/4	SILV	1	SCS	0		7/9	INDY	42	JAX	0	S
5/14	DDA	69	DAY	0		6/4	STL	41	WM	7		7/9	SD	36	BAB	0	S
5/14	ERIE	38	BING	0	I	6/4	UTB	8	PFF	0		7/16	BOSM	46	INDY	18	CC
5/14	GCR	18	TBP	13		6/4	WIW	24	NE	12		7/16	SD	48	DAL	20	CC
5/14	IAX	7	MACH	0		6/4	ZYD	44	TULE	0		7/23	JYNX	34	AZ	20	I
5/14	INDY	34	TOL	0		6/11	ATLH	28	SAV	25		7/30	BOSM	34	SD	19	C
5/14	JAX	49	ORL	0		6/11	BAB	40	LA	0		10/1	WTF	44	ARR	0	IE
5/14	KCS	20	WID	8		6/11	BOSM	27	DC	16							
5/14	KCT	37	STL	34		6/11	CCWA	60	PFF	0							

Independent Women's Football League (IWFL) – 2011 Season

The IWFL, demoted to the #2 spot in women's football thanks to a slew of departures to the WFA, regrouped by dissolving IWFL2 and moving all of its surviving teams back up to the main league. Promoting all of these teams allowed the IWFL to move forward in 2011 with 27 full-member teams. The Atlanta Xplosion, who decided for one season to call themselves the Ravens before reverting back to their Xplosion nickname, won the 2011 IWFL championship by taking out the California Quake, who were making their first league title game appearance since winning the WAFL in 2001. The Atlanta (Ravens) Xplosion won their second IWFL title, adding to their championship from 2006.

Minor National League   Teams: 30 (27)   Games: 117 (106)
Championship game result: Atlanta Ravens 24, California Quake 22
Founders Bowl Championship: Seattle Majestics 20, New England Intensity 0

2011 IWFL Standings

Eastern Conference	W	L	T	PR	Before	After
North Atlantic Division						
Montreal Blitz (MON)	6	1	0	S	Joined from IWFL2	--
New England Intensity (NEI)	7	3	0	BC	Joined from IWFL2	--
Manchester Freedom (MF)	4	4	0	--	Joined from IWFL2	Became New Hampshire Freedom
Maine Rebels (MR)	0	7	0	--	Were IWFL2's Southern Maine Rebels	--
Mid-Atlantic Division						
Carolina Phoenix (CAR)	7	1	0	CC	Joined from IWFL2	--
Baltimore Nighthawks (BNH)	3	4	1	BQ	--	--
Philadelphia Firebirds (PHI)	1	4	1	--	--	--
Mid South Division						
Atlanta Ravens (RAVE)	11	0	0	LC	Were Atlanta Xplosion	Became Atlanta Xplosion
Chattanooga Locomotion (CHAT)	8	3	0	BS	Joined from IWFL2	Deferred until 2013
Clarksville Fox (FOX)	3	5	0	--	Joined from IWFL2	Folded
Memphis Belles (MEMB)	3	6	0	--	Joined from IWFL2	--
Tennessee Valley Tigers (TVT)	1	7	0	--	Joined from IWFL2	Became WSFL's Huntsville Tigers
Georgia Peachez (GAP)	0	7	0	--	Expansion	Folded
South Atlantic Division						
Houston Energy (HOU)	6	3	0	S	--	--
North Texas Knockouts (NTK)	5	4	0	BQ	Expansion	Folded
Monterrey Black Mambas (MBM)	0	4	0	--	Expansion	Folded
Western Conference						
Midwest Division						
Wisconsin Warriors (WI)	9	1	0	CC	Joined from IWFL2	--
Madison Cougars (MADC)	5	4	0	BQ	Expansion	--
Iowa Crush (IA)	3	5	0	--	Joined from IWFL2	--
Minnesota Vixen (MN)	0	8	0	--	Joined from IWFL2	--
Pacific Northwest Division						
Portland Shockwave (POR)	6	3	0	S	--	--
Seattle Majestics (SEA)	7	4	0	BCW	--	--
Pacific West Division						
Sacramento Sirens (SAC)	5	4	0	S	--	--
Modesto Maniax (MODX)	4	5	0	BS	Joined from IWFL2	--
Southern California Breakers (SCB)	0	8	0	--	Joined from IWFL2	Folded
Pacific Southwest Division						
California Quake (CAL)	10	1	0	C	--	--
Tucson Monsoon (TUC)	2	5	0	BQ	Joined from IWFL2	--
Affiliate Teams						
Reno Rattlers (RENO)	2	2	0	--	Expansion	Folded
Nor Cal Red Hawks (NCRH)	1	1	0	--	Joined from IWFL2	Deferred until 2013
Desert Fire Cats (DFC)	0	1	0	--	Expansion	Folded

Independent Women's Football League (IWFL) – 2011 Season (continued)
2011 IWFL Scoreboard

Date	Team1	Score	Team2	Score	Note
4/2	BNH	36	GAP	0	
4/2	CHAT	30	FOX	0	
4/2	HOU	50	NTK	14	
4/2	SEA	14	PFF	0	I
4/9	CAL	60	TUC	6	
4/9	CAR	32	BNH	8	
4/9	IA	20	MN	6	
4/9	MEMB	16	TVT	12	
4/9	MON	12	MF	6	
4/9	NEI	18	MR	0	
4/9	NTK	19	MBM	6	
4/9	POR	21	SEA	0	
4/9	RAVE	35	HOU	15	
4/9	SAC	21	MODX	14	
4/9	WI	36	MADC	0	
4/16	BNH	0	PHI	0	
4/16	CAL	28	POR	0	
4/16	FOX	32	TVT	6	
4/16	MF	8	JJ	0	I
4/16	MODX	41	SCB	6	
4/16	MON	14	NEI	0	
4/16	RAVE	34	CHAT	0	
4/16	SAC	45	JYNX	20	I
4/23	CAL	60	SCB	0	
4/23	CAR	57	PHI	17	
4/23	CHAT	52	MEMB	12	
4/23	HOU	40	NTK	14	
4/23	MADC	16	MN	0	
4/23	NCRH	13	RENO	6	E
4/23	NEI	34	MR	0	
4/23	RAVE	69	FOX	0	
4/23	SEA	40	TUC	8	
4/23	TVT	1	GAP	0	
4/23	WI	43	IA	6	
4/30	BNH	1	GAP	0	
4/30	CAL	42	SAC	13	
4/30	HOU	44	MBM	6	
4/30	MADC	12	IA	6	
4/30	MEMB	20	FOX	12	
4/30	MON	40	MR	0	
4/30	NEI	27	MF	7	
4/30	POR	40	SCB	6	
4/30	WI	45	MN	12	
5/7	CAL	30	SAC	13	
5/7	CHAT	42	FOX	0	
5/7	HOU	34	NTK	12	
5/7	IA	26	MN	14	
5/7	MEMB	32	TVT	6	
5/7	MODX	37	SCB	0	
5/7	MON	25	MF	13	
5/7	PHI	13	BNH	6	
5/7	POR	12	SEA	6	*
5/7	RAVE	1	GAP	0	
5/7	VBW	83	RENO	6	I
5/7	WI	33	MADC	6	
5/14	CAL	1	DFC	0	N
5/14	CAR	54	PHI	7	
5/14	FOX	12	TVT	6	
5/14	MADC	13	IA	6	
5/14	MF	40	MR	8	
5/14	MODX	7	SCB	0	
5/14	MON	30	NEI	0	
5/14	NTK	40	MEMB	6	
5/14	POR	64	TUC	0	
5/14	RAVE	39	HOU	6	
5/14	RENO	19	NCRH	6	
5/14	SAC	15	SEA	0	
5/21	CHAT	26	MEMB	20	
5/21	FOX	22	TVT	6	
5/21	MON	58	MR	0	
5/21	NEI	7	MF	0	
5/21	POR	20	MODX	6	
5/21	RAVE	1	GAP	0	
5/21	RENO	20	VBW	8	I
5/21	SEA	28	TUC	0	
5/21	WI	60	MN	6	
5/28	BNH	8	PHI	0	
5/28	CAL	68	SCB	0	
5/28	CAR	1	GAP	0	
5/28	CHAT	1	TVT	0	
5/28	MADC	7	MN	6	
5/28	NTK	1	MBM	0	
5/28	SAC	16	POR	12	
5/28	WI	41	IA	0	
6/4	CAL	50	SEA	0	
6/4	CAR	42	BNH	0	
6/4	HOU	38	MBM	0	
6/4	IA	38	MN	12	
6/4	MF	37	MR	0	
6/4	NTK	52	MEMB	0	
6/4	RAVE	49	CHAT	0	
6/4	SAC	34	MODX	7	
6/4	TUC	36	SCB	20	
6/4	WI	26	MADC	0	
6/11	CAR	1	GAP	0	
6/11	CHAT	54	MEMB	0	
6/11	HOU	22	JYNX	17	I
6/11	MADC	26	MN	14	
6/11	MF	26	PHI	0	
6/11	NEI	41	MR	0	
6/11	NTK	63	FOX	6	
6/11	POR	9	SAC	0	
6/11	RAVE	1	TVT	0	
6/11	SEA	12	MODX	0	
6/11	TUC	6	SCB	0	
6/11	WI	44	IA	0	
6/18	CHAT	54	MEMB	0	
6/25	CHAT	24	NTK	20	BQ
6/25	MODX	42	TUC	8	BQ
6/25	NEI	25	BNH	0	BQ
6/25	SEA	1	MADC	0	BQ
6/25	CAL	22	SAC	19	S
6/25	CAR	12	MON	7	S
6/25	RAVE	14	HOU	13	S
6/25	WI	13	POR	12	S
7/16	NEI	20	CHAT	0	BS
7/16	SEA	14	MODX	0	BS
7/16	CAL	48	WI	0	CC
7/16	RAVE	24	CAR	6	CC
7/30	SEA	20	NEI	0	BC
7/30	RAVE	24	CAL	22	C

Women's Spring Football League (WSFL) – 2011 Season

The WSFL nearly had eight teams lined up for its 2011 season, but – in a move somewhat reminiscent of the WPFL in 2001 – four of these teams officially defected from the WSFL just before the year started and grouped together to play a schedule outside of the WSFL umbrella. As a result, four teams officially competed in the WSFL in 2011, while four other teams were independent but affiliated with the league. All this league turmoil resulted in the WSFL failing to hold a championship game in 2011, electing instead to declare the Baltimore Burn their champion on the basis of regular season record.

Exhibition Season Teams: 8 (4) Games: 23.5 (15)
Declared Champion (by virtue of regular season record): Baltimore Burn

2011 WSFL Standings

Teams	W	L	PR	Before	After
Baltimore Burn (BAL)	5	0	--	Joined from WFA	--
Arkansas Rampage (ARR)	4	2	--	Expansion	--
Topeka Mudcats (MUD)	2	2	--	--	Folded
Kansas Phoenix (KS)	0	4	--	Were WFA's Missouri Phoenix (2009)	--
Independent Affiliates					
Binghamton Tiger Cats (BING)	5	4	--	Joined from IWFL	--
Three Rivers Xplosion (3RX)	2	5	--	Expansion	Left for W8FL
Jersey Justice (JJ)	1	4	--	Joined from IWFL2	Folded
Kansas City Storm (STM)	0	1	--	--	Left for IWFL (2013)

2011 WSFL Scoreboard

Date						Date						Date					
4/2	NE	52	MUD	0	IE	4/30	BAL	12	JJ	8		5/28	WTF	36	ARR	0	I
						4/30	BING	22	3RX	8							
4/9	BING	40	3RX	12		4/30	MUD	34	STM	30		6/4	BAL	46	BING	0	
4/16	BAL	22	BING	0		5/7	3RX	1	JJ	0		6/11	BAL	54	3RX	0	
4/16	MF	8	JJ	0	I	5/7	ARR	36	MUD	6		6/11	BING	1	NEN	0	I
4/23	BAL	48	3RX	6		5/14	ARR	1	KS	0		6/18	ARR	34	KS	14	
4/23	JJ	36	BING	8		5/14	ERIE	38	BING	0	I	6/18	BING	1	3RX	0	
4/23	MUD	30	KS	6		5/21	ARR	1	KS	0		6/25	3RX	28	WVB	16	
						5/21	BING	1	JJ	0		10/1	WTF	44	ARR	0	IE

Women's Eights Football League (W8FL) – 2011 Season

Five teams competed in the eights division of the WSFL in 2011. The Cape Fear Thunder were named the first W8FL champions on the basis of regular season record.

Exhibition Season   Teams: 5 (4)   Games: 13
Declared Champion (by virtue of regular season record): Cape Fear Thunder

2011 W8FL Standings

Teams	W	L	T	PR	Before	After
Cape Fear Thunder (CFT)	4	2	1	--	Joined from IWFL2 (2009)	--
West Virginia Bruisers (WVB)	4	2	0	--	Joined from WSFL	Became WSFL's Tri-State Bruisers
Ventura Black Widows (VBW)	1	4	0	--	Joined from WSFL	--
West Virginia Wildfire (WV)	0	5	1	--	Expansion	--

Affiliate Team

Nevada Storm (NV)	1	1	0	--	Expansion	--

2011 W8FL Scoreboard

Date						Date						Date					
4/9	WVB	8	CFT	6		5/7	VBW	83	RENO	6	I	6/4	CFT	6	WV	6	
4/16	CFT	32	WVB	13		5/14	WVB	34	CFT	0		6/11	CFT	14	WV	6	
4/23	CFT	40	WV	0		5/21	RENO	20	VBW	8	I	6/11	NV	50	VBW	18	
4/23	JYNX	50	VBW	6	I	5/28	WVB	13	WV	6		6/18	WVB	16	WV	6	
4/30	CFT	47	WV	0								6/25	3RX	28	WVB	16	
												7/9	JYNX	60	VBW	0	I
												7/16	JYNX	33	NV	12	I

Independent Teams – 2011 Season

The expansion Utah Jynx completed the first full, truly independent season in women's football history in 2011. The Jynx played eight games – three against WFA opponents, three against WSFL/W8FL opponents, and two against IWFL opponents. The Jynx would join the WFA the following season.

Major Independent   Teams: 1   Games: 4

2011 Independent Standings

Team	W	L	PR	Before	After
Utah Jynx (JYNX)	5	3	--	Expansion	Left for WFA

2011 Independent Scoreboard

3/26	LV	12	JYNX	8	IE
4/16	SAC	45	JYNX	20	I
4/23	JYNX	50	VBW	6	I
5/28	JYNX	43	LV	22	I
6/11	HOU	22	JYNX	17	I
7/9	JYNX	60	VBW	0	I
7/16	JYNX	33	NV	12	I
7/23	JYNX	34	AZ	20	I

2012 Season Review

In the WFA title game, a dramatic comeback took the consensus national championship to the West Coast for the first time. Meanwhile, an IWFL dynasty was being built abroad, with a third league title in the last five years leaving the U.S. for the Great White North. The WSFL held its inaugural championship game since its resurrection, but the W8FL championship didn't go as smoothly.

Leagues: 4   Teams: 103 (97)   Games: 432 (398)

Women's Football Alliance (WFA) – 2012 Season

Remarkably, the WFA retained 57 full-member teams to compete in their 2012 season. The Chicago Force, who lost in overtime in the 2008 national title game, made the 2012 WFA championship game and were seeking their first league title in team history. The Force faced the San Diego Surge, who made the WFA championship game for the second consecutive year. In a dramatic rally, the Surge scored two late touchdowns to bring the consensus national championship to the West Coast for the first time.

Major National League   Teams: 58 (57)   Games: 252 (238.5)
Championship game result: San Diego Surge 40, Chicago Force 36

2012 WFA Standings

National Conference	W	L	PR	Before	After
Division 1 (Northeast)					
Keystone Assault (KEY)	7	2	W	--	Left for IWFL
New England Nightmare (NEN)	3	5	--	--	Left for IWFL
Maine Lynx (MLNX)	1	6	--	Expansion	Folded
Division 2 (North)					
Boston Militia (BOSM)	10	1	CC	--	--
New York Sharks (NY)	5	5	Q	--	--
Philadelphia Liberty Belles (II) (PLB2)	2	6	--	--	Folded
Division 3 (Mid-Atlantic)					
D.C. Divas (DC)	6	4	S	--	--
Pittsburgh Passion (PITT)	8	2	Q	--	--
Columbus Comets (COL)	2	6	--	--	--
Division 4 (Mideast)					
Detroit Dark Angels (DDA)	8	1	W	--	--
Cleveland Fusion (CLE)	2	6	--	--	--
Pittsburgh Force (PITF)	1	7	--	--	Deferred until 2014
Division 5 (North Central)					
Toledo Reign (TOL)	3	6	W	--	--
Derby City Dynamite (DCD)	4	4	--	Expansion	--
Cincinnati Sizzle (CIN)	0	8	--	--	--
Division 6 (Great Lakes)					
Chicago Force (CHI)	11	1	C	--	--
Indy Crash (INDY)	6	4	Q	--	--
West Michigan Mayhem (WM)	4	4	--	--	--
Division 7 (Southeast)					
Atlanta Phoenix (ATL)	8	2	Q	Expansion	--
Savannah Sabers (SAV)	5	3	--	--	--
Carolina Raging Wolves (CRW)	0	8	--	--	Folded
Division 8 (Gulf Coast)					
Tallahassee Jewels (TALL)	6	3	W	Expansion	--
Acadiana Zydeco (ZYD)	4	4	--	--	--
Gulf Coast Riptide (GCR)	1	7	--	--	Folded
Division 9 (South Atlantic)					
Jacksonville Dixie Blues (JAX)	9	1	S	--	--
Tampa Bay Inferno (TB)	7	1	--	Were Tampa Bay Pirates	--
Palm Beach Punishers (PALM)	4	4	--	--	Folded
Orlando Anarchy (ORL)	2	6	--	--	--
Miami Fury (MIA)	0	8	--	--	--

Women's Football Alliance (WFA) – 2012 Season (continued)
2012 WFA Standings (continued)

American Conference
Division 10 (Upper Midwest)
Minnesota Machine (MACH)	6	3	W	--		--
Wisconsin Wolves (WIW)	4	4	--	--		Folded
Nebraska Stampede (NE)	4	4	--	--		--
Wisconsin Dragons (WID)	1	7	--	--		Folded

Division 11 (Midwest)
Kansas City Tribe (KCT)	8	2	S	--		Folded
St. Louis Slam (STL)	6	4	Q	--		--
Kansas City Spartans (KCS)	2	6	--	--		Folded

Division 12 (Southwest)
Dallas Diamonds (DAL)	10	1	CC	--		--
Lone Star Mustangs (LSM)	7	3	Q	--		--
Houston Power (HPOW)	4	4	--	--		--
Austin Outlaws (OUT)	1	7	--	--		--

Division 13 (South Central)
Arkansas Wildcats (ARK)	5	4	W	Were Little Rock Wildcats		Became Little Rock Wildcats
Memphis Dynasty (MEM)	4	5	--	Were Memphis WTF		Left for WSFL
Tulsa Threat (TUL)	2	6	--	Were Tulsa Eagles		--

Division 14 (Pacific Northwest)
Utah Jynx (JYNX)	8	1	W	Joined from Indy		--
Portland Fighting Fillies (PFF)	4	3	--	--		--
Utah Blitz (UTB)	0	7	--	--		--

Division 15 (Pacific West)
Las Vegas Showgirlz (LV)	7	4	W	--		--
San Diego Sting (SDS)	5	3	--	--		--
Los Angeles Amazons (LA)	0	8	--	--		Folded

Division 16 (North Pacific)
Bay Area Bandits (BAB)	8	2	S	--		Folded
Central Cal War Angels (CCWA)	7	3	Q	--		--
West Coast Lightning (WCL)	2	6	--	Expansion		--
Valley Vipers (VV)	1	7	--	Expansion		Folded

Division 17 (South Pacific)
San Diego Surge (SD)	12	0	LC	--		--
Pacific Warriors (PAC)	6	4	Q	--		--
Silver State Legacy (SILV)	4	5	--	--		Folded
Arizona Assassins (AZ)	0	8	--	--		--

Affiliate Team
Iowa Xplosion (IAX)	0	1	--	--		Folded

2012 WFA Scoreboard

Date	Away	Sc	Home	Sc		Date	Away	Sc	Home	Sc		Date	Away	Sc	Home	Sc
3/10	PHX	30	LV	8 IE		4/14	NE	29	WID	0		4/21	CLE	33	PITF	6
3/24	LV	8	PHX	7 IE		4/14	OUT	7	TUL	6		4/21	DAL	90	LSM	0
3/31	JYNX	28	SILV	27 E		4/14	PAC	48	SDS	0		4/21	DDA	35	TOL	0
4/7	NE	82	KS	0 I		4/14	PITT	35	DC	34		4/21	GCR	22	ZYD	0
						4/14	PLB2	14	NEN	0		4/21	JAX	31	ORL	3
4/14	ATL	48	CRW	7		4/14	SAV	33	PALM	28		4/21	JYNX	49	UTB	23
4/14	BAB	33	PFF	6		4/14	SILV	20	UTB	0		4/21	KCT	33	STL	14
4/14	BOSM	64	NY	6		4/14	STL	59	MACH	0		4/21	KEY	50	NEN	0
4/14	CCWA	46	LA	0		4/14	TALL	8	ZYD	6		4/21	LV	48	LA	0
4/14	CHI	21	KCT	14		4/14	TB	25	ORL	0		4/21	MACH	35	WIW	6
4/14	DDA	35	PITF	6		4/14	TOL	68	CIN	14		4/21	MEM	18	TUL	6
4/14	HPOW	31	GCR	0		4/14	WCL	6	VV	0		4/21	NE	9	KCS	6
4/14	INDY	2	DCD	0		4/14	WM	23	CLE	7		4/21	NY	1	MLNX	0
4/14	JAX	20	MIA	0								4/21	PAC	54	AZ	0
4/14	KCS	21	WIW	15		4/21	ATL	48	MIA	32		4/21	PALM	14	TALL	6
4/14	KEY	54	MLNX	0		4/21	BAB	46	WCL	0		4/21	SAV	28	CRW	0
4/14	LSM	33	DFW	0 I		4/21	BOSM	59	PLB2	0		4/21	SD	42	SILV	0
4/14	LV	32	AZ	7		4/21	CCWA	66	VV	0		4/21	WM	52	CIN	8
4/14	MEM	32	ARK	0		4/21	CHI	47	COL	0						

Continued on next page

Women's Football Alliance (WFA) – 2012 Season (continued)
2012 WFA Scoreboard (continued)

Date	Team1	Score	Team2	Score	Note
4/28	ARK	18	ZYD	8	
4/28	ATL	57	SAV	13	
4/28	BAB	63	VV	0	
4/28	BOSM	31	KEY	0	
4/28	CCWA	42	WCL	7	
4/28	CHI	72	INDY	0	
4/28	DAL	54	HPOW	8	
4/28	DC	41	NY	12	
4/28	DCD	6	CIN	0	
4/28	DDA	14	CLE	6	
4/28	JAX	49	GCR	6	
4/28	JYNX	20	PFF	13	
4/28	KCT	94	TUL	0	
4/28	LSM	12	OUT	0	
4/28	LV	44	UTB	12	
4/28	MACH	14	NE	6	
4/28	MEM	16	HUNT	6	I
4/28	NEN	51	MLNX	7	
4/28	ORL	34	MIA	8	
4/28	PAC	22	SILV	14	
4/28	PITT	37	COL	14	
4/28	SD	64	AZ	0	
4/28	SDS	8	LA	0	
4/28	STL	59	KCS	0	
4/28	TALL	42	CRW	21	
4/28	TB	40	PALM	0	
4/28	WIW	30	WID	21	
4/28	WM	41	TOL	13	
5/5	ATL	62	CRW	0	
5/5	CHI	57	STL	14	
5/5	DAL	109	ARK	0	
5/5	DC	49	COL	0	
5/5	DCD	8	PITF	2	
5/5	DDA	26	WM	14	
5/5	HPOW	28	OUT	0	
5/5	INDY	56	CIN	0	
5/5	JAX	35	TB	6	
5/5	KCT	67	KCS	6	
5/5	KEY	34	BAL	6	I
5/5	LV	30	SDS	7	
5/5	MACH	41	WID	6	
5/5	NY	25	PLB2	8	
5/5	PALM	1	MIA	0	
5/5	PFF	26	UTB	14	
5/5	PITT	49	CLE	0	
5/5	SD	69	PAC	12	
5/5	SILV	44	AZ	0	
5/5	TALL	26	GCR	20	
5/5	WCL	48	VV	0	
5/5	WIW	24	NE	8	
5/5	ZYD	12	MEM	6	
5/12	ARK	36	TUL	16	
5/12	ATL	19	MEM	6	
5/12	BAB	20	CCWA	18	
5/12	BOSM	62	PLB2	0	
5/12	CHI	54	WM	0	
5/12	CLE	14	PITF	6	
5/12	COL	64	CIN	6	
5/12	DAL	60	OUT	0	
5/12	DC	41	NY	13	
5/12	DDA	60	WID	0	
5/12	INDY	18	DCD	14	
5/12	JYNX	38	LV	28	
5/12	KEY	46	BAL	8	I
5/12	LSM	24	HPOW	8	
5/12	MACH	38	NE	0	
5/12	NEN	34	BING	0	I
5/12	PALM	14	ORL	13	
5/12	PFF	42	VV	0	
5/12	PITT	71	TOL	14	
5/12	SD	55	WCL	0	
5/12	SDS	14	LA	0	
5/12	TALL	16	MIA	8	
5/12	TB	46	SAV	0	
5/12	ZYD	28	GCR	0	
5/19	ARK	1	ARR	0	
5/19	BOSM	44	DC	7	
5/19	CCWA	30	PAC	12	
5/19	CHI	48	CLE	0	
5/19	DAL	69	HPOW	0	
5/19	DCD	20	TOL	18	
5/19	DDA	7	COL	0	
5/19	JAX	33	ORL	6	
5/19	JYNX	62	LA	22	
5/19	KCS	1	ARR	0	
5/19	KCT	13	MACH	0	
5/19	KEY	20	PLB2	0	
5/19	LSM	45	OUT	0	
5/19	MLNX	31	MC	6	I
5/19	BAL	20	NEN	14	I
5/19	PALM	44	MIA	28	
5/19	PFF	22	UTB	0	
5/19	PITT	66	PITF	0	
5/19	SAV	47	CRW	0	
5/19	SD	57	BAB	0	
5/19	SDS	13	AZ	0	
5/19	SILV	28	LV	12	
5/19	STL	1	IAX	0	N
5/19	TALL	1	GCR	0	
5/19	TB	26	ATL	25	
5/19	TUL	14	MEM	6	
5/19	WIW	54	WID	0	
5/19	WM	39	INDY	33	
5/26	DAL	59	LSM	8	
5/26	SDS	13	WCL	8	
6/2	ATL	1	GCR	0	
6/2	BAB	38	WCL	0	
6/2	BOSM	65	MLNX	0	
6/2	CCWA	46	VV	0	
6/2	CHI	71	INDY	0	
6/2	COL	22	CLE	0	
6/2	DAL	83	DFW	12	I
6/2	DC	43	PITT	28	
6/2	DDA	54	PITF	6	
6/2	JAX	46	CRW	0	
6/2	JYNX	33	PFF	13	
6/2	KCT	53	NE	6	
6/2	KEY	42	NEN	0	
6/2	LSM	28	HPOW	14	
6/2	LV	20	LA	6	
6/2	MEM	12	DCD	6	*
6/2	NY	31	PLB2	0	
6/2	PAC	61	AZ	0	
6/2	SAV	34	ORL	20	
6/2	SD	48	SILV	0	
6/2	STL	32	KCS	0	
6/2	TB	1	MIA	0	
6/2	TOL	14	CIN	6	
6/2	TUL	21	OUT	19	
6/2	WID	27	WIW	6	
6/2	ZYD	16	ARK	8	
6/9	ARK	34	TUL	14	
6/9	BAB	57	VV	0	
6/9	BOSM	32	DC	25	
6/9	CCWA	40	WCL	0	
6/9	DAL	79	OUT	6	
6/9	DDA	17	CLE	14	
6/9	HPOW	14	ZYD	8	
6/9	INDY	34	WM	7	
6/9	JAX	1	PALM	0	
6/9	JYNX	50	UTB	0	
6/9	KCT	83	KCS	0	
6/9	MACH	34	WIW	24	
6/9	NE	27	WID	6	
6/9	NY	72	NEN	14	
6/9	PAC	27	SILV	7	
6/9	PITF	21	CIN	16	
6/9	PITT	22	COL	6	
6/9	PLB2	1	MLNX	0	
6/9	SAV	41	CRW	14	
6/9	SD	62	AZ	0	
6/9	SDS	7	LA	0	
6/9	STL	49	MEM	0	
6/9	TALL	1	GCR	0	
6/9	TB	42	ORL	20	
6/9	TOL	32	DCD	22	
6/16	ARK	22	MEM	14	
6/16	ATL	41	SAV	14	
6/16	BAB	26	CCWA	20	**
6/16	BOSM	55	NY	12	
6/16	CHI	55	WM	6	
6/16	DC	42	COL	0	
6/16	DCD	52	CIN	16	
6/16	HPOW	30	OUT	0	
6/16	INDY	28	TOL	7	
6/16	JAX	1	MIA	0	
6/16	JYNX	1	COS	0	I
6/16	KCT	63	STL	42	
6/16	KEY	50	PITF	15	
6/16	LSM	40	TUL	0	
6/16	LV	24	SDS	14	
6/16	MACH	34	WID	0	
6/16	NEN	48	MLNX	0	
6/16	ORL	41	CRW	8	
6/16	PFF	27	UTB	6	
6/16	PITT	50	PLB2	0	
6/16	SD	49	PAC	0	
6/16	SILV	19	AZ	8	
6/16	TB	1	PALM	0	
6/16	VV	12	LA	6	
6/16	WIW	1	KCS	0	
6/16	ZYD	18	TALL	6	

Continued on next page

Women's Football Alliance (WFA) – 2012 Season (continued)
2012 WFA Scoreboard (continued)

6/23	ATL	55	TALL	0	W	6/30	BAB	34	CCWA	8	Q	7/7	BOSM	55	DC	34 S
6/23	CCWA	36	JYNX	26	W	6/30	BOSM	47	NY	6	Q	7/7	CHI	67	JAX	14 S
6/23	INDY	52	TOL	35	W	6/30	CHI	70	INDY	14	Q	7/7	DAL	55	KCT	35 S
6/23	LSM	70	ARK	0	W	6/30	DAL	76	LSM	0	Q	7/7	SD	42	BAB	7 S
6/23	NY	24	KEY	19	W	6/30	DC	45	PITT	30	Q					
6/23	PAC	27	LV	20	W	6/30	JAX	49	ATL	41	Q	7/21	CHI	35	BOSM	34 CC
6/23	PITT	34	DDA	0	W	6/30	KCT	42	STL	17	Q	7/21	SD	56	DAL	29 CC
6/23	STL	42	MACH	6	W	6/30	SD	48	PAC	0	Q	8/4	SD	40	CHI	36 C

Independent Women's Football League (IWFL) – 2012 Season

The Sacramento Sirens qualified for their sixth league championship game in team history, advancing to the 2012 IWFL title game. They faced the Montreal Blitz, who had won IWFL2 championships in 2008 and 2010. A close, hard-fought contest went the way of the Blitz, denying the Sirens their first championship since 2005. It was the Blitz' third league championship in five years and a striking victory for the only Canadian team competing in an American women's football league.

Minor National League   Teams: 29 (26)   Games: 125.5 (116)
Championship game result: Montreal Blitz 28, Sacramento Sirens 27
Founders Bowl Championship: Carolina Phoenix 27, Portland Shockwave 0
Tier III Bowl: Carolina Queens 18, Colorado Sting 0

2012 IWFL Standings

Eastern Conference	W	L	PR	Before	After
North Atlantic Division					
Montreal Blitz (MON)	11	0	LC	--	--
New England Intensity (NEI)	7	3	BS	--	--
New Hampshire Freedom (NH)	3	5	--	Were Manchester Freedom	Folded
Northeastern Nitro (NTRO)	2	6	--	Joined from WFA	Folded
Mid-Atlantic Division					
Baltimore Nighthawks (BNH)	7	2	S	--	--
Philadelphia Firebirds (PHI)	4	5	BQ	--	--
Erie Illusion (ERIE)	4	4	--	Joined from WFA	--
Connecticut Wreckers (CT)	0	8	--	Expansion	--
Mid South Division					
Atlanta Xplosion (ATLX)	5	2	S	Were Atlanta Ravens	--
Carolina Phoenix (CAR)	7	1	BCW	--	--
Memphis Belles (MEMB)	0	7	--	--	Folded
South Atlantic Division					
Houston Energy (HOU)	7	1	CC	--	--
Arlington Impact (ARL)	6	3	BQ	Expansion	--
Arkansas Banshees (ARB)	3	4	--	Expansion	Left for WSFL

Independent Women's Football League (IWFL) – 2012 Season (continued)
2012 IWFL Standings (continued)

Western Conference

Midwest Division

Team	W	L				
Wisconsin Warriors (WI)	9	1	CC	--		--
Madison Cougars (MADC)	7	3	BS	--		Folded
Iowa Crush (IA)	4	5	BQ	--		--
Minnesota Vixen (MN)	2	6	--	--		--
Rockford Riveters (ROCK)	0	8	--	Expansion		--

Pacific Northwest Division

Team	W	L				
Seattle Majestics (SEA)	6	3	S	--		Left for WFA
Portland Shockwave (POR)	5	6	BC	--		Left for WFA

Pacific West Division

Team	W	L				
Sacramento Sirens (SAC)	9	2	C	--		Left for WFA
Modesto Maniax (MODX)	3	5	--	--		Folded

Pacific Southwest Division

Team	W	L				
Phoenix Phantomz (PHX)	8	3	S	Expansion		--
California Quake (CAL)	3	6	BQ	--		--
Tucson Monsoon (TUC)	0	8	--	--		--

Affiliate Teams

Team	W	L			
Carolina Queens (CARQ)	6	1	BW	Joined from IWFL2 (2010)	--
Colorado Sting (COS)	1	6	B	Expansion	Became Rocky Mountain Thunderkatz
Maine Rebels (MR)	0	8	--	--	--

2012 IWFL Scoreboard

Date	Team	Score	Team	Score		Date	Team	Score	Team	Score		Date	Team	Score	Team	Score	
3/10	PHX	30	LV	8	IE	4/28	MON	28	NTRO	0		5/26	COS	1	SCAA	0	I
3/24	LV	8	PHX	7	IE	4/28	NEI	14	NH	7		5/26	HOU	38	ARL	22	
						4/28	PHX	72	TUC	0		5/26	IA	36	MN	30	
4/7	CAR	26	PHI	0		4/28	SAC	22	POR	6		5/26	MADC	39	ROCK	0	
4/7	MON	20	NEI	11		4/28	WI	74	ROCK	0		5/26	MODX	38	CAL	0	
4/7	NTRO	50	MR	0								5/26	POR	27	TUC	6	
4/7	SEA	34	MODX	12		5/5	ARL	42	MEMB	0							
						5/5	ATLX	39	CARQ	14		6/2	ARB	1	MEMB	0	
4/14	ARL	44	ARB	18		5/5	BNH	20	ERIE	0		6/2	ARL	14	COS	2	
4/14	BNH	32	PHI	23		5/5	HOU	52	ARB	14		6/2	BNH	29	ERIE	12	
4/14	CAR	36	ATLX	31		5/5	MADC	20	IA	12		6/2	CARQ	1	CFT	0	I
4/14	CARQ	56	CFT	0	I	5/5	MN	32	ROCK	0		6/2	MADC	25	IA	0	
4/14	MN	44	ROCK	0		5/5	MON	42	NTRO	0		6/2	NEI	31	MR	0	
4/14	MODX	22	POR	0		5/5	NH	62	MR	0		6/2	NH	20	NTRO	6	
4/14	MON	61	MR	0		5/5	PHI	28	CT	12		6/2	PHI	34	CT	0	
4/14	NEI	36	CT	0		5/5	PHX	66	CAL	6		6/2	PHX	1	TUC	0	
4/14	PHX	70	CAL	0		5/5	SEA	14	SAC	7		6/2	POR	1	MODX	0	
4/14	SEA	41	TUC	0								6/2	SAC	24	SEA	0	
4/14	WI	28	IA	8		5/12	ARL	1	ARB	0		6/2	WI	54	ROCK	0	
						5/12	ATLX	26	MEMB	0							
4/21	ARB	60	KS	8	I	5/12	BNH	28	NTRO	0		6/9	ARL	30	COS	0	
4/21	ATLX	13	MEMB	6		5/12	CAL	38	TUC	30		6/9	ATLX	1	MEMB	0	
4/21	BNH	34	CT	0		5/12	CARQ	22	HUNT	19	I	6/9	BNH	21	PHI	0	
4/21	CAL	48	TUC	31		5/12	ERIE	27	MR	0		6/9	HOU	30	DFW	0	I
4/21	CARQ	44	TSB	6	I	5/12	MADC	20	MN	0		6/9	IA	29	MN	12	
4/21	ERIE	24	NH	20		5/12	NEI	41	NH	14		6/9	MON	35	NEI	6	
4/21	HOU	35	ARL	0		5/12	SAC	31	MODX	6		6/9	NH	20	CT	14	
4/21	IA	66	ROCK	0		5/12	SEA	14	POR	6		6/9	NTRO	34	ERIE	12	
4/21	MON	80	MR	0		5/12	WI	50	IA	26		6/9	PHX	35	CAL	14	
4/21	PHI	8	NTRO	7								6/9	SAC	60	TUC	7	
4/21	PHX	75	COS	0		5/19	ARB	40	MEMB	30		6/9	WI	14	MADC	12	
4/21	SAC	20	MODX	6		5/19	ATLX	23	CAR	10							
4/21	SEA	13	POR	7		5/19	BNH	22	CT	0							
4/21	WI	16	MADC	0		5/19	IA	58	ROCK	6							
						5/19	MON	42	NH	0							
4/28	CAR	22	BNH	0		5/19	NEI	21	NTRO	0							
4/28	CARQ	58	WV	0	I	5/19	PHI	32	ERIE	8							
4/28	ERIE	14	CT	7		5/19	PHX	37	COS	0							
4/28	HOU	19	DFW	14	I	5/19	SAC	41	POR	20							
4/28	MADC	15	MN	0		5/19	SEA	29	MODX	0							
4/28	MODX	22	CAL	6		5/19	WI	40	MN	6							

Continued on next page

Independent Women's Football League (IWFL) – 2012 Season (continued)
2012 IWFL Scoreboard (continued)

Date	Away	Pts	Home	Pts	Note		Date	Away	Pts	Home	Pts	Note		Date	Away	Pts	Home	Pts	Note
6/16	ARL	1	MEMB	0			6/23	BING	22	MR	8	I		7/14	CAR	7	NEI	0	BS
6/16	CAL	32	TUC	15										7/14	POR	43	MADC	6	BS
6/16	CAR	20	PHI	14			6/30	CAR	33	ARL	6	BQ		7/14	MON	28	HOU	16	CC
6/16	JYNX	1	COS	0	I		6/30	MADC	34	IA	0	BQ		7/14	SAC	45	WI	12	CC
6/16	ERIE	1	CT	0			6/30	NEI	30	PHI	13	BQ							
6/16	HOU	56	ARB	30			6/30	POR	1	CAL	0	BQ		7/28	CARQ	18	COS	0	B
6/16	MADC	49	ROCK	0			6/30	HOU	21	ATLX	20	S		7/28	CAR	27	POR	0	BC
6/16	MON	47	NH	0			6/30	MON	33	BNH	6	S		7/28	MON	28	SAC	27	C
6/16	NEI	58	MR	0			6/30	SAC	7	SEA	0	S							
6/16	POR	13	SEA	7			6/30	WI	40	PHX	37	S							
6/16	SAC	62	PHX	22															
6/16	WI	36	MN	6															

Women's Spring Football League (WSFL) – 2012 Season

The WSFL featured seven regulation teams vying for the league title, and for the first time, the WSFL pulled off a league championship game. The New Jersey Titans, who had last played in the WFA in 2010, were pitted against the expansion DFW Xtreme. The Titans won the first WSFL championship game since the league's relaunch and promptly folded.

Regional League Teams: 8 (7) Games: 30.5 (25)
Championship game result: New Jersey Titans 67, DFW Xtreme 6

2012 WSFL Standings

American Conference	W	L	PR	Before	After
New Jersey Titans (NJ)	8	1	LC	Joined from WFA (2010)	Folded
Huntsville Tigers (HUNT)	6	3	CC	Were IWFL's Tennessee Valley Tigers	--
Baltimore Burn (BAL)	3	5	S	--	--
Binghamton Tiger Cats (BING)	4	4	--	--	Left for W8FL

National Conference	W	L	PR	Before	After
DFW Xtreme (DFW)	4	5	C	Expansion	Left for IWFL
Arkansas Rampage (ARR)	2	7	CC	--	Folded
Kansas Phoenix (KS)	0	5	--	--	Folded

Affiliate Team	W	L	PR	Before	After
Tri-State Bruisers (TSB)	0	3	--	Were W8FL's West Virginia Bruisers	Folded

2012 WSFL Scoreboard

Date	Away	Pts	Home	Pts	Note		Date	Away	Pts	Home	Pts	Note		Date	Away	Pts	Home	Pts	Note
4/7	NE	82	KS	0	I		5/12	KEY	46	BAL	8	I		6/23	ARR	8	KS	0	
							5/12	NEN	34	BING	0	I		6/23	BING	22	MR	8	I
4/14	BAL	20	NJ	18			5/12	CARQ	22	HUNT	19	I		6/23	HUNT	50	CFT	0	
4/14	LSM	33	DFW	0	I														
							5/19	BAL	20	NEN	14	I		6/30	DFW	52	ARR	8	
4/21	BING	1	BAL	0			5/19	NJ	59	BING	0			6/30	HUNT	1	TSB	0	
4/21	DFW	48	ARR	0										6/30	NJ	1	MC	0	
4/21	ARB	60	KS	8	I		6/2	BAL	76	BING	0								
4/21	CARQ	44	TSB	6	I		6/2	DAL	83	DFW	12	I		7/7	ARR	22	KS	12	
							6/2	HUNT	41	ARR	0			7/7	HUNT	1	TSB	0	
4/28	BING	30	MC	0			6/2	NJ	1	MC	0			7/7	NJ	37	BAL	8	
4/28	HOU	19	DFW	14	I														
4/28	MEM	16	HUNT	6	I		6/9	HOU	30	DFW	0	I		7/21	NJ	31	BAL	6	S
							6/9	HUNT	40	CFT	0			7/21	DFW	54	ARR	8	CC
5/5	KEY	34	BAL	6	I		6/9	NJ	46	BING	8								
5/5	BING	1	3RX	0										7/28	NJ	25	HUNT	7	CC
5/5	HUNT	32	ARR	0			6/16	DFW	68	KS	0								
														8/11	NJ	67	DFW	6	C

Women's Eights Football League (W8FL) – 2012 Season

The West Virginia Wildfire were supposed to face the Nevada Storm in the first W8FL championship game, but the Storm had already announced their intention to leave the league at the end of the season and declined the invitation. The Wildfire accepted the league title by forfeit and spent the championship weekend scrimmaging against a W8FL all-star team; impressively, the Wildfire took down the all-stars in an exhibition match as they claimed the title.

Regional League   Teams: 8   Games: 24 (18.5)
Championship game result: West Virginia Wildfire 1, Nevada Storm 0

2012 W8FL Standings

Eastern Conference	W	L	PR	Before	After
West Virginia Wildfire (WV)	8	2	LC	--	--
Cape Fear Thunder (CFT)	3	8	--	--	--
Three Rivers Xplosion (3RX)	2	7	CC	Joined from WSFL	--
Mass Chaos (MC)	1	6	--	Expansion	Folded
Western Conference					
Nevada Storm (NV)	3	1	C	--	Left for IWFL
Ventura Black Widows (VBW)	1	3	--	--	--
Salt City Arch Angels (SCAA)	0	3	--	Expansion	Folded
Independent Affiliate					
Tulare County Villainz (TCV)	1	0	--	Expansion	Folded

2012 W8FL Scoreboard

Date						Date						Date					
4/14	3RX	36	MC	12		5/19	MLNX	31	MC	6	I	6/30	WV	42	CFT	20	
4/14	CARQ	56	CFT	0	I	5/19	WV	8	CFT	0		7/7	WV	40	3RX	0	
4/14	VBW	48	SCAA	12		5/26	COS	1	SCAA	0	I	7/14	TCV	47	VBW	12	
4/21	CFT	30	3RX	0		6/2	CARQ	1	CFT	0	I	7/21	3RX	1	MC	0	
4/21	NV	80	SCAA	20		6/2	WV	50	3RX	6		7/21	WV	1	CFT	0	
4/28	CFT	36	3RX	6		6/9	NV	68	VBW	12		7/28	WV	46	3RX	0	CC
4/28	CARQ	58	WV	0	I	6/16	WV	36	CFT	6		8/11	WV	1	NV	0	C
5/5	CFT	46	WV	0		6/23	MC	20	3RX	14							
						6/23	NV	60	VBW	0							

2013 Season Review

A historic team finally broke through for its first championship in the WFA in 2013. Meanwhile, for the second straight season, a one-time small-market team found big-market success in the IWFL. A former WFA squad settled on a name to engrave on the WSFL championship trophy, and the W8FL held its first true title contest.

Leagues: 4   Teams: 94 (81)   Games: 370 (343)

Women's Football Alliance (WFA) – 2013 Season

For the third time in team history, the Chicago Force advanced to the national championship game in 2013. This time, they once again met the Dallas Diamonds, who had defeated them in overtime in the 2008 national title game. The Diamonds were seeking their fifth national championship (and their first since 2008), but the third time was the charm for the Force, who used a record scoring output to secure the first national championship in their illustrious history.

Major National League   Teams: 49   Games: 220.5 (217.5)
Championship game result: Chicago Force 81, Dallas Diamonds 34

2013 WFA Standings

National Conference	W	L	PR	Before	After
Division 1 (Northeast)					
Boston Militia (BOSM)	10	1	CC	--	--
New York Sharks (NY)	4	5	W	--	Left for IWFL
Central Maryland Seahawks (CMS)	0	6	--	Expansion	--
Division 2 (Mid-Atlantic)					
D.C. Divas (DC)	6	4	S	--	--
Pittsburgh Passion (PITT)	7	3	Q	--	Left for IWFL
Columbus Comets (COL)	6	5	Q	--	--
Division 3 (North Central)					
Cleveland Fusion (CLE)	9	1	Q	--	--
Cincinnati Sizzle (CIN)	4	5	W	--	--
Derby City Dynamite (DCD)	3	5	--	--	--
Toledo Reign (TOL)	1	7	--	--	--
Division 4 (Great Lakes)					
Chicago Force (CHI)	12	0	LC	--	--
West Michigan Mayhem (WM)	4	5	W	--	--
Detroit Dark Angels (DDA)	2	6	--	--	--
Indy Crash (INDY)	2	6	--	--	--
Division 5 (Southeast)					
Atlanta Phoenix (ATL)	10	1	S	--	--
Savannah Sabers (SAV)	3	6	W	--	--
Tennessee Train (TNT)	1	7	--	Expansion	--
Division 6 (South Atlantic)					
Miami Fury (MIA)	9	1	Q	--	--
Tampa Bay Inferno (TB)	6	3	W	--	--
Tallahassee Jewels (TALL)	3	5	--	--	Folded
Jacksonville Dixie Blues (JAX)	3	5	--	--	--
Orlando Anarchy (ORL)	0	8	--	--	--

Women's Football Alliance (WFA) – 2013 Season (continued)
2013 WFA Standings (continued)

American Conference
Division 7 (Gulf Coast)
Little Rock Wildcats (LRW)	5	4	W	Were Arkansas Wildcats	Became Arkansas Wildcats (2015)
Acadiana Zydeco (ZYD)	3	6	W	--	--
Tulsa Threat (TUL)	3	5	--	--	--
New Orleans Mojo (NOM)	1	7	--	Expansion	Folded

Division 8 (Midwest)
Kansas City Titans (KC)	6	2	Q	Expansion	--
St. Louis Slam (STL)	7	4	S	--	Deferred until 2015
Minnesota Machine (MACH)	3	4	--	--	--
Nebraska Stampede (NE)	0	8	--	--	--

Division 9 (Southwest)
Dallas Diamonds (DAL)	11	1	C	--	Folded
Austin Outlaws (OUT)	7	3	Q	--	--
Lone Star Mustangs (LSM)	4	4	--	--	Folded
Houston Power (HPOW)	1	7	--	--	--

Division 10 (Pacific Northwest)
Seattle Majestics (SEA)	8	1	W	Joined from IWFL	--
Portland Shockwave (POR)	5	3	W	Joined from IWFL	--
Portland Fighting Fillies (PFF)	4	3	--	--	--
Everett Reign (ER)	4	7	--	Expansion	--
Tacoma Trauma (TAC)	1	7	--	Expansion	--

Division 11 (Pacific West)
Utah Jynx (JYNX)	10	3	Q	--	Left for IWFL
Las Vegas Showgirlz (LV)	7	4	W	--	--
Utah Blitz (UTB)	0	7	--	--	--

Division 12 (North Pacific)
Central Cal War Angels (CCWA)	11	1	CC	--	--
Sacramento Sirens (SAC)	5	4	Q	Joined from IWFL	Left for IWFL (2015)

Division 13 (South Pacific)
San Diego Surge (SD)	9	2	S	--	--
West Coast Lightning (WCL)	3	3	--	--	--
Pacific Warriors (PAC)	3	5	W	--	Deferred until 2015
San Diego Sting (SDS)	2	6	--	--	Folded
Arizona Assassins (AZ)	0	7	--	--	--

2013 WFA Scoreboard

Date	Team	Score	Team	Score		Date	Team	Score	Team	Score		Date	Team	Score	Team	Score	
3/2	LV	28	EVER	0	E	4/6	POR	16	EVER	3		4/20	ATL	42	TNT	0	
3/16	JYNX	54	EVER	6	E	4/6	SD	28	PAC	8		4/20	BOSM	56	MON	22	I
3/23	JYNX	38	PHX	10	IE	4/6	SEA	47	JYNX	18		4/20	CCWA	55	PAC	0	
						4/6	TB	40	SAV	14		4/20	CHI	66	INDY	6	
3/30	ER	50	RCRZ	0	IE	4/6	WCL	40	AZ	0		4/20	CIN	24	DCD	20	
3/30	JYNX	55	RMTK	18	IE	4/6	ZYD	40	NOM	0		4/20	CLE	36	TOL	6	
3/30	LV	18	PHX	12	IE							4/20	COL	52	SMSH	0	I
						4/13	ATL	48	NOM	0		4/20	DAL	68	HPOW	8	
4/6	ATL	61	TALL	14		4/13	BOSM	70	NY	0		4/20	DC	40	CMS	0	
4/6	CCWA	42	LV	6		4/13	CCWA	24	SAC	6		4/20	ER	22	UTB	6	
4/6	CHI	62	DDA	0		4/13	CLE	44	DCD	0		4/20	JAX	48	ORL	13	
4/6	CIN	36	TOL	14		4/13	DAL	49	OUT	0		4/20	JYNX	38	LV	28	
4/6	COL	28	WM	16		4/13	DC	53	COL	20		4/20	KC	59	NE	14	
4/6	DAL	41	HPOW	6		4/13	HPOW	52	ZYD	0		4/20	LRW	28	NOM	0	
4/6	DC	42	PITT	31		4/13	INDY	22	DDA	6		4/20	LSM	54	TUL	10	
4/6	INDY	48	DCD	6		4/13	JYNX	73	TAC	6		4/20	PITT	35	NY	0	
4/6	JAX	67	TNT	12		4/13	LV	48	SDS	19		4/20	SD	69	AZ	6	
4/6	KC	35	STL	14		4/13	MIA	22	JAX	10		4/20	SEA	40	TAC	0	
4/6	LSM	20	LRW	14		4/13	PAC	66	AZ	8		4/20	STL	35	MACH	0	
4/6	MACH	35	NE	34		4/13	PITT	42	TOL	0		4/20	TB	62	TALL	22	
4/6	MIA	32	ORL	0		4/13	SAV	28	TNT	20		4/20	WCL	17	SDS	0	
4/6	NY	20	CMS	6		4/13	SD	51	WCL	0		4/20	WM	40	DDA	0	
4/6	OUT	50	TUL	10		4/13	SEA	34	PFF	0							
4/6	PFF	42	TAC	0		4/13	TB	34	ORL	14							
						4/13	WM	52	CIN	0							

Continued on next page

Women's Football Alliance (WFA) – 2013 Season (continued)
2013 WFA Scoreboard (continued)

Date	Team 1	Score	Team 2	Score		Date	Team 1	Score	Team 2	Score		Date	Team 1	Score	Team 2	Score	
4/27	ATL	48	SAV	0		5/18	ATL	48	TNT	0		6/8	ATL	64	SAV	0	
4/27	BOSM	56	DC	35		5/18	BOSM	81	DC	54		6/8	BOSM	50	MON	0	I
4/27	CHI	50	STL	7		5/18	CCWA	42	SDS	0		6/8	CCWA	55	SAC	6	
4/27	CLE	40	DCD	0		5/18	CHI	82	INDY	20		6/8	CHI	56	WM	7	
4/27	DAL	48	LSM	0		5/18	CLE	50	TOL	0		6/8	CIN	20	TOL	12	
4/27	ER	46	TAC	6		5/18	DAL	68	NOM	0		6/8	CLE	48	CMS	0	
4/27	KC	61	MACH	0		5/18	DCD	58	CIN	56		6/8	DAL	82	LSM	6	
4/27	LV	40	UTB	2		5/18	DDA	19	WM	13		6/8	DC	42	COL	20	
4/27	MIA	38	TALL	8		5/18	JAX	39	ORL	0		6/8	DCD	14	TNT	0	
4/27	NOM	32	ZYD	12		5/18	JYNX	47	NV	22	I	6/8	ER	14	PFF	13	
4/27	NY	18	BAL	0	I	5/18	LRW	56	TUL	28		6/8	JYNX	60	UTB	6	
4/27	OUT	19	HPOW	14		5/18	LSM	20	HPOW	14		6/8	KC	27	STL	15	
4/27	PITT	49	COL	0		5/18	MACH	10	NE	3		6/8	LRW	20	NOM	0	
4/27	SAC	40	SD	18		5/18	MIA	22	TB	6		6/8	MACH	27	NE	0	
4/27	SDS	28	AZ	0		5/18	PFF	33	UTB	14		6/8	MIA	28	TB	0	
4/27	SEA	27	POR	7		5/18	PITT	35	COL	14		6/8	OUT	43	HPOW	0	
4/27	TB	60	ORL	7		5/18	POR	32	TAC	0		6/8	PITT	31	DDA	0	
4/27	TUL	28	LRW	8		5/18	SAV	24	TALL	12		6/8	SD	41	PAC	12	
4/27	WM	17	INDY	12		5/18	SD	32	LV	22		6/8	SDS	22	AZ	0	
												6/8	SEA	42	TAC	0	
5/4	ATL	30	JAX	14		5/25	ATL	56	SAV	18		6/8	TALL	26	JAX	14	
5/4	BOSM	47	NY	0		5/25	KC	51	NE	6		6/8	ZYD	26	TUL	8	
5/4	CCWA	20	PAC	8		5/25	LRW	30	ZYD	0							
5/4	CHI	67	WM	13		5/25	LV	56	JYNX	50		6/15	ATL	24	TB	19	W
5/4	CIN	38	TNT	6		5/25	NY	28	CMS	20		6/15	CCWA	34	POR	0	W
5/4	CLE	42	CMS	0		5/25	OUT	38	LSM	0		6/15	CLE	35	WM	6	W
5/4	COL	56	TOL	7		5/25	POR	18	PFF	0		6/15	COL	22	NY	20	W
5/4	DAL	55	OUT	0		5/25	SAC	45	NV	0	I	6/15	JYNX	36	SEA	26	W
5/4	DDA	6	INDY	0		5/25	SEA	35	EVER	0		6/15	MIA	1	SAV	0	W
5/4	JYNX	80	AZ	6		5/25	STL	69	MACH	0		6/15	OUT	35	LRW	0	W
5/4	MIA	52	ORL	0		5/25	TALL	47	ORL	20		6/15	PITT	63	CIN	0	W
5/4	PFF	16	EVER	6		5/25	TB	21	JAX	12		6/15	SAC	25	PAC	6	W
5/4	POR	25	UTB	7								6/15	SD	78	LV	14	W
5/4	SAC	61	NV	8	I	6/1	BOSM	56	CMS	0		6/15	STL	72	ZYD	0	W
5/4	STL	62	NE	27		6/1	CCWA	1	NV	0	I						
5/4	TUL	37	NOM	0		6/1	CHI	51	KC	7		6/22	ATL	28	MIA	24	Q
5/4	WCL	13	SDS	0		6/1	CLE	55	CIN	6		6/22	BOSM	63	PITT	28	Q
5/4	ZYD	30	LRW	22		6/1	COL	24	DDA	0		6/22	CCWA	65	JYNX	6	Q
						6/1	DCD	14	TOL	0		6/22	CHI	65	CLE	7	Q
5/11	BOSM	42	PITT	28		6/1	LRW	28	TUL	16		6/22	DAL	61	OUT	6	Q
5/11	CCWA	49	NV	22	I	6/1	LSM	26	HPOW	12		6/22	DC	40	COL	12	Q
5/11	CHI	61	DDA	0		6/1	LV	49	UTB	0		6/22	SD	39	SAC	13	Q
5/11	CLE	47	CIN	6		6/1	MIA	46	ORL	0		6/22	STL	58	KC	55	Q
5/11	COL	26	INDY	7		6/1	NY	32	BAL	0	I						
5/11	DAL	1	HPOW	0		6/1	OUT	48	ZYD	0		7/13	BOSM	58	DC	34	S
5/11	DC	49	NY	6		6/1	PAC	22	WCL	0		7/13	CCWA	40	SD	14	S
5/11	JYNX	66	UTB	22		6/1	PITT	36	DC	27		7/13	CHI	84	ATL	0	S
5/11	KC	68	NE	0		6/1	SAC	1	RCRZ	0	I	7/13	DAL	35	STL	20	S
5/11	LV	65	AZ	8		6/1	SAV	40	TNT	32							
5/11	MIA	14	JAX	5		6/1	SD	49	SDS	0		7/20	CHI	46	BOSM	27	CC
5/11	OUT	28	LSM	14		6/1	SEA	26	POR	14		7/20	DAL	27	CCWA	6	CC
5/11	PAC	36	SDS	8		6/1	STL	34	NE	0							
5/11	PFF	33	TAC	14		6/1	TAC	24	EVER	0		8/3	CHI	81	DAL	34	C
5/11	POR	44	EVER	8		6/1	TALL	47	NOM	6							
5/11	SD	63	WCL	0		6/1	WM	16	INDY	10							
5/11	SEA	42	SAC	21													
5/11	STL	47	MACH	0													
5/11	TB	47	TALL	0													
5/11	TNT	34	SAV	16													
5/11	TOL	26	DCD	24													
5/11	TUL	9	ZYD	8													

Independent Women's Football League (IWFL) – 2013 Season

The Houston Energy, who won three championships and played in five league title games in the WPFL, qualified for the 2013 IWFL championship game; it was their first championship game appearance since joining the league in 2008. The Carolina Phoenix, on the other hand, had spent 2008-2010 in IWFL2 as a small-market team. But the Phoenix joined the Montreal Blitz as the second straight former IWFL2 team to capture the IWFL title, shutting out the historic Energy on their way to their first league championship.

Minor National League   Teams: 32 (23)   Games: 122.5 (100)
Championship game result: Carolina Phoenix 14, Houston Energy 0
Founders Bowl Championship: Montreal Blitz 55, Arlington Impact 8
Tier III Bowl: Carolina Queens 28, San Antonio Regulators 14

2013 IWFL Standings

Eastern Conference	W	L	PR	Before	After
North Atlantic Division					
New England Intensity (NEI)	8	2	CC	--	Folded
Montreal Blitz (MON)	8	3	BCW	--	--
Northeast Division					
New York Knockout (NYK)	5	3	--	Expansion	--
New England Nightmare (NEN)	4	5	S	Joined from WFA	--
Connecticut Wreckers (CT)	0	7	--	--	--
Mid-Atlantic Division					
Philadelphia Firebirds (PHI)	6	2	S	--	--
Keystone Assault (KEY)	7	2	BS	Joined from WFA	--
Washington Prodigy (WP)	4	5	BQ	Expansion	--
Baltimore Nighthawks (BNH)	0	7	--	--	--
Southeast Division					
Carolina Phoenix (CAR)	11	0	LC	--	--
Atlanta Xplosion (ATLX)	3	1	--	--	Folded
Atlanta Rage (ATLR)	1	3	BQ	Expansion	Folded
Chattanooga Locomotion (CHAT)	1	6	--	Returned from 2011	--
Western Conference					
Midwest Division					
Madison Blaze (MAD)	7	2	S	Expansion	--
Wisconsin Warriors (WI)	6	3	BQ	--	--
Minnesota Vixen (MN)	6	4	BS	--	--
Iowa Crush (IA)	2	6	--	--	--
Rockford Riveters (ROCK)	0	8	--	--	Folded
Southwest Division					
Houston Energy (HOU)	9	1	C	--	--
Arlington Impact (ARL)	6	4	BC	--	--
DFW Xtreme (DFW)	0	7	--	Joined from WSFL	Left for WSFL
Pacific West Division					
California Quake (CAL)	3	5	S	--	--
Pacific Southwest Division					
Phoenix Phantomz (PHX)	6	3	CC	--	--
Tucson Monsoon (TUC)	0	6	BQ	--	--
Affiliate Teams					
Carolina Queens (CARQ)	5	4	BW	--	--
Rocky Mountain Thunderkatz (RMTK)	4	3	--	Were Colorado Sting	Left for WSFL
San Antonio Regulators (SA)	3	5	B	Expansion	--
Nevada Storm (NV)	2	5	--	Joined from W8FL	Left for WFA
Erie Illusion (ERIE)	1	4	--	--	--
Nor Cal Red Hawks (NCRH)	0	1	--	Returned from 2011	Folded
Maine Rebels (MR)	0	8	--	--	Became Northeast Rebels
Independent Affiliate					
Kansas City Storm (STM)	0	2	--	Joined from WSFL (2011)	Left for WSFL

Independent Women's Football League (IWFL) – 2013 Season (continued)
2013 IWFL Scoreboard

Date	Team1	Score	Team2	Score	Note
3/23	JYNX	38	PHX	10	IE
3/30	LV	18	PHX	12	IE
3/30	JYNX	55	RMTK	18	IE
4/20	BOSM	56	MON	22	I
4/20	NEN	40	MR	0	
4/27	ARL	40	DFW	32	
4/27	CAR	12	ATLX	6	
4/27	CARQ	30	CHAT	8	
4/27	KEY	12	WP	6	
4/27	MN	1	ROCK	0	N
4/27	MON	21	NEN	0	
4/27	NV	28	CAL	12	
4/27	NYK	34	MR	0	
4/27	PHI	14	BNH	0	
4/27	PHX	50	RMTK	16	
4/27	WI	35	IA	6	
5/4	ATLX	52	CARQ	8	
5/4	CAR	58	CHAT	0	
5/4	HOU	73	ARL	8	
5/4	KEY	20	BNH	0	
5/4	MAD	41	IA	0	
5/4	MON	14	NEI	0	
5/4	NEN	66	MR	0	
5/4	SAC	61	NV	8	I
5/4	NYK	14	CT	13	
5/4	PHI	14	WP	3	
5/4	PHX	72	CAL	0	
5/4	SA	44	DFW	12	
5/4	WI	26	MN	20	
5/11	ATLX	64	HUNT	0	I
5/11	CAL	38	TUC	19	
5/11	CAR	54	CARQ	0	
5/11	CHAT	34	ERIE	0	
5/11	HOU	56	SA	0	
5/11	IA	1	ROCK	0	N
5/11	MON	49	NYK	0	
5/11	NEI	33	NEN	6	
5/11	CCWA	49	NV	22	I
5/11	RMTK	88	STM	0	
5/11	WI	29	MAD	15	
5/11	WP	14	BNH	0	
5/18	ATLX	66	CHAT	0	
5/18	CAR	46	WP	7	
5/18	HOU	55	ARL	8	
5/18	KEY	7	BNH	6	
5/18	MAD	26	MN	0	
5/18	NEI	14	MON	13	
5/18	NEN	50	MR	0	
5/18	JYNX	47	NV	22	I
5/18	PHI	44	CT	0	
5/18	RMTK	20	TUC	7	
5/18	SA	6	DFW	0	
5/18	WI	1	ROCK	0	N
5/25	ARL	48	DFW	6	
5/25	CAL	1	NCRH	0	N
5/25	MAD	1	ROCK	0	N
5/25	MN	6	IA	0	
5/25	SAC	45	NV	0	I
5/25	NYK	6	CT	0	
6/1	ARL	28	SA	0	
6/1	CAR	42	WP	0	
6/1	CARQ	60	CHAT	0	
6/1	HOU	1	DFW	0	
6/1	KEY	40	CT	0	
6/1	MN	1	ROCK	0	N
6/1	MON	1	ERIE	0	
6/1	NEI	53	MR	0	
6/1	CCWA	1	NV	0	I
6/1	PHI	42	BNH	8	
6/1	PHX	67	RMTK	6	
6/1	WI	30	IA	0	
6/8	HOU	35	SA	0	
6/8	IA	1	ROCK	0	N
6/8	MAD	40	WI	7	
6/8	BOSM	50	MON	0	I
6/8	NEI	16	NEN	6	
6/8	NYK	42	MR	0	
6/15	ARL	36	SA	0	
6/15	ATLR	66	CHAT	0	
6/15	CAL	56	TUC	6	
6/15	CAR	64	CARQ	8	
6/15	ERIE	26	MR	6	
6/15	KEY	65	CT	0	
6/15	MAD	41	IA	6	
6/15	MN	51	WI	7	
6/15	MON	41	NYK	0	
6/15	NEI	20	PHI	6	
6/15	WP	22	BNH	0	
6/22	CAR	14	ATLR	0	
6/22	CARQ	42	BNH	28	
6/22	HOU	52	ARL	8	
6/22	MAD	40	MN	6	
6/22	NEI	49	CT	0	
6/22	NV	56	CAL	0	
6/22	NYK	28	NEN	14	
6/22	PHI	22	KEY	13	
6/22	PHX	1	TUC	0	
6/22	SA	1	DFW	0	
6/22	WI	1	ROCK	0	N
6/22	WP	1	ERIE	0	
6/29	CAR	1	CHAT	0	
6/29	HOU	1	DFW	0	
6/29	KEY	49	ERIE	0	
6/29	MAD	1	ROCK	0	N
6/29	MN	26	IA	6	
6/29	NEI	1	MR	0	
6/29	NEN	12	NYK	6	
6/29	PHI	1	CT	0	
6/29	PHX	21	CAL	8	
6/29	RMTK	14	TUC	7	
6/29	WP	48	CARQ	0	
7/6	CARQ	26	ATLR	12	
7/13	ARL	1	TUC	0	BQ
7/13	KEY	1	ATLR	0	BQ
7/13	MN	1	WI	0	BQ
7/13	MON	1	WP	0	BQ
7/13	CAR	32	PHI	0	S
7/13	HOU	30	MAD	0	S
7/13	NEI	33	NEN	0	S
7/13	PHX	18	CAL	0	S
7/13	RMTK	6	STM	0	***
7/20	ARL	18	MN	14	BS
7/20	MON	47	KEY	22	BS
7/20	CAR	18	NEI	6	CC
7/20	HOU	56	PHX	0	CC
8/2	CARQ	28	SA	14	B
8/2	MON	55	ARL	8	BC
8/3	CAR	14	HOU	0	C

Women's Spring Football League (WSFL) – 2013 Season

The Memphis Dynasty played three seasons in the WFA from 2010-2012 under three different names, including in 2011, when they famously went the entire season without choosing a nickname. The Dynasty jumped from the major league in the sport to the #3 league in 2013, and the result was not unexpected – they trumped the Arkansas Banshees on their way to a WSFL championship.

Regional League   Teams: 7 (5)   Games: 14
Championship game result: Memphis Dynasty 32, Arkansas Banshees 12

2013 WSFL Standings

Teams	W	L	PR	Before	After
Memphis Dynasty (MEM)	7	0	LC	Joined from WFA	--
Arkansas Banshees (ARB)	2	2	C	Joined from IWFL	--
Huntsville Tigers (HUNT)	2	3	--	--	Left for IWFL
Atlanta Heartbreakers (ATLH)	0	3	--	Joined from WFA (2011)	--
Nashville Smashers (SMSH)	0	5	--	Expansion	Left for W8FL
Affiliate Teams					
Tri-State Warriors (TSW)	1	0	--	Expansion	Folded
Baltimore Burn (BAL)	0	3	--	--	--

2013 WSFL Scoreboard

4/6	HUNT	20	SMSH	0		4/27	NY	18	BAL	0	I	5/11	ARB	46	SMSH	12
4/6	MEM	46	ATLH	0		4/27	HUNT	19	ATLH	16		5/11	ATLX	64	HUNT	0 I
4/13	MEM	22	HUNT	0		4/27	MEM	32	SMSH	0		5/18	MEM	18	SMSH	0
4/20	ARB	34	HUNT	8		5/4	MEM	34	ARB	26		6/1	NY	32	BAL	0 I
4/20	MEM	50	ATLH	6								6/29	MEM	32	ARB	12 C
4/20	COL	52	SMSH	0 I												
4/20	TSW	26	BAL	0												

Women's Eights Football League (W8FL) – 2013 Season

The West Virginia Wildfire won the 2012 W8FL championship by forfeit. In 2013, they qualified for the title game again, and this time, their opponents showed up. But the Binghamton Tiger Cats were no match for the Wildfire, who claimed their second straight W8FL championship.

Regional League   Teams: 6 (4)   Games: 13 (11.5)
Championship game result: West Virginia Wildfire 44, Binghamton Tiger Cats 8

2013 W8FL Standings

Teams	W	L	PR	Before	After
West Virginia Wildfire (WV)	6	0	LC	--	--
Binghamton Tiger Cats (BING)	4	2	C	Joined from WSFL	--
Cape Fear Thunder (CFT)	1	4	--	--	--
Three Rivers Xplosion (3RX)	0	5	--	--	Deferred until 2015
Affiliate Teams					
Ventura Black Widows (VBW)	1	0	--	--	Left for IWFL (2015)
River City Raiderz (RCRZ)	0	3	--	Expansion	Folded

2013 W8FL Scoreboard

3/30	EVER	50	RCRZ	0 IE		4/27	CFT	20	3RX	16		5/18	BING	28	CFT	8
4/6	WV	30	CFT	0		4/27	WV	50	BING	8		5/18	WV	1	3RX	0
4/13	BING	20	CFT	14		5/4	BING	38	3RX	30 *		6/1	SAC	1	RCRZ	0 I
4/20	VBW	44	RCRZ	8		5/4	WV	30	CFT	0		6/29	WV	44	BING	8 C
4/20	WV	46	3RX	6		5/11	BING	34	3RX	0						

2014 Season Review

The 2014 WFA season marked the end of a dynasty and a shocking discontinuation, and a prominent defection from the WFA made the 2014 IWFL championship all but preordained before the year even began. The WSFL season also held few surprises, but the W8FL championship threw fans a curveball. Finally, for just the second time in the sport's history, an independent team – from a familiar place – completed a full schedule and did so without a blemish.

Leagues: 4   Teams: 85 (77)   Games: 345 (298)

Women's Football Alliance (WFA) – 2014 Season

The top league in women's football had another competitive season in 2014, capped by a championship contest that was a rematch of the 2011 national title game between the Boston Militia and the San Diego Surge. The outcome in 2014 was the same as it had been three years prior – the Militia held off the Surge for their third consensus national championship in five years. But in a stunning offseason announcement, the reigning national champion Militia were then discontinued, becoming the first franchise in women's football history to win a major national championship and subsequently fold without playing another game.

Major National League   Teams: 42 (40)   Games: 187 (169)
Championship game result: Boston Militia 69, San Diego Surge 34
Alliance Bowl: Indy Crash 26, Seattle Majestics 12

2014 WFA Standings

National Conference	W	L	PR	Before	After
Northeast Division					
Boston Militia (BOSM)	11	0	LC	--	Folded
Cleveland Fusion (CLE)	7	3	Q	--	--
Pittsburgh Force (PITF)	3	2	--	Returned from 2012	Folded
Mid-Atlantic Division					
D.C. Divas (DC)	5	4	S	--	--
Columbus Comets (COL)	5	5	Q	--	--
Central Maryland Seahawks (CMS)	0	6	--	--	--
Southeast Division					
Atlanta Phoenix (ATL)	7	3	Q	--	--
Jacksonville Dixie Blues (JAX)	5	3	--	--	--
Tennessee Train (TNT)	5	3	--	--	Left for IWFL
Savannah Sabers (SAV)	0	8	--	--	Folded
South Atlantic Division					
Miami Fury (MIA)	7	3	S	--	--
Tampa Bay Inferno (TB)	7	2	W	--	--
Daytona Breakers (DB)	2	6	--	Expansion	Folded
Orlando Anarchy (ORL)	1	7	--	--	--
Mideast Division					
Toledo Reign (TOL)	6	3	W	--	Left for IWFL
Derby City Dynamite (DCD)	4	6	W	--	--
Cincinnati Sizzle (CIN)	0	8	--	--	Left for WSFL
Great Lakes Division					
Chicago Force (CHI)	8	2	CC	--	--
Indy Crash (INDY)	6	4	W-BW	--	--
Detroit Dark Angels (DDA)	4	4	--	--	--
West Michigan Mayhem (WM)	3	7	Q	--	--

Women's Football Alliance (WFA) – 2014 Season (continued)
2014 WFA Standings (continued)

American Conference

Midwest Division
Team	W	L			
Kansas City Titans (KC)	10	1	CC	--	--
Nebraska Stampede (NE)	6	3	W	--	Left for IWFL
Minnesota Machine (MACH)	3	8	Q	--	--
Iowa Steamrollers (IAS)	0	4	--	Expansion	Folded

Gulf Coast Division
Team	W	L			
Tulsa Threat (TUL)	3	6	W	--	--
Acadiana Zydeco (ZYD)	3	5	--	--	--
Louisiana Jazz (JAZZ)	0	7	--	Expansion	Folded

Southwest Division
Team	W	L			
Austin Outlaws (OUT)	8	2	S	--	--
Houston Power (HPOW)	6	4	Q	--	--

Northwest Division
Team	W	L			
Seattle Majestics (SEA)	8	3	S-B	--	--
Portland Shockwave (POR)	6	2	--	--	--
Everett Reign (ER)	4	7	W	--	--
Utah Blitz (UTB)	4	5	--	--	--
Portland Fighting Fillies (PFF)	3	6	W	--	--
Tacoma Trauma (TAC)	0	8	--	--	--

Pacific West Division
Team	W	L			
Central Cal War Angels (CCWA)	5	3	Q	--	--
Las Vegas Showgirlz (LV)	10	3	Q	--	Folded
Nevada Storm (NV)	0	6	--	Joined from IWFL	Left for IWFL

Pacific South Division
Team	W	L			
San Diego Surge (SD)	11	1	C	--	--
West Coast Lightning (WCL)	2	6	--	--	--
Arizona Assassins (AZ)	0	7	--	--	--

2014 WFA Scoreboard

Date						Date						Date					
3/1	LV	24	EVER	0	E	4/12	MIA	48	JAX	8		4/26	DC	39	COL	0	
3/8	LV	74	JYNX	38	IE	4/12	HOU	56	OUT	3	I	4/26	DDA	52	DCD	22	
3/22	UT	52	ER	0	IE	4/12	PITF	1	CMS	0	N	4/26	ER	8	PFF	7	
3/29	UT	59	UTB	0	IE	4/12	POR	20	PFF	14		4/26	LV	54	AZ	0	
						4/12	SD	62	WCL	0		4/26	MIA	50	SAV	12	
4/5	BOSM	36	DC	32		4/12	SEA	46	TAC	0		4/26	NE	45	MACH	13	
4/5	CCWA	46	NV	0		4/12	TB	55	SAV	6		4/26	POR	28	TAC	8	
4/5	CHI	70	DDA	0		4/12	UTB	14	EVER	12		4/26	SD	1	WCL	0	
4/5	CLE	20	COL	6		4/12	WM	15	DCD	6		4/26	TB	68	ORL	0	
4/5	ER	19	TAC	12								4/26	TNT	26	DB	21	
4/5	JAX	62	DB	0		4/19	ATL	12	MIA	8		4/26	TOL	33	CIN	0	
4/5	KC	1	IAS	0	N	4/19	BOSM	47	CLE	7		4/26	TUL	34	JAZZ	6	
4/5	MIA	56	ORL	0		4/19	CCWA	60	WCL	8							
4/5	NE	54	MACH	12		4/19	CHI	42	DC	27		5/3	BOSM	48	CLE	7	
4/5	OUT	17	HPOW	8		4/19	COL	42	DCD	0		5/3	CHI	36	INDY	6	
4/5	PFF	37	UTB	0		4/19	DB	32	ORL	13		5/3	COL	1	CMS	0	N
4/5	PITF	30	BAL	8	I	4/19	HPOW	39	JAZZ	0		5/3	DC	43	BAL	0	I
4/5	SD	59	LV	6		4/19	INDY	36	DDA	6		5/3	DDA	28	WM	25	
4/5	SEA	33	POR	12		4/19	KC	42	MACH	2		5/3	ER	23	UTB	8	
4/5	TB	32	ATL	25		4/19	NE	1	IAS	0		5/3	HPOW	50	JAZZ	0	
4/5	TNT	22	SAV	20		4/19	PFF	21	TAC	0		5/3	JAX	27	TNT	14	
4/5	TOL	26	DCD	6		4/19	SD	68	AZ	0		5/3	KC	62	MACH	0	
4/5	WCL	34	AZ	6		4/19	SEA	41	EVER	0		5/3	LV	60	NCS	0	I
4/5	WM	75	CIN	0		4/19	TNT	30	CIN	6		5/3	NE	56	TUL	32	
4/5	ZYD	18	JAZZ	6		4/19	TOL	1	CMS	0		5/3	ORL	20	SAV	14	
						4/19	TUL	30	ZYD	8		5/3	OUT	34	ZYD	0	
4/12	ATL	34	TNT	0		4/19	UTB	18	NV	8		5/3	SD	56	NV	6	
4/12	CCWA	32	LV	28								5/3	SEA	32	POR	0	
4/12	CHI	48	INDY	6		4/26	ATL	12	JAX	10		5/3	TB	77	DB	0	
4/12	HPOW	47	ZYD	8		4/26	BOSM	1	CMS	0	N	5/3	TOL	35	PITF	6	
4/12	KC	48	TUL	8		4/26	CHI	30	WM	0							
4/12	MACH	1	IAS	0	N	4/26	CLE	7	INDY	0							

Continued on next page

Women's Football Alliance (WFA) – 2014 Season (continued)
2014 WFA Scoreboard (continued)

Date	Team1	Score	Team2	Score	Note	Date	Team1	Score	Team2	Score	Note	Date	Team1	Score	Team2	Score	Note
5/10	ATL	56	SAV	6		5/24	DCD	72	ERIE	0	I	6/7	IA	34	MACH	29	I
5/10	BOSM	1	BAL	0	I	5/24	JAX	41	DB	12		6/7	MIA	14	TB	2	
5/10	CCWA	40	WCL	0		5/24	KC	50	TUL	6		6/7	OUT	8	HPOW	7	
5/10	CLE	71	CIN	0		5/24	LV	1	NV	0		6/7	PFF	57	TAC	0	
5/10	COL	48	TOL	0		5/24	OUT	1	SA	0	I	6/7	POR	32	UTB	0	
5/10	DCD	22	DDA	20		5/24	PITF	26	CIN	0		6/7	SD	35	CCWA	6	
5/10	HPOW	42	SA	0	I	5/24	POR	30	UTB	18		6/7	SEA	43	EVER	0	
5/10	INDY	33	WM	13		5/24	UT	72	TAC	0	I	6/7	TNT	24	ORL	14	
5/10	KC	33	NE	14		5/24	TB	14	MIA	13		6/7	TOL	1	CMS	0	N
5/10	LV	56	NV	0		5/24	WCL	54	AZ	0		6/7	ZYD	28	TUL	27	
5/10	MACH	1	IAS	0	N	5/24	ZYD	1	JAZZ	0		6/14	ATL	15	TB	7	W
5/10	MIA	41	ORL	0		5/31	ATL	1	JAZZ	0		6/14	CCWA	44	PFF	0	W
5/10	OUT	28	ARL	18	I	5/31	MHB	51	AZ	0	I	6/14	CLE	38	INDY	32	W
5/10	POR	36	PFF	16		5/31	CLE	23	COL	12		6/14	COL	22	TOL	0	W
5/10	SD	101	AZ	0		5/31	DB	41	SAV	22		6/14	HPOW	35	NE	0	W
5/10	UT	39	SEA	20	I	5/31	DC	1	CMS	0	N	6/14	LV	50	EVER	0	W
5/10	TB	49	JAX	0		5/31	DCD	40	TNT	12		6/14	MACH	35	TUL	13	W
5/10	TUL	1	JAZZ	0		5/31	DDA	12	WM	10		6/14	WM	30	DCD	22	W
5/10	UTB	28	TAC	7		5/31	HOU	35	HPOW	13	I						
5/17	BOSM	35	CHI	18		5/31	INDY	68	CIN	0		6/21	BOSM	47	CLE	6	Q
5/17	CLE	46	TOL	0		5/31	JAX	48	ORL	7		6/21	CHI	66	WM	0	Q
5/17	COL	20	WM	12		5/31	KC	20	MACH	7		6/21	DC	69	COL	8	Q
5/17	DC	44	ATL	0		5/31	LV	50	WCL	6		6/21	KC	43	HPOW	2	Q
5/17	DDA	54	CIN	0		5/31	NE	59	STM	0	I	6/21	MIA	9	ATL	7	Q
5/17	ER	47	TAC	12		5/31	OUT	46	ZYD	6		6/21	OUT	14	MACH	3	Q
5/17	HPOW	1	ZYD	0		5/31	POR	8	EVER	3		6/21	SD	48	LV	16	Q
5/17	INDY	19	DCD	0		5/31	SEA	48	PFF	3		6/21	SEA	13	CCWA	12	Q
5/17	LV	38	WCL	6		5/31	TOL	37	PITF	0							
5/17	MIA	47	DB	0		5/31	UTB	1	NV	0		7/5	BOSM	72	DC	56	S
5/17	NE	20	MACH	13		6/7	ATL	53	DB	13		7/5	CHI	66	MIA	8	S
5/17	OUT	14	TUL	0		6/7	BOSM	29	DC	28		7/5	KC	41	OUT	0	S
5/17	SD	64	CCWA	0		6/7	CHI	72	COL	8		7/5	SD	36	SEA	20	S
5/17	SEA	42	PFF	14		6/7	CLE	43	WM	8		7/19	BOSM	63	CHI	14	CC
5/17	TB	57	ORL	0		6/7	DCD	74	CIN	0		7/19	SD	59	KC	14	CC
5/17	TNT	28	SAV	0		6/7	INDY	35	DDA	7		8/2	INDY	26	SEA	12	B
						6/7	JAX	46	SAV	16		8/3	BOSM	69	SD	34	C
						6/7	KC	57	NE	0							
						6/7	LV	22	AZ	12							

Independent Women's Football League (IWFL) – 2014 Season

In 2008, a clear hierarchy was established in women's football with the emergence of a consensus #1 competitive league in the sport. Since that time, the Pittsburgh Passion had consistently competed at the highest level, strongly contending but never quite breaking through for a title. In 2014, rather than continue in the WFA – the #1 competitive league in the sport – the Passion moved to the IWFL, the #2 league. The results were predictable: the Pittsburgh Passion overwhelmed the smaller league and easily cruised to the IWFL championship by dispatching the Houston Energy, who were making their seventh appearance in a league title game. The Passion became the first team since the hierarchy was established in 2008 to drop down from the top league in the sport and immediately celebrate a title in the #2 league.

Minor National League   Teams: 30 (25)   Games: 118.5 (95)
Championship game result: Pittsburgh Passion 41, Houston Energy 7
Founders Bowl: Madison Blaze 31, Baltimore Nighthawks 14
Legacy Bowl: Carolina Queens 28, Minnesota Vixen 22

Independent Women's Football League (IWFL) – 2014 Season (continued)
2014 IWFL Standings

Eastern Conference	W	L	PR	Before	After
North Atlantic Division					
New York Sharks (NY)	7	3	CC	Joined from WFA	--
Montreal Blitz (MON)	6	2	--	--	--
New York Knockout (NYK)	4	2	--	--	Left for W8FL
Connecticut Wreckers (CT)	4	4	--	--	--
New England Nightmare (NEN)	3	5	--	--	Left for WSFL
Mid-Atlantic Division					
PITTSBURGH PASSION (PITT)	11	0	LC	Joined from WFA	--
KEYSTONE ASSAULT (KEY)	8	1	S	--	Left for WSFL
Baltimore Nighthawks (BNH)	4	5	B	--	--
Washington Prodigy (WP)	3	5	--	--	--
Philadelphia Firebirds (PHI)	2	6	--	--	--
South Atlantic Division					
Carolina Phoenix (CAR)	4	5	S	--	--
Carolina Queens (CARQ)	6	3	BW	--	--
Huntsville Tigers (HUNT)	2	3	--	Joined from WSFL	--
Chattanooga Locomotion (CHAT)	0	7	--	--	Folded

Western Conference	W	L	PR	Before	After
Midwest Division					
Madison Blaze (MAD)	8	2	CC-BW	--	--
Minnesota Vixen (MN)	6	3	B	--	--
Wisconsin Warriors (WI)	4	4	--	--	--
Iowa Crush (IA)	3	5	--	--	--
Southwest Division					
Houston Energy (HOU)	9	2	C	--	--
Arlington Impact (ARL)	5	3	--	--	Left for WFA
Pacific West Division					
Phoenix Phantomz (PHX)	6	2	S	--	--
California Quake (CAL)	5	2	--	--	--
North County Stars (NCS)	2	5	--	Expansion	--
Utah Jynx (JYNX)	3	5	--	Joined from WFA	Folded
Tucson Monsoon (TUC)	1	5	--	--	Folded

Affiliate Teams	W	L	PR	Before	After
San Antonio Regulators (SA)	1	6	--	--	--
Hillsboro Hammerheads (HILL)	0	2	--	Expansion	Folded
Erie Illusion (ERIE)	0	6	--	--	Folded
Missouri Thundercats (MOT)	0	7	--	Expansion	Folded
Northeast Rebels (NER)	0	8	--	Were Maine Rebels	--

2014 IWFL Scoreboard

Date	Team	Score	Team	Score	Note
3/8	LV	74	JYNX	38	IE
4/12	ARL	61	SA	0	
4/12	CAL	64	NCS	0	
4/12	HOU	56	OUT	3	I
4/12	HUNT	30	CHAT	16	
4/12	JYNX	44	RMTK	0	I
4/12	KEY	13	BNH	6	
4/12	MAD	7	IA	6	
4/12	MON	40	NEN	8	
4/12	PHI	20	WP	6	
4/12	PITT	29	CAR	6	
4/12	WI	1	MOT	0	N
4/19	CAL	20	JYNX	15	
4/19	CARQ	32	HUNT	30	
4/19	HOU	41	ARL	12	
4/19	KEY	37	NEN	8	
4/19	MN	1	MOT	0	N
4/19	NY	50	CT	0	
4/19	NYK	14	NER	0	
4/19	PITT	42	PHI	0	
4/19	SA	12	TUC	0	
4/19	WI	20	IA	8	
4/19	WP	27	CAR	20	
4/26	ARL	50	MEM	0	I
4/26	BNH	28	CARQ	22	*
4/26	CAR	47	CHAT	6	
4/26	MAD	1	MOT	0	N
4/26	MN	12	WI	6	
4/26	MON	53	CT	0	
4/26	NEN	32	NER	6	
4/26	PHI	18	WP	6	
4/26	PHX	41	JYNX	12	
4/26	PITT	31	NY	6	
5/3	BNH	14	PHI	12	
5/3	CARQ	52	CHAT	0	
5/3	HOU	24	ARL	14	
5/3	IA	1	MOT	0	N
5/3	KEY	31	NEN	0	
5/3	MAD	14	MN	0	
5/3	MON	51	NER	0	
5/3	LV	60	NCS	0	I
5/3	NY	29	CAR	28	
5/3	NYK	16	CT	6	
5/3	PHX	40	CAL	14	

Continued on next page

Independent Women's Football League (IWFL) – 2014 Season (continued)
2014 IWFL Scoreboard (continued)

Date	Team	Score	Team	Score	Note
5/10	OUT	28	ARL	18	I
5/10	BNH	1	PHI	0	
5/10	CAL	52	TUC	0	
5/10	CAR	26	CARQ	6	
5/10	CT	21	NER	0	
5/10	HOU	62	PHX	13	
5/10	HUNT	34	CHAT	16	
5/10	IA	14	MN	6	
5/10	JYNX	1	HILL	0	N
5/10	KEY	40	NYK	0	
5/10	MAD	29	WI	12	
5/10	NY	41	WP	24	
5/10	PITT	35	MON	0	
5/10	HPOW	42	SA	0	I
5/17	ARL	1	MOT	0	N
5/17	CARQ	1	CHAT	0	
5/17	CT	21	NEN	20	
5/17	HOU	1	SA	0	
5/17	KEY	62	ERIE	0	
5/17	MON	55	NER	0	
5/17	NCS	40	TUC	6	
5/17	PITT	51	CAR	0	
5/17	WI	18	IA	13	
5/17	WP	15	BNH	0	
5/24	CAL	48	TUC	0	
5/24	DCD	72	ERIE	0	I
5/24	MAD	1	MOT	0	N
5/24	MN	14	WI	0	
5/24	PHX	1	NCS	0	
5/24	PITT	21	NY	6	
5/24	OUT	1	SA	0	I
5/31	ARL	1	SA	0	
5/31	BNH	32	CARQ	8	
5/31	CAR	1	CHAT	0	
5/31	CT	1	ERIE	0	
5/31	HOU	35	HPOW	13	I
5/31	JYNX	1	HILL	0	N
5/31	KEY	21	PHI	0	
5/31	MAD	27	IA	0	
5/31	MN	1	MOT	0	N
5/31	MON	55	NYK	0	
5/31	NCS	48	TUC	8	
5/31	NEN	38	NER	0	
5/31	NY	31	WP	18	
5/31	PHX	21	CAL	6	
6/7	ARL	26	HOU	7	
6/7	CARQ	64	CHAT	6	
6/7	IA	34	MACH	29	I
6/7	KEY	34	NER	0	
6/7	MN	18	MAD	14	
6/7	NY	40	MON	9	
6/7	PHX	76	NCS	28	
6/7	PITT	31	PHI	0	
6/7	TUC	1	JYNX	0	
6/7	WI	1	ERIE	0	
6/7	WP	26	BNH	14	
6/8	NEN	27	CT	14	
6/14	CAL	30	NCS	14	
6/14	CAR	52	HUNT	0	
6/14	CT	20	NER	0	
6/14	HOU	1	SA	0	
6/14	KEY	39	WP	20	
6/14	MAD	40	WI	0	
6/14	MN	12	IA	6	*
6/14	MON	1	NEN	0	
6/14	NY	31	PHI	6	
6/14	NYK	40	ERIE	0	
6/14	PHX	1	JYNX	0	
6/14	PITT	38	BNH	6	
6/21	CARQ	1	HUNT	0	
6/21	NYK	54	ERIE	0	
6/28	HOU	90	PHX	26	S
6/28	NY	60	CAR	12	S
6/28	PITT	42	KEY	12	S
7/12	HOU	53	MAD	0	CC
7/12	PITT	26	NY	12	CC
7/25	CARQ	28	MN	22	B
7/25	MAD	31	BNH	14	B
7/26	PITT	41	HOU	7	C

Women's Spring Football League (WSFL) – 2014 Season

The WSFL was sold a week before the 2014 regular season began, resulting in a chaotic year for the league. The Memphis Dynasty again won all of their games against WSFL competition, including a second straight victory in the WSFL championship game over the Arkansas Banshees. But then, like the Boston Militia in the WFA, the Dynasty abruptly folded that offseason without playing another game.

Regional League   Teams: 8 (7)   Games: 21.5 (18)
Championship game result: Memphis Dynasty 34, Arkansas Banshees 12

2014 WSFL Standings

Eastern Conference	W	L	PR	Before	After
Memphis Dynasty (MEM)	6	1	LC	--	Folded
Baltimore Burn (BAL)	1	4	CC	--	--
Atlanta Heartbreakers (ATLH)	0	4	--	--	--

Western Conference	W	L	PR	Before	After
Arkansas Banshees (ARB)	3	4	C	--	Folded
Mile High Blaze (MHB)	4	2	--	Expansion	Left for IWFL
DFW Xtreme (DFW)	2	3	CC	Joined from IWFL	--
Rocky Mountain Thunderkatz (RMTK)	1	5	--	Joined from IWFL	Left for IWFL

Independent Affiliate	W	L	PR	Before	After
Kansas City Storm (STM)	0	3	--	Joined from IWFL	Folded

U.S. Women's Football Leagues – Year-By-Year Results, 1999-2015

Women's Spring Football League (WSFL) – 2014 Season (continued)

2014 WSFL Scoreboard

Date	Team	Score	Team	Score		Date	Team	Score	Team	Score		Date	Team	Score	Team	Score	
3/30	MHB	40	RMTK	0		4/26	BAL	1	ARB	0		5/31	MHB	51	AZ	0	I
4/5	PITF	30	BAL	8	I	4/26	DFW	60	ATLH	0		5/31	UT	63	RMTK	0	I
4/5	MEM	1	ATLH	0		4/26	ARL	50	MEM	0	I	5/31	NE	59	STM	0	I
4/5	UT	58	RMTK	0	I	5/3	DC	43	BAL	0	I	6/7	ARB	42	DFW	6	
4/12	DFW	30	ATLH	14		5/3	MEM	30	ARB	14		6/7	MHB	42	STM	0	
4/12	MEM	38	ARB	32	*	5/3	UT	55	MHB	17	I	6/14	MHB	34	RMTK	0	
4/12	UT	64	MHB	0	I	5/10	BOSM	1	BAL	0	I	7/19	ARB	1	DFW	0	CC
4/12	JYNX	44	RMTK	0	I	5/17	MEM	44	DFW	8		7/19	MEM	20	BAL	8	CC
4/19	ARB	65	ATLH	26		5/17	RMTK	28	STM	0		7/26	MEM	34	ARB	12	C

Women's Eights Football League (W8FL) – 2014 Season

Though limited to only four teams, the W8FL championship game was the most competitive of the four league championship contests in 2014. The West Virginia Wildfire were gunning for their third straight W8FL title, but they were narrowly upset in the championship game by the Cape Fear Thunder, who gained a second W8FL title to go along with the one they won on the basis of regular season record in 2011.

Regional League Teams: 4 Games: 14 (12)

Championship game result: Cape Fear Thunder 36, West Virginia Wildfire 28

2014 W8FL Standings

Teams	W	L	PR	Before	After
West Virginia Wildfire (WV)	6	2	C	--	Left for WSFL
Nashville Smashers (SMSH)	3	3	CC	Joined from WSFL	Folded
Cape Fear Thunder (CFT)	3	5	LC	--	--
Binghamton Tiger Cats (BING)	2	4	CC	--	Folded

2014 W8FL Scoreboard

Date	Team	Score	Team	Score		Date	Team	Score	Team	Score		Date	Team	Score	Team	Score	
4/5	BING	1	CFT	0		5/3	SMSH	34	BING	0		6/21	WV	26	CFT	20	
4/12	CFT	28	SMSH	0		5/10	WV	22	SMSH	2		7/12	CFT	32	SMSH	20	CC
4/19	WV	20	BING	8		5/17	SMSH	12	CFT	9		7/12	WV	1	BING	0	CC
4/26	BING	16	CFT	6		6/7	WV	30	CFT	0		7/26	CFT	36	WV	28	C
4/26	SMSH	25	WV	8		6/14	WV	34	BING	20							

Independent Teams – 2014 Season

In 2011, the Utah Jynx were the first team to complete a full, truly independent schedule. When several members of the Jynx defected in 2014 and formed a new team, the Utah Falconz, the Falconz embarked upon their own independent schedule in their first season. The Falconz split their schedule between WFA and WSFL teams and were heralded as one of the top franchises in the sport when they rolled through that very strong schedule with an undefeated record. The Falconz would join the IWFL the following season.

Major Independent Teams: 1 Games: 4

2014 Independent Standings

Team	W	L	PR	Before	After
Utah Falconz (UT)	8	0	--	Expansion	Left for IWFL

2014 Independent Scoreboard

Date	Team	Score	Team	Score		Date	Team	Score	Team	Score		Date	Team	Score	Team	Score	
3/22	UT	52	EVER	0	IE	4/12	UT	64	MHB	0	I	5/24	UT	72	TAC	0	I
3/29	UT	59	UTB	0	IE	5/3	UT	55	MHB	17	I	5/31	UT	63	RMTK	0	I
4/5	UT	58	RMTK	0	I	5/10	UT	39	SEA	20	I							

2015 Season Review

The 2015 WFA season saw a familiar face return to the top of the women's football world after nearly a decade away. The IWFL had a repeat champion, but a new entry to the league made them work a little harder for it this time. In the WSFL, Bluff City fell just shy of a third straight championship, which gave a longtime franchise their first trophy, and the W8FL saw a former eleven-player team rip the title away from the defending champ.

Leagues: 4   Teams: 90 (80)   Games: 345 (318)

Women's Football Alliance (WFA) – 2015 Season

The WFA completed half a decade as the premier league in women's football in 2015. In the East, the D.C. Divas topped the Chicago Force for their first national title game appearance in six years. The expansion Dallas Elite, taking over the territory of the defunct Dallas Diamonds, captured the title in the West in their first season. The D.C. Divas – who won the 2006 national championship in the NWFA – narrowly held off the Elite for their second national championship and their first consensus title. The nine-year gap between the Divas' two national championships in 2006 and 2015 was the longest for any team in women's football history.

Major National League   Teams: 40   Games: 173 (156.5)
Championship game result: D.C. Divas 30, Dallas Elite 26
Alliance Bowl: Central Cal War Angels 28, Atlanta Phoenix 8
Midwest Regional Alliance Bowl: Houston Power 18, Acadiana Zydeco 6

2015 WFA Standings

National Conference	W	L	PR	Before	After
New England Division					
Boston Renegades (BOS)	4	3	S	Expansion	Current
Mid-Atlantic Division					
D.C. Divas (DC)	12	0	LC	--	Current
Cleveland Fusion (CLE)	6	3	Q	--	Current
Columbus Comets (COL)	2	6	--	--	Current
Central Maryland Seahawks (CMS)	0	5	--	--	Folded
North Atlantic Division					
Jacksonville Dixie Blues (JAX)	6	3	Q	--	Current
Atlanta Phoenix (ATL)	6	5	S-B	--	Current
South Atlantic Division					
Miami Fury (MIA)	6	3	Q	--	Current
Tampa Bay Inferno (TB)	5	3	--	--	Current
Daytona Waverunners (DWR)	2	6	--	Expansion	Current
Orlando Anarchy (ORL)	0	8	--	--	Current
Great Lakes Division					
Chicago Force (CHI)	9	2	CC	--	Current
West Michigan Mayhem (WM)	6	3	Q	--	Current
Indy Crash (INDY)	5	3	--	--	Current
Detroit Dark Angels (DDA)	2	6	--	--	Current
Derby City Dynamite (DCD)	0	8	--	--	Current

Women's Football Alliance (WFA) – 2015 Season (continued)
2015 WFA Standings (continued)

American Conference
Great Plains Division
St. Louis Slam (STL)   6   3   Q   Returned from 2013   Current
Kansas City Titans (KC)   6   4   S   --   Current
Minnesota Machine (MACH)   0   8   --   --   Current

Gulf Coast Division
Acadiana Zydeco (ZYD)   5   4   B   --   Current
Tulsa Threat (TUL)   3   5   --   --   Current
Arkansas Wildcats (ARK)   2   6   --   Were Little Rock Wildcats (2013)   Current

Southwest Division
Dallas Elite (ELTE)   11   1   C   Expansion   Current
Arlington Impact (ARL)   6   3   Q   Joined from IWFL   Current
Houston Power (HPOW)   6   3   BW   --   Current
Austin Outlaws (OUT)   2   6   --   --   Current
South Texas Lady Crushers (STLC)   0   8   --   Expansion   Current

Pacific Northwest Division
Seattle Majestics (SEA)   9   1   S   --   Current
Tacoma Trauma (TAC)   7   2   Q   --   Current
Portland Shockwave (POR)   4   3   --   --   Current
Everett Reign (ER)   2   6   --   --   Current
Portland Fighting Fillies (PFF)   1   7   --   --   Current
Utah Blitz (UTB)   0   7   --   --   Current

Pacific West Division
San Diego Surge (SD)   9   2   CC   --   Current
Central Cal War Angels (CCWA)   6   3   Q-BW   --   Current
Pacific Warriors (PAC)   6   2   --   Returned from 2013   Current
Sin City Sun Devils (SCSD)   5   4   --   Expansion   Current

Pacific South Division
West Coast Lightning (WCL)   3   5   --   --   Current
Arizona Assassins (AZ)   3   5   --   --   Current
Ventura County Wolfpack (VCW)   0   8   --   Expansion   Current

2015 WFA Scoreboard

Date					Date					Date				
4/11	ATL	34	DCD	10	4/18	TB	21	MIA	13	5/2	SEA	82	UTB	0
4/11	AZ	26	VCW	6	4/18	WCL	40	VCW	0	5/2	TAC	20	PFF	10
4/11	CCWA	69	WCL	0	4/18	WM	35	MACH	13	5/2	TB	54	DWR	0
4/11	CHI	64	WM	0	4/18	ZYD	14	TUL	12	5/2	TUL	28	MHB	0 I
4/11	CLE	35	CMS	0						5/2	WM	12	DDA	0
4/11	DC	40	COL	6	4/25	ARK	28	ZYD	6					
4/11	ELTE	47	ARL	6	4/25	ARL	63	OUT	0	5/9	ATL	26	TB	19
4/11	HPOW	42	OUT	0	4/25	CCWA	75	VCW	0	5/9	AZ	20	WCL	6
4/11	INDY	18	DDA	14	4/25	CHI	70	MACH	0	5/9	CHI	62	INDY	7
4/11	MIA	61	DWR	0	4/25	CLE	35	INDY	0	5/9	CLE	46	COL	6
4/11	POR	47	EVER	20	4/25	DC	1	CMS	0	5/9	DC	1	CMS	0
4/11	SCSD	31	PHX	20 I	4/25	ELTE	78	KC	6	5/9	DDA	38	DCD	8
4/11	SD	73	PAC	31	4/25	JAX	70	DWR	10	5/9	ELTE	66	ARL	0
4/11	SEA	20	PFF	0	4/25	MIA	42	ORL	0	5/9	HPOW	28	ARK	8
4/11	STL	27	MACH	18	4/25	PAC	46	SCSD	0	5/9	JAX	1	ORL	0
4/11	TB	17	JAX	9	4/25	SEA	56	PFF	6	5/9	KC	66	TUL	14
4/11	TUL	7	ARK	0	4/25	STL	49	TUL	16	5/9	MIA	33	DWR	19
4/11	ZYD	1	STLC	0	4/25	TAC	62	UTB	0	5/9	OUT	56	STLC	0
					4/25	WM	36	DCD	0	5/9	SCSD	1	VCW	0
4/18	ARL	16	HPOW	0						5/9	SD	66	CCWA	26
4/18	BOS	57	CMS	0	5/2	ARL	82	STLC	0	5/9	SEA	56	EVER	0
4/18	CHI	67	DDA	0	5/2	ATL	1	ORL	0	5/9	STL	50	MACH	39
4/18	CLE	49	COL	0	5/2	CCWA	46	SCSD	6					
4/18	DWR	22	ORL	6	5/2	PITT	35	COL	8 I					
4/18	ELTE	53	STLC	0	5/2	DC	32	BOS	27					
4/18	ER	18	PFF	13	5/2	ELTE	76	OUT	0					
4/18	INDY	31	DCD	6	5/2	HPOW	43	ZYD	0					
4/18	JAX	24	ATL	10	5/2	INDY	32	MACH	6					
4/18	KC	35	ARK	0	5/2	KC	27	STL	17					
4/18	PAC	77	AZ	0	5/2	PAC	88	WCL	2					
4/18	SD	54	SCSD	12	5/2	POR	21	EVER	8					
4/18	TAC	39	POR	18	5/2	SD	90	AZ	6					

Continued on next page

Women's Football Alliance (WFA) – 2015 Season (continued)
2015 WFA Scoreboard (continued)

Date	Away	Pts	Home	Pts		Date	Away	Pts	Home	Pts		Date	Away	Pts	Home	Pts	
5/16	ARK	6	OUT	0		5/30	STL	52	TUL	19		6/13	ELTE	59	OUT	0	
5/16	BOS	24	CLE	20		5/30	TAC	35	EVER	0		6/13	HPOW	72	STLC	0	
5/16	CHI	74	KC	8		5/30	TB	35	DWR	0		6/13	INDY	41	DCD	0	
5/16	DC	60	COL	0		5/30	WCL	64	AZ	46		6/13	KC	54	MACH	6	
5/16	ELTE	70	HPOW	0		5/30	WM	15	DCD	0		6/13	MIA	26	TB	0	
5/16	ER	8	UTB	0		5/30	ZYD	40	ARK	0		6/13	PAC	84	AZ	6	
5/16	INDY	29	DDA	6								6/13	SCSD	12	UTB	0	
5/16	JAX	37	TB	6		6/6	ARL	46	OUT	8		6/13	SEA	44	POR	6	
5/16	MIA	12	ATL	6	*	6/6	ATL	66	DWR	0		6/13	TAC	24	EVER	13	
5/16	PAC	1	VCW	0		6/6	AZ	36	VCW	6		6/13	WCL	36	VCW	6	
5/16	POR	20	PFF	17		6/6	CCWA	59	SCSD	12		6/13	ZYD	28	TUL	20	
5/16	SCSD	57	AZ	8		6/6	CHI	60	INDY	7							
5/16	SD	65	WCL	6		6/6	DC	27	CLE	7		6/27	ATL	48	JAX	9	Q
5/16	STL	26	DCD	8		6/6	DDA	26	DCD	18		6/27	BOS	59	WM	12	Q
5/16	WM	35	MACH	13		6/6	ELTE	1	STLC	0		6/27	CHI	71	CLE	14	Q
5/16	ZYD	56	STLC	0		6/6	HPOW	22	ZYD	0		6/27	DC	48	MIA	12	Q
5/17	SEA	49	TAC	18		6/6	JAX	23	MIA	9		6/27	ELTE	54	STL	3	Q
						6/6	POR	30	PFF	12		6/27	KC	22	ARL	12	Q
5/23	JAX	1	ORL	0		6/6	SD	48	PAC	8		6/27	SD	27	CCWA	7	Q
5/23	SCSD	41	WCL	6		6/6	SEA	56	EVER	0		6/27	SEA	34	TAC	0	Q
5/23	TAC	28	PFF	13		6/6	STL	35	KC	22							
						6/6	TAC	24	UTB	0		7/11	HPOW	18	ZYD	6	B
5/30	ARL	14	HPOW	6		6/6	TB	1	ORL	0		7/11	CHI	49	BOS	18	S
5/30	BOS	30	CHI	24	*	6/6	TUL	1	ARK	0		7/11	DC	40	ATL	6	S
5/30	CLE	35	DDA	0		6/6	WM	43	COL	8		7/11	ELTE	70	KC	14	S
5/30	COL	1	CMS	0								7/11	SD	57	SEA	27	S
5/30	DC	54	ATL	0		6/13	ARL	1	ARK	0							
5/30	KC	36	MACH	22		6/13	ATL	13	JAX	6		7/25	DC	43	CHI	24	CC
5/30	MIA	1	ORL	0		6/13	CCWA	23	SD	14		7/25	ELTE	56	SD	28	CC
5/30	OUT	57	STLC	0		6/13	CHI	57	STL	0							
5/30	PAC	38	CCWA	34		6/13	CLE	42	WM	12		8/8	CCWA	28	ATL	8	B
5/30	PFF	49	UTB	22		6/13	COL	26	DDA	12		8/8	DC	30	ELTE	26	C
5/30	SD	1	VCW	0		6/13	DC	56	BOS	28							
5/30	SEA	32	POR	0		6/13	DWR	1	ORL	0							

Independent Women's Football League (IWFL) – 2015 Season

The Pittsburgh Passion continued their winning streak in the IWFL and rolled to a second straight undefeated season, but unlike the previous year, the 2015 Passion had to fight much harder to get there. In particular, the Utah Falconz, who played their inaugural 2014 season as an independent, rolled through the Western Conference and gave Pittsburgh a strong challenge in the IWFL title game. But the Pittsburgh Passion ultimately celebrated their second straight minor national championship, titles that had eluded them while playing against the sport's top competition from 2008-2013.

Minor National League   Teams: 36 (28)   Games: 132.5 (125)
Championship game result: Pittsburgh Passion 41, Utah Falconz 37
Founders Bowl: Carolina Phoenix 32, Madison Blaze 9
Affiliate Bowl: Detroit Pride 24, San Antonio Regulators 22

Independent Women's Football League (IWFL) – 2015 Season (continued)
2015 IWFL Standings

Eastern Conference	W	L	PR	Before	After
North Atlantic Division					
New York Sharks (NY)	6	3	S	--	Current
Montreal Blitz (MON)	5	2	--	--	Current
Connecticut Wreckers (CT)	2	6	--	--	Current
Mid-Atlantic Division					
Pittsburgh Passion (PITT)	11	0	LC	--	Current
Philadelphia Firebirds (PHI)	6	2	--	--	Current
Baltimore Nighthawks (BNH)	3	4	--	--	Current
Washington Prodigy (WP)	1	6	--	--	Current
South Atlantic Division					
Carolina Phoenix (CAR)	8	3	CC-BW	--	Current
Carolina Queens (CARQ)	7	3	S	--	Current
Huntsville Tigers (HUNT)	5	3	--	--	Current
Tennessee Train (TNT)	3	5	--	Joined from WFA	Current
Great Lakes Division					
Toledo Reign (TOL)	3	6	Q	Joined from WFA	Current
Wisconsin Warriors (WI)	0	7	--	--	Current
Western Conference					
Midwest Division					
Madison Blaze (MAD)	8	3	CC-B	--	Current
Minnesota Vixen (MN)	6	2	--	--	Current
Nebraska Stampede (NE)	4	3	--	Joined from WFA	Current
Iowa Crush (IA)	2	6	--	--	Current
Southwest Division					
Houston Energy (HOU)	6	1	S	--	Current
Austin Yellow Jackets (AYJ)	4	2	--	Expansion	Current
New Orleans Krewe (NOK)	0	6	--	Expansion	Current
Mountain West Division					
Utah Falconz (UT)	11	1	C	Joined from Indy	Current
Rocky Mountain Thunderkatz (RMTK)	4	3	Q	Joined from WSFL	Current
Colorado Springs Voodoo (CSV)	0	5	--	Expansion	Current
Pacific West Division					
Sacramento Sirens (SAC)	8	1	S	Joined from WFA (2013)	Current
Phoenix Phantomz (PHX)	3	4	--	--	Current
Nevada Storm (NV)	3	5	--	Joined from WFA	Current
North County Stars (NCS)	2	5	--	--	Current
California Quake (CAL)	1	6	--	--	Current
Affiliate Teams					
Detroit Pride (DETP)	3	2	BW	Expansion	Current
San Antonio Regulators (SA)	2	5	B	--	Current
Colorado Freeze (COF)	3	4	--	Expansion	Current
Central Valley Mustangs (CVM)	1	1	--	Expansion	Current
Ventura Black Widows (VBW)	0	1	--	Joined from W8FL (2013)	Current
Northeast Rebels (NER)	0	5	--	--	Folded
Knoxville Lightning (KNOX)	0	8	--	Expansion	Current
Independent Affiliate					
Mile High Blaze (MHB)	1	4	--	Joined from WSFL	Current

2015 IWFL Scoreboard

4/4	UT	32	RMTK	0	E	4/11	SCSD	31	PHX	20	I	4/18	MN	38	WI	7
						4/11	PITT	66	TOL	0		4/18	NE	28	IA	0
4/11	CAL	34	NCS	14		4/11	SA	14	NOK	0		4/18	PHX	14	NCS	0
4/11	CARQ	18	TNT	8		4/11	SAC	41	NV	6		4/18	PITT	55	PHI	8
4/11	COF	20	CSV	6		4/11	UT	1	UTB	0		4/18	RMTK	21	COF	0
4/11	HOU	45	AYJ	0								4/18	SAC	49	CAL	0
4/11	HUNT	55	KNOX	8		4/18	AYJ	30	NOK	0						
4/11	MAD	26	IA	20		4/18	BNH	29	TOL	18						
4/11	MN	22	NE	6		4/18	CAR	45	KNOX	0						
4/11	MON	36	NER	0		4/18	CARQ	16	HUNT	0						
4/11	NY	37	WP	8		4/18	CT	26	NER	0						
4/11	PHI	20	CAR	0		4/18	MHB	60	CSV	0						

Continued on next page

Independent Women's Football League (IWFL) – 2015 Season (continued)
2015 IWFL Scoreboard (continued)

Date	Away	Pts	Home	Pts	Note
4/25	CAR	19	WP	0	
4/25	DETP	17	TOL	13	
4/25	HOU	14	SA	0	
4/25	MAD	56	WI	0	
4/25	MN	14	IA	8	
4/25	NV	33	CAL	6	
4/25	NY	26	MON	19	
4/25	PHI	34	BNH	6	
4/25	RMTK	58	CSV	6	
4/25	SAC	41	PHX	0	
4/25	TNT	35	KNOX	12	
4/25	UT	57	MHB	12	
5/2	AYJ	40	SA	14	
5/2	CAR	14	CARQ	0	
5/2	HOU	54	NOK	0	
5/2	HUNT	34	TNT	16	
5/2	MAD	16	NE	8	
5/2	TUL	28	MHB	0	I
5/2	MON	42	CT	14	
5/2	NY	19	WP	0	
5/2	PHI	30	NER	0	
5/2	PITT	35	COL	8	I
5/2	SAC	59	NCS	0	
5/2	TOL	28	WI	0	
5/2	UT	60	NV	0	
5/9	CAR	40	TNT	0	
5/9	CARQ	26	BNH	0	
5/9	CT	6	NER	0	
5/9	HUNT	46	KNOX	0	
5/9	IA	44	WI	0	
5/9	MAD	14	MN	8	*
5/9	NE	49	RMTK	6	
5/9	PHI	19	WP	7	
5/9	PITT	32	NY	18	
5/9	SAC	47	CAL	0	
5/9	UT	68	NV	8	
5/16	BNH	28	CT	13	
5/16	CARQ	14	TNT	0	
5/16	DETP	26	TOL	21	
5/16	HOU	14	AYJ	12	
5/16	HUNT	52	KNOX	0	
5/16	MAD	48	IA	14	
5/16	MON	57	NER	0	
5/16	NE	14	MN	0	
5/16	NV	28	PHX	14	
5/16	PITT	41	CAR	6	
5/16	RMTK	18	COF	6	
5/16	SA	42	NOK	6	
5/16	SAC	60	NCS	0	
5/23	HUNT	42	TNT	22	
5/23	MN	40	WI	0	
5/23	MON	56	DETP	0	
5/23	NY	38	CT	0	
5/23	PHX	1	CAL	0	
5/30	AYJ	37	NOK	0	
5/30	CAR	33	WP	0	
5/30	CARQ	20	HUNT	18	
5/30	IA	36	COF	6	
5/30	MN	12	MAD	7	
5/30	MON	1	CT	0	
5/30	PHI	63	DETP	0	
5/30	PHX	28	NCS	0	
5/30	PITT	21	NY	14	
5/30	RMTK	18	MHB	13	
5/30	SAC	54	NV	7	
5/30	TNT	28	KNOX	6	
5/30	TOL	20	BNH	14	
5/30	UT	81	CAL	0	
6/6	CARQ	1	KNOX	0	
6/6	COF	26	CSV	0	
6/6	HOU	53	SA	14	
6/6	MAD	60	WI	0	
6/6	NCS	1	CAL	0	
6/6	NE	56	IA	0	
6/6	NV	43	CVM	0	
6/6	NY	14	MON	7	
6/6	PHI	33	CT	0	
6/6	PITT	63	TOL	0	
6/6	UT	67	MHB	6	
6/6	WP	24	BNH	0	
6/13	AYJ	22	SA	8	
6/13	BNH	14	CT	13	
6/13	CAR	28	CARQ	0	
6/13	CVM	1	VBW	0	N
6/13	HOU	1	NOK	0	
6/13	MAD	27	NE	24	
6/13	MN	28	IA	14	
6/13	NCS	24	NV	22	
6/13	NY	28	PHI	20	
6/13	PITT	49	WP	0	
6/13	SAC	21	PHX	18	
6/13	TNT	32	HUNT	6	
6/13	TOL	1	WI	0	
6/13	UT	58	COF	0	
6/20	COF	17	CSV	6	
6/20	TCT	66	KNOX	6	I
6/20	CARQ	20	TOL	6	Q
6/20	UT	63	RMTK	0	Q
6/27	CAR	20	CARQ	0	S
6/27	MAD	41	HOU	7	S
6/27	PITT	35	NY	28	S
6/27	UT	61	SAC	0	S
7/11	PITT	41	CAR	12	CC
7/11	UT	73	MAD	0	CC
7/24	CAR	32	MAD	9	B
7/24	DETP	24	SA	22	B
7/25	PITT	41	UT	37	C

Women's Spring Football League (WSFL) – 2015 Season

The WSFL had one of their best and most organized seasons in years in 2015, with ten clubs split into two conferences. The Tennessee Legacy, based out of Memphis, took over the territory of the defunct two-time defending champion Memphis Dynasty and immediately continued their tradition. The Legacy blew through the Southern Conference and represented Memphis in the WSFL title game for the third straight year. Yet it was the Keystone Assault, playing in their third league in four seasons, who finally reached the mountaintop and captured the first league championship in their seven-year history.

Regional League   Teams: 10 (9)   Games: 32 (29)
Championship game result: Keystone Assault 9, Tennessee Legacy 7
Freedom Bowl: Cincinnati Sizzle 26, West Virginia Wildfire 20

Women's Spring Football League (WSFL) – 2015 Season (continued)

2015 WSFL Standings

Northern Conference	W	L	PR	Before	After
Keystone Assault (KEY)	9	0	LC	Joined from IWFL	Current
New England Nightmare (NEN)	4	3	CC	Joined from IWFL	Current
Cincinnati Sizzle (CIN)	3	4	BW	Joined from WFA	Current
West Virginia Wildfire (WV)	1	6	B	Joined from W8FL	Current
Baltimore Burn (BAL)	1	4	--	--	Current

Southern Conference	W	L	PR	Before	After
TRI-CITIES THUNDER (TCT)	8	1	CC	Expansion	Current
TENNESSEE LEGACY (TNL)	7	1	C	Expansion	Current
DFW Xtreme (DFW)	2	2	--	--	Current
Atlanta Heartbreakers (ATLH)	0	6	--	--	Current

Affiliate Team	W	L	PR	Before	After
Arkansas Assassins (ARA)	0	2	--	Expansion	Current

2015 WSFL Scoreboard

Date					Date					Date					
4/18	DFW	14	ARA	8	5/16	TNL	60	ATLH	0	6/20	KEY	49	BAL	0	
4/18	TCT	84	ATLH	6	5/16	WV	24	CIN	0	6/20	NEN	39	NYK	0	
										6/20	TCT	66	KNOX	6	I
4/25	CIN	37	VALK	12	5/30	CIN	26	WV	2	6/20	TNL	64	ATLH	0	
4/25	KEY	41	BAL	0	5/30	KEY	27	NEN	6	6/27	KEY	27	CIN	0	
					5/30	TCT	58	ATLH	8	6/27	NEN	26	NYK	8	
5/2	KEY	58	WV	0						6/27	TCT	1	ATLH	0	
5/2	TCT	82	VALK	12	6/6	NEN	1	BAL	0	6/27	TNL	48	DFW	0	
5/2	TNL	57	ARA	6	6/6	TCT	1	WV	0						
					6/6	TNL	46	DFW	12	7/11	CIN	26	WV	20	B
5/9	BAL	22	WV	6	6/13	DFW	56	ATLH	44						
5/9	KEY	24	NEN	6	6/13	KEY	28	WV	0	7/18	KEY	34	NEN	0	CC
5/9	TNL	48	CIN	0	6/13	TCT	68	CIN	30	7/18	TNL	46	TCT	30	CC
5/16	NEN	36	BAL	6											
5/16	TCT	70	VALK	14						8/1	KEY	9	TNL	7	C

Women's Eights Football League (W8FL) – 2015 Season

The W8FL once again struggled with membership, competing with just four teams in 2015. The defending league champion Cape Fear Thunder made it back to the title game to face the New York Knockout, who had played the previous two seasons in the IWFL. The Knockout snapped a four-game losing streak in the W8FL title game, shutting out Cape Fear on their way to the league title.

Regional League   Teams: 4 (3)   Games: 7.5

2015 W8FL Standings

Teams	W	L	PR	Before	After
Cape Fear Thunder (CFT)	2	2	C	--	Current
New York Knockout (NYK)	2	4	LC	Joined from IWFL	Current
Southern Valkyrie (VALK)	1	3	--	Expansion	Current

Affiliate Team	W	L	PR	Before	After
Three Rivers Xplosion (3RX)	0	1	--	Returned from 2013	Current

2015 W8FL Scoreboard

Date						Date					Date				
4/18	VALK	42	CFT	14		5/2	CFT	18	NYK	12	6/20	NEN	39	NYK	0
4/25	NYK	20	3RX	18	**	5/2	TCT	82	VALK	12	6/27	NEN	26	NYK	8
4/25	CIN	37	VALK	12		5/16	TCT	70	VALK	14	8/1	NYK	28	CFT	0 C
						6/6	CFT	12	NYK	0					

All-Star Game Results

The WPFL held an all-star game in Miami after their initial barnstorming tour in 1999, but all-star games in women's football were a trend that was slow to catch on. The WAFL held what it billed as an "all-star game" in advance of their fall 2001 season, but the second postseason all-star game on record wasn't held until the WPFL organized one in 2006, a tradition they may have continued had the league not folded a year later.

The IWFL has held their annual all-star game since 2009, and the WFA followed suit the following year. This list may be incomplete, but here are 16 known all-star game results:

WPFL
1/22/2000	Central All-Stars 30, South All-Stars 6	Miami, FL
11/5/2006	American Conference 21, National Conference 14	Roswell, GA

WAFL
8/4/2001	Atlantic Coast 19, Pacific Coast 0	Henderson, NV

IWFL
7/26/2009	Eastern Conference 48, Western Conference 26	Round Rock, TX
7/25/2010	Western Conference 43, Eastern Conference 6	Round Rock, TX
7/31/2011	Eastern Conference 20, Western Conference 0	Round Rock, TX
7/28/2012	Eastern Conference 20, Western Conference 18	Round Rock, TX
8/3/2013	Western Conference 27, Eastern Conference 20	Round Rock, TX
7/26/2014	Eastern Conference 12, Western Conference 7	Rock Hill, SC
7/25/2015	Eastern Conference 29, Western Conference 12	Rock Hill, SC

WFA
7/31/2010	American Conference 13, National Conference 7	Las Vegas, NV
7/30/2011	National Conference 13, American Conference 6	Bedford, TX
8/4/2012	National Conference 21, American Conference 20	Pittsburgh, PA
8/3/2013	National Conference 48, American Conference 31	San Diego, CA
8/2/2014	National Conference 24, American Conference 7	Chicago, IL
8/8/2015	National Conference 26, American Conference 0	Los Angeles, CA

Franchise Database Legend

Every traditional women's football franchise since 1999 is listed alphabetically in the following chapter. Each franchise listing begins with a season-by-season section, and every line represents a team's season in ten columns.

The first column of season data lists the year, while the second column indicates the league in which the team participated that season. The third column states the name under which the franchise competed that season, which may be different than the overall franchise name.

When a franchise changed names, it was often a judgment call as to whether it remained the same franchise with a name change or whether it was a completely new franchise. Several factors were considered in these cases, including whether there was an ownership change and whether the newly-named team claimed the history of the previously-named team, to reach an ultimate decision. Every franchise has a distinct name except for the two editions of the Philadelphia Liberty Belles: the original Belles competed from 2001-2003, and a second (but unrelated) franchise with the same name later emerged in 2009. These two franchises are differentiated as (I) and (II).

The fourth column tallies the team's total number of wins that season, the fifth column tabulates losses, while the sixth column indicates the number of ties. If a franchise has never had a tie game in its history, the sixth column is omitted. The fourth, fifth, and sixth (if applicable) columns are totaled at the bottom of the season-by-season table to give all-time franchise win/loss records.

The seventh column of the season-by-season table displays the conference in which the team competed that season (if applicable), and the eighth column indicates the division in which the team played (if applicable). The ninth column tallies the team's finish within their division that season; if the team did not compete within a division that season, the division finish is not displayed. Occasionally, the team's conference (or even the entire league) functions as a division, in which case a team may have a division finish displayed despite having no listed division that season.

The final column in the season-by-season table notes the team's postseason results for that season. These codes are similar to those listed in the league database, but there is some additional detail where national champions are concerned. The following codes are used to indicate a team's postseason results:

NC	won major national league championship game
NC	won minor national league championship game
LC	won league championship game
C	made league championship game
CC	made conference championship game (or league semifinals)
S	made conference semifinals (or league quarterfinals)
Q	made conference quarterfinals
W	made conference wild card game
BCW	won bowl tournament
BC	made bowl tournament championship
BS	made bowl tournament semifinals
BQ	made bowl tournament quarterfinals
BW	won bowl game
B	made bowl game
--	did not make postseason

These codes can be used in combination using a hyphen, which occurs when bowl games feature teams that were previously eliminated from the playoffs. For example, the 2014 Madison Blaze are listed as CC-BW, which means they lost their conference championship game before playing in (and winning) a postseason bowl game.

After the season-by-season table, there are up to two lines of additional data. The first line indicates the city in which the team is based (which is not necessarily the exact city in which they play their home games). If a team has played any games in their history at a neutral site, their home city is then followed by a listing of the neutral sites where the team has played, with each neutral site given a separate code that is displayed in the game-by-game results table below.

The second line (if applicable) lists any additional miscellaneous notes about the franchise. These notes can include if the team is a non-existent franchise (defined as a team that forfeited all their games in team history, which means that the team existed in name only) or if the team forfeited all of its games in a given season.

Predecessor and successor franchises are also indicated in the notes section. These are instances where a team in a particular area folds and a new team quickly launches within the same geographical territory. Currently, teams are only listed as predecessors or successors if there is no overlap between the existences of the two franchises; for example, the San Diego Surge are not listed as a successor to the So Cal Scorpions, because both teams competed during the 2011 season.

The two major mergers in women's football history are also listed in the franchise notes section: the Massachusetts Mutiny-Boston Rampage merger that formed the Boston Militia, and the Kansas City Tribe-Kansas City Spartans merger that created the Kansas City Titans. A third major merger between the Portland Fighting Fillies and Portland Shockwave to form the Portland Fighting Shockwave has been announced for the 2016 season.

Every franchise then has a table that lists all-time game-by-game results. Each line represents a game, and lines have been blocked where possible to indicate seasons. Every game line has up to seven columns.

The first game line column lists the date of the game, while the second column indicates if the game was played at home (H), away (A), or at a neutral location (if game location information is available). If the same was played at a neutral site, it is coded (N) and the location of the game is included in the franchise notes section above.

The third column lists the name of the opponent; the name the opposing team used that season is what is listed, not necessarily the name of the franchise overall. The fourth column notes whether the game was a win (W), loss (L), or tie (T); the fifth column tallies the team's points scored; and the sixth column indicates the number of points allowed.

Franchise Database Legend

The final game line column provides additional detail about the contest (where applicable) using a game code, similar to the codes listed in the league database. The following game codes are used in the last column of the game-by-game results table:

*	indicates overtime
**	indicates double overtime
***	indicates triple overtime
E	indicates preseason exhibition game
I	indicates interleague game
N	indicates forfeit by a team that forfeited all of its games that season
C	indicates league championship game
CC	indicates conference championship game (or league semifinal game)
S	indicates conference semifinal game (or league quarterfinal game)
Q	indicates conference quarterfinal game
W	indicates conference wild card game
B	indicates bowl game
BC	indicates bowl tournament championship game
BS	indicates bowl tournament semifinal game
BQ	indicates bowl tournament quarterfinal game

These codes can also be used in combination. For example, IE indicates a preseason interleague exhibition, and CC* denotes a conference championship game that was decided in overtime.

Finally, where available, franchise listings conclude with all-time player registers. These player registers alphabetically list the women who were publicly included on a roster for that team in a given season. Publicly available information was used to construct the team rosters; most 2015 rosters have been obtained, while player rosters from previous seasons vary by the information made available by teams and leagues.

The NWFA listed player rosters from 2004-2008 (although the 2004 rosters may be incomplete). The WFA has player rosters available for most teams dating back to the league's founding in 2009. The IWFL only displays player rosters for the 2014 and 2015 seasons, and several IWFL teams lack rosters even from those seasons. Finally, several individual teams have maintained player rosters on their individual websites. All this information has been aggregated into franchise player registers.

Nicknames have only been included when it might be needed to aid in player identification. Player registers include all players listed by teams on their roster for a given season, not players who actually suited up for the team that season. Teams often list a retired player on its roster to secure her spot should she rejoin the team later in the year, and in many instances, more than one team in an area will list the same player on both of their rosters as they compete for a player's services. Player registers are constrained in their accuracy by the information provided by the teams and leagues themselves.

Misspellings of player names have been corrected to the best of the author's ability, but all errors and omissions of both games and players are his and his alone. While not every women's football roster could be located, the following player registers list more than 10,000 women who have graced the roster of a women's football team over the past two decades. Without question, these athletes deserve to be recognized and remembered as pioneers of the burgeoning sport of women's football.

Alternate Franchise Name List

There have been 292 women's football franchises that have competed in major U.S women's football; these teams are listed alphabetically in the following section. However, some of these franchises have operated under multiple names. Here is a listing of the women's football teams that are listed under a different franchise name:

Antelope Valley Bombers *(see All Valley Attack)*
Antelope Valley Attack *(see All Valley Attack)*
Arizona Venom *(see Tucson Wildfire)*
Arizona Wildfire *(see Tucson Wildfire)*
Atlanta Ravens *(see Atlanta Xplosion)*
Baton Rouge Wildcats *(see Louisiana Fuel)*
Biloxi Herricanes *(see Gulf Coast Herricanes)*
Boston Rampage *(see Bay State Warriors)*
California Lynx *(see Pacific Warriors)*
Central Florida Anarchy *(see Orlando Anarchy)*
Colorado Sting *(see Rocky Mountain Thunderkatz)*
Columbus Flames *(see Columbus Comets)*
Connecticut Crushers *(see Connecticut Crush)*
Des Moines Courage *(see Iowa Crush)*
Detroit Danger *(see Detroit Demolition)*
East Tennessee Rhythm *(see Tennessee Venom)*
Emerald Coast Sharks *(see Emerald Coast Barracudas)*
Fayetteville Thunder *(see Cape Fear Thunder)*
Gulf Coast Riptide *(see Pensacola Power)*
Harrisburg Angels *(see Central PA Vipers)*
Kentucky Valkyries *(see Kentucky Force)*
Knoxville Summit *(see Knoxville Tornadoes)*
Little Rock Wildcats *(see Arkansas Wildcats)*
Maine Rebels *(see Southern Maine Rebels)*
Memphis Soul *(see Memphis Dynasty)*
Memphis WTF *(see Memphis Dynasty)*
Minnesota Vixens *(see Minnesota Vixen)*
Missouri Avengers *(see Missouri Prowlers)*
Missouri Phoenix *(see Kansas Phoenix)*
New Hampshire Freedom *(see Manchester Freedom)*
New Orleans Spice *(see New Orleans Blaze)*
North Texas Fury *(see Dallas Rage)*
Northeast Rebels *(see Southern Maine Rebels)*
Orange County Breakers *(see Southern California Breakers)*
Orlando Starz *(see Orlando Mayhem)*
Panama City Beach Rumble *(see Emerald Coast Barracudas)*
Philadelphia Phoenix *(see Philadelphia Firebirds)*
Rhode Island Intensity *(see New England Intensity)*
Rhode Island Riptide *(see New England Intensity)*
Shreveport Shockhers *(see Shreveport Aftershock)*
South Bend Hawks *(see Indiana Thunder)*
Southwest Michigan Jaguars *(see West Michigan Mayhem)*
Tacoma Majestics *(see Seattle Majestics)*
Tampa Bay Pirates *(see Tampa Bay Inferno)*
Tennessee Valley Tigers *(see Huntsville Tigers)*
Tree Town Spitfire *(see Toledo Spitfire)*
Tri-State Bruisers *(see West Virginia Bruisers)*
Tulsa Eagles *(see Tulsa Threat)*

Franchise Game-By-Game Records, 1999-2015

Acadiana Zydeco

Year	League	Name	W	L	Conference	Division	DF	PR
2010	WFA	Acadiana Zydeco	0	8	American	South	3	--
2011	WFA	Acadiana Zydeco	1	7	American	Gulf	3	--
2012	WFA	Acadiana Zydeco	4	4	National	Division 8 (Gulf Coast)	2	--
2013	WFA	Acadiana Zydeco	3	6	American	Division 7 (Gulf Coast)	2	W
2014	WFA	Acadiana Zydeco	3	5	American	Gulf Coast	2	--
2015	WFA	Acadiana Zydeco	5	4	American	Gulf Coast	1	B
		Total	**16**	**34**				

Based in: Opelousas, LA

Date	H/A	Opponent	Result	Score		Date	H/A	Opponent	Result	Score	
4/17/2010	A	New Orleans Blaze	L	0	33	4/6/2013	H	New Orleans Mojo	W	40	0
4/24/2010	A	Memphis Soul	L	6	30	4/13/2013	A	Houston Power	L	0	52
5/1/2010	H	Austin Outlaws	L	0	68	4/27/2013	A	New Orleans Mojo	L	12	32
5/8/2010	H	New Orleans Blaze	L	0	27	5/4/2013	H	Little Rock Wildcats	W	30	22
5/15/2010	A	Houston Power	L	0	63	5/11/2013	A	Tulsa Threat	L	8	9
5/22/2010	H	Memphis Soul	L	0	34	5/25/2013	A	Little Rock Wildcats	L	0	30
6/5/2010	A	Memphis Soul	L	6	20	6/1/2013	H	Austin Outlaws	L	0	48
6/19/2010	H	New Orleans Blaze	L	6	17	6/8/2013	H	Tulsa Threat	W	26	8
						6/15/2013	A	St. Louis Slam	L	0	72 W
4/9/2011	H	New Orleans Blaze	L	8	14						
4/16/2011	H	Memphis WTF	L	14	54	4/5/2014	A	Louisiana Jazz	W	18	6
4/30/2011	A	New Orleans Blaze	L	0	19	4/12/2014	H	Houston Power	L	8	47
5/7/2011	A	Little Rock Wildcats	L	8	38	4/19/2014	A	Tulsa Threat	L	8	30
5/21/2011	H	Houston Power	L	0	1	5/3/2014	A	Austin Outlaws	L	0	34
6/4/2011	A	Tulsa Eagles	W	44	0	5/17/2014	A	Houston Power	L	0	1
6/11/2011	H	Austin Outlaws	L	0	1	5/24/2014	H	Louisiana Jazz	W	1	0
6/18/2011	A	Houston Power	L	0	33	5/31/2014	H	Austin Outlaws	L	6	46
						6/7/2014	H	Tulsa Threat	W	28	27
4/14/2012	A	Tallahassee Jewels	L	6	8						
4/21/2012	H	Gulf Coast Riptide	L	0	22	4/11/2015	A	South Texas Lady Crushers	W	1	0
4/28/2012	A	Arkansas Wildcats	L	8	18	4/18/2015	H	Tulsa Threat	W	14	12
5/5/2012	H	Memphis Dynasty	W	12	6	4/25/2015	A	Arkansas Wildcats	L	6	28
5/12/2012	A	Gulf Coast Riptide	W	28	0	5/2/2015	A	Houston Power	L	0	43
6/2/2012	H	Arkansas Wildcats	W	16	8	5/16/2015	H	South Texas Lady Crushers	W	56	0
6/9/2012	A	Houston Power	L	8	14	5/30/2015	H	Arkansas Wildcats	W	40	0
6/16/2012	H	Tallahassee Jewels	W	18	6	6/6/2015	H	Houston Power	L	0	22
						6/13/2015	A	Tulsa Threat	W	28	20
						7/11/2015	A	Houston Power	L	6	18 B

Acadiana Zydeco Player Register (2010-2015)

Alexander, Amber (2012-2014)
Alexander, Kenitha (2010)
Anderson, Nicole (2015)
Arceneaux, Eugena (2014)
Avory, Clare (2012-2013)
Baptiste, Jalessa Jean (2012-2013)
Ben, Mia (2010-2015)
Benefield, Lisa (2015)
Bernard, Shannon (2010-2011, 2014)
Bickham, Shonetel (2014)
Bonnet, Paulaina (2014)
Brittingham, Kadedra (2010-2011)
Broussard, Shelia (2011)
Carney, Dana (2014)
Chaisson, Nia (2014)
Charles, Michelle (2013)
Charles, Tasha (2014-2015)
Clark, Yolanda (2015)
Collins, Latasha (2011)
Conques, Megan (2012)
Crimmins, Amanda (2014)
Davis, Natasha (2013)
Dixon, Renata (2010)
Eastling, Toni (2015)
Edgerson, Cashara (2010)
Edwards, Hannah (2013)
Edwards, Roshundra (2010)
Ford, Mecca (2014)
Francis, Alethea (2014)
Freeman Jones, Shelly (2012-2015)
Gabriel, Tiffany (2014-2015)
Gallien, Trahnieceia (2012)
Garatie, Esther (2010)
George, Talanna (2014-2015)
Goins, Kimberly "Kim" (2014-2015)
Greene, Jennifer (2014-2015)
Gregoire, Lisa (2015)
Guidry, Anika (2010)
Guillory, Kim (2012-2013)
Hardy, Allison (2010)
Hardy, Justine (2010)
Haynes, Tyra (2010)
Heisser, Tiffany (2014-2015)
Housley, Cotina (2014-2015)
Housley, Rachael (2013-2015)
Iglus, Keyanna (2013)
Irvine, Marquisha (2012-2013, 2015)
Jackson, Shandrell (2014)
Jackson, Stephanie (2015)
John, Crystal (2013)
Johnson, Erika (2014-2015)
Johnson, Lauren (2010-2011)
Johnson, Shameka (2014)
Jones, Kewanna (2010)
Jones, Kimberly (2015)
Jones, Shelly (2011)
Jordan, Apphia (2014)
Judice, Molly (2012)
Lang, Cassandra (2010)

Continued on next page

Acadiana Zydeco Player Register (continued)

Lazare, Nikki (2012)
Lemalle, Nikki (2014)
Lemelle, Jessie (2010-2011)
Lewis, Takeisha "Keisha" (2011-13, '15)
Little, Maureen (2013)
Lomas, Temika (2010)
Mair, Talia (2010)
Manning, Tamra (2011-2014)
Martinez, Anequa (2010-2014)
Mason, Anastacia (2010)
Mason, Jeannine (2010)
McCoy, Lauren (2010)
Mitchell, Nicole (2010)
Mouton, Amber (2011-2015)
Noel, Jada (2013)
Ortego, Lauren (2012)
Palmer, Leslie (2015)
Pawlovsky, Sandy (2011-2015)
Perry, Jessica (2012)
Philips, Courtney (2013)
Primeaux, Ashley (2015)
Rosette, Madelyn (2012-2013)
Sassnet, Bridget (2010)
Senegal, Becky (2013-2015)
Senegal, Vanessa (2010)
Sias, Allison (2012-2013)
Singleton, Azelia (2011)
Slaughter, Ayana (2012-2015)
Smith, Chaun (2015)
Smith, Deidra (2015)
Smith, Deondra (2012-2013)
Smith, Sirrena (2015)
Spivey, Erica (2010-2013)
Stafford, Audry (2015)
Stansberry, Dashanti (2011-2013)
Steward, Ashley (2012)
Sumlar, Cherise (2010-2015)
Thigpen, Monica (2010-2014)
Thompson, Sheronica (2012-2013, 2015)
Turner, Tristian (2010)
Vaughan, Jordyn (2015)
Volter, Tia (2013)
Walker, Ashley (2013)
Washington, Sherriate (2010)
White, Stacie (2010)
Wilson, Shondalynn (2013-2014)
Woods, April (2014-2015)
Woods, Ebony (2013)
Wright, Ayla (2014)
Young, Artenzia (2010)

Alabama Renegades

Year	League	Name	W	L	Conference	Division	DF	PR
2000	NWFA	Alabama Renegades	3	3	--	--	--	--
2001	NWFA	Alabama Renegades	5	3	Southern	--	2	--
2002	NWFA	Alabama Renegades	7	2	--	Central	1	S
2003	NWFA	Alabama Renegades	7	4	Southern	Central	2	S
2004	NWFA	Alabama Renegades	6	3	Southern	Gulf Coast	2	--
2005	NWFA	Alabama Renegades	5	3	Southern	--	7	--
2006	NWFA	Alabama Renegades	4	4	Southern	Southeast	3	--
2007	NWFA	Alabama Renegades	3	5	Southern	Central	3	--
2008	NWFA	Alabama Renegades	2	6	Southern	East	4	--
		Total	**42**	**33**				

Based in: Huntsville, AL
Notes: Succeeded by IWFL2's Tennessee Valley Tigers [Huntsville Tigers]

Date	H/A	Opponent	W/L	PF	PA	
10/21/2000	A	Nashville Dream	L	15	30	
4/21/2001	A	Pensacola Power	L	0	20	
4/28/2001	H	Nashville Dream	W	46	6	
5/12/2001	A	Tennessee Venom	W	20	13	
5/19/2001	H	Tennessee Venom	W	27	6	
5/26/2001	H	Chattanooga Locomotion	W	32	12	
6/2/2001	A	Pensacola Power	L	6	7	
6/9/2001	A	Nashville Dream	W	28	21	
6/23/2001	H	Pensacola Power	L	0	3	
4/20/2002		Chattanooga Locomotion	W	40	12	
5/4/2002		Nashville Dream	L	14	24	
5/18/2002		Knoxville Summit	W	74	0	
5/25/2002		Atlanta Leopards	W	32	21	
6/8/2002		Chattanooga Locomotion	W	22	12	
6/15/2002		Knoxville Summit	W	54	12	
6/22/2002		Nashville Dream	W	34	19	
6/29/2002		Atlanta Leopards	W	22	21	
7/6/2002	A	Pensacola Power	L	8	12	S
3/22/2003		Chattanooga Locomotion	L	8	10	E
4/12/2003	H	Nashville Dream	W	8	6	
4/19/2003	H	Atlanta Leopards	W	30	0	
4/26/2003	A	Chattanooga Locomotion	L	26	28	
5/3/2003	H	Asheville Assault	W	20	19	
5/17/2003	A	Knoxville Summit	W	41	0	
5/24/2003	A	Atlanta Leopards	W	42	6	
5/31/2003	H	Tennessee Venom	W	49	0	
6/14/2003	A	Pensacola Power	L	0	35	
6/28/2003	H	Asheville Assault	W	27	13	Q
7/12/2003	A	Pensacola Power	L	12	34	S
4/17/2004	A	Pensacola Power	L	7	56	
4/24/2004	A	New Orleans Blaze	L	7	28	
5/1/2004	H	Muscle Shoals Smashers	W	19	0	
5/8/2004	H	Gulf Coast Herricanes	W	46	0	
5/15/2004	A	Atlanta Leopards	W	55	0	
5/22/2004	H	Pensacola Power	L	18	42	
5/29/2004	A	Muscle Shoals Smashers	W	56	10	
6/5/2004	A	Gulf Coast Herricanes	W	35	7	
6/12/2004	H	New Orleans Blaze	W	21	12	

Continued on next page

Alabama Renegades Game-By-Game Results (continued)

Date	H/A	Opponent	Result	Score		Date	H/A	Opponent	Result	Score	
4/16/2005	A	Nashville Dream	L	6	20	4/21/2007	A	East Tennessee Rhythm	L	8	14
4/30/2005	A	Asheville Assault	W	7	0	4/28/2007	A	Chattanooga Locomotion	L	0	52
5/14/2005	H	Tennessee Venom	W	36	6	5/5/2007	H	Nashville Dream	W	21	7
5/21/2005	H	Chattanooga Locomotion	L	6	20	5/19/2007	A	Dallas Rage	L	8	35
5/28/2005	A	Pensacola Power	L	6	59	5/26/2007	H	East Tennessee Rhythm	W	33	0
6/4/2005	H	Knoxville Tornadoes	W	38	2	6/2/2007	H	Chattanooga Locomotion	L	0	62
6/11/2005	A	Atlanta Leopards	W	1	0	6/9/2007	H	Dallas Rage	W	1	0
6/18/2005	H	Emerald Coast Sharks	W	48	0	6/16/2007	A	Nashville Dream	L	0	6
4/22/2006	A	Emerald Coast Barracudas	W	48	0	4/19/2008	A	Chattanooga Locomotion	L	0	44
4/29/2006	A	Knoxville Tornadoes	W	1	0	4/26/2008	A	Pensacola Power	W	60	58
5/6/2006	H	Pensacola Power	L	6	22	5/3/2008	H	Cincinnati Sizzle	W	46	14
5/13/2006	A	Kentucky Karma	L	0	14	5/17/2008	A	Kentucky Karma	L	26	27
5/27/2006	H	Emerald Coast Barracudas	W	30	8	5/24/2008	H	Chattanooga Locomotion	L	6	34
6/10/2006	A	Pensacola Power	L	0	18	5/31/2008	H	Pensacola Power	L	8	40
6/17/2006	H	Kentucky Karma	W	6	2	6/14/2008	H	Kentucky Karma	L	0	14
6/24/2006	A	Chattanooga Locomotion	L	6	35	6/21/2008	A	Cincinnati Sizzle	L	6	43

Alabama Renegades Player Register (2004-2008)

Alber, Marty (2006-2008)
Arlain, Nicole (2005)
Azode, Jamie (2007-2008)
Banghart, Ella (2008)
Barfield, Carly (2005-2006)
Beasley, Darina (2007-2008)
Boon, Sarah (2008)
Borden, Kim (2006)
Buckley, Katie (2004-2005)
Byas, Michelle (2005)
Byrd, Nancy (2004-2008)
Campbell, Lori (2005-2008)
Chillers, Nancy (2004, 2006)
Clark, Kim (2007)
Colbert, Tiffany (2008)
Cousar, Tera (2006-2007)
Cutting, Meredith (2005-2006)
Cyr, Char (2005-2008)
Dobbs, Leslie (2006-2007)
Eatman, Dionne (2005-2008)
Everett, Wendy (2004-2005, 2007)
Fields, Ashley (2008)
Finley, Teresa (2004-2007)
Flynt, Jamie (2005-2006)
Fossett, Faye (2007)
Frazier, Jamey (2007-2008)
Futrell, Megan (2005)
Gadson, Monika (2004-2005)
Garth, Janai (2007)
Gholston, Bird (2005-2008)
Green, Link (2008)
Hammond, Shana (2005)
Hardeman, Amy (2006-2008)
Hardy, Kelly (2005-2008)
Hardy, Kira (2006-2008)
Harvey, Stephanie (2005-2008)
Haun, Destarte (2008)
Henderson, Candiss (2005)
Hendrix, Danielle (2005-2006)
Herrin, Jane (2007-2008)
Hill, Elizabeth (2005, 2007-2008)
Howard, Hayley (2008)
Hughes, Kira (2007)
Hunter, Nikie (2004-2008)
Kennedy, Vicki (2004-2007)
Kerby, Sandra (2005-2008)
Lott, Michelle (2008)
Massey, Sonya (2005-2008)
Moody, Ashley (2005-2008)
Moore, Kimberly (2005)
Murray, Sarah (2007-2008)
Nall, Nicole (2004-2005)
Nickey, Tina (2007)
Palmer, Stephanie (2008)
Patton, Jennifer (2005-2008)
Phillips, Cheronda (2008)
Porch, Karen (2005)
Pruett, Sherry (2006-2008)
Sanders, Dana (2005-2008)
Sansom, Lori Bob (2005)
Scarvey, Kim (2005)
Smith, J.D. (2008)
Solomon, Shante (2005-2006)
Steger, Kim (2007)
Sullivan, Carmela (2007)
Sullivan, Carmelesia (2007-2008)
Summers, Amber (2007)
Terry, Tammy (2006)
Thomas, Kris (2008)
Tindle, Michelle (2004-2005)
Uselton, Tricia (2007)
Wakefield, Carson (2008)
Williams, Ryan (2004)
Wissel, Tammy (2004, 2006)

Alabama Slammers

Year	League	Name	W	L	Conference	Division	DF	PR
2001	WAFL	Alabama Slammers	2	7	Atlantic	Central	2	--

Based in: Birmingham, AL
Notes: Succeeded by WAFL-WFA's Birmingham Steel Magnolias

Date	H/A	Opponent	Result	Score		Date	H/A	Opponent	Result	Score	
10/27/2001	H	New Orleans Voodoo Dolls	L	0	6	12/15/2001	A	Indianapolis Vipers	L	8	44
11/10/2001	A	New Orleans Voodoo Dolls	L	0	14	12/22/2001	H	Jacksonville Dixie Blues	L	8	43
11/17/2001	A	Indianapolis Vipers	L	6	52	1/12/2002	H	Tampa Bay Force	W	1	0
12/1/2001	H	New Orleans Voodoo Dolls	W	12	6	1/19/2002	H	Indianapolis Vipers	L	0	36
12/8/2001	A	Orlando Fire	L	0	36						

Albany Ambush

Year	League		Name	W	L	Conference	Division	DF	PR
2004	WPFL	X	Albany Ambush	4	0	--	--	--	--
2005	WPFL		Albany Ambush	4	6	National	East	2	--
2006	WPFL	X	Albany Ambush	0	3	--	--	--	--
			Total	**8**	**9**				

Based in: Albany, NY
Notes: Preceded by IWFL's Albany Night-Mares

8/7/2004	H	New York Dazzles	W	53	0
8/22/2004	H	New York Dazzles	W	33	0
10/2/2004	A	New York Dazzles	W	23	0
10/16/2004	A	Syracuse Sting	W	10	6
7/30/2005	H	Delaware Griffins	W	35	24
8/13/2005	H	Empire State Roar	W	14	13
8/20/2005	H	Delaware Griffins	W	38	22
8/27/2005	A	Empire State Roar	L	0	21
9/10/2005	A	Toledo Reign	L	6	48
9/17/2005	A	Cape Fear Thunder	L	8	20
9/24/2005	H	New York Dazzles	L	16	33
10/1/2005	A	New York Dazzles	L	6	20
10/8/2005	A	Delaware Griffins	L	0	6
10/15/2005	H	Toledo Reign	W	20	14
7/22/2006	A	New England Intensity	L	0	26
7/29/2006	H	Empire State Roar	L	0	36
8/5/2006	A	Carolina Queens	L	0	1

Albany Night-Mares

Year	League	Name	W	L	Conference	Division	DF	PR
2002	IWFL	Albany Night-Mares	1	6	Eastern	--	7	--
2003	IWFL	Albany Night-Mares	1	5	Eastern	Mid-Atlantic	3	--
		Total	**2**	**11**				

Based in: Albany, NY
Notes: Succeeded by WPFL's Albany Ambush

5/4/2002	Montreal Blitz	L	13	24
5/11/2002	Bay State Warriors	L	9	14
5/18/2002	Bay State Warriors	L	6	14
6/1/2002	New York Sharks	L	6	34
6/8/2002	Montreal Blitz	L	13	21
6/15/2002	Detroit Blaze	W	22	0
6/22/2002	New Hampshire Freedom	L	7	12
4/26/2003	H	Philadelphia Liberty Belles (I)	L	0	14
5/3/2003	A	New Hampshire Freedom	L	0	19
5/10/2003	H	New York Sharks	L	0	98
5/17/2003	H	Detroit Blaze	W	34	28
5/31/2003	A	New York Sharks	L	0	41
6/14/2003	H	New Hampshire Freedom	L	0	29

All Valley Attack

Year	League		Name	W	L	Conference	Division	DF	PR
2005	NWFA	X	Antelope Valley Bombers	0	1	--	--	--	--
2006	NWFA	X	Antelope Valley Attack	4	4	--	Western	2	--
2007	NWFA		All Valley Attack	3	5	Southern	West	3	--
			Total	**7**	**10**				

Based in: Long Beach, CA

5/21/2005	H	Orange County Breakers	L	12	18	
4/22/2006	H	Tucson Wildfire	W	42	0	
4/29/2006	A	Orange County Breakers	L	28	38	
5/20/2006	H	Orange County Breakers	L	12	14	
6/3/2006	A	Orange County Breakers	L	7	44	
6/10/2006	H	Tucson Wildfire	W	20	6	
6/24/2006	A	Tucson Wildfire	W	28	16	
7/1/2006	H	Orange County Breakers	L	6	19	
7/8/2006	A	Tucson Wildfire	W	30	6	
4/14/2007	A	Orange County Breakers	L	6	29	
4/21/2007	H	Phoenix Prowlers	L	0	62	
4/28/2007		Arizona Venom	W	1	0	N
5/12/2007	A	Orange County Breakers	L	0	32	
5/19/2007	A	Phoenix Prowlers	L	0	52	
5/26/2007		Arizona Venom	W	1	0	N
6/9/2007	H	Orange County Breakers	L	0	40	
6/16/2007		Arizona Venom	W	1	0	N

All Valley Attack Player Register (2005-2007)

Adams, Sarah (2005-2007)
Bailey, Tracy (2005-2006)
Bennett, Cyndee (2007)
Bermudas, Jibriallah (2006)
Berthiaume, Johnnie (2007)
Billet, Valerie (2005-2007)
Biscoe, Brittaney (2006)
Blackwell, Sheila (2006-2007)
Blair, Shayla (2005-2007)
Bowman, Dalphana (2005-2007)
Coke, Tiffany (2006)
Courseault, Telana (2005-2006)
Dolberry, Christina (2005-2006)
Freeman, Alicia (2005-2007)
Fujarte, Maria (2006-2007)
Gamble, Jessica (2007)
Garcia, Angie (2006)
Gonzalez, Elizabeth (2006)
Hall, Michelle (2007)
Harris, Kelli (2005)
Henry, Kim (2007)
Hollingsworth, Jennifer (2005-2007)
Johnson, Courtney (2006-2007)
Kennett, Kathy (2005)
Kolvoord, Jennifer (2005-2006)
Koury-Stoop, Trisha (2007)
Kulesza, Amber (2005)
Larson, Christy (2005)
Ligon, Suzy (2005-2007)
Loete, Stephanie (2007)
Luna, Armida (2005-2007)
MacLeod, Nancy (2006)
Maglione, Jackie (2005)
McGee, Esther (2005-2007)
Medlock, Rena (2006-2007)
Monroe, Susan (2007)
Mosher, Jeni (2006-2007)
Osby, Rhonda (2005)
Phipps, Margie (2005-2007)
Podesta, Joni (2007)
Reid, Linda (2007)
Reinard, Malia (2005-2007)
Ripley, Rhonda (2007)
Robinson, Blair (2005-2006)
Shields, Ayesha (2005-2006)
Simpkins, Ashley (2007)
Speir, Kristi (2006)
Stegall, Jenn (2007)
Stokes, Estella (2005-2006)
Sugleris, Lizz (2007)
Suzuki, Hiroko "Betty" (2006-2007)
Tenbrink, Chris (2006-2007)
Turner, Michelle (2006-2007)
Webb, Robin (2005-2006)
Young, Cherrita (2005-2007)

Arizona Assassins

Year	League	Name	W	L	Conference	Division	DF	PR
2010	WFA	Arizona Assassins	3	5	American	South Pacific	3	--
2011	WFA	Arizona Assassins	6	3	American	Southwest	2	--
2012	WFA	Arizona Assassins	0	8	American	Division 17 (South Pacific)	4	--
2013	WFA	Arizona Assassins	0	7	American	Division 13 (South Pacific)	5	--
2014	WFA	Arizona Assassins	0	7	American	Pacific South	3	--
2015	WFA	Arizona Assassins	3	5	American	Pacific South	2	--
		Total	**12**	**35**				

Based in: Phoenix, AZ
Notes: Preceded by Phoenix Prowlers

Date	H/A	Opponent	Result	PF	PA
4/17/2010	H	Las Vegas Showgirlz	L	6	26
4/24/2010	A	San Diego Sting	W	52	0
5/1/2010	A	Pacific Warriors	L	26	34
5/8/2010	H	San Diego Sting	W	42	0
5/15/2010	A	Las Vegas Showgirlz	L	8	48
5/22/2010	H	Pacific Warriors	L	8	20
6/5/2010	H	San Diego Sting	W	24	6
6/19/2010	A	Las Vegas Showgirlz	L	0	31
4/9/2011	H	Silver State Legacy	W	21	8
4/16/2011	A	So Cal Scorpions	W	39	0
4/30/2011	H	San Diego Sting	W	47	6
5/7/2011	A	San Diego Surge	L	20	55
5/21/2011	H	So Cal Scorpions	W	1	0
6/4/2011	A	San Diego Sting	W	41	6
6/11/2011	A	Silver State Legacy	L	7	22
6/18/2011	H	Pacific Warriors	W	26	6
7/23/2011	A	Utah Jynx	L	20	34 I
4/14/2012	A	Las Vegas Showgirlz	L	7	32
4/21/2012	H	Pacific Warriors	L	0	54
4/28/2012	H	San Diego Surge	L	0	64
5/5/2012	A	Silver State Legacy	L	0	44
5/19/2012	H	San Diego Sting	L	0	13
6/2/2012	A	Pacific Warriors	L	0	61
6/9/2012	A	San Diego Surge	L	0	62
6/16/2012	H	Silver State Legacy	L	8	19
4/6/2013	A	West Coast Lightning	L	0	40
4/13/2013	H	Pacific Warriors	L	8	66
4/20/2013	A	San Diego Surge	L	6	69
4/27/2013	H	San Diego Sting	L	0	28
5/4/2013	H	Utah Jynx	L	6	80
5/11/2013	A	Las Vegas Showgirlz	L	8	65
6/8/2013	A	San Diego Sting	L	0	22
4/5/2014	H	West Coast Lightning	L	6	34
4/19/2014	H	San Diego Surge	L	0	68
4/26/2014	A	Las Vegas Showgirlz	L	0	54
5/10/2014	A	San Diego Surge	L	0	101
5/24/2014	A	West Coast Lightning	L	0	54
5/31/2014	H	Mile High Blaze	L	0	51 I
6/7/2014	H	Las Vegas Showgirlz	L	12	22
4/11/2015	H	Ventura County Wolfpack	W	26	6
4/18/2015	A	Pacific Warriors	L	0	77
5/2/2015	A	San Diego Surge	L	6	90
5/9/2015	H	West Coast Lightning	W	20	6
5/16/2015	H	Sin City Sun Devils	L	8	57
5/30/2015	A	West Coast Lightning	L	46	64
6/6/2015	A	Ventura County Wolfpack	W	36	6
6/13/2015	H	Pacific Warriors	L	6	84

Arizona Assassins Player Register (2010-2015)

Aguilar, Jessica (2010)
Allen, Adrianne (2012)
Allen, Crystal (2013)
Altaha, Taeyana (2014-2015)
Anderson, Miranda (2015)
Anderson, Susan (2010)
Atkinson, Ashley (2011)
Augustine, Dallas (2011)
Avila, Daniela (2012)
Baker, Jeannine (2012)
Barkman, Elise (2011)
Beaty, LaQuanda (2012)
Begay, Carm (2015)
Bell, Shonna (2010-2011)
Belliard, Desiree (2010-2011)
Benjamin, Tiana (2015)
Brunson, Twanna (2010-2011)
Bryan, Beth (2013)
Calusine, Jennifer (2011)
Canty, Charlene (2010)
Canty, Selina (2010)
Carpenter, Debra (2012)
Cerventes, Melissa (2013)
Chandler, Jai (2011)
Cipres, Isela (2015)
Clay, Johleda (2010)
Coffman, Shana (2012)
Cole, Allison (2012)
Coleman, Zhanelle (2015)
Cortese, Elle (2012-2014)
Curley, Geri (2013)
Defer, Julia (2011)
DeLaTorre, Chris (2015)
Denetdeel, Kim (2012)
DeSha, Lyla (2012)
Devane, Averil (2014)
Dodge, Dechelle (2015)
Doefer, Kalenne (2013)
Domenicucci, Debbie (2010-2012)
Donnelly, Glennis (2010-2011)
Drago, Kyi (2011)
D'Rossi, Angel (2011)
Duarte, Andrea (2013)
Earl, Dontranee (2015)
Ehiman, Owen (2015)
Enriquez, Carmen (2014)
Espinoza, Christina (2014-2015)
Feretti, Omega (2014)
Fierro, Yvonne (2015)
Foley, Danielle (2012)
Fonseca, Katie (2010-2011)
Forman, Dev (2013-2014)
Fragozo, Dalia (2014)
Fuentes, Jamie (2013)
Gamble, Becky (2010, 2012)
Garcia, Brianna (2014)
Gault, Anna (2014)
Gonzalez, Arlene (2010)
Grayson, Quewanda (2012)
Graziano, Leigha (2013)
Guerra, Andi (2015)
Hahn, Stephanie (2011)
Hall, Latonya (2015)
Hartley, Amber (2011)
Henry, Chris (2015)
Hodge, Brittany (2011)
Hoke, Kim (2010, 2012)
Huerta, Claudia (2010-2012)
Jackson, B.J. (2015)
Johnson, Cari (2015)
Kagi, Jenny (2011)
Khaivilay, Soulinh (2013)
King, Portia (2013)
Laubert, Amber (2011)
Leerhoff, Grace (2014-2015)
Liciaga, Erika (2012)
Lombardo, Maureen (2010)
Long, Heidi (2010-2012)
Lozano, Mary (2013)
Luckett, Lorena (2014)
Lukavsky, Sabrina (2012, 2014)
Lusk, Jennifer (2012)
Madrid, Daniela (2012)
Martinez, Maria (2010)
Martinez, Rebecca (2012)
McCawley, Shana (2010)
McLaughlin, Tami (2012-2014)
McNickles, Prestina (2013)
Mendoza, Georgina (2013)
Miley, Cynthia (2012)
Mongold, Brenda (2015)
Montiel, Nicole (2013)
Moreno, Katherine (2013)
Mousseaux, Amanda (2015)
Mullings, Alicia (2013)
Munksgard, Michelle (2010-2011)
Munoz, Christina (2014)
Nevell, Annie (2012)
O'Bryan, Erin (2011)
Ogunware, Caroline (2011)
Oliphant, Mariah (2014)
Olson, Tammi (2014)
Omo, Desrae (2010)
Ortiz, Imani (2013-2014)
Paredes, Wendy (2013)
Peter, Lala (2012)
Peterson, Diana (2012-2013)
Phillips, Cherri (2011)
Pritikin, Michelle (2010, 2012)
Refuerzo, Mimi (2010-2011)
Reyes, Angela (2010)
Richards, Dee (2010-2015)
Rodis, Mel (2012)
Rodriguez, Sonya (2012-2014)
Romero, Georgina (2015)
Rushforth, Jessica (2010)
Rushing, Kelly (2010)
Salazar, Jasmin (2014)
Schoolcraft, Yvonne (2010)
Schudt, Angelic (2010-2012)
Silvas, Andrea (2013)
Smith, LaShelle (2011)
Smith, Melissa (2013)
Soto, Monica (2015)
Stewart, Alana (2015)
Suchta, Rochelle (2012)
Swanson, Andrea (2015)
Taecker, Jeseyria (2012)
Tafoya, Victoria "Vic" (2014-2015)
Tanski, Shannon (2014)
Thompson, LeeAnn (2011)
Thompson, Taryn (2012-2013)
Torres, Amanda (2014)
Trevino, Summer (2014)
Tuffield, Michelle (2012)
Ubina, Paloma (2014)
Utley, Sara (2011)
Walker, Asiah (2015)
Walker, Shena (2012)
Wallace, Angel (2014)
Waln, Troi (2015)
Weber, Amanda (2010-2011)
West, Sarah (2010)
Whitlemore, Cassandra (2013)
Wildman, Lianna (2014)
Wiley, Abby (2014)
Williams, Raquel (2014)
Wise, Tamea (2013)
Wright, Monique (2013)
Yonnie, Lavinia (2010, 2012)

Arizona Caliente

Year	League	Name	W	L	Conference	Division	DF	PR
2001	WAFL	Arizona Caliente	8	4	Pacific	South	2	CC
2002	WAFC	Arizona Caliente	8	2	Southern	--	1	C
2003	WPFL	Arizona Caliente	8	2	American	West	3	--
2004	WPFL	Arizona Caliente	6	4	American	West	2	--
2005	WPFL	Arizona Caliente	3	4	American	West	3	--
		Total	**33**	**16**				

Based in: Phoenix, AZ
Notes: Succeeded by NWFA's Phoenix Prowlers

Franchise Game-By-Game Records, 1999-2015

Arizona Caliente Game-By-Game Results

Date	H/A	Opponent	Result	PF	PA	Notes
11/3/2001	A	San Diego Sunfire	L	12	14	
11/10/2001	H	Minnesota Vixen	W	12	7	I
11/17/2001	H	California Quake	L	6	19	
11/24/2001	H	San Diego Sunfire	L	7	24	
12/8/2001	A	Los Angeles Lasers	W	6	0	
12/15/2001	H	San Diego Sunfire	W	12	10	
12/29/2001	H	Los Angeles Lasers	W	50	28	
1/5/2002	A	San Francisco Tsunami	W	14	12	
1/12/2002	A	California Quake	W	26	22	
1/19/2002	A	Sacramento Sirens	W	18	15	
2/2/2002	A	Seattle Warbirds	W	24	16	S
2/10/2002	A	California Quake	L	12	16	CC
9/14/2002	H	Oakland Banshees	W	36	12	
9/21/2002	A	California Quake	W	32	16	
9/28/2002	H	San Diego Nitrous	W	56	0	
10/5/2002	H	San Francisco Stingrayz	W	27	0	
10/17/2002	A	Pacific Blast	L	12	36	
10/19/2002	A	Pacific Blast	W	23	6	
11/9/2002	H	California Quake	W	26	0	
11/16/2002	A	San Diego Nitrous	W	1	0	
11/23/2002	H	Pacific Blast	W	1	0	CC
12/7/2002	A	Sacramento Sirens	L	20	59	C
8/9/2003	A	Los Angeles Amazons	W	45	0	
8/16/2003	A	So Cal Scorpions	W	16	14	
8/23/2003	A	Arizona Knighthawks	W	27	6	
8/30/2003	H	San Diego Sunfire	W	38	20	
9/6/2003	H	So Cal Scorpions	W	14	0	
9/13/2003	A	Long Beach Aftershock	L	19	25	
9/20/2003	H	Los Angeles Amazons	W	46	0	
9/27/2003	H	Long Beach Aftershock	L	27	32	
10/4/2003	H	Arizona Knighthawks	W	44	12	
10/18/2003	A	San Diego Sunfire	W	41	24	
7/31/2004	A	So Cal Scorpions	W	41	6	
8/14/2004	A	Los Angeles Amazons	W	35	0	
8/21/2004	H	Long Beach Aftershock	L	14	27	
8/28/2004	A	So Cal Scorpions	W	14	7	
9/4/2004	A	Long Beach Aftershock	L	21	24	
9/11/2004	H	Long Beach Aftershock	W	17	12	
9/18/2004	A	Dallas Diamonds	L	30	56	
9/25/2004	H	So Cal Scorpions	W	22	6	
10/2/2004	H	Dallas Diamonds	L	13	35	
10/9/2004	H	Los Angeles Amazons	W	14	3	
8/20/2005	H	Los Angeles Amazons	L	8	20	
8/27/2005	A	New Mexico Burn	W	38	0	
9/10/2005	A	So Cal Scorpions	L	0	43	
9/17/2005	A	Los Angeles Amazons	L	0	20	
10/1/2005	H	Los Angeles Amazons	L	14	20	
10/15/2005	A	Long Beach Aftershock	W	38	0	
10/22/2005	H	New Mexico Burn	W	50	7	

Arizona Knighthawks

Year	League	Name	W	L	Conference	Division	DF	PR
2002	WPFL	Arizona Knighthawks	8	2	American	--	2	CC
2003	WPFL	Arizona Knighthawks	1	8	American	West	7	--
		Total	9	10				

Based in: Phoenix, AZ

Date	H/A	Opponent	Result	PF	PA	Notes
4/13/2002	A	Boise Xtreme	W	57	0	IE
8/3/2002		Los Angeles Amazons	W	46	6	
8/10/2002		Austin Rage	W	48	33	
8/17/2002		Houston Energy	L	0	1	
8/31/2002		Dallas Diamonds	W	21	19	
9/7/2002		Los Angeles Amazons	W	27	0	
9/28/2002		Austin Outlaws	W	1	0	I
10/5/2002		Los Angeles Amazons	W	41	0	
10/12/2002		Los Angeles Amazons	W	16	0	
10/26/2002		Houston Energy	L	0	6	CC
8/9/2003	H	Long Beach Aftershock	L	6	33	
8/16/2003	A	Los Angeles Amazons	L	6	26	
8/23/2003	H	Arizona Caliente	L	6	27	
8/30/2003	A	Long Beach Aftershock	L	0	54	
9/13/2003	H	Los Angeles Amazons	W	14	7	
9/20/2003	A	So Cal Scorpions	L	14	27	
9/27/2003	A	San Diego Sunfire	L	0	50	
10/4/2003	A	Arizona Caliente	L	12	44	
10/11/2003	H	San Diego Sunfire	L	14	20	

Arizona Titans

Year	League	Name	W	L	Conference	Division	DF	PR
2001	IWFL	Arizona Titans	0	2	--	--	--	--
2002	AFWL	Arizona Titans	2	10	--	--	4	CC
		Total	2	12				

Based in: Phoenix, AZ

Arizona Titans Game-By-Game Results

Date	H/A	Opponent	W/L	PF	PA	Note
9/8/2001	H	New York Sharks	L	0	20	I
10/7/2001	A	Houston Energy	L	7	55	I
8/10/2002		Houston Energy	L	0	39	I
9/14/2002		Austin Rage	W	1	0	I
9/21/2002	H	Los Angeles Lasers	L	0	66	
9/28/2002		Dallas Diamonds	L	22	27	I
9/28/2002	A	Long Beach Aftershock	L	0	63	
10/12/2002	H	San Diego Sunfire	L	6	42	
10/19/2002	A	San Francisco Tsunami	L	0	1	
11/2/2002	H	Long Beach Aftershock	L	0	12	
11/9/2002	A	San Diego Sunfire	L	0	30	
11/16/2002	H	San Francisco Tsunami	W	1	0	
11/23/2002	A	Los Angeles Lasers	L	0	56	
12/7/2002	A	San Diego Sunfire	L	0	55	CC

Arkansas Assassins

Year	League	Name		W	L	Conference	Division	DF	PR
2015	WSFL	X	Arkansas Assassins	0	2	--	--	--	--

Based in: Little Rock, AR
Notes: Preceded by Arkansas Banshees

Date	H/A	Opponent	W/L	PF	PA
4/18/2015	A	DFW Xtreme	L	8	14
5/2/2015	H	Tennessee Legacy	L	6	57

Arkansas Banshees

Year	League	Name	W	L	Conference	Division	DF	PR
2012	IWFL	Arkansas Banshees	3	4	Eastern	South Atlantic	3	--
2013	WSFL	Arkansas Banshees	2	2	--	--	2	C
2014	WSFL	Arkansas Banshees	3	4	Western	--	1	C
		Total	**8**	**10**				

Based in: Little Rock, AR **Neutral site:** Little Rock, AR (N)
Notes: Succeeded by Arkansas Assassins

Date	H/A	Opponent	W/L	PF	PA	Note
4/14/2012	A	Arlington Impact	L	18	44	
4/21/2012		Kansas Phoenix	W	60	8	I
5/5/2012	A	Houston Energy	L	14	52	
5/12/2012	H	Arlington Impact	L	0	1	
5/19/2012	A	Memphis Belles	W	40	30	
6/2/2012	H	Memphis Belles	W	1	0	
6/16/2012		Houston Energy	L	30	56	
4/20/2013	H	Huntsville Tigers	W	34	8	
5/4/2013	H	Memphis Dynasty	L	26	34	
5/11/2013	A	Nashville Smashers	W	46	12	
6/29/2013	A	Memphis Dynasty	L	12	32	C
4/12/2014	H	Memphis Dynasty	L	32	38	*
4/19/2014	A	Atlanta Heartbreakers	W	65	26	
4/26/2014	H	Baltimore Burn	L	0	1	
5/3/2014	A	Memphis Dynasty	L	14	30	
6/7/2014	A	DFW Xtreme	W	42	6	
7/19/2014	H	DFW Xtreme	W	1	0	CC
7/26/2014	N	Memphis Dynasty	L	12	34	C

Arkansas Rampage

Year	League	Name	W	L	Conference	Division	DF	PR
2011	WSFL	Arkansas Rampage	4	2	--	--	--	--
2012	WSFL	Arkansas Rampage	2	7	National	--	2	CC
		Total	**6**	**9**				

Based in: Rogers, AR

Date	H/A	Opponent	W/L	PF	PA	Note
5/7/2011	H	Topeka Mudcats	W	36	6	
5/14/2011	A	Kansas Phoenix	W	1	0	
5/21/2011	H	Kansas Phoenix	W	1	0	
5/28/2011	H	Memphis WTF	L	0	36	I
6/18/2011	A	Kansas Phoenix	W	34	14	
10/1/2011		Memphis WTF	L	0	44	IE
4/21/2012	A	DFW Xtreme	L	0	48	
5/5/2012	A	Huntsville Tigers	L	0	32	
5/19/2012	A	Arkansas Wildcats	L	0	1	
5/19/2012	A	Kansas City Spartans	L	0	1	
6/2/2012	H	Huntsville Tigers	L	0	41	
6/23/2012	A	Kansas Phoenix	W	8	0	
6/30/2012	H	DFW Xtreme	L	8	52	
7/7/2012	H	Kansas Phoenix	W	22	12	
7/21/2012	A	DFW Xtreme	L	8	54	CC

Arkansas Wildcats

Year	League	Name	W	L	Conference	Division	DF	PR
2011	WFA	Little Rock Wildcats	3	5	American	Southeast	2	--
2012	WFA	Arkansas Wildcats	5	4	American	Division 13 (South Central)	1	W
2013	WFA	Little Rock Wildcats	5	4	American	Division 7 (Gulf Coast)	1	W
2015	WFA	Arkansas Wildcats	2	6	American	Gulf Coast	3	--
		Total	15	19				

Based in: Little Rock, AR

Date	H/A	Opponent	W/L	PF	PA		Date	H/A	Opponent	W/L	PF	PA	
4/2/2011	H	Tulsa Eagles	W	44	0		4/6/2013	A	Lone Star Mustangs	L	14	20	
4/9/2011	A	Memphis WTF	L	14	38		4/20/2013	H	New Orleans Mojo	W	28	0	
4/16/2011	A	New Orleans Blaze	L	14	22		4/27/2013	H	Tulsa Threat	L	8	28	
5/7/2011	H	Acadiana Zydeco	W	38	8		5/4/2013	A	Acadiana Zydeco	L	22	30	
5/14/2011	H	Dallas Diamonds	L	0	64		5/18/2013	H	Tulsa Threat	W	56	28	
6/4/2011	A	Lone Star Mustangs	L	0	40		5/25/2013	H	Acadiana Zydeco	W	30	0	
6/11/2011	H	Memphis WTF	L	8	30		6/1/2013	A	Tulsa Threat	W	28	16	
6/18/2011	A	Tulsa Eagles	W	1	0		6/8/2013	A	New Orleans Mojo	W	20	0	
							6/15/2013	A	Austin Outlaws	L	0	35	W
4/14/2012	A	Memphis Dynasty	L	0	32								
4/28/2012	H	Acadiana Zydeco	W	18	8		4/11/2015	A	Tulsa Threat	L	0	7	
5/5/2012	A	Dallas Diamonds	L	0	109		4/18/2015	H	Kansas City Titans	L	0	35	
5/12/2012	H	Tulsa Threat	W	36	16		4/25/2015	H	Acadiana Zydeco	W	28	6	
5/19/2012	H	Arkansas Rampage	W	1	0		5/9/2015	H	Houston Power	L	8	28	
6/2/2012	A	Acadiana Zydeco	L	8	16		5/16/2015	A	Austin Outlaws	W	6	0	
6/9/2012	A	Tulsa Threat	W	34	14		5/30/2015	A	Acadiana Zydeco	L	0	40	
6/16/2012	H	Memphis Dynasty	W	22	14		6/6/2015	H	Tulsa Threat	L	0	1	
6/23/2012	A	Lone Star Mustangs	L	0	70	W	6/13/2015	A	Arlington Impact	L	0	1	

Arkansas Wildcats Player Register (2011-2013, 2015)

Alfred, Charmaine (2011-2013, 2015)
Anderson, Latoya (2015)
Anderson, Valencia (2011)
Appleberry, Kady (2013)
Bady, Starry (2013, 2015)
Bailey, Raquel (2012)
Ball, Dana (2011)
Beaver, Jessica (2012-2013)
Blaylock, Lisa (2015)
Brewer, Keidra (2015)
Broadway, Nicole (2015)
Brown, Brandi (2013)
Bruce, Crystal (2011-2012)
Bumpous, Lydia (2012-2013)
Butram, Madison (2013)
Carney, Summer (2015)
Clegg, April (2015)
Crowe, Lolisa (2011)
Curtis, Stacy (2015)
Daniels, Ashley (2012)
Davis, LaRhonda "Rhonda" (2012-13, '15)
Davis, Shantella (2012-2013, 2015)
Dawdy, Elisa (2012-2013)
Dennler, Jennifer (2012)
Dukes, Brandy (2015)
Dupree, Amanda (2011-2013)
Eakin, Sarah (2013, 2015)
Ellis, Brandi (2013)
Foster, Jackie (2011)
Freeman, Jasmine (2015)
Glaze, Tracee (2011)
Goldie, Deidre (2011)
Goode, Kelsey (2012-2013, 2015)
Gregson, Carmen (2013)
Griffin, Shanice (2011)
Gulley, Carmen (2012)
Harmon, Amanda (2013)
Hawkins, Erika (2015)
Hayes, Sommer (2011-2013)
Hil, Loryn (2011)
Hill, Whitney (2011-2013)
Hopkins, Brittany (2015)
Horton, Cortnei (2011-2013)
Jernigan, Kerri (2012-2013)
Johns, Ursula (2015)
Keele, April (2015)
King, Jennifer (2011-2013)
Larkin, Orlonda (2011-2012)
Lewis, Misty (2011-2013, 2015)
Marshall, Tawanta (2015)
Massey, Vickie (2011)
Mauldin, Nova-Dawn (2012)
McGuire, Judy Beth (2012)
McKinney, Andrea (2011)
Meyer, Heather (2011)
Miller, Starlyte (2012)
Mills, Alex (2011)
Moore, Shawn (2015)
Nooner, Tisha (2012)
Norman, Hannah (2015)
Norman, L.J. (2015)
Patterson, Dee Dee (2015)
Potter, Jennifer (2011-2012)
Reinbolt, Brittany (2011, 2013)
Romero, Brittani (2015)
Scott, Jerricka (2015)
Scott, Kimberly (2012)
Scott, Sadie (2015)
Shorter, Melissa (2012)
Sims, Latoya (2015)
Smith, Kaila (2012-2013)
Stone, Portia (2013)
Thomas, Hannah (2011-2013)
Tyler, Yesenia (2012)
Vega, Mari (2011)
Walker, Barbara (2011)
Walters, Paige (2012-2013)
Weldon, Holly (2015)
White, Dominique (2011)
Williams, Erica (2012-2013, 2015)
Williams, Raquel (2013, 2015)
Williamson, Monique (2011)
Wilson, Amy (2015)
Wood, Max (2012-2013, 2015)
Workman, Rachel (2012)
Young, Kendra (2012-2013)

Arlington Impact

Year	League	Name	W	L	Conference	Division	DF	PR
2012	IWFL	Arlington Impact	6	3	Eastern	South Atlantic	2	BQ
2013	IWFL	Arlington Impact	6	4	Western	Southwest	2	BC
2014	IWFL	Arlington Impact	5	3	Western	Southwest	2	--
2015	WFA	Arlington Impact	6	3	American	Southwest	2	Q
		Total	23	13				

Based in: Arlington, TX

Neutral site: Round Rock, TX (N)

Date	H/A	Opponent	Result	Score	Notes
4/14/2012	H	Arkansas Banshees	W	44 18	
4/21/2012	A	Houston Energy	L	0 35	
5/5/2012	H	Memphis Belles	W	42 0	
5/12/2012	A	Arkansas Banshees	W	1 0	
5/26/2012	H	Houston Energy	L	22 38	
6/2/2012	A	Colorado Sting	W	14 2	
6/9/2012		Colorado Sting	W	30 0	
6/16/2012		Memphis Belles	W	1 0	
6/30/2012		Carolina Phoenix	L	6 33	BQ
4/27/2013	A	DFW Xtreme	W	40 32	
5/4/2013	H	Houston Energy	L	8 73	
5/18/2013	A	Houston Energy	L	8 55	
5/25/2013	H	DFW Xtreme	W	48 6	
6/1/2013	A	San Antonio Regulators	W	28 0	
6/15/2013	H	San Antonio Regulators	W	36 0	
6/22/2013	H	Houston Energy	L	8 52	
7/13/2013	H	Tucson Monsoon	W	1 0	BQ
7/20/2013	H	Minnesota Vixen	W	18 14	BS
8/2/2013	N	Montreal Blitz	L	8 55	BC
4/12/2014	A	San Antonio Regulators	W	61 0	
4/19/2014	H	Houston Energy	L	12 41	
4/26/2014	H	Memphis Dynasty	W	50 0	I
5/3/2014	A	Houston Energy	L	14 24	
5/10/2014	A	Austin Outlaws	L	18 28	I
5/17/2014	H	Missouri Thundercats	W	1 0	N
5/31/2014	A	San Antonio Regulators	W	1 0	
6/7/2014	A	Houston Energy	W	26 7	
4/11/2015	H	Dallas Elite	L	6 47	
4/18/2015	A	Houston Power	W	16 0	
4/25/2015	A	Austin Outlaws	W	63 0	
5/2/2015	A	South Texas Lady Crushers	W	82 0	
5/9/2015	A	Dallas Elite	L	0 66	
5/30/2015	H	Houston Power	W	14 6	
6/6/2015	H	Austin Outlaws	W	46 8	
6/13/2015	H	Arkansas Wildcats	W	1 0	
6/27/2015	H	Kansas City Titans	L	12 22	Q

Arlington Impact Player Register (2014-2015)

Allen, Desiree (2014)
Blakely, Kinickie (2014-2015)
Bland, Sharron (2014)
Bridges, Courtney (2015)
Cooper, Shawn (2014)
Davis, Darby (2014)
Dixon, Renata (2015)
Dye, Takesha (2014)
Dyer, Valarie (2014)
Esparza, Fabiana (2015)
Ford, Amira (2014-2015)
Foster, Charnika (2014-2015)
Fruean, Renee "Lilo" (2014)
Gardner, Brandi (2014)
Gill, LaTerrany (2015)
Grant, Yolanda (2014)
Guy, T.J. (2015)
Haley, Courtney (2014-2015)
Hardwell, DeTesha (2015)
Heilman, Amanda (2014)
Hill, Cassidy (2015)
Hill, Tiffany (2014)
Ikeda, Chelsea (2014)
Johnson, Nakia (2014)
Johnson, Nikita (2014-2015)
Kania, Francinea (2015)
Kelley, Tamra (2014)
Landry, Elizabeth "Liz" (2014)
Law, Katelynn (2015)
Lawless, Ashley (2015)
Lawless, Autumn (2015)
Lee, Whitney (2014-2015)
May, Rachel (2014)
Maytubby, Etta (2014-2015)
McDonald, Teoka (2014)
Morrisette, Remeisha (2014-2015)
Oliver, Allison (2014)
Peck, Missy (2014)
Penn, Natasha (2014)
Perez, Fabiana (2014)
Polk, Teresa (2014-2015)
Richardson, Amber (2014-2015)
Ricks, D'Angela (2014-2015)
Roach, Krystal (2014)
Robinson, Fancy (2014-2015)
Rogers, Jeaniel "Jai" (2014-2015)
Rutlin, Courtnei (2014-2015)
Smith, Jasmine (2014)
Southall, Stephanie (2014-2015)
Stout, Lyndi (2014)
Thompson, Tiffany (2014)
Toney, Sydell (2015)
Walker, Lucinda (2014)
Ware, Shane "Betina" (2014-2015)
Warner, Yumi (2014)
Warren, Jasmine (2015)
Washington, Ashley (2014)
Weyman, Jessie (2014)
Williams, Marquita (2015)
Williams, Tracie (2014)
Wynn, Tanika (2015)
Young, Tatanisha (2015)

Asheville Assault

Year	League	Name	W	L	Conference	Division	DF	PR
2002	NWFA	Asheville Assault	4	4	--	Mid-Atlantic	3	--
2003	NWFA	Asheville Assault	5	4	Southern	Central	3	Q
2004	NWFA	Asheville Assault	5	3	Southern	South	3	Q
2005	NWFA	Asheville Assault	4	4	Southern	--	8	--
		Total	18	15				

Based in: Asheville, NC

Asheville Assault Game-By-Game Results

Date	H/A	Opponent	W/L	Score		Date	H/A	Opponent	W/L	Score	
4/20/2002		Tennessee Venom	W	36 14		4/24/2004	A	Tennessee Venom	W	19 6	
4/27/2002	H	D.C. Divas	L	0 22		5/1/2004	A	Atlanta Leopards	W	25 0	
5/4/2002		Tennessee Venom	W	48 28		5/8/2004	H	Nashville Dream	L	14 35	
5/18/2002		Baltimore Burn	L	0 21		5/15/2004	A	Tennessee Venom	W	25 12	
5/25/2002	A	D.C. Divas	L	0 54		5/29/2004	H	Tennessee Venom	W	13 12	
6/8/2002		Tennessee Venom	W	22 0		6/5/2004	A	Chattanooga Locomotion	L	0 49	
6/15/2002		Baltimore Burn	L	0 40		6/12/2004	H	Atlanta Leopards	W	19 0	
6/22/2002		Tennessee Venom	W	1 0		6/26/2004	A	Pensacola Power	L	0 60	Q
4/12/2003	A	Chattanooga Locomotion	L	12 15	*	4/16/2005	H	Chattanooga Locomotion	L	6 12	*
4/19/2003	H	Tennessee Venom	W	26 0		4/23/2005	A	Knoxville Tornadoes	W	39 0	
5/3/2003	A	Alabama Renegades	L	19 20		4/30/2005	H	Alabama Renegades	L	0 7	
5/10/2003	H	Atlanta Leopards	W	47 0		5/21/2005	H	Knoxville Tornadoes	W	46 0	
5/17/2003	A	Tennessee Venom	W	54 0		5/28/2005	A	Chattanooga Locomotion	L	0 20	
5/24/2003	H	Knoxville Summit	W	48 21		6/4/2005	A	Nashville Dream	L	0 42	
5/31/2003	A	Nashville Dream	W	21 20		6/11/2005	H	Tennessee Venom	W	22 14	
6/14/2003	H	Chattanooga Locomotion	L	15 22		6/18/2005	A	Atlanta Leopards	W	1 0	
6/28/2003	A	Alabama Renegades	L	13 27	Q						

Asheville Assault Player Register (2004-2005)

Aiken, Shannon (2005)
Arnold, Rebecca (2005)
Ashe, Shannon (2005)
Bogdal, Mo (2005)
Bruegger, Laura (2004)
Buchanan, Sandra (2004-2005)
Cantrell, Renee (2004-2005)
Cox, Charley (2004-2005)
Dakoski, Jennifer (2005)
Darby, Angela (2004)
Dill, Amy (2004-2005)
English, Sarah (2005)
Goins, Heather (2004-2005)
Guffey, Nicki (2004)
Hartman, Eva (2004)
Hollifield, Heidi (2004-2005)
Hurt, Karoline (2005)
Lantz, Sue (2005)
Long, Anita (2005)
McCoy, Jay (2005)
McGinnis, Nikki (2004-2005)
Niedermaier, Amy (2005)
Ramey, Angel (2005)
Roberts, Dawn (2005)
Scott, Rita (2005)
Searcy, Christina (2005)
Shepard, Tracy (2005)
Smith, Traci (2004)
Thompson, Sonja (2004-2005)
Vasquez, Danny (2005)
Wells, Ashley (2005)
Womack, Jamie (2004)

Atlanta Heartbreakers

Year	League	Name	W	L	Conference	Division	DF	PR
2011	WFA	Atlanta Heartbreakers	4	5	National	Atlantic	1	Q
2013	WSFL	Atlanta Heartbreakers	0	3	--	--	4	--
2014	WSFL	Atlanta Heartbreakers	0	4	Eastern	--	3	--
2015	WSFL	Atlanta Heartbreakers	0	6	Southern	--	4	--
		Total	**4**	**18**				

Based in: Atlanta, GA

Date	H/A	Opponent	W/L	Score		Date	H/A	Opponent	W/L	Score	
4/2/2011	H	Gulf Coast Riptide	L	6 64		4/5/2014	A	Memphis Dynasty	L	0 1	
4/16/2011	H	Miami Fury	L	0 72		4/12/2014	H	DFW Xtreme	L	14 30	
4/30/2011	A	Carolina Raging Wolves	W	28 14		4/19/2014	H	Arkansas Banshees	L	26 65	
5/14/2011	H	Savannah Sabers	W	22 19		4/26/2014	H	DFW Xtreme	L	0 60	
5/21/2011	H	Carolina Raging Wolves	W	32 14							
6/4/2011	A	Palm Beach Punishers	L	6 34		4/18/2015	H	Tri-Cities Thunder	L	6 84	
6/11/2011	A	Savannah Sabers	W	28 25		5/16/2015	H	Tennessee Legacy	L	0 60	
6/18/2011	A	Orlando Anarchy	L	0 28		5/30/2015	A	Tri-Cities Thunder	L	8 58	
6/25/2011	A	Indy Crash	L	0 47	Q	6/13/2015	H	DFW Xtreme	L	44 56	
						6/20/2015	A	Tennessee Legacy	L	0 64	
4/6/2013	A	Memphis Dynasty	L	0 46		6/27/2015	A	Tri-Cities Thunder	L	0 1	
4/20/2013	H	Memphis Dynasty	L	6 50							
4/27/2013	H	Huntsville Tigers	L	16 19							

Atlanta Heartbreakers Player Register (2011, 2013, 2015)

Asbury, Yvonne (2013)
Barnes, Sabrina (2011)
Barton, Alexandria (2011)
Binford, Verna (2011)
Brown, Jalana (2015)
Clark, Blair (2011)
Dailey, Moneka (2015)
Davis, Angalique (2013, 2015)
Dunn-Shropshire, Anita (2015)
Echols, Tatyana (2013, 2015)
Edwards-Houston, Shannon (2013, 2015)
Griffin, Maya (2015)
Hargraves, Lanisha (2011)
Harps, Quintessa (2011)
Heard, Shawn (2013, 2015)
Henderson, Barbara (Rogers) (2013, 2015)
Hines, Deitra (2011)
Hornberger, Kelli (2011)
Howard, Shatora (2013, 2015)
James, Chashaveyon (2013, 2015)
Jones, Ashley (2013, 2015)
Jones, Corliss (2013, 2015)
Jones, Julisa (2013, 2015)
Klier-Bouler, Bena (2011)
Knox, Marchail (2013)
Lyman, Jenny (2011)
Maloney, Onecia (2013)
Marshall, Keyatta (2013)
McCullum, Topaz (2013, 2015)
McDuffie, Opal "Opie" (2011)
McLeod, Mia (2011)
Morales, Christine (2011)
Murphy, Tishia (2015)
Pitts, Quintella (2013)
Rainey, Mesha (2015)
Rittenberry, Brittany (2015)
Warnell, Wilnesha (2015)
Welch, Nik (2011)
White, Lawanna (2015)
Williams, Shantrell (2011)
Yarbough, Theresa (2011)

Atlanta Leopards

Year	League	Name	W	L	Conference	Division	DF	PR
2002	NWFA	Atlanta Leopards	2	6	--	Central	4	--
2003	NWFA	Atlanta Leopards	0	8	Southern	Central	7	--
2004	NWFA	Atlanta Leopards	0	7	Southern	South	5	--
2005	NWFA	Atlanta Leopards	0	7	Southern	--	16	--
		Total	**2**	**28**				

Based in: Atlanta, GA

Date	H/A	Opponent	Result	PF	PA
4/20/2002		Nashville Dream	L	12	26
4/27/2002		Chattanooga Locomotion	L	6	8
5/18/2002		Chattanooga Locomotion	L	0	14
5/25/2002		Alabama Renegades	L	21	32
6/1/2002		Knoxville Summit	W	79	0
6/8/2002		Knoxville Summit	W	77	0
6/15/2002		Nashville Dream	L	14	16
6/29/2002		Alabama Renegades	L	21	22
4/12/2003	H	Knoxville Summit	L	0	34
4/19/2003	A	Alabama Renegades	L	0	30
4/26/2003	H	Pensacola Power	L	0	81
5/3/2003	H	Chattanooga Locomotion	L	0	56
5/10/2003	A	Asheville Assault	L	0	47
5/24/2003	H	Alabama Renegades	L	6	42
6/7/2003	A	Tennessee Venom	L	14	46
6/14/2003	A	Nashville Dream	L	0	54
4/3/2004	H	Chattanooga Locomotion	L	0	68
4/24/2004	A	Nashville Dream	L	0	65
5/1/2004	H	Asheville Assault	L	0	25
5/15/2004	H	Alabama Renegades	L	0	55
5/22/2004	A	Chattanooga Locomotion	L	0	62
6/5/2004	H	Tennessee Venom	L	13	29
6/12/2004	A	Asheville Assault	L	0	19
4/23/2005	H	Tennessee Venom	L	0	50
4/30/2005	A	Knoxville Tornadoes	L	8	30
5/21/2005	A	Gulf Coast Herricanes	L	0	1
5/28/2005	H	Nashville Dream	L	0	1
6/4/2005	A	Chattanooga Locomotion	L	0	1
6/11/2005	H	Alabama Renegades	L	0	1
6/18/2005	H	Asheville Assault	L	0	1

Atlanta Leopards Player Register (2004-2005)

Ashrita, Samyyah (2005)
Balenciaga, Budah (2005)
Bridges, Morneike (2004)
Burton, Keyondra (2005)
Chambers, Monica (2005)
Corley, Sherry (2004)
Farmer, Ashanti (2004)
Floyd, Darlene (2005)
Gennovario, Jack (2004)
Harvey, Nikki (2005)
Jackson, Mary (2005)
Jackson, Michelle (2005)
Jones, Kathy (2005)
Jones, Kenya (2004)
Knight, Keisha (2004)
McDonald, Jenenne (2005)
Miller, Janique (2005)
Moore, Martha (2005)
OlSkool, Yrese (2005)
Phillips, Cheronda (2004)
Phillips, Lox (2005)
Preyer, Torie (2004)
Reynolds, Bridge (2004)
Richardson, Misti (2005)
Rivera, Vicki (2005)
Siget, Kristen (2004)
Stephens, Angeline (2005)
Taylor, Jo (2004)
Thompson, Lakeshia (2005)
Thorp, Samantha (2005)
Tugler, Keysha (2004)
Watters, LaTonya (2005)
Wilford, Diania (2005)
Woodward, Terri (2004)
Wynn, Desmona (2005)
Yarn, Janelle (2005)

Atlanta Phoenix

Year	League	Name	W	L	Conference	Division	DF	PR
2012	WFA	Atlanta Phoenix	8	2	National	Division 7 (Southeast)	1	Q
2013	WFA	Atlanta Phoenix	10	1	National	Division 5 (Southeast)	1	S
2014	WFA	Atlanta Phoenix	7	3	National	Southeast	1	Q
2015	WFA	Atlanta Phoenix	6	5	National	North Atlantic	2	S-B
		Total	**31**	**11**				

Based in: Atlanta, GA **Neutral site:** Los Angeles, CA (N)

Date	H/A	Opponent	Result				Date	H/A	Opponent	Result			
4/14/2012	H	Carolina Raging Wolves	W	48	7		4/5/2014	H	Tampa Bay Inferno	L	25	32	
4/21/2012	A	Miami Fury	W	48	32		4/12/2014	A	Tennessee Train	W	34	0	
4/28/2012	H	Savannah Sabers	W	57	13		4/19/2014	H	Miami Fury	W	12	8	
5/5/2012	A	Carolina Raging Wolves	W	62	0		4/26/2014	A	Jacksonville Dixie Blues	W	12	10	
5/12/2012	A	Memphis Dynasty	W	19	6		5/10/2014	H	Savannah Sabers	W	56	6	
5/19/2012	H	Tampa Bay Inferno	L	25	26		5/17/2014	A	D.C. Divas	L	0	44	
6/2/2012	H	Gulf Coast Riptide	W	1	0		5/31/2014	H	Louisiana Jazz	W	1	0	
6/16/2012	A	Savannah Sabers	W	41	14		6/7/2014	A	Daytona Breakers	W	53	13	
6/23/2012	H	Tallahassee Jewels	W	55	0	W	6/14/2014	A	Tampa Bay Inferno	W	15	7	W
6/30/2012	A	Jacksonville Dixie Blues	L	41	49	Q	6/21/2014	H	Miami Fury	L	7	9	Q
4/6/2013	H	Tallahassee Jewels	W	61	14		4/11/2015	A	Derby City Dynamite	W	34	10	
4/13/2013	A	New Orleans Mojo	W	48	0		4/18/2015	H	Jacksonville Dixie Blues	L	10	24	
4/20/2013	A	Tennessee Train	W	42	0		5/2/2015	A	Orlando Anarchy	W	1	0	
4/27/2013	H	Savannah Sabers	W	48	0		5/9/2015	H	Tampa Bay Inferno	W	26	19	
5/4/2013	A	Jacksonville Dixie Blues	W	30	14		5/16/2015	A	Miami Fury	L	6	12	*
5/18/2013	H	Tennessee Train	W	48	0		5/30/2015	H	D.C. Divas	L	0	54	
5/25/2013	A	Savannah Sabers	W	56	18		6/6/2015	H	Daytona Waverunners	W	66	0	
6/8/2013	H	Savannah Sabers	W	64	0		6/13/2015	A	Jacksonville Dixie Blues	W	13	6	
6/15/2013	H	Tampa Bay Inferno	W	24	19	W	6/27/2015	A	Jacksonville Dixie Blues	W	48	9	Q
6/22/2013	H	Miami Fury	W	28	24	Q	7/11/2015	A	D.C. Divas	L	6	40	S
7/13/2013	A	Chicago Force	L	0	84	S	8/8/2015	N	Central Cal War Angels	L	8	28	B

Atlanta Phoenix Player Register (2012-2015)

Adams, Richelle (2013)
Akinyemi, Sade (2014)
Armstrong, Mikia (2015)
Asbury, Crystal (2015)
Aviles, Cherese (2013)
Barnes, Sabrina (2012-2014)
Barton, Alexandria (2012-2015)
Bingham, Kimberly (2013)
Blair, Shayla (2012-2015)
Braxton, Sheila (2013, 2015)
Briggs, Tanysha (2012)
Brown, Ashlie (2015)
Brown, Latoya (2013-2014)
Brown, Tammy (2012)
Brown-English, Natarsha (2013)
Calderon, Ashley (2015)
Carlton, Tanea (2014-2015)
Casas, Adela (2015)
Champion, Kareemah (2014-2015)
Childress, Brandi (2014-2015)
Clark, Blair (2012-2015)
Clements, Shawn (2013)
Collins, Alisha (2013-2015)
Collymore, Lavonna (2013-2015)
Cooper, Kristina (2014-2015)
Crawford, Whitney (2014)
Davis, LaShane (2014)
Davis, Sylvana (2012-2015)
Deramus, Davida (2013)
Dozier, Mickieon (2014)
Ebrahim, Alyshah (2014)
Ervin, Shawnie (2014-2015)
Fannin, Anita (2015)
Folry, Ronette (2014-2015)

Fontaine, Nargis (2012)
Ford, Janiah (2013, 2015)
Franklin, Traci (2012-2013)
Gardner, Nyasha (2015)
Gillis, Jillian (2012)
Goodman, Michelle (2013)
Gordon, Tracy (2015)
Green, Dana (2014-2015)
Hamilton, Angela (2012, 2014)
Hargraves, Lanisha (2012-2015)
Hasan, Saudia (2012-2015)
Holmes, Shonna (2012)
Hornberger, Kelli (2012-2013)
Hursey, Dawn (2015)
James, Monique (2013)
Jamison, Jessica (2015)
Jiles, Teretha (2015)
Key, Chanee (2015)
Lane, Elizabeth (2014-2015)
Lewis, Amanda (2012-2015)
London, Kristen (2014-2015)
Lyman, Jenny (2012)
Mabrie, Angela (2012-2013)
Mabutas, Sarah (2014)
Marks, Arnetha (2014-2015)
May, Michelle (2012-2013)
McCaskill, Amy (2012)
McDonald, Kim (2014-2015)
McDuffie, Opal "Opie" (2012-2015)
McLeod, Mia (2012, 2014)
Mitchell, Kandice (2014)
Moore, Jocelyn (2014)
Morales, Christine (2012)
Morris, Sharina (2012)

Nelson, Tammy (2014-2015)
Odom, Carla (2014-2015)
Oxendine, Kelly (2013)
Peterman, Rona (2014-2015)
Prichett-Mitchell, Kandice (2015)
Pringle, Brandi (2013-2015)
Provost, Adrianna (2015)
Reed, Chasmon (2014-2015)
Rivers, Shantrell (2014-2015)
Sampson, Shelly (2013)
Searcy, Cyerius (2012-2013)
Senna, Kelly (2013)
Sheppard, Nikki (2012-2013)
Shields, Jenitra (2014-2015)
Showman, Jihrleah (2013)
Simmons, Sasha (2015)
Sims, Launa (2012-2013)
Smith, Brittney (2013)
Smith, Ramiah (2014-2015)
Smith, Whitney (2012)
Stefanelli, Francesca (2015)
Strohman, Nikki (2013)
Taylor, Keresa (2012-2015)
Thomas, AlNisa (2014-2015)
Thompson, Tameka (2014-2015)
Tompkins, Wendy (2015)
Tyus, Kristy (2012)
Van, Brenda (2013)
Wahkeleh, Nenplenseh (2014)
Welch, Nik (2012-2013)
Williams, Jeffone (2015)
Williams, Shantrell (2012-2013)
Williams-Jones, Brittany (2015)
Yarbough, Theresa (2012-2015)

Atlanta Rage

Year	League	Name	W	L	Conference	Division	DF	PR
2013	IWFL	Atlanta Rage	1	3	Eastern	Southeast	3	BQ

Based in: Atlanta, GA
Notes: Midseason replacement for Atlanta Xplosion

6/15/2013	A	Chattanooga Locomotion	W	66	0		7/6/2013	A	Carolina Queens	L	12	26	
6/22/2013	A	Carolina Phoenix	L	0	14		7/13/2013	A	Keystone Assault	L	0	1	BQ

Atlanta Xplosion

Year	League		Name	W	L	Conference	Division	DF	PR
2003	IWFL	X	Atlanta Xplosion	9	1	--	--	--	--
2004	IWFL		Atlanta Xplosion	5	4	Eastern	South Atlantic	2	S
2005	IWFL		Atlanta Xplosion	12	1	Eastern	Southern Central	1	C
2006	IWFL		Atlanta Xplosion	10	1	Eastern	South Atlantic	1	**NC**
2007	IWFL		Atlanta Xplosion	10	1	Eastern	South Atlantic	1	C
2008	IWFL		Atlanta Xplosion	6	2	Eastern	South Atlantic	2	--
2009	IWFL		Atlanta Xplosion	7	1	Eastern	South Atlantic	2	--
2010	IWFL		Atlanta Xplosion	7	2	Eastern	Southeast	2	S
2011	IWFL		Atlanta Ravens	11	0	Eastern	Mid South	1	NC
2012	IWFL		Atlanta Xplosion	5	2	Eastern	Mid South	1	S
2013	IWFL		Atlanta Xplosion	3	1	Eastern	Southeast	2	--
			Total	**85**	**16**				

Based in: Atlanta, GA   **Neutral sites:** Manchester, NH (N1); Long Beach, CA (N2); Round Rock, TX (N3)

4/19/2003	H	Orlando Starz	W	39	0	
5/3/2003	A	Tampa Bay Terminators	W	25	6	
5/10/2003	H	Miami Fury	L	21	26	
5/17/2003	H	Tampa Bay Terminators	W	28	14	
5/24/2003		Tennessee Heat	W	35	6	I
5/31/2003	A	Orlando Starz	W	39	0	
6/7/2003		Fayetteville Thunder	W	34	8	I
6/14/2003	A	Miami Fury	W	40	6	
6/21/2003		Tennessee Heat	W	50	0	I
6/28/2003	H	Memphis Maulers	W	34	14	I
4/3/2004	A	New York Sharks	L	21	28	
4/17/2004	H	Knoxville Summit	W	47	0	
4/24/2004	A	Tampa Bay Terminators	L	6	7	
5/1/2004	H	Jacksonville Dixie Blues	W	14	12	
5/15/2004	A	Knoxville Summit	W	1	0	
5/22/2004	H	Orlando Mayhem	W	52	13	
5/29/2004	H	Tampa Bay Terminators	L	8	22	
6/5/2004	A	Orlando Mayhem	W	22	0	
6/26/2004	A	Tampa Bay Terminators	L	8	21	S

4/2/2005	H	Jacksonville Dixie Blues	W	41	16	
4/9/2005	H	Dallas Revolution	W	1	0	N
4/16/2005	H	Chicago Force	W	29	0	
4/23/2005	A	Baton Rouge Wildcats	W	63	0	
4/30/2005	A	Orlando Mayhem	W	40	6	
5/14/2005	H	Baton Rouge Wildcats	W	43	0	
5/28/2005	A	Miami Fury	W	34	0	
6/4/2005	A	Jacksonville Dixie Blues	W	39	18	
6/11/2005	H	Tampa Bay Terminators	W	49	0	
6/25/2005	A	Chicago Force	W	12	0	
7/9/2005	H	Jacksonville Dixie Blues	W	26	12	S
7/23/2005	A	New York Sharks	W	3	0	CC
8/6/2005	N1	Sacramento Sirens	L	7	9	C
4/29/2006	A	Sacramento Sirens	W	67	20	
5/6/2006	H	Baton Rouge Wildcats	W	77	0	
5/13/2006	H	Orlando Mayhem	W	41	0	
5/20/2006	A	Tampa Bay Terminators	W	46	0	
6/3/2006	A	Baton Rouge Wildcats	W	36	0	
6/10/2006	H	Miami Fury	W	41	6	
6/17/2006	H	Tampa Bay Terminators	W	1	0	
6/24/2006	H	Detroit Demolition	L	7	42	
7/8/2006	A	Bay State Warriors	W	41	0	S
7/15/2006	A	New York Sharks	W	35	14	CC
7/29/2006	N2	Detroit Demolition	W	21	14	C

Continued on next page

Atlanta Xplosion Game-By-Game Results (continued)

Date	H/A	Opponent	W/L	PF	PA	Note
4/28/2007	A	Baton Rouge Wildcats	W	60	0	
5/5/2007	H	Miami Fury	W	36	0	
5/19/2007	H	Orlando Mayhem	W	14	7	
5/26/2007	H	Palm Beach Punishers	W	62	0	
6/9/2007	A	Shreveport Aftershock	W	65	0	
6/16/2007	A	Orlando Mayhem	W	7	0	
6/23/2007	H	Baton Rouge Wildcats	W	1	0	
6/30/2007	A	Miami Fury	W	1	0	
7/14/2007	H	D.C. Divas	W	28	18	S
7/28/2007	H	New York Sharks	W	10	7	CC
8/11/2007	H	Detroit Demolition	L	7	17	C
4/12/2008	A	Orlando Mayhem	L	7	13	*
4/26/2008	A	Dallas Diamonds	L	14	37	
5/3/2008	A	Miami Fury	W	44	0	
5/10/2008	H	Palm Beach Punishers	W	37	0	
5/17/2008	A	Orlando Mayhem	W	17	14	
5/24/2008	H	Miami Fury	W	35	0	
6/7/2008	H	Carolina Phoenix	W	42	0	
6/14/2008	A	Carolina Queens	W	40	0	
4/11/2009	H	Clarksville Fox	W	43	0	
4/18/2009	A	Houston Energy	W	38	7	
4/25/2009	H	Chattanooga Locomotion	W	28	6	
5/2/2009	H	Dallas Diamonds	L	7	32	
5/16/2009	H	Palm Beach Punishers	W	77	7	
5/23/2009	A	Miami Fury	W	16	12	
6/6/2009	A	Tennessee Valley Tigers	W	63	0	
6/13/2009	A	Orlando Mayhem	W	19	14	
4/3/2010	A	Chattanooga Locomotion	W	65	0	
4/10/2010	A	Carolina Queens	W	54	7	
4/24/2010	H	Miami Fury	W	39	0	
5/1/2010	H	Houston Energy	W	21	20	
5/8/2010	A	Dallas Diamonds	L	3	23	
5/15/2010	H	Carolina Queens	W	50	0	
5/22/2010	A	Miami Fury	W	1	0	
5/29/2010	H	Clarksville Fox	W	56	0	
6/12/2010	A	D.C. Divas	L	7	35	S
4/9/2011	A	Houston Energy	W	35	15	
4/16/2011	H	Chattanooga Locomotion	W	34	0	
4/23/2011	H	Clarksville Fox	W	69	0	
5/7/2011	A	Georgia Peachez	W	1	0	
5/14/2011	H	Houston Energy	W	39	6	
5/21/2011	H	Georgia Peachez	W	1	0	
6/4/2011	A	Chattanooga Locomotion	W	49	0	
6/11/2011	A	Tennessee Valley Tigers	W	1	0	
6/25/2011	H	Houston Energy	W	14	13	S
7/16/2011	H	Carolina Phoenix	W	24	6	CC
7/30/2011	N3	California Quake	W	24	22	C
4/14/2012	H	Carolina Phoenix	L	31	36	
4/21/2012	H	Memphis Belles	W	13	6	
5/5/2012	H	Carolina Queens	W	39	14	
5/12/2012	A	Memphis Belles	W	26	0	
5/19/2012	H	Carolina Phoenix	W	23	10	
6/9/2012	H	Memphis Belles	W	1	0	
6/30/2012	A	Houston Energy	L	20	21	S
4/27/2013	H	Carolina Phoenix	L	6	12	
5/4/2013	H	Carolina Queens	W	52	8	
5/11/2013	A	Huntsville Tigers	W	64	0	I
5/18/2013	H	Chattanooga Locomotion	W	66	0	

Austin Outlaws

Year	League		Name	W	L	Conference	Division	DF	PR
2001	IWFL		Austin Outlaws	5	1	--	--	--	--
2002	IWFL		Austin Outlaws	8	4	Western	--	2	C
2003	NWFA	X	Austin Outlaws	1	1	--	--	--	--
2004	NWFA		Austin Outlaws	5	3	Southern	Southwest	2	--
2005	NWFA		Austin Outlaws	4	4	Southern	--	9	--
2006	NWFA		Austin Outlaws	6	3	Southern	Southwest	2	Q
2007	NWFA		Austin Outlaws	5	3	Southern	West	2	--
2008	NWFA		Austin Outlaws	5	3	Southern	Central	3	--
2009	WFA		Austin Outlaws	7	2	American	Southwest	1	S
2010	WFA		Austin Outlaws	6	4	American	Southwest	2	S
2011	WFA		Austin Outlaws	3	5	American	South Central	3	--
2012	WFA		Austin Outlaws	1	7	American	Division 12 (Southwest)	4	--
2013	WFA		Austin Outlaws	7	3	American	Division 9 (Southwest)	2	Q
2014	WFA		Austin Outlaws	8	2	American	Southwest	1	S
2015	WFA		Austin Outlaws	2	6	American	Southwest	4	--
			Total	**73**	**51**				

Based in: Austin, TX   **Neutral site:** Tulsa, OK (N)

Austin Outlaws Game-By-Game Results

Date	H/A	Opponent	W/L	PF	PA	Note
5/9/2001	N	Memphis Maulers	W	28	0	E
6/2/2001	H	Memphis Maulers	W	42	12	
6/23/2001	H	Memphis Maulers	W	56	0	
6/30/2001	H	Tennessee Heat	W	22	6	I
7/21/2001	A	Tennessee Heat	L	0	6	I*
8/18/2001	A	Orlando Lightning	W	32	6	I
4/6/2002		Memphis Maulers	L	14	24	
4/13/2002		Oklahoma City Avengers	W	24	7	
4/20/2002		Tulsa Tornadoes	W	45	0	
4/27/2002		Memphis Maulers	W	28	0	
5/11/2002		Tulsa Tornadoes	W	55	0	
5/18/2002		Oklahoma City Avengers	L	6	25	
5/25/2002		Memphis Maulers	W	29	6	
6/8/2002		Oklahoma City Avengers	W	7	6	
6/15/2002		Tulsa Tornadoes	W	1	0	
6/22/2002		Corvallis Pride	W	42	14	CC
7/6/2002		New York Sharks	L	4	24	C
9/28/2002		Arizona Knighthawks	L	0	1	I
4/5/2003		Denton Stampede	W	47	0	E
5/31/2003		Oklahoma City Lightning	L	0	14	
4/3/2004	H	Dallas Dragons	L	31	32	
4/17/2004	A	Oklahoma City Lightning	L	6	32	
4/24/2004	H	Denton Stampede	W	78	0	
5/1/2004	A	Denton Stampede	W	64	0	
5/8/2004	H	Dallas Dragons	W	28	6	
5/22/2004	A	Dallas Dragons	W	22	16	
5/29/2004	H	Oklahoma City Lightning	L	6	42	
6/12/2004	A	Dallas Dragons	W	52	6	
4/16/2005	H	Denton Stampede	W	43	0	
4/23/2005	A	Dallas Rage	L	38	40	
4/30/2005	A	Oklahoma City Lightning	L	7	69	
5/14/2005	H	Dallas Rage	W	39	24	
5/21/2005	A	Denton Stampede	W	19	6	
5/28/2005	H	Oklahoma City Lightning	L	3	34	
6/4/2005	H	Dallas Rage	L	0	8	
6/11/2005	A	Denton Stampede	W	42	0	
4/22/2006	H	Shreveport Shockhers	W	36	8	
4/29/2006	A	Pensacola Power	W	24	8	
5/6/2006	H	Oklahoma City Lightning	L	20	41	
5/13/2006	A	Dallas Rage	W	43	40	
5/27/2006	A	Shreveport Shockhers	W	55	13	
6/3/2006	H	Pensacola Power	W	24	0	
6/10/2006	A	Oklahoma City Lightning	L	17	38	
6/17/2006	H	Dallas Rage	W	31	29	
7/1/2006	A	Chattanooga Locomotion	L	6	23	Q
4/14/2007	H	Gulf Coast Herricanes	W	49	6	
4/28/2007	H	Dallas Rage	W	68	24	
5/5/2007	H	Oklahoma City Lightning	L	20	32	
5/12/2007	A	Pensacola Power	L	14	20	
5/26/2007	A	Oklahoma City Lightning	L	7	37	
6/2/2007	A	Gulf Coast Herricanes	W	57	8	
6/9/2007	H	Pensacola Power	W	32	12	
6/16/2007	A	Dallas Rage	W	1	0	
4/19/2008	A	H-Town Texas Cyclones	L	20	27	
4/26/2008	A	North Texas Fury	W	33	0	
5/10/2008	H	New Orleans Blaze	W	42	6	
5/17/2008	A	Oklahoma City Lightning	W	28	22	
5/24/2008	H	H-Town Texas Cyclones	L	14	35	
6/7/2008	A	New Orleans Blaze	W	48	0	
6/14/2008	H	North Texas Fury	W	41	0	
6/21/2008	H	Oklahoma City Lightning	L	3	30	
4/18/2009	A	H-Town Texas Cyclones	W	40	34	
4/25/2009	A	Lone Star Mustangs	W	14	13	
5/2/2009	A	East Texas Saberkats	W	1	0	N
5/9/2009	H	Lone Star Mustangs	W	28	14	
5/30/2009	A	Lone Star Mustangs	L	14	28	
6/6/2009	H	H-Town Texas Cyclones	W	42	20	
6/20/2009	H	East Texas Saberkats	W	1	0	N
6/27/2009	H	H-Town Texas Cyclones	W	29	7	
7/11/2009	A	Jacksonville Dixie Blues	L	14	55	S
4/10/2010	H	Houston Power	W	7	6	
4/17/2010	H	Monterrey Royal Eagles	W	53	0	
5/1/2010	A	Acadiana Zydeco	W	68	0	
5/8/2010	H	Lone Star Mustangs	L	16	38	
5/22/2010	H	New Orleans Blaze	W	51	0	
6/5/2010	A	Houston Power	L	13	34	
6/12/2010	A	Lone Star Mustangs	L	7	38	
6/19/2010	H	Houston Power	W	48	15	
6/26/2010	A	Memphis Soul	W	35	0	Q
7/10/2010	H	Las Vegas Showgirlz	L	21	27	S
4/2/2011	H	Lone Star Mustangs	L	0	16	
4/9/2011	H	Tulsa Eagles	W	68	8	
4/16/2011	A	Lone Star Mustangs	L	3	33	
4/30/2011	A	Houston Power	L	6	16	
5/7/2011	A	Dallas Diamonds	L	21	31	
5/21/2011	H	New Orleans Blaze	W	52	0	
6/11/2011	A	Acadiana Zydeco	W	1	0	
6/18/2011	H	Dallas Diamonds	L	0	56	
4/14/2012	H	Tulsa Threat	W	7	6	
4/28/2012	A	Lone Star Mustangs	L	0	12	
5/5/2012	A	Houston Power	L	0	28	
5/12/2012	H	Dallas Diamonds	L	0	60	
5/19/2012	H	Lone Star Mustangs	L	0	45	
6/2/2012	A	Tulsa Threat	L	19	21	
6/9/2012	A	Dallas Diamonds	L	6	79	
6/16/2012	H	Houston Power	L	0	30	
4/6/2013	H	Tulsa Threat	W	50	10	
4/13/2013	H	Dallas Diamonds	L	0	49	
4/27/2013	A	Houston Power	W	19	14	
5/4/2013	A	Dallas Diamonds	L	0	55	
5/11/2013	H	Lone Star Mustangs	W	28	14	
5/25/2013	A	Lone Star Mustangs	W	38	0	
6/1/2013	A	Acadiana Zydeco	W	48	0	
6/8/2013	H	Houston Power	W	43	0	
6/15/2013	H	Little Rock Wildcats	W	35	0	W
6/22/2013	A	Dallas Diamonds	L	6	61	Q
4/5/2014	A	Houston Power	W	17	8	
4/12/2014	H	Houston Energy	L	3	56	I
5/3/2014	A	Acadiana Zydeco	W	34	0	
5/10/2014	A	Arlington Impact	W	28	18	I
5/17/2014	A	Tulsa Threat	W	14	0	
5/24/2014	A	San Antonio Regulators	W	1	0	I
5/31/2014	A	Acadiana Zydeco	W	46	6	
6/7/2014	H	Houston Power	W	8	7	
6/21/2014	H	Minnesota Machine	W	14	3	Q
7/5/2014	A	Kansas City Titans	L	0	41	S
4/11/2015	A	Houston Power	L	0	42	
4/25/2015	H	Arlington Impact	L	0	63	
5/2/2015	A	Dallas Elite	L	0	76	
5/9/2015	A	South Texas Lady Crushers	W	56	0	
5/16/2015	H	Arkansas Wildcats	L	0	6	
5/30/2015	H	South Texas Lady Crushers	W	57	0	
6/6/2015	A	Arlington Impact	L	8	46	
6/13/2015	H	Dallas Elite	L	0	59	

Austin Outlaws Player Register (2004-2015)

Alexander, Tara (2015)
Allen, Alexis (2005-2006)
Allen, Mary (2014)
Ammerman, Stevie ('07-09, '11, '14-15)
Andrickson, Tara (2012, 2014)
Arceneaux, Nicolette (2007, 2009)
Arispe, Jessica "J.J." (2007-2009)
Avery, Marq (2011-2013, 2015)
Avila, Sasha (2010, 2012-2015)
Baker, Jessica (2010-2011, 2013-2015)
Barber, Jennifer (2014)
Barrington, Jennifer (2004, 2006-2009)
Barry, Joy (2013-2014)
Batson, Amber (2009)
Bayer, Rebecca (2009-2010)
Beaumont, Jennifer (2007-2009)
Bell, Stephanie (2005)
Benitez, Lucinda (2006-2015)
Berg, Amy (2007)
Berry, Lou Ellen (2004-2006)
Boss, Deadre (2011)
Brooks, Cheryl (2009, 2012-2013)
Brown, Angela (2006)
Brown, Bridgette (2007-11, 2013-15)
Buckley, Lisa (2005)
Bueno, Evelyn (2015)
Cadena, Laurie (2013-2014)
Capers-Cristobal, Maile (2010-2015)
Capers-Cristobal, Malia (2011-2015)
Cardile, Diane (2008)
Carpenter, Rebecca (2014)
Carver, Esther (2012)
Castro, Melanie (2014-2015)
Chaffin, Billy Jo (2004)
Chancellor, Jennifer (2012-2013)
Choate, Nate (2009)
Clay, Tanea (2012)
Coleman, Marci (2007-2008)
Collins, Diana (2004)
Collins, Melissa (2010)
Contreras, Katie (2015)
Crash, Tiffany (2012)
Crayton, Jennifer (2012)
Crouch, Antonita (2011-2012)
Darlington, Symone (2008)
Dikibo, Sotonye (2009-2012, 2014)
Dillard, Lori (2004-2005, 2010)
Dixon, Dena (2004)
Dixon, Nichol (2005)
Dobbins, Laquita (2014)
Dobkowski, Alexandra (2008)
Dominguez, Sandy (2010)
Eddy, Laura (2005-2007)
Elliott, Jill (2006-2008)
Essien, Earlie (2005-2006)
Fiedler, Melissa (2007-2010, 2015)
Fien, Melanie (2006-2007)
Foxworth, Gina (2013-2015)
Freeman, Tiney (2009, 2011)
Fuller, Toni (2011-2014)
Futrell, Adriene (2012, 2014)
Gallegos, Vanessa (2011)
Garvin, Tiffany (2004-2005)
Gauck, Monica (2004-2011)
Gipson, Cindy (2005)
Green, Emily (2008)
Greybeck, Jennifer (2005-2006)
Griffith, Melissa (2005-2012, 2014)

Hancock, Laura (2008-2011)
Harris, Myra (2005-2006, 2010)
Hebert, Kelly (2012-2013)
Helton, Laurie (2015)
Herrera, Josie (2005, 2007)
Hill, Krys (2015)
Hines, Dorothy (2005-2009, 2011)
Hoke, LaKesha (2013)
Holewyne, Lisa (2012-2014)
Holland, Deidra (2011-2014)
Hooper, Lindsey (2007-2011)
Howard, Ereka (2012)
Hurd, Shadana (2006-2011, 2013)
Jackson, Charmeine (2009-2014)
Jackson, Krystal (2015)
James, Bobbie (2005)
James, Tiffany (2006-2007)
Jessup, Lisa (2005)
Johnson, Jazmine (2011)
Johnson, Tina (2008-2009)
Jones, Lakisha (2008-2015)
Jovel, Minori (2005-2006, 2010)
Jurek, Kris (2004-2006, 2008, 2010)
Keehn, Kysha (2010)
Kemp, Julaine (2004)
Kendall, Nissa (2010)
Kincheon, Patricia (2009-11, 2013-15)
Kirkpatrick, Cara (2013)
Klotz, Holly (2007-2008)
Knight, Dana (2005)
Lacy, Demetrice (2014)
Laga, Ariane (2007)
Lahmann, Rebecca "Becky" (2008, 2010)
Lametrie, Christine (2006-2007)
Langford, Jessica (2013-2014)
Laursen, Victoria (2005)
LaViola, Tasha (2006, 2013-2015)
Lewis, Verice (2011)
Lish, Lori (2009-2010)
Lopez, Liz (2010)
Lopez, Marina (2015)
Lyons, Amber (2007-2012)
Maher, Sophia (2008)
Marshall, Stephanie (2009-10, 2012-15)
Martin, Chantele (2011-2012)
Martin, Nancy (2009)
Martinez, Christina (2010-2012)
Mays, Kazia (2010)
McEntire, Heather (2015)
McKinney, Brooke (2015)
McKinney, Hannah (2015)
Melton, Stephanie (2004)
Merced, Marta (2004)
Messina, Lily (2005-2012)
Miner, Jess (2006)
Mitchell, Danyell (2011)
Mitchell, Jennifer (2012)
Morgan, Danica (2014-2015)
Morris, Carolyn (2015)
Morris, Davida (2013-2014)
Narvaez, Veronica (2005-2011)
Nguyen, Mary (2005-2007)
Nihart, Shawna (2008, 2010)
Novar, Eva (2005)
O'Halleran, Christina (2004-2005)
Olloway, LaTonia (2008, 2011)
Pafford, Amber (2012)
Pearmon, Jay (2005)

Perry, Monique (2009)
Phillips, Juli (2004-2007)
Pickens, Velma (2005-2008)
Plumley, Rebecca (2005)
Preston, Q.T. (2012-2015)
Read, Michelle (2008)
Regalbuti, Veronica (2008)
Rendon, Nancy (2010)
Reyna, Ruby (2012-2014)
Rhodes, Holly (2005-2006)
Riley, Megan (2012)
Rivas, Marisa (2009-2014)
Romero, Angelic (2014)
Romero, Rebecca (2014)
Ross, Tommy (2010-2014)
Rowland, Erika (2011)
Russano, Becky (2006-2007)
Saenz, Erica (2012)
Salter, Wendy (2009)
Sander, Sherice (2010)
Sandoval, Victoria (2011)
Saucedo, Janie (2004)
Savell, Ty (2008)
Scheib, K.J. (2004-2006)
Schindle, Kristen (2008)
Shagam, Patricia (2013)
Simmons, Dominique (2015)
Simmons, Elanda (2004-2005, 2007)
Simmons, Jamie (2008)
Smith, Jillian (2005)
Smith, Lorin (2004, 2006-2010)
Smith, Nikki (2015)
Snyder, Sarah (2007)
Sparrowhawk, Laurie (2005)
Spedden, Jamie (2009)
Stabel, Francesca (2013-2014)
Standridge, Haley (2014)
Stewart, Ashley (2015)
Stewart, Rene (2007)
Suire, Tracey (2004-2010)
Sullivan, Melanie (2005-2007)
Swanson, April (2014)
Taylor, Jennifer (2013-2014)
Tejeda, Sekethia (2004-2014)
Thiele, Anna (2009)
Thomas, DeeAnn (2009-2010)
Tillman-Brooks, Chenell "Soho" ('09-10, '14)
Turner, Holly (2009)
Urban, Amanda (2004)
Villa, Mary (2013)
Walker, Tonya (2013)
Waller, Janet (2007)
Walters, Lisa (2005)
Warner, Theresa (2004)
Waters, Lisa (2006-2007)
Westbrook, Debra (2009)
Whalen, Jeanette (2006)
White, Alexis (2013-2014)
Wilke, Julie (2005-2008)
Williams, Heather (2008)
Williams, Justine (2012)
Williamsen, Suzie (2011)
Wolfanger, Justine (2005, 2008-2011)
Womack, Tiffany (2014)
Wood, Sherry (2009)
Wright, Mary (2015)
Ysasi, Erin (2007-2008)

Continued on next page

Austin Outlaws Player Register (continued)

Zelee, Treyah (2012) Zerda, Debra (2005) Zunker, Teresa (2005)

Austin Rage

Year	League	Name	W	L	Conference	Division	DF	PR
2000	WPFL	Austin Rage	2	5	American	West	2	--
2001	WPFL	Austin Rage	4	4	--	--	2	C
2002	WPFL	Austin Rage	2	5	American	--	4	--
		Total	8	14				

Based in: Austin, TX

Date	H/A	Opponent	W/L	Score			Date	H/A	Opponent	W/L	Score		
10/14/2000	H	Houston Energy	L	25	52		8/10/2002		Arizona Knighthawks	L	33	48	
10/21/2000	A	Houston Energy	L	20	30		8/17/2002		Dallas Diamonds	L	21	26	
10/28/2000	A	Minnesota Vixen	L	19	35		9/7/2002		Dallas Diamonds	W	34	26	
11/4/2000	H	Colorado Valkyries	L	0	53		9/14/2002		Arizona Titans	L	0	1	I
11/11/2000	A	Houston Energy	L	21	35		9/21/2002		Houston Energy	L	26	59	
11/25/2000	H	Oklahoma City Wildcats	W	13	12		9/28/2002		Missouri Prowlers	W	74	0	
12/2/2000	A	Oklahoma City Wildcats	W	14	8		10/5/2002		Houston Energy	L	7	42	
7/28/2001	H	Houston Energy	L	13	27								
8/4/2001	A	Houston Energy	L	0	25								
8/11/2001	A	Tampa Tempest	W	21	0								
8/25/2001	H	New England Storm	W	32	16								
9/8/2001	A	New England Storm	W	30	18								
9/22/2001	H	Tampa Tempest	W	1	0								
10/6/2001	A	Orlando Fire	L	7	8	I							
10/20/2001	A	Houston Energy	L	14	47	C							

Austin Yellow Jackets

Year	League	Name	W	L	Conference	Division	DF	PR
2015	IWFL	Austin Yellow Jackets	4	2	Western	Southwest	2	--

Based in: Austin, TX

Date	H/A	Opponent	W/L	Score		Date	H/A	Opponent	W/L	Score	
4/11/2015	A	Houston Energy	L	0	45	5/16/2015	H	Houston Energy	L	12	14
4/18/2015	H	New Orleans Krewe	W	30	0	5/30/2015	A	New Orleans Krewe	W	37	0
5/2/2015	H	San Antonio Regulators	W	40	14	6/13/2015	A	San Antonio Regulators	W	22	8

Austin Yellow Jackets Player Register (2015)

Allen, Kelly (2015)
Andrickson, Tara (2015)
Barry, Joy (2015)
Bryant, Felexis (2015)
Dobbins, Laquita (2015)
Fuller, Sioneesha (2015)
Fuller, Toni (2015)
Futrell, Adriene (2015)
Griffith, Melissa (2015)
Hancock, Laura (2015)
Hines, Dorothy (2015)
Holewyne, Lisa (2015)
Jackson, Charmaine (2015)
Langford, Jessica (2015)
Lewis, Latreese (2015)
Miranda, Diana (2015)
Morris, Davida (2015)
Murray, Lacresha (2015)
Neely-Otts, Hope (2015)
Reyna, Ruby (2015)
River, Naveen (2015)
Romero, Angelic (2015)
Ruland, Michelle (2015)
Scott, Victoria (2015)
Standridge, Haley (2015)
Swanson, April (2015)
Taylor, Jennifer (2015)
Thornton, Olivia (2015)
Thrower, Chaquitta (2015)
Tillman-Brooks, Chenell "Soho" (2015)
Turner, Juliette (Baker-Brice) (2015)
Womack, Tiffany (2015)

Baltimore Burn

Year	League		Name	W	L	Conference	Division	DF	PR
2001	NWFA		Baltimore Burn	0	7	Northern	--	5	--
2002	NWFA		Baltimore Burn	9	2	--	Mid-Atlantic	1	S
2003	NWFA		Baltimore Burn	7	3	Northern	Mid-Atlantic	2	Q
2004	NWFA		Baltimore Burn	4	4	Northern	Mid-Atlantic	3	--
2005	NWFA		Baltimore Burn	4	4	Northern	--	11	--
2006	NWFA		Baltimore Burn	4	4	Northern	North Atlantic	2	--
2007	NWFA		Baltimore Burn	4	5	Northern	South	1	Q
2008	NWFA		Baltimore Burn	2	6	Northern	East	3	--
2009	WFA		Baltimore Burn	5	4	National	Northeast	3	--
2010	WFA		Baltimore Burn	6	3	National	East	1	Q
2011	WSFL		Baltimore Burn	6	0	--	--	--	--
2012	WSFL		Baltimore Burn	3	5	American	Northeast	2	S
2013	WSFL	X	Baltimore Burn	0	3	--	--	--	--
2014	WSFL		Baltimore Burn	1	4	Eastern	--	2	CC
2015	WSFL		Baltimore Burn	1	4	Northern	--	5	--
			Total	56	58				

Based in: Baltimore, MD

Date		Opponent				
5/5/2001	H	Philadelphia Liberty Belles (I)	L	0	46	
5/12/2001	A	Massachusetts Mutiny	L	0	35	
5/19/2001	A	Connecticut Crush	L	0	24	
5/26/2001		D.C. Divas	L	8	20	
6/2/2001	A	Philadelphia Liberty Belles (I)	L	0	47	
6/9/2001	H	Connecticut Crush	L	12	18	
6/23/2001	H	Massachusetts Mutiny	L	22	90	
3/23/2002		Rochester Raptors	W	20	0	E
3/30/2002		Rochester Raptors	W	39	0	E
4/20/2002	A	D.C. Divas	W	7	2	
4/27/2002		Tennessee Venom	W	30	0	
5/4/2002	H	D.C. Divas	L	6	7	
5/18/2002		Asheville Assault	W	21	0	
5/25/2002		Tennessee Venom	W	57	0	
6/1/2002	H	D.C. Divas	W	12	6	
6/15/2002		Asheville Assault	W	40	0	
6/22/2002	A	D.C. Divas	W	6	0	
7/6/2002	H	Philadelphia Liberty Belles (I)	L	20	21	S
3/29/2003		Knoxville Summit	W	45	0	E
4/12/2003	A	Pittsburgh Passion	W	7	0	
4/19/2003	A	D.C. Divas	L	0	24	
4/26/2003	H	Columbus Flames	W	13	7	
5/10/2003	H	Erie Illusion	W	58	3	
5/17/2003	A	Columbus Flames	L	0	13	
5/24/2003	H	Pittsburgh Passion	W	21	15	
6/7/2003	A	Erie Illusion	W	28	21	
6/14/2003	H	D.C. Divas	W	22	14	
6/28/2003	A	Cleveland Fusion	L	19	28	Q
4/3/2004	A	Pittsburgh Passion	L	19	22	
4/17/2004	H	D.C. Divas	L	14	26	
4/24/2004	A	Erie Illusion	W	36	0	
5/1/2004	H	Pittsburgh Passion	L	14	20	
5/15/2004	H	Erie Illusion	W	32	0	
5/22/2004	H	Roanoke Revenge	W	56	6	
5/29/2004	A	Roanoke Revenge	W	24	8	
6/12/2004	A	D.C. Divas	L	16	52	
4/16/2005	A	Tidewater Floods	W	38	8	
4/23/2005	H	Columbus Comets	L	20	22	
4/30/2005	A	Toledo Spitfire	W	46	0	
5/14/2005	H	Philadelphia Phoenix	W	14	0	
5/21/2005	A	Pittsburgh Passion	L	12	26	
6/4/2005	H	Tidewater Floods	W	68	0	
6/11/2005	A	Cleveland Fusion	L	14	34	
6/18/2005	H	D.C. Divas	L	0	36	
4/22/2006	A	D.C. Divas	L	6	13	
4/29/2006	H	Harrisburg Angels	W	50	0	
5/6/2006	H	Tidewater Floods	W	49	0	
5/20/2006	A	Massachusetts Mutiny	L	0	35	
5/27/2006	H	D.C. Divas	L	0	30	
6/3/2006	A	Harrisburg Angels	W	56	0	
6/10/2006	A	Tidewater Floods	W	48	12	
6/17/2006	H	Massachusetts Mutiny	L	16	20	
4/14/2007	H	Philadelphia Phoenix	W	6	0	
4/21/2007	A	Massachusetts Mutiny	L	0	21	
4/28/2007	H	Cleveland Fusion	L	8	24	
5/5/2007	H	Richmond Spirit	W	1	0	N
5/19/2007	A	Philadelphia Phoenix	W	14	8	*
5/26/2007	H	Massachusetts Mutiny	L	14	34	
6/9/2007	A	Cleveland Fusion	L	0	39	
6/16/2007	A	Richmond Spirit	W	1	0	N
6/23/2007	A	West Michigan Mayhem	L	14	33	Q
4/26/2008	A	Connecticut Crush	L	24	55	
5/3/2008	H	Philadelphia Phoenix	L	8	50	
5/10/2008	H	New York Nemesis	L	8	42	
5/17/2008	A	New Jersey Titans	L	6	26	
5/31/2008	A	Philadelphia Phoenix	L	0	49	
6/7/2008	H	Connecticut Crush	W	24	21	
6/14/2008	H	New Jersey Titans	W	28	22	
6/21/2008	A	New York Nemesis	L	18	40	
4/4/2009	H	Columbus Comets	L	16	21	E
4/18/2009	A	Connecticut Cyclones	W	1	0	N
4/25/2009	H	Philadelphia Liberty Belles (II)	L	8	43	
5/9/2009	A	Keystone Assault	W	20	16	
5/16/2009	H	Connecticut Cyclones	W	1	0	N
5/30/2009	A	Philadelphia Liberty Belles (II)	L	10	13	
6/6/2009	H	Keystone Assault	W	46	22	
6/13/2009	A	Binghamton Tiger Cats	W	56	6	
6/20/2009	H	New Jersey Titans	L	0	1	

Continued on next page

Baltimore Burn Game-By-Game Results (continued)

Date	H/A	Opponent	W/L	Score		Note
4/10/2010	H	New England Nightmare	W	54	14	
4/17/2010	A	New Jersey Titans	W	62	36	
5/1/2010	A	Philadelphia Liberty Belles (II)	L	6	26	
5/15/2010	H	Southern Tier Spitfire	W	1	0	
5/22/2010	H	Keystone Assault	L	24	34	
6/5/2010	A	New England Nightmare	W	28	20	
6/12/2010	H	New Jersey Titans	W	16	0	
6/19/2010	A	Keystone Assault	W	36	24	
6/26/2010	A	Columbus Comets	L	8	67	Q
4/16/2011	A	Binghamton Tiger Cats	W	22	0	
4/23/2011	H	Three Rivers Xplosion	W	48	6	
4/30/2011	A	Jersey Justice	W	12	8	
6/4/2011	H	Jersey Justice	W	1	0	
6/4/2011	H	Binghamton Tiger Cats	W	46	0	
6/11/2011	A	Three Rivers Xplosion	W	54	0	
4/14/2012	H	New Jersey Titans	W	20	18	
4/21/2012	H	Binghamton Tiger Cats	L	0	1	
5/5/2012	A	Keystone Assault	L	6	34	I
5/12/2012	H	Keystone Assault	L	8	46	I
5/19/2012	H	New England Nightmare	W	20	14	I
6/2/2012	A	Binghamton Tiger Cats	W	76	0	
7/7/2012	A	New Jersey Titans	L	8	37	
7/21/2012	A	New Jersey Titans	L	6	31	S
4/20/2013	H	Tri-State Warriors	L	0	26	
4/27/2013	H	New York Sharks	L	0	18	I
6/1/2013	A	New York Sharks	L	0	32	I
4/5/2014	A	Pittsburgh Force	L	8	30	I
4/26/2014	A	Arkansas Banshees	W	1	0	
5/3/2014	H	D.C. Divas	L	0	43	I
5/10/2014	A	Boston Militia	L	0	1	I
7/19/2014	H	Memphis Dynasty	L	8	20	CC
4/25/2015	A	Keystone Assault	L	0	41	
5/9/2015	H	West Virginia Wildfire	W	22	6	
5/16/2015	H	New England Nightmare	L	6	36	
6/6/2015	A	New England Nightmare	L	0	1	
6/20/2015	H	Keystone Assault	L	0	49	

Baltimore Burn Player Register (2004-2010, 2015)

Adams, Kiara (2006-2007)
Anderson, Patrice (2008-2010)
Anderson, Sherri (2015)
Artis, Toleah (2010)
Arvin, Shannon (2009)
Askew, Pleshette (2007)
Barnes, Lakia (2009-2010)
Bates, Kendra (2007)
Beam, Tina (2004)
Beasley, Laura (2004)
Bolling, Allicia (2008-2010)
Bolling, Alysa (2010)
Bovell, Kristian (2005-2007)
Boykins, Teresia (2007-2009)
Brown, Aretha (2004-2007)
Brown, Jocelyn (2005)
Brown, Karen (2007)
Brown, Necole (2007)
Bryant, Iymaani (2005)
Burgess, Melanie (2005-2006)
Campbell, Sherrie (2004-2006)
Cappi, Gina (2004-05, 2007-08)
Carson, Corinne (2004-2006)
Church, Viola (2005-2006)
Clark, Dawn (2006)
Clark, Jasmine (2009)
Clark, Mandakova (2009)
Cleveland, Angela (2009)
Cooper, Tiara (2006)
Copeland, Kris (2006)
Copelin, Christina (2007, '09, '15)
Crabbe, Renee (2005)
Craig, Jacqueline (2004-2005)
Curry, Brittany (2008)
Cutchin, Cheryl (2004)
Damaio, Cheri (2008)
Dameron, Rikkia (2008-2010, 2015)
Darby, Krystal (2005-2007)
Dash, Amanda (2008)
Davis, Takishia (2004-2006)
DeCosta, Deanne (2008)
Deuber, Tracey (2009)
Dixon, Sheena (2007-2009)
Doll, Maddie (2008-2009)
Dorsey, Brehon (2015)
Dorsey, Tekemia (2005-2006)
Dudley, Clarissa (2004-2006)
Dukes, Rayna (2009-2010, 2015)
Edwards, Monica (2009)
Eifler, Mary (2004)
Fain, Tarsha (2004-2007)
Fisher, Kelly (2008)
Fitzgerald, Shay (2005-2006)
Floyd, Dee (2005)
Franklin, Pamela (2015)
Freeman, Teneka (2005-2007)
Frye, Mandy (2009)
Gardner, Kelly (2005)
Gaylor, Jamey (2010)
Green, Cheri (2004)
Green, Nikia (2004-2007)
Griffin, Keisha (2007)
Griffin, Margaret (2005-2010)
Grigsby, Kenyetta (2004-2007)
Harding, Antoinette (2004-2005)
Harris, Chantey "C.J." (2009-2010)
Harris, Kim (2007-2008)
Harrison, Kelly (2009-2010)
Harvey, LaByanca "Byanca" (2008-10, '15)
Hawkins, Ganee (2008)
Hayward, Brandy (2015)
Heffington, Kim (2008-2009)
Helm, Kristen (2005)
Herasingh, Pamela "Pam" (2008)
Hicks, Tyeshawn (2015)
Hill, Tanya (2004)
Hockaday, Monica (2004-2005)
Howard, Heather (2007)
Howard, Torre (2007)
Hubbell, Leslie (2004-2005, 2008)
Hughes, Sheenika (2015)
Imbragulio, Alissa (2005-2006)
Isaacs, Charquette (2004-2006)
Jackson, Akiba (2008)
Jackson, Precious (2015)
James, Janae (2015)
Jeanerret, Carrie (2007)
Jeffcoat, Jamilah (2009)
Johnson, Cortney (2009)
Johnson, Erica (2015)
Johnson, Maya (2004)
Johnson, Tamara (2004-07, 2009-10)
Jones, Erica (2006)
Jude, China (2005)
Kinney, Angelique (2010)
Leaf, Jennifer (2010, 2015)
Lyde, Carmen (2004-2005)
Mackall, Sade (2008)
Maclin, Kamil (2010)
Marion, Teresa (2004-2008)
Marshall, Shamika (2009)
Matthews, Brandis (2004)
Mayo, Tydesha (2008-2010, 2015)
McCauley, Tee (2004-2007, 2009)
McDowney, Debra (2008-2010)
McLean, Carla (2009)
McLeod, Trina (2015)
Miller, Christina (2008)
Miller, Debra (2004-2007, 2009, 2015)
Millett, Jaime (2004-2005)
Millius, Cassandra (2015)
Milly, Dobson (2008)
Moore, Jacquin (2007)
Morton, Yasmin (2009-2010)
Mouzone, Nina (2004-2005)
Muhammed, Amatullah (2010)
Munford, Robyn (2009)
Muscato, Dawn (2004)
Nolan, Regina (2004-2007)
Palmer, Sheranda (2004-2007)
Parham, Takeisha (2007)
Platt, Amanda (2006)
Porter, Faneca (2015)
Presberry, Angelia (2005-2007)
Randall, Key (2006)
Reedy, Raven (2005)
Robinson, LaDonna (2008)
Robinson, Lakeisia (2007)
Rogers, Nicole (2004)
Rogers, Tamika (2008-2009)
Roman, Marqita (2006-2007)

Continued on next page

Baltimore Burn Player Register (continued)

Salmeron, Bettie Joe "B.J." (2008-2009)
Savage, Tanya (2009, 2015)
Schell, Allegra (2007, 2009)
Sheckells, Cheryl (2004)
Shettle, Janet (2004)
Shumate, Lisa (2008)
Smith, Keeley (2005-2007, 2009)
Smith, Yasmeen (2008)
Spence, Lisa (2005-2006)
Stevens, Leslie (2008)
Streeter, Jennifer (2005-2006)
Strong, Jimmien (2004-2007)
Strong, Maciah (2005-2006)
Sturtz, Brandy (2005-2006)
Taylor, Brandis (2010)
Taylor, Heather (2009-2010)
Taylor, Tanza (2010)
Taylor, Toneika (2015)
Thomas, Sabrina (2004-2007)
Tozzi, Ann (2004, 2006)
Tucker, Sherry (2008-2009)
Tyson, Cynthia (2004-07, 2009-10, '15)
Walker, Ayrica (2007)
Walker, Stephanie (2008-2010)
Waller, Jessica (2008)
Watanathai, Tara (2006)
West, Karida (2004)
White, Lynda (2004-2005)
Williams, Candis (2010, 2015)
Williams, Shaquita (2008-2010)
Wise, Tamika (2009)
Wollschlager, Tonya (2005-2007)
Wynn, Nate (2005-2006)
Young, Courtney (2015)
Young, Renita (2006)
Young, Tami (2004)

Baltimore Nighthawks

Year	League	Name	W	L	T	Conference	Division	DF	PR
2008	IWFL	Baltimore Nighthawks	2	6	0	Eastern	North Atlantic	5	--
2009	IWFL	Baltimore Nighthawks	3	5	0	Eastern	Mid-Atlantic	4	--
2010	IWFL	Baltimore Nighthawks	3	5	0	Eastern	Southeast	4	--
2011	IWFL	Baltimore Nighthawks	3	4	1	Eastern	Mid-Atlantic	2	BQ
2012	IWFL	Baltimore Nighthawks	7	2	0	Eastern	Mid-Atlantic	1	S
2013	IWFL	Baltimore Nighthawks	0	7	0	Eastern	Mid-Atlantic	4	--
2014	IWFL	Baltimore Nighthawks	4	5	0	Eastern	Mid-Atlantic	3	B
2015	IWFL	Baltimore Nighthawks	3	4	0	Eastern	Mid-Atlantic	3	--
		Total	**25**	**38**	**1**				

Based in: Baltimore, MD

Neutral site: Rock Hill, SC (N)

Date	H/A	Opponent	Result	Score		Note
4/12/2008	H	Central PA Vipers	W	55	0	
4/19/2008	A	New York Sharks	L	6	26	
4/26/2008	A	D.C. Divas	L	6	35	
5/3/2008	H	New York Sharks	L	28	54	
5/17/2008	H	Pittsburgh Passion	L	0	28	
5/31/2008	A	D.C. Divas	L	6	41	
6/7/2008	A	Manchester Freedom	W	49	0	
6/14/2008	H	Boston Militia	L	6	28	
4/11/2009	H	D.C. Divas	L	0	33	
4/18/2009	A	Philadelphia Firebirds	W	22	15	
4/25/2009	A	Pittsburgh Passion	L	0	49	
5/2/2009	H	Detroit Demolition	L	0	13	
5/16/2009	H	Jersey Justice	W	32	6	
5/23/2009	A	D.C. Divas	L	14	70	
5/30/2009	H	Boston Militia	L	0	66	
6/6/2009	A	Connecticut Crushers	W	30	8	
4/3/2010	H	Philadelphia Firebirds	W	54	0	
4/10/2010	A	D.C. Divas	L	6	54	
4/24/2010	H	New York Nemesis	W	7	6	
5/1/2010	A	Carolina Queens	W	21	0	
5/8/2010	H	D.C. Divas	L	7	28	
5/15/2010	A	Pittsburgh Passion	L	6	34	
5/22/2010	A	New York Sharks	L	6	38	
6/5/2010	H	Carolina Phoenix	L	20	22	*
4/2/2011	A	Georgia Peachez	W	36	0	
4/9/2011	H	Carolina Phoenix	L	8	32	
4/16/2011	A	Philadelphia Firebirds	T	0	0	
4/30/2011	H	Georgia Peachez	W	1	0	
5/7/2011	H	Philadelphia Firebirds	L	6	13	
5/28/2011	A	Philadelphia Firebirds	W	8	0	
6/4/2011	A	Carolina Phoenix	L	0	42	
6/25/2011	A	New England Intensity	L	0	25	BQ
4/14/2012	H	Philadelphia Firebirds	W	32	23	
4/21/2012	H	Connecticut Wreckers	W	34	0	
4/28/2012	H	Carolina Phoenix	L	0	22	
5/5/2012	A	Erie Illusion	W	20	0	
5/12/2012	H	Northeastern Nitro	W	28	0	
5/19/2012	A	Connecticut Wreckers	W	22	0	
6/2/2012	H	Erie Illusion	W	29	12	
6/9/2012	A	Philadelphia Firebirds	W	21	0	
6/30/2012	A	Montreal Blitz	L	6	33	S
4/27/2013	H	Philadelphia Firebirds	L	0	14	
5/4/2013	A	Keystone Assault	L	0	20	
5/11/2013	A	Washington Prodigy	L	0	14	
5/18/2013	H	Keystone Assault	L	6	7	
6/1/2013	A	Philadelphia Firebirds	L	8	42	
6/15/2013	H	Washington Prodigy	L	0	22	
6/22/2013	H	Carolina Queens	L	28	42	
4/12/2014	H	Keystone Assault	L	6	13	
4/26/2014	A	Carolina Queens	W	28	22	*
5/3/2014	H	Philadelphia Firebirds	W	14	12	
5/10/2014	A	Philadelphia Firebirds	W	1	0	
5/17/2014	A	Washington Prodigy	L	0	15	
5/31/2014	H	Carolina Queens	W	32	8	
6/7/2014	H	Washington Prodigy	L	14	26	
6/14/2014	H	Pittsburgh Passion	L	6	38	
7/25/2014	N	Madison Blaze	L	14	31	B
4/18/2015	H	Toledo Reign	W	29	18	
4/25/2015	A	Philadelphia Firebirds	L	6	34	
5/9/2015	H	Carolina Queens	L	0	26	
5/16/2015	A	Connecticut Wreckers	W	28	13	
5/30/2015	A	Toledo Reign	L	14	20	
6/6/2015	A	Washington Prodigy	L	0	24	
6/13/2015	H	Connecticut Wreckers	W	14	13	

Baltimore Nighthawks Player Register (2010, 2014-2015)

Aldridge, Jennifer (2010)
Ashby-Gamble, Tova (2015)
Badgett, Kayla (2015)
Barlag, Jessica (2015)
Bates, Kendra (2010, 2014)
Beadles, Ashley (2010, 2015)
Benny, Dustilynn (2014-2015)
Branch, Ashley (2010, 2014)
Brown, Jesseca (2015)
Brown, Kaily (2015)
Brown, Tanya (2014)
Buchanan, Naeemah (2014-2015)
Clay, Jawana (2010)
Countess, Tykisha (2010)
Cousins, Leslie (2014-2015)
Davis, Rolanda (2014-2015)
Dixon, Sameda (2014)
Drumgold, Lillian "Lil" (2010, 2014)
Elliott, Delores (2015)
Elliott, Nikia (2015)
Fain, Tarsha (2010)
Few, Carolyn (2010, 2014-2015)
Fitzgerald, Shay (2010, 2015)
Goldsmith, DeVon (2010)
Green, Krichan (2015)
Green, Nikia (2010)
Hamlet, Shae (2010)
Harrington, Kaylan (2015)
Henninger, Andrea (2015)
Howard, Torre (2010)
James, Sandi (2015)
Jennings, Cynthia (2010)
Johnson, Audene (2010)
Jones, Arieka (2015)
Jones, Kelli (2014)
Jordan, Terharsa "T.J." (2010, '14-15)
Juang, Amy (2014-2015)
King, Kellie (2010)
Lange, Lauren (2015)
Laudenschlager, Suzanna (2014-15)
Letman, India (2015)
Maclin, Kamil (2014)
McClain, Ondrea (2014-2015)
McKay, Onette (2014)
Meinert, Megan (2015)
Melendez, Suyapa (2014-2015)
Mossanen, Ghoncheh (2014-2015)
Murrill, Chimere (2010)
Nolan, Regina (2010)
Olson, Laura (2014)
Oparaocha, Cathy (2010)
Powell, Tracy (2015)
Presberry, Angelia (2010)
Ratliff, Jamila (2014)
Reecht, Lindsey (2015)
Reyes, Sophia (2014)
Roser, Elysia (2010)
Sauter, Katherine (2010)
Savage, Tanya (2010)
Smiler, Cheryl (2010, 2014)
Smith, Alexa (2014)
Smith, Tamara (2010)
Spencer, Steeley (2014)
Steele, Hope (2015)
Stevens, Symone (2015)
Stokes, Danielle (2014)
Thomas, Rebekka (2010)
Thomas, Sherrie (2015)
Walker, Ayrica (2010)
Watkins, Tia (2014)
Williams, Mildred (2010, 2014)
Wilson, Alicia (2014)
Wingfield, Tanya (2010, 2014)
Wright, Alexa (2015)

Bay Area Bandits

Year	League	Name	W	L	Conference	Division	DF	PR
2010	IWFL2	Bay Area Bandits	7	4	Western	Pacific West	1	C
2011	WFA	Bay Area Bandits	7	3	American	North Pacific	1	S
2012	WFA	Bay Area Bandits	8	2	American	Division 16 (North Pacific)	1	S
		Total	22	9				

Based in: Freemont, CA
Neutral site: Round Rock, TX (N)
Notes: Preceded by IWFL's Oakland Banshees

4/3/2010	A	Sacramento Sirens	L	13	33		4/14/2012	H	Portland Fighting Fillies	W	33	6
4/10/2010	H	Portland Shockwave	W	13	0		4/21/2012	A	West Coast Lightning	W	46	0
4/17/2010	A	Southern California Breakers	W	42	7		4/28/2012	A	Valley Vipers	W	63	0
5/1/2010	H	Southern California Breakers	W	26	6		5/12/2012	H	Central Cal War Angels	W	20	18
5/15/2010	A	Los Angeles Amazons	W	33	22		5/19/2012	A	San Diego Surge	L	0	57
5/22/2010	H	Modesto Maniax	W	47	8		6/2/2012	H	West Coast Lightning	W	38	0
5/29/2010	A	So Cal Scorpions	L	6	43		6/9/2012	H	Valley Vipers	W	57	0
6/5/2010	H	So Cal Scorpions	L	22	26		6/16/2012	A	Central Cal War Angels	W	26	20 **
6/12/2010	H	Modesto Maniax	W	46	0 S		6/30/2012	H	Central Cal War Angels	W	34	8 Q
7/10/2010	H	Wisconsin Warriors	W	35	2 CC		7/7/2012	A	San Diego Surge	L	7	42 S
7/24/2010	N	Montreal Blitz	L	2	9 C							
4/2/2011	A	Los Angeles Amazons	W	53	0							
4/9/2011	H	Portland Fighting Fillies	W	36	0							
4/30/2011	A	Central Cal War Angels	W	11	6							
5/7/2011	A	Portland Fighting Fillies	W	36	0							
5/14/2011	H	Central Cal War Angels	W	19	0							
6/4/2011	H	San Diego Surge	L	13	42							
6/11/2011	H	Los Angeles Amazons	W	40	0							
6/18/2011	A	Central Cal War Angels	L	15	24							
6/25/2011	H	Portland Fighting Fillies	W	39	0 Q							
7/9/2011	A	San Diego Surge	L	0	36 S							

Bay Area Bandits Player Register (2011-2012)

Albanese, Justus (2011)
Amirault, K. (2011)
Avila, Sasha (2011)
Block, Donelle (2011-2012)
Brinkerhoff, Sam (2011)
Brown, LaStar (2011-2012)
Brown, Rowena (2011)
Cordell, Dana (2011-2012)
Cuore, Rosaria Del (2011-2012)
Darrow, Rachel (2011-2012)
Deering, Jen (2011-2012)
Dolcini, Ashlynn (2011-2012)
Edison, Breonna (2011-2012)
Evans, Cori (2012)
Garcia, Michelle (2012)
Golay, Danielle (2011-2012)
Gudiel, Monica (2011)
Hernandez, Sandra (2011-2012)
Higgins, Valencia (2011-2012)
Howe, Jodi (2011-2012)
Jackson, Latisha (2012)
Jahnigen, Karenina (2011)
Jalalat, Julia (2011-2012)
Johnson, Latrice (2011-2012)
Jones, Amber (2011-2012)
Kendall, Anne (2011-2012)
Kimble, Shalom (2011)
Kimmel, Kara (2011-2012)
Larsen, Angela (2012)
Marshall, Aspen (2012)
Marshall, Stephanie (2011)
McCoid, Kelly (2012)
Melendez, Marlene (2011)
Mendoza, Esmi (2011-2012)
Mitchell, Kandice (2011-2012)
Mosley, Kimberly (2011-2012)
Muti, Valu (2011-2012)
Paraiso, April (2011)
Payton, Casey (2011)
Piellusch, Anastasia (2011)
Pine, Farris (2011-2012)
Reed, Dominique (2011-2012)
Riggs, Kelli (2011-2012)
Romanini, Jen (2011-2012)
Santos, Sharon (2011)
Sarieh, Nancy (2012)
Smith, Dakura (2011-2012)
Stephens, Irene (2011)
Strom, Lanecia (2011-2012)
Takapu, Loisi (2011-2012)
Tan, Melanie (2011)
Taylor, Jackie (2011-2012)
Vaeao, Lelatasio (2011)
Villa, Sheri (2012)
Williams, Jenny (2011)
Wong, Jocelyn (2011)
Zarnowiecki, Joy (2011-2012)

Bay State Warriors

Year	League	Name	W	L	Conference	Division	DF	PR
2002	IWFL	Bay State Warriors	5	4	Eastern	--	4	--
2003	IWFL	Bay State Warriors	9	1	Eastern	North Atlantic	1	CC
2004	IWFL	Bay State Warriors	0	8	Eastern	North Atlantic	2	--
2005	IWFL	Bay State Warriors	4	7	Eastern	North Atlantic	3	--
2006	IWFL	Bay State Warriors	7	2	Eastern	North Atlantic	1	S
2007	IWFL	Boston Rampage	4	4	Eastern	North Atlantic	2	--
		Total	**29**	**26**				

Based in: Boston, MA
Notes: Merged with NWFA's Massachusetts Mutiny to form Boston Militia

Date	H/A	Opponent	Result			
4/20/2002		New Hampshire Freedom	W	48	0	
4/27/2002		New York Sharks	L	0	40	
5/4/2002		New Hampshire Freedom	W	34	8	
5/11/2002		Albany Night-Mares	W	14	9	
5/18/2002		Albany Night-Mares	W	14	6	
6/1/2002		Montreal Blitz	L	24	33	
6/8/2002		New York Sharks	L	0	26	
6/15/2002		Montreal Blitz	W	18	12	
6/22/2002		New York Sharks	L	2	22	
4/12/2003	H	Rhode Island Riptide	W	12	0	
4/19/2003	H	Montreal Blitz	W	30	6	
5/3/2003	H	Philadelphia Liberty Belles (I)	W	34	6	
5/10/2003	A	New Hampshire Freedom	W	30	0	
5/17/2003	A	Montreal Blitz	W	35	0	
5/31/2003	H	New Hampshire Freedom	W	34	0	
6/7/2003	A	Rhode Island Riptide	W	26	0	
6/14/2003	A	Philadelphia Liberty Belles (I)	W	28	8	
6/21/2003	H	Miami Fury	W	1	0	S
6/28/2003	A	New York Sharks	L	6	20	CC
4/24/2004	H	Rhode Island Intensity	L	6	7	
5/1/2004	A	Rhode Island Intensity	L	14	30	
5/8/2004	A	New Hampshire Freedom	L	0	20	
5/15/2004	A	New York Sharks	L	0	45	
5/22/2004	H	New Hampshire Freedom	L	0	7	
5/29/2004	A	Montreal Blitz	L	0	28	
6/5/2004	H	Montreal Blitz	L	6	20	
6/12/2004	H	New York Sharks	L	0	35	
4/2/2005	A	Chicago Force	L	7	12	
4/9/2005	H	New York Sharks	L	12	41	
4/16/2005	A	Rhode Island Intensity	W	21	6	
4/23/2005	H	Manchester Freedom	W	18	0	
4/30/2005	H	Southern Maine Rebels	L	0	8	
5/14/2005	H	Chicago Force	L	0	16	
5/21/2005	A	New York Sharks	L	0	9	
6/4/2005	H	Rhode Island Intensity	W	20	0	
6/11/2005	A	Southern Maine Rebels	L	0	8	
6/18/2005	A	Connecticut Lightning	L	0	19	
6/25/2005		Manchester Freedom	W	18	0	
4/29/2006	H	Montreal Blitz	W	32	6	
5/6/2006	A	Southern Maine Rebels	W	41	6	
5/13/2006	H	Delaware Griffins	W	32	0	
5/20/2006	A	Montreal Blitz	W	9	0	
6/3/2006	A	Manchester Freedom	W	7	0	
6/10/2006	H	Manchester Freedom	W	7	6	
6/17/2006	H	Carolina Cardinals	W	1	0	
6/24/2006	H	New York Sharks	L	16	24	
7/8/2006	H	Atlanta Xplosion	L	0	41	S
4/28/2007	H	Southern Maine Rebels	W	13	0	
5/12/2007	A	New England Intensity	L	7	13	
5/19/2007	H	New York Sharks	L	6	26	
5/26/2007	A	Montreal Blitz	L	0	7	
6/9/2007	A	D.C. Divas	L	0	70	
6/16/2007	A	Cape Fear Thunder	W	17	7	
6/23/2007	H	Delaware Griffins	W	28	0	
6/30/2007	H	Southern Maine Rebels	W	13	8	

Binghamton Tiger Cats

Year	League		Name	W	L	Conference	Division	DF	PR
2009	WFA		Binghamton Tiger Cats	2	6	National	Northeast	5	--
2010	IWFL2		Binghamton Tiger Cats	0	8	Eastern	Northeast	8	--
2011	WSFL	IX	Binghamton Tiger Cats	6	4	--	--	--	--
2012	WSFL		Binghamton Tiger Cats	4	4	American	Northeast	3	--
2013	W8FL		Binghamton Tiger Cats	4	2	--	--	2	C
2014	W8FL		Binghamton Tiger Cats	2	4	--	--	3	CC
			Total	18	28				

Based in: Binghamton, NY **Neutral site:** Memphis, TN (N)

Date		Opponent				
4/18/2009	A	New Jersey Titans	L	0	21	
4/25/2009	H	Keystone Assault	L	20	34	
5/9/2009	H	Connecticut Cyclones	W	1	0	N
5/16/2009	H	New Jersey Titans	L	6	26	
5/30/2009	A	Keystone Assault	L	6	32	
6/6/2009	A	Connecticut Cyclones	W	1	0	N
6/13/2009	H	Baltimore Burn	L	6	56	
6/20/2009	A	Philadelphia Liberty Belles (II)	L	0	53	
4/3/2010	H	Montreal Blitz	L	0	76	
4/10/2010	A	Erie Illusion	L	0	57	
4/17/2010	H	Erie Illusion	L	0	55	
4/24/2010	A	Jersey Justice	L	0	40	
5/8/2010	H	Jersey Justice	L	0	38	
5/15/2010	A	Philadelphia Firebirds	L	0	49	
5/22/2010	A	Jersey Justice	L	8	38	
6/5/2010	H	Southern Maine Rebels	L	8	21	
4/9/2011	H	Three Rivers Xplosion	W	40	12	
4/16/2011	H	Baltimore Burn	L	0	22	
4/23/2011	A	Jersey Justice	L	8	36	
4/30/2011	A	Three Rivers Xplosion	W	22	8	
5/14/2011	A	Erie Illusion	L	0	38	I
5/21/2011	H	Jersey Justice	W	1	0	
5/21/2011	H	Three Rivers Xplosion	W	1	0	
6/4/2011	A	Baltimore Burn	L	0	46	
6/11/2011	H	New England Nightmare	W	1	0	I
6/18/2011	H	Three Rivers Xplosion	W	1	0	
4/21/2012	A	Baltimore Burn	W	1	0	
4/28/2012	H	Mass Chaos	W	30	0	
5/5/2012	H	Three Rivers Xplosion	W	1	0	
5/12/2012	A	New England Nightmare	L	0	34	I
5/19/2012	H	New Jersey Titans	L	0	59	
6/2/2012	H	Baltimore Burn	L	0	76	
6/9/2012	A	New Jersey Titans	L	8	46	
6/23/2012	A	Maine Rebels	W	22	8	I
4/13/2013	A	Cape Fear Thunder	W	20	14	
4/27/2013	H	West Virginia Wildfire	L	8	50	
5/4/2013	A	Three Rivers Xplosion	W	38	30	*
5/11/2013	H	Three Rivers Xplosion	W	34	0	
5/18/2013	H	Cape Fear Thunder	W	28	8	
6/29/2013	N	West Virginia Wildfire	L	8	44	C
4/5/2014	H	Cape Fear Thunder	W	1	0	
4/19/2014	A	West Virginia Wildfire	L	8	20	
4/26/2014	H	Cape Fear Thunder	W	16	6	
5/3/2014	A	Nashville Smashers	L	0	34	
6/14/2014	H	West Virginia Wildfire	L	20	34	
7/12/2014	A	West Virginia Wildfire	L	0	1	CC

Binghamton Tiger Cats Player Register (2009)

Abruzzi, Jessica (2009)
Andrascik, Kristin (2009)
Bachofer, Tabitha (2009)
Bahnuk, Jackie (2009)
Benjamin, Chris (2009)
Black, Mandi (2009)
Bobroff, Ilana (2009)
Bunker, Kristen (2009)
Burnham, Kelly (2009)
Chapman, Jen (2009)
Clicquennoi, Meghan (2009)
Collins, Julie (2009)
Czimback, Carol (2009)
Dean, Jennifer (2009)
DeJesus, Tamyra (2009)
Dunbar, Brittanny (2009)
English, Julianne (2009)
Fenton, Katie (2009)
Hall, Amy (2009)
Henley, Donna (2009)
House, Tracy (2009)
Jansen, Dawn (2009)
Jensen, Sarah (2009)
Johnston, Jami (2009)
Knox, Ashley (2009)
Mallory, Nicole (2009)
Meyers, Linda (2009)
Mundy, Cheryl (2009)
Onuska, Michelle (2009)
Pasto, Beth (2009)
Patten, Rachel (2009)
Peck, Heather (2009)
Poole, Jessica (2009)
Ranelli, Nancy (2009)
Shaffer, Gisella (2009)
Telfer, Denise (2009)
Tomlinson, Amanda (2009)
Townsend, Ashley (2009)
Turner, Mindy (2009)
White, Cheri (2009)
Wright, Julie (2009)
Zuber, Kishan (2009)

Birmingham Steel Magnolias

Year	League	Name	W	L	Conference	Division	DF	PR
2002	WAFL-WFA	Birmingham Steel Magnolias	5	6	Central	--	2	CC

Based in: Birmingham, AL
Notes: Preceded by WAFL's Alabama Slammers

10/12/2002	H	Indianapolis Vipers	L	14	20		11/23/2002	A	New Orleans Voodoo Dolls	W	1	0 N
10/19/2002	A	Georgia Enforcers	W	20	8		12/7/2002	H	Georgia Enforcers	W	1	0
10/26/2002	H	New Orleans Voodoo Dolls	W	1	0 N		12/14/2002	A	Tampa Bay Force	W	1	0
11/2/2002	H	Jacksonville Dixie Blues	L	16	40		12/21/2002	A	Orlando Fire	L	0	1
11/9/2002	A	Indianapolis Vipers	L	8	14		1/11/2003	A	Indianapolis Vipers	L	6	38 CC
11/16/2002	H	Orlando Fire	L	0	35							

Blaze'n Canes

Year	League	Name	W	L	Conference	Division	DF	PR
2006	NWFA	X Blaze'n Canes	1	0	--	--	--	--

Based in: New Orleans, LA
Notes: One-year merger of New Orleans Blaze and Gulf Coast Herricanes (Hurricane Katrina)

5/13/2006   A   Emerald Coast Barracudas   W   16   12

Boise Xtreme

Year	League	Name	W	L	Conference	Division	DF	PR
2002	WSFL	Boise Xtreme	1	5	--	--	3	--
2003	IWFL	Boise Xtreme	2	8	Western	Pacific Northwest	5	--
2004	IWFL	Boise Xtreme	2	6	Western	Pacific Northwest	4	--
2005	IWFL	Boise Xtreme	2	8	Western	Pacific Northwest	4	--
		Total	7	27				

Based in: Boise, ID

4/13/2002	H	Arizona Knighthawks	L	0	57	IE	4/3/2004	A	Tacoma Majestics	L	0	27
4/20/2002		Tacoma Majestics	L	8	34		4/24/2004	H	Eugene Edge	W	20	14
4/27/2002		Portland Shockwave	L	12	18	*	5/1/2004	A	Corvallis Pride	L	8	20
5/4/2002		Oregon Unforgiven	W	39	0		5/8/2004	A	Portland Shockwave	L	14	21
5/18/2002		Portland Shockwave	L	13	20		5/15/2004	H	Tacoma Majestics	L	6	27
5/26/2002		Tacoma Majestics	L	0	38		5/29/2004	A	Eugene Edge	W	45	40
							6/5/2004	H	Corvallis Pride	L	0	34
3/22/2003	A	Portland Shockwave	L	8	32		6/12/2004	H	Portland Shockwave	L	14	21
4/5/2003	H	Tacoma Majestics	L	6	26							
4/12/2003	H	Eugene Edge	L	16	18		4/2/2005	H	Corvallis Pride	L	6	41
4/19/2003	A	Santa Rosa Scorchers	W	14	6		4/9/2005	A	Portland Shockwave	L	7	52
4/26/2003	H	Corvallis Pride	L	0	12		4/23/2005	H	Tacoma Majestics	L	6	26
5/3/2003	H	Portland Shockwave	L	12	34		4/30/2005	A	Corvallis Pride	L	6	34
5/17/2003	A	Tacoma Majestics	L	8	47		5/7/2005	A	Santa Rosa Scorchers	L	6	20
5/24/2003	H	Santa Rosa Scorchers	W	1	0		5/21/2005	H	Corvallis Pride	L	6	43
5/31/2003	A	Eugene Edge	L	0	39		5/28/2005	A	Tacoma Majestics	L	0	26
6/7/2003	A	Corvallis Pride	L	6	38		6/4/2005	H	Santa Rosa Scorchers	L	8	38
							6/11/2005	H	Eugene Edge	W	1	0
							6/18/2005	A	Eugene Edge	W	1	0

Boston Militia

Year	League	Name	W	L	Conference	Division	DF	PR
2008	IWFL	Boston Militia	6	2	Eastern	North Atlantic	2	--
2009	IWFL	Boston Militia	9	1	Eastern	North Atlantic	1	CC
2010	IWFL	Boston Militia	11	0	Eastern	Northeast	1	**NC**
2011	WFA	Boston Militia	11	1	National	North	1	**NC**
2012	WFA	Boston Militia	10	1	National	Division 2 (North)	1	CC
2013	WFA	Boston Militia	10	1	National	Division 1 (Northeast)	1	CC
2014	WFA	Boston Militia	11	0	National	Northeast	1	**NC**
		Total	**68**	**6**				

Based in: Boston, MA   **Neutral sites:** Round Rock, TX (N1); Bedford, TX (N2); Pittsburgh, PA (N3); Chicago, IL (N4)
Notes: Merger of Boston Rampage [Bay State Warriors] and NWFA's Massachusetts Mutiny; Succeeded by Boston Renegades

Date	H/A	Opponent	Result			
4/12/2008	H	D.C. Divas	W	27	22	
4/26/2008	A	Pittsburgh Passion	L	8	34	
5/3/2008	A	Central PA Vipers	W	48	0	
5/10/2008	H	New York Sharks	L	24	26	
5/17/2008	A	New York Sharks	W	28	14	
5/31/2008	H	Manchester Freedom	W	38	7	
6/7/2008	H	Montreal Blitz	W	30	20	
6/14/2008	A	Baltimore Nighthawks	W	28	6	
4/18/2009	H	Manchester Freedom	W	42	0	
4/25/2009	A	New York Sharks	W	21	7	
5/2/2009	H	Connecticut Crushers	W	47	0	
5/9/2009	A	Montreal Blitz	W	39	0	
5/16/2009	H	Philadelphia Firebirds	W	60	0	
5/30/2009	A	Baltimore Nighthawks	W	66	0	
6/6/2009	H	New York Nemesis	W	49	12	
6/13/2009	A	New England Intensity	W	60	0	
6/27/2009	H	Dallas Diamonds	W	34	14	S
7/11/2009	H	D.C. Divas	L	21	27	CC
4/3/2010	A	New York Nemesis	W	56	6	
4/10/2010	H	Connecticut Crushers	W	59	10	
4/24/2010	H	Pittsburgh Passion	W	27	0	
5/1/2010	A	D.C. Divas	W	42	35	
5/8/2010	A	New York Nemesis	W	40	0	
5/15/2010	H	New York Sharks	W	31	0	
5/22/2010	A	Philadelphia Firebirds	W	1	0	
6/5/2010	H	D.C. Divas	W	52	36	
6/12/2010	H	New York Sharks	W	26	6	S
7/10/2010	H	D.C. Divas	W	28	0	CC
7/24/2010	N1	Sacramento Sirens	W	39	7	C
4/2/2011	A	D.C. Divas	L	20	35	
4/16/2011	H	New York Sharks	W	28	7	
4/30/2011	H	Northeastern Nitro	W	72	0	
5/7/2011	A	New England Nightmare	W	62	0	
5/14/2011	A	Northeastern Nitro	W	42	0	
5/21/2011	A	New York Sharks	W	43	6	
6/4/2011	H	Philadelphia Liberty Belles (II)	W	70	8	
6/11/2011	H	D.C. Divas	W	27	16	
6/25/2011	A	D.C. Divas	W	37	24	Q
7/9/2011	A	Chicago Force	W	50	23	S
7/16/2011	H	Indy Crash	W	46	18	CC
7/30/2011	N2	San Diego Surge	W	34	19	C
4/14/2012	H	New York Sharks	W	64	6	
4/21/2012	A	Philadelphia Liberty Belles (II)	W	59	0	
4/28/2012	A	Keystone Assault	W	31	0	
5/12/2012	A	Philadelphia Liberty Belles (II)	W	62	0	
5/19/2012	H	D.C. Divas	W	44	7	
6/2/2012	H	Maine Lynx	W	65	0	
6/9/2012	A	D.C. Divas	W	32	25	
6/16/2012	A	New York Sharks	W	55	12	
6/30/2012	H	New York Sharks	W	47	6	Q
7/7/2012	H	D.C. Divas	W	55	34	S
7/21/2012	A	Chicago Force	L	34	35	CC
4/13/2013	H	New York Sharks	W	70	0	
4/20/2013	H	Montreal Blitz	W	56	22	I
4/27/2013	A	D.C. Divas	W	56	35	
5/4/2013	A	New York Sharks	W	47	0	
5/11/2013	A	Pittsburgh Passion	W	42	28	
5/18/2013	H	D.C. Divas	W	81	54	
6/1/2013	H	Central Maryland Seahawks	W	56	0	
6/8/2013	A	Montreal Blitz	W	50	0	I
6/22/2013	H	Pittsburgh Passion	W	63	28	Q
7/13/2013	H	D.C. Divas	W	58	34	S
7/20/2013	A	Chicago Force	L	27	46	CC
4/5/2014	H	D.C. Divas	W	36	32	
4/19/2014	H	Cleveland Fusion	W	47	7	
4/26/2014	A	Central Maryland Seahawks	W	1	0	N
5/3/2014	A	Cleveland Fusion	W	48	7	
5/10/2014	H	Baltimore Burn	W	1	0	I
5/17/2014	N3	Chicago Force	W	35	18	
6/7/2014	A	D.C. Divas	W	29	28	
6/21/2014	H	Cleveland Fusion	W	47	6	Q
7/5/2014	H	D.C. Divas	W	72	56	S
7/19/2014	H	Chicago Force	W	63	14	CC
8/3/2014	N4	San Diego Surge	W	69	34	C

Boston Militia Player Register (2011-2014)

Alpert, Amanda (2011-2014)
Banks, Holli (2011-2012)
Battaglia, Nicole (2013)
Baumgartner, Erin (2011)
Bertman, Katy (2011-2013)
Bonds, Chante (2011-2012)
Bowman, Nakita (2012-2014)
Brickhouse, Mia (2011-2013)
Brown, Jennie (2011)
Brown, Torrance (2014)
Burge, Joy (2014)
Cabrera, Jessica (2011-2013)
Cahill, Allison (2011-2014)
Calkins, Elizabeth "Betsy" (2011-2014)
Carden, Chloe (2011-2012)
Carvey, Fatima (2012)
Casey, Charlene (2014)
Chace, Meredith (2011-2012)
Colindres, Stacey (2012)
Conway, Emily (2011, 2013)
Crocker, Heather (2014)
Dawson, Sheila "L.D." (2012-2013)
Diette, Erin (2014)
Donaldson, Dorothy (2011-2014)
Dyment, Natalie (2011)
Eddy, Vicky (2011-2014)
Edwards, Jennifer (2014)
English, Raxan "Roxy" (2011-2014)
Entienne, Marie (2011-2013)
Fillion, Kim (2012-2013)
Gallo, Briannah (2011-2014)
Gibson, Tomi (2014)
Goodwin, Molly (2011-2013)
Greene, Alicia (2011)
Guen, Monica (2012-2013)
Harper, Patricia (2011-2012)
Harris, Alicia (2011-2012)
Hickey, Kim (2011)
Hiort, Deirdre "Dee" (2012-2014)
Hodge, Jeriesha "Jay" (2011-2012)
Holland, Emily (2014)
Jeffers, Stephanie "Steph" (2012-2014)
Kaleta, Beth (2011-2014)
Kelley, Christine (2011-2012)
Kokura, Noriko (2014)
Landrum, Asia (2011-2014)
Lewis, Janet (2011)
Liu, Tiana (2013-2014)
Lowe, Hailee (2013)
Lowe, Meredith (2011)
McFadden, Katie (2013-2014)
McKenley, Sherene (2011-2012)
Nardelli, Riss (2014)
Olivieri, Jennifer "Jenny" (2011-2014)
Oshikoya, Adia (2014)
Oshodi, Kehinda (2011-2014)
Payne, Nakita "Kita" (2011-2013)
Pelletier, Abby (2013-2014)
Penta, Jessica (2011-2012)
Pirog, Jennifer (2013)
Pittman, Kesa (2012)
Ponzo, Gladys (2013-2014)
Ponzo, Tinisha (2013-2014)
Powell, Jen (2011-2012)
Princi, Michelle (2011, 2013)
Resha, Danielle (2011-2013)
Robinson-Griggs, Lucia (2012-2014)
Roderique, Allie (2011)
Rush, Samantha (2011)
Saez, Xaymara (2011-2013)
Sarson, Kristen (2011-2014)
Saur, Amy (2011-2012)
Schwartz, Kathryn (2011)
Segers, Shana (2012-2014)
Slack, Kate (2011-2012)
Smith, Adrienne (2011-2014)
Snow, Ginger (2011)
Snow, Rebecca "Becky" (2012)
Snyder, Ashley (2011-2012)
Stewart, Shauntay (2012-2014)
Tesfaye, Manmenasha (2011-2014)
Thomas, Chris (2012-2013)
Tiamfook, Stacey (2011-2014)
Toal, Rachel (2011)
Torres, Mocha (2014)
Trice, Brandy (2011-2012)
Tylander, Kathryn (2011-2014)
Vachon-Breden, Michelle (2014)
Vincent-Horta, Lisa (2014)
Wachholz, Katherine (2012)
Wacht, Sharyn (2011)
Walsh, Deanna (2013-2014)
Weddell, Amy (2011)
Weinberg, Emily (2011-2014)
Williams, Naiyaka Sade (2011-2012)
Woodfine, Sherese (2011-2014)
Zelee, Whitney (2011-2014)

Boston Renegades

Year	League	Name	W	L	Conference	Division	DF	PR
2015	WFA	Boston Renegades	4	3	National	New England	--	S

Based in: Boston, MA
Notes: Preceded by Boston Militia

4/18/2015	H	Central Maryland Seahawks	W	57	0		6/13/2015	A	D.C. Divas	L	28	56
5/2/2015	H	D.C. Divas	L	27	32		6/27/2015	H	West Michigan Mayhem	W	59	12	Q
5/16/2015	A	Cleveland Fusion	W	24	20		7/11/2015	H	Chicago Force	L	18	49	S
5/30/2015	A	Chicago Force	W	30	24	*						

Boston Renegades Player Register (2015)

Adams, Erica (2015)
Alpert, Amanda (2015)
Asante, Asia (2015)
Beinecke, Emily (2015)
Bonds, Chante (2015)
Boroyan, Kimberly (2015)
Bowman, Nakita (2015)
Brickhouse, Mia (2015)
Brown, Torrance (2015)
Cabrera, Jessica (2015)
Cahill, Allison (2015)
Calkins, Elizabeth "Betsy" (2015)
Casey, Charlene (2015)
Clark, Sarah (2015)
Curd, Kyesha (2015)
Diette, Erin (2015)
Dulski, Jen (2015)
Eddy, Vicky (2015)
English, Raxan "Roxy" (2015)
Etienne, Marie (2015)
Gainey, Jazmine (2015)
Gallo, Briannah (2015)
Gonzalez, Crissy (2015)
Goodman, Brooke (2015)
Hiort, Deirdre "Dee" (2015)
Holland, Emily (2015)
Jeffers, Stephanie "Steph" (2015)
Katz, Kristina (2015)
Kelley, Christine (2015)
Kokura, Noriko (2015)
Liu, Tiana (2015)
McFadden, Katie (2015)
Miechkowski, Kate (2015)
Nardelli, Riss (2015)
Nesbitt, Sandra "Gumby" (2015)
Olivieri, Jennifer "Jenny" (2015)
Payne, Nakita "Kita" (2015)
Pelletier, Abby (2015)
Penta, Jessica (2015)
Powell, Jen (2015)
Quimby, Sue (2015)
Reynolds, Maureen (2015)
Robinson-Griggs, Lucia (2015)
Saez, Xaymara (2015)
Sanderson, Lizzie (2015)
Santiago, Lissette (2015)
Saur, Amy (2015)

Continued on next page

Boston Renegades Player Register (continued)

Segers, Shana (2015)
Smith, Adrienne (2015)
Snyder, Ashley (2015)
Tiamfook, Stacey (2015)
Torres, Mocha (2015)

Tseng, Chiung-Yi (2015)
Tull, Tia (2015)
Tylander, Kathryn (2015)
Vachon-Breden, Michelle (2015)
Vermette, Sera (2015)

Viola, Sarah (2015)
Walsh, Deanna (2015)
Weinberg, Emily (2015)
Zelee, Whitney (2015)

California Quake

Year	League	Name	W	L	T	Conference	Division	DF	PR
2001	WAFL	California Quake	11	2	0	Pacific	South	1	**NC**
2002	WAFC	California Quake	5	5	0	Southern	--	3	--
2003	IWFL	California Quake	3	5	0	Western	Pacific Southwest	3	--
2004	IWFL	California Quake	0	8	0	Western	Pacific Southwest	3	--
2005	IWFL	California Quake	6	3	1	Western	Pacific Southwest	3	--
2006	IWFL	California Quake	4	4	0	Western	Pacific Southwest	3	--
2007	IWFL	California Quake	3	5	0	Western	Pacific Southwest	3	--
2008	IWFL	California Quake	8	1	0	Western	Pacific Southwest	1	S
2009	IWFL	California Quake	4	4	0	Western	Pacific Southwest	3	--
2010	IWFL	California Quake	7	2	0	Western	Pacific West	4	--
2011	IWFL	California Quake	10	1	0	Western	Pacific Southwest	1	C
2012	IWFL	California Quake	3	6	0	Western	Pacific Southwest	2	BQ
2013	IWFL	California Quake	3	5	0	Western	Pacific West	--	S
2014	IWFL	California Quake	5	2	0	Western	Pacific West	2	--
2015	IWFL	California Quake	1	6	0	Western	Pacific West	5	--
		Total	73	59	1				

Based in: Downey, CA   **Neutral sites:** San Diego, CA (N1); Round Rock, TX (N2)

Date		Opponent				
11/3/2001	A	Los Angeles Lasers	L	14	22	
11/14/2001	H	Hawaii Legends	W	21	18	
11/17/2001	A	Arizona Caliente	W	19	6	
12/1/2001	A	San Diego Sunfire	W	20	14	
12/8/2001	A	Rose City Wildcats	W	20	8	
12/15/2001	H	Los Angeles Lasers	W	27	22	
12/29/2001	A	Oakland Banshees	W	32	8	
1/5/2002	H	San Diego Sunfire	W	24	8	
1/12/2002	H	Arizona Caliente	L	22	26	
1/19/2002	H	San Francisco Tsunami	W	36	6	
1/26/2002	H	Sacramento Sirens	W	40	13	S
2/10/2002	H	Arizona Caliente	W	16	12	CC
2/24/2002	N1	Jacksonville Dixie Blues	W	30	14	C
8/29/2002		Los Angeles Amazons	W	20	8	I
9/11/2002	A	Pacific Blast	L	6	46	
9/14/2002	A	Pacific Blast	L	6	72	
9/21/2002	H	Arizona Caliente	L	16	32	
10/5/2002	H	Sacramento Sirens	L	19	52	
10/12/2002	H	San Diego Nitrous	W	41	0	
10/19/2002		Los Angeles Amazons	W	20	14	I*
10/26/2002	A	San Diego Nitrous	W	1	0	
11/2/2002	H	San Francisco Stingrayz	W	1	0	
11/9/2002	A	Arizona Caliente	L	0	26	
3/8/2003	A	Santa Rosa Scorchers	W	8	0	
3/29/2003	H	Oakland Banshees	W	31	14	
4/12/2003	H	San Diego Sea Catz	W	43	0	
4/26/2003	A	Oakland Banshees	L	14	16	
5/3/2003	H	Santa Rosa Scorchers	L	0	6	
5/10/2003	A	Sacramento Sirens	L	14	67	
5/24/2003	H	San Francisco Stingrayz	L	3	80	
5/31/2003	H	Sacramento Sirens	L	21	65	
4/3/2004	H	Oakland Banshees	L	0	41	
4/17/2004	A	Sacramento Sirens	L	0	69	
4/24/2004	A	San Diego Sea Catz	L	13	20	
5/1/2004	A	San Francisco Stingrayz	L	0	1	
5/15/2004	H	Santa Rosa Scorchers	L	0	1	
5/29/2004	H	San Diego Sea Catz	L	0	18	
6/5/2004	A	Oakland Banshees	L	0	38	
6/12/2004	H	Sacramento Sirens	L	0	1	
4/2/2005	H	Santa Rosa Scorchers	W	17	6	
4/9/2005	A	Sacramento Sirens	L	0	72	
4/16/2005	H	Redding Rage	W	33	0	
4/23/2005	A	Santa Rosa Scorchers	L	0	14	
4/30/2005	H	Oakland Banshees	T	0	0	*
5/7/2005	A	So Cal Bandits	W	1	0	
5/14/2005	H	Sacramento Sirens	L	21	52	
5/28/2005	A	Tucson Wildfire	W	32	0	
6/11/2005	A	Oakland Banshees	W	21	6	
6/18/2005	H	Tucson Wildfire	W	59	6	
4/29/2006	A	Santa Rosa Scorchers	L	8	18	
5/6/2006	H	Tucson Monsoon	W	59	6	
5/13/2006	A	Tucson Monsoon	W	49	12	
5/20/2006	A	Sacramento Sirens	L	19	53	
5/27/2006	H	Santa Rosa Scorchers	L	0	46	
6/3/2006	H	Sacramento Sirens	L	0	53	
6/17/2006	A	Tucson Monsoon	W	28	0	
6/24/2006	H	Tucson Monsoon	W	22	0	

Continued on next page

California Quake Game-By-Game Results (continued)

Date	H/A	Opponent	W/L	PF	PA	Note
4/28/2007	A	Tucson Monsoon	L	23	30	
5/5/2007	A	Santa Rosa Scorchers	L	19	23	
5/12/2007	A	Sacramento Sirens	L	6	27	
5/19/2007	H	Santa Rosa Scorchers	W	32	26	*
6/2/2007	H	Sacramento Sirens	L	15	24	
6/16/2007	A	Sacramento Sirens	L	17	39	
6/23/2007	H	Tucson Monsoon	W	20	0	
6/30/2007	H	Redding Rage	W	50	24	
4/12/2008	H	Tucson Monsoon	W	45	14	
4/19/2008	A	Southern California Breakers	W	5	0	
4/26/2008	H	New Mexico Menace	W	64	0	
5/3/2008	A	Las Vegas Showgirlz	W	30	27	
5/10/2008	H	Tucson Monsoon	W	37	0	
5/24/2008	H	Las Vegas Showgirlz	W	41	38	
5/31/2008	A	Southern California Breakers	W	27	0	
6/7/2008	A	New Mexico Menace	W	35	0	
6/28/2008	A	Dallas Diamonds	L	3	69	S
4/11/2009	H	Los Angeles Amazons	L	2	32	
4/18/2009	A	Sacramento Sirens	L	0	46	
4/25/2009	H	New Mexico Menace	W	61	0	
5/2/2009	A	Los Angeles Amazons	L	21	36	
5/9/2009	H	Sacramento Sirens	L	14	34	
5/23/2009	H	Modesto Maniax	W	58	24	
5/30/2009	A	Modesto Maniax	W	42	14	
6/6/2009	A	Southern California Breakers	W	26	20	
4/3/2010	H	Seattle Majestics	W	50	14	
4/10/2010	A	Tucson Monsoon	W	60	20	
4/17/2010	H	Los Angeles Amazons	L	36	48	
4/24/2010	H	So Cal Scorpions	W	42	40	
5/1/2010	A	Tucson Monsoon	W	40	8	
5/8/2010	H	Modesto Maniax	W	62	0	
5/22/2010	A	Southern California Breakers	W	34	14	
6/5/2010	A	Portland Shockwave	L	6	7	
9/11/2010		Nor Cal Red Hawks	W	68	12	E
4/9/2011	A	Tucson Monsoon	W	60	6	
4/16/2011	H	Portland Shockwave	W	28	0	
4/23/2011	A	Southern California Breakers	W	60	0	
4/30/2011	A	Sacramento Sirens	W	42	13	
5/7/2011	H	Sacramento Sirens	W	30	13	
5/14/2011	H	Desert Fire Cats	W	1	0	N
5/28/2011	H	Southern California Breakers	W	68	0	
6/4/2011	A	Seattle Majestics	W	50	0	
6/25/2011	H	Sacramento Sirens	W	22	19	S
7/16/2011	A	Wisconsin Warriors	W	48	0	CC
7/30/2011	N2	Atlanta Ravens	L	22	24	C
4/14/2012	H	Phoenix Phantomz	L	0	70	
4/21/2012	A	Tucson Monsoon	W	48	31	
4/28/2012	A	Modesto Maniax	L	6	22	
5/5/2012	A	Phoenix Phantomz	L	6	66	
5/12/2012	H	Tucson Monsoon	W	38	30	
5/26/2012	H	Modesto Maniax	L	0	38	
6/9/2012	A	Phoenix Phantomz	L	14	35	
6/16/2012	H	Tucson Monsoon	W	32	15	
6/30/2012	A	Portland Shockwave	L	0	1	BQ
4/27/2013	H	Nevada Storm	L	12	28	
5/4/2013	A	Phoenix Phantomz	L	0	72	
5/11/2013	A	Tucson Monsoon	W	38	19	
5/25/2013	H	Nor Cal Red Hawks	W	1	0	N
6/15/2013	H	Tucson Monsoon	W	56	6	
6/22/2013	A	Nevada Storm	L	0	56	
6/29/2013	H	Phoenix Phantomz	L	8	21	
7/13/2013	A	Phoenix Phantomz	L	0	18	S
4/12/2014	H	North County Stars	W	64	0	
4/19/2014	A	Utah Jynx	W	20	15	
5/3/2014	A	Phoenix Phantomz	L	14	40	
5/10/2014	H	Tucson Monsoon	W	52	0	
5/24/2014	A	Tucson Monsoon	W	48	0	
5/31/2014	A	Phoenix Phantomz	L	6	21	
6/14/2014	A	North County Stars	W	30	14	
4/11/2015	H	North County Stars	W	34	14	
4/18/2015	A	Sacramento Sirens	L	0	49	
4/25/2015	A	Nevada Storm	L	6	33	
5/9/2015	H	Sacramento Sirens	L	0	47	
5/23/2015	A	Phoenix Phantomz	L	0	1	
5/30/2015	H	Utah Falconz	L	0	81	
6/6/2015	A	North County Stars	L	0	1	

California Quake Player Register (2014-2015)

Adams, Monique (2014)
Arnold, Chassity (2015)
Bible, Lekeisha (2014-2015)
Black, Clarissa (2014)
Blackwell, April (2014)
Blanchard, Jackie (2015)
Bolden, Cachrelle (2015)
Brannon, Kris (2014)
Brooks, Tiffany (2015)
Calhoun, Veronica (2015)
Castellanos, Mikie (2014)
Christensen, Kim (2014)
Cuenca, Rachel (2014)
De Oca, Glenda Montes (2014)
Derbigny, Sherika (2015)
Dieu, Emily (2015)
Duenas, Nathalie (2014)
Duran, Justina (2014-2015)
Evans-Santiago, BreAnna (2015)
Griffith, Tyee (2014)
Hardiman, Demetrea (2014)
Hayes, Ashleigh (2014)
Hollenshed, Laurisa (2014)
Honani, VaNiesha (2014)
Johnson-McKeown, Jasmine (2014)
Juge, Stephanie (2014)
Kim, Paulina (2015)
Lavann, Paula (2014)
Lester-Jefferson, Nicole (2014)
Luna, Jennifer (2014)
Marquez, Selena (2014)
Mattera, Carrie (2015)
McCoy, Latoya (2015)
McNulty, Jennie (2014-2015)
Monterroso, Helen (2014)
Morse, Sharlene (2015)
Niemi, Micaela (2015)
Quenga, Tina (2014)
Quimby, Malaysia (2014)
Renteria, Francia (2014)
Robancho, Shay (2014)
Robledo, Yvette (2014)
Sandoval, Brenda (2014)
Seabloom, Brittany (2015)
Shuler, Heather (2014)
Singletary, Tami (2014)
Taunauu, Alyshia (2015)
Turner, Mariah (2014)
Urrutia, Melissa (2014)
Villa, Estella (2015)
Vivo, Catherine (2014)
Weston, Leutissuer (2014)
Yahn, Shannon (2015)
Young, Sherika (2014)

Cape Fear Thunder

Year	League		Name	W	L	T	Conference	Division	DF	PR
2003	WFL		Fayetteville Thunder	3	3	0	--	--	--	--
2005	WPFL		Cape Fear Thunder	2	5	0	National	East	4	--
2006	WPFL	X	Cape Fear Thunder	1	1	0	--	--	--	--
2007	IWFL		Cape Fear Thunder	1	7	0	Eastern	Mid-Atlantic	3	--
2008	IWFL2		Cape Fear Thunder	2	6	0	Southern	South Atlantic	3	--
2009	IWFL2		Cape Fear Thunder	1	7	0	--	--	19	--
2011	W8FL		Cape Fear Thunder	4	2	1	--	--	1	--
2012	W8FL		Cape Fear Thunder	3	8	0	Eastern	--	2	--
2013	W8FL		Cape Fear Thunder	1	4	0	--	--	3	--
2014	W8FL		Cape Fear Thunder	3	5	0	--	--	4	LC
2015	W8FL		Cape Fear Thunder	2	2	0	--	--	2	C
			Total	**23**	**50**	**1**				

Based in: Fayetteville, NC
Notes: Preceded by Fayetteville Warriors

Neutral sites: Erie, PA (N1); Atlanta, GA (N2)

Date	H/A	Opponent	W/L	PF	PA	Note
5/31/2003	H	Memphis Maulers	L	0	8	
6/7/2003	A	Atlanta Xplosion	L	8	34	I
6/14/2003	H	Tennessee Heat	W	28	20	
6/21/2003	A	Memphis Maulers	L	0	16	
7/19/2003	A	Tennessee Heat	W	30	6	
7/26/2003	H	Tennessee Heat	W	22	14	CC
7/30/2005	H	Carolina Queens	W	34	0	
8/13/2005	A	Delaware Griffins	L	14	16	
8/20/2005	A	Indiana Speed	L	8	44	
9/17/2005	H	Albany Ambush	W	20	8	
9/24/2005	H	Delaware Griffins	L	8	44	
10/1/2005	A	Toledo Reign	L	0	53	
10/8/2005	A	New York Dazzles	L	0	34	
7/22/2006	H	Carolina Queens	W	32	7	
8/12/2006	A	Carolina Queens	L	8	20	
4/28/2007	H	Delaware Griffins	W	6	0	
5/12/2007	A	Carolina Phoenix	L	6	13	
5/19/2007	H	D.C. Divas	L	0	77	
6/2/2007	A	Delaware Griffins	L	0	21	
6/9/2007	A	Palm Beach Punishers	L	0	13	
6/16/2007	H	Boston Rampage	L	7	17	
6/23/2007	H	Carolina Phoenix	L	6	29	
6/30/2007	H	D.C. Divas	L	3	38	
4/12/2008	A	Carolina Phoenix	L	0	40	
4/19/2008	H	Carolina Queens	L	0	51	
5/3/2008	H	Connecticut Cyclones	W	1	0	N
5/10/2008	A	Carolina Queens	L	12	63	
5/17/2008	A	Connecticut Cyclones	W	1	0	N
5/24/2008	H	Carolina Phoenix	L	0	50	
5/31/2008	H	Carolina Queens	L	6	60	
6/14/2008	A	Carolina Phoenix	L	0	41	
4/11/2009	H	Carolina Queens	L	0	66	
4/18/2009	A	Carolina Queens	L	0	59	
4/25/2009	A	Tennessee Valley Tigers	L	0	68	
5/9/2009	H	Carolina Phoenix	L	0	48	
5/16/2009	A	Chattanooga Locomotion	L	0	60	
5/23/2009	A	Louisville Nightmare	W	34	14	
6/6/2009	H	Carolina Phoenix	L	8	55	
6/13/2009	A	Central PA Vipers	L	6	30	
4/9/2011	A	West Virginia Bruisers	L	6	8	
4/16/2011	H	West Virginia Bruisers	W	32	13	
4/23/2011	A	West Virginia Wildfire	W	40	0	
4/30/2011	A	West Virginia Wildfire	W	47	0	
5/14/2011	H	West Virginia Bruisers	L	0	34	
6/4/2011	A	West Virginia Wildfire	T	6	6	
6/11/2011	H	West Virginia Wildfire	W	14	6	
4/14/2012	H	Carolina Queens	L	0	56	I
4/21/2012	H	Three Rivers Xplosion	W	30	0	
4/28/2012	A	Three Rivers Xplosion	W	36	6	
5/5/2012	H	West Virginia Wildfire	W	46	0	
5/19/2012	A	West Virginia Wildfire	L	0	8	
6/2/2012	A	Carolina Queens	L	0	1	I
6/9/2012	H	Huntsville Tigers	L	0	40	
6/16/2012	A	West Virginia Wildfire	L	6	36	
6/23/2012	A	Huntsville Tigers	L	0	50	
6/30/2012	H	West Virginia Wildfire	L	20	42	
7/21/2012		West Virginia Wildfire	L	0	1	
4/6/2013	A	West Virginia Wildfire	L	0	30	
4/13/2013	H	Binghamton Tiger Cats	L	14	20	
4/27/2013	A	Three Rivers Xplosion	W	20	16	
5/4/2013	H	West Virginia Wildfire	L	0	30	
5/18/2013	A	Binghamton Tiger Cats	L	8	28	
4/5/2014	A	Binghamton Tiger Cats	L	0	1	
4/12/2014	H	Nashville Smashers	W	28	0	
4/26/2014	A	Binghamton Tiger Cats	L	6	16	
5/17/2014	A	Nashville Smashers	L	9	12	
6/7/2014	A	West Virginia Wildfire	L	0	30	
6/21/2014	H	West Virginia Wildfire	L	20	26	
7/12/2014	A	Nashville Smashers	W	32	20	CC
7/26/2014	N1	West Virginia Wildfire	W	36	28	C
4/18/2015	N2	Southern Valkyrie	L	14	42	
5/2/2015	H	New York Knockout	W	18	12	
6/6/2015	H	New York Knockout	W	12	0	
8/1/2015	A	New York Knockout	L	0	28	C

Cape Fear Thunder Player Register (2015)

Buie, Jasmine (2015)	Howard, Denita (2015)	Nelson, Nancy (2015)
Feliciano, Jazmin (2015)	Hudson, Sara (2015)	Quinones, Crystal (2015)
Fralin, Tonya (2015)	James, Dee (2015)	Rye, Misty (2015)
Harris, Vanessa (2015)	Love, Bianca (2015)	Shank, Jen (2015)
Heath, Chelsea (2015)	McDonald, Lakisha (2015)	Washington, Denita (2015)

Carolina Cardinals

Year	League		Name	W	L	Conference	Division	DF	PR
2006	IWFL	X	Carolina Cardinals	0	5	--	--	--	--

Based in: Greensboro, NC
Notes: Succeeded by Carolina Phoenix

5/20/2006	A	Manchester Freedom	L	0	1
5/27/2006	A	Delaware Griffins	L	0	1
6/3/2006	A	Orlando Mayhem	L	0	48
6/10/2006	A	Indianapolis Chaos	L	0	1
6/17/2006	A	Bay State Warriors	L	0	1

Carolina Cougars

Year	League		Name	W	L	Conference	Division	DF	PR
2000	WPFL	X	Carolina Cougars	0	1	--	--	--	--
2001	MIWFA		Carolina Cougars	7	1	--	--	--	--
2002	WFL		Carolina Cougars	4	0	--	--	--	--
			Total	**11**	**2**				

Based in: Greensboro, NC

12/9/2000	A	Tampa Tempest	L	7	8	
7/14/2001	A	Tennessee Heat	W	22	0	I
7/28/2001	H	Tennessee Heat	W	18	0	I
8/4/2001	H	New York Sharks	W	10	8	
8/11/2001	H	Tennessee Heat	W	10	0	I
8/18/2001	H	Miami Fury	W	16	7	
8/25/2001	A	Orlando Lightning	W	12	0	
9/1/2001	A	Miami Fury	L	0	28	
9/29/2001	H	Tennessee Heat	W	43	6	I
7/20/2002		Tennessee Heat	W	27	8	
8/10/2002	H	Tennessee Heat	W	44	0	
8/24/2002	A	Fayetteville Warriors	W	14	12	
9/7/2002	H	Fayetteville Warriors	W	44	8	

Carolina Phoenix

Year	League		Name	W	L	Conference	Division	DF	PR
2007	IWFL	X	Carolina Phoenix	5	1	--	--	--	--
2008	IWFL2		Carolina Phoenix	7	2	Southern	South Atlantic	1	CC
2009	IWFL2		Carolina Phoenix	8	2	--	--	1	CC
2010	IWFL2		Carolina Phoenix	9	1	Eastern	Southeast	1	CC
2011	IWFL		Carolina Phoenix	7	1	Eastern	Mid-Atlantic	1	CC
2012	IWFL		Carolina Phoenix	7	1	Eastern	Mid South	2	BCW
2013	IWFL		Carolina Phoenix	11	0	Eastern	Southeast	1	NC
2014	IWFL		Carolina Phoenix	4	5	Eastern	South Atlantic	1	S
2015	IWFL		Carolina Phoenix	8	3	Eastern	South Atlantic	1	CC-BW
			Total	**66**	**16**				

Based in: Greensboro, NC **Neutral sites:** Round Rock, TX (N1); Rock Hill, SC (N2)
Notes: Preceded by Carolina Cardinals

Carolina Phoenix Game-By-Game Results

Date	H/A	Opponent	W/L	PF	PA	Notes
4/28/2007	A	Shreveport Aftershock	L	6	24	
5/12/2007	H	Cape Fear Thunder	W	13	6	
5/19/2007	H	Detroit Predators	W	19	18	
6/2/2007	A	Detroit Predators	W	36	0	
6/9/2007	A	Delaware Griffins	W	12	0	
6/23/2007	A	Cape Fear Thunder	W	29	6	
4/12/2008	H	Cape Fear Thunder	W	40	0	
4/26/2008	A	Palm Beach Punishers	W	25	7	
5/3/2008	H	Carolina Queens	W	21	12	
5/17/2008	A	Carolina Queens	W	20	14	*
5/24/2008	A	Cape Fear Thunder	W	50	0	
5/31/2008	H	Central PA Vipers	W	41	0	
6/7/2008	A	Atlanta Xplosion	L	0	42	
6/14/2008	H	Cape Fear Thunder	W	41	0	
6/28/2008	A	Montreal Blitz	L	27	41	CC
4/11/2009	H	Louisville Nightmare	W	32	7	
4/18/2009	H	Erie Illusion	W	6	0	
5/2/2009	H	Orlando Mayhem	W	42	15	
5/9/2009	A	Cape Fear Thunder	W	48	0	
5/23/2009	A	Palm Beach Punishers	W	14	9	
5/30/2009	H	Carolina Queens	W	8	0	
6/6/2009	A	Cape Fear Thunder	W	55	8	
6/13/2009	A	Carolina Queens	L	20	36	
6/27/2009	A	Carolina Queens	W	26	16	S
7/11/2009	A	Wisconsin Warriors	L	6	28	CC
4/3/2010	A	Carolina Queens	W	26	2	
4/10/2010	H	Palm Beach Punishers	W	49	0	
4/24/2010	A	Louisville Nightmare	W	58	0	
5/1/2010	H	Chattanooga Locomotion	W	56	0	
5/8/2010	H	Carolina Queens	W	48	0	
5/15/2010	A	Tennessee Valley Tigers	W	72	0	
5/22/2010	A	Palm Beach Punishers	W	71	14	
6/5/2010	A	Baltimore Nighthawks	W	22	20	*
6/12/2010	A	Chattanooga Locomotion	W	42	14	S
7/10/2010	A	Montreal Blitz	L	14	19	CC
4/9/2011	A	Baltimore Nighthawks	W	32	8	
4/23/2011	H	Philadelphia Firebirds	W	57	17	
5/14/2011	A	Philadelphia Firebirds	W	54	7	
5/28/2011	A	Georgia Peachez	W	1	0	
6/4/2011	H	Baltimore Nighthawks	W	42	0	
6/11/2011	H	Georgia Peachez	W	1	0	
6/25/2011	A	Montreal Blitz	W	12	7	S
7/16/2011	A	Atlanta Ravens	L	6	24	CC
4/7/2012	A	Philadelphia Firebirds	W	26	0	
4/14/2012	A	Atlanta Xplosion	W	36	31	
4/28/2012	A	Baltimore Nighthawks	W	22	0	
5/19/2012	A	Atlanta Xplosion	L	10	23	
6/16/2012		Philadelphia Firebirds	W	20	14	
6/30/2012		Arlington Impact	W	33	6	BQ
7/14/2012		New England Intensity	W	7	0	BS
7/28/2012	N1	Portland Shockwave	W	27	0	BC
4/27/2013	A	Atlanta Xplosion	W	12	6	
5/4/2013	H	Chattanooga Locomotion	W	58	0	
5/11/2013	A	Carolina Queens	W	54	0	
5/18/2013	H	Washington Prodigy	W	46	7	
6/1/2013	A	Washington Prodigy	W	42	0	
6/15/2013	H	Carolina Queens	W	64	8	
6/22/2013	H	Atlanta Rage	W	14	0	
6/29/2013	A	Chattanooga Locomotion	W	1	0	
7/13/2013	H	Philadelphia Firebirds	W	32	0	S
7/20/2013	H	New England Intensity	W	18	6	CC
8/3/2013	N1	Houston Energy	W	14	0	C
4/12/2014	H	Pittsburgh Passion	L	6	29	
4/19/2014	A	Washington Prodigy	L	20	27	
4/26/2014	H	Chattanooga Locomotion	W	47	6	
5/3/2014	H	New York Sharks	L	28	29	
5/10/2014	A	Carolina Queens	W	26	6	
5/17/2014	A	Pittsburgh Passion	L	0	51	
5/31/2014	A	Chattanooga Locomotion	W	1	0	
6/14/2014	H	Huntsville Tigers	W	52	0	
6/28/2014	A	New York Sharks	L	12	60	S
4/11/2015	A	Philadelphia Firebirds	L	0	20	
4/18/2015	H	Knoxville Lightning	W	45	0	
4/25/2015	A	Washington Prodigy	W	19	0	
5/2/2015	H	Carolina Queens	W	14	0	
5/9/2015	H	Tennessee Train	W	40	0	
5/16/2015	A	Pittsburgh Passion	L	6	41	
5/30/2015	H	Washington Prodigy	W	33	0	
6/13/2015	A	Carolina Queens	W	28	0	
6/27/2015	H	Carolina Queens	W	20	0	S
7/11/2015	A	Pittsburgh Passion	L	12	41	CC
7/24/2015	N2	Madison Blaze	W	32	9	B

Carolina Phoenix Player Register (2014-2015)

Alison, Mana (2014-2015)
Belle Isle, Beth (2014)
Britton, Kristal (2014-2015)
Byrd, Sheila (2014)
Carr, Angela (2014-2015)
Chappell, Murphie (2014-2015)
Cooke, Alecia (2014-2015)
DeGraffinreed, Hannah (2015)
Floyd, Quicha (2014)
Geselle, Bettina (2014-2015)
Glover, T. (2015)
Hargrove, Kimberly (2014-2015)
Herron, Nikki (2014-2015)
Holmes, Porschia (2014-2015)
Idol, Candice (2014-2015)
Jackson, Sequaya (2014)
James, Terah (2014-2015)
Jarrett, Tamara (2014-2015)
King, Jennifer (2014-2015)
Koontz, Tasha (2015)
McDonald, Jeanine (2014-2015)
Mitchell, Caroline (2015)
Mohler, Mara (2014-2015)
Montgomery, Ebony (2014-2015)
Nolan, Katie (2015)
Ormond, Maria (2014-2015)
Rich, Ronda (2014-2015)
Riley, Sherrell (2015)
Rivera, Maria (2014-2015)
Rivera-Reckley, Lisa (2014)
Sainovich, Katrina "Katie" (2015)
Scott, Kelly (2014-2015)
Sellars, Candyce (2014-2015)
Sims, Aisha (2014-2015)
Smith, Asia (2015)
Snyder, Candice (2014)
Souter, Shenicqua (2015)
Spencer, Frankie (2015)
Tonker, Wendy (2014)
Tucci, Annamarie (2014)
Walden, Amanda (2015)
Walker, Starsha (2014-2015)

Franchise Game-By-Game Records, 1999-2015

Carolina Queens

Year	League		Name	W	L	Conference	Division	DF	PR
2005	WPFL		Carolina Queens	0	6	National	North	4	--
2006	WPFL		Carolina Queens	2	6	National	North	3	--
2007	WPFL		Carolina Queens	1	6	National	North	3	--
2008	IWFL2		Carolina Queens	4	4	Southern	South Atlantic	2	--
2009	IWFL2		Carolina Queens	7	2	--	--	1	S
2010	IWFL2		Carolina Queens	1	7	Eastern	Southeast	6	--
2012	IWFL	X	Carolina Queens	6	1	--	--	--	BW
2013	IWFL	X	Carolina Queens	5	4	--	--	--	BW
2014	IWFL		Carolina Queens	6	3	Eastern	South Atlantic	2	BW
2015	IWFL		Carolina Queens	7	3	Eastern	South Atlantic	2	S
			Total	**39**	**42**				

Based in: Charlotte, NC   **Neutral sites:** Round Rock, TX (N1); Rock Hill, SC (N2)

Date		Opponent				
7/30/2005	A	Cape Fear Thunder	L	0	34	
8/13/2005	A	Toledo Reign	L	0	56	
8/20/2005	H	Toledo Reign	L	0	34	
9/3/2005	H	Indiana Speed	L	6	42	
9/24/2005	A	Indiana Speed	L	8	55	
10/8/2005	H	Indiana Speed	L	8	66	
7/22/2006	A	Cape Fear Thunder	L	7	32	
7/29/2006	A	Toledo Reign	L	0	36	
8/5/2006	H	Albany Ambush	W	1	0	
8/12/2006	H	Cape Fear Thunder	W	20	8	
8/19/2006	A	Empire State Roar	L	8	31	
9/2/2006	H	Toledo Reign	L	0	51	
9/9/2006	A	Indiana Speed	L	0	51	
9/23/2006	H	Indiana Speed	L	0	41	
8/18/2007	A	Toledo Reign	L	0	33	
9/1/2007	H	Toledo Reign	L	0	28	
9/22/2007	H	New Jersey Titans	L	8	49	
9/29/2007	H	Connecticut Cyclones	W	20	2	
10/6/2007	A	Indiana Speed	L	0	53	
10/13/2007	A	New Jersey Titans	L	8	61	
10/20/2007	H	Indiana Speed	L	0	43	
4/12/2008	H	Clarksville Fox	L	0	30	
4/19/2008	A	Cape Fear Thunder	W	51	0	
5/3/2008	A	Carolina Phoenix	L	12	21	
5/10/2008	H	Cape Fear Thunder	W	63	12	
5/17/2008	H	Carolina Phoenix	L	14	20	*
5/31/2008	A	Cape Fear Thunder	W	60	6	
6/7/2008	A	Shreveport Aftershock	W	34	6	
6/14/2008	H	Atlanta Xplosion	L	0	40	
4/11/2009	A	Cape Fear Thunder	W	66	0	
4/18/2009	H	Cape Fear Thunder	W	59	0	
4/25/2009	A	Jersey Justice	W	28	20	
5/2/2009	H	Palm Beach Punishers	W	26	14	
5/9/2009	A	Louisville Nightmare	W	1	0	
5/23/2009	H	Chattanooga Locomotion	W	30	12	
5/30/2009	A	Carolina Phoenix	L	0	8	
6/13/2009	H	Carolina Phoenix	W	36	20	
6/27/2009	H	Carolina Phoenix	L	16	26	S
4/3/2010	H	Carolina Phoenix	L	2	26	
4/10/2010	H	Atlanta Xplosion	L	7	54	
4/17/2010	A	Palm Beach Punishers	W	13	3	
5/1/2010	H	Baltimore Nighthawks	L	0	21	
5/8/2010	A	Carolina Phoenix	L	0	48	
5/15/2010	A	Atlanta Xplosion	L	0	50	
5/22/2010	H	Chattanooga Locomotion	L	6	20	
6/5/2010	A	Chattanooga Locomotion	L	0	22	
4/14/2012	A	Cape Fear Thunder	W	56	0	I
4/21/2012	H	Tri-State Bruisers	W	44	6	I
4/28/2012	A	West Virginia Wildfire	W	58	0	I
5/5/2012	A	Atlanta Xplosion	L	14	39	
5/12/2012	H	Huntsville Tigers	W	22	19	I
6/2/2012	H	Cape Fear Thunder	W	1	0	I
7/28/2012	N1	Colorado Sting	W	18	0	B
4/27/2013	A	Chattanooga Locomotion	W	30	8	
5/4/2013	A	Atlanta Xplosion	L	8	52	
5/11/2013	H	Carolina Phoenix	L	0	54	
6/1/2013	H	Chattanooga Locomotion	W	60	0	
6/15/2013	A	Carolina Phoenix	L	8	64	
6/22/2013	A	Baltimore Nighthawks	W	42	28	
6/29/2013	H	Washington Prodigy	L	0	48	
7/6/2013	H	Atlanta Rage	W	26	12	
8/2/2013	N1	San Antonio Regulators	W	28	14	B
4/19/2014	A	Huntsville Tigers	W	32	30	
4/26/2014	H	Baltimore Nighthawks	L	22	28	*
5/3/2014	A	Chattanooga Locomotion	W	52	0	
5/10/2014	H	Carolina Phoenix	L	6	26	
5/17/2014	H	Chattanooga Locomotion	W	1	0	
5/31/2014	A	Baltimore Nighthawks	L	8	32	
6/7/2014	A	Chattanooga Locomotion	W	64	6	
6/21/2014	H	Huntsville Tigers	W	1	0	
7/25/2014	N2	Minnesota Vixen	W	28	22	B
4/11/2015	A	Tennessee Train	W	18	8	
4/18/2015	H	Huntsville Tigers	W	16	0	
5/2/2015	A	Carolina Phoenix	L	0	14	
5/9/2015	A	Baltimore Nighthawks	W	26	0	
5/16/2015	H	Tennessee Train	W	14	0	
5/30/2015	A	Huntsville Tigers	W	20	18	
6/6/2015	H	Knoxville Lightning	W	1	0	
6/13/2015	H	Carolina Phoenix	L	0	28	
6/20/2015	A	Toledo Reign	W	20	6	Q
6/27/2015	A	Carolina Phoenix	L	0	20	S

Carolina Queens Player Register (2015)

Bolden, Lashon (2015)
Capps, Jenny (2015)
Coley, Denise (2015)
Cousar, Keshia (2015)
Cullins, Monique (2015)
Dixon, Starr (2015)
Ellerbee, Ruth (2015)
Foster, Qua (2015)
Gill, Temekia (2015)
Grant, Denise (2015)
Hall, JoJo (2015)
Hall, Tiffany (2015)
Harden, Azure (2015)
Jackson, Brandi (2015)
Jackson, Tawanda (2015)
Kimbrough, Ebony (2015)
Leduc, Andrea (2015)
Martin, Monique (2015)
Martin, Rosalyn (2015)
McNair, Victoria (2015)
Mencia, Jazmin (2015)
Moore, Lorie (2015)
Ogletree, Aketa (2015)
Parker, Miriam (2015)
Powell, Dom (2015)
Powell, Keeyauna (2015)
Rickenbacker, Diamond (2015)
Scott, Erica (2015)
Sessoms, Kia (2015)
Sherrill, Whitney (2015)
Slade, Darekia (2015)
Thomas, Brittany (2015)
Thompson, Brizi (2015)
Thompson, Patti (2015)
Vaughns, Shamia (2015)
Zeigler, Krista (2015)

Carolina Raging Wolves

Year	League	Name	W	L	Conference	Division	DF	PR
2010	WFA	Carolina Raging Wolves	0	8	National	South Central	4	--
2011	WFA	Carolina Raging Wolves	1	7	National	Atlantic	2	--
2012	WFA	Carolina Raging Wolves	0	8	National	Division 7 (Southeast)	3	--
		Total	**1**	**23**				

Based in: St. Pauls, NC

Date	H/A	Opponent	Result		
4/17/2010	A	Tampa Bay Pirates	L	36	42
4/24/2010	H	Central Florida Anarchy	L	14	35
5/1/2010	A	Jacksonville Dixie Blues	L	6	45
5/8/2010	H	Jacksonville Dixie Blues	L	16	48
5/15/2010	A	Tampa Bay Pirates	L	0	8
5/22/2010	H	Tampa Bay Pirates	L	20	26
6/5/2010	A	Central Florida Anarchy	L	6	26
6/12/2010	H	Jacksonville Dixie Blues	L	6	48
4/2/2011	A	Miami Fury	L	0	62
4/9/2011	H	Tampa Bay Pirates	L	6	26
4/30/2011	H	Atlanta Heartbreakers	L	14	28
5/7/2011	A	Savannah Sabers	L	6	7
5/21/2011	A	Atlanta Heartbreakers	L	14	32
6/4/2011	H	Savannah Sabers	W	32	13
6/11/2011	H	Orlando Anarchy	L	0	30
6/18/2011	A	Gulf Coast Riptide	L	14	36
4/14/2012	A	Atlanta Phoenix	L	7	48
4/21/2012	H	Savannah Sabers	L	0	28
4/28/2012	A	Tallahassee Jewels	L	21	42
5/5/2012	H	Atlanta Phoenix	L	0	62
5/19/2012	A	Savannah Sabers	L	0	47
6/2/2012	H	Jacksonville Dixie Blues	L	0	46
6/9/2012	A	Savannah Sabers	L	14	41
6/16/2012	H	Orlando Anarchy	L	8	41

Carolina Raging Wolves Player Register (2010-2012)

Alexander, La Quanza (2010)
Boone, Nautausha (2010)
Brown, Armetta (2010)
Carter, Amy (2010)
Carter, Tamika (2010)
Collins, Alicia (2012)
Feliciano, Jazmin (2011)
Ferguson, Chanel (2010-2011)
Fields, Demia "Dee" (2010-2012)
Foster-Martin, Stephanie (2011)
Fralin, Tonya (2010)
Franklin, Corynn (2012)
Frison, Ivy Paige (2010)
Gilliard, Dezzire (2010)
Gray, Kendra (2012)
Griffith, Danielle (2010-2011)
Harvey, Angela (2010-2012)
Hileman, Jillian (2010)
Howard, Kassie (2011-2012)
Jenkins, Barbara (2012)
Joines, Sherry (2010-2012)
Jordan, Tiffany (2010-2012)
Kearn, Darci (2010)
Madden, Jessi (2011-2012)
Maiava, Tahirih (2011)
Mask, Maria (2010)
McDonald, Lakisha (2010-2012)
McKoy, Shonda (2010-2012)
Mednis, Chris (2011)
Moore, Sonya (2010-2012)
Mosley, Marquetta "Shon" (2010-2012)
Nelson, Jennifer (2012)
Nelson, Natasha (2010)
Parker, Kristen (2010-2012)
Parker, Tammi Sherrill (2010)
Parks, Kristin (2012)
Reed, Jennifer (2011)
Rivera, Aixa (2012)
Rivera, Angela (2012)
Rothmaier, Jessica (2011)
Sidbury-Dumas, Elizabeth (2010)
Starr, Lisa (2010)
Stone, Mary (2011-2012)
Townsend, Meagan (2011)
Tunisia Johnson, Mary (2010-2011)
Washington, Regina (2010-2012)
White, April (2011)
Williams, Joy (2010)

Franchise Game-By-Game Records, 1999-2015

Carolina Spartans

Year	League		Name	W	L	Conference	Division	DF	PR
2004	IWFL	X	Carolina Spartans	0	4	--	--	--	--

Based in: Myrtle Beach, SC

4/3/2004	A	Orlando Mayhem	L	0	72		5/1/2004	H	Tampa Bay Terminators	L	0	70	
4/24/2004	H	Orlando Mayhem	L	0	54		6/5/2004	A	Tampa Bay Terminators	L	0	1	

Central Cal War Angels

Year	League	Name	W	L	Conference	Division	DF	PR
2010	WFA	Central Cal War Angels	4	5	American	North Pacific	2	--
2011	WFA	Central Cal War Angels	6	2	American	North Pacific	2	--
2012	WFA	Central Cal War Angels	7	3	American	Division 16 (North Pacific)	2	Q
2013	WFA	Central Cal War Angels	11	1	American	Division 12 (North Pacific)	1	CC
2014	WFA	Central Cal War Angels	5	3	American	Pacific West	1	Q
2015	WFA	Central Cal War Angels	6	3	American	Pacific West	3	Q-BW
		Total	**39**	**17**				

Based in: Fresno, CA   **Neutral site:** Los Angeles, CA (N)

4/10/2010	H	San Diego Sting	W	26	18		4/6/2013	H	Las Vegas Showgirlz	W	42	6	
4/17/2010	H	Portland Fighting Fillies	L	21	26		4/13/2013	A	Sacramento Sirens	W	24	6	
4/24/2010	A	Pacific Warriors	L	29	34		4/20/2013	H	Pacific Warriors	W	55	0	
5/1/2010	A	Portland Fighting Fillies	L	8	19		5/4/2013	A	Pacific Warriors	W	20	8	
5/15/2010	H	Utah Blitz	W	26	7		5/11/2013	H	Nevada Storm	W	49	22	I
5/22/2010	A	San Diego Sting	W	1	0		5/18/2013	H	San Diego Sting	W	42	0	
6/5/2010	H	Pacific Warriors	L	18	41		6/1/2013	A	Nevada Storm	W	1	0	I
6/12/2010	A	San Diego Sting	W	1	0		6/8/2013	H	Sacramento Sirens	W	55	6	
6/19/2010	A	Portland Fighting Fillies	L	14	16		6/15/2013	H	Portland Shockwave	W	34	0	W
							6/22/2013	H	Utah Jynx	W	65	6	Q
4/9/2011	A	Utah Blitz	W	38	0		7/13/2013	H	San Diego Surge	W	40	14	S
4/30/2011	H	Bay Area Bandits	L	6	11		7/20/2013	A	Dallas Diamonds	L	6	27	CC
5/7/2011	A	Los Angeles Amazons	W	1	0								
5/14/2011	A	Bay Area Bandits	L	0	19		4/5/2014	H	Nevada Storm	W	46	0	
5/21/2011	H	Los Angeles Amazons	W	68	0		4/12/2014	A	Las Vegas Showgirlz	W	32	28	
6/4/2011	A	Pacific Warriors	W	30	8		4/19/2014	H	West Coast Lightning	W	60	8	
6/11/2011	H	Portland Fighting Fillies	W	60	0		5/10/2014	A	West Coast Lightning	W	40	0	
6/18/2011	H	Bay Area Bandits	W	24	15		5/17/2014	A	San Diego Surge	L	0	64	
							6/7/2014	H	San Diego Surge	L	6	35	
4/14/2012	A	Los Angeles Amazons	W	46	0		6/14/2014	H	Portland Fighting Fillies	W	44	0	W
4/21/2012	H	Valley Vipers	W	66	0		6/21/2014	H	Seattle Majestics	L	12	13	Q
4/28/2012	A	West Coast Lightning	W	42	7								
5/12/2012	A	Bay Area Bandits	L	18	20		4/11/2015	H	West Coast Lightning	W	69	0	
5/19/2012	H	Pacific Warriors	W	30	12		4/25/2015	A	Ventura County Wolfpack	W	75	0	
6/2/2012	A	Valley Vipers	W	46	0		5/2/2015	H	Sin City Sun Devils	W	46	6	
6/9/2012	A	West Coast Lightning	W	40	0		5/9/2015	A	San Diego Surge	L	26	66	
6/16/2012	H	Bay Area Bandits	L	20	26	**	5/30/2015	A	Pacific Warriors	L	34	38	
6/23/2012	A	Utah Jynx	W	36	26	W	6/6/2015	A	Sin City Sun Devils	W	59	12	
6/30/2012	A	Bay Area Bandits	L	8	34	Q	6/13/2015	H	San Diego Surge	W	23	14	
							6/27/2015	A	San Diego Surge	L	7	27	Q
							8/8/2015	N	Atlanta Phoenix	W	28	8	B

Central Cal War Angels Player Register (2010-2015)

Aflauge, Carissa (2014-2015)
Aiken, Angelica (2010-2011)
Alcala, Esmerelda (2013)
Alewine, Ty (2014)
Alvarez, Stephanie (2014-2015)
Anderson, Ali (2013)
Anderson, Vanessa (2010)
Asi, Crystal (2014-2015)
Asi, Lani (2014-2015)
Aviles, Amanda (2015)
Barkley, Jennifer (2010)
Bebb, Kelly (2011)
Beltran, Monet (2013)
Bilgin, Susan (2010-2012)
Bivens, Janelle (2012)
Boone, Amanda (2011)
Brick, Cassey (2011)
Brisky, Lauren (2014-2015)
Brown, LaStar (2013-2015)
Burns, Sis (2010)
Camarena, Melissa (2010-2012)
Campos, Vanessa (2014)
Carter, Iesha (2015)
Casas, Angelica (2011-2013)
Castillo, Nikki (2015)
Castodio, Lisa (2010-2014)
Chavez, Melissa (2010-2012)
Cobb, Ashley (2011)
Coles, Arteca (2010)
Collazo, Charlene (2015)
Collins, Donae (2010)
Coria, Luzana (2010)
Cruz, Cindy (2015)
Davis, Dee (2015)
Davis, Erin (2010)
Deering, Jen (2013)
Dolcini, Ashlynn (2013)
Dredd, Kirby (2012, 2014)
Fornal, Jamie (2011-2013)
Gagnier, Maddison (2015)
Garcia, Alex (2013)
Garrett, Adrae (2010)
Garsa, Antoinette (2014-2015)
Gilson, Amanda (2010-2013)
Golay, Danielle (2013)
Gomes, Leslie (2012)
Gray, Chanel (2010)
Guttierez, Beth (2013)
Hall, Tika (2010-2012)
Hartman, Kenna (2013-2015)
Hearnes, Jen (2010-2011)
Hearnes, Sam (2010-2012, 2015)
Herrera, Guillermina (2011)
Hines, Jasmine (2010)
Honey, Noel (2010-2011)
Jackson, Lavina (2011)
Jimenez, Jeannette (2012-2015)
Jones, Jen (2012)
King, Lisa (2011-2015)
Kircher, Heather (2015)
Kurz, Caressa (2010)
Lamb, Emma (2010)
Larsen, Angela (2013)
Leggroan, Tiffany (2015)
Lewis, Sierra (2015)
Loftis, Kelly (2013-2014)
Loya, Francine (2013-2015)
Luna, Lydia (2010-2011)
Marby, Jasmine (2012-2015)
Marker, Melisa (2010-2012)
Marks, Bonnie (2014)
Marshall, Aspen (2013-2015)
Martinez, Marissa (2011)
Martins, Tiffany (2013-2015)
Matu, Leliega Sue (2010)
McClendon, Ali (2012)
McCowan, Athena (2010-2013)
McDonald, Tamara (2011)
McGill, Morgan (2014)
McNeill, Kim (2013)
McVicar, Sarah (2011)
Medina, Gina (2012-2013)
Mehr, Anna (2012)
Metzler, Deidra (2011-2012)
Millan, Carmen (2015)
Moore, Ty (2015)
Morgan, Erica (2014)
Muti, Valu (2013)
Nasti, Bree (2012)
Olveda, Natalie (2015)
Osuna, Olivia (2012)
Ozuna, Gloria (2011)
Paaluhi, Tanya (2011)
Parker, Brittany (2014-2015)
Payne, Elizabeth (2011-2014)
Perez, Elena (2013-2014)
Perez, Nina Sue (2013-2015)
Phillips, Crystal (2010-2012)
Pomee, Malia (2014)
Ramirez, Gabriela (2013)
Ramirez, Joy (2015)
Regan, Robin (2011-2012)
Renteria, Jessica (2011)
Reynaga, Jo Ann (2010)
Ricks, Deshunna (2014)
Riojas, Adella (2010)
Rios, Maria (2013)
Rivera, Ysaura (2014-2015)
Roberts, Nina (2014)
Rogers, Jenna (2011)
Rotella, Rachelle (2012)
Roy, Savannah (2010)
Rubal, Cindy (2012)
Sagredo, Louise (2013)
Salinas, Amanda (2015)
Sanders, Heather (2010-2011)
Sandoval, Toni (2010)
Santiago, J.J. (2011)
Santiago, Monica (2013)
Savory, Cythia (2013-2014)
Sears, Lakeya (2010-2011)
Serqiuna, Geraldine (2015)
Shuklian, Alysia (2011)
Sievers, Candace (2011-2012)
Silvers, Ashley (2010)
Simmons, Michelle (2015)
Smith, LeAndre (2010-2014)
Smith, LeAnne (2015)
Stanley, Michelle (2013)
Terrell, Denisha (2014-2015)
Thiner, Ashley (2012-2015)
Thor, Vickie (2013)
Villanueva, Jessica (2011)
Villanueva, Maria (2013)
Wake, Denise (2013)
Washington, Moneisha (2011-2015)
Washington, Tiffany (2010-2011)
Wiggins, Chantel Niino (2010-2015)
Williams, Darcy (2011)
Winterhalter, Katherine (2010)
Wray, Sonia (2014-2015)
Wright, Alexis (2013)
Yarbrough, Destanie (2011-2015)
Zhou, Mandy (2010)

Central Maryland Seahawks

Year	League	Name	W	L	Conference	Division	DF	PR
2013	WFA	Central Maryland Seahawks	0	6	National	Division 1 (Northeast)	3	--
2014	WFA	Central Maryland Seahawks	0	6	National	Mid-Atlantic	3	--
2015	WFA	Central Maryland Seahawks	0	5	National	Mid-Atlantic	4	--
		Total	0	17				

Based in: Baltimore, MD
Notes: Forfeited entire 2014 season

Central Maryland Seahawks Game-By-Game Results

Date	H/A	Opponent	Result			Date	H/A	Opponent	Result		
4/6/2013	A	New York Sharks	L	6	20	5/3/2014	A	Columbus Comets	L	0	1
4/20/2013	H	D.C. Divas	L	0	40	5/31/2014	H	D.C. Divas	L	0	1
5/4/2013	A	Cleveland Fusion	L	0	42	6/7/2014	A	Toledo Reign	L	0	1
5/25/2013	H	New York Sharks	L	20	28						
6/1/2013	A	Boston Militia	L	0	56	4/11/2015	H	Cleveland Fusion	L	0	35
6/8/2013	H	Cleveland Fusion	L	0	48	4/18/2015	A	Boston Renegades	L	0	57
						4/25/2015	A	D.C. Divas	L	0	1
4/12/2014	H	Pittsburgh Force	L	0	1	5/9/2015	H	D.C. Divas	L	0	1
4/19/2014	H	Toledo Reign	L	0	1	5/30/2015	H	Columbus Comets	L	0	1
4/26/2014	H	Boston Militia	L	0	1						

Central Maryland Seahawks Player Register (2013)

- Armstrong, Alisha (2013)
- Baldwin, Kendra (2013)
- Barnes, Jasmine (2013)
- Booker, Rebecca (2013)
- Britt, Sherri (2013)
- Cherry, Shanetta (2013)
- Clark, Mandakova (2013)
- Coles, Jessica (2013)
- Countess, Tykisha (2013)
- Davis, Rolanda (2013)
- Eskridge, Marsheta (2013)
- Fain, Tarsha (2013)
- Fitzgerald, Shay (2013)
- Harrison, Kelly (2013)
- Hearn, Erica (2013)
- Hunt, Vonda (2013)
- Hunter, Arcella (2013)
- Jennings, Cynthia (2013)
- Jordan, Terharsa "T.J." (2013)
- Marion, Teresa (2013)
- McLeod, Trina (2013)
- Murray, Kimberly (2013)
- Nolan, Regina (2013)
- Owens, Rayana (2013)
- Randolph, Tiffany (2013)
- Reid, Katrina (2013)
- Scipio, Kenyetta (2013)
- Smart, Simone (2013)
- Staten, Neisha (2013)
- Thomas, Sabrina (2013)
- Timberlake, Amara (2013)
- Venable, Amor (2013)
- Wonders, Alainna (2013)

Central Massachusetts Ravens

Year	League	Name	W	L	Conference	Division	DF	PR
2007	NWFA	Central Massachusetts Ravens	0	8	Northern	North	4	--

Based in: Holyoke, MA
Notes: Succeeded by IWFL2's Holyoke Hurricanes

Date	H/A	Opponent	Result			Date	H/A	Opponent	Result		
4/14/2007	H	Maine Freeze	L	0	26	5/19/2007	H	Massachusetts Mutiny	L	0	49
4/21/2007	H	Connecticut Crush	L	0	48	6/2/2007	A	Erie Illusion	L	0	1
4/28/2007	A	Maine Freeze	L	0	22	6/9/2007	A	Massachusetts Mutiny	L	0	1
5/5/2007	H	Erie Illusion	L	0	41	6/16/2007	A	Connecticut Crush	L	0	1

Central Massachusetts Ravens Player Register (2007)

- Amsden, Natasha (2007)
- Boyce, Memphis (2007)
- Bresnahan, Michelle (2007)
- Brown, Marissa (2007)
- Butler, Jill (2007)
- Chapman, Frankie (2007)
- Chapman, Shari (2007)
- Collette, Julie (2007)
- Devarakonda, Melissa (2007)
- Dumas, Stacy (2007)
- Dwelly, Deline (2007)
- Gouveia, Sara (2007)
- Hunt, Sara (2007)
- Irving, Nicole (2007)
- Kulaw, Laura (2007)
- Leach, Kathy (2007)
- McInnnis, Jen (2007)
- Messier, Heather (2007)
- Midgley, Debra (2007)
- Mullett, Katie (2007)
- Nelson, Carol (2007)
- O'Connor, Jennifer (2007)
- Pappas, Kristy (2007)
- Rex, Melissa (2007)
- Rivera, Rachel (2007)
- Rosier, Jenny (2007)
- Venneri, Erin (2007)
- Windzio, Sylvia (2007)

Central PA Vipers

Year	League	Name	W	L	Conference	Division	DF	PR
2006	NWFA	Harrisburg Angels	0	8	Northern	North Atlantic	4	--
2007	NWFA	Central PA Vipers	2	7	Northern	Central	4	--
2008	IWFL	Central PA Vipers	0	8	Eastern	North Atlantic	6	--
2009	IWFL2	Central PA Vipers	2	6	--	--	18	--
		Total	**4**	**29**				

Based in: Harrisburg, PA

Central PA Vipers Game-By-Game Results

Date	H/A	Opponent	Result	Score		Date	H/A	Opponent	Result	Score
4/22/2006	H	Tidewater Floods	L	6 33		4/12/2008	A	Baltimore Nighthawks	L	0 55
4/29/2006	A	Baltimore Burn	L	0 50		4/19/2008	H	Pittsburgh Passion	L	0 62
5/6/2006	A	D.C. Divas	L	0 76		4/26/2008	A	New York Sharks	L	0 40
5/20/2006	H	Maine Freeze	L	6 20		5/3/2008	H	Boston Militia	L	0 48
6/3/2006	H	Baltimore Burn	L	0 56		5/17/2008	H	D.C. Divas	L	0 43
6/10/2006	H	D.C. Divas	L	0 61		5/24/2008	A	D.C. Divas	L	0 35
6/17/2006	A	Maine Freeze	L	12 21		5/31/2008	A	Carolina Phoenix	L	0 41
6/24/2006	A	Tidewater Floods	L	0 10		6/14/2008	H	New York Sharks	L	0 31
4/14/2007	H	Erie Illusion	L	6 25		4/18/2009	H	New England Intensity	L	14 21
4/21/2007	A	Philadelphia Phoenix	L	0 41		4/25/2009	A	Manchester Freedom	L	0 47
4/28/2007	A	Richmond Spirit	W	1 0 N		5/2/2009	A	Erie Illusion	L	8 61
5/5/2007	H	Pittsburgh Passion	L	0 52		5/9/2009	A	Jersey Justice	L	0 34
5/12/2007	A	Cleveland Fusion	L	0 78		5/23/2009	H	Southern Maine Rebels	L	8 14
5/19/2007	H	Richmond Spirit	W	1 0 N		6/6/2009	H	Holyoke Hurricanes	W	48 0
5/26/2007	A	Erie Illusion	L	0 39		6/13/2009	H	Cape Fear Thunder	W	30 6
6/2/2007	H	Cleveland Fusion	L	0 62		6/20/2009	A	Connecticut Crushers	L	0 1
6/16/2007	A	Pittsburgh Passion	L	0 77						

Central PA Vipers Player Register (2007)

Amrhein, Kendra (2007)
Barnes, Davelle (2007)
Beasley, Laura (2007)
Bermel, Kate (2007)
Brannan, Nicole (2007)
Guerrero, Cassie (2007)
Hankey, Amanda (2007)
Heller, Erica (2007)
Howard, Tuffy (2007)
Johnson, Heidi (2007)
Jordan, Kelli (2007)
Kruise, Jessica (2007)
Locust, Lori "L.L." (2007)
McGee, Karen (2007)
McHenry, Tracy (2007)
Monaghan, Kelly (2007)
Morris, Kelly (2007)
Omo, Desrae (2007)
Pratt, Mary (2007)
Pritchard, Jodi (2007)
Radford, Maurecia (2007)
Sellers, Mackendra (2007)
Shearer, Toshia (2007)
Skelton, Stephanie (2007)
Smith, Terri (2007)
Steele, Fonda (2007)
Stewart, Gwen (2007)
Watts, Shirley (2007)
Wilson, Bree (2007)
Wohlbach, Nicole (2007)
Young, Cori (2007)

Central Valley Mustangs

Year	League	Name	W	L	Conference	Division	DF	PR
2015	IWFL X	Central Valley Mustangs	1	1	--	--	--	--

Based in: Modesto, CA

Date	H/A	Opponent	Result	Score		Date	H/A	Opponent	Result	Score
6/6/2015	A	Nevada Storm	L	0 43		6/13/2015	H	Ventura Black Widows	W	1 0 N

Chattanooga Locomotion

Year	League	Name	W	L	Conference	Division	DF	PR
2001	NWFA	Chattanooga Locomotion	1	7	Southern	--	5	--
2002	NWFA	Chattanooga Locomotion	4	4	--	Central	3	--
2003	NWFA	Chattanooga Locomotion	11	1	Southern	Central	1	S
2004	NWFA	Chattanooga Locomotion	6	2	Southern	South	1	S
2005	NWFA	Chattanooga Locomotion	8	3	Southern	--	4	S
2006	NWFA	Chattanooga Locomotion	6	3	Southern	Southeast	2	S
2007	NWFA	Chattanooga Locomotion	8	1	Southern	Central	1	S
2008	NWFA	Chattanooga Locomotion	5	3	Southern	East	2	--
2009	IWFL2	Chattanooga Locomotion	6	3	--	--	6	S
2010	IWFL2	Chattanooga Locomotion	4	4	Eastern	Southeast	2	S
2011	IWFL	Chattanooga Locomotion	8	3	Eastern	Mid South	2	BS
2013	IWFL	Chattanooga Locomotion	1	6	Eastern	Southeast	4	--
2014	IWFL	Chattanooga Locomotion	0	7	Eastern	South Atlantic	4	--
		Total	68	47				

Based in: Chattanooga, TN

Franchise Game-By-Game Records, 1999-2015

Chattanooga Locomotion Game-By-Game Results

Date	H/A	Opponent	W/L	PF	PA	Note
4/28/2001	H	Pensacola Power	L	7	36	
5/5/2001	A	Tennessee Venom	L	18	24	
5/12/2001	A	Pensacola Power	L	0	48	
5/20/2001	A	Nashville Dream	L	14	15	
5/26/2001	A	Alabama Renegades	L	12	32	
6/9/2001	H	Tennessee Venom	L	6	27	
6/16/2001	H	Nashville Dream	W	7	2	
6/23/2001	H	Nashville Dream	L	7	18	
4/20/2002		Alabama Renegades	L	12	40	
4/27/2002		Atlanta Leopards	W	8	6	
5/4/2002		Knoxville Summit	W	18	0	
5/18/2002		Atlanta Leopards	W	14	0	
6/1/2002		Nashville Dream	L	12	31	
6/8/2002		Alabama Renegades	L	12	22	
6/22/2002		Knoxville Summit	W	80	0	
6/29/2002		Nashville Dream	L	6	36	
3/22/2003		Alabama Renegades	W	10	8	E
3/29/2003		Evansville Express	W	42	0	E
4/5/2003		Evansville Express	W	42	0	E
4/12/2003	H	Asheville Assault	W	15	12	*
4/19/2003	A	Knoxville Summit	W	65	0	
4/26/2003	H	Alabama Renegades	W	28	26	
5/3/2003	A	Atlanta Leopards	W	56	0	
5/17/2003	H	Nashville Dream	W	41	8	
5/24/2003	A	Tennessee Venom	W	85	0	
5/31/2003	H	Knoxville Summit	W	44	0	
6/14/2003	A	Asheville Assault	W	22	15	
7/12/2003	H	Oklahoma City Lightning	L	6	20	S
4/3/2004	A	Atlanta Leopards	W	68	0	
4/17/2004	H	Tennessee Venom	W	49	0	
5/1/2004	H	Nashville Dream	L	24	27	
5/15/2004	A	Nashville Dream	W	21	7	
5/22/2004	A	Atlanta Leopards	W	62	0	
6/5/2004	H	Asheville Assault	W	49	0	
6/12/2004	A	Tennessee Venom	W	28	7	
7/10/2004	H	Pensacola Power	L	20	35	S
4/16/2005	A	Asheville Assault	W	12	6	*
4/23/2005	H	Nashville Dream	L	16	21	
4/30/2005	A	Tennessee Venom	W	16	14	
5/14/2005	H	Pensacola Power	L	0	20	
5/21/2005	A	Alabama Renegades	W	20	6	
5/28/2005	H	Asheville Assault	W	20	0	
6/4/2005	H	Atlanta Leopards	W	1	0	
6/11/2005	H	Shreveport Shockhers	W	38	6	
6/18/2005	A	Tennessee Venom	W	1	0	
6/25/2005	H	Dallas Rage	W	16	14	Q
7/16/2005	A	Pensacola Power	L	12	42	S
4/22/2006	A	Knoxville Tornadoes	W	74	0	
4/29/2006	A	St. Louis Slam	L	7	14	
5/6/2006	H	Fort Wayne Flash	W	33	7	
5/13/2006	A	Nashville Dream	W	16	13	
6/3/2006	H	St. Louis Slam	L	14	34	
6/17/2006	H	Nashville Dream	W	20	6	
6/24/2006	H	Alabama Renegades	W	35	6	
7/1/2006	H	Austin Outlaws	W	23	6	Q
7/8/2006	A	D.C. Divas	L	0	40	S
4/21/2007	H	Nashville Dream	W	36	7	
4/28/2007	H	Alabama Renegades	W	52	0	
5/5/2007	A	East Tennessee Rhythm	W	72	0	
5/12/2007	H	Emerald Coast Barracudas	W	70	0	
5/26/2007	A	Nashville Dream	W	54	0	
6/2/2007	A	Alabama Renegades	W	62	0	
6/9/2007	A	Emerald Coast Barracudas	W	70	6	
6/16/2007	H	East Tennessee Rhythm	W	56	0	
6/30/2007	H	Columbus Comets	L	8	27	S
4/19/2008	H	Alabama Renegades	W	44	0	
4/26/2008	A	Cincinnati Sizzle	W	38	0	
5/3/2008	H	St. Louis Slam	L	7	24	
5/10/2008	A	Kentucky Karma	L	7	13	
5/17/2008	H	Cincinnati Sizzle	W	20	6	
5/24/2008	H	Alabama Renegades	W	34	6	
5/31/2008	A	St. Louis Slam	L	0	21	
6/21/2008	H	Kentucky Karma	W	19	0	
4/11/2009	H	Tennessee Valley Tigers	W	46	0	
4/18/2009	A	Tennessee Valley Tigers	W	32	14	
4/25/2009	A	Atlanta Xplosion	L	6	28	
5/2/2009	H	Shreveport Aftershock	W	62	0	
5/16/2009	H	Cape Fear Thunder	W	60	0	
5/23/2009	A	Carolina Queens	L	12	30	
5/30/2009	A	Clarksville Fox	W	28	0	
6/13/2009	H	Louisville Nightmare	W	1	0	
6/27/2009	A	Wisconsin Warriors	L	6	32	S
4/3/2010	H	Atlanta Xplosion	L	0	65	
4/10/2010	A	Clarksville Fox	L	14	30	
4/17/2010	A	Memphis Belles	W	14	0	
5/1/2010	A	Carolina Phoenix	L	0	56	
5/8/2010	H	Memphis Belles	W	22	16	
5/22/2010	A	Carolina Queens	W	20	6	
6/5/2010	H	Carolina Queens	W	22	0	
6/12/2010	A	Carolina Phoenix	L	14	42	S
4/2/2011	A	Clarksville Fox	W	30	0	
4/16/2011	A	Atlanta Ravens	L	0	34	
4/23/2011	H	Memphis Belles	W	52	12	
5/7/2011	A	Clarksville Fox	W	42	0	
5/21/2011	A	Memphis Belles	W	26	20	
5/28/2011	H	Tennessee Valley Tigers	W	1	0	
6/4/2011	H	Atlanta Ravens	L	0	49	
6/11/2011	H	Memphis Belles	W	54	0	
6/18/2011	H	Memphis Belles	W	54	0	
6/25/2011	H	North Texas Knockouts	W	24	20	BQ
7/16/2011	H	New England Intensity	L	0	20	BS
4/27/2013	H	Carolina Queens	L	8	30	
5/4/2013	A	Carolina Phoenix	L	0	58	
5/11/2013	H	Erie Illusion	W	34	0	
5/18/2013	A	Atlanta Xplosion	L	0	66	
6/1/2013	A	Carolina Queens	L	0	60	
6/15/2013	H	Atlanta Rage	L	0	66	
6/29/2013	H	Carolina Phoenix	L	0	1	
4/12/2014	H	Huntsville Tigers	L	16	30	
4/26/2014	A	Carolina Phoenix	L	6	47	
5/3/2014	H	Carolina Queens	L	0	52	
5/10/2014	A	Huntsville Tigers	L	16	34	
5/17/2014	A	Carolina Queens	L	0	1	
5/31/2014	H	Carolina Phoenix	L	0	1	
6/7/2014	H	Carolina Queens	L	6	64	

Chattanooga Locomotion Player Register (2004-2008, 2014)

Balazs, Katie (2006-2007)
Banghart, Ella (2005-2007)
Bennett, Gracie (2014)
Bivens, Mandy (2007-2008)
Bradley, Jessica (2014)
Brimmer, Monique (2014)
Brock, Erin (2006-2008)
Brookbank, Lisa (2005-2007)
Brooks, Dee (2005)
Buchanan, Tara (2006-2008)
Butler, Jaime (2014)
Cantrell, Jessica (2005)
Carlson, Lynnette (2004)
Carr, Carol (2005-2006)
Cary, Becky (2007)
Catoe, Kim (2008)
Causby, Angie (2004-2008)
Cherry, Sarah (2014)
Clark, Demetris (2007)
Clark, Michelle (2006-2007)
Cook, Donna (2004-2007)
Cunningham, Amanda (2014)
Curtis, Tina (2005-2008)
DeFoor, Becca (2007)
Dulaney, Cara (2004-2008)
Dunbar, Alex (2014)
Essex, Stephanie (2006-2007)
Feagans, Shawn (2008)
Fochler, Donna (2007)
Folds, Shalimar (2004)
Fulton, Laura (2006)
Galyon, Rachel (2005-2006)
Garcia, Katherine (2014)
Glick, Carla (2004)
Gonser, Sheila (2005-2006)
Graham, Katie (2005)
Harden, Misty (2006, 2008)
Harmon, Taylor (2008)
Henry, Nichole (2004, 2006-2008)
Hicks, Michelle (2006-2008)
Hood, Natalie (2014)
Horner, Amanda (2004)
Horton, Starlisa (2005-2008)
Howard, Gwynne (2006)
Hudson, Felicia (2006-2008)
Jackson, Kelli (2007)
Jackson, Lena (2005-2006)
Jeffries, Heather (2005-2006)
Johnson, Cayci (Lambert) (2004-2008)
Jones, Kelli (2007-2008, 2014)
Jones, Zillie (2014)
Kilgore, Linda (2005-2006, 2008)
Kleinschmidt, Gina (2005-2006)
Lebo, Amanda (2004-2008)
Lee, Susan (2007)
Long, Shelley (2008)
Loveless, Schandra (2005-2008)
Loven, Brooke (2007)
Mantooth, Kalsea (2014)
Martin, Christie (2014)
Martin, Serena (2005)
Massey, Anna (2007-2008)
McCranie, Melissa (2004-2005)
McCray, Candiss (2004)
McElroy, Amanda (2006)
Meyers, Denise (2006)
Montanez, Lilli (2014)
Montgomery, Denisha (2005-2008)
Moss, Lori (2006-2008)
Myers, Denise (2005, 2007-2008)
Newcomb, Tiffany (2005-2008)
Oliver, Brandi (2008)
Owens, Melody (2014)
Parker, Jenny (2004-2006)
Parker, Kerrin (2005)
Pate, Jessica (2014)
Pensmith, Dani (2006)
Pritchett, Katey (2014)
Ragan, Emily (2008)
Ratledge, Camille (2008)
Reese, Kristin (2004, 2006)
Russell, Audrey (2004, 2006, 2008)
Sanders, Robin (2006-2008)
Schaer, Mellisa (2007)
Schrupp, Joanna (2005-2008)
Semanco, Jamie (2006-2008)
Sichwart, Nelli (2008)
Storey, Joy (2007-2008)
Stutts, Anna (2006-2008, 2014)
Taylor, Ashley (2006-2008)
Teligades, Cat (2007)
Timon, Karen (2006-2008)
Turner, Crystal (2014)
Turner, Karen (2004-2005)
Vaughn, Crystal (2008)
Watson, Licenda (2014)
Wheeler, Shanice Simba (2014)
Wright, Renae (2014)
Young, Jacqueline (2007)

Cheyenne Dust Devils

Year	League	Name	W	L	Conference	Division	DF	PR
2002	UWFL	Cheyenne Dust Devils	0	6	--	--	--	--

Based in: Cheyenne, WY

4/13/2002	Tri-City Mustangs	L	2	43	5/5/2002	Colorado Springs Koalas	L	14	44
4/20/2002	Sweetwater County Outlaws	L	14	15	5/19/2002	Grand Valley Vipers	L	0	22
4/28/2002	Pueblo Pythons	L	0	6	5/26/2002	Denver Foxes	L	0	74

Chicago Force

Year	League	Name	W	L	Conference	Division	DF	PR
2003	IWFL	Chicago Force	10	1	Western	Southwest	1	CC
2004	IWFL	Chicago Force	6	3	Eastern	Mid-Atlantic	2	S
2005	IWFL	Chicago Force	8	3	Western	Midwest	1	S
2006	IWFL	Chicago Force	6	3	Western	Midwest	2	S
2007	IWFL	Chicago Force	5	3	Western	Midwest	2	--
2008	IWFL	Chicago Force	10	1	Eastern	Midwest	1	C
2009	IWFL	Chicago Force	7	3	Western	Midwest	2	CC
2010	IWFL	Chicago Force	7	2	Western	Midwest	2	S
2011	WFA	Chicago Force	9	1	National	Central	1	S
2012	WFA	Chicago Force	11	1	National	Division 6 (Great Lakes)	1	C
2013	WFA	Chicago Force	12	0	National	Division 4 (Great Lakes)	1	**NC**
2014	WFA	Chicago Force	8	2	National	Great Lakes	1	CC
2015	WFA	Chicago Force	9	2	National	Great Lakes	1	CC
		Total	**108**	**25**				

Based in: Chicago, IL   **Neutral sites:** Pittsburgh, PA (N1); San Diego, CA (N2)

Date	H/A	Opponent	Result	PF	PA	Note
3/29/2003	H	Detroit Blaze	W	49	0	
4/5/2003	A	Memphis Maulers	W	1	0	
4/19/2003	H	Dallas Revolution	W	40	8	
4/26/2003	A	Detroit Blaze	W	41	0	
5/3/2003	H	Detroit Blaze	W	47	0	
5/17/2003	H	Oklahoma City Avengers	W	1	0	
5/25/2003	H	San Diego Sea Catz	W	55	0	
5/31/2003	A	Dallas Revolution	W	41	6	
6/7/2003	A	Oklahoma City Avengers	W	1	0	
6/21/2003	H	Corvallis Pride	W	28	14	S
6/28/2003	A	Sacramento Sirens	L	7	47	CC
4/3/2004	H	Des Moines Courage	W	50	0	
4/17/2004	H	Detroit Predators	W	63	0	
4/24/2004	A	Des Moines Courage	W	40	0	
5/1/2004	H	New Hampshire Freedom	W	42	0	
5/8/2004	H	New York Sharks	L	2	6	
5/15/2004	A	Detroit Predators	W	65	0	
5/22/2004	A	New York Sharks	L	7	27	
6/5/2004	A	New Hampshire Freedom	W	30	0	
6/26/2004	A	New York Sharks	L	0	40	S
4/2/2005	H	Bay State Warriors	W	12	7	
4/9/2005	H	Kansas City Storm	W	42	0	
4/16/2005	A	Atlanta Xplosion	L	0	29	
4/23/2005	A	Des Moines Courage	W	36	0	
4/30/2005	H	Detroit Predators	W	34	0	
5/14/2005	A	Bay State Warriors	W	16	0	
6/4/2005	A	Detroit Predators	W	59	13	
6/11/2005	H	Des Moines Courage	W	58	0	
6/18/2005	A	Kansas City Storm	W	30	0	
6/25/2005	H	Atlanta Xplosion	L	0	12	
7/9/2005	A	Tacoma Majestics	L	0	14	S
4/29/2006	H	Iowa Crush	W	26	8	
5/6/2006	A	Detroit Predators	W	30	0	
5/13/2006	H	Detroit Demolition	L	0	19	
5/20/2006	A	Iowa Crush	W	20	6	
5/27/2006	H	Detroit Predators	W	36	8	
6/10/2006	A	Detroit Demolition	L	0	47	
6/17/2006	A	Kansas City Storm	W	42	0	
6/24/2006	H	Kansas City Storm	W	27	0	
7/8/2006	A	Detroit Demolition	L	0	20	S
4/28/2007	A	Iowa Crush	W	27	6	
5/12/2007	A	Detroit Demolition	L	20	23	
5/19/2007	H	Detroit Demolition	L	6	20	
5/26/2007	H	Kansas City Storm	W	21	0	
6/2/2007	A	Iowa Crush	W	33	0	
6/9/2007	A	Detroit Predators	W	41	0	
6/23/2007	H	Detroit Predators	W	69	0	
6/30/2007	H	Detroit Demolition	L	6	21	
4/12/2008	A	Wisconsin Wolves	W	14	7	
4/19/2008	H	Detroit Demolition	W	18	7	
4/26/2008	A	Wisconsin Warriors	W	26	14	
5/3/2008	H	Columbus Phantoms	W	1	0	
5/17/2008	H	Wisconsin Warriors	W	8	0	
5/24/2008	A	Iowa Crush	W	56	0	
5/31/2008	H	Clarksville Fox	W	40	0	
6/14/2008	A	Wisconsin Wolves	W	42	7	
6/28/2008	H	Detroit Demolition	W	8	7	S
7/12/2008	H	Pittsburgh Passion	W	8	7	CC
7/26/2008	H	Dallas Diamonds	L	29	35	C*
4/11/2009	A	Iowa Crush	W	54	0	
4/18/2009	H	Wisconsin Warriors	W	38	20	
4/25/2009	A	Minnesota Vixen	W	55	0	
5/2/2009	H	Kansas City Tribe	W	28	6	
5/16/2009	A	Detroit Demolition	L	19	21	
5/23/2009	H	Minnesota Vixen	W	53	0	
5/30/2009	A	Kansas City Tribe	L	14	30	
6/13/2009	H	Detroit Demolition	W	26	6	
6/27/2009	A	Seattle Majestics	W	28	14	S
7/11/2009	A	Kansas City Tribe	L	16	40	CC
4/3/2010	H	Wisconsin Warriors	W	42	0	
4/10/2010	H	Wisconsin Wolves	W	62	0	
4/17/2010	A	Wisconsin Warriors	W	30	7	
5/1/2010	H	Kansas City Tribe	W	14	12	
5/8/2010	A	Minnesota Vixen	W	56	0	
5/15/2010	A	Wisconsin Wolves	W	49	0	
5/22/2010	H	Pittsburgh Passion	W	7	0	
6/5/2010	A	Kansas City Tribe	L	12	30	
6/12/2010	A	Dallas Diamonds	L	20	27	S

Continued on next page

Chicago Force Game-By-Game Results (continued)

Date	H/A	Opponent	Result			
4/9/2011	H	Minnesota Machine	W	69	0	
4/16/2011	A	Wisconsin Wolves	W	58	0	
4/30/2011	H	St. Louis Slam	W	29	7	
5/7/2011	H	Kansas City Tribe	W	34	26	
5/14/2011	H	West Michigan Mayhem	W	15	6	
5/21/2011	A	St. Louis Slam	W	55	24	
6/11/2011	A	West Michigan Mayhem	W	76	3	
6/18/2011	A	Indy Crash	W	77	18	
6/25/2011	H	Pittsburgh Passion	W	41	31	Q
7/9/2011	H	Boston Militia	L	23	50	S
4/14/2012	A	Kansas City Tribe	W	21	14	
4/21/2012	H	Columbus Comets	W	47	0	
4/28/2012	A	Indy Crash	W	72	0	
5/5/2012	H	St. Louis Slam	W	57	14	
5/12/2012	H	West Michigan Mayhem	W	54	0	
5/19/2012	A	Cleveland Fusion	W	48	0	
6/2/2012	H	Indy Crash	W	71	0	
6/16/2012	A	West Michigan Mayhem	W	55	6	
6/30/2012	H	Indy Crash	W	70	14	Q
7/7/2012	H	Jacksonville Dixie Blues	W	67	14	S
7/21/2012	H	Boston Militia	W	35	34	CC
8/4/2012	N1	San Diego Surge	L	36	40	C
4/6/2013	H	Detroit Dark Angels	W	62	0	
4/20/2013	H	Indy Crash	W	66	6	
4/27/2013	A	St. Louis Slam	W	50	7	
5/4/2013	A	West Michigan Mayhem	W	67	13	
5/11/2013	A	Detroit Dark Angels	W	61	0	
5/18/2013	A	Indy Crash	W	82	20	
6/1/2013	H	Kansas City Titans	W	51	7	
6/8/2013	H	West Michigan Mayhem	W	56	7	
6/22/2013	H	Cleveland Fusion	W	65	7	Q
7/13/2013	H	Atlanta Phoenix	W	84	0	S
7/20/2013	H	Boston Militia	W	46	27	CC
8/3/2013	N2	Dallas Diamonds	W	81	34	C
4/5/2014	A	Detroit Dark Angels	W	70	0	
4/12/2014	H	Indy Crash	W	48	6	
4/19/2014	A	D.C. Divas	W	42	27	
4/26/2014	H	West Michigan Mayhem	W	30	0	
5/3/2014	A	Indy Crash	W	36	6	
5/17/2014	N1	Boston Militia	L	18	35	
6/7/2014	H	Columbus Comets	W	72	8	
6/21/2014	H	West Michigan Mayhem	W	66	0	Q
7/5/2014	H	Miami Fury	W	66	8	S
7/19/2014	A	Boston Militia	L	14	63	CC
4/11/2015	H	West Michigan Mayhem	W	64	0	
4/18/2015	A	Detroit Dark Angels	W	67	0	
4/25/2015	A	Minnesota Machine	W	70	0	
5/9/2015	H	Indy Crash	W	62	7	
5/16/2015	H	Kansas City Titans	W	74	8	
5/30/2015	H	Boston Renegades	L	24	30	*
6/6/2015	A	Indy Crash	W	60	7	
6/13/2015	H	St. Louis Slam	W	57	0	
6/27/2015	H	Cleveland Fusion	W	71	14	Q
7/11/2015	A	Boston Renegades	W	49	18	S
7/25/2015	A	D.C. Divas	L	24	43	CC

Chicago Force Player Register (2003-2015)

Airaki, Jill (2014-2015)
Alvarez, Yesenia (2014)
Amato, Kristen (2009-2010)
Anderson, Akilah (2015)
Andrasko, Jessica (2006-2007)
Andrews, Andrea (2004-2006)
Aranas, Caryl (2004)
Argenzio, Melissa (2013)
Aschom, Melissa (2003-2004)
Atkins, Sarah (2014)
Bache, Linda (2003-2008)
Bacherta, Elesabeth (2009)
Baine, Lacicia (2015)
Baker, Stacey (2006-2010, 2012)
Bandstra, Angie (2006-2012)
Bank, Patty (2003-2004)
Barajaz, Amanda (2011)
Barba, Chaya (2012)
Barret, Charlotte (2015)
Beaumont, Sally (2003-2007)
Belanger, Emilie (2014)
Bennett, Rosalyn "Roz" (2007-09, '11-15)
Benson, Jennifer (2008-2010)
Berggren, Ashley (2011-2015)
Biel, Kelly (2010-2012)
Bluske, Leeann (2014-2015)
Bords, Jessica (2008)
Bosch, Teresa (2005)
Bravo, Annette (2008)
Braymer, Jessee (2015)
Brennon, Alisha (2010)
Brick, Cassey (2015)
Bridges, Alexandria (2010)
Bridges, Dorian (2010-2015)
Brink, Janel (2014)
Broeck, Shannon (2008-2009)
Brooks, Keesha "Taz" (2006-2013)
Brown, Kina (2011)
Bueso, Gricela (2015)
Burns, Amber (2008-2012)
Buteau, Erin (2007-2009)
Carter, Carmen (2003)
Cartman, Chiquita (2014)
Cascallares, Amanda (2004)
Casey, Kelsey (2014-2015)
Cattouse, Casandra (2008-2010)
Cech, Courtney (2014)
Charbonneau, Tricia (2005-2014)
Choules, Mary (2012-2015)
Coffman, Nancy (2007)
Coleman, Ericka (2006-2007, 2009)
Colon, Christina (2003-2004)
Converse, Catherine "Cat" (2010, '14-15)
Crockett, Meagan (2014-2015)
Cromwell, Nicole (2007)
Dantuma, Martha (2009-2015)
Deering, Jen (2014)
Dempsey, Cynthia (2005)
Detweiler, Sarah (2003-2006)
Diaz, Liseida (2003)
Didier, Diane (2007-2009)
Dollarhite, Amy (2009)
Doring, Vanessa (2011)
Dovantzis, Ellie (2011-2014)
Drangsholt, Sonja (2015)
Duffey, Kim (2003-2006)
Dulski, Jen (2006-2007, 2012-2014)
Durrah, Jazmyne (2015)
Easley, Pia (2008)
Echols, Eve (2010)
Enge, Keno (2007)
Engelman, Tami (2010-2015)
Evans, Bethany (2013)
Fahrner, Bridget (2006-2008)
Fahrner, Colleen (2006)
Felix, Savannah "Sav" (2008)
Figueroa, Mari (2003-2004)
Finestone, Emma (2011-2014)
Finley-Matthews, Tekisha (2013-2014)
Finnegan, Megan (2008-2010)
Fonteyn, Mieke (2011)
Fornal, Jamie (2015)
Fowler, Chrissy (2006-2007)
Fowlkes, April (2012)
Fox, Jennifer (2008)
Freeman, Sara (2010)
Garcia, Sabrina (2008-2009)
Gardner, Traci (2007)
Gesky, Luella "Lue" (2004-05, '07, '14)
Gladfelter, Amy (2008)
Gore, Rachel (2015)
Gottschalk, Michelle (2008, 2011)
Graf, Kris (2003-2004)
Gray, Christa (2004)
Gray, Jeanette (2010-2015)
Griffin, Candace (2009-2013)
Grisafe, Sami (2007-2015)
Grodus, Kim (2014)
Hafer, Cynde (2003-2004, 2006)
Hall, Darleen (2009-2010)
Hamilton, Kat (2011)
Hankus, Jamie (2006)
Harper, Trish (2008-2012, 2014-2015)
Harris, Zabrina (2011)

Continued on next page

Chicago Force Player Register (continued)

Hassell, Shaakira (2004)
Hatcher, Brandy (2010-2015)
Hauter, Savannah (2015)
Hawkins, Taneeka (2013)
Hayden, Shari (2004)
Henigan, Esther (2007-2009)
Hernandez, Veronica (2005-06, 2009-12)
Hundley, Samantha (2011-2012)
Hunter, Tamera (2006-2008)
Hunter, Tiffany (2007-2008)
Intress, Kristin (2007)
Iwans, Elizabeth (2014)
Jacob, Lindsey (2010-2011)
Jaffe, J.J. (2003-2004)
Javelet, Jessica (2013-2014)
Jefferies, Jane (2003-2005)
Jezik, Darci (2004)
Jiles, Nicole (2011)
Johnson, Chris (2010-2012)
Johnson, Leslie (2011)
Johnson, Porcha (2012)
Johnson, Tracy "T.J." (2006, 2008-2010)
Johnston, Kayla (2004)
Kadelak, Lisa (2012-2014)
Kaminski (Lewis), Dianna (2004)
Kania, Michelle (2007-2008)
Kasprzak, Kim (2004)
Kelly, Jen (2012-2013)
Kemp, Cyndi (2003-2005)
Kero, Elina (2014)
Kimbrough, Amber (2014-2015)
Kiner, Latoya (2013)
King, Rheda (2006-2008)
Kirincich, Jessica (2010)
Klugow, Aly (2005)
Kluss, Marie (2006)
Kolin, April (2012)
Kreevich, Maria (2003-2004, 2007)
Kubinski, Kristen (2011)
Kucar, Kristina "Kuku" (2007)
Kunc, Lori (2007-2009)
Kunzendorf, Megan (2015)
Kutzscher, Anke (2015)
Lee, Carolyn (2008-2012, 2014-2015)
Lee, Sharmaine (2007-2008)
Leefers, Connie (2004-2005)
Lehtinen, Paula (2014)
Leslie, Darcy (2008-2015)
Linkinhoker, Mandy (2006)
Logan, Latania "Doc" (2004-2006)
Lowe, Danette (2005)
Maeder, Michele (2003-2006)
Magsino, Krystle (2015)
Mahood, Amy (2007-2009)
Malasanos, Natalie (2010)
Maldonado, Stephanie (2014)
Malloy, Taylor (2010-2014)
Malsch, Amanda (2004-06, 2008-2014)
Manabat, Bridget (2006)
Marks, Kim (2007-2015)
Marshall, Angela (2007)
Mason, Angel (2011)
Matheson, Nicole (2015)
Maxwell, Kim (2010)

May, Gwen (2012)
McCafferty, Kara (2007)
McClain, Joy (2011)
McClain, Shannon (2011)
McLenaghan, Lauren (2013)
McPeake, Jessica (2005-2008)
Mendiola, Michelle (2006)
Menzyk, Jamie (2007-2015)
Mertens, Kristen (2009-2011)
Miller, Stephanie (2009)
Moore, Ashlee (2013)
Moore, Kayla (2013)
Moore, Kelly (2015)
Moore, Nicole (2011)
Morales, Lasha (2008)
Moses, Ashlee (2013)
Moyers, Fonda (2006)
Mulligan, Allie (2009)
Murphy, Maggie (2003-2006)
Myers, Marcie (2008)
Nebbeling, Jeannine (2007-08, '10, '12)
Nelson, Melissa (2013-2015)
Nelson, Trish (2003-2008)
Nolan, Sherry (2005)
Okey, Elizabeth (2009-2014)
Okrey, Elisha (2012-2015)
Olivar, Kerri (2014-2015)
Oliver, Ashley (2015)
Olson, Ingrid (2006-2007)
Orstead, Jessica (2005)
Pajaujis, Linda (2003-2005)
Paller, Stacy (2003-2004)
Parkes, Laura (2009-2010)
Parzygnat, Laura (2003-2004, 2006)
Pearce, Christie (2004)
Pederson, Dawn (2007-2015)
Perry, Tamika "Meeks" (2003-2006)
Peterson, Kayley (2014-2015)
Pfeifer, Kari (2011-2012)
Picha, Shelley (2003-2007)
Powers, Susan (2003)
Precourt, Stephanie (2012, 2014)
Quaritsch, Karlee (2013)
Reed, Kim (2007-2009, 2011)
Rehfeld, Jennifer (2008-2009)
Rehr, Kelly (2014-2015)
Reid, Julie (2004)
Rhea, Konesha (2011-2012)
Riewe, Abby (2006)
Riordan, Katelynn (2014)
Roberts, Hayley (2009)
Robinson, LaQueisha (2015)
Rodger, Aynslee (2015)
Rogers, Sarah (2015)
Rollins, Valencia (2011-2012)
Roman, Venus (2007)
Romano, Katie (2010-2012)
Sanchez, Debbie (2006-07, 2013-14)
Sanford, Anna (2014)
Sansone, Christina (2008)
Santana, Therese (2014-2015)
Sardin, Tiffany (2015)
Sargent, Diana (2004)
Saucedo, Vianny (2015)

Schaffrath, Pam (2003-2008)
Schirrippa, Teresa (2010)
Schultz, J.J. (2003-2004)
Schulz, Jenn (2004-2010)
Scurto, Kylie (2015)
Scurto, Sami (2010-2013)
Shaba, Stella (2008)
Shumpert, Tashaunda (2005-2008)
Shuster, Jain (2005-2006)
Sianez, Sofia (2008-2009)
Silvestri, Karyn (2009)
Simon, Theresa (2003-2008)
Smith, Amber (2015)
Smith, Angelique "Angel" (2013-2015)
Smith, Melissa (2003, 2006-2008, 2012)
Smolarczyk, Katrina "Kat" (2003-2005)
Sochacki, Teresa (2004-2006)
Solis, Sol (2010)
Soper, Veronica (2010-2012)
Southard, Diana (2008)
Spanjer, Dani (2003-2004)
Sperling, Wendy (2003-2004, 2006)
Springer, Jessica (2011-2012)
Srda, Brandi (2008, 2011-2012)
Steel, Nyema (2008)
Stinson, Melanie (2007)
Strozinsky, Elizabeth (2011-2012)
Studley, Erica (2007)
Swain, Niki (2011-2013)
Taillon, Linda (2004-2005)
Tang, Heather (2003-2005)
Tejada, Claudia (2003-2004)
Theodoropoulos, Faith (2005-2006)
Thomas, A.J. (2003)
Thompson, Jen (2011)
Thompson, Robin (2014)
Thuestad, Rebecca (2003-07, 2011-14)
Torres, Linda (2010)
Travis, Rachael (2013-2014)
Traylor, Kenshira (2007-2009)
Tryba, Kyle (2003-2006)
Vaksdal, Trudi (2010)
Valene, Mary (2009)
Van Cuick, Brenda (2011-2012)
Varas, Zenia (2009-2011)
Velez, Leslie (2012)
Vermilye, Dana (2010-2013)
Villalobos, Marcelina "Nani" (2011-2015)
Wabbel, Kara (2008)
Watts, Connie (2011)
Wharton, Timesha (2013)
Wheeler, Christine (2006-2007)
White, Jamine (2010-2012)
Whyms, Melissa (2010-2012)
Wilkins, Desiree (2009)
Winder, Dara (2004)
Witt, Anne (2014-2015)
Young, Sue (2004)
Zak, Bea (2003-2004)
Zhubi, Albiona "Albi" (2008-2015)
Ziegler, Arteria (2011-2015)
Zielke, Jennifer (2004)

Cincinnati Sizzle

Year	League	Name	W	L	Conference	Division	DF	PR
2005	NWFA	Cincinnati Sizzle	2	6	Northern	--	15	--
2006	NWFA	Cincinnati Sizzle	3	5	Northern	Northwest	2	--
2007	NWFA	Cincinnati Sizzle	0	8	Southern	North	4	--
2008	NWFA	Cincinnati Sizzle	4	4	Southern	East	3	--
2009	WFA	Cincinnati Sizzle	1	7	National	Mid-Atlantic	5	--
2010	WFA	Cincinnati Sizzle	0	8	National	Central	4	--
2011	WFA	Cincinnati Sizzle	4	4	National	North Central	3	--
2012	WFA	Cincinnati Sizzle	0	8	National	Division 5 (North Central)	3	--
2013	WFA	Cincinnati Sizzle	4	5	National	Division 3 (North Central)	2	W
2014	WFA	Cincinnati Sizzle	0	8	National	Mideast	3	--
2015	WSFL	Cincinnati Sizzle	3	4	Northern	--	3	BW
		Total	21	67				

Based in: Cincinnati, OH

Date	H/A	Opponent	Result	PF	PA	
4/16/2005	H	Toledo Spitfire	W	43	6	
4/23/2005	A	Indiana Thunder	W	1	0	
4/30/2005	H	Detroit Demolition	L	0	76	
5/14/2005	A	Pittsburgh Passion	L	22	56	
5/21/2005	A	Cleveland Fusion	L	0	61	
5/28/2005	H	Columbus Comets	L	0	64	
6/11/2005	A	D.C. Divas	L	0	54	
6/18/2005	H	Southwest Michigan Jaguars	L	7	54	
4/22/2006	A	West Michigan Mayhem	L	5	14	
4/29/2006	A	Toledo Spitfire	W	46	22	
5/6/2006	H	Milwaukee Momentum	W	46	20	
5/20/2006	H	Pittsburgh Passion	L	0	44	
5/27/2006	H	Toledo Spitfire	W	27	14	
6/3/2006	H	West Michigan Mayhem	L	14	42	
6/10/2006	A	Milwaukee Momentum	L	18	26	
6/17/2006	A	Pittsburgh Passion	L	20	55	
4/21/2007	A	Kentucky Karma	L	6	7	
4/28/2007	H	Pittsburgh Passion	L	7	62	
5/5/2007	H	Columbus Comets	L	0	53	
5/12/2007	A	St. Louis Slam	L	0	61	
5/19/2007	H	Kentucky Karma	L	7	8	
6/2/2007	A	Pittsburgh Passion	L	7	44	
6/9/2007	H	St. Louis Slam	L	0	56	
6/16/2007	A	Columbus Comets	L	0	52	
4/19/2008	H	Kentucky Karma	L	6	39	
4/26/2008	H	Chattanooga Locomotion	L	0	38	
5/3/2008	A	Alabama Renegades	L	14	46	
5/10/2008	H	Dayton Diamonds	W	54	6	
5/17/2008	A	Chattanooga Locomotion	L	6	20	
5/31/2008	A	Kentucky Karma	W	28	14	
6/7/2008	A	Dayton Diamonds	W	61	0	
6/21/2008	H	Alabama Renegades	W	43	6	
4/25/2009	A	Kentucky Karma	L	14	22	
5/2/2009	A	Columbus Comets	L	0	36	
5/9/2009	A	Pittsburgh Force	L	18	36	
5/30/2009	H	Kentucky Karma	L	0	22	
6/6/2009	H	Pittsburgh Force	W	14	8	
6/13/2009	A	Cleveland Fusion	L	18	36	
6/20/2009	H	Columbus Comets	L	8	47	
6/27/2009	H	Cleveland Fusion	L	14	48	
4/10/2010	H	St. Louis Slam	L	0	35	
4/17/2010	H	Indiana Speed	L	0	40	
4/24/2010	A	Kentucky Karma	L	0	6	
5/8/2010	A	St. Louis Slam	L	0	57	
5/22/2010	H	Columbus Comets	L	6	68	
6/5/2010	A	Indiana Speed	L	0	62	
6/12/2010	A	Pittsburgh Force	L	0	48	
6/19/2010	H	Kentucky Karma	L	14	20	
4/2/2011	H	West Michigan Mayhem	L	0	20	
4/9/2011	A	Detroit Dark Angels	L	7	33	
4/23/2011	H	Indy Crash	L	21	60	
4/30/2011	A	Dayton Diamonds	W	51	12	
5/7/2011	H	Indy Crash	L	21	60	
5/14/2011	A	Kentucky Karma	W	42	0	
6/11/2011	H	Kentucky Karma	W	67	6	
6/18/2011	H	Toledo Reign	W	34	25	
4/14/2012	A	Toledo Reign	L	14	68	
4/21/2012	A	West Michigan Mayhem	L	8	52	
4/28/2012	H	Derby City Dynamite	L	0	6	
5/5/2012	A	Indy Crash	L	0	56	
5/12/2012	H	Columbus Comets	L	6	64	
6/2/2012	H	Toledo Reign	L	6	14	
6/9/2012	H	Pittsburgh Force	L	16	21	
6/16/2012	A	Derby City Dynamite	L	16	52	
4/6/2013	H	Toledo Reign	W	36	14	
4/13/2013	A	West Michigan Mayhem	L	0	52	
4/20/2013	H	Derby City Dynamite	W	24	20	
5/4/2013	H	Tennessee Train	W	38	6	
5/11/2013	H	Cleveland Fusion	L	6	47	
5/18/2013	A	Derby City Dynamite	L	56	58	
6/1/2013	A	Cleveland Fusion	L	6	55	
6/8/2013	A	Toledo Reign	W	20	12	
6/15/2013	A	Pittsburgh Passion	L	0	63	W
4/5/2014	A	West Michigan Mayhem	L	0	75	
4/19/2014	A	Tennessee Train	L	6	30	
4/26/2014	A	Toledo Reign	L	0	33	
5/10/2014	H	Cleveland Fusion	L	0	71	
5/17/2014	H	Detroit Dark Angels	L	0	54	
5/24/2014	H	Pittsburgh Force	L	0	26	
5/31/2014	A	Indy Crash	L	0	68	
6/7/2014	H	Derby City Dynamite	L	0	74	
4/25/2015	H	Southern Valkyrie	W	37	12	
5/9/2015	A	Tennessee Legacy	L	0	48	
5/16/2015	A	West Virginia Wildfire	L	0	24	
5/30/2015	H	West Virginia Wildfire	W	26	2	
6/13/2015	H	Tri-Cities Thunder	L	30	68	
6/27/2015	A	Keystone Assault	L	0	27	
7/11/2015	H	West Virginia Wildfire	W	26	20	B

Cincinnati Sizzle Player Register (2005-2007, 2009-2015)

Adams, Diane (2005)
Adams, Linda (2005)
Albers, Emily (2007)
Allen, Ebony (2009)
Allen, Kellie (2011-2012)
Apel, Paige (2013-2015)
Applin, Temeca (2005)
Austin, Shilla (2009-2015)
Baker, Laqueita (2014)
Barnett, Latira (2014)
Beyer, Tina (2005)
Blair, Christina (2015)
Boling, Kristie (2011)
Bonapfel, Charity (2011)
Boone, Sarah (2011)
Boose, Theresa (2005)
Bostwick, Sydney (2011-2014)
Bosworth-Dock, Jena (2005)
Bradford, Mia (2007, 2009-2011)
Brewer, Brianna (2009-2011)
Bridges, Tonkia "Tee" (2005)
Brown, Andrea (2009)
Burks, Ann (2005)
Canyon, Markeeta "Keeta" (2005)
Carter, Jen (2011-2012)
Cleveland, Enjoli (2009)
Collins, Sasha (2009)
Colwell, Mary Jo (2006)
Cranmo, Shaina (2014-2015)
Croley, Briana (2013)
Cunningham, Mercedes (2012-2013)
Cunningham, Shere (2012)
Daugherty, Kourtnie (2011-2015)
Davenport, Ansley (2005-07, 2009-11, '14)
Dennis, Micah (2011)
Deramus, Davida (2011-2012, 2015)
Diaz, Xiomara "Zee" (2005-2006)
Durbin, Tiffany (2010)
Egelston, Amber (2011)
Elder, Sterling (2005-2007, 2012-2015)
Elliott, Buck (2015)
Erickson, Teresa (2005)
Fennell, Ebony (2010-2012)
Fennell, Tamar (2011-2012, 2015)
Figueira, Sarah (2014-2015)
Flanagan, Jessica (2012-2013, 2015)
Flick, Joanna "Joey" (2005)
Forte, Ebony (2005-2007, 2009, 2010)
Foster, Jennifer (2005, 2007)
Franzen, Leslie (2005)
Gardner, Anitra (2009)
Gardner, AnnaMarie (2009)
Gardner, Jo Ann (2009-2010)
Gardner, Melissa (2009)
Garner, Jennifer (2013)
Givens, Morgan (2013-2014)
Glasmeier, Katie (2006-07, 2009-14)
Gleason, Allison (2005)
Glenn, Alana (2014-2015)
Gunsch, Kara (2009)
Harden, Erica (2011-2013)
Harris, Angie (2005)
Harris, Desarae (2012)
Harrison, Kellie (2005-2006)
Headrick, Wendy (2005-2006)
Heinz, Shannon (2006)
Helseth, Shannon (2005-07, 2009-15)
Hildebrand, Diana (2011-2014)
Hobson, Miranda (2005-2006)
Hodges, Jamila (2013)
Holler, Jennifer (2011-2012)
Huff, Karen (2005-2007)
Huffmaster, Kassie (2005, 2010)
Hughes, Karmilla (2009)
Hummons, Jamila (2013-2014)
Jenkins, Jessica (2009)
Jenkins, Senina (2009)
Johnson, Heidi (2007, 2009-2012)
Joiner, Sonji (2005)
Jones, Jessica (2005-2007)
Jordan, Anita (2013-2014)
Kaffenberg, Juli (2006-07, 2011-14)
Keeney, Kenitra "Kay" (2006)
King, Angela (2005)
King, Robyn (2007)
Klesse, Kimberly (2009)
Klofta, Jackie (2007)
Kovacs, Staci (2006)
Kraemer, Tiffany (2006-07, 2010, 2011)
Krebs, Heidi (2015)
Lawson, Alya (2012-2013)
Lee, Jessica (2009-2010)
Long, Amanda (2005)
Longieliere, Jessica (2014)
Louis, Tonia (2012)
Lowe, Chrysten (2005)
Lucas, Marquita (2012)
Mark, Katie (2005)
Matt, Dana (2005)
McCollum, Jessica (2014-2015)
McGowan, Cindy (2005-2007)
McKenzie, Sarah (2014)
Meinhardt, Tina (2005-2007)
Miller, Catharine "C.J." (2006-2007)
Mitchell, Dannyelle (2011)
Mitchell, Tumecia (2014)
Molter, T.J. (2005-2007, 2012-2015)
Moore, Ayanna (2009-2010, 2012-2013)
Moore, Julie (2005-2006)
Morris, Danielle (2012-2013)
Mosley, Dominique (2012)
Mueller, Melinda (2005)
Mullins, Ebony (2011)
Murdock, Deona (2005-2006)
Murray, Porsha (2010-2014)
Norton, Maria (2006-2007)
Nurse, Sheila (2005-2006)
Osborn, Kristin (2009)
Owen, Deborah (2006)
Owens, Liana (2012)
Owens, Michelle (2009)
Palmore, Cathy (2005-2007)
Palmore, Danett (2006)
Paulk-McGinley, Jen (2007)
Peter, Theresa (2005)
Prebble, Erin (2009, 2011)
Ray, Renee (2007)
Rechtin, Jackie (2009)
Red, Johnnae (2013)
Rees, Chantille (2009)
Revelos, Mary (2005)
Rusher, Shayvonne (2005-2006)
Russo, Sara (2009)
Sargent, Mary (2005-2007, 2009-2015)
Schran, Heidi (2005)
Scott, Nacole (2012)
Secen, LeAnn (2009)
Shadle, Amanda (2009)
Sjostrom, Nancy (2007)
Smith, Selena (2011-2012)
Spencer, Kendra (2009-2015)
St. Clair, Tamecka (2007, 2009-2011)
Stevens, Briana (2012-2013)
Stinson, Livia (2005-2006)
Stryker, Kat (2009)
Sutherland, Erica (2006-2007)
Taylor, Robin (2010)
Terrell, Michelle (2005-07, 2009-15)
Thomas, Aundreana (2013-2015)
Thomas, DeShawn (2005)
Thomas, Doria (2005)
Tirschek, Katelin (2011)
Todd, Leah (2010-2011)
Trujillo, Marta (2011-2015)
Tungate, Jennifer (2005)
Uecker, Jackie (2005-2007, 2009-2015)
Valdez, Jennifer (2012-2013)
Valerius, Gina (2005)
Vanderbush, Kristin (2005)
Vanek, Shelley (2005, '07, '12, '14)
VonHolle, Vicky (2005)
Walker, Lindsey (2013)
Walton, Kerry (2005-2007)
Washington, Tamika (2011)
Watkins, Shalonda (2010-2012)
Watson, Kim (2005-07, 2009-13, 2015)
Wilkins, Jarobeca (2009)
Williams, Precious (2014-2015)
Williams, Sue (2005)
Williams, Tammie (2011-2012)
Wilson, Cat (2015)
Woods, Belinda (2005)
Woods, Chandra (2005-06, 2009-11)
Wright, LaMieka (2011-2015)
Wright, Melinda (2006)
Young, Renee (2007)
Younker, Sarah (2011)
Zanders, Selena (2009)
Zimmerle, Cindy (2005-2007)

Clarksville Fox

Year	League	Name	W	L	Conference	Division	DF	PR
2007	WFL	Clarksville Fox	4	3	--	--	2	C
2008	IWFL2	Clarksville Fox	8	2	Southern	Mid South	1	C
2009	IWFL2	Clarksville Fox	4	4	--	--	17	--
2010	IWFL2	Clarksville Fox	5	3	Western	Midwest	3	--
2011	IWFL	Clarksville Fox	3	5	Eastern	Mid South	3	--
		Total	**24**	**17**				

Based in: Clarksville, TN   **Neutral site:** Chicago, IL (N)

6/9/2007	H	Tennessee Heat	W	40	22		6/6/2009	A	Louisville Nightmare	W	12	0
7/14/2007	A	Jacksonville Dixie Blues	L	6	49	C	6/13/2009	H	Iowa Crush	W	22	12
4/12/2008	A	Carolina Queens	W	30	0		4/3/2010	H	Tennessee Valley Tigers	W	36	6
4/19/2008	A	Louisiana Fuel	W	66	6		4/10/2010	A	Chattanooga Locomotion	W	30	14
4/26/2008	H	Shreveport Aftershock	W	28	0		4/17/2010	A	Louisville Nightmare	W	1	0
5/10/2008	H	Shreveport Aftershock	W	28	6		4/24/2010	H	Memphis Belles	L	12	18
5/17/2008	H	Louisiana Fuel	W	14	0		5/1/2010	A	Tennessee Valley Tigers	W	28	12
5/31/2008	A	Chicago Force	L	0	40		5/15/2010	H	Louisville Nightmare	W	40	0
6/7/2008	A	Wisconsin Warriors	W	12	6		5/29/2010	A	Atlanta Xplosion	L	0	56
6/14/2008	H	Columbus Phantoms	W	1	0		6/5/2010	A	Memphis Belles	L	6	8
6/28/2008	H	New England Intensity	W	32	0 CC		4/2/2011	H	Chattanooga Locomotion	L	0	30
7/26/2008	N	Montreal Blitz	L	6	26 C		4/16/2011	H	Tennessee Valley Tigers	W	32	6
4/11/2009	A	Atlanta Xplosion	L	0	43		4/23/2011	A	Atlanta Ravens	L	0	69
4/25/2009	H	Louisville Nightmare	W	37	7		4/30/2011	A	Memphis Belles	L	12	20
5/2/2009	A	Iowa Crush	W	14	0		5/7/2011	H	Chattanooga Locomotion	L	0	42
5/16/2009	A	Kansas City Tribe	L	6	48		5/14/2011	A	Tennessee Valley Tigers	W	12	6
5/23/2009	H	Tennessee Valley Tigers	L	0	23		5/21/2011	A	Tennessee Valley Tigers	W	22	6
5/30/2009	H	Chattanooga Locomotion	L	0	28		6/11/2011	H	North Texas Knockouts	L	6	63

Cleveland Fusion

Year	League	Name	W	L	Conference	Division	DF	PR
2002	NWFA	Cleveland Fusion	6	3	--	Great Lakes	2	S
2003	NWFA	Cleveland Fusion	7	3	Northern	Great Lakes	2	S
2004	NWFA	Cleveland Fusion	3	5	Northern	Great Lakes	4	--
2005	NWFA	Cleveland Fusion	5	3	Northern	--	10	--
2006	NWFA	Cleveland Fusion	8	2	Northern	North Central	1	S
2007	NWFA	Cleveland Fusion	8	3	Northern	Central	3	CC
2008	NWFA	Cleveland Fusion	5	3	Northern	Central	2	--
2009	WFA	Cleveland Fusion	4	4	National	Mid-Atlantic	3	--
2010	WFA	Cleveland Fusion	6	3	National	North Central	2	Q
2011	WFA	Cleveland Fusion	5	3	National	Mid-Atlantic	2	--
2012	WFA	Cleveland Fusion	2	6	National	Division 4 (Mideast)	2	--
2013	WFA	Cleveland Fusion	9	1	National	Division 3 (North Central)	1	Q
2014	WFA	Cleveland Fusion	7	3	National	Northeast	2	Q
2015	WFA	Cleveland Fusion	6	3	National	Mid-Atlantic	2	Q
		Total	**81**	**45**				

Based in: Cleveland, OH

4/20/2002		South Bend Hawks	W	39	0		4/12/2003	A	Detroit Demolition	L	0	7	
5/4/2002		Detroit Danger	L	6	20		4/19/2003	A	Toledo Spitfire	W	66	0	
5/18/2002		Southwest Michigan Jaguars	W	18	0		4/26/2003	H	Southwest Michigan Jaguars	W	56	6	
5/25/2002		Detroit Danger	W	14	3		5/3/2003	H	Indiana Thunder	W	90	0	
6/8/2002		South Bend Hawks	W	40	16		5/17/2003	A	Indiana Thunder	W	78	6	
6/15/2002		Southwest Michigan Jaguars	W	20	14		5/24/2003	H	Toledo Spitfire	W	84	0	
6/22/2002		Detroit Danger	L	20	51		6/7/2003	A	Southwest Michigan Jaguars	W	34	0	
6/29/2002		South Bend Hawks	W	20	0		6/14/2003	H	Detroit Demolition	L	19	33	
7/6/2002	A	Massachusetts Mutiny	L	0	45 S		6/28/2003	H	Baltimore Burn	W	28	19	Q
							7/12/2003	A	Detroit Demolition	L	15	28	S

Continued on next page

Cleveland Fusion Game-By-Game Results (continued)

Date	H/A	Opponent	W/L	PF	PA	Note
4/3/2004	A	Columbus Comets	L	2	19	
4/24/2004	H	Columbus Comets	L	6	27	
5/8/2004	A	Southwest Michigan Jaguars	L	6	39	
5/15/2004	A	Detroit Demolition	L	7	75	
5/22/2004	H	Indiana Thunder	W	46	8	
5/29/2004	A	Toledo Spitfire	W	35	0	
6/5/2004	H	Detroit Demolition	L	0	55	
6/12/2004	H	Wisconsin Riveters	W	62	0	
4/16/2005	A	D.C. Divas	L	0	18	
4/23/2005	H	Indianapolis SaberKatz	W	65	0	
4/30/2005	H	Pittsburgh Passion	W	29	28	*
5/8/2005	A	Detroit Demolition	L	7	55	
5/21/2005	H	Cincinnati Sizzle	W	61	0	
6/4/2005	A	Southwest Michigan Jaguars	L	19	34	
6/11/2005	H	Baltimore Burn	W	34	14	
6/18/2005	A	Indiana Thunder	W	1	0	
4/22/2006	H	Pittsburgh Passion	W	13	12	
4/29/2006	H	Erie Illusion	W	43	0	
5/6/2006	A	Columbus Comets	L	13	21	
5/20/2006	H	Milwaukee Momentum	W	49	0	
5/27/2006	A	Pittsburgh Passion	W	35	33	
6/3/2006	H	Columbus Comets	W	18	7	
6/10/2006	A	Erie Illusion	W	46	0	
6/17/2006	H	Milwaukee Momentum	W	82	0	
7/1/2006	H	Philadelphia Phoenix	W	52	13	Q
7/8/2006	A	Oklahoma City Lightning	L	13	14	S
4/21/2007	A	Pittsburgh Passion	L	14	23	
4/28/2007	A	Baltimore Burn	W	24	8	
5/5/2007	H	West Michigan Mayhem	W	34	6	
5/12/2007	H	Central PA Vipers	W	78	0	
5/26/2007	H	Pittsburgh Passion	L	18	40	
6/2/2007	A	Central PA Vipers	W	62	0	
6/9/2007	H	Baltimore Burn	W	39	0	
6/16/2007	A	West Michigan Mayhem	W	22	6	
6/23/2007	A	Connecticut Crush	W	57	0	Q
6/30/2007	A	Massachusetts Mutiny	W	12	7	S
7/7/2007	A	Pittsburgh Passion	L	15	49	CC
4/19/2008	A	West Virginia Wonders	W	22	0	
4/26/2008	H	Columbus Comets	L	8	20	
5/3/2008	H	Erie Illusion	W	30	0	
5/17/2008	A	Fort Wayne Flash	W	8	6	
5/24/2008	A	Columbus Comets	L	16	22	
5/31/2008	H	West Virginia Wonders	W	1	0	
6/7/2008	A	Erie Illusion	W	26	0	
6/21/2008	H	Fort Wayne Flash	L	0	27	
4/18/2009	H	Kentucky Karma	W	38	14	
4/25/2009	H	Pittsburgh Force	L	28	34	
5/9/2009	A	Columbus Comets	L	12	30	
5/16/2009	A	Kentucky Karma	L	12	20	
5/30/2009	A	Pittsburgh Force	W	34	16	
6/6/2009	H	Columbus Comets	L	7	20	
6/13/2009	H	Cincinnati Sizzle	W	36	18	
6/27/2009	A	Cincinnati Sizzle	W	48	14	
4/10/2010	A	Toledo Reign	W	18	7	
4/17/2010	A	Kentucky Karma	W	54	6	
4/24/2010	H	Pittsburgh Force	W	60	3	
5/1/2010	H	Detroit Dark Angels	W	39	12	
5/8/2010	A	West Michigan Mayhem	L	0	55	
5/15/2010	H	Toledo Reign	W	62	0	
6/5/2010	A	Detroit Dark Angels	W	34	14	
6/12/2010	H	West Michigan Mayhem	L	14	66	
6/26/2010	A	St. Louis Slam	L	23	50	Q
4/2/2011	A	Columbus Comets	L	13	16	
4/16/2011	H	Pittsburgh Passion	L	8	26	
4/30/2011	H	Erie Illusion	W	50	0	
5/7/2011	A	Pittsburgh Force	W	54	0	
5/14/2011	H	Columbus Comets	W	16	6	
5/21/2011	A	Erie Illusion	W	50	0	
6/4/2011	H	Pittsburgh Force	W	76	0	
6/11/2011	A	Pittsburgh Passion	L	0	42	
4/14/2012	H	West Michigan Mayhem	L	7	23	
4/21/2012	H	Pittsburgh Force	W	33	6	
4/28/2012	A	Detroit Dark Angels	L	6	14	
5/5/2012	A	Pittsburgh Passion	L	0	49	
5/12/2012	A	Pittsburgh Force	W	14	6	
5/19/2012	H	Chicago Force	L	0	48	
6/2/2012	A	Columbus Comets	L	0	22	
6/9/2012	H	Detroit Dark Angels	L	14	17	
4/13/2013	H	Derby City Dynamite	W	44	0	
4/20/2013	A	Toledo Reign	W	36	6	
4/27/2013	A	Derby City Dynamite	W	40	0	
5/4/2013	H	Central Maryland Seahawks	W	42	0	
5/11/2013	A	Cincinnati Sizzle	W	47	6	
5/18/2013	H	Toledo Reign	W	50	0	
6/1/2013	H	Cincinnati Sizzle	W	55	6	
6/8/2013	A	Central Maryland Seahawks	W	48	0	
6/15/2013	H	West Michigan Mayhem	W	35	6	W
6/22/2013	A	Chicago Force	L	7	65	Q
4/5/2014	H	Columbus Comets	W	20	6	
4/19/2014	A	Boston Militia	L	7	47	
4/26/2014	H	Indy Crash	W	7	0	
5/3/2014	H	Boston Militia	L	7	48	
5/10/2014	A	Cincinnati Sizzle	W	71	0	
5/17/2014	A	Toledo Reign	W	46	0	
5/31/2014	A	Columbus Comets	W	23	12	
6/7/2014	H	West Michigan Mayhem	W	43	8	
6/14/2014	H	Indy Crash	W	38	32	W
6/21/2014	A	Boston Militia	L	6	47	Q
4/11/2015	A	Central Maryland Seahawks	W	35	0	
4/18/2015	H	Columbus Comets	W	49	0	
4/25/2015	H	Indy Crash	W	35	0	
5/9/2015	A	Columbus Comets	W	46	6	
5/16/2015	H	Boston Renegades	L	20	24	
5/30/2015	A	Detroit Dark Angels	W	35	0	
6/6/2015	A	D.C. Divas	L	7	27	
6/13/2015	H	West Michigan Mayhem	W	42	12	
6/27/2015	A	Chicago Force	L	14	71	Q

Cleveland Fusion Player Register (2002-2015)

Acker, Lauren (2015)
Adams, Tiffany (2002-2003, 2007)
Alex, Olga (2002)
Alexander, Desiree (2006-2015)
Alex-Newsom, Dina (2002, 2007)
Anderson, Shannon (2002, '04-08, '12)
Andrasik, Beth (2012-2015)
Archuleta, Maria (2006)
Austin, Jocelyn (2005-2008)
Bader, Alana (2003-2004, 2006)
Bagola, Carlene (2004)
Balochko, Stephanie (2002-2009)
Baon, Brenda (2004)
Barber, Peru (2003-2008, 2011)
Barrick, Amber (2012)
Bauer, Leanne (2009-2010)
Bell, Caprita (2012-2015)
Bell, Kayla (2014)
Bender, Monica (2005-2006)
Bentler, Maribeth (2002-2003)
Biggers, Chelsea (2014-2015)
Bihari, Michele "Shelly" (2002-2004)
Bileci, Anna (2008)
Bitecofer, Sherry (2004)
Blakemore, Heather (2004)
Boccuzzi, Mary (2005)
Boden, Kaeleen (2013)
Bowman, Diana (2015)
Brown, Lisa (2006)
Buell, Shaun (2006)
Byers, Bridgette (2002, 2011)
Cain, Cat (2013-2014)
Cannon, Michelle (2003-2005)
Carson, Danielle (2002)
Casiano, Rosa (2011)
Coats, Joslyn (2011-2012)
Cole, Teresa (2014-2015)
Conlin, Christy (2012-2014)
Constantino, Tracie (2004)
Cooch, Amanda (2013-2015)
Coward, Kanisha (2013-2015)
Coyner, Kathy (2005)
Cramblett, Jennifer (2010)
Davis, Kristen (2011-2013)
Dean, Monica (2002)
DeCarlo, Cara (2004)
Dennis, Elizabeth (2013)
Dennis, Nancy (2002)
Dietrick, Mary (2002-2003, 2007)
Dillow, Elizabeth (2004, '06-08, '11-15)
DiMichele, Vicky (2005)
Doll, Amanda (2011)
Dougherty, Kathy (2008-2015)
Edwards, Erica (2006)
Elder, Amy (2002)
Elliot, Courtney (2009)
Ephraim, Mercedes (2015)
Erne Jr., Mary (2005-2008, 2010)
Fay, Sarah (2014)
Fifer, Stacey (2002-2003)
Fischer, Becky (2002-03, 2005, 2009-10)
Focarett, Marianne (2003)
Gaggiani, Brandi (2004-2005)
Garner, Lavern (2004)
Garrett, Denise (2006-2008, 2012)
Garrison, Danisha (2008-2011)
Glaspy, Shawna (2003)
Glyptis, Melissa (2005)

Goncalves, Mari (2002-2003, 2005-2006)
Goncalves, Zulmira (2002)
Gonzalez, Maritza (2003-2007)
Grace, Daniella (2012)
Green, Katie (2012-2015)
Greulich, Jen (2010)
Grogan, Kisha (2003)
Hall, Carrie (2009-2011)
Hall, Deb (2006, 2008)
Halloran, Nancy (2005)
Hank, Katie (2004, 2010)
Harris, Cristal (2004-2005)
Harris, Daniece (2010-2015)
Harris, Tawanda (2011)
Harshbarger, Margaret (2006)
Hatem, Sonya (2002)
Heart, Sherry (2002)
Heath, Sandi (2002-2004)
Hedlund-Tunnel, Sandra (2004, 2006)
Heinl, Lisa (2002-2008, 2010-2011)
Herron, Atunyese (2005)
Hillier, Michelle (2008)
Hocevar, Kristie (2013-2014)
Hockman, Chrissy (2004)
Hoff, Lisa (2002)
Hogle, Melissa (2008)
Hongo, Liz (2006)
Horton, Lisa (2011)
House, Michelle (2010)
Hruby, Dorothy (2006)
Hudson, Melanie (2009)
Imler, Dawn (2004-2005)
Irons, Kris (2003-2004)
Jackiewicz, Angela (2012)
Jackson, Maria (2013-2015)
Jaqueth, Christine (2013-2015)
Jesensky, Jolie (2006-2007)
Johnson, Chawnte (2013-2014)
Johnson, Lori (2002-2003, 2005)
Johnson, Tiffany (2012-2015)
Johnston, Sarah (2002)
Jones, Candace (2008-2011, 2013-2014)
Jones, Cathy (2003)
Jordan, Shayla (2004-2006)
Josie, Jolene (2002)
Jurenec, Michelle (2008-2009)
Kalczynski, Colleen (2004)
Kemp, Erin (2004)
Kemp, Lauren (2008-2010)
Kendall, Shanolen (2006-2015)
Kiniel, Quinzell (2007-2011)
Kovach, Kristina (2002-2003)
Koziewicz, Joy (2003)
Koziol, Susan (2002-2003)
Krupka, Vickie (2002-2005)
Krzystan, Amanda (2005-2006)
Kuykendall, Dionne (2012)
Kyle, Yermesha (2015)
Lashley, Heather (2002-2003)
Latessa, Martina (2002-2014)
Law, Andrea (2002-2003)
Lindsey, Carla (2004-2006)
Love, Angela (2011)
Lowe, Amber (2010)
Lurry, Danielle (2004-2007)
Lynn, Rhonda (2006)
Majni, Sheila (2006-2007)
Makovitz, Yvette (2002)

Manley, Molly (2004-2006)
Martin, Jacque (2006-2009, 2011-2015)
Mason, Angela (2013-2015)
Mason, Kelly (2003)
Matsimela, Aysha (2003-2004)
McCorvey, Nicole (2012-2014)
McGaffick, Katie (2010)
McGinnis, Michelle (2004)
McKee, Klaire (2014)
McKee, Leann (2011-2015)
Meyers, Rebecca (2005)
Michalakes, Charleen (2003)
Milhoan, Mandy (2010)
Miller, Gina (2015)
Mitrovic, Maja (2003)
Mixon, Andrea (2015)
Moody, Jada (2014)
Moore, Holly (2011)
Moore, Jocelyn (2011)
Moorer, Joselyn (2012)
Morgan, Rosemary (2003-2005)
Muscatello, Stacy (2013)
Nevel, Shauna (2002-2007)
Nickerson, Traci (2002-2004, 2007)
Norris, Tina (2006)
Novotny, Jennifer (2004)
Ogbomoh, Nieha (2011)
Palma, Keri (2014-2015)
Patrizi, Judi (2002)
Perez, Rene (2013)
Pike, Megyn (2005-2006)
Pizzie, Sarah (2009-2011, 2014)
Plank, Moya (2005)
Pogue, Kim (2002, 2004)
Popka, Pam (2004-2005)
Post, Autumn (2012)
Post, Heather (2005)
Pou, LaTonya (2013)
Racy, Meredith (2002-2004)
Radtke, Faye (2009)
Ramps, Roxanne (2008)
Reed, Denise (2005)
Repa, Vickie (2002)
Rex, Kimberly (2005-2013)
Rhoads, Krystal (2002-2003)
Rice, Rhona (2002-2003)
Richmond, Emily (2011-2013)
Riley, Valerie (2015)
Rininger, Tamara (2005)
Rosa, Tee (2002)
Ross, Wanda (2002-2008)
Rucker, Veronica (2006-2015)
Rush, Kelley (2005-2007)
Rusnak, Laura (2013)
Russo, Stefanie (2004-2007, 2009-2015)
Ryba, Jennifer (2002-2005, 2007-2008)
Saggio, Sam (2004)
Sarratt, Genese (2004)
Sas, Melanie (2008)
Schmid, Susan (2002)
Schriner, Katie (2004-2005)
Schutte, Rachel (2009)
Scotch, Michelle (2002-2003, 2005-2006)
Sheets, Amanda (2011)
Sheldon, Jennifer (2004-2006)
Shofar, Candace (2014)
Simcik, Jackie (2011)

Continued on next page

Cleveland Fusion Player Register (continued)

Simpson, Danielle (2009)
Skiles, Christine (2002-2003)
Skrovan, Stephanie (2012)
Smith, Kelly (2006)
Smith, Marcia (2002)
Soggs, Tiffany (2008-2013, 2015)
Speight, Ashley (2014)
Spencer, Marie (2003-2005, 2007-2008)
St. Cyr, Tiffany (2007-2010)
Stamper, Sune (2014)
Stefan, Danijela (2002-2003)
Stewart, Jillian (2011)
Stewart, Tammy (2003-2005)
Stinson, Casey (2005-2007)
Strebig, Cindy (2002)
Tadych, Jackie (2002-2003, 2007)
Tate, Andrea (2003)
Tatum, Chrissy (2013)
Tibbs, Georgia (2004-2005)
Tigner, Stefanie (2009)
Tobin, Christine (2003)
Torres, Tania (2015)
Unique, Danielle (2009-2010)
VanDyne, Angela (2004)
Vega, Astrid (2002)
Vibbert, Marie (2010-2014)
Wallace, Britney (2012, 2015)
Walsh, Laura (2002)
Ward, Vonda (2007)
Ware, Erica (2006-2008)
Washington, Jamila (2002)
Weber, Traci (2011)
Weiss, Danielle (2002-2004)
Wertz, Donna (2002)
Whiting, Kristie (2004-2006)
Williams, Haizle (2009-2010)
Williams, Laura (2002)
Williams, Stephanie (2009)
Wilson, Nikicha (2006-2010)
Wozniak, Elizabeth (2005-2006)
Yahner, Kelly (2006)
Zane, Lisa (2012)
Zimo, Andrea (2010-2012)
Zofchak, Ann (2002-2003)
Zubko, Maria (2002-2003)

Colorado Freeze

Year	League		Name	W	L	Conference	Division	DF	PR
2015	IWFL	X	Colorado Freeze	3	4	--	--	--	--

Based in: Denver, CO

4/11/2015	A	Colorado Springs Voodoo	W	20	6		6/6/2015	H	Colorado Springs Voodoo	W	26	0
4/18/2015	A	Rocky Mountain Thunderkatz	L	0	21		6/13/2015	A	Utah Falconz	L	0	58
5/16/2015	A	Rocky Mountain Thunderkatz	L	6	18		6/20/2015	H	Colorado Springs Voodoo	W	17	6
5/30/2015	A	Iowa Crush	L	6	36							

Colorado Freeze Player Register (2015)

Apodaca, Reese (2015)
Baca, Barb (2015)
Canez, Lacey (2015)
Clark, Lindsay (2015)
Davis, Ashley (2015)
DeGroat, Kim (2015)
Gebhart, Victoria (2015)
Gusa, Keri (2015)
Heydt, Emily (2015)
Ivey, Jessica (2015)
Jolly, Sarah (2015)
Juarez, Michelle (2015)
Lewis, Nina (2015)
Mansheim, Shae (2015)
Mazzocco, Ericka (2015)
Mendez, Maribel (2015)
Miranda, Callie (2015)
Pounds, Erin (2015)
Quezada, Gabrielle (2015)
Shuster, Summer (2015)
Skinner, Jennifer (2015)
Spalding, Alex (2015)
Torres, Nicole (2015)
Welch, Stephanie (2015)
Williams, Gini (2015)
Young, Nikki (2015)
Zuniga, Isis (2015)

Colorado Springs Koalas

Year	League	Name	W	L	Conference	Division	DF	PR
2002	UWFL	Colorado Springs Koalas	5	1	--	--	--	--

Based in: Colorado Springs, CO

4/14/2002	Sweetwater County Outlaws	W	63	13		5/12/2002	Grand Valley Vipers	W	31	6
4/21/2002	Denver Foxes	W	30	29		5/19/2002	Tri-City Mustangs	W	26	14
5/5/2002	Cheyenne Dust Devils	W	44	14		5/26/2002	Pueblo Pythons	L	46	48

Colorado Springs Voodoo

Year	League	Name	W	L	Conference	Division	DF	PR
2015	IWFL	Colorado Springs Voodoo	0	5	Western	Mountain West	3	--

Based in: Colorado Springs, CO

4/11/2015	H	Colorado Freeze	L	6	20		6/6/2015	A	Colorado Freeze	L	0	26
4/18/2015	A	Mile High Blaze	L	0	60	I	6/20/2015	A	Colorado Freeze	L	6	17
4/25/2015	H	Rocky Mountain Thunderkatz	L	6	58							

Colorado Valkyries

Year	League	Name	W	L	Conference	Division	DF	PR
2000	WPFL	Colorado Valkyries	5	2	American	Central	2	S

Based in: Denver, CO

10/14/2000	A	Minnesota Vixen	L	12	14		11/18/2000	H	New England Storm	W	7 3
10/22/2000	H	Oklahoma City Wildcats	W	58	0		11/26/2000	A	Oregon Sirens	W	54 0
10/29/2000	H	Houston Energy	W	62	6		12/2/2000	A	Houston Energy	L	0 13 S
11/4/2000	A	Austin Rage	W	53	0						

Columbus Comets

Year	League	Name	W	L	Conference	Division	DF	PR
2003	NWFA	Columbus Flames	6	3	Northern	Mid-Atlantic	3	--
2004	NWFA	Columbus Comets	7	3	Northern	Great Lakes	2	S
2005	NWFA	Columbus Comets	6	3	Northern	--	5	Q
2006	NWFA	Columbus Comets	7	4	Northern	North Central	2	CC
2007	NWFA	Columbus Comets	9	4	Southern	North	2	C
2008	NWFA	Columbus Comets	7	3	Northern	Central	1	S
2009	WFA	Columbus Comets	9	1	National	Mid-Atlantic	1	S
2010	WFA	Columbus Comets	11	1	National	Mid-Atlantic	1	C
2011	WFA	Columbus Comets	5	3	National	Mid-Atlantic	3	--
2012	WFA	Columbus Comets	2	6	National	Division 3 (Mid-Atlantic)	3	--
2013	WFA	Columbus Comets	6	5	National	Division 2 (Mid-Atlantic)	3	Q
2014	WFA	Columbus Comets	5	5	National	Mid-Atlantic	2	Q
2015	WFA	Columbus Comets	2	6	National	Mid-Atlantic	3	--
		Total	82	47				

Based in: Columbus, OH   **Neutral sites:** Nashville, TN (N1); Las Vegas, NV (N2)

4/5/2003		Nashville Dream	W	13	0	E	4/7/2006	A	Pittsburgh Passion	L	7 14	E
4/19/2003	H	Pittsburgh Passion	W	21	18		4/22/2006	H	Erie Illusion	W	71 0	
4/26/2003	A	Baltimore Burn	L	7	13		4/29/2006	A	Pittsburgh Passion	L	0 6	
5/3/2003	A	Erie Illusion	W	34	13		5/6/2006	H	Cleveland Fusion	W	21 13	
5/10/2003	H	D.C. Divas	L	22	30		5/20/2006	H	West Michigan Mayhem	W	30 7	
5/17/2003	H	Baltimore Burn	W	13	0		5/27/2006	A	Erie Illusion	W	59 0	
5/31/2003	H	Erie Illusion	W	35	12		6/3/2006	A	Cleveland Fusion	L	7 18	
6/7/2003	A	D.C. Divas	L	7	8		6/10/2006	H	Pittsburgh Passion	W	27 13	
6/14/2003	A	Pittsburgh Passion	W	57	15		6/17/2006	A	West Michigan Mayhem	L	0 10	
							7/1/2006	A	West Michigan Mayhem	W	17 7	Q
4/3/2004	H	Cleveland Fusion	W	19	2		7/8/2006	A	Pensacola Power	W	20 0	S
4/17/2004	A	Detroit Demolition	L	7	20		7/22/2006	A	D.C. Divas	L	7 32	CC
4/24/2004	A	Cleveland Fusion	W	27	6							
5/1/2004	H	Detroit Demolition	L	10	18		4/21/2007	A	St. Louis Slam	L	14 27	
5/8/2004	A	Toledo Spitfire	W	50	0		4/28/2007	H	Fort Wayne Flash	W	35 6	
5/15/2004	A	Wisconsin Riveters	W	69	0		5/5/2007	A	Cincinnati Sizzle	W	53 0	
5/22/2004	H	Southwest Michigan Jaguars	W	34	14		5/12/2007	H	Kentucky Karma	W	44 0	
6/5/2004	H	Indiana Thunder	W	90	0		5/26/2007	H	St. Louis Slam	L	13 26	
6/26/2004	A	Massachusetts Mutiny	W	7	6	Q	6/2/2007	A	Fort Wayne Flash	W	10 0	
7/10/2004	A	Detroit Demolition	L	23	41	S	6/9/2007	A	Kentucky Karma	W	28 0	
							6/16/2007	H	Cincinnati Sizzle	W	52 0	
4/16/2005	H	Detroit Demolition	L	7	10		6/23/2007	A	Pensacola Power	W	10 0	Q
4/23/2005	A	Baltimore Burn	W	22	20		6/30/2007	A	Chattanooga Locomotion	W	27 8	S
4/30/2005	H	Indiana Thunder	W	75	0		7/7/2007	A	Oklahoma City Lightning	W	9 7	CC
5/21/2005	H	Tidewater Floods	W	100	0		7/21/2007	N1	Pittsburgh Passion	L	0 32	C
5/28/2005	A	Cincinnati Sizzle	W	64	0				**Continued on next page**			
6/4/2005	A	Detroit Demolition	L	23	41							
6/11/2005	H	Toledo Spitfire	W	74	0							
6/18/2005	A	Kentucky Karma	W	56	0							
6/25/2005	A	Southwest Michigan Jaguars	L	14	20	Q						

Franchise Game-By-Game Records, 1999-2015

Columbus Comets Game-By-Game Results (continued)

Date	H/A	Opponent	W/L	PF	PA	Note
4/19/2008	H	St. Louis Slam	L	16	18	
4/26/2008	A	Cleveland Fusion	W	20	8	
5/3/2008	H	West Virginia Wonders	W	91	0	
5/10/2008	H	Erie Illusion	W	48	0	
5/24/2008	H	Cleveland Fusion	W	22	16	
5/31/2008	A	Erie Illusion	W	34	0	
6/7/2008	A	West Virginia Wonders	W	104	0	
6/14/2008	A	St. Louis Slam	L	23	48	
6/28/2008	H	Fort Wayne Flash	W	14	7	Q
7/5/2008	A	Philadelphia Phoenix	L	14	15	S
4/4/2009	A	Baltimore Burn	W	21	16	E
4/18/2009	H	Pittsburgh Force	W	49	0	
5/2/2009	H	Cincinnati Sizzle	W	36	0	
5/9/2009	H	Cleveland Fusion	W	30	12	
5/16/2009	A	Pittsburgh Force	W	38	0	
6/6/2009	A	Cleveland Fusion	W	20	7	
6/13/2009	H	Kentucky Karma	W	23	8	
6/20/2009	A	Cincinnati Sizzle	W	47	8	
6/27/2009	A	Kentucky Karma	W	21	12	
7/11/2009	A	West Michigan Mayhem	L	12	41	S
4/17/2010	A	Pittsburgh Force	W	68	0	
4/24/2010	H	Dayton Diamonds	W	43	0	
5/8/2010	H	Pittsburgh Force	W	58	0	
5/15/2010	H	West Michigan Mayhem	W	36	31	
5/22/2010	A	Cincinnati Sizzle	W	68	6	
6/5/2010	H	Kentucky Karma	W	66	0	
6/12/2010	A	Dayton Diamonds	W	48	0	
6/19/2010	A	Toledo Reign	W	65	0	
6/26/2010	H	Baltimore Burn	W	67	8	Q
7/10/2010	H	Philadelphia Liberty Belles (II)	W	36	7	S
7/17/2010	H	St. Louis Slam	W	21	14	CC
7/31/2010	N2	Lone Star Mustangs	L	12	16	C
4/2/2011	H	Cleveland Fusion	W	16	13	
4/9/2011	H	Pittsburgh Force	W	55	0	
4/30/2011	A	Pittsburgh Passion	L	0	17	
5/7/2011	A	Erie Illusion	W	36	7	
5/14/2011	A	Cleveland Fusion	L	6	16	
5/21/2011	H	Pittsburgh Passion	L	6	7	
6/4/2011	H	Erie Illusion	W	1	0	
6/18/2011	A	Pittsburgh Force	W	64	0	
4/21/2012	A	Chicago Force	L	0	47	
4/28/2012	H	Pittsburgh Passion	L	14	37	
5/5/2012	A	D.C. Divas	L	0	49	
5/12/2012	A	Cincinnati Sizzle	W	64	6	
5/19/2012	H	Detroit Dark Angels	L	0	7	
6/2/2012	H	Cleveland Fusion	W	22	0	
6/9/2012	A	Pittsburgh Passion	L	0	22	
6/16/2012	H	D.C. Divas	L	0	42	
4/6/2013	H	West Michigan Mayhem	W	28	16	
4/13/2013	H	D.C. Divas	L	20	53	
4/20/2013	A	Nashville Smashers	W	52	0	I
4/27/2013	A	Pittsburgh Passion	L	0	49	
5/4/2013	H	Toledo Reign	W	56	7	
5/11/2013	A	Indy Crash	W	26	7	
5/18/2013	H	Pittsburgh Passion	L	14	35	
6/1/2013	A	Detroit Dark Angels	W	24	0	
6/8/2013	A	D.C. Divas	L	20	42	
6/15/2013	A	New York Sharks	W	22	20	W
6/22/2013	A	D.C. Divas	L	12	40	Q
4/5/2014	A	Cleveland Fusion	L	6	20	
4/19/2014	H	Derby City Dynamite	W	42	0	
4/26/2014	A	D.C. Divas	L	0	39	
5/3/2014	H	Central Maryland Seahawks	W	1	0	N
5/10/2014	H	Toledo Reign	W	48	0	
5/17/2014	A	West Michigan Mayhem	W	20	12	
5/31/2014	H	Cleveland Fusion	L	12	23	
6/7/2014	A	Chicago Force	L	8	72	
6/14/2014	H	Toledo Reign	W	22	0	W
6/21/2014	A	D.C. Divas	L	8	69	Q
4/11/2015	H	D.C. Divas	L	6	40	
4/18/2015	A	Cleveland Fusion	L	0	49	
5/2/2015	H	Pittsburgh Passion	L	8	35	I
5/9/2015	A	Cleveland Fusion	L	6	46	
5/16/2015	A	D.C. Divas	L	0	60	
5/30/2015	A	Central Maryland Seahawks	W	1	0	
6/6/2015	A	West Michigan Mayhem	L	8	43	
6/13/2015	H	Detroit Dark Angels	W	26	12	

Columbus Comets Player Register (2003-2015)

Alkula, Staci (2007-2013)
Allen, Star (2010)
Allerton, Janet (2003-2004)
Arnold, April (2007-2009)
Auel, Kristen (2010-2011)
Bader, Mari Anne (2003-04, 2008-10, '15)
Bahan, Jennifer (2011-2014)
Bailey, Cari (2008)
Baird, Carly (2012-2015)
Banta, Natalie (2008)
Barnes, Whitney (2003-2013)
Barney, Angie (2005-2006)
Barno, Karla (2003-2004)
Basenback, Angela (2015)
Bates, Samantha (2005-2006)
Bautista, Rebecca (2011-2015)
Beaudry, Shannon (2003, 2011)
Bellamy, Debra (2003)
Bennett, Terri (2003)
Bentler, Maribeth (2004-2005)
Blake, Laura (2003)
Bolin, Nicole (2005)
Boone, Shelley (2006-2007)
Bost, Rebecca (2004-2006)
Bowles, Teaira (2009)
Boyd, Chelsey (2008-2014)
Boyd, Christine (2003)
Boyle, Amber (2011)
Brand, Gerrie (2006)
Brock, Ashley (2009)
Burke, Star (2007, 2009)
Burney, Brittany (2014)
Carlisle, Kasey (2013)
Castle, Tesa (2007)
Castro, Caroline (2014)
Clapham, Margene (2009)
Coley, Kiana (2014-2015)
Colley, Brenda (2008)
Colton, Sara (2007)
Conley, Danyel (2012-2013)
Cooper, Dawn (2011)
Crosby, Shirley (2004-2005)
Crowder, Dawn (2008-2009)
Cullins, Ebony (2009-2011)
Cusick, Shea (2003)
Cutcliff, Ashley (2006-2007)
Daniels, Jessica (2014)
Darr, Elizabeth (2003)
Davis, Crystal (2003-2011, 2013-2014)
Davis, Erica "Shai" (2007)
Dodd, Carolyn (2004-2006)
Doty, Caitlin (2012)
Duke, Jaymi (2010)
Dunton, Megan (2004-2006)
Eckles, Lindsay (2004-2008)
Elmore, Dashjuania (2011-2012)
Englund, Erika (2010-2012)
Erne Jr., Mary (2009)
Everson, Brandie (2008)
Fadis, Shanna (2003)
Favata, Sarah (2006-2011)
Featherstone, Alpha (2006)
Fields, Bridget (2005)
Fleshman, Jeri (2004-2005)
Fontes, Keeahna (2013-2014)
Foreman, Christa (2003)
Forgy, Meghan (2008-2009)
Foster, Sheronda (2003-2004)

Continued on next page

Columbus Comets Player Register (continued)

Fowler, Chrissy (2003-2004)
Freeman, Cynthia (2004-2005)
Frieson, Tajah (2015)
Fusetti-Anderson, Mindy (2005)
Gardner, Jo Ann (2011-2015)
Garnes, Chanelle (2005-2006)
Garnes, Karla (2006)
Gartner, Louise (2004-2006)
Gates, Shelley (2003-2010, 2012-2015)
Gatson, Robyn (2005-2006)
Geiger, Amy (2004-2006)
Goings, Azelia (2005-2010)
Gorby, Tiffany (2006-2007)
Gray, Rachel (2015)
Guffy, Judy (2003)
Hall, Carrie (2015)
Hanchin, Debbie (2003-2004)
Harrington, India (2007-11, 2013-14)
Harris, Antionette (2004-05, 2007-09)
Harris, Cristal (2003)
Harris, LaShelle (2012)
Harris, Leah (2013-2014)
Harris, Lorrain (2004-2015)
Harris, Toni (2003, 2006)
Harter, Cheri (2004)
Hayes, Amanda (2004)
Haynam, Emily (2005)
Henderson, Arianne (2011)
Herbst, Amanda (2014-2015)
Hughes, Kim (2005-2007)
Hughes, Megan (2011)
Hutchinson, Jennifer (2003-2007)
Isaacs, Tabitha (2003)
Jackson, Dorethia (2006-2007)
Jackson, Gigi (2004-2005)
Jackson, Vanessa (2012)
Jeffers, Stephanie "Steph" (2010-2011)
Jenkins, Rachel (2004)
Jewett, Deb (2003-2005)
Johnson, Chelsea (2008-2015)
Johnson, Jershua (2014)
Johnson, Latrice (2004-2010, 2012)
Jones, Ayesha (2009-2014)
Jones, Dionjaleah (2015)
Jordan, Danielle (2007)
Judy, Andrea (2008-2012)
Junies, Darneeka (2008-2015)
Justiniani, Tijuana (2012-2015)
Kaiser, Marlene (2005-2007)
Keeney, Kenitra "Kay" (2014)
Keller, Suzy (2008-2010)
Kerr, Laura (2003-2006, 2012)
Kerr, Samantha (2015)
Kershner, Aerian (2004-2007, 2009)
Klesse, Kimberly (2004, 2010-2013)
Knight, Lashonda (2010)
Krejci, Danielle (2004, 2007)

Lawrence, Eugenia (2006-2007)
Lemke, Tasha (2013)
Lensch, Robin (2003-2004)
Lippke, Kim (2003)
Logan, Tiffany (2004-2005)
Looker, Cherish (2010-2012)
Lowery, Serenia (2015)
Martin, Breeanne (2004-2011, 2013)
Martin, Denise (2004-2006, 2011)
Martinez, Claritza (2012)
Mays, Natasha (2003-2004)
McCollum, Victoria (2015)
McEnaney, Erin (2007-2009)
McFarland, Amy (2003)
McGregor, Shannon (2009-2011)
Merritt, Mandy (2005, 2007)
Merryman, Jill (2005)
Meyer, Kelly (2003-2004)
Miller, Anndrea (2004)
Miller, Sara (2006-2012)
Misseldine, Ava (2005)
Mitchell, Danyel (2006-2007)
Mitchell, Tarnisha (2007)
Moore, Julie (2003)
Moraga, Deb (2003)
Morgan, Ashley (2011-2012)
Morgan, Kelly (2003)
Munson-Dibrell, Savannah (2015)
Nelson, Susan (2003-2005, 2007)
Notestine, Laura (2013-2015)
O'Leary, Carolyn (2007-2015)
Ortiz, Jonna (2015)
Ortman, Ivy (2005-2013, 2015)
Ottey, Tina (2011)
Owens, Amber (2006)
Page, Jaiza (2013)
Pahlas, Sarah (2008-2009, 2011)
Park, Crystal (2008)
Payne, Tonya (2004)
Payne, Trilisa (2004)
Perkins, Myesha (2008-2009, 2013)
Peterson, Jana (2004)
Pettway, Cassandra (2009-2013)
Pierce, KryShana (2013)
Pierson, G. Michelle (2003)
Porter, Amanda (2015)
Povisil, Lori (2006)
Raffuel, Leyla (2005)
Redman, Angie (2003-2005)
Reed, Melissa (2006)
Reese, Chania (2013-2014)
Rice, Lindsay (2007-2015)
Ritter, Nicole (2005)
Roberts, Kim (2007-2013)
Robinson, Jocelyn (2003)
Robinson, Raquel (2010-2011)
Robison, Holly (2009-2012, 2014-2015)

Robison, Sierra (2014-2015)
Rodriquez, Sentora (2011-2012)
Romanello, Jennifer (2006-2008)
Rorick, Liz (2014)
Ross, Kelly (2014-2015)
Sabatucci, Cristie (2003-2015)
Saldivar, Leanna (2013)
Schenck, Darlene (2003)
Schnittger, Emily (2009-2010)
Sciacca, Abigail (2015)
Seymour, Laquita (2011-2012, 2014)
Shaffer, Cassandra (2003-2004)
Sherwin, Dietra (2003-2015)
Shorts, Ashley (2013-2015)
Singleton, Jennifer (2003)
Smith, Erica (2007)
Sollberger, Tiffany (2004-2014)
Solum, Ashley (2003)
Souvannavong, Sally (2003)
Steimel, Jessica (2006)
Stephens, Laura (2008-2010)
Stevens, Stephanie (2007-12, 2014-15)
Stewart, Heather (2006)
Stockton, Heather (2013-2015)
Stumpf, Lisa (2003)
Swafford, Cassandra (2012)
Synder, Sam (2011)
Talley, Deasha (2010, 2014-2015)
Taylor, Erin (2003-2004)
Taylor, Esmeralda (2003-2005)
Theis, Michelle (2005)
Thompson, Dawn (2004-2005)
Tompkins, Christy (2003)
Townsend, Naomi (2007-2008)
Tremayne, Alicia (2003)
Vanatter, Jennifer (2009)
VanHoose, Tanya (2003)
Vernon, Regina (2003-2006)
Walker, Brittany (2015)
Walker, Jacki (2011-2012)
Walko, Kacy (2003)
Wells, Kaeko (2013-2014)
Wheeler, Tiffany (2003-2004)
Wilkes, Tammy (2007-2009)
Williams, Heidi (2004-2005)
Williams, May (2014)
Williams, Sally (2009, 2012)
Winegardner, Stephanie (2003)
Wingard, Shannon (2003)
Wolford, Roxanne (2003)
Wood, Sheila (2003-2006, 2013)
Woods, Bernice (2003-2006)
Wright, Kahle (2006-2007, 2014-2015)
Yard, Ellen (2005-2006)
Yurchick, Leyla (2006-2007)

Columbus Phantoms

Year	League	Name	W	L	Conference	Division	DF	PR
2008	IWFL	Columbus Phantoms	0	7	Eastern	Midwest	5	--

Based in: Columbus, OH

Franchise Game-By-Game Records, 1999-2015 171

Columbus Phantoms Game-By-Game Results

4/12/2008	A	Detroit Demolition	L	0	34
4/26/2008	A	Wisconsin Wolves	L	0	25
5/3/2008	A	Chicago Force	L	0	1
5/10/2008	A	Pittsburgh Passion	L	0	38
5/17/2008	A	Wisconsin Wolves	L	0	1
5/31/2008	H	Wisconsin Warriors	L	0	1
6/14/2008	A	Clarksville Fox	L	0	1

Connecticut Crush

Year	League	Name	W	L	Conference	Division	DF	PR
2001	NWFA	Connecticut Crush	2	6	Northern	--	4	--
2002	NWFA	Connecticut Crush	5	5	--	Northern	3	--
2003	NWFA	Connecticut Crush	7	3	Northern	Northern	2	Q
2004	NWFA	Connecticut Crush	5	3	Northern	Northern	3	--
2005	NWFA	Connecticut Crush	6	3	Northern	--	6	Q
2006	NWFA	Connecticut Crush	4	4	Northern	Northeast	3	--
2007	NWFA	Connecticut Crush	6	3	Northern	North	2	Q
2008	NWFA	Connecticut Crush	3	5	Northern	Northeast	2	--
2009	IWFL	Connecticut Crushers	1	7	Eastern	North Atlantic	5	--
2010	IWFL2	Connecticut Crushers	1	7	Eastern	Northeast	6	--
		Total	**40**	**46**				

Based in: Hartford, CT
Notes: Succeeded by WFA's Northeastern Nitro

4/21/2001	A	Philadelphia Liberty Belles (I)	L	6	20
4/28/2001	H	Massachusetts Mutiny	L	0	19
5/12/2001	A	D.C. Divas	L	6	10
5/19/2001	H	Baltimore Burn	W	24	0
5/26/2001	A	Massachusetts Mutiny	L	6	27
6/9/2001	A	Baltimore Burn	W	18	12
6/16/2001	H	Massachusetts Mutiny	L	0	52
6/23/2001	H	Philadelphia Liberty Belles (I)	L	0	74
4/27/2002		Philadelphia Liberty Belles (I)	L	0	26
5/4/2002		Maine Freeze	W	41	0
5/11/2002		Rochester Raptors	W	19	0
5/18/2002		Massachusetts Mutiny	L	15	47
5/25/2002		Maine Freeze	W	45	0
6/1/2002		Philadelphia Liberty Belles (I)	L	6	25
6/8/2002		Rochester Raptors	W	34	6
6/15/2002		Massachusetts Mutiny	L	19	28
6/22/2002		Maine Freeze	W	49	6
6/29/2002		Philadelphia Liberty Belles (I)	L	6	35
4/5/2003		Maine Freeze	W	30	20 E
4/12/2003	A	Philadelphia Phoenix	W	12	7
4/19/2003	A	Rochester Raptors	W	49	6
5/3/2003	H	Rochester Raptors	W	49	0
5/10/2003	A	Massachusetts Mutiny	W	21	20
5/17/2003	H	Massachusetts Mutiny	L	7	24
5/31/2003	H	Philadelphia Phoenix	L	0	40
6/7/2003	H	Maine Freeze	W	37	12
6/14/2003	A	Maine Freeze	W	18	0
6/28/2003	A	D.C. Divas	L	0	76 Q
4/10/2004	A	Maine Freeze	W	32	8
4/17/2004	A	Philadelphia Phoenix	L	14	42
5/1/2004	A	Rochester Raptors	W	34	0
5/8/2004	H	Rochester Raptors	W	62	0
5/15/2004	A	Massachusetts Mutiny	L	7	27
5/22/2004	H	Maine Freeze	W	23	0
5/29/2004	H	Philadelphia Phoenix	W	18	16
6/12/2004	H	Massachusetts Mutiny	L	7	27
4/23/2005	H	Erie Illusion	W	39	0
4/30/2005	A	Maine Freeze	W	65	0
5/14/2005	H	Massachusetts Mutiny	L	19	22
5/21/2005	H	Erie Illusion	W	44	0
5/28/2005	H	Maine Freeze	W	92	0
6/4/2005	A	Massachusetts Mutiny	L	6	42
6/11/2005	A	Erie Illusion	W	30	0
6/18/2005	A	Philadelphia Phoenix	W	49	27
6/25/2005	A	Massachusetts Mutiny	L	12	34 Q
4/22/2006	A	Maine Freeze	W	61	0
4/29/2006	A	Massachusetts Mutiny	L	0	37
5/6/2006	A	Philadelphia Phoenix	L	0	35
5/20/2006	H	D.C. Divas	L	0	40
5/27/2006	H	Maine Freeze	W	64	12
6/3/2006	H	Massachusetts Mutiny	W	7	0 *
6/10/2006	H	Philadelphia Phoenix	W	7	3
6/17/2006	A	D.C. Divas	L	0	48
4/14/2007	H	Massachusetts Mutiny	L	0	34
4/21/2007	A	Central Massachusetts Ravens	W	48	0
4/28/2007	H	Philadelphia Phoenix	W	20	13
5/12/2007	A	Massachusetts Mutiny	L	7	14
5/19/2007	H	Maine Freeze	W	52	0
5/26/2007	A	Maine Freeze	W	49	6
6/2/2007	A	Philadelphia Phoenix	W	27	14
6/16/2007	H	Central Massachusetts Ravens	W	1	0
6/23/2007	H	Cleveland Fusion	L	0	57 Q
4/19/2008	A	New York Nemesis	L	0	35
4/26/2008	H	Baltimore Burn	W	55	24
5/3/2008	H	Maine Freeze	W	48	0
5/17/2008	A	Philadelphia Phoenix	L	0	19
5/24/2008	H	New York Nemesis	L	0	19
5/31/2008	A	Maine Freeze	W	44	0
6/7/2008	A	Baltimore Burn	L	21	24
6/14/2008	H	Philadelphia Phoenix	L	0	20

Continued on next page

Connecticut Crush Game-By-Game Results (continued)

4/11/2009	H	Manchester Freedom	L	15	27		4/10/2010	A	Boston Militia	L	10	59
4/25/2009	A	Philadelphia Firebirds	L	12	31		4/17/2010	A	New York Nemesis	L	0	25
5/2/2009	A	Boston Militia	L	0	47		4/24/2010	A	New York Sharks	L	14	65
5/9/2009	A	New York Sharks	L	7	40		5/1/2010	A	New England Intensity	L	18	19
5/30/2009	A	Pittsburgh Passion	L	0	76		5/8/2010	H	Montreal Blitz	L	0	22
6/6/2009	H	Baltimore Nighthawks	L	8	30		5/15/2010	H	Jersey Justice	L	6	22
6/13/2009	H	New York Nemesis	L	6	28		5/22/2010	H	Manchester Freedom	W	46	0
6/20/2009	H	Central PA Vipers	W	1	0		6/5/2010	H	Montreal Blitz	L	0	26

Connecticut Crush Player Register (2001, 2004-2008)

Amsden, Michelle (2005-2006)
Baptiste, Candia (2006-2007)
Basilicato, Diane (2007)
Bell, Carolyn (2004-2005)
Bepko, Ashleigh (2007)
Black, Sherrona "Shay" (2005-2008)
Bloam, Heather (2001)
Bogue, Lori (2001)
Breakell, Michaela (2005-2007)
Bruce, Donna (2004)
Bubar, Jennifer (2001)
Buckman, Penny (2001)
Bundock, Heather (2001)
Cappa-Kotulski, Deborah (2001)
Casella, Ashley (2005)
Casolo, Shari (2001, 2006-2007)
Catania, Kelly (2006-2007)
Clarke, Cindy (2001, 2005)
Colon, Evelyn (2008)
Corris, Ann (2001)
Cote, Deb (2001)
Coty, Veronica (2007)
Crosby, Kelly (2004-2005)
Dale, Laurie (2001)
Darling, Nicole (2008)
Davis, Jennifer (2005-2008)
Dawson, Sheila "L.D." (2005-2007)
Debicki, Joanna (2005-2006)
DeFrancesco, Donna (2001)
Dellavalle, Jodi (2006-2008)
DePamphilis, Melanie (2001, 2004-2008)
DiFederico, Sandy (2008)
Dorsey, Heather (2001)
Eddy, Vicky (2001)
Fabian, Renee (2001, 2005)
Foster, Tracy (2001)
Frederickson, Leslee (2001)
Frederickson, Shannon (2001)
Fredine, Nancy (2006-2008)
Futtner, Carrie (2001)
Gallego, Andy (2005-2006)
Garnett, Teresa (2001)
Giansanti, Christina (2001)
Gibson, Tomi (2001, 2004-2008)
Gilchrist, Amy (2004)
Giuliano, Santina (2001)
Griffin, Deshond (2001)
Harrison, Danielle (2007)
Hart, Stephanie (2008)
Harwood, Tennyson (2001)
Head, Dena (2005)
Hedglen, Elise (2005)
Higgins, Jody (2001)
Hilton, Louise (2001, 2004-2008)
Hincks, Carrie (2008)
Hodge, Jeriesha "Jay" (2005-2007)
Holzer, Martina (2005)
Howard, Yvonne (2006-2008)
Huber, Christine (2005-2008)
Jahn, Julie (2001)
Jones, Kimberly (2006-2008)
Jones, Melissa (2001)
Keith, Tammy (2001)
Kelley, Leah (2005)
Kelly, Jerrilyn (2007)
Kenniston, Kristen (2007-2008)
Konzsaki, Khamiko (2005)
Kraynak, Kelly (2001, 2005)
Kulaw, Laura (2005-2006)
Kurtz, Becky (2001)
LaConte, Brenda (2001)
Landess, Stephanie (2001)
Lomelino, Jen (2005)
Lott, Victoria (2001, 2005)
Martin, Holly (2008)
Martin, Kim (2004)
Martin, Laurie (2001)
Martin, Valerie (2008)
McCarthy, Denise (2001)
McFarland, Lisa (2001)
Mendes, Kathleen (2008)
Mertes, Christene (2005-2006)
Meyer, April (2004-2006)
Mitchell, Angela (2004-2008)
Morgatto, Christin (2007-2008)
Morrison, Fay (2007)
Motta, Danielle (2007)
Oliver, Luz (2004-2008)
Olsen, Kimberly (2001)
Palica, Jenna (2008)
Palkimas, Cindy (2001)
Palmer, Kimberly (2004)
Paradis, Nicole (2004-2008)
Parker, Jennifer (2001)
Philibert, Christina (2008)
Plankey, Kristine (2005-2007)
Prail, Nancy (2006-2007)
Punsalan, Elizabeth (2005-2006)
Reidy, Sheila (2001)
Rende, Kathleen (2008)
Rios, Jerica (2005-2006, 2008)
Robinson, Michaela (2001)
Rogers, Erin (2008)
Sanborn, Samantha "Sam" (2008)
Sanchez, Rita (2005-2007)
Saur, Amy (2005)
Schofield, Stacey (2007)
Scott, Phillapa (2004)
Sharp, Veri (2007)
Simpson, Corynthia (2006-2008)
Snow, Rebecca "Becky" (2005-2007)
Stango, Jennifer (2006-2008)
Supino, Sarah (2001)
Theriault, Nicki (2006-2008)
Turner, Margaret (2004-2008)
Villano, Andrea (2001)
Walton, Kim (2005)
Werner, Sheryl (2005)
Whidbee, Lisa (2006-2007)
Winter, Molly (2006-2007)
Woodard, Kelly (2007-2008)
Yacovacci, Nina (2006-2007)
Zannoni, Bonnie (2007-2008)

Connecticut Cyclones

Year	League		Name	W	L	Conference	Division	DF	PR
2006	WPFL		Connecticut Cyclones	0	5	American	East	3	--
2007	WPFL		Connecticut Cyclones	0	7	American	East	3	--
2008	IWFL	X	Connecticut Cyclones	0	4	--	--	--	--
2009	WFA		Connecticut Cyclones	0	8	National	Northeast	6	--
			Total	**0**	**24**				

Based in: Hartford, CT
Notes: Preceded by IWFL's Connecticut Lightning; Forfeited entire 2008 and 2009 seasons

Connecticut Cyclones Game-By-Game Results

Date	H/A	Opponent	W/L	PF	PA
8/5/2006	A	Empire State Roar	L	0	54
8/19/2006	H	New England Intensity	L	0	34
8/26/2006	H	Empire State Roar	L	0	34
9/23/2006	A	New England Intensity	L	6	42
9/30/2006	A	New England Intensity	L	6	49
8/18/2007	A	Empire State Roar	L	0	61
8/25/2007	H	Toledo Reign	L	0	20
9/1/2007	A	New Jersey Titans	L	0	32
9/15/2007	H	Houston Energy	L	0	1
9/29/2007	A	Carolina Queens	L	2	20
10/6/2007	A	Houston Energy	L	0	1
10/20/2007	H	Empire State Roar	L	0	1
5/3/2008	A	Cape Fear Thunder	L	0	1
5/10/2008	H	New England Intensity	L	0	1
5/17/2008	H	Cape Fear Thunder	L	0	1
6/14/2008	A	Holyoke Hurricanes	L	0	1
4/18/2009	H	Baltimore Burn	L	0	1
4/25/2009	H	New Jersey Titans	L	0	1
5/9/2009	A	Binghamton Tiger Cats	L	0	1
5/16/2009	A	Baltimore Burn	L	0	1
5/30/2009	A	New Jersey Titans	L	0	1
6/6/2009	H	Binghamton Tiger Cats	L	0	1
6/13/2009	H	Philadelphia Liberty Belles (II)	L	0	1
6/20/2009	A	Keystone Assault	L	0	1

Connecticut Lightning

Year	League		Name	W	L	Conference	Division	DF	PR
2005	IWFL	X	Connecticut Lightning	6	2	--	--	--	--

Based in: Hartford, CT
Notes: Succeeded by WPFL's Connecticut Cyclones

Date	H/A	Opponent	W/L	PF	PA
4/9/2005	H	Detroit Predators	W	33	6
4/16/2005	A	Manchester Freedom	W	7	0
4/23/2005	A	New York Sharks	L	0	36
4/30/2005	H	Rhode Island Intensity	W	18	0
5/21/2005	A	Detroit Predators	W	12	7
6/4/2005	H	Manchester Freedom	L	12	19
6/11/2005	A	Rhode Island Intensity	W	28	22
6/18/2005	H	Bay State Warriors	W	19	0

Connecticut Wreckers

Year	League	Name	W	L	Conference	Division	DF	PR
2012	IWFL	Connecticut Wreckers	0	8	Eastern	Mid-Atlantic	4	--
2013	IWFL	Connecticut Wreckers	0	7	Eastern	Northeast	3	--
2014	IWFL	Connecticut Wreckers	4	4	Eastern	North Atlantic	4	--
2015	IWFL	Connecticut Wreckers	2	6	Eastern	North Atlantic	3	--
		Total	**6**	**25**				

Based in: Danbury, CT

Date	H/A	Opponent	W/L	PF	PA
4/14/2012	A	New England Intensity	L	0	36
4/21/2012	A	Baltimore Nighthawks	L	0	34
4/28/2012	H	Erie Illusion	L	7	14
5/5/2012	A	Philadelphia Firebirds	L	12	28
5/19/2012	H	Baltimore Nighthawks	L	0	22
6/2/2012	A	Philadelphia Firebirds	L	0	34
6/9/2012	H	New Hampshire Freedom	L	14	20
6/16/2012		Erie Illusion	L	0	1
5/4/2013	H	New York Knockout	L	13	14
5/18/2013	H	Philadelphia Firebirds	L	0	44
5/25/2013	A	New York Knockout	L	0	6
6/1/2013	H	Keystone Assault	L	0	40
6/15/2013	A	Keystone Assault	L	0	65
6/22/2013	A	New England Intensity	L	0	49
6/29/2013	A	Philadelphia Firebirds	L	0	1
4/19/2014	A	New York Sharks	L	0	50
4/26/2014	A	Montreal Blitz	L	0	53
5/3/2014	A	New York Knockout	L	6	16
5/10/2014	H	Northeast Rebels	W	21	0
5/17/2014	A	New England Nightmare	W	21	20
5/31/2014	H	Erie Illusion	W	1	0
6/8/2014	H	New England Nightmare	L	14	27
6/14/2014	A	Northeast Rebels	W	20	0
4/18/2015	A	Northeast Rebels	W	26	0
5/2/2015	A	Montreal Blitz	L	14	42
5/9/2015	A	Northeast Rebels	W	6	0
5/16/2015	H	Baltimore Nighthawks	L	13	28
5/23/2015	H	New York Sharks	L	0	38
5/30/2015	A	Montreal Blitz	L	0	1
6/6/2015	H	Philadelphia Firebirds	L	0	33
6/13/2015	A	Baltimore Nighthawks	L	13	14

Connecticut Wreckers Player Register (2015)

Anderson, Laura (2015)
Camara, Rebecca (2015)
DeJesus, Crystal (2015)
Dixon, Gabby (2015)
Downs, Alyssa (2015)
Elya, Mandy (2015)
Fluskey, Sonya (2015)
Foster, Effie (2015)
Granato, Ria (2015)
Janosko, Christine (2015)
Koukopoulos, Christie "Chris" (2015)
Ladouceur, Sophie (2015)
LaSane, Jessica (2015)
Louis, Ayisha (2015)
Manfred, Lauren (2015)
Moraes, Danielle (2015)
Perri, Michelle (2015)
Plisko, Chantal (2015)
Renko, Jennifer (2015)
Rodrigues, Kim (2015)
Saunders, Marquitta (2015)
Stepp, Kate (2015)
Stow, Jennifer (2015)
Uszakiewicz, Hannah (2015)
Valentine, Janirish (2015)
Whitlock, Lisa (2015)
Wissinger, Emily (2015)

Corvallis Pride

Year	League	Name	W	L	T	Conference	Division	DF	PR
2002	IWFL	Corvallis Pride	8	1	0	Western	--	1	CC
2003	IWFL	Corvallis Pride	6	2	1	Western	Pacific Northwest	2	S
2004	IWFL	Corvallis Pride	7	3	0	Western	Pacific Northwest	2	CC
2005	IWFL	Corvallis Pride	8	3	0	Western	Pacific Northwest	2	S
2006	IWFL	Corvallis Pride	5	3	0	Western	Pacific Northwest	3	--
2007	IWFL	Corvallis Pride	2	6	0	Western	Pacific Northwest	3	--
2008	IWFL	Corvallis Pride	5	4	0	Western	Pacific Northwest	2	S
2009	IWFL	Corvallis Pride	2	6	0	Western	Pacific Northwest	3	--
		Total	**43**	**28**	**1**				

Based in: Corvallis, OR

Date	H/A	Opponent	Result	Score		Note
3/30/2002		Eugene Edge	W	12	0	
4/13/2002		Oregon Thunder	W	41	19	
4/20/2002		Eugene Edge	W	8	7	
5/4/2002		Oregon Thunder	W	46	0	
5/11/2002		Eugene Edge	W	14	6	
5/25/2002		Oregon Thunder	W	21	13	
6/1/2002		Eugene Edge	W	28	0	
6/15/2002		Oregon Thunder	W	1	0	
6/22/2002		Austin Outlaws	L	14	42	CC
3/22/2003	H	Eugene Edge	W	19	8	
3/29/2003	A	Portland Shockwave	T	26	26	
4/12/2003	A	Tacoma Majestics	W	18	0	
4/26/2003	A	Boise Xtreme	W	12	0	
5/3/2003	A	Eugene Edge	W	33	8	
5/10/2003	H	Portland Shockwave	W	20	14	
5/31/2003	H	Tacoma Majestics	L	0	12	
6/7/2003	H	Boise Xtreme	W	38	6	
6/21/2003	A	Chicago Force	L	14	28	S
4/17/2004	A	Portland Shockwave	W	20	7	
4/24/2004	H	Tacoma Majestics	L	14	33	
5/1/2004	H	Boise Xtreme	W	20	8	
5/8/2004	A	Eugene Edge	W	32	6	
5/22/2004	H	Portland Shockwave	W	28	14	
5/29/2004	A	Tacoma Majestics	L	0	7	
6/5/2004	A	Boise Xtreme	W	34	0	
6/12/2004	H	Eugene Edge	W	50	6	
6/26/2004	A	Oakland Banshees	W	22	14	S
7/10/2004	A	Sacramento Sirens	L	8	43	CC
4/2/2005	A	Boise Xtreme	W	41	6	
4/9/2005	A	Tacoma Majestics	L	0	13	
4/16/2005	H	Portland Shockwave	W	9	7	
4/30/2005	H	Boise Xtreme	W	34	6	
5/7/2005	H	Eugene Edge	W	45	6	
5/14/2005	H	Tacoma Majestics	W	21	6	
5/21/2005	A	Boise Xtreme	W	43	6	
5/28/2005	A	Portland Shockwave	W	20	14	
6/4/2005	A	Eugene Edge	W	1	0	
6/18/2005	H	Tacoma Majestics	L	0	28	
7/9/2005	A	Sacramento Sirens	L	22	43	S
4/29/2006	H	Eugene Edge	W	36	8	
5/6/2006	A	Redding Rage	W	28	8	
5/13/2006	A	Seattle Majestics	L	6	21	
5/20/2006	H	Redding Rage	W	30	6	
6/3/2006	A	Portland Shockwave	L	0	6	
6/10/2006	A	Seattle Majestics	L	0	28	
6/17/2006	A	Eugene Edge	W	52	14	
6/24/2006	H	Santa Rosa Scorchers	W	20	18	
4/28/2007	A	Redding Rage	W	46	0	
5/5/2007	H	Seattle Majestics	L	0	15	
5/12/2007	H	Portland Shockwave	L	7	28	
5/26/2007	A	Portland Shockwave	L	6	9	
6/9/2007	A	Seattle Majestics	L	3	28	
6/16/2007	H	Redding Rage	W	42	0	
6/23/2007	H	Seattle Majestics	L	0	23	
6/30/2007	A	Portland Shockwave	L	6	41	
4/12/2008	A	Redding Rage	W	46	0	
4/19/2008	H	Portland Shockwave	W	28	6	
4/26/2008	A	Sacramento Sirens	W	33	13	
5/10/2008	H	Seattle Majestics	L	0	25	
5/17/2008	A	Santa Rosa Scorchers	W	18	6	
5/24/2008	H	Redding Rage	W	21	0	
6/7/2008	A	Portland Shockwave	L	20	23	
6/14/2008	H	Seattle Majestics	L	7	16	
6/28/2008	A	Seattle Majestics	L	0	35	S
4/11/2009	A	Seattle Majestics	L	0	34	
4/25/2009	H	Portland Shockwave	L	7	20	
5/2/2009	A	Sacramento Sirens	L	0	39	
5/16/2009	A	Portland Shockwave	L	0	33	
5/23/2009	H	Redding Rage	W	1	0	N
5/30/2009	H	Sacramento Sirens	L	0	48	
6/6/2009	A	Modesto Maniax	W	20	8	
6/13/2009	H	Portland Shockwave	L	6	26	

Dallas Diamonds

Year	League	Name	W	L	Conference	Division	DF	PR
2002	WPFL	Dallas Diamonds	4	5	American	--	3	--
2003	WPFL	Dallas Diamonds	7	3	American	West	2	CC
2004	WPFL	Dallas Diamonds	12	0	American	South	1	**NC**
2005	WPFL	Dallas Diamonds	11	0	American	South	1	**NC**
2006	WPFL	Dallas Diamonds	8	1	American	West	1	**NC**
2007	WPFL	Dallas Diamonds	5	3	American	West	3	--
2008	IWFL	Dallas Diamonds	11	0	Western	Mid South	1	**NC**
2009	IWFL	Dallas Diamonds	8	1	Eastern	South Atlantic	1	S
2010	IWFL	Dallas Diamonds	8	2	Western	Midwest	1	CC
2011	WFA	Dallas Diamonds	10	1	American	South Central	1	CC
2012	WFA	Dallas Diamonds	10	1	American	Division 12 (Southwest)	1	CC
2013	WFA	Dallas Diamonds	11	1	American	Division 9 (Southwest)	1	C
		Total	**105**	**18**				

Based in: Dallas, TX   **Neutral sites:** Long Beach, CA (N1); Roswell, GA (N2); San Diego, CA (N3)
Notes: Succeeded by Dallas Elite

Date	H/A	Opponent	W/L	PF	PA	Note
8/3/2002		Houston Energy	L	6	46	
8/17/2002		Austin Rage	W	26	21	
8/24/2002		New England Storm	W	39	20	
8/31/2002		Arizona Knighthawks	L	19	21	
9/7/2002		Austin Rage	L	26	34	
9/21/2002		Missouri Prowlers	W	79	0	
9/28/2002		Arizona Titans	W	27	22	I
10/12/2002		Houston Energy	L	0	31	
10/19/2002		Houston Energy	L	7	46	
8/2/2003	A	Missouri Prowlers	W	66	0	
8/9/2003	H	Houston Energy	W	14	12	
8/16/2003	H	Houston Energy	L	14	39	
9/6/2003	H	Missouri Prowlers	W	72	0	
9/20/2003	H	Missouri Prowlers	W	65	0	
9/27/2003	A	Houston Energy	L	27	38	
10/4/2003	A	Missouri Prowlers	W	49	0	
10/11/2003	A	Florida Stingrayz	W	26	22	
10/18/2003	H	Houston Energy	W	10	7	
10/25/2003	H	Florida Stingrayz	L	14	22	CC
7/31/2004	H	Syracuse Sting	W	49	0	
8/14/2004	H	Houston Energy	W	28	26	
8/21/2004	H	Missouri Avengers	W	90	0	
8/28/2004	A	Houston Energy	W	33	13	
9/11/2004	A	New York Dazzles	W	67	0	
9/18/2004	H	Arizona Caliente	W	56	30	
9/25/2004	H	Toledo Reign	W	68	0	
10/2/2004	A	Arizona Caliente	W	35	13	
10/9/2004	A	Missouri Avengers	W	1	0	
10/16/2004	A	So Cal Scorpions	W	44	7	
11/6/2004	H	Houston Energy	W	25	14	CC
11/20/2004	N1	Northern Ice	W	68	13	C
7/30/2005	H	New Mexico Burn	W	76	0	
8/6/2005	H	Georgia Gladiators	W	1	0	N
8/13/2005	A	New Mexico Burn	W	56	0	
8/20/2005	H	Houston Energy	W	21	18	
8/27/2005	A	Houston Energy	W	49	31	
9/17/2005	H	Minnesota Vixen	W	62	6	
10/1/2005	A	Long Beach Aftershock	W	55	0	
10/8/2005	H	Long Beach Aftershock	W	56	0	
10/15/2005	A	Houston Energy	W	38	27	
11/5/2005	H	So Cal Scorpions	W	48	19	CC
11/19/2005	H	New York Dazzles	W	61	8	C
7/22/2006	H	New Mexico Burn	W	97	0	
7/29/2006	A	Los Angeles Amazons	W	42	13	
8/5/2006	A	New Mexico Burn	W	80	0	
8/19/2006	H	Houston Energy	W	31	21	
9/9/2006	A	Houston Energy	L	10	24	
9/16/2006	H	Los Angeles Amazons	W	39	16	
9/23/2006	H	Wisconsin Wolves	W	47	20	
10/21/2006	H	So Cal Scorpions	W	34	3	CC
11/4/2006	N2	Houston Energy	W	34	27	C
8/18/2007	H	Houston Energy	W	14	6	
9/8/2007	H	So Cal Scorpions	L	14	34	
9/15/2007	A	Las Vegas Showgirlz	W	41	10	
9/22/2007	H	New Mexico Burn	W	1	0	
9/29/2007	A	So Cal Scorpions	L	19	21	
10/6/2007	H	Las Vegas Showgirlz	W	50	20	
10/13/2007	A	Houston Energy	L	12	33	
10/20/2007	A	New Mexico Burn	W	1	0	
4/12/2008	H	Kansas City Tribe	W	58	0	
4/19/2008	A	New Mexico Menace	W	91	0	
4/26/2008	H	Atlanta Xplosion	W	37	14	
5/10/2008	A	Miami Fury	W	48	6	
5/17/2008	H	Iowa Crush	W	62	0	
5/31/2008	A	Kansas City Tribe	W	28	13	
6/7/2008	H	Tucson Monsoon	W	50	0	
6/14/2008	H	Miami Fury	W	49	0	
6/28/2008	H	California Quake	W	69	3	S
7/12/2008	A	Seattle Majestics	W	38	6	CC
7/26/2008	A	Chicago Force	W	35	29	C*
4/11/2009	H	Houston Energy	W	69	0	
4/18/2009	A	Louisiana Fuel	W	27	0	
4/25/2009	H	Shreveport Aftershock	W	59	0	
5/2/2009	A	Atlanta Xplosion	W	32	7	
5/16/2009	H	Louisiana Fuel	W	64	0	
5/30/2009	H	Miami Fury	W	41	8	
6/6/2009	A	Houston Energy	W	61	20	
6/13/2009	H	Houston Energy	W	76	7	
6/27/2009	A	Boston Militia	L	14	34	S

Continued on next page

Dallas Diamonds Game-By-Game Results (continued)

Date	H/A	Opponent	W/L	Score		Notes	Date	H/A	Opponent	W/L	Score		Notes
4/3/2010	H	Houston Energy	W	34	12		4/21/2012	H	Lone Star Mustangs	W	90	0	
4/10/2010	A	Kansas City Tribe	L	21	28		4/28/2012	A	Houston Power	W	54	8	
4/24/2010	H	Minnesota Vixen	W	79	0		5/5/2012	H	Arkansas Wildcats	W	109	0	
5/1/2010	A	Memphis Belles	W	49	6		5/12/2012	A	Austin Outlaws	W	60	0	
5/8/2010	H	Atlanta Xplosion	W	23	3		5/19/2012	H	Houston Power	W	69	0	
5/15/2010	A	H-Town Texas Cyclones	W	1	0	N	5/26/2012	A	Lone Star Mustangs	W	59	8	
5/22/2010	H	Kansas City Tribe	W	35	21		6/2/2012	A	DFW Xtreme	W	83	12	I
6/5/2010	A	Houston Energy	W	44	36		6/9/2012	H	Austin Outlaws	W	79	6	
6/12/2010	H	Chicago Force	W	27	20	S	6/30/2012	H	Lone Star Mustangs	W	76	0	Q
7/10/2010	A	Sacramento Sirens	L	43	45	CC	7/7/2012	H	Kansas City Tribe	W	55	35	S
							7/21/2012	A	San Diego Surge	L	29	56	CC
4/9/2011	H	Houston Power	W	39	14								
4/30/2011	A	Lone Star Mustangs	W	16	6		4/6/2013	A	Houston Power	W	41	6	
5/7/2011	H	Austin Outlaws	W	31	21		4/13/2013	A	Austin Outlaws	W	49	0	
5/14/2011	A	Little Rock Wildcats	W	64	0		4/20/2013	H	Houston Power	W	68	8	
5/21/2011	H	Lone Star Mustangs	W	23	12		4/27/2013	A	Lone Star Mustangs	W	48	0	
6/4/2011	A	Memphis WTF	W	44	0		5/4/2013	H	Austin Outlaws	W	55	0	
6/11/2011	H	Tulsa Eagles	W	1	0		5/11/2013	H	Houston Power	W	1	0	
6/18/2011	A	Austin Outlaws	W	56	0		5/18/2013	A	New Orleans Mojo	W	68	0	
6/25/2011	H	Houston Power	W	21	6	Q	6/8/2013	H	Lone Star Mustangs	W	82	6	
7/9/2011	H	Kansas City Tribe	W	23	20	S	6/22/2013	H	Austin Outlaws	W	61	6	Q
7/16/2011	A	San Diego Surge	L	20	48	CC	7/13/2013	A	St. Louis Slam	W	35	20	S
							7/20/2013	H	Central Cal War Angels	W	27	6	CC
							8/3/2013	N3	Chicago Force	L	34	81	C

Dallas Diamonds Player Register (2011-2013)

Alexander, Valerie (2011-2012)
Allen, Desiree (2013)
Bartlett, Meagan (2011)
Beddow, Laura (2011)
Bell, Krishena (2011)
Bender, Niki (2011)
Blackmon, Keke (2013)
Bowman, LaKissha (2011-2013)
Bowman, Shaunte (2012-2013)
Brown, Lashanda "Bo" (2011-2013)
Brown, Sno (2011-2012)
Brydson, Alberta (2011-2013)
Bunton, Tiffany (2011-2012)
Bushman, Brittany (2012-2013)
Champion, Tan (2011-2012)
Childress, Cierra (2013)
Clark, Lindsey (2011)
Coats, Tye (2012)
Coffin, Nicole (2011-2013)
Cutrer, Ashley (2011)
Davis, Katie (2011)
Durham, Morgan (2013)
Ethridge, Amanda (2013)
Ewell, Danesh (2012)
Ferrell, Jennifer (2011)
Ford, Lanie (2013)
Foster, Monica (2011)
Franco, Megan (2013)
Gallegos, Melissa (2013)
Garcia, Lily (2013)
Gardner, Jabrill (2013)
Gerhart, Jessica (2011)
Graves, Marsha (2011, 2013)

Grayson, Angellica (2011-2013)
Green, Danielle (2011-2012)
Harvey, Alex (2013)
Haynes, Addrianne (2013)
Heilman, Amanda (2011-2013)
Hill, Cassidy (2013)
Hill, Tiffany (2011-2013)
Hollis, Amari (2011-2013)
Hontz, Kayla (2012-2013)
Ikeda, Chelsea (2013)
Jenkins, Odessa (2013)
Knight, Daneshia (2013)
Kontz, Kayla (2011)
Land, Tally (2012)
Landry, Elizabeth "Liz" (2012-2013)
Malloy, Nicole (2011)
Martin, Stephanie "Joos" (2013)
May, Rachel (2011-2013)
McClinton, Jamie (2013)
McDonald, Sandy (2012)
McDonald, Teoka (2011-2012)
Meyer, Tiffany (2011)
Million, Rachel (2012)
Mitchell, Ingrid (2011-2012)
Mitchell, Janice (2011-2013)
Murrell, Latricia (2011)
Neal, Kym (2012)
Oliver, Kat (2011)
Ottaiano, Daniela (2012-2013)
Overstreet, Tara (2011)
Ozols, Shannon (2012)
Padgett, Karen (2011)
Parton, Julie (2011)

Penn, Natasha (2012-2013)
Pontray, Alex (2011)
Richardson, Ann (2011-2012)
Rogers, Christia (2011)
Rostenbach, Katie (2011)
Runnels, LaToya (2012)
Russell, Zoia (2012)
Ryan, Tempest (2013)
Saari, Hanna (2011-2013)
Sample, Stephanie (2011)
Sanders, Brittany (2012)
Satterwhite, Brittany (2012-2013)
Shields, Lonnie (2012)
Simmons-Ward, Maggie (2012)
Sims, Brittani (2012-2013)
Smallwood, Toshiba (2011-2013)
Spencer, Maria (2013)
Spiller, Kelanna (2013)
Stenson, Erica (2011)
Summerville, Natasha "Taz" (2013)
Townsell, Shareda (2013)
Walton, Laura (2011)
Warner, Yumi (2013)
Watkins, Lucinda "Blak" (2011-2013)
Webb, Umeki (2011-2013)
Welniak, Danilynn (2011)
Welter, Jen (2011-2013)
Williams, Emily (2011)
Williams, Maddie (2012)
Williams, Tracie (2011-2013)
Wooten, Mary (2011)

Franchise Game-By-Game Records, 1999-2015

Dallas Dragons

Year	League	Name	W	L	Conference	Division	DF	PR
2004	NWFA	Dallas Dragons	3	5	Southern	Southwest	3	--

Based in: Dallas, TX
Notes: Succeeded by Dallas Rage

4/3/2004	A	Austin Outlaws	W	32	31		5/15/2004	A	Denton Stampede	W	57	0
4/17/2004	H	Denton Stampede	W	69	0		5/22/2004	H	Austin Outlaws	L	16	22
5/1/2004	H	Oklahoma City Lightning	L	18	49		6/5/2004	A	Oklahoma City Lightning	L	22	62
5/8/2004	A	Austin Outlaws	L	6	28		6/12/2004	H	Austin Outlaws	L	6	52

Partial Dallas Dragons Player Register (2004)

Brown, Dee (2004)
Correa, Mary (2004)
Golston, Rachel (2004)
Hull, Jennifer (2004)
King, Dyala (2004)
Kirk, Valarie (2004)
Mask, Judy (2004)
McKinney, Brooke (2004)
Welter, Jen (2004)
Wilkinson, Tracy (2004)

Dallas Elite

Year	League	Name	W	L	Conference	Division	DF	PR
2015	WFA	Dallas Elite	11	1	American	Southwest	1	C

Based in: Dallas, TX
Notes: Preceded by Dallas Diamonds
Neutral site: Los Angeles, CA (N)

4/11/2015	A	Arlington Impact	W	47	6		6/6/2015	A	South Texas Lady Crushers	W	1	0	
4/18/2015	H	South Texas Lady Crushers	W	53	0		6/13/2015	A	Austin Outlaws	W	59	0	
4/25/2015	A	Kansas City Titans	W	78	6		6/27/2015	H	St. Louis Slam	W	54	3	Q
5/2/2015	H	Austin Outlaws	W	76	0		7/11/2015	H	Kansas City Titans	W	70	14	S
5/9/2015	H	Arlington Impact	W	66	0		7/25/2015	H	San Diego Surge	W	56	28	CC
5/16/2015	H	Houston Power	W	70	0		8/8/2015	N	D.C. Divas	L	26	30	C

Dallas Elite Player Register (2015)

Allen, Desiree (2015)
Bender, Niki (2015)
Bobo, Erika (2015)
Bowman, Lakissha (2015)
Bowman, Shaunte (2015)
Brydson, Alberta (2015)
Carrillo, Estella (2015)
Coffin, Nicole (2015)
Ford, Shavonne (2015)
Fruean, Renee "Lilo" (2015)
Gerhart, Jessica (2015)
Grayson, Angellica (2015)
Harvey, Alex (2015)
Haynes, Addrianne (2015)
Heilman, Amanda (2015)
Hill, Tiffany (2015)
Holcomb, Gina (2015)
Ikeda, Chelsea (2015)
Jenkins, Amanda (2015)
Jenkins, Odessa (2015)
Jurado, Bruce (2015)
Landry, Elizabeth "Liz" (2015)
Love, Karen (2015)
Martin, Stephanie "Joos" (2015)
May, Rachel (2015)
McDonald, Teoka (2015)
McQueen, Dishambra (2015)
Murrell, Suede (2015)
Peck, Missy (2015)
Richardson, Ann (2015)
Roach, Krystal (2015)
Saari, Hanna (2015)
Satterwhite, Brittany (2015)
Sims, Brittani (2015)
Singleton, Eshombi "Kash" (2015)
Smith, Jazz (2015)
Spiller, KeLanna (2015)
Warner, Yumi (2015)
Watkins, Lucinda "Blak" (2015)
Webb, Umeki (2015)
Williams, Ashley (2015)
Williams, Tracie (2015)

Dallas Rage

Year	League	Name	W	L	T	Conference	Division	DF	PR
2005	NWFA	Dallas Rage	6	3	0	Southern	--	5	Q
2006	NWFA	Dallas Rage	4	4	0	Southern	Southwest	3	--
2007	NWFA	Dallas Rage	2	6	0	Southern	West	3	--
2008	NWFA	North Texas Fury	1	6	1	Southern	Central	4	--
		Total	**13**	**19**	**1**				

Based in: Dallas, TX
Notes: Preceded by Dallas Dragons; Succeeded by WFA's Lone Star Mustangs

Dallas Rage Game-By-Game Results

Date	H/A	Opponent	W/L	PF	PA
4/23/2005	H	Austin Outlaws	W	40	38
4/30/2005	H	Denton Stampede	W	58	0
5/14/2005	A	Austin Outlaws	L	24	39
5/21/2005	A	Oklahoma City Lightning	L	6	47
5/28/2005	H	Kansas City Krunch	W	12	0
6/4/2005	A	Austin Outlaws	W	8	0
6/11/2005	H	Oklahoma City Lightning	W	26	21
6/18/2005	A	Kansas City Krunch	W	24	0
6/25/2005	A	Chattanooga Locomotion	L	14	16 Q
4/22/2006	H	Oklahoma City Lightning	L	20	35
4/29/2006	H	Nashville Dream	W	32	10
5/6/2006	A	Shreveport Shockhers	W	40	8
5/13/2006	H	Austin Outlaws	L	40	43
5/27/2006	A	Oklahoma City Lightning	L	6	44
6/3/2006	A	Nashville Dream	W	38	7
6/10/2006	H	Shreveport Shockhers	W	46	6
6/17/2006	A	Austin Outlaws	L	29	31
4/14/2007	H	New Orleans Blaze	W	34	33 *
4/21/2007	H	Oklahoma City Lightning	L	12	60
4/28/2007	A	Austin Outlaws	L	24	68
5/12/2007	A	Oklahoma City Lightning	L	20	43
5/19/2007	H	Alabama Renegades	W	35	8
6/2/2007	A	New Orleans Blaze	L	0	1
6/9/2007	A	Alabama Renegades	L	0	1
6/16/2007	H	Austin Outlaws	L	0	1
4/19/2008	A	Oklahoma City Lightning	L	0	23
4/26/2008	H	Austin Outlaws	L	0	33
5/10/2008	A	Memphis Belles	T	6	6
5/17/2008	A	H-Town Texas Cyclones	L	6	40
5/24/2008	H	Oklahoma City Lightning	L	18	43
6/7/2008	H	Memphis Belles	W	30	14
6/14/2008	A	Austin Outlaws	L	0	41
6/21/2008	H	H-Town Texas Cyclones	L	6	43

Dallas Rage Player Register (2005-2008)

Albritton, Jerri (2007)
Albritton, Kat (2007)
Bauer, Mary Beth (2008)
Baylor, April (2007)
Beinhauer, Deanna (2006)
Berg, Joanna (2008)
Briscoe, Demekia (2005-2007)
Brown, Dee (2005)
Brown, Kelly (2006-2007)
Brown, Mandisa (2006)
Browning, Becca (2007)
Burdett, Simia (2008)
Butler, Dequerio (2005)
Casley, Jessica (2007)
Corsi, Stacy (2006)
Denman, Delta (2006)
Downs, Lacy (2006, 2008)
Everett, Lori (2007)
Fisher, Melissa (2005-2006)
Flood, Ariell (2006)
Flowers, April (2005-2006)
Fossis, Heather (2007-2008)
Garrett, Theresa (2007)
Godare, Susan (2007)
Golston, Rachel (2005-2008)
Hammonds, Nikki (2005)
Harvey, Alex (2008)
Haymes, Tamara (2005)
Hull, Jennifer (2005-2008)
Jones, Jennifer "Jay Jay" (2006-2008)
Jones, Tanya (2005)
Kellar, Cindy (2005)
Kendall, Mo (2006)
Kettner, Brande (2005)
King, Dyala (2005)
Kirk, Valarie (2005-2006)
Lemon, Amanda (2005, 2007-2008)
Lessa, Kathy (2005-2006)
Luscious, Joose (2008)
Maytubby, Etta (2006)
McKinney, Brooke (2005-2006)
Moore, Jen (2005-2006)
Mueller, Brandice (2008)
Newman, Lorrie (2005-2007)
Ray-Tribble, Casey (2006-2008)
Recine, Reggie (2007)
Requejo, Gretchen (2005)
Reschke, Amanda (2008)
Savage, Dionna (2005)
Selph, Deondra (2006-2007)
Senkayi, Sala (2006)
Shaw, S.S. (2006-2008)
Shepherd, Donna (2005-2007)
Smith, Jackie (2006)
Smith, Tammy (2006)
Smith, Twyla (2005-2006)
Spencer, Maria (2007-2008)
Stanford, Susan (2008)
Stewart, Rene (2005-2006)
Thomas, Talisha (2006)
Tole, Brittany (2005-2006)
Williams, E. (2006)
Williams, M.K. (2006)
Wood, Chris (2006-2008)

Dallas Revolution

Year	League	Name	W	L	Conference	Division	DF	PR
2003	IWFL	Dallas Revolution	4	2	Western	Southwest	2	--
2005	IWFL	Dallas Revolution	0	6	Eastern	Southern Central	3	--
		Total	4	8				

Based in: Dallas, TX
Notes: Also known as Texas Revolution; Forfeited entire 2005 season

Date	H/A	Opponent	W/L	PF	PA
3/22/2003	H	Memphis Maulers	W	36	18
4/5/2003	H	Oklahoma City Avengers	W	16	0
4/12/2003	H	Oklahoma City Avengers	W	24	8
4/19/2003	A	Chicago Force	L	8	40
5/3/2003	A	Oklahoma City Avengers	W	18	6
5/31/2003	H	Chicago Force	L	6	41
4/2/2005	H	Baton Rouge Wildcats	L	0	1
4/9/2005	A	Atlanta Xplosion	L	0	1
5/14/2005	H	Kansas City Storm	L	0	1
6/4/2005	H	Des Moines Courage	L	0	1
6/11/2005	H	Baton Rouge Wildcats	L	0	1
6/18/2005	A	Des Moines Courage	L	0	1

Dayton Diamonds

Year	League	Name	W	L	Conference	Division	DF	PR
2008	NWFA	Dayton Diamonds	1	7	Northern	Midwest	3	--
2009	WFA	Dayton Diamonds	1	7	National	Central	5	--
2010	WFA	Dayton Diamonds	0	8	National	Mid-Atlantic	3	--
2011	WFA	Dayton Diamonds	0	8	National	North Central	6	--
		Total	2	30				

Based in: Dayton, OH

Date	H/A	Opponent	Result	PF	PA
4/19/2008	H	Fort Wayne Flash	L	0	59
5/3/2008	A	West Michigan Mayhem	L	0	82
5/10/2008	A	Cincinnati Sizzle	L	6	54
5/17/2008	H	Indianapolis Chaos	W	14	8
5/24/2008	A	Fort Wayne Flash	L	0	62
6/7/2008	H	Cincinnati Sizzle	L	0	61
6/14/2008	H	West Michigan Mayhem	L	0	68
6/21/2008	A	Indianapolis Chaos	L	6	12
4/18/2009	A	Indiana Speed	L	8	62
5/2/2009	H	West Michigan Mayhem	L	0	56
5/9/2009	H	Fort Wayne Flash	L	0	29
5/30/2009	A	Toledo Reign	L	8	20
6/6/2009	H	Indiana Speed	L	0	56
6/13/2009	A	West Michigan Mayhem	L	0	55
6/20/2009	A	Fort Wayne Flash	L	20	68
6/27/2009	H	Toledo Reign	W	6	0
4/10/2010	A	Pittsburgh Force	L	8	9
4/24/2010	A	Columbus Comets	L	0	43
5/8/2010	H	Toledo Reign	L	0	7
5/15/2010	A	Detroit Dark Angels	L	0	45
5/22/2010	A	Indiana Speed	L	0	54
6/5/2010	H	Pittsburgh Force	L	6	12
6/12/2010	A	Columbus Comets	L	0	48
6/19/2010	H	Pittsburgh Force	L	0	13
4/2/2011	H	Toledo Reign	L	0	61
4/16/2011	A	St. Louis Slam	L	0	70
4/30/2011	H	Cincinnati Sizzle	L	12	51
5/7/2011	A	Toledo Reign	L	0	63
5/14/2011	A	Detroit Dark Angels	L	0	69
5/21/2011	H	West Michigan Mayhem	L	0	63
6/4/2011	A	Kentucky Karma	L	12	28
6/11/2011	H	Detroit Dark Angels	L	0	57

Dayton Diamonds Player Register (2008-2010)

Bailey, Kawanna (2010)
Bailey, Shanice (2010)
Bean, Stephanie (2008)
Blalock, Josie (2008-2009)
Bradford, Robyn (2008)
Brookbank, Lisa (2008-2010)
Bruns, Amy (2009)
Cabugao, Tracy (2008)
Carpenter, Maranda (2008-2009)
Carter, Danielle (2008-2010)
Clagg, Sarah (2009)
Coleman, Coni (2010)
Crews, Jenny (2008-2009)
Dudgeon, Amy (2008)
Duncan, Ashlee (2008-2009)
Fannin, LeAnna (2008)
Gill, Yashika (2008)
Gmuca, Linda (2009)
Haines, Jessica (2009-2010)
Harris, Leah (2009-2010)
Hawkins, Rhyanne (2009)
Hill, Tonya (2008-2010)
Hopson, Joy (2008)
Huff, Karen (2008-2010)
Huffmaster, Kassie (2010)
Jahn, Carol (2008)
Jenkins, Mishelle (2010)
Johnson, Lauran (2009)
Jones, Angela (2010)
Keeney, Kenitra "Kay" (2009-2010)
King, Robyn (2008)
Klosterman, Julie (2009)
Krejci, Danielle (2009)
Leigeber, Brandi (2009)
Lirette, Jacqueline (2010)
Little, Amber (2010)
Massey, Anna (2009)
McCoy, Pisce (2008-2009)
Miller, Linda (2009)
Mohammed, Denee (2009-2010)
Mullins, Nikole (2009-2010)
Niese, Angela (2008-2009)
Pierce, KryShana (2010)
Preston, Shawntae (2008)
Qualls, Tonya (2008-2010)
Robertson, Paige (2008)
Robinson, Tonya (2008)
Salazar, Suzanne (2008)
Scott, Lare (2010)
Sims, Emily (2010)
Sisson, Sheila (2008-2010)
Smith, Ann (2008)
Strahan, Fern (2009)
Thomas, Doria (2008-2010)
Turner, Laura (2008-2009)
Ward, Bonnie (2008)
Weisflock, Jessica (2010)
Welch, Michelle (2009-2010)
Woods, Kawanna (2009)
Wumer, Jen (2008)
Young, Sharon (2010)
Ziemer, Jonica (2008-2010)

Dayton Rebellion

Year	League	Name	W	L	Conference	Division	DF	PR
2003	WPFL	Dayton Rebellion	2	8	National	East	3	--

Based in: Dayton, OH

Date	H/A	Opponent	Result	PF	PA
8/9/2003	A	Northern Ice	L	6	69
8/23/2003	A	Toledo Reign	W	30	18
8/30/2003	H	New England Storm	L	6	28
9/6/2003	H	Syracuse Sting	L	8	41
9/13/2003	A	Indiana Speed	L	6	35
9/20/2003	H	Northern Ice	L	0	48
9/27/2003	A	Syracuse Sting	L	14	48
10/4/2003	H	Indiana Speed	L	20	40
10/11/2003	A	New England Storm	L	8	12
10/18/2003	H	Missouri Prowlers	W	48	0

Daytona Beach Barracudas

Year	League	Name	W	L	Conference	Division	DF	PR
2000	WPFL	Daytona Beach Barracudas	6	1	National	South	1	CC

Based in: Daytona Beach, FL

10/14/2000	A	Miami Fury	W	34	17	11/22/2000	H	Miami Fury	W	21	20
10/22/2000	A	New York Galaxy	W	35	6	11/25/2000	H	Tampa Tempest	W	27	6
10/28/2000	H	Miami Fury	W	27	0	1/6/2001	H	New England Storm	L	26	29 CC*
11/11/2000	H	Tampa Tempest	W	62	6						

Daytona Breakers

Year	League	Name	W	L	Conference	Division	DF	PR
2014	WFA	Daytona Breakers	2	6	National	South Atlantic	3	--

Based in: Daytona Beach, FL
Notes: Succeeded by Daytona Waverunners

4/5/2014	A	Jacksonville Dixie Blues	L	0	62	5/17/2014	H	Miami Fury	L	0	47
4/19/2014	A	Orlando Anarchy	W	32	13	5/24/2014	H	Jacksonville Dixie Blues	L	12	41
4/26/2014	H	Tennessee Train	L	21	26	5/31/2014	A	Savannah Sabers	W	41	22
5/3/2014	A	Tampa Bay Inferno	L	0	77	6/7/2014	H	Atlanta Phoenix	L	13	53

Daytona Breakers Player Register (2014)

Bain, Keiaira (2014)
Boyan, Jamie (2014)
Bursee, Julianne (2014)
Cedieu, Osseline (2014)
Channey, Kristi (2014)
Darrisaw, Samaria (2014)
Davenport, Debra (2014)
Davis, Tekoya (2014)
Fajardo, Brittany (2014)
Flotow, Heidi (2014)
Gordon, Tremisha (2014)
Hamilton, Tyeria (2014)
Hopkins, Reijina (2014)
Howard, Dacia (2014)
Jefferson, Verdell (2014)
Johnson, Antoinette (2014)
Johnson, Cassandra (2014)
Leon, Christina (2014)
Martinez, Adriana (2014)
Mendez, Keymei (2014)
Moran, Kelly (2014)
Oliver, Mary (2014)
Priemer, Amanda (2014)
Prunty, Noel (2014)
Pullen, Akeya (2014)
Ramos, Katlyn (2014)
Rogers, Toni (2014)
Scofield, Ashley (2014)
Seacott, Gabriella (2014)
Shapiro, Kimberly (2014)
Smith, Kaelie (2014)
Stakes, Tammy (2014)
Storey, Jasmine (2014)
Sunseri, Jennifer (2014)
Swen, Jennifer (2014)
Wood, Taylor (2014)

Daytona Waverunners

Year	League	Name	W	L	Conference	Division	DF	PR
2015	WFA	Daytona Waverunners	2	6	National	South Atlantic	3	--

Based in: Daytona Beach, FL
Notes: Preceded by Daytona Breakers

4/11/2015	A	Miami Fury	L	0	61	5/9/2015	H	Miami Fury	L	19	33
4/18/2015	H	Orlando Anarchy	W	22	6	5/30/2015	H	Tampa Bay Inferno	L	0	35
4/25/2015	H	Jacksonville Dixie Blues	L	10	70	6/6/2015	A	Atlanta Phoenix	L	0	66
5/2/2015	A	Tampa Bay Inferno	L	0	54	6/13/2015	A	Orlando Anarchy	W	1	0

Daytona Waverunners Player Register (2015)

Anthony, Michelle (2015)
Arnold, Jen (2015)
Bain, Keiaira (2015)
Ball, Rosa (2015)
Bennett, Latasha (2015)
Cedieu, Osseline (2015)
Cintron, Lillian (2015)
Davenport, Debra (2015)
Ehrhart, Tammy (2015)
Formor, Kyanna (2015)
Green, Shambria (2015)
Harris, Kirsten (2015)
Hopkins, Reijina (2015)
Hunter, Chandice (2015)
Hunter, Stephanie (2015)
Jackson, Paulette (2015)
Jefferson, Verdell (2015)
Jones, Michelle (2015)
Law, Alexis (2015)
Lee, Monica (2015)
Martinez, Adriana (2015)
Miller, Devon (2015)
Moore, Breona (2015)
Oliver, Mary (2015)
Priemer, Amanda (2015)
Raby, Erishawnda (2015)
Searcy, Cyerius (2015)
Searcy, Nicole (2015)
Shaffer, Danielle (2015)
Smith, Kaelie (2015)
Snead, Andrea (2015)
Sunseri, Jennifer (2015)
Truax, Stacie (2015)
Tucker, Veronika (2015)
Wood, Taylor (2015)

D.C. Divas

Year	League	Name	W	L	Conference	Division	DF	PR
2001	NWFA	D.C. Divas	3	4	Northern	--	3	--
2002	NWFA	D.C. Divas	6	3	--	Mid-Atlantic	2	--
2003	NWFA	D.C. Divas	8	2	Northern	Mid-Atlantic	1	S
2004	NWFA	D.C. Divas	9	1	Northern	Mid-Atlantic	1	CC
2005	NWFA	D.C. Divas	9	1	Northern	--	1	CC
2006	NWFA	D.C. Divas	11	0	Northern	North Atlantic	1	**NC**
2007	IWFL	D.C. Divas	8	1	Eastern	Mid-Atlantic	1	S
2008	IWFL	D.C. Divas	4	4	Eastern	North Atlantic	4	--
2009	IWFL	D.C. Divas	10	1	Eastern	Mid-Atlantic	1	C
2010	IWFL	D.C. Divas	6	4	Eastern	Southeast	1	CC
2011	WFA	D.C. Divas	7	2	National	Northeast	1	Q
2012	WFA	D.C. Divas	6	4	National	Division 3 (Mid-Atlantic)	1	S
2013	WFA	D.C. Divas	6	4	National	Division 2 (Mid-Atlantic)	1	S
2014	WFA	D.C. Divas	5	4	National	Mid-Atlantic	1	S
2015	WFA	D.C. Divas	12	0	National	Mid-Atlantic	1	**NC**
		Total	**110**	**35**				

Based in: Washington, DC   **Neutral sites:** Pittsburgh, PA (N1); Round Rock, TX (N2); Los Angeles, CA (N3)

Date	H/A	Opponent	W/L	PF	PA	Note
4/28/2001	A	Philadelphia Liberty Belles (I)	L	0	40	
5/5/2001	A	Massachusetts Mutiny	L	8	15	
5/12/2001	H	Connecticut Crush	W	10	6	
5/26/2001	A	Baltimore Burn	W	20	8	
6/2/2001	H	Massachusetts Mutiny	L	0	12	
6/16/2001	H	Philadelphia Liberty Belles (I)	L	7	14	
6/23/2001	H	Tennessee Venom	W	52	0	
4/6/2002	H	Rochester Raptors	W	46	0	E
4/20/2002	H	Baltimore Burn	L	2	7	
4/27/2002	A	Asheville Assault	W	22	0	
5/4/2002	A	Baltimore Burn	W	7	6	
5/18/2002	H	Tennessee Venom	W	53	0	
5/25/2002	H	Asheville Assault	W	54	0	
6/1/2002	A	Baltimore Burn	L	6	12	
6/15/2002	A	Tennessee Venom	W	60	0	
6/22/2002	H	Baltimore Burn	L	0	6	
4/12/2003	A	Erie Illusion	W	50	0	
4/19/2003	H	Baltimore Burn	W	24	0	
5/3/2003	H	Pittsburgh Passion	W	32	7	
5/10/2003	A	Columbus Flames	W	30	22	
5/24/2003	H	Erie Illusion	W	74	7	
5/31/2003	A	Pittsburgh Passion	W	30	25	
6/7/2003	H	Columbus Flames	W	8	7	
6/14/2003	A	Baltimore Burn	L	14	22	
6/28/2003	H	Connecticut Crush	W	76	0	Q
7/12/2003	A	Philadelphia Phoenix	L	32	36	S
4/3/2004	H	Roanoke Revenge	W	70	0	
4/17/2004	A	Baltimore Burn	W	26	14	
5/1/2004	A	Erie Illusion	W	34	0	
5/8/2004	H	Erie Illusion	W	46	0	
5/15/2004	A	Roanoke Revenge	W	70	0	
5/22/2004	A	Pittsburgh Passion	W	28	14	
6/5/2004	H	Pittsburgh Passion	W	42	14	
6/12/2004	H	Baltimore Burn	W	52	16	
7/10/2004	H	Southwest Michigan Jaguars	W	30	18	S
7/17/2004	H	Detroit Demolition	L	14	20	CC
4/16/2005	H	Cleveland Fusion	W	18	0	
4/23/2005	A	Pittsburgh Passion	W	20	0	
5/14/2005	H	Tidewater Floods	W	51	0	
5/21/2005	A	Massachusetts Mutiny	W	22	12	
5/28/2005	A	Tidewater Floods	W	53	0	
6/4/2005	H	Philadelphia Phoenix	W	37	0	
6/11/2005	H	Cincinnati Sizzle	W	54	0	
6/18/2005	A	Baltimore Burn	W	36	0	
7/9/2005	H	Massachusetts Mutiny	W	36	6	S
7/16/2005	A	Detroit Demolition	L	16	38	CC
4/22/2006	H	Baltimore Burn	W	13	6	
4/29/2006	A	Tidewater Floods	W	45	0	
5/6/2006	H	Harrisburg Angels	W	76	0	
5/20/2006	A	Connecticut Crush	W	40	0	
5/27/2006	A	Baltimore Burn	W	30	0	
6/3/2006	H	Tidewater Floods	W	65	0	
6/10/2006	A	Harrisburg Angels	W	61	0	
6/17/2006	H	Connecticut Crush	W	48	0	
7/8/2006	A	Chattanooga Locomotion	W	40	0	S
7/22/2006	H	Columbus Comets	W	32	7	CC
8/5/2006	N1	Oklahoma City Lightning	W	28	7	C
4/28/2007	H	New England Intensity	W	70	0	
5/5/2007	A	New York Sharks	W	20	14	
5/19/2007	A	Cape Fear Thunder	W	77	0	
6/2/2007	H	Detroit Demolition	W	24	22	
6/9/2007	H	Boston Rampage	W	70	0	
6/16/2007	H	New York Sharks	W	22	0	
6/23/2007	A	New England Intensity	W	51	0	
6/30/2007	A	Cape Fear Thunder	W	38	3	
7/14/2007	A	Atlanta Xplosion	L	18	28	S
4/12/2008	A	Boston Militia	L	22	27	
4/26/2008	H	Baltimore Nighthawks	W	35	6	
5/3/2008	A	Pittsburgh Passion	L	34	38	
5/17/2008	A	Central PA Vipers	W	43	0	
5/24/2008	H	Central PA Vipers	W	35	0	
5/31/2008	H	Baltimore Nighthawks	W	41	6	
6/7/2008	A	New York Sharks	L	8	14	
6/14/2008	H	Pittsburgh Passion	L	12	17	

Continued on next page

D.C. Divas Game-By-Game Results (continued)

Date	H/A	Opponent	Result	Score	Note
4/11/2009	A	Baltimore Nighthawks	W	33 0	
4/25/2009	A	Detroit Demolition	W	35 0	
5/2/2009	H	Pittsburgh Passion	W	27 7	
5/16/2009	A	New York Sharks	W	21 7	
5/23/2009	H	Baltimore Nighthawks	W	70 14	
5/30/2009	A	Philadelphia Firebirds	W	42 0	
6/6/2009	H	New York Sharks	W	34 18	
6/13/2009	H	Philadelphia Firebirds	W	63 0	
6/27/2009	H	Pittsburgh Passion	W	27 17	S
7/11/2009	A	Boston Militia	W	27 21	CC
7/25/2009	N2	Kansas City Tribe	L	18 21	C
4/10/2010	H	Baltimore Nighthawks	W	54 6	
4/17/2010	A	New York Sharks	L	13 19	
4/24/2010	A	Philadelphia Firebirds	W	1 0	
5/1/2010	H	Boston Militia	L	35 42	
5/8/2010	A	Baltimore Nighthawks	W	28 7	
5/22/2010	H	New York Nemesis	W	49 21	
5/29/2010	H	Philadelphia Firebirds	W	49 3	
6/5/2010	A	Boston Militia	L	36 52	
6/12/2010	H	Atlanta Xplosion	W	35 7	S
7/10/2010	A	Boston Militia	L	0 28	CC
4/2/2011	H	Boston Militia	W	35 20	
4/9/2011	H	Keystone Assault	W	55 6	
4/16/2011	H	Philadelphia Liberty Belles (II)	W	20 0	
4/30/2011	A	Keystone Assault	W	49 0	
5/7/2011	H	Northeastern Nitro	W	77 0	
5/21/2011	A	Philadelphia Liberty Belles (II)	W	42 0	
6/11/2011	A	Boston Militia	L	16 27	
6/18/2011	A	New York Sharks	W	38 16	
6/25/2011	H	Boston Militia	L	24 37	Q
4/14/2012	H	Pittsburgh Passion	L	34 35	
4/28/2012	H	New York Sharks	W	41 12	
5/5/2012	H	Columbus Comets	W	49 0	
5/12/2012	A	New York Sharks	W	41 13	
5/19/2012	A	Boston Militia	L	7 44	
6/2/2012	A	Pittsburgh Passion	W	43 28	
6/9/2012	H	Boston Militia	L	25 32	
6/16/2012	A	Columbus Comets	W	42 0	
6/30/2012	H	Pittsburgh Passion	W	45 30	Q
7/7/2012	A	Boston Militia	L	34 55	S
4/6/2013	A	Pittsburgh Passion	W	42 31	
4/13/2013	A	Columbus Comets	W	53 20	
4/20/2013	A	Central Maryland Seahawks	W	40 0	
4/27/2013	H	Boston Militia	L	35 56	
5/11/2013	H	New York Sharks	W	49 6	
5/18/2013	A	Boston Militia	L	54 81	
6/1/2013	H	Pittsburgh Passion	L	27 36	
6/8/2013	H	Columbus Comets	W	42 20	
6/22/2013	H	Columbus Comets	W	40 12	Q
7/13/2013	A	Boston Militia	L	34 58	S
4/5/2014	A	Boston Militia	L	32 36	
4/19/2014	H	Chicago Force	L	27 42	
4/26/2014	H	Columbus Comets	W	39 0	
5/3/2014	A	Baltimore Burn	W	43 0	I
5/17/2014	H	Atlanta Phoenix	W	44 0	
5/31/2014	A	Central Maryland Seahawks	W	1 0	N
6/7/2014	H	Boston Militia	L	28 29	
6/21/2014	H	Columbus Comets	W	69 8	Q
7/5/2014	A	Boston Militia	L	56 72	S
4/11/2015	A	Columbus Comets	W	40 6	
4/25/2015	H	Central Maryland Seahawks	W	1 0	
5/2/2015	A	Boston Renegades	W	32 27	
5/9/2015	A	Central Maryland Seahawks	W	1 0	
5/16/2015	H	Columbus Comets	W	60 0	
5/30/2015	A	Atlanta Phoenix	W	54 0	
6/6/2015	H	Cleveland Fusion	W	27 7	
6/13/2015	H	Boston Renegades	W	56 28	
6/27/2015	H	Miami Fury	W	48 12	Q
7/11/2015	H	Atlanta Phoenix	W	40 6	S
7/25/2015	H	Chicago Force	W	43 24	CC
8/8/2015	N3	Dallas Elite	W	30 26	C

D.C. Divas Player Register (2001-2015)

Abraham, Sondra (2010)
Abrams, Desiree (2007, 2014-2015)
Acevedo, Catherine (2001-2005)
Adams-Jones, Allison (2008)
Aina, Bukola (2010-2012)
Akins, Kelly (2002)
Altema, Sabrina (2009-2010)
Alvarez Flores, Ana Rosa (2012)
Anderson, M'Bwende (2001-2007)
Anyanwu, Crystal (2008-2010)
Aribisala, Lara (2007-2012)
Askew, Cheria (2003)
Atwood, Kristen "K.C." (2001-2002)
Avery, Dyshanda (2009)
Bahena, Shellie (2010)
Barber, Lakia (2011-2013)
Barnes, Alison (2002)
Barnwell, Anne Elyse (2012)
Barta, Laura Jo (2003)
Bates, Kendra (2015)
Battle, Lakeisha (2004)
Beagan, Michelle (2002)
Bedwell, Missy (2010-2015)
Bell, Kim (2008, 2010-2011)
Bembry, Ariana (2015)
Bergner, Jessica (2002)
Bey, Jamila (2007)
Billups, TaQuina (2003-2006)
Blackstone, Lilah (2003-2006)
Bowman, Patrice (2002-2006)
Boyd, Crystal (2006-2009)
Boyle, Kim (2002)
Brach, Alexis (2012)
Branch, Ashley (2015)
Britton, Amy (2003-2006, 2008)
Brown-English, Natarsha (2012)
Brown-Pegues, Donna (2004)
Brownson, Callie (2010-2015)
Bruce, Stacy (2013)
Bruckenthal, Noabeth (2008-2011)
Buermeyer, Nancy (2001-2006)
Burns, Sherry (2001-2002)
Butler, Nichole (2002)
Cabugao, Tracy (2009-2010)
Cajas, Wendy (2006)
Campbell, Markeeta (2002)
Carson, Corinne (2002)
Carter, Karen (2002-2003)
Cates, Alice (2012-2013)
Charles, Shawntese (2011)
Chase, Charmaine (2011-2012, 2014)
Cherry, Lillian (2014-2015)
Chesley, Lauren (2015)
Christiansen, Krista (2004)
Ciccarelli, Julie (2004)
Clark, Lynnette (2011)
Clark, Victoria (2012)
Clements, Amanda (2009-2011)
Cohen, Barbara (2001)
Cola, Shay (2012)
Cole, Jennifer (2011)
Coley, Brooke (2013)
Colton-Bell, Julia (2009)
Cooper, Angela (2003)
Cooper, Rachel (2002)
Cordwell, Berri (2013-2014)
Critzos, Stephanie (2015)
Curtis, Sabrina (2004)
Daniels, Priscilla (2002)
Davis, April (2004)
Davis, Carla (2002)
Davis, Emma (2014)
Davis, Genaya (2013, 2015)
Deer, Helen (2014-2015)
Dennis, Latoya (2005-2006)
DeRiso, Stephanie (2012)
Dilla, Gayle (2001-2008)
Douglas, Cheri (2011)
Dubois, Danielle (2007)
Duckworth, Caroline (2011)

Continued on next page

D.C. Divas Player Register (continued)

Dukes, Tyran (2004-2007)
Elcock, Latriece (2014-2015)
Eley, Cheryl (2001)
Ellickson, Vickie (2002)
Espinoza, Sylvia (2015)
Essenmacher, Jenna (2015)
Fair, Mia (2002)
Farmer, Jacquelyn (2012-2013)
Faulkner, Kandace (2010-2011)
Felix, Savannah "Sav" (2013)
Finnaman, Donnell (2012-2013)
Fischer, Alison (2001-2009, 2011)
Fisk, Nicole (2011)
Flynn, Morgan (2010)
Ford, Quiana (2015)
Foster, Christina (2012)
Foust, LaShawn (2002-2010)
Frye, Debbie (2003-2004)
Fuller, Keri (2012)
Gainey, Shaquanda (2015)
Gamble, Lena (2013)
Gaston, Natalie (2014-2015)
George, Esther (2010)
George, Melanie (2008)
Giles, Anna (2006-2007)
Gittins, Christine (2004)
Glasgow, Rebecca (2003-2005)
Goldsmith, DeVon ('04, '08-09, '13, '15)
Gonzalez, Lisa (2001-2004)
Gray, Jennifer (2012-2015)
Green, Jacqueline (2001-2002)
Green, Nikia (2011-2012, 2015)
Green, T. (2007-2009)
Grigg, Krista (2001-2003)
Grigsby, Kenyetta (2010-2015)
Grimes, Kim (2014)
Grossman, Emily (2014-2015)
Gunton-Rumball, Rose (2003)
Gwanyalla, Feh (2006-2008)
Halicy, Melissa (2002-2003)
Hall, Kimberly (2008)
Hall, Mahogany (2010)
Hall, Meghan (2013)
Hamlin, Allyson (2002-09, 2011-15)
Harding, Jennifer (2005)
Hardy, Asia (2005-2015)
Hargrove, Brooke (2001-2003)
Harrell, Shontese (2002)
Harrington, Jewelyn (2011)
Harris, Earline (2004)
Hartley, Melia (2001)
Hawkins, Demetria (2005)
Hawkins, Regina "Reggie" (2001-2004)
Head, Angela "Angie" (2001-2003)
Heck, Jessica (2007-2008)
Helm, Tiffany (2012)
Hemlock, Kathryn (2004-2011)
Henderson, Tish (2011)
Herasingh, Pamela "Pam" (2011-2012)
Herchelroath, Beth (2007-2008)
Hicks, Beth (2008-2009)
Hill, Lisa (2002-2003)
Hill, Stephanie (2006)
Hillgrove, Labelle (2006-2009)
Hilliard, Kasee (2012-2015)
Hilton, Knyesha (2011)
Hines, Yakeshia (2008-2010)
Hockaday, Monica (2006)
Hodge, Jeriesha "Jay" (2009-2010)
Hogan, Claudia (2002-2009)
Holiday, Stevie (2011)
Holloway, Regina (2003)
Hopkins, Alicia (2013-2015)
Hopkins, Patrice (2002)
Horne, Tiffani (2014)
Howard, Ellen (2010-2015)
Hubbard, Nikita (2006, 2008)
Huhn, Rachel (2008-2015)
Hulme, Karen (2001-2002)
Hunt, Karen (2004-2008)
Imbragulio, Alissa (2007-2012)
Ingram, Zenola (2002)
Izevbigie, Sue (2009)
Jensen, Andrea (2008)
Johnson, Brittney (2012)
Johnson, Kendra (2005-2006)
Johnson, Kucheria (2012)
Johnson, Marica (2010)
Johnson, Marie (2007-2008)
Johnson, Shanterry (2014)
Jordan, Annika (2011)
Juang, Amy (2001-2010)
Kalinowski, Maile (2002)
Kallal, Tara (2001-2009, 2011)
Keller, Kelly (2004)
Kelpy, Dawn (2002)
Kelsey, Emerine (2002-2004)
Kennedy, Josephine (2012-2013)
Kennedy, Kimberly (2012)
Knapp, Jennifer (2008)
Kordish, Konnie (2014)
Kotsis, Eleni (2012-2015)
Kotsis, Vassi (2003-2004)
Krensky, Sarah (2004)
Kutz, Susan (2013-2014)
Lambert, Alana (2005-2006)
Laster, Danielle (2014)
Lathon, Tamyra (2011, 2014)
LeClair, Laura "Livy" (2001-2002)
Lee, Christen (2006)
Lemke, Tasha (2014)
Leopold, Cassandra (2008)
Letman, Katrina (2004-2005)
Lewis, Adrienne (2002-2004)
Lewis, Angel (2013-2014)
Lewis, Chennita "Neitah" (2004-2010)
Lewis, Trecia "Tree" (2010-2015)
Lilley, Jasmine (2013)
Littauer, Danielle (2010)
Livingston, Monica (2002-2007)
Long, Jennifer (2003-2004)
Lough, Kristin (2009)
Love, Candy (2002-2004)
Lucas, Vickie (2003-2009)
Lucia, Kristin (2011)
Maclin, Kamil (2015)
Maher, Linda (2002)
Mahoney, Alisha (2014)
Mahoney, LaTasha (Burney) (2002-06)
Major, Andrea "Drea" (2005-2009)
Mann, Dana (2001-2002)
Marfull, Allysea "Ghost" (2005-2013)
Marshall, Alison (2003)
Marshall, Cherre (2008-2015)
Marshall, Kimberly (2001-2002)
Martinez, Madra (2008)
Massie, Jenne (2014-2015)
Matthews, Tiffany (2004-2012)
McCauley, Tee (2010-2013)
McKinney, Unique (2009, 2011, 2014)
McLain, Antoinette (2003)
McMillon, Monecho (2010-2012)
McMullen, Debra (2001-2003)
McNair, Trigger (2006-2015)
McNeil, Lois (2004, 2009-2013)
McNeill, Shara (2008-2009)
Mead, Rebecca (2001-2005)
Melton, Lydia (2010)
Merritt, Carla (2002)
Michael, Stacey (2003-2008)
Mikolajczak, Melissa (2002)
Millard, Monique (2010)
Minetti, Daniella (2002)
Mitchell, Melissa (2012-2013, 2015)
Mojidi, Safi (2014-2015)
Morris, Debra (2002)
Morrison, Jayme (2003-2006)
Murphy, Kianna (2015)
Musick, Danielle (2013)
Myers, Angela (2013)
Nabie, Kadia (2004)
Nealis, Stephanie (2015)
Nelson, Tessa (2002-2009)
Newkirk, Kia (2013)
Nguyen, Xuan (2014-2015)
Nicholas, Jamie (2001-2004)
Niemi, Tytti (2015)
Nolte, Rochelle (2001-2002)
Oden, Lisa (2001)
Oglesby, Sabrina (2006-2007)
Ogletree, Aketa (2010-2012)
Oseth, Kristina "Kris" (2007-2008)
Ottley, Alda (2010)
Paap, Regina (2002)
Palmer, Diana (2013)
Palmer, Stacy (2001-2006)
Palmer, Tashina (2008)
Pecover, Carrie (2003-2004)
Pecovsky, Rachelle (2006-2009, 2011)
Penn, Teri (2002)
Pennington, Debra (2002)
Perry, Nikieva (2013)
Perry-Guinn, Latisha (2008)
Peterson, Luann (2001-2003)
Pickett, Okiima (2007-2015)
Pittman, Elise (2013-2014)
Poawui, Jessica (Banks) (2005-09, 2011)
Powers, Stephanie (2002)
Pruitt, Lauren (2006)
Quitania, Siena (2009)
Randolph, Natalie (2004-2008)
Redmond, Molly (2013-2014)
Reese, Dameka (2005-2007)
Reid, Linda (2001-2004)
Reith, Michelle (2013)
Reynolds, Jane (2001-2002)
Reynosa, Erica (2007-2009)
Rhodes, Elisha (2006-2008)
Riddle, Michelle (2002-2010)
Rivers, Subrena (2004-2007)
Roach, Renee (2003-2006)
Roberts-White, Adele (2015)
Robinson, Courtney (2006)

Continued on next page

D.C. Divas Player Register (continued)

Robinson, Kira (2015)
Robinson, Mikaela (2013)
Robinson, Syreta (2002)
Rock, Brittany (2014-2015)
Rogers, Jasmine (2012)
Romano, Katie (2006)
Rorie, Raina (2013-2014)
Rothlein, Debbie (2010-2011)
Rowell, Jody (2001-2002)
Rozendaal, Ashley (2013, 2015)
Samuda, Jodi (2011)
Sanders, Narja (2003)
Sanders, Staci (2002)
Savage, Devoralyn "Dee" (2005-2015)
Savoy, Raynette "Ray" (2004-2007)
Savoy, Tatjana (2002)
Schaefer, Alisa (2006)
Scheid, Heather (2001)
Schnarrs, Georgia (2001-2002)
Scott, Candice (2008-2010)
Scott, D'Ajah (2012-2015)
Silk, Natalie (2014)
Simmons, Debbie (2006)
Simms, Whitney (2015)
Simon, Kris (2012-2013)
Smith, Christina (2015)
Smith, Janelle (2008)
Smith, Paris (2015)
Smith, Robyn (2013)
Smith, Tasha (2014-2015)
Snow, Rebecca "Becky" (2008)
Snyder, Tammy (2001-2002)
Sollers, Lindsay (2011-2015)
Spain, Rebecca (2002)
Sprester, Brenda (2006)
St. Martin, Crystal (2015)
Stabel, Francesca (2015)
Starkey, Jennifer (2011)
Stenson, Amy (2002)
Stensrud, Meg (2009)
Stephenson, Malissa (2005)
Stephenson, Tara (2006-2012)
Stewart, Crystal (2002)
Stivers, Rachel (2007-2008, 2011)
Strong, Jimmien (2009-2015)
Studds, Beverly (2001)
Swailes, Allyson (2013-2014)
Tate, Blessing (2010)
Thomas, Doria (2006)
Thomas, Yolanda (2001-2007)
Thompson, Veronica (2011-2012, 2014)
Tillman, Ivy (2001-2009)
Timmons, Mozette (2004-2007)
Timulak, Alana (2009)
Todd, Sacoyia (2014-2015)
Tompkins, Wendy (2005)
Törmänen, Tea (2010-2011)
Troell, Debra "Deb" (2001-2004)
Tu, Christina (2013-2015)
Turner, Juliette (Baker-Brice) (2013)
Vasquez, Ann Marie (2002)
Vyas, Rachelle (2013)
Walker, Amina (2007, 2010)
Walker, Ayrica (2011-2015)
Walker, Denee "Dex" (2014-2015)
Walker, Stephanie (2011-2012)
Walton, Tiffany (2013)
Warren, Shana (2002-2003)
Washington, Melissa (2013-2015)
Washington, Takiyah "T.K." ('03-08, '11-12)
Wasser, Brenda (2002)
Watanathai, Tara (2004)
Watkins, Alison (2004)
Watkins, Reneka (2010-2011)
Watkins, Tia (2015)
Watson, Christal (2002)
Wayne, Tarlesha (2002-2008)
Werries, Christina (2007)
Wessels, Kelly (2005)
Western, Sharina (2003-2009)
Whisonant, Ashley (2011-2015)
White, Jordyn (2007-2012)
Whitehead, Shannon (2015)
Whiting, Jamie (2010)
Wideman, Kristy (2013)
Wilkins, Brianna (2007-2012)
Wilkinson, Donna (2001-2015)
Williams, Ariella (2014-2015)
Williams, Erica "Deni" (2015)
Williams, LaTonia (2003)
Williams, Nikki (2002-09, 2011-12, '14)
Williams, Raquel (2013)
Williams, Rhonda (2005)
Williams, Samantha (2011)
Williams, Tamara (2011)
Willis, Jada (2012)
Wilson, Francesca (2014)
Wilson, Kentrina (2014-2015)
Wilson, Timmae (2008-2009)
Windle, Stacy (2002)
Windsor, Michelle (2008)
Wood, Susannah (2002)
Woodard, Eris (2014-2015)
Worsham, Becky (2008-2015)
Wright, Shannon (2001-2002, 2008)
Zupancic, Alison (2011)

Delaware Griffins

Year	League	Name	W	L	Conference	Division	DF	PR
2004	WPFL	Delaware Griffins	8	4	National	East	1	CC
2005	WPFL	Delaware Griffins	3	6	National	East	3	--
2006	IWFL	Delaware Griffins	2	6	Eastern	Mid-Atlantic	2	--
2007	IWFL	Delaware Griffins	1	5	Eastern	Mid-Atlantic	2	--
		Total	**14**	**21**				

Based in: Wilmington, DE

8/7/2004	H	Syracuse Sting	W	20	16	
8/21/2004	H	Syracuse Sting	W	26	6	
8/28/2004	A	New York Dazzles	W	36	0	
9/11/2004	A	Toledo Reign	W	34	22	
9/18/2004	A	Syracuse Sting	W	18	0	
9/25/2004	A	Houston Energy	L	6	50	
10/2/2004	H	Toledo Reign	W	52	28	
10/9/2004	A	Minnesota Vixen	L	20	30	
10/16/2004	H	Los Angeles Amazons	L	14	20	
10/23/2004	H	New York Dazzles	W	47	0	
10/30/2004	H	Minnesota Vixen	W	8	6	S
11/6/2004	A	Northern Ice	L	12	15	CC
7/30/2005	A	Albany Ambush	L	24	35	
8/6/2005	A	New York Dazzles	L	8	21	
8/13/2005	H	Cape Fear Thunder	W	16	14	
8/20/2005	A	Albany Ambush	L	22	38	
8/27/2005	H	Indiana Speed	L	0	20	
9/10/2005	A	New York Dazzles	L	6	19	
9/24/2005	A	Cape Fear Thunder	W	44	8	
10/8/2005	H	Albany Ambush	W	6	0	
10/16/2005	A	New York Dazzles	L	0	30	

Continued on next page

Delaware Griffins Game-By-Game Results (continued)

Date	H/A	Opponent	W/L	Score		Date	H/A	Opponent	W/L	Score
4/29/2006	H	Detroit Demolition	L	0 1		4/28/2007	A	Cape Fear Thunder	L	0 6
5/6/2006	H	New York Sharks	L	0 48		5/5/2007	A	New England Intensity	L	0 34
5/13/2006	A	Bay State Warriors	L	0 32		6/2/2007	H	Cape Fear Thunder	W	21 0
5/27/2006	H	Carolina Cardinals	W	1 0		6/9/2007	H	Carolina Phoenix	L	0 12
6/3/2006	A	New York Sharks	L	0 47		6/23/2007	A	Boston Rampage	L	0 28
6/10/2006	H	Southern Maine Rebels	W	24 0		6/30/2007	H	New York Sharks	L	0 27
6/17/2006	A	Detroit Predators	L	20 22						
6/24/2006	A	Southern Maine Rebels	L	0 1						

Denton Stampede

Year	League		Name	W	L	Conference	Division	DF	PR
2003	NWFA	X	Denton Stampede	0	3	--	--	--	--
2004	NWFA		Denton Stampede	0	8	Southern	Southwest	4	--
2005	NWFA		Denton Stampede	0	8	Southern	--	15	--
			Total	**0**	**19**				

Based in: Denton, TX

Date	H/A	Opponent	W/L	Score			Date	H/A	Opponent	W/L	Score
4/5/2003		Austin Outlaws	L	0 47	E		4/16/2005	A	Austin Outlaws	L	0 43
4/12/2003		Oklahoma City Lightning	L	0 97			4/23/2005	H	Kansas City Krunch	L	0 47
5/17/2003		Oklahoma City Lightning	L	14 84			4/30/2005	A	Dallas Rage	L	0 58
4/3/2004	H	Kansas City Krunch	L	0 59			5/14/2005	H	Oklahoma City Lightning	L	0 73
4/17/2004	A	Dallas Dragons	L	0 69			5/21/2005	H	Austin Outlaws	L	6 19
4/24/2004	A	Austin Outlaws	L	0 78			6/4/2005	A	Oklahoma City Lightning	L	0 65
5/1/2004	H	Austin Outlaws	L	0 64			6/11/2005	H	Austin Outlaws	L	0 42
5/8/2004	A	Oklahoma City Lightning	L	0 65			6/18/2005	A	Oklahoma City Lightning	L	0 1
5/15/2004	H	Dallas Dragons	L	0 57							
6/5/2004	A	Kansas City Krunch	L	0 59							
6/12/2004	H	Oklahoma City Lightning	L	0 80							

Denton Stampede Player Register (2004-2005)

Anthony, Tonya (2004)
Beach, Melissa (2005)
Brownson, Michelle (2005)
Chordas, Carrie (2004-2005)
Copeland, Shannon (2005)
Crawford, Eugina (2004-2005)
Crawford, Summer (2005)
Davis, Deborah (2004-2005)
Davis, Toya (2004-2005)
Desselles, Alexis (2005)
DiCesare, Talia (2005)
Figueredo, Tammy (2005)
Flowers, Karissa (2005)
Garder, Bridget (2005)
Griffin, Sara (2004)
Jackson, Amber (2005)
Kemp, Trinity (2005)
Lambright, Vanessa (2004)
Loiselle, Lauri (2005)
Maddox, Keisha (2004-2005)
Mathis, LaQuenita (2005)
McCleskey, Chandra (2005)
McConnell, Laura (2004)
Melnick, Jenny (2005)
Melton, Stephanie (2005)
Miller, Tracey (2004)
Mitchell, Crystal (2005)
Nash, Akiba (2005)
Padilla, Athena (2004-2005)
Phillips, Katerina (2005)
Powell, Anna (2005)
Rameriz, Erica (2005)
Roberts, Lisa (2004-2005)
Smith, Areil (2004)
Sweeney, Sarah (2004-2005)
Vasquez, Kimberly (2005)
White, Christi (2005)
Whiting, Arielle (2005)
Williams, Dawn (2004)
Williams, Shana (2004-2005)

Denver Foxes

Year	League	Name	W	L	Conference	Division	DF	PR
2002	UWFL	Denver Foxes	5	1	--	--	--	--

Based in: Denver, CO

Date	Opponent	W/L	Score		Date	Opponent	W/L	Score
4/14/2002	Grand Valley Vipers	W	71 6		5/5/2002	Sweetwater County Outlaws	W	30 0
4/21/2002	Colorado Springs Koalas	L	29 30		5/12/2002	Pueblo Pythons	W	42 19
4/27/2002	Tri-City Mustangs	W	40 7		5/26/2002	Cheyenne Dust Devils	W	74 0

Derby City Dynamite

Year	League	Name	W	L	Conference	Division	DF	PR
2012	WFA	Derby City Dynamite	4	4	National	Division 5 (North Central)	1	--
2013	WFA	Derby City Dynamite	3	5	National	Division 3 (North Central)	3	--
2014	WFA	Derby City Dynamite	4	6	National	Mideast	2	W
2015	WFA	Derby City Dynamite	0	8	National	Great Lakes	5	--
		Total	**11**	**23**				

Based in: Louisville, KY
Notes: Preceded by Kentucky Karma

Date	H/A	Opponent	Result	PF	PA	Note
4/14/2012	A	Indy Crash	L	0	2	
4/28/2012	A	Cincinnati Sizzle	W	6	0	
5/5/2012	H	Pittsburgh Force	W	8	2	
5/12/2012	H	Indy Crash	L	14	18	
5/19/2012	H	Toledo Reign	W	20	18	
6/2/2012	A	Memphis Dynasty	L	6	12	*
6/9/2012	A	Toledo Reign	L	22	32	
6/16/2012	H	Cincinnati Sizzle	W	52	16	
4/6/2013	H	Indy Crash	L	6	48	
4/13/2013	A	Cleveland Fusion	L	0	44	
4/20/2013	A	Cincinnati Sizzle	L	20	24	
4/27/2013	H	Cleveland Fusion	L	0	40	
5/11/2013	A	Toledo Reign	L	24	26	
5/18/2013	H	Cincinnati Sizzle	W	58	56	
6/1/2013	H	Toledo Reign	W	14	0	
6/8/2013	A	Tennessee Train	W	14	0	
4/5/2014	H	Toledo Reign	L	6	26	
4/12/2014	H	West Michigan Mayhem	L	6	15	
4/19/2014	A	Columbus Comets	L	0	42	
4/26/2014	A	Detroit Dark Angels	L	22	52	
5/10/2014	H	Detroit Dark Angels	W	22	20	
5/17/2014	A	Indy Crash	L	0	19	
5/24/2014	H	Erie Illusion	W	72	0	I
5/31/2014	H	Tennessee Train	W	40	12	
6/7/2014	A	Cincinnati Sizzle	W	74	0	
6/14/2014	A	West Michigan Mayhem	L	22	30	W
4/11/2015	H	Atlanta Phoenix	L	10	34	
4/18/2015	A	Indy Crash	L	6	31	
4/25/2015	A	West Michigan Mayhem	L	0	36	
5/9/2015	A	Detroit Dark Angels	L	8	38	
5/16/2015	A	St. Louis Slam	L	8	26	
5/30/2015	H	West Michigan Mayhem	L	0	15	
6/6/2015	H	Detroit Dark Angels	L	18	26	
6/13/2015	A	Indy Crash	L	0	41	

Derby City Dynamite Player Register (2012-2015)

Anderson, Elizabeth (2012)
Anderson, Kendra (2012-2014)
Anthony, Kylee (2015)
Baker, Latisha "Tish" (2012-2015)
Banks, Thelma "Tee" (2012-2015)
Barrett, Marthea (2013-2014)
Belle, Jaimme (2015)
Best, Danielle (2012-2015)
Bins, Sheldon (2014-2015)
Blacksshear, Brandy (2015)
Boone, Shanequa "Nikki" (2014-2015)
Botelho, Antoinette (2012)
Brito, Cheryl (2012)
Brown, Breona (2013)
Brown, Simone (2013)
Bryant, Mari (2012)
Carter, Laura (2012)
Chapman, Katie (2014)
Chavis, Shonna (2013)
Coakley, Victoria (2012-2013, 2015)
Cobler, Chelsey (2015)
Cole-Lockett, Nicole (2012-2014)
Coleman, Roneece (2012-2014)
Colvin, Judy (2013)
Conners, Ambra (2012-2014)
Coward, Tabatha (2012)
Crofoot, Carolyn (2013)
Daughtery, Laresha (2012, 2015)
Davis, Taylor (2015)
Deason, Patti (2014)
Embry Jr., Angela "Angie" (2012-15)
Embry, Iesha (2014)
Fears, Brittany (2014)
Feilds, Ashely (2013)
Floyd, Toni (2015)
Forman, Karen (2013-2014)
Gilmer, Jessica (2015)
Gubler, Amy (2015)
Hatfield, Kristina (2013-2015)
Henderson, Amber (2014)
Hill, Saskia (2012)
Holmes, Chelsey (2015)
Houston-Buckner, LaEssence (2015)
Jackson, Chelsea (2013)
Jackson, Shanica "A.J." (2012-2014)
Jewell, Jesse (2015)
Johnson, Karen "K.J." (2012)
Johnson, Macie (2015)
Jones, Danisha "Co Co" (2013)
Kilgore, April (2012-2013)
Koenigsknecht, Michelle (2013-2014)
Lewis, Cynthia (2012-2013)
Lockett, Nicole (2015)
Lockett, Shemika (2012)
Lowe, Layla (2014)
Lynch, Kristy (2012)
Major, Cherrelle "Relle" (2012-2013)
Malone, Lanisha (2015)
Mann, Caitlin (2013)
Martin, Jakesha "Juice" (2014)
McIntyre, Latoschia (2012-13, 2015)
Meyer, Magen (2015)
Mitchell, Lazhia (2015)
Nash, Dani (2015)
Payne, Tierra (2012-2015)
Phelps, Jessica (2015)
Phillips, Malissa (2012)
Rabish, Becky (2012)
Rauen, Shannel (2012, 2014)
Rideout, Alishia (2012)
Roberts, Becca (2012)
Rodriguez, Magen (2014)
Rogers, Tiffany (2014)
Schilling, Katherine (2015)
Scott, Edwina (2014-2015)
Scott, Toya (2012-2014)
Seitz, Sara (2012)
Shepherd, Casey (2012, 2014-2015)
Sissiom, Rashawn (2015)
Smith, Tonie (2014)
Taylor, Shonda (2012)
Thomas, Jessica (2012)
Ward, Shion (2014-2015)
Watkins, Jerrica (2012-2015)
Weaver, Tosha (2012-2015)
White, Crystal (2012, 2014-2015)
Wilson, Gloria (2012-2015)
Woods, Keira (2012-2013)

Desert Fire Cats

Year	League		Name	W	L	Conference	Division	DF	PR
2011	IWFL	X	Desert Fire Cats	0	1	--	--	--	--

Based in: Palm Springs, CA
Notes: Non-existent team

5/14/2011	A	California Quake	L	0	1

Detroit Blaze

Year	League		Name	W	L	Conference	Division	DF	PR
2002	IWFL	X	Detroit Blaze	0	3	--	--	--	--
2003	IWFL	X	Detroit Blaze	0	6	--	--	--	--
			Total	0	9				

Based in: Detroit, MI
Notes: Succeeded by Detroit Predators

5/11/2002		New York Sharks	L	0	73
6/8/2002		New Hampshire Freedom	L	0	22
6/15/2002		Albany Night-Mares	L	0	22
3/29/2003	A	Chicago Force	L	0	49
4/26/2003	H	Chicago Force	L	0	41
5/3/2003	A	Chicago Force	L	0	47
5/17/2003	A	Albany Night-Mares	L	28	34
5/31/2003	A	Montreal Blitz	L	0	1
6/7/2003	H	Orlando Starz	L	14	22

Detroit Dark Angels

Year	League	Name	W	L	Conference	Division	DF	PR
2010	WFA	Detroit Dark Angels	3	5	National	North Central	3	--
2011	WFA	Detroit Dark Angels	6	2	National	North Central	2	--
2012	WFA	Detroit Dark Angels	8	1	National	Division 4 (Mideast)	1	W
2013	WFA	Detroit Dark Angels	2	6	National	Division 4 (Great Lakes)	3	--
2014	WFA	Detroit Dark Angels	4	4	National	Great Lakes	3	--
2015	WFA	Detroit Dark Angels	2	6	National	Great Lakes	4	--
		Total	25	24				

Based in: Detroit, MI
Notes: Preceded by IWFL's Detroit Demolition

4/10/2010	H	West Michigan Mayhem	L	0	52
4/24/2010	A	Toledo Reign	W	7	6
5/1/2010	A	Cleveland Fusion	L	12	39
5/15/2010	H	Dayton Diamonds	W	45	0
5/22/2010	A	Pittsburgh Force	L	14	32
6/5/2010	H	Cleveland Fusion	L	14	34
6/12/2010	H	Toledo Reign	W	20	0
6/19/2010	A	West Michigan Mayhem	L	0	73
4/2/2011	H	Kentucky Karma	W	14	0
4/9/2011	H	Cincinnati Sizzle	W	33	7
4/16/2011	A	Indy Crash	L	6	36
4/30/2011	A	Toledo Reign	L	6	19
5/14/2011	H	Dayton Diamonds	W	69	0
6/4/2011	H	Toledo Reign	W	33	6
6/11/2011	A	Dayton Diamonds	W	57	0
6/18/2011	A	West Michigan Mayhem	W	24	14
4/14/2012	A	Pittsburgh Force	W	35	6
4/21/2012	A	Toledo Reign	W	35	0
4/28/2012	H	Cleveland Fusion	W	14	6
5/5/2012	H	West Michigan Mayhem	W	26	14
5/12/2012	H	Wisconsin Dragons	W	60	0
5/19/2012	A	Columbus Comets	W	7	0
6/2/2012	H	Pittsburgh Force	W	54	6
6/9/2012	A	Cleveland Fusion	W	17	14
6/23/2012	A	Pittsburgh Passion	L	0	34	W
4/6/2013	A	Chicago Force	L	0	62
4/13/2013	A	Indy Crash	L	6	22
4/20/2013	H	West Michigan Mayhem	L	0	40
5/4/2013	H	Indy Crash	W	6	0
5/11/2013	H	Chicago Force	L	0	61
5/18/2013	A	West Michigan Mayhem	W	19	13
6/1/2013	H	Columbus Comets	L	0	24
6/8/2013	A	Pittsburgh Passion	L	0	31

Continued on next page

Detroit Dark Angels Game-By-Game Results (continued)

Date	H/A	Opponent	Result	PF	PA
4/5/2014	H	Chicago Force	L	0	70
4/19/2014	A	Indy Crash	L	6	36
4/26/2014	H	Derby City Dynamite	W	52	22
5/3/2014	A	West Michigan Mayhem	W	28	25
5/10/2014	A	Derby City Dynamite	L	20	22
5/17/2014	A	Cincinnati Sizzle	W	54	0
5/31/2014	H	West Michigan Mayhem	W	12	10
6/7/2014	H	Indy Crash	L	7	35
4/11/2015	A	Indy Crash	L	14	18
4/18/2015	H	Chicago Force	L	0	67
5/2/2015	A	West Michigan Mayhem	L	0	12
5/9/2015	H	Derby City Dynamite	W	38	8
5/16/2015	H	Indy Crash	L	6	29
5/30/2015	H	Cleveland Fusion	L	0	35
6/6/2015	A	Derby City Dynamite	W	26	18
6/13/2015	A	Columbus Comets	L	12	26

Detroit Dark Angels Player Register (2010-2015)

Adams, Caelin (2013)
Adams, Ciara (2010-2011, 2013)
Alford, Rhonda (2012)
Allen, Dominique (2013)
Aniapam, Zakiya (2014-2015)
Azarias, Amy (2010)
Baccus, Jennifer (2011-2014)
Ballard, Jessica (2013)
Barbee, Tiffany (2010-2012, 2015)
Barc, Amanda (2011-2013)
Barney, Monique (2013)
Beier, Nicole (2013-2015)
Belog, Joanne (2011)
Bennington, Jacquie (2014-2015)
Billington, Raychal (2015)
Blahnik, Sydney (2014-2015)
Bradley, Amanda (2010)
Brandon, Kristie (2015)
Brewer, Brandy (2010-2015)
Brown, Darlene (2014-2015)
Burse, Chez (2011)
Butts, Emily (2014-2015)
Carter, Keontay (2012-2014)
Castillo, Alyssa (2013-2014)
Cherry, Yolanda (2011-2013)
Clarke, Stacia (2012-2013)
Corby, Mindy (2010-2014)
Cox, Ramona (2010-2012)
Crosby, Erika (2013)
Currie, Tracie (2012)
Davidson, Enika (2010-2013)
Davis, Cassandra (2010)
Davis, Rachel (2012)
Davis-Wilson, Kim Leeta (2014-2015)
Deaibes, Nina (2015)
Dewey, Annie (2012-2014)
Dietrich, Brianna (2012-2014)
Doughty, Delainey (2012)
Dunwoody, Shameakia (2010)
El, Kia (2011)
Elder, Kayla (2015)
Fagan, Erika (2012)
Farkas, Stephanie (2011-2012)
Findlay, Misty (2010)
Fishaw, Kali (2011)
Floyd, LaToyia (2011-2013)
Forro, Anne (2010)
Gentile, Kara (2015)
George, Takanta (2010-2013)
Godair, Danielle (2015)
Grace, Tori (2015)
Graham, Amber (2011)
Green, Rainelle (2010)
Gregg, Jaime (2011)
Guyton, Cheron (2011-2013)
Hakim, Suzanne (2015)
Hall, Julia (2014-2015)
Halle, Emilie (2015)
Head, DayJanas (2015)
Henry, Yarlen (2010-2014)
Holloway, Ebony (2013)
Hugan, Jennifer (2011-2012)
Johnson, Marva (2010)
Jones, Joz (2010)
Kelly, Lindsay (2014)
Kemp, Nefertiti (2011-2012)
Kerse, Danyelle (2010-2012)
Khul, Dawn (2014)
Kosanic, Brooke (2010-2014)
Kreutzkamp, Holly (2010)
Kuhl, Dawn (2013)
Lachlainn, Sabreena (2010-2014)
LaFrance, Deirdre (2011-2013)
Leduc, Andrea (2013)
Lee, Jamara (2010, 2012)
Lenaway, Diana (2014-2015)
Loyst, Allison (2015)
Luther, Cheryl (2011, 2013)
Lynn, Chelsie (2015)
Maher, Sophia (2011)
Mallory, Neisha (2010)
Mann, Cornice (2013-2014)
Matthews, Dominique (2013)
Mays, Candace (2015)
McCloskey, Morgan (2014)
McGowan, Erin (2012-2013)
McKay, Laquetia (2011, 2013, 2015)
Menchaca, Ashley (2015)
Micheals, Ellen (2015)
Michel, Deb (2011)
Miles, Lisa (2010)
Miline, Christina (2015)
Miller, Chelsea (2014)
Miller, Felicia (2014)
Minter, Ebony (2015)
Mooney, Kirsten (2012-2013)
Moss, Catherine (2010-2013)
Mundy, Annqunetta (2013)
Napiantek, Susan (2010-2011)
Negro, Ali (2015)
Newton, Crystal (2012)
Nobles, Karla (2015)
Noel, Alexis (2010)
Nugent, Andrea (2013)
Otto, Kellie (2010)
Payne, Crystina (2011)
Payne, Junita (2010-2011)
Phelps, Tristan (2015)
Poindexter, Andrea (2010)
Raboczkay, Melissa (2013)
Renaud, Chantelle (2011)
Riggs, Yolanda (2010)
Robinson, Celeste (2012-2014)
Rucker, Labresha (2010)
Russell, Leilani (2012-2015)
Salkeld, Konstantine (2012-2014)
Sargeant, Joyce (2013)
Schinske, Ashley (2013-2014)
Schobey, Jennifer (2014)
Seay, Maricka (2013, 2015)
Shelton, Shontelle (2010-2012, 2015)
Sherman, Tessa (2015)
Shipp, Valeria (2011)
Simpson, Alysia (2010-2011)
Smith, Kaitelin (2012)
Snellen, Tina (2010)
Stelma, Jillian (2011)
Struab, Elyse (2014)
Sundman, Sheri (2010-2011)
Sweeney, Alecia (2010-2015)
Tate, Lanita (2015)
Torre, Lisa (2011-2013)
Touma, Heather (2011)
Tucker, Cortney (2010-2013)
Ulbrich, Dee Dee (2010-2011)
Vidojevski, Kristine (2010-2014)
Vossen, Leah (2012)
Walters, Kim (2010)
Whilby, Jennie (2014)
Wilber, Kendra (2013)
Williams, Ajaesha (2013-2014)
Williams, Amber (2011)
Williams, Ellen (2011)
Williams, Leann (2015)
Williams, Stephanie (2010)
Williams, Tayana (2010)
Witchen, Kelly (2012-2014)
Witt, Heather (2011)
Wright, Kimberly (2015)
Wunderlich, Jana (2013)
Wyatt, Julie (2010-2012)
Zirkle, Stacy (2012)

Detroit Demolition

Year	League	Name	W	L	Conference	Division	DF	PR
2002	NWFA	Detroit Danger	10	1	--	Great Lakes	1	**NC**
2003	NWFA	Detroit Demolition	11	0	Northern	Great Lakes	1	**NC**
2004	NWFA	Detroit Demolition	11	0	Northern	Great Lakes	1	**NC**
2005	NWFA	Detroit Demolition	11	0	Northern	--	1	**NC**
2006	IWFL	Detroit Demolition	10	1	Western	Midwest	1	C
2007	IWFL	Detroit Demolition	10	1	Western	Midwest	1	**NC**
2008	IWFL	Detroit Demolition	7	2	Eastern	Midwest	2	S
2009	IWFL	Detroit Demolition	4	4	Eastern	Mid-Atlantic	3	--
		Total	**74**	**9**				

Based in: Detroit, MI   **Neutral sites:** Pittsburgh, PA (N1); Nashville, TN (N2); Louisville, KY (N3); Long Beach, CA (N4)
Notes: Succeeded by WFA's Detroit Dark Angels

Date		Opponent	Result			Date		Opponent	Result		
4/20/2002		Southwest Michigan Jaguars	W 34	16		4/29/2006	A	Delaware Griffins	W 1	0	
5/4/2002		Cleveland Fusion	W 20	6		5/6/2006	H	Iowa Crush	W 60	8	
5/18/2002		South Bend Hawks	W 41	16		5/13/2006	A	Chicago Force	W 19	0	
5/25/2002		Cleveland Fusion	L 3	14		5/27/2006	H	Kansas City Storm	W 74	6	
6/8/2002		Southwest Michigan Jaguars	W 48	6		6/3/2006	A	Detroit Predators	W 64	0	
6/15/2002		South Bend Hawks	W 33	0		6/10/2006	H	Chicago Force	W 47	0	
6/22/2002		Cleveland Fusion	W 51	20		6/17/2006	H	Iowa Crush	W 65	0	
6/29/2002		Southwest Michigan Jaguars	W 48	6		6/24/2006	A	Atlanta Xplosion	W 42	7	
7/6/2002	H	Nashville Dream	W 47	0	S	7/8/2006	H	Chicago Force	W 20	0	S
7/13/2002	A	Pensacola Power	W 14	7	CC	7/15/2006	H	Sacramento Sirens	W 52	20	CC
7/27/2002	N1	Massachusetts Mutiny	W 48	30	C	7/29/2006	N4	Atlanta Xplosion	L 14	21	C
4/12/2003	H	Cleveland Fusion	W 7	0		4/28/2007	H	Detroit Predators	W 83	0	
4/19/2003	A	Southwest Michigan Jaguars	W 45	9		5/5/2007	A	Iowa Crush	W 59	0	
4/26/2003	A	Indiana Thunder	W 90	18		5/12/2007	H	Chicago Force	W 23	20	
5/10/2003	H	Toledo Spitfire	W 95	0		5/19/2007	A	Chicago Force	W 20	6	
5/24/2003	H	Southwest Michigan Jaguars	W 70	6		6/2/2007	A	D.C. Divas	L 22	24	
5/31/2003	A	Toledo Spitfire	W 81	0		6/9/2007	H	Iowa Crush	W 69	0	
6/7/2003	H	Indiana Thunder	W 105	0		6/16/2007	H	Kansas City Storm	W 63	0	
6/14/2003	A	Cleveland Fusion	W 33	19		6/30/2007	A	Chicago Force	W 21	6	
7/12/2003	H	Cleveland Fusion	W 28	15	S	7/14/2007	H	Kansas City Storm	W 1	0	S
7/19/2003	H	Philadelphia Phoenix	W 58	14	CC	7/28/2007	H	Sacramento Sirens	W 49	0	CC
8/2/2003	N2	Pensacola Power	W 28	21	C	8/11/2007	A	Atlanta Xplosion	W 17	7	C
4/17/2004	H	Columbus Comets	W 20	7		4/12/2008	H	Columbus Phantoms	W 34	0	
4/24/2004	A	Southwest Michigan Jaguars	W 28	0		4/19/2008	A	Chicago Force	L 7	18	
5/1/2004	A	Columbus Comets	W 18	10		4/26/2008	H	Iowa Crush	W 53	0	
5/15/2004	H	Cleveland Fusion	W 75	7		5/10/2008	A	Wisconsin Wolves	W 14	0	
5/22/2004	H	Wisconsin Riveters	W 67	0		5/17/2008	A	Kansas City Tribe	W 38	0	
5/29/2004	A	Indiana Thunder	W 82	0		5/31/2008	H	Wisconsin Wolves	W 34	7	
6/5/2004	A	Cleveland Fusion	W 55	0		6/7/2008	A	Iowa Crush	W 73	0	
6/12/2004	H	Toledo Spitfire	W 93	0		6/14/2008	H	Wisconsin Warriors	W 37	0	
7/10/2004	H	Columbus Comets	W 41	23	S	6/28/2008	A	Chicago Force	L 7	8	S
7/17/2004	A	D.C. Divas	W 20	14	CC						
7/31/2004	N3	Oklahoma City Lightning	W 52	0	C	4/11/2009	H	Wisconsin Warriors	W 34	6	
						4/18/2009	A	Pittsburgh Passion	L 6	29	
4/16/2005	A	Columbus Comets	W 10	7		4/25/2009	H	D.C. Divas	L 0	35	
4/30/2005	A	Cincinnati Sizzle	W 76	0		5/2/2009	A	Baltimore Nighthawks	W 13	0	
5/8/2005	H	Cleveland Fusion	W 55	7		5/16/2009	H	Chicago Force	W 21	19	
5/21/2005	H	Southwest Michigan Jaguars	W 42	6		5/23/2009	H	Pittsburgh Passion	L 12	34	
5/28/2005	A	Milwaukee Momentum	W 31	0		6/6/2009	A	Erie Illusion	W 33	7	
6/4/2005	H	Columbus Comets	W 41	23		6/13/2009	A	Chicago Force	L 6	26	
6/11/2005	A	Pittsburgh Passion	W 40	14							
6/18/2005	H	Indianapolis SaberKatz	W 1	0							
7/9/2005	H	Southwest Michigan Jaguars	W 49	6	S						
7/16/2005	H	D.C. Divas	W 38	16	CC						
7/30/2005	N3	Pensacola Power	W 74	0	C						

Detroit Demolition Player Register (2003-2005)

Aaron, Laurie (2003-2004)
Adams, Dawn (2004-2005)
Alexander, Heather (2003-2005)
Andrykew, Sue (2003)
Barnes, Stephanie (2004-2005)
Bouchard, Sharon (2003)
Bousson, Theresa (2003)
Brooks, Lauren (2004-2005)
Brown, Aisha (2004-2005)
Cady, Nikki (2003)
Calvin, Julia (2004-2005)
Cherry, Yolanda (2004-2005)
Clark-Patterson, Catherine (2003-2004)
Cox, Ramona (2003-2005)
Cunningham, Rebecca (2003-2005)
Davidson, Enika (2004-2005)
Davis, Naomi (2005)
Deal, Rebecca (2005)
Dennis, Kiana (2004-2005)
Desentz, Erica (2003)
Drake, DeLisa (2004)
Easley, Felicia (2003)
Edwards, Tenisha (2004-2005)
Ellis, Marvene (2003)
Findlay, Misty (2003-2005)
Fowlkes, April (2004-2005)
Frazier, Christi (2003)
Gavin, Danielle (2003-2005)
Gdula, Michelle (2004)
George, Takanta (2004-2005)
Gerrity, Sue (2004)
Gillman, Mary (2003)
Girolami, Toni (2004)
Grace, Lisa (2004)
Griffin, Angela (2003-2005)
Grodus, Kim (2003-2005)
Harris, LaTasha (2005)
Hartman, Niki (2004)
Heckman, Mary Kay (2003)
Hunt, Lucretia (2003)
Jefferson-Faison, Trecia (2003)
Johnson, Deidra (2005)
Johnson, Mia (2005)
Johnson, Porcha (2003-2005)
Johnson, Roslyn (2003)
Jones, Tekela (2004)
Jones-Keys, Mary (2003-2004)
June, Kim (2004)
Kalczynski, Colleen (2005)
Kanski, Jennifer (2003-2004)
Kasischke, Sarah (2003-2005)
Kemp, Davina (2004)
Kemp, Nefertiti (2005)
Kendrick, Chris (2003)
Kolan, Anneliese (2003-2004)
Kreutzkamp, Holly (2004-2005)
Lamb, Bria (2005)
Lattiere, Daniere (2003-2005)
Lee, Jamara (2004-2005)
Lincoln, Terri (2005)
Luther, Cheryl (2004)
Malak, Anne (2003-2005)
Mansfield, Jennifer (2003-2004)
Martin, Amy (2003-2005)
McGough, Kristine (2004)
McLean, Tiffany (2005)
McManus, Bev (2003)
McQuigg, Laura (2003-2005)
Mears, Dawn (2004)
Menzie, Joanna (2003-2004)
Miles, Lisa (2004-2005)
Moseley, Lakina (2004)
Moss, Catherine (2005)
Nugent, Andrea (2003-2005)
Ossowski, Mary (2005)
Parker, Brandi (2004)
Phelps, Melinda (2003-2004)
Porter, Bridget (2003-2005)
Raines, Jilian (2003)
Randolph, Nicole (2003-2005)
Ratliff, Latrice (2004)
Rogers, Andrea (2005)
Rubin, Traci (2003-2005)
Sargent, Sherida (2003-2005)
Smith, Cynthia (2004)
Smith, Justina (2005)
Smith, Maria (2003-2005)
Streit, Leslie (2003-2004)
Suter, Sarah (2005)
Swanderski, Stacy (2005)
Thomas, Aisha (2003)
Thomas, Rita (2004)
Tolbert, Edna (2003)
Tolbert, Miaya (2003-2005)
Tulik, Marcy (2003-2004)
Twining, Kami (2004)
Twomey, Ellen (2004)
Tyler, Audra (2003)
Ulman, Carol (2004)
VanderMarliere, Anna (2005)
Vidojevski, Kristine (2003-2005)
Vinson, Ruth (2003-2004)
Walters, Kim (2003-2005)
Wilcox, Jennifer (2004)
Williams, LaShonda (2003-2004)
Yoches, Annie (2003-2005)
Zeolla, Crystal (2004)

Detroit Predators

Year	League		Name	W	L	T	Conference	Division	DF	PR
2004	IWFL	X	Detroit Predators	0	3	0	--	--	--	--
2005	IWFL		Detroit Predators	4	5	1	Western	Midwest	3	--
2006	IWFL		Detroit Predators	2	6	0	Western	Midwest	4	--
2007	IWFL		Detroit Predators	0	8	0	Western	Midwest	4	--
			Total	6	22	1				

Based in: Detroit, MI
Notes: Preceded by Detroit Blaze

Date	H/A	Opponent	Result		
4/17/2004	A	Chicago Force	L	0	63
5/15/2004	H	Chicago Force	L	0	65
5/29/2004	H	Des Moines Courage	L	6	30
4/9/2005	A	Connecticut Lightning	L	6	33
4/16/2005	H	Des Moines Courage	W	20	12
4/23/2005	A	Kansas City Storm	W	20	14
4/30/2005	A	Chicago Force	L	0	34
5/7/2005	A	Des Moines Courage	W	26	14
5/14/2005	H	Des Moines Courage	W	25	0
5/21/2005	H	Connecticut Lightning	L	7	12
6/4/2005	H	Chicago Force	L	13	59
6/11/2005	A	Kansas City Storm	L	0	20
6/25/2005	H	Kansas City Storm	T	6	6 *
4/29/2006	H	Kansas City Storm	W	14	8
5/6/2006	H	Chicago Force	L	0	30
5/13/2006	A	Iowa Crush	L	6	14
5/20/2006	A	Kansas City Storm	L	0	1
5/27/2006	A	Chicago Force	L	8	36
6/3/2006	H	Detroit Demolition	L	0	64
6/17/2006	H	Delaware Griffins	W	22	20
6/24/2006	A	Iowa Crush	L	0	48
4/28/2007	A	Detroit Demolition	L	0	83
5/19/2007	A	Carolina Phoenix	L	18	19
5/26/2007	A	Iowa Crush	L	8	26
6/2/2007	A	Carolina Phoenix	L	0	36
6/9/2007	H	Chicago Force	L	0	41
6/16/2007	H	Iowa Crush	L	6	14
6/23/2007	A	Chicago Force	L	0	69
6/30/2007	A	Montreal Blitz	L	0	1

Detroit Pride

Year	League		Name	W	L	Conference	Division	DF	PR
2015	IWFL	X	Detroit Pride	3	2	--	--	--	BW

Based in: Detroit, MI
Neutral site: Rock Hill, SC (N)

4/25/2015	H	Toledo Reign	W	17	13		5/30/2015	A	Philadelphia Firebirds	L	0	63	
5/16/2015	H	Toledo Reign	W	26	21		7/24/2015	N	San Antonio Regulators	W	24	22	B
5/23/2015	A	Montreal Blitz	L	0	56								

Detroit Pride Player Register (2015)

Aniapam, Zakiya (2015)
Beam, Amanda (2015)
Beeks, Megan (2015)
Bennett, Sherita (2015)
Brown, Jayla (2015)
Budzynski, Shelby (2015)
Carter-Berry, Khey (2015)
Connell, Roxanne (2015)
Denson, Asia (2015)
Derrick, Karlee (2015)
Dooley, Alexandra (2015)
Florence, Carmen (2015)
Honeycutt, Sheila (2015)
Horn, Pamela (2015)
Hudson, Netta (2015)
Jameson, Danetta (2015)
Kelly, Kiara (2015)
Kincannon, Bianca (2015)
Miller, Carrie (2015)
Miller, Kamry (2015)
Ogadinma, Louise (2015)
Parker, Pam (2015)
Pickett, NaTashia (2015)
Pollock, Jenalyn (2015)
Racine, Bianca (2015)
Roberson, Marionna (2015)
Robinson, Janiel (2015)
Sauls, Joselynn (2015)
Smith, India (2015)
Stover, Lindsey (2015)
Vasquez, Mica (2015)
Wells, Tiffany (2015)
Werts, Dasia (2015)
Weyhing, Shelby (2015)
Whitner, Adranna (2015)
Youngblood, Patricia (2015)

DFW Xtreme

Year	League	Name	W	L	Conference	Division	DF	PR
2012	WSFL	DFW Xtreme	4	5	National	--	1	C
2013	IWFL	DFW Xtreme	0	7	Western	Southwest	3	--
2014	WSFL	DFW Xtreme	2	3	Western	--	3	CC
2015	WSFL	DFW Xtreme	2	2	Southern	--	3	--
		Total	8	17				

Based in: Dallas, TX
Neutral site: Towanda, PA (N)
Notes: Preceded by IWFL's North Texas Knockouts

4/14/2012	H	Lone Star Mustangs	L	0	33	I	6/1/2013	H	Houston Energy	L	0	1	
4/21/2012	H	Arkansas Rampage	W	48	0		6/22/2013	H	San Antonio Regulators	L	0	1	
4/28/2012	H	Houston Energy	L	14	19	I	6/29/2013	A	Houston Energy	L	0	1	
6/2/2012	H	Dallas Diamonds	L	12	83	I							
6/9/2012	H	Houston Energy	L	0	30	I	4/12/2014	A	Atlanta Heartbreakers	W	30	14	
6/16/2012		Kansas Phoenix	W	68	0		4/26/2014	A	Atlanta Heartbreakers	W	60	0	
6/30/2012	A	Arkansas Rampage	W	52	8		5/17/2014	A	Memphis Dynasty	L	8	44	
7/21/2012	H	Arkansas Rampage	W	54	8	CC	6/7/2014	H	Arkansas Banshees	L	6	42	
8/11/2012	N	New Jersey Titans	L	6	67	C	7/19/2014	A	Arkansas Banshees	L	0	1	CC
4/27/2013	H	Arlington Impact	L	32	40		4/18/2015	H	Arkansas Assassins	W	14	8	
5/4/2013	A	San Antonio Regulators	L	12	44		6/6/2015	A	Tennessee Legacy	L	12	46	
5/18/2013	H	San Antonio Regulators	L	0	6		6/13/2015	A	Atlanta Heartbreakers	W	56	44	
5/25/2013	A	Arlington Impact	L	6	48		6/27/2015	A	Tennessee Legacy	L	0	48	

DFW Xtreme Player Register (2012)

Boothe, Raycham (2012)
Butler, Psyche (2012)
Carroll, Courtney (2012)
Carroll, Nicole (2012)
Douthit, Jacki (2012)
Ford, Amira (2012)
Guy, Tiffany (2012)
Hinson, Jessica (2012)
Johnson, Gabby (2012)
Jones, Ebony (2012)
Malone, Montrelle (2012)
Manthe, Jamie (2012)
McCray, Ali (2012)
Morgan, Brooklyn (2012)
Nunn, Monica (2012)
Sanders, Erica (2012)
Sumners, Heather (2012)
Tyler, Dawanya (2012)
Walker, Asta (2012)
Williams, Lovie (2012)

East Texas Saberkats

Year	League	Name	W	L	Conference	Division	DF	PR
2009	WFA	East Texas Saberkats	0	6	American	Southwest	4	--

Based in: Marshall, TX
Notes: Non-existent team

Date	H/A	Opponent	Result			Date	H/A	Opponent	Result		
4/18/2009	H	Lone Star Mustangs	L	0	1	5/30/2009	A	H-Town Texas Cyclones	L	0	1
4/25/2009	H	H-Town Texas Cyclones	L	0	1	6/13/2009	A	Lone Star Mustangs	L	0	1
5/2/2009	H	Austin Outlaws	L	0	1	6/20/2009	A	Austin Outlaws	L	0	1

Emerald Coast Barracudas

Year	League	Name	W	L	Conference	Division	DF	PR
2002	NWFA	Panama City Beach Rumble	1	7	--	Southern	4	--
2003	NWFA	Panama City Beach Rumble	4	4	Southern	Gulf Coast	3	--
2005	NWFA	Emerald Coast Sharks	0	8	Southern	--	14	--
2006	NWFA	Emerald Coast Barracudas	1	7	Southern	Southeast	4	--
2007	NWFA	Emerald Coast Barracudas	0	8	Southern	South	4	--
2008	NWFA	Emerald Coast Barracudas	0	8	Southern	Southeast	4	--
2009	WFA	Emerald Coast Barracudas	0	8	American	Southeast	5	--
		Total	**6**	**50**				

Based in: Panama City, FL

Date	H/A	Opponent	Result			Date	H/A	Opponent	Result		
4/20/2002		Pensacola Power	L	6	56	4/21/2007	A	Pensacola Power	L	0	40
5/4/2002		New Orleans Spice	L	38	48	4/28/2007	A	New Orleans Blaze	L	0	30
5/18/2002		Pensacola Power	L	0	61	5/5/2007	H	Gulf Coast Herricanes	L	13	22
5/25/2002		Biloxi Herricanes	L	6	34	5/12/2007	A	Chattanooga Locomotion	L	0	70
6/8/2002		New Orleans Spice	L	8	36	5/19/2007	H	New Orleans Blaze	L	6	55
6/15/2002		Biloxi Herricanes	L	14	36	6/2/2007	H	Pensacola Power	L	0	54
6/22/2002		New Orleans Spice	W	24	16	6/9/2007	H	Chattanooga Locomotion	L	6	70
6/29/2002		Biloxi Herricanes	L	6	30	6/16/2007	A	Gulf Coast Herricanes	L	0	32
4/12/2003	H	Pensacola Power	L	0	54	4/26/2008	H	New Orleans Blaze	L	7	38
4/19/2003	A	Gulf Coast Herricanes	W	60	8	5/3/2008	A	Memphis Belles	L	0	52
4/26/2003	H	New Orleans Spice	W	35	34	5/10/2008	H	Pensacola Power	L	24	64
5/3/2003	A	New Orleans Spice	L	27	44	5/17/2008	A	Gulf Coast Herricanes	L	12	50
5/17/2003	H	Gulf Coast Herricanes	W	55	6	5/31/2008	H	Memphis Belles	L	33	36
5/24/2003	A	Pensacola Power	L	7	41	6/7/2008	A	Pensacola Power	L	12	38
5/31/2003	H	New Orleans Spice	L	14	39	6/14/2008	H	Gulf Coast Herricanes	L	14	30
6/7/2003	A	Gulf Coast Herricanes	W	28	8	6/21/2008	A	New Orleans Blaze	L	0	34
4/16/2005	H	Gulf Coast Herricanes	L	25	58	4/18/2009	H	Jacksonville Dixie Blues	L	16	64
4/23/2005	H	Pensacola Power	L	7	81	4/25/2009	A	Memphis Belles	L	0	50
4/30/2005	A	New Orleans Blaze	L	0	48	5/2/2009	H	Gulf Coast Riptide	L	8	66
5/14/2005	A	Gulf Coast Herricanes	L	0	22	5/16/2009	H	New Orleans Blaze	L	20	39
5/21/2005	A	Pensacola Power	L	0	55	5/30/2009	H	Memphis Belles	L	12	44
5/28/2005	H	New Orleans Blaze	L	0	28	6/6/2009	A	Jacksonville Dixie Blues	L	0	1
6/4/2005	H	Gulf Coast Herricanes	L	15	22	6/20/2009	A	Gulf Coast Riptide	L	0	1
6/18/2005	A	Alabama Renegades	L	0	48	6/27/2009	A	New Orleans Blaze	L	0	1
4/15/2006	H	Pensacola Power	L	12	56						
4/22/2006	H	Alabama Renegades	L	0	48						
4/29/2006	A	Shreveport Shockhers	L	0	6						
5/13/2006	H	Blaze'n Canes	L	12	16						
5/20/2006	A	Pensacola Power	L	0	48						
5/27/2006	A	Alabama Renegades	L	8	30						
6/3/2006	H	Shreveport Shockhers	W	28	26						
6/17/2006	A	Pensacola Power	L	0	58						

Emerald Coast Barracudas Player Register (2005-2009)

Adams, Katie (2005)
Anderson, Lisa (2007)
Andrews, Morshelle (2005)
Bagshaw, Stephanie (2005)
Battles, Clisha (2008-2009)
Beach, Bebee (2006)
Boyce, Lisa (2005-2006, 2008)
Brown, Julie (2009)
Brown, Kim (2005)
Burleson, Amy (2006)
Cabrillas, Carman (2007)
Campbell, Deanne (2006-2008)
Clack, Kenisha (2007-2009)
Cook, Lynn (2008)
Crawford, Nicki (2007)
Cummings, Sandra (2009)
Daniels, Regina (2005)
DeVaney, Bridgette (2007)
Edmondson, Mashell (2009)
Evangelista, Angie (2006)
Faustin, Kim (2008-2009)
Fellows, Hannah (2006)
Fellows, Jessica (2005-2006)
Grainger, Ellen (2006)
Haley, Curtice (2007-2009)
Hampton, Margaret (2008)
Harrell, Katy (2007-2009)
Holmes, Monique (2005)
Holt, Shequita (2008-2009)
Honeycutt, Tanya (2007)
Hunt, Amber (2005)
Jackson, Caroline (2005-2006)
Johnson, Megan (2005-2009)
Jones, Aisha (2005-2006, 2008-2009)
Jones, Robin (2007)
Katowich, Lori (2005)
Kennedy, Lydia (2006-2009)
LaFrance, Teborah (2006, 2008-2009)
Larrimor, Mandy (2005)
Lawson, Natalie (2006)
Little, Rhonda (2006-2007)
Lopez, Gloria (2005)
Lowe, Sonya (2008)
McCune, Beth (2006)
McGowan, Brylecia (2006)
McKenzie, Erin (2005)
Meade, Tish (2006)
Meadows, Tina (2008-2009)
Miller, Patrice (2007)
Minchew, Stephanie (2006-2009)
Nabor, Stacy (2008)
Pannell, Lanedra (2008-2009)
Parks, Nakia (2005)
Peckham, Katherine (2007)
Persons, Mel (2006)
Postell, Cassandra (2008-2009)
Rainelli, JoAnn (2005-2009)
Rausa, Kathy (2005)
Redden, Jessica (2006)
Reed, Charuae (2007)
Reed, Chevy (2009)
Reed, DeeDee (2006)
Simmons, Nicey (2005-2006)
Smith, Queena (2008-2009)
Spooner, Jessie (2006-2007)
Sutton, Janet (2005-2006)
Sutton, Janice (2005-2006)
Terry, Katrina (2005-2006)
Troupe, Kiamani (2009)
Turner, Minnie (2006-2007, 2009)
Van Camp, Holli (2007)
VanSandt, Stacy (2005)
Vines, Lacey (2008)
Walker, Jeannette (2008-2009)
Waltman, DeeDee (2005)
Watson, Ruth (2007)
West, Jessie (2006, 2008)
Wojtysiak, Brenda (2006)

Empire State Roar

Year	League		Name	W	L	Conference	Division	DF	PR
2005	WPFL	X	Empire State Roar	2	4	--	--	--	--
2006	WPFL		Empire State Roar	4	3	American	East	2	--
2007	WPFL		Empire State Roar	8	1	American	East	1	CC
			Total	**14**	**8**				

Based in: Rochester, NY
Notes: Preceded by NWFA's Rochester Raptors

Date	H/A	Opponent	Result		
7/30/2005	H	New York Dazzles	L	0	6
8/13/2005	A	Albany Ambush	L	13	14
8/20/2005	H	New York Dazzles	L	8	12
8/27/2005	H	Albany Ambush	W	21	0
9/3/2005	A	New York Dazzles	W	30	13
10/8/2005	A	Minnesota Vixen	L	14	39
7/29/2006	A	Albany Ambush	W	36	0
8/5/2006	H	Connecticut Cyclones	W	54	0
8/12/2006	H	New England Intensity	L	0	20
8/19/2006	H	Carolina Queens	W	31	8
8/26/2006	A	Connecticut Cyclones	W	34	0
9/16/2006	A	New England Intensity	L	0	6
9/30/2006	A	Wisconsin Wolves	L	0	24
8/18/2007	H	Connecticut Cyclones	W	61	0
8/25/2007	H	New Jersey Titans	W	20	6
9/1/2007	H	Indiana Speed	W	28	0
9/15/2007	A	So Cal Scorpions	W	28	6
9/22/2007	A	Toledo Reign	W	40	0
9/29/2007	A	New Jersey Titans	W	22	7
10/6/2007	H	Toledo Reign	W	51	7
10/20/2007	A	Connecticut Cyclones	W	1	0
11/17/2007	H	So Cal Scorpions	L	6	42 CC

Erie Illusion

Year	League	Name	W	L	Conference	Division	DF	PR
2003	NWFA	Erie Illusion	0	8	Northern	Mid-Atlantic	5	--
2004	NWFA	Erie Illusion	1	7	Northern	Mid-Atlantic	4	--
2005	NWFA	Erie Illusion	3	5	Northern	--	14	--
2006	NWFA	Erie Illusion	1	7	Northern	North Central	4	--
2007	NWFA	Erie Illusion	7	2	Northern	Central	2	Q
2008	NWFA	Erie Illusion	4	4	Northern	Central	3	--
2009	IWFL2	Erie Illusion	3	5	--	--	12	--
2010	IWFL2	Erie Illusion	3	5	Eastern	Northeast	4	--
2011	WFA	Erie Illusion	3	6	National	Mid-Atlantic	4	--
2012	IWFL	Erie Illusion	4	4	Eastern	Mid-Atlantic	3	--
2013	IWFL X	Erie Illusion	1	4	--	--	--	--
2014	IWFL X	Erie Illusion	0	6	--	--	--	--
		Total	30	63				

Based in: Erie, PA

Date	H/A	Opponent	Result	Score		Date	H/A	Opponent	Result	Score	
4/12/2003	H	D.C. Divas	L	0	50	4/26/2008	A	Tree Town Spitfire	W	15	0
4/26/2003	A	Pittsburgh Passion	L	7	14	5/3/2008	A	Cleveland Fusion	L	0	30
5/3/2003	H	Columbus Flames	L	13	34	5/10/2008	A	Columbus Comets	L	0	48
5/10/2003	A	Baltimore Burn	L	3	58	5/17/2008	A	West Virginia Wonders	W	54	0
5/17/2003	H	Pittsburgh Passion	L	18	20	5/31/2008	H	Columbus Comets	L	0	34
5/24/2003	A	D.C. Divas	L	7	74	6/7/2008	H	Cleveland Fusion	L	0	26
5/31/2003	A	Columbus Flames	L	12	35	6/14/2008	H	West Virginia Wonders	W	1	0
6/7/2003	H	Baltimore Burn	L	21	28	6/21/2008	H	Tree Town Spitfire	W	29	0
4/17/2004	A	Roanoke Revenge	L	6	12	4/11/2009	H	Jersey Justice	L	6	8
4/24/2004	H	Baltimore Burn	L	0	36	4/18/2009	A	Carolina Phoenix	L	0	6
5/1/2004	H	D.C. Divas	L	0	34	5/2/2009	H	Central PA Vipers	W	61	8
5/8/2004	A	D.C. Divas	L	0	46	5/23/2009	A	Montreal Blitz	L	10	41
5/15/2004	A	Baltimore Burn	L	0	32	5/30/2009	A	Manchester Freedom	W	20	13
5/29/2004	H	Pittsburgh Passion	L	0	28	6/6/2009	H	Detroit Demolition	L	7	33
6/5/2004	H	Roanoke Revenge	W	21	0	6/7/2009	H	Holyoke Hurricanes	W	1	0
6/12/2004	A	Pittsburgh Passion	L	0	46	6/13/2009	A	Jersey Justice	L	16	36
4/23/2005	A	Connecticut Crush	L	0	39	4/3/2010	H	Pittsburgh Passion	L	0	32
4/30/2005	A	Massachusetts Mutiny	L	0	42	4/10/2010	H	Binghamton Tiger Cats	W	57	0
5/14/2005	A	Maine Freeze	W	30	6	4/17/2010	H	Binghamton Tiger Cats	W	55	0
5/21/2005	A	Connecticut Crush	L	0	44	4/24/2010	A	Wisconsin Warriors	L	0	19
5/28/2005	H	Massachusetts Mutiny	L	0	27	5/1/2010	A	Pittsburgh Passion	L	2	40
6/4/2005	H	Maine Freeze	W	34	14	5/8/2010	H	Louisville Nightmare	W	47	8
6/11/2005	H	Connecticut Crush	L	0	30	5/22/2010	A	New England Intensity	L	8	28
6/18/2005	H	Toledo Spitfire	W	44	0	6/5/2010	H	New England Intensity	L	20	27
4/15/2006	A	Toledo Spitfire	W	8	0	4/9/2011	H	Pittsburgh Passion	L	14	56
4/22/2006	A	Columbus Comets	L	0	71	4/16/2011	A	Pittsburgh Force	W	20	8
4/29/2006	A	Cleveland Fusion	L	0	43	4/30/2011	A	Cleveland Fusion	L	0	50
5/6/2006	A	Pittsburgh Passion	L	0	45	5/7/2011	H	Columbus Comets	L	7	36
5/27/2006	H	Columbus Comets	L	0	59	5/14/2011	H	Binghamton Tiger Cats	W	38	0 I
6/3/2006	H	Pittsburgh Passion	L	0	54	5/21/2011	H	Cleveland Fusion	L	0	50
6/10/2006	H	Cleveland Fusion	L	0	46	6/4/2011	A	Columbus Comets	L	0	1
6/17/2006	H	Toledo Spitfire	L	7	8	6/11/2011	H	Pittsburgh Force	W	20	0
						6/18/2011	A	Pittsburgh Passion	L	7	47
4/7/2007	A	Tree Town Spitfire	L	0	6 *						
4/14/2007	A	Central PA Vipers	W	25	6	4/21/2012	H	New Hampshire Freedom	W	24	20
5/5/2007	A	Central Massachusetts Ravens	W	41	0	4/28/2012	A	Connecticut Wreckers	W	14	7
5/12/2007	A	Maine Freeze	W	14	13	5/5/2012	H	Baltimore Nighthawks	L	0	20
5/26/2007	H	Central PA Vipers	W	39	0	5/12/2012	H	Maine Rebels	W	27	0
6/2/2007	H	Central Massachusetts Ravens	W	1	0	5/19/2012	A	Philadelphia Firebirds	L	8	32
6/9/2007	H	Tree Town Spitfire	W	12	8	6/2/2012	A	Baltimore Nighthawks	L	12	29
6/16/2007	H	Maine Freeze	W	42	0	6/9/2012	A	Northeastern Nitro	L	12	34
6/23/2007	A	Pittsburgh Passion	L	7	63 Q	6/16/2012		Connecticut Wreckers	W	1	0

Continued on next page

Erie Illusion Game-By-Game Results (continued)

Date	H/A	Opponent	W/L	PF	PA
5/11/2013	A	Chattanooga Locomotion	L	0	34
6/1/2013	A	Montreal Blitz	L	0	1
6/15/2013	H	Maine Rebels	W	26	6
6/22/2013	A	Washington Prodigy	L	0	1
6/29/2013	H	Keystone Assault	L	0	49
5/17/2014	A	Keystone Assault	L	0	62
5/24/2014	A	Derby City Dynamite	L	0	72 I
5/31/2014	A	Connecticut Wreckers	L	0	1
6/7/2014	A	Wisconsin Warriors	L	0	1
6/14/2014	A	New York Knockout	L	0	40
6/21/2014	H	New York Knockout	L	0	54

Erie Illusion Player Register (2003-2005, 2010-2011)

Ali, Yasmin (2010)
Beardsley, Aleatha (2003)
Bowerman, Margo (2004)
Britt, Colleen (2011)
Brown, Stephanie (2004)
Burkett, Shawna (2010)
Butler, Mary (2003, 2011)
Callaghan, Stacy (2005)
Carey, Sameania (2003)
Carr, Wendy (2003)
Clark, Heather (2003, 2005)
Cole, Mona (2003)
Coleman, Sharon (2004-2005)
Cooper, Missy (2011)
Cray, Erin (2004-2005)
Domholdt, Megan (2005)
Ellis, Darci (2005)
Fernandez, Lisa (2003, '05, 2010-11)
Ford, Lindey (2003)
Frawley, Mellisa (2003)
Glazier, Allison (2010)
Gore, Kesha (2011)
Haefner, Shelly (2010)
Hall, Liz (2003-2004)
Hawryliw, Nicole (2003)
Henderson, Melanie (2003)
Hoover, Jill (2005)
Huston, OreLecia (2011)
Illig, Stacy (2003, 2011)
Johnson, Rebecca (2010)
Jones, Brenda (2003)
Joyner, Tiffany (2010-2011)
Kemling, Julie (2003)
Kephart, Michelle (2004-05, 2010-11)
Kinder, Jamie (2011)
Klinek, Shelly (2003-2005, 2010)
Knight, Jen (2011)
Krupa, Dorothy (2010)
Kulesza, Carol (2010)
Leet, Tracy (2004-2005, 2011)
Lenken, Elizabeth (2010-2011)
Leone, Judy (2003)
Lindsey, Carla (2003)
Madigan, Melody (2004)
Mastalaki, Lindsey (2003)
McCabe, Karen (2003)
McCullough, Kerri Leigh (2003, 2005)
McDade, Mary (2003-05, 2010-11)
Mee, Stacey (2010)
Michalski, Julie (2010)
Middleton, Susanne (2003)
Miller, Casey (2005)
Munksgard, Michelle (2003, 2005)
Nesbitt, Sandra "Gumby" (2011)
Niskanen, Kelly (2003-2005)
Olson, Laura (2010-2011)
Orlop, Marianne (2010)
Owens, Carrie (2011)
Palaimo, Mary (2011)
Palmer, Lakea (2011)
Pastrick, Emma (2003, 2005, 2010)
Payne, Wendy (2003, 2005)
Pelger, Joy (2003)
Peterson, Tiffany (2003, 2005)
Polinick, Brandy (2005, 2010-2011)
Puff, Angela (2011)
Rankin, Jen (2003)
Reed, Rebecca (2010)
Robson, Kim (2003)
Rogers, Trumane (2005)
Santana, Kamille (2003)
Sapko, Stacy (2003)
Schaeffer, Corrine (2003, '05, '10-11)
Simitoski, Mikenzie (2011)
Smith, Amy (2004)
Sommers, Jen (2011)
Stachura, Jen (2011)
Stephenson, Cindy (2011)
Swick, Martha (2010-2011)
Theisen, Jamie (2003)
Tomeo, Amanda (2003-2005)
VanHorne, Tara (2003, 2010-2011)
Vaughn, B.J. (2010)
Vilardo, Alexa (2011)
Villagonzola, Marife (2010)
Weibel, Victoria (2005, 2010)
Williams, Kim (2005)
Wingerter, Judy (2003)
Wurst, Martha (2005)
Zacherl, Marci (2005)
Zomcik, Jessica (2005)

Eugene Edge

Year	League	Name	W	L	Conference	Division	DF	PR
2002	IWFL	Eugene Edge	4	4	Western	--	5	--
2003	IWFL	Eugene Edge	2	6	Western	Pacific Northwest	4	--
2004	IWFL	Eugene Edge	1	7	Western	Pacific Northwest	5	--
2005	IWFL	Eugene Edge	1	9	Western	Pacific Northwest	5	--
2006	IWFL	Eugene Edge	0	8	Western	Pacific Northwest	4	--
		Total	8	34				

Based in: Eugene, OR

Date	H/A	Opponent	W/L	PF	PA
3/30/2002		Corvallis Pride	L	0	12
4/6/2002		Oregon Thunder	W	35	20
4/20/2002		Corvallis Pride	L	7	8
4/27/2002		Oregon Thunder	W	31	14
5/11/2002		Corvallis Pride	L	6	14
5/18/2002		Oregon Thunder	W	20	8
6/1/2002		Corvallis Pride	L	0	28
6/8/2002		Oregon Thunder	W	1	0
3/22/2003	A	Corvallis Pride	L	8	19
3/29/2003	A	Tacoma Majestics	L	0	42
4/5/2003	H	Portland Shockwave	L	0	6
4/12/2003	A	Boise Xtreme	W	18	16
5/3/2003	H	Corvallis Pride	L	8	33
5/10/2003	H	Tacoma Majestics	L	7	26
5/17/2003	A	Portland Shockwave	L	14	18
5/31/2003	H	Boise Xtreme	W	39	0
4/3/2004	H	Portland Shockwave	W	6	0
4/17/2004	H	Tacoma Majestics	L	13	42
4/24/2004	A	Boise Xtreme	L	14	20
5/8/2004	H	Corvallis Pride	L	6	32
5/15/2004	A	Portland Shockwave	L	13	28
5/22/2004	A	Tacoma Majestics	L	0	49
5/29/2004	H	Boise Xtreme	L	40	45
6/12/2004	A	Corvallis Pride	L	6	50

Continued on next page

Eugene Edge Game-By-Game Results (continued)

Date	H/A	Opponent	W/L	Score		Date	H/A	Opponent	W/L	Score
4/2/2005	A	Redding Rage	L	19 20		4/29/2006	A	Corvallis Pride	L	8 36
4/16/2005	A	Tacoma Majestics	L	0 42		5/13/2006	A	Portland Shockwave	L	0 48
4/23/2005	H	Portland Shockwave	L	20 39		5/20/2006	H	Santa Rosa Scorchers	L	0 41
4/30/2005	H	Redding Rage	W	7 0		5/27/2006	A	Redding Rage	L	6 20
5/7/2005	A	Corvallis Pride	L	6 45		6/3/2006	H	Seattle Majestics	L	0 48
5/14/2005	A	Portland Shockwave	L	12 42		6/10/2006	A	Portland Shockwave	L	0 55
5/21/2005	H	Tacoma Majestics	L	0 20		6/17/2006	H	Corvallis Pride	L	14 52
6/4/2005	H	Corvallis Pride	L	0 1		6/24/2006	H	Portland Shockwave	L	14 46
6/11/2005	A	Boise Xtreme	L	0 1						
6/18/2005	H	Boise Xtreme	L	0 1						

Evansville Express

Year	League	Name	W	L	Conference	Division	DF	PR
2003	NWFA	Evansville Express	0	7	Southern	Midwest	4	--
2004	NWFA	Evansville Express	0	8	Southern	Midwest	3	--
		Total	**0**	**15**				

Based in: Evansville, IN

Date	Opponent	W/L	Score			Date	H/A	Opponent	W/L	Score
3/29/2003	Chattanooga Locomotion	L	0 42	E		4/3/2004	A	St. Louis Slam	L	0 29
4/5/2003	Chattanooga Locomotion	L	0 42	E		4/17/2004	A	Nashville Dream	L	0 33
4/19/2003	Kansas City Krunch	L	0 20			4/24/2004	H	Kansas City Krunch	L	6 36
4/26/2003	St. Louis Slam	L	20 27			5/1/2004	A	Kansas City Krunch	L	0 32
5/10/2003	Kansas City Krunch	L	0 16			5/15/2004	H	Kansas City Krunch	L	0 27
6/7/2003	Kansas City Krunch	L	7 34			5/22/2004	H	Nashville Dream	L	12 48
6/14/2003	St. Louis Slam	L	14 35			6/5/2004	A	St. Louis Slam	L	6 29
						6/12/2004	H	St. Louis Slam	L	0 12

Evansville Express Player Register (2004)

Ambrose, Dana (2004)
Barrett, Joni (2004)
Beaty, Laurel (2004)
Csukas, Beth (2004)
Garrett, Kim (2004)
Gilley, Sarah (2004)
Hall, Natalie (2004)
Hamlet, Kim (2004)
Huley, Jennifer (2004)
Leslie, Laura (2004)
Maynard, Krista (2004)
Miles, Seyonna (2004)
Reynolds, Stephanie (2004)

Everett Reign

Year	League	Name	W	L	Conference	Division	DF	PR
2013	WFA	Everett Reign	4	7	American	Division 10 (Pacific Northwest)	4	--
2014	WFA	Everett Reign	4	7	American	Northwest	3	W
2015	WFA	Everett Reign	2	6	American	Pacific Northwest	4	--
		Total	**10**	**20**				

Based in: Everett, WA

Date	H/A	Opponent	W/L	Score			Date	H/A	Opponent	W/L	Score	
3/2/2013	H	Las Vegas Showgirlz	L	0 28	E		4/19/2014	A	Seattle Majestics	L	0 41	
3/16/2013	H	Utah Jynx	L	6 54	E		4/26/2014	H	Portland Fighting Fillies	W	8 7	
3/30/2013	H	River City Raiderz	W	50 0	IE		5/3/2014	H	Utah Blitz	W	23 8	
4/6/2013	H	Portland Shockwave	L	3 16			5/17/2014	A	Tacoma Trauma	W	47 12	
4/20/2013	A	Utah Blitz	W	22 6			5/31/2014	A	Portland Shockwave	L	3 8	
4/27/2013	H	Tacoma Trauma	W	46 6			6/7/2014	H	Seattle Majestics	L	0 43	
5/4/2013	A	Portland Fighting Fillies	L	6 16			6/14/2014	A	Las Vegas Showgirlz	L	0 50	W
5/11/2013	A	Portland Shockwave	L	8 44								
5/25/2013	H	Seattle Majestics	L	0 35			4/11/2015	A	Portland Shockwave	L	20 47	
6/1/2013	A	Tacoma Trauma	L	0 24			4/18/2015	H	Portland Fighting Fillies	W	18 13	
6/8/2013	H	Portland Fighting Fillies	W	14 13			5/2/2015	H	Portland Shockwave	L	8 21	
							5/9/2015	H	Seattle Majestics	L	0 56	
3/1/2014	A	Las Vegas Showgirlz	L	0 24	E		5/16/2015	A	Utah Blitz	W	8 0	
3/22/2014	H	Utah Falconz	L	0 52	IE		5/30/2015	H	Tacoma Trauma	L	0 35	
4/5/2014	H	Tacoma Trauma	W	19 12			6/6/2015	A	Seattle Majestics	L	0 56	
4/12/2014	A	Utah Blitz	L	12 14			6/13/2015	A	Tacoma Trauma	L	13 24	

Everett Reign Player Register (2013-2015)

Allen, Alyssa (2013-2015)
Allen, Kayla (2013)
Alyea, Janell (2013-2015)
Autrey, Kathleen (2013)
Barto, Marika (2013-2014)
Beltz, Caitlin (2014)
Blurton, Emily (2014)
Bonilla, Maricela (2015)
Burns, Brit (2013-2015)
Cannales, Brynn (2014)
Champoux, Doria (2015)
Chau, Linda (2013)
Christin-Nelson, Maritza (2013)
Cimmer, Megan (2014)
Cooper, Sarah (2015)
Curdy, Cheri (2014-2015)
Curdy, Courtney (2014-2015)
Davidson, B.J. (2015)
Delgado, Yolly (2014-2015)
Eden, Kia (2013)
Ensley, Lore (2013)
Escamilla, Alexia (2013)
Felder, Lynzee (2013-2015)
Hendren, Melissa (2014)
Holland, Shania (2015)
Holton, Brooklyn (2013-2015)
Howard, Toni (2013-2014)
Hutchinson, Christine (2015)
Ito-Simpkins, Lena (2014)
Johnson, Tammie (2013-2014)
Kahr, Amelia (2015)
Keoho, Bridget (2013)
Kreide, Shannon (2013)
Larsen, Foreste (2013-2015)
Laures, Chrissy (2013)
Lawson, Jamie (2013-2015)
Layman, Leann (2013-2015)
Lind, Jen (2014)
Madison, Britta (2013-2014)
McCormack, Megan (2013)
Morgan, Darian (2013)
Myers, Mandy (2013-2014)
Pelham, Nikki (2015)
Reda, Nomie (2015)
Rice, Jordan (2013)
Richardson, Julez (2013-2014)
Richardson, Sam (2013-2014)
Ripley, Stephany (2014-2015)
Roy, Reanna (2015)
Schade, Alanna (2013-2014)
Schlachter, Stella (2015)
Schy, Jeri (2015)
Selia, Amy (2013-2015)
Serrano, Mimi (2015)
Sims, Joleen (2013)
Smyers, Sha (2015)
Spencer, Keisha (2014-2015)
Stutsman, Austen (2014-2015)
Thomas, Naia (2015)
Todd, Riley (2014)
Trinka-Hoard, Theresa (2013)
Vancil, Abbie (2013-2014)
Walsh, Michele (2014-2015)
Ward, Tauna (2014)
Westbrooks, Jae (2013-2015)
Wilson, Nancy (2013)
Winningham, Pat (2015)
Winsor, Brynn (2013)
Wood, Kristin (2015)
Wride, Brandy (2013-2015)

Fayetteville Warriors

Year	League	Name	W	L	Conference	Division	DF	PR
2002	WFL	Fayetteville Warriors	0	2	--	--	--	--

Based in: Fayetteville, NC
Notes: Succeeded by Cape Fear Thunder

8/24/2002	H	Carolina Cougars	L	12	14		9/7/2002	A	Carolina Cougars	L	8	44

Florida Stingrayz

Year	League	Name	W	L	Conference	Division	DF	PR
2003	WPFL	Florida Stingrayz	8	3	National	South	1	C

Based in: Miami, FL

8/9/2003	H	Missouri Prowlers	W	87	0		9/27/2003	H	Minnesota Vixen	W	33	15	
8/16/2003	H	Syracuse Sting	W	6	0		10/4/2003	H	New England Storm	W	84	6	
8/23/2003	A	New England Storm	W	14	0		10/11/2003	H	Dallas Diamonds	L	22	26	
9/6/2003	A	Los Angeles Amazons	W	14	2		10/25/2003	A	Dallas Diamonds	W	22	14	CC
9/13/2003	A	Houston Energy	L	20	57		11/8/2003	A	Northern Ice	L	12	53	C
9/20/2003	A	Indiana Speed	W	44	21								

Fort Wayne Flash

Year	League		Name	W	L	Conference	Division	DF	PR
2006	NWFA	X	Fort Wayne Flash	0	3	--	--	--	--
2007	NWFA		Fort Wayne Flash	4	4	Northern	West	2	--
2008	NWFA		Fort Wayne Flash	5	4	Northern	Midwest	1	Q
2009	WFA		Fort Wayne Flash	4	4	National	Central	3	--
			Total	**13**	**15**				

Based in: Fort Wayne, IN

Fort Wayne Flash Game-By-Game Results

Date	H/A	Opponent	W/L	Score		Date	H/A	Opponent	W/L	Score	
5/6/2006	A	Chattanooga Locomotion	L	7	33	4/19/2008	A	Dayton Diamonds	W	59	0
5/13/2006	H	Toledo Spitfire	L	0	6	4/26/2008	H	West Michigan Mayhem	L	6	7 *
6/3/2006	A	Kentucky Karma	L	6	18	5/10/2008	A	Indianapolis Chaos	W	58	0
						5/17/2008	H	Cleveland Fusion	L	6	8
4/14/2007	H	West Michigan Mayhem	L	0	6	5/24/2008	H	Dayton Diamonds	W	62	0
4/21/2007	H	Milwaukee Momentum	W	36	0	6/7/2008	A	West Michigan Mayhem	L	14	19
4/28/2007	A	Columbus Comets	L	6	35	6/14/2008	H	Indianapolis Chaos	W	67	6
5/12/2007	A	Tree Town Spitfire	W	16	14	6/21/2008	A	Cleveland Fusion	W	27	0
5/19/2007	A	West Michigan Mayhem	L	5	14	6/28/2008	A	Columbus Comets	L	7	14 Q
6/2/2007	H	Columbus Comets	L	0	10						
6/9/2007	A	Milwaukee Momentum	W	22	0	4/18/2009	A	West Michigan Mayhem	L	0	41
6/16/2007	H	Tree Town Spitfire	W	28	0	4/25/2009	H	Indiana Speed	L	0	52
						5/9/2009	A	Dayton Diamonds	W	29	0
						5/16/2009	A	Toledo Reign	W	47	0
						5/30/2009	A	Indiana Speed	L	7	14
						6/6/2009	H	West Michigan Mayhem	L	0	35
						6/13/2009	H	Toledo Reign	W	38	0
						6/20/2009	H	Dayton Diamonds	W	68	20

Fort Wayne Flash Player Register (2007-2009)

Adam, Alica (2007-2008)
Allen, Nicole (2007-2009)
Anderson, Heather (2007-2009)
Baker, Rachel (2007-2009)
Beck, Amber (2007-2009)
Beck, Amy (2007-2008)
Bennett, Kellie (2007-2008)
Booth, DeAnn (2007)
Brand, Gerrie (2007-2009)
Budenz, Heather (2007-2008)
Carney, Kathy (2007-2009)
Conley, Danyel (2008-2009)
Couch, Candy (2007-2008)
Curneal, Andrea (2007-2008)
Davis, Stacey (2008-2009)
Dickover, Lori (2007)
Dreibelbis, Courtney (2008)
Duff, Keitra (2007-2008)
Dunham, Jeanne (2007-2008)
Freds, Becky (2007)
Fultz, Kara (2009)
Gartner, Louise (2007, 2009)
Geiger, Amy (2007-2009)
Gemmer, Jill (2007-2009)
Gerber, LeAnn (2007-2008)
Harrison, Bethany (2007-2008)
Hartle, Monique (2007-2009)
Heaton, Lisa (2009)
Heffernan, Jennifer (2007-2009)
Heinzen, Michelle (2009)
Hughes, Kim (2009)
Jasinski, Nicole (2007-2008)
Keffaber, Tina (2007-2008)
Kerr, Laura (2007-2009)
Knight, Katie (2007)
Lancaster, Stacie (2007-2008)
Macke, Kate (2007-2008)
Marble, Tara (2007-2009)
Martin, Jill (2007)
Meeks, Cindy (2007-2009)
Mettler, Sonia (2008)
Morgan, Trisha (2007-2009)
Napierkowski, Amanda (2007-2009)
Neal, Jayme (2009)
O'Boyle, Karen (2008-2009)
Pais, Kim (2007)
Pernsteiner, Tessa (2008-2009)
Powers, Regina (2007-2009)
Raupfer, Kim (2008)
Rzasa, Teri (2007-2009)
Shuman, Stephanie (2007)
Smith, Tammy (2009)
Stevens, Jaci (2009)
Tarnow, Karen (2007-2008)
Taylor, Deb (2007-2009)
Wade, Cheryl (2007-2009)
Wierenga, Kipp (2007)
Wright, Heidi (2007-2009)

Georgia Enforcers

Year	League	Name	W	L	Conference	Division	DF	PR
2002	WAFL-WFA	Georgia Enforcers	2	8	Central	--	3	--

Based in: Atlanta, GA

Date	H/A	Opponent	W/L	Score			Date	H/A	Opponent	W/L	Score		
10/12/2002	H	New Orleans Voodoo Dolls	W	1	0	N	11/16/2002	H	New Orleans Voodoo Dolls	W	1	0	N
10/19/2002	H	Birmingham Steel Magnolias	L	8	20		11/23/2002	A	Indianapolis Vipers	L	0	1	
10/26/2002	H	Indianapolis Vipers	L	0	1		12/7/2002	A	Birmingham Steel Magnolias	L	0	1	
11/2/2002	A	Tampa Bay Force	L	0	1		12/14/2002	A	South Carolina Crusaders	L	0	1	
11/9/2002	A	Jacksonville Dixie Blues	L	6	35		12/21/2002	H	South Carolina Crusaders	L	0	1	

Georgia Gladiators

Year	League	Name	W	L	Conference	Division	DF	PR
2005	WPFL	X	Georgia Gladiators	0	1	--	--	--	--

Based in: Macon, GA
Notes: Non-existent team

| 8/6/2005 | A | Dallas Diamonds | L | 0 | 1 |

Georgia Peachez

Year	League	Name	W	L	Conference	Division	DF	PR
2011	IWFL	Georgia Peachez	0	7	Eastern	Mid South	6	--

Based in: Savannah, GA

4/2/2011	H	Baltimore Nighthawks	L	0	36
4/23/2011	A	Tennessee Valley Tigers	L	0	1
4/30/2011	A	Baltimore Nighthawks	L	0	1
5/7/2011	H	Atlanta Ravens	L	0	1
5/21/2011	A	Atlanta Ravens	L	0	1
5/28/2011	H	Carolina Phoenix	L	0	1
6/11/2011	A	Carolina Phoenix	L	0	1

Grand Valley Vipers

Year	League	Name	W	L	Conference	Division	DF	PR
2002	UWFL	Grand Valley Vipers	2	3	--	--	--	--

Based in: Grand Junction, CO

4/14/2002	Denver Foxes	L	6	71
4/28/2002	Sweetwater County Outlaws	W	42	14
5/5/2002	Pueblo Pythons	L	8	29
5/12/2002	Colorado Springs Koalas	L	6	31
5/19/2002	Cheyenne Dust Devils	W	22	0

Gulf Coast Herricanes

Year	League	Name	W	L	Conference	Division	DF	PR
2002	NWFA	Biloxi Herricanes	5	3	--	Southern	2	--
2003	NWFA	Gulf Coast Herricanes	0	8	Southern	Gulf Coast	4	--
2004	NWFA	Gulf Coast Herricanes	0	8	Southern	Gulf Coast	5	--
2005	NWFA	Gulf Coast Herricanes	4	4	Southern	--	10	--
2007	NWFA	Gulf Coast Herricanes	2	6	Southern	South	3	--
2008	NWFA	Gulf Coast Herricanes	2	6	Southern	Southeast	3	--
		Total	**13**	**35**				

Based in: Biloxi, MS

4/20/2002		New Orleans Spice	W	40	34
5/4/2002		Pensacola Power	L	6	42
5/18/2002		New Orleans Spice	W	22	14
5/25/2002		Panama City Beach Rumble	W	34	6
6/8/2002		Pensacola Power	L	0	30
6/15/2002		Panama City Beach Rumble	W	36	14
6/22/2002		Pensacola Power	L	0	63
6/29/2002		Panama City Beach Rumble	W	30	6
4/12/2003	A	New Orleans Spice	L	22	26
4/19/2003	H	Panama City Beach Rumble	L	8	60
5/3/2003	A	Pensacola Power	L	0	82
5/17/2003	A	Panama City Beach Rumble	L	6	55
5/24/2003	H	New Orleans Spice	L	0	24
5/31/2003	H	Pensacola Power	L	0	84
6/7/2003	H	Panama City Beach Rumble	L	8	28
6/14/2003	A	New Orleans Spice	L	0	34
4/3/2004	A	New Orleans Blaze	L	0	67
4/17/2004	A	Muscle Shoals Smashers	L	0	46
4/24/2004	H	Pensacola Power	L	0	62
5/8/2004	A	Alabama Renegades	L	0	46
5/15/2004	H	New Orleans Blaze	L	0	26
5/29/2004	A	Pensacola Power	L	0	49
6/5/2004	H	Alabama Renegades	L	7	35
6/12/2004	H	Muscle Shoals Smashers	L	12	21
4/16/2005	A	Emerald Coast Sharks	W	58	25
4/23/2005	H	New Orleans Blaze	L	0	42
4/30/2005	A	Pensacola Power	L	6	44
5/14/2005	H	Emerald Coast Sharks	W	22	0
5/21/2005	H	Atlanta Leopards	W	1	0
6/4/2005	A	Emerald Coast Sharks	W	22	15
6/11/2005	H	Pensacola Power	L	8	47
6/18/2005	A	New Orleans Blaze	L	0	27
4/14/2007	A	Austin Outlaws	L	6	49
4/28/2007	H	Pensacola Power	L	0	48
5/5/2007	A	Emerald Coast Barracudas	W	22	13
5/12/2007	H	New Orleans Blaze	L	6	27
5/19/2007	A	Pensacola Power	L	8	56
6/2/2007	H	Austin Outlaws	L	8	57
6/9/2007	A	New Orleans Blaze	L	12	19
6/16/2007	H	Emerald Coast Barracudas	W	32	0
4/26/2008	A	H-Town Texas Cyclones	L	0	46
5/3/2008	A	New Orleans Blaze	L	0	36
5/17/2008	H	Emerald Coast Barracudas	W	50	12
5/24/2008	A	Pensacola Power	L	22	28
5/31/2008	H	New Orleans Blaze	L	16	27
6/7/2008	H	H-Town Texas Cyclones	L	0	41
6/14/2008	A	Emerald Coast Barracudas	W	30	14
6/21/2008	H	Pensacola Power	L	0	36

Gulf Coast Herricanes Player Register (2004-2005, 2007-2008)

Andrews, Traci (2007)
Barner, Roslyn "Roz" (2004-2005)
Beach, Bebee (2004-2005, 2007)
Benjamin, Kim (2008)
Bishop, Kim (2005)
Black, Naomi (2005)
Bodden, Beth (2004-2005)
Bolden, La Toya (2005)
Boswell, Valencia "Jay" (2007-2008)
Bradford, Robbie (2004-2005, 2007)
Brantley, Jessica (2007)
Burke, Debbie (2004-2005)
Catchings, A.C. (2005)
Christian, Simone (2007)
Colvin, Teryn (2007-2008)
Copeland, Jeannie (2007-2008)
Cribb, Rachael (2008)
Daley, Stephanie (2007-2008)
Davis, LaShane (2004-2005, 2007-2008)
Davis, Mindy (2004-2005)
Donald, Roslyn (2007)
Dortch, Tiffany "Tip" (2007-2008)
Dutton, Heather (2005)
Ellison, Frankie (2005, 2007-2008)
Faulkner, Melanie (2007-2008)
Fellows, Hannah (2004-2005, 2007-2008)
Fellows, Jessica (2007-2008)
Germany, Sara (2008)
Gingerella, Shannon (2005)
Grabowsky, Stephanie (2005)
Green, Lee (2008)
Griffin, Alisha (2008)
Harlow, Chantel (2005)
Hill, Kathy (2008)
Hughes, Danielle (2007)
Hunter, Essie (2004-2005)
Hurtado, Leequnita (2005)
Jackson, Kee (2008)
James, Casandra (2004-2005)
Johnson, Angel (2007-2008)
Johnson, Megan (2004)
Jones, Tania (2007-2008)
Kinton, Sherrie (2004)
Lacy, Colleen (2004)
Lawley, Rae (2007)
McDuffie, Carrie (2004-2005)
McGee, Carla (2005)
McNeil, Jessie (2008)
McPhetridge, Cathy (2005)
Montigny, Mary (2005)
Moore, Tina "Boo" (2005)
Neal, Jen (2004-2005)
Owens, Donna (2007-2008)
Price, Nicee (2008)
Redden, Jessica (2005, 2007)
Reed, DeeDee (2007-2008)
Reon, Sidney (2004-2005, 2007)
Reusser, Konni (2007-2008)
Savage, Amanda (2007-2008)
Smith, DeeDee (2004-2005, 2007)
Smith, Melinda (2005)
Steward, Neccee (2008)
Stockstill, Helen (2004-2005, 2007-2008)
Stokes, Pam (2007)
Strickland, Chris (2005, 2007)
Swartzmiller, Bobby (2007-2008)
Tapley, Mallory (2007)
Taylor, April (2005)
Taylor, Lauren (2004)
Thigpen, Monica (2007-2008)
Thomas, Kisha (2004-2005, 2007)
Wagner, Teresa (2005)
Walton, Mary (2004-2005)
Wiggins, Shannon (2007-2008)
Williams, Ella (2007-2008)
Wright, Skyler (2008)
Zirlott, Erika (2007)

Harlan Red Devils

Year	League	Name	W	L	Conference	Division	DF	PR
2003	AWFL	Harlan Red Devils	0	2	--	--	--	--

Based in: Harlan, KY

4/19/2003	A	Lee County Predators	L	0	6	4/26/2003	H	Tennessee Mountaincats	L	0	36

Hawaii Legends

Year	League	Name	W	L	Conference	Division	DF	PR
2001	WAFL	Hawaii Legends	6	4	Pacific	Northwest	2	--
2002	WAFC	Hawaii Legends	1	0	--	--	--	--

Based in: Honolulu, HI

11/14/2001	A	California Quake	L	18	21		1/3/2002	A	Seattle Warbirds	L	7	14	
11/17/2001	A	San Diego Sunfire	L	10	20		1/5/2002	A	Rose City Wildcats	W	16	8	
11/29/2001	H	Los Angeles Lasers	W	34	28	*	1/13/2002	H	San Diego Sunfire	W	57	29	
12/2/2001	H	Los Angeles Lasers	W	7	6								
12/13/2001	H	Oakland Banshees	W	40	6		10/27/2002	H	Pacific Blast	W	72	7	E
12/16/2001	H	Oakland Banshees	W	35	8								
12/29/2001	A	Seattle Warbirds	L	0	22								

Hawaii Kaua'i Thunder

Year	League	Name	W	L	Conference	Division	DF	PR
1999	HWFL	Hawaii Kaua'i Thunder	0	1	--	--	--	--
2000	HWFL	Hawaii Kaua'i Thunder	0	1	--	--	--	--
		Total	0	2				

Based in: Lihue, HI

11/27/1999	H	Hawaiian Waves	L	0	61	5/13/2000	A	Hawaii Storm	L	0	44

Hawaii Storm

Year	League	Name	W	L	Conference	Division	DF	PR
1999	HWFL	Hawaiian Waves	1	0	--	--	--	--
2000	HWFL	Hawaii Storm	1	0	--	--	--	--
		Total	**2**	**0**				

Based in: Honolulu, HI

11/27/1999	A	Hawaii Kaua'i Thunder	W	61	0	5/13/2000	H	Hawaii Kaua'i Thunder	W	44	0

Hillsboro Hammerheads

Year	League		Name	W	L	Conference	Division	DF	PR
2014	IWFL	X	Hillsboro Hammerheads	0	2	--	--	--	--

Based in: Hillsboro, OR
Notes: Non-existent team

5/10/2014	A	Utah Jynx	L	0	1	5/31/2014	H	Utah Jynx	L	0	1

Holyoke Hurricanes

Year	League		Name	W	L	Conference	Division	DF	PR
2008	IWFL2		Holyoke Hurricanes	2	6	Northern	North Atlantic	4	--
2009	IWFL2		Holyoke Hurricanes	0	8	--	--	22	--
2010	IWFL2	X	Holyoke Hurricanes	0	2	--	--	--	--
			Total	**2**	**16**				

Based in: Holyoke, MA
Notes: Preceded by NWFA's Central Massachusetts Ravens; Forfeited entire 2010 season

4/12/2008	H	Montreal Blitz	L	10	47		4/11/2009	A	New England Intensity	L	0	34	
4/26/2008	H	Southern Maine Rebels	W	38	30		4/25/2009	H	Southern Maine Rebels	L	0	14	
5/3/2008	A	New England Intensity	L	0	48		5/2/2009	H	Montreal Blitz	L	0	48	
5/10/2008	A	Manchester Freedom	L	0	68		5/16/2009	H	New England Intensity	L	0	53	
5/17/2008	A	Montreal Blitz	L	6	41		5/17/2009	A	Montreal Blitz	L	0	1	
5/31/2008	A	Southern Maine Rebels	L	14	20		6/6/2009	A	Central PA Vipers	L	0	48	
6/7/2008	A	Pittsburgh Passion	L	6	54		6/7/2009	A	Erie Illusion	L	0	1	
6/14/2008	H	Connecticut Cyclones	W	1	0	N	6/13/2009	H	Montreal Blitz	L	0	1	
							4/24/2010	A	Montreal Blitz	L	0	1	
							5/1/2010	A	Manchester Freedom	L	0	1	

Houston Energy

Year	League	Name	W	L	Conference	Division	DF	PR
2000	WPFL	Houston Energy	7	2	American	West	1	**NC**
2001	WPFL	Houston Energy	8	0	--	--	1	NC
2002	WPFL	Houston Energy	11	0	American	--	1	**NC**
2003	WPFL	Houston Energy	7	2	National	South	2	--
2004	WPFL	Houston Energy	8	4	American	South	2	CC
2005	WPFL	Houston Energy	4	4	American	South	2	--
2006	WPFL	Houston Energy	7	2	National	Central	1	C
2007	WPFL	Houston Energy	8	2	National	Central	1	C
2009	IWFL	Houston Energy	2	6	Eastern	South Atlantic	4	--
2010	IWFL	Houston Energy	5	3	Western	Midwest	4	--
2011	IWFL	Houston Energy	6	3	Eastern	South Atlantic	1	S
2012	IWFL	Houston Energy	7	1	Eastern	South Atlantic	1	CC
2013	IWFL	Houston Energy	9	1	Western	Southwest	1	C
2014	IWFL	Houston Energy	9	2	Western	Southwest	1	C
2015	IWFL	Houston Energy	6	1	Western	Southwest	1	S
		Total	**104**	**33**				

Based in: Houston, TX   **Neutral sites:** Roswell, GA (N1); Round Rock, TX (N2); Rock Hill, SC (N3)

Houston Energy Game-By-Game Results

Date	H/A	Opponent	Result			
10/14/2000	A	Austin Rage	W	52	25	
10/21/2000	H	Austin Rage	W	30	20	
10/29/2000	A	Colorado Valkyries	L	6	62	
11/4/2000	A	Minnesota Vixen	L	8	30	
11/11/2000	H	Austin Rage	W	35	21	
11/18/2000	H	Oklahoma City Wildcats	W	21	0	
12/2/2000	H	Colorado Valkyries	W	13	0	S
12/16/2000	A	Minnesota Vixen	W	35	14	CC
1/20/2001	H	New England Storm	W	39	7	C
7/28/2001	A	Austin Rage	W	27	13	
8/4/2001	H	Austin Rage	W	25	0	
8/11/2001	H	New England Storm	W	1	0	
8/25/2001	A	Tampa Tempest	W	53	0	
9/8/2001	H	Tampa Tempest	W	51	0	
9/22/2001	A	New England Storm	W	33	0	
10/7/2001	H	Arizona Titans	W	55	7	I
10/20/2001	H	Austin Rage	W	47	14	C
8/3/2002		Dallas Diamonds	W	46	6	
8/10/2002		Arizona Titans	W	39	0	I
8/17/2002		Arizona Knighthawks	W	1	0	
9/7/2002		Syracuse Sting	W	40	6	
9/21/2002		Austin Rage	W	59	26	
9/28/2002		Los Angeles Amazons	W	1	0	
10/5/2002		Austin Rage	W	42	7	
10/12/2002		Dallas Diamonds	W	31	0	
10/19/2002		Dallas Diamonds	W	46	7	
10/26/2002		Arizona Knighthawks	W	6	0	CC
11/9/2002		Wisconsin Riveters	W	56	7	C
8/9/2003	A	Dallas Diamonds	L	12	14	
8/16/2003	A	Dallas Diamonds	W	39	14	
8/23/2003	A	So Cal Scorpions	W	41	0	
9/6/2003	H	San Diego Sunfire	W	62	22	
9/13/2003	H	Florida Stingrayz	W	57	20	
9/27/2003	H	Dallas Diamonds	W	38	27	
10/4/2003	A	Missouri Prowlers	W	1	0	
10/12/2003	H	So Cal Scorpions	W	75	14	
10/18/2003	A	Dallas Diamonds	L	7	10	
7/31/2004	A	Missouri Avengers	W	1	0	
8/14/2004	A	Dallas Diamonds	L	26	28	
8/21/2004	A	Indiana Speed	W	64	6	
8/28/2004	H	Dallas Diamonds	L	13	33	
9/11/2004	H	Missouri Avengers	W	38	8	
9/18/2004	A	New York Dazzles	W	68	0	
9/25/2004	H	Delaware Griffins	W	50	6	
10/9/2004	A	Long Beach Aftershock	L	9	18	
10/16/2004	H	Long Beach Aftershock	W	28	8	
10/23/2004	H	Northern Ice	W	21	14	
10/30/2004	A	Long Beach Aftershock	W	22	8	S
11/6/2004	A	Dallas Diamonds	L	14	25	CC
7/30/2005	A	Minnesota Vixen	W	40	0	
8/13/2005	A	So Cal Scorpions	L	13	28	
8/20/2005	A	Dallas Diamonds	L	18	21	
8/27/2005	H	Dallas Diamonds	L	31	49	
9/3/2005	H	So Cal Scorpions	W	14	13	
9/10/2005	H	New Mexico Burn	W	58	6	
10/8/2005	A	New Mexico Burn	W	76	6	
10/15/2005	H	Dallas Diamonds	L	27	38	
8/5/2006	A	So Cal Scorpions	W	28	6	
8/19/2006	A	Dallas Diamonds	L	21	31	
8/26/2006	H	Las Vegas Showgirlz	W	53	6	
9/2/2006	A	Minnesota Vixen	W	41	0	
9/9/2006	H	Dallas Diamonds	W	24	10	
9/16/2006	H	So Cal Scorpions	W	45	17	
9/23/2006	H	Minnesota Vixen	W	66	0	
10/21/2006	H	Wisconsin Wolves	W	68	0	CC
11/4/2006	N1	Dallas Diamonds	L	27	34	C
8/18/2007	A	Dallas Diamonds	L	6	14	
8/25/2007	A	New Mexico Burn	W	77	0	
9/8/2007	H	New Mexico Burn	W	63	0	
9/15/2007	A	Connecticut Cyclones	W	1	0	
9/29/2007	H	Wisconsin Wolves	W	27	6	
10/6/2007	H	Connecticut Cyclones	W	1	0	
10/13/2007	H	Dallas Diamonds	W	33	12	
10/20/2007	A	Wisconsin Wolves	W	33	0	
11/17/2007	H	Wisconsin Wolves	W	35	8	CC
12/1/2007	A	So Cal Scorpions	L	7	14	C

Continued on next page

Houston Energy Game-By-Game Results (continued)

Date	H/A	Opponent	Result			Date	H/A	Opponent	Result			
4/11/2009	A	Dallas Diamonds	L	0	69	5/4/2013	A	Arlington Impact	W	73	8	
4/18/2009	H	Atlanta Xplosion	L	7	38	5/11/2013	A	San Antonio Regulators	W	56	0	
4/25/2009	A	Orlando Mayhem	L	7	28	5/18/2013	H	Arlington Impact	W	55	8	
5/2/2009	H	Miami Fury	L	0	21	6/1/2013	A	DFW Xtreme	W	1	0	
5/9/2009	A	Shreveport Aftershock	W	40	6	6/8/2013	H	San Antonio Regulators	W	35	0	
5/23/2009	H	Shreveport Aftershock	W	49	0	6/22/2013	A	Arlington Impact	W	52	8	
6/6/2009	H	Dallas Diamonds	L	20	61	6/29/2013	A	DFW Xtreme	W	1	0	
6/13/2009	A	Dallas Diamonds	L	7	76	7/13/2013	H	Madison Blaze	W	30	0	S
4/3/2010	A	Dallas Diamonds	L	12	34	7/20/2013	H	Phoenix Phantomz	W	56	0	CC
4/10/2010	H	Louisiana Fuel	W	60	0	8/3/2013	N2	Carolina Phoenix	L	0	14	C
4/24/2010	A	H-Town Texas Cyclones	W	1	0	N	4/12/2014	A	Austin Outlaws	W	56	3	I
5/1/2010	A	Atlanta Xplosion	L	20	21	4/19/2014	A	Arlington Impact	W	41	12	
5/8/2010	H	Miami Fury	W	1	0	5/3/2014	H	Arlington Impact	W	24	14	
5/15/2010	A	Louisiana Fuel	W	30	0	5/10/2014	A	Phoenix Phantomz	W	62	13	
5/29/2010	H	H-Town Texas Cyclones	W	1	0	N	5/17/2014	H	San Antonio Regulators	W	1	0	
6/5/2010	H	Dallas Diamonds	L	36	44	5/31/2014	H	Houston Power	W	35	13	I
4/2/2011	H	North Texas Knockouts	W	50	14	6/7/2014	H	Arlington Impact	L	7	26	
4/9/2011	H	Atlanta Ravens	L	15	35	6/14/2014	A	San Antonio Regulators	W	1	0	
4/23/2011	A	North Texas Knockouts	W	40	14	6/28/2014	H	Phoenix Phantomz	W	90	26	S
4/30/2011	A	Monterrey Black Mambas	W	44	6	7/12/2014	A	Madison Blaze	W	53	0	CC
5/7/2011	H	North Texas Knockouts	W	34	12	7/26/2014	N3	Pittsburgh Passion	L	7	41	C
5/14/2011	A	Atlanta Ravens	L	6	39	4/11/2015	H	Austin Yellow Jackets	W	45	0	
6/4/2011	H	Monterrey Black Mambas	W	38	0	4/25/2015	H	San Antonio Regulators	W	14	0	
6/11/2011	H	Utah Jynx	W	22	17	I	5/2/2015	A	New Orleans Krewe	W	54	0	
6/25/2011	A	Atlanta Ravens	L	13	14	S	5/16/2015	A	Austin Yellow Jackets	W	14	12	
4/21/2012	H	Arlington Impact	W	35	0	6/6/2015	A	San Antonio Regulators	W	53	14	
4/28/2012	A	DFW Xtreme	W	19	14	I	6/13/2015	H	New Orleans Krewe	W	1	0	
5/5/2012	H	Arkansas Banshees	W	52	14	6/27/2015	H	Madison Blaze	L	7	41	S
5/26/2012	A	Arlington Impact	W	38	22							
6/9/2012	A	DFW Xtreme	W	30	0	I							
6/16/2012		Arkansas Banshees	W	56	30							
6/30/2012	H	Atlanta Xplosion	W	21	20	S							
7/14/2012		Montreal Blitz	L	16	28	CC							

Houston Energy Player Register (2014)

Ajayi, Shalon "A.J." (2014)
Bankett, Tysha (2014)
Bates, Johnika (2014)
Bender, Niki (2014)
Brown, Bo (2014)
Bryant, Tangie (2014)
Brydson, Alberta (2014)
Cantu, Laura (2014)
Cole, Tara (2014)
Criswell, Erica (2014)
Davis, Erma (2014)
De La Garza, Ashley (2014)
Ford, Emeral (2014)
Grayson, Angellica (2014)
Harris, Ebony (2014)
Ivey, Brandy (2014)
Jenkins, Odessa (2014)
Jones, Jay (2014)
King, Aundria (2014)
Lansdell, Laura (2014)
Little, Robin (2014)
Long, Camisha (2014)
Long, Julia (2014)
Martinez, April (2014)
Mitchell, Janice (2014)
Morris, Nicole (2014)
Newman, Kaci (2014)
Nickerson, Tonya (2014)
Prejean, Cindy (2014)
Rakestraw, Giovanni (2014)
Ricketts, Dez (2014)
Robinson, Holly (2014)
Ruelas, Shari (2014)
Shirley, Tana Shay (2014)
Singleton, Eshombi "Kash" (2014)
Smallwood, Toshiba (2014)
Summerville, Natasha "Taz" (2014)
Tatum, Jessica (2014)
Turner, Tiesha (2014)
Villa, Maria (2014)
Webb, Umeki (2014)
Williams, Mia (2014)
Winters, Kinesha (2014)

Houston Power

Year	League	Name	W	L	Conference	Division	DF	PR
2010	WFA	Houston Power	5	4	American	Southwest	3	--
2011	WFA	Houston Power	6	3	American	Gulf	1	Q
2012	WFA	Houston Power	4	4	American	Division 12 (Southwest)	3	--
2013	WFA	Houston Power	1	7	American	Division 9 (Southwest)	4	--
2014	WFA	Houston Power	6	4	American	Southwest	2	Q
2015	WFA	Houston Power	6	3	American	Southwest	3	BW
		Total	**28**	**25**				

Based in: Houston, TX
Notes: Preceded by H-Town Texas Cyclones

Houston Power Game-By-Game Results

Date	H/A	Opponent	W/L	PF	PA	Note
4/10/2010	A	Austin Outlaws	L	6	7	
4/17/2010	H	Lone Star Mustangs	L	13	32	
4/24/2010	A	New Orleans Blaze	W	39	6	
5/1/2010	A	Lone Star Mustangs	L	0	32	
5/8/2010	H	Monterrey Royal Eagles	W	53	7	
5/15/2010	H	Acadiana Zydeco	W	63	0	
5/22/2010	H	Monterrey Royal Eagles	W	43	0	
6/5/2010	H	Austin Outlaws	W	34	13	
6/19/2010	A	Austin Outlaws	L	15	48	
4/2/2011	H	New Orleans Blaze	W	40	0	
4/9/2011	A	Dallas Diamonds	L	14	39	
4/30/2011	H	Austin Outlaws	W	16	6	
5/14/2011	A	Lone Star Mustangs	L	6	14	
5/21/2011	A	Acadiana Zydeco	W	1	0	
6/4/2011	A	New Orleans Blaze	W	38	6	
6/11/2011	H	Lone Star Mustangs	W	12	0	
6/18/2011	H	Acadiana Zydeco	W	33	0	
6/25/2011	A	Dallas Diamonds	L	6	21	Q
4/14/2012	A	Gulf Coast Riptide	W	31	0	
4/28/2012	H	Dallas Diamonds	L	8	54	
5/5/2012	H	Austin Outlaws	W	28	0	
5/12/2012	A	Lone Star Mustangs	L	8	24	
5/19/2012	A	Dallas Diamonds	L	0	69	
6/2/2012	H	Lone Star Mustangs	L	14	28	
6/9/2012	H	Acadiana Zydeco	W	14	8	
6/16/2012	A	Austin Outlaws	W	30	0	
4/6/2013	H	Dallas Diamonds	L	6	41	
4/13/2013	H	Acadiana Zydeco	W	52	0	
4/20/2013	A	Dallas Diamonds	L	8	68	
4/27/2013	H	Austin Outlaws	L	14	19	
5/11/2013	A	Dallas Diamonds	L	0	1	
5/18/2013	H	Lone Star Mustangs	L	14	20	
6/1/2013	A	Lone Star Mustangs	L	12	26	
6/8/2013	A	Austin Outlaws	L	0	43	
4/5/2014	H	Austin Outlaws	L	8	17	
4/12/2014	A	Acadiana Zydeco	W	47	8	
4/19/2014	H	Louisiana Jazz	W	39	0	
5/3/2014	A	Louisiana Jazz	W	50	0	
5/10/2014	H	San Antonio Regulators	W	42	0	I
5/17/2014	H	Acadiana Zydeco	W	1	0	
5/31/2014	A	Houston Energy	L	13	35	I
6/7/2014	A	Austin Outlaws	L	7	8	
6/14/2014	H	Nebraska Stampede	W	35	0	W
6/21/2014	A	Kansas City Titans	L	2	43	Q
4/11/2015	H	Austin Outlaws	W	42	0	
4/18/2015	H	Arlington Impact	L	0	16	
5/2/2015	H	Acadiana Zydeco	W	43	0	
5/9/2015	A	Arkansas Wildcats	W	28	8	
5/16/2015	A	Dallas Elite	L	0	70	
5/30/2015	H	Arlington Impact	L	6	14	
6/6/2015	A	Acadiana Zydeco	W	22	0	
6/13/2015	H	South Texas Lady Crushers	W	72	0	
7/11/2015	H	Acadiana Zydeco	W	18	6	B

Houston Power Player Register (2010-2015)

Agee, Stacy (2011)
Alaniz, Corena (2014-2015)
Alexander, Tawana (2011-2012)
Ayotte, Donita (2015)
Babers, Rita (2012-2013)
Barbee, Lauren (2011)
Baxter, Anisha (2012-2015)
Baxter, Donna (2012-2014)
Bighorse, Courtney (2015)
Boyce, Amy (2010)
Boyd, Shaun (2012-2015)
Bravo, Tiffany (2010)
Broussard, Lessie (2014)
Brown, Claudia (2010-2015)
Brown, Cristie (2015)
Brown, Tobi (2011-2015)
Buck, Tyrhonda (2014)
Burnley, Catherine (2011-2012)
Bush, Ashley (2015)
Butterfield, Byrnne (2010)
Cain, Lauren (2012)
Campbell, Tam (2010)
Chavarria, Laura (2011-2012)
Clarke, Sheryl (2010-2011)
Claudio, Camesha (2013)
Collins, R.C. (2011)
Conway, Dita (2011)
Corpening, Kiyona (2010-2012)
Costello, Sarah (2012)
Cousins, Deaysha (2013)
Covin, Ruby (2010)
Davenport, Heather (2011)
Davidson, Davae (2010)
De Jongh, Hannah (2010)
Dennis, Thyra (2012-2013)
Dickerson, Amanda (2011)
Drennan, Amy (2010-2011)
Eitel, Alexis (2011)
Felder, Montoya (2015)
Foret, Jennifer (2010-2011)
Francis, Benita (2015)
Fugler, Conner (2010)
Garcia, Maria (2013)
Glass, Megan (2010-2015)
Gonzales, Racquel (2015)
Hackney, Charolette (2010)
Hall, Tawanna (2010)
Hamilton, Alphadeesha (2010-2012)
Hampton, Barbara (2013)
Hanks, Janay (2012)
Harper, Sharon (2012, 2014)
Hawkins, Halima (2011)
Hawkins, Taneeka (2014)
Hernandez, Stephanie (2013)
Hill, Ayanna (2014-2015)
Hill, Cheoka (2012)
Holcomb, Gina (2014)
Holiam, Emily (2010)
Holts, Tracy (2011)
Jacobs, Amanda (2010-2011)
Jenkins, Tamara (2015)
Jones, Stacey (2010)
Juarez, Cassie (2015)
Kadlitz, Jennifer (2010-2015)
Kellum, Andi (2011)
Kenney, Michele (2013-2014)
Kettle, Kate (2011)
Kullum, Andi (2010)
Lametrie, Christine (2010-2012)
Lee, Glenda (2013)
Leon, Liz (2011)
Lewis, Patrice (2010, 2013)
Matthews, Kisha (2011)
McPherson, Sparkle (2013-2014)
Moncada, Kellyn (2012)
Morris, Alicia (2015)
Morrow, Andrea (2010-2012)
Mulligan, Tina (2011)
Negrete, Sara (2013-2014)
Negron, Leslie (2011)
Newton, Tonya (2011-2012, 2014)
Nowlin, LaQuesha (2013)
Patrick, Miriam (2013)
Patterson, Karrion (2013)
Phillips, Tiffany (2010-2011, 2013-2015)
Pilgrim, Frankie (2010)
Pipkin, Johneicia (2014-2015)
Polk, Tabitha (2012, 2015)
Prater, Cindy (2012-2013)
Prytle, Tam (2011)
Roberts, Sue (2010)
Rock, Tiffany (2013)
Rogers, Tawana (2010, 2013, 2015)
Roquemore, Andrea (2013)
Rosemin, Ronda (2011)
Rosenthal, Nike (2011)
Salas, Evelyn (2010-2012)
Sanders, Patricia (2013-2014)
Sawyer, Charlene (2012-2015)
Shayib, Najat (2011)
Sjohdahl, Elin (2015)
Smallwood, Kim (2010-2013)
Smith, Tiffany (2012-2013)
Speakman, Sarah (2013)
Stephanson, Kiyana (2010-2013)
Stewart, Sarah (2015)
Stockton, Jummanah (2011)
Strong, Cat (2011-2012)
Strong, Kristeon (2011-2015)
Sutton, Alicia (2013-2015)

Continued on next page

Houston Power Player Register (continued)

Tate, Blessing (2014-2015)
Tatum, Jessica (2014)
Thibodeaux, Lisa (2011)
Thomas, A.J. (2010)
Thomas, Shacoya (2015)
Thomas, Tahari (2010-2015)
Thompson, Deundreia (2010)
Thompson, Frankey (2010)
Tolbert, Atim (2011-2012, 2014)
Townsend, Sissy (2011)
Tyler, Toni (2010)
Tyler, Valerie (2013-2015)
Untz, Brandi (2014)
Vasquez, April (2015)
Walker, Monique (2011)
Walker, Pauline (2011-2015)
Ward, Melissa (2011)
Ware, Tiffany (2015)
Washington, Byrena (2011-2015)
Watkins, Syreeta (2014)
Williams, Chechrystal (2015)
Williams, Kayla (2014)
Wilson, Jannelle (2011)
Winters, Natasha (2010-2011)
Wolf, Brandy (2012)
Woods, Kyshia (2013)
Yanko, Susie (2013)
Young, Bernice (2015)
Young, Tracy (2013)
Zabawa, Rachel (2015)
Zboril, Christine (2010-2011)

H-Town Texas Cyclones

Year	League	Name	W	L	Conference	Division	DF	PR
2008	NWFA	H-Town Texas Cyclones	11	1	Southern	Central	1	NC
2009	WFA	H-Town Texas Cyclones	2	6	American	Southwest	3	--
2010	IWFL	H-Town Texas Cyclones	0	8	Western	Midwest	5	--
		Total	**13**	**15**				

Based in: Houston, TX
Neutral site: Memphis, TN (N)
Notes: Forfeited entire 2010 season; Succeeded by Houston Power

4/19/2008	H	Austin Outlaws	W	27	20	
4/26/2008	H	Gulf Coast Herricanes	W	46	0	
5/10/2008	A	Oklahoma City Lightning	L	13	21	
5/17/2008	H	North Texas Fury	W	40	6	
5/24/2008	A	Austin Outlaws	W	35	14	
6/7/2008	A	Gulf Coast Herricanes	W	41	0	
6/14/2008	H	Oklahoma City Lightning	W	21	15	
6/21/2008	A	North Texas Fury	W	43	6	
6/28/2008	H	Oklahoma City Lightning	W	26	0	Q
7/5/2008	A	St. Louis Slam	W	25	13	S
7/12/2008	A	Los Angeles Amazons	W	34	14	CC
7/26/2008	N	West Michigan Mayhem	W	39	10	C

4/18/2009	H	Austin Outlaws	L	34	40	
4/25/2009	A	East Texas Saberkats	W	1	0	N
5/2/2009	A	Lone Star Mustangs	L	12	20	
5/16/2009	H	Lone Star Mustangs	L	12	14	
5/30/2009	H	East Texas Saberkats	W	1	0	N
6/6/2009	A	Austin Outlaws	L	20	42	
6/20/2009	H	Lone Star Mustangs	L	0	31	
6/27/2009	A	Austin Outlaws	L	7	29	
4/3/2010	H	Louisiana Fuel	L	0	1	
4/17/2010	A	Miami Fury	L	0	1	
4/24/2010	H	Houston Energy	L	0	1	
5/1/2010	H	Louisiana Fuel	L	0	1	
5/15/2010	H	Dallas Diamonds	L	0	1	
5/22/2010	A	Memphis Belles	L	0	1	
5/29/2010	A	Houston Energy	L	0	1	
6/5/2010	A	Louisiana Fuel	L	0	1	

H-Town Texas Cyclones Player Register (2008-2009)

Barnes, Ashley (2008-2009)
Bean, B. (2009)
Boyce, Amy (2009)
Bradley, Chiquita (2008-2009)
Bravo, Tiffany (2009)
Brett, Ethel (2008)
Brown, Claudia (2008-2009)
Brown, Tobi (2008-2009)
Butterfield, Byrnne (2009)
Campbell, Tam (2008)
Cates, Alice (2009)
Chandler, G. (2009)
Clark, G. (2009)
Closs, C. (2009)
Crosby, Renee (2008)
Davidson, Davae (2008)
Dixon, Candice (2008)
Dorsey, K. (2009)
Eitel, Alexis (2009)
Francis, Benita (2008)
Gallagher, Michelle (2008)
Gray, Lucretia (2008-2009)
Greenwood, Shonta (2008)
Griffin, Machalle (2008)
Griffin, Roxy (2008-2009)
Guillory, Chris (2008)
Gunter, E. (2009)
Gustave, Tricia (2008)
Hampton, Barbara (2009)
Harrison, M. (2009)
Hawkins, W. (2009)
Hill, Sabreen (2008)
Hobbs, A. (2009)
Holiam, Emily (2009)
Howard, J. (2009)
Hutchinson, Christina (2008)
Jones, Brandy (2008)
Jones, Stacey (2009)
Kadlitz, Jennifer (2008-2009)
Kindred, Pat (2008)
King, K. (2009)
Lametrie, Christine (2008-2009)
Lelo, Linda (2008)
Luna, Liz (2008)
Madu, Renita (2008-2009)
Major, C. (2009)
Matthews, Kisha (2009)
Mayden, E. (2009)
McCreary, S. (2009)
McCuin, Ashley (2008)
McIntosh, Raasin (2008-2009)
Mendietta, Melissa (2008)
Morris, Nicole (2008)
Peethnmnongsin, E. (2009)
Pierson, M. (2009)
Polk, Tabitha (2008-2009)
Price-Hardeman, Angela (2008)
Raven, Stacey (2008-2009)
Rogers, Tawana (2008-2009)
Roper, B. (2009)
Rusch, Deborah (2008)
Sawyer, Charlene (2008-2009)
Sharpe, J. (2009)
Smallwood, Kim (2008)
Smith, Celina (2008)
Sustaita, C. (2009)
Swannegan, Susanna (2008)
Thibodeaux, Lisa (2009)
Thomas, Tahari (2009)
Thrash, M. (2009)
Tyler, Toni (2008)
Ward, Melissa (2008-2009)
Wilson, Jannelle (2008)
Winters, Natasha (2008)
Zboril, Christine (2009)

Huntsville Tigers

Year	League	Name	W	L	Conference	Division	DF	PR
2009	IWFL2	Tennessee Valley Tigers	5	3	--	--	10	--
2010	IWFL2	Tennessee Valley Tigers	3	4	Eastern	Southeast	3	--
2011	IWFL	Tennessee Valley Tigers	1	7	Eastern	Mid South	5	--
2012	WSFL	Huntsville Tigers	6	3	American	South	1	CC
2013	WSFL	Huntsville Tigers	2	3	--	--	3	--
2014	IWFL	Huntsville Tigers	2	3	Eastern	South Atlantic	3	--
2015	IWFL	Huntsville Tigers	5	3	Eastern	South Atlantic	3	--
		Total	**24**	**26**				

Based in: Huntsville, AL
Notes: Preceded by NWFA's Alabama Renegades

Date	H/A	Opponent	W/L	PF	PA	
4/11/2009	A	Chattanooga Locomotion	L	0	46	
4/18/2009	H	Chattanooga Locomotion	L	14	32	
4/25/2009	H	Cape Fear Thunder	W	68	0	
5/2/2009	A	Louisiana Fuel	W	32	27	
5/16/2009	H	Louisville Nightmare	W	53	0	
5/23/2009	A	Clarksville Fox	W	23	0	
5/30/2009	A	Louisville Nightmare	W	54	0	
6/6/2009	H	Atlanta Xplosion	L	0	63	
4/3/2010	A	Clarksville Fox	L	6	36	
4/10/2010	H	Memphis Belles	L	0	28	
5/1/2010	H	Clarksville Fox	L	12	28	
5/8/2010	A	Louisiana Fuel	W	30	22	
5/15/2010	H	Carolina Phoenix	L	0	72	
5/22/2010	A	Louisville Nightmare	W	1	0	
5/29/2010	H	Louisville Nightmare	W	25	8	
4/9/2011	A	Memphis Belles	L	12	16	
4/16/2011	A	Clarksville Fox	L	6	32	
4/23/2011	H	Georgia Peachez	W	1	0	
5/7/2011	H	Memphis Belles	L	6	32	
5/14/2011	H	Clarksville Fox	L	6	12	
5/21/2011	H	Clarksville Fox	L	6	22	
5/28/2011	A	Chattanooga Locomotion	L	0	1	
6/11/2011	H	Atlanta Ravens	L	0	1	
4/28/2012	H	Memphis Dynasty	L	6	16	I
5/5/2012	H	Arkansas Rampage	W	32	0	
5/12/2012	A	Carolina Queens	L	19	22	I
6/2/2012	A	Arkansas Rampage	W	41	0	
6/9/2012	A	Cape Fear Thunder	W	40	0	
6/23/2012	H	Cape Fear Thunder	W	50	0	
6/30/2012	A	Tri-State Bruisers	W	1	0	
7/7/2012	H	Tri-State Bruisers	W	1	0	
7/28/2012	A	New Jersey Titans	L	7	25	CC
4/6/2013	H	Nashville Smashers	W	20	0	
4/13/2013	H	Memphis Dynasty	L	0	22	
4/20/2013	A	Arkansas Banshees	L	8	34	
4/27/2013	A	Atlanta Heartbreakers	W	19	16	
5/11/2013	H	Atlanta Xplosion	L	0	64	I
4/12/2014	A	Chattanooga Locomotion	W	30	16	
4/19/2014	H	Carolina Queens	L	30	32	
5/10/2014	A	Chattanooga Locomotion	W	34	16	
6/14/2014	A	Carolina Phoenix	L	0	52	
6/21/2014	A	Carolina Queens	L	0	1	
4/11/2015	A	Knoxville Lightning	W	55	8	
4/18/2015	A	Carolina Queens	L	0	16	
5/2/2015	A	Tennessee Train	W	34	16	
5/9/2015	H	Knoxville Lightning	W	46	0	
5/16/2015	A	Knoxville Lightning	W	52	0	
5/23/2015	A	Tennessee Train	W	42	22	
5/30/2015	H	Carolina Queens	L	18	20	
6/13/2015	H	Tennessee Train	L	6	32	

Huntsville Tigers Player Register (2014-2015)

Atkins, Franchesca (2014)
Brady, Jhanae (2015)
Buchanan, Aujzhane (2014)
Campbell, Amanda (2014)
Clements, Brittany (2014)
Conley, Kayla (2014)
Darnell, Natalie (2014)
Ebert, Kirsten (2015)
Ellis, Amanda (2014)
Garcia, Megan (2015)
Garner, Chelsey (2014)
Graham, Crystal (2014-2015)
Hardge, Brittany (2014)
Herron, Chasity (2014)
Jackson, Monique (2014)
Ketcham, Ruth (2014-2015)
McCord, Domonique (2014)
McRath, Jessica (2015)
Nelson, Aquie (2015)
Nobles, Asia (2014)
Palmer, Whitney (2014-2015)
Parker, Ashlee (2014-2015)
Patton, Margaret (2014)
Peebles, Tiffany (2015)
Perkins, Enjoli (2014)
Phillips, Skylar (2015)
Richardson, Andrea Bailey (2015)
Richardson, Molly (2015)
Simon, Nichelle (2014)
Smith, Brandie (2015)
Truitt, Jayme (2014)
Truss, Olivia (2014)
Tupulua, Jacqueline (2015)
Vann, Ashley (2014)
Wheeler, Shanice Simba (2015)
Wright, Renae (2015)

Indiana Speed

Year	League	Name	W	L	Conference	Division	DF	PR
2002	WPFL	Indiana Speed	4	4	National	--	3	--
2003	WPFL	Indiana Speed	6	3	American	North	2	--
2004	WPFL	Indiana Speed	3	7	National	North	4	--
2005	WPFL	Indiana Speed	7	4	National	North	1	S
2006	WPFL	Indiana Speed	7	2	National	North	1	S
2007	WPFL	Indiana Speed	4	5	National	North	1	S
2009	WFA	Indiana Speed	6	3	National	Central	2	S
2010	WFA	Indiana Speed	5	3	National	Central	2	--
		Total	**42**	**31**				

Based in: Indianapolis, IN
Notes: Succeeded by Indy Crash

Date	H/A	Opponent	Result	Score	
8/17/2002		Syracuse Sting	L	0	30
8/24/2002		Minnesota Vixen	W	11	6
8/31/2002		New England Storm	L	28	29
9/7/2002		Missouri Prowlers	W	61	0
9/14/2002		Wisconsin Riveters	L	13	26
9/21/2002		Wisconsin Riveters	L	6	27
10/12/2002		New England Storm	W	37	0
10/19/2002		Missouri Prowlers	W	55	0
8/2/2003	A	Minnesota Vixen	W	26	0
8/9/2003	H	Minnesota Vixen	W	46	13
8/16/2003	H	Northern Ice	L	10	24
8/23/2003	A	Missouri Prowlers	W	1	0
8/30/2003	H	Syracuse Sting	W	22	7
9/13/2003	H	Dayton Rebellion	W	35	6
9/20/2003	H	Florida Stingrayz	L	21	44
10/4/2003	A	Dayton Rebellion	W	40	20
10/11/2003	A	Northern Ice	L	13	58
7/31/2004	H	Minnesota Vixen	W	14	12
8/7/2004	A	Minnesota Vixen	L	24	26
8/14/2004	A	Toledo Reign	L	26	28
8/21/2004	H	Houston Energy	L	6	64
8/28/2004	A	Northern Ice	L	0	71
9/4/2004	H	Syracuse Sting	W	46	16
9/11/2004	H	Northern Ice	L	20	42
9/18/2004	A	Missouri Avengers	W	1	0
10/2/2004	A	Syracuse Sting	L	0	25
10/16/2004	H	Northern Ice	L	19	35
7/30/2005	A	Toledo Reign	L	20	26 *
8/13/2005	H	Minnesota Vixen	L	6	7
8/20/2005	H	Cape Fear Thunder	W	44	8
8/27/2005	A	Delaware Griffins	W	20	0
9/3/2005	A	Carolina Queens	W	42	6
9/10/2005	A	Minnesota Vixen	L	13	18
9/17/2005	H	Toledo Reign	W	21	10
9/24/2005	H	Carolina Queens	W	55	8
10/8/2005	A	Carolina Queens	W	66	8
10/15/2005	H	Minnesota Vixen	W	26	14
10/28/2005	H	Minnesota Vixen	L	14	19 S
7/22/2006	H	Wisconsin Wolves	L	0	20
7/29/2006	H	Minnesota Vixen	W	14	0
8/12/2006	A	Minnesota Vixen	W	14	7
8/19/2006	A	Toledo Reign	W	13	6
9/2/2006	A	Wisconsin Wolves	W	13	0
9/9/2006	H	Carolina Queens	W	51	0
9/16/2006	H	Toledo Reign	W	18	8
9/23/2006	A	Carolina Queens	W	41	0
10/7/2006	H	Wisconsin Wolves	L	18	20 S
8/18/2007	H	Minnesota Vixen	W	16	0
8/25/2007	A	Wisconsin Wolves	L	0	34
9/1/2007	A	Empire State Roar	L	0	28
9/15/2007	H	Wisconsin Wolves	L	0	29
9/29/2007	A	Toledo Reign	W	20	7
10/6/2007	H	Carolina Queens	W	53	0
10/13/2007	A	Minnesota Vixen	L	0	7
10/20/2007	A	Carolina Queens	W	43	0
11/3/2007	A	Wisconsin Wolves	L	8	27 S
4/18/2009	H	Dayton Diamonds	W	62	8
4/25/2009	A	Fort Wayne Flash	W	52	0
5/2/2009	A	Toledo Reign	W	60	0
5/16/2009	H	West Michigan Mayhem	L	15	20
5/30/2009	H	Fort Wayne Flash	W	14	7
6/6/2009	A	Dayton Diamonds	W	56	0
6/20/2009	H	Toledo Reign	W	58	0
6/27/2009	A	West Michigan Mayhem	L	0	21
7/11/2009	A	Philadelphia Liberty Belles (II)	L	9	19 S
4/10/2010	H	Kentucky Karma	W	41	0
4/17/2010	A	Cincinnati Sizzle	W	40	0
4/24/2010	H	St. Louis Slam	L	6	13
5/1/2010	A	West Michigan Mayhem	L	13	45
5/8/2010	A	Kentucky Karma	W	54	6
5/22/2010	H	Dayton Diamonds	W	54	0
6/5/2010	H	Cincinnati Sizzle	W	62	0
6/19/2010	A	St. Louis Slam	L	14	16

Indiana Speed Player Register (2009-2010)

Abraham, Terri (2010)
Anderson, Jamie (2010)
Anderson, Jenessa (2010)
Bagg, Danielle (2009-2010)
Beisel, Ellen (2009-2010)
Beverly, DaNaesha (2009)
Cash, Ebony (2009-2010)
Crossland, Annie (2010)
Diggle, Laura (2009)
Evans, Frances (2010)
Filburn, Jennifer (2010)
Flood, Kate (2009)
Flores, Nicho (2009)
Fultz, Kara (2010)
Furman, Angelita (2009-2010)
Grosvenor, Eileen (2009-2010)
Hall, Crystal (2009)
Hedgspeth, April (2009)
Hicks, Virginia "Vee" (2009-2010)
Johnson, Ashley (2010)

Continued on next page

Indiana Speed Player Register (continued)

Johnson, Erika (2009-2010)
Kaszas, Lea (2009-2010)
LeShore, Chasity (2009-2010)
List, Kylee (2010)
Longcore, Cassie (2009-2010)
Madden, Tiffany (2010)
Martini, Christa (2009-2010)
McAfee, Molly (2009)
McDowell, Ashley (2009-2010)
McKiernan-Allen, Moriah (2009-2010)
Meinhold, Jill (2010)
Messenger, Cayla (2009-2010)
Miller, Dana (2009-2010)
Mills, Melissa (2009)
Morgan, Asia (2009-2010)
Morgan, Holly (2010)
Officer, Lisa (2010)
Pardue, Alicia (2010)
Pierce, Caitlyn (2010)
Pilkington, Nikole (2009)
Priest, April (2009-2010)
Rorick, Liz (2009-2010)
Schmidt, Cynthia (2010)
Shrum, Danielle (2009)
Sklar, Lisa (2009-2010)
Smith, Jen (2010)
St. Andrew, Candise (2010)
Stringfellow, Chris (2009-2010)
Sturm, Chris (2009)
Taylor, Adrienne (2010)
Thomas, Kiva (2009-2010)
Walker, Alicia (2009)
Watson, Cassandra (2010)
Watson, Lisa (2009)
Wolfe, Rochelle (2009)
Wright, Shanon (2009)

Indiana Thunder

Year	League	Name	W	L	Conference	Division	DF	PR
2002	NWFA	South Bend Hawks	0	8	--	Great Lakes	4	--
2003	NWFA	Indiana Thunder	0	8	Northern	Great Lakes	5	--
2004	NWFA	Indiana Thunder	2	6	Northern	Great Lakes	6	--
2005	NWFA	Indiana Thunder	0	5	Northern	--	16	--
		Total	2	27				

Based in: South Bend, IN

4/20/2002		Cleveland Fusion	L	0	39	4/3/2004	H	Southwest Michigan Jaguars	L	0	1
5/4/2002		Southwest Michigan Jaguars	L	0	30	4/24/2004	A	Toledo Spitfire	L	14	32
5/18/2002		Detroit Danger	L	16	41	5/1/2004	H	Wisconsin Riveters	W	30	0
5/25/2002		Southwest Michigan Jaguars	L	0	20	5/8/2004	A	Wisconsin Riveters	W	31	0
6/8/2002		Cleveland Fusion	L	16	40	5/15/2004	H	Toledo Spitfire	L	8	18
6/15/2002		Detroit Danger	L	0	33	5/22/2004	A	Cleveland Fusion	L	8	46
6/22/2002		Southwest Michigan Jaguars	L	8	33	5/29/2004	H	Detroit Demolition	L	0	82
6/29/2002		Cleveland Fusion	L	0	20	6/5/2004	A	Columbus Comets	L	0	90
4/12/2003	H	Toledo Spitfire	L	28	32	4/23/2005	H	Cincinnati Sizzle	L	0	1
4/26/2003	H	Detroit Demolition	L	18	90	4/30/2005	A	Columbus Comets	L	0	75
5/3/2003	A	Cleveland Fusion	L	0	90	5/14/2005	A	Kentucky Karma	L	0	1
5/10/2003	A	Southwest Michigan Jaguars	L	12	81	6/4/2005	H	Milwaukee Momentum	L	0	1
5/17/2003	H	Cleveland Fusion	L	6	78	6/18/2005	H	Cleveland Fusion	L	0	1
5/31/2003	H	Southwest Michigan Jaguars	L	0	57						
6/7/2003	A	Detroit Demolition	L	0	105						
6/14/2003	A	Toledo Spitfire	L	8	30						

Partial Indiana Thunder Player Register (2004)

Amor, Sarah (2004)
Brooker, Tonual (2004)
Carpenter, Amber (2004)
Cincoski, Katie (2004)
Glanders, Larra (2004)
Johnson, Keshia (2004)
Knepper, Rhonda (2004)
Levenhagen, Jane (2004)
Murray, Ashley (2004)
Parker, Valerie (2004)
Williams, Kari (2004)

Indianapolis Chaos

Year	League		Name	W	L	Conference	Division	DF	PR
2006	IWFL	X	Indianapolis Chaos	1	6	--	--	--	--
2008	NWFA		Indianapolis Chaos	1	7	Northern	Midwest	2	--
			Total	2	13				

Based in: Indianapolis, IN
Notes: Preceded by NWFA's Indianapolis SaberKatz

Indianapolis Chaos Game-By-Game Results

Date	H/A	Opponent	W/L	PF	PA		Date	H/A	Opponent	W/L	PF	PA
4/29/2006	A	New York Sharks	L	0	73		4/19/2008	H	Tree Town Spitfire	L	0	1
5/6/2006	A	Kansas City Storm	L	0	77		4/26/2008	H	Minnesota Vixen	L	0	40
5/20/2006	A	Baton Rouge Wildcats	L	12	36		5/10/2008	H	Fort Wayne Flash	L	0	58
5/27/2006	H	Iowa Crush	L	12	50		5/17/2008	A	Dayton Diamonds	L	8	14
6/3/2006	A	Kansas City Storm	L	0	85		5/24/2008	A	Tree Town Spitfire	L	0	12
6/10/2006	H	Carolina Cardinals	W	1	0		5/31/2008	A	Minnesota Vixen	L	6	62
6/17/2006	A	Baton Rouge Wildcats	L	0	1		6/14/2008	A	Fort Wayne Flash	L	6	67
							6/21/2008	H	Dayton Diamonds	W	12	6

Indianapolis Chaos Player Register (2008)

Adams, Angel (2008)
Arnold, Stephanie (2008)
Conway, Angela (2008)
Cullens, Sonja (2008)
Daniels, Pam (2008)
Eldridge, Donya (2008)
Farman, Angelique (2008)
Forest, Shamika (2008)
Hale, Katina (2008)
Huntzinger, Briana (2008)
Jackson, Josette (2008)
Johnson, Erika (2008)
McDowell, Ashley (2008)
Motz, Kristen (2008)
Rorick, Liz (2008)
Sanders, Keri (2008)
Shrum, Danielle (2008)
Shupe, Crystal (2008)
Sisler, Dawn (2008)
Tyler, Becky (2008)
Watson, Cassandra (2008)
Williams, Regina (2008)
Wydock, Valarie (2008)

Indianapolis SaberKatz

Year	League	Name	W	L	Conference	Division	DF	PR
2005	NWFA	Indianapolis SaberKatz	0	8	Northern	--	20	--

Based in: Indianapolis, IN
Notes: Succeeded by IWFL's Indianapolis Chaos

Date	H/A	Opponent	W/L	PF	PA		Date	H/A	Opponent	W/L	PF	PA
4/16/2005	H	Pittsburgh Passion	L	0	54		5/21/2005	H	Kansas City Krunch	L	0	52
4/23/2005	A	Cleveland Fusion	L	0	65		5/28/2005	A	Southwest Michigan Jaguars	L	0	60
4/30/2005	H	St. Louis Slam	L	0	46		6/4/2005	A	St. Louis Slam	L	0	102
5/14/2005	A	Milwaukee Momentum	L	0	65		6/18/2005	A	Detroit Demolition	L	0	1

Indianapolis Saberkatz Player Register (2005)

Arns, Laura (2005)
Carter, Crystal (2005)
Carter, Rana (2005)
Caruthers, Jenetta (2005)
Clark, Sherri (2005)
Conway, Angela (2005)
Crawford, Clarinda (2005)
Cullens, Sonja (2005)
Duncan, Anne (2005)
Farmer, Kelly (2005)
Gordy, Christy (2005)
Grier, Danielle (2005)
Hawes-Tooke, Sharon (2005)
Hicks, LaJuana (2005)
Hyche, Holli (2005)
Keyes, Charmin (2005)
Lewis, Angie (2005)
Malone, Jamica (2005)
Mann, Laurie (2005)
Miller, Tiffany (2005)
Mitchell, Christie (2005)
Phillips, Deanna (2005)
Reed, Lori (2005)
Rogers, Lori (2005)
Rorick, Liz (2005)
Sanders, Keri (2005)
Sharp, LaTrice (2005)
Shupe, Crystal (2005)
Simmons, Kinyana (2005)
Sisler, Dawn (2005)
Stringham, Missy (2005)
Taylor, Chiena (2005)
Wagner, Tammy (2005)
Whitaker, Kelly (2005)
Witherspoon, Lakeia (2005)

Indianapolis Vipers

Year	League	Name	W	L	Conference	Division	DF	PR
2001	WAFL	Indianapolis Vipers	6	4	Atlantic	Central	1	S
2002	WAFL-WFA	Indianapolis Vipers	9	3	Central	--	1	C
		Total	**15**	**7**				

Based in: Indianapolis, IN   **Neutral site:** Birmingham, AL (N)

Indianapolis Vipers Game-By-Game Results

Date	H/A	Opponent	W/L	PF	PA	Note
10/27/2001	A	Minnesota Vixen	L	14	21	I
11/3/2001	H	Minnesota Vixen	W	18	7	I
11/17/2001	H	Alabama Slammers	W	52	6	
11/24/2001	H	Jacksonville Dixie Blues	W	1	0	
12/1/2001	A	Orlando Fire	L	20	42	
12/15/2001	H	Alabama Slammers	W	44	8	
12/22/2001	A	New Orleans Voodoo Dolls	W	44	6	
1/5/2002	H	Orlando Fire	L	14	38	
1/19/2002	A	Alabama Slammers	W	36	0	
1/26/2002	H	Jacksonville Dixie Blues	L	32	38	S
10/12/2002	A	Birmingham Steel Magnolias	W	20	14	
10/19/2002	A	New Orleans Voodoo Dolls	W	1	0	N
10/26/2002	A	Georgia Enforcers	W	1	0	
11/3/2002	H	South Carolina Crusaders	L	34	54	
11/9/2002	H	Birmingham Steel Magnolias	W	14	8	
11/16/2002	A	South Carolina Crusaders	W	20	15	
11/23/2002	H	Georgia Enforcers	W	1	0	
12/7/2002	H	New Orleans Voodoo Dolls	W	1	0	N
12/14/2002	A	Jacksonville Dixie Blues	L	6	33	
12/21/2002	H	Tampa Bay Force	W	1	0	
1/11/2003	H	Birmingham Steel Magnolias	W	38	6	CC
1/18/2003	N	Jacksonville Dixie Blues	L	20	68	C

Indy Crash

Year	League	Name	W	L	Conference	Division	DF	PR
2011	WFA	Indy Crash	8	3	National	North Central	1	CC
2012	WFA	Indy Crash	6	4	National	Division 6 (Great Lakes)	2	Q
2013	WFA	Indy Crash	2	6	National	Division 4 (Great Lakes)	4	--
2014	WFA	Indy Crash	6	4	National	Great Lakes	2	W-BW
2015	WFA	Indy Crash	5	3	National	Great Lakes	3	--
		Total	**27**	**20**				

Based in: Indianapolis, IN
Neutral site: Chicago, IL (N)
Notes: Preceded by Indiana Speed

Date	H/A	Opponent	W/L	PF	PA	Note
4/9/2011	A	St. Louis Slam	L	6	43	
4/16/2011	H	Detroit Dark Angels	W	36	6	
4/23/2011	A	Cincinnati Sizzle	W	60	21	
4/30/2011	H	Kentucky Karma	W	77	0	
5/7/2011	A	Cincinnati Sizzle	W	60	21	
5/14/2011	A	Toledo Reign	W	34	0	
5/21/2011	A	Kentucky Karma	W	77	0	
6/18/2011	H	Chicago Force	L	18	77	
6/25/2011	H	Atlanta Heartbreakers	W	47	0	Q
7/9/2011	A	Jacksonville Dixie Blues	W	42	0	S
7/16/2011	A	Boston Militia	L	18	46	CC
4/14/2012	H	Derby City Dynamite	W	2	0	
4/28/2012	H	Chicago Force	L	0	72	
5/5/2012	H	Cincinnati Sizzle	W	56	0	
5/12/2012	A	Derby City Dynamite	W	18	14	
5/19/2012	A	West Michigan Mayhem	L	33	39	
6/2/2012	A	Chicago Force	L	0	71	
6/9/2012	H	West Michigan Mayhem	W	34	7	
6/16/2012	A	Toledo Reign	W	28	7	
6/23/2012	H	Toledo Reign	W	52	35	W
6/30/2012	A	Chicago Force	L	14	70	Q
4/6/2013	A	Derby City Dynamite	W	48	6	
4/13/2013	H	Detroit Dark Angels	W	22	6	
4/20/2013	A	Chicago Force	L	6	66	
4/27/2013	H	West Michigan Mayhem	L	12	17	
5/4/2013	A	Detroit Dark Angels	L	0	6	
5/11/2013	H	Columbus Comets	L	7	26	
5/18/2013	H	Chicago Force	L	20	82	
6/1/2013	A	West Michigan Mayhem	L	10	16	
4/12/2014	A	Chicago Force	L	6	48	
4/19/2014	H	Detroit Dark Angels	W	36	6	
4/26/2014	A	Cleveland Fusion	L	0	7	
5/3/2014	H	Chicago Force	L	6	36	
5/10/2014	A	West Michigan Mayhem	W	33	13	
5/17/2014	H	Derby City Dynamite	W	19	0	
5/31/2014	H	Cincinnati Sizzle	W	68	0	
6/7/2014	A	Detroit Dark Angels	W	35	7	
6/14/2014	A	Cleveland Fusion	L	32	38	W
8/2/2014	N	Seattle Majestics	W	26	12	B
4/11/2015	H	Detroit Dark Angels	W	18	14	
4/18/2015	A	Derby City Dynamite	W	31	6	
4/25/2015	A	Cleveland Fusion	L	0	35	
5/2/2015	H	Minnesota Machine	W	32	6	
5/9/2015	A	Chicago Force	L	7	62	
5/16/2015	A	Detroit Dark Angels	W	29	6	
6/6/2015	H	Chicago Force	L	7	60	
6/13/2015	H	Derby City Dynamite	W	41	0	

Indy Crash Player Register (2011-2015)

Abraham, Terri (2011-2014)
Adams, Megan (2012)
Allen, Jen (2011, 2013)
Anderson, Jenessa (2011-2015)
Babb, Katrina (2015)
Barth, Claire (2011-2013)
Beeler, Jessica (2012-2015)
Beisel, Ellen (2011-2015)
Chang, Joice (2012-2013)
Christiansen, Brandi (2014)
Cloyd, Brittany (2013)
Coan, Tammy (2013)
Creed, Konnie (2011)
Crenshaw, Anzia (2015)
Crossland, Annie (2011-2012, 2014)
Davis, Bryce (2013-2014)
Davis, Katrina (2012-2014)
Davis, Kristen (2015)
Day, Jen (2015)
Deckard, Abby (2014)
Del Rio Gabiola, Irune (2015)
Ervin, Jennipher (2012)
Fox, Christy (2011-2015)
Fultz, Kara (2011-2015)
Furman, Angelita (2011-2015)
Greene, Courtney (2012)
Harris, Marie (2014-2015)
Harris, Tekoa (2011-2012)
Heinrich, Nicole (2012-2013, 2015)

Continued on next page

Indy Crash Player Register (continued)

Hicks, Ashley (2012)
Hicks, Virginia "Vee" (2011-2012, 2014)
Holcomb, Brittany (2013)
Horton, Cobre (2011)
Hulse, Shelby (2015)
Jensen, Audrey (2015)
Johnson, Erika (2011-2015)
Johnson, Sasha (2011)
Jones, Danielle (2012)
Kaszas, Brooke (2011)
Kaszas, Lea (2011-2015)
King, Aundrea (2012)
Langley, Brittany (2012-2015)
Lauray, Alexandria (2014)
Madden, Tiffany (2011)
Martini, Christa (2012, 2015)

McDaniel, Emily (2011-2013)
McDowell, Ashley (2014-2015)
McKiernan-Allen, Moriah (2011-2012)
Meinhold, Jill (2011-2013)
Mermelstein, Sharon (2014)
Messenger, Cayla (2011)
Miller, Aspree (2015)
Miller, Dana (2011, 2013-2015)
Moore, Sara (2013)
Morgan, Asia (2011, 2014-2015)
Morgan, Trisha (2013-2015)
Nance, Leslie (2014-2015)
Powell, Courtney (2011, 2013-2015)
Priest, April (2011-2013)
Rorick, Liz (2011-2012)
Rupp, Mimi (2011)

Sanders, Tawanna "Tee" (2013-2015)
Schmidt, Cynthia (2012)
Sklar, Lisa (2011)
Smith, Alexis (2013)
Smith, Rachel (2013-2014)
St. Andrew, Candise (2011)
Thomas, Kiva (2012-2015)
Vautaw, Emily (2013)
Watkins, Jenn (2011-2015)
Watson, Lisa (2011-2015)
Wells, Mandisha (2012)
Whitson, Lalaynva (2013)
Whitted, Julia (2012)
Wilson, Anna (2012-2013)
Wilson, Roxy (2012-2015)

Iowa Crush

Year	League		Name	W	L	Conference	Division	DF	PR
2004	IWFL	X	Des Moines Courage	1	3	--	--	--	--
2005	IWFL	X	Des Moines Courage	4	6	--	--	--	--
2006	IWFL	X	Iowa Crush	4	4	--	--	--	--
2007	IWFL		Iowa Crush	2	6	Western	Midwest	3	--
2008	IWFL		Iowa Crush	0	8	Western	Mid South	3	--
2009	IWFL2		Iowa Crush	0	8	--	--	21	--
2010	IWFL2		Iowa Crush	3	5	Western	Midwest	5	--
2011	IWFL		Iowa Crush	3	5	Western	Midwest	3	--
2012	IWFL		Iowa Crush	4	5	Western	Midwest	3	BQ
2013	IWFL		Iowa Crush	2	6	Western	Midwest	4	--
2014	IWFL		Iowa Crush	4	5	Western	Midwest	4	--
2015	IWFL		Iowa Crush	2	6	Western	Midwest	4	--
			Total	**29**	**67**				

Based in: Des Moines, IA

Date		Opponent				
4/3/2004	A	Chicago Force	L	0	50	
4/17/2004	H	Memphis Matrix	L	0	30	
4/24/2004	H	Chicago Force	L	0	40	
5/29/2004	A	Detroit Predators	W	30	6	
4/2/2005	H	Kansas City Storm	W	50	20	
4/16/2005	A	Detroit Predators	L	12	20	
4/23/2005	H	Chicago Force	L	0	36	
4/30/2005	H	Kansas City Storm	W	30	18	
5/7/2005	H	Detroit Predators	L	14	26	
5/14/2005	A	Detroit Predators	L	0	25	
5/28/2005	A	Kansas City Storm	L	6	25	
6/4/2005	A	Dallas Revolution	W	1	0	N
6/11/2005	A	Chicago Force	L	0	58	
6/18/2005	H	Dallas Revolution	W	1	0	N
4/29/2006	A	Chicago Force	L	8	26	
5/6/2006	A	Detroit Demolition	L	8	60	
5/13/2006	H	Detroit Predators	W	14	6	
5/20/2006	H	Chicago Force	L	6	20	
5/27/2006	A	Indianapolis Chaos	W	50	12	
6/10/2006	H	Kansas City Storm	W	28	6	
6/17/2006	A	Detroit Demolition	L	0	65	
6/24/2006	H	Detroit Predators	W	48	0	
4/28/2007	H	Chicago Force	L	6	27	
5/5/2007	H	Detroit Demolition	L	0	59	
5/12/2007	A	Kansas City Storm	L	12	25	
5/26/2007	H	Detroit Predators	W	26	8	
6/2/2007	A	Chicago Force	L	0	33	
6/9/2007	H	Detroit Demolition	L	0	69	
6/16/2007	A	Detroit Predators	W	14	6	
6/23/2007	H	Kansas City Storm	L	0	19	
4/12/2008	H	Wisconsin Warriors	L	7	30	
4/19/2008	A	Kansas City Tribe	L	6	19	
4/26/2008	A	Detroit Demolition	L	0	53	
5/3/2008	H	Kansas City Tribe	L	0	6	
5/17/2008	A	Dallas Diamonds	L	0	62	
5/24/2008	H	Chicago Force	L	0	56	
6/7/2008	H	Detroit Demolition	L	0	73	
6/14/2008	A	Kansas City Tribe	L	0	49	
4/11/2009	H	Chicago Force	L	0	54	
4/18/2009	A	Kansas City Tribe	L	0	62	
4/25/2009	A	Wisconsin Warriors	L	0	30	
5/2/2009	H	Clarksville Fox	L	0	14	
5/16/2009	A	Minnesota Vixen	L	20	38	
5/23/2009	A	Wisconsin Warriors	L	0	42	
6/6/2009	H	Minnesota Vixen	L	9	14	
6/13/2009	A	Clarksville Fox	L	12	22	

Continued on next page

Iowa Crush Game-By-Game Results (continued)

Date	H/A	Opponent	Result	PF	PA	Note
4/3/2010	H	Kansas City Tribe	L	0	77	
4/10/2010	A	Minnesota Vixen	W	35	14	
4/17/2010	A	Louisiana Fuel	W	16	14	
5/1/2010	H	Minnesota Vixen	W	37	0	
5/8/2010	H	Wisconsin Wolves	L	6	12	
5/15/2010	A	Wisconsin Warriors	L	0	40	
5/22/2010	A	Wisconsin Wolves	L	16	22	
6/5/2010	H	Wisconsin Warriors	L	0	28	
4/9/2011	A	Minnesota Vixen	W	20	6	
4/23/2011	A	Wisconsin Warriors	L	6	43	
4/30/2011	H	Madison Cougars	L	6	12	
5/7/2011	H	Minnesota Vixen	W	26	14	
5/14/2011	A	Madison Cougars	L	6	13	
5/28/2011	H	Wisconsin Warriors	L	0	41	
6/4/2011	H	Minnesota Vixen	W	38	12	
6/11/2011	A	Wisconsin Warriors	L	0	44	
4/14/2012	H	Wisconsin Warriors	L	8	28	
4/21/2012	A	Rockford Riveters	W	66	0	
5/5/2012	H	Madison Cougars	L	12	20	
5/12/2012	A	Wisconsin Warriors	L	26	50	
5/19/2012	H	Rockford Riveters	W	58	6	
5/26/2012	A	Minnesota Vixen	W	36	30	
6/2/2012	A	Madison Cougars	L	0	25	
6/9/2012	H	Minnesota Vixen	W	29	12	
6/30/2012		Madison Cougars	L	0	34	BQ
4/27/2013	H	Wisconsin Warriors	L	6	35	
5/4/2013	A	Madison Blaze	L	0	41	
5/11/2013	A	Rockford Riveters	W	1	0	N
5/25/2013	H	Minnesota Vixen	L	0	6	
6/1/2013	A	Wisconsin Warriors	L	0	30	
6/8/2013	H	Rockford Riveters	W	1	0	N
6/15/2013	H	Madison Blaze	L	6	41	
6/29/2013	A	Minnesota Vixen	L	6	26	
4/12/2014	H	Madison Blaze	L	6	7	
4/19/2014	A	Wisconsin Warriors	L	8	20	
5/3/2014	H	Missouri Thundercats	W	1	0	N
5/10/2014	A	Minnesota Vixen	W	14	6	
5/17/2014	H	Wisconsin Warriors	L	13	18	
5/31/2014	A	Madison Blaze	L	0	27	
6/7/2014	H	Missouri Thundercats	W	1	0	N
6/7/2014	A	Minnesota Machine	W	34	29	I
6/14/2014	H	Minnesota Vixen	L	6	12	*
4/11/2015	H	Madison Blaze	L	20	26	
4/18/2015	H	Nebraska Stampede	L	0	28	
4/25/2015	A	Minnesota Vixen	L	8	14	
5/9/2015	H	Wisconsin Warriors	W	44	0	
5/16/2015	A	Madison Blaze	L	14	48	
5/30/2015	H	Colorado Freeze	W	36	6	
6/6/2015	A	Nebraska Stampede	L	0	56	
6/13/2015	H	Minnesota Vixen	L	14	28	

Iowa Crush Player Register (2014-2015)

Allison, Alicia (2014-2015)
Allison, Amber (2014-2015)
Anderson-Lee, Julia (2015)
Battin, Ashleigh (2015)
Brandner, Andrea (2015)
Butts, Amanda (2015)
Coffman, Amber (2015)
Dameron, Ashley (2014-2015)
Dickenson, Ashley (2014)
Dorenkamp, Christine (2014-2015)
Fast, Nicole (2015)
Hamm, Rachel (2015)
Handy, Melia (2015)
Javaux, Nancy (2014-2015)
Jensen, Jenna (2014)
Keoouthai, LuLu (2014)
Key, Mackenzie (2014-2015)
Koger, Lynn (2014)
Lamfers, Heather (2014)
Larpenter, Kelly (2014-2015)
Lavalais, Kayla (2015)
Manning, Tiara (2015)
McClellan, Kristen (2015)
McIntire, Jenifer (2014-2015)
McMillan, Katie (2014)
Mozee, Johnelle (2014)
Palmer, Charity (2015)
Parrish, Latice (2014-2015)
Reiter, Abby (2014-2015)
Rice, Renate (2015)
Rios, Marilynn (2014)
Robinson, Brianna (2014)
Salazar, Racquel (2014-2015)
Schultz, Aeja (2015)
Shinn, Lisa (2014-2015)
Slykhuis, Mary (2014)
Sutton, Jazmine (2015)
Umsted, Morgan (2014)
Waggoner, Amy (2014-2015)
Wepking, Jo (2014-2015)
Williams, Jen (2014-2015)
Wolgamott, Cheria (2015)

Iowa Steamrollers

Year	League	Name	W	L	Conference	Division	DF	PR
2014	WFA	Iowa Steamrollers	0	4	American	Midwest	4	--

Based in: Des Moines, IA
Notes: Non-existent team

Date	H/A	Opponent	Result	PF	PA
4/5/2014	H	Kansas City Titans	L	0	1
4/12/2014	H	Minnesota Machine	L	0	1
4/19/2014	H	Nebraska Stampede	L	0	1
5/10/2014	A	Minnesota Machine	L	0	1

Iowa Thunder

Year	League	Name	W	L	Conference	Division	DF	PR
2009	WFA	Iowa Thunder	5	3	American	Midwest	3	--
2010	WFA	Iowa Thunder	7	3	American	Midwest	2	S
		Total	**12**	**6**				

Based in: Des Moines, IA
Notes: Succeeded by Iowa Xplosion

Iowa Thunder Game-By-Game Results

Date	H/A	Opponent	W/L	PF	PA		Date	H/A	Opponent	W/L	PF	PA	
4/18/2009	A	Missouri Phoenix	W	54	0		4/17/2010	A	Kansas City Spartans	W	22	8	
4/25/2009	H	Minnesota Machine	W	16	6		4/24/2010	H	Nebraska Stampede	W	47	0	
5/2/2009	H	Kansas City Storm	W	74	0		5/1/2010	H	Minnesota Machine	L	7	21	
5/16/2009	A	St. Louis Slam	L	7	35		5/8/2010	A	Nebraska Stampede	W	28	6	
5/30/2009	H	Missouri Phoenix	W	65	0		5/15/2010	H	Kansas City Spartans	W	24	0	
6/13/2009	A	Minnesota Machine	L	0	20		6/5/2010	H	St. Louis Slam	L	14	37	
6/20/2009	A	Kansas City Storm	W	54	0		6/12/2010	A	Minnesota Machine	W	21	13	
6/27/2009	H	St. Louis Slam	L	10	40		6/19/2010	A	Kansas City Spartans	W	33	14	
							6/26/2010	A	Minnesota Machine	W	20	12	Q
							7/10/2010	H	Lone Star Mustangs	L	20	30	S

Iowa Thunder Player Register (2009-2010)

Alden, Amanda (2010)
Axline, Courtney (2009-2010)
Bagbey, Danielle (2009)
Bascomb, Mook (2010)
Blackford, Ashley (2010)
Boling, Jennifer (2009-2010)
Brakke, Amanda (2010)
Brown, Love (2009-2010)
Chipman, Angela (2010)
Cowan, Cindy (2009)
Daugherty, Tiffany (2010)
Dorenkamp, Christine (2010)
Egli, Megan (2009-2010)
Eilterson, Andy (2009)
Elam, Jeanne (2009-2010)
Fleischmann, Sarah (2009)
Gray, Brandy (2009)
Gray, Kerri (2009-2010)
Grimes, Melissa (2009-2010)
Heinemann, Jacy (2009)
Hirakawa, Jennifer (2009-2010)
Hirakawa, Taylor (2010)
Hixson, Karla (2009)
Horn, DeeAnna (2009-2010)
Jones, Robin (2009-2010)
Keoouthai, LuLu (2009-2010)
Langstraat, Steph (2010)
McCloney, Jennifer (2009)
Milheiser, Kristina (2010)
Millonig, Allie (2010)
Morgan, Rachel (2010)
Moss, Teresa (2009-2010)
Parker, Kendra (2010)
Paul, Kendra (2009)
Pearson, Cindy (2009)
Pena, Alexis (2010)
Robinson, Brianna (2009-2010)
Ross, Stephanie (2010)
Savitski, Bevy (2009)
Schraeder, Angela (2009-2010)
Septer, Tiffany (2010)
Smith, Misty (2010)
Somers, Kasandra (2010)
Sorg, Kristy (2009-2010)
Steffy, Chantalla (2009-2010)
Stokka, Rachel (2009)
Strong, Nicole (2010)
Sumner, Ashley (2009)
Taft, Cindy (2009-2010)
Trammell, Sara (2009-2010)
Watkins, Torie (2009)
Wilson, Erin (2009)
Wilson, Marcie (2010)
Yoder, Lori (2009-2010)

Iowa Xplosion

Year	League		Name	W	L	Conference	Division	DF	PR
2011	WFA		Iowa Xplosion	5	3	American	Midwest	2	--
2012	WFA	X	Iowa Xplosion	0	1	--	--	--	--
			Total	5	4				

Based in: Des Moines, IA
Notes: Preceded by Iowa Thunder

Date	H/A	Opponent	W/L	PF	PA		Date	H/A	Opponent	W/L	PF	PA
4/9/2011	H	Kansas City Tribe	L	0	82		6/4/2011	A	Kansas City Tribe	L	0	77
4/16/2011	A	Nebraska Stampede	W	14	13		6/11/2011	A	Minnesota Machine	W	20	17
4/30/2011	A	Wisconsin Dragons	W	20	0		6/18/2011	H	Nebraska Stampede	L	14	19
5/14/2011	H	Minnesota Machine	W	7	0		5/19/2012	H	St. Louis Slam	L	0	1
5/21/2011	H	Kansas City Spartans	W	44	22							

Iowa Xplosion Player Register (2011)

Axline, Courtney (2011)
Bascomb, Mook (2011)
Boling, Jennifer (2011)
Brown, Love (2011)
Chapman, Michelle (2011)
Daugherty, Tiffany (2011)
Dickenson, Ashley (2011)
Dorenkamp, Christine (2011)
Eggert, Echo (2011)
Egli, Megan (2011)
Elam, Jeanne (2011)
Gray, Kerri (2011)
Horn, DeeAnna (2011)
Keoouthai, LuLu (2011)
Magill, Mollie (2011)
Millonig, Allie (2011)
Morgan, Rachel (2011)
Richeson, Juanita (2011)
Septer, Tiffany (2011)
Smith, Misty (2011)
Sorg, Kristy (2011)
Steffy, Chantalla (2011)
Taft, Cindy (2011)
Warner, Mary Lou (2011)
Wilson, Erin (2011)
Wilson, Marcie (2011)
Ziola, Olivia (2011)

Jacksonville Dixie Blues

Year	League	Name		W	L	Conference	Division	DF	PR
2001	WAFL	Jacksonville Dixie Blues		6	6	Atlantic	South	3	C
2002	WAFL-WFA	Jacksonville Dixie Blues		11	1	Southern	--	1	LC
2004	IWFL	X	Jacksonville Dixie Blues	5	1	--	--	--	--
2005	IWFL	Jacksonville Dixie Blues		8	3	Eastern	South Atlantic	1	S
2006	WFL	Jacksonville Dixie Blues		10	0	--	--	1	LC
2007	WFL	Jacksonville Dixie Blues		6	0	--	--	1	LC
2009	WFA	Jacksonville Dixie Blues		9	1	American	Southeast	1	CC
2010	WFA	Jacksonville Dixie Blues		9	1	National	South Central	1	S
2011	WFA	Jacksonville Dixie Blues		9	1	National	South Atlantic	1	S
2012	WFA	Jacksonville Dixie Blues		9	1	National	Division 9 (South Atlantic)	1	S
2013	WFA	Jacksonville Dixie Blues		3	5	National	Division 6 (South Atlantic)	4	--
2014	WFA	Jacksonville Dixie Blues		5	3	National	Southeast	2	--
2015	WFA	Jacksonville Dixie Blues		6	3	National	North Atlantic	1	Q
		Total		**96**	**26**				

Based in: Jacksonville, FL   **Neutral sites:** San Diego, CA (N1); Birmingham, AL (N2)

Date		Opponent		Result			
11/3/2001	A	Orlando Fire	L	22	28	*	
11/17/2001	H	Orlando Fire	W	21	10		
11/24/2001	A	Indianapolis Vipers	L	0	1		
12/1/2001	A	Tampa Bay Force	L	14	31		
12/15/2001	H	Orlando Fire	L	9	20		
12/22/2001	A	Alabama Slammers	W	43	8		
1/5/2002	H	Tampa Bay Force	L	49	56		
1/12/2002	H	New Orleans Voodoo Dolls	W	47	7		
1/19/2002	A	New Orleans Voodoo Dolls	W	36	12		
1/26/2002	A	Indianapolis Vipers	W	38	32	S	
2/2/2002	A	Tampa Bay Force	W	26	6	CC	
2/24/2002	N1	California Quake	L	14	30	C	
10/12/2002		Orlando Fire	L	30	33		
10/19/2002		Tampa Bay Force	W	41	8		
10/26/2002	H	South Carolina Crusaders	W	40	13		
11/2/2002	A	Birmingham Steel Magnolias	W	40	16		
11/9/2002	H	Georgia Enforcers	W	35	6		
11/16/2002		Tampa Bay Force	W	1	0		
11/23/2002	A	South Carolina Crusaders	W	59	13		
12/7/2002		Orlando Fire	W	20	0		
12/14/2002	H	Indianapolis Vipers	W	33	6		
12/21/2002	A	New Orleans Voodoo Dolls	W	1	0	N	
1/11/2003		Orlando Fire	W	38	18	CC	
1/18/2003	N2	Indianapolis Vipers	W	68	20	C	
4/3/2004	A	Tampa Bay Terminators	W	34	20		
5/1/2004	A	Atlanta Xplosion	L	12	14		
5/8/2004	H	Memphis Matrix	W	46	16		
5/15/2004	A	Orlando Mayhem	W	1	0		
5/22/2004	H	Tampa Bay Terminators	W	34	23		
5/29/2004	H	Orlando Mayhem	W	53	0		
4/2/2005	A	Atlanta Xplosion	L	16	41		
4/9/2005	A	Orlando Mayhem	W	40	6		
4/16/2005	H	Baton Rouge Wildcats	W	57	13		
4/23/2005	H	Tampa Bay Terminators	W	58	27		
4/30/2005	A	Baton Rouge Wildcats	W	33	13		
5/14/2005	A	Orlando Mayhem	W	46	9		
5/21/2005	H	Miami Fury	W	64	12		
6/4/2005	A	Atlanta Xplosion	L	18	39		
6/11/2005	H	Orlando Mayhem	W	43	19		
6/18/2005	A	Baton Rouge Wildcats	W	40	14		
7/9/2005	A	Atlanta Xplosion	L	12	26	S	
5/6/2006	A	Mississippi Rapids	W	63	22		
5/13/2006	H	Kentucky Force	W	1	0		
6/24/2006	A	Kentucky Force	W	1	0		
7/15/2006	H	Tennessee Heat	W	54	25	C	
7/14/2007	H	Clarksville Fox	W	49	6	C	
4/18/2009	A	Emerald Coast Barracudas	W	64	16		
5/2/2009	A	New Orleans Blaze	W	46	0		
5/9/2009	H	Memphis Belles	W	34	20		
5/30/2009	A	Gulf Coast Riptide	W	49	36		
6/6/2009	H	Emerald Coast Barracudas	W	1	0		
6/13/2009	H	New Orleans Blaze	W	42	0		
6/20/2009	A	Memphis Belles	W	34	6		
6/27/2009	H	Gulf Coast Riptide	W	37	14		
7/11/2009	H	Austin Outlaws	W	55	14	S	
7/25/2009	A	St. Louis Slam	L	32	40	CC	
4/10/2010	A	Central Florida Anarchy	W	41	13		
4/17/2010	H	Central Florida Anarchy	W	29	7		
4/24/2010	A	Tampa Bay Pirates	W	63	0		
5/1/2010	H	Carolina Raging Wolves	W	45	6		
5/8/2010	A	Carolina Raging Wolves	W	48	16		
5/15/2010	A	Central Florida Anarchy	W	47	13		
6/5/2010	H	Tampa Bay Pirates	W	42	6		
6/12/2010	A	Carolina Raging Wolves	W	48	6		
6/26/2010	H	Central Florida Anarchy	W	47	13	Q	
7/10/2010	H	St. Louis Slam	L	26	52	S	
4/2/2011	A	Savannah Sabers	W	52	6		
4/9/2011	H	Palm Beach Punishers	W	42	12		
4/16/2011	A	Orlando Anarchy	W	42	7		
4/30/2011	A	Gulf Coast Riptide	W	21	14		
5/14/2011	H	Orlando Anarchy	W	49	0		
5/21/2011	H	Gulf Coast Riptide	W	43	0		
6/11/2011	H	Miami Fury	W	45	24		
6/18/2011	A	Tampa Bay Pirates	W	34	7		
6/25/2011	H	Miami Fury	W	20	18	Q	
7/9/2011	H	Indy Crash	L	0	42	S	

Continued on next page

Jacksonville Dixie Blues Game-By-Game Results (continued)

Date	H/A	Opponent	W/L	Score			Date	H/A	Opponent	W/L	Score		
4/14/2012	A	Miami Fury	W	20	0		4/5/2014	H	Daytona Breakers	W	62	0	
4/21/2012	H	Orlando Anarchy	W	31	3		4/12/2014	A	Miami Fury	L	8	48	
4/28/2012	H	Gulf Coast Riptide	W	49	6		4/26/2014	H	Atlanta Phoenix	L	10	12	
5/5/2012	A	Tampa Bay Inferno	W	35	6		5/3/2014	A	Tennessee Train	W	27	14	
5/19/2012	A	Orlando Anarchy	W	33	6		5/10/2014	H	Tampa Bay Inferno	L	0	49	
6/2/2012	A	Carolina Raging Wolves	W	46	0		5/24/2014	A	Daytona Breakers	W	41	12	
6/9/2012	H	Palm Beach Punishers	W	1	0		5/31/2014	H	Orlando Anarchy	W	48	7	
6/16/2012	H	Miami Fury	W	1	0		6/7/2014	A	Savannah Sabers	W	46	16	
6/30/2012	H	Atlanta Phoenix	W	49	41	Q							
7/7/2012	A	Chicago Force	L	14	67	S	4/11/2015	A	Tampa Bay Inferno	L	9	17	
							4/18/2015	A	Atlanta Phoenix	W	24	10	
4/6/2013	H	Tennessee Train	W	67	12		4/25/2015	A	Daytona Waverunners	W	70	10	
4/13/2013	H	Miami Fury	L	10	22		5/9/2015	H	Orlando Anarchy	W	1	0	
4/20/2013	A	Orlando Anarchy	W	48	13		5/16/2015	H	Tampa Bay Inferno	W	37	6	
5/4/2013	H	Atlanta Phoenix	L	14	30		5/23/2015	A	Orlando Anarchy	W	1	0	
5/11/2013	A	Miami Fury	L	5	14		6/6/2015	H	Miami Fury	W	23	9	
5/18/2013	H	Orlando Anarchy	W	39	0		6/13/2015	H	Atlanta Phoenix	L	6	13	
5/25/2013	A	Tampa Bay Inferno	L	12	21		6/27/2015	H	Atlanta Phoenix	L	9	48	Q
6/8/2013	A	Tallahassee Jewels	L	14	26								

Jacksonville Dixie Blues Player Register (2009-2015)

Adams, Meti (2010, 2014)
Alexander, Nikki (2015)
Allen, Kimberly (2010)
Alvarado, Lynnette (2009-2011, 2014)
Anderson, Shenoa (2013)
Aupont, Daniella (2012)
Bailey, Charnesia (2012-2013)
Barnes, Renvia (2015)
Bass, Brandi (2010-2015)
Bell, Kristann (2009-2015)
Bishop, Heather (2012-2013)
Brigman, Kayla "Storm" (2012-2015)
Brigman, Mackenzie "Rain" (2015)
Brouhard, Stephanie (2013)
Brown, Anya (2015)
Brown, Kim "Rocky" (2009-2015)
Bryant, Santina (2012-2015)
Casaletto, Jessie (2013)
Casaletto, Nicole (2013)
Castellano, Regina (2013)
Castillo, Raquel (2012-2014)
Church, Lauren (2010-2015)
Clark, Jody (2009)
Clausen, Kim (2010)
Cook, Marcia (2009)
Crober, Joanie (2013)
Daughtry, Ternithia (2015)
Davis, Natasha (2013-2014)
Dawson, Jen (2012-2013)
Defeo, Marissa (2015)
Del Cogliano, Ida (2009-12, 2014-15)
Dewald, April (2010-2012, 2015)
Dickert, Jennifer (2009-2011)
Dunlap, Jamie (2011-2014)
Easter, Anita (2013)
Embry, D.J. (2010)

Evans, Betsy (2009-2011)
Faucette, Farrah (2009-2011)
Fowler, Rachel (2012-2015)
Gaines, Tracy (2010-2012)
German, Georgina (2009-2010)
Gibson, Jessica (2009-2011)
Gilbert, Ellea (2010-2013)
Glisson, Joanna (2012)
Gonser, Sheila (2009-2010)
Gonzalez, Jocelyn (2013)
Hamilton, Geri (2011-2015)
Harrison, Becky (2013)
Hartzog, Leeza (2013)
Henry, Aisha (2013)
Hewitt, Rochelle "Chelley" (2009-2012)
Hice, Jessica (2009)
Hice-Jones, Kristy (2009, 2014-2015)
Higgs, Ali (2015)
Holick, Brittany (2010)
Hopper, Erin (2009-2011)
Hotten, Alisha (2011-2013)
Hubbell, Leslie (2013-2015)
Huffman, Jackie (2014-2015)
Jenkins, Heather (2013)
Jones, Monique (2015)
Jones, Paige (2014-2015)
Jones, Wonndra (2009-2010)
Kelley, Madeleine (2012)
Kilfoyle, Helen (2010)
Kirkland, Phoenda (2012-2015)
Langston, Octavia (2015)
Lay, Ishika (2009-2011)
LeDuc, Allison (2015)
Lee, Kelly (2009)
Littler, Bettina (2013)
Loatman, Alissa (2009-2010)

Mack, Brantley (2009-2010)
Maroon, Erin (2012-2015)
Maroon, Jaime (2009-2013)
McFarland, Sheila (2011-2014)
McKinley, Kelly (2015)
McKinney, Stephanie (2013-2015)
McPhilomy, Annalee (2009-2010)
Mincey, Lou (2012)
Monkoski, Susan (2012-2015)
Moody, Jennifer (2009-2010)
Morton, Emily (2014)
Nelson, Lindsey (2009, 2013-2014)
Nickolas, Janay (2013)
Patton, Angie (2013-2014)
Phillips-Bosshart, Vanessa (2009)
Pomeroy, Jessie (2009-2011)
Pond, Sandy (2010-2012)
Price, Kathryn (2009-2012)
Robinson, Michelle (2009-2015)
Rodriguez Gonsalez, Jocelyn (2011-2012)
Rodriguez, Elaine (2009)
Rosario, Cristina (2013-2015)
Schoolcraft, Melissa (2009-2011)
Schwinghammer, April (2013-2014)
Smith, Mercedes (2009-2011)
Stebbins, Traci Rae (2013-2014)
Thompson, Nikki (2013)
Tomlinson, Paige (2009)
Tuten, Amanda (2009)
Walker, Tabitha (2014-2015)
Webb, Lucy (2011)
West, LeShae (2009-2011)
Williams, Monique (2012)
Willis, Brook (2013-2014)
Wilson, Keely (2011-2014)

Jersey Justice

Year	League	Name	W	L	Conference	Division	DF	PR
2009	IWFL2	Jersey Justice	6	4	--	--	7	CC
2010	IWFL2	Jersey Justice	6	1	Eastern	Northeast	3	--
2011	WSFL IX	Jersey Justice	1	6	--	--	--	--
		Total	13	11				

Based in: Carteret, NJ

Date	H/A	Opponent	Result			
4/11/2009	A	Erie Illusion	W	8	6	
4/18/2009	A	New York Nemesis	L	0	40	
4/25/2009	H	Carolina Queens	L	20	28	
5/2/2009	A	Southern Maine Rebels	W	40	14	
5/9/2009	H	Central PA Vipers	W	34	0	
5/16/2009	A	Baltimore Nighthawks	L	6	32	
5/30/2009	H	Southern Maine Rebels	W	28	8	
6/13/2009	H	Erie Illusion	W	36	16	
6/27/2009	A	New England Intensity	W	30	7	S
7/11/2009	A	Montreal Blitz	L	8	9	CC
4/3/2010	H	Manchester Freedom	W	32	0	
4/10/2010	A	Southern Maine Rebels	W	26	8	
4/24/2010	H	Binghamton Tiger Cats	W	40	0	
5/1/2010	H	New York Sharks	L	8	50	
5/8/2010	A	Binghamton Tiger Cats	W	38	0	
5/15/2010	A	Connecticut Crushers	W	22	6	
5/22/2010	H	Binghamton Tiger Cats	W	38	8	
4/16/2011	A	Manchester Freedom	L	0	8	I
4/23/2011	H	Binghamton Tiger Cats	W	36	8	
4/30/2011	H	Baltimore Burn	L	8	12	
5/7/2011	H	Three Rivers Xplosion	L	0	1	
5/21/2011	A	Binghamton Tiger Cats	L	0	1	
6/4/2011	A	Baltimore Burn	L	0	1	
6/11/2011	A	Three Rivers Xplosion	L	0	1	

Kansas City Krunch

Year	League	Name	W	L	Conference	Division	DF	PR
2003	NWFA	Kansas City Krunch	5	3	Southern	Midwest	2	--
2004	NWFA	Kansas City Krunch	7	3	Southern	Midwest	1	S
2005	NWFA	Kansas City Krunch	3	5	Southern	--	11	--
		Total	15	11				

Based in: Kansas City, KS

Date	H/A	Opponent	Result			
4/12/2003	A	St. Louis Slam	W	12	6	**
4/19/2003		Evansville Express	W	20	0	
4/26/2003	A	Oklahoma City Lightning	L	18	19	*
5/10/2003		Evansville Express	W	16	0	
5/17/2003	H	St. Louis Slam	L	6	7	
5/24/2003	H	Oklahoma City Lightning	W	8	7	
6/7/2003		Evansville Express	W	34	7	
6/14/2003	H	Oklahoma City Lightning	L	14	35	
4/3/2004	A	Denton Stampede	W	59	0	
4/17/2004	H	St. Louis Slam	L	0	6	
4/24/2004	A	Evansville Express	W	36	6	
5/1/2004	H	Evansville Express	W	32	0	
5/8/2004	A	St. Louis Slam	L	14	20	
5/15/2004	A	Evansville Express	W	27	0	
5/29/2004	H	St. Louis Slam	W	28	18	
6/5/2004	H	Denton Stampede	W	59	0	
6/26/2004	H	Nashville Dream	W	20	19	Q
7/10/2004	A	Oklahoma City Lightning	L	7	21	S
4/16/2005	H	Oklahoma City Lightning	L	0	47	
4/23/2005	A	Denton Stampede	W	47	0	
5/14/2005	H	St. Louis Slam	W	16	6	
5/21/2005	A	Indianapolis SaberKatz	W	52	0	
5/28/2005	A	Dallas Rage	L	0	12	
6/4/2005	H	Kentucky Karma	L	12	36	
6/11/2005	A	St. Louis Slam	L	8	42	
6/18/2005	H	Dallas Rage	L	0	24	

Kansas City Krunch Player Register (2004-2005)

Barr, Terri (2005)
Bonthius, Denise (2005)
Bross, Vanessa (2004)
Burton, Dorinda (2004-2005)
Butler, LaCreta (2005)
Cade, Yvonne (2005)
Campbell, Stephanie (2004)
Cheirs, Monica (2005)
Cheirs, Nyala (2004)
Collins, Darlene (2005)
Combs, Sara (2004)
Copeland, Ursula (2004)
Danley, Courtney (2005)
Davis, Sara (2005)
DePreiest, Rochelle (2004)
Fish, Daashia (2005)
Franklin, Ann (2004-2005)
Graves, Camille (2005)
Guinn, Dana (2004-2005)
Harlin, Sonya (2004)
Harvey, Liz (2005)
Haughton, Dorothy "Dee" (2004-2005)
Jackson, Janeece (2005)
Janasz, Jenny (2004)
Jones, Krystle (2004-2005)
Jones, Micki (2004-2005)
Kastilahn, Kim (2004)
Lawrence, Jody (2005)
Mitchell, Mindy (2005)
Morris, Tequella (2004-2005)
Musgrave, Diane (2005)
Neal, Krista (2005)
O'Neal, Andrea (2005)
Pankey, Linda (2004)
Patton, Theresa (2004)
Ramirez, Yolanda (2004-2005)
Sheldon, Laura (2004)
Shoemaker, Brandy (2005)
Skaham, Kris (2004)
Smith, Latanya (2005)
Solomon, Tamara (2004)
Stack, Gale (2005)
Stansbery, Cathie (2004)
Steemken, Missy (2004)
Suttington, Careena (2005)
Sutton, Tempie (2005)
Thomas, A.J. (2004)
Thornton, Aisha (2004-2005)
Wernes, Nance (2004)
Zeller, Jessica (2005)

Kansas City Spartans

Year	League	Name	W	L	Conference	Division	DF	PR
2010	WFA	Kansas City Spartans	3	5	American	Midwest	3	--
2011	WFA	Kansas City Spartans	3	5	American	Midwest	4	--
2012	WFA	Kansas City Spartans	2	6	American	Division 11 (Midwest)	3	--
		Total	**8**	**16**				

Based in: Kansas City, KS
Notes: Merged with Kansas City Tribe to form Kansas City Titans

Date	H/A	Opponent	Result		
4/17/2010	H	Iowa Thunder	L	8	22
5/1/2010	A	Nebraska Stampede	W	32	18
5/8/2010	H	Minnesota Machine	L	12	13
5/15/2010	A	Iowa Thunder	L	0	24
5/22/2010	A	Nebraska Stampede	W	32	6
6/5/2010	A	Minnesota Machine	L	8	22
6/12/2010	H	Nebraska Stampede	W	28	6
6/19/2010	H	Iowa Thunder	L	14	33
4/2/2011	H	Kansas City Tribe	L	0	77
4/9/2011	H	Nebraska Stampede	W	14	12
4/16/2011	A	Kansas City Tribe	L	0	76
5/7/2011	H	Wisconsin Wolves	L	8	20
5/14/2011	A	Wisconsin Dragons	W	20	8
5/21/2011	A	Iowa Xplosion	L	22	44
6/11/2011	A	Nebraska Stampede	L	18	32
6/18/2011	H	Wisconsin Dragons	W	30	0
4/14/2012	H	Wisconsin Wolves	W	21	15
4/21/2012	A	Nebraska Stampede	L	6	9
4/28/2012	H	St. Louis Slam	L	0	59
5/5/2012	A	Kansas City Tribe	L	6	67
5/19/2012	H	Arkansas Rampage	W	1	0
6/2/2012	A	St. Louis Slam	L	0	32
6/9/2012	H	Kansas City Tribe	L	0	83
6/16/2012	A	Wisconsin Wolves	L	0	1

Kansas City Spartans Player Register (2010-2012)

Anthony, Kendra (2011)
Benson, Consuela (2012)
Blue, Linda (2010-2012)
Boling, Morgan (2011)
Bonthius, Denise (2011)
Bosley, Coleen (2011)
Bowden, Tam (2011)
Brake, Christina (2010-2011)
Brewer, Candice (2011-2012)
Brim, Cadena (2012)
Briseno, Erika (2010-2011)
Buford, Rashedia (2011)
Bulock, Nyala (2010-2012)
Burden, Ashley (2010)
Calderon, Illiana (2012)
Caldwell, Sabrina (2012)
Campbell, Stephanie (2010-2011)
Cheirs, Monica (2010-2011)
Curtis, Ah Kia (2010-2011)
Danley, Courtney (2010-2012)
Ford, Shannon (2011-2012)
Garcia, Drea (2010-2011)
Gorres-Martens, Brittany (2010-2011)
Goss, Tanika "T.J." (2010-2011)
Harrison, Keyon (2012)
Hoover, Billie (2011-2012)
Johnson, Ashley (2010-2012)
Johnson, Sharis (2011)
Jones, Sarah (2010)
Jones, Shonna (2011)
Lee, Teona (2011)
Leonard, Nicole (2010-2011)
Logan, Brook (2010)
McCrary, Lisa (2010-2012)
McLaster, Consuela (2011)
Moses, Princess (2011)
Murtha, Christine (2010-2011)
Nelson, Nicci (2010-2012)
Nichols, Victoria (2012)
Patton, Destanie (2012)
Pennon, Maeisha (2010-2012)
Perkins, Marla (2010-2012)
Ragsdale, Crystal (2010-2012)
Reed, Christina (2012)
Richardson, Cherie (2012)
Roath, Tanesha (2010)
Roland, Elara (2011-2012)
Rowe, Gena (2010)
Rowe, Javona (2010-2012)
Ryals, Janielle (2011-2012)
Smith, Brenda (2012)
Stephens, ReQuecia (2010)
Taylor, Danielle (2011-2012)
Thomas, Keira (2010)
Thomas, LaShawne (2010)
Tu, Vailgalepa (2011)
Vaughn, Julie (2010-2012)
Veal, Rhonda (2012)
Walker, Natasha (2010-2012)
West, Amanda (2011-2012)
Weston, India (2012)
Wiggins, Jamiene (2010-2012)
Wilson, Lakisha (2012)
Zeller, Jessica (2010-2011)

Kansas City Storm

Year	League		Name	W	L	T	Conference	Division	DF	PR
2005	IWFL		Kansas City Storm	4	5	1	Western	Midwest	2	--
2006	IWFL		Kansas City Storm	3	5	0	Western	Midwest	3	--
2007	IWFL		Kansas City Storm	6	3	0	Western	Mid South	1	S
2008	NWFA		Kansas City Storm	1	7	0	Southern	Midwest	3	--
2009	WFA		Kansas City Storm	2	6	0	American	Midwest	4	--
2010	WSFL		Kansas City Storm	7	0	0	--	--	--	--
2011	WSFL	IX	Kansas City Storm	0	1	0	--	--	--	--
2013	IWFL	IX	Kansas City Storm	0	2	0	--	--	--	--
2014	WSFL	IX	Kansas City Storm	0	3	0	--	--	--	--
			Total	**23**	**32**	**1**				

Based in: Kansas City, MO

Date	H/A	Opponent	Result			
4/2/2005	A	Des Moines Courage	L	20	50	
4/9/2005	A	Chicago Force	L	0	42	
4/16/2005	H	Tucson Wildfire	W	63	6	
4/23/2005	H	Detroit Predators	L	14	20	
4/30/2005	A	Des Moines Courage	L	18	30	
5/14/2005	A	Dallas Revolution	W	1	0	N
5/28/2005	H	Des Moines Courage	W	25	6	
6/11/2005	H	Detroit Predators	W	20	0	
6/18/2005	H	Chicago Force	L	0	30	
6/25/2005	A	Detroit Predators	T	6	6	*
4/29/2006	A	Detroit Predators	L	8	14	
5/6/2006	H	Indianapolis Chaos	W	77	0	
5/20/2006	A	Detroit Predators	W	1	0	
5/27/2006	A	Detroit Demolition	L	6	74	
6/3/2006	H	Indianapolis Chaos	W	85	0	
6/10/2006	A	Iowa Crush	L	6	28	
6/17/2006	H	Chicago Force	L	0	42	
6/24/2006	A	Chicago Force	L	0	27	
5/5/2007	A	Shreveport Aftershock	W	12	6	
5/12/2007	H	Iowa Crush	W	25	12	
5/19/2007	H	Shreveport Aftershock	W	27	0	
5/26/2007	A	Chicago Force	L	0	21	
6/2/2007	H	Baton Rouge Wildcats	W	47	0	
6/16/2007	A	Detroit Demolition	L	0	63	
6/23/2007	A	Iowa Crush	W	19	0	
6/30/2007	H	Shreveport Aftershock	W	1	0	
7/14/2007	A	Detroit Demolition	L	0	1	S
4/19/2008	H	Memphis Belles	W	20	16	
4/26/2008	H	Oklahoma City Lightning	L	0	67	
5/10/2008	A	Minnesota Vixen	L	0	58	
5/17/2008	A	St. Louis Slam	L	0	54	
5/31/2008	A	Oklahoma City Lightning	L	0	1	
6/7/2008	H	St. Louis Slam	L	0	1	
6/14/2008	H	Minnesota Vixen	L	0	1	
6/21/2008	A	Memphis Belles	L	0	52	
4/18/2009	H	St. Louis Slam	L	0	77	
5/2/2009	A	Iowa Thunder	L	0	74	
5/9/2009	A	Missouri Phoenix	W	1	0	
5/16/2009	H	Minnesota Machine	L	0	50	
5/30/2009	A	St. Louis Slam	L	0	88	
6/6/2009	H	Missouri Phoenix	W	1	0	
6/20/2009	A	Iowa Thunder	L	0	54	
6/27/2009	A	Minnesota Machine	L	0	1	
5/1/2010	H	Topeka Mudcats	W	21	0	
5/15/2010	H	River City Raiders	W	66	0	
5/22/2010	A	River City Raiders	W	21	15	
6/5/2010	A	Topeka Mudcats	W	36	0	
6/12/2010	A	River City Raiders	W	52	8	
6/19/2010	H	Topeka Mudcats	W	30	7	
6/26/2010	A	Topeka Mudcats	W	30	6	
4/30/2011	A	Topeka Mudcats	L	30	34	
5/11/2013	A	Rocky Mountain Thunderkatz	L	0	88	
7/13/2013	H	Rocky Mountain Thunderkatz	L	0	6	***
5/17/2014	H	Rocky Mountain Thunderkatz	L	0	28	
5/31/2014	A	Nebraska Stampede	L	0	59	I
6/7/2014	H	Mile High Blaze	L	0	42	

Kansas City Storm Player Register (2005-2006, 2008-2009)

Agbaje, Adejoke (2005-2006)
Allbaugh, Alexandra (2005)
Archer, Jasmine (2008)
Austin, Tamara (2005)
Barth, Susan (2005-2006)
Becken, Lisa (2005-2006)
Benson, Consuela (2009)
Blackmon, Keke (2008)
Blake, Whitney (2008)
Blann, Tamra (2006)
Bonneau, Tishia (2005)
Bosley, Coleen (2008)
Brake, Christina (2008)
Bross, Vanessa (2005)
Burton, Sharon (2005-2006)
Callahan, Bree (2008)
Campbell, Stephanie (2005-2006)
Cimpl, Selina (2008)
Collins, Darlene (2006)
Combs, Sara (2006)
Copeland, Ursula (2009)
Coppenberger, Kristi (2009)
Cubie, Angie (2005-2006, 2009)
Curry, Stephanni (2009)
Danley, Courtney (2006)
Davis, Lindsay (2005-2006)
Denney, Leilani (2008)
Dixon, Kitina (2005)
Dresen, Carrie (2005)
Edwards, Emily (2005)
Fawks, Angie (2006)
Federick, Katie (2009)
Ferguson, Jena (2008)
Findley, Anna (2006)
Franz, Christine (2005)
George, Tammy (2009)
Golightly, Brandy (2008)
Graves, Larisha (2008)
Griffith, Logan (2009)
Grogan, Kelly (2008)
Grosshart, Monika (2009)
Groves, Cami (2005)
Harakas, Leanne (2005-'06, 2008-'09)
Harris, Ashlee (2005)
Harris, Lei (2009)
Harvey, Liz (2006)
Hedrick, Amber (2009)
Hensley, Christine (2009)
Hoover, Billie (2009)
Hoppenstedt, Holly (2005)
House, Jennifer (2005-2006)
Howell, Candice (2008)
Husted, Nicole (2008)

Continued on next page

Kansas City Storm Player Register (continued)

Hyten, Ami (2009)
Jacobsson, Tailyre (2009)
Jemison, Latoya (2005)
Johnson, Robyn (2008)
Kastilahn, Kim (2005-2006)
King, Deborah (2009)
Kinzler, Gail (2009)
LaMarra-Hill, Sarah (2008)
Landers, Jennifer (2008)
Landis, Jennifer (2005)
Lawrence, Jody (2006)
Leeds, Laura (2005-2006)
Leonard, Nicole (2008)
Logsdon, Christy (2005)
Lonergan, Molly (2008)
Long, Tricia (2005)
Loya, Destiny (2008)
Lundquist, Kara (2008)
Martin, Mel (2008)
Martinez, Lora (2005-2006)
Mason, Amber (2006)
Maxwell, Karen (2009)
McCampbell, Emily (2009)
McCreary, Ruthanne (2006)

Melendez, Candace (2009)
Messmer, Pam (2009)
Mitchell, Nikki (2009)
Mountain, Stephanie (2005-2006)
Murphy, Jamie (2006)
Nickel, Kimberly (2008)
Obiefule, Magdalen (2008)
Palelei, Shawnna-Lei (2005-2006)
Parsons, Julie (2009)
Peck, Jacki (2006)
Pemberton, Semone (2006)
Perkins, Marla (2008)
Poe, Angela "Angie" (2005-'06, 2008-'09)
Randle, Ashley (2008)
Ritzer, Melody (2009)
Roberts, Leslie (2005)
Roe, Jennifer (2008)
Rush, Pam (2009)
Schneller, Shannon (2009)
Schroeder, Beth (2009)
Sheldon, Laura (2005-2006)
Shull, Julie (2006)
Sloan, Angie (2005-2006)
Smith, Angela (2009)

Sowers, Rusty (2005)
Sprewell, Sher (2008)
Stack, Erica (2005)
Stack, Gale (2006)
Steemken, Melissa "Missy" (2005)
Stewart, Tessa (2006)
Stuhr, Shawnna (2005-2006)
Summers, Deneane (2005)
Thomas, A.J. (2005)
Trugillo, Michelle (2008)
Van Tassel, Melissa (2009)
Vance, Trina (2009)
VanSandt, Kristi (2008)
Vestal, Abby (2008)
Villegas, Vanezza (2008)
Vivers, Andrea (2009)
Wernes, Nance (2005-2006, 2008-2009)
White, Mindy (2005-2006)
Willcox, Candace (2008-2009)
Williams, Angela (2008)
Williams, Tonille (2005)
Worley, Sandy (2005-2006)
Zeller, Jessica (2006)

Kansas City Titans

Year	League	Name	W	L	Conference	Division	DF	PR
2013	WFA	Kansas City Titans	6	2	American	Division 8 (Midwest)	1	Q
2014	WFA	Kansas City Titans	10	1	American	Midwest	1	CC
2015	WFA	Kansas City Titans	6	4	American	Great Plains	2	S
		Total	**22**	**7**				

Based in: Kansas City, KS
Notes: Merger of Kansas City Spartans and Kansas City Tribe

Date	H/A	Opponent	Result		
4/6/2013	H	St. Louis Slam	W	35	14
4/20/2013	A	Nebraska Stampede	W	59	14
4/27/2013	H	Minnesota Machine	W	61	0
5/11/2013	H	Nebraska Stampede	W	68	0
5/25/2013	H	Nebraska Stampede	W	51	6
6/1/2013	A	Chicago Force	L	7	51
6/8/2013	A	St. Louis Slam	W	27	15
6/22/2013	H	St. Louis Slam	L	55	58	Q
4/5/2014	A	Iowa Steamrollers	W	1	0	N
4/12/2014	H	Tulsa Threat	W	48	8
4/19/2014	H	Minnesota Machine	W	42	2
5/3/2014	H	Minnesota Machine	W	62	0
5/10/2014	A	Nebraska Stampede	W	33	14
5/24/2014	A	Tulsa Threat	W	50	6
5/31/2014	A	Minnesota Machine	W	20	7
6/7/2014	H	Nebraska Stampede	W	57	0
6/21/2014	H	Houston Power	W	43	2	Q
7/5/2014	H	Austin Outlaws	W	41	0	S
7/19/2014	A	San Diego Surge	L	14	59	CC
4/18/2015	A	Arkansas Wildcats	W	35	0
4/25/2015	H	Dallas Elite	L	6	78
5/2/2015	H	St. Louis Slam	W	27	17
5/9/2015	H	Tulsa Threat	W	66	14
5/16/2015	A	Chicago Force	L	8	74
5/30/2015	A	Minnesota Machine	W	36	22
6/6/2015	A	St. Louis Slam	L	22	35
6/13/2015	H	Minnesota Machine	W	54	6
6/27/2015	A	Arlington Impact	W	22	12	Q
7/11/2015	A	Dallas Elite	L	14	70	S

Kansas City Titans Player Register (2013-2015)

Adams, Dawn (2015)
Anderson, Rachel (2013)
Bates, Emily (2013-2014)
Bates, Tina (2013-2015)
Bello, Fatima (2013)
Benson, Consuela (2013)
Bichel, Jennifer (2014-2015)
Blackmon, Keke (2014)
Blue, Linda (2013-2015)
Brewer, Candice (2013)
Brim, Cadena (2013-2015)
Bulock, Nyala (2013)
Burns, Tinika (2014-2015)

Cason-Randle, Jamie (2013)
Castillo, Sica (2015)
Childress, Cierra (2014-2015)
Cillie, Heloise (2013)
Daniels, Lauren (2014)
Danley, Courtney (2013)
DeClue, Shannon (2013-2015)
Demmit, Melissa (2013)
Durham, Morgan (2014-2015)
Edmo, Chamisa (2014)
Elliott, Kerry (2013-2015)
Fields, Alana (2014)
Ford, Lanie (2014-2015)

Ford, Shannon (2013, 2015)
Foreman, Ashlee (2015)
Frenchers, Aisha (2013-2014)
Funk, Sara (2015)
Graves, Larisha "Ree" (2013-2014)
Green, Ebony (2014)
Grollmes, Danielle (2013)
Guscott, Lara (2013)
Hall, Dyon (2015)
Hampton, Courtney (2013)
Harlow, Amanda (2015)
Harring, Kechelle (2013)

Continued on next page

Kansas City Titans Player Register (continued)

Harvey, Brooklyn (2013)
Hawkins, Devin (2013)
Hawkins, Sierra (2013)
Hay, Taylor (2014)
Herber, Crystal (2013)
Horton, Allison (2013)
Jackson, Jenny (2013-2015)
Johnson, Ashley (2013)
Johnson, Robyn (2013)
Jones, Benita (2015)
Jones, Maryssa (2013)
Kent, Brooke (2014)
Lyle, Janiece (2014)
Marrero, Cicely (2013)
Martin, Brittany (2013)
McCrary, Lisa (2013)
Morrison, India (2013)
Moten, Juanita (2013-2014)
Myers, Amanda (2014)
Neutzling, Kaylee (2014)
Nichols, Victoria (2013-2014)
Paschal, Janet (2015)
Pennington, Hanna (2015)
Piper, Melissa (2013, 2015)
Pittman, Jenise (2015)
Pittman, Jeri-Lynn Lehua (2015)
Ragsdale, Crystal (2013)
Ramirez, Yolanda (2013-2014)
Raukur, Morgan (2015)
Reed, Christina (2013-2014)
Reyes, Karina (2015)
Roland, Elara (2013)
Rowe, Javona (2013-2015)
Schmidt, Jenny (2013)
Smallwood, Toshiba (2014)
Smith, Emily (2013)
Sowers, Katie (2013-2015)
Sowers, Liz (2013-2015)
Tackett, Ashlee (2015)
Valvero, Berkley (2015)
Vaughn, Julie (2013-2015)
Veal, Rhonda (2013-2014)
Washington, Antonnia (2014)
Webb, Christina (2014)
Weilert, Linzi (2013)
Weiseman, Cara Jo (2015)
West, Amanda (2013)
Weston, India (2013-2015)
Wiggins, Jamiene (2013)
Willis, Katherine (2015)
Zeller, Jessica (2013)

Kansas City Tribe

Year	League	Name	W	L	Conference	Division	DF	PR
2008	IWFL	Kansas City Tribe	4	4	Western	Mid South	2	--
2009	IWFL	Kansas City Tribe	10	1	Western	Midwest	1	**NC**
2010	IWFL	Kansas City Tribe	6	2	Western	Midwest	3	--
2011	WFA	Kansas City Tribe	8	2	American	Midwest	1	S
2012	WFA	Kansas City Tribe	8	2	American	Division 11 (Midwest)	1	S
		Total	36	11				

Based in: Kansas City, MO **Neutral site:** Round Rock, TX (N)
Notes: Merged with Kansas City Spartans to form Kansas City Titans

4/12/2008	A	Dallas Diamonds	L	0	58		5/8/2010	H	Wisconsin Warriors	W	44	0
4/19/2008	H	Iowa Crush	W	19	6		5/15/2010	A	Minnesota Vixen	W	80	0
5/3/2008	A	Iowa Crush	W	6	0		5/22/2010	A	Dallas Diamonds	L	21	35
5/10/2008	A	Wisconsin Warriors	W	20	12		6/5/2010	H	Chicago Force	W	30	12
5/17/2008	H	Detroit Demolition	L	0	38							
5/31/2008	H	Dallas Diamonds	L	13	28		4/2/2011	A	Kansas City Spartans	W	77	0
6/7/2008	A	Wisconsin Wolves	L	7	13		4/9/2011	A	Iowa Xplosion	W	82	0
6/14/2008	H	Iowa Crush	W	49	0		4/16/2011	H	Kansas City Spartans	W	76	0
							4/30/2011	A	Nebraska Stampede	W	88	0
4/11/2009	H	Minnesota Vixen	W	45	8		5/7/2011	A	Chicago Force	L	26	34
4/18/2009	A	Iowa Crush	W	62	0		5/14/2011	H	St. Louis Slam	W	37	34
5/2/2009	A	Chicago Force	L	6	28		5/21/2011	H	Wisconsin Wolves	W	57	0
5/9/2009	H	Wisconsin Warriors	W	58	0		6/4/2011	H	Iowa Xplosion	W	77	0
5/16/2009	H	Clarksville Fox	W	48	6		6/25/2011	H	Minnesota Machine	W	51	0 Q
5/30/2009	H	Chicago Force	W	30	14		7/9/2011	A	Dallas Diamonds	L	20	23 S
6/6/2009	A	Wisconsin Warriors	W	19	12							
6/13/2009	A	Minnesota Vixen	W	65	0		4/14/2012	H	Chicago Force	L	14	21
6/27/2009	H	Los Angeles Amazons	W	19	14 S		4/21/2012	H	St. Louis Slam	W	33	14
7/11/2009	H	Chicago Force	W	40	16 CC		4/28/2012	A	Tulsa Threat	W	94	0
7/25/2009	N	D.C. Divas	W	21	18 C		5/5/2012	H	Kansas City Spartans	W	67	6
							5/19/2012	A	Minnesota Machine	W	13	0
4/3/2010	A	Iowa Crush	W	77	0		6/2/2012	H	Nebraska Stampede	W	53	6
4/10/2010	H	Dallas Diamonds	W	28	21		6/9/2012	A	Kansas City Spartans	W	83	0
4/24/2010	H	Wisconsin Wolves	W	55	0		6/16/2012	A	St. Louis Slam	W	63	42
5/1/2010	A	Chicago Force	L	12	14		6/30/2012	H	St. Louis Slam	W	42	17 Q
							7/7/2012	A	Dallas Diamonds	L	35	55 S

Kansas City Tribe Player Register (2011-2012)

Adams, Dawn (2011)
Ashton, Samantha (2012)
Barbarick, Pamela (2011)
Barnett, Meagan (2012)
Bates, Emily (2011-2012)
Bates, Kristina (2012)
Bello, Fatima (2012)
Blackmon, Keke (2011-2012)
Bourland, Liz (2011)
Burns, Tiara (2011-2012)
Campbell, Regan (2011)
Cartwright, Tiffany (2012)
Childress, Cierra (2012)
DeClue, Shannon (2012)
Denetdeel, Kim (2011)
Dimmitt, Melissa (2012)
Downs, Lindsay (2012)
Due, April (2011)
Durham, Morgan (2011-2012)
Elliott, Kerry (2011-2012)
Ford, Lanie (2011-2012)
Franco, Megan (2012)
Furr, Ginger (2012)

Continued on next page

Kansas City Tribe Player Register (continued)

Gent, Leslie (2011-2012)
Goddard, Erica (2011)
Graves, Larisha (2011-2012)
Guscott, Lara (2011-2012)
Hampton, Courtney (2012)
Harris, Cindel (2012)
Hatcher, Carissa (2012)
Horton, Allison (2011-2012)
Hudson, Shantrell (2011)
Ingels, Brianna (2011)
Johnson, DeShanta (2011)
Johnson, Robyn (2012)
Kent, Brooke (2012)
Kingcannon, Jasmine (2011-2012)
Major, Carmela (2012)
Marrero, Cicely (2011-2012)
McCune, K.J. (2011-2012)
Miller, Crista (2011)
Morris, Tequella (2011-2012)
Moten, Juanita (2011-2012)
Obiefule, Magdalen (2011-2012)
Piper, Melissa (2011-2012)
Ramirez, Yolanda (2011-2012)
Rankin, Jeanne (2011)
Ray, Jacki (2011-2012)
Scates, Janetta (2011)
Schmidt, Jenny (2011-2012)
Shell, Amanda (2012)
Smith, Angela (2012)
Smith, Jill (2012)
Sowers, Katie (2011-2012)
Sowers, Liz (2011-2012)
Sweeten, Amanda (2011)
Thuman, Heather (2012)
Walker, Kennisha (2011)
Weilert, Linzi (2011-2012)
White, Mindy (2011-2012)
Young, Stacy (2012)

Kansas Phoenix

Year	League	Name	W	L	Conference	Division	DF	PR
2009	WFA	Missouri Phoenix	0	8	American	Midwest	5	--
2011	WSFL	Kansas Phoenix	0	4	--	--	--	--
2012	WSFL	Kansas Phoenix	0	5	National	--	3	--
		Total	**0**	**17**				

Based in: Kansas City, KS

Date	H/A	Opponent	Result			Date	H/A	Opponent	Result			
4/18/2009	H	Iowa Thunder	L	0	54	4/23/2011	H	Topeka Mudcats	L	6	30	
4/25/2009	H	St. Louis Slam	L	0	1	5/14/2011	H	Arkansas Rampage	L	0	1	
5/2/2009	A	Minnesota Machine	L	0	56	5/21/2011	A	Arkansas Rampage	L	0	1	
5/9/2009	H	Kansas City Storm	L	0	1	6/18/2011	H	Arkansas Rampage	L	14	34	
5/30/2009	A	Iowa Thunder	L	0	65	4/7/2012	A	Nebraska Stampede	L	0	82	I
6/6/2009	A	Kansas City Storm	L	0	1	4/21/2012		Arkansas Banshees	L	8	60	I
6/13/2009	A	St. Louis Slam	L	0	51	6/16/2012		DFW Xtreme	L	0	68	
6/20/2009	H	Minnesota Machine	L	0	61	6/23/2012	H	Arkansas Rampage	L	0	8	
						7/7/2012	A	Arkansas Rampage	L	12	22	

Kansas Phoenix Player Register (2009)

Blue, Linda (2009)
Boise, Jessie (2009)
Bosley, Coleen (2009)
Brake, Christina (2009)
Callahan, Bree (2009)
Cambron, Laura (2009)
Crosby, Marlena (2009)
Dempsey, Mariann (2009)
Denetdeel, Kim (2009)
Denney, Leilani (2009)
Findley, Anna (2009)
George, Tammy (2009)
Grace, Beverlee (2009)
Howell, Candice (2009)
Husted, Nicole (2009)
Jones, Sarah (2009)
Kinzler, Gail (2009)
Kohl, Racheal (2009)
LaMarra-Hill, Sarah (2009)
Loya, Destiny (2009)
Luckan, Paula (2009)
Lundquist, Kara (2009)
Lundvall, Jessie (2009)
McCampbell, Emily (2009)
Mitchell, Dawn (2009)
Nickel, Kimberly (2009)
Peterson, Tina (2009)
Poe, Angie (2009)
Schneller, Shannon (2009)
Stevens, Marlee (2009)
Strahan, Gayle (2009)
Thomas, Keira (2009)
Thomas, Sarah (2009)
Vaughn, Julie (2009)
Vestal, Abby (2009)

Kentucky Force

Year	League		Name	W	L	Conference	Division	DF	PR
2005	WFL		Kentucky Force	0	3	--	--	--	--
2006	WFL		Kentucky Force	0	4	--	--	--	--
2007	WPFL	X	Kentucky Valkyries	0	1	--	--	--	--
			Total	**0**	**8**				

Based in: Oak Grove, KY
Notes: Forfeited entire 2007 season

Date	H/A	Opponent	Result			Date	H/A	Opponent	Result		
5/21/2005		Tennessee Heat	L	0	14	4/29/2006	H	Mississippi Rapids	L	7	38
6/18/2005		Mississippi Rapids	L	0	1	5/13/2006	A	Jacksonville Dixie Blues	L	0	1
6/25/2005		Tennessee Heat	L	0	33	6/10/2006	H	Tennessee Heat	L	12	28
						6/24/2006	H	Jacksonville Dixie Blues	L	0	1
						8/18/2007	H	Wisconsin Wolves	L	0	1

Kentucky Karma

Year	League	Name	W	L	Conference	Division	DF	PR
2005	NWFA	Kentucky Karma	5	4	Northern	--	8	--
2006	NWFA	Kentucky Karma	4	4	Southern	South Central	2	Q
2007	NWFA	Kentucky Karma	4	4	Southern	North	3	--
2008	NWFA	Kentucky Karma	7	3	Southern	East	1	S
2009	WFA	Kentucky Karma	5	3	National	Mid-Atlantic	2	--
2010	WFA	Kentucky Karma	2	6	National	Central	3	--
2011	WFA	Kentucky Karma	1	7	National	North Central	5	--
		Total	**28**	**31**				

Based in: Louisville, KY
Notes: Succeeded by Derby City Dynamite

Date	H/A	Opponent	Result		
4/16/2005	H	St. Louis Slam	W	20	0
4/23/2005	A	Milwaukee Momentum	L	12	21
4/30/2005	H	Southwest Michigan Jaguars	L	8	22
5/14/2005	H	Indiana Thunder	W	1	0
5/21/2005	A	St. Louis Slam	L	6	34
5/28/2005	A	Toledo Spitfire	W	37	0
6/4/2005	A	Kansas City Krunch	W	36	12
6/11/2005	H	Milwaukee Momentum	W	20	14
6/18/2005	H	Columbus Comets	L	0	56
4/15/2006	A	St. Louis Slam	L	14	36
5/6/2006	A	Nashville Dream	W	8	3
5/13/2006	H	Alabama Renegades	W	14	0
5/27/2006	H	St. Louis Slam	L	0	22
6/3/2006	H	Fort Wayne Flash	W	18	6
6/10/2006	H	Nashville Dream	W	23	0
6/17/2006	A	Alabama Renegades	L	2	6
7/1/2006	A	St. Louis Slam	L	8	27 Q
4/21/2007	H	Cincinnati Sizzle	W	7	6
4/28/2007	H	Milwaukee Momentum	W	33	0
5/5/2007	A	St. Louis Slam	L	0	62
5/12/2007	A	Columbus Comets	L	0	44
5/19/2007	A	Cincinnati Sizzle	W	8	7
6/2/2007	H	St. Louis Slam	L	0	26
6/9/2007	H	Columbus Comets	L	0	28
6/16/2007	A	Milwaukee Momentum	W	14	6
4/19/2008	A	Cincinnati Sizzle	W	39	6
4/26/2008	H	West Virginia Wonders	W	79	0
5/10/2008	H	Chattanooga Locomotion	W	13	7
5/17/2008	H	Alabama Renegades	W	27	26
5/24/2008	A	West Virginia Wonders	W	70	0
5/31/2008	H	Cincinnati Sizzle	L	14	28
6/14/2008	A	Alabama Renegades	W	14	0
6/21/2008	A	Chattanooga Locomotion	L	0	19
6/28/2008	H	Pensacola Power	W	6	0 Q
7/5/2008	A	Los Angeles Amazons	L	0	1 S
4/18/2009	A	Cleveland Fusion	L	14	38
4/25/2009	H	Cincinnati Sizzle	W	22	14
5/16/2009	H	Cleveland Fusion	W	20	12
5/23/2009	A	Pittsburgh Force	W	8	6
5/30/2009	A	Cincinnati Sizzle	W	22	0
6/13/2009	A	Columbus Comets	L	8	23
6/20/2009	H	Pittsburgh Force	W	46	20
6/27/2009	H	Columbus Comets	L	12	21
4/10/2010	A	Indiana Speed	L	0	41
4/17/2010	H	Cleveland Fusion	L	6	54
4/24/2010	H	Cincinnati Sizzle	W	6	0
5/1/2010	A	St. Louis Slam	L	0	50
5/8/2010	H	Indiana Speed	L	6	54
5/22/2010	H	St. Louis Slam	L	6	70
6/5/2010	A	Columbus Comets	L	0	66
6/19/2010	A	Cincinnati Sizzle	W	20	14
4/2/2011	A	Detroit Dark Angels	L	0	14
4/9/2011	A	Toledo Reign	L	0	23
4/30/2011	A	Indy Crash	L	0	77
5/14/2011	H	Cincinnati Sizzle	L	0	42
5/21/2011	H	Indy Crash	L	0	77
6/4/2011	H	Dayton Diamonds	W	28	12
6/11/2011	A	Cincinnati Sizzle	L	6	67
6/18/2011	H	St. Louis Slam	L	0	1

Kentucky Karma Player Register (2005-2009, 2011)

Aimers, Erica (2007-2009)
Aitken, Helen (2007)
Arrington, Melinda (2005)
Bair, Beth (2005)
Baker, Latisha "Tish" (2005-06, '08-09, '11)
Baker, Lauren (2005)
Banks, Thelma "Tee" (2005-2009, 2011)
Barnett, Kris (2011)
Baxter, Tina (2005)
Bell, Ebony (2005-2006)
Best, Danielle (2011)
Bickers, Bernie (2009)
Bishop, Becky (2009)
Blazak, Heidi (2005)
Bonilla, B.J. (2008)
Bonilla, Victoria (2008)
Bradley, Morgan (2008-2009)
Bradley, Terry (2005)
Braun, Lisa (2005)
Brown, Vicky (2006)
Bruner, Beth (2009)
Burris, Sheretta (2011)
Carney, Vicky (2005-2009)
Carter, Laura (2007-2009, 2011)
Carter, Tina (2006-2007)
Chamberlain, Jessica (2005-2009)
Childs, Jamile (2011)
Clark, Mary (2005-2008)
Coakley, Victoria (2011)
Cole-Lockett, Nicole (2011)
Collins, Adele (2007-2009)
Comodeca, Cindy (2008-2009)
Conner, Karen (2006, 2008)
Cook, Valeria (2005)
Cross, Latasha (2005, 2009)
Csukas, Beth (2005-2006)
Daniels, Angela (2006)
Davis, Natashi (2007)
Delagnis, Pat (2011)
Drake, Dontashia (2008)
Durham, Michelle (2006-2009)
Ellison, Rachel (2005)
Evans, Emily (2011)
Evans, Tee (2009)
Fears, Brittany (2011)
Fisher, Liz (2011)
Fitzgerald, Lori (2005-2006)

Continued on next page

Kentucky Karma Player Register (continued)

Fuelling, Deidre (2011)
Futrell, Susan (2009)
Gattis, Lisa (2009, 2011)
Grace, Peggy (2005)
Gubler, Amy (2005-2007, 2011)
Hadley, Sara (2005-2006)
Hall, Darleen (2008)
Hall, Kristen (2007)
Hampton, Kimber (2005-2008)
Hardin, Liz (2005)
Harlamert, Andrea (2005-2006)
Harmon, Jesalyn (2011)
Hartlage, Allison (2008)
Herron, Keturah (2005)
Jackson, Khadijah (2009)
Jaudon, Shadonna (2005)
Johnson, Angie (2006)
Johnson, Kathy (2008)
Jolley, A.J. (2005-2006)
Jones, Danisha "Co Co" (2011)
Jones, Sara (2006-2009)
Kelly, Shelley (2009)
Kendall, Terri (2006-2007)
Kilgore, April (2009, 2011)
Koenigsknecht, Michelle (2006)
Kohorst, Jana (2005)
Krampe, Trish (2006)
Landrum, Donen (2007)
Lemon, Carla (2005)
Lewis, Danielle (2006)
Lynch, Kristy (2011)
Major, Cherrelle "Relle" (2011)
Malika, Jameela (2009)
Marks, Latasha (2005-2006)
Martin, Nancy (2005)
McClanahan, Melanie (2005)
McDavitt, Carmen (2009)
McKenzie, Erin (2007)
Mehr, Anna (2009)
Miles, Chaz (2006)
Miller, Brittany (2007)
Mink, Amber (2008-2009, 2011)
Mischler, Paula (2005)
Moore, Jessica (2005-2006)
Moore, Keneath (2009)
Nett, Beth (2005-2006)
Pamler, Charlotte (2008)
Payne, Tierra (2008-2009, 2011)
Penny, Collene (2005-2009, 2011)
Perry, Brooke (2011)
Perry, Christie (2005-2006)
Pettaway, Jaliza (2011)
Phillips, Malissa (2011)
Pigneri, Andi (2008)
Poindexter, Stacy (2005)
Profitt, Kelly (2006)
Rabish, Becky (2005-2009)
Rauen, Shannel (2011)
Reardon, Dana (2011)
Rhodes, Leigh-Ann (2005)
Riggens, Sonja (2009, 2011)
Rowan, Rico (2011)
Rowe, Keke (2005-2006)
Santiago, Lisa (2005-2006)
Saxon, Bobbi Jo (2007)
Schmidt, Julie (2006)
Scott, Jessica (2005, 2008)
Scott, Toya (2011)
Seitz, Sara (2007-2009, 2011)
Shannon, Lissette (2005-2006)
Shepherd, Casey (2008-2009, 2011)
Skillman, Val (2005-2007)
Slinker, Kindra (2011)
Smith, Allie (2008)
Stewart, Tamara (2006-2009)
Stults, Shannel (2005)
Thayer, Kat (2011)
Thompson, Erin (2006)
Tilghman, Alyce (2005)
Torres, Anitra (2008)
Trembley, Christina (2005, 2007)
Trindeitmar, Sarah (2005)
Vance, Jamie (2011)
Vannatter, Kristen (2005, 2007)
Villerreal, Noelia (2005)
Walker, Catrena (2006)
Ward, P.J. (2005)
Westfall, Kiera (2008)
Whitson, Lalaynva (2011)
Wile, Jackie (2006-2009)
Williams, Kim (2011)
Williamson, Lisa (2011)
Wilson, Gloria (2009)
Wright, LaQuita (2008)
Wright, Lasheka (2009)

Keystone Assault

Year	League	Name	W	L	Conference	Division	DF	PR
2009	WFA	Keystone Assault	4	4	National	Northeast	4	--
2010	WFA	Keystone Assault	6	2	National	East	2	--
2011	WFA	Keystone Assault	3	5	National	Northeast	2	--
2012	WFA	Keystone Assault	7	2	National	Division 1 (Northeast)	1	W
2013	IWFL	Keystone Assault	7	2	Eastern	Mid-Atlantic	2	BS
2014	IWFL	Keystone Assault	8	1	Eastern	Mid-Atlantic	1	S
2015	WSFL	Keystone Assault	9	0	Northern	--	1	LC
		Total	44	16				

Based in: Harrisburg, PA

Date	H/A	Opponent	W/L	Score			Date	H/A	Opponent	W/L	Score	
4/18/2009	A	Philadelphia Liberty Belles (II)	L	24	47		5/22/2010	A	Baltimore Burn	W	34	24
4/25/2009	A	Binghamton Tiger Cats	W	34	20		6/5/2010	H	New Jersey Titans	W	28	8
5/9/2009	H	Baltimore Burn	L	16	20		6/12/2010	A	Southern Tier Spitfire	W	38	0
5/16/2009	H	Philadelphia Liberty Belles (II)	L	12	14		6/19/2010	H	Baltimore Burn	L	24	36
5/30/2009	H	Binghamton Tiger Cats	W	32	6							
6/6/2009	A	Baltimore Burn	L	22	46		4/9/2011	A	D.C. Divas	L	6	55
6/13/2009	A	New Jersey Titans	W	28	6		4/16/2011	H	Northeastern Nitro	L	0	6
6/20/2009	H	Connecticut Cyclones	W	1	0	N	4/30/2011	H	D.C. Divas	L	0	49
							5/7/2011	A	Philadelphia Liberty Belles (II)	L	12	28
4/10/2010	A	New Jersey Titans	W	30	16		5/14/2011	H	New England Nightmare	W	27	0
4/24/2010	H	Southern Tier Spitfire	W	54	0		6/4/2011	A	Northeastern Nitro	L	6	12
5/1/2010	A	New England Nightmare	W	56	6		6/11/2011	H	Philadelphia Liberty Belles (II)	W	14	8
5/15/2010	H	Philadelphia Liberty Belles (II)	L	12	35		6/18/2011	H	New England Nightmare	W	26	8

Continued on next page

Keystone Assault Game-By-Game Results (continued)

Date	H/A	Opponent	W/L	PF	PA	Note	Date	H/A	Opponent	W/L	PF	PA	Note
4/14/2012	H	Maine Lynx	W	54	0		4/12/2014	A	Baltimore Nighthawks	W	13	6	
4/21/2012	A	New England Nightmare	W	50	0		4/19/2014	H	New England Nightmare	W	37	8	
4/28/2012	H	Boston Militia	L	0	31		5/3/2014	A	New England Nightmare	W	31	0	
5/5/2012	H	Baltimore Burn	W	34	6	I	5/10/2014	A	New York Knockout	W	40	0	
5/12/2012	A	Baltimore Burn	W	46	8	I	5/17/2014	H	Erie Illusion	W	62	0	
5/19/2012	A	Philadelphia Liberty Belles (II)	W	20	0		5/31/2014	A	Philadelphia Firebirds	W	21	0	
6/2/2012	H	New England Nightmare	W	42	0		6/7/2014	H	Northeast Rebels	W	34	0	
6/16/2012	A	Pittsburgh Force	W	50	15		6/14/2014	H	Washington Prodigy	W	39	20	
6/23/2012	A	New York Sharks	L	19	24	W	6/28/2014	A	Pittsburgh Passion	L	12	42	S
4/27/2013	A	Washington Prodigy	W	12	6		4/25/2015	H	Baltimore Burn	W	41	0	
5/4/2013	H	Baltimore Nighthawks	W	20	0		5/2/2015	H	West Virginia Wildfire	W	58	0	
5/18/2013	A	Baltimore Nighthawks	W	7	6		5/9/2015	H	New England Nightmare	W	24	6	
6/1/2013	A	Connecticut Wreckers	W	40	0		5/30/2015	H	New England Nightmare	W	27	6	
6/15/2013	H	Connecticut Wreckers	W	65	0		6/13/2015	A	West Virginia Wildfire	W	28	0	
6/22/2013	H	Philadelphia Firebirds	L	13	22		6/20/2015	A	Baltimore Burn	W	49	0	
6/29/2013	A	Erie Illusion	W	49	0		6/27/2015	H	Cincinnati Sizzle	W	27	0	
7/13/2013	H	Atlanta Rage	W	1	0	BQ	7/18/2015	H	New England Nightmare	W	34	0	CC
7/20/2013	H	Montreal Blitz	L	22	47	BS	8/1/2015	H	Tennessee Legacy	W	9	7	C

Keystone Assault Player Register (2009-2012, 2014-2015)

Amrhein, Kendra (2009-2012)
Beam, Jamie (2012)
Beard, Melissa (2014)
Becknauld, Alicia (2009)
Berry, Jen (2009, 2014)
Brown, Janelle (2009-2010)
Brown, Ruth (2014)
Burd, Laura (2010)
Cambria, Bridget (2012, 2015)
Cardile, Diane (2011)
Carr, Sheemea (2012)
Chase, Sydelle (2009-2012, 2015)
Clemons, Faye (2011-2012, 2015)
DiMaio, Cherie (2009, 2011)
DiPietro, Rebecca "Becca" ('09, '11-12, '14-15)
Dolbin, Christian (2015)
Early, Amber (2012, 2015)
Engelsman, Sarah (2014)
Finkbeiner, Sherri (2012)
Fischer, Rachel (2009-2012, 2014-2015)
Frye, Jane (2009-2010)
Gauthier, Jody (2012)
Gianni-Bradford, Meghan (2014-2015)
Glowzenski, Lauren (2012)
Good, Sarah (2015)
Gordan, Kayla (2010)
Grafmyer, Melissa (2014-2015)
Green, Mariah (2014-2015)
Greishaw, Jessica (2014-2015)
Harmon, Kimberly (2012)
Heller, Erica (2010, 2012)
Hindman, Maria (2010-2011)
Hogg, Carri (2014-2015)
Howard, Tuffy (2009-12, 2014-15)
Jacob, Jodilynn (2009-2010)
Johnson, Heidi (2009-2012, 2015)
Koehler, Justeen (2015)
Kretz, Tracy (2009-2012)
Lacey, Juelz (2009-2010)
Lamie, Shannon (2011-2012, 2015)
Landes, Brittanny (2015)
Lauchle, Mary (2009-2012)
Legg, Jennifer (2011)
Leonard, Tre (2009-2011, 2014)
Liesch, Becky (2010)
McMurray, Sue (2014-2015)
McWhite, Ti (2014)
Nicholas, Joey (2014)
Noon, Nicole (2014-2015)
Peete, Ashley (2012)
Pfender, Rene (2012)
Pratt, Mary (2009-2012)
Price, Linda (2009)
Pritchard, Jodi (2009-2010)
Proper, Lauren (2014)
Rector, Lori (2011)
Reid, Danielle (2012)
Rivers, Maria (2012, 2014)
Roach, Marirose (2014)
Robertson, Jennifer "Jen" (2009-10)
Rogers, Laura (2015)
Rosario, Jennifer "Rico" (2012, 2014)
Ross, Christine (2010-12, 2014-15)
Runk, Katie (2009-2011)
Schraeder, Machelle (2011)
Sheaffer, Emily (2014-2015)
Shertzer, Missy (2014)
Shull, Lara (2015)
Shultz, Christine (2010-2012)
Sorber, Hannah (2014)
Spurgeon, Laura (2010)
Starr, Emi (2012)
Stine, M.J. (2009-2011)
Stinney, Marcia (2012, 2015)
Swinnerton, Karen (2009, 2011)
Tharkur, Shanice (2011-2012, 2015)
Thomas, Kenya (2015)
Tormonen, Taina (2010)
Torres, Eve (2012)
Tosheff, Lisa (2009)
Trinidad, Latravia (2015)
Vereb, Sammie (2014)
Walker, Alexis (2014-2015)
Walker, Denee "Dex" (2012)
Walker, Jacki (2010)
Watts, Shirley (2010)
Watts, Stephanie (2012, 2014-2015)
Weir, Jess (2009-2012)
Whitworth, Breah (2012)
Wilson, Chrissy (2014)
Wohlbach, Nicole (2009)
Wright, Danica (2011-2012)
Young, Cori (2010-2012, 2015)

Knoxville Lightning

Year	League		Name	W	L	Conference	Division	DF	PR
2015	IWFL	X	Knoxville Lightning	0	8	--	--	--	--

Based in: Knoxville, TN

Date	H/A	Opponent	W/L	PF	PA	Note	Date	H/A	Opponent	W/L	PF	PA	Note
4/11/2015	H	Huntsville Tigers	L	8	55		5/16/2015	H	Huntsville Tigers	L	0	52	
4/18/2015	A	Carolina Phoenix	L	0	45		5/30/2015	A	Tennessee Train	L	6	28	
4/25/2015	H	Tennessee Train	L	12	35		6/6/2015	A	Carolina Queens	L	0	1	
5/9/2015	A	Huntsville Tigers	L	0	46		6/20/2015	H	Tri-Cities Thunder	L	6	66	I

Knoxville Lightning Player Register (2015)

Alford, Laurice (2015)
Basham, Trista (2015)
Bennett, Lena (2015)
Brady, Anne (2015)
Cervino, Brenna (2015)
Crutcher, Nikki (2015)
Edwards, Wyeshia (2015)
Erickson, Natasha (2015)
Heidmann, Lisa (2015)
Kiestler, Cassie (2015)
Marlett, Denise (2015)
Murr, Chas (2015)
Otero, Jenn (2015)
Partin, Melissa (2015)
Reyes, Melissa (2015)
Roberts, Heather (2015)
Sickau, Sheila (2015)
Smiley, A.J. (2015)
Sutton, Cindy (2015)
Thomas, Erin (2015)
Vierstra, Thea (2015)
White, Donna (2015)

Knoxville Summit

Year	League		Name	W	L	Conference	Division	DF	PR
2002	NWFA		Knoxville Summit	0	8	--	Central	5	--
2003	NWFA		Knoxville Summit	2	7	Southern	Central	6	--
2004	IWFL	X	Knoxville Summit	0	2	--	--	--	--
2005	NWFA		Knoxville Tornadoes	1	7	Southern	--	13	--
2006	NWFA	X	Knoxville Tornadoes	0	2	--	--	--	--
			Total	**3**	**26**				

Based in: Knoxville, TN

Date		Opponent				Date		Opponent			
4/27/2002		Nashville Dream	L	8	48	4/17/2004	A	Atlanta Xplosion	L	0	47
5/4/2002		Chattanooga Locomotion	L	0	18	5/15/2004	H	Atlanta Xplosion	L	0	1
5/18/2002		Alabama Renegades	L	0	74						
5/25/2002		Nashville Dream	L	0	51	4/16/2005	A	Tennessee Venom	L	0	38
6/1/2002		Atlanta Leopards	L	0	79	4/23/2005	H	Asheville Assault	L	0	39
6/8/2002		Atlanta Leopards	L	0	77	4/30/2005	H	Atlanta Leopards	W	30	8
6/15/2002		Alabama Renegades	L	12	54	5/14/2005	A	Nashville Dream	L	0	51
6/22/2002		Chattanooga Locomotion	L	0	80	5/21/2005	A	Asheville Assault	L	0	46
						5/28/2005	H	Tennessee Venom	L	24	28
3/29/2003		Baltimore Burn	L	0	45 E	6/4/2005	A	Alabama Renegades	L	2	38
4/12/2003	A	Atlanta Leopards	W	34	0	6/18/2005	H	Nashville Dream	L	0	30
4/19/2003	H	Chattanooga Locomotion	L	0	65						
4/26/2003	A	Tennessee Venom	L	0	26	4/22/2006	H	Chattanooga Locomotion	L	0	74
5/3/2003	H	Nashville Dream	L	0	50	4/29/2006	H	Alabama Renegades	L	0	1
5/17/2003	H	Alabama Renegades	L	0	41						
5/24/2003	A	Asheville Assault	L	21	48						
5/31/2003	A	Chattanooga Locomotion	L	0	44						
6/14/2003	H	Tennessee Venom	W	13	6						

Knoxville Tornadoes Player Register (2005)

Barrow, Frankie (2005)
Burris, Robin (2005)
Daughter, Lisa (2005)
Delapp, Mary (2005)
Eakins, Melissa (2005)
Gaither, Ebony (2005)
Hall, Meghan (2005)
Hawn, Nicole (2005)
Jackson, Natalie (2005)
Jackson, Ronance (2005)
Kritch, Ashley (2005)
Macias, Amy (2005)
Medina, Ariyueis (2005)
Moore, Joyce (2005)
Myers, Melissa (2005)
Patrick, Tanicka (2005)
Pennington, Sue (2005)
Ruch, Sierra (2005)
Scott, Bridget (2005)
Whitcomb, Shari (2005)
Wilson, Erica (2005)
Woodward, Terri (2005)

Lake Michigan Minx

Year	League	Name	W	L	Conference	Division	DF	PR
1999	WPFL	Lake Michigan Minx	5	0	--	--	1	NC

Based in: Green Bay, WI   **Neutral site:** Naperville, IL (N)

Date		Opponent				Date		Opponent			
10/9/1999	A	Minnesota Vixens	W	33	6	11/9/1999	A	Minnesota Vixens	W	23	21
10/16/1999	N	Minnesota Vixens	W	31	19	1/22/2000	A	Minnesota Vixens	W	30	27 C
10/23/1999	H	Minnesota Vixens	W	41	37						

Las Vegas Showgirlz

Year	League	Name	W	L	Conference	Division	DF	PR
2006	WPFL	Las Vegas Showgirlz	2	5	American	West	4	--
2007	WPFL	Las Vegas Showgirlz	2	6	American	West	4	--
2008	IWFL	Las Vegas Showgirlz	5	3	Western	Pacific Southwest	2	--
2009	WFA	Las Vegas Showgirlz	8	1	American	Pacific	1	S
2010	WFA	Las Vegas Showgirlz	10	2	American	South Pacific	1	CC
2011	WFA	Las Vegas Showgirlz	4	6	American	South Pacific	3	--
2012	WFA	Las Vegas Showgirlz	7	4	American	Division 15 (Pacific West)	1	W
2013	WFA	Las Vegas Showgirlz	7	4	American	Division 11 (Pacific West)	2	W
2014	WFA	Las Vegas Showgirlz	10	3	American	Pacific West	2	Q
		Total	55	34				

Based in: Las Vegas, NV
Notes: Succeeded by Sin City Sun Devils

Date	H/A	Opponent	W/L	PF	PA	Note
7/29/2006	H	So Cal Scorpions	L	0	41	
8/5/2006	H	Los Angeles Amazons	L	14	20	
8/19/2006	H	New Mexico Burn	W	30	0	
8/26/2006	A	Houston Energy	L	6	53	
9/9/2006	A	So Cal Scorpions	L	8	35	
9/16/2006	A	New Mexico Burn	W	36	0	
9/23/2006	A	Los Angeles Amazons	L	2	26	
8/18/2007	H	So Cal Scorpions	L	14	36	
8/25/2007	A	Los Angeles Amazons	L	14	33	
9/1/2007	H	New Mexico Burn	W	41	8	
9/15/2007	H	Dallas Diamonds	L	10	41	
9/29/2007	A	New Mexico Burn	W	1	0	
10/6/2007	A	Dallas Diamonds	L	20	50	
10/13/2007	A	So Cal Scorpions	L	18	35	
10/20/2007	H	Los Angeles Amazons	L	0	28	
4/12/2008	H	Southern California Breakers	W	22	12	
4/19/2008	A	Tucson Monsoon	W	35	16	
5/3/2008	H	California Quake	L	27	30	
5/17/2008	A	New Mexico Menace	W	27	7	
5/24/2008	A	California Quake	L	38	41	
5/31/2008	H	Sacramento Sirens	L	14	21	
6/7/2008	A	Southern California Breakers	W	24	6	
6/14/2008	H	New Mexico Menace	W	55	0	
4/18/2009	H	California Lynx	W	19	6	
5/9/2009	A	Marana She-Devils	W	1	0	N
5/23/2009	A	Phoenix Prowlers	W	26	14	
5/30/2009	H	Phoenix Prowlers	W	47	8	
6/6/2009	H	Marana She-Devils	W	1	0	N
6/13/2009	H	California Lynx	W	28	20	
6/20/2009	A	Phoenix Prowlers	W	35	8	
6/27/2009	A	California Lynx	W	40	22	
7/11/2009	A	St. Louis Slam	L	12	30	S
4/10/2010	A	Utah Blitz	W	27	0	
4/17/2010	A	Arizona Assassins	W	26	6	
5/1/2010	H	Utah Blitz	W	41	0	
5/8/2010	H	Pacific Warriors	W	34	6	
5/15/2010	H	Arizona Assassins	W	48	8	
5/22/2010	A	Utah Blitz	W	55	0	
6/5/2010	H	Portland Fighting Fillies	W	17	6	
6/12/2010	A	Pacific Warriors	L	21	33	
6/19/2010	H	Arizona Assassins	W	31	0	
6/26/2010	H	Portland Fighting Fillies	W	34	6	Q
7/10/2010	A	Austin Outlaws	W	27	21	S
7/17/2010	H	Lone Star Mustangs	L	6	8	CC
3/26/2011	H	Utah Jynx	W	12	8	IE
4/9/2011	A	San Diego Surge	L	0	84	
4/16/2011	H	Pacific Warriors	L	0	36	
4/30/2011	H	Los Angeles Amazons	W	16	0	
5/7/2011	A	Pacific Warriors	L	6	56	
5/14/2011	A	Utah Blitz	W	14	0	
5/21/2011	H	San Diego Surge	L	0	55	
5/28/2011	A	Utah Jynx	L	22	43	I
6/4/2011	A	Los Angeles Amazons	W	1	0	
6/11/2011	H	San Diego Sting	L	6	20	
3/10/2012	H	Phoenix Phantomz	L	8	30	IE
3/24/2012	A	Phoenix Phantomz	W	8	7	IE
4/14/2012	H	Arizona Assassins	W	32	7	
4/21/2012	H	Los Angeles Amazons	W	48	0	
4/28/2012	A	Utah Blitz	W	44	12	
5/5/2012	A	San Diego Sting	W	30	7	
5/12/2012	A	Utah Jynx	L	28	38	
5/19/2012	H	Silver State Legacy	L	12	28	
6/2/2012	A	Los Angeles Amazons	W	20	6	
6/16/2012	H	San Diego Sting	W	24	14	
6/23/2012	A	Pacific Warriors	L	20	27	W
3/2/2013	A	Everett Reign	W	28	0	E
3/30/2013	A	Phoenix Phantomz	W	18	12	IE
4/6/2013	A	Central Cal War Angels	L	6	42	
4/13/2013	H	San Diego Sting	W	48	19	
4/20/2013	H	Utah Jynx	L	28	38	
4/27/2013	A	Utah Blitz	W	40	2	
5/11/2013	H	Arizona Assassins	W	65	8	
5/18/2013	A	San Diego Surge	L	22	32	
5/25/2013	A	Utah Jynx	W	56	50	
6/1/2013	H	Utah Blitz	W	49	0	
6/15/2013	A	San Diego Surge	L	14	78	W
3/1/2014	H	Everett Reign	W	24	0	E
3/8/2014	H	Utah Jynx	W	74	38	IE
4/5/2014	A	San Diego Surge	L	6	59	
4/12/2014	H	Central Cal War Angels	L	28	32	
4/26/2014	H	Arizona Assassins	W	54	0	
5/3/2014	H	North County Stars	W	60	0	I
5/10/2014	H	Nevada Storm	W	56	0	
5/17/2014	A	West Coast Lightning	W	38	6	
5/24/2014	A	Nevada Storm	W	1	0	
5/31/2014	H	West Coast Lightning	W	50	6	
6/7/2014	A	Arizona Assassins	W	22	12	
6/14/2014	H	Everett Reign	W	50	0	W
6/21/2014	A	San Diego Surge	L	16	48	Q

Las Vegas Showgirlz Player Register (2006-2014)

Acacio, Christi (2006-2010, 2013-2014)
Adamson, Shyra (2010)
Agao, Jennifer (2006-2010)
Ahuna-Larrison, Summer (2006-07, '09)
Alexander, Kari (2007-2009)
Alston, Casandra (2006-2008)
Altman, Vernessa (2011)
Anderson, Shante (2006)
Anderson, Tatina (2006)
Andrade, Pamela (2011)
Ayala, Salina (2014)
Banks, Colleen (2007)
Barton, Wendy (2011-2014)
Becton, Felicia (2006)
Beltz, Kirstie (2008)
Beverly, Krista (2006-2007, 2009)
Beynon-Russo, Jacqueline (2006-2007)
Bodine, Margret (2007)
Bright, Ronnece (2010)
Britt, Cheryl (2010-2011)
Brouchet, Kristina (2007-2010)
Brown, Jessica (2010-2011)
Brownlee, Shamika (2007-2010)
Bryan-White, Annise (2006-2008)
Burrell, LaTeish (2012)
Burrow, Shawn (2006)
Camacho, Lisa (2009)
Cannon, Jodie (2007-2008)
Carter, DustyDawn (2011-2014)
Cattlett, Michelle (2006-2007)
Chase, Brittany (2012)
Chester, Moniqua (2011-2012)
Clemons, Wakesha (2010)
Coignard, Emma (2012)
Coley, Misty (2012)
Collins, Erika (2013)
Cowan, Jennifer (2012-2013)
Cox, Charley (2010)
Cunningham, Katrina (2010)
Cusato, Jonelle (2006)
Denton, Erin (2006)
Dickson, Nicole (2011-2014)
Doll, Madie (2013)
Dunbar, Calena (2006)
Dye, Joyce (2008)
Edwards, MyKeesha (2011-2014)
Ellis, Alisha (2013)
Estes, Jackie (2006-2007)
Estrada, Jenei (2009)
Fair, Jenisha (2010)
Finks, Shameka (2008-2010, 2013-2014)
Flanagan, Katina (2009, 2013)
Forrest, Cynthia (2010)
Freeman, Shay (2013)
Garcia, Denise (2009)
Gemar, Stephanie (2006-2010)
Gentry, Eboni (2006-2007)
Giorgione, Summer (2013)
Grayson, Krystle (2007)
Grayson, Rachel "Rocky" (2006-07, 2009)
Hailey, Shannon (2007, 2009, 2013)
Hall, Taylor (2009-2010, 2014)
Harper-Mosby, Leticia (2011-2012)
Harris, C'mon (2010)
Hart, Brye (2011)
Hawwass, Maha (2010-14)
Heath, Faith (2011, 2013-2014)
Henderson, Brittany (2014)
Hernandez, Nickecia (2010)
Hernandez, Vanessa (2007-10, 2012-14)
Hewing, Azuree (2012)
Hildebrandt, Mary (2010-2013)
Holland, Ashli (2014)
Houser, Dena (2007-2008)
Jackson, Angela (2006)
Jackson, Ocean (2007-2008)
Jamerson, LaShanna (2006)
Johnson, Nikki (2009-2010, 2014)
Jones, Jennifer (2014)
Jones, Kowanna (2006)
Joot, Karin (2006-2009)
Kalua, Kelinani (2011)
Katris, Kristina (2013)
Kean, Kelly (2006)
Kennelly, Shawna (2006-2007)
Knight, Cynthia (2007)
La'a, Leana (2011)
Lacey, Jackie (2006)
Ladue, Christina (2007-2008)
Lancaster, Alicia (2010-2012)
Landing, Khaliah (2012-2013)
Leuma, Christina (2011)
Loau-Salgado, Suitupe (2006-2007)
Lorenzo, Gina (2011-2012)
Lula, Christina (2012-2013)
Maldonado, Stephanie (2006-2010)
Mallon, Kathrine (2013-2014)
Martinez, Samantha (2011)
McConnell, Ashley (2011)
McDowell, Lorriane (2006)
Merriman, Simone (2011)
Mohler, Rachel (2006)
Montgomery, Romona (2006-10, 2013-14)
Morris, Akia "Kiki" (2006-2007, 2009)
Murature, Aubrey (2012)
Murillo, Trina (2011)
Mytych, Kerri (2007-2010)
Nehf, Sara (2014)
Nishikawa, Tricia (2009-2010)
Nolan, Sunny (2007-2008, 2010-2014)
Norman, LaJoya (2007-2010)
Nunez, Elsa (2006-2008, 2010)
Nuno, Genevia (2013)
Olsen, Sharisse (2010)
Pale, Olivia (2014)
Palenapa, Marlena "Lena" ('06-07, '09, '13)
Parson-Rimsey, Willena (2008)
Perez, Nelly (2006)
Perkins, Junise (2011)
Phillips, Trea (2007)
Pitts, Simone (2013-2014)
Porter, Alicia (2014)
Ramos, Alicia (2006-2009, 2013-2014)
Rathbone, Norine (2008-2009)
Ray, Valerie (2012)
Rhemm, Colleen (2006)
Richardson, Misty (2006)
Rodgers, Brandi (2013-2014)
Rodriquez, Thaycha "Ty" (2008-2014)
Ronczka, Randie (2006)
Rozek, Becky (2010-11)
Rushing, Amy (2007)
Salinas, Angel (2013-2014)
Samson, Tori (2013)
Santiago, Kendrell (2012-2013)
Sasarita, Sandy (2006)
Saunders, Ebony (2006-08, 2010, 2014)
Savea, Moana (2011)
Scarlett, Shannon (2009)
Schudt, Angelic (2007-2009, 2013-2014)
Schultz, Jennifer (2007)
Schwenke, Kelesi (2013)
Simanu, Lua'ipou Afo (2012-2013)
Sims, ShaQuana (2011)
Smith, Cicely (2006-2007)
Sochachi, Teresa (2007)
Stanley, Barb (2014)
Stevenson, Jade (2012-2013)
Sull, Mandeep (2007, 2009)
Swenson, Erin (2008)
Tanasale, Veronique (2006-09, 2012-14)
Tanner, Yvette (2012-2014)
Teitsma, Cindy (2010-14)
Temple, Vicky (2007)
To'o To'o, Pearl (2011-2012)
Trejo, Lupe (2006-2007, 2009)
Turner, Romya (2012)
Turner, Wendy (2012-2013)
Vernon, Amanda (2011)
Villaflores, Vanessa (2012-2014)
Von Herbulis, Michele (2010)
Walter, Angela (2011-2012)
Walters, Brittney (2006)
Walters, Carrie (2006-2014)
Washington, La Tina (2010)
Washington, LaDonna (2013)
Wayman, Octavia (2006)
Weindenbosch, Charessee (2009-2010)
Williams, Alecsys (2011-2013)
Williams, Alonda (2007)
Wolridge, Edrecka (2010)
Wright, Robbye (2006-2007)

Lee County Predators

Year	League	Name	W	L	Conference	Division	DF	PR
2003	AWFL	Lee County Predators	1	2	--	--	--	--

Based in: Pennington Gap, VA

Lee County Predators Game-By-Game Results

Date	H/A	Opponent	Result		Date	H/A	Opponent	Result
4/12/2003	A	Tennessee Mountaincatz	L 0 16		5/3/2003	H	Tennessee Mountaincatz	L 0 40
4/19/2003	H	Harlan Red Devils	W 6 0					

Lone Star Mustangs

Year	League	Name	W	L	Conference	Division	DF	PR
2009	WFA	Lone Star Mustangs	6	2	American	Southwest	2	--
2010	WFA	Lone Star Mustangs	13	0	American	Southwest	1	NC
2011	WFA	Lone Star Mustangs	5	3	American	South Central	2	--
2012	WFA	Lone Star Mustangs	7	3	American	Division 12 (Southwest)	2	Q
2013	WFA	Lone Star Mustangs	4	4	American	Division 9 (Southwest)	3	--
		Total	35	12				

Based in: Bedford, TX
Neutral site: Las Vegas, NV (N)
Notes: Preceded by NWFA's Dallas Rage

Date	H/A	Opponent	Result		Date	H/A	Opponent	Result
4/18/2009	A	East Texas Saberkats	W 1 0 N		5/7/2011	A	Tulsa Eagles	W 40 0
4/25/2009	H	Austin Outlaws	L 13 14		5/14/2011	H	Houston Power	W 14 6
5/2/2009	H	H-Town Texas Cyclones	W 20 12		5/21/2011	A	Dallas Diamonds	L 12 23
5/9/2009	A	Austin Outlaws	L 14 28		6/4/2011	H	Little Rock Wildcats	W 40 0
5/16/2009	A	H-Town Texas Cyclones	W 14 12		6/11/2011	A	Houston Power	L 0 12
5/30/2009	H	Austin Outlaws	W 28 14					
6/13/2009	H	East Texas Saberkats	W 1 0 N		4/14/2012	A	DFW Xtreme	W 33 0 I
6/20/2009	A	H-Town Texas Cyclones	W 31 0		4/21/2012	A	Dallas Diamonds	L 0 90
					4/28/2012	H	Austin Outlaws	W 12 0
4/10/2010	H	Oklahoma City Lightning	W 62 0		5/12/2012	H	Houston Power	W 24 8
4/17/2010	A	Houston Power	W 32 13		5/19/2012	A	Austin Outlaws	W 45 0
5/1/2010	H	Houston Power	W 32 0		5/26/2012	H	Dallas Diamonds	L 8 59
5/8/2010	A	Austin Outlaws	W 38 16		6/2/2012	A	Houston Power	W 28 14
5/15/2010	H	Memphis Soul	W 55 0		6/16/2012	H	Tulsa Threat	W 40 0
5/22/2010	A	Oklahoma City Lightning	W 1 0		6/23/2012	H	Arkansas Wildcats	W 70 0 W
6/5/2010	A	New Orleans Blaze	W 51 0		6/30/2012	A	Dallas Diamonds	L 0 76 Q
6/12/2010	H	Austin Outlaws	W 38 7					
6/19/2010	H	Monterrey Royal Eagles	W 1 0		4/6/2013	H	Little Rock Wildcats	W 20 14
6/26/2010	H	Pacific Warriors	W 38 14 Q		4/20/2013	A	Tulsa Threat	W 54 10
7/10/2010	A	Iowa Thunder	W 30 20 S		4/27/2013	H	Dallas Diamonds	L 0 48
7/17/2010	A	Las Vegas Showgirlz	W 8 6 CC		5/11/2013	A	Austin Outlaws	L 14 28
7/31/2010	N	Columbus Comets	W 16 12 C		5/18/2013	A	Houston Power	W 20 14
					5/25/2013	H	Austin Outlaws	L 0 38
4/2/2011	A	Austin Outlaws	W 16 0		6/1/2013	H	Houston Power	W 26 12
4/16/2011	H	Austin Outlaws	W 33 3		6/8/2013	A	Dallas Diamonds	L 6 82
4/30/2011	H	Dallas Diamonds	L 6 16					

Lone Star Mustangs Player Register (2009-2013)

Abrego, Yvette (2010)
Alexander, Krystal (2011)
Allen, Christina (2012)
Alonso, Jennifer (2009-2010)
Alonzo, Tawny (2013)
Atencio, C.J. (2012)
Atkins, April (2011)
Avants, Taylor (2012)
Bauer, Mary Beth (2009-2013)
Beach, Melissa (2010-2012)
Bearden, Jamie "Red" (2009-2011)
Berg, Joanna (2009)
Bland, Sharron (2013)
Boaz-Anderson, Loni (2012)
Boney, Jona (2009-2010)
Borchardt, Schannia (2010)
Bowman, K.B. (2010)
Boyle, Aimi (2011)
Bresnehan, Rhonda (2012)
Broussard, Kristen (2009, 2011)
Brown, Elisha (2009)
Brown, Kiamesha (2009-2010)
Brundidge, Haleigh (2013)
Bushman, Brittany (2010-2011)
Cain, Brittany (2012)
Calhoun, Mercedes (2013)
Canales, Jamie (2011)
Carrillo, Estella (2012)
Carter, Bethany (2011)
Carter, Catlin (2011)
Carter, D.C. (2013)
Cherry, Dominique (2012-2013)
Childs, Ashley (2011)
Collins, Ashley (2010)
Colmer, Courtney (2012)
Connolly, Teresa (2012)
Crayton, Christina (2013)
Crow, Leslie (2009-2010)
Dixon, Lindsey (2009, 2011-2012)
Doan, Melissa (2009)
Downs, Lacy (2010-2011, 2013)
Dye, Takesha (2012-2013)
Dyer, Valarie (2013)
Edmondson, Dominique (2013)
Erhart, Crystal (2012)
Escamilla, Flower (2013)
Fossis, Shug (2009)
Fuentes, Rea (2009)
Garcia, Lily (2012)
Garrett, Skye (2011)
Gay, D.J. (2009-2010)
Gil, Rosa (2009-2010)
Golston, Rachel (2009)
Grant, Yolanda (2009-2011)
Grayson, Shelise (2009)
Haley, Courtney (2012-2013)
Harris, Nate (2012)
Hart, T.K. (2010)
Harvey, Alex (2009-2011)

Continued on next page

Lone Star Mustangs Player Register (continued)

Hayes, Jocelynn (2013)
Haynes, Kim (2013)
Henry, T.K. (2010-2011)
Hill, Cassidy (2010)
Hull, Jennifer (2009-2011)
Hunter, Natasha (2009)
Irvin, Ginger (2013)
Jenkins, Odessa (2010)
Johnson, Iris (2011-2012)
Jones, Dia (2012-2013)
Jones, Ebony (2009, 2012-2013)
Jones, Jennifer "Jay Jay" (2009-2013)
Kelley, Tamra (2009-2013)
Kenney, Michele (2012)
Kirven, C.D. (2012)
Kohle, Amber (2011)
Korywchak, Cassie (2011)
Korywchak, Kelsey (2009)
Larson, Cadie (2009)
Law, Katelynn (2012)
Lemon, Amanda (2009)
Lyles, Kristen (2010)
Mack, J. (2011)
Martin, Stephanie "Joos" (2009-2012)
Martinez, Venessa (2009-2011)
Matthews, Shinnette (2012-2013)
Maytubby, Eboni (2011)
Maytubby, Etta (2009-2011, 2013)
McCuin, Ashley (2009-2011)
McQueen, DeeBaby (2010, 2012)
Merlino, Mary (2012-2013)
Minton, Jillian (2011)
Mueller, Brandice (2009-2010, 2012)
Newkirk, Joy (2009-2010)
Newman, Lorrie (2010)
Newsom, Kay (2013)
Nunsant, Shauntia "Tia" (2009-10, 2012)
Ottaiano, Daniela (2009-2011)
Parkman, Carmon (2010)
Pena, Genn (2012)
Perkins, Veronica (2012-2013)
Pietras, Amy (2012-2013)
Puente-Garza, Marlo (2012)
Ramos, Pattie (2009, 2012)
Ray-Tribble, Casey (2009-2010)
Reece, R. (2010)
Reid, Courtney (2013)
Rivers, Rachael (2012-2013)
Roach, Krystal (2012-2013)
Robinson, Fancy (2012-2013)
Rogers, Jai (2012-2013)
Rojas, Marisa (2010)
Sabeh, Jillian (2012)
Salazar, Jennifer (2011)
Satterwhite, Brittany (2009-2011)
Saville, Mary (2009-2012)
Scott, Constance (2013)
Selph, Deondra (2009-2010)
Shaw, S.S. (2011)
Simmons, Melissa (2009-2010)
Smith, Julie (2013)
Smith, Terri (2010)
Smith, Twyla (2012)
Spencer, Stuff (2009-2011)
Spiller, Kelanna (2010-2011)
Stepich, Kortney (2013)
Stewart, Tia (2013)
Stout, Lyndi (2012)
Summerville, Natasha "Taz" (2011-2012)
Thurmon, Monique (2013)
Vallejo, Cathy (2012)
Vincentti, Eboni (2009-2010, 2013)
Wakefield, Stephanie (2009-2011)
Waller, Janet (2011)
Walters, Tasha (2012)
Ward, Shion (2009-2013)
Washington, Whitney (2010)
Weyman, Jessie (2012-2013)
White, Brittany (2011)
Whitney, Shon (2012)
Wiesner, Kimberley (2012)
Williams, Maddie (2009-2011)
Williams, Michelle (2012)
Woods, Shan (2012-2013)

Long Beach Aftershock

Year	League	Name	W	L	Conference	Division	DF	PR
2002	AFWL	Long Beach Aftershock	8	3	--	--	2	LC
2003	WPFL	Long Beach Aftershock	8	1	American	West	1	CC
2004	WPFL	Long Beach Aftershock	8	3	American	West	1	S
2005	WPFL	Long Beach Aftershock	1	8	American	West	4	--
		Total	25	15				

Based in: Long Beach, CA

Date	H/A	Opponent	W/L	PF	PA	Note
9/21/2002		Los Angeles Amazons	W	1	0	I
9/28/2002	H	Arizona Titans	W	63	0	
10/5/2002	A	San Diego Sunfire	L	28	34	
10/12/2002	A	San Francisco Tsunami	W	46	0	
10/19/2002	H	Los Angeles Lasers	W	14	0	
10/26/2002	H	San Diego Sunfire	L	8	27	
11/2/2002	A	Arizona Titans	W	12	0	
11/9/2002	H	San Francisco Tsunami	W	1	0	
11/17/2002	A	Los Angeles Lasers	L	6	35	
12/7/2002	A	Los Angeles Lasers	W	8	6	CC
12/14/2002	A	San Diego Sunfire	W	12	7	C
8/3/2003	H	San Diego Sunfire	W	18	6	
8/9/2003	A	Arizona Knighthawks	W	33	6	
8/16/2003	A	San Diego Sunfire	W	34	13	
8/30/2003	H	Arizona Knighthawks	W	54	0	
9/13/2003	H	Arizona Caliente	W	25	19	
9/27/2003	A	Arizona Caliente	W	32	27	
10/4/2003	A	So Cal Scorpions	W	41	10	
10/11/2003	H	Los Angeles Amazons	W	40	6	
10/25/2003	A	Northern Ice	L	30	37	CC
7/31/2004	A	Los Angeles Amazons	W	36	7	
8/14/2004	A	So Cal Scorpions	W	36	0	
8/21/2004	A	Arizona Caliente	W	27	14	
9/4/2004	H	Arizona Caliente	W	24	21	
9/11/2004	A	Arizona Caliente	L	12	17	
9/25/2004	H	Los Angeles Amazons	W	57	15	
10/2/2004	H	So Cal Scorpions	W	42	6	
10/9/2004	H	Houston Energy	W	18	9	
10/16/2004	A	Houston Energy	L	8	28	
10/23/2004	H	Los Angeles Amazons	W	20	0	
10/30/2004	H	Houston Energy	L	8	22	S
7/30/2005	A	So Cal Scorpions	L	0	14	
8/6/2005	H	So Cal Scorpions	L	16	33	
8/27/2005	A	San Francisco Stingrayz	W	1	0	
9/10/2005	A	Los Angeles Amazons	L	0	32	
9/17/2005	H	So Cal Scorpions	L	0	39	
10/1/2005	H	Dallas Diamonds	L	0	55	
10/8/2005	A	Dallas Diamonds	L	0	56	
10/15/2005	H	Arizona Caliente	L	0	38	
10/22/2005	A	Los Angeles Amazons	L	6	12	

Los Angeles Amazons

Year	League	Name	W	L	Conference	Division	DF	PR
2002	WPFL	Los Angeles Amazons	2	9	American	--	5	--
2003	WPFL	Los Angeles Amazons	2	8	American	West	6	--
2004	WPFL	Los Angeles Amazons	4	6	American	West	3	--
2005	WPFL	Los Angeles Amazons	7	4	American	West	2	S
2006	WPFL	Los Angeles Amazons	4	4	American	West	3	--
2007	WPFL	Los Angeles Amazons	7	2	American	West	1	S
2008	NWFA	Los Angeles Amazons	9	1	Southern	West	1	CC
2009	IWFL	Los Angeles Amazons	8	1	Western	Pacific Southwest	1	S
2010	IWFL	Los Angeles Amazons	4	4	Western	Pacific West	5	--
2011	WFA	Los Angeles Amazons	1	7	American	North Pacific	3	--
2012	WFA	Los Angeles Amazons	0	8	American	Division 15 (Pacific West)	3	--
		Total	48	54				

Based in: Los Angeles, CA

Date		Opponent		W/L	PF	PA	Note
7/27/2002		Santa Rosa Scorchers		L	0	6	I
8/3/2002		Arizona Knighthawks		L	6	46	
8/29/2002		California Quake		L	8	20	I
9/7/2002		Arizona Knighthawks		L	0	27	
9/14/2002		Santa Rosa Scorchers		W	14	13	I
9/21/2002		Long Beach Aftershock		L	0	1	I
9/28/2002		Houston Energy		L	0	1	
10/5/2002		Arizona Knighthawks		L	0	41	
10/12/2002		Arizona Knighthawks		L	0	16	
10/19/2002		California Quake		L	14	20	I*
11/10/2002	A	Pacific Blast		W	8	0	I
8/2/2003	A	So Cal Scorpions		W	8	7	
8/9/2003	H	Arizona Caliente		L	0	45	
8/16/2003	H	Arizona Knighthawks		W	26	6	
8/23/2003	A	San Diego Sunfire		L	12	20	
9/6/2003	H	Florida Stingrayz		L	2	14	
9/13/2003	A	Arizona Knighthawks		L	7	14	
9/20/2003	A	Arizona Caliente		L	0	46	
9/27/2003	H	So Cal Scorpions		L	14	24	
10/4/2003	H	San Diego Sunfire		L	14	58	
10/11/2003	A	Long Beach Aftershock		L	6	40	
7/31/2004	H	Long Beach Aftershock		L	7	36	
8/14/2004	H	Arizona Caliente		L	0	35	
8/21/2004	H	So Cal Scorpions		W	3	0	
8/28/2004	H	Minnesota Vixen		W	15	0	
9/11/2004	A	So Cal Scorpions		L	0	3	
9/18/2004	H	So Cal Scorpions		W	6	3	
9/25/2004	A	Long Beach Aftershock		L	15	57	
10/9/2004	A	Arizona Caliente		L	3	14	
10/16/2004	A	Delaware Griffins		W	20	14	
10/23/2004	A	Long Beach Aftershock		L	0	20	
7/30/2005	A	San Francisco Stingrayz		W	42	0	
8/6/2005	H	San Francisco Stingrayz		W	1	0	
8/20/2005	A	Arizona Caliente		W	20	8	
8/27/2005	H	So Cal Scorpions		L	0	14	
9/10/2005	H	Long Beach Aftershock		W	32	0	
9/17/2005	H	Arizona Caliente		W	20	0	
10/1/2005	A	Arizona Caliente		W	20	14	
10/8/2005	A	So Cal Scorpions		L	0	35	
10/15/2005	H	So Cal Scorpions		L	14	24	
10/22/2005	H	Long Beach Aftershock		W	12	6	
10/28/2005	A	So Cal Scorpions		L	14	27	S
7/22/2006	A	So Cal Scorpions		L	0	13	
7/29/2006	H	Dallas Diamonds		L	13	42	
8/5/2006	A	Las Vegas Showgirlz		W	20	14	
8/12/2006	A	New Mexico Burn		W	62	0	
8/19/2006	H	So Cal Scorpions		L	12	34	
9/9/2006	H	New Mexico Burn		W	50	0	
9/16/2006	A	Dallas Diamonds		L	16	39	
9/23/2006	H	Las Vegas Showgirlz		W	26	2	
8/18/2007	A	New Mexico Burn		W	64	0	
8/25/2007	H	Las Vegas Showgirlz		W	33	14	
9/1/2007	A	So Cal Scorpions		W	15	13	
9/8/2007	H	Minnesota Vixen		W	52	6	
9/22/2007	A	So Cal Scorpions		L	12	23	
9/29/2007	A	Minnesota Vixen		W	35	0	
10/6/2007	H	New Mexico Burn		W	1	0	
10/20/2007	A	Las Vegas Showgirlz		W	28	0	
11/3/2007	H	So Cal Scorpions		L	6	7	S
4/19/2008	H	Phoenix Prowlers		W	47	14	
4/26/2008	H	Modesto Magic		W	90	0	
5/3/2008	A	Arizona Wildfire		W	62	0	
5/17/2008	A	Phoenix Prowlers		W	42	0	
5/24/2008	H	Arizona Wildfire		W	75	6	
5/31/2008	A	Modesto Magic		W	1	0	
6/7/2008	A	Arizona Wildfire		W	1	0	
6/21/2008	H	Phoenix Prowlers		W	41	14	
7/5/2008	H	Kentucky Karma		W	1	0	S
7/12/2008	H	H-Town Texas Cyclones		L	14	34	CC
4/11/2009	A	California Quake		W	32	2	
4/25/2009	A	Southern California Breakers		W	42	0	
5/2/2009	H	California Quake		W	36	21	
5/9/2009	H	Modesto Maniax		W	64	0	
5/16/2009	H	New Mexico Menace		W	50	0	
5/23/2009	H	Southern California Breakers		W	33	0	
5/30/2009	A	Tucson Monsoon		W	57	0	
6/13/2009	A	Sacramento Sirens		W	20	19	
6/27/2009	A	Kansas City Tribe		L	14	19	S
4/3/2010	A	So Cal Scorpions		W	37	26	
4/17/2010	A	California Quake		W	48	36	
4/24/2010	H	Sacramento Sirens		L	26	27	
5/8/2010	A	Portland Shockwave		W	17	0	
5/15/2010	H	Bay Area Bandits		L	22	33	
5/22/2010	A	Sacramento Sirens		L	6	10	
5/29/2010	H	Portland Shockwave		L	6	20	
6/5/2010	H	Southern California Breakers		W	39	14	

Continued on next page

Los Angeles Amazons Game-By-Game Results (continued)

Date	H/A	Opponent	W/L	Score		Date	H/A	Opponent	W/L	Score
4/2/2011	H	Bay Area Bandits	L	0 53		4/14/2012	H	Central Cal War Angels	L	0 46
4/16/2011	H	San Diego Surge	L	0 74		4/21/2012	A	Las Vegas Showgirlz	L	0 48
4/30/2011	A	Las Vegas Showgirlz	L	0 16		4/28/2012	A	San Diego Sting	L	0 8
5/7/2011	H	Central Cal War Angels	L	0 1		5/12/2012	H	San Diego Sting	L	0 14
5/21/2011	A	Central Cal War Angels	L	0 68		5/19/2012	H	Utah Jynx	L	22 62
6/4/2011	H	Las Vegas Showgirlz	L	0 1		6/2/2012	H	Las Vegas Showgirlz	L	6 20
6/11/2011	A	Bay Area Bandits	L	0 40		6/9/2012	A	San Diego Sting	L	0 7
6/18/2011	A	So Cal Scorpions	W	1 0		6/16/2012	A	Valley Vipers	L	6 12

Los Angeles Amazons Player Register (2008, 2011-2012)

Adams, Sarah (2008)
Agnew, Odja (2012)
Alvarado, Dianna (2011-2012)
Anderson, Rebekkah Chanel (2012)
Banks, Tenisha (2011)
Bhakta, Sweta (2008)
Blanchard, Rashynda (2012)
Blueford, Nicole (2008)
Castellanos, Mikie (2011-2012)
Castro, Emilia (2008)
Castro, Maria (2012)
Cervantes, Anel (2011)
Cola, Shay (2011)
Crim, Dawn (2012)
Dabul, Diana (2011)
Davis, Lauren (2008)
De Leon, Dorothy (2012)
Delgado, Patricia (2011)
Estrada, Nicole (2008, 2011-2012)
Federico, Diane (2008, 2011)
Galarza, Valarie (2012)
Garcia, Crystal (2012)
Gibbons, Lisa (2008)
Glenn, Alexis (2008)
Glover, Shardae (2011-2012)
Golde, Sadjah (2011)
Gomez, Araceli (2011)
Gordon, Donna (2008, 2011-2012)
Guidry, Deana (2008)
Gutierrez, Michelle (2008)
Guzman, Jessica (2008)
Hairell, Meg (2012)
Hall, Danielle (2008)
Hanson, Valerie (2008)
Hardiman, Demetrea (2012)
Henry, Kim (2008)
Hill, Lorraine (2008, 2011-2012)
Holland, Quelsie (2012)
Honani, VaNiesha (2012)
Jaso, Lisa (2008)
Jaso, Regina (2008)
Jovel, Zahira (2008)
Kozlowski, Stephanie (2008)
Lester-Jefferson, Nicole (2012)
Mack, Justine (2008, 2011-2012)
Mancille, Marina (2011)
Martin, Jasmine (2008)
McDonald, Tamara (2008)
Mendez, Salena (2011)
Mills, Veronica (2008, 2011-2012)
Miranda, Alice (2011-2012)
Moffett-White, Amber (2008)
Moody, Ashley (2008)
Moore, Lorie (2008)
Morin, Alexis (2008)
Nix, Brianna (2012)
Patino, Delinda (2008)
Paxton, La-Isa (2008, 2011)
Pereda, Melissa (2008)
Podesta, Joni (2008)
Potts, Christian Mychal (2012)
Reyes, Rose Marie (2012)
Rincon, Roberta (2011)
Rivera, Deeann (2008)
Rodriguez, Christina (2008, 2011)
Rodriguez, Maria (2008)
Rodriguez, Rayleen (2008)
Romo, Miriam (2011)
Rosselle, Charmaige (2008)
Royal, Erin (2008)
Salazar, Asia (2012)
Sanchez, Alejandra (2012)
Satterfield, Amy (2008)
Seabloom, Brittany (2011-2012)
Serrato, Michelle (2011-2012)
Starnes, Tammy (2012)
Steward, Adrienne (2008)
Sumpter, Banea (2008, 2012)
Taylor, Jody (2012)
Taylor, Rebecca (2008)
Thomson, Chandra (2008)
Villareal, Frances (2011)
Williams, Alice (2012)

Los Angeles Lasers

Year	League	Name	W	L	Conference	Division	DF	PR
2001	WAFL	Los Angeles Lasers	3	7	Pacific	South	4	--
2002	AFWL	Los Angeles Lasers	5	4	--	--	3	CC
		Total	8	11				

Based in: Los Angeles, CA

Date	H/A	Opponent	W/L	Score		Date	H/A	Opponent	W/L	Score	
11/3/2001	H	California Quake	W	22 14		9/21/2002	A	Arizona Titans	W	66 0	
11/10/2001	H	San Diego Sunfire	L	6 12		9/28/2002	H	San Diego Sunfire	L	14 17	*
11/29/2001	A	Hawaii Legends	L	28 34	*	10/5/2002	A	San Francisco Tsunami	W	48 6	
12/2/2001	A	Hawaii Legends	L	6 7		10/19/2002	A	Long Beach Aftershock	L	0 14	
12/8/2001	H	Arizona Caliente	L	0 6		10/26/2002	H	San Francisco Tsunami	W	1 0	
12/15/2001	A	California Quake	L	22 27		11/2/2002	A	San Diego Sunfire	L	26 33	
12/22/2001	A	San Diego Sunfire	L	13 28		11/17/2002	H	Long Beach Aftershock	W	35 6	
12/29/2001	A	Arizona Caliente	L	28 50		11/23/2002	H	Arizona Titans	W	56 0	
1/5/2002	H	Oakland Banshees	W	46 6		12/7/2002	H	Long Beach Aftershock	L	6 8	CC
1/12/2002	H	San Francisco Tsunami	W	20 19							

Louisiana Fuel

Year	League	Name	W	L	Conference	Division	DF	PR
2005	IWFL	Baton Rouge Wildcats	2	8	Eastern	Southern Central	2	--
2006	IWFL	Baton Rouge Wildcats	3	5	Eastern	South Atlantic	4	--
2007	IWFL	Baton Rouge Wildcats	1	6	Western	Mid South	3	--
2008	IWFL2	Louisiana Fuel	1	7	Southern	Mid South	3	--
2009	IWFL2	Louisiana Fuel	0	6	--	--	19	--
2010	IWFL2	Louisiana Fuel	3	5	Eastern	Southeast	4	--
		Total	**10**	**37**				

Based in: Baton Rouge, LA

4/2/2005	A	Dallas Revolution	W	1	0	N	4/12/2008	H	Shreveport Aftershock	W	12	8
4/9/2005	H	Tampa Bay Terminators	L	6	62		4/19/2008	H	Clarksville Fox	L	6	66
4/16/2005	A	Jacksonville Dixie Blues	L	13	57		4/26/2008	H	Orlando Mayhem	L	0	55
4/23/2005	H	Atlanta Xplosion	L	0	63		5/3/2008	A	Shreveport Aftershock	L	6	36
4/30/2005	H	Jacksonville Dixie Blues	L	13	33		5/17/2008	A	Clarksville Fox	L	0	14
5/14/2005	A	Atlanta Xplosion	L	0	43		5/31/2008	H	Shreveport Aftershock	L	0	14
5/21/2005	H	Tucson Wildfire	L	6	12		6/7/2008	A	Orlando Mayhem	L	0	42
6/4/2005	A	Tampa Bay Terminators	L	0	63		6/14/2008	A	Shreveport Aftershock	L	0	56
6/11/2005	A	Dallas Revolution	W	1	0	N						
6/18/2005	H	Jacksonville Dixie Blues	L	14	40		4/11/2009	A	Shreveport Aftershock	L	18	32
							4/18/2009	H	Dallas Diamonds	L	0	27
4/29/2006	H	Miami Fury	L	0	1		5/2/2009	H	Tennessee Valley Tigers	L	27	32
5/6/2006	A	Atlanta Xplosion	L	0	77		5/9/2009	A	Palm Beach Punishers	L	0	28
5/13/2006	A	Tampa Bay Terminators	L	0	62		5/16/2009	A	Dallas Diamonds	L	0	64
5/20/2006	H	Indianapolis Chaos	W	36	12		5/30/2009	A	Shreveport Aftershock	L	36	65
5/27/2006	H	Tucson Monsoon	W	21	14							
6/3/2006	A	Atlanta Xplosion	L	0	36		4/3/2010	A	H-Town Texas Cyclones	W	1	0	N
6/17/2006	H	Indianapolis Chaos	W	1	0		4/10/2010	A	Houston Energy	L	0	60
6/24/2006	A	Orlando Mayhem	L	3	34		4/17/2010	H	Iowa Crush	L	14	16
							4/24/2010	H	Palm Beach Punishers	L	20	26
4/28/2007	H	Atlanta Xplosion	L	0	60		5/1/2010	A	H-Town Texas Cyclones	W	1	0	N
5/5/2007	A	Orlando Mayhem	L	0	55		5/8/2010	H	Tennessee Valley Tigers	L	22	30
5/12/2007	A	Shreveport Aftershock	L	24	28		5/15/2010	H	Houston Energy	L	0	30
6/2/2007	A	Kansas City Storm	L	0	47		6/5/2010	H	H-Town Texas Cyclones	W	1	0	N
6/9/2007	H	Orlando Mayhem	L	0	54							
6/16/2007	H	Shreveport Aftershock	W	42	6							
6/23/2007	A	Atlanta Xplosion	L	0	1							

Louisiana Jazz

Year	League	Name	W	L	Conference	Division	DF	PR
2014	WFA	Louisiana Jazz	0	7	American	Gulf Coast	3	--

Based in: New Orleans, LA
Notes: Preceded by New Orleans Mojo

4/5/2014	H	Acadiana Zydeco	L	6	18		5/10/2014	A	Tulsa Threat	L	0	1
4/19/2014	A	Houston Power	L	0	39		5/24/2014	A	Acadiana Zydeco	L	0	1
4/26/2014	H	Tulsa Threat	L	6	34		5/31/2014	A	Atlanta Phoenix	L	0	1
5/3/2014	H	Houston Power	L	0	50							

Louisiana Jazz Player Register (2014)

Barconey, Keioaka (2014)
Blount, Daysha (2014)
Bott, Allison (2014)
Bowens, Lillie (2014)
Butler, Anndrelle (2014)
Caston, Jesyka (2014)
Davenport, Imogene (2014)
Disotell, Brenda (2014)
Duncan, Marquia (2014)
Farmer, Analyn (2014)
Harper, Kylie (2014)
Harris, Shannon (2014)
Johnson, D. (2014)
Jones, Victoria (2014)
Morales, Tianne (2014)
Morgan, Rebecca "Beck" (2014)
Nguyen, Jennifer (2014)
Nguyen, Jodie (2014)
Patterson, Keshawn (2014)
Prevost, Erin (2014)
Robinson, Dantrelle (2014)
Russell, Magan (2014)
Schunert, Yvette (2014)
Spencer, Tiffany (2014)
Troulliet, Richelle (2014)
Wilson, Tonisha (2014)

Louisville Nightmare

Year	League	Name	W	L	Conference	Division	DF	PR
2009	IWFL2	Louisville Nightmare	0	8	--	--	25	--
2010	IWFL2	Louisville Nightmare	0	7	Western	Midwest	7	--
		Total	0	15				

Based in: Louisville, KY

4/11/2009	A	Carolina Phoenix	L	7	32
4/25/2009	A	Clarksville Fox	L	7	37
5/9/2009	H	Carolina Queens	L	0	1
5/16/2009	A	Tennessee Valley Tigers	L	0	53
5/23/2009	H	Cape Fear Thunder	L	14	34
5/30/2009	H	Tennessee Valley Tigers	L	0	54
6/6/2009	H	Clarksville Fox	L	0	12
6/13/2009	A	Chattanooga Locomotion	L	0	1
4/3/2010	H	Memphis Belles	L	0	1
4/17/2010	H	Clarksville Fox	L	0	1
4/24/2010	H	Carolina Phoenix	L	0	58
5/8/2010	A	Erie Illusion	L	8	47
5/15/2010	A	Clarksville Fox	L	0	40
5/22/2010	H	Tennessee Valley Tigers	L	0	1
5/29/2010	A	Tennessee Valley Tigers	L	8	25

Madison Blaze

Year	League	Name	W	L	Conference	Division	DF	PR
2013	IWFL	Madison Blaze	7	2	Western	Midwest	1	S
2014	IWFL	Madison Blaze	8	2	Western	Midwest	1	CC-BW
2015	IWFL	Madison Blaze	8	3	Western	Midwest	1	CC-B
		Total	23	7				

Based in: Madison, WI
Neutral site: Rock Hill, SC (N)
Notes: Preceded by Madison Cougars

5/4/2013	H	Iowa Crush	W	41	0	
5/11/2013	A	Wisconsin Warriors	L	15	29	
5/18/2013	A	Minnesota Vixen	W	26	0	
5/25/2013	A	Rockford Riveters	W	1	0	N
6/8/2013	H	Wisconsin Warriors	W	40	7	
6/15/2013	A	Iowa Crush	W	41	0	
6/22/2013	H	Minnesota Vixen	W	40	6	
6/29/2013	H	Rockford Riveters	W	1	0	N
7/13/2013	A	Houston Energy	L	0	30	S
4/12/2014	A	Iowa Crush	W	7	6	
4/26/2014	A	Missouri Thundercats	W	1	0	N
5/3/2014	H	Minnesota Vixen	W	14	0	
5/10/2014	A	Wisconsin Warriors	W	29	12	
5/24/2014	H	Missouri Thundercats	W	1	0	N
5/31/2014	H	Iowa Crush	W	27	0	
6/7/2014	A	Minnesota Vixen	L	14	18	
6/14/2014	H	Wisconsin Warriors	W	40	0	
7/12/2014	H	Houston Energy	L	0	53	CC
7/25/2014	N	Baltimore Nighthawks	W	31	14	B
4/11/2015	A	Iowa Crush	W	26	20	
4/25/2015	A	Wisconsin Warriors	W	56	0	
5/2/2015	H	Nebraska Stampede	W	16	8	
5/9/2015	A	Minnesota Vixen	W	14	8	*
5/16/2015	H	Iowa Crush	W	48	14	
5/30/2015	A	Minnesota Vixen	L	7	12	
6/6/2015	H	Wisconsin Warriors	W	60	0	
6/13/2015	A	Nebraska Stampede	W	27	24	
6/27/2015	A	Houston Energy	W	41	7	S
7/11/2015	A	Utah Falconz	L	0	73	CC
7/24/2015	N	Carolina Phoenix	L	9	32	B

Madison Blaze Player Register (2014-2015)

Alexander, Akiya (2015)
Alt, Chelsea (2014-2015)
Bailey, Jen (2015)
Bjelopetrovich, Ali (2014-2015)
Brettingen-Nash, Natalie (2015)
Brettingen-Nash, Stefanie (2015)
Brown, Anita (2015)
Clark, Erin (2014)
Close, Pam (2014-2015)
Derden, Tiffany (2014)
Durfee, Alia (2015)
Edlebeck, Teri (2014)
Fowlkes, Sarah (2014-2015)
Funck, Nicole (2014)
Geisler, Briana (2014-2015)
Gibson, Sara (2014)
Gott, Laurie (2014-2015)
Gregor, Lindsey (2014-2015)
Grose, Fayla (2014-2015)
Grulke, Jennifer (2014-2015)
Haines, Kara (2014-2015)
Havens, Becky (2014-2015)
Heizman, Karen (2014)
Hirschfield, Sheena (2014-2015)
Hochschild, Lisa (2014)
Jayce, Katie (2015)
Justice, Stormy-Kito (2015)
Justin, Kelsey (2014)
Kirk, Robbin (2014-2015)
Leatherberry, Amy (2014-2015)
Lein, Tiffany (2014)
Leverington, Stephanie (2015)
Loomis, Heather (2014-2015)
Loomis, Tiffany (2014-2015)
Maier, Ellie (2015)
Mier, Katie (2014)
Milbrath, Brenda (2014-2015)
Monroe, Jessica (2015)
Moore, Jennifer (2015)
Niemczyk, Melissa (2014)
O'Neil, Gabrielle (2015)
Precourt, Stephanie (2015)
Reith, Cori (2014)
Robinson, Katie (2015)
Rodriguez, Melissa (2015)
Rojas, Liz (2014)
Seggerman, Brenda (2014-2015)
Shaver, Tonya (2015)
Smith, Brianna (2014-2015)
Stamer, Chris (2014-2015)
Sujewicz, Lydia (2014-2015)
Taggart, Janet (2014)
Vaksdal, Trudi (2015)
Vechinski, Val (2014)
Viscuso, Michelle (2014)
White, Jamine (2015)

Madison Cougars

Year	League	Name	W	L	Conference	Division	DF	PR
2011	IWFL	Madison Cougars	5	4	Western	Midwest	2	BQ
2012	IWFL	Madison Cougars	7	3	Western	Midwest	2	BS
		Total	**12**	**7**				

Based in: Madison, WI
Notes: Succeeded by Madison Blaze

Date	H/A	Opponent	W/L	Score		Date	H/A	Opponent	W/L	Score	
4/9/2011	H	Wisconsin Warriors	L	0	36	4/21/2012	A	Wisconsin Warriors	L	0	16
4/23/2011	H	Minnesota Vixen	W	16	0	4/28/2012	A	Minnesota Vixen	W	15	0
4/30/2011	A	Iowa Crush	W	12	6	5/5/2012	A	Iowa Crush	W	20	12
5/7/2011	A	Wisconsin Warriors	L	6	33	5/12/2012		Minnesota Vixen	W	20	0
5/14/2011	H	Iowa Crush	W	13	6	5/26/2012	H	Rockford Riveters	W	39	0
5/28/2011	H	Minnesota Vixen	W	7	6	6/2/2012	H	Iowa Crush	W	25	0
6/4/2011	H	Wisconsin Warriors	L	0	26	6/9/2012	H	Wisconsin Warriors	L	12	14
6/11/2011	A	Minnesota Vixen	W	26	14	6/16/2012		Rockford Riveters	W	49	0
6/25/2011	A	Seattle Majestics	L	0	1 BQ	6/30/2012		Iowa Crush	W	34	0 BQ
						7/14/2012		Portland Shockwave	L	6	43 BS

Maine Freeze

Year	League	Name	W	L	Conference	Division	DF	PR
2002	NWFA	Maine Freeze	1	9	--	Northern	4	--
2003	NWFA	Maine Freeze	3	7	Northern	Northern	4	--
2004	NWFA	Maine Freeze	1	7	Northern	Northern	4	--
2005	NWFA	Maine Freeze	0	8	Northern	--	19	--
2006	NWFA	Maine Freeze	2	6	Northern	Northeast	4	--
2007	NWFA	Maine Freeze	2	6	Northern	North	3	--
2008	NWFA	Maine Freeze	0	8	Northern	Northeast	3	--
		Total	**9**	**51**				

Based in: Portland, ME

Date	Opponent	W/L	Score			Date	H/A	Opponent	W/L	Score	
4/13/2002	Rochester Raptors	L	0	12	E	4/23/2005	H	Philadelphia Phoenix	L	0	41
4/20/2002	Rochester Raptors	W	13	7	E	4/30/2005	H	Connecticut Crush	L	0	65
4/27/2002	Massachusetts Mutiny	L	0	62		5/14/2005	H	Erie Illusion	L	6	30
5/4/2002	Connecticut Crush	L	0	41		5/21/2005	A	Philadelphia Phoenix	L	0	62
5/18/2002	Philadelphia Liberty Belles (I)	L	14	55		5/28/2005	A	Connecticut Crush	L	0	92
5/25/2002	Connecticut Crush	L	0	45		6/4/2005	A	Erie Illusion	L	14	34
6/1/2002	Massachusetts Mutiny	L	12	68		6/11/2005	H	Massachusetts Mutiny	L	0	48
6/15/2002	Philadelphia Liberty Belles (I)	L	0	60		6/18/2005	A	Massachusetts Mutiny	L	0	60
6/22/2002	Connecticut Crush	L	6	49							
6/29/2002	Massachusetts Mutiny	L	0	55		4/22/2006	H	Connecticut Crush	L	0	61
						4/29/2006	A	Philadelphia Phoenix	L	0	54
3/29/2003	Rochester Raptors	W	7	0	E	5/6/2006	H	Massachusetts Mutiny	L	0	75
4/5/2003	Connecticut Crush	L	20	30	E	5/20/2006	A	Harrisburg Angels	W	20	6
4/19/2003	A Massachusetts Mutiny	L	9	32		5/27/2006	A	Connecticut Crush	L	12	64
4/26/2003	A Philadelphia Phoenix	L	0	34		6/3/2006	H	Philadelphia Phoenix	L	7	35
5/3/2003	H Philadelphia Phoenix	L	0	34		6/10/2006	A	Massachusetts Mutiny	L	0	48
5/17/2003	H Rochester Raptors	W	15	7		6/17/2006	H	Harrisburg Angels	W	21	12
5/24/2003	A Rochester Raptors	W	19	6							
6/1/2003	H Massachusetts Mutiny	L	0	42		4/14/2007	A	Central Massachusetts Ravens	W	26	0
6/7/2003	A Connecticut Crush	L	12	37		4/28/2007	H	Central Massachusetts Ravens	W	22	0
6/14/2003	H Connecticut Crush	L	0	18		5/5/2007	A	Massachusetts Mutiny	L	0	60
						5/12/2007	H	Erie Illusion	L	13	14
4/3/2004	H Rochester Raptors	W	12	8		5/19/2007	A	Connecticut Crush	L	0	52
4/10/2004	H Connecticut Crush	L	8	32		5/26/2007	H	Connecticut Crush	L	6	49
4/24/2004	H Philadelphia Phoenix	L	0	57		6/2/2007	H	Massachusetts Mutiny	L	0	52
5/1/2004	A Philadelphia Phoenix	L	0	55		6/16/2007	A	Erie Illusion	L	0	42
5/8/2004	H Massachusetts Mutiny	L	0	40				**Continued on next page**			
5/22/2004	A Connecticut Crush	L	0	23							
5/29/2004	A Rochester Raptors	L	14	22							
6/5/2004	A Massachusetts Mutiny	L	0	57							

Maine Freeze Game-By-Game Results (continued)

Date	H/A	Opponent	Result	PF	PA	Date	H/A	Opponent	Result	PF	PA
4/19/2008	A	New Jersey Titans	L	0	50	5/24/2008	H	New Jersey Titans	L	0	40
5/3/2008	A	Connecticut Crush	L	0	48	5/31/2008	H	Connecticut Crush	L	0	44
5/10/2008	H	Philadelphia Phoenix	L	0	56	6/14/2008	H	New York Nemesis	L	8	58
5/17/2008	A	New York Nemesis	L	0	60	6/21/2008	A	Philadelphia Phoenix	L	0	1

Maine Freeze Player Register (2004-2007)

Bailey, Jennifer (2005)
Baker, Natalie (2006-2007)
Berube, Angela (2005)
Blanchard, Ashley (2007)
Cameron, Kelly (2005-2006)
Capriani, Vanessa (2007)
Comier, Becky (2006)
Connolly, Erin (2006-2007)
Courtney, Andrea (2007)
Crosby, B.J. (2006)
Cross, Priscilla (2006)
Curtis, Lori (2004)
Deering, Kim (2005)
Desley, Rachel (2005-2007)
Deyesso, Lisa (2005)
Doe, Jen (2005-2006)
Drown, Mandy (2005-2006)
Dubourdieu, Shauna (2005-2007)
Durgan, Penny (2004-2006)
Farda, Courtney (2005-2007)
Farda, Emily (2006)
Farrin, Lena (2004-2006)
Fecteau, Brenda (2007)
Fink, Robyn (2006-2007)
Frazier, Peg (2005)
Goodrich, Melissa (2006-2007)
Graves, Kat (2005-2006)
Greene, Hillary (2006)
Harris, Brooke (2005-2007)
Herring, Dawn (2004)
Hollauer, Helena (2004)
Huntington, Cheryl (2005-2007)
Jesky, Amber (2005-2006)
Jewitt, Devin (2006-2007)
Jones, Tori (2005)
Lizotte, Sue (2005-2007)
Lopez, Jessikah (2004-2007)
McKechnie, Kathy (2004)
McKenny, Elizabeth (2005)
Moran, Katie (2004)
Moreau, Kelcey (2006-2007)
Murphy, Rachel (2007)
Nahar, Darcie (2006)
Neild, Tara (2005)
Page, Alicia (2007)
Pearson, Amber (2005)
Pesente, Carley (2006-2007)
Petkus, Joanne (2005-2007)
Plourde, Kim (2005-2007)
Powell, Angela (2007)
Preston, Suzy (2004-2005)
Reeves, Merrell (2007)
Ricci, Jen (2007)
Rice, Annie (2007)
Rivera, Wilnet (2005)
Silver, Christy (2004-2006)
Small, Sarah (2007)
Sprague, Heather (2006)
Staires, Julie (2005)
Thomas, Kris (2006)
Thompson, Stacy (2005-2007)
Trainor, Lisa (2004)
Vachon-Breden, Michelle (2005-2007)
Wadsworth, Danielle (2006)
Watson, Jennifer (2007)
Weatherbie, Donna (2007)
Welch, Betty (2005)
White, Courtney (2007)
Wilbur, Lori (2005)

Maine Lynx

Year	League	Name	W	L	Conference	Division	DF	PR
2012	WFA	Maine Lynx	1	6	National	Division 1 (Northeast)	3	--

Based in: Portland, ME

Date	H/A	Opponent	Result	PF	PA		Date	H/A	Opponent	Result	PF	PA	
4/14/2012	A	Keystone Assault	L	0	54		6/2/2012	A	Boston Militia	L	0	65	
4/21/2012	H	New York Sharks	L	0	1		6/9/2012	H	Philadelphia Liberty Belles (II)	L	0	1	
4/28/2012	A	New England Nightmare	L	7	51		6/16/2012	H	New England Nightmare	L	0	48	
5/19/2012	A	Mass Chaos	W	31	6	I							

Manchester Freedom

Year	League	Name	W	L	T	Conference	Division	DF	PR
2002	IWFL	New Hampshire Freedom	2	7	0	Eastern	--	6	--
2003	IWFL	New Hampshire Freedom	3	5	0	Eastern	North Atlantic	3	--
2004	IWFL	New Hampshire Freedom	4	3	1	Eastern	Mid-Atlantic	3	--
2005	IWFL	Manchester Freedom	3	8	0	Eastern	North Atlantic	4	--
2006	IWFL	Manchester Freedom	4	4	0	Eastern	North Atlantic	2	--
2007	IWFL	Manchester Freedom	6	3	0	Eastern	Northeast	1	S
2008	IWFL2	Manchester Freedom	4	4	0	Northern	North Atlantic	3	--
2009	IWFL2	Manchester Freedom	4	5	0	--	--	8	S
2010	IWFL2	Manchester Freedom	2	6	0	Eastern	Northeast	5	--
2011	IWFL	Manchester Freedom	4	4	0	Eastern	North Atlantic	3	--
2012	IWFL	New Hampshire Freedom	3	5	0	Eastern	North Atlantic	3	--
		Total	**39**	**54**	**1**				

Based in: Manchester, NH

Manchester Freedom Game-By-Game Results

Date	H/A	Opponent	Result	PF	PA	
4/20/2002		Bay State Warriors	L	0	48	
4/27/2002		Montreal Blitz	L	0	12	
5/4/2002		Bay State Warriors	L	8	34	
5/11/2002		Montreal Blitz	L	22	47	
5/31/2002		Tampa Tempest	L	0	26	
6/2/2002		Orlando Starz	L	6	27	
6/8/2002		Detroit Blaze	W	22	0	
6/15/2002		New York Sharks	L	0	64	
6/22/2002		Albany Night-Mares	W	12	7	
4/19/2003	H	Rhode Island Riptide	L	0	21	
4/26/2003	A	Montreal Blitz	L	0	40	
5/3/2003	H	Albany Night-Mares	W	19	0	
5/10/2003	H	Bay State Warriors	L	0	30	
5/17/2003	A	Rhode Island Riptide	W	20	14	*
5/31/2003	A	Bay State Warriors	L	0	34	
6/7/2003	H	Montreal Blitz	L	6	14	
6/14/2003	A	Albany Night-Mares	W	29	0	
4/17/2004	A	New York Sharks	L	0	26	
4/24/2004	A	Southern Maine Rebels	T	0	0	*
5/1/2004	A	Chicago Force	L	0	42	
5/8/2004	H	Bay State Warriors	W	20	0	
5/15/2004	H	Southern Maine Rebels	W	14	8	
5/22/2004	A	Bay State Warriors	W	7	0	
6/5/2004	H	Chicago Force	L	0	30	
6/12/2004	H	Rhode Island Intensity	W	36	6	
4/9/2005	A	Rhode Island Intensity	W	26	0	
4/16/2005	H	Connecticut Lightning	L	0	7	
4/23/2005	A	Bay State Warriors	L	0	18	
4/30/2005	H	New York Sharks	L	0	28	
5/7/2005	H	Southern Maine Rebels	L	13	18	
5/14/2005	A	Southern Maine Rebels	L	12	22	
5/21/2005	H	Rhode Island Intensity	W	18	7	
6/4/2005	A	Connecticut Lightning	W	19	12	
6/11/2005	A	New York Sharks	L	0	43	
6/18/2005	H	Southern Maine Rebels	L	3	36	
6/25/2005		Bay State Warriors	L	0	18	
4/29/2006	A	Southern Maine Rebels	W	26	6	
5/6/2006	A	Montreal Blitz	W	9	0	
5/13/2006	A	New York Sharks	L	0	20	
5/20/2006	H	Carolina Cardinals	W	1	0	
6/3/2006	H	Bay State Warriors	L	0	7	
6/10/2006	A	Bay State Warriors	L	6	7	
6/17/2006	H	Southern Maine Rebels	W	32	0	
6/24/2006	H	Montreal Blitz	L	22	36	
4/28/2007	A	Montreal Blitz	L	6	20	
5/12/2007	H	Montreal Blitz	W	27	7	
5/19/2007	A	Southern Maine Rebels	W	36	6	
6/2/2007	H	Southern Maine Rebels	W	26	2	
6/9/2007	A	Southern Maine Rebels	W	36	14	
6/16/2007	A	New England Intensity	L	15	24	
6/23/2007	H	Montreal Blitz	W	28	6	
6/30/2007	H	New England Intensity	W	41	12	
7/14/2007	H	New York Sharks	L	0	28	S
4/19/2008	A	Montreal Blitz	L	12	14	
5/3/2008	A	Southern Maine Rebels	W	70	8	
5/10/2008	H	Holyoke Hurricanes	W	68	0	
5/17/2008	H	New England Intensity	W	49	8	
5/31/2008	A	Boston Militia	L	7	38	
6/7/2008	H	Baltimore Nighthawks	L	0	49	
6/14/2008	A	New England Intensity	L	7	14	
6/21/2008	H	Southern Maine Rebels	W	53	0	
4/11/2009	A	Connecticut Crushers	W	27	15	
4/18/2009	A	Boston Militia	L	0	42	
4/25/2009	H	Central PA Vipers	W	47	0	
5/2/2009	A	New England Intensity	L	0	13	
5/9/2009	H	New England Intensity	L	8	20	
5/16/2009	A	Southern Maine Rebels	W	13	8	
5/30/2009	H	Erie Illusion	L	13	20	
6/13/2009	H	Southern Maine Rebels	W	19	6	
6/27/2009	A	Montreal Blitz	L	0	68	S
4/3/2010	A	Jersey Justice	L	0	32	
4/10/2010	A	New England Intensity	L	6	25	
4/17/2010	A	Montreal Blitz	L	14	41	
5/1/2010	H	Holyoke Hurricanes	W	1	0	N
5/8/2010	H	New England Intensity	L	8	20	
5/15/2010	H	Southern Maine Rebels	W	21	6	
5/22/2010	A	Connecticut Crushers	L	0	46	
6/5/2010	H	New York Nemesis	L	0	38	
4/9/2011	A	Montreal Blitz	L	6	12	
4/16/2011	H	Jersey Justice	W	8	0	I
4/30/2011	A	New England Intensity	L	7	27	
5/7/2011	H	Montreal Blitz	L	13	25	
5/14/2011	A	Maine Rebels	W	40	8	
5/21/2011	H	New England Intensity	L	0	7	
6/4/2011	H	Maine Rebels	W	37	0	
6/11/2011	H	Philadelphia Firebirds	W	26	0	
4/21/2012	A	Erie Illusion	L	20	24	
4/28/2012	A	New England Intensity	L	7	14	
5/5/2012	H	Maine Rebels	W	62	0	
5/12/2012	H	New England Intensity	L	14	41	
5/19/2012	A	Montreal Blitz	L	0	42	
6/2/2012	H	Northeastern Nitro	W	20	6	
6/9/2012	A	Connecticut Wreckers	W	20	14	
6/16/2012		Montreal Blitz	L	0	47	

Marana She-Devils

Year	League	Name	W	L	Conference	Division	DF	PR
2009	WFA	Marana She-Devils	0	8	American	Pacific	4	--

Based in: Marana, AZ
Notes: Non-existent team

Date	H/A	Opponent	Result	PF	PA
4/18/2009	H	Phoenix Prowlers	L	0	1
4/25/2009	H	California Lynx	L	0	1
5/9/2009	H	Las Vegas Showgirlz	L	0	1
5/16/2009	A	Phoenix Prowlers	L	0	1
5/30/2009	A	California Lynx	L	0	1
6/6/2009	A	Las Vegas Showgirlz	L	0	1
6/13/2009	H	Phoenix Prowlers	L	0	1
6/20/2009	A	California Lynx	L	0	1

Mass Chaos

Year	League	Name	W	L	Conference	Division	DF	PR
2012	W8FL	Mass Chaos	1	6	Eastern	--	4	--

Based in: Ware, MA

Date	H/A	Opponent	Result	PF	PA		Date	H/A	Opponent	Result	PF	PA	
4/14/2012	A	Three Rivers Xplosion	L	12	36		6/23/2012		Three Rivers Xplosion	W	20	14	
4/28/2012	A	Binghamton Tiger Cats	L	0	30		6/30/2012	H	New Jersey Titans	L	0	1	
5/19/2012	H	Maine Lynx	L	6	31	I	7/21/2012		Three Rivers Xplosion	L	0	1	
6/2/2012	A	New Jersey Titans	L	0	1								

Massachusetts Mutiny

Year	League	Name	W	L	Conference	Division	DF	PR
2001	NWFA	Massachusetts Mutiny	8	1	Northern	--	2	--
2002	NWFA	Massachusetts Mutiny	9	2	--	Northern	1	C
2003	NWFA	Massachusetts Mutiny	5	3	Northern	Northern	3	--
2004	NWFA	Massachusetts Mutiny	6	3	Northern	Northern	2	Q
2005	NWFA	Massachusetts Mutiny	8	2	Northern	--	3	S
2006	NWFA	Massachusetts Mutiny	8	2	Northern	Northeast	1	CC
2007	NWFA	Massachusetts Mutiny	8	1	Northern	North	1	S
		Total	**52**	**14**				

Based in: Lawrence, MA **Neutral site:** Pittsburgh, PA (N)
Notes: Merged with IWFL's Boston Rampage [Bay State Warriors] to form IWFL's Boston Militia

Date	H/A	Opponent	Result	PF	PA		Date	H/A	Opponent	Result	PF	PA	
4/28/2001	A	Connecticut Crush	W	19	0		5/22/2004	A	Philadelphia Phoenix	L	7	14	
5/5/2001	H	D.C. Divas	W	15	8		6/5/2004	H	Maine Freeze	W	57	0	
5/12/2001	H	Baltimore Burn	W	35	0		6/12/2004	A	Connecticut Crush	W	27	7	
5/19/2001	A	Philadelphia Liberty Belles (I)	L	0	27		6/26/2004	H	Columbus Comets	L	6	7	Q
5/26/2001	H	Connecticut Crush	W	27	6								
6/2/2001	A	D.C. Divas	W	12	0		4/16/2005	A	Philadelphia Phoenix	W	17	0	
6/9/2001	H	Philadelphia Liberty Belles (I)	W	13	7		4/30/2005	H	Erie Illusion	W	42	0	
6/16/2001	A	Connecticut Crush	W	52	0		5/14/2005	A	Connecticut Crush	W	22	19	
6/23/2001	A	Baltimore Burn	W	90	22		5/21/2005	H	D.C. Divas	L	12	22	
							5/28/2005	A	Erie Illusion	W	27	0	
4/27/2002		Maine Freeze	W	62	0		6/4/2005	H	Connecticut Crush	W	42	6	
5/4/2002		Philadelphia Liberty Belles (I)	L	20	21		6/11/2005	A	Maine Freeze	W	48	0	
5/18/2002		Connecticut Crush	W	47	15		6/18/2005	H	Maine Freeze	W	60	0	
5/25/2002		Philadelphia Liberty Belles (I)	W	17	12		6/25/2005	H	Connecticut Crush	W	34	12	Q
6/1/2002		Maine Freeze	W	68	12		7/9/2005	A	D.C. Divas	L	6	36	S
6/15/2002		Connecticut Crush	W	28	19								
6/22/2002		Philadelphia Liberty Belles (I)	W	35	21		4/22/2006	H	Philadelphia Phoenix	W	7	0	
6/29/2002		Maine Freeze	W	55	0		4/29/2006	A	Connecticut Crush	W	37	0	
7/6/2002	H	Cleveland Fusion	W	45	0	S	5/6/2006	A	Maine Freeze	W	75	0	
7/13/2002	H	Philadelphia Liberty Belles (I)	W	27	16	CC	5/20/2006	H	Baltimore Burn	W	35	0	
7/27/2002	N	Detroit Danger	L	30	48	C	5/27/2006	A	Philadelphia Phoenix	W	14	7	
							6/3/2006	A	Connecticut Crush	L	0	7	*
4/12/2003	H	Rochester Raptors	W	48	0		6/10/2006	H	Maine Freeze	W	48	0	
4/19/2003	H	Maine Freeze	W	32	9		6/17/2006	A	Baltimore Burn	W	20	16	
4/26/2003	A	Rochester Raptors	W	47	0		7/8/2006	H	St. Louis Slam	W	42	14	S
5/10/2003	H	Connecticut Crush	L	20	21		7/22/2006	A	Oklahoma City Lightning	L	16	21	CC
5/17/2003	A	Connecticut Crush	W	24	7								
5/24/2003	A	Philadelphia Phoenix	L	12	34		4/14/2007	A	Connecticut Crush	W	34	0	
6/1/2003	A	Maine Freeze	W	42	0		4/21/2007	H	Baltimore Burn	W	21	0	
6/7/2003	H	Philadelphia Phoenix	L	7	26		5/5/2007	H	Maine Freeze	W	60	0	
							5/12/2007	H	Connecticut Crush	W	14	7	
4/3/2004	H	Philadelphia Phoenix	L	19	34		5/19/2007	A	Central Massachusetts Ravens	W	49	0	
4/17/2004	A	Rochester Raptors	W	56	0		5/26/2007	A	Baltimore Burn	W	34	14	
4/24/2004	A	Rochester Raptors	W	40	0		6/2/2007	A	Maine Freeze	W	52	0	
5/8/2004	A	Maine Freeze	W	40	0		6/9/2007	H	Central Massachusetts Ravens	W	1	0	
5/15/2004	H	Connecticut Crush	W	27	7		6/30/2007	H	Cleveland Fusion	L	7	12	S

Massachusetts Mutiny Player Register (2004-2007)

Atwood, Aja (2005-2007)
Barker, Kelly (2004-2007)
Berman, Stephanie (2006)
Bowie, Lynette (2006)
Boyd, Kimi (2005-2007)
Brickhouse, Mia (2005-2007)
Bruce, Donna (2006-2007)
Burtoft, Sue (2005-2007)
Bushman, Brittany (2006-2007)
Cahill, Allison (2005-2007)
Caruso, Linda (2004-2005)
Casey, Charlene (2006)
Cestone, Kendra (2004-2006)
Chang, Showna (2004)
Deltoro, Deb (2004-2007)
Depew, Kris (2004-2005)
Devin, Mary (2004-2006)
DiEduardo, Patricia (2007)
Domini, Karolyn (2004)
Donaldson, Dorothy (2007)
Eddy, Vicky (2004-2007)
Epstein, Heidi (2005-2007)
Farfaras, Toni (2005-2006)
Fay, Tara (2004)
Geanacopoulos, Denise (2005)
Gilden, Rebecca (2005)
Gooding, Tania (2006)
Goodwin, Molly (2006-2007)
Grealy, Erin (2004)
Harrington, Joyce (2004-2005)
Harris, Alicia (2006-2007)
Helm, Leah (2006)
Henehan, Jovee (2007)
Hibbett, Chris (2005-2007)
Hickey, Kim (2004-2007)
Holder, Monique (2005-2007)
Joyce, Heather (2005)
Kraynak, Kelly (2006)
Lizotte, Sue (2004)
Manning, Heather (2005)
Mecado, Jess (2005)
Messuri, Chrissie (2005)
Milinazzo, Veronica (2004-2007)
Mitchell, Nora (2005-2007)
Nelson, Heather (2005)
O'Hara, Jen (2004)
Payne, Nakita "Kita" (2005-2007)
Pettingill, Cobie (2006-2007)
Pillsbury, Terri (2005-2007)
Powell, Jen (2007)
Robbins, Anastasia (2005)
Roderique, Allie (2006-2007)
Rossell, Jill (2005)
Saur, Amy (2006-2007)
Schofield, Stacey (2005-2006)
Schondelmayer, Tammy (2006)
Sestini, Jill (2006-2007)
Sherman, Katherine (2005)
Shoemaker, Candi (2004-2005)
Smith, Jeanette (2004-2005)
Snow, Ginger (2004-2007)
Szyszka, Jess (2006)
Toal, Rachel (2006-2007)
Walker, Stacy (2005, 2007)
Ward, Sarah (2006)
Zousoumas, Michelle (2004)

Memphis Belles

Year	League	Name	W	L	T	Conference	Division	DF	PR
2008	NWFA	Memphis Belles	3	4	1	Southern	Midwest	2	--
2009	WFA	Memphis Belles	4	4	0	American	Southeast	3	--
2010	IWFL2	Memphis Belles	5	4	0	Western	Midwest	2	S
2011	IWFL	Memphis Belles	3	6	0	Eastern	Mid South	4	--
2012	IWFL	Memphis Belles	0	7	0	Eastern	Mid South	3	--
		Total	**15**	**25**	**1**				

Based in: Memphis, TN

Date	H/A	Opponent	Result		
4/19/2008	A	Kansas City Storm	L	16	20
4/26/2008	A	St. Louis Slam	L	0	51
5/3/2008	H	Emerald Coast Barracudas	W	52	0
5/10/2008	H	North Texas Fury	T	6	6
5/24/2008	H	St. Louis Slam	L	0	42
5/31/2008	A	Emerald Coast Barracudas	W	36	33
6/7/2008	A	North Texas Fury	L	14	30
6/21/2008	H	Kansas City Storm	W	52	0
4/18/2009	H	New Orleans Blaze	W	46	7
4/25/2009	H	Emerald Coast Barracudas	W	50	0
5/9/2009	A	Jacksonville Dixie Blues	L	20	34
5/16/2009	A	Gulf Coast Riptide	L	8	50
5/30/2009	A	Emerald Coast Barracudas	W	44	12
6/6/2009	A	New Orleans Blaze	W	32	26
6/13/2009	H	Gulf Coast Riptide	L	20	54
6/20/2009	H	Jacksonville Dixie Blues	L	6	34
4/3/2010	A	Louisville Nightmare	W	1	0
4/10/2010	A	Tennessee Valley Tigers	W	28	0
4/17/2010	H	Chattanooga Locomotion	L	0	14
4/24/2010	A	Clarksville Fox	W	18	12
5/1/2010	H	Dallas Diamonds	L	6	49
5/8/2010	A	Chattanooga Locomotion	L	16	22
5/22/2010	H	H-Town Texas Cyclones	W	1	0 N
6/5/2010	H	Clarksville Fox	W	8	6
6/12/2010	A	Wisconsin Warriors	L	6	36 S
4/9/2011	H	Tennessee Valley Tigers	W	16	12
4/23/2011	A	Chattanooga Locomotion	L	12	52
4/30/2011	H	Clarksville Fox	W	20	12
5/7/2011	A	Tennessee Valley Tigers	W	32	6
5/14/2011	A	North Texas Knockouts	L	6	40
5/21/2011	H	Chattanooga Locomotion	L	20	26
6/4/2011	H	North Texas Knockouts	L	0	52
6/11/2011	A	Chattanooga Locomotion	L	0	54
6/18/2011	A	Chattanooga Locomotion	L	0	54
4/21/2012	A	Atlanta Xplosion	L	6	13
5/5/2012	A	Arlington Impact	L	0	42
5/12/2012	H	Atlanta Xplosion	L	0	26
5/19/2012	H	Arkansas Banshees	L	30	40
6/2/2012	A	Arkansas Banshees	L	0	1
6/9/2012	A	Atlanta Xplosion	L	0	1
6/16/2012		Arlington Impact	L	0	1

Memphis Belles Player Register (2008-2009)

Anderson, Paula (2008-2009)
Bady, Starry (2008)
Barry, Marriam (2008-2009)
Barton, Rhonda (2008)
Benbow-Scarborough, Ashley (2009)
Blacknell, Shea (2009)
Bowen, Theresa (2008-2009)
Boyd, Jessica (2009)
Brewer, Lee Ann (2008-2009)
Brightwell, Angela (2008)
Burns, Melissa (2008)
Butler, Allison (2008)
Cain, Jennifer (2008-2009)
Christian, Tay (2009)
Conklin, Lori (2009)
Conley, Brooke (2009)
Crane, Cheryelle (2008-2009)
Durham, Andrea (2008)
Ellis, Stacy (2008-2009)
Flewelling, Nici (2008-2009)
Gatlin, Stacy (2009)
Gibson, Elizabeth (2008-2009)
Gilchrist, Terri (2009)
Henry, Cindy (2009)
Hills, Abby (2009)
Hoover, Stacie (2009)
Husband, LaTasha (2009)
Johnson, Shelli (2008)
Kennon, Ashley (2009)
King, Susan (2009)
Kinney, Michelle (2008-2009)
Krell, Evonne (2008-2009)
Krell, Leanne (2008)
Lawrence, Rebecca (2008-2009)
Lewis, Shonda (2008)
Liggins, Caressa (2009)
Mack, Shelia (2008-2009)
Marcinko, Bonnie (2009)
Mills, Caitlin (2008-2009)
Morman, Andrea (2009)
Nielsen, Suzanne (2008)
Patterson, Renee (2009)
Pickett, Leslie (2008)
Plunkett, Jessica (2009)
Pope, Dominique (2009)
Pratcher, Andra (2008-2009)
Preyer, Alexandria (2008)
Robertson, Christina (2009)
Roe, Mary Elizabeth (2008-2009)
Scales, Katina (2008-2009)
Shappley, Brandi (2008-2009)
Small, Kim (2008-2009)
Smith, Angela (2009)
Suttles, G.T. (2008)
Tatum, Sharon (2008-2009)
Thompson, Kristina (2008)
Tibbels, Ginny (2009)
Walls, Minkey (2008-2009)
Williams, Tracy (2009)
Wilson, Angelica (2009)

Memphis Dynasty

Year	League	Name	W	L	Conference	Division	DF	PR
2010	WFA	Memphis Soul	6	2	American	South	1	Q
2011	WFA	Memphis WTF	8	2	American	Southeast	1	--
2012	WFA	Memphis Dynasty	4	5	American	Division 13 (South Central)	2	--
2013	WSFL	Memphis Dynasty	7	0	--	--	1	LC
2014	WSFL	Memphis Dynasty	6	1	Eastern	--	1	LC
		Total	**31**	**10**				

Based in: Memphis, TN **Neutral site:** Erie, PA (N)
Notes: Went through the entire 2011 season without choosing a team nickname, so were nicknamed "Memphis WTF" by outsiders (with WTF ostensibly standing for Women's Tackle Football, although it could have also represented the acronym's more conventional interpretation); Succeeded by Tennessee Legacy

Date	H/A	Opponent	Result		
4/10/2010	A	New Orleans Blaze	W	34	32
4/17/2010	H	Oklahoma City Lightning	W	1	0
4/24/2010	H	Acadiana Zydeco	W	30	6
5/15/2010	A	Lone Star Mustangs	L	0	55
5/22/2010	A	Acadiana Zydeco	W	34	0
6/5/2010	H	Acadiana Zydeco	W	20	6
6/12/2010	A	New Orleans Blaze	W	8	6
6/26/2010	H	Austin Outlaws	L	0	35 Q
4/9/2011	H	Little Rock Wildcats	W	38	14
4/16/2011	A	Acadiana Zydeco	W	54	14
4/30/2011	H	Tulsa Eagles	W	66	6
5/14/2011	A	New Orleans Blaze	L	8	9
5/21/2011	H	Tulsa Eagles	W	56	0
5/28/2011	A	Arkansas Rampage	W	36	0 I
6/4/2011	H	Dallas Diamonds	L	0	44
6/11/2011	A	Little Rock Wildcats	W	30	8
6/18/2011	H	New Orleans Blaze	W	1	0
10/1/2011		Arkansas Rampage	W	44	0 IE
4/14/2012	H	Arkansas Wildcats	W	32	0
4/21/2012	H	Tulsa Threat	W	18	6
4/28/2012	A	Huntsville Tigers	W	16	6 I
5/5/2012	A	Acadiana Zydeco	L	6	12
5/12/2012	H	Atlanta Phoenix	L	6	19
5/19/2012	A	Tulsa Threat	L	6	14
6/2/2012	H	Derby City Dynamite	W	12	6 *
6/9/2012	A	St. Louis Slam	L	0	49
6/16/2012	A	Arkansas Wildcats	L	14	22
4/6/2013	H	Atlanta Heartbreakers	W	46	0
4/13/2013	A	Huntsville Tigers	W	22	0
4/20/2013	A	Atlanta Heartbreakers	W	50	6
4/27/2013	H	Nashville Smashers	W	32	0
5/4/2013	A	Arkansas Banshees	W	34	26
5/18/2013	A	Nashville Smashers	W	18	0
6/29/2013	H	Arkansas Banshees	W	32	12 C
4/5/2014	H	Atlanta Heartbreakers	W	1	0
4/12/2014	A	Arkansas Banshees	W	38	32 *
4/26/2014	A	Arlington Impact	L	0	50 I
5/3/2014	H	Arkansas Banshees	W	30	14
5/17/2014	H	DFW Xtreme	W	44	8
7/19/2014	A	Baltimore Burn	W	20	8 CC
7/26/2014	N	Arkansas Banshees	W	34	12 C

Memphis Dynasty Player Register (2011-2012)

Akbari, Raumina (2011)
Bady, Starry (2011-2012)
Benbow-Scarborough, Ashley (2011-2012)
Blacknell, Shea (2011-2012)
Booth, Naomi (2011)
Boyd, Jessica (2011-2012)
Brown, Brandi (2012)
Charles, Kimberly (2012)
Conklin, Lori (2011-2012)
Davis, Nicole (2012)
Dean, Tanya (2011-2012)
Dodd, Daisy (2012)
Ellis, Stacy (2012)
Evans, Cincelia (2011-2012)
Evans, Oleisha (2012)
Gilchrist, Terri (2011-2012)
Harmon, Amanda (2012)
Harris, Anita (2012)
Haynes, Cherene (2011-2012)
Henry, Cindy (2011-2012)
Jennings, Samone (2012)
Kenney, Ashawnte (2011-2012)
Kennon, Ashley (2011-2012)
Krell, Evonne (2011)
Laguna, Sugey (2011-2012)
Lucca, Bryanna (2012)
Mackey, Kaylissa "K.K." (2011)
Marcinko, Bonnie (2011-2012)
Phillips, Jayne (2011)
Plunkett, Jessica (2011-2012)
Pope, Dominique (2011-2012)
Roe, Mary Elizabeth (2011-2012)
Small, Kim (2012)
Smith, Angela (2011)
Stiff, Serena (2011-2012)
Tatum, Sharon (2011-2012)
Taylor, Jasmine (2011-2012)
Turner, Angelica (2011)
Wheeler, Kim (2011)
Wheeler, Suzi (2011-2012)
Wood, Brandy (2011)

Memphis Matrix

Year	League		Name	W	L	Conference	Division	DF	PR
2004	IWFL	X	Memphis Matrix	1	1	--	--	--	--

Based in: Memphis, TN
Notes: Preceded by WFL's Memphis Maulers

4/17/2004	A	Des Moines Courage	W	30	0	5/8/2004	A	Jacksonville Dixie Blues	L	16	46

Memphis Maulers

Year	League		Name	W	L	T	Conference	Division	DF	PR
2001	IWFL		Memphis Maulers	0	3	1	--	--	--	--
2002	IWFL		Memphis Maulers	5	4	0	Western	--	4	--
2003	IWFL	X	Memphis Maulers	1	3	0	--	--	--	--
2003	WFL		Memphis Maulers	4	1	0	--	--	--	--
			Total	**10**	**11**	**1**				

Based in: Memphis, TN **Neutral site:** Tulsa, OK (N)
Notes: Left IWFL midway through 2003 season and finished season in the WFL; Succeeded by IWFL's Memphis Matrix

5/9/2001	N	Austin Outlaws	L	0	28	E	3/22/2003	A	Dallas Revolution	L	18	36
6/2/2001	A	Austin Outlaws	L	12	42		3/29/2003	H	Oklahoma City Avengers	W	16	0
6/23/2001	A	Austin Outlaws	L	0	56		4/5/2003	H	Chicago Force	L	0	1
8/25/2001		Tulsa Tornadoes	T	0	0		4/26/2003	A	Oklahoma City Avengers	L	0	1
4/6/2002		Austin Outlaws	W	24	14		5/17/2003	H	Tennessee Heat	W	34	6
4/13/2002		Tulsa Tornadoes	W	60	8		5/31/2003	A	Fayetteville Thunder	W	8	0
4/20/2002		Oklahoma City Avengers	W	28	13		6/7/2003	A	Tennessee Heat	W	14	6
4/27/2002		Austin Outlaws	L	0	28		6/21/2003	H	Fayetteville Thunder	W	16	0
5/11/2002		Oklahoma City Avengers	L	16	59		6/28/2003	A	Atlanta Xplosion	L	14	34	I
5/18/2002		Tulsa Tornadoes	W	39	0							
5/25/2002		Austin Outlaws	L	6	29							
6/8/2002		Tulsa Tornadoes	W	1	0							
6/15/2002		Oklahoma City Avengers	L	0	44							

Miami Fury

Year	League		Name	W	L	Conference	Division	DF	PR
2000	WPFL		Miami Fury	3	4	National	South	2	--
2001	MIWFA		Miami Fury	3	1	--	--	--	--
2002	IWFL	X	Miami Fury	2	1	--	--	--	--
2003	IWFL		Miami Fury	6	3	Eastern	South Atlantic	1	S
2005	IWFL	X	Miami Fury	4	4	--	--	--	--
2006	IWFL		Miami Fury	7	2	Eastern	South Atlantic	2	S
2007	IWFL		Miami Fury	3	5	Eastern	South Atlantic	3	--
2008	IWFL		Miami Fury	3	5	Eastern	South Atlantic	3	--
2009	IWFL		Miami Fury	6	2	Eastern	South Atlantic	3	--
2010	IWFL		Miami Fury	5	3	Eastern	Southeast	3	--
2011	WFA		Miami Fury	7	2	National	Coastal	1	Q
2012	WFA		Miami Fury	0	8	National	Division 9 (South Atlantic)	5	--
2013	WFA		Miami Fury	9	1	National	Division 6 (South Atlantic)	1	Q
2014	WFA		Miami Fury	7	3	National	South Atlantic	1	S
2015	WFA		Miami Fury	6	3	National	South Atlantic	1	Q
			Total	**71**	**47**				

Based in: Miami, FL

Date	H/A	Opponent	Result			
10/14/2000	H	Daytona Beach Barracudas	L	17	34	
10/28/2000	A	Daytona Beach Barracudas	L	0	27	
11/4/2000	A	Tampa Tempest	W	34	22	
11/11/2000	A	New York Sharks	L	12	19	
11/18/2000	H	Tampa Tempest	W	33	0	
11/22/2000	A	Daytona Beach Barracudas	L	20	21	
12/2/2000	A	Tampa Tempest	W	28	12	
8/18/2001	A	Carolina Cougars	L	7	16	
8/25/2001		Tennessee Heat	W	16	6	I
9/1/2001	H	Carolina Cougars	W	28	0	
9/8/2001	A	Orlando Lightning	W	48	0	
5/11/2002		Orlando Starz	L	0	1	
5/18/2002		Tampa Tempest	W	34	0	
5/25/2002		Tampa Tempest	W	48	0	
4/26/2003	H	Tampa Bay Terminators	W	26	13	
5/3/2003	H	Orlando Starz	W	30	6	
5/10/2003	A	Atlanta Xplosion	W	26	21	
5/17/2003	A	Orlando Starz	W	20	0	
5/25/2003	H	Orlando Starz	W	44	14	
5/31/2003	A	Tampa Bay Terminators	W	20	15	
6/7/2003	H	New York Sharks	L	6	20	
6/14/2003	H	Atlanta Xplosion	L	6	40	
6/21/2003	A	Bay State Warriors	L	0	1	S
4/23/2005	H	Orlando Mayhem	W	24	0	
5/7/2005	A	Tampa Bay Terminators	L	8	25	
5/14/2005	H	Tampa Bay Terminators	W	22	6	
5/21/2005	A	Jacksonville Dixie Blues	L	12	64	
5/28/2005	H	Atlanta Xplosion	L	0	34	
6/4/2005	A	Orlando Mayhem	W	22	13	
6/18/2005	A	Orlando Mayhem	W	14	7	
6/25/2005	A	Tampa Bay Terminators	L	14	21	
4/29/2006	A	Baton Rouge Wildcats	W	1	0	
5/6/2006	A	Orlando Mayhem	W	40	6	
5/20/2006	H	Orlando Mayhem	W	22	13	
5/27/2006	A	Tampa Bay Terminators	W	14	12	
6/3/2006	H	Tampa Bay Terminators	W	22	19	
6/10/2006	A	Atlanta Xplosion	L	6	41	
6/17/2006	H	Orlando Mayhem	W	20	14	
6/24/2006	H	Tampa Bay Terminators	W	1	0	
7/8/2006	A	New York Sharks	L	8	14	S
4/28/2007	H	New York Sharks	L	33	48	
5/5/2007	A	Atlanta Xplosion	L	0	36	
5/19/2007	H	Palm Beach Punishers	W	63	0	
6/2/2007	A	Orlando Mayhem	L	13	27	
6/9/2007	A	New York Sharks	L	18	41	
6/16/2007	H	Palm Beach Punishers	W	22	7	
6/23/2007	A	Palm Beach Punishers	W	7	0	
6/30/2007	H	Atlanta Xplosion	L	0	1	
4/12/2008	A	Palm Beach Punishers	W	6	2	
4/19/2008	H	Orlando Mayhem	L	0	21	
5/3/2008	H	Atlanta Xplosion	L	0	44	
5/10/2008	H	Dallas Diamonds	L	6	48	
5/17/2008	A	Palm Beach Punishers	W	22	0	
5/24/2008	A	Atlanta Xplosion	L	0	35	
6/7/2008	H	Palm Beach Punishers	W	52	2	
6/14/2008	A	Dallas Diamonds	L	0	49	
4/11/2009	A	Orlando Mayhem	W	21	0	
4/24/2009	H	Palm Beach Punishers	W	44	0	
5/2/2009	A	Houston Energy	W	21	0	
5/16/2009	H	Orlando Mayhem	W	27	6	
5/23/2009	A	Atlanta Xplosion	L	12	16	
5/30/2009	A	Dallas Diamonds	L	8	41	
6/6/2009	H	Orlando Mayhem	W	18	0	
6/13/2009	A	Palm Beach Punishers	W	53	0	
4/3/2010	A	Palm Beach Punishers	W	40	9	
4/17/2010	H	H-Town Texas Cyclones	W	1	0	N
4/24/2010	A	Atlanta Xplosion	L	0	39	
5/1/2010	H	Palm Beach Punishers	W	41	0	
5/8/2010	A	Houston Energy	L	0	1	
5/15/2010	H	Palm Beach Punishers	W	55	0	
5/22/2010	A	Atlanta Xplosion	L	0	1	
6/5/2010	A	Palm Beach Punishers	W	14	6	

Continued on next page

Miami Fury Game-By-Game Results (continued)

Date	H/A	Opponent	Result	PF	PA	Note
4/2/2011	H	Carolina Raging Wolves	W	62	0	
4/9/2011	H	Gulf Coast Riptide	W	52	14	
4/16/2011	A	Atlanta Heartbreakers	W	72	0	
4/30/2011	A	Tampa Bay Pirates	W	32	0	
5/14/2011	H	Palm Beach Punishers	W	12	9	
5/21/2011	H	Tampa Bay Pirates	W	34	21	
6/11/2011	A	Jacksonville Dixie Blues	L	24	45	
6/18/2011	A	Palm Beach Punishers	W	14	0	
6/25/2011	A	Jacksonville Dixie Blues	L	18	20	Q
4/14/2012	H	Jacksonville Dixie Blues	L	0	20	
4/21/2012	H	Atlanta Phoenix	L	32	48	
4/28/2012	A	Orlando Anarchy	L	8	34	
5/5/2012	H	Palm Beach Punishers	L	0	1	
5/12/2012	A	Tallahassee Jewels	L	8	16	
5/19/2012	A	Palm Beach Punishers	L	28	44	
6/2/2012	H	Tampa Bay Inferno	L	0	1	
6/16/2012	A	Jacksonville Dixie Blues	L	0	1	
4/6/2013	H	Orlando Anarchy	W	32	0	
4/13/2013	A	Jacksonville Dixie Blues	W	22	10	
4/27/2013	H	Tallahassee Jewels	W	38	8	
5/4/2013	A	Orlando Anarchy	W	52	0	
5/11/2013	H	Jacksonville Dixie Blues	W	14	5	
5/18/2013	A	Tampa Bay Inferno	W	22	6	
6/1/2013	A	Orlando Anarchy	W	46	0	
6/8/2013	H	Tampa Bay Inferno	W	28	0	
6/15/2013	H	Savannah Sabers	W	1	0	W
6/22/2013	A	Atlanta Phoenix	L	24	28	Q
4/5/2014	H	Orlando Anarchy	W	56	0	
4/12/2014	H	Jacksonville Dixie Blues	W	48	8	
4/19/2014	A	Atlanta Phoenix	L	8	12	
4/26/2014	H	Savannah Sabers	W	50	12	
5/10/2014	A	Orlando Anarchy	W	41	0	
5/17/2014	A	Daytona Breakers	W	47	0	
5/24/2014	A	Tampa Bay Inferno	L	13	14	
6/7/2014	H	Tampa Bay Inferno	W	14	2	
6/21/2014	A	Atlanta Phoenix	W	9	7	Q
7/5/2014	A	Chicago Force	L	8	66	S
4/11/2015	H	Daytona Waverunners	W	61	0	
4/18/2015	A	Tampa Bay Inferno	L	13	21	
4/25/2015	H	Orlando Anarchy	W	42	0	
5/9/2015	A	Daytona Waverunners	W	33	19	
5/16/2015	H	Atlanta Phoenix	W	12	6	*
5/30/2015	A	Orlando Anarchy	W	1	0	
6/6/2015	A	Jacksonville Dixie Blues	L	9	23	
6/13/2015	H	Tampa Bay Inferno	W	26	0	
6/27/2015	A	D.C. Divas	L	12	48	Q

Miami Fury Player Register (2011-2015)

Anderson, Yashima (2013)
Apey, Claudia (2011)
Ballard, Natrasha (2011-2012, 2014)
Baptiste, Sabrina (2011, 2013-2014)
Barbosa, Deniele (2011-2012)
Bethel, Gilda (2014-2015)
Blackwell, Seneka (2013)
Boykin, Jeri (2011-2015)
Brent-Harris, Dionne (2014-2015)
Brown, Jazmine (2013)
Carey, Tammy (2011-2012)
Carias, Melissa (2013-2015)
Chatman, Darline (2011)
Childers, Jessica (2013-2015)
Cleveland, Camilla (2014-2015)
Cofield, Ternisha (2012-2015)
Cordova, Blanca (2012-2014)
Cortes, Jennifer (2012-2015)
Dunne, Allison (2011, 2014-2015)
Dwyer, Stacy (2011-2015)
Epstein, Miriam (2012-2013)
Fanakos, Sandi (2011, 2014)
Freitas, Priscilla (2011-2013)
Gray, Mellissa (2014)
Gray, Rebekah (2011)
Greer, Keondra (2011-2015)
Harrington, Gayla (2011-2012)
Harris, Alexandra (2013, 2015)
Harris, Lenora (2011)
Hill, Terica (2011)
Jenkins, Muranda (2012)
Johnson, Brittani (2013-2015)
Kendrick, Medallion (2013)
Levy, Caroline (2011-2012)
Malcolm, Tonian (2011)
Maple, Sally (2014-2015)
McDonald, Keisha (2011-2015)
McKenzie, Kalondra (2011)
Melvin, Shamieka (2011-2012, 2014)
Miller, KeShia (2011)
Moise, Shirley (2011-2012)
Montanez, Jessica (2011, 2014-2015)
Moody, Malika (2013)
Moore, Kourtni (2015)
Moore, Natasha (2012, 2014)
Norton, Jessica (2015)
Palmer, Barbara Lee (2011)
Paul, Etta (2013-2015)
Peterman, Lucretia (2012)
Rex, Sheila (2012)
Rivers, Shambrya (2013-2014)
Rogers, Danitra (2011-2015)
Rossin, Monica (2014)
Ruiz, Chelsy (2014)
Scales, Andraki (2015)
Selm, Marabeth (2012)
Sharp, Nicolette (2014)
Sinkfield, Alexis (2014)
Sumpter, Shawnee (2011, 2014)
Tarver, Angelina (2015)
Thomas, Dominique (2013)
Thomas, JeNay (2015)
Thomas, Monika (2012-2014)
Toombs, Ronkia (2011-2015)
Trody, Jazmine (2012)
Truitt, Chastity (2014)
Velez, Jenna (2012)
Walker, Cheryl (2011-2012, 2014)
Watson, Alessandra (2012-2015)
White, Sharlene (2011)
White, Sherry (2012-2015)
Williams, Antionette (2014)
Williams, Kristina (2013-2015)
Wilson, Alexis (2011)
Wilson, Lacharmer (2014)
Wilson, Shaedricka (2014)
Wright, Nicole (2013-2015)

Mile High Blaze

Year	League		Name	W	L	Conference	Division	DF	PR
2014	WSFL		Mile High Blaze	4	2	Western	--	2	--
2015	IWFL	IX	Mile High Blaze	1	4	--	--	--	--
			Total	5	6				

Based in: Denver, CO

Mile High Blaze Game-By-Game Results

Date	H/A	Opponent	W/L	Score			Date	H/A	Opponent	W/L	Score		
3/30/2014	A	Rocky Mountain Thunderkatz	W	40	0		4/18/2015	H	Colorado Springs Voodoo	W	60	0	I
4/12/2014	A	Utah Falconz	L	0	64	I	4/25/2015	A	Utah Falconz	L	12	57	I
5/3/2014	H	Utah Falconz	L	17	55	I	5/2/2015	A	Tulsa Threat	L	0	28	I
5/31/2014	A	Arizona Assassins	W	51	0	I	5/30/2015	A	Rocky Mountain Thunderkatz	L	13	18	I
6/7/2014	A	Kansas City Storm	W	42	0	I	6/6/2015	H	Utah Falconz	L	6	67	I
6/14/2014	H	Rocky Mountain Thunderkatz	W	34	0								

Mile High Blaze Player Register (2015)

Bates, Sable (2015)
Berlin, Josette (2015)
Braxton, Katrina (2015)
Brigham, Shaun (2015)
Dombovy, Lucy (2015)
Esparza, Cassandra (2015)
Hamlet, Sydeny (2015)
Hernandez, Chantel (2015)
Hockaday, Coco (2015)
Lewis, D.J. (2015)
Lohman, Megann (2015)
Lowe, Sheilah (2015)
Lowery, Tyesha (2015)
Martinez, Beth (2015)
Mike, Nelly (2015)
Otero, Celena (2015)
Santistevan, Kim (2015)
Searcy, Yolanda (2015)
Stone, Libby (2015)
Stovik-Seatvet, Laurie (2015)
Warren, Sara (2015)
Williams, Stacey (2015)

Milwaukee Momentum

Year	League	Name	W	L	Conference	Division	DF	PR
2005	NWFA	Milwaukee Momentum	4	4	Northern	--	13	--
2006	NWFA	Milwaukee Momentum	3	5	Northern	Northwest	3	--
2007	NWFA	Milwaukee Momentum	1	7	Northern	West	4	--
		Total	**8**	**16**				

Based in: Milwaukee, WI
Notes: Preceded by Wisconsin Riveters; Succeeded by IWFL's Wisconsin Warriors

Date	H/A	Opponent	W/L	Score		Date	H/A	Opponent	W/L	Score	
4/16/2005	A	Southwest Michigan Jaguars	L	0	48	5/27/2006	A	West Michigan Mayhem	L	0	53
4/23/2005	H	Kentucky Karma	W	21	12	6/3/2006	A	Toledo Spitfire	W	20	6
5/14/2005	H	Indianapolis SaberKatz	W	65	0	6/10/2006	H	Cincinnati Sizzle	W	26	18
5/21/2005	A	Toledo Spitfire	W	14	6	6/17/2006	H	Cleveland Fusion	L	0	82
5/28/2005	H	Detroit Demolition	L	0	31						
6/4/2005	A	Indiana Thunder	W	1	0	4/21/2007	A	Fort Wayne Flash	L	0	36
6/11/2005	A	Kentucky Karma	L	14	20	4/28/2007	A	Kentucky Karma	L	0	33
6/18/2005	H	St. Louis Slam	L	7	12	5/5/2007	H	Tree Town Spitfire	W	13	6
						5/12/2007	A	West Michigan Mayhem	L	0	51
4/22/2006	H	Toledo Spitfire	W	42	8	5/19/2007	A	Tree Town Spitfire	L	10	30
4/29/2006	H	West Michigan Mayhem	L	20	21	6/2/2007	H	West Michigan Mayhem	L	0	49
5/6/2006	A	Cincinnati Sizzle	L	20	46	6/9/2007	H	Fort Wayne Flash	L	0	22
5/20/2006	A	Cleveland Fusion	L	0	49	6/16/2007	H	Kentucky Karma	L	6	14

Milwaukee Momentum Player Register (2005-2007)

Aasterud, Susanne (2005-2007)
Alvarez, Tisha (2005)
Ansorge, Laurie (2005)
Ashley, Amanda (2005-2006)
Auer, Jessica (2006)
Bassie, Jami (2005)
Biker, Nancy (2005)
Caddell, Angela (2007)
Chuchman, Valerie (2005)
Cochran, Lisa (2007)
Cook, Tiffany (2005-2006)
Coons, Abbey (2005, 2007)
Criss, Theresa (2005)
Davey, Sarah (2007)
Delimat, Kolette (2005-2006)
DeRosia, Jessica (2005)
Dieck, Sheri (2005-2006)
Filbrandt, Nicole (2005)
Gonya, Elaine (2006-2007)
Henry, Sarah (2006-2007)
Herrmann, Desiree (2006-2007)
Hochschild, Lisa (2006-2007)
Hubing, Bridget (2005-2007)
Johnson, Jenny (2005-2006)
Johnson, Tammy (2007)
Kludtke, Audrey (2007)
Kostuch, Amber (2006-2007)
Krueger, Jamie (2005)
Krueger, Mickey (2005)
Laack, Angela (2005-2007)
LaDuron, Kelli (2005)
Lambrecht, Laurie (2006)
Maurer, Stefanie (2006)
Moore, Jennifer (2007)
Mortimer, Shannon (2005-2007)
O'Grady, Saren (2006-2007)
Ollila, Laurie (2005)
Owens, Vicki (2006)
Pattillo, Fredericka (2007)
Reinheimer, Carol (2006)
Roberts, Elizabeth "Liz" (2005-2007)
Robinson, Deb (2005-2007)
Shepardson, Lesley (2007)
Simon, Kelly (2005)
Simon, Rose (2005-2007)
Steffes, McGee (2005)
Stoltenburg, Rebekah (2005-2006)
Stratman, Nichol (2005)
Strozinsky, Elizabeth (2007)
Swenson, Beth (2006-2007)
Thomas, Carmella (2005)
Turner, Jovanta (2005)
Twining, Kami (2007)
Vande Zande, Laurie (2006)
Vaughner, Clover (2005)
vonSpreckelsen, Jodi (2005-2007)
Wagner, Anne (2005)
Walker, Chris (2005-2007)
Weisensel, Jill (2005)
Zamiatowski, Lisa (2005-2006)
Zettel, Melissa (2005, 2007)

Minnesota Machine

Year	League	Name	W	L	Conference	Division	DF	PR
2009	WFA	Minnesota Machine	5	3	American	Midwest	2	--
2010	WFA	Minnesota Machine	6	3	American	Midwest	1	Q
2011	WFA	Minnesota Machine	5	4	American	Upper Midwest	1	Q
2012	WFA	Minnesota Machine	6	3	American	Division 10 (Upper Midwest)	1	W
2013	WFA	Minnesota Machine	3	4	American	Division 8 (Midwest)	3	--
2014	WFA	Minnesota Machine	3	8	American	Midwest	3	Q
2015	WFA	Minnesota Machine	0	8	American	Great Plains	3	--
		Total	**28**	**33**				

Based in: St. Paul, MN

Date	H/A	Opponent	Result	PF	PA	Note
4/25/2009	A	Iowa Thunder	L	6	16	
5/2/2009	H	Missouri Phoenix	W	56	0	
5/9/2009	H	St. Louis Slam	L	0	28	
5/16/2009	A	Kansas City Storm	W	50	0	
6/6/2009	A	St. Louis Slam	L	7	42	
6/13/2009	H	Iowa Thunder	W	20	0	
6/20/2009	A	Missouri Phoenix	W	61	0	
6/27/2009	H	Kansas City Storm	W	1	0	
4/10/2010	H	Nebraska Stampede	W	50	0	
4/17/2010	A	St. Louis Slam	L	0	34	
5/1/2010	A	Iowa Thunder	W	21	7	
5/8/2010	A	Kansas City Spartans	W	13	12	
5/15/2010	H	Nebraska Stampede	W	34	0	
6/5/2010	H	Kansas City Spartans	W	22	8	
6/12/2010	H	Iowa Thunder	L	13	21	
6/19/2010	A	Nebraska Stampede	W	13	12	
6/26/2010	H	Iowa Thunder	L	12	20	Q
4/9/2011	A	Chicago Force	L	0	69	
4/16/2011	H	Wisconsin Dragons	W	21	7	
4/30/2011	A	Wisconsin Wolves	W	27	6	
5/7/2011	H	Nebraska Stampede	W	6	0	
5/14/2011	A	Iowa Xplosion	L	0	7	
6/4/2011	A	Wisconsin Dragons	W	46	0	
6/11/2011	H	Iowa Xplosion	L	17	20	
6/18/2011	H	Wisconsin Wolves	W	33	8	
6/25/2011	A	Kansas City Tribe	L	0	51	Q
4/14/2012	A	St. Louis Slam	L	0	59	
4/21/2012	H	Wisconsin Wolves	W	35	6	
4/28/2012	A	Nebraska Stampede	W	14	6	
5/5/2012	H	Wisconsin Dragons	W	41	0	
5/12/2012	H	Nebraska Stampede	W	38	0	
5/19/2012	H	Kansas City Tribe	L	0	13	
6/9/2012	A	Wisconsin Wolves	W	34	24	
6/16/2012	A	Wisconsin Dragons	W	34	0	
6/23/2012	A	St. Louis Slam	L	6	42	W
4/6/2013	A	Nebraska Stampede	W	35	34	
4/20/2013	H	St. Louis Slam	L	0	35	
4/27/2013	A	Kansas City Titans	L	0	61	
5/11/2013	H	St. Louis Slam	L	0	47	
5/18/2013	A	Nebraska Stampede	W	10	3	
5/25/2013	A	St. Louis Slam	L	0	69	
6/8/2013	H	Nebraska Stampede	W	27	0	
4/5/2014	A	Nebraska Stampede	L	12	54	
4/12/2014	A	Iowa Steamrollers	W	1	0	N
4/19/2014	A	Kansas City Titans	L	2	42	
4/26/2014	H	Nebraska Stampede	L	13	45	
5/3/2014	A	Kansas City Titans	L	0	62	
5/10/2014	H	Iowa Steamrollers	W	1	0	N
5/17/2014	H	Nebraska Stampede	L	13	20	
5/31/2014	H	Kansas City Titans	L	7	20	
6/7/2014	H	Iowa Crush	L	29	34	I
6/14/2014	H	Tulsa Threat	W	35	13	W
6/21/2014	A	Austin Outlaws	L	3	14	Q
4/11/2015	A	St. Louis Slam	L	18	27	
4/18/2015	H	West Michigan Mayhem	L	13	35	
4/25/2015	H	Chicago Force	L	0	70	
5/2/2015	A	Indy Crash	L	6	32	
5/9/2015	H	St. Louis Slam	L	39	50	
5/16/2015	A	West Michigan Mayhem	L	13	35	
5/30/2015	H	Kansas City Titans	L	22	36	
6/13/2015	A	Kansas City Titans	L	6	54	

Minnesota Machine Player Register (2010-2015)

Acevedo, Melissa (2010)
Alman, Angela (2010-2012)
Alt, Maggie (2010-2011)
Anderson, Christal (2013)
Baker, Heather (2010-2012)
Bastien, Lisa (2010, 2014)
Bishop, Sarah (2010-2012)
Bjerke, Laura (2013-2014)
Blake, Cumah (2015)
Blakely, Danielle (2010)
Bouwman, Becky (2011-2013)
Boyles, Jessie (2011)
Brent, Mattie (2011)
Brooks, Susan (2011)
Byram, Sam (2010)
Cabral, Jenoveba (2012-2015)
Campbell, Adria (2015)
Campos, Brett (2010-2012)
Cheese, Hannah (2011)
Christian, Tiashia (2012-2014)
Clark, Amanda (2015)
Clausen, Krista (2012-2015)
Cocchiarella, Nina (2011, 2013)
Elliott, Danielle (2014-2015)
Eubanks, Shayla (2010)
Favors, Arlene (2013-2015)
Fietz, Nicole (2010-2012)
Flynn, Katy (2011)
Gelhaus, Nell (2011-2013)
Gilbert, Tanisha (2011)
Gillispie, Kelli (2014)
Goodman, Michelle (2011-2012)
Graham, Diorelle (2015)
Graham, Olivia (2015)
Gutierrez, Delia (2011)
Harris, Bree (2015)
Hicks, Virginia "Vee" (2012)
Hofschulte, Desiree (2011)
Horton, Allison (2014-2015)
Huls, Megan (2013)
Johnson, Alyssa (2012-2013)
Kamba, Babette (2013)
Kilpatrick, Kendra (2010-2011)
Knox, Chandell (2012)
Kopas, Selena (2011)
Krause, Abby (2010)
Krause, Lesley (2011)
Kvilhaug, Jackie (2011)
Lee, Rachel (2010, 2012)
Linberg, Sami (2014-2015)

Continued on next page

Minnesota Machine Player Register (continued)

Marchioni, Alicia (2014)
Mateo, Regina (2011)
McCloud, Swana (2011)
Means, Jackie (2010)
Mena, Alicia (2012-2013, 2015)
Merriman, Mandy (2010-2012)
Miller, Kim (2010-2011)
Mitchell, Julianne (2011)
Mois, Erica (2013-2015)
Morrison, Laurie Jo (2014)
Mulvehill-Rogers, Tequilla (2011)
Murphy, Bree (2014-2015)
Olson, Lisa (2010-2011)
Patnode, Jessica (2010-2012, 2014-2015)
Petsch, Cassie (2010)
Pikula, Emily (2011)
Plaskett, Phoenix (2013)
Prince, Amber (2015)
Ragozzino, Lia (2015)
Ramirez, Fia (2013-2015)
Richardson, Carmen (2010-2011)
Richardson, Ramona (2010-2011)
Ritzer, Amanda (2014-2015)
Rivera, Lydia (2013-2014)
Roberts, Lacy (2010-2012)
Sawyer, Lorin (2010)
Schlueter, Melisa (2010)
Schmidt, Dawn (2011)
Searcy, Yolanda (2010-2011)
Seeger, Amanda (2014)
Sell, Amanda (2013)
Sell, Ashley (2013)
Sirek, Neina (2010)
Smith, Abigail (2011-2013)
Spencer, Shauna (2015)
Stehula, Abby (2013-2014)
Stewart, Katrina (2011)
Stone, Jennifer "Jenn" (2014-2015)
Stork, Ashley (2014-2015)
Stout, Janelle (2013)
Thompson, Danielle (2010-2015)
Tully, Lexi (2011-2012)
Unverferth, Stefani (2010)
Vang, Julie (2014-2015)
Wallraff, Mary (2010-2014)
Washington, Zan (2014-2015)
Weyer, Erin (2013)
Willard, Leela (2011)
Williams, Shalonda (2011)
Williamson, Charlie (2011)
Wilson, Catima (2010-2011, 2015)
Wolf, Sara (2011-2013)
Youngers, Allison (2011)

Minnesota Vixen

Year	League	Name	W	L	Conference	Division	DF	PR
1999	WPFL	Minnesota Vixens	0	6	--	--	2	C
2000	WPFL	Minnesota Vixen	5	1	American	Central	1	CC
2001	MIWFA	Minnesota Vixen	1	2	--	--	--	--
2002	WPFL	Minnesota Vixen	2	3	National	--	4	--
2003	WPFL	Minnesota Vixen	3	7	American	North	3	--
2004	WPFL	Minnesota Vixen	6	5	National	North	2	S
2005	WPFL	Minnesota Vixen	6	5	National	North	2	CC
2006	WPFL	Minnesota Vixen	1	6	National	Central	3	--
2007	WPFL	Minnesota Vixen	3	5	National	Central	3	--
2008	NWFA	Minnesota Vixen	6	3	Northern	North	2	Q
2009	IWFL	Minnesota Vixen	2	6	Western	Midwest	3	--
2010	IWFL2	Minnesota Vixen	0	8	Western	Midwest	6	--
2011	IWFL	Minnesota Vixen	0	8	Western	Midwest	4	--
2012	IWFL	Minnesota Vixen	2	6	Western	Midwest	4	--
2013	IWFL	Minnesota Vixen	6	4	Western	Midwest	3	BS
2014	IWFL	Minnesota Vixen	6	3	Western	Midwest	2	B
2015	IWFL	Minnesota Vixen	6	2	Western	Midwest	2	--
		Total	**55**	**80**				

Based in: Minneapolis, MN **Neutral sites:** Naperville, IL (N1); Rock Hill, SC (N2)

Date		Opponent					Date		Opponent			
10/9/1999	H	Lake Michigan Minx	L	6	33		8/10/2002		Missouri Prowlers	W	54	0
10/16/1999	N1	Lake Michigan Minx	L	19	31		8/17/2002		Wisconsin Riveters	L	14	33
10/23/1999	A	Lake Michigan Minx	L	37	41		8/24/2002		Indiana Speed	L	6	11
11/9/1999	H	Lake Michigan Minx	L	21	23		8/31/2002		Missouri Prowlers	W	53	0
12/11/1999	A	New York Sharks	L	6	12		9/7/2002		Wisconsin Riveters	L	14	44
1/22/2000	H	Lake Michigan Minx	L	27	30 C							
							8/2/2003	H	Indiana Speed	L	0	26
10/14/2000	H	Colorado Valkyries	W	14	12		8/9/2003	A	Indiana Speed	L	13	46
10/21/2000	H	Tampa Tempest	W	63	0		8/16/2003	A	Missouri Prowlers	W	1	0
10/28/2000	H	Austin Rage	W	35	19		8/24/2003	H	Northern Ice	L	6	61
11/4/2000	H	Houston Energy	W	30	8		9/6/2003	A	Northern Ice	L	7	63
11/11/2000	A	Oklahoma City Wildcats	W	28	0		9/20/2003	H	Toledo Reign	W	61	0
12/16/2000	H	Houston Energy	L	14	35 CC		9/27/2003	A	Florida Stingrayz	L	15	33
							10/4/2003	A	Syracuse Sting	L	19	28
10/27/2001	H	Indianapolis Vipers	W	21	14 I		10/11/2003	H	Missouri Prowlers	W	61	12
11/3/2001	A	Indianapolis Vipers	L	7	18 I		10/18/2003	H	Northern Ice	L	13	61
11/10/2001	A	Arizona Caliente	L	7	12 I							

Continued on next page

Minnesota Vixen Game-By-Game Results (continued)

Date	H/A	Opponent	W/L	PF	PA	Note
7/31/2004	A	Indiana Speed	L	12	14	
8/7/2004	H	Indiana Speed	W	26	24	
8/14/2004	A	Northern Ice	L	0	27	
8/28/2004	A	Los Angeles Amazons	L	0	15	
9/4/2004	H	Toledo Reign	W	27	0	
9/25/2004	H	Northern Ice	L	25	32	
10/2/2004	H	Missouri Avengers	W	35	20	
10/9/2004	H	Delaware Griffins	W	30	20	
10/16/2004	A	Missouri Avengers	W	1	0	
10/23/2004	A	Toledo Reign	W	14	8	
10/30/2004	A	Delaware Griffins	L	6	8	S
7/30/2005	H	Houston Energy	L	0	40	
8/6/2005	A	Toledo Reign	W	27	22	
8/13/2005	A	Indiana Speed	W	7	6	
9/10/2005	H	Indiana Speed	W	18	13	
9/17/2005	A	Dallas Diamonds	L	6	62	
9/24/2005	H	Toledo Reign	W	30	8	
10/8/2005	H	Empire State Roar	W	39	14	
10/15/2005	A	Indiana Speed	L	14	26	
10/22/2005	H	Toledo Reign	L	22	36	
10/28/2005	A	Indiana Speed	W	19	14	S
11/5/2005	A	New York Dazzles	L	12	14	CC
7/22/2006	H	Toledo Reign	W	32	8	
7/29/2006	A	Indiana Speed	L	0	14	
8/5/2006	A	Wisconsin Wolves	L	0	20	
8/12/2006	H	Indiana Speed	L	7	14	
9/2/2006	H	Houston Energy	L	0	41	
9/16/2006	H	Wisconsin Wolves	L	6	32	
9/23/2006	A	Houston Energy	L	0	66	
8/18/2007	A	Indiana Speed	L	0	16	
9/1/2007	H	Wisconsin Wolves	L	10	13	
9/8/2007	A	Los Angeles Amazons	L	6	52	
9/15/2007	H	Toledo Reign	W	13	6	
9/22/2007	A	Wisconsin Wolves	L	7	42	
9/29/2007	H	Los Angeles Amazons	L	0	35	
10/13/2007	H	Indiana Speed	W	7	0	
10/20/2007	A	Toledo Reign	W	18	6	
4/26/2008	A	Indianapolis Chaos	W	40	0	
5/3/2008	H	Tree Town Spitfire	W	40	0	
5/10/2008	H	Kansas City Storm	W	58	0	
5/17/2008	A	West Michigan Mayhem	L	7	51	
5/31/2008	H	Indianapolis Chaos	W	62	6	
6/7/2008	A	Tree Town Spitfire	W	41	0	
6/14/2008	A	Kansas City Storm	W	1	0	
6/21/2008	H	West Michigan Mayhem	L	13	21	
6/28/2008	A	West Michigan Mayhem	L	7	31	Q
4/11/2009	A	Kansas City Tribe	L	8	45	
4/25/2009	H	Chicago Force	L	0	55	
5/2/2009	H	Wisconsin Warriors	L	16	54	
5/16/2009	H	Iowa Crush	W	38	20	
5/23/2009	A	Chicago Force	L	0	53	
5/30/2009	A	Wisconsin Warriors	L	8	38	
6/6/2009	A	Iowa Crush	W	14	9	
6/13/2009	H	Kansas City Tribe	L	0	65	
4/3/2010	A	Wisconsin Wolves	L	30	73	
4/10/2010	H	Iowa Crush	L	14	35	
4/24/2010	A	Dallas Diamonds	L	0	79	
5/1/2010	A	Iowa Crush	L	0	37	
5/8/2010	H	Chicago Force	L	0	56	
5/15/2010	H	Kansas City Tribe	L	0	80	
5/22/2010	A	Wisconsin Warriors	L	0	55	
6/5/2010	H	Wisconsin Wolves	L	18	20	
4/9/2011	H	Iowa Crush	L	6	20	
4/23/2011	A	Madison Cougars	L	0	16	
4/30/2011	H	Wisconsin Warriors	L	12	45	
5/7/2011	A	Iowa Crush	L	14	26	
5/21/2011	A	Wisconsin Warriors	L	6	60	
5/28/2011	A	Madison Cougars	L	6	7	
6/4/2011	A	Iowa Crush	L	12	38	
6/11/2011	H	Madison Cougars	L	14	26	
4/14/2012	H	Rockford Riveters	W	44	0	
4/28/2012	H	Madison Cougars	L	0	15	
5/5/2012	A	Rockford Riveters	W	32	0	
5/12/2012		Madison Cougars	L	0	20	
5/19/2012	H	Wisconsin Warriors	L	6	40	
5/26/2012	H	Iowa Crush	L	30	36	
6/9/2012	A	Iowa Crush	L	12	29	
6/16/2012		Wisconsin Warriors	L	6	36	
4/27/2013	H	Rockford Riveters	W	1	0	N
5/4/2013	A	Wisconsin Warriors	L	20	26	
5/18/2013	H	Madison Blaze	L	0	26	
5/25/2013	A	Iowa Crush	W	6	0	
6/1/2013	A	Rockford Riveters	W	1	0	N
6/15/2013	H	Wisconsin Warriors	W	51	7	
6/22/2013	A	Madison Blaze	L	6	40	
6/29/2013	H	Iowa Crush	W	26	6	
7/13/2013	A	Wisconsin Warriors	W	1	0	BQ
7/20/2013	A	Arlington Impact	L	14	18	BS
4/19/2014	H	Missouri Thundercats	W	1	0	N
4/26/2014	A	Wisconsin Warriors	W	12	6	
5/3/2014	A	Madison Blaze	L	0	14	
5/10/2014	H	Iowa Crush	L	6	14	
5/24/2014	H	Wisconsin Warriors	W	14	0	
5/31/2014	A	Missouri Thundercats	W	1	0	N
6/7/2014	H	Madison Blaze	W	18	14	
6/14/2014	A	Iowa Crush	W	12	6	*
7/25/2014	N2	Carolina Queens	L	22	28	B
4/11/2015	A	Nebraska Stampede	W	22	6	
4/18/2015	H	Wisconsin Warriors	W	38	7	
4/25/2015	H	Iowa Crush	W	14	8	
5/9/2015	H	Madison Blaze	L	8	14	*
5/16/2015	H	Nebraska Stampede	L	0	14	
5/23/2015	A	Wisconsin Warriors	W	40	0	
5/30/2015	H	Madison Blaze	W	12	7	
6/13/2015	A	Iowa Crush	W	28	14	

Minnesota Vixen Player Register (2008, 2014-2015)

Acciari, Nicole (2008)
Acevedo, Melissa (2008)
Alman, Angela (2008)
Arnold, Grace (2015)
Baker, Heather (2008)
Barber, Drue (2008, 2014-2015)
Bartoletti, Maria (2008, 2014)
Berkstaller, Julia (2014)
Beyer, Nikki (2014-2015)
Bishop, Sarah (2008)
Bostick, Kandace (2014)
Braun, Michele (2008, 2014)
Brown, Laura (2014)
Bryant, Cynthia (2014-2015)
Burkstaller, Julia (2015)
Campos, Brett (2008)
Castaldi, Monica (2008)
Charnell, Beth (2014)
Christensen, Yvonne (2014)
Cochran, Tonita (2008)

Continued on next page

Minnesota Vixen Player Register (continued)

Cox, Chelsea (2014)
Darden, Jazmine (2014-2015)
Evans, Emily (2008, 2014-2015)
Fason, Yolanda (2008)
Fickle, Erin (2008)
Fjetland, Bryce (2015)
Geismann, Jessica (2014)
Gibson-Thomas, Courtney (2014)
Gosa, Iesha (2015)
Grabau, Molly (2014)
Graf, Nikki (2015)
Griffin, Angela (2014-2015)
Hakamaa, Jennifer (2008)
Haman, Megan (2014-2015)
Hartman, Sarah (2008)
Heimbecher, Lyssa (2008)
Heimer, Kasie (2014)
Hoglum, Jodi (2008)
Huls, Megan (2008)
Jensen, Jamie (2008)
Jorgenson, Aimie (2014-2015)
Kile, Jannie (2014)
Koffler, Lisa (2008)
Kreger, Tasha (2015)
Lee, Bea (2015)
Lee, Kat (2014)
Lee, Rachel (2008)
Levasseur, Sherry (2008)
May, Michelle (2008)
Means, Jackie (2008)
Merriman, Mandy (2008)
Miller, Kim (2008)
Mindestrom, Heidi (2014)
Mois, Erica (2008)
Mudd, Roxi (2014)
Mugaas, Amy (2015)
Nelson, Jeanie (2015)
Nord, Jeanette (2008)
Olson, Lisa (2008)
Palomares, Dulce (2014)
Patnode, Jessica (2008)
Pearson, Bre (2014)
Phillips, Whitney (2014-2015)
Rehlander, Jodi (2014-2015)
Rounsville, Janet (2008)
Sander, Becky (2015)
Schmatz, Madison (2014-2015)
Schoen, Sara (2008)
Schwartz, Katie (2008)
Shannon, Markeeta (2015)
Shegstad, Nicolette (2014)
Sheppard, Angie (2014)
Sklors, Stephanie (2014)
Skogsberg, Claire (2015)
Smith, Kate (2008)
Stener, Tessa (2015)
Stewart, Natasha (2008)
Thompson, Danielle (2008)
Tilford, Erin (2014-2015)
Tomczak, Amanda (2014)
Umana, Ini (2014)
Vang, Koula (2008)
Voracek, Regina (2008)
Wagner, Kristi (2015)
Weisner, Lindsey (2015)
Williamson, Charlie (2008)
Wilson, Catima (2008)

Mississippi Rapids

Year	League	Name	W	L	Conference	Division	DF	PR
2005	WFL	Mississippi Rapids	2	0	--	--	--	LC
2006	WFL	Mississippi Rapids	1	1	--	--	--	--
		Total	3	1				

Based in: Horn Lake, MS

6/18/2005		Kentucky Force	W	1	0		4/29/2006	A	Kentucky Force	W	38	7
7/30/2005	A	Tennessee Heat	W	8	6	C	5/6/2006	H	Jacksonville Dixie Blues	L	22	63

Missouri Prowlers

Year	League	Name	W	L	Conference	Division	DF	PR
2002	WPFL	Missouri Prowlers	0	7	National	--	6	--
2003	WPFL	Missouri Prowlers	0	11	National	South	3	--
2004	WPFL	Missouri Avengers	0	10	American	South	3	--
		Total	0	28				

Based in: Springfield, MO

Date	H/A	Opponent	W/L	PF	PA		Date	H/A	Opponent	W/L	PF	PA
8/10/2002		Minnesota Vixen	L	0	54		10/4/2003	H	Houston Energy	L	0	1
8/31/2002		Minnesota Vixen	L	0	53		10/4/2003	H	Dallas Diamonds	L	0	49
9/7/2002		Indiana Speed	L	0	61		10/11/2003	A	Minnesota Vixen	L	12	61
9/21/2002		Dallas Diamonds	L	0	79		10/18/2003	A	Dayton Rebellion	L	0	48
9/28/2002		Austin Rage	L	0	74							
10/12/2002		Wisconsin Riveters	L	0	67		7/31/2004	H	Houston Energy	L	0	1
10/19/2002		Indiana Speed	L	0	55		8/7/2004	A	Toledo Reign	L	12	88
							8/21/2004	A	Dallas Diamonds	L	0	90
8/2/2003	H	Dallas Diamonds	L	0	66		8/28/2004	H	Toledo Reign	L	0	1
8/9/2003	A	Florida Stingrayz	L	0	87		9/4/2004	A	Northern Ice	L	12	49
8/16/2003	H	Minnesota Vixen	L	0	1		9/11/2004	A	Houston Energy	L	8	38
8/23/2003	H	Indiana Speed	L	0	1		9/18/2004	H	Indiana Speed	L	0	1
9/6/2003	A	Dallas Diamonds	L	0	72		10/2/2004	A	Minnesota Vixen	L	20	35
9/20/2003	A	Dallas Diamonds	L	0	65		10/9/2004	H	Dallas Diamonds	L	0	1
9/27/2003	A	Northern Ice	L	0	77		10/16/2004	H	Minnesota Vixen	L	0	1

Missouri Thundercats

Year	League		Name	W	L	Conference	Division	DF	PR
2014	IWFL	X	Missouri Thundercats	0	8	--	--	--	--

Based in: Kansas City, MO
Notes: Non-existent team

4/12/2014	H	Wisconsin Warriors	L	0	1	5/17/2014	A	Arlington Impact	L	0	1
4/19/2014	A	Minnesota Vixen	L	0	1	5/24/2014	A	Madison Blaze	L	0	1
4/26/2014	H	Madison Blaze	L	0	1	5/31/2014	H	Minnesota Vixen	L	0	1
5/3/2014	A	Iowa Crush	L	0	1	6/7/2014	A	Iowa Crush	L	0	1

Modesto Magic

Year	League	Name	W	L	Conference	Division	DF	PR
2008	NWFA	Modesto Magic	1	5	Southern	West	3	--

Based in: Modesto, CA
Notes: Succeeded by IWFL2's Modesto Maniax

4/19/2008	H	Arizona Wildfire	W	20	6	5/24/2008	H	Phoenix Prowlers	L	0	64
4/26/2008	A	Los Angeles Amazons	L	0	90	5/31/2008	H	Los Angeles Amazons	L	0	1
5/3/2008	A	Phoenix Prowlers	L	0	67	6/7/2008	A	Phoenix Prowlers	L	0	1

Modesto Magic Player Register (2008)

Alldredge, Stacey (2008)
Alton, Christy (2008)
Barber, Jenny (2008)
Bauer, Jen (2008)
Cabelera, Erin (2008)
Carver, Thelma (2008)
Cervantes, Rosa (2008)
Couch, Jamie (2008)
Dawson, Michelle (2008)
De Wane, Kelleigh (2008)
Estrada, Salena "Sal" (2008)
Foutz, Carol (2008)
Galvan, Angela (2008)
Genest, Maggie (2008)
Gilbert, Meggie (2008)
Goodwin, Dineen (2008)
Gray, Jessica (2008)
Hannula, Jennifer (2008)
Harwood, Ashley (2008)
Hodges, Marlo (2008)
Levie, Nicole (2008)
McNeill, Courtney (2008)
McNeill, Kim (2008)
Medeiros, Cassie (2008)
Ojeda, Rose (2008)
Paminsan, Cyless (2008)
Patterson, Jenny (2008)
Princevalle, Kim (2008)
Selby, Gerry (2008)
Sheppard, Amy (2008)
Walker, Kesha (2008)
Wears, Debbie (2008)
Wears, Kellie (2008)
White, Michele (2008)
Wright, Shanna (2008)

Modesto Maniax

Year	League	Name	W	L	Conference	Division	DF	PR
2009	IWFL2	Modesto Maniax	0	8	--	--	22	--
2010	IWFL2	Modesto Maniax	1	8	Western	Pacific West	3	S
2011	IWFL	Modesto Maniax	4	5	Western	Pacific West	2	BS
2012	IWFL	Modesto Maniax	3	5	Western	Pacific West	2	--
		Total	**8**	**26**				

Based in: Modesto, CA
Notes: Preceded by NWFA's Modesto Magic

4/11/2009	H	Sacramento Sirens	L	0	71	4/17/2010	H	Portland Shockwave	L	8	22	
4/25/2009	H	Tucson Monsoon	L	8	12	4/24/2010	H	Southern California Breakers	W	12	0	
5/2/2009	A	Southern California Breakers	L	0	55	5/1/2010	H	Sacramento Sirens	L	0	68	
5/9/2009	A	Los Angeles Amazons	L	0	64	5/8/2010	A	California Quake	L	0	62	
5/23/2009	A	California Quake	L	24	58	5/15/2010	H	Sacramento Sirens	L	0	55	
5/30/2009	H	California Quake	L	14	42	5/22/2010	A	Bay Area Bandits	L	8	47	
6/6/2009	H	Corvallis Pride	L	8	20	5/29/2010	A	Seattle Majestics	L	0	52	
6/13/2009	H	Southern California Breakers	L	6	21	6/5/2010	A	Sacramento Sirens	L	0	60	
						6/12/2010	A	Bay Area Bandits	L	0	46	S

Continued on next page

Modesto Maniax Game-By-Game Results (continued)

Date	H/A	Opponent	W/L	Score		Date	H/A	Opponent	W/L	Score	
4/9/2011	H	Sacramento Sirens	L	14	21	4/7/2012	A	Seattle Majestics	L	12	34
4/16/2011	H	Southern California Breakers	W	41	6	4/14/2012	H	Portland Shockwave	W	22	0
5/7/2011	A	Southern California Breakers	W	37	0	4/21/2012	H	Sacramento Sirens	L	6	20
5/14/2011	H	Southern California Breakers	W	7	0	4/28/2012	H	California Quake	W	22	6
5/21/2011	A	Portland Shockwave	L	6	20	5/12/2012	A	Sacramento Sirens	L	6	31
6/4/2011	A	Sacramento Sirens	L	7	34	5/19/2012	H	Seattle Majestics	L	0	29
6/11/2011	H	Seattle Majestics	L	0	12	5/26/2012	A	California Quake	W	38	0
6/25/2011	H	Tucson Monsoon	W	42	8 BQ	6/2/2012	A	Portland Shockwave	L	0	1
7/16/2011	A	Seattle Majestics	L	0	14 BS						

Monterrey Black Mambas

Year	League	Name	W	L	Conference	Division	DF	PR
2011	IWFL	Monterrey Black Mambas	0	4	Eastern	South Atlantic	3	--

Based in: Monterrey, Mexico
Notes: Preceded by WFA's Monterrey Royal Eagles

Date	H/A	Opponent	W/L	Score		Date	H/A	Opponent	W/L	Score	
4/9/2011	A	North Texas Knockouts	L	6	19	5/28/2011	A	North Texas Knockouts	L	0	1
4/30/2011	H	Houston Energy	L	6	44	6/4/2011	A	Houston Energy	L	0	38

Monterrey Royal Eagles

Year	League		Name	W	L	Conference	Division	DF	PR
2009	WFA	X	Monterrey Royal Eagles	0	1	--	--	--	B
2010	WFA		Monterrey Royal Eagles	0	4	American	Southwest	4	--
			Total	**0**	**5**				

Based in: Monterrey, Mexico
Notes: Succeeded by IWFL's Monterrey Black Mambas

Date	H/A	Opponent	W/L	Score		Date	H/A	Opponent	W/L	Score
8/15/2009	A	New Orleans Blaze	L	0	12 B	4/17/2010	A	Austin Outlaws	L	0	53
						5/8/2010	A	Houston Power	L	7	53
						5/22/2010	A	Houston Power	L	0	43
						6/19/2010	A	Lone Star Mustangs	L	0	1

Montreal Blitz

Year	League		Name	W	L	Conference	Division	DF	PR
2002	IWFL		Montreal Blitz	5	3	Eastern	--	3	--
2003	IWFL		Montreal Blitz	4	4	Eastern	North Atlantic	2	--
2004	IWFL		Montreal Blitz	6	2	Eastern	North Atlantic	1	--
2005	IWFL	X	Montreal Blitz	0	4	--	--	--	--
2006	IWFL		Montreal Blitz	3	5	Eastern	North Atlantic	3	--
2007	IWFL		Montreal Blitz	6	2	Eastern	Northeast	2	--
2008	IWFL2		Montreal Blitz	9	1	Northern	North Atlantic	1	LC
2009	IWFL2		Montreal Blitz	7	4	--	--	3	C
2010	IWFL2		Montreal Blitz	11	0	Eastern	Northeast	1	NC
2011	IWFL		Montreal Blitz	6	1	Eastern	North Atlantic	1	S
2012	IWFL		Montreal Blitz	11	0	Eastern	North Atlantic	1	NC
2013	IWFL		Montreal Blitz	8	3	Eastern	North Atlantic	2	BCW
2014	IWFL		Montreal Blitz	6	2	Eastern	North Atlantic	2	--
2015	IWFL		Montreal Blitz	5	2	Eastern	North Atlantic	2	--
			Total	**87**	**33**				

Based in: Montreal, Canada   **Neutral sites:** Chicago, IL (N1); Round Rock, TX (N2)

Montreal Blitz Game-By-Game Results

Date	H/A	Opponent	W/L	PF	PA	Note
4/20/2002		New York Sharks	L	6	45	
4/27/2002		New Hampshire Freedom	W	12	0	
5/4/2002		Albany Night-Mares	W	24	13	
5/11/2002		New Hampshire Freedom	W	47	22	
5/18/2002		New York Sharks	L	0	44	
6/1/2002		Bay State Warriors	W	33	24	
6/8/2002		Albany Night-Mares	W	21	13	
6/15/2002		Bay State Warriors	L	12	18	
4/12/2003	A	New York Sharks	L	0	52	
4/19/2003	A	Bay State Warriors	L	6	30	
4/26/2003	H	New Hampshire Freedom	W	40	0	
5/3/2003	A	Rhode Island Riptide	W	15	12	
5/17/2003	H	Bay State Warriors	L	0	35	
5/31/2003	H	Detroit Blaze	W	1	0	
6/7/2003	A	New Hampshire Freedom	W	14	6	
6/14/2003	A	Rhode Island Riptide	L	10	26	
4/17/2004	A	Southern Maine Rebels	L	0	22	
4/24/2004	A	New York Sharks	L	0	20	
5/1/2004	H	Southern Maine Rebels	W	20	14	
5/15/2004	H	Rhode Island Intensity	W	26	13	
5/22/2004	A	Rhode Island Intensity	W	12	7	
5/29/2004	H	Bay State Warriors	W	28	0	
6/5/2004	A	Bay State Warriors	W	20	6	
6/12/2004	A	Southern Maine Rebels	W	24	14	
4/9/2005	A	Southern Maine Rebels	L	6	16	
5/21/2005	A	Southern Maine Rebels	L	0	30	
6/12/2005	A	Rhode Island Intensity	L	0	19	
6/25/2005	A	New York Sharks	L	7	41	
4/29/2006	A	Bay State Warriors	L	6	32	
5/6/2006	H	Manchester Freedom	L	0	9	
5/13/2006	A	Southern Maine Rebels	W	34	0	
5/20/2006	H	Bay State Warriors	L	0	9	
6/3/2006	H	Southern Maine Rebels	W	31	12	
6/10/2006	A	New York Sharks	L	7	53	
6/17/2006	H	New York Sharks	L	27	42	
6/24/2006	A	Manchester Freedom	W	36	22	
4/28/2007	H	Manchester Freedom	W	20	6	
5/5/2007	A	Southern Maine Rebels	W	36	6	
5/12/2007	A	Manchester Freedom	L	7	27	
5/26/2007	H	Boston Rampage	W	7	0	
6/9/2007	H	New England Intensity	W	28	21	
6/16/2007	A	Southern Maine Rebels	W	27	0	
6/23/2007	A	Manchester Freedom	L	6	28	
6/30/2007	H	Detroit Predators	W	1	0	
4/12/2008	A	Holyoke Hurricanes	W	47	10	
4/19/2008	H	Manchester Freedom	W	14	12	
4/26/2008	A	New England Intensity	W	28	0	
5/10/2008	A	Southern Maine Rebels	W	53	0	
5/17/2008	H	Holyoke Hurricanes	W	41	6	
5/31/2008	H	New England Intensity	W	40	14	
6/7/2008	A	Boston Militia	L	20	30	
6/14/2008	H	Southern Maine Rebels	W	70	0	
6/28/2008	H	Carolina Phoenix	W	41	27	CC
7/26/2008	N1	Clarksville Fox	W	26	6	C
4/18/2009	A	Southern Maine Rebels	W	55	6	
4/25/2009	H	New York Nemesis	L	6	14	
5/2/2009	A	Holyoke Hurricanes	W	48	0	
5/9/2009	H	Boston Militia	L	0	39	
5/17/2009	H	Holyoke Hurricanes	W	1	0	
5/23/2009	H	Erie Illusion	W	41	10	
5/30/2009	A	New York Nemesis	L	12	13	
6/13/2009	A	Holyoke Hurricanes	W	1	0	
6/27/2009	H	Manchester Freedom	W	68	0	S
7/11/2009	H	Jersey Justice	W	9	8	CC
7/25/2009	H	Wisconsin Warriors	L	14	42	C
4/3/2010	A	Binghamton Tiger Cats	W	76	0	
4/17/2010	H	Manchester Freedom	W	41	14	
4/24/2010	H	Holyoke Hurricanes	W	1	0	N
5/1/2010	A	Southern Maine Rebels	W	41	6	
5/8/2010	A	Connecticut Crushers	W	22	0	
5/15/2010	H	New York Nemesis	W	20	0	
5/22/2010	H	Southern Maine Rebels	W	34	0	
6/5/2010	A	Connecticut Crushers	W	26	0	
6/12/2010	H	New England Intensity	W	53	14	S
7/10/2010	H	Carolina Phoenix	W	19	14	CC
7/24/2010	N2	Bay Area Bandits	W	9	2	C
4/9/2011	H	Manchester Freedom	W	12	6	
4/16/2011	H	New England Intensity	W	14	0	
4/30/2011	A	Maine Rebels	W	40	0	
5/7/2011	A	Manchester Freedom	W	25	13	
5/14/2011	A	New England Intensity	W	30	0	
5/21/2011	H	Maine Rebels	W	58	0	
6/25/2011	H	Carolina Phoenix	L	7	12	S
4/7/2012	A	New England Intensity	W	20	11	
4/14/2012	H	Maine Rebels	W	61	0	
4/21/2012	A	Maine Rebels	W	80	0	
4/28/2012	A	Northeastern Nitro	W	28	0	
5/5/2012	H	Northeastern Nitro	W	42	0	
5/19/2012	H	New Hampshire Freedom	W	42	0	
6/9/2012	H	New England Intensity	W	35	6	
6/16/2012		New Hampshire Freedom	W	47	0	
6/30/2012	H	Baltimore Nighthawks	W	33	6	S
7/14/2012		Houston Energy	W	28	16	CC
7/28/2012	N2	Sacramento Sirens	W	28	27	C
4/20/2013	A	Boston Militia	L	22	56	I
4/27/2013	A	New England Nightmare	W	21	0	
5/4/2013	A	New England Intensity	W	14	0	
5/11/2013	H	New York Knockout	W	49	0	
5/18/2013	H	New England Intensity	L	13	14	
6/1/2013	H	Erie Illusion	W	1	0	
6/8/2013	H	Boston Militia	L	0	50	I
6/15/2013	A	New York Knockout	W	41	0	
7/13/2013	H	Washington Prodigy	W	1	0	BQ
7/20/2013	A	Keystone Assault	W	47	22	BS
8/2/2013	N2	Arlington Impact	W	55	8	BC
4/12/2014	A	New England Nightmare	W	40	8	
4/26/2014	H	Connecticut Wreckers	W	53	0	
5/3/2014	A	Northeast Rebels	W	51	0	
5/10/2014	A	Pittsburgh Passion	L	0	35	
5/17/2014	H	Northeast Rebels	W	55	0	
5/31/2014	H	New York Knockout	W	55	0	
6/7/2014	A	New York Sharks	L	9	40	
6/14/2014	H	New England Nightmare	W	1	0	
4/11/2015	H	Northeast Rebels	W	36	0	
4/25/2015	A	New York Sharks	L	19	26	
5/2/2015	H	Connecticut Wreckers	W	42	14	
5/16/2015	A	Northeast Rebels	W	57	0	
5/23/2015	H	Detroit Pride	W	56	0	
5/30/2015	H	Connecticut Wreckers	W	1	0	
6/6/2015	H	New York Sharks	L	7	14	

Montreal Blitz Player Register (2014-2015)

Archer, Jennifer (2014-2015)
Ashraf, Saadia (2014)
Auger, Myriam (2015)
Barron, Alexa (2015)
Belanger, Emilie (2015)
Brodeur, Sonia (2015)
Brunet, Rose-Amelie (2015)
Cantave, Amanda (2014)
Caron, Marilyse (2015)
Chevrier, Annabelle (2014-2015)
Drouin, Dominique (2015)
Duchesneau, Joanie (2015)
Duguay, Erika (2014)
Dykeman, Melissa (2014)
Flanagan, Lyndee (2014-2015)
Fuamba, Ngalula (2014-2015)
Gagne, Chantal (2014)
Germain, Cloee (2015)
Giaccobbe, Rachel Victoria (2015)
Hayes, Amber (2014)
Henault, Sabrina (2014)
Jalbert, Joelle (2015)
Janson, Amelie (2014-2015)
Kalafatidis, Joy (2014)
Lacasse, Maude (2014-2015)
Laframboise, Marie-Claude (2015)
Lefebvre, Alexandra (2014-2015)
Masse-Lefebvre, Pascale (2015)
Morin, Lysane (2015)
Newman, Denikah (2014)
O'Driscoll, Brigitte (2014-2015)
Parent, Andreanne Dupont (2014)
Parisien-Cameron, Elyse (2015)
Paull, Georgina (2014)
Phan, Lan Anh (2014-2015)
Pontbriand, Laurence (2014)
Posch, Stacey (2014)
Poulin, Sabrina (2014)
Ranger, Erika (2015)
Roberge, Virginie (2014-2015)
Roussel, Virginie (2014-2015)
Royet, Cassandre (2015)
Saint-Jean, Genevieve (2015)
Vallieres, Stephanie (2014)
Vincent, Marie-Claude (2014-2015)
Warnet, Maude (2014-2015)

Muscle Shoals Smashers

Year	League	Name	W	L	Conference	Division	DF	PR
2004	NWFA	Muscle Shoals Smashers	2	7	Southern	Gulf Coast	4	--

Based in: Muscle Shoals, AL

4/3/2004	H	Pensacola Power	L	0	56
4/17/2004	H	Gulf Coast Herricanes	W	46	0
5/1/2004	A	Alabama Renegades	L	0	19
5/8/2004	H	New Orleans Blaze	L	0	60
5/15/2004	A	Pensacola Power	L	0	70
5/22/2004	A	New Orleans Blaze	L	0	55
5/29/2004	H	Alabama Renegades	L	10	56
6/5/2004	A	Nashville Dream	L	0	50
6/12/2004	A	Gulf Coast Herricanes	W	21	12

Muscle Shoals Smashers Player Register (2004)

Barfield, Carly (2004)
Borden, Kim (2004)
Brown, Ashley (2004)
Dobbs, Leslie (2004)
Ford, Kosha (2004)
Gibson, Amanda (2004)
Hammond, Kim (2004)
Hampton, Lisa (2004)
Harvey, Kelly (2004)
Johnson, Julianne (2004)
Linville, Gina (2004)
Matlock, Amy (2004)
McCutchen, Mollie (2004)
Osbourne, Christie (2004)
Underwood, Dawn (2004)

Nashville Dream

Year	League	Name	W	L	Conference	Division	DF	PR
2000	NWFA	Nashville Dream	3	3	--	--	--	--
2001	NWFA	Nashville Dream	2	7	Southern	--	4	--
2002	NWFA	Nashville Dream	7	2	--	Central	2	S
2003	NWFA	Nashville Dream	5	6	Southern	Central	4	Q
2004	NWFA	Nashville Dream	7	2	Southern	South	2	Q
2005	NWFA	Nashville Dream	8	1	Southern	--	1	S
2006	NWFA	Nashville Dream	0	8	Southern	South Central	3	--
2007	NWFA	Nashville Dream	2	6	Southern	Central	4	--
		Total	**34**	**35**				

Based in: Nashville, TN

10/21/2000	H	Alabama Renegades	W	30	15
4/21/2001	H	Tennessee Venom	L	14	20
4/28/2001	A	Alabama Renegades	L	6	46
5/5/2001	H	Pensacola Power	L	12	40
5/20/2001	H	Chattanooga Locomotion	W	15	14
5/26/2001	A	Pensacola Power	L	9	22
6/2/2001	A	Tennessee Venom	L	8	14
6/9/2001	H	Alabama Renegades	L	21	28
6/16/2001	A	Chattanooga Locomotion	L	2	7
6/23/2001	A	Chattanooga Locomotion	W	18	7
4/20/2002	A	Atlanta Leopards	W	26	12
4/27/2002	A	Knoxville Summit	W	48	8
5/4/2002	H	Alabama Renegades	W	24	14
5/25/2002	H	Knoxville Summit	W	51	0
6/1/2002	A	Chattanooga Locomotion	W	31	12
6/15/2002	H	Atlanta Leopards	W	16	14
6/22/2002	A	Alabama Renegades	L	19	34
6/29/2002	H	Chattanooga Locomotion	W	36	6
7/6/2002	A	Detroit Danger	L	0	47	S

Continued on next page

Nashville Dream Game-By-Game Results (continued)

Date	H/A	Opponent	W/L	PF	PA	Note		Date	H/A	Opponent	W/L	PF	PA	Note
3/29/2003		Pensacola Power	L	0	24	E		5/21/2005	A	Tennessee Venom	W	28	0	
4/5/2003		Columbus Flames	L	0	13	E		5/28/2005	A	Atlanta Leopards	W	1	0	
4/12/2003	A	Alabama Renegades	L	6	8			6/4/2005	H	Asheville Assault	W	42	0	
4/19/2003	H	St. Louis Slam	W	20	6			6/11/2005	H	New Orleans Blaze	W	17	6	
5/3/2003	A	Knoxville Summit	W	50	0			6/18/2005	A	Knoxville Tornadoes	W	30	0	
5/10/2003	H	Tennessee Venom	W	60	0			7/9/2005	H	Oklahoma City Lightning	L	7	42	S
5/17/2003	A	Chattanooga Locomotion	L	8	41									
5/24/2003	A	St. Louis Slam	W	27	7			4/22/2006	H	St. Louis Slam	L	14	22	
5/31/2003	H	Asheville Assault	L	20	21			4/29/2006	A	Dallas Rage	L	10	32	
6/14/2003	H	Atlanta Leopards	W	54	0			5/6/2006	H	Kentucky Karma	L	3	8	
6/28/2003	A	Oklahoma City Lightning	L	21	28	Q		5/13/2006	H	Chattanooga Locomotion	L	13	16	
								5/20/2006	A	St. Louis Slam	L	0	48	
4/3/2004	A	Tennessee Venom	W	31	0			6/3/2006	H	Dallas Rage	L	7	38	
4/17/2004	H	Evansville Express	W	33	0			6/10/2006	A	Kentucky Karma	L	0	23	
4/24/2004	H	Atlanta Leopards	W	65	0			6/17/2006	A	Chattanooga Locomotion	L	6	20	
5/1/2004	A	Chattanooga Locomotion	W	27	24									
5/8/2004	A	Asheville Assault	W	35	14			4/21/2007	A	Chattanooga Locomotion	L	7	36	
5/15/2004	H	Chattanooga Locomotion	L	7	21			4/28/2007	H	East Tennessee Rhythm	W	28	22	
5/22/2004	A	Evansville Express	W	48	12			5/5/2007	A	Alabama Renegades	L	7	21	
6/5/2004	H	Muscle Shoals Smashers	W	50	0			5/19/2007	H	Oklahoma City Lightning	L	6	48	
6/26/2004	A	Kansas City Krunch	L	19	20	Q		5/26/2007	H	Chattanooga Locomotion	L	0	54	
								6/2/2007	A	East Tennessee Rhythm	L	12	32	
4/16/2005	H	Alabama Renegades	W	20	6			6/9/2007	A	Oklahoma City Lightning	L	0	59	
4/23/2005	A	Chattanooga Locomotion	W	21	16			6/16/2007	H	Alabama Renegades	W	6	0	
5/14/2005	H	Knoxville Tornadoes	W	51	0									

Nashville Dream Player Register (2001-2007)

Afotey, Chris (2006)
Alessandrini, Kathlene (2007)
Armstrong, LaSonya (2003)
Banfield, Carrie (2007)
Barron, Frankie (2006)
Beard, Q. (2007)
Bolyard, Shelley (2003)
Bouldin, Stacy (2001)
Boyd, Raven (2007)
Buckley, Jennifer (2006)
Buerstetta, Avrill (2007)
Burris, Alice (2001, 2007)
Busbee, Chana (2006-2007)
Carr, Ginger (2001-2002)
Coffey, Ahndi (2001-2005)
Copenhaver, Stacey (2003)
Dassel, Missy (2004-2007)
Davis, Marquisha (2005-2006)
Davis, Rhonda (2004-2007)
DeNoto, Katt (2006)
Doyle, Laura (2005-2006)
Driskell, Rejetta (2004)
Eddins, Leigh (2006-2007)
Edwards, Jeri (2007)
Fielding, Chris (2001, 2003)
Fosbinder, Laura (2001)
Foster, Dawn (2003-2007)
Fox, Angie (2005)
Freeman, Paula (2005)
Fulbright, Amy (2003)
Garrison, Tina (2002, 2006-2007)
Gasho, Debbie (2006-2007)
Gerling, Mandy (2004)
Gibbs, C.J. (2001)
Glick, Carla (2005-2006)
Goodwin, Fran (2003-2004)
Goodwin, Laura (2006)
Grady, Carolyn (2002-2003)
Grubb, Robin (2001)
Guoan, Morgan (2002-2004)

Hall, Andrea (2005)
Harper, Lakisha (2004-2006)
Hatmaker, Amy (2004)
Haynes, Danielle (2001)
Henderson, Amy (2001)
Henderson, Bridgette (2003-2007)
Hines, Donita (2005-2007)
Hooper, Chelsey (2002)
Howard, Rhonda (2001-2002)
Hull, Christy (2002-2005)
Hunter, Jamie (2007)
Jackson, Sherri (2007)
Jenkins, Ebony (2003)
Johnson, Carrie (2001)
Johnson, Red (2001)
Jones, Brandie (2007)
Kane, Debbie (2001)
Kardokus, Janet (2001)
Kastl, Carla (2003)
Kennedy, Amelia (2001-2003)
Kilpatrick, Jamie (2003)
Kroemer, Joy (2005-2007)
Lawson, Angelique (2002-2006)
Ledbetter, Dorothy (2005-2007)
Lilley, Jennifer (2003-2004)
Lowe, Michele (2001)
Lucas, Mikell (2003-2007)
Machado, Stacy (2003)
McCreary, Leah (2003-2004)
McGuire, Heidi (2005-2007)
McKenzie, Sarah (2002)
Mench, Lisa (2001)
Mize, Nikki (2001)
Moore, Lorna (2001-2002)
Moore, Rochelle (2002)
Mullice, Erica (2006)
Murphy, Amy (2006)
Nickelberry, Denise (2003)
Noe, Jennifer (2004)
Overstreet, Mona (2002-2005)

Pace, Jennifer (2003)
Patton, Chernal (2005)
Philips, Michelle (2004)
Quick, Resa (2001)
Ramirez, Deborah (2001)
Roberson, Lorri (2002, 2004-2007)
Roberts, Tiffany (2005-2006)
Roderick, Debbie (2002-2004, 2006)
Roe, Denise (2001)
Rogers, Beth (2001)
Rogers, Debbie (2003-2007)
Rogers, Lisa (2004)
Sain, Johnna (2001)
Shandor, Vicky (2002)
Simms, Tamara (2007)
Sisson, Tricia (2001-2005)
Smith, Autumn (2004)
Smith, Nikki (2003)
Stamm, Katie (2001)
Stevenson, Jenny (2001-2003)
Thomas, Cassie (2005-2006)
Thomas, Christie (2001)
Thompson, Karen (2004-2007)
Thompson, Megyn (2006-2007)
Torres, Lori (2004)
Trapp, Patti (2002-2003)
Trent, Pamela (2001)
Trost, Christie (2002-2005)
Trost, Michele (2002)
Tubville, Angie (2003)
Uchida, Missy (2001-2007)
Villegas, Andrea (2003-2004)
Weddell, Shelley (2006)
West, Melinda (2001)
White, Lindsay (2006)
Wilcox, Christina (2001)
Wilson, Kimmey (2003)
Woodcock, Kim (2002)
Young, Jennifer (2001-2003)

Nashville Smashers

Year	League	Name	W	L	Conference	Division	DF	PR
2013	WSFL	Nashville Smashers	0	5	--	--	5	--
2014	W8FL	Nashville Smashers	3	3	--	--	2	CC
		Total	**3**	**8**				

Based in: Nashville, TN
Notes: Succeeded by Southern Valkyrie

4/6/2013	A	Huntsville Tigers	L	0	20		4/12/2014	A	Cape Fear Thunder	L	0	28
4/20/2013	H	Columbus Comets	L	0	52	I	4/26/2014	H	West Virginia Wildfire	W	25	8
4/27/2013	A	Memphis Dynasty	L	0	32		5/3/2014	H	Binghamton Tiger Cats	W	34	0
5/11/2013	H	Arkansas Banshees	L	12	46		5/10/2014	A	West Virginia Wildfire	L	2	22
5/18/2013	H	Memphis Dynasty	L	0	18		5/17/2014	H	Cape Fear Thunder	W	12	9
							7/12/2014	H	Cape Fear Thunder	L	20	32 CC

Nebraska Stampede

Year	League	Name	W	L	Conference	Division	DF	PR
2010	WFA	Nebraska Stampede	0	8	American	Midwest	4	--
2011	WFA	Nebraska Stampede	4	5	American	Midwest	3	--
2012	WFA	Nebraska Stampede	4	4	American	Division 10 (Upper Midwest)	3	--
2013	WFA	Nebraska Stampede	0	8	American	Division 8 (Midwest)	4	--
2014	WFA	Nebraska Stampede	6	3	American	Midwest	2	W
2015	IWFL	Nebraska Stampede	4	3	Western	Midwest	3	--
		Total	**18**	**31**				

Based in: Omaha, NE

4/10/2010	A	Minnesota Machine	L	0	50		4/6/2013	H	Minnesota Machine	L	34	35
4/24/2010	A	Iowa Thunder	L	0	47		4/20/2013	H	Kansas City Titans	L	14	59
5/1/2010	H	Kansas City Spartans	L	18	32		5/4/2013	A	St. Louis Slam	L	27	62
5/8/2010	H	Iowa Thunder	L	6	28		5/11/2013	A	Kansas City Titans	L	0	68
5/15/2010	A	Minnesota Machine	L	0	34		5/18/2013	H	Minnesota Machine	L	3	10
5/22/2010	H	Kansas City Spartans	L	6	32		5/25/2013	A	Kansas City Titans	L	6	51
6/12/2010	A	Kansas City Spartans	L	6	28		6/1/2013	H	St. Louis Slam	L	0	34
6/19/2010	H	Minnesota Machine	L	12	13		6/8/2013	A	Minnesota Machine	L	0	27
4/2/2011	H	Topeka Mudcats	W	52	0 IE	4/5/2014	H	Minnesota Machine	W	54	12
4/9/2011	A	Kansas City Spartans	L	12	14		4/19/2014	A	Iowa Steamrollers	W	1	0
4/16/2011	H	Iowa Xplosion	L	13	14		4/26/2014	A	Minnesota Machine	W	45	13
4/30/2011	H	Kansas City Tribe	L	0	88		5/3/2014	H	Tulsa Threat	W	56	32
5/7/2011	A	Minnesota Machine	L	0	6		5/10/2014	H	Kansas City Titans	L	14	33
5/21/2011	H	Wisconsin Dragons	W	48	0		5/17/2014	A	Minnesota Machine	W	20	13
6/4/2011	A	Wisconsin Wolves	L	12	24		5/31/2014	H	Kansas City Storm	W	59	0 I
6/11/2011	H	Kansas City Spartans	W	32	18		6/7/2014	A	Kansas City Titans	L	0	57
6/18/2011	A	Iowa Xplosion	W	19	14		6/14/2014	A	Houston Power	L	0	35 W
4/7/2012	H	Kansas Phoenix	W	82	0 I	4/11/2015	H	Minnesota Vixen	L	6	22
4/14/2012	H	Wisconsin Dragons	W	29	0		4/18/2015	A	Iowa Crush	W	28	0
4/21/2012	H	Kansas City Spartans	W	9	6		5/2/2015	A	Madison Blaze	L	8	16
4/28/2012	H	Minnesota Machine	L	6	14		5/9/2015	H	Rocky Mountain Thunderkatz	W	49	6
5/5/2012	A	Wisconsin Wolves	L	8	24		5/16/2015	A	Minnesota Vixen	W	14	0
5/12/2012	A	Minnesota Machine	L	0	38		6/6/2015	H	Iowa Crush	W	56	0
6/2/2012	A	Kansas City Tribe	L	6	53		6/13/2015	H	Madison Blaze	L	24	27
6/9/2012	A	Wisconsin Dragons	W	27	6							

Nebraska Stampede Player Register (2010-2015)

Adams-Novak, April (2013)
Archer, Megan (2012)
Ausbie, Dominick "Dom" (2013-2015)
Baker, Tiffany (2015)
Balistreri, Adriana (2014)
Barents, Kim (2010)
Barrett, Kelly (2012)
Beacom, Miquela (2010-2014)
Benak, Jessica (2015)
Bennett, Angie (2015)
Blackstone, Charlotte (2011)
Bohaboj, Kelley (2013-2015)
Book, Kelly (2012-2013)
Boucher, Mandy (2012)
Box, Ashley (2010-2015)
Bristol, Resha (2012)
Broksle, Kayla (2015)
Brown, Katie (2011-2012)
Bunte, Kristi "Kris" (2010-2015)
Bussing, Natalie (2012)
Cabrera, Katie (2011)
Carroll, Lindsay (2010-2015)
Cartier, Inette (2014)
Champaign, Tori (2013)
Cherney, Abbey (2010-2012)
Cooper, Sarah (2013)
Crouch, Ali (2011-2012)
De La Cruz-Kaiser, Monica (2012-2013)
Diehm, Ashley (2010)
Esquivel, Tabby "Tab" (2014-2015)
Felner, Katy (2010, 2014-2015)
Filipowicz, Jenny "Flip" (2014-2015)
Flores, Angi (2013)
Forman, Tracy (2014-2015)
Gamblin, Elizabeth "Liz" (2014-2015)
Greenhill, Monica (2010)
Hampton, Brenda (2010-2011)
Hanbrough, Kourtnee (2015)
Hanner, Deb (2011-2013, 2015)
Hardrich, Shelagh (2015)
Harris, Crystal (2010)
Haworth, Melissa (2010)
Head, Michelle (2014-2015)
Honeycutt, Theresa (2014-2015)
Horn, Shay (2010-2015)
Hudson, Beth (2010)
Johnson, Beth (2011-2015)
Johnson, Julie (2010)
Johnson, Tina (2010-2015)
Jones, Nellie (2011)
Kania, Francinea (2014)
Kelly, Emma (2010-2011)
Kiernan, Delaney (2014)
Kirkpatrick, Erika (2014-2015)
Kniewel, LeAnne (2013)
Kruse, Katie (2012)
Kwiatkowski, Cindy (2010)
Laughlin, Rita (2012)
LeDroit, Michelle (2010-2011)
Leeds, Laura (2011)
Lewiston, Ashley (2012)
Maeder, Krystle (2010)
McGlothlin, Ariel (2010-2013)
McKeone, Desiree (2012)
Meidlinger, Sara (2011)
Melendres, Joselyn (2011)
Miller, Brittany (2010-2011)
Mills, C.J. (2011)
Murphy, Niccole (2011)
Nickisch, Teresa (2010-2012)
Noland, Nikie (2015)
O'Neil, Keara (2012-2013)
Oyler, Sam (2012, 2014)
Paczosa, Trena (2014)
Patterson, Tanisha (2012)
Pearson, Cindy (2011-2015)
Pender, Emily (2011-2015)
Pender, Rachal (2015)
Peters, Trina (2012)
Pittaway, Kimberly (2010-2011)
Posey, LaShawnda (2010-2011)
Pridie, Stephanie (2013)
Quintana, Kaitlin (2010)
Reed, Chelsea (2012-2013, 2015)
Reed, Rachal (2010-2013)
Ruppert-Archer, Shelsie (2012)
Schram, Lori (2011)
Secor, Victoria (2010-2015)
Seewald, Steph (2011)
Sheridan, Mandi (2013)
Sherman, Sylvia (2013)
Shestak, Tiffany (2010-2013, 2015)
Sok, Karen (2013)
Solomon, Starr (2015)
Swinton, Sharyn (2010-2012)
Taylor, Kamisha (2012)
Thomson, Amber (2012-2014)
Thomson, Jessica (2012-2014)
Thurston, Sara (2010-2011, 2014-2015)
Urich, Ann (2010)
Van Camp, Brittany (2014-2015)
VanSchoiack, Taryn (2014)
Vaughn, Snoop (2011-2015)
Verbeek, Heather (2010)
Walker, Whitney (2010)
Walter, Nicole (2010)
Westbrook, Demetria (2011, 2013-2014)
Winters, Victoria (2013-2014)
Wood, Cindy (2010)
Zelenka, Jenn (2010-2015)
Zelenka, Mary (2010-2011)

Nevada Storm

Year	League		Name	W	L	Conference	Division	DF	PR
2011	W8FL	X	Nevada Storm	1	1	--	--	--	--
2012	W8FL		Nevada Storm	3	1	Western	--	1	C
2013	IWFL	X	Nevada Storm	2	5	--	--	--	--
2014	WFA		Nevada Storm	0	6	American	Pacific West	3	--
2015	IWFL		Nevada Storm	3	5	Western	Pacific West	3	--
			Total	**9**	**18**				

Based in: Reno, NV **Neutral site:** Towanda, PA (N)

Date	H/A/N	Opponent	W/L	PF	PA	
6/11/2011	A	Ventura Black Widows	W	50	18	
7/16/2011	A	Utah Jynx	L	12	33	I
4/21/2012	H	Salt City Arch Angels	W	80	20	
6/9/2012	A	Ventura Black Widows	W	68	12	
6/23/2012		Ventura Black Widows	W	60	0	
8/11/2012	N	West Virginia Wildfire	L	0	1	C
4/27/2013	A	California Quake	W	28	12	
5/4/2013	H	Sacramento Sirens	L	8	61	I
5/11/2013	A	Central Cal War Angels	L	22	49	I
5/18/2013	A	Utah Jynx	L	22	47	I
5/25/2013	A	Sacramento Sirens	L	0	45	I
6/1/2013	H	Central Cal War Angels	L	0	1	I
6/22/2013	H	California Quake	W	56	0	
4/5/2014	A	Central Cal War Angels	L	0	46	
4/19/2014	H	Utah Blitz	L	8	18	
5/3/2014	H	San Diego Surge	L	6	56	
5/10/2014	A	Las Vegas Showgirlz	L	0	56	
5/24/2014	H	Las Vegas Showgirlz	L	0	1	
5/31/2014	A	Utah Blitz	L	0	1	
4/11/2015	H	Sacramento Sirens	L	6	41	
4/25/2015	A	California Quake	W	33	6	
5/2/2015	H	Utah Falconz	L	0	60	
5/9/2015	A	Utah Falconz	L	8	68	
5/16/2015	H	Phoenix Phantomz	W	28	14	
5/30/2015	A	Sacramento Sirens	L	7	54	
6/6/2015	H	Central Valley Mustangs	W	43	0	
6/13/2015	A	North County Stars	L	22	24	

Nevada Storm Player Register (2014)

Aguayo, Megan (2014)	Ke-a, Momi (2014)	Peed, Shannon (2014)
Arett, April (2014)	Kennedy, Lisa (2014)	Reiff, Kaitlyn (2014)
Atkinson, Ashley (2014)	Mackey, Carrie (2014)	Ruiz, Pitts (2014)
Bodo, Janine (2014)	Martinez, Vanessa (2014)	Rupert, Amanda (2014)
Brinkley, Christina (2014)	Martino, Jamie (2014)	Russell, Leah (2014)
Ettinger, Bobbie (2014)	McMicken, Holly (2014)	Seirer, Sharon (2014)
Houston, Christine (2014)	Moore, Amber (2014)	Simms, Kristen (2014)
Hunt, Sarah (2014)	Moore, Marieleah (2014)	Smith, Chari (2014)
Jacobo, Angela (2014)	Morris, Melissa (2014)	Taufa, Ola (2014)
Jones, Shauna (2014)	Osborne, Ashley (2014)	Taufa, Vika (2014)
Kaho, Lusiola (2014)	Palmer, Amanda (2014)	Wilson, Anna (2014)

New England Intensity

Year	League		Name	W	L	Conference	Division	DF	PR
2003	IWFL		Rhode Island Riptide	2	7	Eastern	North Atlantic	4	--
2004	IWFL	X	Rhode Island Intensity	3	5	--	--	--	--
2005	IWFL		Rhode Island Intensity	1	9	Eastern	North Atlantic	5	--
2006	WPFL		New England Intensity	6	2	American	East	1	S
2007	IWFL		New England Intensity	3	5	Eastern	North Atlantic	3	--
2008	IWFL2		New England Intensity	5	4	Northern	North Atlantic	2	CC
2009	IWFL2		New England Intensity	6	3	--	--	5	S
2010	IWFL2		New England Intensity	8	1	Eastern	Northeast	1	S
2011	IWFL		New England Intensity	7	3	Eastern	North Atlantic	2	BC
2012	IWFL		New England Intensity	7	3	Eastern	North Atlantic	2	BS
2013	IWFL		New England Intensity	8	2	Eastern	North Atlantic	1	CC
			Total	56	44				

Based in: Medway, MA (2006-2013); Providence, RI (2003-2005) **Neutral site:** Round Rock, TX (N)

Date	H/A	Opponent	W/L	PF	PA	
4/12/2003	A	Bay State Warriors	L	0	12	
4/19/2003	A	New Hampshire Freedom	W	21	0	
4/26/2003	A	New York Sharks	L	0	62	
5/3/2003	H	Montreal Blitz	L	12	15	
5/10/2003	H	Philadelphia Liberty Belles (I)	L	14	16	
5/17/2003	H	New Hampshire Freedom	L	14	20	*
5/31/2003	A	Philadelphia Liberty Belles (I)	L	0	8	
6/7/2003	H	Bay State Warriors	L	0	26	
6/14/2003	H	Montreal Blitz	W	26	10	
4/24/2004	A	Bay State Warriors	W	7	6	
5/1/2004	H	Bay State Warriors	W	30	14	
5/8/2004	A	Southern Maine Rebels	W	21	14	
5/15/2004	A	Montreal Blitz	L	13	26	
5/22/2004	H	Montreal Blitz	L	7	12	
5/29/2004	H	Southern Maine Rebels	L	19	38	
6/5/2004	H	New York Sharks	L	16	41	
6/12/2004	A	New Hampshire Freedom	L	6	36	
4/9/2005	H	Manchester Freedom	L	0	26	
4/16/2005	H	Bay State Warriors	L	6	21	
4/23/2005	A	Southern Maine Rebels	L	7	14	
4/30/2005	A	Connecticut Lightning	L	0	18	
5/14/2005	H	New York Sharks	L	6	40	
5/21/2005	A	Manchester Freedom	L	7	18	
6/4/2005	A	Bay State Warriors	L	0	20	
6/11/2005	H	Connecticut Lightning	L	22	28	
6/12/2005	H	Montreal Blitz	W	19	0	
6/18/2005	A	New York Sharks	L	0	59	
7/22/2006	H	Albany Ambush	W	26	0	
8/5/2006	A	Toledo Reign	L	22	34	
8/12/2006	A	Empire State Roar	W	20	0	
8/19/2006	A	Connecticut Cyclones	W	34	0	
9/16/2006	H	Empire State Roar	W	6	0	
9/23/2006	H	Connecticut Cyclones	W	42	6	
9/30/2006	H	Connecticut Cyclones	W	49	6	
10/7/2006	A	So Cal Scorpions	L	0	30	S
4/28/2007	A	D.C. Divas	L	0	70	
5/5/2007	H	Delaware Griffins	W	34	0	
5/12/2007	H	Boston Rampage	W	13	7	
6/2/2007	A	New York Sharks	L	0	19	
6/9/2007	A	Montreal Blitz	L	21	28	
6/16/2007	H	Manchester Freedom	W	24	15	
6/23/2007	H	D.C. Divas	L	0	51	
6/30/2007	A	Manchester Freedom	L	12	41	
4/19/2008	A	Southern Maine Rebels	W	37	6	
4/26/2008	H	Montreal Blitz	L	0	28	
5/3/2008	H	Holyoke Hurricanes	W	48	0	
5/10/2008	A	Connecticut Cyclones	W	1	0	N
5/17/2008	A	Manchester Freedom	L	8	49	
5/31/2008	A	Montreal Blitz	L	14	40	
6/7/2008	H	Southern Maine Rebels	W	44	0	
6/14/2008	H	Manchester Freedom	W	14	7	
6/28/2008	A	Clarksville Fox	L	0	32	CC
4/11/2009	H	Holyoke Hurricanes	W	34	0	
4/18/2009	A	Central PA Vipers	W	21	14	
5/2/2009	H	Manchester Freedom	W	13	0	
5/9/2009	A	Manchester Freedom	W	20	8	
5/16/2009	A	Holyoke Hurricanes	W	53	0	
5/30/2009	H	New York Sharks	L	0	44	
6/6/2009	A	Southern Maine Rebels	W	19	0	
6/13/2009	H	Boston Militia	L	0	60	
6/27/2009	H	Jersey Justice	L	7	30	S

Continued on next page

New England Intensity Game-By-Game Results (continued)

Date	H/A	Opponent	Result	Score		Date	H/A	Opponent	Result	Score	
4/3/2010	H	Southern Maine Rebels	W	28 0		4/7/2012	H	Montreal Blitz	L	11 20	
4/10/2010	H	Manchester Freedom	W	25 6		4/14/2012	H	Connecticut Wreckers	W	36 0	
4/24/2010	A	Southern Maine Rebels	W	22 0		4/28/2012	H	New Hampshire Freedom	W	14 7	
5/1/2010	H	Connecticut Crushers	W	19 18		5/12/2012	A	New Hampshire Freedom	W	41 14	
5/8/2010	A	Manchester Freedom	W	20 8		5/19/2012	A	Northeastern Nitro	W	21 0	
5/22/2010	H	Erie Illusion	W	28 8		6/2/2012	A	Maine Rebels	W	31 0	
5/29/2010	A	Southern Maine Rebels	W	56 7		6/9/2012	A	Montreal Blitz	L	6 35	
6/5/2010	A	Erie Illusion	W	27 20		6/16/2012		Maine Rebels	W	58 0	
6/12/2010	A	Montreal Blitz	L	14 53	S	6/30/2012		Philadelphia Firebirds	W	30 13	BQ
						7/14/2012		Carolina Phoenix	L	0 7	BS
4/9/2011	A	Maine Rebels	W	18 0							
4/16/2011	A	Montreal Blitz	L	0 14		5/4/2013	H	Montreal Blitz	L	0 14	
4/23/2011	H	Maine Rebels	W	34 0		5/11/2013	A	New England Nightmare	W	33 6	
4/30/2011	H	Manchester Freedom	W	27 7		5/18/2013	A	Montreal Blitz	W	14 13	
5/14/2011	H	Montreal Blitz	L	0 30		6/1/2013	H	Maine Rebels	W	53 0	
5/21/2011	A	Manchester Freedom	W	7 0		6/8/2013	H	New England Nightmare	W	16 6	
6/11/2011	A	Maine Rebels	W	41 0		6/15/2013	A	Philadelphia Firebirds	W	20 6	
6/25/2011	H	Baltimore Nighthawks	W	25 0	BQ	6/22/2013	H	Connecticut Wreckers	W	49 0	
7/16/2011	A	Chattanooga Locomotion	W	20 0	BS	6/29/2013	A	Maine Rebels	W	1 0	
7/30/2011	N	Seattle Majestics	L	0 20	BC	7/13/2013	H	New England Nightmare	W	33 0	S
						7/20/2013	A	Carolina Phoenix	L	6 18	CC

New England Nightmare

Year	League	Name	W	L	Conference	Division	DF	PR
2010	WFA	New England Nightmare	2	6	National	Northeast	2	--
2011	WFA	New England Nightmare	0	9	National	North	4	--
2012	WFA	New England Nightmare	3	5	National	Division 1 (Northeast)	2	--
2013	IWFL	New England Nightmare	4	5	Eastern	Northeast	2	S
2014	IWFL	New England Nightmare	3	5	Eastern	North Atlantic	5	--
2015	WSFL	New England Nightmare	4	3	Northern	--	2	CC
		Total	**16**	**33**				

Based in: New Haven, CT

Date	H/A	Opponent	Result	Score		Date	H/A	Opponent	Result	Score	
4/10/2010	A	Baltimore Burn	L	14 54		4/20/2013	H	Maine Rebels	W	40 0	
4/24/2010	H	Philadelphia Liberty Belles (II)	L	6 70		4/27/2013	H	Montreal Blitz	L	0 21	
5/1/2010	H	Keystone Assault	L	6 56		5/4/2013	A	Maine Rebels	W	66 0	
5/8/2010	A	Southern Tier Spitfire	W	26 8		5/11/2013	H	New England Intensity	L	6 33	
5/15/2010	A	New Jersey Titans	L	6 47		5/18/2013	A	Maine Rebels	W	50 0	
6/5/2010	H	Baltimore Burn	L	20 28		6/8/2013	A	New England Intensity	L	6 16	
6/12/2010	A	Philadelphia Liberty Belles (II)	L	6 62		6/22/2013	H	New York Knockout	L	14 28	
6/19/2010	H	Southern Tier Spitfire	W	32 0		6/29/2013	A	New York Knockout	W	12 6	
						7/13/2013	A	New England Intensity	L	0 33	S
4/2/2011	A	Northeastern Nitro	L	0 13							
4/9/2011	A	Philadelphia Liberty Belles (II)	L	0 52		4/12/2014	H	Montreal Blitz	L	8 40	
4/30/2011	A	New York Sharks	L	12 48		4/19/2014	A	Keystone Assault	L	8 37	
5/7/2011	H	Boston Militia	L	0 62		4/26/2014	H	Northeast Rebels	W	32 6	
5/14/2011	H	Keystone Assault	L	0 27		5/3/2014	H	Keystone Assault	L	0 31	
5/21/2011	H	Northeastern Nitro	L	0 8		5/17/2014	H	Connecticut Wreckers	L	20 21	
6/4/2011	H	New York Sharks	L	8 28		5/31/2014	A	Northeast Rebels	W	38 0	
6/11/2011	A	Binghamton Tiger Cats	L	0 1	I	6/8/2014	A	Connecticut Wreckers	W	27 14	
6/18/2011	A	Keystone Assault	L	8 26		6/14/2014	A	Montreal Blitz	L	0 1	
4/14/2012	H	Philadelphia Liberty Belles (II)	L	0 14		5/9/2015	A	Keystone Assault	L	6 24	
4/21/2012	H	Keystone Assault	L	0 50		5/16/2015	A	Baltimore Burn	W	36 6	
4/28/2012	H	Maine Lynx	W	51 7		5/30/2015	A	Keystone Assault	L	6 27	
5/12/2012	H	Binghamton Tiger Cats	W	34 0	I	6/6/2015	H	Baltimore Burn	W	1 0	
5/19/2012	A	Baltimore Burn	L	14 20	I	6/20/2015	H	New York Knockout	W	39 0	
6/2/2012	A	Keystone Assault	L	0 42		6/27/2015	A	New York Knockout	W	26 8	
6/9/2012	A	New York Sharks	L	14 72		7/18/2015	A	Keystone Assault	L	0 34	CC
6/16/2012	A	Maine Lynx	W	48 0							

New England Nightmare Player Register (2010-2012, 2014-2015)

Altman, Marlaina (2011)
Avery, Caite (2015)
Baldwin, Traci (2011-2012, 2014)
Bermudez, Jerica (2010-12, 2014-15)
Betters, Hollie (2010)
Black, Sherrona "Shay" (2011)
Boulware, Amelia (2014)
Bray, Jackie (2010-2012, 2014)
Bray, Shawn (2010)
Brooks, Molly (Roldan) (2014-2015)
Canady, Devonne (2010)
Capriglione, Lori (2011-2012, 2014)
Coles, Suzy (2010-2011)
Collette, Julie (2014)
Cruz, Nicole (2015)
Dauphin, Ana (2010-2011)
Davern, Lauren (2010)
Davis, Raven (2012)
Donahue, Jennifer (2010-2012)
Doughtie, Athena (2014-2015)
Dumas, Meghan (2014-2015)
Evans, Kenya (2012)
Falbo, Erin (2011-2012)
Farquharson, KamaraOwana (2012)
Freeman, Taneka (2010-2012)
Genereux, Allie (2015)
Gonzalez, Mayo (2015)
Guyer, Jessylynn (2015)
Hardcaltle, Ciera (2011)
Harlow, Chella (2011-2012, 2014-2015)
Harrell, Sopheis (2011)
Harrison, Dee (2010)
Hathaway, Meghan (2012)
Hincks, Carrie (2014)
Holloway, Raynette (2014)
Howard, Yvonne "Hype" (2010-12, '14-15)
Hynes, Elizabeth "Bizzie" (2012)
Kalstrom, Kira (2010)
Kelly, Jerrilyn (2012)
Kenniston, Kristen (2011-2012)
King-Smith, Donnell (2012, 2014)
Knowlen, Kelly (2011-2012)
Kraatz, Faith (2015)
Lindo, Lorie (2010-2012, 2014-2015)
Martell, Megan (2011)
Maulucci, Dina (2010-2011)
McCallister, Chelsea (2014)
Mendes, Jazminn (2015)
Mendes, Kathleen (2011, 2014-2015)
Messier, Heather (2010-2011)
Messier, Hollie Ann (2011)
Mitchell, Angela (2010-2011)
Montanez, Yanira (2014)
Morales, Yanaira (2011)
Murdock, Kristen (2014)
Napier, Shaneca (2012, 2014)
Paradis, Nicole (2010)
Petit-Frere, Alexandria (2014)
Pfeffer, Laura (2010-2011)
Pittman, Elizabeth (2011-2012)
Quatanta, Marissa (2011)
Rex, Melissa (2011)
Robles-Claudio, Toni (2010)
Sanborn, Samantha "Sam" (2010-12, '15)
Sickler, Sierra (2010)
Silvestri, Kristan (2012)
Smith, Brigitte (2014)
Smith, Heather (2015)
Sprague, Sandy (2011)
Stango, Jennifer (2014-2015)
Sullivan, Carly (2012)
Theriault, Nicki (2010-2012)
Toledo, Tanya (2014)
Toohey, Stephanie (2014-2015)
Trice, Letrice (2011, 2014-2015)
Valie, Christine (2010)
Vossen, Stephanie (2012)
Watson, Lovette (2010-2012, 2014-2015)
Williams, Ashley (2014-2015)
Yacovacci, Nina (2010)
Young, Candace (2010-2012, 2014)
Zannoni, Bonnie (2010-2012, 2014-2015)

New England Storm

Year	League	Name	W	L	Conference	Division	DF	PR
2000	WPFL	New England Storm	6	3	National	East	1	C
2001	WPFL	New England Storm	2	6	--	--	3	--
2002	WPFL	New England Storm	1	7	National	--	5	--
2003	WPFL	New England Storm	3	6	National	East	2	--
		Total	**12**	**22**				

Based in: Boston, MA (2001-2003); Providence, RI (2000)

Date	H/A	Opponent	W/L	PF	PA	Note
10/14/2000	A	New York Galaxy	W	28	0	
10/22/2000	H	New York Sharks	L	8	16	
10/28/2000	A	New York Sharks	W	3	0	
11/5/2000	H	New York Galaxy	W	32	0	
11/18/2000	A	Colorado Valkyries	L	3	7	
12/2/2000	H	New York Sharks	W	48	12	
12/9/2000	H	New York Sharks	W	10	7	S
1/6/2001	A	Daytona Beach Barracudas	W	29	26	CC*
1/20/2001	A	Houston Energy	L	7	39	C
7/28/2001	H	New York Sharks	L	0	20	I
8/11/2001	A	Houston Energy	L	0	1	
8/18/2001	H	Syracuse Sting	W	20	0	I
8/25/2001	A	Austin Rage	L	16	32	
9/1/2001	H	Tampa Tempest	W	41	0	
9/8/2001	H	Austin Rage	L	18	30	
9/22/2001	H	Houston Energy	L	0	33	
10/7/2001	A	New York Sharks	L	0	19	I
8/3/2002		Wisconsin Riveters	L	0	32	
8/10/2002		Syracuse Sting	L	3	6	
8/24/2002		Dallas Diamonds	L	20	39	
8/31/2002		Indiana Speed	W	29	28	
9/14/2002		Syracuse Sting	L	13	14	
9/21/2002		Syracuse Sting	L	7	40	
9/28/2002		Wisconsin Riveters	L	0	1	
10/12/2002		Indiana Speed	L	0	37	
8/2/2003	A	Northern Ice	L	0	47	
8/9/2003	H	Syracuse Sting	L	6	12	
8/23/2003	H	Florida Stingrayz	L	0	14	
8/30/2003	A	Dayton Rebellion	W	28	6	
9/13/2003	H	Syracuse Sting	L	8	28	
9/20/2003	A	Syracuse Sting	L	12	41	
9/27/2003	H	Toledo Reign	W	30	14	
10/4/2003	A	Florida Stingrayz	L	6	84	
10/11/2003	H	Dayton Rebellion	W	12	8	

New Jersey Titans

Year	League	Name	W	L	Conference	Division	DF	PR
2007	WPFL	New Jersey Titans	3	2	American	East	2	--
2008	NWFA	New Jersey Titans	3	5	Northern	East	2	--
2009	WFA	New Jersey Titans	5	3	National	Northeast	2	--
2010	WFA	New Jersey Titans	2	6	National	East	3	--
2012	WSFL	New Jersey Titans	8	1	American	Northeast	1	LC
		Total	**21**	**17**				

Based in: Clifton, NJ
Neutral site: Towanda, PA (N)
Notes: Succeeded by Tri-State Warriors

Date	H/A	Opponent	Result	PF	PA	
8/25/2007	A	Empire State Roar	L	6	20	
9/1/2007	H	Connecticut Cyclones	W	32	0	
9/22/2007	A	Carolina Queens	W	49	8	
9/29/2007	H	Empire State Roar	L	7	22	
10/13/2007	H	Carolina Queens	W	61	8	
4/19/2008	H	Maine Freeze	W	50	0	
4/26/2008	A	Philadelphia Phoenix	L	0	40	
5/3/2008	H	New York Nemesis	L	12	19	
5/17/2008	H	Baltimore Burn	W	26	6	
5/24/2008	A	Maine Freeze	W	40	0	
5/31/2008	A	New York Nemesis	L	6	46	
6/7/2008	H	Philadelphia Phoenix	L	0	28	
6/14/2008	A	Baltimore Burn	L	22	28	
4/18/2009	H	Binghamton Tiger Cats	W	21	0	
4/25/2009	A	Connecticut Cyclones	W	1	0	N
5/9/2009	H	Philadelphia Liberty Belles (II)	L	12	14	
5/16/2009	A	Binghamton Tiger Cats	W	26	6	
5/30/2009	H	Connecticut Cyclones	W	1	0	N
6/6/2009	A	Philadelphia Liberty Belles (II)	L	0	59	
6/13/2009	H	Keystone Assault	L	6	28	
6/20/2009	A	Baltimore Burn	W	1	0	
4/10/2010	H	Keystone Assault	L	16	30	
4/17/2010	H	Baltimore Burn	L	36	62	
5/1/2010	A	Southern Tier Spitfire	W	47	2	
5/8/2010	A	Philadelphia Liberty Belles (II)	L	12	25	
5/15/2010	H	New England Nightmare	W	47	6	
6/5/2010	A	Keystone Assault	L	8	28	
6/12/2010	A	Baltimore Burn	L	0	16	
6/19/2010	H	Philadelphia Liberty Belles (II)	L	0	42	
4/14/2012	A	Baltimore Burn	L	18	20	
5/19/2012	A	Binghamton Tiger Cats	W	59	0	
6/2/2012	H	Mass Chaos	W	1	0	
6/9/2012	H	Binghamton Tiger Cats	W	46	8	
6/30/2012	A	Mass Chaos	W	1	0	
7/7/2012	H	Baltimore Burn	W	37	8	
7/21/2012	H	Baltimore Burn	W	31	6	S
7/28/2012	H	Huntsville Tigers	W	25	7	CC
8/11/2012	N	DFW Xtreme	W	67	6	C

New Jersey Titans Player Register (2009-2010)

Alexis, Tarah (2010)
Barthold, Sarah (2009)
Bradford, Melissa (2009-2010)
Brown, Keanna (2009)
Bubryckie, Nicole (2009)
Burke, Marsha (2010)
Campbell, June (2009)
Carbonara, Robyn (2009-2010)
Champion, Kesha (2010)
Colon, Amy (2009-2010)
Decrenza, Kerissa (2010)
Dunkelman, Jodi (2009-2010)
Duska, Kristen (2009)
Edwards, Simone (2009-2010)
Flood, Al-Nisa (2009-2010)
Frey, Lisa (2009)
Garner, Latorri (2010)
Garrison, April (2009)
Green, Danielle (2009-2010)
Hamill, Kelly (2010)
Harrison, Seleta (2009-2010)
Hazel, Cynthia (2009-2010)
Henderson, Aja (2010)
Huskey, Talesha (2010)
Johnson, Nasira (2009-2010)
Johnson, Shaniqua (2010)
Kulaw, Laura (2009-2010)
Leach, Amy (2010)
Lesniak, Jennifer (2010)
Lombana, Lissette (2009-2010)
Lykes, Mo (2010)
McCargo, Margaret (2009)
McDonnell, Kari (2009-2010)
Messemer, Melissa (2010)
Montague, Caniece (2010)
Pahuliz, Brenda (2009-2010)
Renko, Jennifer (2009-2010)
Reyes, Iris (2010)
Rodriguez, Anabell (2009-2010)
Scharpnick, Carrie (2009)
Stefanidis, Rita (2009)
Stopherd, Renee (2009-2010)
Stravato, Maria (2009)
Townsend, Stacy (2009-2010)
VanDevere, Victoria (2010)
Wilcox, Kim (2009)
Woods, Crystal (2010)

New Mexico Burn

Year	League	Name	W	L	Conference	Division	DF	PR
2005	WPFL	New Mexico Burn	0	7	American	South	3	--
2006	WPFL	New Mexico Burn	0	8	American	West	5	--
2007	WPFL	New Mexico Burn	0	8	American	West	5	--
		Total	**0**	**23**				

Based in: Albuquerque, NM
Notes: Succeeded by IWFL's New Mexico Menace

New Mexico Burn Game-By-Game Results

Date	H/A	Opponent	W/L	Score		Date	H/A	Opponent	W/L	Score
7/30/2005	A	Dallas Diamonds	L	0 76		9/2/2006	H	So Cal Scorpions	L	0 54
8/13/2005	H	Dallas Diamonds	L	0 56		9/9/2006	A	Los Angeles Amazons	L	0 50
8/27/2005	H	Arizona Caliente	L	0 38		9/16/2006	H	Las Vegas Showgirlz	L	0 36
9/10/2005	A	Houston Energy	L	6 58		9/23/2006	A	So Cal Scorpions	L	7 77
10/1/2005	A	So Cal Scorpions	L	0 69						
10/8/2005	H	Houston Energy	L	6 76		8/18/2007	H	Los Angeles Amazons	L	0 64
10/22/2005	A	Arizona Caliente	L	7 50		8/25/2007	H	Houston Energy	L	0 77
						9/1/2007	A	Las Vegas Showgirlz	L	8 41
7/22/2006	A	Dallas Diamonds	L	0 97		9/8/2007	A	Houston Energy	L	0 63
8/5/2006	H	Dallas Diamonds	L	0 80		9/22/2007	A	Dallas Diamonds	L	0 1
8/12/2006	H	Los Angeles Amazons	L	0 62		9/29/2007	H	Las Vegas Showgirlz	L	0 1
8/19/2006	A	Las Vegas Showgirlz	L	0 30		10/6/2007	A	Los Angeles Amazons	L	0 1
						10/20/2007	H	Dallas Diamonds	L	0 1

New Mexico Menace

Year	League	Name	W	L	Conference	Division	DF	PR
2008	IWFL	New Mexico Menace	0	8	Western	Pacific Southwest	5	--
2009	IWFL2	New Mexico Menace	0	6	--	--	24	--
		Total	**0**	**14**				

Based in: Albuquerque, NM
Notes: Preceded by WPFL's New Mexico Burn

Date	H/A	Opponent	W/L	Score		Date	H/A	Opponent	W/L	Score
4/19/2008	H	Dallas Diamonds	L	0 91		4/11/2009	A	Tucson Monsoon	L	0 8
4/26/2008	A	California Quake	L	0 64		4/18/2009	H	Southern California Breakers	L	0 33
5/3/2008	H	Tucson Monsoon	L	7 20		4/25/2009	A	California Quake	L	0 61
5/10/2008	A	Southern California Breakers	L	0 48		5/2/2009	H	Tucson Monsoon	L	0 54
5/17/2008	H	Las Vegas Showgirlz	L	7 27		5/16/2009	A	Los Angeles Amazons	L	0 50
5/24/2008	A	Tucson Monsoon	L	13 14		5/23/2009	H	Tucson Monsoon	L	7 55
6/7/2008	H	California Quake	L	0 35						
6/14/2008	A	Las Vegas Showgirlz	L	0 55						

New Orleans Blaze

Year	League	Name	W	L	Conference	Division	DF	PR
2002	NWFA	New Orleans Spice	2	6	--	Southern	3	--
2003	NWFA	New Orleans Spice	5	3	Southern	Gulf Coast	2	--
2004	NWFA	New Orleans Blaze	5	3	Southern	Gulf Coast	3	--
2005	NWFA	New Orleans Blaze	5	4	Southern	--	6	Q
2007	NWFA	New Orleans Blaze	5	4	Southern	South	2	Q
2008	NWFA	New Orleans Blaze	5	3	Southern	Southeast	2	--
2009	WFA	New Orleans Blaze	3	6	American	Southeast	4	BW
2010	WFA	New Orleans Blaze	3	5	American	South	2	--
2011	WFA	New Orleans Blaze	4	4	American	Gulf	2	--
		Total	**37**	**38**				

Based in: New Orleans, LA
Notes: Succeeded by New Orleans Mojo

Date	Opponent	W/L	Score		Date	H/A	Opponent	W/L	Score
4/20/2002	Biloxi Herricanes	L	34 40		4/12/2003	H	Gulf Coast Herricanes	W	26 22
5/4/2002	Panama City Beach Rumble	W	48 38		4/19/2003	A	Pensacola Power	L	3 49
5/18/2002	Biloxi Herricanes	L	14 22		4/26/2003	A	Panama City Beach Rumble	L	34 35
5/25/2002	Pensacola Power	L	7 50		5/3/2003	H	Panama City Beach Rumble	W	44 27
6/8/2002	Panama City Beach Rumble	W	36 8		5/17/2003	H	Pensacola Power	L	0 49
6/15/2002	Pensacola Power	L	0 41		5/24/2003	A	Gulf Coast Herricanes	W	24 0
6/22/2002	Panama City Beach Rumble	L	16 24		5/31/2003	A	Panama City Beach Rumble	W	39 14
6/29/2002	Pensacola Power	L	0 59		6/14/2003	H	Gulf Coast Herricanes	W	34 0

Continued on next page

New Orleans Blaze Game-By-Game Results (continued)

Date	H/A	Opponent	Result	PF	PA	Note
4/3/2004	H	Gulf Coast Herricanes	W	67	0	
4/24/2004	H	Alabama Renegades	W	28	7	
5/1/2004	A	Pensacola Power	L	12	35	
5/8/2004	A	Muscle Shoals Smashers	W	60	0	
5/15/2004	A	Gulf Coast Herricanes	W	26	0	
5/22/2004	H	Muscle Shoals Smashers	W	55	0	
6/5/2004	H	Pensacola Power	L	20	28	
6/12/2004	A	Alabama Renegades	L	12	21	
4/16/2005	A	Pensacola Power	L	26	31	
4/23/2005	A	Gulf Coast Herricanes	W	42	0	
4/30/2005	H	Emerald Coast Sharks	W	48	0	
5/14/2005	H	Shreveport Shockhers	W	33	0	
5/28/2005	A	Emerald Coast Sharks	W	28	0	
6/4/2005	H	Pensacola Power	L	8	35	
6/11/2005	A	Nashville Dream	L	6	17	
6/18/2005	H	Gulf Coast Herricanes	W	27	0	
6/25/2005	A	Oklahoma City Lightning	L	14	61	Q
4/14/2007	A	Dallas Rage	L	33	34	*
4/28/2007	H	Emerald Coast Barracudas	W	30	0	
5/5/2007	H	Pensacola Power	L	7	22	
5/12/2007	A	Gulf Coast Herricanes	W	27	6	
5/19/2007	A	Emerald Coast Barracudas	W	55	6	
6/2/2007	H	Dallas Rage	W	1	0	
6/9/2007	H	Gulf Coast Herricanes	W	19	12	
6/16/2007	A	Pensacola Power	L	28	37	
6/23/2007	A	Oklahoma City Lightning	L	12	42	Q
4/19/2008	H	Pensacola Power	W	20	0	
4/26/2008	A	Emerald Coast Barracudas	W	38	7	
5/3/2008	H	Gulf Coast Herricanes	W	36	0	
5/10/2008	A	Austin Outlaws	L	6	42	
5/17/2008	A	Pensacola Power	L	6	16	
5/31/2008	A	Gulf Coast Herricanes	W	27	16	
6/7/2008	H	Austin Outlaws	L	0	48	
6/21/2008	H	Emerald Coast Barracudas	W	34	0	
4/18/2009	A	Memphis Belles	L	7	46	
4/25/2009	A	Gulf Coast Riptide	L	0	28	
5/2/2009	H	Jacksonville Dixie Blues	L	0	46	
5/9/2009	H	Gulf Coast Riptide	L	10	20	
5/16/2009	A	Emerald Coast Barracudas	W	39	20	
6/6/2009	H	Memphis Belles	L	26	32	
6/13/2009	A	Jacksonville Dixie Blues	L	0	42	
6/27/2009	H	Emerald Coast Barracudas	W	1	0	
8/15/2009	H	Monterrey Royal Eagles	W	12	0	B
4/10/2010	H	Memphis Soul	L	32	34	
4/17/2010	H	Acadiana Zydeco	W	33	0	
4/24/2010	H	Houston Power	L	6	39	
5/8/2010	A	Acadiana Zydeco	W	27	0	
5/22/2010	A	Austin Outlaws	L	0	51	
6/5/2010	H	Lone Star Mustangs	L	0	51	
6/12/2010	H	Memphis Soul	L	6	8	
6/19/2010	A	Acadiana Zydeco	W	17	6	
4/2/2011	A	Houston Power	L	0	40	
4/9/2011	A	Acadiana Zydeco	W	14	8	
4/16/2011	H	Little Rock Wildcats	W	22	14	
4/30/2011	H	Acadiana Zydeco	W	19	0	
5/14/2011	H	Memphis WTF	W	9	8	
5/21/2011	A	Austin Outlaws	L	0	52	
6/4/2011	H	Houston Power	L	6	38	
6/18/2011	A	Memphis WTF	L	0	1	

New Orleans Blaze Player Register (2004-2005, 2007-2011)

Agee, Simone (2011)
Allen, Akesha (2004-2005, 2008-2011)
Allen, Crystal (2008-2010)
Babin, Casey (2009)
Banks, Natasha (2005, 2009)
Barto, Marika (2007-2011)
Bergeron, Chere (2009)
Black, Naomi (2007)
Bott, Allison (2010-2011)
Boudreaux, Jackie (2004-05, 2007-11)
Bradley, Arrie (2010)
Breaux, Danie (2010-2011)
Bree, Miss (2005)
Brewer, Pat (2011)
Bundrick, Stacey (2010-2011)
Carnley, Hope (2007-2009)
Carr, Bridgett (2011)
Carrier, Liz (2009-2010)
Causin, Dawn (2004-2005)
Champagne, Brooke (2008-2011)
Cinquemano, Ashley (2008-2009)
Cocroft, Tamara (2005)
Coleman, Danielle (2004-05, 2007-08)
Cook, Channa (2010)
Covington, Jasmine (2011)
D'Antoni, Miko (2008-2010)
Davenport, E.J. (2004-05, 2007-08, '11)
Davenport, Imogene (2010)
Decoteau, Anya (2007)
Del Castillo, Chris (2004-2005, 2007)
Delellis, Diana (2011)
Dixon, Shantell (2010-2011)
Doll, Madelaine (2007)
Domangue, Katherine (2004)
Douglas, Mandy (2008-2011)
Duhon, Tonya (2007-2009)
Dunham, Kristy (2007-2009)
Dunn, Jasmine (2010-2011)
Dupre, Brandy (2011)
Dutton, Heather (2007)
Edwards, Melissa "Mook" ('04-05, '07, '09)
Elder, Dawn (2004-2005)
Farrell, Jill (2004-2005)
Federline, Alex (2009)
Fisher, Amanda (2007, 2009)
Franco, Bernie (2004)
Franklin, Raven (2005)
Frisard, Candace (2004-05, 2007-08)
Fugler, Conner (2004-2005, 2007)
Gamble, Lena (2005)
Gantt (Brie), Laurin (2004-2005)
Garatie, Esther (2011)
Garrett, Lori (2004-2005)
Gimma, Victoria (2011)
Gordon, Betty Ann (2008-2010)
Gordon, Kim (2004)
Guilliot, Dixie (2009)
Hadley, Jenn (2007, 2009-2010)
Hadley, Roxanne (2004-2005, 2007-2008)
Hernandez, Laura (2011)
Hilliard, Sandy (2008)
Holland, Dani (2010-2011)
Jacobi, Catherine (2008, 2010)
Johnson, Chemetra (2010-2011)
Johnson, Demetria (2007)
Jones, Camelia (2005)
Jones, Schantalyn (2009)
Jones, Shay (2010-2011)
Keegan, Jillian (2009)
Kerns, Linda (2007-2009)
King, Destiny (2010-2011)
King, Julie (2007)
Kokemor, Lynette (2004-05, 2007-08)
Lockhart, CoCo (2011)
Lofton, Sonja (2005)
Ludwicki, Jen (2004-2005, 2007-2008)
Lunsford, Lisa (2004-2005, 2007-2008)
Magnuson, Lynn (2011)
McCartney, Sue (2005, 2007-2008)
McDuffie, Carrie (2007)
McDuffie, Opal "Opie" (2005, 2007-08)
McLuckie, Mandy (2008-2009)
McNamara, Kelly (2004)
Mischler, Paula (2007, 2009-2010)
Monteleone, Athena (2004-05, '07-08)
Morales, Tianne "Yanni" (2005, '07-11)
Morgan, Rebecca "Beck" (2005, '07-11)
Myers, Mandy (2008-2011)
Neunzig, Sara (2007)
Noel, Michelle (2005)
Norton, Kathy (2007)
Parquet, Tashika (2004-2005, 2007)
Parvino, Cheri (2004-2005)
Piatt, Tiffany (2005)
Pichon, Evanne (2005)

Continued on next page

New Orleans Blaze Player Register (continued)

Plummer, Tammy (2007-2008)
Powell, Nicole (2004)
Ransaw, Kerri (2004-2005)
Reeder, Brittney (2010-2011)
Richards, Angela (2011)
Rivet, Nicole (2007)
Robertson, Christina (2004)
Robino, Kristal (2005, 2007)
Rodriguez, Natalie (2004)
Ruffin, Lisa (2011)
Schmitt, Amy (2009-2011)
Shirer, Tricia (2010)
Simon, Danielle (2008-2010)
Slaughter, Ayana (2011)
Smith, Ellen (2004)
Smith, Jane (2005)
Smith, Melinda (2007)
Stepter, Melissa (2004)
Stewart, Tiffany (2009)
Stockton, Jummanah (2007-2008)
Stovall, Nicole (2004-2005)
Sylve, Ariel (2009-2011)
Szyller, Nicole (2005)
Thibodeaux, Lisa (2007-2008)
Thibodeaux, Nicole (2007)
Thompson, Naomia (2008-2009)
Tranchina, Lacy (2007)
Trosclair, Jenny (2007-2009)
Wensel, April (2009)
West, Nicole (2005)
Williams, Rontashala (2004-2005)
Williams, Shana (2007-2008)
Willie, Knyisha (2011)
Wunderland, Alicin (2005)
Zboril, Christine (2004-2005, 2007-2008)
Zeeb, Lisa (2010-2011)

New Orleans Krewe

Year	League	Name	W	L	Conference	Division	DF	PR
2015	IWFL	New Orleans Krewe	0	6	Western	Southwest	3	--

Based in: New Orleans, LA

4/11/2015	A	San Antonio Regulators	L	0	14
4/18/2015	A	Austin Yellow Jackets	L	0	30
5/2/2015	H	Houston Energy	L	0	54
5/16/2015	H	San Antonio Regulators	L	6	42
5/30/2015	H	Austin Yellow Jackets	L	0	37
6/13/2015	A	Houston Energy	L	0	1

New Orleans Mojo

Year	League	Name	W	L	Conference	Division	DF	PR
2013	WFA	New Orleans Mojo	1	7	American	Division 7 (Gulf Coast)	4	--

Based in: New Orleans, LA
Notes: Preceded by New Orleans Blaze; Succeeded by Louisiana Jazz

4/6/2013	A	Acadiana Zydeco	L	0	40
4/13/2013	H	Atlanta Phoenix	L	0	48
4/20/2013	A	Little Rock Wildcats	L	0	28
4/27/2013	H	Acadiana Zydeco	W	32	12
5/4/2013	A	Tulsa Threat	L	0	37
5/18/2013	H	Dallas Diamonds	L	0	68
6/1/2013	A	Tallahassee Jewels	L	6	47
6/8/2013	H	Little Rock Wildcats	L	0	20

New Orleans Mojo Player Register (2013)

Allen, Paula (2013)
Andrews, Deidra (2013)
Batiste, Malika (2013)
Bott, Allison (2013)
Bowens, Lillie (2013)
Bruce, Faith (2013)
Callaway, Ayesha (2013)
Chestnut, Coy (2013)
Chiasson, Brandi (2013)
Davenport, Imogene (2013)
Doyle, Nichole (2013)
Ernst, Ashley (2013)
Felix, Pat (2013)
Guichard, Carla (2013)
Harper, Kylie (2013)
Harris, Shannon (2013)
Hewitt, Jade (2013)
Honore, Jennifer (2013)
Iglus, Rochella (2013)
Johnson, Shavone (2013)
Jones, Javanti (2013)
Menzies, Vyntrella (2013)
Miller, Donna (2013)
Morales, Tianne (2013)
Morgan, Rebecca "Beck" (2013)
Myers, Andrea (2013)
Nelson, Renoitta (2013)
Ortolano, Staci (2013)
Parker, Jonderick (2013)
Patterson, Keshawn (2013)
Pax, Elizabeth (2013)
Prevost, Erin (2013)
Robichaux, Dakota (2013)
Ruffin, Lisa (2013)
Scherberger, Sandra (2013)
Schubert, Yvette (2013)
Scott, Tamika (2013)
Shirer, Tricia (2013)
Tassin, Corlesha (2013)
Thomas, Dominique (2013)
Troulliet, Richelle (2013)
White, Darlene (2013)
Williams, Regina (2013)

New Orleans Voodoo Dolls

Year	League	Name	W	L	Conference	Division	DF	PR
2001	WAFL	New Orleans Voodoo Dolls	2	8	Atlantic	Central	3	--
2002	WAFL-WFA	New Orleans Voodoo Dolls	0	10	Central	--	4	--
		Total	**2**	**18**				

Based in: New Orleans, LA
Notes: Forfeited entire 2002 season

10/27/2001	A	Alabama Slammers	W	6	0	10/12/2002	A	Georgia Enforcers	L	0	1
11/3/2001	A	Tampa Bay Force	L	0	58	10/19/2002	H	Indianapolis Vipers	L	0	1
11/10/2001	H	Alabama Slammers	W	14	0	10/26/2002	A	Birmingham Steel Magnolias	L	0	1
11/17/2001	H	Tampa Bay Force	L	0	52	11/3/2002	A	Orlando Fire	L	0	1
12/1/2001	A	Alabama Slammers	L	6	12	11/9/2002	H	Tampa Bay Force	L	0	1
12/15/2001	A	Tampa Bay Force	L	0	26	11/16/2002	A	Georgia Enforcers	L	0	1
12/22/2001	H	Indianapolis Vipers	L	6	44	11/23/2002	H	Birmingham Steel Magnolias	L	0	1
12/29/2001	H	Orlando Fire	L	0	44	12/7/2002	A	Indianapolis Vipers	L	0	1
1/12/2002	A	Jacksonville Dixie Blues	L	7	47	12/14/2002	H	Orlando Fire	L	0	1
1/19/2002	H	Jacksonville Dixie Blues	L	12	36	12/21/2002	H	Jacksonville Dixie Blues	L	0	1

New York Dazzles

Year	League	Name	W	L	Conference	Division	DF	PR
2004	WPFL	New York Dazzles	0	10	National	East	3	--
2005	WPFL	New York Dazzles	10	2	National	East	1	C
		Total	**10**	**12**				

Based in: Long Island, NY

8/7/2004	A	Albany Ambush	L	0	53	7/30/2005	A	Empire State Roar	W	6	0	
8/14/2004	H	Syracuse Sting	L	0	20	8/6/2005	H	Delaware Griffins	W	21	8	
8/22/2004	A	Albany Ambush	L	0	33	8/13/2005	A	San Francisco Stingrayz	W	27	8	
8/28/2004	H	Delaware Griffins	L	0	36	8/20/2005	A	Empire State Roar	W	12	8	
9/11/2004	H	Dallas Diamonds	L	0	67	9/3/2005	H	Empire State Roar	L	13	30	
9/18/2004	H	Houston Energy	L	0	68	9/10/2005	H	Delaware Griffins	W	19	6	
9/25/2004	A	Syracuse Sting	L	0	47	9/24/2005	A	Albany Ambush	W	33	16	
10/2/2004	H	Albany Ambush	L	0	23	10/1/2005	H	Albany Ambush	W	20	6	
10/9/2004	A	Syracuse Sting	L	8	40	10/8/2005	H	Cape Fear Thunder	W	34	0	
10/23/2004	A	Delaware Griffins	L	0	47	10/16/2005	H	Delaware Griffins	W	30	0	
						11/5/2005	H	Minnesota Vixen	W	14	12	CC
						11/19/2005	A	Dallas Diamonds	L	8	61	C

New York Galaxy

Year	League	Name	W	L	Conference	Division	DF	PR
2000	WPFL	New York Galaxy	0	4	National	East	3	--

Based in: Rochester, NY
Notes: Succeeded by MIWFA's Syracuse Sting

10/14/2000	H	New England Storm	L	0	28	11/5/2000	A	New England Storm	L	0	32
10/22/2000	H	Daytona Beach Barracudas	L	6	35	11/18/2000	A	New York Sharks	L	0	41

New York Gems

Year	League	Name	W	L	Conference	Division	DF	PR
2000	WCFL	New York Gems	0	1	--	--	--	--

Based in: New York, NY

12/1/2000	A	New York Sharks	L	12	50	I

New York Knockout

Year	League	Name	W	L	Conference	Division	DF	PR
2013	IWFL	New York Knockout	5	3	Eastern	Northeast	1	--
2014	IWFL	New York Knockout	4	2	Eastern	North Atlantic	3	--
2015	W8FL	New York Knockout	2	4	--	--	3	LC
		Total	**11**	**9**				

Based in: Schenectady, NY

4/27/2013	H	Maine Rebels	W	34	0		5/31/2014	A	Montreal Blitz	L	0	55	
5/4/2013	A	Connecticut Wreckers	W	14	13		6/14/2014	H	Erie Illusion	W	40	0	
5/11/2013	A	Montreal Blitz	L	0	49		6/21/2014	A	Erie Illusion	W	54	0	
5/25/2013	H	Connecticut Wreckers	W	6	0		4/25/2015	A	Three Rivers Xplosion	W	20	18	**
6/8/2013	A	Maine Rebels	W	42	0		5/2/2015	A	Cape Fear Thunder	L	12	18	
6/15/2013	H	Montreal Blitz	L	0	41		6/6/2015	A	Cape Fear Thunder	L	0	12	
6/22/2013	A	New England Nightmare	W	28	14		6/20/2015	A	New England Nightmare	L	0	39	
6/29/2013	H	New England Nightmare	L	6	12		6/27/2015	H	New England Nightmare	L	8	26	
4/19/2014	A	Northeast Rebels	W	14	0		8/1/2015	H	Cape Fear Thunder	W	28	0	C
5/3/2014	H	Connecticut Wreckers	W	16	6								
5/10/2014	H	Keystone Assault	L	0	40								

New York Knockout Player Register (2014)

Bauer, Chantal (2014)
Bolton, Yvonne (2014)
Crawford, Cindy (2014)
Demarest, Kayla (2014)
Faga, Heather (2014)
Fitzgerald, Shaysha (2014)
Halesworth, Val (2014)
Hall, Lauren (2014)
Hamilton, Renee (2014)
Hansler, Jessica (2014)
Hull, Katie (2014)
Lanfear, Els (2014)
Lubba, Madyson (2014)
Marmorale, Missy (2014)
Messemer, Melissa (2014)
Mills, Kimberly (2014)
Nolan, Regina (2014)
Norero, Justina (2014)
Oswald, Lucy (2014)
Rivette, Kyle (2014)
Sauls, Karessa (2014)
Savage, Tanya (2014)
Silver, Elizabeth (2014)
Tymeson, Lynda (2014)
Veillette, Sarah (2014)
Vigiard, Emily (2014)
Westbrook, Maria (2014)

New York Nemesis

Year	League	Name	W	L	Conference	Division	DF	PR
2008	NWFA	New York Nemesis	8	1	Northern	Northeast	1	S
2009	IWFL	New York Nemesis	5	3	Eastern	North Atlantic	2	--
2010	IWFL	New York Nemesis	3	5	Eastern	Northeast	4	--
		Total	**16**	**9**				

Based in: Schenectady, NY

4/19/2008	H	Connecticut Crush	W	35	0		5/16/2009	A	Pittsburgh Passion	L	0	41	
5/3/2008	A	New Jersey Titans	W	19	12		5/30/2009	H	Montreal Blitz	W	13	12	
5/10/2008	A	Baltimore Burn	W	42	8		6/6/2009	A	Boston Militia	L	12	49	
5/17/2008	H	Maine Freeze	W	60	0		6/13/2009	A	Connecticut Crushers	W	28	6	
5/24/2008	A	Connecticut Crush	W	19	0								
5/31/2008	H	New Jersey Titans	W	46	6		4/3/2010	H	Boston Militia	L	6	56	
6/14/2008	A	Maine Freeze	W	58	8		4/17/2010	H	Connecticut Crushers	W	25	0	
6/21/2008	H	Baltimore Burn	W	40	18		4/24/2010	A	Baltimore Nighthawks	L	6	7	
7/5/2008	H	West Michigan Mayhem	L	7	34	S	5/1/2010	H	Philadelphia Firebirds	W	33	0	
							5/8/2010	H	Boston Militia	L	0	40	
4/11/2009	H	New York Sharks	L	7	21		5/15/2010	A	Montreal Blitz	L	0	20	
4/18/2009	H	Jersey Justice	W	40	0		5/22/2010	A	D.C. Divas	L	21	49	
4/25/2009	A	Montreal Blitz	W	14	6		6/5/2010	A	Manchester Freedom	W	38	0	
5/9/2009	H	Philadelphia Firebirds	W	34	3								

New York Nemesis Player Register (2008)

Acosta, Michelle (2008)
Amedio, Stacie (2008)
Benoit, Lindsay (2008)
Bepko, Ashleigh (2008)
Bruce, Donna (2008)
Cannella, Kim (2008)
Carter, Angela (2008)
Choi, Asook (2008)
Deltoro, Deb (2008)
Diaz, Xiomara "Zee" (2008)
Dunn, Jessica (2008)
Eddy, Vicky (2008)
Fromm, Talia (2008)
Gable, Miriam (2008)
Graziano, Alana (2008)
Green, Tashia (2008)
Halesworth, Val (2008)
Johnson, Nadine (2008)
King, Emily (2008)
Kobos, Jane (2008)
Koosa, Maggie (2008)
Kroepfl, Jessica (2008)
Lamie, Shannon (2008)
Leo, Lauren (2008)
Lighthart, Aurora (2008)
Manfred, Amy (2008)
Manfred, Lauren (2008)
Marmorale, Missy (2008)
Millbyer, Lynn (2008)
Monaco, Val (2008)
Nardelli, Riss (2008)
Nesbitt, Sandra "Gumby" (2008)
Oswald, Lucy (2008)
Palmer, Kim (2008)
Pesente, Carley (2008)
Phillip, Tasha (2008)
Roker, Tony (2008)
Rupp, Mimi (2008)
Scott, Phillapa (2008)
Sears, Cathy (2008)
Slack, Kate (2008)
Sloan, Jessica (2008)
Speed, Nikia (2008)
Suggs, Cynthia (2008)
Vongvorachoti, Jane (2008)
Williams, Rokia (2008)
Williams, Tamara (2008)
Workman, Heather (2008)
Yacovacci, Nina (2008)
Yasso, Liz (2008)
Ying, Pei (2008)

New York Sharks

Year	League	Name	W	L	Conference	Division	DF	PR
1999	WPFL IX	New York Sharks	1	0	--	--	--	--
2000	WPFL	New York Sharks	5	3	National	East	2	S
2001	MIWFA	New York Sharks	6	1	--	--	--	--
2002	IWFL	New York Sharks	9	0	Eastern	--	1	**NC**
2003	IWFL	New York Sharks	9	1	Eastern	Mid-Atlantic	1	C
2004	IWFL	New York Sharks	10	1	Eastern	Mid-Atlantic	1	C
2005	IWFL	New York Sharks	11	1	Eastern	North Atlantic	1	CC
2006	IWFL	New York Sharks	9	1	Eastern	Mid-Atlantic	1	CC
2007	IWFL	New York Sharks	7	3	Eastern	North Atlantic	1	CC
2008	IWFL	New York Sharks	6	2	Eastern	North Atlantic	3	--
2009	IWFL	New York Sharks	4	4	Eastern	North Atlantic	3	--
2010	IWFL	New York Sharks	7	2	Eastern	Northeast	2	S
2011	WFA	New York Sharks	5	3	National	North	2	--
2012	WFA	New York Sharks	5	5	National	Division 2 (North)	2	Q
2013	WFA	New York Sharks	4	5	National	Division 1 (Northeast)	2	W
2014	IWFL	New York Sharks	7	3	Eastern	North Atlantic	1	CC
2015	IWFL	New York Sharks	6	3	Eastern	North Atlantic	1	S
		Total	**111**	**38**				

Based in: Brooklyn, NY

Date	H/A	Opponent	W/L	Score		Note
12/11/1999	H	Minnesota Vixens	W	12	6	
10/22/2000	A	New England Storm	W	16	8	
10/28/2000	H	New England Storm	L	0	3	
11/4/2000	A	Oklahoma City Wildcats	W	26	6	
11/11/2000	H	Miami Fury	W	19	12	
11/18/2000	H	New York Galaxy	W	41	0	
12/1/2000	H	New York Gems	W	50	12	I
12/2/2000	A	New England Storm	L	12	48	
12/9/2000	A	New England Storm	L	7	10	S
7/28/2001	A	New England Storm	W	20	0	I
8/4/2001	A	Carolina Cougars	L	8	10	
8/11/2001	H	Syracuse Sting	W	34	6	
8/18/2001	A	Tampa Tempest	W	25	0	I
9/1/2001	A	Syracuse Sting	W	21	14	
9/8/2001	A	Arizona Titans	W	20	0	I
10/7/2001	H	New England Storm	W	19	0	I
4/20/2002		Montreal Blitz	W	45	6	
4/27/2002		Bay State Warriors	W	40	0	
5/11/2002		Detroit Blaze	W	73	0	
5/18/2002		Montreal Blitz	W	44	0	
6/1/2002		Albany Night-Mares	W	34	6	
6/8/2002		Bay State Warriors	W	26	0	
6/15/2002		New Hampshire Freedom	W	64	0	
6/22/2002		Bay State Warriors	W	22	2	
7/6/2002		Austin Outlaws	W	24	4	C
4/12/2003	H	Montreal Blitz	W	52	0	
4/19/2003	A	Philadelphia Liberty Belles (I)	W	48	0	
4/26/2003	H	Rhode Island Riptide	W	62	0	
5/10/2003	A	Albany Night-Mares	W	98	0	
5/17/2003	H	Philadelphia Liberty Belles (I)	W	58	0	
5/31/2003	H	Albany Night-Mares	W	41	0	
6/7/2003	A	Miami Fury	W	20	6	
6/9/2003	A	Tampa Bay Terminators	W	36	0	
6/28/2003	H	Bay State Warriors	W	20	6	CC
7/12/2003	H	Sacramento Sirens	L	30	41	C

Continued on next page

New York Sharks Game-By-Game Results (continued)

Date	H/A	Opponent	W/L	PF	PA	Note
4/3/2004	H	Atlanta Xplosion	W	28	21	
4/17/2004	H	New Hampshire Freedom	W	26	0	
4/24/2004	H	Montreal Blitz	W	20	0	
5/8/2004	A	Chicago Force	W	6	2	
5/15/2004	H	Bay State Warriors	W	45	0	
5/22/2004	H	Chicago Force	W	27	7	
6/5/2004	A	Rhode Island Intensity	W	41	16	
6/12/2004	A	Bay State Warriors	W	35	0	
6/26/2004	H	Chicago Force	W	40	0	S
7/10/2004	H	Tampa Bay Terminators	W	29	7	CC
7/24/2004	A	Sacramento Sirens	L	27	29	C
4/9/2005	A	Bay State Warriors	W	41	12	
4/16/2005	A	Southern Maine Rebels	W	32	6	
4/23/2005	H	Connecticut Lightning	W	36	0	
4/30/2005	A	Manchester Freedom	W	28	0	
5/14/2005	A	Rhode Island Intensity	W	40	6	
5/21/2005	H	Bay State Warriors	W	9	0	
6/4/2005	H	Southern Maine Rebels	W	28	6	
6/11/2005	H	Manchester Freedom	W	43	0	
6/18/2005	H	Rhode Island Intensity	W	59	0	
6/25/2005	H	Montreal Blitz	W	41	7	
7/9/2005	H	Southern Maine Rebels	W	26	0	S
7/23/2005	H	Atlanta Xplosion	L	0	3	CC
4/29/2006	H	Indianapolis Chaos	W	73	0	
5/6/2006	A	Delaware Griffins	W	48	0	
5/13/2006	H	Manchester Freedom	W	20	0	
5/20/2006	A	Southern Maine Rebels	W	55	0	
6/3/2006	H	Delaware Griffins	W	47	0	
6/10/2006	H	Montreal Blitz	W	53	7	
6/17/2006	A	Montreal Blitz	W	42	27	
6/24/2006	A	Bay State Warriors	W	24	16	
7/8/2006	H	Miami Fury	W	14	8	S
7/15/2006	H	Atlanta Xplosion	L	14	35	CC
4/28/2007	A	Miami Fury	W	48	33	
5/5/2007	H	D.C. Divas	L	14	20	
5/19/2007	A	Boston Rampage	W	26	6	
6/2/2007	H	New England Intensity	W	19	0	
6/9/2007	H	Miami Fury	W	41	18	
6/16/2007	A	D.C. Divas	L	0	22	
6/23/2007	H	Southern Maine Rebels	W	1	0	
6/30/2007	A	Delaware Griffins	W	27	0	
7/14/2007	H	Manchester Freedom	W	28	0	S
7/28/2007	A	Atlanta Xplosion	L	7	10	CC
4/19/2008	H	Baltimore Nighthawks	W	26	6	
4/26/2008	H	Central PA Vipers	W	40	0	
5/3/2008	A	Baltimore Nighthawks	W	54	28	
5/10/2008	A	Boston Militia	W	26	24	
5/17/2008	H	Boston Militia	L	14	28	
5/31/2008	A	Pittsburgh Passion	L	21	28	
6/7/2008	H	D.C. Divas	W	14	8	
6/14/2008	A	Central PA Vipers	W	31	0	
4/11/2009	A	New York Nemesis	W	21	7	
4/25/2009	A	Boston Militia	L	7	21	
5/2/2009	A	Philadelphia Firebirds	W	33	14	
5/9/2009	H	Connecticut Crushers	W	40	7	
5/16/2009	H	D.C. Divas	L	7	21	
5/30/2009	A	New England Intensity	W	44	0	
6/6/2009	A	D.C. Divas	L	18	34	
6/13/2009	H	Pittsburgh Passion	L	33	34	
4/10/2010	A	Philadelphia Firebirds	W	64	0	
4/17/2010	H	D.C. Divas	W	19	13	
4/24/2010	H	Connecticut Crushers	W	65	14	
5/1/2010	A	Jersey Justice	W	50	8	
5/8/2010	H	Pittsburgh Passion	W	12	8	
5/15/2010	A	Boston Militia	L	0	31	
5/22/2010	H	Baltimore Nighthawks	W	38	6	
6/5/2010	A	Pittsburgh Passion	W	27	10	
6/12/2010	A	Boston Militia	L	6	26	S
4/2/2011	A	Philadelphia Liberty Belles (II)	W	34	20	
4/16/2011	A	Boston Militia	L	7	28	
4/30/2011	H	New England Nightmare	W	48	12	
5/14/2011	H	Philadelphia Liberty Belles (II)	W	27	21	
5/21/2011	H	Boston Militia	L	6	43	
6/4/2011	A	New England Nightmare	W	28	8	
6/11/2011	A	Northeastern Nitro	W	46	7	
6/18/2011	H	D.C. Divas	L	16	38	
4/14/2012	A	Boston Militia	L	6	64	
4/21/2012	A	Maine Lynx	W	1	0	
4/28/2012	A	D.C. Divas	L	12	41	
5/5/2012	H	Philadelphia Liberty Belles (II)	W	25	8	
5/12/2012	H	D.C. Divas	L	13	41	
6/2/2012	A	Philadelphia Liberty Belles (II)	W	31	0	
6/9/2012	H	New England Nightmare	W	72	14	
6/16/2012	A	Boston Militia	L	12	55	
6/23/2012	H	Keystone Assault	W	24	19	W
6/30/2012	A	Boston Militia	L	6	47	Q
4/6/2013	H	Central Maryland Seahawks	W	20	6	
4/13/2013	A	Boston Militia	L	0	70	
4/20/2013	H	Pittsburgh Passion	L	0	35	
4/27/2013	A	Baltimore Burn	W	18	0	I
5/4/2013	H	Boston Militia	L	0	47	
5/11/2013	A	D.C. Divas	L	6	49	
5/25/2013	A	Central Maryland Seahawks	W	28	20	
6/1/2013	H	Baltimore Burn	W	32	0	I
6/15/2013	H	Columbus Comets	L	20	22	W
4/19/2014	H	Connecticut Wreckers	W	50	0	
4/26/2014	H	Pittsburgh Passion	L	6	31	
5/3/2014	A	Carolina Phoenix	W	29	28	
5/10/2014	H	Washington Prodigy	W	41	24	
5/24/2014	A	Pittsburgh Passion	L	6	21	
5/31/2014	A	Washington Prodigy	W	31	18	
6/7/2014	H	Montreal Blitz	W	40	9	
6/14/2014	A	Philadelphia Firebirds	W	31	6	
6/28/2014	H	Carolina Phoenix	W	60	12	S
7/12/2014	A	Pittsburgh Passion	L	12	26	CC
4/11/2015	A	Washington Prodigy	W	37	8	
4/25/2015	H	Montreal Blitz	W	26	19	
5/2/2015	A	Washington Prodigy	W	19	0	
5/9/2015	A	Pittsburgh Passion	L	18	32	
5/23/2015	A	Connecticut Wreckers	W	38	0	
5/30/2015	H	Pittsburgh Passion	L	14	21	
6/6/2015	A	Montreal Blitz	W	14	7	
6/13/2015	H	Philadelphia Firebirds	W	28	20	
6/27/2015	A	Pittsburgh Passion	L	28	35	S

New York Sharks Player Register (1999-2003, 2005, 2008, 2011-2015)

Abrook, Melodie "Mel" (2011-12, 2014)
Addison, Rose (2000-2001, 2003, 2005)
Aigotti, Chris (2001)
Albano, Joan (2003)
Alberty, Vivian ('03, '05, '08, '11-12, '14)
Alcantara, Olga (2011)
Allen, Taisha (2011)
Anderson, Alissa (2012)
Antonucci, Megan (2005, 2008)
Aponte, Alison (2001)
Armstrong, Desiree (2001-2002)
Auguste, Cherelle (2014)
Ayoub, Lucy (2013)
Baden, Laura (2011-2015)
Bankston, Claire (2013)
Barnard, Andrea (2001)
Bauer, Chantal (2003, 2005)
Baum, Rachel (2013-2014)
Bernard, Carmelle (2014)
Biscardi, Sue (1999)
Bishop, Kimberly (2000-2002, 2005)
Black, Karen (2002)
Bluhm, Isabella "Bella" (2011-2012)
Blum, Jennifer (1999, '03, '05, '08, '11)
Bobcombe, Cheryl (1999)
Boone, Frances (2013)
Bresnahan, Michelle (2012, 2014)
Brooks, Jamie (1999)
Brown, Kareen (2008)
Brown, Michelle (2000, 2003, 2005)
Brown, Nhandi (2014-2015)
Brown, Telisha (2013-2015)
Brzozowski, Leeann (2008)
Burnett, Tyara (2000-2001)
Butler, Erica (2011-2012)
Butler, Jaclyn (2000)
Butts, Hadisha (2015)
Butz-Houghton, Cyndi (2000)
Caddy, Danielle (2008)
Cadenillas, Jenny (2005)
Cantave, Amanda (2013)
Cartabiano, Elle (2013)
Carvey, Fatima (2008)
Casner, Alana (2014-2015)
Cerrato, Nikki (1999-2002)
Chichester, Janet (2002)
Christopher, Denicka (2011)
Cinque, Shelly (2000-2001)
Colangelo, Julia (2013-2015)
Collazo, Lynette (2015)
Colon, Amy (2005, 2011)
Colon, Jacqueline (1999-2000)
Cottle, Erika (2012-2015)
Crotty, Julie (2000)
Crumley, Suzette (2002-2003, 2005)
Cruz, Teresa (2013)
Curtis, Michelle (2001)
Dailey, Ann (2008)
Daniels, Phylicia (2013)
Dantzler, Jay "J.D." (2008, 2011-2012)
Darby, Danielle (2014-2015)
Davis, Kimberly (2001)
Davis, Larissa (2008, 2012-2014)
Davitt, Kelliann (2003)
Dawson, Ione (2001)
Deal, Amy (2012-2015)
DeGarr, Ariadne (2001-2003)
Dejesus, Kareen (2015)

DeLeon, Natasha (2014)
Desiano, Jill (2000)
Devellis, Marae (2002)
Devito, Beth (2002)
DeVivio, Lori (1999-2002, 2005)
Dignam, Veronica (2002)
DiMatteo, Kathie (2008)
DiNuzzio, Jackie (2008)
Dock, Leslie (2005, 2008)
Dollison, Joy (2011)
Donahue Sparling, Dana (2005)
Doran, Lisa (2005, 2008)
Douglas, Andra (1999-2003, 2005)
Douglas, Tracy (2003)
Drayton, Denise (2014)
Eaton, Courtney (2001-2003, 2005)
Eckstein, Kellie (2000-2002)
Eleazer, Cheri (2008, 2011-2012)
Elliott, Kymm (2011-2015)
Elmore, Kristine (2011-2013)
Ely, Regina (2008)
Emerson, Sarah (2005)
Engels, Stefanie (2014-2015)
Farol, Leilani (2003)
Farrell, Gabriella (2015)
Fields, Brilynn (2014-2015)
Fields, Brooklyn (2015)
Figueroa, Angela (2011)
Finestone, Emma (2015)
Firore, Rosemary (1999)
Floria, Michele (2003)
Forrester, Sabrina (2014)
Gaidusek, Corie (2008)
Gaudet, Beth (2000)
Gibson, Jessica (2014-2015)
Goldsack, Jenna (2014-2015)
Goldsack, Paige (2014-2015)
Gonzalez, Siobhan (2013)
Granados, Elizabeth (2013)
Grant, Jerkieda (2013)
Grant, Lakisha (2001-2003, 2005)
Gray, Caprece (2013-2014)
Gray, Lisa (2000-2001)
Greene, Lori (2005, 2008, 2011)
Gregg, Joan (2008)
Grim, Debo (2001)
Grimsley, Jewelle (2014-2015)
Gwinnett, Nicole (2003, 2005)
Halesworth, Val (1999-2003, 2005, 2011)
Hall, Darleen (2000-2003, 2011-2014)
Harden, Sabrina (2002)
Harris, Stacey (2005)
Harrison, Seleta (2008, 2012-2014)
Harrison, Yvonne (2008)
Height, Patti (2002)
Hemphill, Soyna (2000)
Herrera, Fabiola (2001)
Hilla, Christine (2002-2003)
Hilliard, Amalia (2001)
Hilton, Michelle (2001)
Holloman, Kathy (2001, 2011)
Hopkins, Yatia "Tia" (2011-2015)
Howell, Deborah (2000)
Jackson, Nicole (2014)
Jaryno, Stacey (2008)
Jaso, Regina (2014)
Jenkins, Odessa (2011-2012)
Jones, Indica (2015)

Joseph, Manouchka "Nikki" (2008, 2011-15)
Jufer, Natalie (1999-2000)
Kelly, Roshawn (2011, 2015)
Kieltyka, Nichole (2013-2014)
Knepp, Veronica (2000)
Kowalski, Marcie (2008)
Kulaw, Laura (2012)
Kureczka, Lisa (2008)
Kutner, Jenny (1999)
La Nier, Evelyn (2002)
Lambiase, Katrina (2003)
Larson, Tracy (2002)
Lawrence, Shriene (2008)
Leary, Jennifer (2000)
Leary, Marion (2000)
LeBlanc, Monique (2003)
Leon, Virginia (2001-2003, 2005)
Leone, Jessica (2001)
Lesniak, Jennifer (2005)
Levi, Leah (2011)
Levine, Cheryl (2000)
Lewis, Lynn (1999-2002)
Lighthart, Aurora (2000-2002)
Locke, Tracy (2001)
Lombana, Lissette (2008)
Lueck, Jen (2001)
Maher, Leah (2012-2014)
Manning, Dawn (1999-2001)
Marisseau, Simone (2000)
Markowitz, Liane (2005)
Marmorale, Missy (1999-2003, 2005)
Marsh, Monica (2000-2003, 2005)
Marshall, Raven (2001-2002)
Martinez, Ruth (2011-2012)
Mastanduno, Josephine (2000-2001)
McCarthy, Theresa (1999)
McGuire, Bonnie (2005)
McKinney, Brooke (2008)
McTamaney, Kriste (2008)
Melendez, Jennifer (2013-2015)
Metrocavich, Jessica (2000)
Milland, Melanie (2011)
Minena, Linda (2005)
Mira, Gabriela "Gabby" (2013, 2015)
Mitchell, Alinda (1999-2001)
Mitchell, Faith (2003, 2005)
Molina, Krystal (2013-2015)
Monaco, Val (1999-2003)
Mondie, Nicole (2005)
Moneta, Dayna (2013-2015)
Montrose, Shelly (2005)
Moretti, Kristen (2000, 2002)
Morris, Shanon (2015)
Mulligan, Karen (2003, 2005, 2008, 2011-15)
Myers, Cornelia (2012-2014)
Myers, Danielle (2012)
Natell, Maggie (2014-2015)
Nazaire, Gabrielle (2008, 2012)
Nelson, Klassik (2005)
Nugent, Beth (1999-2003, 2005)
Olivencia, Jessica (2014-2015)
Oppel, Mandy (2005)
Orliss, Beth (2001)
Ortiz, Priscilla (2011)
Pagan, Christina (2008)
Palmer, Penny (2005)
Pascale, Sharon (1999-2001)

Continued on next page

New York Sharks Player Register (continued)

Passarell, Stephanie (2000)
Passoni, Tara (2001-2002)
Patterson, Janes (2003)
Peace, Desire (2008)
Pearsall, Joan (1999-2000)
Pender, Nayah (2015)
Perez, Erica (2011)
Perissi, Anne (2005)
Pettigano, Gina (2014-2015)
Phillips, M.J. (2015)
Pickett, Melissa (2008, 2011-2012, 2014)
Pinckney, Shayna (2005, 2008)
Plasek, Nish (2003)
Pohl, Fay (1999-2001)
Porder, Sarah (2013)
Presto, Liz (2001-2003, 2005)
Preus, Karen (2005)
Priestly, Tonia (1999)
Pringle, Lauren (2008, 2011-2013)
Rainson-Rose, Carol (1999)
Ray, Courtney (2008)
Reece, Delmara (2015)
Reyes, Duece (2014)
Rhock, Kim (2000)
Robinson, Celeste (2008)
Robinson, Shana (2011)
Robinson, Tiffany (2008)
Roche, Maureen (2001)
Rochlitz, Melanie (2000)
Rodriguez, Anabell (2008)
Rose, Carol (2000, 2002)
Rose, Katie (2011-2014)

Roy, Selina (1999)
Rudolph, Sherrilyn (2000)
Russell, Nicole (2005)
Russo, Kate (2001-2002)
Salfelder, Alex (2014)
Salvatore, Toni (2001-03, '05, '08, '11-12)
Santizo, Lesie (2011)
Schaub, Erika (2003)
Schirrippa, Teresa (2003, 2005)
Schkeeper, Sarah (2011-2013)
Schneider, Tracy (1999)
Segers, Shana (2005, 2008)
Shabunia, Carolyn (1999)
Shepardson, Monty (2000-2002)
Sibblies, Cynthia (2002-2003)
Siegal, Lisa (1999)
Simerly-Paddock, Sally (2001)
Simmons, Veronica (2002, 2012)
Smith, Adrienne (2008)
Smith, Collette (2012, 2014)
Smith, Samantha (2001)
Smitherman, Tracy (1999-2000)
Smith-Malave, Josie (2000-2002)
Sosa, Edeline (2015)
Sparling, Dana (2001-2002)
Sperling, Ridley (2002-2003, 2005)
Spilotras, Donna (1999-2001, '05, '08)
Stephney, Cheryl (1999-2001)
Stewart, Shauntay (2005, 2008)
Stone, Heather (2000-2001, 2005)
Sullivan, Carol (1999-2000)
Sumnicht, Anais (2011-2012)

Sutton, Charonn (2011-2014)
Szabo, Samantha (1999)
Szmilewska, Magda (2015)
Tanida, Junko (2005)
Tankeng, Lenahndem (2011-2015)
Tate, Anna (1999-2003)
Taylor, Monica (2015)
Teague, Nikki (1999-2000)
Terrell, Amber (2014-2015)
Thompson, Leslie (2011-2012)
Tighe, Ellie (2011)
Trautz, Lynn (2003, 2005, 2008)
Urena, Vikky (2008)
Valenti, Michelle (2001)
Vasta, Jennifer (2015)
Wasilewski, Debra (2001-2003)
Wasilewski, Denise (2001-2002)
Webb, Keturah (2002)
White, Courtney (2015)
White, Crystal (2011)
Wilkerson, Janea (2011-12, 2014-15)
Williams, Letitia (2011)
Williams, Lisa (2002)
Williams, Marie (2012)
Williams, Robin (2002)
Williams, Wanda (2000-03, '05, '08, '11)
Wilson, Shiante (2013)
Wong, Alice (2005)
Xikis, Faith (2013-2014)
Yarn, Janelle (2012)
Zaffarese, Marg (1999)

Nor Cal Red Hawks

Year	League	Name	W	L	Conference	Division	DF	PR
2010	IWFL2	X Nor Cal Red Hawks	0	3	--	--	--	--
2011	IWFL	X Nor Cal Red Hawks	1	1	--	--	--	--
2013	IWFL	X Nor Cal Red Hawks	0	1	--	--	--	--
		Total	1	5				

Based in: Sacramento, CA
Notes: Forfeited entire 2013 season

5/29/2010	A	Ventura Black Widows	L	8	46	I
9/11/2010		California Quake	L	12	68	E
10/2/2010		Ventura Black Widows	L	0	46	IE
4/23/2011		Reno Rattlers	W	13	6	E
5/14/2011	A	Reno Rattlers	L	6	19	
5/25/2013	A	California Quake	L	0	1	

North County Stars

Year	League	Name	W	L	Conference	Division	DF	PR
2014	IWFL	North County Stars	2	5	Western	Pacific West	3	--
2015	IWFL	North County Stars	2	5	Western	Pacific West	4	--
		Total	4	10				

Based in: San Diego, CA
Notes: Preceded by WFA's San Diego Sting

4/12/2014	A	California Quake	L	0	64	
5/3/2014	H	Las Vegas Showgirlz	L	0	60	I
5/17/2014	A	Tucson Monsoon	W	40	6	
5/24/2014	A	Phoenix Phantomz	L	0	1	
5/31/2014	H	Tucson Monsoon	W	48	8	
6/7/2014	H	Phoenix Phantomz	L	28	76	
6/14/2014	H	California Quake	L	14	30	
4/11/2015	A	California Quake	L	14	34	
4/18/2015	H	Phoenix Phantomz	L	0	14	
5/2/2015	H	Sacramento Sirens	L	0	59	
5/16/2015	A	Sacramento Sirens	L	0	60	
5/30/2015	A	Phoenix Phantomz	L	0	28	
6/6/2015	H	California Quake	W	1	0	
6/13/2015	H	Nevada Storm	W	24	22	

North County Stars Player Register (2014-2015)

Austin, Robyn (2014)
Banks, Latifah (2014)
Barbra, Charlie (2015)
Baston, CeCe (2014)
Brinkman, Janet (2014)
Brinkman, Redd (2015)
Carlson, Laurie (2015)
Cavalcanti, Marcela (2014)
Cooper, Sam (2015)
Cortez, Gigi (2014-2015)
Cuffie, Toni (2015)
Dowling, Pamela (2014)
Drayton, Chandra (2014)
Duenas, Carla (2014-2015)
Franklin, Icy (2014-2015)
Gilbert, Natasha (2014-2015)
Grierson, Kacey (2015)
Haney, Michelle (2015)
Harris, Gram (2015)
Hernandez, Christine "Chris" (2014)
Hickman, Renea (2015)
Jones, Monica "Mo" (2014-2015)
Kaleopa, Iolani "Lani" (2014-2015)
Laie, Alofa (2015)
Lee, Brittany (2015)
Lemasters, Mary (2014-2015)
Limon, Champagne (2015)
McClain, Patricia (2014-2015)
McGuinness, Crystle (2015)
Melvin, Ashley (2015)
Moak, Terese (2014-2015)
Mota, Delfina (2014)
Perez, Laura (2014-2015)
Quenell, Diedre (2015)
Remick, Angie (2014-2015)
Ricca, Jessica (2014)
Roche, Shaula (2015)
Rodriguez, Sara (2015)
Sadri, Mariam (2014)
Sanchez, Becca (2015)
Thomas, Tommy (2014)
Traut, Vanessa (2015)
Ulukita, Annaleii (2014-2015)
Vaeo, Leila (2014)
Whitaker-Cuffie, Toni (2014)
Wright, Christine (2014-2015)
Zarty-Moore, Cheree (2014)

North Texas Knockouts

Year	League	Name	W	L	Conference	Division	DF	PR
2011	IWFL	North Texas Knockouts	5	4	Eastern	South Atlantic	2	BQ

Based in: Dallas, TX
Notes: Succeeded by WSFL's DFW Xtreme

4/2/2011	A	Houston Energy	L	14	50	5/28/2011	H	Monterrey Black Mambas	W	1	0
4/9/2011	H	Monterrey Black Mambas	W	19	6	6/4/2011	A	Memphis Belles	W	52	0
4/23/2011	H	Houston Energy	L	14	40	6/11/2011	A	Clarksville Fox	W	63	6
5/7/2011	A	Houston Energy	L	12	34	6/25/2011	A	Chattanooga Locomotion	L	20	24 BQ
5/14/2011	H	Memphis Belles	W	40	6						

Northeastern Nitro

Year	League	Name	W	L	Conference	Division	DF	PR
2011	WFA	Northeastern Nitro	4	4	National	North	3	--
2012	IWFL	Northeastern Nitro	2	6	Eastern	North Atlantic	4	--
		Total	**6**	**10**				

Based in: Danbury, CT
Notes: Preceded by IWFL2's Connecticut Crushers [Connecticut Crush]

4/2/2011	H	New England Nightmare	W	13	0	4/7/2012	A	Maine Rebels	W	50	0
4/16/2011	A	Keystone Assault	W	6	0	4/21/2012	H	Philadelphia Firebirds	L	7	8
4/30/2011	A	Boston Militia	L	0	72	4/28/2012	H	Montreal Blitz	L	0	28
5/7/2011	A	D.C. Divas	L	0	77	5/5/2012	A	Montreal Blitz	L	0	42
5/14/2011	H	Boston Militia	L	0	42	5/12/2012	A	Baltimore Nighthawks	L	0	28
5/21/2011	A	New England Nightmare	W	8	0	5/19/2012	H	New England Intensity	L	0	21
6/4/2011	H	Keystone Assault	W	12	6	6/2/2012	A	New Hampshire Freedom	L	6	20
6/11/2011	H	New York Sharks	L	7	46	6/9/2012	H	Erie Illusion	W	34	12

Northeastern Nitro Player Register (2011)

Amsden, Natasha (2011)
Anderson, Laura (2011)
Artale, Cori (2011)
Bepko, Ashleigh (2011)
Breakell, Michaela (2011)
Bresnahan, Michelle (2011)
Cambell, Margaret (2011)
Caruso, Christie (2011)
Davis, Jennifer (2011)
Dawson, Sheila "L.D." (2011)
DiDio, Katie (2011)
Diette, Erin (2011)
Dombroski, Alyssa (2011)
Dunkelman, Jodi (2011)
Falk, Gretchen (2011)
Hartford, Lisa (2011)
Herstell, Anne (2011)
Hincks, Carrie (2011)
Huber, Christine (2011)
Kavanaugh, Megan (2011)
Koosa, Maggie (2011)
Koukopoulos, Christie "Chris" (2011)
Kovack, Lynn (2011)
Krasnoff, Stacy (2011)
Kulaw, Laura (2011)
Manfred, Amy (2011)
Manfred, Lauren (2011)
Marmorale, Missy (2011)
Martin-Peele, Holly (2011)
Mohr, Kelly (2011)
Monaco, Val (2011)
Morgatto, Christin (2011)
Perkins, Sonya (2011)
Pesente, Carley (2011)
Philibert, Christina (2011)

Continued on next page

Northeastern Nitro Player Register (continued)

Profenno, Erika (2011)
Renko, Jennifer (2011)
Rodrigues, Kim (2011)
Ruocco, Brianna (2011)
Ryan, Holly (2011)

Sabio, Stephany (2011)
Sanchez, Stephanie (2011)
Schang, Lisa (2011)
Shupe, Annie (2011)
Stango, Jennifer (2011)

Stepp, Kate (2011)
Valenti, Michelle (2011)
Webster, Melissa (2011)
Woodard, Kelly (2011)

Northern Ice

Year	League	Name	W	L	Conference	Division	DF	PR
2003	WPFL	Northern Ice	12	0	American	North	1	**NC**
2004	WPFL	Northern Ice	10	2	National	North	1	C
		Total	**22**	**2**				

Based in: Kenosha, WI
Neutral site: Long Beach, CA (N)

Date	H/A	Opponent	W/L	PF	PA	Note	Date	H/A	Opponent	W/L	PF	PA	Note
8/2/2003	H	New England Storm	W	47	0		7/31/2004	A	Toledo Reign	W	43	6	
8/9/2003	H	Dayton Rebellion	W	69	6		8/7/2004	H	So Cal Scorpions	W	33	27	
8/16/2003	A	Indiana Speed	W	24	10		8/14/2004	A	Minnesota Vixen	W	27	0	
8/24/2003	A	Minnesota Vixen	W	61	6		8/28/2004	H	Indiana Speed	W	71	0	
9/6/2003	H	Minnesota Vixen	W	63	7		9/4/2004	H	Missouri Avengers	W	49	12	
9/13/2003	A	Toledo Reign	W	80	0		9/11/2004	A	Indiana Speed	W	42	20	
9/20/2003	A	Dayton Rebellion	W	48	0		9/18/2004	H	Toledo Reign	W	49	8	
9/27/2003	H	Missouri Prowlers	W	77	0		9/25/2004	A	Minnesota Vixen	W	32	25	
10/11/2003	H	Indiana Speed	W	58	13		10/16/2004	A	Indiana Speed	W	35	19	
10/18/2003	A	Minnesota Vixen	W	61	13		10/23/2004	A	Houston Energy	L	14	21	
10/25/2003	H	Long Beach Aftershock	W	37	30	CC	11/6/2004	H	Delaware Griffins	W	15	12	CC
11/8/2003	H	Florida Stingrayz	W	53	12	C	11/20/2004	N	Dallas Diamonds	L	13	68	C

Oakland Banshees

Year	League		Name	W	L	T	Conference	Division	DF	PR
2001	WAFL		Oakland Banshees	2	7	0	Pacific	Central	2	--
2002	WAFC		Oakland Banshees	5	6	0	Northern	--	2	CC
2003	IWFL		Oakland Banshees	5	5	0	Western	Pacific Southwest	2	--
2004	IWFL		Oakland Banshees	8	1	0	Western	Pacific Southwest	1	S
2005	IWFL		Oakland Banshees	5	4	1	Western	Pacific Southwest	4	--
2006	IWFL	X	Oakland Banshees	0	2	0	--	--	--	--
2008	IWFL	X	Oakland Banshees	0	3	0	--	--	--	--
2009	IWFL	X	Oakland Banshees	0	1	0	--	--	--	--
			Total	**25**	**29**	**1**				

Based in: Oakland, CA
Notes: Forfeited entire 2009 season; Succeeded by IWFL2's Bay Area Bandits

Date	H/A	Opponent	W/L	PF	PA	Note	Date	H/A	Opponent	W/L	PF	PA	Note
11/3/2001	H	Seattle Warbirds	L	0	41		8/3/2002		Sacramento Sirens	L	20	41	E
11/10/2001	H	Sacramento Sirens	L	0	42		8/10/2002		San Francisco Stingrayz	W	26	6	E
11/17/2001	A	San Francisco Tsunami	W	34	14		9/8/2002	A	Santa Rosa Scorchers	W	31	6	
11/24/2001	A	San Francisco Tsunami	W	34	6		9/14/2002	A	Arizona Caliente	L	12	36	
12/8/2001	H	Sacramento Sirens	L	8	28		9/21/2002	H	Santa Rosa Scorchers	W	20	14	
12/13/2001	A	Hawaii Legends	L	6	40		9/28/2002	A	San Francisco Stingrayz	W	34	14	
12/16/2001	A	Hawaii Legends	L	8	35		10/5/2002	H	Pacific Blast	L	20	56	
12/29/2001	H	California Quake	L	8	32		10/19/2002	A	Sacramento Sirens	L	32	53	
1/5/2002	A	Los Angeles Lasers	L	6	46		10/26/2002	H	San Francisco Stingrayz	W	24	20	
							11/10/2002	H	Sacramento Sirens	L	0	55	
							11/23/2002	A	Sacramento Sirens	L	0	69	CC

Continued on next page

Oakland Banshees Game-By-Game Results (continued)

Date	H/A	Opponent	W/L	Score		Date	H/A	Opponent	W/L	Score	
3/8/2003	A	Sacramento Sirens	L	14	64	4/2/2005	A	Sacramento Sirens	L	0	43
3/15/2003	H	Santa Rosa Scorchers	W	28	12	4/9/2005	H	Santa Rosa Scorchers	W	22	12
3/29/2003	A	California Quake	L	14	31	4/16/2005	A	So Cal Bandits	W	50	0
4/5/2003	H	Sacramento Sirens	L	8	67	4/23/2005	H	Redding Rage	W	32	7
4/12/2003	H	Portland Shockwave	W	16	14	4/30/2005	A	California Quake	T	0	0 *
4/26/2003	H	California Quake	W	16	14	5/7/2005	H	Sacramento Sirens	L	12	62
5/3/2003	A	San Francisco Stingrayz	L	0	1	5/21/2005	A	Redding Rage	W	18	12
5/10/2003	H	San Diego Sea Catz	W	58	0	5/28/2005	A	Santa Rosa Scorchers	L	20	32
5/17/2003	A	Santa Rosa Scorchers	W	14	0	6/4/2005	H	So Cal Bandits	W	1	0
5/31/2003	A	Portland Shockwave	L	12	32	6/11/2005	H	California Quake	L	6	21
4/3/2004	A	California Quake	W	41	0	6/17/2006	A	Redding Rage	L	7	12
4/17/2004	H	San Diego Sea Catz	W	40	0	6/24/2006	H	Sacramento Sirens	L	0	1
4/24/2004	A	Redding Rage	W	54	6						
5/1/2004	A	Santa Rosa Scorchers	W	34	0	5/24/2008	H	Seattle Majestics	L	0	20
5/8/2004	H	Redding Rage	W	68	0	6/7/2008	A	Seattle Majestics	L	0	22
5/15/2004	A	San Diego Sea Catz	W	42	0	6/14/2008	H	Portland Shockwave	L	2	9
5/29/2004	H	Santa Rosa Scorchers	W	34	19						
6/5/2004	H	California Quake	W	38	0	5/2/2009	A	Portland Shockwave	L	0	1
6/26/2004	H	Corvallis Pride	L	14	22 S						

Oklahoma City Avengers

Year	League	Name	W	L	Conference	Division	DF	PR
2002	IWFL	Oklahoma City Avengers	5	3	Western	--	3	--
2003	IWFL	Oklahoma City Avengers	1	7	Western	Southwest	3	--
		Total	**6**	**10**				

Based in: Oklahoma City, OK
Notes: Preceded by WPFL's Oklahoma City Wildcats

Date	Opponent	W/L	Score		Date	H/A	Opponent	W/L	Score	
4/6/2002	Tulsa Tornadoes	W	44	0	3/29/2003	A	Memphis Maulers	L	0	16
4/13/2002	Austin Outlaws	L	7	24	4/5/2003	A	Dallas Revolution	L	0	16
4/20/2002	Memphis Maulers	L	13	28	4/12/2003	A	Dallas Revolution	L	8	24
4/27/2002	Tulsa Tornadoes	W	46	0	4/26/2003	H	Memphis Maulers	W	1	0
5/11/2002	Memphis Maulers	W	59	16	5/3/2003	H	Dallas Revolution	L	6	18
5/18/2002	Austin Outlaws	W	25	6	5/17/2003	A	Chicago Force	L	0	1
6/8/2002	Austin Outlaws	L	6	7	5/24/2003	H	Tampa Bay Terminators	L	14	43
6/15/2002	Memphis Maulers	W	44	0	6/7/2003	H	Chicago Force	L	0	1

Oklahoma City Lightning

Year	League		Name	W	L	Conference	Division	DF	PR
2003	NWFA		Oklahoma City Lightning	9	2	Southern	Midwest	1	CC
2004	NWFA		Oklahoma City Lightning	10	1	Southern	Southwest	1	C
2005	NWFA		Oklahoma City Lightning	9	2	Southern	--	3	CC
2006	NWFA		Oklahoma City Lightning	10	1	Southern	Southwest	1	C
2007	NWFA		Oklahoma City Lightning	9	2	Southern	West	1	CC
2008	NWFA		Oklahoma City Lightning	6	3	Southern	Central	2	Q
2010	WFA	X	Oklahoma City Lightning	0	3	--	--	--	--
			Total	**53**	**14**				

Based in: Oklahoma City, OK
Neutral sites: Louisville, KY (N1); Pittsburgh, PA (N2)

Oklahoma City Lightning Game-By-Game Results

Date	H/A	Opponent	W/L	PF	PA	Note
4/12/2003		Denton Stampede	W	97	0	
4/26/2003	H	Kansas City Krunch	W	19	18	*
5/10/2003	A	St. Louis Slam	W	21	6	
5/17/2003		Denton Stampede	W	84	14	
5/24/2003	A	Kansas City Krunch	L	7	8	
5/31/2003		Austin Outlaws	W	14	0	
6/7/2003	H	St. Louis Slam	W	48	13	
6/14/2003	A	Kansas City Krunch	W	35	14	
6/28/2003	H	Nashville Dream	W	28	21	Q
7/12/2003	A	Chattanooga Locomotion	W	20	6	S
7/19/2003	A	Pensacola Power	L	14	26	CC
4/17/2004	H	Austin Outlaws	W	32	6	
4/24/2004	A	St. Louis Slam	W	32	18	
5/1/2004	A	Dallas Dragons	W	49	18	
5/8/2004	H	Denton Stampede	W	65	0	
5/22/2004	H	St. Louis Slam	W	43	12	
5/29/2004	A	Austin Outlaws	W	42	6	
6/5/2004	H	Dallas Dragons	W	62	22	
6/12/2004	A	Denton Stampede	W	80	0	
7/10/2004	H	Kansas City Krunch	W	21	7	S
7/17/2004	H	Pensacola Power	W	37	13	CC
7/31/2004	N1	Detroit Demolition	L	0	52	C
4/16/2005	A	Kansas City Krunch	W	47	0	
4/30/2005	H	Austin Outlaws	W	69	7	
5/14/2005	A	Denton Stampede	W	73	0	
5/21/2005	H	Dallas Rage	W	47	6	
5/28/2005	A	Austin Outlaws	W	34	3	
6/4/2005	H	Denton Stampede	W	65	0	
6/11/2005	A	Dallas Rage	L	21	26	
6/18/2005	H	Denton Stampede	W	1	0	
6/25/2005	H	New Orleans Blaze	W	61	14	Q
7/9/2005	A	Nashville Dream	W	42	7	S
7/23/2005	A	Pensacola Power	L	14	17	CC*
4/15/2006	H	Shreveport Shockhers	W	70	0	
4/22/2006	A	Dallas Rage	W	35	20	
5/6/2006	A	Austin Outlaws	W	41	20	
5/13/2006	H	St. Louis Slam	W	35	12	
5/20/2006	A	Shreveport Shockhers	W	45	0	
5/27/2006	H	Dallas Rage	W	44	6	
6/10/2006	H	Austin Outlaws	W	38	17	
6/17/2006	A	St. Louis Slam	W	21	16	
7/8/2006	H	Cleveland Fusion	W	14	13	S
7/22/2006	H	Massachusetts Mutiny	W	21	16	CC
8/5/2006	N2	D.C. Divas	L	7	28	C
4/21/2007	A	Dallas Rage	W	60	12	
4/28/2007	H	St. Louis Slam	W	21	6	
5/5/2007	A	Austin Outlaws	W	32	20	
5/12/2007	H	Dallas Rage	W	43	20	
5/19/2007	A	Nashville Dream	W	48	6	
5/26/2007	H	Austin Outlaws	W	37	7	
6/9/2007	H	Nashville Dream	W	59	0	
6/16/2007	A	St. Louis Slam	L	0	7	
6/23/2007	H	New Orleans Blaze	W	42	12	Q
6/30/2007	H	St. Louis Slam	W	33	7	S
7/7/2007	H	Columbus Comets	L	7	9	CC
4/19/2008	H	North Texas Fury	W	23	0	
4/26/2008	A	Kansas City Storm	W	67	0	
5/10/2008	H	H-Town Texas Cyclones	W	21	13	
5/17/2008	H	Austin Outlaws	L	22	28	
5/24/2008	A	North Texas Fury	W	43	18	
5/31/2008	H	Kansas City Storm	W	1	0	
6/14/2008	A	H-Town Texas Cyclones	L	15	21	
6/21/2008	A	Austin Outlaws	W	30	3	
6/28/2008	A	H-Town Texas Cyclones	L	0	26	Q
4/10/2010	A	Lone Star Mustangs	L	0	62	
4/17/2010	A	Memphis Soul	L	0	1	
5/22/2010	H	Lone Star Mustangs	L	0	1	

Oklahoma City Lightning Player Register (2004-2008)

Allen, April (2006)
Arbuckle, Mary (2007)
Archer, Jenny (2007-2008)
Belcher, Lindsay (2007)
Bowden, Tam (2004-2008)
Bowen, Jennifer (2007)
Branstetter, Aly (2006)
Briseno, Erika (2004-2008)
Britt, Jennifer (2008)
Brown, LaShane (2004-2007)
Bryce, Amanda (2007)
Calderon, Illiana (2004-2008)
Carter, Krisna (2004-2008)
Cheirs, Monica (2006-2008)
Cheirs, Nyala (2004-2008)
Cowan, Patty (2008)
Ealy, Michelle (2004-2005)
Fabrizio, Margie (2008)
Ford, Shannon (2004-2008)
Freese, Helen (2007)
Freitick, Amy (2004-2005)
Godwin, Kayce (2008)
Goss, Tanika "T.J." (2004-2008)
Gothard, Ashley (2006)
Graves, Destiny (2004-2005)
Hemry, Lauren (2008)
Henneman, Lina (2007)
Hennesy, Anita (2004-2005)
Hudgens, Lisa (2004-2005)
Hutton, Brighton (2008)
Jackson, Hannah (2006)
Jackson, Yasmin (2007)
Johnson, Cali (2007)
Johnson, Kristi (2004-2005)
Johnson, Molli (2006-2007)
Jones, Deanna "Dee" (2004-2005)
Jones, Shonna (2004-2008)
Kelley-Arndt, Sarah (2004-2005)
Leonard, Danielle (2004-2006)
Long, Laura (2006)
Malena, Kandace (2007)
Malone, Malinda (2007-2008)
Mason, Jayme (2004-2008)
Mathews, Cocoa (2004-2005)
Maytubby, Etta (2004-05, 2007-08)
Mitchell, Kim (2004-2006)
Mobley, Angela (2006)
Muhammad, Venecia (2004-2006)
Murray, Mary (2004-2006)
Nayphe, Kristal (2006)
Nichols, Lorena (2004-2006, 2008)
O'Conner, Patricia (2007)
Pennington, Alisha (2007-2008)
Pennon, Maeisha (2007-2008)
Pennon, Nacole (2004-2008)
Raiber, Tammy (2004-2007)
Redburn, Abbey (2008)
Roland, Lameshia (2004-2005)
Rorick, Lisa (2004-2007)
Schafer, Dana (2008)
Schulz, Lacey (2004-05, 2007-08)
Sims, Rachel (2007)
Sipes, Sara (2007)
Smith, Kristie (2004-05, 2007-08)
Smith, Patricia (2004-2005)
Sperry, Candace (2004-2005)
Thompson, Lacie (2008)
Thurman, Phoebe (2004-05, 2007-08)
Vick, Orianna (2004-2005)
Walker, Joni (2007)
Walker, Mindy (2007-2008)
Ware, Rochelle (2004-2005)
Webber, Jana (2004)
Wehr, Jennifer (2007)
Williams, Christie (2004-05, 2007-08)
Williams, Kris (2004-05, 2007-08)
Winston, Angela (2004)
Woody, Alisha (2007-2008)
Woody, Gloricia (2007)
Worthy, Jessie (2004-2005, 2008)

Oklahoma City Wildcats

Year	League	Name	W	L	Conference	Division	DF	PR
2000	WPFL	Oklahoma City Wildcats	0	6	American	West	3	--

Based in: Oklahoma City, OK
Notes: Succeeded by IWFL's Oklahoma City Avengers

10/22/2000	A	Colorado Valkyries	L	0	58	11/18/2000	A	Houston Energy	L	0	21
11/4/2000	H	New York Sharks	L	6	26	11/25/2000	A	Austin Rage	L	12	13
11/11/2000	H	Minnesota Vixen	L	0	28	12/2/2000	H	Austin Rage	L	8	14

Oregon Sirens

Year	League		Name	W	L	Conference	Division	DF	PR
2000	WPFL	X	Oregon Sirens	0	1	--	--	--	--

Based in: Portland, OR

11/26/2000　H　Colorado Valkyries　L　0　54

Oregon Thunder

Year	League	Name	W	L	Conference	Division	DF	PR
2002	IWFL	Oregon Thunder	0	8	Western	--	6	--

Based in: Portland, OR

4/6/2002	Eugene Edge	L	20	35	5/18/2002	Eugene Edge	L	8	20
4/13/2002	Corvallis Pride	L	19	41	5/25/2002	Corvallis Pride	L	13	21
4/27/2002	Eugene Edge	L	14	31	6/8/2002	Eugene Edge	L	0	1
5/4/2002	Corvallis Pride	L	0	46	6/15/2002	Corvallis Pride	L	0	1

Oregon Unforgiven

Year	League	Name	W	L	Conference	Division	DF	PR
2002	WSFL	Oregon Unforgiven	0	5	--	--	4	--

Based in: Eugene, OR

4/21/2002	Portland Shockwave	L	0	42	5/12/2002	Portland Shockwave	L	0	63
4/27/2002	Tacoma Majestics	L	0	49	5/18/2002	Tacoma Majestics	L	0	1
5/4/2002	Boise Xtreme	L	0	39					

Orlando Anarchy

Year	League	Name	W	L	Conference	Division	DF	PR
2010	WFA	Central Florida Anarchy	4	5	National	South Central	2	Q
2011	WFA	Orlando Anarchy	5	3	National	South Atlantic	2	--
2012	WFA	Orlando Anarchy	2	6	National	Division 9 (South Atlantic)	4	--
2013	WFA	Orlando Anarchy	0	8	National	Division 6 (South Atlantic)	5	--
2014	WFA	Orlando Anarchy	1	7	National	South Atlantic	4	--
2015	WFA	Orlando Anarchy	0	8	National	South Atlantic	4	--
		Total	12	37				

Based in: Orlando, FL
Notes: Preceded by IWFL2's Orlando Mayhem

Orlando Anarchy Game-By-Game Results

Date	H/A	Opponent	W/L	Score			Date	H/A	Opponent	W/L	Score	
4/10/2010	H	Jacksonville Dixie Blues	L	13	41		4/6/2013	A	Miami Fury	L	0	32
4/17/2010	A	Jacksonville Dixie Blues	L	7	29		4/13/2013	H	Tampa Bay Inferno	L	14	34
4/24/2010	A	Carolina Raging Wolves	W	35	14		4/20/2013	H	Jacksonville Dixie Blues	L	13	48
5/8/2010	A	Tampa Bay Pirates	W	14	0		4/27/2013	A	Tampa Bay Inferno	L	7	60
5/15/2010	A	Jacksonville Dixie Blues	L	13	47		5/4/2013	H	Miami Fury	L	0	52
6/5/2010	H	Carolina Raging Wolves	W	26	6		5/18/2013	A	Jacksonville Dixie Blues	L	0	39
6/12/2010	H	Tampa Bay Pirates	L	9	14		5/25/2013	A	Tallahassee Jewels	L	20	47
6/19/2010	H	Tampa Bay Pirates	W	19	0		6/1/2013	H	Miami Fury	L	0	46
6/26/2010	A	Jacksonville Dixie Blues	L	13	47 Q							
							4/5/2014	A	Miami Fury	L	0	56
4/2/2011	A	Tampa Bay Pirates	L	0	6		4/19/2014	H	Daytona Breakers	L	13	32
4/9/2011	H	Savannah Sabers	W	36	14		4/26/2014	H	Tampa Bay Inferno	L	0	68
4/16/2011	H	Jacksonville Dixie Blues	L	7	42		5/3/2014	A	Savannah Sabers	W	20	14
5/7/2011	H	Gulf Coast Riptide	W	41	14		5/10/2014	H	Miami Fury	L	0	41
5/14/2011	A	Jacksonville Dixie Blues	L	0	49		5/17/2014	A	Tampa Bay Inferno	L	0	57
6/4/2011	A	Gulf Coast Riptide	W	26	14		5/31/2014	A	Jacksonville Dixie Blues	L	7	48
6/11/2011	A	Carolina Raging Wolves	W	30	0		6/7/2014	H	Tennessee Train	L	14	24
6/18/2011	H	Atlanta Heartbreakers	W	28	0							
							4/18/2015	A	Daytona Waverunners	L	6	22
4/14/2012	H	Tampa Bay Inferno	L	0	25		4/25/2015	A	Miami Fury	L	0	42
4/21/2012	A	Jacksonville Dixie Blues	L	3	31		5/2/2015	H	Atlanta Phoenix	L	0	1
4/28/2012	H	Miami Fury	W	34	8		5/9/2015	A	Jacksonville Dixie Blues	L	0	1
5/12/2012	A	Palm Beach Punishers	L	13	14		5/23/2015	H	Jacksonville Dixie Blues	L	0	1
5/19/2012	H	Jacksonville Dixie Blues	L	6	33		5/30/2015	H	Miami Fury	L	0	1
6/2/2012	H	Savannah Sabers	L	20	34		6/6/2015	A	Tampa Bay Inferno	L	0	1
6/9/2012	A	Tampa Bay Inferno	L	20	42		6/13/2015	H	Daytona Waverunners	L	0	1
6/16/2012	A	Carolina Raging Wolves	W	41	8							

Orlando Anarchy Player Register (2010-2015)

Albert, Heather (2013-2014)
Anthony, Michelle (2015)
Arner, Amanda (2011-2013, 2015)
Austin, Amy (2010-2013)
Baehne, Jennifer (2010-2013)
Banks, Alexandria (2010-2011)
Barbour, Eboni (2012)
Bell, Rebeka (2014)
Berardo, Tabitha (2013-2015)
Betancourth, Jennifer (2015)
Bozeman, Tiffany (2010-2014)
Cadeau, Monet (2011)
Cafaso, Joey (2012-2013)
Cardenas, Marielyn "Mex" (2010-2014)
Christoff, Dawn (2011)
Coogle, Shatoya (2011, 2013)
Dixon, Lightning (2010-2011)
Elliott, Denisha (2013)
Farrow, Tamara (2015)
Fischetti, Shalimar (2014)
FlintRoyal, Ashley (2015)
Fryer, Beth (2012-2013)
Gagne, Courtney (2014-2015)
Gonzalez, Idilia (2010)
Greenwood, Mimi (2010-2015)
Griffin, Brittney (2014)
Heath, Chelsea (2010)
Heath, Nancy (2012)
Heinz, Shannon (2010)
Holmes, Kristal (2015)
Holt, Ashley (2013)
Hooker, Karen (2013-2014)
Hunter, Chandice (2015)
Jackson, Paulette (2010-2015)
Jeune, Tamara (2010-2011)
Johnson, Raveendra "Vee Val" ('11, '13-14)
Jones, Vhontrese (2011)
Keesee, Melissa (2010-2014)
Kenemuth, Jennifer (2011)
Lastra, Liz (2013-2014)
Loesel, Lee (2010, 2012)
Mackey, Kaylissa "K.K." (2015)
Martin, Kimberly (2010)
Marvin, Jenifer (2014)
McCallion, Kerri (2010-2012)
McCullough, Kerri (2013)
McKnight, Erica (2014)
McNaughton, Kayla (2012-2013)
Mercado, Lisette (2010)
Meredith, Tana (2010)
Morgan, Kaycie (2015)
Nelson, Amanda (2014)
O'Keefe, Staci Rae (2012)
Padilla, Maria (2013-2014)
Paschall, Jada (2011-2012)
Pawol, Jen (2011)
Perry, Jessica (2011)
Plowden, Sue (2010-2011)
Pringle, Brandi (2010-2012)
Promchana, Kwan Juthamard (2015)
Roberson, Kambi (2011, 2013-2014)
Robinson, Evette (2011)
Rodriguez, Janessa (2010, 2014)
Sanderson, Des (2010, 2013-2014)
Searcy, Elisicia (2014-2015)
Shaw, Christine (2010, 2012-2014)
Shaw, Porsche (2015)
Sheppard, Nicole "Nikki" (2014-2015)
Smith, Diana (2014)
Snead, Andrea (2010-2014)
Sobers, Constance (2015)
Sparks, Melinda (2010-2015)
Stallworth, LaSheena "Rena" (2014-15)
Stephens, Tracy (2012-2013)
Stinebaugh, Joleen (2010)
Stinson, Britney (2015)
Stratman, Nichol (2010)
Sullivan, Caitlin (2012-2013)
Tejada, Angie (2014)
Thomas, Chatara (2015)
Tryon, Gail (2010)
White, Cheri (2011)
White, Lana (2010-2014)
Williams, Angie (2013-2014)
Williams, Melissia (2012)
Wright, Jenelle (2015)

Orlando Fire

Year	League	Name	W	L	Conference	Division	DF	PR
2001	WAFL	Orlando Fire	7	6	Atlantic	South	2	S
2002	WAFL-WFA	Orlando Fire	9	2	Southern	--	2	CC
		Total	16	8				

Based in: Orlando, FL

9/8/2001	A	Syracuse Sting	L	13	26	I	10/5/2002		Tampa Bay Force	W	53	6
10/6/2001	H	Austin Rage	W	8	7	I	10/12/2002		Jacksonville Dixie Blues	W	33	30
10/27/2001	H	Tampa Bay Force	L	6	18		10/19/2002	A	South Carolina Crusaders	W	18	12
11/3/2001	H	Jacksonville Dixie Blues	W	28	22	*	11/3/2002	H	New Orleans Voodoo Dolls	W	1	0	N
11/10/2001	A	Tampa Bay Force	L	6	50		11/9/2002	H	South Carolina Crusaders	W	35	0
11/17/2001	A	Jacksonville Dixie Blues	L	10	21		11/16/2002	A	Birmingham Steel Magnolias	W	35	0
12/1/2001	H	Indianapolis Vipers	W	42	20		11/23/2002		Tampa Bay Force	W	40	0
12/8/2001	H	Alabama Slammers	W	36	0		12/7/2002		Jacksonville Dixie Blues	L	0	20
12/15/2001	A	Jacksonville Dixie Blues	W	20	9		12/14/2002	A	New Orleans Voodoo Dolls	W	1	0	N
12/22/2001	H	Tampa Bay Force	L	14	20		12/21/2002	H	Birmingham Steel Magnolias	W	1	0
12/29/2001	A	New Orleans Voodoo Dolls	W	44	0		1/11/2003		Jacksonville Dixie Blues	L	18	38	CC
1/5/2002	A	Indianapolis Vipers	W	38	14							
1/26/2002	A	Tampa Bay Force	L	20	31	S						

Orlando Lightning

Year	League	Name	W	L	Conference	Division	DF	PR
2001	MIWFA	Orlando Lightning	1	4	--	--	--	--

Based in: Orlando, FL
Notes: Succeeded by IWFL's Orlando Starz [Orlando Mayhem]

8/4/2001	H	Tennessee Heat	L	0	6	I	9/1/2001	A	Tennessee Heat	W	14	3	I
8/18/2001	H	Austin Outlaws	L	6	32	I	9/8/2001	H	Miami Fury	L	0	48
8/25/2001	H	Carolina Cougars	L	0	12							

Orlando Mayhem

Year	League		Name	W	L	Conference	Division	DF	PR
2002	IWFL		Orlando Starz	6	1	Eastern	--	2	--
2003	IWFL		Orlando Starz	1	8	Eastern	South Atlantic	3	--
2004	IWFL	X	Orlando Mayhem	2	6	--	--	--	--
2005	IWFL		Orlando Mayhem	0	10	Eastern	South Atlantic	3	--
2006	IWFL		Orlando Mayhem	3	5	Eastern	South Atlantic	3	--
2007	IWFL		Orlando Mayhem	6	2	Eastern	South Atlantic	2	--
2008	IWFL		Orlando Mayhem	7	2	Eastern	South Atlantic	1	S
2009	IWFL2		Orlando Mayhem	2	6	--	--	9	--
			Total	27	40				

Based in: Orlando, FL
Notes: Preceded by MIWFA's Orlando Lightning; Changed name from Orlando Starz to Orlando Mayhem midseason 2004; Succeeded by WFA's Central Florida Anarchy [Orlando Anarchy]

4/27/2002		Tampa Tempest	W	34	6		4/12/2003	H	Tampa Bay Terminators	L	0	8
5/4/2002		Tampa Tempest	W	20	6		4/19/2003	A	Atlanta Xplosion	L	0	39
5/11/2002		Miami Fury	W	1	0		5/3/2003	A	Miami Fury	L	6	30
5/25/2002		Tampa Bay Force	W	48	0	I	5/10/2003	H	Tampa Bay Terminators	L	14	20
6/2/2002		New Hampshire Freedom	W	27	6		5/17/2003	H	Miami Fury	L	0	20
6/8/2002		Tampa Tempest	L	6	14		5/25/2003	A	Miami Fury	L	14	44
6/22/2002		Tampa Tempest	W	9	6		5/31/2003	H	Atlanta Xplosion	L	0	39
							6/7/2003	A	Detroit Blaze	W	22	14
							6/14/2003	A	Tampa Bay Terminators	L	0	34

Continued on next page

Orlando Mayhem Game-By-Game Results (continued)

Date	H/A	Opponent	W/L	Score		Date	H/A	Opponent	W/L	Score	
4/3/2004	H	Carolina Spartans	W	72	0	4/28/2007	H	Palm Beach Punishers	W	43	13
4/17/2004	A	Tampa Bay Terminators	L	0	14	5/5/2007	H	Baton Rouge Wildcats	W	55	0
4/24/2004	A	Carolina Spartans	W	54	0	5/12/2007	A	Palm Beach Punishers	W	37	0
5/8/2004	A	Tampa Bay Terminators	L	0	49	5/19/2007	A	Atlanta Xplosion	L	7	14
5/15/2004	H	Jacksonville Dixie Blues	L	0	1	6/2/2007	H	Miami Fury	W	27	13
5/22/2004	A	Atlanta Xplosion	L	13	52	6/9/2007	A	Baton Rouge Wildcats	W	54	0
5/29/2004	A	Jacksonville Dixie Blues	L	0	53	6/16/2007	H	Atlanta Xplosion	L	0	7
6/5/2004	H	Atlanta Xplosion	L	0	22	6/30/2007	A	Palm Beach Punishers	W	65	0
4/2/2005	H	Tampa Bay Terminators	L	6	24	4/12/2008	H	Atlanta Xplosion	W	13	7 *
4/9/2005	H	Jacksonville Dixie Blues	L	6	40	4/19/2008	A	Miami Fury	W	21	0
4/16/2005	A	Tampa Bay Terminators	L	0	27	4/26/2008	A	Louisiana Fuel	W	55	0
4/23/2005	A	Miami Fury	L	0	24	5/3/2008	H	Palm Beach Punishers	W	43	0
4/30/2005	H	Atlanta Xplosion	L	6	40	5/17/2008	A	Atlanta Xplosion	L	14	17
5/14/2005	H	Jacksonville Dixie Blues	L	9	46	5/31/2008	H	Palm Beach Punishers	W	39	0
5/21/2005	A	Tampa Bay Terminators	L	3	14	6/7/2008	H	Louisiana Fuel	W	42	0
6/4/2005	H	Miami Fury	L	13	22	6/14/2008	A	Palm Beach Punishers	W	33	0
6/11/2005	A	Jacksonville Dixie Blues	L	19	43	6/28/2008	A	Pittsburgh Passion	L	6	41 S
6/18/2005	H	Miami Fury	L	7	14	4/11/2009	H	Miami Fury	L	0	21
4/29/2006	H	Tampa Bay Terminators	L	13	41	4/18/2009	A	Palm Beach Punishers	L	6	21
5/6/2006	H	Miami Fury	L	6	40	4/25/2009	H	Houston Energy	W	28	7
5/13/2006	A	Atlanta Xplosion	L	0	41	5/2/2009	A	Carolina Phoenix	L	15	42
5/20/2006	A	Miami Fury	L	13	22	5/16/2009	A	Miami Fury	L	6	27
6/3/2006	H	Carolina Cardinals	W	48	0	5/30/2009	H	Palm Beach Punishers	W	41	25
6/10/2006	A	Tampa Bay Terminators	W	21	8	6/6/2009	A	Miami Fury	L	0	18
6/17/2006	A	Miami Fury	L	14	20	6/13/2009	H	Atlanta Xplosion	L	14	19
6/24/2006	H	Baton Rouge Wildcats	W	34	3						

Pacific Blast

Year	League	Name	W	L	Conference	Division	DF	PR
2002	WAFC	Pacific Blast	6	5	Southern	--	2	CC

Based in: Honolulu, HI

Date	H/A	Opponent	W/L	Score		Date	H/A	Opponent	W/L	Score	
9/11/2002	H	California Quake	W	46	6	10/27/2002	A	Hawaii Legends	L	7	72 E
9/14/2002	H	California Quake	W	72	6	11/6/2002	A	Sacramento Sirens	L	26	47
10/2/2002	A	San Francisco Stingrayz	W	22	12	11/9/2002	A	San Francisco Stingrayz	W	1	0
10/5/2002	A	Oakland Banshees	W	56	20	11/10/2002	H	Los Angeles Amazons	L	0	8 I
10/17/2002	H	Arizona Caliente	W	36	12	11/23/2002	A	Arizona Caliente	L	0	1 CC
10/19/2002	H	Arizona Caliente	L	6	23						

Pacific Warriors

Year	League	Name	W	L	Conference	Division	DF	PR
2009	WFA	California Lynx	5	3	American	Pacific	2	--
2010	WFA	Pacific Warriors	7	2	American	South Pacific	2	Q
2011	WFA	Pacific Warriors	4	4	American	South Pacific	2	--
2012	WFA	Pacific Warriors	6	4	American	Division 17 (South Pacific)	2	Q
2013	WFA	Pacific Warriors	3	5	American	Division 13 (South Pacific)	3	W
2015	WFA	Pacific Warriors	6	2	American	Pacific West	2	--
		Total	**31**	**20**				

Based in: Hermosa Beach, CA

Date	H/A	Opponent	W/L	Score			Date	H/A	Opponent	W/L	Score		
4/18/2009	A	Las Vegas Showgirlz	L	6	19		6/6/2009	A	Phoenix Prowlers	W	41	6	
4/25/2009	A	Marana She-Devils	W	1	0	N	6/13/2009	A	Las Vegas Showgirlz	L	20	28	
5/9/2009	H	Phoenix Prowlers	W	27	20		6/20/2009	H	Marana She-Devils	W	1	0	N
5/30/2009	H	Marana She-Devils	W	1	0	N	6/27/2009	H	Las Vegas Showgirlz	L	22	40	

Continued on next page

Pacific Warriors Game-By-Game Results (continued)

Date	H/A	Opponent	Result			
4/17/2010	H	San Diego Sting	W	41	0	
4/24/2010	H	Central Cal War Angels	W	34	29	
5/1/2010	H	Arizona Assassins	W	34	26	
5/8/2010	A	Las Vegas Showgirlz	L	6	34	
5/15/2010	A	San Diego Sting	W	1	0	
5/22/2010	A	Arizona Assassins	W	20	8	
6/5/2010	A	Central Cal War Angels	W	41	18	
6/12/2010	H	Las Vegas Showgirlz	W	33	21	
6/26/2010	A	Lone Star Mustangs	L	14	38	Q
4/9/2011	A	San Diego Sting	W	40	0	
4/16/2011	A	Las Vegas Showgirlz	W	36	0	
4/30/2011	A	San Diego Surge	L	0	82	
5/7/2011	H	Las Vegas Showgirlz	W	56	6	
5/14/2011	H	So Cal Scorpions	W	21	6	
6/4/2011	A	Central Cal War Angels	L	8	30	
6/11/2011	H	San Diego Surge	L	6	43	
6/18/2011	A	Arizona Assassins	L	6	26	
4/14/2012	H	San Diego Sting	W	48	0	
4/21/2012	A	Arizona Assassins	W	54	0	
4/28/2012	A	Silver State Legacy	W	22	14	
5/5/2012	H	San Diego Surge	L	12	69	
5/19/2012	A	Central Cal War Angels	L	12	30	
6/2/2012	H	Arizona Assassins	W	61	0	
6/9/2012	H	Silver State Legacy	W	27	7	
6/16/2012	A	San Diego Surge	L	0	49	
6/23/2012	H	Las Vegas Showgirlz	W	27	20	W
6/30/2012	A	San Diego Surge	L	0	48	Q
4/6/2013	H	San Diego Surge	L	8	28	
4/13/2013	A	Arizona Assassins	W	66	8	
4/20/2013	A	Central Cal War Angels	L	0	55	
5/4/2013	H	Central Cal War Angels	L	8	20	
5/11/2013	H	San Diego Sting	W	36	8	
6/1/2013	H	West Coast Lightning	W	22	0	
6/8/2013	A	San Diego Surge	L	12	41	
6/15/2013	A	Sacramento Sirens	L	6	25	W
4/11/2015	A	San Diego Surge	L	31	73	
4/18/2015	H	Arizona Assassins	W	77	0	
4/25/2015	A	Sin City Sun Devils	W	46	0	
5/2/2015	A	West Coast Lightning	W	88	2	
5/16/2015	H	Ventura County Wolfpack	W	1	0	
5/30/2015	H	Central Cal War Angels	W	38	34	
6/6/2015	H	San Diego Surge	L	8	48	
6/13/2015	A	Arizona Assassins	W	84	6	

Pacific Warriors Player Register (2009-2013, 2015)

Adams, Monique (2012-2013, 2015)
Alexander, Ryane (2013)
Asi, Crystal (2012-2013)
Asi, Lani (2012-2013)
Bagley, Lauren (2015)
Baker, Jeannine (2009)
Bartholomew, Shanna (2011)
Bolton, Shawn (2012)
Bowden, Jeanine (2010)
Bowman, Dalphana (2010)
Brannon, Kris (2012-2013, 2015)
Brick, Cassey (2009-2010)
Centeno, Carmen (2010)
Chan, Magnolia (2011)
Cheeks, Jessica (2012)
Christian, LaSheree (2012)
Cisneros, Jacqueline "Jackie" (2012, '15)
Clapp, Karlene (2011)
Clay, Travonia (2011)
Costner, Nelda (2009-2013)
Crook-Williams, Alondra (2013)
Davis, Lauren (2011-2013)
Fardmanesh, Newsha (2010)
Filoialii, Mata (2010)
Flynn, Jameelah (2010-2011)
Francis, Cynthia (2011)
Freeman, Alicia (2012-2013)
French-Love, Jhamara (2011)
Galarza, Valarie (2010)
Garcia, Michelle (2009)
Gardner, Priscilla (2015)
Glenn, Alexis (2011-2013)
Gnekow, Erin (2009-2011, 2013)
Gonzalez, Chrystal (2010)
Green, Kim (2012, 2015)
Griffith, Tyee (2015)
Guerrero, Jeanine (2009-2010)
Gutierrez, Shannon (2009-2010)
Hardiman, Demetrea (2015)
Harper, Dawn (2009-2013)
Harrison, Whitney (2015)

Hayes, Ashleigh (2010-2013, 2015)
Heath, Faith (2015)
Henry, Kim (2011-2013)
Hollenshed, Laurisa (2015)
Honani, VaNiesha (2015)
Hosea, Ranae (2015)
Houston, LaShay (2011)
Humphrey, Tiffany (2011-2013)
Insular, Betsy (2009)
Iose, Ashley (2009-2011)
Iose, Audrey (2009-2011)
Iose, Selah (2009-2011, 2013)
Jackson, Melissa Jo (2009-2010)
Jetter, Tara (2009)
Joyce, Jessica (2015)
Kenney, Michele (2015)
King, Lisa (2009-2010)
Kirby, Alex (2012)
Laguna, Harlan (2012-2013)
Lakei, Sonya (2011-2012)
Leilua, Susan (2010-2011)
Linn, Suzanne (2015)
Lokeni, Rowena (2011)
Long, Maleka (2010-2011)
Lopez, Angie (2010-2011)
Lopez, Stephanie (2011-2012, 2015)
Luna, Rhonda (2013)
MacLeod, Nancy (2012)
Manning, Lanika (2011-2013)
Martinez, Cecilia (2015)
Marvin, Andrea Nicole (2009)
Maxwell, Taffany (2011-2012)
McDonald, Tamara (2009-2010)
McDonough, Jasmine (2015)
McVicar, Sarah (2009-2010)
Micheau, Kelli (2012)
Mims, Angela (2015)
Monsod, Amparo (2015)
Morgan, Erica (2013)
Morin, Alexis (2012-2013)
Mulatu, Phieban (2009)

Munoa, Amanda (2012-2013, 2015)
Munoa, Rebecca "Becky" (2012-13, 2015)
Nehrenberg, Andrea (2009)
Nerey, Annette (2009)
Newman, Kristina (2011)
Nieves, Bianca (2012-2013)
Paaluhi, Tanya (2009-2010, 2013)
Park, Debbie (2009)
Patino, Delinda (2010)
Perez, Yvette (2015)
Peterson, Melody (2009-2010)
Philpott, Tarrah (2013)
Podesta, Joni (2010)
Pomee, Malia (2013)
Pouli, Salah (2010)
Riley, Sandra (2012-2013)
Rivas, Kasey (2011)
Robinson, Blair (2013)
Robledo, Yvette (2015)
Romero, Nataki (2015)
Schiro, Lisa (2009)
Sherman, Mariana (2009-2010)
Shuler, Heather (2015)
Singletary, Tami (2012-2013, 2015)
Smith, Ashley (2009)
Smith, Dana (2010)
Smith, Tatiana (2015)
Soakai, Ellen (2009-2010)
Southwell, Simone (2012)
Spann, Sabrina (2009)
Sula, Reta (2011)
Suzuki, Hiroko "Betty" (2013, 2015)
Tagaloa, Tepora (2011)
Tavai, Nafanua "Nua" (2010-2013)
Taylor, Stephanie (2011-2013)
Terrell, Denisha (2012-2013)
Trotter, Design (2012)
Tupuivao, Lisa (2010)
Turner, Mariah (2015)
Uni, Ester (2009-2010, 2012-2013)

Continued on next page

Pacific Warriors Player Register (continued)

Unzueta, Marissa (2013)
Valencia, Monica (2010)
Vanschoelandt, Annelise (2009)
Velasquez, Mary (2010)
Whitlock, Aubrey (2011)
Wickman, Leslie (2009)
Williams, Niesha (2012)
Wilson, Amber (2012)
Wilson, Timmae (2012-2013)
Wright, Bryann (2010)

Palm Beach Punishers

Year	League	Name	W	L	Conference	Division	DF	PR
2007	IWFL	Palm Beach Punishers	1	7	Eastern	South Atlantic	4	--
2008	IWFL	Palm Beach Punishers	0	8	Eastern	South Atlantic	4	--
2009	IWFL2	Palm Beach Punishers	2	6	--	--	11	--
2010	IWFL2	Palm Beach Punishers	1	7	Eastern	Southeast	5	--
2011	WFA	Palm Beach Punishers	5	3	National	Coastal	2	--
2012	WFA	Palm Beach Punishers	4	4	National	Division 9 (South Atlantic)	3	--
		Total	**13**	**35**				

Based in: Wellington, FL

Date	H/A	Opponent	Result	PF	PA
4/28/2007	A	Orlando Mayhem	L	13	43
5/12/2007	H	Orlando Mayhem	L	0	37
5/19/2007	A	Miami Fury	L	0	63
5/26/2007	A	Atlanta Xplosion	L	0	62
6/9/2007	H	Cape Fear Thunder	W	13	0
6/16/2007	A	Miami Fury	L	7	22
6/23/2007	H	Miami Fury	L	0	7
6/30/2007	H	Orlando Mayhem	L	0	65
4/12/2008	H	Miami Fury	L	2	6
4/26/2008	H	Carolina Phoenix	L	7	25
5/3/2008	A	Orlando Mayhem	L	0	43
5/10/2008	A	Atlanta Xplosion	L	0	37
5/17/2008	H	Miami Fury	L	0	22
5/31/2008	A	Orlando Mayhem	L	0	39
6/7/2008	A	Miami Fury	L	2	52
6/14/2008	H	Orlando Mayhem	L	0	33
4/18/2009	H	Orlando Mayhem	W	21	6
4/24/2009	A	Miami Fury	L	0	44
5/2/2009	A	Carolina Queens	L	14	26
5/9/2009	H	Louisiana Fuel	W	28	0
5/16/2009	A	Atlanta Xplosion	L	7	77
5/23/2009	H	Carolina Phoenix	L	9	14
5/30/2009	A	Orlando Mayhem	L	25	41
6/13/2009	H	Miami Fury	L	0	53
4/3/2010	H	Miami Fury	L	9	40
4/10/2010	A	Carolina Phoenix	L	0	49
4/17/2010	H	Carolina Queens	L	3	13
4/24/2010	A	Louisiana Fuel	W	26	20
5/1/2010	A	Miami Fury	L	0	41
5/15/2010	A	Miami Fury	L	0	55
5/22/2010	H	Carolina Phoenix	L	14	71
6/5/2010	H	Miami Fury	L	6	14
4/9/2011	A	Jacksonville Dixie Blues	L	12	42
4/16/2011	H	Savannah Sabers	W	38	0
5/7/2011	H	Tampa Bay Pirates	W	16	8
5/14/2011	A	Miami Fury	L	9	12
5/21/2011	A	Savannah Sabers	W	35	0
6/4/2011	H	Atlanta Heartbreakers	W	34	6
6/11/2011	A	Tampa Bay Pirates	W	20	14
6/18/2011	H	Miami Fury	L	0	14
4/14/2012	A	Savannah Sabers	L	28	33
4/21/2012	H	Tallahassee Jewels	W	14	6
4/28/2012	A	Tampa Bay Inferno	L	0	40
5/5/2012	A	Miami Fury	W	1	0
5/12/2012	H	Orlando Anarchy	W	14	13
5/19/2012	H	Miami Fury	W	44	28
6/9/2012	A	Jacksonville Dixie Blues	L	0	1
6/16/2012	H	Tampa Bay Inferno	L	0	1

Palm Beach Punishers Player Register (2011-2012)

Accetturo, Domnique (2011)
Beauchamp, Sarah (2011-2012)
Bell, Keia (2011-2012)
Cintron, Margaret-Ann "Maggie" (2011-12)
Coles, Jennifer (2011-2012)
Deveaux, Lashaunda (2011)
Footman, Cardiece (2011)
Footman, Sam (2012)
Francis, Caitlin (2012)
Francis, Kathleen (2012)
Freybe, Hileia (2011-2012)
Hand, Jessica (2011-2012)
Hargreaves, Becca (2011-2012)
Hazel, Rita (2011)
Hernandez, Iris (2011)
Jackson, Yashica (2011-2012)
Jones, S. Micki (2012)
Konttinen, Elisa Johanna (2012)
Kwiatkowski, Amanda (2011)
Leggett, Lageri (2011)
Louis, Abigail (2011-2012)
Maple, Sally (2011-2012)
Marsh, Lyndsey (2012)
McKenzie, Valerie (2011)
Mitchell, Natasha (2011)
Moody, Dani (2011-2012)
Morris, Melissa (2011-2012)
Napier, Toccara (2011)
Newbold, S. Ashley (2012)
Norris, Jennifer (2012)
Osment, Khristy (2011-2012)
Rhone, Sarina (2011-2012)
Saunders, Ann Marshall (2012)
Savage, Melissa (2011-2012)
Schwinn, Kaytlin (2011-2012)
Sinkfield, Alexis (2011-2012)
Sinkfield, Alicia (2011)
Tatum, Valerie (2012)
Tryon, Gail (2012)
Wehnes, Ashley (2012)
Wisemane, Alcema (2011)

Pensacola Power

Year	League	Name	W	L	Conference	Division	DF	PR
2001	NWFA	Pensacola Power	8	1	Southern	--	1	C
2002	NWFA	Pensacola Power	9	1	--	Southern	1	CC
2003	NWFA	Pensacola Power	11	1	Southern	Gulf Coast	1	C
2004	NWFA	Pensacola Power	10	1	Southern	Gulf Coast	1	CC
2005	NWFA	Pensacola Power	10	1	Southern	--	1	C
2006	NWFA	Pensacola Power	5	3	Southern	Southeast	1	S
2007	NWFA	Pensacola Power	7	2	Southern	South	1	Q
2008	NWFA	Pensacola Power	6	3	Southern	Southeast	1	Q
2009	WFA	Gulf Coast Riptide	6	2	American	Southeast	2	--
2011	WFA	Gulf Coast Riptide	3	5	National	South Atlantic	3	--
2012	WFA	Gulf Coast Riptide	1	7	National	Division 8 (Gulf Coast)	3	--
		Total	**76**	**27**				

Based in: Pensacola, FL   **Neutral sites:** Nashville, TN (N1); Louisville, KY (N2)

Date	H/A	Opponent	W/L	PF	PA	Note
4/21/2001	H	Alabama Renegades	W	20	0	
4/28/2001	A	Chattanooga Locomotion	W	36	7	
5/5/2001	A	Nashville Dream	W	40	12	
5/12/2001	H	Chattanooga Locomotion	W	48	0	
5/26/2001	H	Nashville Dream	W	22	9	
6/2/2001	H	Alabama Renegades	W	7	6	
6/16/2001	A	Tennessee Venom	W	20	6	
6/23/2001	A	Alabama Renegades	W	3	0	
7/14/2001	H	Philadelphia Liberty Belles (I)	L	7	40	C
4/20/2002		Panama City Beach Rumble	W	56	6	
5/4/2002		Biloxi Herricanes	W	42	6	
5/18/2002		Panama City Beach Rumble	W	61	0	
5/25/2002		New Orleans Spice	W	50	7	
6/8/2002		Biloxi Herricanes	W	30	0	
6/15/2002		New Orleans Spice	W	41	0	
6/22/2002		Biloxi Herricanes	W	63	0	
6/29/2002		New Orleans Spice	W	59	0	
7/6/2002	H	Alabama Renegades	W	12	8	S
7/13/2002	H	Detroit Danger	L	7	14	CC
3/29/2003		Nashville Dream	W	24	0	E
4/12/2003	A	Panama City Beach Rumble	W	54	0	
4/19/2003	H	New Orleans Spice	W	49	3	
4/26/2003	A	Atlanta Leopards	W	81	0	
5/3/2003	H	Gulf Coast Herricanes	W	82	0	
5/17/2003	A	New Orleans Spice	W	49	0	
5/24/2003	H	Panama City Beach Rumble	W	41	7	
5/31/2003	A	Gulf Coast Herricanes	W	84	0	
6/14/2003	H	Alabama Renegades	W	35	0	
7/12/2003	H	Alabama Renegades	W	34	12	S
7/19/2003	H	Oklahoma City Lightning	W	26	14	CC
8/2/2003	N1	Detroit Demolition	L	21	28	C
4/3/2004	A	Muscle Shoals Smashers	W	56	0	
4/17/2004	H	Alabama Renegades	W	56	7	
4/24/2004	A	Gulf Coast Herricanes	W	62	0	
5/1/2004	H	New Orleans Blaze	W	35	12	
5/15/2004	H	Muscle Shoals Smashers	W	70	0	
5/22/2004	A	Alabama Renegades	W	42	18	
5/29/2004	H	Gulf Coast Herricanes	W	49	0	
6/5/2004	A	New Orleans Blaze	W	28	20	
6/26/2004	H	Asheville Assault	W	60	0	Q
7/10/2004	A	Chattanooga Locomotion	W	35	20	S
7/17/2004	A	Oklahoma City Lightning	L	13	37	CC
4/16/2005	H	New Orleans Blaze	W	31	26	
4/23/2005	A	Emerald Coast Sharks	W	81	7	
4/30/2005	H	Gulf Coast Herricanes	W	44	6	
5/14/2005	A	Chattanooga Locomotion	W	20	0	
5/21/2005	H	Emerald Coast Sharks	W	55	0	
5/28/2005	H	Alabama Renegades	W	59	6	
6/4/2005	A	New Orleans Blaze	W	35	8	
6/11/2005	A	Gulf Coast Herricanes	W	47	8	
7/16/2005	H	Chattanooga Locomotion	W	42	12	S
7/23/2005	H	Oklahoma City Lightning	W	17	14	CC*
7/30/2005	N2	Detroit Demolition	L	0	74	C
4/15/2006	A	Emerald Coast Barracudas	W	56	12	
4/29/2006	H	Austin Outlaws	L	8	24	
5/6/2006	A	Alabama Renegades	W	22	6	
5/20/2006	H	Emerald Coast Barracudas	W	48	0	
6/3/2006	A	Austin Outlaws	L	0	24	
6/10/2006	A	Alabama Renegades	W	18	0	
6/17/2006	H	Emerald Coast Barracudas	W	58	0	
7/8/2006	H	Columbus Comets	L	0	20	S
4/21/2007	H	Emerald Coast Barracudas	W	40	0	
4/28/2007	A	Gulf Coast Herricanes	W	48	0	
5/5/2007	A	New Orleans Blaze	W	22	7	
5/12/2007	H	Austin Outlaws	W	20	14	
5/19/2007	H	Gulf Coast Herricanes	W	56	8	
6/2/2007	A	Emerald Coast Barracudas	W	54	0	
6/9/2007	A	Austin Outlaws	L	12	32	
6/16/2007	H	New Orleans Blaze	W	37	28	
6/23/2007	H	Columbus Comets	L	0	10	Q
4/19/2008	A	New Orleans Blaze	L	0	20	
4/26/2008	H	Alabama Renegades	L	58	60	
5/10/2008	A	Emerald Coast Barracudas	W	64	24	
5/17/2008	H	New Orleans Blaze	W	16	6	
5/24/2008	H	Gulf Coast Herricanes	W	28	22	
5/31/2008	A	Alabama Renegades	W	40	8	
6/7/2008	H	Emerald Coast Barracudas	W	38	12	
6/21/2008	A	Gulf Coast Herricanes	W	36	0	
6/28/2008	A	Kentucky Karma	L	0	6	Q
4/25/2009	H	New Orleans Blaze	W	28	0	
5/2/2009	A	Emerald Coast Barracudas	W	66	8	
5/9/2009	A	New Orleans Blaze	W	20	10	
5/16/2009	H	Memphis Belles	W	50	8	
5/30/2009	H	Jacksonville Dixie Blues	L	36	49	
6/13/2009	A	Memphis Belles	W	54	20	
6/20/2009	H	Emerald Coast Barracudas	W	1	0	
6/27/2009	A	Jacksonville Dixie Blues	L	14	37	

Continued on next page

Pensacola Power Game-By-Game Results (continued)

Date	H/A	Opponent	W/L	Score		Date	H/A	Opponent	W/L	Score	
4/2/2011	A	Atlanta Heartbreakers	W	64	6	4/14/2012	H	Houston Power	L	0	31
4/9/2011	A	Miami Fury	L	14	52	4/21/2012	A	Acadiana Zydeco	W	22	0
4/30/2011	H	Jacksonville Dixie Blues	L	14	21	4/28/2012	A	Jacksonville Dixie Blues	L	6	49
5/7/2011	A	Orlando Anarchy	L	14	41	5/5/2012	H	Tallahassee Jewels	L	20	26
5/14/2011	H	Tampa Bay Pirates	W	18	13	5/12/2012	H	Acadiana Zydeco	L	0	28
5/21/2011	A	Jacksonville Dixie Blues	L	0	43	5/19/2012	A	Tallahassee Jewels	L	0	1
6/4/2011	H	Orlando Anarchy	L	14	26	6/2/2012	A	Atlanta Phoenix	L	0	1
6/18/2011	H	Carolina Raging Wolves	W	36	14	6/9/2012	H	Tallahassee Jewels	L	0	1

Pensacola Power Player Register (2003-2009, 2011-2012)

Aezel, Mina (2006)
Aguiar, Kim (2012)
Amato, Cassie (2003-2005)
Antone, Brittany (2008)
Artym, Candice (2006-2007)
Bailey, Kim (2004)
Baillie, Chontal (2004)
Benoit, Laura (2005)
Bonal-Smith, Wendy (2003-2005, 2009)
Bonfanti, Leigh (2005)
Brady, Shanna (2003-2004)
Brashier, Sandra (2004)
Bray, Angela (2006-2008)
Bray, Karen (2003)
Brocks, Tamara (2006-2007, 2009)
Brosky, Melinda (2003)
Brothers, Tiffany (2011)
Burleson, Brittney (2008)
Cain, Kara (2011-2012)
Carver, Kate (2007, 2012)
Clary, Tiffany (2004)
Clem, Maggie (2007)
Colum, Helen (2004)
Coop, Erica (2009)
Cooper, Kim (2005-2007)
Copeland, Jeannie (2009, 2011)
Crews, Linda (2008)
Cutts, Heather (2005)
Davalt, Ashlee (2007)
Dawson, Melissa (2005-2006)
Deeb, Valerie (2003-2008, 2012)
Densel, Dawn (2005)
Dickerson, Jen (2007)
Dickey, Olivia (2004-06, 2008, 2011-12)
Durant, Stefanie (2008-2009)
Dutton, Heather (2009)
Ellis, Janie (2005)
Ellison, Frankie (2009)
Fellows, Hannah (2009)
Freeman, Jamie (2009, 2011-2012)
Gamewell, Amanda (2005)
Glaze, Deb (2003-2009)
Gonzalez, Regina (2008)
Goode, Zaveria (2008-2009, 2011-2012)
Green, Heather (2008-2009)
Griffin, Shanthenia (2008, 2012)
Grubbs, Brittney (2011-2012)
Guy, Victoria (2011)
Hall, Clara (2005, 2009)
Halverson, Erica (2003)
Hines, Pat (2003-2004)
Hobbs, Cathy (2003)
Hodge, Lee (2008-2009)
Holi, Zelie (2009)

Holmes, Gail (2003)
Hoodless, Skye (2005-2007, 2009)
Ingram, Sarah (2008)
Jackson, Deanna (2004)
James, Rose (2003)
Jenkins, Prescilla (2005)
Jernigan, Keeyana (2008)
Johnson, Angel (2009)
Johnson, Jennifer "J.J." (2003-2007)
Johnson, LaKeisha (2005-2009)
Johnson, Shelette (2003-2006)
Jones, Dominique (2009)
Jones, Tania (2009, 2011-2012)
Kagan, Shauna (2011)
Kidd, Audrey (2003-2009)
King, Denise (2003)
Kipu, Lei (2011)
Kirchharr, Sonia (2003-2005, 2007-2008)
Kniffen, Josette (2004)
Knight, Dee Dee (2008-2009, 2011-2012)
Lambeth, Kristie (2003, 2005)
Lewis, Kieara (2008)
Lewis, Rekena (2008)
Lindsey, Therese (2004, 2009)
Lowrey-Ridgley, Tammy (2003)
Lunsford, Libby (2005-2007)
Lynch, Kelly (2006)
Machovec, Deb ('03-04, '06-07, '09, '11-12)
Martinez, Stacy (2005)
McCarthy, Missy (2004)
McCary, Daniele (2004)
McCole, Laura (2005)
McElroy, Raquel (2003-2004)
Merritt, Jay (2011)
Mitchell, Sara (2008)
Moore, Brittany (2008-2009)
Moore, Jamie (2003-2007)
Moore, Kimberly (2003, 2006)
Morgan, Emily (2003-2004)
Morris, Heather (2003)
Morris, Shea (2008-2009)
Nickerson, Tisha (2003-2004)
Omundsen, Nina (2012)
Opielowski, Tara (2003)
Padgett, Julie (2009)
Palmer, Amanda (2006-2007)
Patterson, Donzaleigh (2003-2009)
Perkins, Lottie (2007)
Perko, Katie (2008)
Powell, Debbie "Deb" (2003-04, '07, '12)
Prather, Belinda (2003)
Prescott, Karrie (2004-2005)
Price, Casey (2003)
Price, Nicee (2009)

Prim, Clarrissa (2012)
Pro, Juliette (2004, 2007)
Reid, Nicole (2008, 2011)
Riker, Tracy (2007)
Roberson, Celeste (2011)
Rouillard, Tiffany (2012)
Rutherford, Jessica (2003-2007)
Savage, Amanda (2009)
Scarvey, Kim (2003)
Serrano, Lima (2005)
Severns, Shanney (2008)
Shamhart, Bobbi (2003)
Shelly, Christina (2006)
Skelton, Melissa (2003-2004)
Slyvester, Katie (2008)
Smith, Jessica (2004-2005)
Steely, Kellie (2003)
Stockstill, Helen (2009, 2011-2012)
Street, Kim (2004)
Strickland, Chris (2012)
Strother, Monica (2006-2007)
Swartzmiller, Bobby (2009, 2011)
Taylor, Stephanie (2003)
Temple, Jennifer (2005-2007)
Thorrington, Stacy (2003-2005)
Tipton, Shauna (2007)
Tisa, Christina (2011-2012)
Tucker, Tia (2008)
Turner, Valene (2008)
Valentine, Tikiha (2005-2007)
Van Der Werf, Anya (2006)
Van Houten, Kim (2005-07, 2009)
Varney, Amanda (2012)
Waters, Angie (2004-2005)
Wells, Tonia (2003-2009)
Wert, Dana (2003-2007)
Wert, Michelle (2004-2008)
West, Sara (2012)
Whidden, Lindsay (2004-2008)
White, Rachael (2005, 2007)
Wiggins, Jodi (2003-2009, 2011-2012)
Williams, Anjel (2011)
Williams, Ella (2009)
Williams, Kieshwanda (2009)
Williams, LaToya (2003-2006)
Williams, Monique (2004)
Williford, Tracie (2005-2007)
Wilson, Yvonne (2003-2009)
Wood, Jenni (2007)
Wright, Bri-Ann (2005-2009)
Wright, Skyler (2009, 2011)
Wylie, Annelyse (2004)

Philadelphia Firebirds

Year	League	Name	W	L	T	Conference	Division	DF	PR
2003	NWFA	Philadelphia Phoenix	8	2	0	Northern	Northern	1	CC
2004	NWFA	Philadelphia Phoenix	7	2	0	Northern	Northern	1	Q
2005	NWFA	Philadelphia Phoenix	4	4	0	Northern	--	12	--
2006	NWFA	Philadelphia Phoenix	5	4	0	Northern	Northeast	2	Q
2007	NWFA	Philadelphia Phoenix	2	6	0	Northern	South	2	--
2008	NWFA	Philadelphia Phoenix	9	1	0	Northern	East	1	CC
2009	IWFL	Philadelphia Firebirds	1	7	0	Eastern	North Atlantic	4	--
2010	IWFL	Philadelphia Firebirds	1	7	0	Eastern	Northeast	5	--
2011	IWFL	Philadelphia Firebirds	1	4	1	Eastern	Mid-Atlantic	3	--
2012	IWFL	Philadelphia Firebirds	4	5	0	Eastern	Mid-Atlantic	2	BQ
2013	IWFL	Philadelphia Firebirds	6	2	0	Eastern	Mid-Atlantic	1	S
2014	IWFL	Philadelphia Firebirds	2	6	0	Eastern	Mid-Atlantic	5	--
2015	IWFL	Philadelphia Firebirds	6	2	0	Eastern	Mid-Atlantic	2	--
		Total	**56**	**52**	**1**				

Based in: Philadelphia, PA

Date	H/A	Opponent	Result	PF	PA	Note
4/12/2003	H	Connecticut Crush	L	7	12	
4/26/2003	H	Maine Freeze	W	34	0	
5/3/2003	A	Maine Freeze	W	34	0	
5/10/2003	H	Rochester Raptors	W	51	0	
5/24/2003	H	Massachusetts Mutiny	W	34	12	
5/31/2003	A	Connecticut Crush	W	40	0	
6/7/2003	A	Massachusetts Mutiny	W	26	7	
6/14/2003	A	Rochester Raptors	W	34	0	
7/12/2003	H	D.C. Divas	W	36	32	S
7/19/2003	A	Detroit Demolition	L	14	58	CC
4/3/2004	A	Massachusetts Mutiny	W	34	19	
4/17/2004	H	Connecticut Crush	W	42	14	
4/24/2004	A	Maine Freeze	W	57	0	
5/1/2004	H	Maine Freeze	W	55	0	
5/15/2004	A	Rochester Raptors	W	48	0	
5/22/2004	H	Massachusetts Mutiny	W	14	7	
5/29/2004	A	Connecticut Crush	L	16	18	
6/12/2004	H	Rochester Raptors	W	58	0	
6/26/2004	H	Southwest Michigan Jaguars	L	6	26	Q
4/16/2005	H	Massachusetts Mutiny	L	0	17	
4/23/2005	A	Maine Freeze	W	41	0	
4/30/2005	A	Tidewater Floods	W	47	0	
5/14/2005	A	Baltimore Burn	L	0	14	
5/21/2005	H	Maine Freeze	W	62	0	
6/4/2005	A	D.C. Divas	L	0	37	
6/11/2005	H	Tidewater Floods	W	48	12	
6/18/2005	H	Connecticut Crush	L	27	49	
4/22/2006	A	Massachusetts Mutiny	L	0	7	
4/29/2006	H	Maine Freeze	W	54	0	
5/6/2006	H	Connecticut Crush	W	35	0	
5/20/2006	A	Tidewater Floods	W	28	8	
5/27/2006	H	Massachusetts Mutiny	L	7	14	
6/3/2006	A	Maine Freeze	W	35	7	
6/10/2006	A	Connecticut Crush	L	3	7	
6/17/2006	H	Tidewater Floods	W	50	0	
7/1/2006	A	Cleveland Fusion	L	13	52	Q
4/14/2007	A	Baltimore Burn	L	0	6	
4/21/2007	H	Central PA Vipers	W	41	0	
4/28/2007	A	Connecticut Crush	L	13	20	
5/12/2007	A	Pittsburgh Passion	L	7	53	
5/19/2007	H	Baltimore Burn	L	8	14	*
5/26/2007	A	Richmond Spirit	W	1	0	N
6/2/2007	H	Connecticut Crush	L	14	27	
6/9/2007	H	Pittsburgh Passion	L	0	40	
4/26/2008	H	New Jersey Titans	W	40	0	
5/3/2008	A	Baltimore Burn	W	50	8	
5/10/2008	A	Maine Freeze	W	56	0	
5/17/2008	H	Connecticut Crush	W	19	0	
5/31/2008	H	Baltimore Burn	W	49	0	
6/7/2008	A	New Jersey Titans	W	28	0	
6/14/2008	A	Connecticut Crush	W	20	0	
6/21/2008	H	Maine Freeze	W	1	0	
7/5/2008	H	Columbus Comets	W	15	14	S
7/12/2008	H	West Michigan Mayhem	L	0	21	CC
4/18/2009	H	Baltimore Nighthawks	L	15	22	
4/25/2009	H	Connecticut Crushers	W	31	12	
5/2/2009	H	New York Sharks	L	14	33	
5/9/2009	A	New York Nemesis	L	3	34	
5/16/2009	A	Boston Militia	L	0	60	
5/30/2009	H	D.C. Divas	L	0	42	
6/6/2009	H	Pittsburgh Passion	L	0	53	
6/13/2009	A	D.C. Divas	L	0	63	
4/3/2010	A	Baltimore Nighthawks	L	0	54	
4/10/2010	H	New York Sharks	L	0	64	
4/17/2010	A	Pittsburgh Passion	L	0	49	
4/24/2010	H	D.C. Divas	L	0	1	
5/1/2010	A	New York Nemesis	L	0	33	
5/15/2010	H	Binghamton Tiger Cats	W	49	0	
5/22/2010	H	Boston Militia	L	0	1	
5/29/2010	A	D.C. Divas	L	3	49	
4/16/2011	H	Baltimore Nighthawks	T	0	0	
4/23/2011	A	Carolina Phoenix	L	17	57	
5/7/2011	A	Baltimore Nighthawks	W	13	6	
5/14/2011	H	Carolina Phoenix	L	7	54	
5/28/2011	H	Baltimore Nighthawks	L	0	8	
6/11/2011	A	Manchester Freedom	L	0	26	

Continued on next page

Philadelphia Firebirds Game-By-Game Results (continued)

Date	H/A	Opponent	Result	PF	PA	Note		Date	H/A	Opponent	Result	PF	PA
4/7/2012	H	Carolina Phoenix	L	0	26			4/12/2014	A	Washington Prodigy	W	20	6
4/14/2012	A	Baltimore Nighthawks	L	23	32			4/19/2014	H	Pittsburgh Passion	L	0	42
4/21/2012	A	Northeastern Nitro	W	8	7			4/26/2014	H	Washington Prodigy	W	18	6
5/5/2012	H	Connecticut Wreckers	W	28	12			5/3/2014	A	Baltimore Nighthawks	L	12	14
5/19/2012	H	Erie Illusion	W	32	8			5/10/2014	H	Baltimore Nighthawks	L	0	1
6/2/2012	A	Connecticut Wreckers	W	34	0			5/31/2014	H	Keystone Assault	L	0	21
6/9/2012	H	Baltimore Nighthawks	L	0	21			6/7/2014	A	Pittsburgh Passion	L	0	31
6/16/2012		Carolina Phoenix	L	14	20			6/14/2014	H	New York Sharks	L	6	31
6/30/2012		New England Intensity	L	13	30	BQ							
								4/11/2015	H	Carolina Phoenix	W	20	0
4/27/2013	A	Baltimore Nighthawks	W	14	0			4/18/2015	A	Pittsburgh Passion	L	8	55
5/4/2013	H	Washington Prodigy	W	14	3			4/25/2015	H	Baltimore Nighthawks	W	34	6
5/18/2013	A	Connecticut Wreckers	W	44	0			5/2/2015	H	Northeast Rebels	W	30	0
6/1/2013	H	Baltimore Nighthawks	W	42	8			5/9/2015	A	Washington Prodigy	W	19	7
6/15/2013	H	New England Intensity	L	6	20			5/30/2015	H	Detroit Pride	W	63	0
6/22/2013	A	Keystone Assault	W	22	13			6/6/2015	A	Connecticut Wreckers	W	33	0
6/29/2013	H	Connecticut Wreckers	W	1	0			6/13/2015	A	New York Sharks	L	20	28
7/13/2013	A	Carolina Phoenix	L	0	32	S							

Philadelphia Firebirds Player Register (2004-2008, 2015)

Adams-Jones, Allison (2007)
Albrecht, Danielle (2007-2008)
Allen, Sarah (2006)
Angelikas, Zeffi (2004-2006)
Archer, Ryann (2006)
Avvento, Amanda (2015)
Bell, Satoria (2015)
Bradley, Rebecca "Becky" (2006-2007)
Brandemarte, Alicia (2007)
Brickhouse, Mia (2004)
Brooks, Rasheeda (2007)
Burcan, Laurie (2006)
Butler, Jennifer (2008)
Capaccio, Roseanne (2007-2008)
Carney, Charniece (2015)
Carr, Sheemea (2015)
Carroll, Rhonda (2006)
Castellini, Ali (2006-2007)
Catlin, Sarah (2006)
Clark, Jen (2005)
Clark, Lisa (2006)
Cody, Colleen (2015)
Colleluori, Diana (2007-2008)
Congialdi, Amanda (2015)
Cooper, Janet (2015)
Corisdeo, Cynthia (2004-2008)
Crego, Dalisia (2004)
Cushman, Christine (2007)
Daisey, Mary (2006)
Dean-Campbell, Chrystellendria (2007-08)
Deaton, Katrina (2007)
DeMuro, Theresa (2008)
DiCicco, Melissa (2005-2006)
Donnelly, Chris (2004-2007)
Dorsey, Zorita (2006)
Drumgoole, Caroline (2015)
Dudick, Sheena (2007)
Edwards, Simone (2004-2006)
Ellam, Stacy (2008)
Fagnani, Annamarie (2015)
Fife, Malinda (2008)
Fitzsimmons, Erin (2004-2005)
Fortsch, Robyn (2004-2006)
Gaeta, Lauren (2008)
Gamble, Spring (2015)
Gerber, Megan (2007-2008)

Gonzalez, Sabrina (2008)
Graham, Deb (2008)
Grayson, Tawana (2006)
Gregory, Coleen (2015)
Grubb, Carol (2006-2008)
Hamill, Kelly (2005-2006)
Hertel, Erika (2007)
Higby, Heather (2004-2007)
Hill, Nielle (2008)
Hogan, Shannon (2006)
Hopkins, Danika (2006-2007)
Ingalls, Shacrea (2007)
Jack, Andrea (2007)
Jennings, Kim (2004)
Johnstone, Kia (2004-2006)
Kirkendall, Shaina (2008)
Krouse, Critty (2008)
Kurzrok, Becky (2007)
Landau, Sara (2007)
Larry, April (2005-2008)
Lawson, Shameca (2008, 2015)
Loutey, Kim (2008)
Love, Amy (2004)
Mackaravitz, Beth (2007-2008)
Majchrzak, Cheryl (2008)
Martin, Heather (2005)
Matteis, Jen (2008)
McCoy, Megan (2008)
McIntyre, Chria (2006)
McKeefery, Mo (2005-2006)
Mesaros, Julie (2007)
Mills, Tiffany (2015)
Montgomery, Stacey (2005)
Morrison, Carla (2005)
Mueller, Machelle (2005)
Murdy, Dee (2008)
Murray, Angie (2004-2005)
Murray, Brandi (2004-2005)
Naifeh, Joy (2008)
Nugent, Cathy (2004)
Ottinger, Jill (2007-2008)
Overton, Deonna (2015)
Parker, Kimberly (2015)
Pecovsky, Rachelle (2004-2005)
Perkins, Becky (2005)
Petrini, Chrissy (2007)

Petty, Christine (2004-2006)
Pfender, Rene (2004-2005, 2007)
Phan, Michelle (2008)
Pinckney, Tasha (2008)
Poole, Colleen (2008)
Powell, Jen (2004-2005)
Punderson, Sarah (2008)
Rankin, Jen (2006-2008)
Reeves, Ann (2004-2006)
Rideout, Meredith (2004, 2006-2007)
Rider, Stephanie (2006)
Robinson, Deidre "Dee" (2008)
Robinson, Kelly (2007)
Rogers, Amanda (2006)
Rosario, Jennifer (2015)
Seymour, Paige (2006)
Shunk, Kelly (2005-2007)
Simms, Samirah (2004, 2006)
Skelton, Brianna (2015)
Speakman, Beth (2008)
Spearman, Brooke (2007)
Stanford, NaTaza (2008)
Stein, Jane (2008)
Street, Kim (2004-2006)
Strong, Deann (2005)
Sullivan, Kate (2008)
Taylor, Jessica (2015)
Thompson, Amber (2004-2005)
Trippett, Dot (2007-2008)
Turman, Cindy (2004-2005)
Turrentine, Tiffany (2007-2008)
Villante, Nancy (2008)
Wartman, Sarah (2008)
Waszena, Stephanie (2007)
Weand, Tracy (2005-2006)
Wells, Angela (2015)
White, Jordyn (2004-2006)
Williams, Synae (2015)
Williams, Tyra (2015)
Wilson, Christine (2015)
Womack, Omariyana (2015)
Wright, Nikki (2004)
Yergey, Dawn (2007-2008)
Young, Sakera (2015)

Philadelphia Liberty Belles (I)

Year	League	Name	W	L	Conference	Division	DF	PR
2001	NWFA	Philadelphia Liberty Belles (I)	8	1	Northern	--	1	**NC**
2002	NWFA	Philadelphia Liberty Belles (I)	7	3	--	Northern	2	CC
2003	IWFL	Philadelphia Liberty Belles (I)	3	4	Eastern	Mid-Atlantic	2	--
		Total	18	8				

Based in: Philadelphia, PA

Date	H/A	Opponent	Result			
4/21/2001	H	Connecticut Crush	W	20	6	
4/28/2001	H	D.C. Divas	W	40	0	
5/5/2001	A	Baltimore Burn	W	46	0	
5/19/2001	H	Massachusetts Mutiny	W	27	0	
6/2/2001	H	Baltimore Burn	W	47	0	
6/9/2001	A	Massachusetts Mutiny	L	7	13	
6/16/2001	A	D.C. Divas	W	14	7	
6/23/2001	A	Connecticut Crush	W	74	0	
7/14/2001	A	Pensacola Power	W	40	7	C
4/27/2002		Connecticut Crush	W	26	0	
5/4/2002		Massachusetts Mutiny	W	21	20	
5/18/2002		Maine Freeze	W	55	14	
5/25/2002		Massachusetts Mutiny	L	12	17	
6/1/2002		Connecticut Crush	W	25	6	
6/15/2002		Maine Freeze	W	60	0	
6/22/2002		Massachusetts Mutiny	L	21	35	
6/29/2002		Connecticut Crush	W	35	6	
7/6/2002	A	Baltimore Burn	W	21	20	S
7/13/2002	A	Massachusetts Mutiny	L	16	27	CC
4/19/2003	H	New York Sharks	L	0	48	
4/26/2003	A	Albany Night-Mares	W	14	0	
5/3/2003	A	Bay State Warriors	L	6	34	
5/10/2003	A	Rhode Island Riptide	W	16	14	
5/17/2003	A	New York Sharks	L	0	58	
5/31/2003	H	Rhode Island Riptide	W	8	0	
6/14/2003	H	Bay State Warriors	L	8	28	

Philadelphia Liberty Belles (I) Player Register (2001)

Alsdorf, Joan (2001)
Angelikas, Zeffi (2001)
Bender, Kathy (2001)
Betz, Elise (2001)
Brambrink, Jill (2001)
Brown, Chris (2001)
Butz-Houghton, Cyndi (2001)
Carolan, Meg (2001)
Curcio, Tarrah (2001)
David-Kryszczak, Susan (2001)
Donnelly, Chris (2001)
Ericsson, Karen (2001)
Fatiga, Annette (2001)
Fernandez, Liza (2001)
Fortsch, Robyn (2001)
Fowler, Kelly (2001)
Frederick, Donna (2001)
Garrett, Donna (2001)
Griffin, Tricia (2001)
Grubb, Carol (2001)
Higby, Heather (2001)
Jakubowicz, Cindy (2001)
Kohler, Tina (2001)
Kraft, Anne (2001)
Krauter, Mariah (2001)
Leary, Jennifer (2001)
Leary, Marion (2001)
Love, Amy (2001)
Marcial, Julie (2001)
Montgomery, Tamara (2001)
Mulvihill, Karen (2001)
Ormsby, Marianne (2001)
Pastore, Jen (2001)
Pecovsky, Rachelle (2001)
Priano, Janeen (2001)
Rentz, Julie (2001)
Ricketts, Trina (2001)
Saravo, Jan (2001)
Scannell, Karen (2001)
Schnieders, Robyn (2001)
Settle, Tracy (2001)
Taubman, Beth (2001)
Titano, Angela (2001)
Weaver, Nicole (2001)
Wieland, Karen (2001)
Wykes, Alissa (2001)

Philadelphia Liberty Belles (II)

Year	League	Name	W	L	Conference	Division	DF	PR
2009	WFA	Philadelphia Liberty Belles (II)	9	1	National	Northeast	1	CC
2010	WFA	Philadelphia Liberty Belles (II)	9	1	National	Northeast	1	S
2011	WFA	Philadelphia Liberty Belles (II)	2	6	National	Northeast	3	--
2012	WFA	Philadelphia Liberty Belles (II)	2	6	National	Division 2 (North)	3	--
		Total	22	14				

Based in: Philadelphia, PA

Date	H/A	Opponent	Result			
4/18/2009	H	Keystone Assault	W	47	24	
4/25/2009	A	Baltimore Burn	W	43	8	
5/9/2009	A	New Jersey Titans	W	14	12	
5/16/2009	A	Keystone Assault	W	14	12	
5/30/2009	H	Baltimore Burn	W	13	10	
6/6/2009	H	New Jersey Titans	W	59	0	
6/13/2009	A	Connecticut Cyclones	W	1	0	N
6/20/2009	H	Binghamton Tiger Cats	W	53	0	
7/11/2009	H	Indiana Speed	W	19	9	S
7/25/2009	A	West Michigan Mayhem	L	21	28	CC
4/10/2010	A	Southern Tier Spitfire	W	63	0	
4/24/2010	A	New England Nightmare	W	70	6	
5/1/2010	H	Baltimore Burn	W	26	6	
5/8/2010	H	New Jersey Titans	W	25	12	
5/15/2010	A	Keystone Assault	W	35	12	
5/22/2010	H	Southern Tier Spitfire	W	71	0	
6/12/2010	H	New England Nightmare	W	62	6	
6/19/2010	A	New Jersey Titans	W	42	0	
6/26/2010	H	West Michigan Mayhem	W	35	33	Q
7/10/2010	A	Columbus Comets	L	7	36	S

Continued on next page

Philadelphia Liberty Belles (II) Game-By-Game Results (continued)

Date	H/A	Opponent	W/L	PF	PA	Date	H/A	Opponent	W/L	PF	PA
4/2/2011	H	New York Sharks	L	20	34	4/14/2012	A	New England Nightmare	W	14	0
4/9/2011	H	New England Nightmare	W	52	0	4/21/2012	H	Boston Militia	L	0	59
4/16/2011	A	D.C. Divas	L	0	20	5/5/2012	A	New York Sharks	L	8	25
5/7/2011	H	Keystone Assault	W	28	12	5/12/2012	A	Boston Militia	L	0	62
5/14/2011	A	New York Sharks	L	21	27	5/19/2012	H	Keystone Assault	L	0	20
5/21/2011	H	D.C. Divas	L	0	42	6/2/2012	H	New York Sharks	L	0	31
6/4/2011	A	Boston Militia	L	8	70	6/9/2012	A	Maine Lynx	W	1	0
6/11/2011	A	Keystone Assault	L	8	14	6/16/2012	H	Pittsburgh Passion	L	0	50

Philadelphia Liberty Belles (II) Player Register (2009-2012)

Albrecht, Danielle (2009)
Anderson, Christine (2010)
Austin, Mikaelyn (2009-2012)
Bennett, Khalifah (2011-2012)
Broome, Vanessa (2009)
Bunn, Stephanie (2012)
Burns, Rasheena (2009, 2012)
Butler, Jennifer (2009-2010)
Butz-Houghton, Cyndi (2010-2011)
Carangelo, Sarah (2011)
Carlin, Colleen (2010-2011)
Carr, Sheemea (2009-2011)
Chapman, Danielle (2009-2010)
Colyar, Kimberly (2010-2012)
Crockett, Brittanie (2012)
Dandar, Kristen (2009)
Davis, Aisha (2012)
DeMuro, Theresa (2009-2010)
Dwyer, Kate (2012)
Echevarria, Jaya (2009-2010)
Evans, MaLeka (2011)
Fitzpatrick, Laurie (2012)
Flood, Al-Nisa (2011)
Grubb, Carol (2009)
Heavlow, Joy (2010)
Hertel, Erika (2010-2011)
Hibbs, Jeanette (2009-2011)
Hopkins, Danika (2009-2012)
Hurley, Katherine (2009)
Irvin, Jamie (2010-2011)
Jackson, Allison (2010-2012)
Jones, Diamond (2010-2011)
Kappler, Deborah (2011-2012)
Katchi, Vanessa (2010-2011)
Kirkendall, Shaina (2009)
Landau, Sara (2009-2012)
Loutey, Kim (2009)
Mackaravitz, Beth (2009-2011)
McCulligan, Bridget (2011)
Mendez, Noel (2010-2011)
Merkel, Jay (2011-2012)
Mitchell, Dana (2012)
Moran, Bridget (2012)
Muhammad, Jaliyla (2012)
Murray, Brandi (2011)
Paige, Barbara (2009)
Peete, Ashley (2009-2011)
Pfender, Rene (2009-2011)
Phan, Michelle (2009)
Pinones, Tonya (2011)
Pittman, Mecca (2011)
Poole, Kelly (2009)
Purcell, Tara (2010-2011)
Reid, Danielle (2011)
Roach, Marirose (2009-2011)
Robinson, Deidre "Dee" (2009-2011)
Rosario, Jennifer (2009-2011)
Rylander, Alisha (2010)
Seiple, Elizabeth (2009-2012)
Shaw, Tiffany (2012)
Sithens, Denise (2009-2010)
Slattery, Caitlin (2010)
Solomon, Laurionne (2012)
Stanford, NaTaza (2009-2012)
Staniskis, Kathleen (2009)
Stewart, Kathryn (2009)
Stinney, Marcia (2009-2011)
Sullivan, Kate (2009)
Tankelewicz, Jessica (2010)
Turrentine, Tiffany (2009)
Upshur, Myisha (2009-2012)
Villone, Victoria (2011-2012)
Walker, Denee "Dex" (2009-2011)
Wheeler, Tanishea (2010-2011)
Williams, Venita (2012)
Wilson, Chrissy (2009-2012)
Yergey, Dawn (2009-2012)

Phoenix Phantomz

Year	League	Name	W	L	Conference	Division	DF	PR
2012	IWFL	Phoenix Phantomz	8	3	Western	Pacific Southwest	1	S
2013	IWFL	Phoenix Phantomz	6	3	Western	Pacific Southwest	1	CC
2014	IWFL	Phoenix Phantomz	6	2	Western	Pacific West	1	S
2015	IWFL	Phoenix Phantomz	3	4	Western	Pacific West	2	--
		Total	23	12				

Based in: Phoenix, AZ

Date	H/A	Opponent	W/L	PF	PA	Note	Date	H/A	Opponent	W/L	PF	PA	Note
3/10/2012	A	Las Vegas Showgirlz	W	30	8	IE	3/23/2013	A	Utah Jynx	L	10	38	IE
3/24/2012	H	Las Vegas Showgirlz	L	7	8	IE	3/30/2013	H	Las Vegas Showgirlz	L	12	18	IE
4/14/2012	A	California Quake	W	70	0		4/27/2013	H	Rocky Mountain Thunderkatz	W	50	16	
4/21/2012	H	Colorado Sting	W	75	0		5/4/2013	H	California Quake	W	72	0	
4/28/2012	A	Tucson Monsoon	W	72	0		6/1/2013	A	Rocky Mountain Thunderkatz	W	67	6	
5/5/2012	H	California Quake	W	66	6		6/22/2013	H	Tucson Monsoon	W	1	0	
5/19/2012	A	Colorado Sting	W	37	0		6/29/2013	A	California Quake	W	21	8	
6/2/2012	H	Tucson Monsoon	W	1	0		7/13/2013	H	California Quake	W	18	0	S
6/9/2012	H	California Quake	W	35	14		7/20/2013	A	Houston Energy	L	0	56	CC
6/16/2012		Sacramento Sirens	L	22	62								
6/30/2012		Wisconsin Warriors	L	37	40	S							

Continued on next page

Phoenix Phantomz Game-By-Game Results (continued)

4/26/2014	H	Utah Jynx	W	41	12		4/11/2015	H	Sin City Sun Devils	L	20	31	I
5/3/2014	H	California Quake	W	40	14		4/18/2015	A	North County Stars	W	14	0	
5/10/2014	H	Houston Energy	L	13	62		4/25/2015	A	Sacramento Sirens	L	0	41	
5/24/2014	H	North County Stars	W	1	0		5/16/2015	A	Nevada Storm	L	14	28	
5/31/2014	H	California Quake	W	21	6		5/23/2015	H	California Quake	W	1	0	
6/7/2014	A	North County Stars	W	76	28		5/30/2015	H	North County Stars	W	28	0	
6/14/2014	H	Utah Jynx	W	1	0		6/13/2015	H	Sacramento Sirens	L	18	21	
6/28/2014	A	Houston Energy	L	26	90	S							

Phoenix Phantomz Player Register (2012-2015)

Ahrens, Mary (2012)
Alonzo, Erin (2013-2014)
Arroyo-Monteon, Gaby (2012-2013)
Augustine, Dallas (2012)
Barkman, Elise (2012)
Bell, Shonna (2012-2014)
Belliard, Desiree (2012-2015)
Benjamin, Joniece (2015)
Brown, Kim (2013)
Brunson, Twanna (2014)
Bryan, Beth (2014-2015)
Bryan, Erin (2014)
Cantrell, Lana (2014-2015)
Crayton, Sabriya (2015)
Crosby, Faith (2012)
Curley, Geri (2014-2015)
Dauphinais, Anne (2013)
Davidson, Amanda (2014-2015)
Dayondon, Lehua (2012)
Defer, Julia (2012-2014)
Dennis-Shaw, Micah (2012)
Devane, Averil (2015)
Donnelly, Glennis (2013-2015)
Douglas, Kelly (2012, 2014-2015)
Drago, Kyi (2012)
D'Rossi, Angel (2012, 2014)
Dutton, Heather (2012-2014)
Edward, Cindy (2012-2015)
Feretti, Omega (2015)
Fonseca, Katie (2012, 2014-2015)
Foster, Kristyn (2012)
Glasper, Adena (2014)
Grimm, Corinna (2015)
Hahn, Stephanie (2012)
Hartley, Amber (2012-2015)
Higgerson, Kris (2012-2015)
Hinton, Deloriann (2013)
Jackson, Tiffany (2015)
Jenkins, Red (2012)
Johnson, LaToya (2014-2015)
Kibodeaux, Parnee (2013)
Kocher, Sue (2013-2014)
Laubert, Amber (2012)
Martinez, Jennifer (2013)
Martinez, Melissa (2013)
Munksgard, Michelle (2012, 2014)
Nordgulen, Regi (2012-2015)
O'Bryan, Erin (2012-2013)
Ogunware, Caroline (2012, 2014)
Parker, Trynaty (2012)
Perez, Salina (2014)
Peterson, Diana (2014-2015)
Phillips, Cherri (2012-2013)
Price, Lorraine (2012, 2015)
Refuerzo, Mimi (2013-2014)
Reyes, Angela (2015)
Rodriguez, Christine (2013-2015)
Rodriguez, Sonya (2015)
Roth, Kyla (2013-2014)
Schudt, Angelic (2015)
Sinclair, Monica (2014-2015)
Smith, Andrea (2013-2015)
Smith, LaShelle (2012)
Smith, Serena (2014-2015)
Snyder, Alexis (2012-2013)
Suchta, Rochelle (2013-2014)
Taylor, Nichole (2013-2014)
Thomas, Dansby (2013-2014)
Thompson, LeeAnn (2013-2014)
Toft, Elaina (2014)
Villaverde, Billie Jo (2013)
Walker, Breanna (2014)
Weber, Amanda (2012)
Williams, Bridgette (2012-2013, 2015)
Wright, Monique (2014-2015)

Phoenix Prowlers

Year	League	Name	W	L	Conference	Division	DF	PR
2007	NWFA	Phoenix Prowlers	8	1	Southern	West	1	Q
2008	NWFA	Phoenix Prowlers	5	3	Southern	West	2	--
2009	WFA	Phoenix Prowlers	3	5	American	Pacific	3	--
		Total	16	9				

Based in: Phoenix, AZ
Notes: Preceded by WPFL's Arizona Caliente; Succeeded by Arizona Assassins

4/14/2007		Arizona Venom	W	1	0	N	5/24/2008	A	Modesto Magic	W	64	0	
4/21/2007	A	All Valley Attack	W	62	0		5/31/2008	A	Arizona Wildfire	W	49	8	
4/28/2007	H	Orange County Breakers	W	36	0		6/7/2008	H	Modesto Magic	W	1	0	
5/12/2007		Arizona Venom	W	1	0	N	6/21/2008	A	Los Angeles Amazons	L	14	41	
5/19/2007	H	All Valley Attack	W	52	0								
5/26/2007	A	Orange County Breakers	W	50	0		4/18/2009	A	Marana She-Devils	W	1	0	N
6/9/2007		Arizona Venom	W	1	0	N	5/9/2009	A	California Lynx	L	20	27	
6/16/2007	H	Orange County Breakers	W	35	0		5/16/2009	H	Marana She-Devils	W	1	0	N
6/23/2007	A	St. Louis Slam	L	29	33	Q	5/23/2009	H	Las Vegas Showgirlz	L	14	26	
							5/30/2009	A	Las Vegas Showgirlz	L	8	47	
4/19/2008	A	Los Angeles Amazons	L	14	47		6/6/2009	H	California Lynx	L	6	41	
4/26/2008	H	Arizona Wildfire	W	72	0		6/13/2009	A	Marana She-Devils	W	1	0	N
5/3/2008	H	Modesto Magic	W	67	0		6/20/2009	H	Las Vegas Showgirlz	L	8	35	
5/17/2008	H	Los Angeles Amazons	L	0	42								

Phoenix Prowlers Player Register (2007-2009)

Aguilar, Valerie (2009)
Alonzo, Erin (2008-2009)
Anderson, Darla (2009)
Anderson, Susan (2008)
Arnold, Amy (2007-2008)
Bell, Shonna (2007-2008)
Belliard, Desiree (2007-2009)
Boccia, Valoria (2008)
Brown, Kelly (2007-2008)
Brunson, Twanna (2008-2009)
Calusine, Jennifer (2007-2009)
Canty, Charlene (2007)
Canty, Selina (2007-2008)
Chavez, April (2009)
Clay, Johleda (2008-2009)
Curley, Geri (2007-2009)
Darnel, Angie (2007-2008)
Doi, Tammy (2007-2008)
Donnelly, Glennis (2008-2009)
Drago, Kyi (2007-2008)
D'Rossi, Angel (2007-2008)
Edenburgs, Falonia (2007-2008)
Edenburgs, LaTanya (2007-2008)
Floyd, Sarah (2008)
Fonseca, Katie (2009)
Franco, Angelica (2009)
Gamble, Becky (2007-2008)
Grimes, Kim (2008)
Hawkins, Karmen (2007-2008)
Hedlund, Kristine (2009)
Hill, Jae (2008)
Hoke, Kim (2007-2009)
Huerta, Claudia (2008-2009)
Jarabek, Jackie (2008)
Johnson, Cari (2008-2009)
Kruise, Elecia (2007-2009)
Larue, Mindi (2008)
Lewis, Amy (2007-2009)
Lewis, Debra Jo (2007-2009)
Locklin, Arlene (2007)
Lowe, Tracey (2007)
Maggiore, Brianne (2008)
Marcus, Brandy (2007-2009)
Martin, Debbie (2007-2008)
Martinez, Maria (2008)
McMillian, Levada (2008)
Moore, Jennifer (2008)
Munksgard, Michelle (2007-2008)
Newton, Crystal (2008-2009)
O'Bryan, Erin (2009)
Omo, Desrae (2008)
Quaranta, Mary (2007-2009)
Refuerzo, Mimi (2008-2009)
Reyes, Angela (2008)
Richards, Dee (2007-2008)
Rushforth, Jessica (2008)
Rushing, Kelly (2008-2009)
Smith, Kelly (2009)
Stewart, Becky (2007)
Thompson, Alicia (2008)
Tucker, Elizabeth (2009)
Walinska, Daria (2009)
Walls, Tamika (2009)
Weber, Amanda (2009)
West, Sarah (2008)
Yonnie, Lavinia (2007-2008)

Pittsburgh Force

Year	League	Name	W	L	Conference	Division	DF	PR
2009	WFA	Pittsburgh Force	2	6	National	Mid-Atlantic	4	--
2010	WFA	Pittsburgh Force	5	3	National	Mid-Atlantic	2	--
2011	WFA	Pittsburgh Force	0	8	National	Mid-Atlantic	5	--
2012	WFA	Pittsburgh Force	1	7	National	Division 4 (Mideast)	3	--
2014	WFA	Pittsburgh Force	3	2	National	Northeast	3	--
		Total	**11**	**26**				

Based in: Pittsburgh, PA

Date	H/A	Opponent	Result		
4/18/2009	A	Columbus Comets	L	0	49
4/25/2009	A	Cleveland Fusion	W	34	28
5/9/2009	H	Cincinnati Sizzle	W	36	18
5/16/2009	H	Columbus Comets	L	0	38
5/23/2009	H	Kentucky Karma	L	6	8
5/30/2009	H	Cleveland Fusion	L	16	34
6/6/2009	A	Cincinnati Sizzle	L	8	14
6/20/2009	A	Kentucky Karma	L	20	46
4/10/2010	H	Dayton Diamonds	W	9	8
4/17/2010	H	Columbus Comets	L	0	68
4/24/2010	A	Cleveland Fusion	L	3	60
5/8/2010	A	Columbus Comets	L	0	58
5/22/2010	H	Detroit Dark Angels	W	32	14
6/5/2010	A	Dayton Diamonds	W	12	6
6/12/2010	H	Cincinnati Sizzle	W	48	0
6/19/2010	A	Dayton Diamonds	W	13	0
4/2/2011	H	Pittsburgh Passion	L	0	30
4/9/2011	A	Columbus Comets	L	0	55
4/16/2011	H	Erie Illusion	L	8	20
5/7/2011	H	Cleveland Fusion	L	0	54
5/14/2011	A	Pittsburgh Passion	L	0	45
6/4/2011	H	Cleveland Fusion	L	0	76
6/11/2011	A	Erie Illusion	L	0	20
6/18/2011	H	Columbus Comets	L	0	64
4/14/2012	H	Detroit Dark Angels	L	6	35
4/21/2012	A	Cleveland Fusion	L	6	33
5/5/2012	A	Derby City Dynamite	L	2	8
5/12/2012	H	Cleveland Fusion	L	6	14
5/19/2012	H	Pittsburgh Passion	L	0	66
6/2/2012	A	Detroit Dark Angels	L	6	54
6/9/2012	A	Cincinnati Sizzle	W	21	16
6/16/2012	H	Keystone Assault	L	15	50
4/5/2014	H	Baltimore Burn	W	30	8 I
4/12/2014	A	Central Maryland Seahawks	W	1	0 N
5/3/2014	A	Toledo Reign	L	6	35
5/24/2014	A	Cincinnati Sizzle	W	26	0
5/31/2014	H	Toledo Reign	L	0	37

Pittsburgh Force Player Register (2009-2012, 2014)

Anantarow, Lisa (2009, 2014)
Andrews, Heather (2009-2011)
Avery, Tressia (2009-2012)
Barnes, Davelle (2011)
Battaglia, Heather (2011-2012)
Berarducci, Debbie (2009)
Bernard, Kendra (2014)
Berry, Tonyarae (2014)
Bizub, Melissa Lucy (2009)
Boyd, Tamara (2009-2012)
Brandstadter, Nicole (2009)
Brestensky, Veronica (2009)
Brieck, Olivia (2010-2012)
Buzard, Michele (2009-2011)
Christian, LaShawn (2012)
Clark, Tiffany (2009-2011)
Clifford, Shannon Nikki (2009)
Clifton, Jennifer (2009-2010)
Coley, Brooke (2009)
Coluccio, Dana (2009)

Continued on next page

Pittsburgh Force Player Register (continued)

Courtney, Sarah (2014)
Cox, Denise (2009-2010)
Crump, Debra (2009-2012)
Dais, Dana (2011-2012)
Davidson, Ashley (2011-2012)
Davidson, Janet (2011-2012)
Davis, Jennifer (2009-2011)
Demarco, Brandi (2011)
Dippold, Nancy (2009-2010)
Donahoo, Rhonda (2011)
Dorsett, Desiree (2009-2010)
Double, Barbara (2010)
Doyle, Jaime (2009-2011)
Eggeman, Jamie (2012)
Ellison, Nia (2010)
Englert, Christina (2014)
Engles, Marlene (2011)
Ferrari, Kathy (2009-2012)
Fezar, Kristin (2009-2011)
Figurel, Darcy (2010)
Gaster, Jaimee (2009)
Golnazarian, Emily (2009)
Good, Abby (2010)
Greene, Brittany (2011-2012)
Henley, Torina (2009-2010)
Hollibaugh, Tiffany (2014)
Holmes, Kayla (2011)
Honaker, Adrienne (2014)
Horew, Nikki (2009-2010)
Horn, Dana (2009-2011)
Howard, Constance "Connie" (2011-12, '14)
Howell, Kristina (2009-2012, 2014)
Hudson, Sandra (2009)
Hunter, Carrie (2009)
Jackson, Eve (2009-2011)
Jackson, Tanya (2014)
Jeanette, Jessica (2009)
Jeffers, Beth Ann (2009-2010)
Johnson, Brittany (2014)
Jones, Rhiannon (2011-2012, 2014)
Kennelly, Kerrieann (2012)
Kinsey, Kim (2009)
Lasure, Amy (2010)
Lawrence, Joyce (2010-2012)
Lefcowitz, Tamara (2009-2010)
Lewis, Darlaina (2011)
Lewis, Tatijana (2010-2012, 2014)
Lilley, Amber (2009)
Lollo, Nicole (2014)
Lyons, Megan (2010)
Malovich, Kelley (2014)
Marcum, Krystal (2011-2012)
Marshall, Cherish (2010-2012)
McGregor, Shannon (2012)
McKivitz, Lisa (2009)
McLellan-Miller, Laurie (2011)
McQueen, Dana (2009)
Mitchell, Siroya (2012, 2014)
Montgomery, Tia (2011-2012)
Muldrow, Kandice (2012)
Murphy, Yanique (2011-2012)
Nanni, Betsy (2009)
Nixon, Justice (2014)
Nocito, Joei (2009)
O'Laughlin, Darlene (2009-2011)
Orbin, Kristie (2010)
Owens, Katrina (2014)
Pauvlinch, Kayla (2014)
Payne, Alyssa (2011)
Peer, Deidra (2012, 2014)
Pitruzzella, Salvatrice (2009)
Pitts, Latoya (2009-2012, 2014)
Prioleau, Ashlie (2012)
Ransaw, Cheronda (2010-2012, 2014)
Reddick, Kia (2014)
Rivers, Brittney (2014)
Roberts, Victoria (2014)
Sainovich, Katrina "Katie" (2009-2012)
Sallard, Sophronia (2014)
Sashin, Shelby (2012)
Schleicher, Rachel (2010-2012)
Setmire, Jessica (2010)
Shields, Goldette (2014)
Shields, Sheila (2014)
Shuck, Lee Ann (2009)
Slagle, Jessica (2009-2010)
Smiley, Dawn (2010-2011)
Smith, Miashanti (2012, 2014)
Snyder, Candice (2010-2012)
Sopata, Ashley (2014)
Stiles, Lorri (2010-2012)
Stillwell, Joan (2010-2011)
Stoner, Kelly (2009)
Thompson, Victoria (2012)
Tinklepaugh, Shelby (2014)
Van Eck, Carola (2010-2011)
Vanderpool, Kelequien (2012)
Verrico, Alonna (2010)
Wallace, Melina (2009)
Walsh, Kris (2014)
Walton, Wilma (2011)
Wells, Equaill (2012)
Whitlock, Brittany (2014)
Williams, Denise (2012, 2014)
Wojtaszek, Jessica (2009)
Wolfe, Amanda (2010)
Zatezalo, Stacey (2011-2012)
Zigler, Cynthia (2012, 2014)

Pittsburgh Passion

Year	League	Name	W	L	Conference	Division	DF	PR
2003	NWFA	Pittsburgh Passion	2	6	Northern	Mid-Atlantic	4	--
2004	NWFA	Pittsburgh Passion	6	2	Northern	Mid-Atlantic	2	--
2005	NWFA	Pittsburgh Passion	5	3	Northern	--	9	--
2006	NWFA	Pittsburgh Passion	5	3	Northern	North Central	3	--
2007	NWFA	Pittsburgh Passion	13	0	Northern	Central	1	NC
2008	IWFL	Pittsburgh Passion	9	1	Eastern	North Atlantic	1	CC
2009	IWFL	Pittsburgh Passion	7	2	Eastern	Mid-Atlantic	2	S
2010	IWFL	Pittsburgh Passion	4	4	Eastern	Northeast	3	--
2011	WFA	Pittsburgh Passion	8	1	National	Mid-Atlantic	1	Q
2012	WFA	Pittsburgh Passion	8	2	National	Division 3 (Mid-Atlantic)	2	Q
2013	WFA	Pittsburgh Passion	7	3	National	Division 2 (Mid-Atlantic)	2	Q
2014	IWFL	Pittsburgh Passion	11	0	Eastern	Mid-Atlantic	1	NC
2015	IWFL	Pittsburgh Passion	11	0	Eastern	Mid-Atlantic	1	NC
		Total	96	27				

Based in: Pittsburgh, PA   **Neutral sites:** Nashville, TN (N1); Rock Hill, SC (N2)

Pittsburgh Passion Game-By-Game Results

Date	H/A	Opponent	Result	PF	PA	Note
4/12/2003	H	Baltimore Burn	L	0	7	
4/19/2003	A	Columbus Flames	L	18	21	
4/26/2003	H	Erie Illusion	W	14	7	
5/3/2003	A	D.C. Divas	L	7	32	
5/17/2003	A	Erie Illusion	W	20	18	
5/24/2003	A	Baltimore Burn	L	15	21	
5/31/2003	H	D.C. Divas	L	25	30	
6/14/2003	H	Columbus Flames	L	15	57	
4/3/2004	H	Baltimore Burn	W	22	19	
4/24/2004	A	Roanoke Revenge	W	34	26	
5/1/2004	A	Baltimore Burn	W	20	14	
5/8/2004	H	Roanoke Revenge	W	49	0	
5/22/2004	H	D.C. Divas	L	14	28	
5/29/2004	A	Erie Illusion	W	28	0	
6/5/2004	A	D.C. Divas	L	14	42	
6/12/2004	H	Erie Illusion	W	46	0	
4/16/2005	A	Indianapolis SaberKatz	W	54	0	
4/23/2005	H	D.C. Divas	L	0	20	
4/30/2005	A	Cleveland Fusion	L	28	29	*
5/14/2005	H	Cincinnati Sizzle	W	56	22	
5/21/2005	H	Baltimore Burn	W	26	12	
6/4/2005	A	Toledo Spitfire	W	53	0	
6/11/2005	H	Detroit Demolition	L	14	40	
6/18/2005	A	Tidewater Floods	W	49	0	
4/7/2006	H	Columbus Comets	W	14	7	E
4/22/2006	A	Cleveland Fusion	L	12	13	
4/29/2006	H	Columbus Comets	W	6	0	
5/6/2006	H	Erie Illusion	W	45	0	
5/20/2006	A	Cincinnati Sizzle	W	44	0	
5/27/2006	H	Cleveland Fusion	L	33	35	
6/3/2006	A	Erie Illusion	W	54	0	
6/10/2006	A	Columbus Comets	L	13	27	
6/17/2006	H	Cincinnati Sizzle	W	55	20	
4/21/2007	H	Cleveland Fusion	W	23	14	
4/28/2007	A	Cincinnati Sizzle	W	62	7	
5/5/2007	A	Central PA Vipers	W	52	0	
5/12/2007	H	Philadelphia Phoenix	W	53	7	
5/26/2007	A	Cleveland Fusion	W	40	18	
6/2/2007	H	Cincinnati Sizzle	W	44	7	
6/9/2007	A	Philadelphia Phoenix	W	40	0	
6/16/2007	H	Central PA Vipers	W	77	0	
6/23/2007	H	Erie Illusion	W	63	7	Q
6/30/2007	H	West Michigan Mayhem	W	34	6	S
7/7/2007	H	Cleveland Fusion	W	49	15	CC
7/21/2007	N1	Columbus Comets	W	32	0	C
4/19/2008	A	Central PA Vipers	W	62	0	
4/26/2008	H	Boston Militia	W	34	8	
5/3/2008	H	D.C. Divas	W	38	34	
5/10/2008	H	Columbus Phantoms	W	38	0	
5/17/2008	A	Baltimore Nighthawks	W	28	0	
5/31/2008	H	New York Sharks	W	28	21	
6/7/2008	H	Holyoke Hurricanes	W	54	6	
6/14/2008	A	D.C. Divas	W	17	12	
6/28/2008	H	Orlando Mayhem	W	41	6	S
7/12/2008	A	Chicago Force	L	7	8	CC
4/18/2009	H	Detroit Demolition	W	29	6	
4/25/2009	H	Baltimore Nighthawks	W	49	0	
5/2/2009	A	D.C. Divas	L	7	27	
5/16/2009	H	New York Nemesis	W	41	0	
5/23/2009	A	Detroit Demolition	W	34	12	
5/30/2009	H	Connecticut Crushers	W	76	0	
6/6/2009	A	Philadelphia Firebirds	W	53	0	
6/13/2009	A	New York Sharks	W	34	33	
6/27/2009	A	D.C. Divas	L	17	27	S
4/3/2010	A	Erie Illusion	W	32	0	
4/17/2010	H	Philadelphia Firebirds	W	49	0	
4/24/2010	A	Boston Militia	L	0	27	
5/1/2010	H	Erie Illusion	W	40	2	
5/8/2010	A	New York Sharks	L	8	12	
5/15/2010	H	Baltimore Nighthawks	W	34	6	
5/22/2010	A	Chicago Force	L	0	7	
6/5/2010	H	New York Sharks	L	10	27	
4/2/2011	A	Pittsburgh Force	W	30	0	
4/9/2011	A	Erie Illusion	W	56	14	
4/16/2011	A	Cleveland Fusion	W	26	8	
4/30/2011	H	Columbus Comets	W	17	0	
5/14/2011	H	Pittsburgh Force	W	45	0	
5/21/2011	A	Columbus Comets	W	7	6	
6/11/2011	H	Cleveland Fusion	W	42	0	
6/18/2011	H	Erie Illusion	W	47	7	
6/25/2011	A	Chicago Force	L	31	41	Q
4/14/2012	A	D.C. Divas	W	35	34	
4/28/2012	A	Columbus Comets	W	37	14	
5/5/2012	H	Cleveland Fusion	W	49	0	
5/12/2012	H	Toledo Reign	W	71	14	
5/19/2012	A	Pittsburgh Force	W	66	0	
6/2/2012	H	D.C. Divas	L	28	43	
6/9/2012	H	Columbus Comets	W	22	0	
6/16/2012	A	Philadelphia Liberty Belles (II)	W	50	0	
6/23/2012	H	Detroit Dark Angels	W	34	0	W
6/30/2012	A	D.C. Divas	L	30	45	Q
4/6/2013	H	D.C. Divas	L	31	42	
4/13/2013	A	Toledo Reign	W	42	0	
4/20/2013	A	New York Sharks	W	35	0	
4/27/2013	H	Columbus Comets	W	49	0	
5/11/2013	H	Boston Militia	L	28	42	
5/18/2013	A	Columbus Comets	W	35	14	
6/1/2013	A	D.C. Divas	W	36	27	
6/8/2013	H	Detroit Dark Angels	W	31	0	
6/15/2013	H	Cincinnati Sizzle	W	63	0	W
6/22/2013	A	Boston Militia	L	28	63	Q
4/12/2014	A	Carolina Phoenix	W	29	6	
4/19/2014	A	Philadelphia Firebirds	W	42	0	
4/26/2014	A	New York Sharks	W	31	6	
5/10/2014	H	Montreal Blitz	W	35	0	
5/17/2014	H	Carolina Phoenix	W	51	0	
5/24/2014	A	New York Sharks	W	21	6	
6/7/2014	H	Philadelphia Firebirds	W	31	0	
6/14/2014	A	Baltimore Nighthawks	W	38	6	
6/28/2014	H	Keystone Assault	W	42	12	S
7/12/2014	H	New York Sharks	W	26	12	CC
7/26/2014	N2	Houston Energy	W	41	7	C
4/11/2015	A	Toledo Reign	W	66	0	
4/18/2015	H	Philadelphia Firebirds	W	55	8	
5/2/2015	A	Columbus Comets	W	35	8	I
5/9/2015	H	New York Sharks	W	32	18	
5/16/2015	H	Carolina Phoenix	W	41	6	
5/30/2015	A	New York Sharks	W	21	14	
6/6/2015	H	Toledo Reign	W	63	0	
6/13/2015	H	Washington Prodigy	W	49	0	
6/27/2015	H	New York Sharks	W	35	28	S
7/11/2015	H	Carolina Phoenix	W	41	12	CC
7/25/2015	N2	Utah Falconz	W	41	37	C

Pittsburgh Passion Player Register (2003-2007, 2011-2015)

Adams, Haley (2013-2014)
Allen, Angelina (2007)
Allen, Michelle (2015)
Amato, Beth (2003, 2005-07, 2011-14)
Anderson, Stacey (2005)
Anderson, Tracy (2013)
Aston, Brittany (2014-2015)
Austin, Stephanie (2013)
Bajus, Melissa (2003)
Baker, Angela (2012-2015)
Balochko, Stephanie (2011-2013, 2015)
Barrow, Jean (2011)
Basick, Kim (2012)
Baxter, Ashley (2011)
Beachom, Talisa ('06-07, '11-12, '14-15)
Bean, Emily (2011)
Beanner, Lori (2013)
Beauchamp, Sarah (2006-2007)
Beaver, Kim (2015)
Bentley, Tina (2013)
Berke, Jen (2011)
Berry, Tonyarae (2015)
Bertges, B.J. (2007)
Betterton, Amy (2013)
Blocker, Debi (2006)
Bombash, Melinda (2013)
Bowman, Paige (2014-2015)
Bracco, Lauren (2012)
Brand, Gerrie (2003-2004)
Brenning, Jessica (2011)
Brestensky, Veronica (2006)
Brevard-Peters, Michelle ('07, '11-12, '14)
Brown, Cortlyn (2011)
Brown, Hillary (2004)
Brown, Shirell (2014)
Burkes, Sharon (2012-2014)
Burkholder, Lori (2003, '05-07, '11-13)
Burress, Veronica (2007, 2011-2015)
Burton, Tammy (2003)
Byers, Kellie (2003, 2005-2007)
Byrne, Natalie (2003, 2006)
Cain, Hope (2011-2013)
Cain, Lindsey (2013-2014)
Cairns, Jen (2003-2007, 2011)
Camerota, Katie (2003, 2005)
Cardillo, Lori (2013-2014)
Carkuff, Paige (2015)
Carter, Devona (2006)
Carvelli, Carrie (2005)
Cary, Ava (2007)
Casciani, Deborah (2003)
Catone, Tara (2015)
Chic, Ciara (2011-2015)
Christian, Rosie (2014-2015)
Clark, Kadesha (2013-2014)
Clayboss, Mandy (2007)
Clifford, Shannon Nikki (2005)
Coley, Brooke (2006-2007)
Conchran, Krista (2015)
Conn, Teresa (2003, 2005-07, 2012-14)
Cook, Michelle (2011)
Cotton, Rosie (2014)
Cox, Umeika (2011)
Cozzo, Krystal (2011-2015)
Crawford, Hope (2015)
Croce, Jill (2015)
Danko, Brianne (2012)
Davis, Rebecca (2014)

Dawicki, Helen (2011)
Debo, Stacey (2003)
DeCouto, Kimberly (2005)
Del Prete, Doria (2013)
Dennison, Keri (2011)
Denniston, Carol (2003, 2005, 2007)
DeWald, April (2003)
DiBucci, Diedra (2011, 2013)
Dillaman, Autumn (2007, 2011-2013)
Dman, Hannah (2015)
Donahoo, Rhonda (2005, 2007)
Dowd, Deirdre (2005)
Doyle, Jaime (2007)
Drake, Jennifer (2003)
Dreischalick, Kimberly (2011, 2013-2015)
Drieling, Heather (2015)
Dugas, Kelsey (2011)
Dulski, Jen (2011)
Duncan, Amanda (2013-2014)
Eaton, Jacklyn (2011-2014)
Edmonds, Krissy (2007, 2014)
Engles, Marlene (2003, 2007)
Evans, Meg (2014)
Fallon, Amy (2011-2015)
Ferragonio, Lauren (2013-2015)
Ferrari, Kathy (2003, 2005-2006)
Filmore, Jaharia (2014-2015)
Folta, Nicole (2013)
Ford, Raven (2003, 2005-2007)
Galbreath, Kendra (2011-2015)
Gasdick, Melissa (2011, 2013)
Gaster, Jaimee (2006-2007)
George, Courtney (2013)
Getz, Kathy Jo (2011)
Gold, Jennifer (2005)
Goodson, Cathy (2007)
Graba, Michelle (2014)
Griffith-Taylor, Denise (2006-07, '11-12)
Griswold, Octavia (2011-12, 2014-15)
Griswold, Olivia (2007, 2011-2015)
Grogan, Rochelle (2005)
Guerico, Linda (2005)
Gunde, Janet (2003)
Haeg, Amanda (2011-2015)
Hammond, Melanie "Mel" (2012-2015)
Handra, Kate (2012-2013)
Hatfield, Kasey (2015)
Hauser, Ellen (2003-2004)
Henderson, Melinda (2006, '11-13, '15)
Henley, Torina (2003, 2005-2007)
Hessom, Jessica (2012)
Hoffman, Jenn (2011-2012)
Holt, Dira (2015)
Holzer, Kristin (2013-2014)
Horak, Shelby (2011-2015)
Horew, Nikki (2003, 2005, 2007)
Horn, Dana (2003, 2005, 2007, 2012)
Horton, Lisa (2003-2007, 2012-2015)
Hughes, Lyndsi (2006-2007, 2011-2013)
Hulse, Gretchen (2012)
Humes, Dee (2003)
Illig, Kristalyn (2005)
Issac, Lailah (2006)
Ivy, Ebony (2011-2013)
Jackson, Brittany (2006-2007)
Jackson, Eve (2006)
Jenkins, Amanda (2011)
Jennings, Crystal (2013)

Johnson, Emily (2014)
Johnson, Lori (2006-2007)
Johnson-Bey, Nicole (2003)
Jones, Elisha (2013)
Kacinko, Katie (2015)
Keefer, Tracy (2003, 2005)
Kelly, Tina (2011-2013)
Kennis, Julia (2012)
Kimmen, Lori (2014)
Kinsey, Kim (2007)
Kopelic, Tina (2012)
Kramer, Autumn (2012-2014)
Kring, Sherry (2003-2007, 2011-2013)
Kurawa, Erika (2011-2013)
Lander, Lauren (2011-2012)
Laudadio, Cristy (2007)
Law, Chris (2003, 2005)
Lieberman, Jen (2007)
Linnabary, Christie (2013)
Lips, Danielle (2005-2007)
Long, Tiffany (2011)
Lowrey-Ridgley, Tammy (2005)
Mackey, Kaitlyn (2015)
Marshall, Megan (2013-2014)
Martin, Kim (2015)
Masters, Janice (2007, 2011-2015)
Matthews, Cyndey (2012-2014)
McAtee, Alex (2011-2014)
McCormick, Becky (2003-2005)
McCoy, Tobi (2003-2007)
McCurdy, Carrie (2015)
McGrath, Allie (2011-2013)
McHenry, Michelle (2005)
McIntosh, Tera (2007, 2011-2013)
McLuckie, Mandy (2003)
McPherson, Madeline (2011-2012)
Medley, Christina (2012)
Melodia, Jessica (2015)
Meredith, Louann (2013)
Mershimer, Nikki (2003)
Miller, Maria (2004)
Miller, Vicki (2012)
Mills, Ashley (2007)
Montgomery, Tia (2005-2007, 2013-2015)
Moody, Jen (2003-2007)
Murphy, Teri (2005, 2007)
Myers, Kerri (2004-2005)
Nacin, Cindy (2003)
Natale, Stacey (2006)
Nelko, Jessica (2012-2015)
Nelson, Melissa (2005-2006)
Neuber, Michelle (2012-2013)
New, Deanna (2011-2015)
Nickens, Ava (2006-2007)
Niedermeyer, Kaitlain (2011-2015)
Niedermeyer, Sarah (2013-2015)
Nissel, Jan (2004-2007)
Nocito, Joei (2012-2015)
O'Connell, Mary (2007)
O'Farrell, Tanya (2005-2006)
Ogunlesi, Rhonda (2013)
Olinzock, Remy (2015)
Osselborn, Sonya (2011-2014)
O'Toole, Briana (2006-2007)
Owen, Rachel (2013)
Peary-Rahm, Katie (2011)
Peffer, Cathy Lee (2012)

Continued on next page

Pittsburgh Passion Player Register (continued)

Peters, Michelle (2015)
Pirce, Taiha (2013)
Pletcher, Alicia (2014)
Pleva, Eden (2003-2007)
Prentice, Kara (2005-2007, 2011-2015)
Preston, Tanea (2011)
Price, Lindsay (2005)
Ragins, Necla (2015)
Rankin, Felicia (2005-2006)
Read, Sue (2012-2014)
Reasey, Emily (2012)
Reblock, Kim (2005, 2007)
Redney, Samantha (2014)
Reed, Jennifer (2014)
Rembisz, Justine (2012)
Reynolds, Gabby (2015)
Reynolds, Jacqueline (2012-2013)
Riley, Valerie (2013-2014)
Rizzo, Val (2011-2013)
Roberts, Cynthia (2013)
Roberts, Laurie (2006-2007)
Rodriguez, Yolanda (2013)
Roeschenthaler, Rochelle (2012-2013)
Rogers, Trumane (2007, 2011-2012)
Rojtas, Tina (2011-2013)
Rouse, Shawna (2011-2012)
Rowles, Ambra (2014)
Ruzicka, Kristen (2011-2013)
Sainovich, Katrina "Katie" (2013-2014)
Salzman, Kristie (2007)
Sanchez, Debbie (2011)
Scalo, Christina (2005-2006)
Schultz, Ruth (2012)
Scialabba, Nicole (2007)
Sciulli, Jess (2015)
Scott, Nikina (2014)
Shearer, Whitney (2011)
Shrawn, Ashley (2014)
Silvestri, Kristan (2005)
Simeone, Sam (2012-2015)
Skinkis, Diane (2004-2005)
Slater, Maria (2007)
Smith, Jenn (2003-2005)
Snyder, Candice (2013)
Sopko, Heather (2012)
Spencer-Bey, Tammy (2011-2015)
Stanek, Lorraine (2011-2013)
Steele, Nicole (2011)
Steffee, Kayla (2011-2013)
Sterling, Desiree (2011-2013)
Stiles, Lorri (2007)
Stoner, Amy (2003)
Stoner, Kelly (2003-2007)
Strawn, Ashley (2015)
Sullivan, Kate (2003-2007, 2011-2015)
Suprano, Jenine (2007)
Sylvestri, Kristan (2006)
Symmonds, Jen (2006-2007)
Taylor, Brittany (2013, 2015)
Taylor, Denise (2015)
Thomas, Rae (2013, 2015)
Thompson, Monica (2007)
Timmerman, Suzanne (2003)
Tinklepaugh, Shelby (2011)
Toal, Rachel (2005)
Tolomeo, Angela (2005)
Torba, Kristi (2011-2012)
Truitt, Krissy (2013)
Varelas, Priscilla (2005-2007)
Vasquez, Sharon (2007, 2011-2015)
Victor, Shelley (2011-2014)
Vivian, Brittany (2006)
Waha, Casey (2011-2013)
Wain, Shelley (2003)
Walker, Jessica (2006-2007)
Walker, Letitia (2012-2013)
Wallace, Rachel (2006)
Walters, Alexis (2013)
Walton, Wilma (2005-2007)
Warner, JoJo (2003, 2005-2007, 2011)
Washington, Cindy (2013-2015)
White, Sonita (2011)
Wilkerson, Ceree (2015)
Wilkerson, Michelle (2005-2006)
Williams, Letitia (2007)
Williams, Monica (2013-2015)
Wofford, Kweilin (2012-2013)
Wojdowski, Rachel (2011-2015)
Woods, Paris (2015)
Yates, Deanne (2005)
Yeck, Melissa (2003, 2005-2007)
Yoder, Lori (2003)
Young, Jamisha (2012)
Young, Sarah (2005, 2007, 2011-2012)
Zahn, Chelsea (2015)
Zavolta, Renee (2011)
Zeunges, Jordan (2012-2014)
Zoelle, Shelley (2006-2007)
Zubovic, Kim (2005-2007, 2011-2015)

Portland Fighting Fillies

Year	League	Name	W	L	Conference	Division	DF	PR
2010	WFA	Portland Fighting Fillies	8	2	American	North Pacific	1	Q
2011	WFA	Portland Fighting Fillies	4	6	American	Northwest	1	Q
2012	WFA	Portland Fighting Fillies	4	3	American	Division 14 (Pacific Northwest)	2	--
2013	WFA	Portland Fighting Fillies	4	3	American	Division 10 (Pacific Northwest)	3	--
2014	WFA	Portland Fighting Fillies	3	6	American	Northwest	5	W
2015	WFA	Portland Fighting Fillies	1	7	American	Pacific Northwest	5	--
		Total	24	27				

Based in: Portland, OR
Notes: Announced 2016 merger with Portland Shockwave to become Portland Fighting Shockwave

Date	H/A	Opponent	Result			
4/10/2010		Ventura Black Widows	W	74	6	I
4/17/2010	A	Central Cal War Angels	W	26	21	
4/24/2010	H	Utah Blitz	W	30	0	
5/1/2010	H	Central Cal War Angels	W	19	8	
5/8/2010	A	Utah Blitz	W	14	7	
5/22/2010	A	Ventura Black Widows	W	42	0	I
6/5/2010	A	Las Vegas Showgirlz	L	6	17	
6/12/2010	A	Utah Blitz	W	18	10	
6/19/2010	H	Central Cal War Angels	W	16	14	
6/26/2010	A	Las Vegas Showgirlz	L	6	34	Q
4/2/2011	A	Seattle Majestics	L	0	14	I
4/9/2011	A	Bay Area Bandits	L	0	36	
4/16/2011	H	Utah Blitz	W	6	0	
4/30/2011	A	Spokane Scorn	W	12	0	
5/7/2011	H	Bay Area Bandits	L	0	36	
5/14/2011	H	Spokane Scorn	W	22	12	
6/4/2011	A	Utah Blitz	L	0	8	
6/11/2011	A	Central Cal War Angels	L	0	60	
6/18/2011	H	Spokane Scorn	W	1	0	
6/25/2011	A	Bay Area Bandits	L	0	39	Q
4/14/2012	A	Bay Area Bandits	L	6	33	
4/28/2012	A	Utah Jynx	L	13	20	
5/5/2012	H	Utah Blitz	W	26	14	
5/12/2012	H	Valley Vipers	W	42	0	
5/19/2012	H	Utah Blitz	W	22	0	
6/2/2012	H	Utah Jynx	L	13	33	
6/16/2012	A	Utah Blitz	W	27	6	

Continued on next page

Portland Fighting Fillies Game-By-Game Results (continued)

Date	H/A	Opponent	W/L	PF	PA		Date	H/A	Opponent	W/L	PF	PA	
4/6/2013	H	Tacoma Trauma	W	42	0		5/17/2014	H	Seattle Majestics	L	14	42	
4/13/2013	H	Seattle Majestics	L	0	34		5/31/2014	A	Seattle Majestics	L	3	48	
5/4/2013	H	Everett Reign	W	16	6		6/7/2014	H	Tacoma Trauma	W	57	0	
5/11/2013	A	Tacoma Trauma	W	33	14		6/14/2014	A	Central Cal War Angels	L	0	44	W
5/18/2013	A	Utah Blitz	W	33	14								
5/25/2013	H	Portland Shockwave	L	0	18		4/11/2015	H	Seattle Majestics	L	0	20	
6/8/2013	A	Everett Reign	L	13	14		4/18/2015	A	Everett Reign	L	13	18	
							4/25/2015	A	Seattle Majestics	L	6	56	
4/5/2014	H	Utah Blitz	W	37	0		5/2/2015	A	Tacoma Trauma	L	10	20	
4/12/2014	H	Portland Shockwave	L	14	20		5/16/2015	A	Portland Shockwave	L	17	20	
4/19/2014	A	Tacoma Trauma	W	21	0		5/23/2015	H	Tacoma Trauma	L	13	28	
4/26/2014	A	Everett Reign	L	7	8		5/30/2015	H	Utah Blitz	W	49	22	
5/10/2014	A	Portland Shockwave	L	16	36		6/6/2015	H	Portland Shockwave	L	12	30	

Portland Fighting Fillies Player Register (2010-2015)

Aguirre, Andrea (2010)
Aliimatafitafi, Ruby (2014-2015)
Aliimatafitafi, Stephanie (2014-2015)
Allen, Melanie (2012-2013)
Alton, Jessica (2015)
Asahniiruff, Nikia (2015)
Bacastow, Kelsea (2015)
Ball, Nevi (2015)
Barron, Haelynn (2011)
Bissell, Terina (2010, 2014)
Boga, Shay (2013)
Boyd, Heather (2011)
Brajcich, Jenna (2012-2013)
Brown, Monica (2014)
Cantu, Jessica Yates (2012)
Chee, Rebekah (2013)
Chiong, Rhea (2014)
Craig, Chelsea (2010-2011)
Custis, Holly (2010-2014)
Derry, Michelle (2013)
Dinu, Andreea (2012)
Diurba, Erin (2011)
Dixon, Tori (2015)
Doolittle, Sonya (2013-2015)
Dunsire, Cassie (2011-2015)
Dunsire, Nikki (2015)
Elliott, Lisa (2010-2011, 2014-2015)
Ellis, Tamara (2010-2011)
Ferchland, Nikki (2013-2014)
Fial, Tamsyn (2014-2015)
Fisher, Karla (2010-2011)
Gallucci, Julaine (2010)
Genter, Aimee (2010)
Gerdes, Jessica (2010-2015)
Giavia, Chrissy (2013)
Graham, A.J. (2014-2015)
Green, Barbara (2010)
Grundy, Tiffany (2012-2013)
Harms, Lauren (2012)
Harris, Monique (2014)
Henneman, Jamie (2015)
Herbert, Ollie (2012)
Herzog, Katie (2014-2015)
Holness, Tracy-Ann (2015)
Householder, Chelsea (2012)
Hulslander, Alyssa (2014)
Janousek, Ronnie (2013)
Johnson, Christina (2010-2012)
Johnson, Jayne (2013)
Kali, Wendi (2010)
Kienborts, Kristi (2010-2011)
Kindig, Gretchen (2012)
King, Gwendolyn (2015)
Kondziela, Ashley (2011-2014)
La Vine, Kristen (2012)
LaDuke, Tori (2014-2015)
Landgraver, Meri (2015)
Little, Tyree (2013-2014)
Lopez-Redford, Tori (2010-2015)
Maddox, Angie (2012-2013)
Maier, Kadence (2013)
Malone, Sarah (2014-2015)
Martin, Crissy (2013)
Martzall, Christina (2010-2012)
Mason, Emily (2013)
Mathis, Autumn (2014-2015)
McAtee, Christy (2010-2013)
McLawhorn, Jenny (2015)
Meisner, Krystal (2010)
Miklos, Anne Marie (2011)
Miller, Courtney (2011)
Miller, Erin (2014-2015)
Mitchell, Latasha (2013-2014)
Muncy, Teresa (2014)
Noah, Teresa (2015)
Odowick, Jody (2013)
Osborn, Julia (2012)
Partridge, Joann (2013)
Perkins, Amanda (2012)
Petrie, Hollie (2014-2015)
Pugh, Nora (2010)
Punteney, Christi (2011-2012)
Riding, Jeanette (2010-2012)
Robideau, Lauren (2012)
Robinette, Shalynn (2010)
Rossos, Elizabeth (2011)
Ruff, Nikia Asahnii (2013-2014)
Salazar, Katie (2010-2014)
Sand, Tracy (2010-2011)
Sanford, Rebecca (2015)
Santistevan, Yolanda (2014)
Sato, Jennifer (2010-2011)
Schade, Shaffryn (2010-2011)
Schmidt, Laura (2010-2011)
Serricchio, Maru (2013)
Shipley, Mariah (2010-2011)
Steadman, Terra (2015)
Steiger, Roni (2015)
Sweeney, Maddy (2011)
Talbutt, Tori (2014-2015)
Teters, Jasmine (2010-2013)
Torres, Anetra (2012-2013)
Treasure, Amy (2011-2012)
Tucker, Alicia (2010)
Vanden Berg, Megan (2012)
Wachter, Nevi (2014)
Wentzek, Jessica (2014)
Westover, Carley (2014-2015)
Wheeler, Wendy (2010-2012)
Wilson, C.J. (2015)
Wilson, Christina (2014)
Wilson, Shannon (2010-2012, 2014)
Wisecarver, Asia (2011-2012)
Wood, Heather (2014-2015)
Wood, Tina (2015)
Wright, Asa (2015)
Yates, Jessica (2010-2011)

Portland Shockwave

Year	League	Name	W	L	T	Conference	Division	DF	PR
2002	WSFL	Portland Shockwave	4	3	0	--	--	2	C
2003	IWFL	Portland Shockwave	5	4	1	Western	Pacific Northwest	3	--
2004	IWFL	Portland Shockwave	3	5	0	Western	Pacific Northwest	3	--
2005	IWFL	Portland Shockwave	3	7	0	Western	Pacific Northwest	3	--
2006	IWFL	Portland Shockwave	7	2	0	Western	Pacific Northwest	1	S
2007	IWFL	Portland Shockwave	6	2	0	Western	Pacific Northwest	2	--
2008	IWFL	Portland Shockwave	5	3	0	Western	Pacific Northwest	3	--
2009	IWFL	Portland Shockwave	4	4	0	Western	Pacific Northwest	2	--
2010	IWFL	Portland Shockwave	6	2	0	Western	Pacific West	3	--
2011	IWFL	Portland Shockwave	6	3	0	Western	Pacific Northwest	1	S
2012	IWFL	Portland Shockwave	5	6	0	Western	Pacific Northwest	2	BC
2013	WFA	Portland Shockwave	5	3	0	American	Division 10 (Pacific Northwest)	2	W
2014	WFA	Portland Shockwave	6	2	0	American	Northwest	2	--
2015	WFA	Portland Shockwave	4	3	0	American	Pacific Northwest	3	--
		Total	**69**	**49**	**1**				

Based in: Portland, OR
Neutral site: Round Rock, TX (N)
Notes: Announced 2016 merger with Portland Fighting Fillies to become Portland Fighting Shockwave

Date	H/A	Opponent	Result			
4/21/2002		Oregon Unforgiven	W	42	0	
4/27/2002		Boise Xtreme	W	18	12	*
5/4/2002		Tacoma Majestics	L	6	20	
5/12/2002		Oregon Unforgiven	W	63	0	
5/18/2002		Boise Xtreme	W	20	13	
6/1/2002		Tacoma Majestics	L	12	15	
6/15/2002		Tacoma Majestics	L	0	14	C
3/22/2003	H	Boise Xtreme	W	32	8	
3/29/2003	H	Corvallis Pride	T	26	26	
4/5/2003	A	Eugene Edge	W	6	0	
4/12/2003	A	Oakland Banshees	L	14	16	
4/26/2003	H	Tacoma Majestics	L	0	12	
5/3/2003	A	Boise Xtreme	W	34	12	
5/10/2003	A	Corvallis Pride	L	14	20	
5/17/2003	H	Eugene Edge	W	18	14	
5/31/2003	H	Oakland Banshees	W	32	12	
6/7/2003	A	Tacoma Majestics	L	20	28	
4/3/2004	A	Eugene Edge	L	0	6	
4/17/2004	H	Corvallis Pride	L	7	20	
5/1/2004	H	Tacoma Majestics	L	28	34	
5/8/2004	H	Boise Xtreme	W	21	14	
5/15/2004	H	Eugene Edge	W	28	13	
5/22/2004	A	Corvallis Pride	L	14	28	
6/5/2004	A	Tacoma Majestics	L	0	27	
6/12/2004	A	Boise Xtreme	W	21	14	
4/2/2005	A	Tacoma Majestics	L	6	38	
4/9/2005	H	Boise Xtreme	W	52	7	
4/16/2005	A	Corvallis Pride	L	7	9	
4/23/2005	A	Eugene Edge	W	39	20	
4/30/2005	H	Tacoma Majestics	L	24	39	
5/14/2005	H	Eugene Edge	W	42	12	
5/21/2005	H	Sacramento Sirens	L	13	56	
5/28/2005	H	Corvallis Pride	L	14	20	
6/4/2005	A	Tacoma Majestics	L	0	42	
6/11/2005	A	Sacramento Sirens	L	7	41	
4/29/2006	A	Redding Rage	W	39	0	
5/13/2006	H	Eugene Edge	W	48	0	
5/20/2006	H	Seattle Majestics	W	32	6	
5/27/2006	A	Seattle Majestics	W	19	13	
6/3/2006	H	Corvallis Pride	W	6	0	
6/10/2006	H	Eugene Edge	W	55	0	
6/17/2006	A	Santa Rosa Scorchers	L	27	33	
6/24/2006	A	Eugene Edge	W	46	14	
7/8/2006	H	Sacramento Sirens	L	27	37	S
4/28/2007	H	Seattle Majestics	L	2	19	
5/12/2007	A	Corvallis Pride	W	28	7	
5/19/2007	A	Redding Rage	W	46	0	
5/26/2007	H	Corvallis Pride	W	9	6	
6/2/2007	A	Seattle Majestics	L	13	33	
6/9/2007	A	Redding Rage	W	43	0	
6/23/2007	H	Redding Rage	W	60	0	
6/30/2007	H	Corvallis Pride	W	41	6	
4/12/2008	A	Seattle Majestics	L	0	14	
4/19/2008	A	Corvallis Pride	L	6	28	
5/3/2008	H	Sacramento Sirens	W	26	6	
5/10/2008	H	Santa Rosa Scorchers	W	33	12	
5/24/2008	A	Sacramento Sirens	L	9	13	
5/31/2008	H	Redding Rage	W	45	7	
6/7/2008	H	Corvallis Pride	W	23	20	
6/14/2008	A	Oakland Banshees	W	9	2	
4/18/2009	H	Seattle Majestics	L	7	20	
4/25/2009	A	Corvallis Pride	W	20	7	
5/2/2009	H	Oakland Banshees	W	1	0	N
5/9/2009	A	Seattle Majestics	L	7	35	
5/16/2009	H	Corvallis Pride	W	33	0	
5/23/2009	H	Seattle Majestics	L	12	14	
6/6/2009	A	Seattle Majestics	L	7	20	
6/13/2009	A	Corvallis Pride	W	26	6	
4/10/2010	A	Bay Area Bandits	L	0	13	
4/17/2010	A	Modesto Maniax	W	22	8	
4/24/2010	H	Seattle Majestics	W	22	7	
5/1/2010	A	Seattle Majestics	W	20	14	
5/8/2010	H	Los Angeles Amazons	L	0	17	
5/15/2010	H	Seattle Majestics	W	20	14	
5/29/2010	A	Los Angeles Amazons	W	20	6	
6/5/2010	H	California Quake	W	7	6	

Continued on next page

Portland Shockwave Game-By-Game Results (continued)

Date	H/A	Opponent	W/L	PF	PA	Note
4/9/2011	H	Seattle Majestics	W	21	0	
4/16/2011	A	California Quake	L	0	28	
4/30/2011	H	Southern California Breakers	W	40	6	
5/7/2011	A	Seattle Majestics	W	12	6	*
5/14/2011	A	Tucson Monsoon	W	64	0	
5/21/2011	H	Modesto Maniax	W	20	6	
5/28/2011	A	Sacramento Sirens	L	12	16	
6/11/2011	H	Sacramento Sirens	W	9	0	
6/25/2011	A	Wisconsin Warriors	L	12	13	S
4/14/2012	A	Modesto Maniax	L	0	22	
4/21/2012	H	Seattle Majestics	L	7	13	
4/28/2012	A	Sacramento Sirens	L	6	22	
5/12/2012	H	Seattle Majestics	L	6	14	
5/19/2012	H	Sacramento Sirens	L	20	41	
5/26/2012	A	Tucson Monsoon	W	27	6	
6/2/2012	H	Modesto Maniax	W	1	0	
6/16/2012		Seattle Majestics	W	13	7	
6/30/2012	H	California Quake	W	1	0	BQ
7/14/2012		Madison Cougars	W	43	6	BS
7/28/2012	N	Carolina Phoenix	L	0	27	BC
4/6/2013	A	Everett Reign	W	16	3	
4/27/2013	A	Seattle Majestics	L	7	27	
5/4/2013	H	Utah Blitz	W	25	7	
5/11/2013	H	Everett Reign	W	44	8	
5/18/2013	A	Tacoma Trauma	W	32	0	
5/25/2013	A	Portland Fighting Fillies	W	18	0	
6/1/2013	H	Seattle Majestics	L	14	26	
6/15/2013	A	Central Cal War Angels	L	0	34	W
4/5/2014	H	Seattle Majestics	L	12	33	
4/12/2014	A	Portland Fighting Fillies	W	20	14	
4/26/2014	A	Tacoma Trauma	W	28	8	
5/3/2014	A	Seattle Majestics	L	0	32	
5/10/2014	H	Portland Fighting Fillies	W	36	16	
5/24/2014	A	Utah Blitz	W	30	18	
5/31/2014	H	Everett Reign	W	8	3	
6/7/2014	H	Utah Blitz	W	32	0	
4/11/2015	H	Everett Reign	W	47	20	
4/18/2015	H	Tacoma Trauma	L	18	39	
5/2/2015	A	Everett Reign	W	21	8	
5/16/2015	H	Portland Fighting Fillies	W	20	17	
5/30/2015	A	Seattle Majestics	L	0	32	
6/6/2015	A	Portland Fighting Fillies	W	30	12	
6/13/2015	H	Seattle Majestics	L	6	44	

Portland Shockwave Player Register (2013-2015)

Albrook, Melodie (2015)
Bailey, Katelyn (2013-2015)
Bair, Tess (2013-2015)
Barcroft, Desiree (2015)
Barton, Mysty (2014)
Bissell, Terina (2015)
Brisson, Rebecca (2013-2014)
Castro, Jenna (2013-2015)
Dawson, Rebecca (2013-2015)
Dumistrescu, Oana (2015)
Duren, Keky (2014-2015)
Edmiston, Ashly (2013-2015)
Edmiston, Kathy (2013-2015)
Ferguson, Veronica (2013-2015)
Fisken, Emily (2015)
Freel, Heather (2013-2014)
Griggs, Breana (2015)
Hahn, Kim (2013)
Hand, Christie (2013)
Hinkle, Leah (2013-2015)
Johnson, Pat (2013, 2015)
Krugel, Tara (2013-2015)
Landers, Chris (2015)
Loebach, Heidi (2013-2015)
McKenna, Rachel (2014-2015)
Mohr, Hilleary (2013)
Peters, Chelsey (2015)
Petty, Michelle (2013-2014)
Phillips, Krysta (2013)
Pineda, Milly (2013-2014)
Rallings, Coco (2013-2015)
Reeder, Josephine (2014)
Reyna, Liani (2013-2015)
Roberts, Amy (2013-2015)
Rowe, Jessica (2015)
Santistevan, Yolanda (2015)
Sargent, Charise (2013)
Sharp, Angela (2013)
Shepherd, Simone (2013-2014)
Sherman, Katherine (2014)
Siekawitch, Maylee (2015)
Simmons, Frayanna (2014)
Skrudland, Kelsey (2015)
Smith, Analise (2013-2014)
Steinmueller, Crystal (2014-2015)
Thomas, Shecola (2014-2015)
Torres, Michelle (2014-2015)
Vanden Berg, Megan (2014-2015)
Vilarino, Nicole (2013-2015)
White, Heather (2013)

Pueblo Pythons

Year	League	Name	W	L	Conference	Division	DF	PR
2002	UWFL	Pueblo Pythons	4	1	--	--	--	--

Based in: Pueblo, CO

Date	Opponent	W/L	PF	PA
4/21/2002	Tri-City Mustangs	W	35	6
4/28/2002	Cheyenne Dust Devils	W	6	0
5/5/2002	Grand Valley Vipers	W	29	8
5/12/2002	Denver Foxes	L	19	42
5/26/2002	Colorado Springs Koalas	W	48	46

Franchise Game-By-Game Records, 1999-2015

Redding Rage

Year	League		Name	W	L	Conference	Division	DF	PR
2004	IWFL	X	Redding Rage	0	4	--	--	--	--
2005	IWFL		Redding Rage	3	7	Western	Pacific Southwest	5	--
2006	IWFL		Redding Rage	2	6	Western	Pacific Southwest	4	--
2007	IWFL		Redding Rage	0	8	Western	Pacific Northwest	4	--
2008	IWFL		Redding Rage	0	8	Western	Pacific Northwest	5	--
2009	IWFL	X	Redding Rage	0	1	--	--	--	--
			Total	5	34				

Based in: Redding, CA
Notes: Forfeited entire 2009 season

Date	H/A	Opponent	Result		
4/17/2004	A	Santa Rosa Scorchers	L	0	43
4/24/2004	H	Oakland Banshees	L	6	54
5/8/2004	A	Oakland Banshees	L	0	68
6/12/2004	H	San Francisco Stingrayz	L	0	92
4/2/2005	H	Eugene Edge	W	20	19
4/9/2005	H	Tucson Wildfire	W	41	0
4/16/2005	A	California Quake	L	0	33
4/23/2005	A	Oakland Banshees	L	7	32
4/30/2005	A	Eugene Edge	L	0	7
5/14/2005	H	Santa Rosa Scorchers	L	13	21
5/21/2005	H	Oakland Banshees	L	12	18
5/28/2005	A	Sacramento Sirens	L	10	53
6/11/2005	A	Tucson Wildfire	W	36	0
6/18/2005	A	Santa Rosa Scorchers	L	0	26
4/29/2006	H	Portland Shockwave	L	0	39
5/6/2006	H	Corvallis Pride	L	8	28
5/20/2006	A	Corvallis Pride	L	6	30
5/27/2006	H	Eugene Edge	W	20	6
6/3/2006	A	Santa Rosa Scorchers	L	0	52
6/10/2006	A	Sacramento Sirens	L	6	53
6/17/2006	H	Oakland Banshees	W	12	7
6/24/2006	A	Seattle Majestics	L	6	48
4/28/2007	H	Corvallis Pride	L	0	46
5/12/2007	A	Seattle Majestics	L	0	61
5/19/2007	H	Portland Shockwave	L	0	46
6/2/2007	H	Santa Rosa Scorchers	L	0	55
6/9/2007	H	Portland Shockwave	L	0	43
6/16/2007	A	Corvallis Pride	L	0	42
6/23/2007	A	Portland Shockwave	L	0	60
6/30/2007	A	California Quake	L	24	50
4/12/2008	H	Corvallis Pride	L	0	46
4/19/2008	H	Santa Rosa Scorchers	L	0	28
4/26/2008	A	Seattle Majestics	L	12	36
5/3/2008	A	Santa Rosa Scorchers	L	6	60
5/17/2008	H	Southern California Breakers	L	6	14
5/24/2008	A	Corvallis Pride	L	0	21
5/31/2008	A	Portland Shockwave	L	7	45
6/14/2008	H	Sacramento Sirens	L	0	34
5/23/2009	A	Corvallis Pride	L	0	1

Reno Rattlers

Year	League		Name	W	L	Conference	Division	DF	PR
2011	IWFL	X	Reno Rattlers	2	2	--	--	--	--

Based in: Reno, NV

Date	H/A	Opponent	Result			
4/23/2011		Nor Cal Red Hawks	L	6	13	E
5/7/2011	H	Ventura Black Widows	L	6	83	I
5/14/2011	H	Nor Cal Red Hawks	W	19	6	
5/21/2011	A	Ventura Black Widows	W	20	8	I

Richmond Spirit

Year	League	Name	W	L	Conference	Division	DF	PR
2007	NWFA	Richmond Spirit	0	7	Northern	South	3	--

Based in: Richmond, VA
Notes: Non-existent team

Date	H/A	Opponent	Result		
4/28/2007	H	Central PA Vipers	L	0	1
5/5/2007	A	Baltimore Burn	L	0	1
5/12/2007	H	East Tennessee Rhythm	L	0	1
5/19/2007	A	Central PA Vipers	L	0	1
5/26/2007	H	Philadelphia Phoenix	L	0	1
6/9/2007	A	East Tennessee Rhythm	L	0	1
6/16/2007	H	Baltimore Burn	L	0	1

River City Raiders

Year	League	Name	W	L	Conference	Division	DF	PR
2010	WSFL	River City Raiders	0	6	--	--	--	--

Based in: Omaha, NE

5/8/2010	H	Topeka Mudcats	L	0	1		5/29/2010	A	Topeka Mudcats	L	0	27
5/15/2010	A	Kansas City Storm	L	0	66		6/12/2010	H	Kansas City Storm	L	8	52
5/22/2010	H	Kansas City Storm	L	15	21		7/10/2010	A	Topeka Mudcats	L	6	27

River City Raiderz

Year	League		Name	W	L	Conference	Division	DF	PR
2013	W8FL	X	River City Raiderz	0	3	--	--	--	--

Based in: Portland, OR

| 3/30/2013 | A | Everett Reign | L | 0 | 50 | IE | | 6/1/2013 | A | Sacramento Sirens | L | 0 | 1 | I |
| 4/20/2013 | H | Ventura Black Widows | L | 8 | 44 | | | | | | | | | |

Roanoke Revenge

Year	League	Name	W	L	Conference	Division	DF	PR
2004	NWFA	Roanoke Revenge	1	7	Northern	Mid-Atlantic	5	--

Based in: Roanoke, VA

4/3/2004	A	D.C. Divas	L	0	70		5/15/2004	H	D.C. Divas	L	0	70
4/17/2004	H	Erie Illusion	W	12	6		5/22/2004	A	Baltimore Burn	L	6	56
4/24/2004	H	Pittsburgh Passion	L	26	34		5/29/2004	H	Baltimore Burn	L	8	24
5/8/2004	A	Pittsburgh Passion	L	0	49		6/5/2004	A	Erie Illusion	L	0	21

Partial Roanoke Revenge Player Register (2004)

Baker, Hilary (2004)
Harmon, Amanda (2004)
Harrison, Michelle (2004)
Hawley, Michelle (2004)
Johnson, Ashaki (2004)
Jones, Elisha (2004)
Nelson, Bridget (2004)
Smith, Becky (2004)
Teubert, Lori (2004)

Rochester Raptors

Year	League		Name	W	L	Conference	Division	DF	PR
2002	NWFA	X	Rochester Raptors	1	6	--	--	--	--
2003	NWFA		Rochester Raptors	0	9	Northern	Northern	5	--
2004	NWFA		Rochester Raptors	1	7	Northern	Northern	5	--
			Total	2	22				

Based in: Rochester, NY
Notes: Succeeded by WPFL's Empire State Roar

3/23/2002		Baltimore Burn	L	0	20	E		5/10/2003	A	Philadelphia Phoenix	L	0	51
3/30/2002		Baltimore Burn	L	0	39	E		5/17/2003	A	Maine Freeze	L	7	15
4/6/2002	A	D.C. Divas	L	0	46	E		5/24/2003	H	Maine Freeze	L	6	19
4/13/2002		Maine Freeze	W	12	0	E		6/14/2003	H	Philadelphia Phoenix	L	0	34
4/20/2002		Maine Freeze	L	7	13	E							
5/11/2002		Connecticut Crush	L	0	19			4/3/2004	A	Maine Freeze	L	8	12
6/8/2002		Connecticut Crush	L	6	34			4/17/2004	H	Massachusetts Mutiny	L	0	56
								4/24/2004		Massachusetts Mutiny	L	0	40
3/29/2003		Maine Freeze	L	0	7	E		5/1/2004	H	Connecticut Crush	L	0	34
4/12/2003	A	Massachusetts Mutiny	L	0	48			5/8/2004	A	Connecticut Crush	L	0	62
4/19/2003	H	Connecticut Crush	L	6	49			5/15/2004	H	Philadelphia Phoenix	L	0	48
4/26/2003	H	Massachusetts Mutiny	L	0	47			5/29/2004	H	Maine Freeze	W	22	14
5/3/2003	A	Connecticut Crush	L	0	49			6/12/2004	A	Philadelphia Phoenix	L	0	58

Partial Rochester Raptors Player Register (2004)

Dunn, Jessica (2004)
Kobos, Jane (2004)
Landahl, Lisa (2004)
Lincourt, Hillary (2004)
Long, Amie (2004)
Odit, Kelly (2004)
Rietmann, Dawn (2004)
Wilkie, Michele (2004)

Rockford Riveters

Year	League	Name	W	L	Conference	Division	DF	PR
2012	IWFL	Rockford Riveters	0	8	Western	Midwest	5	--
2013	IWFL	Rockford Riveters	0	8	Western	Midwest	5	--
		Total	0	16				

Based in: Rockford, IL
Notes: Forfeited entire 2013 season

Date	H/A	Opponent	Result	Score		Date	H/A	Opponent	Result	Score
4/14/2012	A	Minnesota Vixen	L	0 44		4/27/2013	A	Minnesota Vixen	L	0 1
4/21/2012	H	Iowa Crush	L	0 66		5/11/2013	H	Iowa Crush	L	0 1
4/28/2012	H	Wisconsin Warriors	L	0 74		5/18/2013	H	Wisconsin Warriors	L	0 1
5/5/2012	H	Minnesota Vixen	L	0 32		5/25/2013	H	Madison Blaze	L	0 1
5/19/2012	A	Iowa Crush	L	6 58		6/1/2013	H	Minnesota Vixen	L	0 1
5/26/2012	A	Madison Cougars	L	0 39		6/8/2013	A	Iowa Crush	L	0 1
6/2/2012	A	Wisconsin Warriors	L	0 54		6/22/2013	A	Wisconsin Warriors	L	0 1
6/16/2012		Madison Cougars	L	0 49		6/29/2013	A	Madison Blaze	L	0 1

Rocky Mountain Thunderkatz

Year	League		Name	W	L	Conference	Division	DF	PR
2012	IWFL	X	Colorado Sting	1	6	--	--	--	B
2013	IWFL	X	Rocky Mountain Thunderkatz	4	3	--	--	--	--
2014	WSFL		Rocky Mountain Thunderkatz	1	5	Western	--	4	--
2015	IWFL		Rocky Mountain Thunderkatz	4	3	Western	Mountain West	2	Q
			Total	10	17				

Based in: Colorado Springs, CO   **Neutral site:** Round Rock, TX (N)

Date	H/A	Opponent	Result	Score	Note		Date	H/A	Opponent	Result	Score	Note
4/21/2012	A	Phoenix Phantomz	L	0 75			3/30/2014	H	Mile High Blaze	L	0 40	
5/19/2012	H	Phoenix Phantomz	L	0 37			4/5/2014	H	Utah Falconz	L	0 58	I
5/26/2012	H	Salt City Arch Angels	W	1 0	I		4/12/2014	A	Utah Jynx	L	0 44	I
6/2/2012	H	Arlington Impact	L	2 14			5/17/2014	A	Kansas City Storm	W	28 0	I
6/9/2012		Arlington Impact	L	0 30			5/31/2014	A	Utah Falconz	L	0 63	I
6/16/2012	A	Utah Jynx	L	0 1	I		6/14/2014	A	Mile High Blaze	L	0 34	
7/28/2012	N	Carolina Queens	L	0 18	B							
							4/4/2015	A	Utah Falconz	L	0 32	E
3/30/2013	A	Utah Jynx	L	18 55	IE		4/18/2015	H	Colorado Freeze	W	21 0	
4/27/2013	A	Phoenix Phantomz	L	16 50			4/25/2015	A	Colorado Springs Voodoo	W	58 6	
5/11/2013	H	Kansas City Storm	W	88 0	I		5/9/2015	A	Nebraska Stampede	L	6 49	
5/18/2013	H	Tucson Monsoon	W	20 7			5/16/2015	H	Colorado Freeze	W	18 6	
6/1/2013	H	Phoenix Phantomz	L	6 67			5/30/2015	H	Mile High Blaze	W	18 13	I
6/29/2013	A	Tucson Monsoon	W	14 7			6/20/2015	A	Utah Falconz	L	0 63	Q
7/13/2013	A	Kansas City Storm	W	6 0	I***							

Rocky Mountain Thunderkatz Player Register (2015)

Anderson, Tamika (2015)
Baker, Justina (2015)
Benson, Toni (2015)
Brokaw, Alicia (2015)
Decosta, Maricel (2015)
Dixon, Ronnie (2015)
Foe, Ashley (2015)
Fox, Sherrice (2015)
Gonzales, Alisa (2015)
Gustafson, Tiffany (2015)
Gutierrez, Laura (2015)
Hawk, Cathy (2015)
Johnson, Hannah (2015)
Johnson, Shanice (2015)
Jorgenson, Abby (2015)
King, Kylee (2015)
Landi, Andrea (2015)
Quintana, Brea (2015)
Renee, Briana (2015)
Riley, Jess (2015)
Sloan, Sarah (2015)
Smith, Cierra (2015)
Vellejo, Salina (2015)
Watson, Ritta (2015)

Rose City Wildcats

Year	League	Name	W	L	Conference	Division	DF	PR
2001	WAFL	Rose City Wildcats	0	8	Pacific	Northwest	3	--

Based in: Portland, OR

10/27/2001	A	Seattle Warbirds	L	0	37		12/1/2001	A	Seattle Warbirds	L	0	34
11/3/2001	A	Sacramento Sirens	L	22	43		12/8/2001	H	California Quake	L	8	20
11/10/2001	H	Seattle Warbirds	L	8	28		12/15/2001	H	Seattle Warbirds	L	0	12
11/17/2001	H	Sacramento Sirens	L	16	35		1/5/2002	H	Hawaii Legends	L	8	16

Sacramento Sirens

Year	League	Name	W	L	T	Conference	Division	DF	PR
2001	WAFL	Sacramento Sirens	7	3	1	Pacific	Central	1	S
2002	WAFC	Sacramento Sirens	11	0	0	Northern	--	1	LC
2003	IWFL	Sacramento Sirens	12	0	0	Western	Pacific Southwest	1	**NC**
2004	IWFL	Sacramento Sirens	10	1	0	Western	Pacific West	1	**NC**
2005	IWFL	Sacramento Sirens	13	0	0	Western	Pacific Southwest	1	**NC**
2006	IWFL	Sacramento Sirens	7	3	0	Western	Pacific Southwest	1	CC
2007	IWFL	Sacramento Sirens	8	2	0	Western	Pacific Southwest	1	CC
2008	IWFL	Sacramento Sirens	4	4	0	Western	Pacific Northwest	4	--
2009	IWFL	Sacramento Sirens	5	3	0	Western	Pacific Southwest	2	--
2010	IWFL	Sacramento Sirens	10	1	0	Western	Pacific West	1	C
2011	IWFL	Sacramento Sirens	5	4	0	Western	Pacific West	1	S
2012	IWFL	Sacramento Sirens	9	2	0	Western	Pacific West	1	C
2013	WFA	Sacramento Sirens	5	4	0	American	Division 12 (North Pacific)	2	Q
2015	IWFL	Sacramento Sirens	8	1	0	Western	Pacific West	1	S
		Total	**114**	**28**	**1**				

Based in: Sacramento, CA   **Neutral sites:** Manchester, NH (N1); Round Rock, TX (N2)

10/27/2001	A	San Francisco Tsunami	W	29	0		3/8/2003	H	Oakland Banshees	W	64	14	
11/3/2001	H	Rose City Wildcats	W	43	22		3/15/2003	A	San Francisco Stingrayz	W	62	26	
11/10/2001	A	Oakland Banshees	W	42	0		3/22/2003	H	Santa Rosa Scorchers	W	67	6	
11/17/2001	A	Rose City Wildcats	W	35	16		4/5/2003	A	Oakland Banshees	W	67	8	
12/8/2001	A	Oakland Banshees	W	28	8		4/12/2003	A	Santa Rosa Scorchers	W	42	6	
12/15/2001	H	San Francisco Tsunami	W	57	18		4/26/2003	H	San Francisco Stingrayz	W	68	22	
12/22/2001	H	Seattle Warbirds	T	0	0	*	5/3/2003	H	San Diego Sea Catz	W	81	0	
12/29/2001	A	San Diego Sunfire	W	21	12		5/10/2003	H	California Quake	W	67	14	
1/12/2002	A	Seattle Warbirds	L	14	17	**	5/31/2003	A	California Quake	W	65	21	
1/19/2002	H	Arizona Caliente	L	15	18		6/14/2003	H	Tacoma Majestics	W	45	0	S
1/26/2002	A	California Quake	L	13	40	S	6/28/2003	H	Chicago Force	W	47	7	CC
							7/12/2003	A	New York Sharks	W	41	30	C
8/3/2002		Oakland Banshees	W	41	20	E							
9/7/2002	H	San Francisco Stingrayz	W	45	0		4/3/2004	H	Santa Rosa Scorchers	W	68	0	
9/28/2002	H	Santa Rosa Scorchers	W	62	0		4/17/2004	H	California Quake	W	69	0	
10/5/2002	A	California Quake	W	52	19		5/1/2004	H	San Diego Sea Catz	W	68	0	
10/12/2002	A	Santa Rosa Scorchers	W	36	9		5/8/2004	A	San Diego Sea Catz	W	62	6	
10/19/2002	H	Oakland Banshees	W	53	32		5/15/2004	A	San Francisco Stingrayz	L	20	36	
11/6/2002	H	Pacific Blast	W	47	26		5/29/2004	H	San Francisco Stingrayz	W	36	30	
11/10/2002	A	Oakland Banshees	W	55	0		6/5/2004	A	Santa Rosa Scorchers	W	33	0	
11/16/2002	A	San Francisco Stingrayz	W	48	12		6/12/2004	A	California Quake	W	1	0	
11/23/2002	H	Oakland Banshees	W	69	0	CC	6/26/2004	A	Tacoma Majestics	W	49	20	S
12/7/2002	H	Arizona Caliente	W	59	20	C	7/10/2004	H	Corvallis Pride	W	43	8	CC
							7/24/2004	H	New York Sharks	W	29	27	C

Continued on next page

Sacramento Sirens Game-By-Game Results (continued)

Date	H/A	Opponent	Result		
4/2/2005	H	Oakland Banshees	W 43	0	
4/9/2005	H	California Quake	W 72	0	
4/16/2005	A	Santa Rosa Scorchers	W 68	0	
4/23/2005	H	So Cal Bandits	W 115	0	
5/7/2005	A	Oakland Banshees	W 62	12	
5/14/2005	A	California Quake	W 52	21	
5/21/2005	A	Portland Shockwave	W 56	13	
5/28/2005	H	Redding Rage	W 53	10	
6/11/2005	H	Portland Shockwave	W 41	7	
6/18/2005	A	So Cal Bandits	W 1	0	
7/9/2005	H	Corvallis Pride	W 43	22	S
7/23/2005	H	Tacoma Majestics	W 36	14	CC
8/6/2005	N1	Atlanta Xplosion	W 9	7	C
4/29/2006	H	Atlanta Xplosion	L 20	67	
5/6/2006	H	Seattle Majestics	L 21	22	
5/13/2006	A	Santa Rosa Scorchers	W 56	14	
5/20/2006	H	California Quake	W 53	19	
6/3/2006	A	California Quake	W 53	0	
6/10/2006	H	Redding Rage	W 53	6	
6/17/2006	A	Seattle Majestics	W 42	20	
6/24/2006	A	Oakland Banshees	W 1	0	
7/8/2006	A	Portland Shockwave	W 37	27	S
7/15/2006	A	Detroit Demolition	L 20	52	CC
4/28/2007	A	Santa Rosa Scorchers	W 13	6	
5/5/2007	H	Tucson Monsoon	W 48	16	
5/12/2007	H	California Quake	W 27	6	
5/19/2007	A	Tucson Monsoon	W 32	20	
6/2/2007	A	California Quake	W 24	15	
6/9/2007	H	Santa Rosa Scorchers	L 0	6	
6/16/2007	H	California Quake	W 39	17	
6/30/2007	A	Santa Rosa Scorchers	W 25	0	
7/14/2007	A	Seattle Majestics	W 29	12	S
7/28/2007	A	Detroit Demolition	L 0	49	CC
4/12/2008	H	Santa Rosa Scorchers	W 41	27	
4/19/2008	H	Seattle Majestics	L 7	14	
4/26/2008	H	Corvallis Pride	L 13	33	
5/3/2008	A	Portland Shockwave	L 6	26	
5/17/2008	A	Seattle Majestics	L 0	27	
5/24/2008	H	Portland Shockwave	W 13	9	
5/31/2008	A	Las Vegas Showgirlz	W 21	14	
6/14/2008	A	Redding Rage	W 34	0	
4/11/2009	A	Modesto Maniax	W 71	0	
4/18/2009	H	California Quake	W 46	0	
4/25/2009	A	Seattle Majestics	L 8	33	
5/2/2009	H	Corvallis Pride	W 39	0	
5/9/2009	A	California Quake	W 34	14	
5/16/2009	H	Seattle Majestics	L 20	21	
5/30/2009	A	Corvallis Pride	W 48	0	
6/13/2009	H	Los Angeles Amazons	L 19	20	
4/3/2010	H	Bay Area Bandits	W 33	13	
4/10/2010	A	Seattle Majestics	W 35	14	
4/24/2010	A	Los Angeles Amazons	W 27	26	
5/1/2010	A	Modesto Maniax	W 68	0	
5/15/2010	A	Modesto Maniax	W 55	0	
5/22/2010	H	Los Angeles Amazons	W 10	6	
5/29/2010	H	Tucson Monsoon	W 73	0	
6/5/2010	H	Modesto Maniax	W 60	0	
6/12/2010	H	So Cal Scorpions	W 60	26	S
7/10/2010	H	Dallas Diamonds	W 45	43	CC
7/24/2010	N2	Boston Militia	L 7	39	C
4/9/2011	A	Modesto Maniax	W 21	14	
4/16/2011	H	Utah Jynx	W 45	20	I
4/30/2011	H	California Quake	L 13	42	
5/7/2011	A	California Quake	L 13	30	
5/14/2011	A	Seattle Majestics	W 15	0	
5/28/2011	H	Portland Shockwave	W 16	12	
6/4/2011	H	Modesto Maniax	W 34	7	
6/11/2011	A	Portland Shockwave	L 0	9	
6/25/2011	A	California Quake	L 19	22	S
4/21/2012	A	Modesto Maniax	W 20	6	
4/28/2012	H	Portland Shockwave	W 22	6	
5/5/2012	A	Seattle Majestics	L 7	14	
5/12/2012	H	Modesto Maniax	W 31	6	
5/19/2012	A	Portland Shockwave	W 41	20	
6/2/2012	H	Seattle Majestics	W 24	0	
6/9/2012	A	Tucson Monsoon	W 60	7	
6/16/2012		Phoenix Phantomz	W 62	22	
6/30/2012		Seattle Majestics	W 7	0	S
7/14/2012		Wisconsin Warriors	W 45	12	CC
7/28/2012	N2	Montreal Blitz	L 27	28	C
4/13/2013	H	Central Cal War Angels	L 6	24	
4/27/2013	H	San Diego Surge	W 40	18	
5/4/2013	A	Nevada Storm	W 61	8	I
5/11/2013	A	Seattle Majestics	L 21	42	
5/25/2013	H	Nevada Storm	W 45	0	I
6/1/2013	H	River City Raiderz	W 1	0	I
6/8/2013	A	Central Cal War Angels	L 6	55	
6/15/2013	H	Pacific Warriors	W 25	6	W
6/22/2013	A	San Diego Surge	L 13	39	Q
4/11/2015	A	Nevada Storm	W 41	6	
4/18/2015	H	California Quake	W 49	0	
4/25/2015	H	Phoenix Phantomz	W 41	0	
5/2/2015	A	North County Stars	W 59	0	
5/9/2015	A	California Quake	W 47	0	
5/16/2015	H	North County Stars	W 60	0	
5/30/2015	H	Nevada Storm	W 54	7	
6/13/2015	A	Phoenix Phantomz	W 21	18	
6/27/2015	A	Utah Falconz	L 0	61	S

Sacramento Sirens Player Register (2013, 2015)

Adamo, Chiara (2013, 2015)
Aldana, Lyn (2013)
Anderson, Sarah (2015)
Atkinson, Ashley (2013, 2015)
Axiak, Katherine (2015)
Baar, Brei (2013)
Bradshaw, Kimberly (2015)
Bryant, Mari (2015)
Clark, Erica (2013, 2015)
Dunnington, Chelsea (2013)
Ellis, A.J. (2015)
Fassler, Desirae (2013, 2015)
Giblin, Lisa (2013)
Gipson, Giannie (2013)
Hahn, Stephanie (2013)
Harris, Chantal (2013, 2015)
Jbeily, Samia (2013, 2015)
Khalil, Jessica (2015)
Kokura, Noriko (2013)
Koziura, Amy (2013)
Lewis, Tamisha (2013, 2015)
Machado, Michelle (2013, 2015)
McCombs, Melissa (2013, 2015)
McLemore, Ashley (2013, 2015)
Medinger, Christy (2013, 2015)
Milanese, Kristy (2013, 2015)
Nolan, Zionya (2013, 2015)
O'Leary, Caille (2015)
O'Neal, Nic (2013)
Otto, Morgan (2015)
Peterson, Holly (2013)
Reiff, Kaitlyn (2013)
Semrau, Kerry (2015)
Sheffield, Aisha (2015)
Trujillo, Maria (2015)

Continued on next page

Sacramento Sirens Player Register (continued)

Turner, Mariah (2013)
Valele, Siokapesi (2013)
Vierra, Alexis (2013, 2015)
Ward, Violet (2015)
Wheeler, Alyssa (2013)
Wiederhold, Michelle (2013, 2015)
Williams, Kortnee (2015)
Wolfe, Trewdy (2013)

Salt City Arch Angels

Year	League	Name	W	L	Conference	Division	DF	PR
2012	W8FL	Salt City Arch Angels	0	3	Western	--	3	--

Based in: Salt Lake City, UT

4/14/2012	A	Ventura Black Widows	L	12	48		5/26/2012	A	Colorado Sting	L	0	1	I
4/21/2012	A	Nevada Storm	L	20	80							

San Antonio Regulators

Year	League		Name	W	L	Conference	Division	DF	PR
2013	IWFL	X	San Antonio Regulators	3	5	--	--	--	B
2014	IWFL	X	San Antonio Regulators	1	6	--	--	--	--
2015	IWFL	X	San Antonio Regulators	2	5	--	--	--	B
			Total	6	16				

Based in: San Antonio, TX **Neutral sites:** Round Rock, TX (N1); Rock Hill, SC (N2)

5/4/2013	H	DFW Xtreme	W	44	12		5/17/2014	A	Houston Energy	L	0	1	
5/11/2013	H	Houston Energy	L	0	56		5/24/2014	H	Austin Outlaws	L	0	1	I
5/18/2013	A	DFW Xtreme	W	6	0		5/31/2014	H	Arlington Impact	L	0	1	
6/1/2013	H	Arlington Impact	L	0	28		6/14/2014	H	Houston Energy	L	0	1	
6/8/2013	A	Houston Energy	L	0	35								
6/15/2013	A	Arlington Impact	L	0	36		4/11/2015	H	New Orleans Krewe	W	14	0	
6/22/2013	A	DFW Xtreme	W	1	0		4/25/2015	A	Houston Energy	L	0	14	
8/2/2013	N1	Carolina Queens	L	14	28	B	5/2/2015	A	Austin Yellow Jackets	L	14	40	
							5/16/2015	A	New Orleans Krewe	W	42	6	
4/12/2014	H	Arlington Impact	L	0	61		6/6/2015	H	Houston Energy	L	14	53	
4/19/2014	H	Tucson Monsoon	W	12	0		6/13/2015	H	Austin Yellow Jackets	L	8	22	
5/10/2014	A	Houston Power	L	0	42	I	7/24/2015	N2	Detroit Pride	L	22	24	B

San Antonio Regulators Player Register (2015)

Arriaga, Valerie (2015)
Chladek, Joanie (2015)
Esparza, Veronica (2015)
Facey, Marissa (2015)
Ferguson, Alana (2015)
Ferguson, Tyneshia (2015)
Garcia, Alma (2015)
Garcia, Laura (2015)
Guzman, D.J. (2015)
Hardaway, Kristen (2015)
Hardaway, Lashan (2015)
Hernandez, Darian (2015)
Johnson, Billette (2015)
Kirk, Mo (2015)
Knight, Tracee (2015)
Lett, Brianne (2015)
Mata, Alex (2015)
Meyer, Amy (2015)
Patino, Kristina (2015)
Salinas, Claudia (2015)
Samuels, Kartazz (2015)
Sandidge, Emelie (2015)
Scott, Katie (2015)
Shepard, Brenda (2015)
Smock, Danielle (2015)
White, Tiffany (2015)
Wolfe, Adriann (2015)

San Diego Nitrous

Year	League		Name	W	L	Conference	Division	DF	PR
2002	WAFC	X	San Diego Nitrous	0	4	Southern	--	--	--

Based in: San Diego, CA
Notes: Succeeded by IWFL's San Diego Sea Catz

9/28/2002	A	Arizona Caliente	L	0	56		10/26/2002	H	California Quake	L	0	1
10/12/2002	A	California Quake	L	0	41		11/16/2002	H	Arizona Caliente	L	0	1

Franchise Game-By-Game Records, 1999-2015

San Diego Sea Catz

Year	League		Name	W	L	Conference	Division	DF	PR
2003	IWFL	X	San Diego Sea Catz	0	4	--	--	--	--
2004	IWFL		San Diego Sea Catz	3	5	Western	Pacific Southwest	2	--
			Total	**3**	**9**				

Based in: San Diego, CA
Notes: Preceded by WAFC's San Diego Nitrous

4/12/2003	A	California Quake	L	0	43		4/24/2004	H	California Quake	W	20	13
5/3/2003	A	Sacramento Sirens	L	0	81		5/1/2004	A	Sacramento Sirens	L	0	68
5/10/2003	A	Oakland Banshees	L	0	58		5/8/2004	H	Sacramento Sirens	L	6	62
5/25/2003	A	Chicago Force	L	0	55		5/15/2004	H	Oakland Banshees	L	0	42
							5/29/2004	A	California Quake	W	18	0
4/3/2004	H	San Francisco Stingrayz	L	0	94		6/5/2004	A	San Francisco Stingrayz	W	1	0
4/17/2004	A	Oakland Banshees	L	0	40							

San Diego Sting

Year	League	Name	W	L	Conference	Division	DF	PR
2010	WFA	San Diego Sting	0	8	American	South Pacific	4	--
2011	WFA	San Diego Sting	1	7	American	Southwest	4	--
2012	WFA	San Diego Sting	5	3	American	Division 15 (Pacific West)	2	--
2013	WFA	San Diego Sting	2	6	American	Division 13 (South Pacific)	4	--
		Total	**8**	**24**				

Based in: San Diego, CA
Notes: Succeeded by IWFL's North County Stars

4/10/2010	A	Central Cal War Angels	L	18	26		4/14/2012	A	Pacific Warriors	L	0	48
4/17/2010	A	Pacific Warriors	L	0	41		4/28/2012	H	Los Angeles Amazons	W	8	0
4/24/2010	H	Arizona Assassins	L	0	52		5/5/2012	H	Las Vegas Showgirlz	L	7	30
5/8/2010	A	Arizona Assassins	L	0	42		5/12/2012	A	Los Angeles Amazons	W	14	0
5/15/2010	H	Pacific Warriors	L	0	1		5/19/2012	A	Arizona Assassins	W	13	0
5/22/2010	H	Central Cal War Angels	L	0	1		5/26/2012	H	West Coast Lightning	W	13	8
6/5/2010	A	Arizona Assassins	L	6	24		6/9/2012	A	Los Angeles Amazons	W	7	0
6/12/2010	H	Central Cal War Angels	L	0	1		6/16/2012	A	Las Vegas Showgirlz	L	14	24
4/2/2011	H	So Cal Scorpions	L	0	16		4/13/2013	A	Las Vegas Showgirlz	L	19	48
4/9/2011	H	Pacific Warriors	L	0	40		4/20/2013	H	West Coast Lightning	L	0	17
4/16/2011	H	Silver State Legacy	L	0	42		4/27/2013	A	Arizona Assassins	W	28	0
4/30/2011	A	Arizona Assassins	L	6	47		5/4/2013	A	West Coast Lightning	L	0	13
5/7/2011	A	So Cal Scorpions	L	6	12		5/11/2013	A	Pacific Warriors	L	8	36
5/21/2011	A	Silver State Legacy	L	0	35		5/18/2013	H	Central Cal War Angels	L	0	42
6/4/2011	H	Arizona Assassins	L	6	41		6/1/2013	H	San Diego Surge	L	0	49
6/11/2011	A	Las Vegas Showgirlz	W	20	6		6/8/2013	H	Arizona Assassins	W	22	0

San Diego Sting Player Register (2010-2013)

Acosta, Anggie (2013)
Acosta, Layla (2010)
Alden, Cathy (2010)
Anderson, Michelle (2013)
Ballew, Kara (2011)
Barba, Cecilia (2013)
Barba, Cristina (2013)
Barr, Rosa (2011)
Behlman, Brigitte (2013)
Blunt, Taylor (2010-2011)
Blythe, Oprah (2011-2013)
Blythe, Shellmadean (2011)
Boyce, Kellyann (2010)
Brinkman, Jane (2011)
Cabugao, Tracy (2012)
Cash, Marie (2010)
Castle, Desirae (2012)
Cavalcanti, Marcela (2013)
Chavez, Carisa (2012)
Clarke, Brandy (2011)
Daniel, Katelyn (2010-2013)
DeVilla, Melissa (2011)
Duran, Sasha (2011)
Edge-Lobsinger, Tamara (2012)
Fletcher, Tracy (2010)
Foster, Natasha (2012-2013)
Gaitan, Angie (2010)
Green, Akilah (2011-2013)
Haney, Michelle (2012-2013)
Harris, Alayna (2013)
Hernandez, Christine "Chris" (2012-2013)
Hernandez, Kassandra (2011)
Herrera, Wendy (2011)
Hubbell, Leslie (2012)
Jacobucci, Sage (2010-2011)
January, Tamara (2012-2013)
Jones, Ella (2010-2011)
Jones, Monica "Mo" (2012-2013)
Jose, Josie (2013)
Laie, Alofa (2010-2012)
Laie, Sina (2010-2011)
Lara, Lesly (2011)
Lawless, Ashley (2011)
LeMasters, Mary (2012-2013)

Continued on next page

San Diego Sting Player Register (continued)

Lologo, Celia (2012)
Louis, LaDana (2012)
Mangrum, Nicole (2013)
Manzanares, Christina (2012-2013)
McClain, Patricia (2011-2013)
McKinney, Stephanie (2010)
Meneray, Jennifer (2011)
Miller-Perdue, Ilene (2012)
Mills, Bobbi (2010)
Moak, Terese (2013)
Moreno, Yadira (2011-2012)
Morin, Katrina (2011)
Nerey, Annette (2010-2012)
Owens, Caryn (2010)

Parcel, Leigh (2011)
Perez, Laura (2013)
Quest, Aniko "Nikki" (2010)
Ricca, Jessica (2013)
Rios, Jasmin (2013)
Ripley, Jessica (2011)
Roman, Nicole (2013)
Roney, Kimie (2010)
Sadri, Mariam (2013)
Schwartz, Jessica (2011)
Sjursen, Lauren (2011)
Stephany, Trish (2010)
Swatzell, Rachelle (2013)
Temple, Ashley (2011)

Thomas, Denise (2012)
Thorsch, Kelly (2010)
Toppings, Trish (2011)
Torres, Cassandra (2011)
Ulukita, Annaleii (2010-2013)
Valencia, Daisy (2013)
Vandereb, Amara (2010)
Villalobos, Janet (2010)
Washington, Sharne (2010-2011)
Wiley-Gatewood, Sade (2010)
Wilt, Ashlie (2012)
Wright, Autumn (2011)
Wright, Christine (2010-2013)
Zarty-Moore, Cheree (2010-2012)

San Diego Sunfire

Year	League	Name	W	L	Conference	Division	DF	PR
2001	WAFL	San Diego Sunfire	5	5	Pacific	South	3	--
2002	AFWL	San Diego Sunfire	9	1	--	--	1	C
2003	WPFL	San Diego Sunfire	5	5	American	West	4	--
		Total	19	11				

Based in: San Diego, CA

Date	H/A	Opponent	W/L	PF	PA	
11/3/2001	H	Arizona Caliente	W	14	12	
11/10/2001	A	Los Angeles Lasers	W	12	6	
11/17/2001	H	Hawaii Legends	W	20	10	
11/24/2001	A	Arizona Caliente	W	24	7	
12/1/2001	H	California Quake	L	14	20	
12/15/2001	A	Arizona Caliente	L	10	12	
12/22/2001	H	Los Angeles Lasers	W	28	13	
12/29/2001	H	Sacramento Sirens	L	12	21	
1/5/2002	A	California Quake	L	8	24	
1/13/2002	A	Hawaii Legends	L	29	57	
9/21/2002	H	San Francisco Tsunami	W	27	0	
9/28/2002	A	Los Angeles Lasers	W	17	14	*
10/5/2002	H	Long Beach Aftershock	W	34	28	
10/12/2002	A	Arizona Titans	W	42	6	
10/26/2002	A	Long Beach Aftershock	W	27	8	
11/2/2002	H	Los Angeles Lasers	W	33	26	
11/9/2002	H	Arizona Titans	W	30	0	
11/23/2002	A	San Francisco Tsunami	W	1	0	
12/7/2002	H	Arizona Titans	W	55	0	CC
12/14/2002	H	Long Beach Aftershock	L	7	12	C
8/3/2003	A	Long Beach Aftershock	L	6	18	
8/16/2003	H	Long Beach Aftershock	L	13	34	
8/23/2003	H	Los Angeles Amazons	W	20	12	
8/30/2003	A	Arizona Caliente	L	20	38	
9/6/2003	A	Houston Energy	L	22	62	
9/13/2003	H	So Cal Scorpions	W	36	14	
9/27/2003	H	Arizona Knighthawks	W	50	0	
10/4/2003	A	Los Angeles Amazons	W	58	14	
10/11/2003	A	Arizona Knighthawks	W	20	14	
10/18/2003	H	Arizona Caliente	L	24	41	

San Diego Surge

Year	League	Name	W	L	Conference	Division	DF	PR
2011	WFA	San Diego Surge	11	1	American	South Pacific	1	C
2012	WFA	San Diego Surge	12	0	American	Division 17 (South Pacific)	1	**NC**
2013	WFA	San Diego Surge	9	2	American	Division 13 (South Pacific)	1	S
2014	WFA	San Diego Surge	11	1	American	Pacific South	1	C
2015	WFA	San Diego Surge	9	2	American	Pacific West	1	CC
		Total	52	6				

Based in: San Diego, CA   **Neutral sites:** Bedford, TX (N1); Pittsburgh, PA (N2); Chicago, IL (N3)

San Diego Surge Game-By-Game Results

Date	H/A	Opponent	Result	PF	PA	Note
4/9/2011	H	Las Vegas Showgirlz	W	84	0	
4/16/2011	A	Los Angeles Amazons	W	74	0	
4/30/2011	H	Pacific Warriors	W	82	0	
5/7/2011	H	Arizona Assassins	W	55	20	
5/14/2011	H	Silver State Legacy	W	48	15	
5/21/2011	A	Las Vegas Showgirlz	W	55	0	
6/4/2011	A	Bay Area Bandits	W	42	13	
6/11/2011	A	Pacific Warriors	W	43	6	
6/25/2011	H	Silver State Legacy	W	41	7	Q
7/9/2011	H	Bay Area Bandits	W	36	0	S
7/16/2011	H	Dallas Diamonds	W	48	20	CC
7/30/2011	N1	Boston Militia	L	19	34	C
4/21/2012	H	Silver State Legacy	W	42	0	
4/28/2012	A	Arizona Assassins	W	64	0	
5/5/2012	A	Pacific Warriors	W	69	12	
5/12/2012	A	West Coast Lightning	W	55	0	
5/19/2012	H	Bay Area Bandits	W	57	0	
6/2/2012	A	Silver State Legacy	W	48	0	
6/9/2012	H	Arizona Assassins	W	62	0	
6/16/2012	H	Pacific Warriors	W	49	0	
6/30/2012	H	Pacific Warriors	W	48	0	Q
7/7/2012	H	Bay Area Bandits	W	42	7	S
7/21/2012	H	Dallas Diamonds	W	56	29	CC
8/4/2012	N2	Chicago Force	W	40	36	C
4/6/2013	A	Pacific Warriors	W	28	8	
4/13/2013	H	West Coast Lightning	W	51	0	
4/20/2013	H	Arizona Assassins	W	69	6	
4/27/2013	A	Sacramento Sirens	L	18	40	
5/11/2013	A	West Coast Lightning	W	63	0	
5/18/2013	H	Las Vegas Showgirlz	W	32	22	
6/1/2013	A	San Diego Sting	W	49	0	
6/8/2013	H	Pacific Warriors	W	41	12	
6/15/2013	H	Las Vegas Showgirlz	W	78	14	W
6/22/2013	H	Sacramento Sirens	W	39	13	Q
7/13/2013	A	Central Cal War Angels	L	14	40	S
4/5/2014	H	Las Vegas Showgirlz	W	59	6	
4/12/2014	A	West Coast Lightning	W	62	0	
4/19/2014	A	Arizona Assassins	W	68	0	
4/26/2014	H	West Coast Lightning	W	1	0	
5/3/2014	A	Nevada Storm	W	56	6	
5/10/2014	H	Arizona Assassins	W	101	0	
5/17/2014	H	Central Cal War Angels	W	64	0	
6/7/2014	A	Central Cal War Angels	W	35	6	
6/21/2014	H	Las Vegas Showgirlz	W	48	16	Q
7/5/2014	A	Seattle Majestics	W	36	20	S
7/19/2014	H	Kansas City Titans	W	59	14	CC
8/3/2014	N3	Boston Militia	L	34	69	C
4/11/2015	H	Pacific Warriors	W	73	31	
4/18/2015	A	Sin City Sun Devils	W	54	12	
5/2/2015	H	Arizona Assassins	W	90	6	
5/9/2015	H	Central Cal War Angels	W	66	26	
5/16/2015	A	West Coast Lightning	W	65	6	
5/30/2015	H	Ventura County Wolfpack	W	1	0	
6/6/2015	A	Pacific Warriors	W	48	8	
6/13/2015	A	Central Cal War Angels	L	14	23	
6/27/2015	H	Central Cal War Angels	W	27	7	Q
7/11/2015	H	Seattle Majestics	W	57	27	S
7/25/2015	A	Dallas Elite	L	28	56	CC

San Diego Surge Player Register (2011-2015)

Alexander, Traci (2011)
Arnaud, Linda (2011)
Bandstra, Angie (2015)
Benjamin, Joniece (2012, 2015)
Betts, Kassie (2015)
Brick, Cassey (2012-2013)
Buckholz, Rylie (2012)
Bush, Adriana (2015)
Bush, Sheree (2012)
Cable, Jessica (2011-2015)
Carrillo, Christina (2011-12, 2014-15)
Chambers, Eboni (2012-2015)
Chriss, Erica (2013-2014)
Clark, Kaycee (2011-2012, 2014-2015)
Cotton, Brittany (2011, 2013)
Cruz, Carmen (2011-2012, 2014)
Davis, Lauren (2014-2015)
Deal, Amy (2011)
Dickinson, Ashley (2012)
Duran, Amanda (2013)
Edwards, Joniece (2011)
Elliott, Courtney (2012)
Elton-Hanlon, Crystal (2011-2012, 2015)
Estes, Taylor (2015)
Evans, Alexandria "Alex" (2014-2015)
Floto, Liz (2011-2013)
Ford, Meghan (2015)
Freeman, Alicia (2014-2015)
Gallegos, Melissa (2011-12, 2014-15)
Garza, Elizabeth (2011)
Gates, Renisha (2011-2012)
Glenn, Alexis (2014)
Goggins, Aleeza (2011-2013)
Gonzalez, Tiffany (2013)
Grant, Andrea (2011, 2013)
Graves, Cilena (2011)
Grier, Keshona (2013)
Guidry, Deana (2011-2012, 2014-2015)
Hanlon, Wendy (2011-2012)
Hartman, Kenna (2012)
Henry, Kim (2014-2015)
Hicks, Katie (2012-2013)
Holland, Quelsie (2014)
Hood, Lindsay (2011)
Horton, Amanda (2013)
Hubbell, Leslie (2011)
Humphrey, Tiffany (2014)
Jackson, Samantha (2014)
Jaso, Regina (2011-2012)
Javelet, Jessica (2011-2012)
Johnson, Natasha (2012-2015)
Kyle, Lea (2012)
Lamie, Rebekah (2015)
Lawson, Kalilah (2011-2012)
Lehnhoff, Jennell (2012)
Lilo, Felicia (2012)
Love, Kristin (2012)
Magnuson, Kelly (2011-2012)
Manning, Dominique (2012)
Manning, Lanika (2014-2015)
Marin, Diana (2013)
Martin, Jessica (2014)
Martin, Kimberly (2012)
Martin, Knengi (2012-2015)
Moody, Ashley (2011-2012, 2014-2015)
Moore, Lorie (2012, 2014)
Morin, Alexis (2014-2015)
Mosley, Cilena Tanaya (2011-2012)
Mucullough, Meghan (2013)
Nava-Esparza, Dora (2011)
Orr, Melissa (2013, 2015)
Ott, Katie (2014-2015)
Paaluhi, Tanya (2012, 2014-2015)
Palmer, Yessica (2011)
Parker, Stephanie (2012)
Patterson, Tanisha (2013)
Perez, Yaritza (2011)
Peterson, Holly (2011-2012, 2014)
Philpott, Tarrah (2012)
Plogger, Karen (2015)
Quest, Aniko "Nikki" (2011-2015)
Reyes, Duece (2011)
Roberson, Sonfre (2014-2015)
Rodriguez, Maria (2012-2013)
Ruffo, Aisha Nicole (2011-2012)
Sablan, Jordaine (2013-2014)
Sanford, Anna (2012-2013)
Schroth, Jana (2011-2012)
Scott, Nachelle (2015)
Shenault, LaQueena (2013)
Snyder, Alexis (2014-2015)
Springer, Jessica (2015)
Starks, Michelle (2011-2012)
Stokes, Crystal (2011-2014)
Strother, Melissa (2012-2015)
Sumpter, Banea (2015)
Suzuki, Hiroko "Betty" (2012, 2014)
Tafao, Mauri (2011)
Taylor, Stephanie (2014-2015)
Thomson, Chandra (2011)
Tomlinson, Stephanie (2012)

Continued on next page

San Diego Surge Player Register (continued)

Tyler, Mercedes (2015)	Webb, Christina (2015)	Williamson, Taiesha (2014)
Vaeao, Lelatasio (2012)	Weimann, Desiree (2011-2012)	Wilson, Sabrina (2011-2012)
Van Natten, Carol (2011)	Westman, Whitney (2013-2014)	Wong, Tracy (2011-2014)
Vasques, Courtney (2011-2012)	White, Jennifer "Jen" (2011-2015)	Zaky, Monique (2012)
Vega, Yasmine (2014)	White, Samantha (2011-2012)	Zito, Sarah (2015)
Walter, Katrina (2011-2015)	Williams, Kesia (2014-2015)	
Walters, Brittney (2012)	Williams, Shinobu (2011-2015)	

San Francisco Stingrayz

Year	League		Name	W	L	Conference	Division	DF	PR
2002	WAFC		San Francisco Stingrayz	0	11	Northern	--	4	--
2003	IWFL	X	San Francisco Stingrayz	4	2	--	--	--	--
2004	IWFL		San Francisco Stingrayz	6	2	Western	Pacific West	2	--
2005	WPFL	X	San Francisco Stingrayz	0	4	--	--	--	--
			Total	**10**	**19**				

Based in: San Francisco, CA

6/29/2002		Santa Rosa Scorchers	L	0	52	E	4/3/2004	A	San Diego Sea Catz	W	94	0
7/20/2002		Santa Rosa Scorchers	L	0	6	E	4/24/2004	H	Santa Rosa Scorchers	W	86	0
8/10/2002		Oakland Banshees	L	6	26	E	5/1/2004	H	California Quake	W	1	0
9/7/2002	A	Sacramento Sirens	L	0	45		5/15/2004	H	Sacramento Sirens	W	36	20
9/28/2002	H	Oakland Banshees	L	14	34		5/22/2004	A	Santa Rosa Scorchers	W	34	19
10/2/2002	H	Pacific Blast	L	12	22		5/29/2004	A	Sacramento Sirens	L	30	36
10/5/2002	A	Arizona Caliente	L	0	27		6/5/2004	H	San Diego Sea Catz	L	0	1
10/26/2002	A	Oakland Banshees	L	20	24		6/12/2004	A	Redding Rage	W	92	0
11/2/2002	A	California Quake	L	0	1							
11/9/2002	H	Pacific Blast	L	0	1		7/30/2005	H	Los Angeles Amazons	L	0	42
11/16/2002	H	Sacramento Sirens	L	12	48		8/6/2005	A	Los Angeles Amazons	L	0	1
							8/13/2005	H	New York Dazzles	L	8	27
3/15/2003	H	Sacramento Sirens	L	26	62		8/27/2005	H	Long Beach Aftershock	L	0	1
3/29/2003	A	Santa Rosa Scorchers	W	42	13							
4/26/2003	A	Sacramento Sirens	L	22	68							
5/3/2003	H	Oakland Banshees	W	1	0							
5/10/2003	H	Santa Rosa Scorchers	W	50	0							
5/24/2003	A	California Quake	W	80	3							

San Francisco Tsunami

Year	League	Name	W	L	Conference	Division	DF	PR
2001	WAFL	San Francisco Tsunami	0	8	Pacific	Central	3	--
2002	AFWL	San Francisco Tsunami	1	7	--	--	5	--
		Total	**1**	**15**				

Based in: San Francisco, CA

10/27/2001	H	Sacramento Sirens	L	0	29		9/21/2002	A	San Diego Sunfire	L	0	27
11/17/2001	H	Oakland Banshees	L	14	34		10/5/2002	H	Los Angeles Lasers	L	6	48
11/24/2001	A	Oakland Banshees	L	6	34		10/12/2002	H	Long Beach Aftershock	L	0	46
12/8/2001	H	Seattle Warbirds	L	0	41		10/19/2002	H	Arizona Titans	W	1	0
12/15/2001	A	Sacramento Sirens	L	18	57		10/26/2002	A	Los Angeles Lasers	L	0	1
1/5/2002	H	Arizona Caliente	L	12	14		11/9/2002	A	Long Beach Aftershock	L	0	1
1/12/2002	A	Los Angeles Lasers	L	19	20		11/16/2002	A	Arizona Titans	L	0	1
1/19/2002	A	California Quake	L	6	36		11/23/2002	H	San Diego Sunfire	L	0	1

Santa Rosa Scorchers

Year	League		Name	W	L	Conference	Division	DF	PR
2002	WAFC		Santa Rosa Scorchers	3	5	Northern	--	3	--
2003	IWFL		Santa Rosa Scorchers	1	9	Western	Pacific Southwest	4	--
2004	IWFL		Santa Rosa Scorchers	2	6	Western	Pacific West	3	--
2005	IWFL		Santa Rosa Scorchers	7	3	Western	Pacific Southwest	2	--
2006	IWFL		Santa Rosa Scorchers	6	2	Western	Pacific Southwest	2	--
2007	IWFL		Santa Rosa Scorchers	5	3	Western	Pacific Southwest	2	--
2008	IWFL	X	Santa Rosa Scorchers	2	3	--	--	--	--
			Total	**26**	**31**				

Based in: Santa Rosa, CA

6/29/2002		San Francisco Stingrayz	W	52	0	E	4/2/2005	A	California Quake	L	6	17
7/20/2002		San Francisco Stingrayz	W	6	0	E	4/9/2005	A	Oakland Banshees	L	12	22
7/27/2002		Los Angeles Amazons	W	6	0	I	4/16/2005	H	Sacramento Sirens	L	0	68
9/8/2002	H	Oakland Banshees	L	6	31		4/23/2005	H	California Quake	W	14	0
9/14/2002		Los Angeles Amazons	L	13	14	I	5/7/2005	H	Boise Xtreme	W	20	6
9/21/2002	A	Oakland Banshees	L	14	20		5/14/2005	A	Redding Rage	W	21	13
9/28/2002	A	Sacramento Sirens	L	0	62		5/21/2005	H	So Cal Bandits	W	1	0
10/12/2002	H	Sacramento Sirens	L	9	36		5/28/2005	H	Oakland Banshees	W	32	20
							6/4/2005	A	Boise Xtreme	W	38	8
3/8/2003	H	California Quake	L	0	8		6/18/2005	H	Redding Rage	W	26	0
3/15/2003	A	Oakland Banshees	L	12	28							
3/22/2003	A	Sacramento Sirens	L	6	67		4/29/2006	H	California Quake	W	18	8
3/29/2003	H	San Francisco Stingrayz	L	13	42		5/13/2006	H	Sacramento Sirens	L	14	56
4/12/2003	H	Sacramento Sirens	L	6	42		5/20/2006	A	Eugene Edge	W	41	0
4/19/2003	H	Boise Xtreme	L	6	14		5/27/2006	A	California Quake	W	46	0
5/3/2003	A	California Quake	W	6	0		6/3/2006	H	Redding Rage	W	52	0
5/10/2003	A	San Francisco Stingrayz	L	0	50		6/10/2006	A	Tucson Monsoon	W	46	0
5/17/2003	H	Oakland Banshees	L	0	14		6/17/2006	H	Portland Shockwave	W	33	27
5/24/2003	A	Boise Xtreme	L	0	1		6/24/2006	A	Corvallis Pride	L	18	20
4/3/2004	A	Sacramento Sirens	L	0	68		4/28/2007	H	Sacramento Sirens	L	6	13
4/17/2004	H	Redding Rage	W	43	0		5/5/2007	H	California Quake	W	23	19
4/24/2004	A	San Francisco Stingrayz	L	0	86		5/12/2007	A	Tucson Monsoon	W	27	6
5/1/2004	H	Oakland Banshees	L	0	34		5/19/2007	A	California Quake	L	26	32 *
5/15/2004	A	California Quake	W	1	0		6/2/2007	A	Redding Rage	W	55	0
5/22/2004	H	San Francisco Stingrayz	L	19	34		6/9/2007	A	Sacramento Sirens	W	6	0
5/29/2004	A	Oakland Banshees	L	19	34		6/16/2007	H	Tucson Monsoon	W	58	6
6/5/2004	H	Sacramento Sirens	L	0	33		6/30/2007	H	Sacramento Sirens	L	0	25
							4/12/2008	A	Sacramento Sirens	L	27	41
							4/19/2008	A	Redding Rage	W	28	0
							5/3/2008	H	Redding Rage	W	60	6
							5/10/2008	A	Portland Shockwave	L	12	33
							5/17/2008	H	Corvallis Pride	L	6	18

Savannah Sabers

Year	League	Name	W	L	Conference	Division	DF	PR
2011	WFA	Savannah Sabers	1	7	National	Atlantic	3	--
2012	WFA	Savannah Sabers	5	3	National	Division 7 (Southeast)	2	--
2013	WFA	Savannah Sabers	3	6	National	Division 5 (Southeast)	2	W
2014	WFA	Savannah Sabers	0	8	National	Southeast	4	--
		Total	**9**	**24**				

Based in: Savannah, GA

Savannah Sabers Game-By-Game Results

Date	H/A	Opponent	Result	PF	PA		Date	H/A	Opponent	Result	PF	PA	
4/2/2011	H	Jacksonville Dixie Blues	L	6	52		4/6/2013	H	Tampa Bay Inferno	L	14	40	
4/9/2011	A	Orlando Anarchy	L	14	36		4/13/2013	A	Tennessee Train	W	28	20	
4/16/2011	A	Palm Beach Punishers	L	0	38		4/27/2013	A	Atlanta Phoenix	L	0	48	
5/7/2011	H	Carolina Raging Wolves	W	7	6		5/11/2013	A	Tennessee Train	L	16	34	
5/14/2011	A	Atlanta Heartbreakers	L	19	22		5/18/2013	H	Tallahassee Jewels	W	24	12	
5/21/2011	H	Palm Beach Punishers	L	0	35		5/25/2013	H	Atlanta Phoenix	L	18	56	
6/4/2011	A	Carolina Raging Wolves	L	13	32		6/1/2013	H	Tennessee Train	W	40	32	
6/11/2011	H	Atlanta Heartbreakers	L	25	28		6/8/2013	A	Atlanta Phoenix	L	0	64	
							6/15/2013	A	Miami Fury	L	0	1	W
4/14/2012	H	Palm Beach Punishers	W	33	28								
4/21/2012	A	Carolina Raging Wolves	W	28	0		4/5/2014	H	Tennessee Train	L	20	22	
4/28/2012	A	Atlanta Phoenix	L	13	57		4/12/2014	A	Tampa Bay Inferno	L	6	55	
5/12/2012	A	Tampa Bay Inferno	L	0	46		4/26/2014	A	Miami Fury	L	12	50	
5/19/2012	H	Carolina Raging Wolves	W	47	0		5/3/2014	H	Orlando Anarchy	L	14	20	
6/2/2012	A	Orlando Anarchy	W	34	20		5/10/2014	A	Atlanta Phoenix	L	6	56	
6/9/2012	H	Carolina Raging Wolves	W	41	14		5/17/2014	A	Tennessee Train	L	0	28	
6/16/2012	H	Atlanta Phoenix	L	14	41		5/31/2014	H	Daytona Breakers	L	22	41	
							6/7/2014	H	Jacksonville Dixie Blues	L	16	46	

Savannah Sabers Player Register (2012-2014)

Andrew, Deirdra (2012-2013)
Ash, Yolanda (2012-2013)
Blue, Teresa (2012-2014)
Booth, Jenny (2014)
Bostic, Chelsea (2013)
Bryant, Bri (2013)
Chandler, Jessica (2012)
Daniels, Lauren (2013)
Davis, Amber (2012)
Dean, Ashley (2012)
Fowler, Shadera (2013)
Glover, Ebony (2012-2013)
Grimsley, Jewelle "TeeJae" (2012-2013)
Harrison, Dai Dai (2012)
Herndon, Robin (2012)
Jackson, Monique (2013)
Kenty, Joy (2013)
Lowe, T. (2012)
McNair, Kadana (2013)
Merritt, Edy (2012)
Michels, Kiley (2014)
Middleton, Malika (2014)
Milton, Tania "Yella" (2012-2013)
Moody, Stevi (2014)
Moore, Dee Sade (2012)
Olson, Erica (2012-2013)
Pigneri, Andi (2012)
Pinkney, Trina (2012-2014)
Robinson, Kenaya (2012-2014)
Russell, Jenell (2012-2014)
Schaaf, Kyndal (2012)
Seabrook, Mika (2013-2014)
Smith, Brittney (2014)
Sosa, Edeline (2013-2014)
Taylor, Tabitha (2012-2013)
Taylor, Tiara (2013)
Terry, Tanya (2012-2014)
Thomas, Ericka (2012-2013)
Thomas, Sabrina (2014)
Thon, Angel (2012-2014)
Van Valkenburgh, Yessica (2013-2014)
Vasquez, Christina (2012)
Walker, Dominique (2013)
Washington, Thessa (2014)
Williams, CeeLo (2012)
Williams, Keisha (2012)
Young, Kim (2012-2014)
Young, Kris (2012)

Seattle Majestics

Year	League	Name	W	L	Conference	Division	DF	PR
2002	WSFL	Tacoma Majestics	7	0	--	--	1	LC
2003	IWFL	Tacoma Majestics	7	2	Western	Pacific Northwest	1	S
2004	IWFL	Tacoma Majestics	8	1	Western	Pacific Northwest	1	S
2005	IWFL	Tacoma Majestics	10	2	Western	Pacific Northwest	1	CC
2006	IWFL	Seattle Majestics	5	3	Western	Pacific Northwest	2	--
2007	IWFL	Seattle Majestics	8	1	Western	Pacific Northwest	1	S
2008	IWFL	Seattle Majestics	9	1	Western	Pacific Northwest	1	CC
2009	IWFL	Seattle Majestics	8	1	Western	Pacific Northwest	1	S
2010	IWFL	Seattle Majestics	2	6	Western	Pacific West	6	--
2011	IWFL	Seattle Majestics	7	4	Western	Pacific Northwest	2	BCW
2012	IWFL	Seattle Majestics	6	3	Western	Pacific Northwest	1	S
2013	WFA	Seattle Majestics	8	1	American	Division 10 (Pacific Northwest)	1	W
2014	WFA	Seattle Majestics	8	3	American	Northwest	1	S-B
2015	WFA	Seattle Majestics	9	1	American	Pacific Northwest	1	S
		Total	102	29				

Based in: Seattle, WA (2006-2015); Tacoma, WA (2002-2005)   **Neutral sites:** Round Rock, TX (N1); Chicago, IL (N2)

Seattle Majestics Game-By-Game Results

Date	H/A	Opponent	W/L	PF	PA	Note
4/20/2002		Boise Xtreme	W	34	8	
4/27/2002		Oregon Unforgiven	W	49	0	
5/4/2002		Portland Shockwave	W	20	6	
5/18/2002		Oregon Unforgiven	W	1	0	
5/26/2002		Boise Xtreme	W	38	0	
6/1/2002		Portland Shockwave	W	15	12	
6/15/2002		Portland Shockwave	W	14	0	C
3/29/2003	H	Eugene Edge	W	42	0	
4/5/2003	A	Boise Xtreme	W	26	6	
4/12/2003	H	Corvallis Pride	L	0	18	
4/26/2003	A	Portland Shockwave	W	12	0	
5/10/2003	A	Eugene Edge	W	26	7	
5/17/2003	H	Boise Xtreme	W	47	8	
5/31/2003	A	Corvallis Pride	W	12	0	
6/7/2003	H	Portland Shockwave	W	28	20	
6/14/2003	A	Sacramento Sirens	L	0	45	S
4/3/2004	H	Boise Xtreme	W	27	0	
4/17/2004	A	Eugene Edge	W	42	13	
4/24/2004	A	Corvallis Pride	W	33	14	
5/1/2004	A	Portland Shockwave	W	34	28	
5/15/2004	A	Boise Xtreme	W	27	6	
5/22/2004	H	Eugene Edge	W	49	0	
5/29/2004	H	Corvallis Pride	W	7	0	
6/5/2004	H	Portland Shockwave	W	27	0	
6/26/2004	H	Sacramento Sirens	L	20	49	S
4/2/2005	H	Portland Shockwave	W	38	6	
4/9/2005	H	Corvallis Pride	W	13	0	
4/16/2005	H	Eugene Edge	W	42	0	
4/23/2005	A	Boise Xtreme	W	26	6	
4/30/2005	A	Portland Shockwave	W	39	24	
5/14/2005	A	Corvallis Pride	L	6	21	
5/21/2005	A	Eugene Edge	W	20	0	
5/28/2005	H	Boise Xtreme	W	26	0	
6/4/2005	H	Portland Shockwave	W	42	0	
6/18/2005	A	Corvallis Pride	W	28	0	
7/9/2005	H	Chicago Force	W	14	0	S
7/23/2005	A	Sacramento Sirens	L	14	36	CC
5/6/2006	A	Sacramento Sirens	W	22	21	
5/13/2006	H	Corvallis Pride	W	21	6	
5/20/2006	A	Portland Shockwave	L	6	32	
5/27/2006	H	Portland Shockwave	L	13	19	
6/3/2006	A	Eugene Edge	W	48	0	
6/10/2006	A	Corvallis Pride	W	28	0	
6/17/2006	H	Sacramento Sirens	L	20	42	
6/24/2006	H	Redding Rage	W	48	6	
4/28/2007	A	Portland Shockwave	W	19	2	
5/5/2007	A	Corvallis Pride	W	15	0	
5/12/2007	H	Redding Rage	W	61	0	
5/26/2007	H	Tucson Monsoon	W	53	6	
6/2/2007	H	Portland Shockwave	W	33	13	
6/9/2007	H	Corvallis Pride	W	28	3	
6/23/2007	A	Corvallis Pride	W	23	0	
6/30/2007	A	Tucson Monsoon	W	16	0	
7/14/2007	H	Sacramento Sirens	L	12	29	S
4/12/2008	H	Portland Shockwave	W	14	0	
4/19/2008	A	Sacramento Sirens	W	14	7	
4/26/2008	H	Redding Rage	W	36	12	
5/10/2008	A	Corvallis Pride	W	25	0	
5/17/2008	H	Sacramento Sirens	W	27	0	
5/24/2008	A	Oakland Banshees	W	20	0	
6/7/2008	H	Oakland Banshees	W	22	0	
6/14/2008	A	Corvallis Pride	W	16	7	
6/28/2008	H	Corvallis Pride	W	35	0	S
7/12/2008	H	Dallas Diamonds	L	6	38	CC
4/11/2009	H	Corvallis Pride	W	34	0	
4/18/2009	A	Portland Shockwave	W	20	7	
4/25/2009	H	Sacramento Sirens	W	33	8	
5/9/2009	H	Portland Shockwave	W	35	7	
5/16/2009	A	Sacramento Sirens	W	21	20	
5/23/2009	A	Portland Shockwave	W	14	12	
6/6/2009	H	Portland Shockwave	W	20	7	
6/13/2009	A	Tucson Monsoon	W	55	0	
6/27/2009	H	Chicago Force	L	14	28	S
4/3/2010	A	California Quake	L	14	50	
4/10/2010	H	Sacramento Sirens	L	14	35	
4/24/2010	A	Portland Shockwave	L	7	22	
5/1/2010	H	Portland Shockwave	L	14	20	
5/8/2010	A	So Cal Scorpions	L	14	41	
5/15/2010	A	Portland Shockwave	L	14	20	
5/29/2010	H	Modesto Maniax	W	52	0	
6/5/2010	H	Tucson Monsoon	W	56	6	
4/2/2011	H	Portland Fighting Fillies	W	14	0	I
4/9/2011	A	Portland Shockwave	L	0	21	
4/23/2011	H	Tucson Monsoon	W	40	8	
5/7/2011	H	Portland Shockwave	L	6	12	*
5/14/2011	H	Sacramento Sirens	L	0	15	
5/21/2011	A	Tucson Monsoon	W	28	0	
6/4/2011	H	California Quake	L	0	50	
6/11/2011	A	Modesto Maniax	W	12	0	
6/25/2011	H	Madison Cougars	W	1	0	BQ
7/16/2011	H	Modesto Maniax	W	14	0	BS
7/30/2011	N1	New England Intensity	W	20	0	BC
4/7/2012	H	Modesto Maniax	W	34	12	
4/14/2012	H	Tucson Monsoon	W	41	0	
4/21/2012	A	Portland Shockwave	W	13	7	
5/5/2012	H	Sacramento Sirens	W	14	7	
5/12/2012	A	Portland Shockwave	W	14	6	
5/19/2012	A	Modesto Maniax	W	29	0	
6/2/2012	A	Sacramento Sirens	L	0	24	
6/16/2012		Portland Shockwave	L	7	13	
6/30/2012		Sacramento Sirens	L	0	7	S
4/6/2013	H	Utah Jynx	W	47	18	
4/13/2013	A	Portland Fighting Fillies	W	34	0	
4/20/2013	A	Tacoma Trauma	W	40	0	
4/27/2013	H	Portland Shockwave	W	27	7	
5/11/2013	H	Sacramento Sirens	W	42	21	
5/25/2013	A	Everett Reign	W	35	0	
6/1/2013	A	Portland Shockwave	W	26	14	
6/8/2013	H	Tacoma Trauma	W	42	0	
6/15/2013	H	Utah Jynx	L	26	36	W
4/5/2014	A	Portland Shockwave	W	33	12	
4/12/2014	H	Tacoma Trauma	W	46	0	
4/19/2014	H	Everett Reign	W	41	0	
5/3/2014	H	Portland Shockwave	W	32	0	
5/10/2014	A	Utah Falconz	L	20	39	I
5/17/2014	A	Portland Fighting Fillies	W	42	14	
5/31/2014	H	Portland Fighting Fillies	W	48	3	
6/7/2014	A	Everett Reign	W	43	0	
6/21/2014	A	Central Cal War Angels	W	13	12	Q
7/5/2014	H	San Diego Surge	L	20	36	S
8/2/2014	N2	Indy Crash	L	12	26	B

Continued on next page

Seattle Majestics Game-By-Game Results (continued)

Date	H/A	Opponent	Result			Date	H/A	Opponent	Result			
4/11/2015	A	Portland Fighting Fillies	W	20	0	5/30/2015	H	Portland Shockwave	W	32	0	
4/25/2015	H	Portland Fighting Fillies	W	56	6	6/6/2015	H	Everett Reign	W	56	0	
5/2/2015	H	Utah Blitz	W	82	0	6/13/2015	A	Portland Shockwave	W	44	6	
5/9/2015	A	Everett Reign	W	56	0	6/27/2015	H	Tacoma Trauma	W	34	0	Q
5/17/2015	A	Tacoma Trauma	W	49	18	7/11/2015	A	San Diego Surge	L	27	57	S

Seattle Majestics Player Register (2013-2015)

Armendariz, Domenique (2015)
Benjamin, Jeanne (2015)
Blackwood, Nicole (2013)
Bland, Jametta (2014)
Broulette, Jesica (2013)
Brown, Edwina (2015)
Bryant, Vanessa (2013-2014)
Buchholz, Crystal (2013)
Burr, Maya (2015)
Butz-Houghton, Cyndi (2013)
Campolo, Andreana (2013)
Caskey, Vanessa (2015)
Castor, Melissa (2013-2015)
Connor, Krystella (2014-2015)
Costa, Brooke (2013)
Crisman, Maddie (2014)
Custis, Holly (2015)
Deleon, Emony (2014)
Doerr, Kerrie (2013)
Edlen, Elisha (2013-2015)
Farstad, Randi (2013)
Fenimore, Ashley (2013)
Firstrider, Kalena (2013-2015)
Flint, Kass (2013)
Fook, Sarah (2015)
Fornal, Jamie (2014)
Fortson, Mikaile (2015)
Fraser, Tanisha (2013-2014)
Gallemore, Heather (2013)
Geil, Kathy (2014)
Gore, Rachel (2013-2014)
Guzman, Tina (2014)
Haag, Holiann (2015)
Hawkins, Jessica (2013)
Haycock, Anastasia (2015)
Hernandez, Christina (2015)
Hernandez, Christine "Chris" (2015)
Hoffman, Courtney (2013)
Howard, Stephanie (2015)
Hughes, Michelle (2013-2014)
Johnson, Ashley (2014)
Karlek, Sarah (2013-2015)
Koroshes, Kaihla (2013-2015)
Laird, Brandee (2015)
Laird, Karen (2013)
Lawton, Karen (2013-2014)
Layton, Kristy (2014)
Little, Sam (2013)
Lord, Shannon (2013-2015)
Macauley, Quisha (2013)
Madison, Britta (2015)
May, Theresa (2013)
McCall, Jackie (2013-2015)
McComas, Julia (2013-2015)
Murazzo, Aubrey (2013)
Nelson, Irene (2013)
Nipp, Holly (2013-2014)
Pelham, Nikki (2013-2014)
Pomee, MaLia (2015)
Rennie, Tessla (2015)
Rodak, Renee (2013-2014)
Russell, Jazzimyn "Jazz" (2013-2014)
Salas-Lorraine, Rayna (2015)
Samuelson, Rebecca (2015)
Sanderson, Crystal (2013)
Scrivner, Val (2013-2014)
Shively, Tara (2013-2015)
Smith, Dellyn (2014)
Syverson, Shelly (2013)
Tan, Megan (2013)
Tauvela, Tevaite (2013-2014)
Thornton, Karla (2014)
Tolliver, McKenzie (2015)
Trew, Katie (2013)
Tukutau, Toakase "Kase" (2014-2015)
Viinikainen, Otteliina (2013)
Volk, Michel (2015)
Wachsnicht, Theresa (2013-2014)
Waddington, Heather (2014)
Weigel, Regan (2015)
Wheeler, Carnisha (2014)
Williams, Kiki (2013-2015)
Wilson, Adrienne (2013-2015)
Woods, Rachel (2013-2015)
Zahalka, Anne (2015)
Zuniga, Diana (2015)

Seattle Warbirds

Year	League	Name	W	L	T	Conference	Division	DF	PR
2001	WAFL	Seattle Warbirds	9	1	1	Pacific	Northwest	1	S

Based in: Seattle, WA

Date	H/A	Opponent	Result			Date	H/A	Opponent	Result			
10/27/2001	H	Rose City Wildcats	W	37	0	12/22/2001	A	Sacramento Sirens	T	0	0	*
11/3/2001	A	Oakland Banshees	W	41	0	12/29/2001	H	Hawaii Legends	W	22	0	
11/10/2001	A	Rose City Wildcats	W	28	8	1/3/2002	H	Hawaii Legends	W	14	7	
12/1/2001	H	Rose City Wildcats	W	34	0	1/12/2002	H	Sacramento Sirens	W	17	14	**
12/8/2001	A	San Francisco Tsunami	W	41	0	2/2/2002	H	Arizona Caliente	L	16	24	S
12/15/2001	A	Rose City Wildcats	W	12	0							

Shreveport Aftershock

Year	League		Name	W	L	Conference	Division	DF	PR
2005	NWFA	X	Shreveport Shockhers	0	2	--	--	--	--
2006	NWFA		Shreveport Shockhers	1	7	Southern	Southwest	4	--
2007	IWFL		Shreveport Aftershock	2	5	Western	Mid South	2	--
2008	IWFL2		Shreveport Aftershock	3	4	Southern	Mid South	2	--
2009	IWFL2		Shreveport Aftershock	2	4	--	--	15	--
			Total	8	22				

Based in: Shreveport, LA

Shreveport Aftershock Game-By-Game Results

Date	H/A	Opponent	W/L	Score		Date	H/A	Opponent	W/L	Score	
5/14/2005	A	New Orleans Blaze	L	0	33	4/12/2008	A	Louisiana Fuel	L	8	12
6/11/2005	A	Chattanooga Locomotion	L	6	38	4/26/2008	A	Clarksville Fox	L	0	28
						5/3/2008	H	Louisiana Fuel	W	36	6
4/15/2006	A	Oklahoma City Lightning	L	0	70	5/10/2008	A	Clarksville Fox	L	6	28
4/22/2006	A	Austin Outlaws	L	8	36	5/31/2008	A	Louisiana Fuel	W	14	0
4/29/2006	H	Emerald Coast Barracudas	W	6	0	6/7/2008	H	Carolina Queens	L	6	34
5/6/2006	H	Dallas Rage	L	8	40	6/14/2008	H	Louisiana Fuel	W	56	0
5/20/2006	H	Oklahoma City Lightning	L	0	45						
5/27/2006	H	Austin Outlaws	L	13	55	4/11/2009	H	Louisiana Fuel	W	32	18
6/3/2006	A	Emerald Coast Barracudas	L	26	28	4/25/2009	A	Dallas Diamonds	L	0	59
6/10/2006	A	Dallas Rage	L	6	46	5/2/2009	A	Chattanooga Locomotion	L	0	62
						5/9/2009	H	Houston Energy	L	6	40
4/28/2007	H	Carolina Phoenix	W	24	6	5/23/2009	A	Houston Energy	L	0	49
5/5/2007	H	Kansas City Storm	L	6	12	5/30/2009	H	Louisiana Fuel	W	65	36
5/12/2007	H	Baton Rouge Wildcats	W	28	24						
5/19/2007	A	Kansas City Storm	L	0	27						
6/9/2007	H	Atlanta Xplosion	L	0	65						
6/16/2007	A	Baton Rouge Wildcats	L	6	42						
6/30/2007	A	Kansas City Storm	L	0	1						

Shreveport Aftershock Player Register (2006)

Adams, Sydney (2006)
Blackshire, Sonja (2006)
Brewer, Kelly (2006)
Brooks, Carla (2006)
Cawthon, Heather (2006)
Coleman, Morgan (2006)
Davidson, Jody (2006)
Davis, Chanda (2006)
Disotell, Brenda (2006)
Dunlap, Beth (2006)
Edwards, Jenn (2006)
Ewing, Sheena (2006)
Free, Courtney (2006)
Fruean, Renee "Lilo" (2006)
Garner, Sheritta (2006)
Godfrey, Cora (2006)
Hampton, Rosie (2006)
Hill, Cristin (2006)
King, Chelsea (2006)
Knopf, Jennifer (2006)
Lipp, Jill (2006)
Love, Tiona (2006)
McCray, Brossett (2006)
Morre, Tonia (2006)
Palmer, Rosemary (2006)
Patterson, Nicole (2006)
Peyton, Drew (2006)
Quintana-Mosher, Jessica (2006)
Reeves, Bonnie (2006)
Robinson, Errin (2006)
Scott, April (2006)
Sepalvado, Christy (2006)
Slaughter, Ayana (2006)
Stanley, Claire (2006)
Thomas, Paula (2006)
Turner, Evelyn (2006)
White, Shenna (2006)
Wilhite, Angie (2006)
Wolfork, Nordica (2006)

Silver State Legacy

Year	League	Name	W	L	Conference	Division	DF	PR
2011	WFA	Silver State Legacy	6	3	American	Southwest	1	Q
2012	WFA	Silver State Legacy	4	5	American	Division 17 (South Pacific)	3	--
		Total	**10**	**8**				

Based in: Las Vegas, NV

Date	H/A	Opponent	W/L	Score			Date	H/A	Opponent	W/L	Score		
4/9/2011	A	Arizona Assassins	L	8	21		3/31/2012	A	Utah Jynx	L	27	28	E
4/16/2011	A	San Diego Sting	W	42	0		4/14/2012	H	Utah Blitz	W	20	0	
4/30/2011	H	So Cal Scorpions	W	27	3		4/21/2012	A	San Diego Surge	L	0	42	
5/7/2011	H	Utah Blitz	W	44	0		4/28/2012	H	Pacific Warriors	L	14	22	
5/14/2011	A	San Diego Surge	L	15	48		5/5/2012	H	Arizona Assassins	W	44	0	
5/21/2011	H	San Diego Sting	W	35	0		5/19/2012	A	Las Vegas Showgirlz	W	28	12	
6/4/2011	A	So Cal Scorpions	W	1	0		6/2/2012	H	San Diego Surge	L	0	48	
6/11/2011	H	Arizona Assassins	W	22	7		6/9/2012	A	Pacific Warriors	L	7	27	
6/25/2011	A	San Diego Surge	L	7	41	Q	6/16/2012	A	Arizona Assassins	W	19	8	

Silver State Legacy Player Register (2011-2012)

Acacio, Christi (2011-2012)
Brouchet, Kristina (2011)
Brownlee, Shamika (2011)
Buckley, Airiona (2012)
Cannon, Jodie (2011-2012)
Clark, Megan (2011)
Clinkscales, Lenora (2011)
Cox, Charley (2011)
Cunningham, Katrina (2011)
Dixon, Alana (2011)
Estrada, Chelo (2011)
Estrada, Jenei (2011)
Finks, Shameka (2011-2012)
Forrest, Cynthia (2011)
Gemar, Stephanie (2011-2012)
Grayson, Rochuel "Rocky" (2011)
Hall, Taylor (2012)
Haro, Isabel (2012)
Heath, Faith (2012)
Hernandez, Vanessa (2011)
Johnson, Nikki (2011)
Joot, Karin (2011)
Kleinwaks, Rachel (2012)
Krause, Raquel (2012)
Lam, Nguyen (2012)
Maldonado, Stephanie (2011-2012)
Mallon, Kathrine (2012)
Matelau, Kelesi (2012)
McLuckie, Mandy (2012)

Continued on next page

Silver State Legacy Player Register (continued)

Melton, Jennifer (2012)
Montgomery, Romona (2011-2012)
Morris, Kiki (2011)
Mytych, Kerri (2011)
Navin, Erin (2011)
Nishikawa, Tricia (2011)
Norman, Joy (2011)
Nunez, Elsa (2012)
Olivar, Kerri (2012)

Olsen, Sharisse (2011-2012)
Page, Ronne (2011)
Palenapa, Leina (2012)
Pitts, Simone (2012)
Principe, Jaime (2012)
Ramos, Alicia (2011-2012)
Ridley, Vertrinia (2012)
Rodriguez, Maria (2011-2012)
Santarossa, Julie (2012)

Scarlett, Shannon (2011-2012)
Schroeder, Kelley (2012)
Trejo, Lupe (2011)
Utt, Casey (2012)
Velasquez, Emily (2011-2012)
Warren, Andree (2012)
Wayman, Octavia (2011)

Sin City Sun Devils

Year	League	Name	W	L	Conference	Division	DF	PR
2015	WFA	Sin City Sun Devils	5	4	American	Pacific West	4	--

Based in: Las Vegas, NV
Notes: Preceded by Las Vegas Showgirlz

Date	H/A	Opponent	Result			Date	H/A	Opponent	Result		
4/11/2015	A	Phoenix Phantomz	W	31	20	5/16/2015	A	Arizona Assassins	W	57	8
4/18/2015	H	San Diego Surge	L	12	54	5/23/2015	H	West Coast Lightning	W	41	6
4/25/2015	H	Pacific Warriors	L	0	46	6/6/2015	H	Central Cal War Angels	L	12	59
5/2/2015	A	Central Cal War Angels	L	6	46	6/13/2015	A	Utah Blitz	W	12	0
5/9/2015	A	Ventura County Wolfpack	W	1	0						

Sin City Sun Devils Player Register (2015)

Acacio, Christi (2015)
Bedgood, Wendy (2015)
Canfield, Zshalyn (2015)
Carter, Dustydawn (2015)
Dickson, Nichole (2015)
Edwards, MyKeesha (2015)
Fahr, Kelsi (2015)
Gomez, Felicia (2015)
Harper-Mosby, Leticia (2015)
Harrington, Lakeisha (2015)

Hawwass, Maha (2015)
Jones, Jennifer (2015)
Landing, Khalilah (2015)
Moylan, Amanda (2015)
Mulipola, Kristiana (2015)
Naranjo, Sara (2015)
Nolan, Sunny (2015)
Pineda, Kayla (2015)
Price, Trey (2015)
Ramos, Alicia (2015)

Rodgers, Brandi (2015)
Rodriguez, Maria (2015)
Rodriguez, Thaycha "Ty" (2015)
Santiago, Kendrell (2015)
Sini, Fetineiai (2015)
Stanley, Barb (2015)
Teitsma, Cindy (2015)
Tobin, Treasure (2015)
Walters, Carrie (2015)

So Cal Bandits

Year	League		Name	W	L	Conference	Division	DF	PR
2005	IWFL	X	So Cal Bandits	0	9	--	--	--	--

Based in: Los Angeles, CA

Date	H/A	Opponent	Result			Date	H/A	Opponent	Result		
4/2/2005	A	Tucson Wildfire	L	8	12	5/14/2005	A	Tucson Wildfire	L	0	1
4/16/2005	H	Oakland Banshees	L	0	50	5/21/2005	A	Santa Rosa Scorchers	L	0	1
4/23/2005	A	Sacramento Sirens	L	0	115	6/4/2005	A	Oakland Banshees	L	0	1
4/30/2005	H	Tucson Wildfire	L	0	1	6/18/2005	H	Sacramento Sirens	L	0	1
5/7/2005	H	California Quake	L	0	1						

Franchise Game-By-Game Records, 1999-2015

So Cal Scorpions

Year	League	Name	W	L	Conference	Division	DF	PR
2003	WPFL	So Cal Scorpions	2	7	American	West	5	--
2004	WPFL	So Cal Scorpions	1	9	American	West	4	--
2005	WPFL	So Cal Scorpions	10	2	American	West	1	CC
2006	WPFL	So Cal Scorpions	7	3	American	West	2	CC
2007	WPFL	So Cal Scorpions	9	2	American	West	2	**NC**
2010	IWFL	So Cal Scorpions	6	3	Western	Pacific West	2	S
2011	WFA	So Cal Scorpions	2	6	American	Southwest	3	--
		Total	**37**	**32**				

Based in: San Diego, CA

Date	H/A	Opponent	W/L	PF	PA	
8/2/2003	H	Los Angeles Amazons	L	7	8	
8/16/2003	H	Arizona Caliente	L	14	16	
8/23/2003	H	Houston Energy	L	0	41	
9/6/2003	A	Arizona Caliente	L	0	14	
9/13/2003	A	San Diego Sunfire	L	14	36	
9/20/2003	H	Arizona Knighthawks	W	27	14	
9/27/2003	A	Los Angeles Amazons	W	24	14	
10/4/2003	H	Long Beach Aftershock	L	10	41	
10/12/2003	A	Houston Energy	L	14	75	
7/31/2004	H	Arizona Caliente	L	6	41	
8/7/2004	A	Northern Ice	L	27	33	
8/14/2004	H	Long Beach Aftershock	L	0	36	
8/21/2004	A	Los Angeles Amazons	L	0	3	
8/28/2004	H	Arizona Caliente	L	7	14	
9/11/2004	H	Los Angeles Amazons	W	3	0	
9/18/2004	A	Los Angeles Amazons	L	3	6	
9/25/2004	A	Arizona Caliente	L	6	22	
10/2/2004	A	Long Beach Aftershock	L	6	42	
10/16/2004	H	Dallas Diamonds	L	7	44	
7/30/2005	H	Long Beach Aftershock	W	14	0	
8/6/2005	A	Long Beach Aftershock	W	33	16	
8/13/2005	H	Houston Energy	W	28	13	
8/27/2005	A	Los Angeles Amazons	W	14	0	
9/3/2005	A	Houston Energy	L	13	14	
9/10/2005	H	Arizona Caliente	W	43	0	
9/17/2005	A	Long Beach Aftershock	W	39	0	
10/1/2005	H	New Mexico Burn	W	69	0	
10/8/2005	H	Los Angeles Amazons	W	35	0	
10/15/2005	A	Los Angeles Amazons	W	24	14	
10/28/2005	H	Los Angeles Amazons	W	27	14	S
11/5/2005	A	Dallas Diamonds	L	19	48	CC
7/22/2006	H	Los Angeles Amazons	W	13	0	
7/29/2006	A	Las Vegas Showgirlz	W	41	0	
8/5/2006	H	Houston Energy	L	6	28	
8/19/2006	A	Los Angeles Amazons	W	34	12	
9/2/2006	A	New Mexico Burn	W	54	0	
9/9/2006	H	Las Vegas Showgirlz	W	35	8	
9/16/2006	A	Houston Energy	L	17	45	
9/23/2006	H	New Mexico Burn	W	77	7	
10/7/2006	H	New England Intensity	W	30	0	S
10/21/2006	A	Dallas Diamonds	L	3	34	CC
8/18/2007	A	Las Vegas Showgirlz	W	36	14	
9/1/2007	H	Los Angeles Amazons	L	13	15	
9/8/2007	A	Dallas Diamonds	W	34	14	
9/15/2007	H	Empire State Roar	L	6	28	
9/22/2007	A	Los Angeles Amazons	W	23	12	
9/29/2007	H	Dallas Diamonds	W	21	19	
10/6/2007	A	Wisconsin Wolves	W	35	14	
10/13/2007	H	Las Vegas Showgirlz	W	35	18	
11/3/2007	A	Los Angeles Amazons	W	7	6	S
11/17/2007	A	Empire State Roar	W	42	6	CC
12/1/2007	H	Houston Energy	W	14	7	C
4/3/2010	H	Los Angeles Amazons	L	26	37	
4/10/2010	A	Southern California Breakers	W	22	0	
4/17/2010	H	Tucson Monsoon	W	54	0	
4/24/2010	A	California Quake	L	40	42	
5/8/2010	H	Seattle Majestics	W	41	14	
5/22/2010	A	Tucson Monsoon	W	41	0	
5/29/2010	H	Bay Area Bandits	W	43	6	
6/5/2010	A	Bay Area Bandits	W	26	22	
6/12/2010	A	Sacramento Sirens	L	26	60	S
4/2/2011	A	San Diego Sting	W	16	0	
4/16/2011	H	Arizona Assassins	L	0	39	
4/30/2011	A	Silver State Legacy	L	3	27	
5/7/2011	H	San Diego Sting	W	12	6	
5/14/2011	A	Pacific Warriors	L	6	21	
5/21/2011	A	Arizona Assassins	L	0	1	
6/4/2011	H	Silver State Legacy	L	0	1	
6/18/2011	H	Los Angeles Amazons	L	0	1	

So Cal Scorpions Player Register (2011)

Adames, Sandra (2011)
Austria, Eva (2011)
Bosarge, Olvia (2011)
Bridges, Crystal (2011)
Burney, Juanita (2011)
Bush, Danielle (2011)
Crim, Dawn (2011)
Daniels, Danielle (2011)
De Guzman, Paige (2011)
DeJerez, Alexa (2011)
Franklin, Aishama (2011)
Garcia, Mary (2011)
Gary, Kelly (2011)
Germann, Dailene (2011)
Glenn, Ahna (2011)
Gomez, Apple (2011)
Gorman, Natalie (2011)
Grant, Ashley (2011)
Hansen, Randi (2011)
Hash, Rebekah (2011)
Hatcher, Veronica (2011)
Hogue, Patricia (2011)
Jolly, Tawny (2011)
Joyner, Shawnna (2011)
Kharlamova, Anna (2011)
Kuumba, Tiliza (2011)
LaMie, Rebekah (2011)
Medina, Christina (2011)
Morgan, Keisha (2011)
Nunez, Trish (2011)
Parkison, Rachael (2011)
Renick, Marita (2011)
Renteria, Marisa (2011)
Reynoso, Gabby (2011)
Roberson, Sonfre (2011)
Ruffin, Shanae (2011)
Salazar, Elizabeth (2011)
Sandoval, Amy (2011)

Continued on next page

So Cal Scorpions Player Register (continued)

Saulo, Natasha (2011)
Scott, Leigha (2011)
Sessoms, Jacqueline (2011)
Sveum, Jasmin (2011)
Taylor, Jody (2011)
Taylor, Leizel (2011)
Thomas, Mona Lisa (2011)
Tomlin, Tiffany (2011)
Torrance, Melissa (2011)
Waller, Latefah (2011)
Westman, Whitney (2011)

South Carolina Crusaders

Year	League	Name	W	L	Conference	Division	DF	PR
2002	WAFL-WFA	South Carolina Crusaders	5	5	Southern	--	3	--

Based in: Greenville, SC

10/12/2002	H	Tampa Bay Force	W	24	14		11/16/2002	H	Indianapolis Vipers	L	15	20
10/19/2002	H	Orlando Fire	L	12	18		11/23/2002	H	Jacksonville Dixie Blues	L	13	59
10/26/2002	A	Jacksonville Dixie Blues	L	13	40		12/7/2002	A	Tampa Bay Force	W	1	0
11/3/2002	A	Indianapolis Vipers	W	54	34		12/14/2002	H	Georgia Enforcers	W	1	0
11/9/2002	A	Orlando Fire	L	0	35		12/21/2002	A	Georgia Enforcers	W	1	0

South Texas Lady Crushers

Year	League	Name	W	L	Conference	Division	DF	PR
2015	WFA	South Texas Lady Crushers	0	8	American	Southwest	5	--

Based in: Corpus Christi, TX

4/11/2015	H	Acadiana Zydeco	L	0	1		5/16/2015	A	Acadiana Zydeco	L	0	56
4/18/2015	A	Dallas Elite	L	0	53		5/30/2015	A	Austin Outlaws	L	0	57
5/2/2015	H	Arlington Impact	L	0	82		6/6/2015	H	Dallas Elite	L	0	1
5/9/2015	H	Austin Outlaws	L	0	56		6/13/2015	A	Houston Power	L	0	72

South Texas Lady Crushers Player Register (2015)

Alexander, Kahla (2015)
Almora, Jessica (2015)
Alvarez, Audrey (2015)
Anzaldua, Elizabeth (2015)
Ayala, Sherrian (2015)
Benavides, Esther (2015)
Benavides, Leean (2015)
Benavides, Roxanne (2015)
Berryhill, Beverly (2015)
Boyd, Jennifer (2015)
Cabrera, Michelle (2015)
Cervantes, Brigitte (2015)
Cruz, Laura (2015)
Cueva, Kim (2015)
DeLeon, Jackie (2015)
Dyer, Christina (2015)
Figueroa, Marissa (2015)
Franco, Priscilla (2015)
Garcia, Dangelique (2015)
Garcia, Sonia (2015)
Garza, Sandy (2015)
Gipson, Sierra (2015)
Gomez, Maui (2015)
Gutierrez, Becky (2015)
Hernandez, Ruby (2015)
Higuera-Beseril, Melissa (2015)
Hurtado, Claudia (2015)
James, Mari (2015)
LeBlanc-Arthur, Arieals (2015)
Lopez, Barbara (2015)
Luna, Cassandra (2015)
Martinez, Ashley (2015)
McHenry, Tameika (2015)
Mendoza, Ruby (2015)
Nieto, Carly (2015)
Ochoa, Amy (2015)
Pena, Rena (2015)
Perez, Monica (2015)
Perez, Ruby (2015)
Puga, Roxy (2015)
Quiroz, Ana (2015)
Robles, Crystal (2015)
Salinas, Veronica (2015)
Sepulveda, Marie (2015)
Solis, Cynthia (2015)
Soto, Melissa (2015)
Trevino, Janie (2015)
Wallace, Kimberly (2015)
Willis, Vanessa (2015)
Ybarra, Monika (2015)
Zimmerman, Stephanie (2015)

Southern California Breakers

Year	League		Name	W	L	Conference	Division	DF	PR
2005	NWFA	X	Orange County Breakers	1	0	--	--	--	--
2006	NWFA	X	Orange County Breakers	8	0	--	Western	1	--
2007	NWFA		Orange County Breakers	5	3	Southern	West	2	--
2008	IWFL		Southern California Breakers	4	4	Western	Pacific Southwest	3	--
2009	IWFL2		Southern California Breakers	4	4	--	--	12	--
2010	IWFL2		Southern California Breakers	1	7	Western	Pacific West	4	--
2011	IWFL		Southern California Breakers	0	8	Western	Pacific West	3	--
			Total	**23**	**26**				

Based in: Garden Grove, CA

Date	H/A	Opponent	Result		
5/21/2005	A	Antelope Valley Bombers	W	18	12
4/15/2006	A	Tucson Wildfire	W	32	0
4/29/2006	H	Antelope Valley Attack	W	38	28
5/6/2006	H	Tucson Wildfire	W	20	6
5/20/2006	A	Antelope Valley Attack	W	14	12
5/27/2006	A	Tucson Wildfire	W	28	8
6/3/2006	H	Antelope Valley Attack	W	44	7
6/17/2006	H	Tucson Wildfire	W	31	0
7/1/2006	A	Antelope Valley Attack	W	19	6
4/14/2007	H	All Valley Attack	W	29	6
4/21/2007		Arizona Venom	W	1	0 N
4/28/2007	A	Phoenix Prowlers	L	0	36
5/12/2007	H	All Valley Attack	W	32	0
5/19/2007		Arizona Venom	W	1	0 N
5/26/2007	H	Phoenix Prowlers	L	0	50
6/9/2007	A	All Valley Attack	W	40	0
6/16/2007	A	Phoenix Prowlers	L	0	35
4/12/2008	A	Las Vegas Showgirlz	L	12	22
4/19/2008	H	California Quake	L	0	5
4/26/2008	A	Tucson Monsoon	W	35	15
5/10/2008	H	New Mexico Menace	W	48	0
5/17/2008	A	Redding Rage	W	14	6
5/31/2008	H	California Quake	L	0	27
6/7/2008	H	Las Vegas Showgirlz	L	6	24
6/14/2008	A	Tucson Monsoon	W	24	6
4/18/2009	A	New Mexico Menace	W	33	0
4/25/2009	H	Los Angeles Amazons	L	0	42
5/2/2009	H	Modesto Maniax	W	55	0
5/9/2009	A	Tucson Monsoon	L	13	14
5/16/2009	H	Tucson Monsoon	W	32	6
5/23/2009	A	Los Angeles Amazons	L	0	33
6/6/2009	H	California Quake	L	20	26
6/13/2009	A	Modesto Maniax	W	21	6
4/3/2010	A	Tucson Monsoon	L	0	3
4/10/2010	H	So Cal Scorpions	L	0	22
4/17/2010	H	Bay Area Bandits	L	7	42
4/24/2010	A	Modesto Maniax	L	0	12
5/1/2010	A	Bay Area Bandits	L	6	26
5/8/2010	H	Tucson Monsoon	W	25	0
5/22/2010	H	California Quake	L	14	34
6/5/2010	A	Los Angeles Amazons	L	14	39
4/16/2011	A	Modesto Maniax	L	6	41
4/23/2011	H	California Quake	L	0	60
4/30/2011	A	Portland Shockwave	L	6	40
5/7/2011	H	Modesto Maniax	L	0	37
5/14/2011	A	Modesto Maniax	L	0	7
5/28/2011	A	California Quake	L	0	68
6/4/2011	A	Tucson Monsoon	L	20	36
6/11/2011	H	Tucson Monsoon	L	0	6

Southern California Breakers Player Register (2005-2007)

Armstrong, Tutu (2006-2007)
Bilezikjian, Tanya (2005-2007)
Borden, Nicole (2007)
Briggs, Julie (2005-2007)
Cash, Brenda (2005-2007)
Chung, Stephanie (2006)
Ciccarelli, Julie (2007)
Costner, Nelda (2007)
Crizer, Christy (2007)
Dawson, Kelly Ann (2005-2006)
Duggins, Deb (2005-2007)
Dunbar, Erin (2005-2007)
Elliot, Beth (2005-2006)
Flinn, Lori (2005-2007)
Flores, Esther (2005)
Garcia, Amanda (2006-2007)
Garcia, Michelle (2005-2007)
Garcia-Boddie, Cynthia (2005-2007)
Ghazarossian, Darlene (2006)
Guerrero, Jill (2007)
Hanson, Valerie (2006)
Hein, Rebecca (2006)
Hernandez, Elisa (2005)
Iba, Elaine (2005-2007)
Josey-Torres, Dorothy (2006)
Joyce, Jessica (2006-2007)
Juge, Stephanie (2006)
Koller, Kelli (2005)
Leetch, Becky (2005-2007)
Linn, Suzanne (2005-2007)
Mata, Rina (2005)
Munoz, Denise (2005)
Palmer, Moa (2006)
Patino, Delinda (2005-2007)
Paynter, Lisa (2006)
Peters, Sharyn (2005-2006)
Powalski, Cindi (2005-2006)
Rathswohl, Michelle (2005)
Rodriguez, Linda (2005)
Salazar, Asia (2007)
Santillan, Vanessa (2005-2007)
Snavely, Heather (2006)
Stout, Jessica (2007)
Stuart, Kristen (2006)
Thomas, Cheryl (2005-2006)
Turner, Carmen (2006)
Twehous, Shelly (2006)
Valentine, Kim (2005-2007)
Van De Walker, Gegi (2006)
Van Zanten, Jody (2007)
Vrolyk, Wendy (2005-2007)
White, Dawn (2005)

Southern Maine Rebels

Year	League		Name	W	L	T	Conference	Division	DF	PR
2004	IWFL	X	Southern Maine Rebels	2	4	1	--	--	--	--
2005	IWFL		Southern Maine Rebels	8	3	0	Eastern	North Atlantic	2	S
2006	IWFL		Southern Maine Rebels	1	7	0	Eastern	Mid-Atlantic	3	--
2007	IWFL		Southern Maine Rebels	0	8	0	Eastern	Northeast	3	--
2008	IWFL2		Southern Maine Rebels	1	7	0	Northern	North Atlantic	5	--
2009	IWFL2		Southern Maine Rebels	2	6	0	--	--	15	--
2010	IWFL2		Southern Maine Rebels	1	7	0	Eastern	Northeast	7	--
2011	IWFL		Maine Rebels	0	7	0	Eastern	North Atlantic	4	--
2012	IWFL	X	Maine Rebels	0	8	0	--	--	--	--
2013	IWFL	X	Maine Rebels	0	8	0	--	--	--	--
2014	IWFL	X	Northeast Rebels	0	8	0	--	--	--	--
2015	IWFL	X	Northeast Rebels	0	5	0	--	--	--	--
			Total	**15**	**78**	**1**				

Based in: Portsmouth, NH (2014-2015); Portland, ME (2004-2013)

Date	H/A	Opponent	Result			
4/17/2004	H	Montreal Blitz	W	22	0	
4/24/2004	H	New Hampshire Freedom	T	0	0	*
5/1/2004	A	Montreal Blitz	L	14	20	
5/8/2004	H	Rhode Island Intensity	L	14	21	
5/15/2004	A	New Hampshire Freedom	L	8	14	
5/29/2004	A	Rhode Island Intensity	W	38	19	
6/12/2004	H	Montreal Blitz	L	14	24	
4/9/2005	H	Montreal Blitz	W	16	6	
4/16/2005	H	New York Sharks	L	6	32	
4/23/2005	H	Rhode Island Intensity	W	14	7	
4/30/2005	A	Bay State Warriors	W	8	0	
5/7/2005	A	Manchester Freedom	W	18	13	
5/14/2005	H	Manchester Freedom	W	22	12	
5/21/2005	H	Montreal Blitz	W	30	0	
6/4/2005	A	New York Sharks	L	6	28	
6/11/2005	H	Bay State Warriors	W	8	0	
6/18/2005	A	Manchester Freedom	W	36	3	
7/9/2005	A	New York Sharks	L	0	26	S
4/29/2006	H	Manchester Freedom	L	6	26	
5/6/2006	H	Bay State Warriors	L	6	41	
5/13/2006	H	Montreal Blitz	L	0	34	
5/20/2006	H	New York Sharks	L	0	55	
6/3/2006	A	Montreal Blitz	L	12	31	
6/10/2006	A	Delaware Griffins	L	0	24	
6/17/2006	A	Manchester Freedom	L	0	32	
6/24/2006	H	Delaware Griffins	W	1	0	
4/28/2007	A	Boston Rampage	L	0	13	
5/5/2007	H	Montreal Blitz	L	6	36	
5/19/2007	H	Manchester Freedom	L	6	36	
6/2/2007	A	Manchester Freedom	L	2	26	
6/9/2007	H	Manchester Freedom	L	14	36	
6/16/2007	H	Montreal Blitz	L	0	27	
6/23/2007	A	New York Sharks	L	0	1	
6/30/2007	A	Boston Rampage	L	8	13	
4/19/2008	H	New England Intensity	L	6	37	
4/26/2008	A	Holyoke Hurricanes	L	30	38	
5/3/2008	H	Manchester Freedom	L	8	70	
5/10/2008	H	Montreal Blitz	L	0	53	
5/31/2008	H	Holyoke Hurricanes	W	20	14	
6/7/2008	A	New England Intensity	L	0	44	
6/14/2008	A	Montreal Blitz	L	0	70	
6/21/2008	A	Manchester Freedom	L	0	53	
4/18/2009	H	Montreal Blitz	L	6	55	
4/25/2009	A	Holyoke Hurricanes	W	14	0	
5/2/2009	H	Jersey Justice	L	14	40	
5/16/2009	H	Manchester Freedom	L	8	13	
5/23/2009	A	Central PA Vipers	W	14	8	
5/30/2009	A	Jersey Justice	L	8	28	
6/6/2009	H	New England Intensity	L	0	19	
6/13/2009	A	Manchester Freedom	L	6	19	
4/3/2010	A	New England Intensity	L	0	28	
4/10/2010	H	Jersey Justice	L	8	26	
4/24/2010	A	New England Intensity	L	0	22	
5/1/2010	H	Montreal Blitz	L	6	41	
5/15/2010	A	Manchester Freedom	L	6	21	
5/22/2010	A	Montreal Blitz	L	0	34	
5/29/2010	H	New England Intensity	L	7	56	
6/5/2010	A	Binghamton Tiger Cats	W	21	8	
4/9/2011	H	New England Intensity	L	0	18	
4/23/2011	A	New England Intensity	L	0	34	
4/30/2011	H	Montreal Blitz	L	0	40	
5/14/2011	H	Manchester Freedom	L	8	40	
5/21/2011	A	Montreal Blitz	L	0	58	
6/4/2011	A	Manchester Freedom	L	0	37	
6/11/2011	H	New England Intensity	L	0	41	
4/7/2012	H	Northeastern Nitro	L	0	50	
4/14/2012	A	Montreal Blitz	L	0	61	
4/21/2012	H	Montreal Blitz	L	0	80	
5/5/2012	A	New Hampshire Freedom	L	0	62	
5/12/2012	H	Erie Illusion	L	0	27	
6/2/2012	H	New England Intensity	L	0	31	
6/16/2012		New England Intensity	L	0	58	
6/23/2012	H	Binghamton Tiger Cats	L	8	22	I
4/20/2013	A	New England Nightmare	L	0	40	
4/27/2013	A	New York Knockout	L	0	34	
5/4/2013	H	New England Nightmare	L	0	66	
5/18/2013	H	New England Nightmare	L	0	50	
6/1/2013	A	New England Intensity	L	0	53	
6/8/2013	A	New York Knockout	L	0	42	
6/15/2013	A	Erie Illusion	L	6	26	
6/29/2013	H	New England Intensity	L	0	1	

Continued on next page

Southern Maine Rebels Game-By-Game Results (continued)

Date	H/A	Opponent	W/L	PF	PA
4/19/2014	H	New York Knockout	L	0	14
4/26/2014	A	New England Nightmare	L	6	32
5/3/2014	H	Montreal Blitz	L	0	51
5/10/2014	A	Connecticut Wreckers	L	0	21
5/17/2014	A	Montreal Blitz	L	0	55
5/31/2014	H	New England Nightmare	L	0	38
6/7/2014	A	Keystone Assault	L	0	34
6/14/2014	H	Connecticut Wreckers	L	0	20
4/11/2015	A	Montreal Blitz	L	0	36
4/18/2015	H	Connecticut Wreckers	L	0	26
5/2/2015	A	Philadelphia Firebirds	L	0	30
5/9/2015	H	Connecticut Wreckers	L	0	6
5/16/2015	H	Montreal Blitz	L	0	57

Southern Tier Spitfire

Year	League	Name	W	L	Conference	Division	DF	PR
2010	WFA	Southern Tier Spitfire	0	8	National	Northeast	3	--

Based in: Binghamton, NY

Date	H/A	Opponent	W/L	PF	PA
4/10/2010	H	Philadelphia Liberty Belles (II)	L	0	63
4/24/2010	A	Keystone Assault	L	0	54
5/1/2010	H	New Jersey Titans	L	2	47
5/8/2010	H	New England Nightmare	L	8	26
5/15/2010	A	Baltimore Burn	L	0	1
5/22/2010	A	Philadelphia Liberty Belles (II)	L	0	71
6/12/2010	H	Keystone Assault	L	0	38
6/19/2010	A	New England Nightmare	L	0	32

Southern Tier Spitfire Player Register (2010)

Alexander, Jessica (2010)
Barden, Leah (2010)
Bunker, Kristen (2010)
Canfield, Jess (2010)
Collins, Julie (2010)
Czimback, Carol (2010)
Fenton, Katie (2010)
Grant, Tamara (2010)
Grubb, Carol (2010)
Knox, Ashley (2010)
Loutey, Kim (2010)
Lumsden, Amanda (2010)
Mundy, Cheryl (2010)
Onuska, Michelle (2010)
Patten, Rachel (2010)
Pawol, Jen (2010)
Pitcher, Caroline (2010)
Ranelli, Nancy (2010)
Robertson, Jen (2010)
Salisbury, Nicole (2010)
Senz, Jackie Anne (2010)
Shamberger, Melissa (2010)
Tomkins, Jackie (2010)
Velton-Hernon, Dawn (2010)
White, Cheri (2010)

Southern Valkyrie

Year	League	Name	W	L	Conference	Division	DF	PR
2015	W8FL	Southern Valkyrie	1	3	--	--	1	--

Based in: Nashville, TN
Neutral site: Atlanta, GA (N)
Notes: Preceded by Nashville Smashers

Date	H/A	Opponent	W/L	PF	PA
4/18/2015	N	Cape Fear Thunder	W	42	14
4/25/2015	A	Cincinnati Sizzle	L	12	37
5/2/2015	A	Tri-Cities Thunder	L	12	82
5/16/2015	H	Tri-Cities Thunder	L	14	70

Spokane Scorn

Year	League	Name	W	L	Conference	Division	DF	PR
2011	WFA	Spokane Scorn	1	5	American	Northwest	3	--

Based in: Spokane, WA

Date	H/A	Opponent	W/L	PF	PA
4/2/2011	A	Utah Blitz	L	0	40
4/30/2011	H	Portland Fighting Fillies	L	0	12
5/14/2011	A	Portland Fighting Fillies	L	12	22
5/21/2011	H	Utah Blitz	W	26	20
6/11/2011	H	Utah Blitz	L	22	30
6/18/2011	A	Portland Fighting Fillies	L	0	1

Spokane Scorn Player Register (2011)

Armstrong, Ashley (2011)
Buckholz, Rylie (2011)
Cameron, Margaux (2011)
Carter, Amber (2011)
Cowin, Amy (2011)
Cunningham, Leann (2011)
Dobson, Sara (2011)
Frieske, Mallorie (2011)
Funderburg, Tara (2011)
Halverson-Loringer, Courtney (2011)
Johnson, Janay (2011)
Johnson, Savannah (2011)
Landgraver, Meri (2011)
Loparco, Danielle (2011)
Melloni, Vanna (2011)
Morgan, Megan (2011)
Ng, Barbara (2011)
Raley-Jones, Katie (2011)
Rosato, Allison (2011)
Schelin, Jamie (2011)
Skoog, Louisa (2011)
Tiffany, Ruth (2011)

St. Louis Slam

Year	League	Name	W	L	Conference	Division	DF	PR
2003	NWFA	St. Louis Slam	3	5	Southern	Midwest	3	--
2004	NWFA	St. Louis Slam	5	3	Southern	Midwest	2	--
2005	NWFA	St. Louis Slam	5	3	Northern	--	7	--
2006	NWFA	St. Louis Slam	7	3	Southern	South Central	1	S
2007	NWFA	St. Louis Slam	8	2	Southern	North	1	S
2008	NWFA	St. Louis Slam	8	1	Southern	Midwest	1	S
2009	WFA	St. Louis Slam	11	0	American	Midwest	1	NC
2010	WFA	St. Louis Slam	10	1	National	Central	1	CC
2011	WFA	St. Louis Slam	5	3	National	Central	2	--
2012	WFA	St. Louis Slam	6	4	American	Division 11 (Midwest)	2	Q
2013	WFA	St. Louis Slam	7	4	American	Division 8 (Midwest)	2	S
2015	WFA	St. Louis Slam	6	3	American	Great Plains	1	Q
		Total	**81**	**32**				

Based in: St. Louis, MO

Neutral site: New Orleans, LA (N)

4/12/2003	H	Kansas City Krunch	L	6	12	**
4/19/2003	A	Nashville Dream	L	6	20	
4/26/2003		Evansville Express	W	27	20	
5/10/2003	H	Oklahoma City Lightning	L	6	21	
5/17/2003	A	Kansas City Krunch	W	7	6	
5/24/2003	H	Nashville Dream	L	7	27	
6/7/2003	A	Oklahoma City Lightning	L	13	48	
6/14/2003		Evansville Express	W	35	14	
4/3/2004	H	Evansville Express	W	29	0	
4/17/2004	A	Kansas City Krunch	W	6	0	
4/24/2004	H	Oklahoma City Lightning	L	18	32	
5/8/2004	H	Kansas City Krunch	W	20	14	
5/22/2004	A	Oklahoma City Lightning	L	12	43	
5/29/2004	A	Kansas City Krunch	L	18	28	
6/5/2004	H	Evansville Express	W	29	6	
6/12/2004	A	Evansville Express	W	12	0	
4/16/2005	A	Kentucky Karma	L	0	20	
4/23/2005	H	Southwest Michigan Jaguars	L	6	47	
4/30/2005	A	Indianapolis SaberKatz	W	46	0	
5/14/2005	A	Kansas City Krunch	L	6	16	
5/21/2005	H	Kentucky Karma	W	34	6	
6/4/2005	H	Indianapolis SaberKatz	W	102	0	
6/11/2005	H	Kansas City Krunch	W	42	8	
6/18/2005	A	Milwaukee Momentum	W	12	7	
4/15/2006	H	Kentucky Karma	W	36	14	
4/22/2006	A	Nashville Dream	W	22	14	
4/29/2006	H	Chattanooga Locomotion	W	14	7	
5/13/2006	A	Oklahoma City Lightning	L	12	35	
5/20/2006	H	Nashville Dream	W	48	0	
5/27/2006	A	Kentucky Karma	W	22	0	
6/3/2006	A	Chattanooga Locomotion	W	34	14	
6/17/2006	H	Oklahoma City Lightning	L	16	21	
7/1/2006	H	Kentucky Karma	W	27	8	Q
7/8/2006	A	Massachusetts Mutiny	L	14	42	S
4/21/2007	H	Columbus Comets	W	27	14	
4/28/2007	A	Oklahoma City Lightning	L	6	21	
5/5/2007	H	Kentucky Karma	W	62	0	
5/12/2007	H	Cincinnati Sizzle	W	61	0	
5/26/2007	A	Columbus Comets	W	26	13	
6/2/2007	A	Kentucky Karma	W	26	0	
6/9/2007	A	Cincinnati Sizzle	W	56	0	
6/16/2007	H	Oklahoma City Lightning	W	7	0	
6/23/2007	H	Phoenix Prowlers	W	33	29	Q
6/30/2007	A	Oklahoma City Lightning	L	7	33	S
4/19/2008	A	Columbus Comets	W	18	16	
4/26/2008	H	Memphis Belles	W	51	0	
5/3/2008	A	Chattanooga Locomotion	W	24	7	
5/17/2008	H	Kansas City Storm	W	54	0	
5/24/2008	A	Memphis Belles	W	42	0	
5/31/2008	H	Chattanooga Locomotion	W	21	0	
6/7/2008	A	Kansas City Storm	W	1	0	
6/14/2008	H	Columbus Comets	W	48	23	
7/5/2008	H	H-Town Texas Cyclones	L	13	25	S
4/18/2009	A	Kansas City Storm	W	77	0	
4/25/2009	A	Missouri Phoenix	W	1	0	
5/9/2009	A	Minnesota Machine	W	28	0	
5/16/2009	H	Iowa Thunder	W	35	7	
5/30/2009	H	Kansas City Storm	W	88	0	
6/6/2009	H	Minnesota Machine	W	42	7	
6/13/2009	H	Missouri Phoenix	W	51	0	
6/27/2009	A	Iowa Thunder	W	40	10	
7/11/2009	H	Las Vegas Showgirlz	W	30	12	S
7/25/2009	H	Jacksonville Dixie Blues	W	40	32	CC
8/15/2009	N	West Michigan Mayhem	W	21	14	C
4/10/2010	A	Cincinnati Sizzle	W	35	0	
4/17/2010	H	Minnesota Machine	W	34	0	
4/24/2010	A	Indiana Speed	W	13	6	
5/1/2010	H	Kentucky Karma	W	50	0	
5/8/2010	H	Cincinnati Sizzle	W	57	0	
5/22/2010	A	Kentucky Karma	W	70	6	
6/5/2010	A	Iowa Thunder	W	37	14	
6/19/2010	H	Indiana Speed	W	16	14	
6/26/2010	H	Cleveland Fusion	W	50	23	Q
7/10/2010	A	Jacksonville Dixie Blues	W	52	26	S
7/17/2010	A	Columbus Comets	L	14	21	CC

Continued on next page

Franchise Game-By-Game Records, 1999-2015

St. Louis Slam Game-By-Game Results (continued)

Date	H/A	Opponent	Result			Date	H/A	Opponent	Result			
4/9/2011	H	Indy Crash	W	43	6	4/6/2013	A	Kansas City Titans	L	14	35	
4/16/2011	H	Dayton Diamonds	W	70	0	4/20/2013	A	Minnesota Machine	W	35	0	
4/30/2011	A	Chicago Force	L	7	29	4/27/2013	H	Chicago Force	L	7	50	
5/7/2011	A	West Michigan Mayhem	W	36	6	5/4/2013	H	Nebraska Stampede	W	62	27	
5/14/2011	A	Kansas City Tribe	L	34	37	5/11/2013	A	Minnesota Machine	W	47	0	
5/21/2011	H	Chicago Force	L	24	55	5/25/2013	H	Minnesota Machine	W	69	0	
6/4/2011	H	West Michigan Mayhem	W	41	7	6/1/2013	A	Nebraska Stampede	W	34	0	
6/18/2011	A	Kentucky Karma	W	1	0	6/8/2013	H	Kansas City Titans	L	15	27	
						6/15/2013	H	Acadiana Zydeco	W	72	0	W
4/14/2012	H	Minnesota Machine	W	59	0	6/22/2013	A	Kansas City Titans	W	58	55	Q
4/21/2012	A	Kansas City Tribe	L	14	33	7/13/2013	H	Dallas Diamonds	L	20	35	S
4/28/2012	A	Kansas City Spartans	W	59	0							
5/5/2012	A	Chicago Force	L	14	57	4/11/2015	H	Minnesota Machine	W	27	18	
5/19/2012	A	Iowa Xplosion	W	1	0	N	4/25/2015	A	Tulsa Threat	W	49	16
6/2/2012	H	Kansas City Spartans	W	32	0	5/2/2015	A	Kansas City Titans	L	17	27	
6/9/2012	H	Memphis Dynasty	W	49	0	5/9/2015	A	Minnesota Machine	W	50	39	
6/16/2012	H	Kansas City Tribe	L	42	63	5/16/2015	H	Derby City Dynamite	W	26	8	
6/23/2012	H	Minnesota Machine	W	42	6	W	5/30/2015	H	Tulsa Threat	W	52	19
6/30/2012	A	Kansas City Tribe	L	17	42	Q	6/6/2015	H	Kansas City Titans	W	35	22
						6/13/2015	A	Chicago Force	L	0	57	
						6/27/2015	A	Dallas Elite	L	3	54	Q

St. Louis Slam Player Register (2004-2013, 2015)

Ackles, Carmen (2015)
Ackles, Nicola (2015)
Ackles, Tanzie (2015)
Allen, Kim (2004-2007)
Allrich, Leslie (2010-2011)
Artis, Brittany (2012-2013)
Bacher, Candi (2009-2010)
Barks, Kim (2012)
Bastain, Brooklynn (2015)
Betz, Tracy (2011)
Brown, Toya (2004-2005, 2007-2011)
Bruce, Kuleya (2013)
Buckner, Trecia (2009-2011)
Burrell, Christy (2007-2008)
Carr, Melodie (2009-2012)
Carter, Tiffany (2007-2008, 2010)
Chatman, Dana (2009-2011)
Clay, Chelsea (2015)
Clough, Tawnya (2009)
Cockrell, Candice (2015)
Collins, Megan (2009)
Corbin, Stacy (2009-2012)
Corman, Courtney (2006)
Cullen, Danielle (2008-2010)
Daniels, Patrice (2005-2006)
Darden, Meschele (2004, 2006)
Daughenbaugh, Celeste (2006)
Davis, Christine (2005)
Davis, Kristin (2006-2007)
Davis, Myrt (2004-2013)
Dickerson, Nicole (2011-2012)
Dickerson, Quianna (2015)
Dixson, Tinika (2010)
Duffy, Lindsey (2009)
Dunihoo, Brooklyn (2010-2013, 2015)
Durr, Ashley (2008)
Edwards, Tori (2015)
Erickson, Caitlin (2011-2013, 2015)
Evers, Kate (2009-2013)
Ezenwa, Brenda (2010-2011)
Fields, Alana (2011-2013, 2015)
Fish, Daashia (2006)
FitzPatrick, Dana (2005)
Foote, Jessica (2015)

Forgy, Meghan (2007)
Fugman, Trila (2006)
Garcia-Allen, Sadie (2009-2010)
Garden, Athena (2010-2011)
Gardner, Brittani (2012-2013)
Garner, Porsha (2012)
Gelis-Diaz, Laure (2005-2009)
Graff, Gail (2004-2012)
Hall, Theresa (2007)
Hampton, Chris (2005-2011)
Harrison, Lindsey (2010-2011)
Hay, Taylor (2010-2013, 2015)
Hazelwood, Melissa (2008)
Heim, Caitlin (2013)
Henson, Angie (2009-2013)
Hergemueller, Kim (2008-2011)
Hershberger, Kara (2007)
Hinkle, Rachael (2009-2013)
Hollinshed, Vanessa (2004)
Hopper, Tracy (2010-2011)
Hughes, Natalie (2006)
Jackson, Tammy (2009-2010)
Jackson, Tonya (2005-2008)
Jeffries, Latoya (2011)
Johns, Hannah (2012)
Johnson, Stephanie (2005)
Jones, Kellie (2004)
Jones, Lovecia (2006)
Keen, Kelly (2009-2010)
Kelly, Jelani (2013, 2015)
Kenneda, Amber (2006)
Ketchum, Alana (2011)
Key, Omega (2010)
King, Jackie (2011)
Kozlen, Kelly (2004-2013)
Kyles, Melanie (2009-2010)
Lacy, Liz (2004-2011)
Laduron, Jessica (2015)
Laduron, Samantha (2015)
Lane, Lacreshia (2007-2011)
Laster, Sydney (2009)
Lee, Amanda (2013, 2015)
Loftus, Amy (2006)
Lopez, Amy (2011-2012)

Lowell, Anne (2005)
Luedde, Tara (2009-2011, 2013)
Madison, Lanette (2005-2008, 2010)
Malone, Tiara (2009)
Mansker, Amy (2005)
Marcus, Michelle (2005-06, 2008-11)
Mariama, Jairus (2008-2009)
Marshall, Mia (2005)
Martin, Willeesa (2010-2011)
Matoushek, Elizabeth (2006, '08, '13)
McGee, Alecia (2010-2011)
Merriweather, Jocelyn (2005-10, '12-13)
Metcalfe, Inge (2004-2005, 2009-2013)
Miller, Jessica (2009-2010)
Mitchell, Michelle (2009)
Morrow, Robin (2005-2013, 2015)
Murphy, Mollie (2011)
Neutzling, Kaylee (2013, 2015)
Newsome, Alicia (2015)
Nichols, Victoria (2015)
Notorangelo, Nicole (2011)
Obajtek, Rachel (2010)
Ode, Katie (2008-2010)
Ogunware, Caroline (2008)
Overacker, Kristine (2013)
Park, Kendall (2008-2011, 2013, 2015)
Patterson, Heather (2007-2008)
Pawnell, Andrea (2004)
Pettis, Tiara (2007-2011)
Pratt, Stephanie (2008)
Pugh, Tiffany (2010-2013, 2015)
Quisenberry, Lisa (2004)
Ransom, Niekina (2005)
Ray, Jacki (2005-2008)
Riggins, Pat (2004-2010)
Robinson, Chiara (2010-2011, 2015)
Rodgers, Ashley (2011)
Rodman, Tanya (2005-06, 2008-12)
Russel, Kamilah (2011)
Schroeder, Julie (2004)
Shannon, Sherrie (2004)
Sims, Afton (2009-2010)
Smith, Keyonna (2012-2013, 2015)

Continued on next page

St. Louis Slam Player Register (continued)

Smith, Tayona (2009-2011)
Snow, Juanita "Juan" ('05-06, '08-13, '15)
Steen, Sharice (2005-2007)
Steinkamp, Kristen (2013, 2015)
Strong, Emily (2010-2012, 2015)
Stuebgan, Sara (2006)
Taylor, Nikki (2010-2012)
Terry, Sandra (2009)
Toman, Jacki (2004)
Tomlinson, Tracy (2006-2007)
Troupe, Brandi (2015)
Tucker, Sue (2007)
Tyner, Jeanette (2005-2006)
Vales-Smith, Shaunta (2009)
Van Apeldoorn, Jessie (2004-2006)
Verbeck, Chris (2005-2006)
Walker, Carri (2005)
Walker, Chimere (2009-2010)
Ward, Terri (2015)
Washington, Antonnia (2011-13, '15)
Washington, Tina (2005-2008)
Webb, Christina (2013)
Wilke, Lonna (2005-2008)
Williams, Elizabeth (2006-2009)
Williams, Melinda (2004, 2008)
Williams, Raven (2015)
Williams, Sekayi (2011)
Williams-Buckley, Tiffany (2011-2012)
Williams-Kelley, Tracy (2011)
Wilson, Sha (2009)

Steel City Renegades

Year	League	Name	W	L	Conference	Division	DF	PR
2010	WSFL	X Steel City Renegades	2	0	--	--	--	--

Based in: Pittsburgh, PA
Notes: Succeeded by Three Rivers Xplosion

5/15/2010		West Virginia Bruisers	W	22	0	6/26/2010	A	West Virginia Bruisers	W 18 6

Sweetwater County Outlaws

Year	League	Name	W	L	Conference	Division	DF	PR
2002	UWFL	Sweetwater County Outlaws	1	4	--	--	--	--

Based in: Rock Springs, WY

4/14/2002	Colorado Springs Koalas	L	13	63	5/5/2002	Denver Foxes	L	0 30
4/20/2002	Cheyenne Dust Devils	W	15	14	5/12/2002	Tri-City Mustangs	L	7 25
4/28/2002	Grand Valley Vipers	L	14	42				

Syracuse Sting

Year	League	Name	W	L	Conference	Division	DF	PR
2001	MIWFA	Syracuse Sting	1	3	--	--	--	--
2002	WPFL	Syracuse Sting	4	4	National	--	2	CC
2003	WPFL	Syracuse Sting	7	2	National	East	1	--
2004	WPFL	Syracuse Sting	4	6	National	East	2	--
		Total	16	15				

Based in: Syracuse, NY
Notes: Preceded by WPFL's New York Galaxy

8/11/2001	A	New York Sharks	L	6	34		9/6/2003	A	Dayton Rebellion	W	41	8
8/18/2001	A	New England Storm	L	0	20	I	9/13/2003	A	New England Storm	W	28	8
9/1/2001	H	New York Sharks	L	14	21		9/20/2003	H	New England Storm	W	41	12
9/8/2001	H	Orlando Fire	W	26	13	I	9/27/2003	H	Dayton Rebellion	W	48	14
							10/4/2003	H	Minnesota Vixen	W	28	19
8/10/2002		New England Storm	W	6	3		10/11/2003	H	Toledo Reign	W	55	12
8/17/2002		Indiana Speed	W	30	0							
8/31/2002		Wisconsin Riveters	L	8	34		7/31/2004	A	Dallas Diamonds	L	0	49
9/7/2002		Houston Energy	L	6	40		8/7/2004	A	Delaware Griffins	L	16	20
9/14/2002		New England Storm	W	14	13		8/14/2004	A	New York Dazzles	W	20	0
9/21/2002		New England Storm	W	40	7		8/21/2004	A	Delaware Griffins	L	6	26
10/5/2002		Wisconsin Riveters	L	22	26		9/4/2004	A	Indiana Speed	L	16	46
10/26/2002		Wisconsin Riveters	L	6	31	CC	9/18/2004	H	Delaware Griffins	L	0	18
							9/25/2004	H	New York Dazzles	W	47	0
8/9/2003	A	New England Storm	W	12	6		10/2/2004	H	Indiana Speed	W	25	0
8/16/2003	A	Florida Stingrayz	L	0	6		10/9/2004	H	New York Dazzles	W	40	8
8/30/2003	A	Indiana Speed	L	7	22		10/16/2004	H	Albany Ambush	L	6	10

Tacoma Trauma

Year	League	Name	W	L	Conference	Division	DF	PR
2013	WFA	Tacoma Trauma	1	7	American	Division 10 (Pacific Northwest)	5	--
2014	WFA	Tacoma Trauma	0	8	American	Northwest	6	--
2015	WFA	Tacoma Trauma	7	2	American	Pacific Northwest	2	Q
		Total	8	17				

Based in: Tacoma, WA

Date	H/A	Opponent	Result		
4/6/2013	A	Portland Fighting Fillies	L	0	42
4/13/2013	A	Utah Jynx	L	6	73
4/20/2013	H	Seattle Majestics	L	0	40
4/27/2013	A	Everett Reign	L	6	46
5/11/2013	H	Portland Fighting Fillies	L	14	33
5/18/2013	H	Portland Shockwave	L	0	32
6/1/2013	H	Everett Reign	W	24	0
6/8/2013	A	Seattle Majestics	L	0	42
4/5/2014	A	Everett Reign	L	12	19
4/12/2014	A	Seattle Majestics	L	0	46
4/19/2014	H	Portland Fighting Fillies	L	0	21
4/26/2014	H	Portland Shockwave	L	8	28
5/10/2014	A	Utah Blitz	L	7	28
5/17/2014	H	Everett Reign	L	12	47
5/24/2014	H	Utah Falconz	L	0	72 I
6/7/2014	A	Portland Fighting Fillies	L	0	57
4/18/2015	A	Portland Shockwave	W	39	18
4/25/2015	H	Utah Blitz	W	62	0
5/2/2015	H	Portland Fighting Fillies	W	20	10
5/17/2015	H	Seattle Majestics	L	18	49
5/23/2015	A	Portland Fighting Fillies	W	28	13
5/30/2015	A	Everett Reign	W	35	0
6/6/2015	A	Utah Blitz	W	24	0
6/13/2015	H	Everett Reign	W	24	13
6/27/2015	A	Seattle Majestics	L	0	34 Q

Tacoma Trauma Player Register (2013-2015)

Anderson, Amanda (2013)
Barto, Marika (2015)
Beasley, Tory (2015)
Blassman, Shirley (2015)
Blomberg, Christina (2013)
Bottenberg, Maria (2015)
Burgett, Olesya (2013)
Buschmann, April (2014)
Bush-Johnson, Mikisa (2015)
Cabalse, Selena (2014-2015)
Cannon, Amber (2015)
Caskey, Vanessa (2014)
Chenault, Quinia (2015)
Christoffersen, Kristi (2013)
Coleman, Teresa (2015)
Connors, Alex (2014-2015)
Corey, Heidi (2014-2015)
Crady, Chantell (2014)
De Le Torre, Brenna (2013)
Douglass, Millicent (2014)
Dutcher, Candice (2014-2015)
Escubar, Rachelle (2013)
Fraser, Tanisha (2015)
Guerra, Katrina (2013-2015)
Henn-James, Alicia (2015)
Hill, Sherrie (2013-2015)
Hogate, Jennifer (2013)
Ilgenfritz, Reagan (2015)
Jamison, Jasmine (2015)
Jenkins, Veronica (2015)
Johnson, Mikisa (2013-2014)
Keaton, Phaedra (2013-2015)
Kienholz, Kerianne "Keri" (2014-2015)
Leomiti, Tauva (2015)
Martin-Gunderson, Jessie Jo (2014-2015)
McClure, Elizabeth (2013)
McFerran, Lindsay (2015)
McGill, Christian (2015)
Myers, Amanda (2015)
Ockenfels, Brandi (2013-2015)
O'Connell, Bridgette (2013-2015)
O'Connell, Patricia (2013-2015)
Paddock, Taralynn (2013-2014)
Pascoe, Ashley (2014-2015)
Petterson, Sandee (2015)
Pugh, Crystal (2013-2015)
Reda, Nomie (2013-2014)
Rodak, Renee (2015)
Rodak, Vanessa (2015)
Russell, Jazzimyn "Jazz" (2015)
Scott, Jackie (2013)
Sesepasara, Faatuiese (2013)
Shaw, Zakiya (2013)
Silva, Tinai (2013-2014)
Smith, Leslie (2013)
Smithingell, Dee (2013-2014)
Szymczak, Rena (2013)
Tann, Veronica Jenkins (2013)
Taumade Budgett, Vaisina (2015)
Tauvela, Tevaite (2015)
Turner, Joy (2013-2014)
Vernoy, Amanda (2013-2014)
Volk, Michel (2014)
Wachsnicht, Theresa (2015)
Walker, Matal (2015)
Wansley, Boni (2013-2014)
Westwick, Shanon (2014-2015)
Wilson, Chalice (2014-2015)
Wilson, Maycie (2014-2015)
Young, Tiffani (2014-2015)
Zuniga, Diana (2014)

Tallahassee Jewels

Year	League	Name	W	L	Conference	Division	DF	PR
2012	WFA	Tallahassee Jewels	6	3	National	Division 8 (Gulf Coast)	1	W
2013	WFA	Tallahassee Jewels	3	5	National	Division 6 (South Atlantic)	3	--
		Total	9	8				

Based in: Tallahassee, FL

Tallahassee Jewels Game-By-Game Results

4/14/2012	H	Acadiana Zydeco	W	8	6	4/6/2013	A	Atlanta Phoenix	L	14	61
4/21/2012	A	Palm Beach Punishers	L	6	14	4/20/2013	H	Tampa Bay Inferno	L	22	62
4/28/2012	H	Carolina Raging Wolves	W	42	21	4/27/2013	A	Miami Fury	L	8	38
5/5/2012	A	Gulf Coast Riptide	W	26	20	5/11/2013	A	Tampa Bay Inferno	L	0	47
5/12/2012	H	Miami Fury	W	16	8	5/18/2013	A	Savannah Sabers	L	12	24
5/19/2012	H	Gulf Coast Riptide	W	1	0	5/25/2013	H	Orlando Anarchy	W	47	20
6/9/2012	A	Gulf Coast Riptide	W	1	0	6/1/2013	H	New Orleans Mojo	W	47	6
6/16/2012	A	Acadiana Zydeco	L	6	18	6/8/2013	H	Jacksonville Dixie Blues	W	26	14
6/23/2012	A	Atlanta Phoenix	L	0	55 W						

Tallahassee Jewels Player Register (2012-2013)

Aaron, Gabrielle (2012-2013)
Alford, Christina (2012)
Alvarado, Lynnette (2012-2013)
Anderson, Tynease (2013)
Arbogast, Rebecca (2012)
Ates, Keinna (2012-2013)
Battles, Giovonnie (2013)
Bellamy, Kimberly (2013)
Boyd, Keterah (2012)
Braxton, Morgan (2013)
Brown, Kalia (2012)
Campbell, Caleigh (2013)
Cook, Marcia (2012)
Cook, Shelly (2013)
Davis, Mona (2013)
Denmark, DeeDee (2013)
Destine, Ashley (2013)
El-Far, Christina (2012)
Elliott, Kiesha (2012-2013)
Fahnestock, Della (2012)
Folson, Chelsya (2012-2013)
George, Latoria "Tori" (2012-2013)
Givens, Nikki (2012-2013)
Jackson, Joy (2012)
Jefferson, Ella (2012-2013)
Johnson, Rokisha (2013)
Jones, Roshandra (2013)
King, Marketa (2012-2013)
Lamb, Selena (2012-2013)
Larkin, Rosalinda (2012)
Lopez, Jennifer (2012-2013)
Love, Tykia (2012)
Martin, Ashlee (2012-2013)
Mathison, Christie (2012)
Matthews, Jennifer (2013)
McDonald, Carla (2012)
McNealy, Mitzi (2013)
Olaoye, Foluke (2013)
Presley, Twanisha (2012-2013)
Range, Wanda Jackson (2012)
Rossman, Stephanie (2013)
Sapp, Shavonna (2013)
Scialabba, Nicole (2013)
Sehgal, Angela (2012)
Smith, Angie (2013)
Smith, Deborah (2013)
Somerset, Teirra (2012)
Speicher, Whitney (2012-2013)
Steffen, Gay (2012)
Wahkeleh, Nenplenseh (2013)
Waters, Shaulana (2012)
Wiley, Yasika (2012)
Williams, Kaylin (2012-2013)
Wise, Saundra (2013)

Tampa Bay Force

Year	League	Name	W	L	Conference	Division	DF	PR
2001	WAFL	Tampa Bay Force	10	2	Atlantic	South	1	CC
2002	WAFL-WFA	Tampa Bay Force	2	9	Southern	--	4	--
		Total	12	11				

Based in: Tampa, FL

6/9/2001	H	Tennessee Heat	W	60	0 IE	5/25/2002		Orlando Starz	L	0	48 I
10/27/2001	A	Orlando Fire	W	18	6	10/5/2002		Orlando Fire	L	6	53
11/3/2001	H	New Orleans Voodoo Dolls	W	58	0	10/12/2002	A	South Carolina Crusaders	L	14	24
11/10/2001	H	Orlando Fire	W	50	6	10/19/2002		Jacksonville Dixie Blues	L	8	41
11/17/2001	A	New Orleans Voodoo Dolls	W	52	0	11/2/2002	H	Georgia Enforcers	W	1	0
12/1/2001	H	Jacksonville Dixie Blues	W	31	14	11/9/2002	A	New Orleans Voodoo Dolls	W	1	0 N
12/15/2001	H	New Orleans Voodoo Dolls	W	26	0	11/16/2002		Jacksonville Dixie Blues	L	0	1
12/22/2001	A	Orlando Fire	W	20	14	11/23/2002		Orlando Fire	L	0	40
1/5/2002	A	Jacksonville Dixie Blues	W	56	49	12/7/2002	H	South Carolina Crusaders	L	0	1
1/12/2002	A	Alabama Slammers	L	0	1	12/14/2002	H	Birmingham Steel Magnolias	L	0	1
1/26/2002	H	Orlando Fire	W	31	20 S	12/21/2002	A	Indianapolis Vipers	L	0	1
2/2/2002	H	Jacksonville Dixie Blues	L	6	26 CC						

Tampa Bay Inferno

Year	League	Name	W	L	Conference	Division	DF	PR
2010	WFA	Tampa Bay Pirates	4	4	National	South Central	3	--
2011	WFA	Tampa Bay Pirates	2	6	National	Coastal	3	--
2012	WFA	Tampa Bay Inferno	7	1	National	Division 9 (South Atlantic)	2	--
2013	WFA	Tampa Bay Inferno	6	3	National	Division 6 (South Atlantic)	2	W
2014	WFA	Tampa Bay Inferno	7	2	National	South Atlantic	2	W
2015	WFA	Tampa Bay Inferno	5	3	National	South Atlantic	2	--
		Total	31	19				

Based in: Tampa, FL

Franchise Game-By-Game Records, 1999-2015

Tampa Bay Inferno Game-By-Game Results

Date	H/A	Opponent	W/L	PF	PA		Date	H/A	Opponent	W/L	PF	PA	
4/17/2010	H	Carolina Raging Wolves	W	42	36		4/6/2013	A	Savannah Sabers	W	40	14	
4/24/2010	H	Jacksonville Dixie Blues	L	0	63		4/13/2013	A	Orlando Anarchy	W	34	14	
5/8/2010	H	Central Florida Anarchy	L	0	14		4/20/2013	A	Tallahassee Jewels	W	62	22	
5/15/2010	H	Carolina Raging Wolves	W	8	0		4/27/2013	H	Orlando Anarchy	W	60	7	
5/22/2010	A	Carolina Raging Wolves	W	26	20		5/11/2013	H	Tallahassee Jewels	W	47	0	
6/5/2010	A	Jacksonville Dixie Blues	L	6	42		5/18/2013	H	Miami Fury	L	6	22	
6/12/2010	A	Central Florida Anarchy	W	14	9		5/25/2013	H	Jacksonville Dixie Blues	W	21	12	
6/19/2010	A	Central Florida Anarchy	L	0	19		6/8/2013	A	Miami Fury	L	0	28	
							6/15/2013	A	Atlanta Phoenix	L	19	24	W
4/2/2011	H	Orlando Anarchy	W	6	0								
4/9/2011	A	Carolina Raging Wolves	W	26	6		4/5/2014	A	Atlanta Phoenix	W	32	25	
4/30/2011	H	Miami Fury	L	0	32		4/12/2014	H	Savannah Sabers	W	55	6	
5/7/2011	A	Palm Beach Punishers	L	8	16		4/26/2014	A	Orlando Anarchy	W	68	0	
5/14/2011	A	Gulf Coast Riptide	L	13	18		5/3/2014	H	Daytona Breakers	W	77	0	
5/21/2011	A	Miami Fury	L	21	34		5/10/2014	A	Jacksonville Dixie Blues	W	49	0	
6/11/2011	H	Palm Beach Punishers	L	14	20		5/17/2014	H	Orlando Anarchy	W	57	0	
6/18/2011	H	Jacksonville Dixie Blues	L	7	34		5/24/2014	H	Miami Fury	W	14	13	
							6/7/2014	A	Miami Fury	L	2	14	
4/14/2012	A	Orlando Anarchy	W	25	0		6/14/2014	H	Atlanta Phoenix	L	7	15	W
4/28/2012	H	Palm Beach Punishers	W	40	0								
5/5/2012	H	Jacksonville Dixie Blues	L	6	35		4/11/2015	H	Jacksonville Dixie Blues	W	17	9	
5/12/2012	H	Savannah Sabers	W	46	0		4/18/2015	H	Miami Fury	W	21	13	
5/19/2012	A	Atlanta Phoenix	W	26	25		5/2/2015	H	Daytona Waverunners	W	54	0	
6/2/2012	A	Miami Fury	W	1	0		5/9/2015	A	Atlanta Phoenix	L	19	26	
6/9/2012	H	Orlando Anarchy	W	42	20		5/16/2015	A	Jacksonville Dixie Blues	L	6	37	
6/16/2012	A	Palm Beach Punishers	W	1	0		5/30/2015	A	Daytona Waverunners	W	35	0	
							6/6/2015	H	Orlando Anarchy	W	1	0	
							6/13/2015	A	Miami Fury	L	0	26	

Tampa Bay Inferno Player Register (2010-2015)

Acevedo, Melissa (2013)
Alman, Angela (2013)
Amey, Hope (2012-2015)
Anderson, Britney (2014)
Anderson, Kechia (2012)
Armstrong, LeKesha "Kesha" (2010-2015)
Aubourg, Elise (2013-2015)
Bacon, Antoinette (2012)
Baker, Beth (2013, 2015)
Baker, Stacey (2011-2015)
Baldwin, Ty (2012-2014)
Baxter, Kesha (2012-2015)
Bolognino, Amanda (2015)
Brady, Candace (2013-2015)
Bratton, Kamille (2014-2015)
Briggs, Latonya (2015)
Brown, Elaina (2012-2014)
Brown, Latoya (2010)
Brown, Telisha (2010-2011)
Brundage, Kristen (2013-2015)
Bryant, Lynne (2014-2015)
Burage, Crystal (2014)
Bush, Taylor (2011)
Carroll, Tara (2012)
Chavez, Marcelina (2014-2015)
Coffee, Ella (2010-2015)
Colon, Camille (2011-2012)
Commodore, LeChele (2010)
Conley, Shantivia (2015)
Conner, Carmelita (2013-2014)
Copeland, Bonita (2010, 2012)
Correa, Jazmine (2013-2015)
Crawford, Stephanie (2012-2015)
Curd, Kyesha (2012)
Daniels, Dominique (2011-2013, 2015)
Dawson, Jen (2014-2015)
Douglas, Kadian (2012-2015)
Ferguson, Alexandra (2013)
Fernandez, Jackie (2014-2015)
Fietz, Nicole (2013)
Gordon, Shakerra (2013)
Gray, Catina (2012)
Green, Elaina (2015)
Green, Lee (2011-2012)
Griffin, Margaret (2013)
Hammonds, Rosa (2011-2015)
Harbour, Amber (2014)
Harper, Amy (2014)
Hicks, Rachel (2010)
Hodge, Kobi (2010)
Holloman, Marissa (2011-2013)
Holmes, Connie (2012-2013)
Hopkins, Hallie (2015)
Howard, Anita (2014-2015)
Huntley, Camille (2015)
Jacobs, Dominique (2015)
James, Fernella (2011)
Johnson, Virginia (2010)
Jones, Maureen (2015)
Keene, Tricia (2012)
Kelly, Sabrina (2012-2014)
Kennon, Ciara (2012-2013)
Krause, Abby (2013-2014)
Langlais, Renee (2010-2015)
Lopez, Rebecca (2013-2014)
Marshall, Valerie (2011-2014)
Martinez, Nelly (2010)
Mercado, Kris (2012)
Meredith, LaShawn (2010)
Mills, Angala (2012)
Moore, Breona (2011)
Myers, Janell (2012)
Nappier, Misty (2015)
Niemuth, Jenny (2010)
Olson, Lisa (2013)
Parker, Kim (2013)
Pistole, Shirley (2014-2015)
Purvis, Sandra (2010-2015)
Robinson, Ebony (2014-2015)
Rochon, Monica (2015)
Rodriguez, Paco (2012)
Rutland, Sheylia (2010-2015)
Ryan, Leah (2010)
Schmitt, Sabrina (2012, 2015)
Schultz, Aminnda (2012, 2014)
Seago, Sonya (2011)
Sellers, Tashawanna (2010-2011, 2014)
Shamburger, Kera (2013)
Shaw, Kim (2010-2015)
Shields, Goldette (2013)
Simmons, Chastity (2014)
Smith, Jasmine (2015)
Smith, Krenishia (2012)
Smith, Michelle (2013-2014)
Smith, Rita (2010, 2012)
Smith, Terelle (2013-2015)
Solomon, Cieasha (2012-2013)
Teeters, Jennifer (2014-2015)
Thompson, Candi (2010-2015)
Thompson, Kathryn (2014)
Townsend, Sharee (2013)
Tribble, Aiyisha (2010-2013)
Trowbridge, Meredithe (2013)
Viliere, Cherrelle (2010)
Walker, Chris (2013-2015)
Webb, Brandy (2011, 2013)
Williamson, Khameiah "Meiah" (2014-15)
Wilson, Elizabeth (2015)
Wright, Phylicia (2010, 2012-2013)
Yule, Christine (2015)

Tampa Bay Terminators

Year	League	Name	W	L	Conference	Division	DF	PR
2003	IWFL	Tampa Bay Terminators	4	5	Eastern	South Atlantic	2	--
2004	IWFL	Tampa Bay Terminators	7	3	Eastern	South Atlantic	1	CC
2005	IWFL	Tampa Bay Terminators	7	3	Eastern	South Atlantic	2	--
2006	IWFL	Tampa Bay Terminators	2	6	Eastern	South Atlantic	5	--
		Total	20	17				

Based in: Tampa, FL

Notes: Preceded by Tampa Tempest

Date	H/A	Opponent	Result	Score		Date	H/A	Opponent	Result	Score	
4/12/2003	A	Orlando Starz	W	8	0	4/2/2005	A	Orlando Mayhem	W	24	6
4/26/2003	A	Miami Fury	L	13	26	4/9/2005	A	Baton Rouge Wildcats	W	62	6
5/3/2003	H	Atlanta Xplosion	L	6	25	4/16/2005	H	Orlando Mayhem	W	27	0
5/10/2003	A	Orlando Starz	W	20	14	4/23/2005	A	Jacksonville Dixie Blues	L	27	58
5/17/2003	A	Atlanta Xplosion	L	14	28	5/7/2005	H	Miami Fury	W	25	8
5/24/2003	A	Oklahoma City Avengers	W	43	14	5/14/2005	A	Miami Fury	L	6	22
5/31/2003	H	Miami Fury	L	15	20	5/21/2005	H	Orlando Mayhem	W	14	3
6/9/2003	H	New York Sharks	L	0	36	6/4/2005	H	Baton Rouge Wildcats	W	63	0
6/14/2003	H	Orlando Starz	W	34	0	6/11/2005	A	Atlanta Xplosion	L	0	49
						6/25/2005	H	Miami Fury	W	21	14
4/3/2004	H	Jacksonville Dixie Blues	L	20	34						
4/17/2004	H	Orlando Mayhem	W	14	0	4/29/2006	A	Orlando Mayhem	W	41	13
4/24/2004	H	Atlanta Xplosion	W	7	6	5/13/2006	H	Baton Rouge Wildcats	W	62	0
5/1/2004	A	Carolina Spartans	W	70	0	5/20/2006	H	Atlanta Xplosion	L	0	46
5/8/2004	H	Orlando Mayhem	W	49	0	5/27/2006	H	Miami Fury	L	12	14
5/22/2004	A	Jacksonville Dixie Blues	L	23	34	6/3/2006	A	Miami Fury	L	19	22
5/29/2004	A	Atlanta Xplosion	W	22	8	6/10/2006	H	Orlando Mayhem	L	8	21
6/5/2004	H	Carolina Spartans	W	1	0	6/17/2006	A	Atlanta Xplosion	L	0	1
6/26/2004	H	Atlanta Xplosion	W	21	8 S	6/24/2006	A	Miami Fury	L	0	1
7/10/2004	A	New York Sharks	L	7	29 CC						

Tampa Tempest

Year	League	Name	W	L	Conference	Division	DF	PR
2000	WPFL	Tampa Tempest	1	6	National	South	3	--
2001	WPFL	Tampa Tempest	0	6	--	--	4	--
2002	IWFL	Tampa Tempest	2	5	Eastern	--	5	--
		Total	3	17				

Based in: Tampa, FL

Notes: Succeeded by Tampa Bay Terminators

Date	H/A	Opponent	Result	Score		Date	Opponent	Result	Score	
10/21/2000	A	Minnesota Vixen	L	0	63	4/27/2002	Orlando Starz	L	6	34
11/4/2000	H	Miami Fury	L	22	34	5/4/2002	Orlando Starz	L	6	20
11/11/2000	A	Daytona Beach Barracudas	L	6	62	5/18/2002	Miami Fury	L	0	34
11/18/2000	A	Miami Fury	L	0	33	5/25/2002	Miami Fury	L	0	48
11/25/2000	A	Daytona Beach Barracudas	L	6	27	5/31/2002	New Hampshire Freedom	W	26	0
12/2/2000	H	Miami Fury	L	12	28	6/8/2002	Orlando Starz	W	14	6
12/9/2000	H	Carolina Cougars	W	8	7	6/22/2002	Orlando Starz	L	6	9
8/11/2001	H	Austin Rage	L	0	21					
8/18/2001	H	New York Sharks	L	0	25 I					
8/25/2001	H	Houston Energy	L	0	53					
9/1/2001	A	New England Storm	L	0	41					
9/8/2001	A	Houston Energy	L	0	51					
9/22/2001	A	Austin Rage	L	0	1					

Tennessee Heat

Year	League	Name	W	L	Conference	Division	DF	PR
2001	WFL	Tennessee Heat	2	8	--	--	--	--
2002	WFL	Tennessee Heat	0	2	--	--	--	--
2003	WFL	Tennessee Heat	0	7	--	--	--	CC
2005	WFL	Tennessee Heat	2	1	--	--	--	C
2006	WFL	Tennessee Heat	1	1	--	--	--	C
2007	WFL	Tennessee Heat	0	1	--	--	--	--
		Total	**5**	**20**				

Based in: Nashville, TN

6/9/2001	A	Tampa Bay Force	L	0	60	IE	5/17/2003	A	Memphis Maulers	L	6	34
6/30/2001	A	Austin Outlaws	L	6	22	I	5/24/2003	H	Atlanta Xplosion	L	6	35 I
7/14/2001	H	Carolina Cougars	L	0	22	I	6/7/2003	H	Memphis Maulers	L	6	14
7/21/2001	H	Austin Outlaws	W	6	0	I*	6/14/2003	A	Fayetteville Thunder	L	20	28
7/28/2001	A	Carolina Cougars	L	0	18	I	6/21/2003	A	Atlanta Xplosion	L	0	50 I
8/4/2001	A	Orlando Lightning	W	6	0	I	7/19/2003	H	Fayetteville Thunder	L	6	30
8/11/2001	A	Carolina Cougars	L	0	10	I	7/26/2003	A	Fayetteville Thunder	L	14	22 CC
8/25/2001		Miami Fury	L	6	16	I	5/21/2005		Kentucky Force	W	14	0
9/1/2001	H	Orlando Lightning	L	3	14	I	6/25/2005		Kentucky Force	W	33	0
9/29/2001	A	Carolina Cougars	L	6	43	I	7/30/2005	H	Mississippi Rapids	L	6	8 C
7/20/2002		Carolina Cougars	L	8	27		6/10/2006	A	Kentucky Force	W	28	12
8/10/2002	A	Carolina Cougars	L	0	44		7/15/2006	A	Jacksonville Dixie Blues	L	25	54 C
							6/9/2007	A	Clarksville Fox	L	22	40

Tennessee Legacy

Year	League	Name	W	L	Conference	Division	DF	PR
2015	WSFL	Tennessee Legacy	7	1	Southern	--	1	C

Based in: Memphis, TN
Notes: Preceded by Memphis Dynasty

5/2/2015	A	Arkansas Assassins	W	57	6		6/20/2015	H	Atlanta Heartbreakers	W	64	0
5/9/2015	H	Cincinnati Sizzle	W	48	0		6/27/2015	H	DFW Xtreme	W	48	0
5/16/2015	A	Atlanta Heartbreakers	W	60	0		7/18/2015	A	Tri-Cities Thunder	W	46	30 CC
6/6/2015	H	DFW Xtreme	W	46	12		8/1/2015	A	Keystone Assault	L	7	9 C

Tennessee Mountaincatz

Year	League	Name	W	L	Conference	Division	DF	PR
2003	AWFL	Tennessee Mountaincatz	3	0	--	--	--	--

Based in: Blountville, TN

4/12/2003	H	Lee County Predators	W	16	0	5/3/2003	A	Lee County Predators	W	40	0
4/26/2003	A	Harlan Red Devils	W	36	0						

Tennessee Train

Year	League	Name	W	L	Conference	Division	DF	PR
2013	WFA	Tennessee Train	1	7	National	Division 5 (Southeast)	3	--
2014	WFA	Tennessee Train	5	3	National	Southeast	3	--
2015	IWFL	Tennessee Train	3	5	Eastern	South Atlantic	4	--
		Total	**9**	**15**				

Based in: Chattanooga, TN

Tennessee Train Game-By-Game Results

Date	H/A	Opponent	W/L	PF	PA
4/6/2013	A	Jacksonville Dixie Blues	L	12	67
4/13/2013	H	Savannah Sabers	L	20	28
4/20/2013	H	Atlanta Phoenix	L	0	42
5/4/2013	A	Cincinnati Sizzle	L	6	38
5/11/2013	H	Savannah Sabers	W	34	16
5/18/2013	A	Atlanta Phoenix	L	0	48
6/1/2013	A	Savannah Sabers	L	32	40
6/8/2013	H	Derby City Dynamite	L	0	14
4/5/2014	A	Savannah Sabers	W	22	20
4/12/2014	H	Atlanta Phoenix	L	0	34
4/19/2014	H	Cincinnati Sizzle	W	30	6
4/26/2014	A	Daytona Breakers	W	26	21
5/3/2014	H	Jacksonville Dixie Blues	L	14	27
5/17/2014	H	Savannah Sabers	W	28	0
5/31/2014	A	Derby City Dynamite	L	12	40
6/7/2014	A	Orlando Anarchy	W	24	14
4/11/2015	H	Carolina Queens	L	8	18
4/25/2015	A	Knoxville Lightning	W	35	12
5/2/2015	H	Huntsville Tigers	L	16	34
5/9/2015	A	Carolina Phoenix	L	0	40
5/16/2015	A	Carolina Queens	L	0	14
5/23/2015	H	Huntsville Tigers	L	22	42
5/30/2015	H	Knoxville Lightning	W	28	6
6/13/2015	A	Huntsville Tigers	W	32	6

Tennessee Train Player Register (2013-2015)

Balazs, Katie (2013-2014)
Barbour, Kayla (2013-2015)
Basham Smith, Trista (2013-2014)
Basham, Kristie (2013-2014)
Beene, Libby (2013-2014)
Bennett, Lena (2014)
Bischer, Corri (2013-2015)
Bowers, Amanda (2015)
Butler, Catrice (2014-2015)
Causby, Angie (2013-2015)
Cherry, Sarah (2015)
Couthron, Baylee (2015)
Crow, Casey (2013)
Dabbs, Chasity (2015)
Dabbs, Faith (2014)
Daniel, Trisha (2013)
Davis, Kacee (2014-2015)
Davis, Rometrice Ruiboi (2015)
Fletcher, Genise "Muffy" (2014-2015)
Goodner, Amy (2013-2014)
Heinrich, Stephanie (2013-2014)
Hicks, Michelle (2013-2015)
Hiett, Kendra (2014-2015)
Horton, Starlisa (2013-2015)
Hudson, Felicia (2013-2015)
Hurtson, Dequana (2014-2015)
Johnson, Jennifer (2013)
Johnson, Leandra (2014-2015)
Laminack, Amanda "Mandy" (2013-2014)
Lancaster, Candace "Luckii" (2013-2015)
Landry, Erica (2014-2015)
Lange, Lauren (2013)
Lawhorn, Margie (2015)
Lloyd, Alexis (2015)
Lofty, Crystal (2015)
Martin, Holly (2013-2015)
McCahill, Hannah (2013-2015)
McCaleb, Michelle (2013-2014)
McCall, Ashley (2015)
McColley, Misheal (2015)
Meister-Hughes, Chris (2013)
Miller, Brittney (2014)
Montanez, Lilli (2015)
Montgomery, Denisha (2013-2015)
Moore, Jessica (2015)
Myers, Denise (2013-2014)
Newton, Casey (2015)
Oliver, Brandi (2013-2015)
Powell, Lee (2015)
Rich, Melissa (2013-2015)
Rogers, Alicia (2013)
Roush, Rachelle (2015)
Russell, Shereese (2013-2014)
Sanders, Nelli (2015)
Sanders, Robin (2013-2014)
Sheppard, Tasha (2014-2015)
Sichwart, Nelli (2014)
Singleton, Latoya (2015)
Stewart, Kirien (2015)
Stokes, Jackie (2015)
Trivett, Ashley (2015)
Wade, Amanda (2013-2014)
Wright, Jennifer (2015)

Tennessee Venom

Year	League	Name	W	L	Conference	Division	DF	PR
2001	NWFA	Tennessee Venom	4	4	Southern	--	3	--
2002	NWFA	Tennessee Venom	0	8	--	Mid-Atlantic	4	--
2003	NWFA	Tennessee Venom	2	6	Southern	Central	5	--
2004	NWFA	Tennessee Venom	1	6	Southern	South	4	--
2005	NWFA	Tennessee Venom	3	5	Southern	--	12	--
2007	NWFA	East Tennessee Rhythm	4	4	Southern	Central	2	--
		Total	**14**	**33**				

Based in: Bristol, TN

Date	H/A	Opponent	W/L	PF	PA
4/21/2001	A	Nashville Dream	W	20	14
5/5/2001	H	Chattanooga Locomotion	W	24	18
5/12/2001	H	Alabama Renegades	L	13	20
5/19/2001	A	Alabama Renegades	L	6	27
6/2/2001	H	Nashville Dream	W	14	8
6/9/2001	A	Chattanooga Locomotion	W	27	6
6/16/2001	H	Pensacola Power	L	6	20
6/23/2001	A	D.C. Divas	L	0	52
4/20/2002		Asheville Assault	L	14	36
4/27/2002		Baltimore Burn	L	0	30
5/4/2002		Asheville Assault	L	28	48
5/18/2002	A	D.C. Divas	L	0	53
5/25/2002		Baltimore Burn	L	0	57
6/8/2002		Asheville Assault	L	0	22
6/15/2002	H	D.C. Divas	L	0	60
6/22/2002		Asheville Assault	L	0	1

Continued on next page

Tennessee Venom Game-By-Game Results (continued)

Date	H/A	Opponent	W/L	Score		Date	H/A	Opponent	W/L	Score	
4/19/2003	A	Asheville Assault	L	0	26	4/16/2005	H	Knoxville Tornadoes	W	38	0
4/26/2003	H	Knoxville Summit	W	26	0	4/23/2005	A	Atlanta Leopards	W	50	0
5/10/2003	A	Nashville Dream	L	0	60	4/30/2005	H	Chattanooga Locomotion	L	14	16
5/17/2003	H	Asheville Assault	L	0	54	5/14/2005	A	Alabama Renegades	L	6	36
5/24/2003	H	Chattanooga Locomotion	L	0	85	5/21/2005	H	Nashville Dream	L	0	28
5/31/2003	A	Alabama Renegades	L	0	49	5/28/2005	A	Knoxville Tornadoes	W	28	24
6/7/2003	H	Atlanta Leopards	W	46	14	6/11/2005	A	Asheville Assault	L	14	22
6/14/2003	A	Knoxville Summit	L	6	13	6/18/2005	H	Chattanooga Locomotion	L	0	1
4/3/2004	H	Nashville Dream	L	0	31	4/21/2007	H	Alabama Renegades	W	14	8
4/17/2004	A	Chattanooga Locomotion	L	0	49	4/28/2007	A	Nashville Dream	L	22	28
4/24/2004	H	Asheville Assault	L	6	19	5/5/2007	H	Chattanooga Locomotion	L	0	72
5/15/2004	H	Asheville Assault	L	12	25	5/12/2007	A	Richmond Spirit	W	1	0 N
5/29/2004	A	Asheville Assault	L	12	13	5/26/2007	A	Alabama Renegades	L	0	33
6/5/2004	A	Atlanta Leopards	W	29	13	6/2/2007	H	Nashville Dream	W	32	12
6/12/2004	H	Chattanooga Locomotion	L	7	28	6/9/2007	H	Richmond Spirit	W	1	0 N
						6/16/2007	A	Chattanooga Locomotion	L	0	56

Tennessee Venom Player Register (2002, 2004-2005, 2007)

Baker, Laura (2005, 2007)
Barrett, Christy (2007)
Blankenship, Shelly (2007)
Bowers, Kristen (2002, 2004)
Brandolini, Brenda (2005)
Brown, Kim (2004-2005, 2007)
Buckingham, Lynsey (2004-2005)
Burke, Vanessa (2002)
Calloway, Shauna (2002)
Canter, Kembley (2002, 2005)
Cordle, Jennifer (2002)
Cothern, Vickie (2007)
Craighead, Cari (2007)
Davis, Jill (2005, 2007)
Delapp, Mary (2007)
Eakin, Deana (2004, 2007)
Estes, Annette (2005, 2007)
Fisher, Vanessa (2004)
Freeman, Summer (2004-2005, 2007)
Garland, Nikki (2004)
Gilliam, Jennifer (2002, 2005)
Graves, Bridget (2002, 2004-2005)
Greene, Kim (2005)
Greenway, Susan (2002, 2004-2005)
Gregory, Neysa (2005)
Groff, Michelle (2005)
Guffey, Nicki (2007)
Hall, Meghan (2002, 2007)
Harper, Christy (2002)
Hart, Terri (2007)
Hartman, Diana (2005)
Helton, Deb (2004-2005)
Henderson, Amy (2002)
Herbert, Malinda (2002)
Hess, Chris (2007)
Howell, Shara (2005, 2007)
Hurt, Caroline (2002)
Johnson, Dean (2002, 2005, 2007)
Johnson, Jo (2005)
Keeling, Stacey (2005)
Keen, Kesha (2002)
Lapitan, Gaily (2007)
Law, Joni (2004-2005, 2007)
Laws, Rosa (2002)
Loving, Lisa (2002)
Macias, Amy (2002)
Main, Teena (2002, 2005, 2007)
Marks, Tameasha (2002)
Masoner, Suzanne (2007)
Mayberry, Jennifer (2002, 2004-05, 2007)
McClanahan, Natasha (2002)
Meade, Celeste (2002)
Meister-Hughes, Chris (2002, 2004-2005)
Morefield, Sheila (2007)
Mottern, Gemma (2002)
Mounce, Leann (2005)
Naumann, Tanya (2004-2005)
Niedermaier, Amy (2007)
Patrick, Tanicka (2002)
Pennington, Sue (2007)
Peters, Robyn (2005)
Powell, Vernice (2002, 2005)
Ray, Kim (2002)
Reece, Stacey (2005, 2007)
Saunders, Nakya (2004)
Smith, Tammy (2002)
St. Louis, Catlin (2002)
Stratton, Megan (2002)
Swarthout, Nikki (2004)
Thompson, Emily Anne (2005, 2007)
Townsend, Jessica (2007)
Turner, Cindy (2002, 2005)
Wallen, Heather (2002, 2005)
Williford, Tracie (2002)
Woodle, Tammy (2004-2005)
Wooldridge, Jennifer (2007)

Three Rivers Xplosion

Year	League		Name	W	L	Conference	Division	DF	PR
2011	WSFL	IX	Three Rivers Xplosion	3	6	--	--	--	--
2012	W8FL		Three Rivers Xplosion	2	7	Eastern	--	3	CC
2013	W8FL		Three Rivers Xplosion	0	5	--	--	4	--
2015	W8FL	X	Three Rivers Xplosion	0	1	--	--	--	--
			Total	**5**	**19**				

Based in: Pittsburgh, PA
Notes: Preceded by Steel City Renegades

Three Rivers Xplosion Game-By-Game Results

4/9/2011	A	Binghamton Tiger Cats	L	12	40	6/2/2012	A	West Virginia Wildfire	L	6	50	
4/23/2011	A	Baltimore Burn	L	6	48	6/23/2012		Mass Chaos	L	14	20	
4/30/2011	H	Binghamton Tiger Cats	L	8	22	7/7/2012		West Virginia Wildfire	L	0	40	
5/7/2011	A	Jersey Justice	W	1	0	7/21/2012		Mass Chaos	W	1	0	
5/21/2011	A	Binghamton Tiger Cats	L	0	1	7/28/2012		West Virginia Wildfire	L	0	46	CC
6/11/2011	H	Jersey Justice	W	1	0							
6/11/2011	H	Baltimore Burn	L	0	54	4/20/2013	H	West Virginia Wildfire	L	6	46	
6/18/2011	A	Binghamton Tiger Cats	L	0	1	4/27/2013	H	Cape Fear Thunder	L	16	20	
6/25/2011		West Virginia Bruisers	W	28	16	5/4/2013	H	Binghamton Tiger Cats	L	30	38	*
						5/11/2013	A	Binghamton Tiger Cats	L	0	34	
4/14/2012	H	Mass Chaos	W	36	12	5/18/2013	A	West Virginia Wildfire	L	0	1	
4/21/2012	A	Cape Fear Thunder	L	0	30							
4/28/2012	H	Cape Fear Thunder	L	6	36	4/25/2015	H	New York Knockout	L	18	20	**
5/5/2012	A	Binghamton Tiger Cats	L	0	1							

Three Rivers Xplosion Player Register (2015)

Anantarow, Lisa (2015)
Barrett, LaKeitha (2015)
Barrington, Kate (2015)
Berry, Tonyarae (2015)
Gilbert, Queen (2015)
Harris, Sherell (2015)
Howell, Kristina (2015)
Lindsey, Danielle (2015)
Martini, Chasity (2015)
McCullough, Stephanie (2015)
Peer, Dee (2015)
Reddick, Takia (2015)
Sopko, Heather (2015)
Wilson, Sheila (2015)

Tidewater Floods

Year	League	Name	W	L	Conference	Division	DF	PR
2005	NWFA	Tidewater Floods	0	8	Northern	--	18	--
2006	NWFA	Tidewater Floods	2	6	Northern	North Atlantic	3	--
		Total	2	14				

Based in: Norfolk, VA

4/16/2005	H	Baltimore Burn	L	8	38	4/22/2006	A	Harrisburg Angels	W	33	6	
4/30/2005	H	Philadelphia Phoenix	L	0	47	4/29/2006	H	D.C. Divas	L	0	45	
5/14/2005	A	D.C. Divas	L	0	51	5/6/2006	A	Baltimore Burn	L	0	49	
5/21/2005	A	Columbus Comets	L	0	100	5/20/2006	H	Philadelphia Phoenix	L	8	28	
5/28/2005	H	D.C. Divas	L	0	53	6/3/2006	A	D.C. Divas	L	0	65	
6/4/2005	A	Baltimore Burn	L	0	68	6/10/2006	H	Baltimore Burn	L	12	48	
6/11/2005	A	Philadelphia Phoenix	L	12	48	6/17/2006	A	Philadelphia Phoenix	L	0	50	
6/18/2005	H	Pittsburgh Passion	L	0	49	6/24/2006	H	Harrisburg Angels	W	10	0	

Tidewater Floods Player Register (2005-2006)

Adams, Dawn (2006)
Allen, Rowena (2005-2006)
Anderson, Nicole (2006)
Anselmo, Kimberly (2005)
Artis, Tiffany (2005-2006)
Atkinson, Lakeesha (2005-2006)
Awkard, Stacey (2006)
Bagirmvano, Monique (2005)
Barnes, Kim (2005)
Berryhill, Renee (2005)
Bowser, Jovan (2005-2006)
Braxton, Shavonne (2006)
Brooks, Tracy (2005-2006)
Brown, Felisha (2006)
Brown, Tameca (2005)
Buttacavoli, Jennifer (2006)
Clark, Sharon (2005)
Conteras, Heidi (2005)
Corprew, Ginger (2006)
Council, Patricia (2006)
Davis, Gracie (2005-2006)
Erdmann, Luciana (2006)
Farricker, Sam (2006)
Glover, Lynn (2005)
Guadalupe, Ashley (2005)
Haskins, Terry (2005-2006)
Holt, Keyla (2005)
Huntley, Pam (2005-2006)
Jonax, Pam (2005)
Jones, Natasha (2006)
Jones, Sharina (2005)
Keener, Vicki (2005)
Kendall, Jacqueline (2005)
Korba, Allison (2006)
Kurfiss, Heather (2006)
Mathieu, Selina (2005)
Meggs, Angele (2006)
Mims, Tammy (2006)
Neneng, Jasmin (2005-2006)
Noise, Melanie (2006)
Plumeau, Cheryl (2005-2006)
Powell, Joanne (2005-2006)
Price, Kristina (2005)
Puchakski, Regina (2005)
Raine, Ginger (2005)
Ramirez, Angie (2005)
Riddick, Sharon (2005-2006)
Ross, Ylander (2006)
Salgado, Esperanza (2006)
Seymore, Carmenta (2006)
Shaw, Sherice (2005)
Smith, Robin (2005)
Smith, Tammajo (2005)
Spruill, Shaniel (2005)
Summerlin, Ebony (2005)
Tedesco, Angela (2006)
True, Renee (2006)
Turner, Amanda (2006)
Valentine, Brandii (2005-2006)
Walker, Tia (2006)
West, Sarah (2006)
Williams, Candis (2005-2006)
Williams, Dorian (2006)
Wright, Brandy (2006)
Yeuell, Robin (2005)

Toledo Reign

Year	League	Name	W	L	Conference	Division	DF	PR
2003	WPFL	Toledo Reign	0	5	American	North	4	--
2004	WPFL	Toledo Reign	3	7	National	North	3	--
2005	WPFL	Toledo Reign	6	4	National	North	3	--
2006	WPFL	Toledo Reign	4	4	National	North	2	--
2007	WPFL	Toledo Reign	3	5	National	North	2	--
2009	WFA	Toledo Reign	1	7	National	Central	4	--
2010	WFA	Toledo Reign	1	7	National	North Central	4	--
2011	WFA	Toledo Reign	4	4	National	North Central	4	--
2012	WFA	Toledo Reign	3	6	National	Division 5 (North Central)	2	W
2013	WFA	Toledo Reign	1	7	National	Division 3 (North Central)	4	--
2014	WFA	Toledo Reign	6	3	National	Mideast	1	W
2015	IWFL	Toledo Reign	3	6	Eastern	Great Lakes	1	Q
		Total	**35**	**65**				

Based in: Toledo, OH

Date	H/A	Opponent	W/L	PF	PA	
8/23/2003	H	Dayton Rebellion	L	18	30	
9/13/2003	H	Northern Ice	L	0	80	
9/20/2003	A	Minnesota Vixen	L	0	61	
9/27/2003	A	New England Storm	L	14	30	
10/11/2003	A	Syracuse Sting	L	12	55	
7/31/2004	H	Northern Ice	L	6	43	
8/7/2004	H	Missouri Avengers	W	88	12	
8/14/2004	H	Indiana Speed	W	28	26	
8/28/2004	A	Missouri Avengers	W	1	0	
9/4/2004	A	Minnesota Vixen	L	0	27	
9/11/2004	H	Delaware Griffins	L	22	34	
9/18/2004	A	Northern Ice	L	8	49	
9/25/2004	A	Dallas Diamonds	L	0	68	
10/2/2004	A	Delaware Griffins	L	28	52	
10/23/2004	H	Minnesota Vixen	L	8	14	
7/30/2005	H	Indiana Speed	W	26	20	*
8/6/2005	H	Minnesota Vixen	L	22	27	
8/13/2005	H	Carolina Queens	W	56	0	
8/20/2005	A	Carolina Queens	W	34	0	
9/10/2005	H	Albany Ambush	W	48	6	
9/17/2005	A	Indiana Speed	L	10	21	
9/24/2005	A	Minnesota Vixen	L	8	30	
10/1/2005	H	Cape Fear Thunder	W	53	0	
10/15/2005	A	Albany Ambush	L	14	20	
10/22/2005	A	Minnesota Vixen	W	36	22	
7/22/2006	A	Minnesota Vixen	L	8	32	
7/29/2006	H	Carolina Queens	W	36	0	
8/5/2006	H	New England Intensity	W	34	22	
8/12/2006	A	Wisconsin Wolves	L	0	27	
8/19/2006	H	Indiana Speed	L	6	13	
9/2/2006	A	Carolina Queens	W	51	0	
9/9/2006	H	Wisconsin Wolves	W	24	6	
9/16/2006	A	Indiana Speed	L	8	18	
8/18/2007	H	Carolina Queens	W	33	0	
8/25/2007	A	Connecticut Cyclones	W	20	0	
9/1/2007	A	Carolina Queens	W	28	0	
9/15/2007	A	Minnesota Vixen	L	6	13	
9/22/2007	H	Empire State Roar	L	0	40	
9/29/2007	H	Indiana Speed	L	7	20	
10/6/2007	A	Empire State Roar	L	7	51	
10/20/2007	H	Minnesota Vixen	L	6	18	
4/25/2009	H	West Michigan Mayhem	L	0	47	
5/2/2009	H	Indiana Speed	L	0	60	
5/9/2009	A	West Michigan Mayhem	L	0	57	
5/16/2009	H	Fort Wayne Flash	L	0	47	
5/30/2009	H	Dayton Diamonds	W	20	8	
6/13/2009	A	Fort Wayne Flash	L	0	38	
6/20/2009	A	Indiana Speed	L	0	58	
6/27/2009	A	Dayton Diamonds	L	0	6	
4/10/2010	H	Cleveland Fusion	L	7	18	
4/17/2010	A	West Michigan Mayhem	L	0	71	
4/24/2010	H	Detroit Dark Angels	L	6	7	
5/8/2010	A	Dayton Diamonds	W	7	0	
5/15/2010	A	Cleveland Fusion	L	0	62	
5/22/2010	A	West Michigan Mayhem	L	0	64	
6/12/2010	A	Detroit Dark Angels	L	0	20	
6/19/2010	H	Columbus Comets	L	0	65	
4/2/2011	A	Dayton Diamonds	W	61	0	
4/9/2011	H	Kentucky Karma	W	23	0	
4/16/2011	A	West Michigan Mayhem	L	12	54	
4/30/2011	H	Detroit Dark Angels	W	19	6	
5/7/2011	H	Dayton Diamonds	W	63	0	
5/14/2011	H	Indy Crash	L	0	34	
6/4/2011	A	Detroit Dark Angels	L	6	33	
6/18/2011	A	Cincinnati Sizzle	L	25	34	
4/14/2012	H	Cincinnati Sizzle	W	68	14	
4/21/2012	H	Detroit Dark Angels	L	0	35	
4/28/2012	A	West Michigan Mayhem	L	13	41	
5/12/2012	A	Pittsburgh Passion	L	14	71	
5/19/2012	A	Derby City Dynamite	L	18	20	
6/2/2012	A	Cincinnati Sizzle	W	14	6	
6/9/2012	A	Derby City Dynamite	W	32	22	
6/16/2012	H	Indy Crash	L	7	28	
6/23/2012	A	Indy Crash	L	35	52	W
4/6/2013	A	Cincinnati Sizzle	L	14	36	
4/13/2013	H	Pittsburgh Passion	L	0	42	
4/20/2013	H	Cleveland Fusion	L	6	36	
5/4/2013	A	Columbus Comets	L	7	56	
5/11/2013	H	Derby City Dynamite	W	26	24	
5/18/2013	A	Cleveland Fusion	L	0	50	
6/1/2013	A	Derby City Dynamite	L	0	14	
6/8/2013	H	Cincinnati Sizzle	L	12	20	

Continued on next page

Toledo Reign Game-By-Game Results (continued)

Date	H/A	Opponent	Result			Date	H/A	Opponent	Result			
4/5/2014	A	Derby City Dynamite	W	26	6	4/11/2015	H	Pittsburgh Passion	L	0	66	
4/19/2014	A	Central Maryland Seahawks	W	1	0	4/18/2015	A	Baltimore Nighthawks	L	18	29	
4/26/2014	H	Cincinnati Sizzle	W	33	0	4/25/2015	A	Detroit Pride	L	13	17	
5/3/2014	H	Pittsburgh Force	W	35	6	5/2/2015	A	Wisconsin Warriors	W	28	0	
5/10/2014	A	Columbus Comets	L	0	48	5/16/2015	A	Detroit Pride	L	21	26	
5/17/2014	H	Cleveland Fusion	L	0	46	5/30/2015	H	Baltimore Nighthawks	W	20	14	
5/31/2014	A	Pittsburgh Force	W	37	0	6/6/2015	A	Pittsburgh Passion	L	0	63	
6/7/2014	H	Central Maryland Seahawks	W	1	0 N	6/13/2015	H	Wisconsin Warriors	W	1	0	
6/14/2014	A	Columbus Comets	L	0	22 W	6/20/2015	H	Carolina Queens	L	6	20	Q

Toledo Reign Player Register (2009-2015)

Alberts, Maggie (2009-2012, 2014-2015)
Ambrose, Sue (2009-2010)
Applegate, Maegan (2009-2015)
Averesch, Amanda (2010)
Barbee, T. (2009)
Barbernitz, Kristen (2012-2013)
Barker, Jasmine (2010)
Bathrick, Vic (2012-2013)
Belcher, Sam (2014)
Benson, Charmaine (2013)
Billick, Keri Jo (2011-2013)
Blasingim, Angie (2015)
Bowen, Sandra "Sandi" (2009-2015)
Brotherwood, Doris (2013)
Burse, Chez (2009-2010)
Cannon, Kleshona (2009)
Carpenter, Maranda (2013)
Clark, Jacki (2009-2012, 2014-2015)
Clark, Kacey (2010-2015)
Collette, Mitchi (2010)
Collins, Sasha (2012-2013)
Coressel, Amanda (2010-2012)
Cosper, Ruby (2011)
Crabtree, Erin (2010-2013)
Csomos, Kaitlyn (2014)
Davis, Ciera (2009-2010)
Davis, Denise (2015)
Dempster, Julz (2013)
Dempster-Walsh, Kendra (2014-2015)
Dunn, Ella (2010, 2012-2013)
Dupler, Chrystal (2014)
Eipperle, Heather (2011)
Emerson, Beth (2015)
Fannin, LeAnna (2009-2011)
Finley, Jocelyn (2011)
Fonseca, Francesca (2009)
Gehrke, Loren (2015)
Geiger, Megyn (2010-2011)
Gibbs, Courtney (2012)
Gray, Zareth "Zee" (2013-2015)
Green, Latoya (2009)
Griffin, Kristin (2012, 2014)
Griswold, Octavia (2009-2010, 2013)
Gross, Maggie (2009, 2011)
Harris, Toni (2015)
Hatch, Michelle (2009-2013)
Haynes, Shantel "Telly" (2012-13, 2015)
Hodges, Gabby (2011-2015)
Holley, India (2010-2011, 2015)
Hubbard, Angie (2015)
Keller, Haleigh (2012)
Kidd, Wendy (2010, 2013-2015)
Kincaid, Jess (2011-2014)
Knight, Andrea (2013)
Kolan, Anneliese (2012-2013)
Koralewski, Julia (2014)
Krzystan, Amanda (2014)
LaFrance, Deirdre (2010)
Lewis, Marabeth (2009-2015)
Lieto, Stephanie (2012)
Lillie, Kristi (2009-2015)
Lipstraw, Erica (2011)
Lipstraw, Jessica (2010-2011)
Lowery, Sabrina (2009-2011)
Lowery, Serenia (2009)
Lynch, Brandi (2012)
Maiden, Amanda (2009)
McDougall, Amanda (2009, 2011-2012)
McKenzie, Megan (2010-2011)
Meadows, Natalie (2012)
Miller, Tara (2014)
Moore, Daneé (2009)
Munoz, Mirta (2009-2013, 2015)
Nelson, Monica (2014)
Nemecek, Jennifer (2009)
Nisbett, Lauren (2015)
Nobles, Karla (2010)
Patman, Brianna (2010-2015)
Pekalska, Aneta (2012)
Pettaway, Toya (2011-2012)
Porter, Jenne (2009)
Preston, Alicia (2013)
Reams, Rosalind (2015)
Reams, Vicky (2014-2015)
Redford, Brandi (2014)
Reed, Denise (2010-2012, 2014)
Riley, Joyell (2009)
Rizer, Brandi (2013-2015)
Romanowski, Patricia (2009)
Ruman, Gale (2009-2011)
Rupert, Brittney (2009-2012)
Sanchez, Chris (2011)
Schardt, Anggie (2009-2011)
Schreiber, Andrea (2013-2015)
Schweikert, Michele (2009)
Shade, Katie (2014)
Shinaul, Toya (2013-2015)
Slater, Rebecca (2011-2012)
Spangler, Jaime (2011-2012)
Spivey, Kaleena (2011)
Stacey, Jodi (2011-2012)
Stevens, Kim (2010)
Stevens, Sarah (2014)
Summers, Molly (2013-2014)
Swinehart, Heather (2009-2011, 2013)
Tanasale, Veronique (2015)
Thames, Amanda (2010)
Tropf, Jasmin (2009)
Vossen, Leah (2009)
Wagner, Sara (2014)
Wagner, Tina (2013-2014)
Watson, Brittaney (2015)
Weaver, Angela (2009)
Webb, Yemaya (2009-2010)
Weising, Ali (2014)
Welling, Lori (2009)
Whetstone, Pamela (2010)
Williams, Jennifer (2009)
Williams, Tayana (2009)
Willobee, Barb (2014)
Zam, Ashley (2015)

Toledo Spitfire

Year	League	Name	W	L	Conference	Division	DF	PR
2003	NWFA	Toledo Spitfire	2	6	Northern	Great Lakes	4	--
2004	NWFA	Toledo Spitfire	3	5	Northern	Great Lakes	5	--
2005	NWFA	Toledo Spitfire	0	8	Northern	--	17	--
2006	NWFA	Toledo Spitfire	2	7	Northern	Northwest	4	--
2007	NWFA	Tree Town Spitfire	2	6	Northern	West	3	--
2008	NWFA	Tree Town Spitfire	2	6	Northern	North	3	--
		Total	**11**	**38**				

Based in: Ann Arbor, MI (2007-2008); Toledo, OH (2003-2006)

Franchise Game-By-Game Records, 1999-2015

Toledo Spitfire Game-By-Game Results

Date	H/A	Opponent	W/L	PF	PA
4/12/2003	A	Indiana Thunder	W	32	28
4/19/2003	H	Cleveland Fusion	L	0	66
5/3/2003	H	Southwest Michigan Jaguars	L	0	33
5/10/2003	A	Detroit Demolition	L	0	95
5/17/2003	A	Southwest Michigan Jaguars	L	0	41
5/24/2003	A	Cleveland Fusion	L	0	84
5/31/2003	H	Detroit Demolition	L	0	81
6/14/2003	H	Indiana Thunder	W	30	8
4/3/2004	A	Wisconsin Riveters	W	37	0
4/24/2004	H	Indiana Thunder	W	32	14
5/1/2004	H	Southwest Michigan Jaguars	L	6	66
5/8/2004	H	Columbus Comets	L	0	50
5/15/2004	A	Indiana Thunder	W	18	8
5/29/2004	H	Cleveland Fusion	L	0	35
6/5/2004	A	Southwest Michigan Jaguars	L	0	74
6/12/2004	A	Detroit Demolition	L	0	93
4/16/2005	A	Cincinnati Sizzle	L	6	43
4/30/2005	H	Baltimore Burn	L	0	46
5/14/2005	A	Southwest Michigan Jaguars	L	0	40
5/21/2005	H	Milwaukee Momentum	L	6	14
5/28/2005	H	Kentucky Karma	L	0	37
6/4/2005	H	Pittsburgh Passion	L	0	53
6/11/2005	A	Columbus Comets	L	0	74
6/18/2005	A	Erie Illusion	L	0	44
4/15/2006	H	Erie Illusion	L	0	8
4/22/2006	A	Milwaukee Momentum	L	8	42
4/29/2006	H	Cincinnati Sizzle	L	22	46
5/6/2006	A	West Michigan Mayhem	L	0	31
5/13/2006	A	Fort Wayne Flash	W	6	0
5/27/2006	A	Cincinnati Sizzle	L	14	27
6/3/2006	H	Milwaukee Momentum	L	6	20
6/10/2006	A	West Michigan Mayhem	L	0	46
6/17/2006	A	Erie Illusion	W	8	7
4/7/2007	H	Erie Illusion	W	6	0 *
4/21/2007	A	West Michigan Mayhem	L	0	50
5/5/2007	A	Milwaukee Momentum	L	6	13
5/12/2007	H	Fort Wayne Flash	L	14	16
5/19/2007	H	Milwaukee Momentum	W	30	10
5/26/2007	H	West Michigan Mayhem	L	0	41
6/9/2007	A	Erie Illusion	L	8	12
6/16/2007	A	Fort Wayne Flash	L	0	28
4/19/2008	A	Indianapolis Chaos	W	1	0
4/26/2008	H	Erie Illusion	L	0	15
5/3/2008	A	Minnesota Vixen	L	0	40
5/10/2008	H	West Michigan Mayhem	L	0	54
5/24/2008	H	Indianapolis Chaos	W	12	0
5/31/2008	A	West Michigan Mayhem	L	0	76
6/7/2008	H	Minnesota Vixen	L	0	41
6/21/2008	A	Erie Illusion	L	0	29

Toledo Spitfire Player Register (2004-2008)

Adams, Rachelle (2005)
Armstrong, Jennifer (2007)
Banks, Deondra (2004-2006)
Berry, LaJonna (2005-2006)
Bowen, Sandra "Sandi" (2004-2008)
Braxton, Sheila (2004)
Bretz, Tonia (2004-2005)
Buell, Shawn (2004)
Burnett, Katie (2008)
Burton, Catrice (2004)
Byrd, Simone (2004-2005)
Cannon, Kleshona (2004-2006)
Cieslikowski, Maria (2008)
Clawson, Jami (2007)
Cole, Jessie (2007)
Combs, Jamie (2006-2008)
Crabtree, Erin (2006-2007)
Crowe, Lolisa (2004)
Cunningham, Rebecca (2007-2008)
Davis, Amber (2004)
Davis, Cassandra (2004)
Davis, Shirley (2006-2008)
Deaver, Kim (2004)
Dowd, Sarah (2004, 2006)
Downs, Liz (2007)
Duddles, Lynn (2007)
Elliott, Andrea (2008)
Estvanik-Vargas, Angela (2004)
Evans, Ginger (2005, 2007)
FitzGerald, Leah (2008)
Fogo, Cortnie (2005)
Foster, Stephane (2007-2008)
Frisch, Tamesha (2004)
Fucik, Katie (2006)
Gladieux, April (2004)
Gonzales, Christine (2005-2006)
Griswold, Octavia (2006-2007)
Griswold, Olivia (2006)
Hasselbring, Cindy (2006)
Hawkins, Leah (2004)
Hebert, Heather (2004)
Hefner, Jennifer (2004)
Hinojosa, Denice (2006)
Holman, Jackie (2004-2007)
Holt, Angela (2004)
Horodeczny, Holly (2007-2008)
Hyssong, Savannah (2007)
Inderrieden, Heather (2004-2006)
James, Karen (2004)
Kluse, Kim (2004)
Koper, Angie (2007)
Lenart, Jennifer (2008)
Lloyd, Mo (2006-2007)
Matsimela, Aysha (2005)
Miller, Shannon (2004)
Moore, Daneé (2004-2008)
Morris, Eliza (2005-2007)
Nelson, Cathie (2004)
Noble, Yolanda (2006)
Nuesmeyer, Sue (2005)
O'Rourke, Brenda (2007)
Pennington, Pam (2004-2006)
Pettaway, Toya (2006-2008)
Podges, Beth (2006-2007)
Poindexter, Wilene (2004-2005)
Post, Heather (2004)
Powell, Denise (2007-2008)
Redmond, Janelle (2004)
Riley, Stephanie (2004)
Robertson, Shayna (2008)
Robinson, Mandie (2004-2007)
Rodgers, Shasta (2006)
Rowicki, Anne (2004-2006)
Russell, Leilani (2007)
Sharp, Sarah (2007-2008)
Smelser, Donna (2005-2006)
Smith, Brande (2008)
Smith, Kentrah (2004-2007)
Snodgrass, Casey (2008)
Stacer, Cloey (2006)
Stinson, Casey (2004)
Suber, Jessica (2006)
Teegardin, Kris (2004)
Thames, Amanda (2004-2007)
Thompson, Denise (2005-2008)
Torda, Jessie (2004-2007)
Tropf, Jasmin (2008)
Venable, Lynne (2008)
Vinson, Ruth (2008)
Welchans, Jori (2004)
Wilkins, Amy (2004-2005)
Wyscaver, Kris (2007-2008)
Youster, Joy (2004-2006)
Yungmann, Cathy (2005-2007)

Topeka Mudcats

Year	League	Name	W	L	Conference	Division	DF	PR
2010	WSFL	Topeka Mudcats	3	4	--	--	--	--
2011	WSFL	Topeka Mudcats	2	2	--	--	--	--
		Total	**5**	**6**				

Based in: Topeka, KS

5/1/2010	A	Kansas City Storm	L	0	21
5/8/2010	A	River City Raiders	W	1	0
5/29/2010	H	River City Raiders	W	27	0
6/5/2010	H	Kansas City Storm	L	0	36
6/19/2010	A	Kansas City Storm	L	7	30
6/26/2010	H	Kansas City Storm	L	6	30
7/10/2010	H	River City Raiders	W	27	6
4/2/2011	A	Nebraska Stampede	L	0	52	IE
4/23/2011	A	Kansas Phoenix	W	30	6
4/30/2011	H	Kansas City Storm	W	34	30
5/7/2011	A	Arkansas Rampage	L	6	36

Tri-Cities Thunder

Year	League	Name	W	L	Conference	Division	DF	PR
2015	WSFL	Tri-Cities Thunder	8	1	Southern	--	1	CC

Based in: Piney Flats, TN

4/18/2015	A	Atlanta Heartbreakers	W	84	6
5/2/2015	H	Southern Valkyrie	W	82	12
5/16/2015	A	Southern Valkyrie	W	70	14
5/30/2015	H	Atlanta Heartbreakers	W	58	8
6/6/2015	H	West Virginia Wildfire	W	1	0
6/13/2015	A	Cincinnati Sizzle	W	68	30
6/20/2015	A	Knoxville Lightning	W	66	6	I
6/27/2015	H	Atlanta Heartbreakers	W	1	0
7/18/2015	H	Tennessee Legacy	L	30	46	CC

Tri-Cities Thunder Player Register (2015)

Baldwin, Lisa (2015)
Barrett, Christin (2015)
Bennett, Lena (2015)
Cox, Katelyn (2015)
Douglas, Nicole (2015)
Gordon, Tarita (2015)
Greer, Mattie (2015)
Hinkel-Glass, Valerie (2015)
Jensen, Michelle (2015)
Johnson, Jennifer (2015)
Kilgore, Rachel (2015)
Leigh, Naomi (2015)
Lewis, Kayla (2015)
Lyons, Meagan (2015)
Moore, Tammy (2015)
Nelson, Kenzie (2015)
Perkins, Kayla (2015)
Smiley, A.J. (2015)
Thomas, Erin (2015)
White, Donna (2015)

Tri-City Mustangs

Year	League	Name	W	L	Conference	Division	DF	PR
2002	UWFL	Tri-City Mustangs	2	3	--	--	--	--

Based in: Greeley, CO

4/13/2002	Cheyenne Dust Devils	W	43	2
4/21/2002	Pueblo Pythons	L	6	35
4/27/2002	Denver Foxes	L	7	40
5/12/2002	Sweetwater County Outlaws	W	25	7
5/19/2002	Colorado Springs Koalas	L	14	26

Tri-State Warriors

Year	League		Name	W	L	Conference	Division	DF	PR
2013	WSFL	X	Tri-State Warriors	1	0	--	--	--	--

Based in: Clifton, NJ
Notes: Preceded by New Jersey Titans

| 4/20/2013 | A | Baltimore Burn | W | 26 | 0 |

Tucson Monsoon

Year	League		Name	W	L	Conference	Division	DF	PR
2006	IWFL	X	Tucson Monsoon	0	6	--	--	--	--
2007	IWFL		Tucson Monsoon	1	7	Western	Pacific Southwest	4	--
2008	IWFL		Tucson Monsoon	2	6	Western	Pacific Southwest	4	--
2009	IWFL2		Tucson Monsoon	5	3	--	--	14	--
2010	IWFL2		Tucson Monsoon	1	7	Western	Pacific West	2	--
2011	IWFL		Tucson Monsoon	2	5	Western	Pacific Southwest	2	BQ
2012	IWFL		Tucson Monsoon	0	8	Western	Pacific Southwest	3	--
2013	IWFL		Tucson Monsoon	0	6	Western	Pacific Southwest	2	BQ
2014	IWFL		Tucson Monsoon	1	5	Western	Pacific West	5	--
			Total	**12**	**53**				

Based in: Tucson, AZ

Date	H/A	Opponent	Result	Score			Date	H/A	Opponent	Result	Score		
5/6/2006	A	California Quake	L	6	59		5/1/2010	H	California Quake	L	8	40	
5/13/2006	H	California Quake	L	12	49		5/8/2010	A	Southern California Breakers	L	0	25	
5/27/2006	A	Baton Rouge Wildcats	L	14	21		5/22/2010	H	So Cal Scorpions	L	0	41	
6/10/2006	H	Santa Rosa Scorchers	L	0	46		5/29/2010	A	Sacramento Sirens	L	0	73	
6/17/2006	H	California Quake	L	0	28		6/5/2010	A	Seattle Majestics	L	6	56	
6/24/2006	A	California Quake	L	0	22								
							4/9/2011	H	California Quake	L	6	60	
4/28/2007	H	California Quake	W	30	23		4/23/2011	A	Seattle Majestics	L	8	40	
5/5/2007	A	Sacramento Sirens	L	16	48		5/14/2011	H	Portland Shockwave	L	0	64	
5/12/2007	A	Santa Rosa Scorchers	L	6	27		5/21/2011	L	Seattle Majestics	L	0	28	
5/19/2007	H	Sacramento Sirens	L	20	32		6/4/2011	H	Southern California Breakers	W	36	20	
5/26/2007	A	Seattle Majestics	L	6	53		6/11/2011	A	Southern California Breakers	W	6	0	
6/16/2007	A	Santa Rosa Scorchers	L	6	58		6/25/2011	A	Modesto Maniax	L	8	42	BQ
6/23/2007	A	California Quake	L	0	20								
6/30/2007	H	Seattle Majestics	L	0	16		4/14/2012	A	Seattle Majestics	L	0	41	
							4/21/2012	H	California Quake	L	31	48	
4/12/2008	A	California Quake	L	14	45		4/28/2012	H	Phoenix Phantomz	L	0	72	
4/19/2008	H	Las Vegas Showgirlz	L	16	35		5/12/2012	A	California Quake	L	30	38	
4/26/2008	H	Southern California Breakers	L	15	35		5/26/2012	H	Portland Shockwave	L	6	27	
5/3/2008	A	New Mexico Menace	W	20	7		6/2/2012	A	Phoenix Phantomz	L	0	1	
5/10/2008	A	California Quake	L	0	37		6/9/2012	H	Sacramento Sirens	L	7	60	
5/24/2008	H	New Mexico Menace	W	14	13		6/16/2012	A	California Quake	L	15	32	
6/7/2008	A	Dallas Diamonds	L	0	50								
6/14/2008	H	Southern California Breakers	L	6	24		5/11/2013	H	California Quake	L	19	38	
							5/18/2013	A	Rocky Mountain Thunderkatz	L	7	20	
4/11/2009	H	New Mexico Menace	W	8	0		6/15/2013	A	California Quake	L	6	56	
4/25/2009	A	Modesto Maniax	W	12	8		6/22/2013	A	Phoenix Phantomz	L	0	1	
5/2/2009	A	New Mexico Menace	W	54	0		6/29/2013	H	Rocky Mountain Thunderkatz	L	7	14	
5/9/2009	H	Southern California Breakers	W	14	13		7/13/2013	A	Arlington Impact	L	0	1	BQ
5/16/2009	A	Southern California Breakers	L	6	32								
5/23/2009	A	New Mexico Menace	W	55	7		4/19/2014	A	San Antonio Regulators	L	0	12	
5/30/2009	H	Los Angeles Amazons	L	0	57		5/10/2014	A	California Quake	L	0	52	
6/13/2009	H	Seattle Majestics	L	0	55		5/17/2014	H	North County Stars	L	6	40	
							5/24/2014	H	California Quake	L	0	48	
4/3/2010	H	Southern California Breakers	W	3	0		5/31/2014	A	North County Stars	L	8	48	
4/10/2010	H	California Quake	L	20	60		6/7/2014	A	Utah Jynx	W	1	0	
4/17/2010	A	So Cal Scorpions	L	0	54								

Tucson Wildfire

Year	League		Name	W	L	Conference	Division	DF	PR
2005	IWFL	X	Tucson Wildfire	4	5	--	--	--	--
2006	NWFA	X	Tucson Wildfire	0	8	--	Western	3	--
2007	NWFA		Arizona Venom	0	8	Southern	West	4	--
2008	NWFA		Arizona Wildfire	0	6	Southern	West	4	--
			Total	**4**	**27**				

Based in: Tucson, AZ
Notes: Forfeited entire 2007 season

Tucson Wildfire Game-By-Game Results

4/2/2005	H	So Cal Bandits	W	12	8		4/14/2007		Phoenix Prowlers	L	0	1
4/9/2005	A	Redding Rage	L	0	41		4/21/2007		Orange County Breakers	L	0	1
4/16/2005	A	Kansas City Storm	L	6	63		4/28/2007		All Valley Attack	L	0	1
4/30/2005	A	So Cal Bandits	W	1	0		5/12/2007		Phoenix Prowlers	L	0	1
5/14/2005	H	So Cal Bandits	W	1	0		5/19/2007		Orange County Breakers	L	0	1
5/21/2005	A	Baton Rouge Wildcats	W	12	6		5/26/2007		All Valley Attack	L	0	1
5/28/2005	H	California Quake	L	0	32		6/9/2007		Phoenix Prowlers	L	0	1
6/11/2005	H	Redding Rage	L	0	36		6/16/2007		All Valley Attack	L	0	1
6/18/2005	A	California Quake	L	6	59							
							4/19/2008	A	Modesto Magic	L	6	20
4/15/2006	H	Orange County Breakers	L	0	32		4/26/2008	A	Phoenix Prowlers	L	0	72
4/22/2006	A	Antelope Valley Attack	L	0	42		5/3/2008	H	Los Angeles Amazons	L	0	62
5/6/2006	A	Orange County Breakers	L	6	20		5/24/2008	A	Los Angeles Amazons	L	6	75
5/27/2006	H	Orange County Breakers	L	8	28		5/31/2008	H	Phoenix Prowlers	L	8	49
6/10/2006	A	Antelope Valley Attack	L	6	20		6/7/2008	H	Los Angeles Amazons	L	0	1
6/17/2006	A	Orange County Breakers	L	0	31							
6/24/2006	H	Antelope Valley Attack	L	16	28							
7/8/2006	H	Antelope Valley Attack	L	6	30							

Tucson Wildfire Player Register (2006, 2008)

Ahumada, Chris (2008)
Apalategui, Adilene (2006)
Apalategui, Lisa (2006)
Araos, Cristina (2006)
Belliard, Desiree (2006)
Cardenas, Faith (2006, 2008)
Clay, Johleda (2006)
Drasch, Allisa (2008)
Draves, Amber (2006)
Flanders-Doland, Jennifer (2006)
Gant, Gina (2006)
Garner, Heather (2006)
Griffith, Emily (2008)
Hansen, Hollie (2006)
Hoard, Viola (2006)
King, Kim (2006)
Kirksey, Sarah (2006)
Leed, Angela (2006)
Lockwood, Hope (2008)
Lopez, Michelle (2006, 2008)
Manson, Nanetta (2008)
Martin, Debbie (2006)
Martinez, Amber (2008)
McInturf, Jessica (2006)
Moore, Jennifer (2006)
Ortiz, Marta (2008)
Pacheco, Ena (2008)
Poston, Angelita (2008)
Riordon, Maria (2006)
Sabori, Cathy (2008)
Seowtewa, Amber (2008)
Smith, Gina (2008)
Steadman, Tara (2008)
Stevenson, Tonya (2006)
Switzer, Jessica (2008)
Varelas, Josaphine (2006)
Williams, Fawndra (2008)

Tulare County Villainz

Year	League	Name	W	L	Conference	Division	DF	PR
2012	W8FL	IX Tulare County Villainz	1	0	--	--	--	--

Based in: Porterville, CA

7/14/2012		Ventura Black Widows	W	47	12	I

Tulsa Threat

Year	League	Name	W	L	Conference	Division	DF	PR
2011	WFA	Tulsa Eagles	0	8	American	Southeast	3	--
2012	WFA	Tulsa Threat	2	6	American	Division 13 (South Central)	3	--
2013	WFA	Tulsa Threat	3	5	American	Division 7 (Gulf Coast)	3	--
2014	WFA	Tulsa Threat	3	6	American	Gulf Coast	1	W
2015	WFA	Tulsa Threat	3	5	American	Gulf Coast	2	--
		Total	11	30				

Based in: Tulsa, OK

4/2/2011	A	Little Rock Wildcats	L	0	44		4/14/2012	A	Austin Outlaws	L	6	7
4/9/2011	A	Austin Outlaws	L	8	68		4/21/2012	A	Memphis Dynasty	L	6	18
4/30/2011	A	Memphis WTF	L	6	66		4/28/2012	H	Kansas City Tribe	L	0	94
5/7/2011	H	Lone Star Mustangs	L	0	40		5/12/2012	A	Arkansas Wildcats	L	16	36
5/21/2011	A	Memphis WTF	L	0	56		5/19/2012	H	Memphis Dynasty	W	14	6
6/4/2011	H	Acadiana Zydeco	L	0	44		6/2/2012	H	Austin Outlaws	W	21	19
6/11/2011	A	Dallas Diamonds	L	0	1		6/9/2012	H	Arkansas Wildcats	L	14	34
6/18/2011	H	Little Rock Wildcats	L	0	1		6/16/2012	A	Lone Star Mustangs	L	0	40

Continued on next page

Tulsa Threat Game-By-Game Results (continued)

Date	H/A	Opponent	W/L	PF	PA		Date	H/A	Opponent	W/L	PF	PA	
4/6/2013	A	Austin Outlaws	L	10	50		5/17/2014	H	Austin Outlaws	L	0	14	
4/20/2013	H	Lone Star Mustangs	L	10	54		5/24/2014	H	Kansas City Titans	L	6	50	
4/27/2013	A	Little Rock Wildcats	W	28	8		6/7/2014	A	Acadiana Zydeco	L	27	28	
5/4/2013	H	New Orleans Mojo	W	37	0		6/14/2014	A	Minnesota Machine	L	13	35	W
5/11/2013	H	Acadiana Zydeco	W	9	8								
5/18/2013	A	Little Rock Wildcats	L	28	56		4/11/2015	H	Arkansas Wildcats	W	7	0	
6/1/2013	H	Little Rock Wildcats	L	16	28		4/18/2015	A	Acadiana Zydeco	L	12	14	
6/8/2013	A	Acadiana Zydeco	L	8	26		4/25/2015	H	St. Louis Slam	L	16	49	
							5/2/2015	H	Mile High Blaze	W	28	0	I
4/12/2014	A	Kansas City Titans	L	8	48		5/9/2015	A	Kansas City Titans	L	14	66	
4/19/2014	H	Acadiana Zydeco	W	30	8		5/30/2015	A	St. Louis Slam	L	19	52	
4/26/2014	A	Louisiana Jazz	W	34	6		6/6/2015	A	Arkansas Wildcats	W	1	0	
5/3/2014	A	Nebraska Stampede	L	32	56		6/13/2015	H	Acadiana Zydeco	L	20	28	
5/10/2014	H	Louisiana Jazz	W	1	0								

Tulsa Threat Player Register (2011, 2013-2015)

Alford, Erica (2014-2015)
Anderson, Jennifer (2014)
Arkeketa, Alison (2015)
Beaver, Katrina (2013, 2015)
Brandy, Jana (2013)
Brown, Laura (2011, 2013-2014)
Cohens, Nita (2013)
Coleman, Cami (2015)
Colyar, Marlene (2013-2014)
Cranford, Kinsey (2013-2015)
Crisi, Devin (2013-2014)
Desha, Patty (2011)
Diaz, Roseanna (2015)
Dixon, Previona (2013)
Dorman, Brittany (2013)
Duckworth, Jennifer "Jenny" (2014-2015)
Dunlap, Beth (2014-2015)
Durham, Christina (2015)
Ebinger, Joey (2013)
Edwards, Taryn (2014)
Fowble, Stephanie (2011, 2013-2015)
Frost, Amy (2011, 2013)
Gilbert, Terri (2013-2015)
Gilfillan, Karen (2011)
Guerrero, Emily (2015)
Guest, Jo (2011, 2013)
Hacker, Tara (2011, 2013-2014)
Hardamann, Desiree (2011)
Harris, Brandy (2013)
Holden, Cat (2014-2015)
Hughes, Angelique (2015)
Hunsucker, Ashley (2011)
Ikley, Dawn (2011)
Jackson, Tamica (2013-2015)
Jarvis, Lauri (2011)
Johnson, Jodi (2013-2015)
King, Dana (2011)
Knaub, Brenda (2014-2015)
Lunn, Chelsea (2013-2015)
Martin, Kimber (2013-2015)
McClure, Janet (2013)
McGuire, Brandi (2013-2015)
McQueen, Megan (2015)
Means, Valerie (2013)
Mejia, Amy (2013-2015)
Miller, Jenn (2011)
Mills, Karen (2011)
Moon, Adrienne (2013-2015)
Moon, Jade (2015)
Moon, Kindall (2014-2015)
Moore, Nicole (2013)
Moran, Amy (2014-2015)
Moran, Ashley (2011, 2013-2015)
Munson, Miranda (2015)
Myers-Jones, Cherraine (2015)
O'Niell, Tera (2013)
Palacios, Roseanna (2014)
Robertson, Meagan (2014-2015)
Rolle, Keera (2015)
Ropeta, Meg (2013)
Rothermel, Tracy (2013)
Showman, Jihrleah (2014)
Sorensen, Katie (2015)
Sowell, Kim (2011)
Stuckey, Stephanie (2013)
Sullivan, Katie (2011)
Thomas, Kerri (2013)
Tottress, Tricia (2014-2015)
Townes, Lamesha (2011)
Walters, Paige (2014)
Wigent, Terri (2013-2014)
Williams, Diane "D.J." (2013-2015)
Williams, Sunny (2011)
Williams, Tambra (2014)
Winters, Sarah (2011, 2013)
Young, Melissa (2015)

Tulsa Tornadoes

Year	League		Name	W	L	T	Conference	Division	DF	PR
2001	IWFL	X	Tulsa Tornadoes	0	0	1	--	--	--	--
2002	IWFL		Tulsa Tornadoes	0	8	0	Western	--	7	--
			Total	**0**	**8**	**1**				

Based in: Tulsa, OK

Date	Opponent	W/L	PF	PA
8/25/2001	Memphis Maulers	T	0	0
4/6/2002	Oklahoma City Avengers	L	0	44
4/13/2002	Memphis Maulers	L	8	60
4/20/2002	Austin Outlaws	L	0	45
4/27/2002	Oklahoma City Avengers	L	0	46
5/11/2002	Austin Outlaws	L	0	55
5/18/2002	Memphis Maulers	L	0	39
6/8/2002	Memphis Maulers	L	0	1
6/15/2002	Austin Outlaws	L	0	1

Utah Blitz

Year	League	Name	W	L	Conference	Division	DF	PR
2010	WFA	Utah Blitz	0	7	American	North Pacific	3	--
2011	WFA	Utah Blitz	3	5	American	Northwest	2	--
2012	WFA	Utah Blitz	0	7	American	Division 14 (Pacific Northwest)	3	--
2013	WFA	Utah Blitz	0	7	American	Division 11 (Pacific West)	3	--
2014	WFA	Utah Blitz	4	5	American	Northwest	4	--
2015	WFA	Utah Blitz	0	7	American	Pacific Northwest	6	--
		Total	7	38				

Based in: Salt Lake City, UT

Date	H/A	Opponent	W/L	PF	PA	
4/10/2010	H	Las Vegas Showgirlz	L	0	27	
4/24/2010	A	Portland Fighting Fillies	L	0	30	
5/1/2010	A	Las Vegas Showgirlz	L	0	41	
5/8/2010	H	Portland Fighting Fillies	L	7	14	
5/15/2010	A	Central Cal War Angels	L	7	26	
5/22/2010	A	Las Vegas Showgirlz	L	0	55	
6/12/2010	H	Portland Fighting Fillies	L	10	18	
4/2/2011	H	Spokane Scorn	W	40	0	
4/9/2011	H	Central Cal War Angels	L	0	38	
4/16/2011	A	Portland Fighting Fillies	L	0	6	
5/7/2011	A	Silver State Legacy	L	0	44	
5/14/2011	H	Las Vegas Showgirlz	L	0	14	
5/21/2011	A	Spokane Scorn	L	20	26	
6/4/2011	H	Portland Fighting Fillies	W	8	0	
6/11/2011	A	Spokane Scorn	W	30	22	
4/14/2012	A	Silver State Legacy	L	0	20	
4/21/2012	H	Utah Jynx	L	23	49	
4/28/2012	H	Las Vegas Showgirlz	L	12	44	
5/5/2012	A	Portland Fighting Fillies	L	14	26	
5/19/2012	A	Portland Fighting Fillies	L	0	22	
6/9/2012	A	Utah Jynx	L	0	50	
6/16/2012	H	Portland Fighting Fillies	L	6	27	
4/20/2013	H	Everett Reign	L	6	22	
4/27/2013	H	Las Vegas Showgirlz	L	2	40	
5/4/2013	A	Portland Shockwave	L	7	25	
5/11/2013	H	Utah Jynx	L	22	66	
5/18/2013	H	Portland Fighting Fillies	L	14	33	
6/1/2013	A	Las Vegas Showgirlz	L	0	49	
6/8/2013	A	Utah Jynx	L	6	60	
3/29/2014	A	Utah Falconz	L	0	59	IE
4/5/2014	A	Portland Fighting Fillies	L	0	37	
4/12/2014	H	Everett Reign	W	14	12	
4/19/2014	A	Nevada Storm	W	18	8	
5/3/2014	A	Everett Reign	L	8	23	
5/10/2014	H	Tacoma Trauma	W	28	7	
5/24/2014	H	Portland Shockwave	L	18	30	
5/31/2014	H	Nevada Storm	W	1	0	
6/7/2014	A	Portland Shockwave	L	0	32	
4/11/2015	H	Utah Falconz	L	0	1	
4/25/2015	H	Tacoma Trauma	L	0	62	
5/2/2015	A	Seattle Majestics	L	0	82	
5/16/2015	H	Everett Reign	L	0	8	
5/30/2015	A	Portland Fighting Fillies	L	22	49	
6/6/2015	H	Tacoma Trauma	L	0	24	
6/13/2015	H	Sin City Sun Devils	L	0	12	

Utah Blitz Player Register (2010-2015)

Ammerman, Stevie (2010)
Anderson, Kristy (2011)
Apple, Chris (2010)
Ashman, Marinda (2010)
Ballard, Brianne (2012)
Baron, Mikell (2013-2014)
Barton, Kimberlee (2015)
Bean, Louise (2010)
Beebe, April (2013)
Bennett, Kim (2010)
Bennion, Tara (2010)
Berente, Lisa (2010)
Berry, Nicole (2010)
Betterley, Heather (2010)
Boelter, Megan (2014-2015)
Bradbury, Niki (2011)
Bradley, Vee (2010)
Bradshaw, Calli (2012-2014)
Brimhall, Camille (2014-2015)
Brooks, Monica (2013)
Brown, Amanda (2010)
Brown, Ruby (2010)
Carrell, Nicole (2010)
Carter, Kami (2012-2013)
Castro, Tara (2012)
Cates, Brittnee (2013)
Cervantes, Cha (2010-2011)
Chapman, Dana (2010)
Charles, Lindsey (2014-2015)
Cherry, Rachel (2012)
Clayton, Chris (2011-2013)
Conover, Amber (2011)
Conrad, Vanessa (2010)
Cooper, Calli (2011)
Cox, Angela (2010)
Crook, Christy (2012-2014)
Curtis, Shar (2010-2011)
Dahl, Adessa (2013)
Danielson, Denette (2010-2011)
Defa, Concetta (2010-2013)
Dyer, Aimee (2011)
Eckley, Marian (2010)
Elliott, Lisa (2013)
England, Angie (2010-2012)
Evans, Linda (2015)
Fernandes, Shara (2013-2014)
Foley, Kindra (2014)
Foutz, Alyssa (2010-2012)
Frank, Erin (2013-2014)
Frank, Natalie (2011)
Galica, Sara (2012-2014)
Gaolga, Lurlynne (2011-2012)
Gaston, Gabi (2014)
Gebbia, Shannon (2012-2013)
George, Ashlyn (2012)
Giles, Kari (2012)
Gines, Britney (2013)
Goff, Jennifer (2012-2014)
Gomez, Angelmarie (2014)
Gonino, Karissa (2012)
Hall, Ema (2010)
Hamby, Angel (2012-2013, 2015)
Henrie, Brandi (2010)
Heskett, Jennifer (2011-2015)
Hislop, Hilary (2011-2012)
Hohrein, Soothie (2010-2015)
Howard, Jessica (2010)
Jackman, Lyndsey (2010)
Jensen, Lisa (2010-2012)
Jensen, Myken (2011)
Johnson, Araelea (2011)
Kaneko, Pepper (2010-2011)
Kerfoot, Chrystle (2010-2012)
Kimball, Nicole (2013-2014)
Kuster, Ashley (2011-2012)
Lafaela, Elena (2013-2014)
Laird, Michele (2012-2014)
Lammi, Ashley (2012)
Lamone, Yolanda (2010)
Lamoureaux, Ashleigh (2014)

Continued on next page

Utah Blitz Player Register (continued)

Lightner, Jamie (2010)
Lightner, Kendra (2015)
Liu, Denise (2013)
Llewelyn, Michelle (2013-2014)
Loftin, Shauna (2010)
Logan, Kirsten (2014)
Luke, Chanon (2015)
Lynde, Wendi (2012)
Mae, Tessie (2015)
Magnuson, Kelly (2010)
Martinelli, Kristie (2010)
Maycock, Adah (2010)
McCracken, Haylee (2012)
Meek, Shawna (2011-2012)
Meisner, Krystal (2011)
Michon, Nield (2014)
Morse, Brooke (2012-2014)
Mower, Daizy (2011)
Nelson, Katelyn (2012)
Neofitos, Melina (2013-2015)
Ngahe, Tepola (2012)
Olsen, Dayna (2015)
Olsen, Laura (2015)
Parrish, Angie (2013)

Pedersen, Cassity (2013)
Peery, Kimberly (2010)
Perkins, Brooke (2010-2012)
Pratt, Jeanne (2011)
Price, Britanie (2015)
Price, Jaclyn "Jackie" (2011-2012, 2015)
Reese, Beckie (2014-2015)
Rich, Judy (2010-2011)
Ricks, Callie (2014-2015)
Ricks, CodyAnn (2014)
Robinson, Christy (2011)
Robinson, Tamitha (2013)
Rodriguez, Jessica (2012)
Romero, Ingrid (2010-2011)
Rounds, Candice (2010, 2012)
Sage, Jennasea (2011)
Salazar, Elisa (2012-2014)
Salazar, Theresa (2014)
Sewell, Mindi (2010)
Shelburg, Madi (2014)
Shipmon, Stacey (2015)
Siepker, Donna (2010)
Sinnott, Carrissa (2011, 2015)
Smith, Annie (2011)

Smith, Ashley (2012)
Smith, Whitney (2010-2012)
Smith-Pizzo, Vickie (2014-2015)
Snead, Cynthia (2011)
Soaia, Daisy (2013)
Soaia, Foketi (2013)
Sorensen, Alicia (2011)
Sorensen, Toni (2012, 2015)
Sphar, Stephanie (2013)
Stone, Lia (2015)
Tafolla, Monica (2015)
Thomasberg, Kris (2012)
Tilo, Saumolia (2011)
Tucker, Alicia (2011)
Vea, Quentina (2014)
Waddell, Jennie (2011)
Wall, Danielle (2010)
Wesley, Quinn (2011-2012)
Wilkins, Sarah (2012)
Williamsen, Suzanna (2010)
Wolfe, Jessica (2013)
Wylie, Shanna (2010)
Young, Melissa (2012)
Zoutomou, Tonette (2015)

Utah Falconz

Year	League	Name	W	L	Conference	Division	DF	PR
2014	Indy	Utah Falconz	8	0	--	--	--	--
2015	IWFL	Utah Falconz	11	1	Western	Mountain West	1	C
		Total	**19**	**1**				

Based in: Salt Lake City, UT **Neutral site:** Rock Hill, SC (N)

Date	H/A	Opponent	W/L	PF	PA	Note
3/22/2014	A	Everett Reign	W	52	0	IE
3/29/2014	H	Utah Blitz	W	59	0	IE
4/5/2014	A	Rocky Mountain Thunderkatz	W	58	0	I
4/12/2014	H	Mile High Blaze	W	64	0	I
5/3/2014	A	Mile High Blaze	W	55	17	I
5/10/2014	H	Seattle Majestics	W	39	20	I
5/24/2014	A	Tacoma Trauma	W	72	0	I
5/31/2014	H	Rocky Mountain Thunderkatz	W	63	0	I
4/4/2015	H	Rocky Mountain Thunderkatz	W	32	0	E
4/11/2015	A	Utah Blitz	W	1	0	
4/25/2015	H	Mile High Blaze	W	57	12	I
5/2/2015	A	Nevada Storm	W	60	0	
5/9/2015	H	Nevada Storm	W	68	8	
5/30/2015	A	California Quake	W	81	0	
6/6/2015	A	Mile High Blaze	W	67	6	I
6/13/2015	H	Colorado Freeze	W	58	0	
6/20/2015	H	Rocky Mountain Thunderkatz	W	63	0	Q
6/27/2015	H	Sacramento Sirens	W	61	0	S
7/11/2015	H	Madison Blaze	W	73	0	CC
7/25/2015	N	Pittsburgh Passion	L	37	41	C

Utah Falconz Player Register (2015)

Alcala, Maira (2015)
Bean, Louise (2015)
Benson, Brenda (2015)
Beynon, Whitney (2015)
Bilbao, Deb (2015)
Bruner, Kayla (2015)
Buns, Abby (2015)
Calchera, Barbara (2015)
Chance, Brenda (2015)
Cherry, Rachel (2015)
Colobella, Kelly (2015)
Cooper, Lorette (2015)
Cox, Keeshya (2015)
Crook, Christy (2015)
Crosland, Stephanie (2015)
Floor, Lexi (2015)
Galica, Sara (2015)

Gebbia, Shannon (2015)
Gommerman, Katlyn (2015)
Guerrero, Julia (2015)
Hall, Kendra (2015)
Hillhouse, BreAnn (2015)
Holdaway, Crystal (2015)
Iese, Renica (2015)
Jolley, Hiroko (2015)
Larson, Shana (2015)
Lewis, Lanu (2015)
Loftin, Shauna (2015)
Mangum, Tina (2015)
Martinez, Crystal (2015)
Moyes, Dani (2015)
Musick, Danielle (2015)
Olson, Nicole (2015)
Prestgard, Lyndi (2015)

Raney, Emmy (2015)
Robertson, Desa-Rae (2015)
Roby, A.J. (2015)
Siqueiros, Veronica (2015)
Solomon, Kim (2015)
Tanner, KayCee (2015)
Taylor, Andrea (2015)
Taylor, Sam (2015)
Tela, Tina (2015)
Teters, Jasmine (2015)
Thomasberg, Kris (2015)
Walden, Krisie (2015)
Ware, Memory (2015)
Wesley, Quinn (2015)
Widdison, Susan (2015)
Willis, Jordan (2015)

Utah Jynx

Year	League	Name	W	L	Conference	Division	DF	PR
2011	Indy	Utah Jynx	5	3	--	--	--	--
2012	WFA	Utah Jynx	8	1	American	Division 14 (Pacific Northwest)	1	W
2013	WFA	Utah Jynx	10	3	American	Division 11 (Pacific West)	1	Q
2014	IWFL	Utah Jynx	3	5	Western	Pacific West	4	--
		Total	**26**	**12**				

Based in: Salt Lake City, UT

Date	H/A	Opponent	W/L	PF	PA	Note
3/26/2011	A	Las Vegas Showgirlz	L	8	12	IE
4/16/2011	A	Sacramento Sirens	L	20	45	I
4/23/2011	A	Ventura Black Widows	W	50	6	I
5/28/2011	H	Las Vegas Showgirlz	W	43	22	I
6/11/2011	A	Houston Energy	L	17	22	I
7/9/2011	H	Ventura Black Widows	W	60	0	I
7/16/2011	H	Nevada Storm	W	33	12	I
7/23/2011	H	Arizona Assassins	W	34	20	I
3/31/2012	H	Silver State Legacy	W	28	27	E
4/21/2012	A	Utah Blitz	W	49	23	
4/28/2012	H	Portland Fighting Fillies	W	20	13	
5/12/2012	H	Las Vegas Showgirlz	W	38	28	
5/19/2012	A	Los Angeles Amazons	W	62	22	
6/2/2012	A	Portland Fighting Fillies	W	33	13	
6/9/2012	H	Utah Blitz	W	50	0	
6/16/2012	H	Colorado Sting	W	1	0	I
6/23/2012	H	Central Cal War Angels	L	26	36	W
3/16/2013	A	Everett Reign	W	54	6	E
3/23/2013	H	Phoenix Phantomz	W	38	10	IE
3/30/2013	H	Rocky Mountain Thunderkatz	W	55	18	IE
4/6/2013	A	Seattle Majestics	L	18	47	
4/13/2013	H	Tacoma Trauma	W	73	6	
4/20/2013	A	Las Vegas Showgirlz	W	38	28	
5/4/2013	A	Arizona Assassins	W	80	6	
5/11/2013	A	Utah Blitz	W	66	22	
5/18/2013	H	Nevada Storm	W	47	22	I
5/25/2013	H	Las Vegas Showgirlz	L	50	56	
6/8/2013	H	Utah Blitz	W	60	6	
6/15/2013	A	Seattle Majestics	W	36	26	W
6/22/2013	A	Central Cal War Angels	L	6	65	Q
3/8/2014	A	Las Vegas Showgirlz	L	38	74	IE
4/12/2014	H	Rocky Mountain Thunderkatz	W	44	0	I
4/19/2014	H	California Quake	L	15	20	
4/26/2014	A	Phoenix Phantomz	L	12	41	
5/10/2014	H	Hillsboro Hammerheads	W	1	0	N
5/31/2014	A	Hillsboro Hammerheads	W	1	0	N
6/7/2014	H	Tucson Monsoon	L	0	1	
6/14/2014	A	Phoenix Phantomz	L	0	1	

Utah Jynx Player Register (2012-2013)

Alcala, Maira (2013)
Anguilau, Dee (2012)
Baker, Rachelle (2012)
Bean, Louise (2012-2013)
Bergstrom, Britta (2013)
Berry, Nicole (2012-2013)
Bigler, Andrea (2012)
Bigney, Cat (2012)
Bradley, Alissa (2012)
Bradley, Vee (2012)
Broadbent, Amy (2013)
Brown, Amanda (2012)
Cherry, Rachel (2013)
Clugston, Jessica (2013)
Colobella, Kelly (2012-2013)
Cox, Angela (2012)
Crockett, Meagan (2012-2013)
Crosland, Stephanie (2012)
Cushing, Tessie (2012-2013)
Declou, Sarah (2013)
Delaney, Elexis (2013)
Fiack, Denise (2013)
Grady, Crystal (2012-2013)
Green, Mamie (2012)
Gressman, Jodie (2012)
Guerrero, Julia (2012-2013)
Hall, Ema (2012-2013)
Hardman, Jennifer (2013)
Headrick, Nevelyn (2013)
Henrie, Brandi (2012)
Hruby, Courtney (2013)
Jacobsen, Jo (2012-2013)
Johnson, Nicole (2012)
Jolley, Amanda (2012-2013)
Jolley, Hiroko (2012-2013)
Jones, Jayna (2012)
Judd, Shayna (2013)
Kafi, Mixsa (2012-2013)
Lealaogata, Tusiga (2013)
Leggroan, Destiny (2013)
Leikam, Kathleen (2012)
Lewis, Lanu (2012-2013)
Lightner, Kendra (2012-2013)
Loftin, Shauna (2012-2013)
Lopez, Andrea (2012)
Lucero, Marie (2013)
Mair, Brandi (2013)
Mason, Emily (2012-2013)
Mason, Melanie (2013)
Miller, Erin (2012)
Mondragon, Gina (2013)
Moyes, Dani (2013)
Murray, Sherri (2012)
Nelson, Christianne (2012)
Petersen, Kayley (2012)
Petruska, Beth (2013)
Pimentel, Jessica (2012-2013)
Prestgard, Lyndi (2012-2013)
Price, Jackie (2013)
Richins, Beverly (2012-2013)
Robertson, Desa-Rae (2012-2013)
Roby, A.J. (2012)
Rounds, Candice (2013)
Sacco, Crystal (2012)
Schmiett, Jennifer (2012)
Shedden, Kim (2012-2013)
Shipmon, Stacey (2012-2013)
Simler, Kristen (2013)
Simmons, Jessica (2012)
Sitake, Numa (2012)
Smith, Monique (2013)
Soelberg, Lavern (2013)
Speer, Allison (2012-2013)
Taylor, Sam (2012)
Tela, Tina (2012-2013)
Thomasberg, Kris (2013)
Thompson, Dani (2012)
Tuiono, Kathrina (2012)
Vanderlinden, Melissa (2012)
Ware, Memory (2012-2013)
Wesley, Quinn (2013)
Wright, Lizy (2012)
Yakemovic, Melanie (2013)
Young, Ally (2012)

Valley Vipers

Year	League	Name	W	L	Conference	Division	DF	PR
2012	WFA	Valley Vipers	1	7	American	Division 16 (North Pacific)	4	--

Based in: Stockton, CA

Date	H/A	Opponent	W/L	PF	PA
4/14/2012	A	West Coast Lightning	L	0	6
4/21/2012	A	Central Cal War Angels	L	0	66
4/28/2012	H	Bay Area Bandits	L	0	63
5/5/2012	H	West Coast Lightning	L	0	48
5/12/2012	A	Portland Fighting Fillies	L	0	42
6/2/2012	H	Central Cal War Angels	L	0	46
6/9/2012	A	Bay Area Bandits	L	0	57
6/16/2012	H	Los Angeles Amazons	W	12	6

Valley Vipers Player Register (2012)

- Acosta, Kristen (2012)
- Alves, Tracy (2012)
- Armstrong, Natalia (2012)
- Berry, Reyoot (2012)
- Brown, Noel (2012)
- Bye, Lisa (2012)
- Campbell, Nikki (2012)
- Cardenas, Felicia (2012)
- Cortez, Sonya (2012)
- Daniel, Jessica (2012)
- Dawson, Michelle (2012)
- Garcia, Joann (2012)
- Garrido, Vickie (2012)
- Hannula, Jennifer (2012)
- Howard, Brandy (2012)
- Jones, Angie (2012)
- Lamb, Kim (2012)
- McNeill, Kim (2012)
- Roen, Lacy (2012)
- Roman, Nicole (2012)
- Ruiz, Yecenia (2012)
- Smith, Tina (2012)
- Talbot, Shaun (2012)
- Terrel, Julie (2012)
- Valles, Ashley (2012)
- Velasquez, Rita (2012)
- Warren, Liz (2012)
- Wilks, Stephanie (2012)
- Wilson, Candace (2012)
- Wise, Gina (2012)

Ventura Black Widows

Year	League	X	Name	W	L	Conference	Division	DF	PR
2010	WSFL	X	Ventura Black Widows	2	2	--	--	--	--
2011	W8FL		Ventura Black Widows	1	4	--	--	3	--
2012	W8FL		Ventura Black Widows	1	3	Western	--	2	--
2013	W8FL	X	Ventura Black Widows	1	0	--	--	--	--
2015	IWFL	X	Ventura Black Widows	0	1	--	--	--	--
			Total	**5**	**10**				

Based in: Ventura, CA
Notes: Forfeited entire 2015 season

Date	H/A	Opponent	W/L	PF	PA	Note
4/10/2010		Portland Fighting Fillies	L	6	74	I
5/22/2010	H	Portland Fighting Fillies	L	0	42	I
5/29/2010	H	Nor Cal Red Hawks	W	46	8	I
10/2/2010		Nor Cal Red Hawks	W	46	0	IE
4/23/2011	H	Utah Jynx	L	6	50	I
5/7/2011	A	Reno Rattlers	W	83	6	I
5/21/2011	H	Reno Rattlers	L	8	20	I
6/11/2011	H	Nevada Storm	L	18	50	
7/9/2011	A	Utah Jynx	L	0	60	I
4/14/2012	H	Salt City Arch Angels	W	48	12	
6/9/2012	H	Nevada Storm	L	12	68	
6/23/2012		Nevada Storm	L	0	60	
7/14/2012		Tulare County Villainz	L	12	47	I
4/20/2013	A	River City Raiderz	W	44	8	
6/13/2015	A	Central Valley Mustangs	L	0	1	

Ventura County Wolfpack

Year	League	Name	W	L	Conference	Division	DF	PR
2015	WFA	Ventura County Wolfpack	0	8	American	Pacific South	3	--

Based in: Ventura, CA

Date	H/A	Opponent	W/L	PF	PA
4/11/2015	A	Arizona Assassins	L	6	26
4/18/2015	A	West Coast Lightning	L	0	40
4/25/2015	H	Central Cal War Angels	L	0	75
5/9/2015	H	Sin City Sun Devils	L	0	1
5/16/2015	A	Pacific Warriors	L	0	1
5/30/2015	A	San Diego Surge	L	0	1
6/6/2015	H	Arizona Assassins	L	6	36
6/13/2015	H	West Coast Lightning	L	6	36

Ventura County Wolfpack Player Register (2015)

Angulo, Norma (2015)
Avilla, Valintina (2015)
Deputee, Sonia (2015)
Evans, Megan (2015)
Gonzales, Kris (2015)
Goodnight, Misty (2015)
Gutierrez, Rebecca (2015)
Jaimes, Jessica (2015)
Jimenez, Diana (2015)
King, Jennifer (2015)
Kraszewski, Barbara (2015)
Langford, Faye (2015)
Lawson, Kimberly (2015)
Mallory, Tina (2015)
Montes, Gladys (2015)
Ornsbey, Victoria (2015)
Ortega, Sarah (2015)
Pillado, Brittany (2015)
Reeger, Tawny (2015)
Ruby, Tiffany (2015)
Sanchez, Jacqueline (2015)
Thorp, Alexandria (2015)
Torres, Maria (2015)
Villalobos, Veronica (2015)

Washington Prodigy

Year	League	Name	W	L	Conference	Division	DF	PR
2013	IWFL	Washington Prodigy	4	5	Eastern	Mid-Atlantic	3	BQ
2014	IWFL	Washington Prodigy	3	5	Eastern	Mid-Atlantic	4	--
2015	IWFL	Washington Prodigy	1	6	Eastern	Mid-Atlantic	4	--
		Total	8	16				

Based in: Washington, DC

Date	H/A	Opponent	Result	PF	PA	Note
4/27/2013	H	Keystone Assault	L	6	12	
5/4/2013	A	Philadelphia Firebirds	L	3	14	
5/11/2013	H	Baltimore Nighthawks	W	14	0	
5/18/2013	A	Carolina Phoenix	L	7	46	
6/1/2013	H	Carolina Phoenix	L	0	42	
6/15/2013	A	Baltimore Nighthawks	W	22	0	
6/22/2013	H	Erie Illusion	W	1	0	
6/29/2013	A	Carolina Queens	W	48	0	
7/13/2013	A	Montreal Blitz	L	0	1	BQ
4/12/2014	H	Philadelphia Firebirds	L	6	20	
4/19/2014	H	Carolina Phoenix	W	27	20	
4/26/2014	A	Philadelphia Firebirds	L	6	18	
5/10/2014	A	New York Sharks	L	24	41	
5/17/2014	H	Baltimore Nighthawks	W	15	0	
5/31/2014	H	New York Sharks	L	18	31	
6/7/2014	A	Baltimore Nighthawks	W	26	14	
6/14/2014	A	Keystone Assault	L	20	39	
4/11/2015	H	New York Sharks	L	8	37	
4/25/2015	H	Carolina Phoenix	L	0	19	
5/2/2015	A	New York Sharks	L	0	19	
5/9/2015	H	Philadelphia Firebirds	L	7	19	
5/30/2015	A	Carolina Phoenix	L	0	33	
6/6/2015	H	Baltimore Nighthawks	W	24	0	
6/13/2015	A	Pittsburgh Passion	L	0	49	

West Coast Lightning

Year	League	Name	W	L	Conference	Division	DF	PR
2012	WFA	West Coast Lightning	2	6	American	Division 16 (North Pacific)	3	--
2013	WFA	West Coast Lightning	3	3	American	Division 13 (South Pacific)	2	--
2014	WFA	West Coast Lightning	2	6	American	Pacific South	2	--
2015	WFA	West Coast Lightning	3	5	American	Pacific South	1	--
		Total	10	20				

Based in: Murrieta, CA

Date	H/A	Opponent	Result	PF	PA
4/14/2012	H	Valley Vipers	W	6	0
4/21/2012	H	Bay Area Bandits	L	0	46
4/28/2012	A	Central Cal War Angels	L	7	42
5/5/2012	A	Valley Vipers	W	48	0
5/12/2012	H	San Diego Surge	L	0	55
5/26/2012	A	San Diego Sting	L	8	13
6/2/2012	A	Bay Area Bandits	L	0	38
6/9/2012	H	Central Cal War Angels	L	0	40
4/6/2013	H	Arizona Assassins	W	40	0
4/13/2013	A	San Diego Surge	L	0	51
4/20/2013	A	San Diego Sting	W	17	0
5/4/2013	H	San Diego Sting	W	13	0
5/11/2013	H	San Diego Surge	L	0	63
6/1/2013	A	Pacific Warriors	L	0	22
4/5/2014	A	Arizona Assassins	W	34	6
4/12/2014	H	San Diego Surge	L	0	62
4/19/2014	A	Central Cal War Angels	L	8	60
4/26/2014	A	San Diego Surge	L	0	1
5/10/2014	A	Central Cal War Angels	L	0	40
5/17/2014	H	Las Vegas Showgirlz	L	6	38
5/24/2014	H	Arizona Assassins	W	54	0
5/31/2014	A	Las Vegas Showgirlz	L	6	50
4/11/2015	A	Central Cal War Angels	L	0	69
4/18/2015	H	Ventura County Wolfpack	W	40	0
5/2/2015	H	Pacific Warriors	L	2	88
5/9/2015	A	Arizona Assassins	L	6	20
5/16/2015	H	San Diego Surge	L	6	65
5/23/2015	A	Sin City Sun Devils	L	6	41
5/30/2015	H	Arizona Assassins	W	64	46
6/13/2015	A	Ventura County Wolfpack	W	36	6

Franchise Game-By-Game Records, 1999-2015

West Coast Lightning Player Register (2012-2015)

Allen, Michelle (2014-2015)
Alvarado, Dianna (2013-2015)
Benjamin, Joniece (2013-2014)
Bergren, Jessica (2015)
Boyle, Jacqueline (2012-2013)
Bridges, Crystal (2012-2014)
Brinkman, Deidre (2013)
Brinkman, Jane (2012-2014)
Burney, Juanita (2012)
Calder, Courtney (2013)
Cardenas, Evilene (2012-2013, 2015)
Carrasco, Felisha (2014)
Carraso-Cannon, Lorraine (2015)
Castillo, Sarah (2014-2015)
Caughorn, Saundra (2012)
Chambers, Veronica (2014)
Cundiff-Drouse, Amanda (2015)
Cystrunk, Julia (2015)
Daniels, Danielle (2012-2013)
Davis, Monique (2012)
Davis, Stacy (2015)
Eilhardt, Michelle (2015)
Estrada, Jenei (2012-2013)
Estrada, Nicole (2013-2014)
Franklin, Aishama (2012)
Garcia, Christine (2012)
Gasper, Brittany (2014)
Gomez, Hilda (2014)
Gonsalez, Olivia (2015)
Gordon, Donna (2015)
Gorman, Natalie (2012-2015)
Harmon, Crystal (2015)
Harris, Nicole (2012-2015)
Hayes, Phyllis (2015)
Hearod, DreShawna (2012-2013)
Henry, Maria (2012-2013)
Hess, Michele (2013)
Hill, Lorraine (2013)
Honani, VaNiesha (2014)
Jose, Josie (2012)
Kendall, J. Arcadia (2012)
Kuumba, Tiliza (2012-2014)
LaMie, Rebekah (2012-2013)
Laster, Dinitra (2015)
Lingenfelter-Chacon, Desiree (2015)
Lingenfelter-Chacon, Shawna (2015)
Loreto, Cinthya (2013)
Luna, Tanya (2013)
Maldonaldo, Angel (2012)
Manning, Dominique (2013, 2015)
Martinez, Ballesa (2012)
Mausia, Kilisitina (2012)
McCowen, Shelby (2015)
McKay, Sheylin (2014)
Melvin, Ashley (2013)
Messmer, Kelsey (2012)
Moore, Michelle (2013)
Orr-Jackson, Elizabeth (2012, 2014)
Ott, Amanda (2012)
Parker, Leilani (2012-2013)
Parkison, Rachael (2012-2013)
Phipps, Amonica (2012)
Pirrello, Mary (2013)
Pulido, Gina (2015)
Quintana-Mosher, Jessica (2015)
Rhode, Shantel (2013)
Roberson, Sonfre (2012-2013)
Robinson, Rachel (2015)
Rodriguez, Martha (2013-2015)
Rye, Misty (2013-2014)
Sessoms, Jacqueline (2012)
Soria, Caroline (2012, 2014-2015)
Soto, Claudia (2015)
Stanislowski, Krystina (2014-2015)
Surratt, DeAnna (2014)
Swatzell, Rachelle (2012, 2014)
Vaeao, Lelatasio (2013-2014)
Valadez, Star (2015)
Wayman, Octavia (2012)
Westman, Whitney (2012)
Williams, Kesia (2012-2013)
Zavala, Rebecca (2012-2013)

West Michigan Mayhem

Year	League	Name	W	L	Conference	Division	DF	PR
2002	NWFA	Southwest Michigan Jaguars	3	5	--	Great Lakes	3	--
2003	NWFA	Southwest Michigan Jaguars	4	4	Northern	Great Lakes	3	--
2004	NWFA	Southwest Michigan Jaguars	7	3	Northern	Great Lakes	3	S
2005	NWFA	Southwest Michigan Jaguars	8	2	Northern	--	4	S
2006	NWFA	West Michigan Mayhem	7	2	Northern	Northwest	1	Q
2007	NWFA	West Michigan Mayhem	7	3	Northern	West	1	S
2008	NWFA	West Michigan Mayhem	11	1	Northern	North	1	C
2009	WFA	West Michigan Mayhem	10	1	National	Central	1	C
2010	WFA	West Michigan Mayhem	7	2	National	North Central	1	Q
2011	WFA	West Michigan Mayhem	3	5	National	Central	3	--
2012	WFA	West Michigan Mayhem	4	4	National	Division 6 (Great Lakes)	3	--
2013	WFA	West Michigan Mayhem	4	5	National	Division 4 (Great Lakes)	2	W
2014	WFA	West Michigan Mayhem	3	7	National	Great Lakes	4	Q
2015	WFA	West Michigan Mayhem	6	3	National	Great Lakes	2	Q
		Total	**84**	**47**				

Based in: Kalamazoo, MI   **Neutral sites:** Memphis, TN (N1); New Orleans, LA (N2)

Date		Opponent			
4/20/2002		Detroit Danger	L	16	34
5/4/2002		South Bend Hawks	W	30	0
5/18/2002		Cleveland Fusion	L	0	18
5/25/2002		South Bend Hawks	W	20	0
6/8/2002		Detroit Danger	L	6	48
6/15/2002		Cleveland Fusion	L	14	20
6/22/2002		South Bend Hawks	W	33	8
6/29/2002		Detroit Danger	L	6	48
4/19/2003	H	Detroit Demolition	L	9	45
4/26/2003	A	Cleveland Fusion	L	6	56
5/3/2003	A	Toledo Spitfire	W	33	0
5/10/2003	H	Indiana Thunder	W	81	12
5/17/2003	H	Toledo Spitfire	W	41	0
5/24/2003	A	Detroit Demolition	L	6	70
5/31/2003	A	Indiana Thunder	W	57	0
6/7/2003	H	Cleveland Fusion	L	0	34
4/3/2004	A	Indiana Thunder	W	1	0
4/17/2004	A	Wisconsin Riveters	W	64	0
4/24/2004	H	Detroit Demolition	L	0	28
5/1/2004	A	Toledo Spitfire	W	66	6
5/8/2004	H	Cleveland Fusion	W	39	6
5/22/2004	A	Columbus Comets	L	14	34
5/29/2004	H	Wisconsin Riveters	W	77	0
6/5/2004	H	Toledo Spitfire	W	74	0
6/26/2004	A	Philadelphia Phoenix	W	26	6	Q
7/10/2004	A	D.C. Divas	L	18	30	S

Continued on next page

West Michigan Mayhem Game-By-Game Results (continued)

Date	H/A	Opponent	W/L	PF	PA	Note
4/16/2005	H	Milwaukee Momentum	W	48	0	
4/23/2005	A	St. Louis Slam	W	47	6	
4/30/2005	A	Kentucky Karma	W	22	8	
5/14/2005	H	Toledo Spitfire	W	40	0	
5/21/2005	A	Detroit Demolition	L	6	42	
5/28/2005	H	Indianapolis SaberKatz	W	60	0	
6/4/2005	H	Cleveland Fusion	W	34	19	
6/18/2005	A	Cincinnati Sizzle	W	54	7	
6/25/2005	H	Columbus Comets	W	20	14	Q
7/9/2005	A	Detroit Demolition	L	6	49	S
4/22/2006	H	Cincinnati Sizzle	W	14	5	
4/29/2006	A	Milwaukee Momentum	W	21	20	
5/6/2006	H	Toledo Spitfire	W	31	0	
5/20/2006	A	Columbus Comets	L	7	30	
5/27/2006	H	Milwaukee Momentum	W	53	0	
6/3/2006	A	Cincinnati Sizzle	W	42	14	
6/10/2006	A	Toledo Spitfire	W	46	0	
6/17/2006	H	Columbus Comets	W	10	0	
7/1/2006	H	Columbus Comets	L	7	17	Q
4/14/2007	A	Fort Wayne Flash	W	6	0	
4/21/2007	H	Tree Town Spitfire	W	50	0	
5/5/2007	A	Cleveland Fusion	L	6	34	
5/12/2007	H	Milwaukee Momentum	W	51	0	
5/19/2007	H	Fort Wayne Flash	W	14	5	
5/26/2007	A	Tree Town Spitfire	W	41	0	
6/2/2007	A	Milwaukee Momentum	W	49	0	
6/16/2007	H	Cleveland Fusion	L	6	22	
6/23/2007	H	Baltimore Burn	W	33	14	Q
6/30/2007	A	Pittsburgh Passion	L	6	34	S
4/26/2008	A	Fort Wayne Flash	W	7	6	*
5/3/2008	H	Dayton Diamonds	W	82	0	
5/10/2008	A	Tree Town Spitfire	W	54	0	
5/17/2008	H	Minnesota Vixen	W	51	7	
5/31/2008	A	Tree Town Spitfire	W	76	0	
6/7/2008	H	Fort Wayne Flash	W	19	14	
6/14/2008	A	Dayton Diamonds	W	68	0	
6/21/2008	A	Minnesota Vixen	W	21	13	
6/28/2008	H	Minnesota Vixen	W	31	7	Q
7/5/2008	A	New York Nemesis	W	34	7	S
7/12/2008	A	Philadelphia Phoenix	W	21	0	CC
7/26/2008	N1	H-Town Texas Cyclones	L	10	39	C
4/18/2009	H	Fort Wayne Flash	W	41	0	
4/25/2009	A	Toledo Reign	W	47	0	
5/2/2009	A	Dayton Diamonds	W	56	0	
5/9/2009	H	Toledo Reign	W	57	0	
5/16/2009	A	Indiana Speed	W	20	15	
6/6/2009	A	Fort Wayne Flash	W	35	0	
6/13/2009	H	Dayton Diamonds	W	55	0	
6/27/2009	H	Indiana Speed	W	21	0	
7/11/2009	H	Columbus Comets	W	41	12	S
7/25/2009	H	Philadelphia Liberty Belles (II)	W	28	21	CC
8/15/2009	N2	St. Louis Slam	L	14	21	C
4/10/2010	A	Detroit Dark Angels	W	52	0	
4/17/2010	H	Toledo Reign	W	71	0	
5/1/2010	H	Indiana Speed	W	45	13	
5/8/2010	H	Cleveland Fusion	W	55	0	
5/15/2010	A	Columbus Comets	L	31	36	
5/22/2010	A	Toledo Reign	W	64	0	
6/12/2010	A	Cleveland Fusion	W	66	14	
6/19/2010	A	Detroit Dark Angels	W	73	0	
6/26/2010	A	Philadelphia Liberty Belles (II)	L	33	35	Q
4/2/2011	A	Cincinnati Sizzle	W	20	0	
4/16/2011	H	Toledo Reign	W	54	12	
5/7/2011	H	St. Louis Slam	L	6	36	
5/14/2011	A	Chicago Force	L	6	15	
5/21/2011	A	Dayton Diamonds	W	63	0	
6/4/2011	A	St. Louis Slam	L	7	41	
6/11/2011	H	Chicago Force	L	3	76	
6/18/2011	H	Detroit Dark Angels	L	14	24	
4/14/2012	A	Cleveland Fusion	W	23	7	
4/21/2012	H	Cincinnati Sizzle	W	52	8	
4/28/2012	H	Toledo Reign	W	41	13	
5/5/2012	A	Detroit Dark Angels	L	14	26	
5/12/2012	A	Chicago Force	L	0	54	
5/19/2012	H	Indy Crash	W	39	33	
6/9/2012	A	Indy Crash	L	7	34	
6/16/2012	H	Chicago Force	L	6	55	
4/6/2013	A	Columbus Comets	L	16	28	
4/13/2013	H	Cincinnati Sizzle	W	52	0	
4/20/2013	A	Detroit Dark Angels	W	40	0	
4/27/2013	A	Indy Crash	W	17	12	
5/4/2013	H	Chicago Force	L	13	67	
5/18/2013	H	Detroit Dark Angels	L	13	19	
6/1/2013	H	Indy Crash	W	16	10	
6/8/2013	A	Chicago Force	L	7	56	
6/15/2013	A	Cleveland Fusion	L	6	35	W
4/5/2014	H	Cincinnati Sizzle	W	75	0	
4/12/2014	A	Derby City Dynamite	W	15	6	
4/26/2014	A	Chicago Force	L	0	30	
5/3/2014	H	Detroit Dark Angels	L	25	28	
5/10/2014	H	Indy Crash	L	13	33	
5/17/2014	H	Columbus Comets	L	12	20	
5/31/2014	A	Detroit Dark Angels	L	10	12	
6/7/2014	A	Cleveland Fusion	L	8	43	
6/14/2014	H	Derby City Dynamite	W	30	22	W
6/21/2014	A	Chicago Force	L	0	66	Q
4/11/2015	A	Chicago Force	L	0	64	
4/18/2015	A	Minnesota Machine	W	35	13	
4/25/2015	H	Derby City Dynamite	W	36	0	
5/2/2015	H	Detroit Dark Angels	W	12	0	
5/16/2015	H	Minnesota Machine	W	35	13	
5/30/2015	A	Derby City Dynamite	W	15	0	
6/6/2015	H	Columbus Comets	W	43	8	
6/13/2015	A	Cleveland Fusion	L	12	42	
6/27/2015	A	Boston Renegades	L	12	59	Q

Franchise Game-By-Game Records, 1999-2015

West Michigan Mayhem Player Register (2002-2015)

Adams, Kathy (2012-2013, 2015)
Afreen, Aisha (2006-2007)
Amman, Kendra (2014)
Anderson, Heather (2010-2015)
Andrews, Ashley (2009-2010, 2012-2015)
Andrews, Jenn (2011)
Anthony, Samantha (2006-08, '10, '12)
Arny, Kris (2002)
Badgero, Shannon (2002)
Bailey, Angie (2007-2010)
Baker, Rachel (2009-2010)
Bamiro, Elizabeth Blessing (2006)
Bardin, Shannah (2010)
Beck, Amber (2010-2015)
Beedell, Linny (2005-2012)
Beier, Nicole (2010-2012)
Belew, Isabel (2015)
Belew, Megan (2015)
Bell, Cheyenne (2015)
Bennett, Kellie (2003-2006)
Bennett, Mel (2005-2006)
Bestrom, Katarina (2014)
Blazo, Pam (2012-2015)
Blessing, Elizabeth (2007)
Block, Donelle (2002-2008)
Blocker, Anne (2002)
Bofysil, Bridget (2007)
Booz, Jen (2002)
Boydston, Laurie (2005)
Brammer, Tania (2003-2004, 2006)
Britton, Julie (2002-2006)
Brown, Yana (2006)
Brozovic, Emily (2009-2010)
Burress, Dawn (2015)
Campau, Kris (2002)
Carr, Tracy (2004)
Carriere, Yvette (2002-05, 2007-08, 2010)
Cash, Ebony (2011)
Chase, Micki (2012-2015)
Chianfoni, Jamie (2006-2007)
Claxton, Sarah (2002-2013)
Coe, Kelly (2002)
Colburn, Ashley (2011-2012)
Coleman, DeTashia (2008)
Collis, Diane (2002-2005)
Colon, Christin (2011)
Converse, Catherine "Cat" ('05-09, '11-13)
Converse, Stacey (2002)
Cornieles, Victoria (2004-2006)
Crews, Stephanie (2011)
Daughtry, Danielle (2008-2011)
Davis, Kaylan (2010-2011)
Davis, Nikisha (2008-2010)
Davis, Stacey (2003-2007, 2010)
Delong, Amy (2006-2007, 2009-2010)
Doss, Khaneshia (2013)
Dowd, Sarah (2004-2005)
Ducklow, Stacey (2002)
Dunham, Jeanne (2003-2005)
Dwigans, Azia (2012-2014)
Earl, Krystal (2014-2015)
Eastes, Chelsea (2013)
Ebeling, Brandi (2002-2004)
Eckert, Christina (2013)
Edwards, Angela (2002-2007)
Emsick, Jodi (2002-2003)
Erskine, Patricia (2007)
Eshuis, Anna (2015)
Feasal, Jen (2012-2013)
Fifolt, Dimara (2013)
Fizer, Ladeetra (2011-2012)
Ford, Kim (2007-2015)
Frick, Stacy (2004)
Fulton, Adine (2015)
Gac, Alicia (2007-2010)
Garcia, Chezli (2013)
Gass, Courtney (2008-2009)
Gavin, Danielle (2007)
Gemmer, Jill (2011-2012)
Gifford, Amy (2003-2006, 2008)
Godsey, Stefani (2002-2003, 2005-2006)
Gould, Sarah (2013)
Grevenstuck, Julie (2002)
Griego, Beth (2006)
Griffin, Candace (2014)
Grzybowski, Tiffany (2010, 2012-2015)
Gwaltney, Tricia (2014)
Hackenburg, Megan (2014)
Hall, Julia (2008-2013)
Hall, Nicole (2011)
Hamlin, Rebecca "Bekah" (2007-2010)
Hanley, Jessica (2007, 2009)
Harris, Marla (2011)
Harris, Thynosha (2015)
Harrison, Bethany (2010)
Helsom, Audrey (2005)
Hennings, Kista (2003)
Hernandez, Regina (2002)
Hetzler, Sarah (2009)
Higgins, Princess (2006)
Hileski, Debi (2002)
Hobbs, Brandy (2003, 2005-2010)
Hoffman, Michele (2002-03, 2006-07)
Horodeczny, Holly (2011)
Houghton, Amy (2002-2007, 2009-2010)
Howe, Jodi (2006-2008)
Hsu, Jennifer (2011)
Hudkins, Maggie (2014-2015)
Hutchins, Emily (2002-2003)
Iobe, Angel (2002)
Jackson, Nicole (2006-2007)
Jenelle, Justin (2003)
Johnson, Gia (2014-2015)
Johnson, Jan (2006-2008)
Johnson, Kristie (2013)
Justin, Jeannell (2002)
Kahler, Katelyn (2011-2015)
Kalinowski, Jessica (2004)
Keister, Katelyn (2014-2015)
Kemp, Kayla (2009-2011, 2015)
Kendall, Janel (2009)
Kerr, Laura (2010-2011, 2014-2015)
Klein, Gretchen (2006)
Knepper, Rhonda (2005)
Knight, Stephanine (2002)
Krieger, Emily (2014)
Kurtz, Stephanie (2008)
Kuszmaul, Joy (2002)
Lamb, Samantha (2002)
Lee, Theresa (2007)
Leenhouts, Jessica (2007)
Lehto, Amanda (2002)
Leitz, Trina (2002-2003)
Loftes, Janet (2002)
Long, Pam (2006-2007)
Luedtke, Lisa (2006-2014)
Lundy, Melissa (2006-2007)
Macomber, Susan (2002)
Majdan, Jenn (2010)
Manoulian, Shannon (2002)
Marble, Tara (2003-2006)
Marentette, Jessica (2002-2005)
Marino, Jessica (2013-2015)
Markwart, Jody (2005-2006, 2008-2010)
Maslowski, Ashley (2015)
Maurer, Meagan (2012, 2014-2015)
McMichael, Jenn (2009-10, 2012-13)
McMillan, Marybeth (2009-2011)
Meihls, Deanne (2002)
Menchanca-Canales, Sabrina (2002)
Miller, Michelle (2003)
Mitchell, Kim (2011)
Mitchell, Tironssa (2002)
Moore, Jaime (2002)
Moore, Mallory (2009)
Morris, Sarah (2013-2014)
Narukawa, Stephanie (2011)
Nichols, Heather (2009-2011)
Nichols, Jennie (2005-2006)
Osterbrock, Lisa (2002)
Otto, Kellie (2011-2012)
Palmer, Stephanie (2013)
Pernsteiner, Tessa (2004-2006)
Phillipson, Linda (Perkins) (2009-13, '15)
Plotner, Chelsie (2008-2011)
Plummer, Jennifer (2002-2015)
Price, Stephanie (2007-2008)
Radke, Raegan (2008-2010)
Redd, Shavone (2010-2014)
Reed, Paula (2002-2005)
Renstrom, Ola (2008)
Robinson, Andi (2005)
Robinson, Chantal "Telly" ('08-10, '12-15)
Rocha, Amanda (2015)
Rodriguez, Anne (2010)
Rosier, Tajiah (2015)
Rupp, Robin (2011)
Russell, Kenzie (2013-2014)
Sabo, Natalie (2009-2010)
Sampsel, Laura (2008)
Scheuerman, Kelly (2008-2009)
Schmalfeldt, Nichole (2002, 2005)
Schwerin, Rochelle (2012-2015)
Seales, Holly (2005-2006, 2008)
Sears, Leigh (2003)
Seelman, Sara (2006, 2010)
Seward, Misty (2005-2010, 2012-2015)
Shank, Januarie (2005)
Sharp, Sarah (2011)
Shief, Katherine (2007)
Shoffner, Judy (2010)
Short, Antionette (2002-2012)
Shwarz, Jennifer (2003)
Six, Mary Ellen (2015)
Skaggs, Crystal (2010)
Smead, Chris (2002)
Smith, Andie (2011)
Smith, Heather (2002-2003)
Smith, Tracy (2013)
Sowers, Katie (2009-2010)
Sowers, Liz (2009-2010)
Spatrisano, Jaime (2010)
Stankewicz, Teresa (2013-2015)

Continued on next page

West Michigan Mayhem Player Register (continued)

Stayner, Stephine (2002)
Stelter, Julie (2002-2015)
Stewart, Candy (2006-2007)
Stowell, Jennifer (2002-2006)
Strang, Lisa (2005)
Sullivan, Susan (2015)
Swafford, Deanna (2003, 2006-2012)
Thomas, Donna (2005)
Timmis, Jen (2013-2014)
Tingwald, Megan (2015)
Tipton, Sophia (2004)
Tucker, Teri (2004)

Tuuk, Leanne (2013-2015)
Valadez, Lisa (2011)
Van Sickle, Holly (2002)
Vance, Lindsay (2003-2004)
Vandermeulen, Jeana (2002)
Vansearsma, L.S. (2002)
Veraza, Sabrina (2002, 2004-2006)
Walker, Chana (2014-2015)
Walker, Michelle (2002)
Walthorn-Cooper, Jen (2008)
Weber, Amanda (2006)
Weir, Jess (2014)

Wessell, Jen (2006-2007)
Wetter, Candace (2015)
Wilkie, Melissa (2002)
Wilkie, Michele (2002-2003)
Williams, Stacey (2010-2014)
Wilson, Nichelle (2002)
Wise, Brittany (2008-2009)
Woods, Virginia (2004-2007)
Wyatt, Liz (2008-2010, 2015)
Yoder, Norma (2003)
Young, Angela (2008)
Zimmerman, Julie (2004)

West Virginia Bruisers

Year	League		Name	W	L	Conference	Division	DF	PR
2010	WSFL	X	West Virginia Bruisers	0	2	--	--	--	--
2011	W8FL		West Virginia Bruisers	4	2	--	--	2	--
2012	WSFL	X	Tri-State Bruisers	0	3	--	--	--	--
			Total	**4**	**7**				

Based in: Kenova, WV

5/15/2010		Steel City Renegades	L	0	22	6/18/2011	A	West Virginia Wildfire	W	16	6
6/26/2010	H	Steel City Renegades	L	6	18	6/25/2011		Three Rivers Xplosion	L	16	28
4/9/2011	H	Cape Fear Thunder	W	8	6	4/21/2012	A	Carolina Queens	L	6	44 I
4/16/2011	A	Cape Fear Thunder	L	13	32	6/30/2012	H	Huntsville Tigers	L	0	1
5/14/2011	A	Cape Fear Thunder	W	34	0	7/7/2012	A	Huntsville Tigers	L	0	1
5/28/2011	A	West Virginia Wildfire	W	13	6						

West Virginia Wildfire

Year	League	Name	W	L	T	Conference	Division	DF	PR
2011	W8FL	West Virginia Wildfire	0	5	1	--	--	4	--
2012	W8FL	West Virginia Wildfire	8	2	0	Eastern	--	1	LC
2013	W8FL	West Virginia Wildfire	6	0	0	--	--	1	LC
2014	W8FL	West Virginia Wildfire	6	2	0	--	--	1	C
2015	WSFL	West Virginia Wildfire	1	6	0	Northern	--	4	B
		Total	21	15	1				

Based in: Belle, WV **Neutral sites:** Towanda, PA (N1); Memphis, TN (N2); Erie, PA (N3)
Notes: Preceded by NWFA's West Virginia Wonders

Date		Opponent					Date		Opponent				
4/23/2011	A	Cape Fear Thunder	L	0	40		5/4/2013	A	Cape Fear Thunder	W	30	0	
4/30/2011	A	Cape Fear Thunder	L	0	47		5/18/2013	H	Three Rivers Xplosion	W	1	0	
5/28/2011	H	West Virginia Bruisers	L	6	13		6/29/2013	N2	Binghamton Tiger Cats	W	44	8	C
6/4/2011	H	Cape Fear Thunder	T	6	6		4/19/2014	H	Binghamton Tiger Cats	W	20	8	
6/11/2011	A	Cape Fear Thunder	L	6	14		4/26/2014	A	Nashville Smashers	L	8	25	
6/18/2011	H	West Virginia Bruisers	L	6	16		5/10/2014	H	Nashville Smashers	W	22	2	
4/28/2012	H	Carolina Queens	L	0	58	I	6/7/2014	H	Cape Fear Thunder	W	30	0	
5/5/2012	A	Cape Fear Thunder	L	0	46		6/14/2014	A	Binghamton Tiger Cats	W	34	20	
5/19/2012	H	Cape Fear Thunder	W	8	0		6/21/2014	A	Cape Fear Thunder	W	26	20	
6/2/2012	H	Three Rivers Xplosion	W	50	6		7/12/2014	H	Binghamton Tiger Cats	W	1	0	CC
6/16/2012	H	Cape Fear Thunder	W	36	6		7/26/2014	N3	Cape Fear Thunder	L	28	36	C
6/30/2012	A	Cape Fear Thunder	W	42	20		5/2/2015	A	Keystone Assault	L	0	58	
7/7/2012		Three Rivers Xplosion	W	40	0		5/9/2015	A	Baltimore Burn	L	6	22	
7/21/2012		Cape Fear Thunder	W	1	0		5/16/2015	H	Cincinnati Sizzle	W	24	0	
7/28/2012		Three Rivers Xplosion	W	46	0	CC	5/30/2015	A	Cincinnati Sizzle	L	2	26	
8/11/2012	N1	Nevada Storm	W	1	0	C	6/6/2015	A	Tri-Cities Thunder	L	0	1	
4/6/2013	H	Cape Fear Thunder	W	30	0		6/13/2015	H	Keystone Assault	L	0	28	
4/20/2013	A	Three Rivers Xplosion	W	46	6		7/11/2015	A	Cincinnati Sizzle	L	20	26	B
4/27/2013	A	Binghamton Tiger Cats	W	50	8								

West Virginia Wildfire Player Register (2015)

Balladares, Heather (2015)
Bess, Bobbi (2015)
Burnette, Jessica (2015)
Butler, Kesha (2015)
Carter, Tyanna (2015)
Clapham, Margene (2015)
Collins, Tausha (2015)
Conklin, Taryn (2015)
Farmer, Alicia (2015)
Francois, Kavita (2015)
Grose, Brittanie (2015)
Grose, Samantha (2015)
Jenkins, Krysten (2015)
Lilly, Mindy (2015)
Lovett, Crystal (2015)
Lynch, Kristy (2015)
Marteny, Lisa (2015)
Miller, Tabitha (2015)
Payne, Fanica (2015)
Pettit, Veronica (2015)
Rae, Jackie (2015)
Walker, Kisha (2015)
Ward, Lexi (2015)

West Virginia Wonders

Year	League	Name	W	L	Conference	Division	DF	PR
2008	NWFA	West Virginia Wonders	0	8	Northern	Central	4	--

Based in: Oak Hill, WV
Notes: Succeeded by W8FL's West Virginia Wildfire

Date		Opponent				Date		Opponent			
4/19/2008	H	Cleveland Fusion	L	0	22	5/24/2008	H	Kentucky Karma	L	0	70
4/26/2008	A	Kentucky Karma	L	0	79	5/31/2008	A	Cleveland Fusion	L	0	1
5/3/2008	A	Columbus Comets	L	0	91	6/7/2008	H	Columbus Comets	L	0	104
5/17/2008	H	Erie Illusion	L	0	54	6/14/2008	A	Erie Illusion	L	0	1

West Virginia Wonders Player Register (2008)

Brown, K. (2008)
Burgess, Norma (2008)
Clapham, Margene (2008)
Graves, Brenda (2008)
Ison, Sarah (2008)
Koontz, Kimberly (2008)
Lilly, Mindy (2008)
Pavlik, Jen (2008)
Preast, Crystal (2008)
Russell, Jolaina (2008)
Sharp, Brooke (2008)
Vannatter, Jennifer (2008)
Walker, Keisha (2008)

Wisconsin Dragons

Year	League	Name	W	L	Conference	Division	DF	PR
2011	WFA	Wisconsin Dragons	0	8	American	Upper Midwest	3	--
2012	WFA	Wisconsin Dragons	1	7	American	Division 10 (Upper Midwest)	4	--
		Total	1	15				

Based in: Milwaukee, WI

Date	H/A	Opponent	W/L	PF	PA
4/2/2011	H	Wisconsin Wolves	L	12	20
4/16/2011	A	Minnesota Machine	L	7	21
4/30/2011	H	Iowa Xplosion	L	0	20
5/14/2011	H	Kansas City Spartans	L	8	20
5/21/2011	A	Nebraska Stampede	L	0	48
6/4/2011	H	Minnesota Machine	L	0	46
6/11/2011	A	Wisconsin Wolves	L	0	66
6/18/2011	A	Kansas City Spartans	L	0	30
4/14/2012	A	Nebraska Stampede	L	0	29
4/28/2012	H	Wisconsin Wolves	L	21	30
5/5/2012	A	Minnesota Machine	L	0	41
5/12/2012	A	Detroit Dark Angels	L	0	60
5/19/2012	A	Wisconsin Wolves	L	0	54
6/2/2012	H	Wisconsin Wolves	W	27	6
6/9/2012	H	Nebraska Stampede	L	6	27
6/16/2012	H	Minnesota Machine	L	0	34

Wisconsin Dragons Player Register (2011-2012)

Akinyi, Vera (2011)
Armstrong, Melissa "C.J." (2012)
Barrett, Holly (2011)
Biker, Nancy (2011-2012)
De Jesus, Melissa (2011)
Derrick, Dana (2011)
Dowling, Irish (2011)
Felske, Nicole (2012)
Flynn, Sim (2011)
Harris, Anji (2011-2012)
Hudson, Amy (2011)
Jones, Jennie (2011)
Jones, Lindsay (2011)
Kazilsky, Amy (2011)
Kinnard, Angie (2012)
Kocher, Sue (2012)
Kotras, Caroline (2011-2012)
Kozelka, Natalie (2012)
Laack, Angela (2011)
Latona, Morgan (2011-2012)
Lusty, Pam (2012)
Moore, Valerie (2011)
Olson, Michelle (2011-2012)
Pfeffer, Alicia (2012)
Radliff, Jessica (2011-2012)
Reifsnider, Jill (2011)
Shaver, Tonya (2011-2012)
Shaver, Valerie (2012)
Shuster, Snoopy (2011-2012)
Six, Mary Ellen (2011-2012)
Steffes, McGee (2011-2012)
Sterr, Jenna (2011)
Wade, Ashley (2011)
Weier, Velvet (2012)
Wooden, Faith (2012)
Zettel, Melissa (2011)

Wisconsin Riveters

Year	League	Name	W	L	Conference	Division	DF	PR
2002	WPFL	Wisconsin Riveters	10	1	National	--	1	C
2004	NWFA	Wisconsin Riveters	0	8	Northern	Great Lakes	7	--
		Total	10	9				

Based in: Kenosha, WI
Notes: Succeeded by Milwaukee Momentum

Date	H/A	Opponent	W/L	PF	PA	Notes
8/3/2002		New England Storm	W	32	0	
8/17/2002		Minnesota Vixen	W	33	14	
8/31/2002		Syracuse Sting	W	34	8	
9/7/2002		Minnesota Vixen	W	44	14	
9/14/2002		Indiana Speed	W	26	13	
9/21/2002		Indiana Speed	W	27	6	
9/28/2002		New England Storm	W	1	0	
10/5/2002		Syracuse Sting	W	26	22	
10/12/2002		Missouri Prowlers	W	67	0	
10/26/2002		Syracuse Sting	W	31	6	CC
11/9/2002		Houston Energy	L	7	56	C
4/3/2004	H	Toledo Spitfire	L	0	37	
4/17/2004	H	Southwest Michigan Jaguars	L	0	64	
5/1/2004	A	Indiana Thunder	L	0	30	
5/8/2004	H	Indiana Thunder	L	0	31	
5/15/2004	H	Columbus Comets	L	0	69	
5/22/2004	A	Detroit Demolition	L	0	67	
5/29/2004	A	Southwest Michigan Jaguars	L	0	77	
6/12/2004	A	Cleveland Fusion	L	0	62	

Partial Wisconsin Riveters Player Register (2004)

Cafaso, Joey (2004)
Filrbandt, Nicole (2004)
Lohr, Tanya (2004)
Mansoorabadi, Karen (2004)
Senick-Celmer, Jennifer (2004)
Wenzel, Angie (2004)

Wisconsin Warriors

Year	League	Name	W	L	Conference	Division	DF	PR
2008	IWFL	Wisconsin Warriors	2	6	Eastern	Midwest	4	--
2009	IWFL2	Wisconsin Warriors	7	4	--	--	4	NC
2010	IWFL2	Wisconsin Warriors	6	4	Western	Midwest	1	CC
2011	IWFL	Wisconsin Warriors	9	1	Western	Midwest	1	CC
2012	IWFL	Wisconsin Warriors	9	1	Western	Midwest	1	CC
2013	IWFL	Wisconsin Warriors	6	3	Western	Midwest	2	BQ
2014	IWFL	Wisconsin Warriors	4	4	Western	Midwest	3	--
2015	IWFL	Wisconsin Warriors	0	7	Eastern	Great Lakes	2	--
		Total	**43**	**30**				

Based in: Greendale, WI
Notes: Preceded by NWFA's Milwaukee Momentum

Date	H/A	Opponent	Result	PF	PA	Note
4/12/2008	A	Iowa Crush	W	30	7	
4/19/2008	H	Wisconsin Wolves	L	13	16	
4/26/2008	H	Chicago Force	L	14	26	
5/10/2008	H	Kansas City Tribe	L	12	20	
5/17/2008	A	Chicago Force	L	0	8	
5/31/2008	A	Columbus Phantoms	W	1	0	
6/7/2008	H	Clarksville Fox	L	6	12	
6/14/2008	A	Detroit Demolition	L	0	37	
4/11/2009	A	Detroit Demolition	L	6	34	
4/18/2009	A	Chicago Force	L	20	38	
4/25/2009	H	Iowa Crush	W	30	0	
5/2/2009	A	Minnesota Vixen	W	54	16	
5/9/2009	A	Kansas City Tribe	L	0	58	
5/23/2009	H	Iowa Crush	W	42	0	
5/30/2009	H	Minnesota Vixen	W	38	8	
6/6/2009	H	Kansas City Tribe	L	12	19	
6/27/2009	H	Chattanooga Locomotion	W	32	6	S
7/11/2009	H	Carolina Phoenix	W	28	6	CC
7/25/2009	A	Montreal Blitz	W	42	14	C
4/3/2010	A	Chicago Force	L	0	42	
4/17/2010	H	Chicago Force	L	7	30	
4/24/2010	H	Erie Illusion	W	19	0	
5/1/2010	A	Wisconsin Wolves	W	50	12	
5/8/2010	A	Kansas City Tribe	L	0	44	
5/15/2010	H	Iowa Crush	W	40	0	
5/22/2010	H	Minnesota Vixen	W	55	0	
6/5/2010	A	Iowa Crush	W	28	0	
6/12/2010	H	Memphis Belles	W	36	6	S
7/10/2010	A	Bay Area Bandits	L	2	35	CC
4/9/2011	A	Madison Cougars	W	36	0	
4/23/2011	H	Iowa Crush	W	43	6	
4/30/2011	A	Minnesota Vixen	W	45	12	
5/7/2011	H	Madison Cougars	W	33	6	
5/21/2011	H	Minnesota Vixen	W	60	6	
5/28/2011	A	Iowa Crush	W	41	0	
6/4/2011	A	Madison Cougars	W	26	0	
6/11/2011	H	Iowa Crush	W	44	0	
6/25/2011	H	Portland Shockwave	W	13	12	S
7/16/2011	H	California Quake	L	0	48	CC
4/14/2012	A	Iowa Crush	W	28	8	
4/21/2012	H	Madison Cougars	W	16	0	
4/28/2012	A	Rockford Riveters	W	74	0	
5/12/2012	H	Iowa Crush	W	50	26	
5/19/2012	A	Minnesota Vixen	W	40	6	
6/2/2012	H	Rockford Riveters	W	54	0	
6/9/2012	A	Madison Cougars	W	14	12	
6/16/2012		Minnesota Vixen	W	36	6	
6/30/2012		Phoenix Phantomz	W	40	37	S
7/14/2012		Sacramento Sirens	L	12	45	CC
4/27/2013	A	Iowa Crush	W	35	6	
5/4/2013	H	Minnesota Vixen	W	26	20	
5/11/2013	H	Madison Blaze	W	29	15	
5/18/2013	A	Rockford Riveters	W	1	0	N
6/1/2013	H	Iowa Crush	W	30	0	
6/8/2013	A	Madison Blaze	L	7	40	
6/15/2013	A	Minnesota Vixen	L	7	51	
6/22/2013	H	Rockford Riveters	W	1	0	N
7/13/2013	H	Minnesota Vixen	L	0	1	BQ
4/12/2014	A	Missouri Thundercats	W	1	0	N
4/19/2014	H	Iowa Crush	W	20	8	
4/26/2014	H	Minnesota Vixen	L	6	12	
5/10/2014	H	Madison Blaze	L	12	29	
5/17/2014	A	Iowa Crush	W	18	13	
5/24/2014	A	Minnesota Vixen	L	0	14	
6/7/2014	H	Erie Illusion	W	1	0	
6/14/2014	A	Madison Blaze	L	0	40	
4/18/2015	A	Minnesota Vixen	L	7	38	
4/25/2015	H	Madison Blaze	L	0	56	
5/2/2015	H	Toledo Reign	L	0	28	
5/9/2015	A	Iowa Crush	L	0	44	
5/23/2015	H	Minnesota Vixen	L	0	40	
6/6/2015	A	Madison Blaze	L	0	60	
6/13/2015	A	Toledo Reign	L	0	1	

Wisconsin Wolves

Year	League	Name	W	L	Conference	Division	DF	PR
2006	WPFL	Wisconsin Wolves	6	4	National	Central	2	CC
2007	WPFL	Wisconsin Wolves	6	4	National	Central	2	CC
2008	IWFL	Wisconsin Wolves	4	4	Eastern	Midwest	3	--
2010	IWFL2	Wisconsin Wolves	4	4	Western	Midwest	4	--
2011	WFA	Wisconsin Wolves	4	4	American	Upper Midwest	2	--
2012	WFA	Wisconsin Wolves	4	4	American	Division 10 (Upper Midwest)	2	--
		Total	28	24				

Based in: Wausau, WI (2011-2012); Madison, WI (2006-2010)

Date	H/A	Opponent	Result			
7/22/2006	A	Indiana Speed	W	20	0	
8/5/2006	H	Minnesota Vixen	W	20	0	
8/12/2006	H	Toledo Reign	W	27	0	
9/2/2006	H	Indiana Speed	L	0	13	
9/9/2006	A	Toledo Reign	L	6	24	
9/16/2006	A	Minnesota Vixen	W	32	6	
9/23/2006	A	Dallas Diamonds	L	20	47	
9/30/2006	H	Empire State Roar	W	24	0	
10/7/2006	A	Indiana Speed	W	20	18	S
10/21/2006	A	Houston Energy	L	0	68	CC
8/18/2007	A	Kentucky Valkyries	W	1	0	N
8/25/2007	H	Indiana Speed	W	34	0	
9/1/2007	A	Minnesota Vixen	W	13	10	
9/15/2007	A	Indiana Speed	W	29	0	
9/22/2007	H	Minnesota Vixen	W	42	7	
9/29/2007	A	Houston Energy	L	6	27	
10/6/2007	H	So Cal Scorpions	L	14	35	
10/20/2007	H	Houston Energy	L	0	33	
11/3/2007	H	Indiana Speed	W	27	8	S
11/17/2007	A	Houston Energy	L	8	35	CC
4/12/2008	H	Chicago Force	L	7	14	
4/19/2008	A	Wisconsin Warriors	W	16	13	
4/26/2008	H	Columbus Phantoms	W	25	0	
5/10/2008	H	Detroit Demolition	L	0	14	
5/17/2008	H	Columbus Phantoms	W	1	0	
5/31/2008	A	Detroit Demolition	L	7	34	
6/7/2008	H	Kansas City Tribe	W	13	7	
6/14/2008	A	Chicago Force	L	7	42	
4/3/2010	H	Minnesota Vixen	W	73	30	
4/10/2010	A	Chicago Force	L	0	62	
4/24/2010	A	Kansas City Tribe	L	0	55	
5/1/2010	H	Wisconsin Warriors	L	12	50	
5/8/2010	A	Iowa Crush	W	12	6	
5/15/2010	H	Chicago Force	L	0	49	
5/22/2010	H	Iowa Crush	W	22	16	
6/5/2010	A	Minnesota Vixen	W	20	18	
4/2/2011	A	Wisconsin Dragons	W	20	12	
4/16/2011	H	Chicago Force	L	0	58	
4/30/2011	H	Minnesota Machine	L	6	27	
5/7/2011	A	Kansas City Spartans	W	20	8	
5/21/2011	A	Kansas City Tribe	L	0	57	
6/4/2011	H	Nebraska Stampede	W	24	12	
6/11/2011	H	Wisconsin Dragons	W	66	0	
6/18/2011	A	Minnesota Machine	L	8	33	
4/14/2012	A	Kansas City Spartans	L	15	21	
4/21/2012	A	Minnesota Machine	L	6	35	
4/28/2012	A	Wisconsin Dragons	W	30	21	
5/5/2012	H	Nebraska Stampede	W	24	8	
5/19/2012	H	Wisconsin Dragons	W	54	0	
6/2/2012	A	Wisconsin Dragons	L	6	27	
6/9/2012	H	Minnesota Machine	L	24	34	
6/16/2012	H	Kansas City Spartans	W	1	0	

Wisconsin Wolves Player Register (2011-2012)

Adrians, Tiffany (2011-2012)
Allen, Ashlee (2011-2012)
Andrychowicz, Candi (2011)
Apkarian, Angela (2011-2012)
Arne, Maria (2011)
BigJohn, Leila (2011)
Bourdon, Aissa (2011-2012)
Brantner, Kelly (2011-2012)
Connors, Jenah (2011)
Dahlke, Laurie (2012)
Dearth, Maria (2011-2012)
Edlebeck, Teri (2011-2012)
Finger, Jolene (2012)
Flatoff, Renee (2011)
Fowlkes, Sarah (2012)
Fremming, Angel (2012)
Frick, Misty (2012)
Gilson, Kristine (2011-2012)
Grose, Fayla (2012)
Heine, Andrea (2012)
Hiller, Haley (2011-2012)
Hochschild, Lisa (2011-2012)
Johnson, Peggy (2011-2012)
Jorgensen, Teresa (2011)
Kiedrowski, Jessica (2011)
Koch, Cassandra (2011)
Kollauf, Melissa (2011)
LittleWolf, Alana (2011-2012)
Madosh, Dionne (2012)
Marsh, Sonya (2011-2012)
Massa, Kari (2011-2012)
Miller, Kristi (2011)
Narlock, Bethany (2011)
Nelson, Kristi (2012)
Nelson, Stephanie (2011)
Nix, Jenifer (2011-2012)
Peterson, Alexandra (2011)
Podolak, Athena (2011)
Raczek, Lea (2011-2012)
Rice, Angela (2012)
Sanderson, Emily (2011)
Schroeder, Nicole (2011-2012)
Sorensen, Laura (2011)
Stevenson, Dara (2011-2012)
Stevenson, Zoe (2011)
Tuper, Rosie (2011)
Wachowiak, Roseanna (2012)
Wesely, Aubrey (2011-2012)
Wilcox, Elizabeth (2011-2012)
Wolfgram, Morgan (2012)
Zelewski, Angela (2011)

Classifying Leagues and League Championships

One of the primary purposes of this encyclopedia is to bring clarity to the often confusing world of women's football. Nowhere is this need for coherence more apparent than it is with championships.

Every year, almost every league in women's football declares a league champion through some process, usually a playoff. And almost every single league then proceeds to label its champion as "national champions" or, even more optimistically, "world champions". In order to separate fact from marketing hype, it's time to give these championship titles some sort of standardized meaning.

First of all, the label "world champions" should be discontinued. With the IFAF Women's World Championships, we now have an international tournament in place which helps to crown a true "world champion". In light of this, giving that title to the annual champion of an American-based league is no longer appropriate; instead, members of gold-medal winning teams in the IFAF Women's World Championships are the only true "world champions" in women's football.

(While we are on the subject of terms to avoid, leagues can and should call their championship game whatever they like...except Super Bowl. The NFL is fiercely protective of that term, and while they currently ignore women's football, it just makes sense to steer clear of a term that would be an impediment to their potential support in the future.)

The term "national champion" is the most reasonable title for the champion of a top American women's football league. Even if a U.S. league has a few international franchises (such as the Montreal Blitz), it's still an American-based league...and therefore the term "national champion" fits, even when it is claimed by a non-American team.

However, it doesn't make sense to bestow upon every league's champion the title of "national champion". It's a common story...a small, regional league with only a handful of teams will name its league champion national champs, despite the fact that these "national champs" didn't venture outside of their local region to play during the season. Meanwhile, the major leagues have *divisions* with that many teams. It waters down the term when every single league's champions – no matter how small – claim a national championship.

So it's time to standardize the terms. Every league champion since 1999 has been classified as a major national champion, minor national champion, regional league champion, exhibition league champion, or bowl (or bowl tournament) champion.

Major National Champion: A major national champion is, quite simply, the playoff champion of the top competitive women's football league of any given year and season. It is the premier title that can be bestowed upon a women's football team.

When women's football was split into spring/summer and fall/winter seasons from 2001-2007, separate major national champions were designated for each season. Also, for the spring/summer seasons of 2002-2007, the NWFL/NWFA and IWFL were roughly equivalent leagues competitively, so their champions are treated as co-champs of their respective seasons.

In total, there have been 29 major national champions in women's football from 2000-2015:

2000	WPFL
Spring 2001	NWFL
Fall 2001	WAFL
Spring 2002	NWFL & IWFL (co-champs)
Fall 2002-2007	WPFL
Spring 2003-2007	NWFA & IWFL (co-champs)
2008-2010	IWFL
2011-2015	WFA

Minor National Champion: A minor national champion is the playoff champion of a league that was not the top competitive league during its season (with the exception of the 1999 WPFL champion). These leagues had fewer teams and/or fewer elite teams than the major league of their respective seasons, but they all had at least 25 teams (with two exceptions) and had a national geographic footprint.

The two minor national leagues that had fewer than 25 teams were the 1999 WPFL and 2001 WPFL. The 1999 WPFL represented the birth of modern women's football and is listed as a minor national league in recognition of that status. The 2001 WPFL was just a four-team league, but it was the only women's football league of that size to have a true national (rather than regional) footprint.

In total, there have been 12 minor national champions in the modern era of women's football:

1999	WPFL
2001	WPFL
2008	NWFA
2009-2010	WFA & IWFL2
2011-2015	IWFL

The 41 women's football leagues listed above are the only modern women's football leagues with the national scope required to truly call their champions "national champs".

Regional League Champion: A regional league champion is the playoff champion of a small, regional league. These leagues had 11 teams or less and had a regional (rather than national) geographic footprint. Many regional leagues label their champions as a "national champ". That's fine as a marketing claim, but it doesn't reflect competitive reality on the field.

In total, there have been 16 regional league champions in the modern era of women's football:

Spring 2002	WSFL
Fall 2002	WAFC, WAFL-WFA, & AFWL
2005-2007	WFL
2008	IWFL2
2012-2015	WSFL & W8FL

Exhibition League Champion: An exhibition league champion is named the champion of a small, regional league by virtue of regular season record rather than winning a playoff game. These leagues all had four full-member teams or less and crowned their league champion at the conclusion of the regular season without holding a league playoff that year.

In total, there have been four exhibition league champions in the modern era of women's football:

2001	IWFL
2010	WSFL
2011	WSFL & W8FL

Bowl Champion (or Bowl Tournament Champion): A bowl champion (or bowl tournament champion) is the champion of a league-approved postseason game (or tournament) which is not designed to represent the league champion for that season. For 2011-2013, the IWFL had an entire bowl tournament structure, in which four to eight teams competed in a consolation bracket separate and distinct from the league's regular playoff structure.

In total, there have been 11 bowl game champions and three bowl tournament champions in the modern era of women's football:

2009	WFA International Bowl
2011-2013	IWFL Founders Bowl Tournament
2014-2015	IWFL Founders Bowl
2012-2015	IWFL Affiliate Bowl
2014-2015	WFA Alliance Bowl
2015	WFA Midwest Regional Alliance Bowl
2015	WSFL Freedom Bowl

Pre-Modern Champions: Finally, some pre-modern teams (especially the Toledo Troopers) often tout their "national championships". It's worth noting that while some credit the Troopers with winning seven straight national championships from 1971-1977, the Troopers did not play in a national championship game (or even compete in a league) for several of those seasons.

Roughly following the definitions outlined above, I have identified the following list of league champions from the pre-modern era. Note that the list below is likely incomplete, as data from pre-modern leagues is not always readily available.

1970 WPFL Exhibition League Champions – Cleveland Daredevils
1972 WPFL Exhibition League Champions – Toledo Troopers
1973 WPFL Regional League Champions – Cleveland Daredevils
1974 WPFL Regional League Champions – Cleveland Daredevils
1974 NWFL Exhibition League Champions – Toledo Troopers
1975 WPFL Regional League Champions – Middletown Mavericks
1975 NWFL Exhibition League Champions – Toledo Troopers
1976 NWFL Major National Champions – Toledo Troopers & Oklahoma City Dolls (co-champs)
1977 NWFL Major National Champions – Toledo Troopers
1978 NWFL Major National Champions – Oklahoma City Dolls
1983 NWFL Regional League Champions – Cleveland Brewers
1984 NWFL Regional League Champions – Toledo Furies
1985 NWFL Regional League Champions – Grand Rapids Carpenters

Women's Football Championship Listing

National Champions (41)

Major National Champions (29):
2000 WPFL – Houston Energy
2001 NWFL – Philadelphia Liberty Belles
2001 WAFL – California Quake
2002 NWFL – Detroit (Demolition) Danger
2002 IWFL – New York Sharks
2002 WPFL – Houston Energy
2003 NWFA – Detroit Demolition
2003 IWFL – Sacramento Sirens
2003 WPFL – Northern Ice
2004 NWFA – Detroit Demolition
2004 IWFL – Sacramento Sirens
2004 WPFL – Dallas Diamonds
2005 NWFA – Detroit Demolition
2005 IWFL – Sacramento Sirens
2005 WPFL – Dallas Diamonds
2006 NWFA – D.C. Divas
2006 IWFL – Atlanta Xplosion
2006 WPFL – Dallas Diamonds
2007 NWFA – Pittsburgh Passion
2007 IWFL – Detroit Demolition
2007 WPFL – So Cal Scorpions
2008 IWFL – Dallas Diamonds
2009 IWFL – Kansas City Tribe
2010 IWFL – Boston Militia
2011 WFA – Boston Militia
2012 WFA – San Diego Surge
2013 WFA – Chicago Force
2014 WFA – Boston Militia
2015 WFA – D.C. Divas

Minor National Champions (12):
1999 WPFL – Lake Michigan Minx
2001 WPFL – Houston Energy
2008 NWFA – H-Town Cyclones
2009 WFA – St. Louis Slam
2009 IWFL2 – Wisconsin Warriors
2010 WFA – Lone Star Mustangs
2010 IWFL2 – Montreal Blitz
2011 IWFL – Atlanta (Xplosion) Ravens
2012 IWFL – Montreal Blitz
2013 IWFL – Carolina Phoenix
2014 IWFL – Pittsburgh Passion
2015 IWFL – Pittsburgh Passion

Regional & Exhibition League Champions (20)

Regional League Champions (16):
2002 AFWL – Long Beach Aftershock
2002 WAFC – Sacramento Sirens
2002 WAFL-WFA – Jacksonville Dixie Blues
2002 WSFL – Tacoma (Seattle) Majestics
2005 WFL – Mississippi Rapids
2006 WFL – Jacksonville Dixie Blues
2007 WFL – Jacksonville Dixie Blues
2008 IWFL2 – Montreal Blitz
2012 WSFL – New Jersey Titans
2012 W8FL – West Virginia Wildfire
2013 WSFL – Memphis Dynasty
2013 W8FL – West Virginia Wildfire
2014 WSFL – Memphis Dynasty
2014 W8FL – Cape Fear Thunder
2015 WSFL – Keystone Assault
2015 W8FL – New York Knockout

Exhibition League Champions (4):
2001 IWFL – Austin Outlaws
2010 WSFL – Kansas City Storm
2011 WSFL – Baltimore Burn
2011 W8FL – Cape Fear Thunder

Bowl Champions (14)

WFA Alliance Bowl:
2014 – Indy Crash
2015 – Central Cal War Angels

WFA Midwest Regional Alliance Bowl:
2015 – Houston Power

WFA International Bowl:
2009 – Monterrey Royal Eagles

IWFL Founders Bowl Tournament:
2011 – Seattle Majestics
2012 – Carolina Phoenix
2013 – Montreal Blitz

IWFL Founders Bowl:
2014 – Madison Blaze
2015 – Carolina Phoenix

IWFL Affiliate Bowl:
2012 – Carolina Queens (Tier III Bowl)
2013 – Carolina Queens (Tier III Bowl)
2014 – Carolina Queens (Legacy Bowl)
2015 – Detroit Pride

WSFL Freedom Bowl:
2015 – Cincinnati Sizzle

Women's Football Team Record Book
Overall Team Records

Most Seasons Played
- 17 Minnesota Vixen
  New York Sharks
- 15 Miami Fury
  Houston Energy
  D.C. Divas
  Baltimore Burn
  Austin Outlaws
  California Quake
- 14 Sacramento Sirens
  Cleveland Fusion
  Montreal Blitz
  Seattle Majestics
  West Michigan Mayhem
  Portland Shockwave
- 13 Chattanooga Locomotion
  Jacksonville Dixie Blues
  Chicago Force
  Columbus Comets
  Philadelphia Firebirds
  Pittsburgh Passion
- 12 Dallas Diamonds
  Erie Illusion
  St. Louis Slam
  Iowa Crush
  Southern Maine Rebels
  Toledo Reign
- 11 Pensacola Power
  Manchester Freedom
  Los Angeles Amazons
  New England Intensity
  Atlanta Xplosion
  Cape Fear Thunder
  Cincinnati Sizzle
- 10 Connecticut Crush
  Carolina Queens

Most Major National Championships
- 5 Detroit Demolition
- 4 Dallas Diamonds
- 3 Boston Militia
  Sacramento Sirens
- 2 D.C. Divas
  Houston Energy

Most League Championships
- 5 Detroit Demolition
- 4 Dallas Diamonds
  Sacramento Sirens
- 3 Pittsburgh Passion
  Boston Militia
  Montreal Blitz
  Jacksonville Dixie Blues
  Houston Energy

Most Conference Titles
- 7 Houston Energy
- 6 Sacramento Sirens
  Detroit Demolition
- 5 Dallas Diamonds
- 4 Montreal Blitz
  Atlanta Xplosion
  Jacksonville Dixie Blues
- 3 D.C. Divas
  Pittsburgh Passion
  Boston Militia
  San Diego Surge
  West Virginia Wildfire
  Chicago Force
  Pensacola Power
  New York Sharks

Most Conference Title Game Appearances
- 9 Dallas Diamonds
- 8 Houston Energy
  Sacramento Sirens
- 7 Chicago Force
- 6 D.C. Divas
  Carolina Phoenix
  New York Sharks
  Boston Militia
  Detroit Demolition
- 5 Oklahoma City Lightning

Most Playoff Appearances
- 12 D.C. Divas
  Chicago Force
  New York Sharks
  Sacramento Sirens
- 11 Seattle Majestics
  Houston Energy
- 10 Jacksonville Dixie Blues
  West Michigan Mayhem
  Dallas Diamonds
- 9 Columbus Comets

Most Playoff Victories
- 18 Sacramento Sirens
- 17 Dallas Diamonds
  Detroit Demolition
- 16 D.C. Divas
  Chicago Force
  Boston Militia
- 14 San Diego Surge
  Houston Energy
- 13 Pittsburgh Passion
- 12 Columbus Comets

Most Games Played
- 149 New York Sharks
- 145 D.C. Divas
- 143 Sacramento Sirens
- 137 Houston Energy
- 135 Minnesota Vixen
- 133 Chicago Force
  California Quake
- 131 Seattle Majestics
  West Michigan Mayhem
- 129 Columbus Comets
- 126 Cleveland Fusion
- 124 Austin Outlaws
- 123 Pittsburgh Passion
  Dallas Diamonds
- 120 Montreal Blitz
- 119 Portland Shockwave
- 118 Miami Fury
- 115 Chattanooga Locomotion
- 114 Baltimore Burn
- 113 St. Louis Slam
- 111 Jacksonville Dixie Blues
- 109 Philadelphia Firebirds
- 103 Pensacola Power
- 102 Los Angeles Amazons
- 101 Atlanta Xplosion
- 100 Toledo Reign
  New England Intensity

Most Total Victories
- 114 Sacramento Sirens
- 111 New York Sharks
- 110 D.C. Divas
- 108 Chicago Force
- 105 Dallas Diamonds
- 104 Houston Energy
- 102 Seattle Majestics
- 96 Pittsburgh Passion
- 87 Montreal Blitz
- 85 Jacksonville Dixie Blues
  Atlanta Xplosion
- 84 West Michigan Mayhem
- 82 Columbus Comets
- 81 Cleveland Fusion
  St. Louis Slam
- 76 Pensacola Power
- 74 Detroit Demolition
- 73 Austin Outlaws
  California Quake
- 71 Miami Fury

Highest Winning Percentage (min. 50 games)
91.9%	Boston Militia
89.7%	San Diego Surge
89.2%	Detroit Demolition
85.4%	Dallas Diamonds
84.2%	Atlanta Xplosion
81.2%	Chicago Force
80.5%	Carolina Phoenix
80.1%	Sacramento Sirens
79.1%	Oklahoma City Lightning
78.8%	Massachusetts Mutiny
78.1%	Pittsburgh Passion
77.9%	Seattle Majestics
76.6%	Jacksonville Dixie Blues
75.91%	Houston Energy
75.86%	D.C. Divas
74.5%	New York Sharks
74.5%	Pensacola Power
73.8%	Keystone Assault
72.5%	Montreal Blitz
71.7%	St. Louis Slam
69.6%	Central Cal War Angels
64.3%	Cleveland Fusion
64.1%	West Michigan Mayhem
63.6%	Columbus Comets
62.0%	Tampa Bay Inferno

Most Division Championships
- 12 D.C. Divas
- 11 Seattle Majestics
     Sacramento Sirens
- 10 Houston Energy
- 9   Jacksonville Dixie Blues
     Dallas Diamonds
- 8   Chicago Force
     New York Sharks
- 7   Carolina Phoenix
     Pensacola Power

Most Seasons with a Winning Record
- 14 New York Sharks
- 13 D.C. Divas
     Chicago Force
     Houston Energy
     Sacramento Sirens
     Seattle Majestics
- 11 Cleveland Fusion
     Pittsburgh Passion
     St. Louis Slam
     Jacksonville Dixie Blues
     Montreal Blitz
     Dallas Diamonds
     Atlanta Xplosion

Most Total Victories, Season
- 13 Lone Star Mustangs, 2010
     Pittsburgh Passion, 2007
     Sacramento Sirens, 2005
- 12 D.C. Divas, 2015
     Chicago Force, 2013
     San Diego Surge, 2012
     Atlanta Xplosion, 2005
     Dallas Diamonds, 2004
     Northern Ice, 2003
     Sacramento Sirens, 2003

Most Total Losses, Season
- 11 Missouri Prowlers, 2003
     San Francisco Stingrayz, 2002
- 10 Orlando Mayhem, 2005
     New York Dazzles, 2004
     Missouri Prowlers, 2004
     Arizona Titans, 2002
     New Orleans Voodoo Dolls, 2002

Longest Winning Streaks
- 50* Detroit Demolition (2002-2006)
- 27   Dallas Diamonds (2004-2006)
      Sacramento Sirens (2002-2004)
- 25   Jacksonville Dixie Blues (2006-2009)
- 24   Houston Energy (2000-2002)
- 23   New York Sharks (2001-2003)
- 22   Pittsburgh Passion (2014-2015)
      Pittsburgh Passion (2006-2008)
- 21   Boston Militia (2011-2012)
      St. Louis Slam (2009-2010)

Several media reports indicated that the Demolition's winning streak was 52 games; two of those victories are currently unaccounted for.

Longest Losing Streaks
- 36 Northeast Rebels (2011-2015)
- 28 Missouri Prowlers (2002-2004)
- 25 Emerald Coast Barracudas (2006-2009)
- 24 Connecticut Cyclones (2006-2009)
     Atlanta Leopards (2002-2005)
- 23 Arizona Assassins (2011-2014)
     New Mexico Burn (2005-2007)
- 19 Orlando Mayhem (2004-2006)
     Denton Stampede (2003-2005)
- 18 Connecticut Wreckers (2012-2014)
     Iowa Crush (2007-2010)
     Redding Rage (2006-2009)
     Maine Freeze (2004-2006)
     Indiana Thunder (2002-2004)
     Rochester Raptors (2002-2004)

Most Points Scored
- 5303 Sacramento Sirens
- 5266 Dallas Diamonds
- 5167 D.C. Divas
- 5135 Chicago Force
- 4293 Pittsburgh Passion
- 4249 New York Sharks
- 4246 Houston Energy
- 3868 West Michigan Mayhem
- 3690 Cleveland Fusion
- 3589 Columbus Comets
- 3578 Jacksonville Dixie Blues
- 3481 St. Louis Slam
- 3460 Seattle Majestics
- 3410 Pensacola Power
- 3339 Detroit Demolition
- 3201 Boston Militia
- 3060 Atlanta Xplosion
- 3017 California Quake
- 3001 Montreal Blitz
- 2925 Austin Outlaws

Most Points Scored, Season
- 771 Chicago Force, 2013
- 763 Dallas Diamonds, 2012
- 716 Sacramento Sirens, 2003
- 678 Northern Ice, 2003
- 657 Utah Falconz, 2015
- 655 Dallas Elite, 2015
- 650 Sacramento Sirens, 2005
- 640 Detroit Demolition, 2003
- 633 Chicago Force, 2012
- 632 San Diego Surge, 2012
- 627 San Diego Surge, 2011
- 622 Chicago Force, 2015
-      San Diego Surge, 2014
- 621 Utah Jynx, 2013
- 606 Boston Militia, 2013
- 591 Kansas City Tribe, 2011
- 588 Columbus Comets, 2010
- 583 Pittsburgh Passion, 2007
- 580 Pensacola Power, 2003
- 568 Dallas Diamonds, 2013

Largest Margin of Victory
- 3728 Chicago Force
- 3709 Dallas Diamonds
- 3287 Sacramento Sirens
- 3280 D.C. Divas
- 2784 Pittsburgh Passion
- 2662 Detroit Demolition
- 2450 Houston Energy
- 2311 New York Sharks
- 2275 Atlanta Xplosion
- 2192 San Diego Surge
- 2182 Boston Militia
- 2125 Pensacola Power
- 2094 Seattle Majestics
- 1914 Jacksonville Dixie Blues
- 1728 St. Louis Slam
- 1699 Columbus Comets
- 1673 Cleveland Fusion
- 1645 West Michigan Mayhem
- 1521 Montreal Blitz
- 1512 Oklahoma City Lightning

Largest Margin of Victory, Season
- 643 Chicago Force, 2013
- 638 Dallas Diamonds, 2012
- 590 Utah Falconz, 2015
- 581 Northern Ice, 2003
- 568 Dallas Elite, 2015
- 562 Sacramento Sirens, 2003
- 548 San Diego Surge, 2012
- 544 Sacramento Sirens, 2005
- 538 Detroit Demolition, 2003
- 516 Pensacola Power, 2003
- 512 San Diego Surge, 2011
- 506 Columbus Comets, 2010
- 500 Kansas City Tribe, 2011
- 497 Chicago Force, 2012
- 495 Chicago Force, 2015
-      Pittsburgh Passion, 2007
- 494 Dallas Diamonds, 2008
- 490 Detroit Demolition, 2004
- 485 San Diego Surge, 2014
- 458 D.C. Divas, 2006

Most Points Scored Per Game (min. 50 games)

- 51.5 San Diego Surge
- 45.4 Dallas Diamonds
- 45.1 Boston Militia
- 41.7 Detroit Demolition
- 39.8 Chicago Force
- 38.2 Sacramento Sirens
- 36.7 D.C. Divas
- 36.5 Oklahoma City Lightning
- 35.8 Jacksonville Dixie Blues
- 34.9 Pittsburgh Passion
- 34.8 Houston Energy
- 34.4 Pensacola Power
- 33.8 Central Cal War Angels
- 33.6 Atlanta Xplosion
- 32.1 Massachusetts Mutiny
- 31.9 St. Louis Slam
- 29.76 Cleveland Fusion
- 29.75 West Michigan Mayhem
- 29.1 Carolina Phoenix
- 28.9 New York Sharks

Most Points Scored Per Game, Season (min. 4 games)

- 69.4 Dallas Diamonds, 2012
- 65.4 Tri-Cities Thunder, 2015
- 64.3 Chicago Force, 2013
- 62.0 San Francisco Stingrayz, 2004
- 59.73 Utah Falconz, 2015
- 59.67 Sacramento Sirens, 2003
- 59.6 Dallas Elite, 2015
- 59.1 Kansas City Tribe, 2011
- 58.2 Detroit Demolition, 2003
- 57.8 Utah Falconz, 2014
- 56.6 Chicago Force, 2015
  San Diego Surge, 2014
- 56.5 Northern Ice, 2003
- 55.1 Boston Militia, 2013
- 54.4 West Michigan Mayhem, 2010
- 54.2 Sacramento Sirens, 2005
- 53.3 Chattanooga Locomotion, 2007
- 53.1 Pacific Warriors, 2015
- 53.0 Los Angeles Amazons, 2008
- 52.8 Chicago Force, 2012

Most Points Scored, Game

- 115 Sacramento Sirens vs. So Cal Bandits, 4/23/2005
- 109 Dallas Diamonds vs. Arkansas Wildcats, 5/5/2012
- 105 Detroit Demolition vs. Indiana Thunder, 6/7/2003
- 104 Columbus Comets vs. West Virginia Wonders, 6/7/2008
- 102 St. Louis Slam vs. Indianapolis SaberKatz, 6/4/2005
- 101 San Diego Surge vs. Arizona Assassins, 5/10/2014
- 100 Columbus Comets vs. Tidewater Floods, 5/21/2005
- 98 New York Sharks vs. Albany Night-Mares, 5/10/2003
- 97 Oklahoma City Lightning vs. Denton Stampede, 4/12/2003
  Dallas Diamonds vs. New Mexico Burn, 7/22/2006

Most Points Scored, Playoff Game

- 90 Houston Energy vs. Phoenix Phantomz, 6/28/2014
- 84 Chicago Force vs. Atlanta Phoenix, 7/13/2013
- 81 Chicago Force vs. Dallas Diamonds, 8/3/2013
- 78 San Diego Surge vs. Las Vegas Showgirlz, 6/15/2013
- 76 D.C. Divas vs. Connecticut Crush, 6/28/2003
  Dallas Diamonds vs. Lone Star Mustangs, 6/30/2012
- 74 Detroit Demolition vs. Pensacola Power, 7/30/2005
- 73 Utah Falconz vs. Madison Blaze, 7/11/2015
- 72 St. Louis Slam vs. Acadiana Zydeco, 6/15/2013
  Boston Militia vs. D.C. Divas, 7/5/2014

Largest Margin of Victory, Playoff Game

- 84 Chicago Force vs. Atlanta Phoenix, 7/13/2013
- 76 D.C. Divas vs. Connecticut Crush, 6/28/2003
  Dallas Diamonds vs. Lone Star Mustangs, 6/30/2012
- 74 Detroit Demolition vs. Pensacola Power, 7/30/2005
- 73 Utah Falconz vs. Madison Blaze, 7/11/2015
- 72 St. Louis Slam vs. Acadiana Zydeco, 6/15/2013
- 70 Lone Star Mustangs vs. Arkansas Wildcats, 6/23/2012
- 69 Sacramento Sirens vs. Oakland Banshees, 11/23/2002
- 68 Houston Energy vs. Wisconsin Wolves, 10/21/2006
  Montreal Blitz vs. Manchester Freedom, 6/27/2009

Most Points Scored, Game, Both Teams
135 Boston Militia 81, D.C. Divas 54 – 5/18/2013
128 Boston Militia 72, D.C. Divas 56 – 7/5/2014
118 Alabama Renegades 60, Pensacola Power 58 – 4/26/2008
116 Houston Energy 90, Phoenix Phantomz 26 – 6/28/2014
115 Sacramento Sirens 115, So Cal Bandits 0 – 4/23/2005
    Chicago Force 81, Dallas Diamonds 34 – 8/3/2013
114 Derby City Dynamite 58, Cincinnati Sizzle 56 – 5/18/2013
113 St. Louis Slam 58, Kansas City Titans 55 – 6/22/2013
112 Massachusetts Mutiny 90, Baltimore Burn 22 – 6/23/2001
    Las Vegas Showgirlz 74, Utah Jynx 38 – 3/8/2014
110 West Coast Lightning 64, Arizona Assassins 46 – 5/30/2015
109 Dallas Diamonds 109, Arkansas Wildcats 0 – 5/5/2012
108 Detroit Demolition 90, Indiana Thunder 18 – 4/26/2003
106 Las Vegas Showgirlz 56, Utah Jynx 50 – 5/25/2013
105 Tampa Bay Force 56, Jacksonville Dixie Blues 49 – 1/5/2002
    Detroit Demolition 105, Indiana Thunder 0 – 6/7/2003
    Kansas City Tribe 63, St. Louis Slam 42 – 6/16/2012
104 Columbus Comets 104, West Virginia Wonders 0 – 6/7/2008
    Phoenix Phantomz 76, North County Stars 28 – 6/7/2014
    San Diego Surge 73, Pacific Warriors 31 – 4/11/2015

Most Points Scored, Playoff Game, Both Teams
128 Boston Militia 72, D.C. Divas 56 – 7/5/2014
116 Houston Energy 90, Phoenix Phantomz 26 – 6/28/2014
115 Chicago Force 81, Dallas Diamonds 34 – 8/3/2013
113 St. Louis Slam 58, Kansas City Titans 55 – 6/22/2013
103 Boston Militia 69, San Diego Surge 34 – 8/3/2014
 92 San Diego Surge 78, Las Vegas Showgirlz 14 – 6/15/2013
    Boston Militia 58, D.C. Divas 34 – 7/13/2013
 91 Boston Militia 63, Pittsburgh Passion 28 – 6/22/2013
 90 Jacksonville Dixie Blues 49, Atlanta Phoenix 41 – 6/30/2012
    Dallas Diamonds 55, Kansas City Tribe 35 – 7/7/2012

Fewest Points Allowed Per Game
        (min. 50 games)
7.77   Atlanta Xplosion
8.16   Detroit Demolition
8.98   Massachusetts Mutiny
10.26   Carolina Phoenix
10.43   Seattle Majestics
10.58   Chicago Force
11.83   Keystone Assault
11.95   San Diego Surge
12.08   Oklahoma City Lightning
12.27   Pittsburgh Passion
12.33   Montreal Blitz
12.66   Dallas Diamonds
12.85   Pensacola Power
13.007   New York Sharks
13.014   D.C. Divas
13.1091   Bay State Warriors
13.1095   Houston Energy
13.45   Central Cal War Angels
13.77   Boston Militia
14.10   Sacramento Sirens

Fewest Points Allowed Per Game, Season
        (min. 7 games)
1.82   D.C. Divas, 2006
2.00   New York Sharks, 2002
2.11   Keystone Assault, 2015
2.45   Carolina Phoenix, 2013
3.27   Baltimore Burn, 2002
3.33   New York Sharks, 2005
3.44   D.C. Divas, 2002
3.67   Detroit Demolition, 2008
       Massachusetts Mutiny, 2007
       Philadelphia Liberty Belles (I), 2001
       Phoenix Prowlers, 2007
3.71   Seattle Majestics, 2002
3.80   Houston Energy, 2013
4.00   Bay State Warriors, 2003
4.10   Pensacola Power, 2002
4.25   Houston Energy, 2001
4.29   New York Sharks, 2001
4.30   Philadelphia Firebirds, 2008
4.43   Montreal Blitz, 2011
4.44   Chattanooga Locomotion, 2007

Most Shutouts

55	D.C. Divas
	Chicago Force
	Seattle Majestics
49	Atlanta Xplosion
48	New York Sharks
47	Houston Energy
46	Montreal Blitz
	West Michigan Mayhem
44	Dallas Diamonds
	Pittsburgh Passion
43	Columbus Comets
41	Cleveland Fusion
	Sacramento Sirens
39	Chattanooga Locomotion
38	St. Louis Slam
37	Carolina Phoenix
36	Miami Fury
35	Detroit Demolition
34	Philadelphia Firebirds
33	Austin Outlaws

Most Shutouts, Playoffs

6	Houston Energy
	Detroit Demolition
4	Seattle Majestics
3	Carolina Phoenix
	Utah Falconz
	Columbus Comets
	West Virginia Wildfire
	Pittsburgh Passion
	Sacramento Sirens
	New York Sharks
2	D.C. Divas
	Central Cal War Angels
	Chicago Force
	Austin Outlaws
	San Diego Surge
	Bay Area Bandits
	Indy Crash
	Atlanta Xplosion

Most Shutouts, Season

8	D.C. Divas, 2006
	Utah Falconz, 2015
	San Diego Surge, 2012
	Phoenix Prowlers, 2007
	Atlanta Xplosion, 2005
7	Carolina Phoenix, 2015
	Carolina Phoenix, 2013
	Kansas City Tribe, 2011
	West Michigan Mayhem, 2009
	Philadelphia Firebirds, 2008
	Atlanta Xplosion, 2007
	D.C. Divas, 2005
	Seattle Majestics, 2005
	Chicago Force, 2003
	New York Sharks, 2003
	Pensacola Power, 2003
	Baltimore Burn, 2002
	Seattle Warbirds, 2001

Most Consecutive Non-Forfeit Shutouts

8	D.C. Divas, 2006
6	San Diego Surge, 2012
	New York Sharks, 2003
5	Sacramento Sirens, 2015
	Keystone Assault, 2014
	Montreal Blitz, 2012
	Carolina Phoenix, 2010
	Philadelphia Firebirds, 2008
	Phoenix Prowlers, 2007
	Chattanooga Locomotion, 2007
	New York Sharks, 2006
	Seattle Majestics, 2005
	Seattle Warbirds, 2001

Women in Men's Football

While this book lists over 10,000 women who have played women's football since 1999, there are also a number of women who have made their mark playing men's football. Here are a few notable female athletes who have broken barriers or received national attention in the men's game.

Youth Football

Sam Gordon: This nine-year-old running back's exploits in a youth football league made her a national sensation when her YouTube clips went viral. She is one of the co-founders of the Utah Girls Tackle Football League, the first tackle football league for girls in the United States.

Karlie Harman: As a 14-year-old girl, Harman played football in the Fairfax County youth football league. Harman became a finalist for the NFL's Together We Make Football contest, earning national headlines.

High School Football

Luverne "Toad" Wise (Albert): Believed by many to be the first girl to score in a high school football game, Wise was a kicker on the Escambia (AL) High School football team in 1939 and 1940, earning coverage in *Life Magazine*.

Tami Maida: In 1981, Maida was the junior varsity quarterback as well as the homecoming princess at Philomath (OR) High School. Her story was the basis of a made-for-TV movie called *Quarterback Princess*, starring Helen Hunt.

College Football

Elizabeth "Liz" Heaston (Thompson): On October 18, 1997, Heaston became the first woman to score in a college football game as a placekicker with the Willamette Bearcats of the NAIA.

Ashley Martin: The first woman to score in an NCAA Division I football game, Martin scored as a placekicker on August 30, 2001, for Jacksonville State University; JSU competed in Division 1-AA (now known as the FCS).

Katie Hnida: Hnida became the first woman to score in a Division I-A football game on August 30, 2003, kicking two extra points for the University of New Mexico against Texas State University. She was also the first woman to appear in a bowl game, having an extra point attempt blocked in the 2002 Las Vegas Bowl against UCLA. Hnida later played professional football (see below).

Tonya Butler: Butler was the first woman to make a field goal in an NCAA game with West Alabama College of Division II on September 27, 2003. She scored 87 career points as a player in 2003 and 2004, setting a record for female players in college football.

Ashley Baker: Baker was the second woman (after Tonya Butler) to make a field goal in college football in 2007 as a member of NCAA Division III's Framingham State University.

Brittany Ryan: As a placekicker for NCAA Division III's Lebanon Valley College from 2007-2010, Ryan broke Butler's scoring record and currently holds the mark for most career points by a female college football player with 100.

Professional Football

Patricia Palinkas: The first woman to play professional football, Palinkas made her debut on August 15, 1970, as a placeholder for her kicker husband on the Orlando Panthers of the Atlantic Coast Football League.

Katie Hnida: After playing college football (see above), Hnida became the second woman and first kicker to play professional football as a member of the Fort Wayne FireHawks of the Continental Indoor Football League (CIFL) in 2010. She successfully kicked an extra point, becoming the first woman to score in a men's pro football game.

Julie Harshbarger: In 2010, Harshbarger became the first woman to make a field goal in a professional football game as a member of the CIFL's Chicago Cardinals; ironically, Harbarger's field goal came against Katie Hnida's Fort Wayne Firehawks.

Jen Welter: Welter was the first woman to play men's professional football in a non-kicking position as a running back with the Texas Revolution of the Indoor Football League in 2014. Welter then joined the coaching staff of the Revolution in the spring of 2015 – becoming the first female to coach in a men's pro football league – before being hired by the Arizona Cardinals as an assistant coaching intern, making her the first female coach in NFL history.

The Case Against Lingerie Football

I debated for some time about whether to include a chapter on lingerie football in this book at all, since lingerie football is an abhorrent perversion of the true sport of women's football. However, many fans are not familiar with any kind of women's football other than the lingerie variety, and there has been a concerted effort on behalf of some misguided souls to somehow attempt to "legitimize" lingerie football as a respectable sport. Largely for that reason, I have decided to include this section on lingerie football and the following editorial in the hopes of educating fans on why this sub-genre of women's football is an abomination and an insult to female athletes everywhere.

What is Lingerie Football?

Let's start with what should be an easy question – what is lingerie football, and how is it distinct and different from traditional women's football? It's a seemingly simple question, but as is often the case, there are those who attempt to complicate what should be a straightforward issue for their own benefit.

Lingerie football is a brand of women's football defined by athletes who wear non-standard, incredibly revealing uniforms that resemble lingerie. Three of the key characteristics of a lingerie football uniform are a low neckline designed to make cleavage more visible, an exposed midriff, and volleyball shorts that reveal most of the player's thighs. Any league in which female players wear less clothing than a football standard uniform – especially a uniform that drastically deviates in any of the above three respects from the accepted, standard equipment worn in men's football leagues at all levels – is, in fact, a lingerie league.

Women's football leagues in which the players wear uniforms similar to those in men's football have tried to differentiate themselves from the lingerie leagues by labeling themselves as "traditional leagues" or "full-contact leagues", among other terms. That differentiation is important and needed. Lingerie football is a separate and distinct sub-genre from traditional women's football, and the two should not be combined or confused in any way. It makes no sense to confound the two. A simple look at each type of player in uniform makes the differences immediately apparent.

But here's where things get tricky. The term "lingerie football" has developed such a negative stigma among sports fans that most lingerie leagues have tried to deny what they are and distance themselves from the term. As such, multiple lingerie football leagues have started to market themselves as "full-contact leagues" and otherwise list themselves alongside traditional women's football leagues, attempting to blur the lines between real women's football and lingerie football.

The first and most recognized lingerie league was, not surprisingly, the Lingerie Football League (LFL). Even the LFL has attempted to distance itself from the very lingerie football label it created, officially changing their name to the "Legends Football League" in 2013. Several less-publicized lingerie football leagues have also formed in the past few years, and these leagues, too, almost universally distance themselves from the lingerie football term.

For instance, a women's football league called (kid you not) the Sugar 'n' Spice Football League began play in Texas in 2012 and positioned itself to be a balance between lingerie football and traditional women's football. The SSFL professed to be more like "real football" than the LFL, because nothing says real football like a league called the Sugar 'n' Spice Football League. The SSFL and its member teams have billed themselves as "full-contact" football teams, not lingerie football teams. Yet SSFL uniforms are strikingly similar to the LFL's with the exception of less cleavage. The volleyball shorts and exposed midriffs remain – all in an effort, in SSFL Commissioner Rebecca Garza's words, to have her players "look like women".[1] The SSFL would likely bristle at being classified as a lingerie football league, but without question, that's what they are.

Jumbling traditional women's football with lingerie football is the precise type of obfuscation this encyclopedia seeks to eliminate. Telling the difference between a "traditional" women's football league and a lingerie league is astonishingly simple. If the female athletes are wearing a uniform that looks like what a male football player would wear on the field, it's a traditional women's football league. If not, it's a lingerie league. It's really that easy. The leagues covered in this section of the book compete in lingerie football, which is separate and distinct from "traditional" women's football.

Why Lingerie Football Is Not a Legitimate Competitive Sport

Much of the debate around lingerie football surrounds the skimpy uniforms, but lost in all the discussion of attire is the fact that lingerie football is not a legitimate competitive sport. Many critics denounce lingerie football uniforms as demeaning and objectifying, but they then get sidetracked into a discussion of the appropriateness of said uniforms. While that's a worthwhile point to make, that's not why lingerie football is not a legitimate competitive sport. There's a much, much bigger issue with lingerie football – one that, for some reason, many people often ignore.

Lingerie football players are forced to wear a revealing, non-standard uniform for one simple reason: marketing. The LFL – the longest-running and most publicized lingerie football league – has a long history of excluding women who don't fit the "image" of their league...*regardless of talent.* Mitch Mortaza, the founder of the LFL, doesn't shy away from that reality, telling *CBS News* in 2010, "First and foremost, you have to be beautiful. We have to be able to market you."[2]

That means that the vast majority of athletic women are banned from playing in the LFL simply because they don't meet the LFL's arbitrary standard of "sexiness". The LFL would frown upon, for instance, any woman over 200 pounds playing in their league, because they can't "market" such a woman wearing lingerie to their lecherous fanbase. It negates the marketing appeal of lingerie football to have relatively heavier players publicly parading around in lingerie.

Yet even novice football fans know that for positions like offensive line, defensive line, and linebacker – all else being equal – 200 pounds is vastly superior to 150. It just stands to reason that the most talented players in women's football aren't universally Barbie dolls. Like NFL players, elite women's football players come in all shapes and sizes...and I'm sorry, but there are definitely some NFL offensive and defensive linemen who you wouldn't want to see in lingerie.

Let's get down to brass tacks, here. **When a "sport" rejects female athletes based not on their talent but based – first and foremost – on whether or not a man subjectively thinks she looks sexy in lingerie, it's not a legitimate competitive sport. Period.** No legitimate competitive sport, anywhere, operates that way. It's an arbitrary and non-purposeful standard used to exclude players of legitimate talent, which clearly violates the very premise on which competitive sports are built. No true competitive sports league – on any level – vets players first and foremost on "sexiness". Doesn't happen.

(Some legitimate competitive sports leagues do exclude talented players for various reasons. Leagues like the NFL and NBA and others have an age requirement, for example, stating that talented players below a certain age are not allowed to join the league. However, these exclusions are always both objective and constructive. For instance, the NFL's age restriction is objective (minimum age requirement of three years after graduation of your high school class) and constructive (the NFL does not want to allow a talented but under-developed 19-year-old football player to put themselves at physical risk – not to mention the fact that they don't want to cannibalize college football, which is popular in its own right). Other legitimate sports leagues have similar exclusions of athletes, but again, they are universally objective and constructive.

The LFL's "sexiness" clause, by contrast – "First and foremost, you have to be beautiful. We have to be able to market you" – is neither objective nor constructive. Beauty is the ultimate subjective standard. On an objective level, who decides who is beautiful? It is literally in the eye of the beholder. Furthermore, the stated reason for the restriction is "marketability", which serves no useful purpose. No legitimate sports league rejects talented athletes solely for sexualized marketing purposes. That's absurd.)

Outside of the LFL, other lingerie football leagues may claim to offer a more "family-friendly" version of lingerie football. They may not directly reject players with varying body types as overtly as the LFL. But lingerie football always falls back on a simple premise...the only reason lingerie players wear those uniforms is "marketing". If it wasn't good for "marketing", they wouldn't wear them, and it's only good for marketing if the players wearing them meet a certain popular standard of sexual desirability.

Even in lingerie leagues that claim to have no exclusions on players deemed "not sexy enough", the uniforms themselves needlessly create an atmosphere where players of some body types would clearly feel unwelcome and will naturally self-select themselves out of the league. If a women's football league was truly, honestly welcoming to players of all shapes and sizes, it would give them uniforms that make players of all shapes and sizes feel welcome. It wouldn't deliberately alter the uniform from the widespread standard set by men's football in such a way that would make some athletes feel shunned. In other words, women's football leagues wouldn't force players to wear lingerie if they were truly open to *all* athletes...but then they wouldn't be a lingerie league.

The Fallacy of Supporting the Players

I'll put this out there again, once more, for effect: no legitimate competitive sport excludes athletes based not on her athletic talent but on how sexy others think she looks in lingerie. That's the inviolable reality of sports that lingerie football supporters simply cannot deny.

Yet any defense of lingerie football immediately begins with a defense of the players themselves. Lingerie football supporters relentlessly plead that the women in lingerie football train hard to stay in peak athletic shape and that they don't shy away from contact. While that may be true, it doesn't change the fact that lingerie football isn't a legitimate sport.

It's the default argument championed by those who try to validate lingerie football as a true sport: the players involved are athletes, therefore it must be a sport. A brief reflection of that statement makes the logical fallacy apparent. For instance, I could gather some of the best NFL players at my house and we could make pancakes together. This wouldn't make "pancake-making" a competitive sport just because a group of elite athletes are doing it together in one place. Nor does saying that pancake-making isn't a competitive sport mean that I'm somehow suggesting the NFL players aren't real athletes...of course they are, but they are athletes because of their ability to excel at a real sport, not because of their mad pancake-making skills.

Along those same lines, the WWE is not a true sports league. Like the LFL, the WWE is sport-based theater that utilizes athletic, pre-selected actors. Naturally, I would never assert that someone like, for example, Dwayne "The Rock" Johnson isn't athletic – one look at The Rock's frame makes it pretty apparent that he would excel at any number of legitimate sports. But just because The Rock is an athlete doesn't mean that the WWE is a true competitive sports league.

As clearly noted in the previous section, competitive sports are not defined by the mere presence of athletes. Competitive sports are defined by accessibility, and no legitimate sports league rejects talented athletes for a subjective, non-purposeful reason like perceived sexiness. The fact that the women who do make it into lingerie football are often athletic and committed individuals doesn't negate the fact that they were vetted by the league primarily on appearance and not football talent. Lingerie football is not a legitimate sport, and it's not insulting lingerie football players to point that out. On the contrary, it's insulting for lingerie football players to be compared to female athletes who compete in legitimate women's sports – including traditional women's football – because those athletes earned their stripes totally on athletic merit, not through sex appeal.

Lingerie football supporters also love to suggest that their uniforms are not that much different from sports like track and beach volleyball. That's not entirely true (you see a lot more cleavage from many lingerie football uniforms, for instance), and it's also a false comparison. For one, track and beach volleyball aren't contact sports like football. But more importantly, it's not like women in track and beach volleyball wear uniforms that offer substantially less protection from injury than those worn by their male counterparts. Lingerie football uniforms, on the other hand, are vastly different and inherently less safe than the football uniforms worn by men, solely for the purpose of sexualizing the athletes involved.

And once again, we return to the primary point...track and beach volleyball players may universally fit a certain body type, but that's because success at those sports demands that body type; the athletes weren't vetted to ensure they all fit that profile. Thin, toned athletes tend to have more success in the non-contact sports of track and beach volleyball, while in football – as noted before – a lineman or linebacker would often have more success if they were *less* thin.

Most importantly, no one in track or beach volleyball is telling the players that they'll be benched if they don't lose weight, which is what Mortaza has been known to tell LFL players.[3] In legitimate sports like track and beach volleyball, athletic talent always wins out over a commissioner's weight preferences. A more in-depth review of the checkered history of the LFL and its founder, chairman, and dictator-for-life, Mitch Mortaza, can be found in the next section.

To summarize: You can have respect for the athletic ability and work ethic of lingerie football players and still acknowledge that lingerie football is in no way a real sport, because it is not accessible to all. Lingerie football has understandably benefitted from having an army of gorgeous, athletic-looking women making faulty arguments in support of their faux-sport, but while I often clash with their flawed logic, I mean the players no disrespect personally. In short, I don't hate the players...I hate the game.

The Future of Lingerie Football

Because of the uniform and, more importantly, because it's not a real sport, lingerie football is forever doomed to the fringes of the mainstream sports community. It will remain a curiosity, a spectacle, a punchline, and a reality show. The LFL, in particular, touts their over-the-air television broadcasts, but there's a reason why the LFL is banished to music networks, sharing the airwaves not with programs like *SportsCenter* but with shows like *16 & Pregnant*. Those are their peers. It can never be accepted as true competitive sport, because it violates the key tenet of competitive sports, which is accessibility.

Lingerie football defenders suggest that if you just look past the lingerie, you'd see some wonderful football being played. But that's the issue...there's no taking the lingerie out of lingerie football (no matter what the LFL decides to call itself). You can no more take the lingerie out of lingerie football than take the table out of table tennis. Once you do, you produce something else entirely. Looking past the lingerie in lingerie football is impossible...taking out the lingerie gives you a completely different sport. In this case, it might give you a real sport rather than a salacious spectacle.

One last argument brought up by lingerie football fans is, "This is America! Who are you to say these women can't play?" That's not the point. Personally, I think if women want to wear lingerie on a football field, that seems irresponsible and degrading to me, but ultimately, it's their choice. And some people find such debauchery entertaining, and that's okay, too. I'm not saying they shouldn't be allowed to play lingerie football...I'm saying it isn't a real sport and shouldn't be confused for one. There's a difference.

Moreover, I'm also saying that these women shouldn't be celebrated as some kind of heroes for playing lingerie football. Misguided lingerie football players often view themselves as pioneers, setting an example for young girls to follow. That sentiment would be laughable if it wasn't so sad and out-of-touch. Lingerie football players aren't sending a message to young girls that women can do anything. They're sending a message to young girls that body image and sexual desirability to men should be their "first and foremost" concern...that girls can do anything, provided they grow into one particular body type and show a willingness to flaunt it for cheering, leering fans. That's hardly an inspirational message, particularly directed toward young girls who struggle enough with self-consciousness and body image issues as it is.

Lingerie football supporters sometimes suggest that one day lingerie football might be "legitimized", with fully-clothed women's football hailed as a mainstream sport. Until then, they argue, the ends of lingerie football justify the means, and they believe the popularity of lingerie football is somehow laying the groundwork for the future of women's football. I've already debunked that argument by pointing out that support for lingerie football is wholly contingent upon the partial nudity it provides.

But more importantly, when or if traditional women's football actually reaches mainstream acceptance remains uncertain. Traditional women's football continues to travel a long, hard road to win the attention and support of mainstream sports fans. Will traditional women's football ever gain traction and become a recognized mainstream niche sport? It's impossible to say. But if traditional women's football ever does reach that level, rest assured that recognition as pioneers of the sport will fall to the Jen Welters and Lisa Hortons of the world over the Liz Gormans and Monique Gaxiolas. Folks like Welter and Horton are the true pioneers who are showing young girls that women can do anything.

At the end of the day, if I have to choose between a sport with plenty of credibility but little name recognition or a spectacle with plenty of name recognition but little credibility, I'm taking the sport every time. It's much, much easier to build a fanbase where there was none than to build credibility where there is none. In fact, no league has ever started with the controversial, lewd origins that lingerie football was founded upon and been able to successfully make the transition to true competitive sport. As long as they're vetting players "first and foremost" by sex appeal, lingerie football will never be able to turn that corner – no matter how committed the women are – and if they ever took the sex appeal out of it, lingerie football would morph into something else entirely.

That's why traditional women's football, even as a long shot, is much the better bet. Every women's sport that has ever gained the respect of the mainstream public has done so because it was founded on the principle that the female athletes play the same game the men do, on a legitimately even playing field. Traditional women's football can properly claim its status as the female version of the incredibly popular sport men play, while lingerie football is...well, it is what it is.

1. http://www.livability.com/topics/arts-and-entertainment/sugar-spice-and-pigskin-womens-football-grows-texas-based-league
2. http://www.cbsnews.com/news/lacing-up-for-the-lingerie-bowl/
3. http://grantland.com/features/legends-football-league-womens-lingerie-football-league-mitchell-mortaza/

Mitch Mortaza and the LFL's Exploitation of Female Athletes

The most well-known lingerie football league in the United States is the Legends Football League (LFL), formerly and still commonly known as the Lingerie Football League. The LFL has been a leader in debasing the concept of women's athletics and objectifying female athletes with sexualized marketing and revealing uniforms. This editorial is an inside look at the history of this so-called sports league. Rest assured, whatever assumptions you may have about the LFL, the reality is likely far, far worse than anything you imagined.

A Quick History of the LFL

The concept of the LFL began when Mitchell S. Mortaza, then a young marketing executive, created the Lingerie Bowl in 2004. The Lingerie Bowl, a Super Bowl halftime alternative shown on pay-per-view television, featured models and actresses in revealing uniforms playing something loosely resembling indoor football.[1] Mortaza called it "an incredible lingerie fashion show, with red carpet arrivals and more."[2]

The Lingerie Bowl wasn't Mitch Mortaza's first television exposure, however. The *Broward Palm Beach New Times* described Mortaza's first brush with television fame:[3]

> The slick self-proclaimed millionaire, whose record includes arrests for drunk driving and public intoxication, wasn't new to lowbrow entertainment. In the late '90s, Mortaza appeared on an episode of the show *Blind Date*. With a neon tan that glared under the high-powered lights and a shirt unbuttoned to his diaphragm, he said his nickname was "Razor" and his biggest turn-on was "toe rings." He called himself "the king of one-night stands" and told the camera, "I'm not out there lookin' for nuns." He showed up for his date wearing a black tank top, a shell necklace, a thumb ring, and a pair of designer sunglasses he didn't remove all night – even inside the candlelit restaurant.

The first Lingerie Bowl in 2004 drew widespread condemnation; their biggest sponsor, Chrysler Dodge, and the American Foundation for AIDS Research, which was supposed to receive proceeds from the event, both pulled their associations with the Lingerie Bowl after fierce criticism.[4] Still, a gambling site came in to save the day, and it salvaged enough ratings to make it an annual event.[5] Three more planned Lingerie Bowls were eventually cancelled, most notably Lingerie Bowl VI, which was scrubbed when a dispute arose with the Florida nudist colony where the event was to be held.[6]

Undeterred, Mitch Mortaza expanded on his annual publicity stunt and started the ten-team Lingerie Football League in the fall of 2009. The concept of the league was and has always been simple – hot women in revealing uniforms playing full-contact football. For Mortaza, it was the perfect carnal blend of sex, violence, and something that passes for sports.

A Spectacle, Not a Sport

Lingerie football is not a real sport, obviously, but that's a point that confuses many otherwise intelligent people. It's easy to be fooled...after all, it's often portrayed as a sport, the women look athletic, they're on a football field, and they seem to be playing what resembles football. Sure, the uniforms are revealing, but it's still a sport, right?

Wrong. Completely wrong. The LFL has a long history of excluding women who don't fit the "image" of their league, *regardless of talent*. Mortaza doesn't shy away from that reality, telling *CBS News* in 2010, "First and foremost, you have to be beautiful. We have to be able to market you."[7] Indeed, LFL players are vetted first and foremost by appearance, a fact of which Mortaza and the LFL are very honest (and seemingly proud).[8] The LFL instructs potential recruits to wear "cute gym gear" and bring a headshot of themselves to tryouts, in what is essentially a casting call.[9]

Tryouts are where potential recruits are first exposed to the verbal and psychological abuse of the LFL. Cameramen lie on the ground, taking upward-angled shots of running players. Recruits are judged not on their football skills but on how aggressively they act toward other recruits and, naturally, on how their bodies fill out their uniforms.[10] Mortaza often attends these tryouts, cursing at the recruits and letting players know when he doesn't like their tattoos.[10,11]

At the end of the tryout, new recruits are selected – first and foremost – based on their sex appeal (or "marketability", to borrow Mortaza's euphemism). LFL players then continue to have their appearances harshly judged on an ongoing basis: players are required to send photos of themselves in bikinis to Mortaza and can be rejected solely based on how they look in those photos.[12] This creates a torturous environment where women who should be preparing for fierce, physical contact are instead downing water pills, starving themselves, and resorting to other extreme measures to look skinny enough to fit the league's image.[13]

Too many mainstream stories on the LFL gloss over all this for some reason and still treat lingerie football like it's legitimate sport; most media sources that glorify LFL players try to ignore the reality that it was only by being chosen in a glorified wet T-shirt contest that they made it into the league in the first place. But it's an inviolable tenet of sports:

When a "sport" rejects female athletes based not on their talent but based – first and foremost – on whether or not a man subjectively thinks she looks sexy in lingerie, it's not a legitimate competitive sport. No legitimate sports enterprise, anywhere, operates that way.

Mortaza doesn't apologize for any of this, stating, "We just happen to have an entire league of Tom Brady's and David Beckham's and Maria Sharapova's."[8] That's an absurd comparison, of course: Brady, Beckham, and Sharapova are elite athletes in a sport open to everyone, and on top of that, they *happen* to also have marketable looks. But Tom Brady isn't the starting quarterback of the New England Patriots because of his sex appeal…if Bill Belichick found a toothless hillbilly who could play quarterback more effectively than Brady, the competitive nature of the NFL would compel Belichick to send Brady to the bench. Because that's how a real sport operates…with roster spots earned on merit, not on how athletes look in their underwear.

The extent to which the LFL judges recruits based on appearance borders on comical. Even eventual LFL standouts like Liz Gorman,[10] Danika Brace,[14] Dakota Hughes,[15] Marirose Roach,[1] and Heather Furr,[1] among many others, have had their appearances questioned by Mortaza. The notion that any of these women might have ever been in danger of being kept out of the LFL solely due to appearance should reinforce how restrictive and unnecessary the league's "marketability" standards have been.

For anyone who might argue the LFL is an actual sports league, consider this: Imagine that the greatest women's football player in the entire world shows up at an LFL tryout. Mitch Mortaza can look her up and down, decide she doesn't look good enough in a bikini (or that she is a little too uncontrollable), and ban her for life…just like that. Discriminatory? Yes. Sexist? Absolutely. But most importantly, **that's not how real sports operate**.

Yes, the women who make it through and become LFL players are often athletic, intelligent, and competitive, always stunningly attractive, and naturally loud proponents of the LFL. But that doesn't make lingerie football a sport, nor does it negate any of the above. The LFL is not sports…like the WWE, it's a sport-like spectacle with pre-selected, athletic actors. It's mud-wrestling without the mud.[16] With all due respect to the women of the LFL, a true sports fan cannot simply ignore the existence of women's football players who are just as committed and far more talented than those in the LFL but who have been blackballed from the league because of Mortaza's outrageous marketing tactics.

Follow the Money

The single most important thing you need to know about the LFL is that it is a single-entity league, which means Mitch Mortaza owns not only the league overall but every single team within it. This setup makes Mortaza the league's supreme decision-maker; he alone has the ability to ban players, fire coaches and staff, cancel games, and even fold entire LFL franchises **purely at his discretion**. Furthermore, all the money generated by the league goes directly into his pocket. This arrangement clearly creates an environment ripe for abuses of power.

Mitch Mortaza made a very clever move in 2013. Realizing that he needed to draw attention away from his own questionable behavior, Mortaza rebranded the league and deliberately turned the public focus and emphasis toward the women of the LFL.[17] By essentially hiding behind the female athletes and their dedication, commitment, and all-around good looks, Mortaza hoped to legitimize the LFL in the public's eyes. Criticism of the LFL was interpreted as somehow demeaning to the women; instead, we were told that we should all support these admirable, hard-working athletes in their efforts.

The most amusing aspect of that argument is that Mitch Mortaza – who proudly declares that the LFL has always been profitable – doesn't pay these women a dime.[1] When pressed on the issue, Mortaza declines to disclose his personal salary.[18] But he is a self-proclaimed millionaire who boasts about "his very expensive mortgage up in Hollywood".[13,19] One prominent critic has suggested that Mortaza is like a pimp, exploiting scantily-clad women for personal profit.[20] That's unfair, of course…pimps pay better. At least, I assume they pay *something*.

It's no coincidence that Mortaza has claimed that the LFL has been "barely profitable" for the past six years.[1] If Mortaza said that the league was unprofitable, he wouldn't be able to claim that the LFL is the "nation's fastest growing sports league".[21] On the other hand, if he said the league was very profitable, he'd naturally get asked when he's going to pay the players, and he sure as heck isn't doing that. As such, you can expect the LFL to be "barely profitable" for the foreseeable future.

The LFL paid its players nominal salaries in its first two seasons. Despite the LFL promising successful players on good teams a possible six-figure salary,[22] two top LFL players (including one on the LFL's championship team) reported netting a couple hundred bucks on the year.[1,13] Mortaza then ended the practice of paying the players in 2011, sending them a memo in which he expressed regret at "unknowingly creating a culture" where players expected compensation.[13] Mortaza now claims it is "misleading" to suggest he ever paid the players a salary.[15]

For the past five years, Mortaza has kept LFL players hooked with grand promises that the league will revert back to a compensation model any day now. Several LFL veterans confirmed that the LFL always makes vague allusions to financial compensation just around the corner.[13] Mortaza suggested to players in the past that they'd be paid once the LFL returned to television, but the LFL returned to television in 2015 and the money is not forthcoming.[23]

So if you "take a step toward sexy" and buy a $15 ticket off of Groupon to a local LFL game, where do you think that money winds up?[24] Mortaza loves to accuse his critics of ignorance by staying they "have obviously never been to an LFL game," essentially challenging them to help fund his operation.[25] But the players don't get a dime of the LFL's financial success, so promoting or glorifying the LFL and its players in any way is little more than subsidizing Mitch Mortaza. Simple as that.

"No Less Than Abuse"

LFL players use their sex appeal, athleticism, and earnestness to attract attention and generate revenue for the league, all of which goes to Mitch Mortaza. In appreciation for their unpaid efforts, LFL players are often rewarded with years of abuse at Mortaza's hands. Because he can expel a player from the league for any reason (or no reason at all), he has the power of a cult leader over the players in the LFL. Even top LFL players admit they feel disposable;[1] one former player anonymously admitted that if you make one move Mortaza does not like, he will replace you or find some way to retaliate against you.[26]

Mortaza's verbal abuse is unrelenting.[27] He has both objectified and marginalized his players by repeatedly reminding them, "No one is here to watch you play football."[1] When LFL players have raised concerns to Mortaza – including safety concerns – his response on multiple occasions has been to tell the women to "shut up and play football".[28,29] Former LFL staff member, Pete Richmire, said simply, "What he's doing to these players constitutes no less than abuse."[23]

Mortaza isn't the only one in the LFL known for verbal abuse. Chicago Bliss head coach Keith Hac was seen in an LFL video screaming at a player that he was going to *bleep* her in the face.[30] When outrage grew online over the comment, Mortaza came to the rescue, claiming that the bleeped word was not the f-bomb – as popularly assumed – but rather "punch".[31,32] (It's an extreme stretch to believe that in a clip filled with profanity, the word "punch" would be the one to get censored. Mortaza claimed the word "punch" was bleeped because the LFL doesn't advocate violence against women, but apparently the league's disdain for violence against women wasn't strong enough to keep them from using the edited clip in the first place.) Mortaza's spin-doctoring desperately tried to downgrade Hac's threat of rape to something more tolerable in his eyes, a mere non-sexual threat of violence. Even if we take Mortaza at his word (always risky, especially in this case), Coach Hac was still *threatening to punch a woman in the face*. But he offered a perfunctory apology and stated that he has three incredible daughters, so he faced no meaningful punishment from the league.[32]

Former LFL players acknowledge that Mortaza exploits players for financial gain.[33] The LFL has countered the notion of exploitation by saying, "Remember one very simple point: these athletes chose to compete in the LFL. No athlete has ever been mandated to be part of the LFL, and in fact, [players] can choose to leave their club at any point."[34] Mortaza himself responds to the allegations by touting the league's college graduation rate and saying, "These are intelligent women who come from all types of backgrounds…hardly the type of women that would allow themselves to be exploited."[19,35]

It's not difficult to recognize such statements as the classic misdirection of an abusive person. First, he's not actually denying that he has said or done any of these inappropriate things. Second, it deplorably suggests that intelligent women can't get sucked into abusive relationships. And third, it makes the faulty argument that it's only abuse if the victim openly acknowledges it. That's a very dangerous assumption – particularly in an organization like the LFL, where Mortaza wields absolute power and players are unable to speak their minds without fear of retaliation.

Finding the Players' Motivation

So if the LFL is an abusive environment, why *do* players stay? That's complicated, and there are likely several reasons. But the one most often cited – "these women just love football" – doesn't fly.[15] In truth, there are multiple traditional, legitimate women's football leagues these women could play in, located in every part of the country. If it were only about wanting to play football, there are outlets for them to do so.

Now, the LFL definitely draws more fans in the stands than any traditional women's football league. Some have tried to rationalize LFL players' participation in the league by saying, "This is the only opportunity they've found that they can play [football] *with high exposure*."[15] It's an amusing and perhaps unintentional double entendre…essentially, LFL players trade exposure for exposure, exposing copious amounts of skin in exchange for the exposure of playing to crowds of 2,000 fans as opposed to 200 in traditional leagues. So if fame – such as it is – is your goal, the LFL is indeed your best option.

But many LFL players also have unselfish reasons for remaining with the league. Many cling to the false hope that the LFL is going to one day become widely recognized and respected. They have invested a lot of energy into the league and don't want to walk away with nothing to show for their sacrifices. Mortaza deftly keeps players on the hook with vague promises of better things right around the corner. Moving the goalposts has become a Mortaza specialty, according to several LFL veterans.[13] Media outlets that serve as LFL propaganda are despicable in that they supply Mortaza with a big carrot he can use to dangle in front of his players and new recruits to indoctrinate them into accepting his abusiveness just a little longer.

Many LFL players also choose to tolerate Mortaza's antics because of the camaraderie they feel with their teammates and coaches. Expulsion from the LFL would leave them ostracized from the teammates they admire; the league has threatened ex-players who have spoken negatively about the LFL that any contact with their former teammates and coaches would result in the filing of a restraining order.[29] Indeed, players who consider quitting the LFL are often pulled back in by their teammates, who offer support with statements like, "You're not the only person [in the LFL] who has to go through this."[15] While they could leave at any time, players don't want to leave their teammates behind in such an abusive scenario, either.

LFL defenders often make the case that the public should support the women of the LFL, because – despite the unsavory nature of the league – these women are making their own free choice to participate in the league. It's an interesting argument, until you realize that not all choices deserve to be celebrated and supported and marketed to children. The LFL is blatant sexual exploitation, even if the women involved choose to do it...and even if the women involved suggest it's *not* exploitation.

We've all heard stories about women who suffer from domestic abuse, who show up with bruises and black eyes and yet adamantly insist that they are not being abused. Whether these victims are ready to confess it or not, most reasonable people can see when abuse is taking place. And while we can't stop women from voluntarily subjecting themselves to abusive situations (because this is America, after all), we can refrain from glorifying or celebrating their decision to do so. Instead, we applaud those who display the true strength it takes to get out of those situations and the former victims who then work to prevent others from suffering the same fate by speaking out and sharing their stories and experiences.

The real heroes of the LFL – the women who truly deserve our admiration and support – are those who summon the strength to leave and then take a stand against their former oppressors, because many of these women then face verbal abuse and bullying on the LFL's social media platforms. One former LFL staff member alleges that Mortaza maintains fake online profiles which he can use to discredit former players and staff.[23] Regardless, prominent LFL defectors who have questioned the LFL's lack of concern over player safety have seen their reputations smeared on the LFL's social media platforms.

Former Seattle Mist quarterback Natasha Lindsay was accused on an LFL team Facebook page of having "the personality of a grapefruit".[36] Lindsay was characterized as wanting "someone else to blame for her ineptitude as a football player and as an adult."[37] Another post to an LFL team Facebook page linked 2010 LFL defensive player of the year Deborah Poles to unsubstantiated rumors of steroid use and mocked her as being "man-like" and needing to be checked "to make certain she does not have a 'man-package'." The post described her defensive player of the year award as a "pity award" and declared, "No one would ever place the words pretty and Deborah Poles in the same sentence."[38]

Kelly Leabu and Aleina Mackey were both labeled on an LFL team Facebook page as "irrelevant", having "poor character", and being "glorified clip-board holders and at times equipment managers".[39] Mortaza himself publicly called former LFL standout Nikki Johnson "a cancer" and went on to say, "This is her last fifteen minutes of fame. She'll never be heard from again."[1] Players who have left the LFL and criticized aspects of their former league have faced persistent verbal abuse from the LFL and on its social media outlets, which have relentlessly slurred them as being "wannabe competitors, teammates, and worst of all, athletes" and even "the lowest forms of life".[37]

One anonymous online commenter summarized Mortaza's relationship with the players perfectly:[40]

> It's similar to Stockholm syndrome in certain ways. At first, [Mortaza] will promise riches and glory. Over time, the shiny coat chips away. They get angry and at least one player will throw down, so to speak. When that person is cut and made an example of, the others fall in line. It's not that they like it...it's that most of them have put in time, lost jobs, and experienced personal and family issues over it, and they don't want to lose out after putting the time in. So they hold out as long as possible, enduring the abuse. Most of them believe this could explode into something profitable any day now, and they want to be there to cash in on it. The sad thing is that they are right in some ways. The LFL could blow up at any moment, but they are wrong that *they* would cash in on it.

To remain connected with the league, LFL players have been forced into becoming Mortaza apologists, responding to reporters' questions with answers that may as well be coming from Mortaza himself. Again, Mortaza rules the league like a despot, and players cannot speak their minds without the threat of retaliation. Not surprisingly, LFL players consistently downplay the revealing uniforms, the safety concerns, and their lack of pay.[41] It's not surprising that current LFL players express almost nothing but positive support for everything their league does...if they didn't, they would no longer be current players. After all, dissent is not tolerated: "If it isn't done his way, he gets rid of you," a former LFL coach said.[14]

"I compare it to being in a relationship with a bad boyfriend. He's amazing in the beginning, and then it starts changing and then I'm in a bad relationship," Tessa Barrera, a former captain for the Los Angeles Temptation, said. "You love your significant other even though you know you deserve to be treated better," she added. "You think, 'Oh, I'll stay and things just have to get better,' but eventually you just have to say, 'No, this isn't right.' I would die for football, but I'm not gonna play for a bad person who mistreats people."[42,43]

Read between the lines...if that doesn't sound like abuse and exploitation, I don't know what does.

Pretty.Unsafe.

Nowhere is Mortaza's complete indoctrination over his players more evident than with the LFL's uniforms and total lack of concern over player safety. LFL players wear hockey helmets designed to give fans a better view of the women's faces, flimsy helmets that literally bend in players' hands. Yet Mitch Mortaza laughably defends their use in part by citing a 2013 league survey in which players stated that they preferred the hockey helmets.[1] You can imagine how valid those "survey results" were, given Mortaza's wide opportunity for retaliation against players who refuse to give the answers he wants to hear.

Coach Hac defended the LFL's use of hockey helmets by declaring that "hockey helmets...offer just enough protection."[44] That's the kind of statement that should send shock waves down the spine of any player, coach, or fan who has even the most basic knowledge about the sport of football. **There's no such thing as "just enough" protection. Protection and safety of players isn't something you should ever, ever skimp on for marketing purposes, even a little bit.** The fact that a so-called "football coach", of all people, would advance that narrative in 2015 is stunningly ignorant. I mean, why bother giving players anything more than "just enough" protection, right?

The uniforms, while often cited as controversial for the amount of skin they display, are far more contentious in that they provide almost no protection from serious injury. Deborah Poles, a former LFL defensive player of the year, suffered such severe turf burns that she was hospitalized with a staph infection after an LFL game.[33] These types of injuries are not surprising when women wearing volleyball shorts are exposed to the full contact of lingerie football.

The sub-standard helmets and uniforms create the perfect environment for injuries. Former player Nikki Johnson said, "We had girls who were getting concussions; we had a girl...who shattered her cheekbone. We had ACL injuries. I broke my wrist. I took a late hit...and wound up being put on a stretcher and taken to a hospital. **Stuff like that is preventable.**"[45]

In one of the more publicized incidents in LFL history, nearly the entire Toronto Triumph team quit en masse in 2011. Players detailed how they engaged in full contact at practice before they even had their helmets, resulting in multiple injuries believed to be concussions. When the helmets finally arrived from the league, they were flimsy field hockey helmets totally inappropriate for football. Beyond that, the LFL coaches had them drill holes into the helmets to attach chinstraps and visors, compromising the helmets' integrity. As if all that weren't enough, Mortaza himself arrived the day of their first game and told them to replace their pads with less-substantial models.[46]

When several players complained, four women were released from the team. Mortaza washed his hands of the matter, stating that it's up to team coaches to make personnel decisions and to supply equipment.[28] Remember, any coach that doesn't follow Mortaza's wishes can be fired from the LFL at a moment's notice.

Sixteen players then quit the Toronto team in protest.[28] Mortaza responded by relentlessly insulting the players in the press after they left, calling them "wannabes that are more interested in being celebrities than football players" and belittling their athletic backgrounds.[47] Several players also received "cease-and-desist" letters, warning them about speaking out against the league.[46] It's not an uncommon tactic for the LFL, which repeatedly threatened legal action in 2009 against a group of former players who complained that the league backtracked on promises to pay for medical bills of players injured during practices and games.[29]

In classically abusive fashion, Mortaza also put the safety issue squarely on the Toronto players' shoulders; he responded to their allegations regarding lack of safety in a statement, saying in part, "If they felt unsafe or not protected they could have chosen to end their LFL tenure months ago."[48]

The New Family-Friendly LFL

The laundry list of former LFL standouts who have been saddled with severe injuries is long and illustrious. Besides Poles and Johnson, Melissa Margulies literally "broke her face" after being kneed in the head, fracturing bones in her cheek and around her eye socket.[1,13] Angela Rypien, one of the most recognizable names in the LFL as the daughter of former NFL quarterback Mark Rypien, was one of many LFL players to suffer a concussion, an incident she described as "refreshing".[18] Natasha Lindsey and Kelli Leabu both tore ACLs while covered under the LFL's medical insurance plan and were then stonewalled by the league when they tried to collect compensation for their surgeries.[49,50]

Several players went public on *Inside Edition* in 2013, detailing their injuries. Marirose Roach broke her neck during one game. Sydney Froelich said she suffered a severe shoulder injury. Laurel Creel acknowledged having had four major concussions during her LFL playing days.[43] And then there was Amber Mane, who took a helmet to the face in one game while rushing for a touchdown. She suffered a broken nose that sent blood gushing out onto the field. Minutes later, Mane collapsed in the tunnel of the arena and was left with three thousand dollars of outstanding medical bills.[1]

Critics often get hung up on the sexualized nature of the uniforms, and understandably so. LFL fans wait with baited breath for a wardrobe malfunction and often get it...when a player's panties are ripped down, the scene is replayed on the large screen to the delight of the crowd.[51] In fact, the very first LFL game back in 2009 was "highlighted" by one player having her panties pulled down and another player having the flimsy fabric of her bra ripped off, leaving her topless on the field.[18] Naturally, the crowd loved it and screamed for a replay.[52]

The LFL encouraged all of this, with the league including an "accidental nudity" clause in player contracts in which the women agree "knowingly and voluntarily" to such potential exposure. One ex-player noted that the LFL did not want players wearing additional bras or underwear since that would inhibit instances where players might be exposed when uniforms were ripped off or pulled down during play. The league established a $500 fine for any player caught wearing "additional garments".[29]

The league has tried to reposition itself as a "family-friendly" enterprise in recent years, luring hundreds of women and children into the stands and disgustingly trying to portray themselves as some kind of inspiration for young girls.[15,53] Yet players still engage in antics like twerking on an opponent's head after a play,[54] chugging a beer at midfield after a game,[55] sipping a beer after scoring a touchdown,[56] and making hand signals in the shape of a vagina after scoring plays.[57] It's hardly family-friendly...to the contrary, it's all part of, as one website said (and pardon the language), the LFL's "quest to be the favorite sport of douchebags."[56]

Fixing the Game

For those who might still be under the impression this is somehow a competitive sport, consider that Mitch Mortaza's despotic control of the league includes the ability to fix the outcomes of games. Mortaza has been known to show up on gameday and look over a team's roster. If, in his expert opinion, he decides that a player isn't up to his aesthetic standards, he orders the team's coaches (who know they can be fired by Mortaza for any reason) to bench certain players just before kickoff.[1] You can imagine how it would affect a team's chances to win a game when they discover right before kickoff that several of their key players have been unilaterally benched by the commissioner, a commissioner who has a vested financial interest in who wins and loses.

Suffice it to say, there have been multiple "controversial" outcomes in the LFL's short history. On December 30, 2011, the Orlando Fantasy played the Tampa Breeze with a playoff berth on the line. The Tampa team had much better ticket sales than the Orlando team, so Mortaza would financially benefit in seeing the Breeze come away with the victory to advance to the playoffs.[58]

Tampa scored a touchdown in the final minute to defeat Orlando, 20-18.[59] In truth, the win was assured thanks largely to what was widely reported as a slew of one-sided calls in Tampa's favor by officials who report directly to Mortaza.[60] Within days, the LFL "parted ways" with two staff members who covered the game, their color commentator and one of their unpaid staff writers.[61,62]

The LFL then fired Orlando head coach Doug Miller for "blatant disrespect and unbecoming behavior".[63] Mortaza tried to use "league medical staff" (who also report to Mortaza) to pressure Coach Miller during the game to bench one of his best players...which, naturally, would have been a considerable advantage for Tampa.[62] When Coach Miller refused, he was fired days later. As for the Orlando players, Mortaza retaliated against them by folding their entire team at the conclusion of the season.[64,65]

Mitch Mortaza and Dion Lee

Dion Lee, the former coach of the LFL's Las Vegas Sin, is one of the few former LFL coaches who has been willing to go on record about his LFL experience, given the league's litigious nature. The LFL has sent numerous cease-and-desist letters to former players and even to media outlets that have published satirical articles about the league.[46,66] Sometimes the harassment goes even further. One former LFL staff member, Justin Schoenrock, was met with a threatening phone call from a blocked number shortly after his departure from the LFL. Schoenrock said someone using a voice scrambling device attempted to blackmail him, warning him not to do any interviews unless he wanted to find his name and reputation smeared online.[23]

Coach Lee's experience in the LFL provides a key reference point between lingerie football and the traditional women's game. Several LFL players and coaches have suggested that the LFL is the "highest level" of competitive women's football.[67] That's laughable, of course. While the LFL attracts more fans (for obvious reasons), the overall level of "football talent" is much weaker in lingerie leagues than it is in traditional women's leagues like the WFA and IWFL, thanks largely to the fact that leagues like the LFL are a closed society of women who fit a very specific body type which is not, at many positions, ideal for high-caliber football. The vast majority of the best women's football players in the world play traditional football, because they would either be rejected by the LFL for perceived lack of sex appeal or because they have too much dignity to play football in lingerie in the first place. And since traditional leagues are open to all women of talent while the lingerie leagues self-limit themselves to a small swath of the female population, the most competitive women's football players in the world flock toward the traditional leagues where they can challenge themselves against the best competition in the sport. Meanwhile, the lingerie leagues operate within a protected bubble limited to those who have the appropriate "look".

Many lingerie football players overestimate their athletic prowess and defensively boast about how tough and raw and fearless they are, because they know they will only have to go up against a small subset of female athletes with a very specific body type. Coach Hac declared, "The level of playing in the women's full gear leagues doesn't even equate to the level of playing in the LFL...It's like watching slow motion football."[44]

To be clear, the level of play presented by the top teams in traditional women's football doesn't approach the skill and speed of NFL teams or major college football teams. But the gap in skill level between the LFL and the closest legitimate male comparison – the Arena Football League – is even more massive than the gap between top WFA teams and the NFL. If the top traditional women's football teams play "slow motion football", the LFL is slow motion *arena* football...in panties, of course.

Coach Dion Lee bridged both worlds, and his experience in the LFL provides proof that, contrary to what some LFL players and supporters might suggest, the talent level in traditional women's football is vastly superior to that of the LFL.[1] Lee came to the LFL with a solid track record as the head coach of the Las Vegas Showgirlz in traditional football. The Showgirlz were a solid but not elite team in the traditional women's game, but Lee managed to slip several members of his Showgirlz past Mortaza's image-centric barricade and into the LFL. Armed with just a few of those players, Lee's expansion team dominated the LFL, going undefeated in the regular season and earning the top seed in the playoffs.

Lee related a story about how his Las Vegas team played the Los Angeles Temptation on November 11, 2011. Clinging to a late lead, Lee had his Vegas team run the ball in the hopes of running out the clock. Vegas held off the favored Temptation, 28-20, in a game the league titled as, "Hell Freezes Over".[68]

After the game, Mortaza came into the Las Vegas locker room. Lee was expecting to accept the commissioner's congratulations, but instead, Mortaza ripped into Lee and his coaches for running the ball. "You should be running the two-minute offense!" Lee recalled Mortaza saying. Running the ball was the right football move, but Mortaza was angry over the lack of showmanship. Lee added, "He would say before every game, 'People don't come to see the girls play football. They come to be entertained.'"[14]

Lee finally told Mortaza to get out of his locker room, and Mortaza responded by e-mail a few days later. "First, it is not your locker room nor your team," Mortaza wrote. "Understand who I am and who you are, or you will have the shortest tenure in LFL history. Do not test me again if you wish to remain."[14] The LFL later passed a bizarre rule change, stating that teams must run twice and pass twice every four downs.[69]

Lee went into detail about Mortaza's micromanaging. "His hands are in everything. He's trying to tell me how to run plays...sending me emails on how I need to run this reverse play," Lee said. "He can tell anybody he wants anything."[14]

More Alleged Game-Fixing From Mortaza

The issue of Mitch Mortaza meddling with game officials surfaced once again when the Los Angeles Temptation and Las Vegas Sin had a rematch for the Western Conference championship on January 29, 2012. The conference championships were played as a doubleheader at Citizens Business Bank Arena, and the Las Vegas-Los Angeles tilt was scheduled to take place immediately following the Eastern Conference championship. But the first game ran late, so the Western Conference championship kickoff was delayed.

The undefeated Sin had rolled through the LFL regular season and earned the top seed in the playoffs. However, when the Las Vegas-Los Angeles game began, it became apparent that the officials were not going to call even the most blatant penalties. Late hits, unsportsmanlike conduct...the officials had swallowed their whistles. "Look at that game; there were no calls," Lee said. "I called a timeout and chewed out the head ref. I said, 'Why the heck are you not calling the personal fouls?' [He responded,] 'We're not calling any fouls because we have limited time on the air. That's from the head man.'"[14]

By Lee's account, Mitch Mortaza ordered the officials to move the game along because the first game ran long and he wanted to fit the doubleheader into a television window.[14] More importantly, he again made sure his refs handed him his approved outcome; Los Angeles came away with the win over outspoken Lee's Las Vegas squad.[70] Following the game, Coach Lee was rewarded for taking an expansion team within a sliver of the Lingerie Bowl by being fired by Mortaza after just one season. Mitch Mortaza made the announcement, citing his dissatisfaction with Lee's "poor guidance" of the team.[71]

"No way in hell" was he going to let L.A. lose that playoff game, Lee alleged.[14] It was no secret that the Los Angeles Temptation were Mitch Mortaza's preferred team; Mortaza has been known to shed tears over playoff losses by the Temptation.[23] Los Angeles' third straight LFL championship enabled Mortaza to sell the public on their "dynasty status".[72]

Mortaza's love for the Temptation was eventually trumped by money, however. In the 2015 LFL Western Conference championship game, the Seattle Mist narrowly held off the Los Angeles Temptation after a questionable "official review" awarded them possession of the ball on a possible game-winning Temptation drive. The LFL championship game was already scheduled to be held in Seattle, and a victory by the Temptation would have cost the league thousands of dollars. With the Seattle win, the LFL did not need to spend money on flights and hotels for the Los Angeles team, and it assured the LFL of a much higher fan turnout for the title game with the local team participating.[13]

Still think this is a real sports league?

Orchestrated Gimmicks

Mortaza is well-known for resorting to controversial gimmicks to drive even more attention to the LFL than the partial nudity already generates. Mortaza famously tried to start a youth division of the LFL, because, in his words, "younger and younger girls are starting to dream of playing LFL football." He then contacted Michael Jackson's daughter Paris to recruit her to head the project, a move one site correctly called "a bid to remain ever creepy".[73]

"What's creepier than starting a youth league to prepare little girls to be lingerie football players?" the site continued. "Identifying the specific underage girls (children of celebrities, natch) that you'd like to see play in underwear one day!" Not surprisingly, Michael Jackson's mother Katherine was furious at the proposition made toward her granddaughter. "Katherine views this as a disgusting attack on a minor," a family friend said. "A teenage spokeswoman for a lingerie league? That's just creepy and downright offensive."[74]

The LFL also tries to draw (ludicrous) comparisons to the NFL whenever it can, naming its "film division" LFL Films, for instance. Mortaza loves to link his publicity stunts to the NFL as well: offering notably pious quarterback Tim Tebow an LFL coaching position,[75] injecting himself into the Washington Redskins' name controversy by taking the moral high ground in naming a proposed DC-based LFL team (which has yet to launch),[76] and famously joining in the chorus of public criticism over the NFL's replacement refs in 2012 by suggesting that the LFL had fired some of them in the past (an allegation that garnered a lot of attention but which was never substantiated).[77] Nothing substantive came out of any of these marketing ploys, but they were exactly the type of attention-grabbing gimmicks the league has become known for.

Mortaza's business gimmicks are fine until they go too far, of course. Amber Mane, who suffered a gruesome broken nose and collapsed at an LFL arena, stated that her injuries were entirely preventable if not for the fact that Mitch Mortaza instructed her and other players to adjust their chin straps so they could rip off their helmets to celebrate plays. The league denies that account, even though it is corroborated by a former LFL assistant coach.[1]

Melissa Margulies registered a quarterback sack in a game in 2010 and got up slowly, having suffered a concussion on the play. Mortaza had her immediately benched…not out of concern for her safety, but to punish her for not properly celebrating her sack. "You guys are boring to watch!" Mortaza told the team at halftime. "I had to bench Margulies because she didn't celebrate a big tackle!"[13]

Mortaza would then use Margulies as an example for years, telling players to "ask Margulies" if they didn't think he was serious about being "entertainers" as much as athletes.[13] The league denies that account, too, stating that only head coaches can decide to bench players.[1] Once again, these head coaches report directly to Mortaza and can be fired for any reason if they don't do exactly as he says.

Former players confessed that on-field fights among players were encouraged by the league to get the crowd riled up, and that those fights sometimes led to injuries.[43] The LFL does seem to suffer from an inordinately large number of such incidents. In just one example, a brawl broke out this past season when a defensive player performed a push-up over the player she just tackled.[78]

Mortaza is the micromanaging ringleader of the whole operation. Players acknowledge Mortaza has a presence in the locker room, where he instructs them to give camera-friendly inspirational speeches. Multiple players also admit that

Mortaza has instructed them to trash-talk opponents and devise elaborate touchdown celebrations. Yet Mortaza states that "nobody has pushed the players to do those things."[15]

One more time...if an LFL player does not do exactly as Mortaza instructs, she can be banned from the league for life for any reason at all. For Mortaza to pass off responsibility for these events is patently ridiculous. He controls every aspect of the league, yet he frequently uses players and coaches as a shield to deflect away from taking responsibility for his unprofessionalism.

The Failures of the LFL

Mitch Mortaza is peddling perhaps the easiest product to sell in the history of mankind – sex, violence, and a dash of faux-sport. In the hands of an astute businessperson, it would be a slam dunk. With Mortaza at the helm, however, the LFL has had more than its share of growing pains in its six-year history.

The LFL launched a league in Canada in 2012. After one season, the league collapsed with teams pulling out amid concerns over league disorganization and safety issues. Mortaza then insulted pretty much the entire country, stating, "We've never seen so many out-of-shape players in the offseason as we have on the rosters in Canada." He also pledged to return in 2014 with six teams and an expanded schedule, promises that, naturally, went unfulfilled.[79]

The LFL organized a league in Australia in 2013 amid considerable controversy. The national Minister of Sport, Kate Lundy, blasted the LFL and Mortaza for "hiding behind the guise of LFL being a 'sport'".[80] Mortaza responded by comparing Australia to North Korea,[81] an absurd comparison he already made when the mayor of Oklahoma City denied him an LFL franchise.[82]

Regardless, the LFL lasted just one season in Australia, scrapping its planned second season two weeks before it was set to kick off. The Australians alleged they were owed $30,000 in payments when Mortaza left the continent and that they planned to organize a class action lawsuit in the United States to recoup the money.[83] Though the LFL pledged to return to Australia in 2015,[84] protests by former LFL players outside of a league tryout led to a paltry turnout of just six recruits, and the LFL abandoned the idea.[85]

Mortaza also announced the launch of an LFL league in Europe in 2014, a league that failed to materialize.[86] The master plan was to have national teams from various international leagues compete in an LFL "World Bowl" in Brazil in 2014 during the World Cup.[87] Mortaza confidently predicted anywhere from 30,000 to 50,000 fans for his event, which never took place.[88]

As always, the LFL did its best to put a positive spin on their failings, announcing a new "global strategy" in 2015 that said, essentially, that their "primary focus" for the next few years would be on the development of the LFL in the U.S.[89] It was a dramatic reversal from less than one year earlier, when the LFL vowed to surpass the WWE as a "commercial global sports property".[17] The refocusing of the LFL on the United States was little more than an admission of their total and unmitigated failure to expand the "sport" abroad.

Here in the United States, the LFL's failures are evident. In just six short years, the league has either had teams "suspend operations" or announced plans for teams that failed to launch on time in the following major markets:

Miami,[90] Orlando,[65] Tampa (which was labeled as a "relocation" to Jacksonville),[91] Jacksonville,[92] Charlotte,[93] Baltimore,[94] DC,[95] New York,[96] Boston,[97] Pittsburgh,[98] Philadelphia,[99] Cleveland (which was labeled as a "relocation" to Toledo),[100] Toledo,[92] Green Bay,[92] Milwaukee,[101] Minneapolis,[99] St. Louis,[102] Oklahoma City,[103] Tulsa (which actually pre-emptively shot down the idea),[104] Dallas,[105] Houston,[106] Denver,[107] Las Vegas,[108] and San Diego.[109]

The LFL has announced expectations to have 26 teams in the league within five years.[99] Yet in 2015, the LFL featured just six teams in five markets, with the Las Vegas franchise "temporarily" operating out of Los Angeles before folding.[92] As always, the league continues to unveil aggressive expansion plans, but history shows that LFL franchises last fewer than six games on average before folding.

The LFL recently defaulted in a May 2015 lawsuit in Las Vegas.[110] Mortaza has also refused to respond to or offer any type of defense against a similar lawsuit in California, which may also be headed toward a default judgment against him.[13] Meanwhile, Mortaza has attempted to elude being served with legal papers, going so far as to deny his identity at a recent tryout despite several women identifying him as Mortaza.[15]

The Future of the LFL

As the league's founder, owner, and commissioner, the fate of the LFL is intrinsically tied to Mitch Mortaza. Even if he were to one day name an LFL player to serve as his puppet in the role league commissioner, Mortaza's "hands-on" presence would always be lurking in the background.[13]

Mortaza's ego demands that he will forever remain the LFL's supreme despot, incapable of being overruled. Creating a new level of front office staff would simply be another way for Mortaza to deflect responsibility for what happens in his league onto someone else, as he now does with his players and coaches. You can fully envision a day when some poor pawn inherits the job of LFL Commissioner, with Mortaza retaining his role as "Founder", of course. Then anyone questioning Mortaza's tactics could be told, "The commissioner makes those decisions," when, in fact, said commissioner is fully subordinate to Mortaza's commands and serves at his leisure.

In my opinion, Mortaza will likely continue to try to tinker with peripheral aspects of the league, hoping to gain legitimacy for his enterprise without actually making any substantive changes to the LFL's operation. The LFL has faced overwhelming public criticism toward the league's players being unpaid. You can foresee a time in which Mortaza approaches a handful of his most loyal lieutenants and offers to pay them a paltry annual "salary" of, say, $100 a year, provided they sign a non-disclosure agreement that they never publicly reveal the amount of their salaries.

For the total cost of about $500 annually, Mortaza could then make a dramatic public announcement that the LFL is returning to a "paid compensation model", in which a select few veterans supposedly get the pay they deserve. Because the salaries are undisclosed, Mortaza would be able to tempt incoming recruits with false dreams that LFL veterans are making solid salaries and blunt a widely-held objection to his league's operations. Make no mistake: if Mortaza ever promises "undisclosed" salaries to select LFL players in the future, you'll know why the amounts are undisclosed.

Mortaza will also futilely try to quell the furor over the league's uniforms. Mortaza gives lip service to player safety and is always suggesting that he might "upgrade" the uniforms someday; he's already teasing the possibility of new uniforms in 2016.[111] But when the LFL made a much-ballyhooed change to their uniforms in 2013, Mortaza considered it a "pretty historic" moment because, in his words, "There's no longer garters."[1] The lingerie that made the Lingerie Football League what it is will never truly go away; the partial nudity, not the quality of football displayed, is what keeps fans in the stands, despite what Mortaza claims and what the players are indoctrinated into repeating.

Along those lines, it's not hard to foresee the eventual end of the LFL. Regardless of who runs the league, the safety concerns surrounding the lingerie uniforms will never truly go away; the lack of proper safety equipment will likely bring LFL to its knees sooner or later. Mortaza has repeatedly justified the use of hockey helmets, saying they are superior to traditional helmets, which tend to be "used as a weapon".[1] But at least one prominent doctor has labeled that assertion "absurd", predicting "skull fractures and deaths".[112] While some doctors *could* envision a day where legitimate men's football players cease wearing helmets altogether, such a move would need to be accompanied by drastic rule changes as well.[113] "If there were no helmets and the game was played the way it is today, a lot of people would be dead on day one," one prominent brain trauma researcher noted.[114]

Evidence would seem to be on the side of the medical establishment rather than Mitch Mortaza on the safety issue. The way football is currently played, less protection is dangerous, and Mortaza's assertions to the contrary are clearly warped by his profit motive. The LFL's history of severe injuries has been well-documented, and it's only a matter of time before some ill-equipped player is catastrophically injured, paralyzed, or killed playing in the LFL. And that will be the end of it.

In the meantime, the arenas that host LFL contests would be well-advised to make sure their insurance policies are up-to-date, because when that time comes, the victims won't be coming after Mortaza – who, despite his claims, probably has little money to give them. When a player is tragically hurt or killed during an LFL game – and wearing those uniforms, it will happen – it's the arenas who will be on the hook. They'll be the ones liable for turning a blind eye to the numerous horrifying injuries that have already occurred to LFL players wearing clearly substandard safety equipment, all with the expressed intention of driving up ticket sales. Arenas ignoring the LFL's appalling track record with respect to safety will have the LFL's blood, quite literally, on their hands as well.

This nation's appetite for unbridled violence between scantily-clad, gorgeous women will never fully go away, so lingerie football will always have a certain amount of appeal from certain types of individuals. But the LFL is forever damaged beyond repair, because you cannot erase the past. When the first game in LFL history was "highlighted" by a woman having her bra ripped off and being left topless on the field, that became a permanent part of the LFL's history, no matter how many "rebrands" the league goes through. The LFL will be forever constrained in the sports world by its tarnished past, exploitative present, and controversial future. And at the end of the day, that truth – unlike attorneys – is something even Mitch Mortaza cannot evade.

1. http://grantland.com/features/legends-football-league-womens-lingerie-football-league-mitchell-mortaza/
2. http://www.nytimes.com/2004/01/31/arts/for-the-football-anti-fan-aliens-lovers-lingerie.html
3. http://www.browardpalmbeach.com/news/the-calientes-inaugural-season-had-blood-sweat-broken-bones-and-a-lot-of-lace-6343539
4. http://www.wsj.com/articles/SB1071699634977600
5. http://usatoday30.usatoday.com/money/advertising/2004-01-13-lingerie-bowl-sponsor_x.htm
6. http://www.tampabay.com/sports/football/bucs/lingerie-bowl-canceled-over-dispute-with-caliente-nudist-resort/970537
7. http://www.cbsnews.com/news/lacing-up-for-the-lingerie-bowl/
8. http://abcnews.go.com/Entertainment/lingerie-football-sexy-sexist-female-players-love-game/story?id=20318487
9. http://sports.yahoo.com/blogs/cfl-55-yard-line/lfl-commissioner-mitch-mortaza-says-lingerie-football-eclipse-230042699.html

10. http://melindatankardreist.com/2012/06/abused-yelled-out-called-pussy-and-told-to-pancake-the-shit-out-of-her-my-experience-of-lingerie-football-league-try-outs-in-sydney-last-week/
11. http://www.blogto.com/sports_play/2011/05/ford_makes_the_cut_at_lingerie_football_league_tryouts/
12. http://www.stuff.co.nz/life-style/life/9522786/Not-lean-enough-for-lingerie-football
13. https://sports.vice.com/en_us/article/the-truth-is-not-always-sexy-inside-the-legends-football-league
14. https://www.youtube.com/watch?v=Mi5KG7ETgx8
15. http://mmqb.si.com/mmqb/2015/09/23/legends-football-league-lingerie-football-lfl-dakota-hughes-atlanta-steam
16. http://www.totalprosports.com/2014/08/28/nasty-brawl-lfl-punch-coach-video/
17. http://www.forbes.com/sites/markjburns/2014/09/06/with-series-of-bold-moves-legends-football-league-aims-to-become-global-sports-property/
18. http://www.citypaper.com/news/features/2013/bcp-cms-1-1492931-migrated-story-cp-20130522-featu-20130522-story.html
19. http://www.browardpalmbeach.com/news/lingerie-football-league-founder-mitch-mortaza-got-his-showbiz-start-on-tvs-blind-date-6444282
20. http://clevelandsports360.com/wordpress/2011-the-year-we-found-out-how-mitchell-mortazas-lfl-degrades-women/
21. http://www.lfl360.com/lfl-north-america/usa/lingerie-football-league-re-brands-legends-football-league-lfl360-com/
22. http://sports.espn.go.com/espn/page2/story?page=buckheit/090612
23. http://www.blogtalkradio.com/gridironbeauties/2013/10/06/gridiron-beauties-radio
24. https://www.groupon.com/deals/gl-lingerie-football-showare-center
25. http://www.thelostogle.com/2010/11/18/lost-ogle-qa-lingerie-football-league-chairman-mitchell-mortaza/
26. http://clevelandsports360.com/wordpress/the-nfl-the-nba-has-one-why-not-the-lingerie-football-league/
27. http://clevelandsports360.com/wordpress/lfl-now-charging-women-to-take-mitchell-mortazas-verbal-abuse-i-mean-tryout-no-arena-in-st-louisno-team/
28. http://www.thestar.com/news/gta/2011/10/23/20_leave_toronto_lingerie_football_team_in_dispute_over_safety_coaching.html
29. http://www.thesmokinggun.com/documents/crime/lingerie-league-gets-litigious
30. https://www.youtube.com/watch?v=Vyp5_DtRcw8
31. http://www.buzzfeed.com/jpmoore/lingerie-football-coach-sexually-threatens-a-player#.wb24a54z4v
32. http://www.sportressofblogitude.com/2013/05/22/lfl-issues-statement-about-bliss-coach/
33. http://www.thestar.com/news/gta/2011/10/28/lingerie_football_touchdown_or_fumble.html
34. http://www.theguardian.com/sport/2014/jan/10/lingerie-football-men-watch-women-play
35. http://triblive.com/news/nafarivanaski/3423730-74/women-league-football
36. https://www.facebook.com/MyLasVegasSin/posts/355043934516747
37. https://www.facebook.com/MyMinnesotaValkyrie/posts/331182036929849
38. https://www.facebook.com/MyMinnesotaValkyrie/posts/315530748494978
39. https://www.facebook.com/MyMinnesotaValkyrie/posts/385340388143079
40. http://clevelandsports360.com/wordpress/rumor-has-it-mitchell-mortaza-heather-theisen-dont-trust-lfl-canada-so-they-bring-american-players-to-play-the-game/
41. http://www.fuse.tv/2015/04/legends-football-league-oral-history-interview
42. http://www.vice.com/read/we-spoke-to-an-ex-lingerie-football-league-player
43. http://www.insideedition.com/investigative/7317-lingerie-football-players-revolt
44. http://whereibreathe.com/the-uniforms-get-them-here/
45. http://www.foxsports.com/nfl/story/lfl-says-it-s-taking-off-lingerie-to-focus-on-football-and-safety-112813
46. http://sports.yahoo.com/cfl/blog/cfl_experts/post/the-safety-concerns-behind-the-lfls-toronto-triumph-disaster?urn=cfl,wp1721
47. http://sports.yahoo.com/nfl/blog/shutdown_corner/post/Most-of-Toronto-8217-s-lingerie-football-team-q?urn=nfl-wp10085
48. http://www.lfl360.com/lfl-north-america/usa/lfl-chairman-mitchell-mortaza-issues-statement-toronto-triumph-players/
49. https://marcella58.wordpress.com/2012/06/05/228/
50. https://www.youtube.com/watch?v=zyV7nAxYnYo
51. http://melindatankardreist.com/2012/06/a-sad-day-for-all-women-in-sport-deborah-malcolm-reports-on-weekends-lingerie-football-league-game/
52. http://theimpactnews.com/items-we-barely-use/archives-2009/2012/11/30/lingerie-football-league-has-no-qualms-about-its-intentions/
53. http://www.huffingtonpost.com/entry/what-its-like-to-be-a-woman-playing-competitive-football_56096441e4b0af3706dcf757
54. https://www.youtube.com/watch?v=VizoJ53C8-Q
55. http://bustedcoverage.com/2015/04/29/lingerie-football-league-game-mvp-chugs-beer-at-midfield/
56. http://www.sportsgrid.com/uncategorized/the-lfl-continues-its-quest-to-be-the-favorite-sport-of-douchebags/
57. http://collettsmart.com/the-family-game-lingerie-football-league/
58. http://indoorfootballboard.proboards.com/thread/5431/fires-orlando-coach-miller-staff
59. http://www.lfl360.com/lfl-north-america/usa/game-20-recap-fantasy-at-breeze/
60. http://clevelandsports360.com/wordpress/lingerie-football-league-fires-sean-salisbury-sources-telll-us-mortazas-referees-is-reason-why/
61. http://content.usatoday.com/communities/gameon/post/2012/01/ex-espner-sean-salisbury-out-at-lingerie-football-league-mitchell-mortaza-lfl/1#.Vgqe79TD9p8
62. http://clevelandsports360.com/wordpress/lfl-orlando-coach-fired-for-exposing-mitchell-mortazas-scamwake-up-people/
63. http://www.lfl360.com/lfl-north-america/usa/lfl-releases-orlando-coach-miller/

64. http://clevelandsports360.com/wordpress/mitchell-mortaza-closes-orlando-lfl-team-calls-it-suspension/
65. http://www.lfl360.com/lfl-north-america/usa/league-announces-temporary-suspension-orlando-fantasy-franchise/
66. http://www.theheckler.com/2011/01/26/an-open-letter-to-lingerie-football-league-commissioner-mitch-mortaza/
67. http://www.reviewjournal.com/columns-blogs/ron-kantowski/ex-lingerie-player-stumps-womens-football-safety
68. http://www.lfl360.com/lfl-north-america/usa/hell-freezes-over-sin-defeats-temptation-game-15/
69. http://www.lfl360.com/lfl-north-america/usa/lfl-fantasy-football-watch-play-win/
70. http://www.lfl360.com/articles/western-conference-final-recap/
71. http://www.lfl360.com/lfl-north-america/usa/las-vegas-head-coach-lee-fired/
72. http://www.lfl360.com/lfl-north-america/usa/the-los-angeles-temptation-take-aim-at-a-fourth-lfl-championship/
73. http://jezebel.com/5852652/lingerie-football-league-courts-paris-jackson-as-youth-spokesperson
74. http://www.dailymail.co.uk/tvshowbiz/article-2052106/Michael-Jacksons-mother-Katherine-furious-Lingerie-Football-League-offer-Paris.html
75. http://www.tmz.com/2013/04/29/tim-tebow-lingerie-football-league-legends-quarterback-coach/
76. http://cnsnews.com/mrctv-blog/kelly-lawyer/lingerie-football-team-revokes-redskins-name
77. http://www.nydailynews.com/sports/football/replacement-refs-working-nfl-fired-lingerie-football-league-report-article-1.1167796
78. https://www.youtube.com/watch?v=8rZ0l_W-Nuc
79. http://www.thestarphoenix.com/sports/Sirens+mutiny+helps+halt+2013+season/8924997/story.html
80. http://www.mamamia.com.au/news/why-cant-they-do-this-with-their-clothes-on/
81. http://www.lfl360.com/lfl-north-america/usa/statement-chairman-mortaza-comments-australian-federal-minister-sport/
82. http://newsok.com/article/3513578
83. http://www.watoday.com.au/wa-news/legal-action-aplenty-as-wa-lingerie-football-spat-turns-ugly-20150217-13h9ph.html
84. http://www.dailytelegraph.com.au/newslocal/parramatta/legends-football-league-cancelled-lingerieclad-players-left-searching-for-new-competition/story-fngr8huy-1227078712532
85. http://www.smh.com.au/wa-news/wa-angels-lingerie-football-team-struggles-for-numbers-after-split-between-players-owner-20150225-13otq1.touch.html?skin=smart-phone
86. http://www.lfl360.com/lfl-north-america/usa/breaking-news-lfl-announces-plans-premiere-leagues-europe-canada-australia-league/
87. https://en.wikipedia.org/wiki/LFL_World_Bowl
88. http://www.lfl360.com/lfl-north-america/usa/lfl-secures-host-stadium-brazil-world-bowl-lfl360-com-marcus-de-la-fuente/
89. http://www.lfl360.com/featured/state-of-the-franchise-lfl-global-strategy/
90. http://www.miaminewtimes.com/news/miamis-lingerie-football-team-has-folded-6531590
91. http://www.lfl360.com/lfl-north-america/usa/lfl360-com-breaking-news-storied-lfl-franchise-tampa-breeze-moving-jacksonville/
92. http://www.lfl360.com/lfl-north-america/usa/lfl-usa-announces-state-franchise-games-rivalries/
93. http://www.wsoctv.com/news/news/what-a-tease-charlotte-lingerie-football-team-on-h/nG2Wb/
94. http://articles.baltimoresun.com/2014-06-24/entertainment/bs-ae-legends-football-20140624_1_baltimore-arena-home-game-baltimore-charm
95. http://www.lfl360.com/lfl-north-america/usa/lfl-beats-washington-redskins-to-new-name-washington-warriorettes/
96. http://www.lfl360.com/lfl-north-america/usa/no-gray-area-baltimores-goals-are-krystal-clear/
97. https://www.facebook.com/notes/legends-football-league/congrats-to-the-lfls-newest-team-the-new-england-euphoria/71082586409
98. http://pittsburgh.cbslocal.com/2013/02/28/lingerie-football-wants-to-make-pittsburgh-home-of-its-13th-franchise/
99. http://www.lfl360.com/lfl-north-america/usa/lfl-usa-suspends-operation-2014-season-philadelphia-minnesota/
100. http://www.newsnet5.com/sports/sports-blogs-local/lingerie-football-team-cleveland-crush-bolting-for-toledo
101. http://mobile.onmilwaukee.com/sports/articles/greenbaychillmilwaukee.html
102. http://www.stltoday.com/news/local/stcharles/lingerie-football-won-t-play-at-family-arena-in-st/article_a17b6eae-3543-521b-bf8a-3b827f767d14.html
103. http://newsok.com/article/3513578
104. http://newsok.com/lingerie-football-league-says-no-to-oklahoma-city/article/3515075
105. http://indoorfootballboard.proboards.com/thread/3864/dallas-desire-folding-return-2012
106. http://www.khou.com/story/news/2014/07/10/11156232/
107. http://www.lfl360.com/lfl-north-america/usa/breaking-news-lfl-usa-2013-divisional-playoffs-awarded-denver-colorado-lfl360-com/
108. http://www.lfl360.com/lfl-north-america/usa/americas-fastest-emerging-sport-names-dallas-texas-for-2016-expansion/
109. https://www.facebook.com/notes/san-diego-seduction/dear-san-diego-seduction-fans/10150130859594089
110. http://www.reviewjournal.com/news/las-vegas/legends-lingerie-football-league-defaults-vegas-lawsuit
111. https://www.facebook.com/mylfl/photos/pb.38982157102.-2207520000.1444703022./10153604566762103/?type=3&theater
112. http://www.metro.us/new-york/legends-football-league-formerly-lingerie-league-making-strides-despite-harsh-criticisms/zsJogA---7DGmVslhkPqiY/
113. http://profootballtalk.nbcsports.com/2015/06/18/nfl-health-and-safety-chair-sees-a-future-without-helmets/
114. http://content.time.com/time/nation/article/0,8599,2027053,00.html

Lingerie Football Leagues – Year-By-Year Results

Lingerie Football League (LFL) – 2009 Season

The LFL introduced the world to the sordid "sport" of lingerie football in 2009 with ten teams split into two conferences. Every team played their conference opponents once, with two cancelled games. The Los Angeles Temptation won Lingerie Bowl VII at the end of the season.

2009 LFL Standings

Eastern Conference	W	L	PR	Before	After
Chicago Bliss (CHI)	4	1	C	Expansion	--
Miami Caliente (MIA)	2	3	CC	Expansion	--
Philadelphia Passion (PHI)	2	2	--	Expansion	--
Tampa Breeze (TAM)	2	2	--	Expansion	--
New York Majesty (NY)	0	3	--	Expansion	Folded

Western Conference	W	L	PR	Before	After
Los Angeles Temptation (LA)	5	1	LC	Expansion	--
Dallas Desire (DAL)	3	2	CC	Expansion	--
Seattle Mist (SEA)	3	1	--	Expansion	--
Denver Dream (DEN)	0	3	--	Expansion	Folded
San Diego Seduction (SD)	0	3	--	Expansion	--

2009 LFL Scoreboard

Date					Date					Date					
9/4	CHI	29	MIA	19	11/6	MIA	37	PHI	26	1/1	SEA	28	DAL	12	
9/11	SEA	20	SD	6	11/13	MIA	49	NY	7	1/15	TAM	40	NY	13	
9/18	LA	26	DEN	19	11/27	LA	26	SEA	20	1/22	TAM	28	MIA	18	
9/25	DAL	20	DEN	6	12/4	CHI	27	TAM	18	1/29	LA	53	SD	0	
10/9	SEA	28	DEN	19	12/11	PHI	12	TAM	6	2/4	CHI	20	MIA	7	CC
10/16	DAL	40	SD	6	12/18	CHI	46	PHI	19	2/4	LA	20	DAL	14	CC
10/23	DAL	24	LA	12						2/6	LA	27	CHI	14	C
10/30	PHI	40	NY	6											

Foxxy Football League (FFL) – 2010 Season

The Foxxy Football League might have been an even more lurid lingerie football league than the LFL, if that's possible. The FFL was the creation of Foxxy Sports and Entertainment, which already featured classic sporting events like Foxxy Boxing and, kid you not, Foxxy Oil Wrestling. Based in Colorado, the FFL was their classiest sporting venture yet.

2010 FFL Standings

Teams	W	L	PR	Before	After
Mile High Dynasty (MHD)	4	0	LC	Expansion	Became Mile High Vixen
Denver Stars (DS)	2	1	--	Expansion	Folded
Tri-City Mystique (TCM)	2	3	C	Expansion	--
Pikes Peak Storm (PPS)	0	4	CC	Expansion	--

2010 FFL Scoreboard

Date					Date					Date					
6/12	MHD	19	PPS	12	7/24	DS	32	TCM	6	8/7	TCM	37	PPS	6	CC
6/12	TCM	26	DS	6	7/24	MHD	34	PPS	12	8/21	MHD	19	TCM	13	C*
6/26	DS	19	PPS	0											
6/26	MHD	12	TCM	6											

Lingerie Football League (LFL) – 2010 Season

The LFL held steady with ten teams in 2010, again split evenly into two conferences. The Los Angeles Temptation won their second straight Lingerie Bowl, defeating the Philadelphia Passion in Lingerie Bowl VIII.

2010 LFL Standings

Eastern Conference	W	L	PR	Before	After
Philadelphia Passion (PHI)	5	1	C	--	--
Tampa Breeze (TAM)	3	2	CC	--	--
Miami Caliente (MIA)	2	2	--	--	Folded
Baltimore Charm (BAL)	1	3	--	Expansion	--
Orlando Fantasy (ORL)	0	4	--	Expansion	--
Western Conference					
Los Angeles Temptation (LA)	6	0	LC	--	--
Chicago Bliss (CHI)	3	2	CC	--	--
San Diego Seduction (SD)	2	2	--	--	Folded
Dallas Desire (DAL)	0	3	--	--	Folded
Seattle Mist (SEA)	0	3	--	--	--

2010 LFL Scoreboard

8/27	LA	36	SEA	32	10/22	SD	26	SEA	25	1/1	LA	18	SD	6
9/3	SD	24	DAL	13	10/29	MIA	27	ORL	19	1/7	LA	18	CHI	12 *
9/10	CHI	14	DAL	7	11/5	BAL	42	ORL	19	1/13	PHI	31	TAM	12
9/17	PHI	60	BAL	6	11/13	CHI	50	SD	12					
9/24	TAM	47	ORL	6	11/19	MIA	42	BAL	12	1/29	LA	31	CHI	14 CC
10/1	TAM	33	BAL	0	12/3	LA	40	DAL	6	1/29	PHI	20	TAM	14 CC
10/8	CHI	41	SEA	12	12/10	PHI	35	ORL	26	2/6	LA	26	PHI	25 C
10/15	PHI	27	MIA	26	12/17	TAM	34	MIA	25					

Foxxy Football League (FFL) – 2011 Season

The FFL returned for a second season and even had plans to form a companion league in Pennsylvania and Ohio. But the second league never got off the ground, and the original FFL mercifully collapsed midway through its second season. It is worth noting, however, that much of the Pikes Peak Storm organization would help form the core of the IWFL's Colorado Sting a year later, one of the few instances of a lingerie team transitioning to legitimate football.

2011 FFL Standings

Teams	W	L	PR	Before	After
Pikes Peak Storm (PPS)	2	0	--	--	Folded
Mile High Vixen (MHV)	1	0	--	Were Mile High Dynasty	Folded
Colorado Galaxy (CG)	0	1	--	Expansion	Folded
Tri-City Mystique (TCM)	0	2	--	--	Folded

2011 FFL Scoreboard

5/28	MHV	26	TCM	12
6/4	PPS	12	CG	6
6/11	PPS	1	TCM	0

Lingerie Football League (LFL) – 2011 Season

The LFL was able to expand by two teams to 12 for the 2011 season. Stocked with several players with experience in traditional women's football, the Las Vegas Sin swept through the LFL's regular season and took the top seed in the West. In a "controversial" contest, the Los Angeles Temptation defeated Las Vegas in the conference title game on their way to a third consecutive Lingerie Bowl victory. After the season, the LFL announced a one-year stateside hiatus, with a return to the field in the spring of 2013.

2011 LFL Standings

Eastern Conference	W	L	PR	Before	After
Philadelphia Passion (PHI)	5	1	C	--	--
Tampa Breeze (TAM)	3	2	CC	--	Became Jacksonville Breeze
Orlando Fantasy (ORL)	3	1	--	--	Folded
Baltimore Charm (BAL)	2	2	--	--	--
Cleveland Crush (CLE)	0	4	--	Expansion	--
Toronto Triumph (TOR)	0	4	--	Expansion	Left for LFL-CAN

Western Conference	W	L	PR	Before	After
Los Angeles Temptation (LA)	5	1	LC	--	--
Las Vegas Sin (LV)	4	1	CC	Expansion	--
Seattle Mist (SEA)	2	2	--	--	--
Chicago Bliss (CHI)	1	3	--	--	--
Green Bay Chill (GB)	1	3	--	Expansion	--
Minnesota Valkyrie (MIN)	1	3	--	Expansion	--

2011 LFL Scoreboard

Date					Date					Date					
8/26	MIN	28	GB	25	10/28	BAL	42	TOR	6	1/6	SEA	32	MIN	14	
9/2	LV	32	CHI	20	10/29	PHI	60	CLE	18	1/13	ORL	49	TOR	18	
9/9	PHI	48	TAM	0	11/4	LV	28	SEA	24	1/20	LA	42	CHI	26	
9/16	ORL	36	BAL	12	11/11	LV	28	LA	20	1/21	LV	30	GB	0	
9/17	TAM	48	TOR	14	11/18	PHI	24	BAL	12						
9/23	BAL	20	CLE	19	11/19	CHI	40	MIN	33	1/29	LA	27	LV	18	CC
9/30	SEA	42	GB	8	12/2	ORL	68	CLE	8	1/29	PHI	44	TAM	32	CC
10/7	GB	36	CHI	34	12/9	PHI	74	TOR	0	2/5	LA	28	PHI	6	C
10/14	LA	28	MIN	7	12/16	LA	27	SEA	24						
10/21	TAM	31	CLE	29	12/30	TAM	20	ORL	18						

Leather 'n' Lace Football League (LLFL) – 2011 Season

Originally conceived by Randall Fields as a lingerie division of the WSFL, the fabulously-named LLFL played one season as a separate league in 2011. The LLFL planned on having six teams in the league (including Fields' Kansas City Tease) and the San Antonio Texas Cowgirls, owned by Rebecca Garza. But only three Alabama franchises were able to launch, and the league collapsed after just one season. Garza would create the SSFL a year later, taking her Cowgirls with her.

2011 LLFL Standings

Teams	W	L	PR	Before	After
Grand Bay Ravens (GBR)	5	2	LC	Expansion	Folded
Dauphin Island Dreamz (DID)	3	3	--	Expansion	Folded
Mobile Bay Vixens (MBV)	2	5	C	Expansion	Folded

2011 LLFL Scoreboard

Date					Date					Date					
5/16	MBV	55	GBR	48	6/6	GBR	28	MBV	8	7/4	MBV	1	DID	0	
5/23	GBR	42	DID	20	6/13	DID	46	MBV	22	7/11	GBR	62	DID	12	
5/30	DID	42	MBV	40	6/20	DID	28	GBR	26						
					6/27	GBR	50	MBV	38	7/18	GBR	1	MBV	0	C

Ladies Arena Football League (LAFL) – 2012 Season

The LAFL is best remembered for the participation of Snoop Dogg, who made national headlines when he announced that he would be part-owner of the Los Angeles franchise. The LAFL planned to have eight teams in their inaugural season and take advantage of the one-year hiatus by the LFL to become the biggest name in lingerie football. But only half of the planned eight teams were able to actually launch, and the LAFL crashed down after one unfinished season.

2012 LAFL Standings

Teams	W	L	PR	Before	After
New Orleans Lady Dollz (NOLD)	3	0	--	Expansion	Became WAFL's New Orleans Bayou Queens
Los Angeles Rideretts (LAR)	2	1	--	Expansion	Folded
Texas Mighty Diamonds (TMD)	1	2	--	Expansion	Folded
Lady Houston Panthers (LHP)	0	3	--	Expansion	Folded

2012 LAFL Scoreboard

5/19	LAR	28	LHP	6	5/26	NOLD	1	LHP	0	6/23	NOLD	34	LAR	12
5/19	NOLD	40	TMD	0	5/26	LAR	32	TMD	14	6/23	TMD	6	LHP	0

Sugar 'n' Spice Football League (SSFL) – 2012 Season

Rebecca Garza debuted the SSFL in 2012 with five teams, including the SA Texas Cowgirls she initially tried to place in the LLFL the previous year. The RGV McAllen Mystics captured the SSFL championship in the league's inaugural season.

2012 SSFL Standings

Teams	W	L	PR	Before	After
RGV McAllen Mystics (RMM)	4	0	LC	Expansion	--
Corpus Christi Mermaids (CCM)	3	1	--	Expansion	--
San Antonio Texas Cowgirls (TXC)	3	3	C	Expansion	--
Laredo Roses (LR)	1	3	--	Expansion	--
Austin Angels (AA)	0	4	--	Expansion	--

2012 SSFL Scoreboard

6/9	CCM	30	TXC	28	7/7	LR	15	AA	8	8/4	CCM	13	AA	12
6/15	TXC	19	AA	0	7/14	RMM	8	TXC	6	8/11	RMM	43	LR	9
6/23	CCM	21	LR	14	7/22	TXC	27	LR	26					
6/29	TXC	33	AA	0	7/28	RMM	34	CCM	13	9/15	RMM	33	TXC	31 C

Lingerie Football League – Canada (LFL-CAN) – 2012 Season

The LFL went north of the border in 2012 with a lingerie league in Canada. Three expansion teams joined the Toronto Triumph to create a four-team league. The BC Angels, bolstered by members of the nearby Seattle Mist, took the Canadian title; the Angels then played the Mist in a Pacific Cup exhibition game. A player revolt on the eve of a planned second season led to the folding of LFL-Canada and all its franchises, as well as the cancellation of an announced second edition of the Pacific Cup.

2012 LFL-CAN Standings

Teams	W	L	PR	Before	After
Saskatoon Sirens (SS)	3	2	C	Expansion	Folded
BC Angels (BCA)	3	3	LC	Expansion	Folded
Regina Rage (RR)	2	2	--	Expansion	Folded
Toronto Triumph (TT)	1	3	--	Joined from LFL-US	Folded

2012 LFL-CAN Scoreboard

8/25	BCA	41	RR	18	10/6	RR	26	SS	20	11/17	BCA	25	SS	12	C
9/1	SS	22	BCA	18	10/21	SS	35	RR	33	12/15	SEA	38	BCA	18	I
9/8	RR	40	TT	32	10/27	TT	22	BCA	8					
9/15	SS	44	TT	22										
9/29	BCA	31	TT	27										

Sugar 'n' Spice Football League (SSFL) – 2013 Season

The SSFL expanded to six teams in 2013, with the five teams from 2012 all returning for the league's second season. The reigning champ RGV McAllen Mystics lost their first game to the SA Texas Cowgirls in the regular season but bounced back for their second straight SSFL title.

2013 SSFL Standings

Teams	W	L	PR	Before	After
San Antonio Texas Cowgirls (TXC)	5	1	C	--	--
RGV McAllen Mystics (RMM)	3	1	LC	--	--
Houston Venus (VEN)	2	2	--	Expansion	Folded
Corpus Christi Mermaids (CCM)	1	1	--	--	--
Austin Angels (AA)	2	3	--	--	--
Laredo Roses (LR)	0	5	--	--	--

2013 SSFL Scoreboard

5/11	TXC	53	AA	12	6/15	RMM	46	AA	0	7/20	RMM	32	HV	14	
5/18	CCM	13	LR	12	6/21	VEN	46	LR	13	7/26	TXC	66	LR	0	
5/31	TXC	25	RMM	14	6/22	TXC	60	CCM	7	8/17	VEN	46	AA	0	
6/7	AA	46	LR	19	6/28	AA	36	LR	7	8/17	RMM	27	TXC	13	C
6/8	TXC	45	HV	0											

Lingerie "Legends" Football League (LFL) – 2013 Season

The LFL returned stateside after a one-year suspension of operations and rebranded itself as the "Legends Football League", but fans weren't fooled and have continued to refer to it as the Lingerie Football League anyway. The LFL went ahead with 12 teams in 2013 and divided into four divisions for the first time, holding a six-team playoff culminating in the first "Legends Cup". Legends Cup I was kicked around from Pittsburgh to Philadelphia before finally landing in Las Vegas. The league tried to save face by stating that they had signed a contract to put the Legends Cup in Las Vegas for the next three seasons; the Legends Cup would be held in California and Seattle the next two years. The Chicago Bliss became the first U.S. team other than Los Angeles to win the LFL championship.

2013 LFL Standings

Eastern Conference	W	L	PR	Before	After
Northeast Division					
Philadelphia Passion (PHI)	4	2	C	--	Folded
Baltimore Charm (BAL)	3	2	CC	--	--
Cleveland Crush (CLE)	1	3	--	--	Became Toledo Crush
Southeast Division					
Atlanta Steam (ATL)	2	2	S	Expansion	--
Jacksonville Breeze (JAX)	2	2	--	Were Tampa Breeze	--
Omaha Heart (OMA)	1	3	--	Expansion	--
Western Conference					
Midwest Division					
Chicago Bliss (CHI)	6	1	LC	--	--
Green Bay Chill (GB)	1	3	--	--	--
Minnesota Valkyrie (MIN)	0	3	--	--	Folded
Pacific Division					
Seattle Mist (SEA)	5	1	CC	--	--
Los Angeles Temptation (LA)	2	2	S	--	--
Las Vegas Sin (LV)	1	3	--	--	--

2013 LFL Scoreboard

Date						Date						Date					
12/15	SEA	38	BCA	18	I	6/1	OMA	8	JAX	0		7/28	PHI	33	CLE	26	
3/30	JAX	48	ATL	0		6/8	BAL	20	PHI	19		8/3	BAL	12	OMA	6	
4/6	SEA	55	GB	36		6/14	CLE	12	OMA	0		8/10	CHI	27	GB	18	
4/13	ATL	42	OMA	6		6/15	PHI	21	JAX	19		8/17	CHI	19	LA	12	S
4/19	LA	31	CHI	18		6/22	LV	40	GB	32		8/17	PHI	28	ATL	20	S
5/4	SEA	24	LA	20		6/29	LA	42	LV	26		8/24	CHI	31	SEA	14	CC
5/10	CHI	34	LV	12		7/6	SEA	38	MIN	0		8/24	PHI	20	BAL	19	CC
5/11	GB	40	MIN	8		7/12	BAL	24	CLE	18		9/1	CHI	34	PHI	18	C
5/18	ATL	49	CLE	40		7/20	SEA	52	LV	14							
5/25	JAX	27	BAL	12		7/26	CHI	25	MIN	12							

Women's Arena Football League (WAFL) – 2013 Season

The return of the waffle! Over a decade after the Women's American Football League used the WAFL acronym in traditional women's football, lingerie football took a shot at it in 2013. Lingerie football's WAFL featured three teams and planned a league championship game set for September 21, but the game had to be cancelled. Despite that enormous red flag, the WAFL actually announced a full schedule and expansion plans for a second season in 2014. It wasn't meant to be; the WAFL crashed and burned after just one season.

2013 WAFL Standings

Teams	W	L	PR	Before	After
Dallas Darlings (DD)	2	0	--	Expansion	Folded
Houston Lady Oilers (HLO)	2	1	--	Expansion	Folded
New Orleans Bayou Queens (NOBQ)	0	3	--	Were LAFL's New Orleans Lady Dollz	Folded

2013 WAFL Scoreboard

Date						Date						Date					
6/30	DD	28	NOBQ	8		8/10	DD	33	HLO	0		8/31	HLO	20	NOBQ	14	CC*
						8/17	HLO	33	NOBQ	21							

Lingerie "Legends" Football League – Australia (LFL-AUS) – 2013-14 Season

The LFL headed down under for the 2013-14 season, launching a four-team lingerie league in Australia for the first time. The New South Wales Surge won the inaugural LFL-Australia title. A planned second LFL-Australia season was cancelled shortly before it was expected to begin, the second straight international failure for the LFL. Many of the players and coaches from LFL-Australia left to start their own lingerie league, the Ladies Gridiron League.

2013-14 LFL-AUS Standings

Teams	W	L	PR	Before	After
New South Wales Surge (NSWS)	4	1	LC	Expansion	Folded
Western Australia Angels (WAA)	2	3	C	Expansion	Folded
Queensland Brigade (QB)	2	2	--	Expansion	Folded
Victoria Maidens (VM)	1	3	--	Expansion	Folded

2013-14 LFL-AUS Scoreboard

Date					Date						Date					
12/7	NSWS	44	QB	6		12/28	NSWS	36	VM	12		1/18	QB	18	VM	13	
12/14	VM	32	WAA	26		1/4	WAA	41	QB	0		2/1	QB	26	WAA	19	
12/21	WAA	20	NSWS	18		1/11	NSWS	14	VM	0		2/8	NSWS	36	WAA	15	C

Lingerie "Legends" Football League (LFL) – 2014 Season

The LFL kept their divisions in 2014 but shrank back down to ten teams. Two postponements and two cancellations blighted the LFL's 16-game regular season schedule before the Chicago Bliss claimed their second league title in Legends Cup II.

2014 LFL Standings

Eastern Conference	W	L	T	PR	Before	After
Northeast Division						
Baltimore Charm (BAL)	1	2	0	--	--	Folded
Toledo Crush (TOL)	0	3	0	--	Were Cleveland Crush	Folded
Southeast Division						
Atlanta Steam (ATL)	3	0	0	C	--	--
Jacksonville Breeze (JAX)	2	1	0	CC	--	Folded
Omaha Heart (OMA)	2	2	0	--	--	--
Western Conference						
Midwest Division						
Chicago Bliss (CHI)	4	0	1	LC	--	--
Green Bay Chill (GB)	0	3	0	--	--	Folded
Pacific Division						
Los Angeles Temptation (LA)	2	2	0	CC	--	--
Seattle Mist (SEA)	2	1	1	--	--	--
Las Vegas Sin (LV)	1	3	0	--	--	--

2014 LFL Scoreboard

Date						Date						Date					
4/12	JAX	27	BAL	12		6/7	ATL	20	OMA	13		8/2	LA	34	SEA	12	
4/19	JAX	25	OMA	0		6/13	CHI	34	SEA	34	*	8/9	OMA	19	BAL	12	
4/26	LA	42	LV	14		6/21	BAL	54	TOL	27							
5/2	SEA	38	GB	24		7/3	CHI	27	LV	18		8/16	ATL	20	JAX	14	CC*
5/9	CHI	25	LA	21		7/11	ATL	40	TOL	13		8/23	CHI	40	LA	12	CC
5/15	LV	34	GB	24		7/12	CHI	32	GB	7							
						7/18	OMA	31	TOL	0		9/6	CHI	24	ATL	18	C
						7/26	SEA	29	LV	18							

Sugar 'n' Spice Football League (SSFL) – 2014 Season

Eight teams took the field in the SSFL in 2014, as the league welcomed three expansion clubs to the fold. None of them could slow down the RGV McAllen Mystics, however, as the Mystics joined the LFL's Los Angeles Temptation as the second three-peat champions of lingerie football.

2014 SSFL Standings

Teams	W	L	PR	Before	After
RGV McAllen Mystics (RMM)	4	0	LC	--	--
Austin Angels (AA)	4	1	C	--	--
Valley Vixens (VV)	3	1	--	Expansion	--
Corpus Christi Mermaids (CCM)	2	2	--	--	--
El Paso Envy (EPE)	1	0	--	Expansion	Folded
Oklahoma City Rayn (OCR)	0	2	--	Expansion	--
Laredo Roses (LR)	0	4	--	--	Folded
San Antonio Texas Cowgirls (TXC)	0	4	--	--	--

2014 SSFL Scoreboard

5/17	AA	50	TXC	0		6/21	AA	51	OCR	37		7/19	RMM	58	OCR	6	
6/1	RMM	52	LR	0		6/28	VV	21	TXC	13		7/26	VV	25	CCM	19	**
6/7	AA	40	CCM	39		7/11	VV	20	LR	0		8/2	CCM	45	LR	20	
6/13	RMM	27	VV	6		7/12	CCM	54	TXC	26		8/16	RMM	20	AA	13	C
6/14	EPE	25	TXC	19		7/18	AA	18	LR	14							

Texas Ladies Football League (TLFL) – 2014 Season

The TLFL was founded in 2014 as a four-team league and put together an aggressive schedule. The San Antonio Texas Legacy claimed the TLFL title with a 10-0 record; their ten victories were a single-season record for a lingerie football team. The TLFL then rebranded after one year to the Ultimate Women's Football (UWF) league in 2015.

2014 TTFL Standings

Teams	W	L	PR	Before	After
San Antonio Texas Legacy (TL)	10	0	LC	Expansion	--
Corpus Christi Divas (CCD)	4	5	CC	Expansion	--
Houston Lady Eagles (HLE)	4	6	C	Expansion	Folded
RGV Cheetahs (RC)	1	8	CC	Expansion	--

2014 TTFL Scoreboard

5/31	TL	49	RC	8		7/5	CCD	26	RC	7		8/2	CCD	29	RC	19	
6/1	CCD	38	HLE	32		7/5	TL	78	HLE	20		8/9	HLE	44	CCD	18	CC
6/7	TL	68	CCD	18		7/12	HLE	34	CCD	13		8/9	TL	52	RC	6	CC
6/14	TL	1	HLE	0		7/12	TL	100	RC	6		8/23	TL	33	HLE	18	C
6/21	HLE	31	RC	24		7/19	HLE	27	RC	21							
6/22	TL	69	CCD	25		7/26	RC	47	CCD	30							
6/28	TL	45	HLE	19		7/26	TL	47	HLE	14							
6/29	CCD	20	RC	18													

Lingerie "Legends" Football League (LFL) – 2015 Season

The LFL celebrated their much-publicized return to music television by contracting to six teams for the 2015 season, so the league had to expand each team's schedule to six games for a planned 18-game season. Two games were cancelled and one mysteriously vanished, giving the league a 15-game regular season. With Legends Cup III already scheduled to take place in Seattle, the Seattle Mist "controversially" upset the three-time LFL champion Los Angeles Temptation for the Western Conference title, saving the LFL thousands in transportation costs and ensuring a good home crowd for the LFL title game. The Mist then won their first lingerie title with a victory over the two-time defending league champ Chicago Bliss in Legends Cup III.

2015 LFL Standings

Eastern Conference	W	L	PR	Before	After
Chicago Bliss (CHI)	6	1	C	--	Current
Atlanta Steam (ATL)	3	3	CC	--	Current
Omaha Heart (OMA)	0	6	--	--	Current
Western Conference					
Seattle Mist (SEA)	6	1	LC	--	Current
Los Angeles Temptation (LA)	3	3	CC	--	Current
Las Vegas Sin (LV)	0	4	--	--	Current

2015 LFL Scoreboard

4/11	CHI	27	ATL	24		6/6	SEA	27	LA	26		8/1	SEA	64	LV	19
4/18	ATL	79	OMA	0		6/13	CHI	40	OMA	0		8/8	CHI	26	OMA	0
4/25	CHI	49	OMA	0		6/21	SEA	34	LV	26		8/15	CHI	41	ATL	6	CC
5/2	ATL	62	OMA	0		7/3	SEA	24	LA	13		8/15	SEA	28	LA	24	CC
5/10	CHI	29	ATL	13		7/10	ATL	71	OMA	13		8/23	SEA	24	CHI	21	C
5/16	LA	59	LV	24		7/23	LA	28	LV	14						
5/29	LA	14	SEA	13												

Sugar 'n' Spice Football League (SSFL) – 2015 Season

Four original SSFL franchises returned for the league's fourth season, laying the foundation for a seven-team league in 2015. For the first time, the RGV McAllen Mystics would not capture the SSFL crown; the Texas Lady Jaguars from Houston ran the table in the league in their first season to take home the league championship.

2015 SSFL Standings

Teams	W	L	PR	Before	After
Texas Lady Jaguars (TLJ)	7	0	LC	Expansion	Current
Austin Angels (AA)	5	2	C	--	Current
Valley Vixens (VV)	3	2	--	--	Current
Corpus Christi Mermaids (CCM)	2	3	--	--	Current
San Antonio Texas Cowgirls (TXC)	2	4	--	--	Current
Oklahoma City Rayn (OCR)	0	3	--	--	Current
RGV McAllen Mystics (RMM)	0	5	--	--	Current

2015 SSFL Scoreboard

Date					Date					Date					
5/16	CCM	74	RMM	38	6/5	AA	33	CCM	26	7/3	CCM	56	TXC	51	
5/16	TLJ	61	TXC	0	6/6	TLJ	1	OCR	0	7/11	TLJ	35	RMM	0	
5/22	VV	35	CCM	18	6/12	VV	93	RMM	6	7/18	AA	30	VV	20	
5/23	AA	1	OCR	0	6/13	TXC	1	OCR	0	8/1	AA	48	TXC	8	
5/30	TXC	34	RMM	14	6/19	VV	28	TXC	0	8/15	TLJ	27	AA	9	C
5/30	TLJ	28	VV	13	6/20	AA	40	RMM	18						
					6/20	TLJ	43	CCM	0						
					6/26	TLJ	61	AA	12						

Ultimate Women's Football (UWF) – 2015 Season

The UWF – a rebrand of 2014's Texas Ladies Football League (TLFL) – featured six teams in 2015, including three TLFL teams from the previous year. As was the case in the TLFL, the San Antonio Texas Legacy ran up a 10-0 record in the UWF on their way to a second straight title and a claim as perhaps the best lingerie football team in Texas.

2015 UWF Standings

Teams	W	L	PR	Before	After
San Antonio Texas Legacy (TL)	11	0	LC	--	Current
RGV Cheetahs (RC)	8	3	C	--	Current
Austin Inferno (AI)	5	4	CC	Expansion	Current
Corpus Christi Divas (CCD)	4	7	CC	--	Current
Houston Vanity (HV)	1	7	--	Expansion	Current
Laredo Fantasy (LF)	1	9	S	Expansion	Current

2015 UWF Scoreboard

Date						Date					Date					
4/25	CCD	49	HV	19	E	6/6	RC	68	CCD	33	7/11	TL	76	HV	6	
4/25	RC	56	LF	29	E	6/7	TL	96	LF	7	7/12	RC	90	LF	47	
5/1	TL	82	AI	24	E	6/13	HV	42	LF	41	7/18	CCD	77	LF	73	
5/16	LF	52	HV	39		6/13	TL	70	AI	33	7/19	TL	72	RC	33	
5/16	RC	50	AI	14		6/20	AI	68	LF	13	7/25	AI	56	RC	26	
5/16	TL	86	CCD	12		6/20	RC	46	HV	24	7/25	CCD	42	LF	25	
5/23	AI	68	CCD	61	*	6/20	TL	89	CCD	12	8/1	CCD	40	LF	8	S
5/23	TL	78	HV	24		6/27	AI	78	CCD	28	8/8	RC	52	CCD	28	CC
5/30	AI	89	HV	13		6/27	RC	73	HV	14	8/8	TL	70	AI	27	CC
5/30	TL	102	LF	7							8/15	TL	74	RC	38	C
5/31	RC	65	CCD	32												

The International Growth of Women's Football

Women's football started in the United States in 1967, and women have been playing there continuously since 1999. But one of the most exciting developments over the last half-decade has been the explosive growth of women's football worldwide.

This chapter will take a quick look at the rapid growth of women's football globally. It is an incomplete view of the topic, as there are a few international leagues for which game information is not readily available – or perhaps more accurately, not readily available in English. This section on international women's football, then, covers recent women's football seasons from the following nations and territories: Canada, Australia, Guam, Austria, Finland, Sweden, Spain, and Italy.

Women's football has a long history in several other non-English-speaking countries as well. Germany has the longest history of women's football abroad; their top domestic women's football league, Damenbundesliga, has operated continuously since 1989. Mexico also has a long-running traditional women's football league called Football Xtremo Femenil (FXF). Several other foreign nations have embraced the sport as well to varying extents, but I was unable to find consistent information on the Damenbundesliga, the FXF, or other foreign women's football leagues. However, if there are any bilingual supporters of the sport in those nations reading this, I'd love your help to improve this section in a future edition of this book!

In the meantime, let's take a quick look at the foreign countries and territories covered here, beginning with Canada. Canada has two well-established women's football leagues: the Maritime Women's Football League (MWFL) and the Western Women's Canadian Football League (WWCFL).

The MWFL is the premier women's football league in Eastern Canada and the oldest women's football league in the country. Founded in 2004 with two teams – the teams now known as the Saint John Storm and Capital Area Lady Gladiators of Fredericton – the MWFL added a third team, the Moncton Vipers, in 2005. The Halifax Xplosion joined in 2007, and those four teams have formed the core of the MWFL. The MWFL calls its championship the "SupHer Bowl", while it annually plays a "Friendship Bowl" for third place in the league.

The WWCFL was founded in 2011 as the top women's football league in Western Canada. For the last half-decade, it has been the largest Canadian women's football league with seven to nine teams each year. The Saskatoon Valkyries have established a dynasty in the WWCFL, winning four consecutive titles from 2011-2014.

Australia has seen explosive growth in the women's football game since 2012, mostly on the eastern half of the continent. The first women's football league in Australia was the Female Gridiron League of Queensland (FGLQ). The FGLQ is the top women's football league in Queensland, one of the eight major populated states and territories in Australia; Queenland is the state on the northeast side of the island. The FGLQ started with three teams in its first year but garnered enough support to expand to a seven-team league just two years later. They annually crown their league champion in a title game called the "Summer Bowl".

South of Queensland on Australia's eastern coast is the state of New South Wales. The New South Wales Women's Gridion (NSWWG) league started in 2013 and is currently in its third season. NSWWG has four teams and crowns its champion in a title game dubbed the "Opal Bowl".

Below New South Wales on the southeast corner of Australia is the state of Victoria. The Gridiron Victoria Women's League (GVWL) started with three teams in 2013 but doubled in size the following year. Teams in the GVWL compete to make the league championship game, known as the "Vic Bowl". The GVWL is in the midst of its third season in 2015 as the premier women's football league in Victoria.

Located inside the state of New South Wales is the small Australian Capital Territory (ACT). The first women's football team representing the ACT, the Tuggernong Tornadoes, was established in 2012. In 2014, the ACT had enough interest to create its own four-team league, the ACT Women's Gridiron (ACTWG) league. Sadly, the ACTWG has had to take a hiatus for the 2015 season, but they hope for a return to competition in 2016.

The surge of interest in women's football in Australia was so dramatic that the country organized their first national tournament in 2014. Three teams representing the states of Queensland and New South Wales as well as the ACT competed in the inaugural national tournament, won by Queensland. The dramatic growth of women's football in Australia over the past four years has been extremely impressive and is poised to make the island one of the top nations competing in the sport.

Believe it or not, the tiny island of Guam has become a hotbed of women's football activity the past five years. The small U.S. territory has seen women's football grow considerably over the last half-decade. The Guam Women's Tackle Football League (GWTFL) began in 2012, first using the six-player format followed by a second season using the eight-player format. The GWTFL continued using the eight-player format in 2013 and saw the number of teams in the league double from four to eight.

In 2014, women's football in Guam took another step forward. The GWTFL moved to the 11-player format and was able to organize five teams. Meanwhile, a second women's football league – the Guam Women's Football League (GWFL) – joined the fray for one season. In 2015, the GWTFL absorbed the rival league and expanded to six teams, all playing 11-player football. It's an astonishing amount of growth in the sport for an island nation of just over 160,000 people.

Women's football is growing in Europe as well. In addition to Germany, which has sponsored a league since 1989, other nations also have leagues with lengthy histories. Neighboring Austria started their top women's football league, Austrian Football Division Ladies, in 1997 and has held their championship Ladies Bowl since 2000. Finland started their women's tackle league, Suomen Amerikkalaisen Jalkapallon Liitto Naisten, in 2008 and expanded to the 11-player format in 2014. Meanwhile, Sweden (Svenska Amerikansk Fotbollförbundet – Damer), Spain (Liga Nacional de Futbol Americano Femenina) and Italy (Campionato Italiano Football Americano Femminile) have domestic women's football leagues as well.

The international growth of women's football is welcome news for the sport's signature event – the Women's Championships hosted by the International Federation of American Football (IFAF). The IFAF hosted the first Women's World Championships (WWC) in 2010, essentially serving as the Olympics of women's football. The second WWC tournament was held in 2013, adjusting the calendar for a signature international women's football event to be conducted every four years, with the third tournament planned for 2017.

At the midpoint of the second and third WWC events in 2015, the IFAF hosted the first Women's European Championships (WEC). Seven nations competed for the European crown of women's football, necessitating a qualifying round for the first time in the tournament's history. Over the past five years, nine separate nations have competed in the IFAF Women's Championships, and the rapid expansion of women's football in Australia, Mexico, Japan, Italy, and several other nations not included on that list will set the stage for more and larger international tournaments in years to come.

These developments are very exciting, but they also come with a critical responsibility. It is far easier to document history as it happens than to attempt to reconstruct it after the fact. It is very important, therefore, that we record the proliferation of international leagues, game outcomes, and players involved, keeping up with the dramatic expansion of the sport globally. The women and teams spurring the growth of women's football abroad are part of a pioneering class, and it is imperative that we do not allow them to get lost in the shuffle.

Nevertheless, the blossoming of women's football internationally is inspirational and an extremely encouraging sign for the future of this great sport.

International Women's Football Leagues – Year-By-Year Results

Canadian Leagues

Maritime Women's Football League (MWFL) – 2012 Season

Four teams battled for the MWFL title in 2012. The Moncton Vipers held off the Capital Area Lady Gladiators in a high-scoring shootout to win the 2012 league title.

Previous Maritime Women's Football League champions:
2004 – Capital Area Lady Gladiators
2005 – Saint John Storm
2006 – Capital Area Lady Gladiators

Previous Maritime Women's Football League championship game results:
2007 – Capital Area Lady Gladiators 15, Moncton Vipers 14
2008 – Saint John Storm 24, Moncton Vipers 14
2009 – Moncton Vipers 30, Saint John Storm 24
2010 – Saint John Storm 26, Moncton Vipers 6
2011 – Saint John Storm 31, Capital Area Lady Gladiators 8

Previous Maritime Women's Football League Friendship Bowl results:
2009 – Capital Area Lady Gladiators 18, Halifax Xplosion 0
2010 – Capital Area Lady Gladiators 42, Halifax Xplosion 6
2011 – Capital Area Lady Gladiators 56, Halifax Xplosion 0

2012 championship game result: Moncton Vipers 49, Capital Area Lady Gladiators 42
2012 Friendship Bowl result: Saint John Storm 40, Halifax Xplosion 0

2012 MWFL Standings

Teams	W	L	PR
Moncton Vipers (MV)	7	1	LC
Saint John Storm (SJS)	6	2	CC
Capital Area Lady Gladiators (CALG)	3	5	C
Halifax Xplosion (HX)	0	8	CC

2012 MWFL Scoreboard

Date					Date					Date					
5/26	CALG	50	HX	0	6/16	SJS	35	CALG	1	7/14	MV	41	HX	0	CC
5/26	SJS	22	MV	16	6/16	MV	51	HX	0	7/14	CALG	21	SJS	7	CC
6/2	MV	34	CALG	7	6/23	MV	41	CALG	0	7/21	SJS	40	HX	0	B
6/2	SJS	1	HX	0	6/23	SJS	42	HX	0	7/21	MV	49	CALG	42	C
6/9	SJS	19	CALG	7	7/7	CALG	29	HX	6						
6/9	MV	40	HX	0	7/7	MV	23	SJS	7						

Maritime Women's Football League (MWFL) – 2013 Season

Despite a losing record in the regular season, the Capital Area Lady Gladiators made a stunning turnaround in the playoffs. They defeated the Moncton Vipers and Saint John Storm in the postseason to capture the 2013 MWFL crown, the Gladiators' first championship since winning consecutive titles in 2006 and 2007.

Championship game result: Capital Area Lady Gladiators 26, Saint John Storm 14

2013 MWFL Standings

Teams	W	L	PR
Saint John Storm (SJS)	7	1	C
Moncton Vipers (MV)	4	3	CC
Capital Area Lady Gladiators (CALG)	3	5	LC
Halifax Xplosion (HX)	1	6	CC

2013 MWFL Scoreboard

Date					Date					Date					
5/25	CALG	25	HX	0	6/15	SJS	21	CALG	18	7/13	SJS	55	HX	0	CC
5/25	SJS	21	MV	16	6/15	MV	38	HX	13	7/13	CALG	27	MV	26	CC
6/1	MV	17	CALG	14	6/22	MV	36	CALG	0	7/20	CALG	26	SJS	14	C
6/1	SJS	34	HX	7	6/22	SJS	38	HX	0						
6/8	SJS	21	CALG	6	7/6	HX	33	CALG	12						
6/8	MV	50	HX	14	7/6	SJS	1	MV	0						

Maritime Women's Football League (MWFL) – 2014 Season

Surrendering just 20 points in seven victories with five shutouts, the Saint John Storm rode their terrific defense to the 2014 MWFL crown. The Storm ended the year in appropriate fashion, shutting out the defending champion Lady Gladiators in the title match.

Championship game result: Saint John Storm 21, Capital Area Lady Gladiators 0

2014 MWFL Standings

Teams	W	L	PR
Saint John Storm (SJS)	7	0	LC
Capital Area Lady Gladiators (CALG)	3	4	C
Halifax Xplosion (HX)	0	6	CC

2014 MWFL Scoreboard

Date					Date					Date					
5/3	SJS	25	CALG	13	5/24	SJS	57	CALG	7	6/14	SJS	24	CALG	0	CC
5/10	CALG	35	HX	0	5/31	SJS	66	HX	0	6/14	CALG	41	HX	0	CC
5/18	SJS	44	HX	0	6/7	CALG	54	HX	13	6/14	SJS	1	HX	0	CC
										6/21	SJS	21	CALG	0	C

Maritime Women's Football League (MWFL) – 2015 Season

The Saint John Storm claimed their sixth MWFL title in 2015, a league record. The Storm won the 2015 championship with their second straight undefeated campaign, including a win over the Lady Gladiators in the title game for the second year in a row.

Championship game result: Saint John Storm 28, Capital Area Lady Gladiators 11
Friendship Bowl result: Halifax Xplosion 27, Moncton Vipers 20

2015 MWFL Standings

Teams	W	L	PR
Saint John Storm (SJS)	8	0	LC
Capital Area Lady Gladiators (CALG)	5	3	C
Halifax Xplosion (HX)	3	5	CC
Moncton Vipers (MV)	0	8	CC

2015 MWFL Scoreboard

5/2	CALG	46	HX	6		5/30	SJS	28	CALG	6		6/20	CALG	41	HX	16	CC
5/3	SJS	66	MV	0		5/30	HX	35	MV	22		6/20	SJS	36	MV	0	CC
5/9	SJS	35	HX	8		6/6	SJS	38	HX	1		6/27	HX	27	MV	20	B
5/9	CALG	55	MV	0		6/6	CALG	49	MV	20		6/27	SJS	28	CALG	11	C
5/23	SJS	15	CALG	7		6/13	CALG	33	HX	0							
5/23	HX	30	MV	14		6/13	SJS	50	MV	14							

Western Women's Canadian Football League (WWCFL) – 2011 Season

The WWCFL kicked off their inaugural season with seven teams in 2011. The Saskatoon Valkyries captured the first WWCFL title with a convincing victory over the Edmonton Storm.

Championship game result: Saskatoon Valkyries 35, Edmonton Storm 7

2011 WWCFL Standings

Western Conference	W	L	PR		Prairie Conference	W	L	PR
Edmonton Storm (ES)	5	1	C		Saskatoon Valkyries (SV)	6	0	LC
Calgary Rage (CR)	2	4	CC		Regina Riot (RR)	2	3	CC
Lethbridge Steel (LS)	1	4	S		Manitoba Fearless (MF)	2	2	--
					Winnipeg Nomads (WN)	0	4	--

2011 WWCFL Scoreboard

5/14	CR	28	LS	14		6/11	ES	22	LS	8		7/2	CR	26	LS	14	S
5/15	MF	47	WN	18		6/12	RR	34	MF	20							
						6/12	SV	78	WN	6		7/9	ES	13	CR	9	CC
5/21	ES	34	CR	0								7/10	SV	36	RR	6	CC
5/22	SV	56	RR	6		6/18	ES	23	CR	0							
						6/18	SV	58	MF	0		7/16	SV	35	ES	7	C
5/28	ES	24	LS	0													
5/29	SV	42	RR	2		6/25	LS	34	CR	32							
5/29	MF	34	WN	14		6/26	RR	23	WN	12							

Western Women's Canadian Football League (WWCFL) – 2012 Season

The Saskatoon Valkyries rolled through the WWCFL with another undefeated season in 2012. The Valkyries claimed their second straight league championship, this time over the Western Conference champion Lethbridge Steel.

Championship game result: Saskatoon Valkyries 64, Lethbridge Steel 21

2012 WWCFL Standings

Western Conference	W	L	PR		Prairie Conference	W	L	PR
Lethbridge Steel (LS)	5	1	C		Saskatoon Valkyries (SV)	7	0	LC
Edmonton Storm (ES)	2	4	CC		Regina Riot (RR)	3	3	CC
Calgary Rage (CR)	1	4	S		Manitoba Fearless (MF)	1	4	S
					Winnipeg Nomads (WN)	1	4	S

2012 WWCFL Scoreboard

Date						Date						Date				
5/12	CR	14	ES	0		6/2	LS	19	CR	14		6/23	ES	34	CR	13	S
5/13	SV	36	RR	6		6/3	SV	47	MF	0		6/24	SV	56	MF	0	S
5/13	MF	34	WN	22								6/24	RR	25	WN	7	S
						6/9	LS	41	ES	6							
5/19	LS	19	CR	6		6/10	RR	38	WN	15		7/7	LS	20	ES	0	CC
												7/8	SV	35	RR	21	CC
5/26	LS	16	ES	14		6/16	ES	19	CR	13							
5/27	RR	39	MF	7		6/17	WN	36	MF	24		7/14	SV	64	LS	21	C
5/27	SV	58	WN	12		6/17	SV	35	RR	16							

Western Women's Canadian Football League (WWCFL) – 2013 Season

The Saskatoon Valkyries finally dropped a game, losing in the regular season to the Regina Riot, 15-7. But the Valkyries rebounded in the playoffs, and they defeated the Lethbridge Steel in the title game for the second straight year to win their third WWCFL championship.

Championship game result: Saskatoon Valkyries 27, Lethbridge Steel 13

2013 WWCFL Standings

Western Conference	W	L	PR		Prairie Conference	W	L	PR
Lethbridge Steel (LS)	4	1	C		Saskatoon Valkyries (SV)	5	1	LC
Edmonton Storm (ES)	3	1	CC		Regina Riot (RR)	3	2	CC
Calgary Rage (CR)	2	2	--		Winnipeg Nomads (WN)	2	2	--
Northern Anarchy (NA)	1	3	--		Manitoba Fearless (MF)	0	4	--
Okotoks Lady Outlawz (OLO)	0	4	--					

2013 WWCFL Scoreboard

Date						Date						Date				
5/4	ES	50	NA	14		5/18	CR	1	OLO	0		6/8	NA	44	OLO	0	
5/4	LS	74	OLO	0		5/19	SV	44	MF	0		6/8	LS	32	ES	27	CC
5/5	RR	35	MF	0		5/19	RR	47	WN	0		6/9	SV	55	RR	27	CC
5/5	SV	52	WN	12													
						5/25	LS	47	CR	0		6/15	SV	27	LS	13	C
5/11	CR	33	NA	0		5/26	SV	48	RR	45							
5/11	ES	43	OLO	0													
5/12	WN	16	MF	13		6/1	ES	25	CR	13							
5/12	RR	15	SV	7		6/1	LS	74	NA	6							
						6/2	WN	21	MF	10							

Western Women's Canadian Football League (WWCFL) – 2014 Season

For the fourth year in a row, the story in the WWCFL was the dominance of the Saskatoon Valkyries. The Valkyries cruised to their fourth straight WWCFL championship in 2014, defeating the Western Conference champion Lethbridge Steel in the title game for the third consecutive time.

Championship game result: Saskatoon Valkyries 53, Lethbridge Steel 0

2014 WWCFL Standings

Western Conference	W	L	PR		Prairie Conference	W	L	PR
Lethbridge Steel (LS)	5	2	C		Saskatoon Valkyries (SV)	7	0	LC
Edmonton Storm (ES)	5	1	CC		Regina Riot (RR)	3	3	CC
Northern Anarchy (NA)	1	4	S		Winnipeg Nomads (WN)	2	3	S
Calgary Rage (CR)	0	5	S		Manitoba Fearless (MF)	0	5	S

2014 WWCFL Scoreboard

Date						Date						Date					
5/10	ES	44	CR	8		5/25	RR	13	MF	0		6/14	ES	47	CR	0	S
5/10	LS	65	NA	16		5/25	SV	60	WN	0		6/14	LS	62	NA	12	S
5/11	SV	55	MF	0								6/15	SV	48	MF	6	S
5/11	RR	41	WN	7		5/31	NA	26	CR	19		6/15	RR	27	WN	13	S
						5/31	ES	50	LS	35							
5/17	LS	51	CR	7								6/21	LS	29	ES	26	CC
5/17	ES	56	NA	14		6/7	LS	54	CR	0		6/22	SV	44	RR	15	CC
5/17	SV	49	RR	7		6/7	ES	20	NA	14							
5/18	WN	34	MF	12		6/7	SV	30	RR	0		7/5	SV	53	LS	0	C
						6/8	WN	18	MF	3							

Western Women's Canadian Football League (WWCFL) – 2015 Season

A new champ is here! The Saskatoon Valkyries' quest for a fifth straight title was derailed in the Prairie Conference championship game. The Regina Riot, the only team to defeat the Valkyries in their half-decade of existence, topped Saskatoon in a thrilling contest, 31-29. With the four-time champs vanquished, the Riot blew out the Edmonton Storm for the 2015 WWCFL title, becoming the first non-Saskatoon team to capture the women's football championship of Western Canada.

Championship game result: Regina Riot 53, Edmonton Storm 6

2015 WWCFL Standings

Western Conference	W	L	PR		Prairie Conference	W	L	PR
Edmonton Storm (ES)	3	3	C		Regina Riot (RR)	6	1	LC
Calgary Rage (CR)	2	3	CC		Saskatoon Valkyries (SV)	4	2	CC
Lethbridge Steel (LS)	2	2	S		Winnipeg Wolfpack (WW)	2	3	S
					Manitoba Fearless (MF)	0	5	S

2015 WWCFL Scoreboard

Date						Date						Date					
5/9	LS	7	CR	6		5/30	ES	51	CR	14		6/20	ES	19	LS	14	S
5/10	RR	47	MF	0		5/30	RR	49	SV	9		6/21	RR	73	MF	0	S
5/10	SV	75	WW	0		5/31	WW	17	MF	2		6/21	SV	66	WW	7	S
5/16	CR	20	ES	19		6/6	CR	34	LS	14		6/27	ES	51	CR	14	CC
5/17	WW	19	MF	6		6/7	SV	36	MF	15		6/28	RR	31	SV	29	CC
5/17	SV	28	RR	19		6/7	RR	47	WW	3							
5/23	LS	21	ES	20								7/4	RR	53	ES	6	C

International Women's Football Leagues – Year-By-Year Results

Australian Leagues

Female Gridiron League of Queensland (FGLQ) – 2012 Season

Three teams competed in the 2012 FGLQ season, the first women's gridiron season in Australian history. The Logan City Jets upset the previously undefeated Kenmore Panthers for the first women's football championship awarded down under.

Championship game result: Logan City Jets 38, Kenmore Panthers 20

2012 FGLQ Standings

Teams	W	L	PR
Kenmore Panthers (KP)	5	1	C
Logan City Jets (LCJ)	4	3	LC
Gold Coast Sea Wolves (GCSW)	1	6	CC

2012 FGLQ Scoreboard

Date					Date					Date					
8/24	KP	34	GCSW	32	9/21	LCJ	26	GCSW	14	10/26	LCJ	42	GCSW	12	CC
8/31	LCJ	44	GCSW	22	9/28	KP	34	LCJ	32	11/1	LCJ	38	KP	20	C
9/7	KP	16	LCJ	10	10/5	KP	22	GCSW	8						
9/14	KP	36	GCSW	6	10/12	GCSW	20	LCJ	14						

Female Gridiron League of Queensland (FGLQ) – 2013 Season

The FGLQ expanded to four teams for the 2013 season. The Gold Coast Stingrays claimed the second FGLQ championship by holding off the defending champion Logan City Jets in the league title game.

Championship game result: Gold Coast Stingrays 12, Logan City Jets 8

2013 FGLQ Standings

Teams	W	L	PR
Logan City Jets (LCJ)	8	2	C
Gold Coast Stingrays (GCSR)	8	2	LC
Kenmore Panthers (KP)	2	7	--
Western Jaguars (WJ)	1	8	--

2013 FGLQ Scoreboard

Date					Date					Date					
9/6	GCSR	6	LCJ	0	10/4	LCJ	28	KP	0	11/1	LCJ	6	GCSR	0	
9/6	KP	40	WJ	0	10/11	LCJ	28	GCSR	8	11/1	WJ	8	KP	0	
9/13	GCSR	30	WJ	0	10/11	KP	8	WJ	0	11/8	GCSR	28	KP	0	
9/14	LCJ	28	KP	0	10/18	GCSR	44	KP	0	11/8	LCJ	38	WJ	8	
9/20	LCJ	30	WJ	6	10/18	LCJ	26	WJ	6	11/30	GCSR	12	LCJ	8	C
9/21	GCSR	32	KP	0	10/25	LCJ	30	KP	0						
9/27	GCSR	46	WJ	0	10/25	GCSR	32	WJ	0						

Female Gridiron League of Queensland (FGLQ) – 2014 Season

The Logan City Jets and Gold Coast Stingrays squared off in the FGLQ championship game for the second straight year, but the Jets turned the tables on Gold Coast in 2014. Logan City avenged their title game loss from the previous season, shutting out the Stingrays for their second Summer Bowl championship.

Championship game result: Logan City Jets 6, Gold Coast Stingrays 0

Female Gridiron League of Queensland (FGLQ) – 2014 Season (continued)

2014 FGLQ Standings

Teams	W	L	PR
Logan City Jets (LCJ)	12	0	LC
Gold Coast Stingrays (GCSR)	10	2	C
Kenmore Panthers (KP)	8	5	CC
Western Jaguars (WJ)	4	7	--
Southern Steelers (SS)	3	9	CC
Sunshine Coast Spartans (SCS)	3	8	--
Moreton Bay Ladyhawks (MBLH)	1	10	--

2014 FGLQ Scoreboard

Date	Team	Score	Team	Score		Date	Team	Score	Team	Score		Date	Team	Score	Team	Score	
8/2	LCJ	58	SS	0		9/13	KP	1	MBLH	0		10/25	GCSR	22	KP	0	
8/2	MBLH	6	SCS	0		9/13	GCSR	1	SS	0		10/25	SS	1	MBLH	0	
8/2	KP	1	WJ	0		9/13	SCS	12	WJ	6		10/25	LCJ	42	SCS	6	
8/9	GCSR	54	MBLH	0		9/20	SCS	1	MBLH	0		11/1	LCJ	34	KP	12	
8/9	KP	56	SS	0		9/20	KP	30	WJ	0		11/1	GCSR	20	SCS	6	
8/9	LCJ	56	WJ	0		9/27	GCSR	52	MBLH	0		11/8	KP	1	MBLH	0	
8/16	LCJ	12	GCSR	0		9/27	KP	40	SS	0		11/8	GCSR	40	SS	0	
8/16	WJ	32	SS	6		9/27	LCJ	1	WJ	0		11/8	SCS	1	WJ	0	
8/16	KP	28	SCS	0		10/4	WJ	1	MBLH	0		11/22	GCSR	34	KP	14	CC
8/30	GCSR	26	KP	8		10/11	LCJ	22	KP	6		11/22	LCJ	1	SS	0	CC
8/30	SS	18	MBLH	0		10/11	WJ	20	SS	14		11/29	LCJ	6	GCSR	0	C
8/30	LCJ	36	SCS	0		10/11	GCSR	36	SCS	12							
9/5	LCJ	1	SS	0		10/18	LCJ	1	MBLH	0							
9/6	WJ	30	MBLH	0		10/18	SS	22	SCS	14							
9/6	KP	24	SCS	0		10/18	GCSR	1	WJ	0							

Female Gridiron League of Queensland (FGLQ) – 2015 Season

The FGLQ had a successful fourth season in 2015. The Gold Coast Stingrays made their third straight appearance in the Summer Bowl and became the first two-time champion in FGLQ history with a victory over the Bayside Ravens, adding another title to their league crown from 2013.

Championship game result: Gold Coast Stingrays 20, Bayside Ravens 8

2015 FGLQ Standings

Teams	W	L	T	PR
Gold Coast Stingrays (GCSR)	11	0	1	LC
Bayside Ravens (BR)	8	3	1	C
Logan City Jets (LCJ)	7	4	0	CC
Kenmore Panthers (KP)	4	7	0	CC
Sunshine Coast Spartans (SCS)	2	8	0	--
South Brisbane Wildcats (SBW)	0	10	0	--

2015 FGLQ Scoreboard

Date	Team	Score	Team	Score		Date	Team	Score	Team	Score		Date	Team	Score	Team	Score	
9/4	LCJ	38	KP	0		10/3	BR	42	SCS	12		10/31	GCSR	58	KP	0	
9/5	BR	43	SBW	6		10/3	GCSR	38	LCJ	16		10/31	LCJ	44	BR	18	
9/5	GCSR	50	SCS	0		10/3	KP	44	SBW	0		10/31	SCS	1	SBW	0	
9/12	BR	10	KP	0		10/9	LCJ	72	KP	38		11/7	BR	30	SCS	3	
9/12	GCSR	64	SBW	0		10/10	BR	1	SBW	0		11/7	GCSR	38	LCJ	22	
9/12	LCJ	32	SCS	6		10/10	GCSR	42	SCS	14		11/7	KP	1	SBW	0	
9/19	GCSR	14	BR	14		10/17	BR	42	KP	14		11/14	BR	20	LCJ	6	CC
9/19	LCJ	1	SBW	0		10/17	GCSR	1	SBW	0		11/14	GCSR	1	KP	0	CC
9/19	KP	18	SCS	14		10/17	LCJ	42	SCS	20		11/28	GCSR	20	BR	8	C
9/26	BR	32	LCJ	30		10/24	GCSR	18	BR	12							
9/26	GCSR	26	KP	0		10/24	KP	20	SCS	12							
9/26	SCS	34	SBW	20		10/24	LCJ	1	SBW	0							

New South Wales Women's Gridiron (NSWWG) – 2013 Season

The NSWWG featured four teams in their inaugural 2013 season. The Northwestern Phoenix defeated the Newcastle Lady Cobras in a championship game the league dubbed "Opal Bowl I".

Championship game result: Northwestern Phoenix 28, Newcastle Lady Cobras 12

2013 NSWWG Standings

Teams	W	L	PR
Northwestern Phoenix (NP)	4	3	LC
Newcastle Lady Cobras (NLC)	4	3	C
UTS Lady Gators	4	3	--
Bondi Lady Raiders (BLR)	2	5	--

2013 NSWWG Scoreboard

Date					Date					Date					
9/27	UTS	28	BLR	0	10/25	UTS	16	BLR	12	11/15	BLR	14	UTS	12	
9/27	NP	44	NLC	6	10/25	NLC	18	NP	14	12/14	NP	28	NLC	12	C
10/11	UTS	36	NLC	0	11/1	NP	22	BLR	8						
10/11	BLR	46	NP	6	11/1	NLC	18	UTS	6						
10/18	NLC	34	BLR	32	11/8	NLC	26	BLR	14						
10/18	UTS	42	NP	6	11/8	NP	16	UTS	14						

New South Wales Women's Gridiron (NSWWG) – 2014 Season

The NSWWG had another competitive four-team season in 2014. The Newcastle Lady Cobras advanced to their second straight Opal Bowl, but they fell in the title game again, this time to the UTS Lady Gators.

Championship game result: UTS Lady Gators 42, Newcastle Lady Cobras 26

2014 NSWWG Standings

Teams	W	L	PR
UTS Lady Gators	5	4	LC
Newcastle Lady Cobras (NLC)	5	4	C
Bondi Lady Raiders (BLR)	5	4	--
Northwestern Phoenix (NP)	3	6	--

2014 NSWWG Scoreboard

Date					Date					Date					
10/10	NLC	54	NP	8	10/31	UTS	42	BLR	6	11/22	NP	32	NLC	26	
10/10	BLR	26	UTS	6	10/31	NLC	52	NP	8	11/22	BLR	54	UTS	6	
10/17	NLC	48	BLR	40	11/7	NLC	40	BLR	8	11/29	BLR	24	NLC	22	
10/17	UTS	38	NP	22	11/7	UTS	42	NP	20	11/29	NP	12	UTS	6	
10/24	NP	46	BLR	22	11/14	UTS	34	NLC	18	12/5	BLR	1	NP	0	
10/24	NLC	22	UTS	6	11/15	BLR	34	NP	28	12/13	UTS	42	NLC	26	C

New South Wales Women's Gridiron (NSWWG) – 2015 Season

The NSWWG had their third season in 2015, and the Opal Bowl had a new champion for the third straight year. The UNSW Raiders were the first team to get through the NSWWG without a defeat, toppling the defending champion UTS Gators in Opal Bowl III.

Championship game result: UNSW Raiders 40, UTS Gators 16

2015 NSWWG Standings

Teams	W	L	T	PR
UNSW Raiders	8	0	0	LC
UTS Gators	5	4	0	C
Newcastle Cobras (NC)	2	4	1	--
Northwestern Phoenix (NW)	0	7	1	--

New South Wales Women's Gridiron (NSWWG) – 2015 Season (continued)

2015 NSWWG Scoreboard

9/11	UNSW	36	NC	12	10/24	UNSW	40	NC	16	11/21	UTS	14	NW	8
9/12	UTS	24	NW	16	10/24	UTS	28	NW	14	11/28	NW	24	NC	24
9/19	NC	30	NW	14	10/31	NC	32	NW	14	11/28	UNSW	36	UTS	18
9/26	UNSW	6	UTS	2	10/31	UNSW	36	UTS	0	12/19	UNSW	40	UTS	16 C
10/10	UNSW	30	NW	20	11/14	UNSW	60	NW	8					
10/10	UTS	36	NC	0	11/14	UTS	30	NC	0					

Gridiron Victoria Women's League (GVWL) – 2013 Season

Three teams competed in the inaugural GVWL in 2013. The Western Foxes easily defeated the Northern Lady Raiders in the first women's "Vic Bowl" for the GVWL crown.

Championship game result: Western Foxes 32, Northern Lady Raiders 8

2013 GVWL Standings

Teams	W	L	PR
Western Foxes (WF)	5	0	LC
Northern Lady Raiders (NLR)	3	3	C
Melbourne Uni Chargers (UNI)	0	5	CC

2013 GVWL Scoreboard

10/13	WF	42	UNI	0	11/3	WF	42	UNI	0	11/24	NLR	48	UNI	8	CC
10/20	NLR	26	UNI	6	11/9	NLR	24	UNI	12	11/30	WF	32	NLR	8	C
10/27	WF	32	NLR	0	11/17	WF	1	NLR	0						

Gridiron Victoria Women's League (GVWL) – 2014 Season

The Western Foxes and Northern Lady Raiders met in the Vic Bowl for the second straight year, and although the Lady Raiders put up a much closer fight in the rematch, the Western Foxes once again captured the GVWL title in 2014.

Championship game result: Western Foxes 42, Northern Lady Raiders 34

2014 GVWL Standings

Teams	W	L	PR
Western Foxes (WF)	7	0	LC
Berwick Diamonds (BD)	4	2	CC
Northern Lady Raiders (NLR)	4	3	C
Geelong Buccaneers (GB)	2	4	CC
Melbourne Uni Chargers (UNI)	1	4	--
Ballarat Kestrels (BK)	0	5	--

2014 GVWL Scoreboard

10/4	GB	30	BK	22	11/1	NLR	90	BK	0	11/29	WF	78	UNI	14	
10/4	WF	18	BD	12	11/1	WF	46	GB	0	11/30	BD	72	BK	0	
10/5	NLR	60	UNI	0	11/2	BD	20	UNI	0	11/30	NLR	34	GB	16	
10/18	WF	80	BK	0	11/15	WF	40	NLR	12	12/6	WF	36	GB	0	CC
10/19	GB	26	UNI	14	11/16	UNI	36	BK	0	12/7	NLR	34	BD	6	CC
10/19	BD	20	NLR	8	11/16	BD	28	GB	24	12/14	WF	42	NLR	34	C

Gridiron Victoria Women's League (GVWL) – 2015 Season

The Northern Lady Raiders blew through the regular season undefeated and made their third straight Vic Bowl appearance, but their season ended in heartbreak, as they fell short in their third consecutive Vic Bowl. The Geelong Buccaneers upset the Lady Raiders to capture the GVWL championship in Vic Bowl III.

Championship game result: Geelong Buccaneers 20, Northern Lady Raiders 12

Gridiron Victoria Women's League (GVWL) – 2015 Season (continued)

2015 GVWL Standings

Teams	W	L	PR
Northern Lady Raiders (NLR)	6	1	C
Geelong Buccaneers (GB)	5	2	LC
Croydon Rangers (CR)	4	2	CC
Berwick Miners Diamonds (BMD)	2	4	CC
Ballarat Kestrels (BK)	1	4	--
Melbourne Uni Chargers (UNI)	0	5	--

2015 GVWL Scoreboard

Date					Date					Date				
9/12	CR	18	BMD	6	9/26	CR	24	UNI	18	10/17	CR	30	GB	22
9/12	GB	36	BK	0	9/26	NLR	60	GB	0	10/17	NLR	64	BK	0
9/13	NLR	32	UNI	0	9/27	BMD	50	BK	6	10/18	BMD	14	UNI	8
9/19	CR	82	BK	32	10/10	BK	24	UNI	6	10/24	GB	22	CR	16 CC
9/19	NLR	34	BMD	0	10/11	GB	30	BMD	16	10/24	NLR	26	BMD	6 CC
9/20	GB	60	UNI	22	10/11	NLR	50	CR	8	10/31	GB	20	NLR	12 C

ACT Women's Gridiron (ACTWG) – 2014 Season

The ACTWG had four teams compete in 2014, with each team being known primarily by their nickname. The Spears defeated the Diamonds in a competitive 2014 ACTWG championship game.

Championship game result: Spears 30, Diamonds 22

2014 ACTWG Standings

Teams	W	L
Spears (SP)	6	0
Diamonds (DM)	4	2
Sirens (SI)	2	4
Wildcats (WC)	0	6

2014 ACTWG Scoreboard

Date					Date					Date				
8/23	SP	30	SI	0	9/7	DM	28	SI	0	9/20	SP	21	SI	0
8/23	DM	12	WC	0	9/7	SP	36	WC	6	9/20	DM	21	WC	0
8/30	SP	34	DM	14	9/14	DM	34	SI	6	9/27	SIN	21	WC	0
8/30	SIN	21	WC	0	9/14	SP	24	WC	0	9/27	SP	30	DM	22 C

Australian Gridiron League (AGL) – 2014 Season

By the spring of 2014, three women's football leagues had started in Australia across multiple states and territories. The country decided to have a national tournament, with three teams representing three different states and territories. The Sundevils representing Queensland won the first true Australian national tournament, defeating the Monarchs of the Australian Capital Territory in a competitive title match.

Championship game result: QLD Sundevils 14, ACT Monarchs 6

2014 AGL Standings

Teams	W	L
QLD Sundevils	3	0
ACT Monarchs	1	2
NSW Coyotes	0	2

2014 AGL Scoreboard

Date				
3/29	QLD	42	ACT	0
4/12	ACT	32	NSW	0
4/26	QLD	42	NSW	6
5/3	QLD	14	ACT	6 C

Guam Leagues

Guam Women's Tackle Football League Six-Player (GWTFL6) – 2012 Season

In the six-player portion of the GWTFL season, the undefeated Steel Blazers advanced to the league title game. But the Island Stunnerz lived up to their nickname, avenging a season-opening loss and upsetting the Blazers to win the six-player portion of the GWTFL championship.

Championship game result: Island Stunnerz 50, Steel Blazers 47

2012 GWTFL6 Standings

Teams	W	L	PR
Island Stunnerz (IS)	4	1	LC
Steel Blazers (SB)	4	1	C
Team Legacy (TL)	1	3	CC
Lady Spartans (LS)	0	4	CC

2012 GWTFL6 Scoreboard

Date					Date					Date				
4/14	SB	46	IS	38	4/28	IS	39	LS	6	5/5	SB	58	LS	18	CC
4/14	TL	60	LS	20	4/28	SB	30	TL	20	5/5	IS	24	TL	18	CC
4/21	SB	57	LS	27						5/12	IS	50	SB	47	C
4/21	IS	30	TL	20											

Guam Women's Tackle Football League Eight-Player (GWTFL8) – 2012 Season

Fresh off of a title in the six-player division, the Island Stunnerz cruised to the eight-player championship game of the 2012 GWTFL season. But just as happened in the six-player division, a previously undefeated team was upset in the title game, and this time the Stunnerz were the victims. Team Legacy toppled the Island Stunnerz for the eight-player crown.

Championship game result: Team Legacy 18, Island Stunnerz 8

2012 GWTFL8 Standings

Teams	W	L	PR
Island Stunnerz (IS)	4	1	C
Team Legacy (TL)	3	2	LC
Steel Blazers (SB)	1	2	CC
Lady Spartans (LS)	0	3	CC

2012 GWTFL8 Scoreboard

6/2	TL	54	LS	14		6/16	SB	28	TL	22	*	6/23	IS	40	LS	20	CC
6/2	IS	32	SB	22		6/16	IS	48	LS	24		6/23	TL	22	SB	18	CC
6/9	IS	14	TL	8								6/30	TL	18	IS	8	C

Guam Women's Tackle Football League (GWTFL) – 2013 Season

The GWTFL expanded to eight teams in 2013, and defending league champion Team Legacy again captured the GWTFL title with an undefeated 10-0 record. Team Legacy shut out seven of their ten opponents on their way to the 2013 title.

Championship game result: Team Legacy 47, Island Stunnerz 0

2013 GWTFL Standings

Teams	W	L	PR
Team Legacy (TL)	10	0	LC
Island Stunnerz (IS)	8	2	C
Sindalu (SIN)	6	3	CC
Steel Blazers (SB)	5	4	CC
Ruff Ryders (RR)	3	5	S
Lady Raiders (LR)	2	6	S
Lady Spartans (LS)	1	7	S
Iron Maidens (IM)	0	8	S

2013 GWTFL Scoreboard

Date						Date						Date					
3/23	LS	18	IM	0		4/20	LR	31	LS	14		5/11	TL	49	IM	0	
3/23	TL	13	IS	0		4/20	IS	30	RR	22		5/11	SIN	22	SB	20	
3/24	SB	29	LR	0		4/21	SB	32	IM	0		5/12	RR	42	LR	6	
3/24	SIN	31	RR	0		4/21	TL	47	SIN	12		5/12	IS	48	LS	12	
4/6	SIN	59	IM	0		4/27	LR	20	IM	0		5/18	TL	72	IM	0	S
4/6	TL	27	SB	0		4/27	IS	48	SIN	24		5/18	IS	46	LS	0	S
4/7	IS	75	LR	7		4/28	SB	41	LS	6		5/19	SIN	30	LR	6	S
4/7	RR	40	LS	0		4/28	TL	48	RR	0		5/19	SB	21	RR	20	S
4/13	RR	44	IM	0		5/4	SIN	34	LR	28	*	5/25	IS	46	SIN	27	CC
4/13	IS	30	SB	20		5/4	SB	50	RR	42		5/25	TL	28	SB	21	CC
4/14	TL	39	LR	0		5/5	IS	62	IM	6		6/1	TL	47	IS	0	C
4/14	SIN	68	LS	0		5/5	TL	50	LS	24							

Guam Women's Football League (GWFL) – 2014 Season

Four teams spun off of the GWTFL to form their own four-team league in 2014. Sindalu captured their first league championship, toppling the Island Stunnerz for the 2014 GWFL title. After the season, the league folded and remaining GWFL teams merged back into the GWTFL.

Championship game result: Sindalu 13, Island Stunnerz 8

2014 GWFL Standings

Teams	W	L	PR
Island Stunnerz (IS)	4	1	C
Sindalu (SIN)	3	1	LC
Ruff Ryders (RR)	1	2	CC
Lady Falcons (LF)	0	4	CC

2014 GWFL Scoreboard

Date						Date						Date					
3/8	RR	32	LF	0		3/29	SIN	35	LF	6		4/26	IS	16	LF	7	CC
3/15	IS	12	SIN	6	*	4/5	IS	42	LF	6		5/3	SIN	40	RR	0	CC
3/22	IS	46	RR	0								5/10	SIN	13	IS	8	C

Guam Women's Tackle Football League (GWTFL) – 2014 Season

The GWTFL moved from the eight-player format to the 11-player format in 2014, and several GWTFL teams spun off into a separate league called the GWFL. Those two developments led the GWTFL to contract to just five teams in 2014. Team Legacy remained, however, and they continued their dominance of the GWTFL by capturing their third straight league title.

Championship game result: Team Legacy 12, Steel Blazers 8

2014 GWTFL Standings

Teams	W	L	PR
Team Legacy (TL)	9	1	LC
Lady Raiders (LR)	6	3	CC
Steel Blazers (SB)	6	4	C
Tough Chicks (TC)	1	8	CC
Lady Spartans (LS)	1	7	--

2014 GWTFL Scoreboard

Date					Date					Date				
3/23	SB	30	TC	6	4/27	TL	8	SB	6	6/1	LR	13	SB	8
					4/27	LS	10	TC	0	6/1	TL	44	TC	0
3/30	TL	42	LR	0										
3/30	SB	50	LS	0	5/4	LR	42	LS	0	6/7	TC	18	LS	0
					5/4	SB	1	TC	0	6/7	TL	24	SB	0
4/6	TL	42	LS	0										
4/6	LR	32	TC	0	5/18	SB	32	LS	0	6/14	SB	34	LR	6 CC
					5/18	LR	18	TL	14	6/14	TL	42	TC	0 CC
4/13	SB	16	LR	0	5/25	TL	44	LS	8	6/21	TL	12	SB	8 C
4/13	TL	48	TC	0	5/25	LR	24	TC	0					

Guam Women's Tackle Football League (GWTFL) – 2015 Season

Unfortunately, a complete schedule and standings could not be obtained for the 2015 GWTFL season. The GWTFL absorbed a few of the teams from the defunct GWFL and expanded to six teams for the 2015 season. The fourth season of the GWTFL was once again dominated by Team Legacy, who claimed the league championship for the fourth straight year.

Championship game result: Team Legacy 16, Lady Raiders 7

2015 GWTFL Standings

Teams	PR
Team Legacy (TL)	LC
Lady Raiders (LR)	C
Lady Falcons (LF)	CC
Steel Blazers (SB)	CC
Sindalu (SIN)	--
Tough Chicks (TC)	--

Partial 2015 GWTFL Scoreboard

Date					Date					Date				
3/28	SIN	12	TL	8	4/25	LR	14	SIN	12	5/9	TL	38	SB	6 CC
3/28	LR	16	SB	12	4/26	SB	28	TC	6	5/9	LR	27	LF	8 CC
										5/16	TL	16	LR	7 C

European Leagues

Liga Nacional de Futbol Americano Femenina (LNFAF) – 2015 Season

Spain's top women's football league completed its fifth season in 2015 and marked the occasion with the crowning of a new champion. The Barbera Rookies, who had won the first four LNFAF championships, made it back to the title game with their sights set on five in a row. But 2015 belonged to the Las Rozas Black Demons, who avenged three LNFAF title game losses to the Rookies from 2011-2013 to rip the national championship away from Barbera for the first time.

Championship game result: Las Rozas Black Demons 38, Barbera Rookies 26

2015 LNFAF Standings

Teams	W	L	PR
Las Rozas Black Demons (LRBD)	6	0	LC
Barbera Rookies (BR)	4	2	C
Terrassa Reds (TR)	3	2	--
Barcelona Bufals (BB)	2	3	--
L'Hospitalet Pioneers (LHP)	1	4	--
Zaragoza Hurricanes (ZH)	0	5	--

2015 LNFAF Scoreboard

Date					Date					Date					
2/7	LRBD	25	BR	6	3/7	BR	27	BB	19	5/10	LRBD	19	TR	12	
2/8	BB	43	ZH	13	3/7	LRBD	44	LHP	6	5/10	BR	38	ZH	6	
2/8	TR	33	LHP	6	3/8	TR	26	ZH	12	5/10	BB	41	LHP	6	
2/21	TR	13	BB	12	4/18	LRBD	20	BB	6	6/19	LRBD	38	BR	26	C
2/21	LRBD	19	ZH	0	4/18	LHP	33	ZH	6						
2/21	BR	32	LHP	0	4/19	BR	26	TR	18						

Campionato Italiano Football Americano Femminile (CIFAF) – 2013 Season

Italy started their domestic women's football league in 2013 with five teams. In an exciting title match that required overtime, Lobsters Pescara captured the first Italian national title of women's football by a single point over Furies Cernusco in what the CIFAF refers to as Rose Bowl Italia.

Championship game result: Lobsters Pescara 26, Furies Cernusco 25 (OT)

2013 CIFAF Standings

Teams	W	L	PR
Lobsters Pescara (LP)	4	1	LC
Furies Cernusco (FC)	3	2	C
Black Marines Ferrara (BMF)	3	1	--
Neptunes Bologna (NB)	1	3	--
Storms and Sirens Busto Arsizio (SSBA)	0	4	--

2013 CIFAF Scoreboard

Date					Date					Date					
4/28	FC	21	SSBA	0	5/19	BMF	33	SSBA	0	6/23	NB	27	SSBA	6	
4/28	BMF	12	NB	0	5/19	LP	25	FC	19	6/23	BMF	13	LP	6	
5/12	LP	24	SSBA	12	6/9	FC	32	BMF	20	7/6	LP	26	FC	25	C*
5/12	FC	32	NB	6	6/9	LP	26	NB	12						

Campionato Italiano Football Americano Femminile (CIFAF) – 2014 Season

The CIFAF expanded to seven teams and split into two conferences for their second season in 2014. The Phoenicians Ferrara became the first team to go undefeated through the CIFAF, winning the championship in Rose Bowl Italia II.

Championship game result: Phoenicians Ferrara 32, Neptunes Bologna 13

2014 CIFAF Standings

Northern Conference	W	L	PR		Southern Conference	W	L	PR
Phoenicians Ferrara (PF)	5	0	LC		Neptunes Bologna (NB)	3	1	C
Sirens Milan (SM)	2	2	CC		Marines Lazio (ML)	1	2	CC
Red Rogues Sarzana (RRS)	1	2	--		Lobsters Pescara (LP)	0	2	--
Nyx Cernusco (NYX)	0	3	--					

2014 CIFAF Scoreboard

5/3	PF	46	NYX	6		5/24	RRS	27	NYX	19		6/15	PF	32	ML	18	CC
5/4	NB	23	ML	0								6/15	NB	19	SM	18	CC*
5/4	SM	20	RRS	14		6/1	NB	26	LP	12							
						6/1	PF	26	RRS	2		7/5	PF	32	NB	13	C
5/18	PF	26	SM	14		6/1	SM	76	NYX	31							
5/18	ML	49	LP	25													

Campionato Italiano Football Americano Femminile (CIFAF) – 2015 Season

The CIFAF continued to grow in 2015, expanding to eight teams. Neptunes Bologna advanced to their second straight CIFAF championship game, but they once again came up one win short as One Team Verona steamrolled their way to victory in Rose Bowl Italia III.

Championship game result: One Team Verona 43, Neptunes Bologna 6

2015 CIFAF Standings

Northern Conference	W	L	PR		Southern Conference	W	L	PR
One Team Verona (1TV)	5	0	LC		Marines Lazio (ML)	3	1	CC
Neptunes Bologna (NB)	4	2	C		Phoenicians Ferrara (PF)	3	2	CC
Red Rogues Sarzana (RRS)	1	3	S		Vibrie Salento (VS)	1	3	S
Elfe Florence (EF)	0	3	--		Lobsters Pescara (LP)	0	3	--

2015 CIFAF Scoreboard

4/19	1TV	15	NB	12		5/10	NB	13	RRS	0		5/31	ML	28	VS	20	
4/19	ML	14	PF	6		5/10	ML	20	LP	0							
						5/10	PF	39	VS	6		6/7	NB	34	VS	7	S
4/26	VS	12	LP	2		5/10	1TV	64	EF	6		6/7	PF	34	RRS	7	S
5/3	RRS	21	EF	0		5/23	NB	28	EF	0		6/20	1TV	26	PF	6	CC
						5/23	1TV	25	RRS	18		6/21	NB	31	ML	0	CC
						5/24	PF	33	LP	18		7/4	1TV	43	NB	6	C

Austrian Football Division Ladies (AFDL) – 2015 Season

Austria has nearly as long a history in women's football as neighboring Germany, starting their domestic league in 1997. The AFDL has been hosting their national title game, the Ladies Bowl, since 2000. The Vienna Vikings capped an undefeated season with a national championship victory in Ladies Bowl XVI.

Championship game result: Vienna Vikings 26, Danube Dragons 14
Consolation game result: Budapest Wolves 58, Schwaz Hammers 0

2015 AFDL Standings

Teams	W	L	PR
Vienna Vikings Ladies (VV)	5	0	LC
Danube Dragons Ladies (DD)	3	2	C
Budapest Wolves Ladies (BW)	3	2	BW
Schwaz Hammers Ladies (SH)	1	4	B
Graz Giants Ladies (GG)	0	4	--

2015 AFDL Scoreboard

Date						Date						Date					
9/12	SH	28	GG	9		10/3	VV	53	GG	0		10/25	VV	50	BW	6	
						10/4	DD	49	BW	0		10/25	DD	55	GG	0	
9/20	BW	38	SH	0													
						10/10	DD	50	SH	0		10/31	BW	58	SH	0	B
9/26	BW	60	GG	0								10/31	VV	26	DD	14	C
9/26	VV	65	SH	0		10/18	VV	50	DD	0							

Suomen Amerikkalaisen Jalkapallon Liitto – Naisten (SAJL-N) – 2014 Season

Finland started their women's tackle football league in 2008, but in 2014 their top women's division – the SM-sarja (SM-series) – moved from the nine-player format to the 11-player format. The Helsinki GS Demons, who had won four titles in the previous format from 2008-2010 and again in 2013, won the inaugural 11-player Finland crown by avenging a regular season loss to the Jyväskylä Jaguars on their way to the championship.

Championship game result: Helsinki GS Demons 40, Jyväskylä Jaguars 0

2014 SAJL-N Standings

Teams	W	L	PR
Jyväskylä Jaguars (JJ)	6	2	C
Helsinki GS Demons (GSD)	7	1	LC
Oulu Northern Lights (ONL)	4	3	CC
Turku Trojans (TT)	3	4	CC
Helsinki Roosters (HR)	3	3	--
Seinäjoki Crocodiles (SC)	1	5	--
Raisio Oakladies (OAK)	0	6	--

2014 SAJL-N Scoreboard

Date						Date						Date					
6/7	TT	56	HR	0		7/12	JJ	7	GSD	6		8/9	JJ	16	TT	6	
6/7	GSD	42	SC	0		7/13	ONL	24	SC	6		8/10	HR	12	SC	8	
6/8	ONL	26	JJ	7		7/13	HR	68	OAK	0		8/10	ONL	80	OAK	0	
6/15	GSD	40	HR	0		7/19	GSD	36	ONL	6		8/23	JJ	18	TT	12	CC
6/15	TT	14	SC	0		7/19	TT	88	OAK	0		8/23	GSD	44	ONL	7	CC
6/15	JJ	67	OAK	0		7/20	JJ	7	SC	6							
7/5	HR	34	ONL	26		8/3	GSD	92	OAK	0		8/30	GSD	40	JJ	0	C
7/5	SC	52	OAK	0		8/3	JJ	12	HR	6							
7/6	GSD	56	TT	14		8/3	ONL	26	TT	6							

Suomen Amerikkalaisen Jalkapallon Liitto – Naisten (SAJL-N) – 2015 Season

The big news in the SAJL-N in 2015 was the addition to the league of Russia's St. Petersburg Valkyries, which gave Finland's top league an international flair. Once again, however, nothing could slow the Helsinki GS Demons, who repeated as 11-player champions after an undefeated season.

Championship game result: Helsinki GS Demons 46, Helsinki Roosters 8

2015 SAJL-N Standings

Teams	W	L	PR
Helsinki GS Demons (GSD)	9	0	LC
Helsinki Roosters (HR)	6	3	C
Oulu Northern Lights (ONL)	5	3	CC
Turku Trojans (TT)	5	3	CC
Seinäjoki Crocodiles (SC)	3	4	--
Jyväskylä Jaguars (JJ)	2	5	--
St. Petersburg Valkyries (SPV)	1	6	--
Tampere Saints (TS)	0	7	--

2015 SAJL-N Scoreboard

Date					Date					Date				
6/6	GSD	60	JJ	0	7/12	GSD	74	ONL	20	8/29	GSD	48	SC	0
6/6	HR	38	SC	0	7/12	TT	36	JJ	0	8/29	HR	60	JJ	6
6/7	TT	8	ONL	6	7/12	SC	24	SPV	6	8/29	ONL	90	SPV	0
6/7	SPV	24	TS	2	7/12	HR	77	TS	0	8/30	TT	90	TS	6
6/13	HR	30	TT	0	7/18	ONL	12	HR	0	9/5	HR	44	ONL	7 CC
6/13	GSD	94	SPV	12	7/19	TT	42	SC	7	9/5	GSD	34	TT	12 CC
6/14	ONL	26	JJ	0	7/19	JJ	20	SPV	16	9/19	GSD	46	HR	8 C
6/14	SC	74	TS	0	7/19	GSD	94	TS	6					
7/4	TT	38	SPV	6	8/22	GSD	40	TT	0					
7/4	ONL	83	TS	0	8/22	JJ	26	TS	12					
7/5	GSD	20	HR	14	8/22	ONL	52	SC	0					
7/5	SC	24	JJ	6	8/22	HR	46	SPV	0					

Svenska Amerikansk Fotbollförbundet – Damer (SAFF-D) – 2015 Season

The 2015 SAFF-D season was the fourth season of Sweden's top national women's football league. For the fourth straight time, the Stockholm Mean Machines ran away with the national title, this time shutting out the Orebro Black Knights in the championship game.

Championship game result: Stockholm Mean Machines 21, Orebro Black Knights 0

2015 SAFF-D Standings

Eastern Conference	W	L	T	PR	Western Conference	W	L	T	PR
Orebro Black Knights (OBK)	6	2	1	C	Stockholm Mean Machines (SMM)	8	1	0	LC
Carlstad Crusaders (CC)	2	5	0	--	Arlanda Jets (AJ)	5	3	0	CC
Gothenberg Marvel (GM)	0	7	0	--	Vasteras Roedeers (VR)	2	5	1	CC

2015 SAFF-D Scoreboard

Date					Date					Date				
5/10	SMM	59	VR	0	5/30	SMM	56	GM	0	8/15	AJ	22	GM	6
5/17	AJ	25	VR	0	5/30	VR	22	CC	0	8/22	OBK	22	GM	0
5/17	OBK	55	GM	0	6/6	SMM	41	OBK	6	8/22	AJ	28	VR	0
5/17	SMM	65	CC	12	6/7	AJ	33	CC	0	8/29	AJ	1	SMM	0
5/23	OBK	14	AJ	0	6/14	OBK	6	VR	6	8/30	OBK	22	CC	0
5/24	CC	19	GM	12	6/18	SMM	32	AJ	19	9/5	VR	12	GM	0
5/24	SMM	35	VR	0	6/21	OBK	31	CC	7	9/12	SMM	29	VR	0 CC
					6/28	CC	44	GM	6	9/12	OBK	20	AJ	13 CC
										9/19	SMM	21	OBK	0 C

International Exhibitions

Eight known international exhibition games have been held by the leagues covered in this book. This list does not include the 2009 WFA International Bowl between the New Orleans Blaze and Mexico's Monterrey Royal Eagles; the Royal Eagles would join the WFA the following year as a league member, so the 2009 International Bowl is classified as a WFA league game rather than an international exhibition.

This list may be incomplete, but here are eight known international exhibition game results:

IWFL-WWCFL International Challenge:
The Manitoba Fearless of the Western Women's Canadian Football League squared off against two IWFL teams in 2009 and 2010. In 2009, the Fearless came to the United States to play against the Minnesota Vixen using American rules, and in 2010, the Iowa Crush traveled to Canada to take on the Fearless under Canadian rules. There was a planned exhibition between Manitoba and the Vixen in 2012, but the game did not appear to take place.

7/18/2009   Minnesota Vixen (IWFL) 46, Manitoba Fearless (WWCFL) 6
7/17/2010   Iowa Crush (IWFL) 20, Manitoba Fearless (WWCFL) 14

Team Mexico International Bowl Series:
The Mexican All-Star team traveled to the United States to play the Austin Outlaws in 2014. The following year, the Mexican All-Stars went on an "international bowl series" in the Pacific Northwest, challenging the Seattle Majestics and Tacoma Trauma to two games in the span of two days. Team Mexico holds a 2-1 record in three games in the International Bowl Series.

3/8/2014   Mexican All-Stars 30, Austin Outlaws (WFA) 20
3/7/2015   Seattle Majestics (WFA) 40, Mexican All-Stars 8
3/8/2015   Mexican All-Stars 64, Tacoma Trauma (WFA) 8

Pacific Rim Sun Bowl:
Two Japanese women's football teams – the Tokyo Blaze and the Osaki Wildcats – formed a joint team called the Japanese Blaze Cats that traveled to Guam in 2014 and 2015 to face one of the teams from the GWTFL. The first contest against the perennial GWTFL champion Team Legacy was billed as a "goodwill game", but the 2015 exhibition against the Steel Blazers was dubbed the Pacific Rim Sun Bowl.

3/22/2014   Team Legacy (GWTFL) 18, Japan Blaze Cats 7
7/19/2015   Steel Blazers (GWTFL) 6, Japan Blaze Cats 2

European International Friendly:
In 2013, Great Britain played their first international women's football competition, a five-player contest against Sweden. The following year, Great Britain played its first international contest in the 11-player format, traveling to Stockholm to face Team Sweden.

9/20/2014   Great Britain 26, Sweden 14

IFAF Women's Championships

IFAF Women's World Championships (WWC) – 2010

The Women's World Championships (WWC) were first organized in 2010 by the International Federation of American Football (IFAF). The WWC is the premier international women's football tournament between nations, essentially functioning as the Olympics of women's football. The first event was held in 2010 in Stockholm, Sweden, between six nations. As expected, the United States and Canada finished first and second, respectively, while Finland placed third as the top European nation in the event.

2010 IFAF Group Standings

Group A	W	L	PR		Group B	W	L	PR
United States (USA)	3	0	#1		Canada (CAN)	2	1	#2
Finland (FIN)	2	1	#3		Germany (GER)	1	2	#4
Austria (AUT)	0	3	#6		Sweden (SWE)	1	2	#5

2010 IFAF Scoreboard

Date						Date						Date					
6/27	CAN	12	SWE	6		7/1	CAN	20	GER	12		7/3	SWE	20	AUT	18	M
6/27	USA	63	AUT	0		7/1	USA	72	FIN	0		7/3	FIN	26	GER	18	M
6/29	FIN	50	AUT	16								7/3	USA	66	CAN	0	M
6/29	GER	14	SWE	0													

2010 Team USA Roster

#	Name	Pos	Hometown		#	Name	Pos	Hometown
5	Adams, Tracy	DB	Modesto, CA		6	Pickett, Okiima	RB	Glen Burnie, MD
31	Bandstra, Angela	LB	Chicago, IL		32	Pirog, Jennifer	DB	Derry, NH
75	Barker, Kelly	OL	Dorchester, MA		81	Pringle, Lauren	WR	New York, NY
84	Blum, Jen	WR	Oakland, NJ		88	Reinbolt, Brittany	WR	Los Angeles, CA
18	Brickhouse, Mia	RB	Revere, MA		98	Richardson, Ann	DL	Bedford, TX
53	Brooks, Keesha	OL	Oak Lawn, IL		61	Riddle, Michelle	OL	Washington, DC
24	Brydson, Alberta	DB	Cedar Hill, TX		58	Satterfield, Amy	LB	Los Angeles, CA
57	Carignan, Julie	LB	Manchester, NH		23	Schmidt, Jenny	QB	Mission, KS
64	Fain, Tarsha	OL	Baltimore, MD		20	Sheriff, Erin	DB	Des Moines, IA
62	Fisher, Jeanamarie	DL	Beaverton, OR		27	Shockley, Julie	RB	Roseville, CA
3	Gallegos, Melissa	QB	Chula Vista, CA		10	Smith, Adrienne	WR	New York, NY
43	Golay, Danielle	DL	San Francisco, CA		67	Smith, Roseanna	OL	Bethlehem, GA
59	Goodwin, Molly	LB	Brookline, MA		21	Sowers, Rusty	WR	Melvern, KS
15	Grisafe, Sami	QB	Chicago, IL		46	Springer, Jessica	RB	Haslet, TX
86	Griswold, Olivia	DL	Homestead, PA		7	Stuart, Tegan	WR	Kansas City, MO
30	Hinkle, Leah	LB	Albany, OR		8	Vasquez, Sharon	DB	Pittsburgh, PA
42	Loveless, Schandra	DL	Cleveland, TN		2	Weimann, Desiree	RB	Temecula, CA
17	Maple, Sally	WR	Tequesta, FL		89	Welniak, Danilynn	WR	Keller, TX
85	Marks, Kimberly	DL	Chicago, IL		48	Welter, Jen	DB	Dallas, TX
47	Martin, Knengi	DL	San Luis Obispo, CA		33	Wilkinson, Donna	TE	Wheaton, MD
63	Menzyk, Jamie	OL	Chicago, IL		80	Williams, Emily	P/K	Dallas, TX
71	Mulligan, Karen	QB	Bronx, NY		9	Wilson, Adrienne	WR	Spokane, WA
70	Pederson, Dawn	OL	Harwood Heights, IL		1	Cannon, Onetha	RB	Atlanta, GA
74	Pickett, Melissa	OL	West Caldwell, NJ					

IFAF Women's World Championships (WWC) – 2013

The IFAF hosted the second Women's World Championships in 2013 in Vantaa, Finland. The major story of the 2013 WWC tournament was Team Germany, who scored a touchdown against the United States in group play. They were the first points scored against the U.S., which had won the 2010 IFAF tournament without surrendering a point. The United States again defeated Canada for the gold medal in the WWC, with Finland once again edging Germany for the bronze, this time by a single point.

2013 IFAF Group Standings

Group A	W	L	PR	Group B	W	L	PR
United States (USA)	3	0	#1	Canada (CAN)	2	1	#2
Germany (GER)	1	2	#4	Finland (FIN)	2	1	#3
Sweden (SWE)	1	2	#5	Spain (ESP)	0	3	#6

2013 IFAF Scoreboard

Date					Date					Date					
6/30	FIN	47	ESP	0	7/4	CAN	34	FIN	12	7/6	SWE	64	ESP	0	M
6/30	USA	84	SWE	0	7/4	USA	107	GER	7	7/6	FIN	20	GER	19	M
7/2	CAN	50	ESP	0						7/6	USA	64	CAN	0	M
7/2	GER	25	SWE	14											

2013 Team USA Roster

#	Name	Pos	Hometown	#	Name	Pos	Hometown
80	Berggren, Ashley	WR	Evanston, IL	85	Marks, Kimberly	DL	Chicago, IL
68	Blackmon, Kenoris	DL	Kansas City, MO	50	Marshall, Aspen	DL	Benicia, CA
25	Brick, Cassey	RB	Costa Mesa, CA	47	Martin, Knengi	DL	San Diego, CA
18	Brickhouse, Mia	RB	San Francisco, CA	82	May, Rachel	DL	Haltom City, TX
21	Brownson, Callie	DB	Alexandria, VA	63	Menzyk, Jamie	OL	Portage, IN
24	Brydson, Alberta	DB	Cedar Hill, TX	5	Mulligan, Karen	QB	Brooklyn, NY
2	Bushman, Brittany	QB	Euless, TX	67	Okey, Elizabeth	OL	Chicago, IL
17	Campolo, Andreana	LB	Auburn, WA	79	Pederson, Dawn	OL	Chicago, IL
26	Converse, Catherine	DL	Kalamazoo, MI	83	Peterson, Holly	WR	Elk Grove, CA
81	Deering, Jennifer	DL	Oakland, CA	45	Plummer, Jennifer	LB	Galesburg, MI
44	Eddy, Vicky	LB	Woburn, MA	22	Reyes, Athena	DB	Yonkers, NY
46	Elmore, Kristine	LB	East Orange, NJ	69	Schkeeper, Sarah	OL	Brooklyn, NY
72	Engelman, Tami	OL	Chicago, IL	10	Smith, Adrienne	WR	New York, NY
43	Golay, Danielle	DL	Alameda, CA	19	Snyder, Alexis	RB	San Diego, CA
6	Gore, Rachel	DB	Federal Way, WA	16	Sowers, Katie	DB	Kansas City, MO
9	Gray, Jeanette	WR	Highland, IN	1	Sowers, Liz	WR	Kansas City, MO
15	Grisafe, Sami	QB	Evanston, IL	8	Vasquez, Sharon	DB	Pittsburgh, PA
28	Hatcher, Brandy	RB	Chicago, IL	23	Vilarino, Nicole	WR	Tualatin, OR
30	Hinkle, Leah	LB	Albany, OR	55	Walter, Katrina	OL	Poway, CA
66	Jeffers, Stephanie	OL	Medford, MA	13	Welter, Jen	LB	Dallas, TX
3	Jenkins, Odessa	RB	Prosper, TX	33	Wilkinson, Donna	DL	Wheaton, MD
41	Klesse, Kimberly	WR	Columbus, OH	74	Worsham, Rebecca	OL	Springfield, VA
12	Larsen, Angela	P/K	San Jose, CA				

IFAF Women's European Championships (WEC) – 2015

In 2015, the IFAF organized their first Women's European Championships to crown the top team in Europe. Seven nations petitioned for six slots in the tournament, so newcomers Russia and Great Britain played a one-game qualifier in Herfordshire, England, with Great Britain advancing to the six-team field. The underdog Brits then became the darlings of the 2015 WEC tournament – held in Maracena, Spain – winning their group in their first major international tournament and capturing the silver medal. Favored Finland, who had won bronze as the top European nation in the first two Women's World Championships, captured the first official European crown with a gold medal. Germany won their first international medal, claiming the bronze, while Team Austria and Team Spain picked up their first victories in IFAF women's football competition.

2015 IFAF Qualifiers

Team	W	L
Great Britain (GBR)	1	0
Russia (RUS)	0	1

2015 IFAF Group Standings

Group A	W	L	PR		Group B	W	L	PR
Finland (FIN)	3	0	#1		Great Britain (GBR)	2	1	#2
Austria (AUT)	1	2	#4		Germany (GER)	2	1	#3
Spain (ESP)	1	2	#5		Sweden (SWE)	0	3	#6

2015 IFAF Scoreboard

5/3	GBR	54	RUS	6	Q		**8/4**	GBR	30	SWE	14		**8/8**	ESP	14	SWE	12	M
8/2	GBR	17	GER	6			**8/4**	AUT	21	ESP	6		**8/8**	GER	26	AUT	7	M
8/2	FIN	56	ESP	18			**8/6**	FIN	52	AUT	7		**8/8**	FIN	50	GBR	12	M
							8/6	GER	22	SWE	12							

www.ingramcontent.com/pod-product-compliance
Lightning Source LLC
Chambersburg PA
CBHW080723230426
43665CB00020B/2593